HARMSWORTH
HISTORY
OF THE WORLD

THE SPHINX

HARMSWORTH HISTORY OF THE WORLD

EDITORS

ARTHUR MEE
EDITOR OF HARMSWORTH SELF-EDUCATOR
AND THE CHILDREN'S ENCYCLOPÆDIA

J. A. HAMMERTON

A. D. INNES, M.A.

THIRD VOLUME

BABYLONIA
ASSYRIA · PERSIA
ANCIENT NATIONS
OF THE NEAR EAST
WESTERN ASIA

PUBLISHED AT
CARMELITE HOUSE
LONDON
1908

EGYPT
NORTH AFRICA
TROPICAL AFRICA
SOUTH AFRICA
MADAGASCAR

CONTENTS OF THIS VOLUME

HARMSWORTH HISTORY OF THE WORLD

FOURTH GRAND DIVISION

THE NEAR EAST

FOURTH GRAND DIVISION
THE NEAR EAST

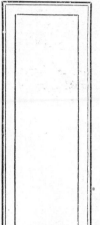

With the Near East we enter upon the regions whose history is in continuous connection with that of Europe from the time when European records begin. Our division covers Persia and all of Asia that lies west of Persia. Geographically, this area is much smaller than that of the preceding divisions ; but it has been the scene of still more tremendous and world-shaking events.

For here the Semitic races developed—the races which gave to the world the religion of the Hebrews, and its offspring, the Christian Faith, and Islam. Here was the cradle of those civilisations of the Tigris and Euphrates, the oldest of which we have record, save Egypt.

Here the Chaldæan learnt the secrets of the stars, Babylon and Nineveh rose and fell ; Solomon raised his Temple ; Aryan conquerors from the East, led first by Cyrus the Persian, fell under the Semite spell ; Aryan conquerors from the West, led first by Alexander of Macedon, yielded to the same enchantment.

Thence the Phœnicians set forth, the pioneers of the greater navigations. From these regions the Apostles spread the Gospel which turned the world upside down ; issuing from them, the successors of the Arabian Prophet made conquest of half Asia and North Africa, and crashed in a thousand years' struggle against the nations of the West. The glory of the Near East is no more ; but it has played a majestic part in human history.

PLAN

THE ANCIENT CIVILISATIONS AND THEIR VANISHED GLORIES
Professor Archibald H. Sayce

ANCIENT EMPIRES OF WESTERN ASIA
Dr. Hugo Winckler, Leonard W. King. M.A.

EARLY NATIONS OF WESTERN ASIA
**Dr. Hugo Winckler, Leonard W. King, M.A.,
Dr. K. G. Brandis, H. R. Hall, M.A.**

WESTERN ASIA FROM THE RISE OF PERSIA TO MAHOMET
**Dr. Hugo Winckler, Leonard W. King, M.A.,
Dr. K. G. Brandis, H. R. Hall, M.A.**

WESTERN ASIA FROM THE TIME OF MAHOMET
Dr. Heinrich Schurtz, Leonard W. King, M.A.

WESTERN ASIA IN OUR OWN TIME
By Angus Hamilton

For full contents and page numbers see Index

THE NEAR EAST

THE ANCIENT CIVILISATIONS
AND THEIR VANISHED GLORIES

BY PROFESSOR A. H. SAYCE

EARLY EMPIRES OF MESOPOTAMIA & EGYPT

Egypt, as regards its early civilisation, is so intimately associated with the ancient empires of Western Asia that in any general survey considerable attention must be devoted to it; but the geographical plan of this History requires that the main treatment of that country should come into the Fifth Grand Division, which deals with the continent of Africa

LESS than a century ago the history of the ancient East could have been compressed into a few pages, and even these few pages would have been a mixture of history and romance. The scanty accounts of the great empires of Oriental antiquity which had drifted down to us from the writers of Greece and Rome were intermingled with myth and fiction, and what the Old Testament had to tell us about them was meagre and fragmentary. A single case was sufficient to hold all the monuments of Assyrian or Babylonian civilisation possessed by the British Museum, and the mummies and other objects of Egyptian antiquity scattered through the museums of Europe were merely so many curiosities the nature and age of which were unknown.

In no department of science has so complete a revolution taken place in our knowledge during the last half-century as in that of Oriental archæology. Thanks to the excavator and decipherer, the ancient world of the East has risen, as it were, from its grave, and has become almost as familiar to us as the European world of the Middle Ages. We can follow the daily life and read the inmost thoughts of the men who lived before Abraham was born; can study the actual letters written by the Babylonian king against whom he fought; can examine the handwriting of Egyptian *littérateurs* who flourished centuries before him; and handle the jewellery and articles of toilette which once belonged to the ladies of the same distant past. The Oriental past, in fact, has ceased to be distant; like a landscape which the telescope brings near to us, the age of Moses or even of Abraham is being unfolded to us in all its minutest details.

The excavator was at work in Egypt before he invaded the valleys of the Tigris and Euphrates. Tombs were ransacked with merciless activity, and the museums of Europe filled with their spoils. But it is only recently that excavation has been conducted with that scientific care and precision which alone can yield satisfactory results. Much of the earlier work was mere spoliation, which ended in destroying material of priceless value to the archæologist of to-day. But there was also much which helped to build up our present knowledge of the history of the past. The artistic skill and patient labour of Sir Gardner Wilkinson recovered for us the life and manners of ancient Egypt, while the Prussian Exploring Expedition, under Professor Lepsius, revealed the extent

Revealers of the Vanished Ages of Egyptian influence in the Sudan, and carried to Berlin the materials for reconstructing the history of the country. Mariette's excavations completed the work of Lepsius on the historical side, and, with the foundation of the Cairo Museum, closed what may be termed the older period of excavation and prepared the way for the more scientific work of to-day.

Meanwhile the ancient cultures of Assyria and Babylonia were also being brought to light. The Frenchman Botta and the Englishman Layard revealed to an astonished world the palaces of Sargon and Sennacherib and other Assyrian kings whose names were new to history. Other expeditions followed; the sites of the forgotten cities of Babylonia were explored, and the libraries of clay books contained in them were sent to Europe and America. Year by year the wonder has grown; year by year, whether it be Egypt or Babylonia, fresh discoveries are being made, each more startling and unexpected than its predecessor, and bringing us into ever closer contact with the culture of the past.

Hand in hand with the work of the excavator has gone the work of the decipherer. From excavation alone we could have learnt only the more material side of ancient Oriental civilisation. The decipherer has given us its history and spiritual side. This is especially the case with Assyria and Babylonia, where so large a proportion of the objects discovered consists of inscribed tablets of clay.

Antiquity of the Art of Writing One result of the discovery and decipherment of these records of the past has been to prove the great antiquity of the art of writing. The art of writing was coeval in the ancient East with the rise of civilisation. It formed an integral part of early Oriental culture, with which it continued to be closely entwined. It was used for literary purposes ages before Abraham was born in "Ur of the Chaldees," and libraries and archive-chambers were established on the banks alike of the Euphrates and the Nile.

One of the earlier fragments of Egyptian literature that have come down to us is a treatise on ethics which was composed in the time of the third dynasty, and some of the epics of Babylonia go back beyond the time of Hammurabi, the contemporary of Abraham. In the age of the eighteenth dynasty the historical novel was already flourishing in Egypt, and Babylonian scientists had written upon astronomy and mathematics before Sargon of Akkad founded the first Semitic empire at the beginning of the third millennium B.C. A postal service had been organised along the roads that intersected Western Asia, and some of the clay seals which took the place of stamps, and bore the name of Sargon's son, are now in the Museum of the Louvre. Many of the original letters of Hammurabi and his immediate successors are preserved in the museums of Europe, and testify to the minute care with which the king attended to the affairs of an empire that extended

Postal Service Before 3000 B.C. from Elam on the east to Palestine on the west. All classes and both sexes took part in a correspondence which went on increasing in activity as the centuries passed, until in the age of the Tell el-Amarna tablets, about a century before the Exodus, it included not only Babylonia and Assyria, Egypt and Canaan, but Asia Minor as well.

The script and language of the correspondence were those of Babylonia, which had become the literary and diplomatic script and language of the day. The Egyptian Government itself had to use them when corresponding with its own officials in Palestine. Even at Boghaz Köi, the capital of the Hittites in distant Cappadocia, the foreign characters were employed, though the language they were called upon to express was the native language of the country whenever home affairs were discussed. But even among the Hittites all subjects of an international nature were written in Assyro-Babylonian. The fact bears witness to the long continuance and profound influence of the Babylonian empire in the West in days which until recently we had been taught to consider "prehistoric."

The culture of Babylonia grew up under similar conditions to that of Egypt.

Both alike developed on the banks of great rivers, whose annual overflow was regulated and directed by engineering science. Both alike rested on the agriculture which was thus made possible, as well as upon a climate with regular seasons and sufficient warmth to allow of social intercourse out-of-doors. The farmer thus knew beforehand what weather to expect, while the people were not separated one from another in isolated households or small communities. In the great plain of Babylonia or the Egyptian delta, there were not even mountain chains to keep them apart. As soon as the rivers had been embanked, and their waters directed over the fields, or diverted into canals, the struggle of man with Nature practically ceased; thenceforth he could settle down to a life of orderly method and leisure. But the regulation of the rivers implied organisation and a directing brain; here, therefore, as in later days in China, organised states first arose, at the head of which was the king.

It is difficult to believe that the engineering science which transformed the trackless swamp into the cultivated field could have grown up independently in two different parts of the ancient world. And since the problem that faced the engineers of Babylonia, where the annual inundation occurred after, and not before, the period of sowing, was more complicated than that with which the irrigation engineers of Egypt had to deal, it is natural to suppose that Egypt would have derived its engineering knowledge from Babylonia.

REVEALERS OF THE PAST

A group of the most notable archæologists, to whose labours so much of our knowledge of the ancient empires is due. 1, Professor A. H. Sayce; 2, Professor W. M. Flinders Petrie; 3, Professor Lepsius; 4, Sir A. H. Layard; 5, Hormuzd Rassam, the chief assistant and successor to Sir A. H. Layard; 6, Sir Gardner Wilkinson.

Photos by Elliott & Fry and Maull & Fox

That there was a close connection between the culture of Babylonia and that of primitive Egypt is now known. The Egyptians of the early " dynastic " era made use of the Babylonian seal-cylinder and impressed the characters engraved upon it on soft clay; in a land of stone they imitated the Babylonians in constructing their buildings of brick; they reckoned time in the Babylonian fashion, and carved vessels of hard stone of Babylonian shape. Even the strange composite monsters of Babylonian invention were reproduced by the artists of Egypt. The Egyptian language itself bears testimony to its Asiatic origin; it belongs fundamentally to the Semitic family of speech, though it has been subjected to a strong African influence. This African influence must be due to the fact that the "dynastic" Egyptians — the Egyptians, that is to say, who drained the marshes, established organised states, and founded what we mean by Egyptian culture — found a population of African origin already existing in the valley of the Nile. Recent excavations have brought the remains of this early population to light, and have allowed us to reconstruct their mode of life. In three essential respects they differed from the Egyptians of history. They were unacquainted with the use of metals, their tools and weapons being of stone; they did not practise the art of writing; and they were herdsmen of the desert rather than agriculturists. But they had attained to a considerable amount of civilisation of their own. Some of their flint implements are exquisite works of art, their vases of hard stone are well made and of artistic shape, and their pottery was of a high order.

There had been a stone age in Babylonia, as in Egypt; but at this early period the greater part of the Babylonian plain was still under water, what settlements

A Land in the Making there were being on the rocky plateaus to the east and west of the Tigris and Euphrates. The plain, called Edina, or the land of Eden, by its inhabitants, was formed by the silt brought by the rivers from the mountains of the north, and it was while it was in course of formation that the discovery of the use of copper was made, and a picture writing was introduced. The copper was imported from abroad, thus carrying back the commercial relations of Babylonia to the very dawn of history, while a running hand or cursive script developed out of the pictorial hieroglyphs. Wood and stone were alike scarce; clay was plentiful, and it was accordingly employed as a writing material. The written characters were impressed upon it by means of a reed pen or metal stylus, the result being that they assumed a wedge-like shape, and became what is known as cuneiform.

The stone age had been of very long duration. At Susa, in Elam, the strata representing it are of great depth, and the pottery that characterises it had time to make its way westward to the Mediterranean, and even to the shores of Spain. But, as in Egypt, so, too, in Babylonia, it is prehistoric; history begins in each country with the use of metals and the art of writing.

In each country, also, history begins with a number of independent states. In Egypt these gradually coalesced into two kingdoms, those of the north and south. The capital of the southern kingdom was at Hieraconpolis, north of Edfu; its

Deification of the Monarchs kings regarded themselves as the successors and vicegerents of Horus, the hawk-god, and divine honours were paid to them. In Babylonia, also, the king was a god. How far back this deification of the Babylonian monarch may go, however, it is at present impossible to say. The first kings of whom we have evidence that they were worshipped during their lifetime were Sargon of Akkad and his son. It has, therefore, been thought

that the belief and custom originated among the Semites, and that the deification needed the sanction of the priests of the great sanctuary of Nippur.

Nippur and Eridu were the two sacred cities of primeval Babylonia. Nippur, now Niffer, stood in the northern part of the Babylonian plain, to the south-west of the later Babylon. The city grew up round the temple of Enlil, the "lord," or Bel, of earth. Here American excavators have been patiently digging year after year. They have made their way through the vast mounds of ruin in which the past history of the temple is recorded down to the virgin soil. But everywhere there is the same tale to tell. Even the lowest strata contain written monuments which show that the primeval hieroglyphs had already passed into the cursive or cuneiform stage. Babylonia was already a land of culture; it possessed organised states under kings or high-priests, and had already reached a comparatively high level of art. Hard stones were cut into seals in the form of cylinders and covered with delicate

Art and Culture in Earliest Babylonia engravings, and at Tello —the ancient Lagash— in Southern Babylonia, French explorers have brought to light a large vase of silver, dedicated in early days by the priest-king Entemena and richly chased with figures of two-headed eagles, heifers, and lions [see tenth illustration on page 1587].

The primitive inhabitants of the Babylonian plain belonged to a beardless, round-headed race, usually termed Sumerian [see pages 266 and 1594]. They spoke an agglutinative language, like that, for instance, of the modern Turks or Finns, which is called in the native inscriptions "the language of Sumer," or Southern Babylonia. To them were due all the elements of Babylonian civilisation. It was they who had drained the marshes, had built the great cities of the country, and invented the cuneiform system of writing. Later ages believed that their culture had come to them from the Persian Gulf. Tradition told how Ea, the culture-god of Eridu, once the seaport of Babylonia, had risen morning by morning from the waters of the sea, bringing with him a knowledge of all the arts and industries of life. The tradition points to intercourse with the incense-bearing lands of Southern Arabia, and the culture that follows in the track of maritime trade. For just as Nippur in the north was the cradle of agriculture and the reclamation of the Babylonian plain, so Eridu was the birthplace of Babylonian navigation. In the days when it was founded—some seven or eight thousand years ago—it was on an inlet of the Persian Gulf; now the growth of the land through the silt annually deposited by the Tigris and Euphrates has made it more than a hundred miles distant from the shore. Even in the historical age of Babylonia it had ceased to be a seaport [see map on page 260].

Babylonian Account of Good and Evil

But its religious influence continued to the last. It was the home of the spells and incantations to which the Babylonians trusted for protection against the demons who were believed to surround them on all sides. While the darker side of Babylonian religion was represented by Nippur, its brighter side was reflected in Eridu. Enlil of Nippur was lord of the demons, whose habitation was in the dark places of the earth, whence they issued to terrify and plague mankind; it was the office of Ea of Eridu and his son " Asari, the good being," to discover how to counteract their malice and communicate the knowledge to man. At Babylon, which seems to have been originally a colony from Eridu, Asari passed into Marduk, the Sun-god who, when his city became the capital of Babylonia, superseded and abolished the older gods of the country, including Ea and Enlil themselves.

But long before this happened a new race had entered the land. Semitic nomads and settlers poured in from the Arabian side of the Euphrates, and established themselves securely in Akkad, the northern half of Babylonia. Thence they made their way northward into the later Assyria, and even into the mountains of Elam to the east. They soon adopted the higher culture of the Sumerians, and gave it a fresh development and a new impulse. Out of the fusion of the Semite and the Sumerian arose the culture and civilisation known to us as Babylonian, which made so profound an impression upon Western Asia, and through Western Asia upon the world. In Akkad the culture, like the language, became predominantly Semitic; in Sumer, on the other hand, the older population succeeded better in holding its own and

Origin of Babylonian Civilisation

in retaining its language down to comparatively modern times.

For a while it seemed as if the Semitic race were to be the ruling power from the shores of the Mediterranean to the deserts of Persia. Like the Arabs in the early days of Islam, they spread in a resistless stream from east to west. Recent excavations in Palestine have shown that at least as early as the third millennium before our era they had dispossessed the older Neolithic people of their territory and were filling Syria with cities surrounded by massive walls. The older people had not been acquainted with the use of metals; they were a long-headed race who lived in caverns, and buried their dead. The Semites brought with them a knowledge of copper, which had long been employed in Babylonia, and it was doubtless the superiority of their weapons of war which enabled them to conquer and hold their new possessions in the west. They burned their dead instead of burying them, and the caverns of the earlier race were replaced by houses of brick and cities built in imitation of those of the Babylonian plain. To the Babylonians these Semites of Palestine and Syria were known as Amorites, and, as trade developed along the high-roads that ran between the Euphrates and the Mediterranean, Amorite merchants passed to and fro between Canaan and Babylonia, and Amorite traders settled in the Babylonian towns.

The First Semitic Imperialist

The time was ripe for the rise of a Semitic empire in Western Asia, and this came with the conquest of Sargon of Akkad. The date of Sargon is given as the beginning of the third millennium B.C. by Nabonidus, who was an antiquarian as well as a Babylonian monarch, and had at his disposal innumerable records which have now perished. Sargon's capital was at Akkad, a suburb of Sippar, north of Babylon, which is mentioned for the first time in the annals of his reign. His first work was to unify Babylonia itself; next he led his victorious army across mountains and deserts, subduing Elam on the one side and the provinces of Syria on the other. His campaigns in " the land of the Amorites " occupied him for three years; then, we are told, he formed his widespread dominions into " a single empire," and assumed the proud title of " King of the Four Zones." Nearly the whole of the known world acknowledged his rule. His policy and conquests were continued by his son and successor Naram-Sin, who marched as far as Magan, or Western Arabia, and there wrenched the copper mines of Sinai from Egyptian hands. The empire was knit together by a system of roads and posts ; at home, literature was encouraged, and libraries of clay books were collected together. The cuneiform script was modified and perfected, and the gem-cutter's art attained a degree of excellence which it never reached again in later ages. Sculpture also made similar progress, and a broken bas-relief of the king found in Mesopotamia is one of the finest examples that have come down to us of the sculptor's art in Babylonia.

Semitic Power at its Greatest Height

But the empire of Sargon and his son represents the apogee of Semitic power in Western Asia. The wave of Semitic progress had already begun to ebb, and it never overpassed the bounds to which it had already attained. In Elam Semitic governors were replaced by native kings, and the language of its capital, Susa, ceased to be Semitic Babylonian and became agglutinative. The provinces of the west regained their independence, though the memory of the empire of Sargon was never lost, and was again and again invoked in later times to enforce the claims of Babylonian supremacy. In Babylonia itself, at all events in the southern part of the country, Sumerian princes once more held rule, and the brilliant epoch which had witnessed the union of Semite and Sumerian was succeeded, as is generally the case in the East, by a long period of stagnation.

Meanwhile, Egypt also had been passing through a period of high attainment, in culture, to be followed by stagnation and decay. Here, too, there had been a fusion of two races. But whereas in Babylonia it had been the non-Semitic race from which the civilising impulse was derived, in Egypt it was the invaders from Asia who had brought with them the elements of a higher civilisation. Later tradition ascribed their conquest of the Nile valley—without doubt, justly—to their possession of metal weapons, and traced their gradual progress from south to north. Near Edfu they had first

Egypt Civilised from Asia

reached the Nile after their passage across the eastern desert, and thence they made their way northward, erecting a sanctuary at each spot where they had been victorious over their foes.

For several centuries Egypt was divided into two kingdoms. It was during this period that the so-called " dynastic " civilisation was matured ; the land was drained and canalised, cities were built, the hieroglyphic script was evolved, and the government organised. Eventually, Menes, the hereditary king of This, in the neighbourhood of the modern Girga, succeeded in uniting " the two lands " of the south and north, and founding the first dynasty of the united monarchy. His own tomb has been discovered at Negada, north of Thebes ; those of his successors close to the reputed sepulchre of the god Osiris at Abydos, the sanctuary of This. The objects disinterred from the tombs prove to how high a level Egyptian culture had already advanced. There was trade with the Red Sea on the one side, and with the Ægean on the other, the obsidian of Melos being worked into exquisitely shaped vases ; the art of the goldsmith and jeweller had attained to high perfection, and household furniture was wrought into artistic forms. A cursive hand had been evolved from the hieroglyphic signs, and massive blocks of granite were hewn out of the quarries of Assuan and floated on rafts down the river to This, there to be shaped for architectural purposes. In the age of Menes Egyptian civilisation was already nearing its bloom.

The Bloom of Egypt's Civilisation

It was in the schools and workshops of Memphis, however, the capital of the united monarchy, that this bloom displayed itself in all its fulness. Memphis had been built on an embankment won by Menes from the Nile, whose original course he had diverted into a new channel some seventy miles in length. Egyptian history thus begins with a stupendous work of engineering, the reality of which has been verified by modern English engineers. It was no wonder, therefore, that under the fourth dynasty, some four thousand years before our era, the development of mechanical science went hand in hand with that of art. The huge granite blocks used in the construction of the great pyramid of Gizeh were cut with tubular drills fitted with points of a stone hard as the diamond—an instrument which was rediscovered only when the Mont Cenis tunnel was half completed. The hardest of hard stones were carved into statuary instinct with life and portraiture; indeed, one of the finest statues in the world is that of Khafra, the builder of the second pyramid at Gizeh, which is of a greenish diorite. The king is seated on his throne with the imperial hawk behind his head, and the face—speaking likeness though it clearly is—wears the divine calm of an omnipotent god. So far as the sculptor's art was concerned, its history in Egypt after the age of the fourth dynasty was that of a continuous decline.

A hawk's head of gold, with obsidian eyes, found at Hieraconpolis, shows that the goldsmith's art was equally advanced. A statue of King Pepi of the sixth dynasty, more than life-size, and made of hammered copper, which was found at the same place, bears similar testimony as regards work in other metals.

But with the sixth dynasty the Old Empire of Egypt comes suddenly to an end. Memphis became the scene of revolution and struggles for power; the political organisation of the country, which had rested on the divinely-derived autocracy of the king, was broken up, and Egypt passed into its feudal stage. The great landowners became a feudal nobility, who acknowledged the authority of the Pharaoh in name, but ignored it in fact, and even the old line of kings ceased to exist. The ninth and tenth dynasties belonged to the provincial city of Heracleopolis; but they possessed neither the power nor the prestige of their predecessors, and after carrying on war for several generations with the rival princes of Thebes, they too passed away. Henceforward, Thebes, which had grown up around the ancient sanctuary of Amon at Karnak, became the leading city in the valley of the Nile.

Egypt in the Feudal Stage

In the strong and capable hands of the three Theban dynasties which constituted " the Middle Empire," Egypt again took its place in the front rank of history and civilisation. The artistic impulse which in the time of the Old Empire had found expression in statuary, now turned to architecture; stately temples of stone arose all over the country, adorned with sculpture and painting, the execution of which, if we may judge from the recently excavated eleventh dynasty temple of Mentu-hotep at Thebes, was exceptionally fine. Great engineering works were undertaken for regulating and distributing the waters of the inundation and for improving the system of irrigation which the political disturbances of the last few centuries had allowed to fall into decay. The Fayyum was reclaimed and a large additional acreage of cultivable land given to the Egyptian agriculturists. But the control also of the river necessitated the control also of the regions in the south through which it flowed. Egypt consequently became, for the first time, a conquering power; the Sudan was added to the dominions of the Pharaoh, and the cataracts were guarded by strongly built fortresses. The armies which had been trained in war with the negroes of the south, were used for service in the north also. The desert, which had hitherto separated Egypt from Asia, was crossed, and the Amorites of Southern Palestine were forced to send tribute to Thebes.

The First Egyptian Conquests

Scarabs and stone vases of the twelfth dynasty have been met with in the excavations at Gezer, west of Jerusalem. Here, too, the tombstone of an Egyptian of the same age has been discovered in the " high-place " of the city—a line of nine great monoliths, surrounded with a platform of stone, under the pavement of which have been found the bones of infants who had been burnt or otherwise sacrificed to the gods of Canaan. The high-place was that of the second city built by the Semitic settlers on the site, the huge stone wall of which was intersected with towers. Objects of bronze occur among the ruins of this second town in harmony with the fact that the earliest bronze of Egypt belongs to the epoch of the twelfth dynasty. A knowledge of the metal, it is probable, had come alike to Egypt and to Canaan from Asia Minor, to which the first use of it has been traced. Was it from Britain that the tin was brought with which the alloy was made? The gold of Asia Minor had already been transported to Egypt in the age of the sixth dynasty.

Egyptian Arts from Asia Minor

The pottery of Asia Minor followed in the wake of the metal trade. Before the second Amorite city at Gezer came to an end, the polychrome pottery of the Hittites, north of the Halys, had not only

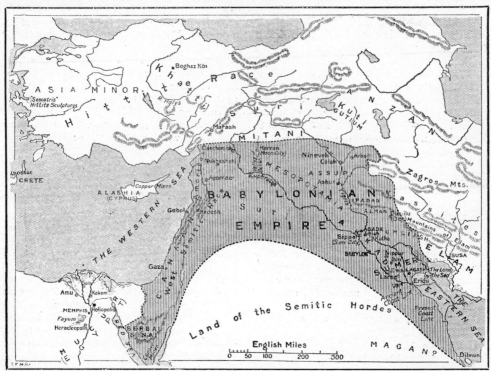

The centres of civilisation in the third millennium B.C., and the Babylonian Empire of Sargon of Akkad, Hammurabi and his successors, until the eve of the Kassite and Hittite domination in the sixteenth and fifteenth centuries B.C.

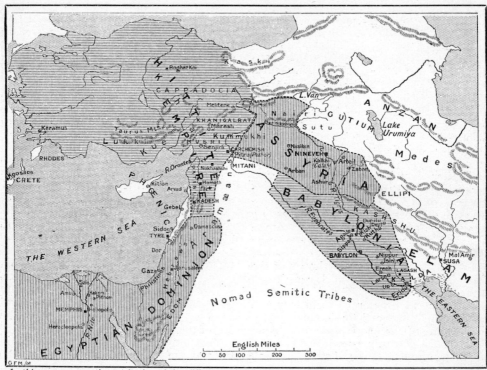

In this map we see the territories of the different empires that developed out of the first Babylonian Empire between B.C. 1500 and 1000, showing the balance of power between the twelfth and tenth centuries B.C.

THE EARLY EMPIRES OF THE ANCIENT NEAR EAST

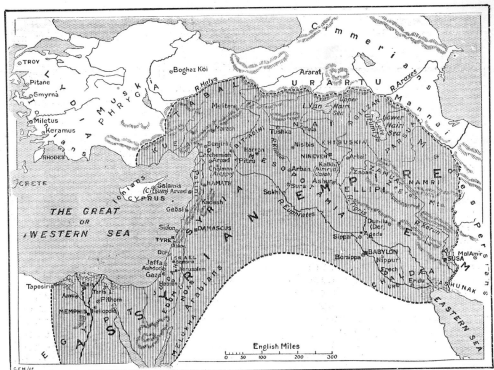

The development of the Assyrian Empire and of the peoples and towns absorbed by its growth, from the tenth century B.C. to the time of its greatest expansion in the seventh century, is illustrated in the above map.

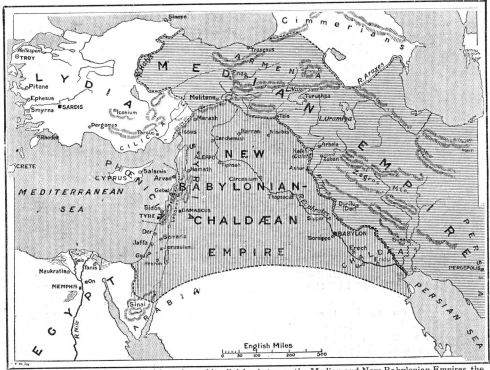

The empires that rose on the fall of Assyria, and its division between the Median and New Babylonian Empires, the whole constituting the Persian Empire until the rise of Alexander, covering the sixth, fifth, and fourth centuries B.C.

THE LATER EMPIRES OF THE ANCIENT NEAR EAST

made its way to Palestine, but had to a large extent superseded the native pottery of the country. It is possible that it had also influenced the arts of the islands in the Greek seas. At all events, excavation in Crete has brought to light vases of egg-shell faience, exquisitely decorated in various colours with flowers and other conventionalised emblems. The faience is generally known as " Kamares ware," from the name of the place where it was first found, and it characterises the period called by Dr. Evans, " Middle Minoan II."

High Culture of Early Crete

The discovery of the highly developed culture of early Crete is one of the most striking revelations of archæological science. There, as elsewhere in the Levant, a neolithic age of long duration was succeeded by one in which copper took the place of stone. The copper was in great measure derived from the mines of Cyprus. How early the latter were worked is shown by the fact that innumerable seals of cylinder shape, made in imitation of those of Babylonia, have been found in Cyprian graves of the early copper age, and that these seals go back to the period of Sargon of Akkad. One of the commonest symbols engraved upon them is the picture of a copper ingot, often accompanied by a bull's head, which in Crete represented a weight. We may thus see in them the signets of the Cyprian exporters of the metal.

The conquest of Sargon of Akkad had carried a knowledge of Babylonian culture to the shores of the Mediterranean. Of this culture, the use of the seal-cylinder and of clay as a writing material formed an integral part, and wherever they are found their presence is a sure witness of Babylonian influence. The Cretan tablets of clay, which have been discovered in such abundance in the ancient palaces of the island, thus point unmistakably towards Babylonia. They make their earliest appearance in what Dr. Evans has termed the first stage in the Middle Minoan period, though the strange hieroglyphs incised upon them go back to the third and last stage of an earlier epoch. This epoch, which followed the neolithic age, is itself divided into three stages, to the last of which belong the seals of button shape, whose original home was in Asia Minor, and which in the time of the

Babylonian Influence in Crete

sixth dynasty replaced the older seal-cylinder in Egypt. To the same stage belong also the geometric designs which distinguish the early Ægean pottery, and which, thanks to recent discoveries, can now be traced back through Asia Minor to Elam on the east of Babylonia. Here, M. De Morgan has found abundance of pottery of exactly the same character which was manufactured in the neolithic ages long before the epoch of Sargon.

The second and third stages in the Middle Minoan period represent the high-water mark of Cretan civilisation. It was then that the splendid palaces of the Cretan kings were first built, with their spacious halls, their frescoed walls, their elaborate drainage, and their luxurious bath-rooms. The absence of walls or forts to protect them proves plainly that those who built them were lords of the sea, with no fear of the invader before their eyes. The beautiful " Kamares " pottery, with which they were filled, was imitated from vessels of gold and silver, while porcelain like that of Egypt was moulded into realistic figures of fish and animals and plants, and a linear or cursive script makes its appearance by the side of the hieroglyphic writing. But the palaces in which all this magnificence and luxury had been displayed were sacked and burned, and for a time Cretan culture passed under eclipse. It revived again at the beginning of the " Late Minoan " period ; the palaces rose once more in their former splendour, and in the south a summer villa was erected whose walls were decorated with the choicest specimens of the painter's art. A change had, however, come over the face of Cretan culture. The old hieroglyphics had made way for linear characters similar to those used in Cyprus and at Troy ; bronze was taking the place of copper, and the long sword was substituted for the dirk. The pottery, moreover, had assumed the form known as " Mycenæan," and was already beginning to degenerate. But wealth was still abundant ; at Cnossos the ruler sat in state on an elaborately fashioned throne and watched the bull-fights and boxing matches in the arena of the theatre where slaves and captives made sport for their Cretan masters. A sword has been found with its pommel formed of translucent agate, and its hilt plated with gold and engraved with delicate designs, while the royal draught-

Cretan Kings as Lords of the Sea

board has been disinterred from its grave of centuries still brilliant with gold and silver, ivory and crystal, and the blue glass paste of which we read in the Homeric poems. The art displayed in some of the objects that have been brought to light was never surpassed, even in the later Greek world. The ivory figure of a diver, or the religious procession exquisitely carved on a vase of black steatite, declares in no uncertain tone that the art of classical Greece was but a renaissance. The lords of Minoan Crete, however, were no Greeks ; that is made clear by their portraits on the Egyptian monuments as well as by the strange composite figures of their religious art—combinations of a man and bull, of an eagle and a woman, or a winged cherub with a lion's legs.

Grecian Art a Cretan Renaissance

The Middle Minoan period of Crete was coincident with a period of decay and foreign rule in both Babylonia and Egypt. The Semitic empire of Sargon and his son Naram-Sin was succeeded by a revival of Sumerian power and influence. The Sumerian princes of Southern Babylonia made themselves independent or founded dynasties which claimed rule over the whole valley of the Euphrates. When the curtain rises once more, it is, however, again a Semitic dynasty, which claims to have inherited the empire of Sargon. But the dynasty has its seat not in Northern Babylonia, but in the south, in " Ur of the Chaldees," on the western bank of the Euphrates, where bodies of Amorites from Canaan and Bedouins from Arabia had long been settled. The dynasty extended over five reigns and lasted for 117 years. Numberless legal documents dated in the reigns of its kings have come down to us, and have made us well acquainted with the social life, the law and commerce, and religious beliefs of the time. The old supremacy of Babylonia in Western Asia, which had once belonged to Sargon, was again asserted, and Syria and Canaan were again laid under tribute. Gudea, the Sumerian high-priest of Lagash, who, vassal though he was of the king of Ur, nevertheless exercised an almost independent authority, ransacked the whole known world for the materials for his buildings. Blocks of limestone and alabaster were brought from Palestine and the Lebanon, beams of cedar from the Gulf of Antioch, gold-dust and acacia

Babylonia Again Triumphant

from the deserts of Northern Arabia, and diorite from the peninsula of Sinai, while other costly stones were quarried in the Taurus Mountains and floated down the Euphrates on rafts. About 2300 B.C. Gudea was viceroy of Dungi, the second king of the dynasty of Ur, who, like his father, the founder of the dynasty, covered Babylonia with his buildings and restorations. The provinces of the empire were carefully organised and taxed, and part of a cadastral survey made by Urimelech, the governor of Canaan, for the purpose of taxation is still in existence. But the dynasty went down in disaster. Its last representative was captured in battle against the Elamites, and the lordship of Babylonia passed to the kings of Isin, whose dynasty lasted for 225 years.

Then evil days fell upon Babylonia. City fought against city ; the Elamites raided it from the east, while Amorite invaders attacked it from the west. The Amorites eventually possessed themselves of the northern half of the country, and made Babylon their capital. For the first time in history it became the leading city in Babylonia, and, eventually—when the kingdom of the Amorite dynasty grew into an empire —the capital and holy city of the civilised Asiatic world. Marduk, its patron-god, followed the fortunes of his city ; he, too, became the supreme Bel, or " Lord," of the Babylonian deities in heaven, as his vicegerent and adopted son, the king of Babylon, was the supreme lord of their worshippers upon earth.

The Holy City of Civilised Asia

But it needed a long struggle before the new dynasty succeeded in overcoming all rival claimants to the throne of Western Asia, and in re-establishing the empire of Sargon. At one time it seemed as if Elam were destined to take the place of Babylonia, and the wave of Semitic influence which had been rolled back from the Elamite mountains would retreat from the Babylonian plain itself. Babylon was taken and plundered by the Elamite monarch, and Esagila, the temple of Bel-Merodach, was burnt with fire. Its king, Sin-muballit, disappears from history, and his son, Hammurabi, or Amraphel, a mere boy, was set on the vacant throne as an Elamite tributary. At the same time Southern Babylonia was transformed into another dependent state and given to an Elamite prince, Eri-Aku— called Rim-Sin by his Semitic subjects

1565

—who fixed his capital at Larsa. Eri-Aku's father was appointed governor of Syria and Palestine, which had passed to Elam with the conquest of Babylonia.

Hammurabi grew up and proved to be one of the ablest rulers that have ever lived. In the thirtieth year of his reign he felt himself strong enough to rise in rebellion against his Elamite suzerain. The forces of Elam were overthrown in a decisive battle, and Larsa forced to surrender. Once more Babylonia was united under a Semitic king, whose authority was acknowledged as far as the shores of the Mediterranean. Indeed, Hammurabi seems never to have forgotten his Amorite descent, and on one of his monuments found in Northern Mesopotamia the only title he bears is that of " King of the land of the Amorites."

With the restoration of peace and the consolidation of his power, Hammurabi set himself to the work of reorganising and administering the provinces of his empire. Nothing seems to have been either too great or too small to escape the notice of the king. Numerous letters of his, written by his own **Hammurabi** hand, have survived to us, **Law-giver** and they show that he took as **and King** much pains to investigate a complaint of bribery or oppression on the part of a petty official as he did to inquire into the administration of the Crown lands or the discipline of the standing army. The compilation of the great code of laws, which was henceforth to be obeyed throughout Western Asia, was his work. Babylonian law, like English law, was " judge-made," and its codification was at once a desirable and a difficult task. One of the most remarkable points about the code is its purely secular character ; the gods may be invoked in the introduction and peroration, but in the code itself it is the civil law as laid down by the judges and sanctioned by the authority of the king that is alone regarded. Equally remarkable is the way in which the old law of blood-revenge is superseded in it by a system of fixed legal penalties, which can be inflicted only by the judge after full and impartial trial.

The publication of the code was doubtless suggested by the efforts Hammurabi was called upon to make for the suppression of crime, and more especially the acts of brigandage, to which the intestine troubles of Babylonia had given

rise. But it was also part of a literary revival which characterises the age of Hammurabi as it had characterised the age of Sargon. The great Chaldæan Epic of Gilgamesh was composed, embodying older poems or traditions, other literary works were re-edited or published for the first time, astronomical and medical treatises were compiled, com- **Literature** mentaries were written upon **4,000** the earlier literature of the **Years Ago** country, and grammars, dictionaries, and reading books were drawn up to facilitate the study of Sumerian. Learned men as well as poets and lawyers were welcomed at the court, and the libraries of Babylonia were again stocked with books on clay. Foremost among these were collections of the letters which passed between the king and his high officials.

The long reign of Hammurabi was followed by that of his son, Samsu-iluna, who, like his successor Abishu, made vain attempts to suppress a revolt which had broken out in the marshy lands at the head of the Persian Gulf, where the Aramæan tribe of Kaldâ, or Chaldæans, afterwards settled. Here an independent dynasty established itself which, on the fall of the house of Hammurabi, may have succeeded in making itself master of the whole of Babylonia. This did not happen, however, until the death of Samsu-ditana, the third successor of Abishua. His power had been weakened, if not shattered, by an invasion of Babylonia by the Hittites from Cappadocia, when it seems probable that Babylon itself was captured and its temple despoiled.

The kings of " the sea-coast " did not long enjoy their possession of the disunited and tottering kingdom. Wild Kassite hordes poured down upon the Babylonian plain from the mountains of Elam, and eventually founded a dynasty at Babylon, which lasted for 576 years. But the spell of Babylonian culture soon passed over the semi-barbarous con- **Barbarians** querors ; the Kassite kings **in** became Babylonian in manners **Babylonia** and customs, even in language and names. Their foreign origin, however, was never forgotten, and in spite of intermarriages with the Semites of Assyria and of Babylonia itself, their right to the inheritance of Sargon of Akkad was never fully recognised. Like the Hanoverians in England, their " right divine " was rejected, and with the rise of the Kassite dynasty the deification of the Babylonian monarch comes practically to an end.

One result of the fall of the Hammurabi dynasty and the Kassite conquest was the loss of the Babylonian empire in the west. It is true that Babylon still claimed to be mistress of western Asia, and the Tell el-Amarna letters are **Babylon Loses its Foreign Power** witness that even when Canaan had become an Egyptian province, Babylonia was still ready to intrigue with its inhabitants against their new masters. But, politically, Syria and Palestine were never again to be Babylonian until the day came when Nebuchadnezzar restored the old glories of his fatherland and created the second Babylonian empire. Babylon, indeed, continued to be the sacred city of Asiatic civilisation; it was revered as the venerable fountain-head of Asiatic culture and theology, but its political supremacy was gone. Babylonian influence ceases to be a living principle outside the valleys of the Tigris and Euphrates, and the Babylonian culture of Western Asia and in the lands of the Mediterranean becomes merely the inheritance of the past.

In Babylonia itself the Kassite conquest completed the work of unifying the Semitic and Sumerian elements in the population which had been begun under the Hammurabi dynasty. Thenceforward there is only one people, the Babylonians of later history, outwardly Semitic, though inwardly Sumerian. The language is Semitic, but, like English, profoundly modified by the foreign element; the religion is also Semitic, but its roots lie far back in Sumerian animism. The spirits of the ancient cult pass into human deities, in accordance with the Semitic belief that man was made in the image of the gods, and conversely the gods revealed themselves in the image of man. The changes that thus passed over the map of Western Asia were reflected **Barbarians in Egypt** in the valley of the Nile. The Pharaohs of the Middle Empire had shown how the desert which separated them from Asia could be crossed, and the lesson was soon learnt by their enemies. The Semites of Canaan and Arabia descended upon Egypt and founded the three successive dynasties known as Hyksos, or Shepherd, which lasted for more than 500 years. Like the Kassites in Babylonia, they were rude warriors armed with the bow and unskilled in the arts of life when they first poured over Egypt like a flood. Its cities were sacked and destroyed, and its temples profaned; but, like the Kassites, they, too, soon passed under the spell of a higher civilisation. The Hyksos court became outwardly Egyptian, the kings assumed the old titles, and even gave themselves Egyptian names. Science and literature were patronised, and one of the Egyptian works on mathematics that has come down to us was written for a Hyksos Pharaoh; but, as in Babylonia, so also in Egypt, the foreign origin of the new line of kings was never forgotten. Up to the last they were compelled to garrison it like a foreign country; and their court was fixed in the Delta, where they could be in touch with their kinsmen in Asia.

As long as the Hyksos rule lasted Egypt was an appanage of Canaan. The desert ceased to be a dividing line between the two countries, just as in Norman days the English Channel ceased to be a dividing line between Normandy and its English province. The **Why Joseph Ruled in Egypt** Semites of Canaan passed to and fro across it, and, like Abraham, found a welcome at the court of their Hyksos kinsfolk. That a Hebrew like Joseph should rise to be Vizier was no marvel; nor was it strange that he should reduce the native population to a state of serfdom, and thereby strengthen the power of their Hyksos masters.

But through all the centuries of Hyksos domination the Egyptians were awaiting their opportunity for revolt. Tradition averred that the opportunity was given by an attack on the native religion. The religious passions of the people of Upper Egypt were aroused, and the Prince of Thebes headed the insurrection. For five generations the struggle was carried on; it ended in the expulsion of the foreigner and the foundation of the native eighteenth dynasty by Ahmes I., about 1600 B.C.

The war which had been begun in Egypt was carried into Asia. Under Ahmes and his successors Canaan was made an Egyptian province, and the boundaries of the Egyptian empire were fixed at the banks of the Euphrates and the ranges of the Taurus. The campaigns of Thothmes III. brought boundless spoil and numberless captives to Egypt, while the gold-mines which were opened in the eastern desert made it the California of the ancient world. Maritime trade was encouraged, and Cyprus and Crete paid tribute to the Pharaoh. Even at distant Mycenæ, on the mainland of Greece, plaques of porcelain were imported from Egypt to adorn the palace of its rulers. Gifts came from the king of Assyria which the Egyptian courtiers construed into tribute. In the south the Sudan was once more conquered, and Egyptian temples were erected on the banks of the Upper Nile.

Egypt Realises the Dangers of Empire

But the Asiatic empire of Egypt brought with it the destruction of the dynasty to which it owed its origin. The court became Asiatised. The Pharaohs married Asiatic wives, and filled the high places of state with Asiatic officials. Eventually a king arose who attempted to overthrow the national faith of which he was the official guardian, and to substitute for it a kind of pantheistic monotheism. He changed his own name from that of Amon-hotep to Khu-n-Aten, "the brilliance of the solar disc"—the visible symbol of the new deity—and for the first time in history there was persecution for religion's sake. But the priesthood of Thebes were too powerful for the king. He was forced to quit Thebes and build a new capital further north, at Tel lel-Amarna, where he gave daily lectures on the articles of his creed, and erected a temple to Aten, as well as a palace for himself, gorgeous with statues and frescoes, and glittering with gilded bronze.

The archives of Thebes were moved at the same time to the foreign office of the new city, where their discovery in 1887 brought about a complete revolution in our conceptions of ancient Oriental history. They consist of letters and despatches written in cuneiform characters and the Babylonian language on tablets of clay. They prove that the culture of Western Asia was so thoroughly Babylonian that even the Egyptian Government had to correspond with its own officials in the foreign language and script. They also prove how widely diffused education must have been. Not only were the educated classes of Canaan, including ladies, able to read and write in Babylonian cuneiform ; it was also the common medium

Education in the Ancient East

of educated intercourse throughout the eastern world. Not only the kings of Assyria and Babylon, but the kings of the Hittites and Cappadocia, of Mesopotamia and the coast of Asia Minor used it as well. The roads must have been kept in good order, for the posts were constantly passing to and fro along them. So, too, were the commercial travellers, for whose benefit a system of international law had been organised.

Canaan was governed much as India is governed to-day. There were protected states as well as cities under Egyptian governors. From time to time Egyptian high commissioners traversed the country, which was garrisoned partly by native troops, partly by a small force of Egyptians. Bodies of Bedouins were in the service of the petty princes and governors, together with numbers of Hittite freelances, who sold their services to the highest bidder. In later days when the authority of the home Government was growing weak, these hired troops and their paymasters fought with one another, and endless were the complaints brought before the Egyptian king by one governor against another. The vassal king of Jerusalem, who seems to have been of Hittite origin, was especially clamorous, and also especially urgent that Egyptian troops should be sent to his help.

Canaan a Parallel to India

But the Egyptian Government was already involved in difficulties at home. Civil and religious war was breaking out in Egypt itself, and when Khu-n-Aten died, leaving only daughters behind him, the doom of the eighteenth dynasty was sealed. A few short reigns followed, and then the nineteenth dynasty was founded in the person of Ramses I., about 1350 B.C. It represented the national reaction against the Canaanite and the foreigner who had captured Khu-n-Aten and his court. The Asiatic strangers were driven from the country or reduced to serfdom, and the high offices of state were again held by native Egyptians. The Asiatic provinces of Egypt had been lost, and it was necessary to reconquer them. To this task Seti I., the son of Ramses I., accordingly set himself, and when he was succeeded by his son, Ramses II., Canaan was once more a province of Egypt. North of Canaan, however, the Syrian province had fallen into the hands of the Hittites, who had established their southern capital at Kadesh, on the Orontes, and were threatening Canaan itself. The struggle for its possession was long and strenuous, but at last, in the twenty-first year of Ramses, the two antagonists, weary and exhausted, agreed to come to terms. A treaty was drawn up, offensive and defensive, recognising the existing boundaries of the two empires, and providing for the pardon and return from exile of all political offenders.

The rest of Ramses' long reign of sixty-seven years was mainly spent in covering Egypt with his buildings or in restoring and usurping the monuments of his predecessors. Of all his own monuments, the most famous is Abu-Simbel, in Nubia, where a temple has been carved out of a mountain. Among the cities built by him were Ramses and Pithom in the Delta, at which the Israelites were compelled to toil.

Ramses II. was succeeded by his son Meneptah. The death of the "Grand Monarque" of Egyptian history was the signal for attack on the part of the surrounding nations. The Libyans from the **The Grand** west overran the Delta, while **Monarque** ships filled with Achæans and **of Egypt** Lycians and other tribes of the eastern basin of the Mediterranean invaded the coast. But in the fifth year of Meneptah the threatened destruction of Egyptian civilisation was averted by a decisive victory which he gained over the invading hordes. The Libyans and their allies were practically exterminated. It was under the cover of this Libyan invasion that the Israelites—called *Israelu* on a monument of the Pharaoh—would seem to have escaped from their Egyptian taskmasters; the land of Goshen was deserted, and three years later we find its pasturage handed over to Edomite herdsmen.

But neither the Egyptian monarchy nor the dynasty that ruled it recovered from the blow which the barbarians from the west and north had dealt it. Its Asiatic empire was lost for ever, and the frontier cities of Canaan which guarded the entrance to Asia fell into the hands of Philistine pirates from Crete. The nineteenth dynasty perished from decay, and after a short interval of anarchy was followed by the twentieth.

Once more Egypt was called upon to repel an attack of the northern tribes. But it was a more formidable confederacy

that Ramses III., the second king of the dynasty, had to face than that which had invaded Egypt half a century before. While the Libyans again entered the valley of the Nile from the west, the Philistines of Crete, the Danaans of Asia Minor, and other Greek and Asiatic tribes, forced their way through the Hittite territory into Syria, and moved **Egypt's Wars** southward, partly on land, **at the Time** partly by sea. After defeating **of the Exodus** the Libyans, Ramses marched into Canaan; the invaders were overthrown in battle, and pursued northwards to the harbour where they had stationed their fleet. Here a great maritime struggle took place, which ended in complete victory for the Egyptians. The ships of the enemy were destroyed, and vast numbers of prisoners taken. On its way back to Egypt, various Canaanitish towns surrendered or were captured; among them were Hebron and Jerusalem. The entrance of the Israelites into Canaan cannot have taken place long after this event.

Ramses III. was the last of the native Egyptian conquerors. His immediate successors became little more than puppets in the hands of the high-priests of Thebes, and when a strong Pharaoh again appeared on the throne it was in the person of Sheshonk or Shishak I., the founder of the twenty-second dynasty and chief of the Libyan bodyguard. But for many centuries Egypt ceased to be a factor in international politics; its influence did not extend beyond its own natural confines, and it needed all its strength to protect itself against the negro princes of the Sudan. One of them eventually overran Egypt, and plundered Memphis, while another succeeded in permanently occupying the country, and establishing a dynasty of Ethiopian kings. The Ethiopian conquest was followed by the Assyrian conquest; for a time Assyrian satraps **Egypt** collected tribute in the cities **Under** of Egypt and Assyrian armies **Eclipse** ruthlessly suppressed revolts against the foreign rule. In 662 B.C. Thebes—the No-Amon of the Old Testament—was sacked and burnt, and the ancient capital of Egypt lived thenceforward upon its past fame. When Egypt recovered its independence under Psammetichus and his successors of the twenty-sixth dynasty, the seat of power was transferred permanently to the north.

For five centuries from the age of Ramses III. to that of the Ethiopian Tirhakah—Egypt thus remained outside the sphere of international politics, in a sort of backwater of the world's history. Babylonia was in like condition ; the leadership had passed to other lands and younger races. At first it was the Hittites who promised to become the leading people in Western Asia.

Rise of the Hittites With their yellow skins, protrusive jaws, and beardless faces they descended from Cappadocia and the Taurus Mountains upon the fertile plains of Syria, and at an early date had possessed themselves of Carchemish, which commanded the ford over the Euphrates and the high-road of commerce from east to west. A kindred race founded a monarchy—that of Mitani—in Northern Mesopotamia, where in the age of the eighteenth Egyptian dynasty they became so powerful as to be allowed to marry into the Royal house of the Pharaohs. Long before this the Hittites had invaded Babylonia, and helped to overthrow the dynasty of Hammurabi, but it was not until the fifteenth century before our era that they founded an empire, which extended to the coasts of the Greek seas, and bid fair to make Canaan what the Assyrians called it, a "Hittite land." Under Khattu-sil I. and his successors the larger part of Asia Minor was transformed into a confederacy of vassal states ; Hittite soldiers poured southward through the passes of the Taurus, and the possession of Syria and Palestine was disputed with the Pharaohs of Egypt. The way had already been prepared by the Hittite freelances, who had hired their services to the Egyptian Government and the petty princes of Canaan ; as the power of Egypt declined the regular forces of the "great king of the Hittites" followed in their rear, and Kadesh on the Orontes was made the southern capital of his empire. The old Hittite capital at Boghaz Köi, north of the Halys, became one of the chief cities of the world ; strong walls of stone, wide in circuit, enclosed stately palaces and temples, which contained libraries of clay books inscribed in cuneiform characters, and written sometimes in the Assyrian language, sometimes in that of the Hittites themselves. A knowledge of the cuneiform script had doubtless been communicated to the Hittites by the Assyrian

Dominance of Hittite Empire

colonies which had been planted in the heart of Cappadocia as early as the age of Hammurabi, the ruins of one of which have been found at Kara Eyuk, near Kaisariyeh. It was the mineral wealth of Asia Minor that had attracted the colonists and raiders of Assyria and Babylonia ; the gold of the sixth Egyptian dynasty was already derived from its mines.

For a time the Hittites dominated the civilised world of the East. Their armies marched to Lydia, and carried their art and culture to Greek lands. The culture itself was of Babylonian origin, but had been modified in a peculiar fashion. Just as the cuneiform signs of Babylonia superseded the native hieroglyphs, except for monumental purposes, so, too, the native art had to give way before the artistic conceptions of the Babylonians, and even the old fetish worship of the country was replaced by the anthropomorphic divinities of Babylon. The Greek centaur and the winged horse Pegasus came from Babylonia to the West through Hittite intermediaries. A treaty between Ramses II. and the Hittite king marks the extreme limit of the Hittite advance. It is probable that the irruption of the northern tribes, which overthrew the foreign power of Egypt and sapped its internal forces, also broke up the Hittite empire. Isolated fragments of this empire alone survived ; there was never again a "great king" who could summon his vassals from the furthest bounds of Asia Minor, and treat on equal terms with one of the mightiest of the Egyptian Pharaohs.

Fall of Crete and the Hittites

It was to the movement of the northern tribes that the downfall of Cretan civilisation seems also to have been due. The maritime supremacy of Crete was lost ; pirates landed from the north and destroyed its palaces, and the dynasty of Minos passed away. The period at which this took place is coeval with that known as "Mycenæan," when a peculiar class of pottery was spread over the Ægean world, and when artists from the Greek seas made goblets and vases for the Egyptian Pharaoh Khu-n-Aten, and painted the floors of his palace at Tell el-Amarna with naturalistic scenes. A century or two later half-civilised Dorians, speaking the Greek language, streamed southward from their northern homes ; Mycenæ, Sparta, Crete, all alike were overwhelmed, and the old Minoan culture was lost and forgotten.

THE LATER EMPIRES

PHŒNICIA, ISRAEL, ASSYRIA AND PERSIA

THE break-up of the powers that had so long been supreme in the Oriental world was the opportunity of Canaan. At first it seemed as if Canaan, the battle-field of the nations, would itself be swallowed up in the cataclysm. The Israelites, fresh from their desert training, and moulded into a compact nationality by the legislation of Sinai and Kadesh, after an unsuccessful endeavour to invade Canaan from the south, overran the country east of the Jordan, and then forced their way into the plains and mountains of the West. The Canaanites, weakened by intestine feuds and the long war between Egypt and the Hittites, were in no condition to resist them; city after city fell into the hands of the rude desert tribes, and for a while became a deserted ruin. The native Canaanites retreated into the north or to the coastland of Phœnicia, or else made terms with the **Phœnicia Becomes a Power** invaders, and, as time went on, intermarried with them. The population of the coast had always been more maritime than agricultural; now they turned entirely to their sea trade. There were no longer either Cretan or Egyptian fleets to bar their enterprise, and the Greek seas soon passed into the possession of the Phœnician merchant-men. The murex was discovered with its purple dye, and Tyre and Sidon, with their companion cities, grew rich with the development of their trade. Phœnicia became the centre of the carrying trade of the civilised world, the intermediary between East and West. The art and culture of Asia was carried as far as Spain and the Straits of Gibraltar, Phœnician colonies were founded on the shores of Africa and Europe, and a new art arose in which Assyrian, Egyptian, and Asiatic elements were mingled together, without, however, any attempt at originality. The old amber trade from the Baltic to the head of the Adriatic passed into Phœnician hands; so, too, did the trade in British tin, which travelled overland to Massilia, the modern Marseilles.

Tyre, secure in its insular position, took the lead among the Phœnician cities. **Tyre, the Island City** Under Abibal and his son, Hiram I., its temple of Melkarth, its royal palace, and its fortifications, were rebuilt and enlarged, and the simpler Phœnician alphabet replaced the cumbrous cuneiform. Along with the change of script went a change in the literary language; the native language of Canaan—Hebrew, as we should call it—was substituted for Assyrian, and papyrus and parchment for the clay tablet.

The development of Israelitish power was synchronous with that of Phœnicia. An abortive attempt to establish an Israelitish monarchy had been made by Abimelech, but the tribes were not yet ripe for organised union. This was forced upon them by the Philistine conquest of the country; resistance to the "uncircumcised" foreigner from Crete developed first a feeling of common origin and worship, and then of the necessity for a leader in war. The destruction of the national sanctuary at Shiloh, with its priesthood and archives, removed what might have been a rival to the royal authority; Saul, indeed, fell in the struggle with the enemy, but under David and his able general, Joab, the Philistines were not only driven back, but compelled to acknowledge the supremacy **David, Emperor of Israel** of the Hebrew king. With an army behind him, composed partly of foreign mercenaries, David found himself strong enough not only to weld the Israelitish tribes into a monarchical state, but to create an empire which extended as far as the Euphrates. There was no other power in Western Asia to dispute his progress; Egypt and the

Hittites were alike effete; so were the Babylonians; and the Aramæans of Mesopotamia had successfully blocked the Assyrian advance.

The consolidation of the kingdom, begun by David, was completed by his son Solomon. Jerusalem had already been made a capital; now a new central sanctuary was erected in it, built by the king and attached like a chapel to the royal palace. As in Assyria, the king took the place of the high-priest. Alliance was made with Tyre, and the Israelitish treasury was replenished with the wealth which Tyrian trade helped to pour into it. But the extravagance of the king knew no bounds. Taxation was increased until the freemen of Israel began to murmur, and the subject territories to rebel. Expenditure was for the most part on palaces and similar luxuries, which brought the state but little profit, and foreign loans were as yet unknown. When Solomon died, the empire was already breaking in pieces, and discontent was seething at home. Without his prestige and experience, his son Rehoboam failed to meet it; the northern tribes burst into revolt, and from thenceforth a kingdom of Israel stood by the side of that of Judah. Of the empire of David all that was left were Edom, which was kept by Judah, and Moab, which went with Israel. Five years later, the Egyptian Pharaoh Shishak invaded Judah; Jerusalem was taken, its palace burned and its archives destroyed. Its short dream of political power was gone for ever; thenceforward it was in the world of religion, and not of politics, that its influence was to be felt.

Israel's Short Dream Ended

The political stage was thus cleared for the advent of Assyria. And for many centuries Assyria had been preparing itself for its future work. At first it had been merely the district surrounding the deified city of Assur, now Kala Sherghat, on the western bank of the Tigris. The names of the early kings and high-priests who had founded or repaired the Temple of Ashur were remembered down to later days, and from the first it had been a stronghold of the Semite. For many centuries it had been included in the Babylonian empire, and a letter of Hammurabi refers to the troops who were stationed there. With the Kassite conquest of Babylonia, Assyria recovered

Military Empire of Assyria

its independence and the high-priest became a king. The sources of his power lay in the north; there Nineveh had been built at the junction of the Tigris and the Upper Zab, and communication was kept up, not only with Southern Armenia, but even with the colonies in distant Cappadocia. Bronze, of which the earliest known examples have been found in Asia Minor, was imported into Palestine and Egypt on the one side, and into Assyria on the other, and the horse followed in the wake of bronze.

From the outset, the Assyrian was a trader rather than an agriculturist. Circumstances forced him to be a soldier as well. The need of keeping the road to the north open obliged Assyria to be from the first a military kingdom, and the neighbourhood of the Kurdish mountains, with their wild and thievish population, kept the Assyrian troops constantly employed. The power of the Assyrian kings, like that of the kings of the northern kingdom of Israel, rested on the army; they were, in fact, military commanders who owed their authority to a successful revolt from Babylonia. Hence in Assyria the head of the state was the king, and not, as in Babylonia, the god; while the Babylonian monarch was subordinate to the priesthood, the Assyrian monarch was himself the high-priest. Like Jahveh in Israel, Ashur in Assyria was a " Lord of Hosts " : without wife or child, he led the Assyrian armies to victory, and destroyed those who would not acknowledge his name.

Assyria Independent of Babylonia

Babylonia was long reluctant to recognise the independence of its rebellious vassal. Burnaburiash, the Babylonian king, in his letters to the Egyptian Pharaoh, still claims sovereignty over the northern kingdom. But facts were too strong for theories, and finally, in the thirteenth century before our era, Tiglath-In-aristi, or Tukulti-Ninib I., king of Assyria, took the sacred city of Babylon by storm and had himself crowned king of Babylonia. His father, Shalmaneser I., the builder of Calah near Nineveh, about 1300 B.C., had carried on campaign after campaign against the Aramæans and Hittites, and had brought Northern Mesopotamia under his rule.

For seven years, Tiglath-In-aristi was lord of Babylon. Then a conspiracy was formed against him at home; he was

IN THE DAYS OF ASSYRIA'S GREATNESS: A KING ISSUING FROM HIS PALACE

assassinated in his palace, and one of his sons seized the crown. A Babylonian king of the Kassite dynasty once more sat on the Babylonian throne. But the political prestige of Babylonia had departed. From thenceforth Assyria, and not Babylonia, was the ruling power in the valleys of the Tigris and Euphrates. The sceptre had passed from the mixed people of Babylonia to the purer Semites of Assyria.

Under Tiglath-pileser I., in 1100 B.C., Assyria resumed its career of foreign conquest. The nations of Northern Asia Minor were driven back from the Assyrian provinces which adjoined Cappadocia, the Armenian highlands were harassed by Assyrian armies, and the command of the high-road from Mesopotamia to Palestine was transferred to Assyrian hands. From the Phœnician coast the Assyrian king sailed out to sea in a ship of Arvad, and there he received presents from the Pharaoh of Egypt, which included a crocodile and a hippopotamus. Perhaps these were intended for a zoological garden, since the king had established botanical gardens at Ashur and Nineveh, planted with the trees and shrubs of foreign lands. An attempt to invade Babylonia was unsuccessful, and the immediate followers of Tiglath-pileser do not seem to have been gifted with high military qualities. At all events for several generations the armies of Assyria remained at home, and by the capture of the Assyrian fortresses at the fords of the Euphrates the Aramæans once more barred the way to the West. Palestine, accordingly, which had been threatened by the Assyrian advance, was allowed a respite ; opportunity was given for the founding of David's empire, and the merchants of Nineveh were compelled to leave the trade of the Mediterranean in the hands of the Phœnicians.

The Assyrian Lion Wakes

Under Ashurnasirpal II., who ruled B.C. 883-858, the Assyrian lion again awoke. Year after year the Assyrian army marched out of the gates of Nineveh, carrying ruin with it wherever it went. The campaigns were largely of the character of raids ; their chief object was plunder. But they not only filled Nineveh with the wealth of other lands and made the name of Assyria one of terror ; they also trained the Assyrian army itself so that it became well-nigh

irresistible. East, west and north it made its way, and the ruthlessness of its king—the cruellest of a cruel race— marked its track with fire and blood.

Ashurnasirpal's son and successor, Shalmaneser II., who reigned B.C. 858-823, maintained the military traditions of his father. But, unlike his father, he aimed at something more than mere raiding. The conquered lands were placed under Assyrian governors and required to pay tribute, which was also exacted from the vassal princes who had submitted to the rule of Ashur. We can thus speak once more of an Assyrian empire, which had a more permanent character than that of Shalmaneser I. or Tiglath-pileser I. And with the establishment of the empire was associated a commercial policy. Every effort was made to open and keep the high-road to the Mediterranean ; the Phœnician cities were made tributary, and for the first time Palestine became an Assyrian battle-ground. Its possession meant the supremacy of Assyria in Western Asia, and therewith its commercial supremacy in the civilised world.

Shalmaneser Establishes an Empire

In B.C. 853 Shalmaneser met at Karkar a confederacy of the Syrian states, which had been formed against him by the king of Hamath. Damascus was represented in it as well as " Ahab of Israel " ; Arabs, Ammorites and Phœnicians had also sent their chariots and infantry. The battle ended in favour of the Assyrians, but Shalmaneser found himself too much weakened to pursue his advantage. Four years later he returned to the attack, and once more the Hamathites and their allies were defeated. The conquest of Syria, however, proved more difficult than he had anticipated, and even when he led 120,000 picked troops of Assyria against Ben-Hadad of Damascus, in B.C. 845, the result was a drawn battle. But events fought for him in the West. Ben-Hadad was murdered by Hazael, and the throne of Ahab usurped by Jehu. When the Assyrian forces again appeared, in B.C. 841, there was no longer the formidable league of a few years earlier to oppose it. Hazael was besieged in Damascus ; Jehu paid homage, and sent tribute by his ambassadors, whose portraits are sculptured on an obelisk of black marble now in the British Museum [see page 1664].

Assyria Gains Syria

The other campaigns of Shalmaneser were directed partly against the Armenian highlands of the north, from which it was always possible for the invader to swoop down upon Assyria, partly against the Hittites on the Orontes and in Cilicia, who stood in the way of his schemes for creating an Assyrian province in Syria. But

Shalmaneser's Son Revolts and Reigns before the schemes could be realised the old king grew too infirm to take the field. The command of his armies was entrusted to a general, and intrigue and conspiracy began at home. First Ashur, the ancient capital, then Nineveh and the neighbouring cities, revolted under his son Ashur-dan-pal, and for five years a rival prince reigned over the divided monarchy. Thanks, however, to the military abilities of another son, Samsi - Raman (Shamshi - Adad), and the veteran soldiers who followed him, the revolt was at last put down; Nineveh was taken and the rebel king perished in the ruins of his palace. Shalmaneser died shortly afterwards, and Samsi-Raman IV. was proclaimed his successor. He reigned for thirteen years, the earlier of which were occupied in campaigns against Armenia and the Medes, who for the first time appear on the horizon of Asiatic history, while the later years were distinguished by a successful invasion of Babylonia.

His son Adad-nirari IV. once more turned his attention to the West. The policy of Shalmaneser was resumed, and an Assyrian army again entered Syria. Damascus surrendered, and its king, Marih, purchased safety by submission and tribute.

But a new power had risen out of the north. While the Assyrians had been engaged in repressing the raiding tendencies of the semi-barbarous Aryan Medes on the eastern side of their territories a new dynasty had established

Armenian Imitation of Assyria itself in Armenia, on the shores of Lake Van, full of life and energy and eager to adopt all the arts and habits of Assyrian civilisation. The cuneiform script of Assyria was introduced in a modified form; cities and palaces were built in imitation of those of Assyria; Assyrian art was adapted to the older art of the country; above all, an army was formed modelled after that of the Assyrian kings. From their capital, on the site

of the modern Van, the Armenian sovereigns went forth to conquer and to establish an empire which extended from Lake Urumiya on the east to Cappadocia on the west, and robbed Assyria of its fairest provinces in the north. The descendants of Ashurnasirpal and Shalmaneser were in no position to resist the new force that had thus suddenly grown up beside them. They became feebler every year, and the revolt of Ashur in B.C. 763 brought matters to a crisis. The revolt spread to the provinces of the empire, and an expedition against Arpad in B.C. 754 was the last expiring effort of the old régime. Eight years later the army itself rebelled; the reigning king, Ashur-nirari II., disappeared from the scene, and on the 13th of Iyyar, or April, B.C. 745, a military adventurer, Pulu, or Pul, seized the crown and assumed the name of Tiglath-pileser IV.

Tiglath-pileser, the founder of the later Assyrian empire, was a man of unusual ability and military skill. His first task was to reorganise the kingdom, his next to create an army which, by the

Pul, an Empire Founder help of superior discipline and arms, should become an irresistible engine of war. Assyria was in a perilous condition. In the north it was threatened by the Armenians; westward its road to the Mediterranean had been cut off; to the south, Babylonia was restless and menacing; while the Medes on the east took advantage of its weakness to recommence their raids. The new ruler of Assyria had not even the prestige of birth and descent; his title had not been legitimised by the priesthood of Babylon, and the Assyrians had just tasted the pleasures of a successful revolt.

The Aramæan nomads of Northern Arabia and the Median raiders were the first to learn that order had been restored in Assyria. They were driven out of the Assyrian territories, and an expedition which reached the Caspian taught the Medes to respect Assyrian power. Then Tiglath-pileser turned to the Armenians and their northern allies. A hard-fought battle, not far from Malatiya, decided the fate of the campaign. Sarduris, the Armenian king, fled from the field, where 72,950 of his soldiers, with his state carriage and a vast amount of spoil fell into the hands of the victors. The Hittite and Phœnician princes hastened to pay

WHEN THE ASSYRIAN EMPIRE WAS AT THE ZENITH OF ITS POWER: HEBREW CAPTIVES BROUGHT BEFORE THE KING

homage to the conqueror, and the merchants of Nineveh found themselves once more able to share in the profits of the Mediterranean trade.

Tiglath-pileser, however, was not content with the almost nominal ties which had hitherto connected the conquered provinces of the Assyrian empire with the governing state. For the first time he introduced into politics the conception of a centralised government. Thenceforward the provinces of the empire were to form a single organism, strictly controlled by a bureaucracy, at the head of which was the king. The amount of taxation each should contribute was carefully defined, and the royal residence became an imperial city into which the wealth of its dependencies was poured. The empire was extended and maintained by a standing army, in the wake of which followed the civil functionaries. The army itself was provided with new weapons and instructed in new tactics. Thoroughly disciplined, and consisting as it did of conscripts raised partly in Assyria, partly in the dependent provinces, it soon became practical master of Western Asia.

Centralised Government Begun With this new instrument at his disposal, Tiglath-pileser undertook what he determined should be a lasting conquest of the West. The king was as keen as his merchants to direct into the coffers of Nineveh the trade of the world, and for this the subjugation of the Phœnician cities was essential. But campaign after campaign was needed before the spirit of the Syrian states could be finally broken, and Tiglath-pileser was forced to have recourse to the new expedient of transporting a troublesome nationality from its home. Hamath vainly tried to preserve its independence by alliance with Azariah of Judah and other Syrian princes; it was taken by storm and reduced to the condition of an Assyrian satrapy. In B.C. 732 the same fate befell Damascus.

Rezon, the Damascene king, and Pekah of Israel had endeavoured to dethrone the young king Ahaz of Israel, and to substitute for him a creature of their own who would join them in the defiance of their Assyrian suzerain. Ahaz appealed to Tiglath-pileser, who, nothing loth, soon made his appearance upon the scene. Samaria and its king were crushed, Rezon fled to his capital, where, after a siege of two years, he was starved out and put to death. Meanwhile, a pretext was found

for exacting a heavy fine from Tyre, and the expenses of the wars in Syria were paid for with the 150 talents of gold—about £400,000—which the merchant princes of that city were compelled to provide.

In B.C. 735 a campaign into the heart of Ararat had effectually put a stop to all immediate danger from that quarter.

Syrian and Armenian Conquests The Armenian king was forced to retreat to his capital and there watch helplessly the wasting of his country by the Assyrian army. Leagues of fertile land were reduced to desert, and Tiglath-pileser added the insult of setting up a memorial of his successes just outside the gate of Van.

Tiglath-pileser had thus justified in deed his right to be king; it was now time that his title should be justified in law. In B.C. 731, accordingly, he marched into Babylonia, and two years later he was crowned king at Babylon, and his right to rule the empire of Sargon of Akkad acknowledged by the priests of Bel. The long struggle between Babylonia and its insurgent vassal Assyria was over; the vassal had prevailed, and the Babylonians, though with an ill grace, had to submit to Assyrian supremacy.

Tiglath-pileser IV. died in December, B.C. 727, and was succeeded by a certain Ulula, who took the name of Shalmaneser IV. While besieging Samaria, he died or was murdered in December 722 B.C., and the throne was seized by another general, who assumed the name of Sargon, "the legitimate king," and subsequently endeavoured to justify his title by claiming to be descended from the ancient kings of Assur. The army was now all-powerful; frequent revolution, as in the northern kingdom of Israel, had destroyed among the people all feeling of veneration for the ruling monarch, and the throne consequently was the prize of the ablest or most influential military commander. Sargon,

Military Regime in Assyria however, proved that he had the ability to conquer and govern, as well as to influence the soldiery, and he also succeeded in doing what his immediate predecessors had failed to accomplish—handing on his power to his descendants.

The year after his accession saw the capture of Samaria. Its leading citizens, 27,280 in number, were carried into exile, and the country placed under an Assyrian governor. In B.C. 717 came the fall of

Carchemish, with which the history of the Hittites finds its end. The city became the seat of an Assyrian satrap, and the ford across the Euphrates was henceforth under Assyrian control. Trade had definitely passed into Assyrian hands.

But the northern kingdoms made one last struggle for resistance. Rusas I. of Van placed himself at the head of a great confederacy which included the Minni of Lake Urumiya and Midas the Moschian in Asia Minor. Year after year the war lasted with varying fortunes. At last the time came when the Assyrians were victorious all along the line; their armies penetrated the barrier of the northern mountains, and the strongest fortresses of the enemy fell into their hands. Even the Medic tribes had to submit to the conqueror. The power of Ararat was broken for ever; the Assyrian king had nothing further to fear from its rivalry.

Sargon was now free to turn his face southward. The revolution which had placed him on the throne had cost Assyria the possession of Babylonia. Merodach-baladan, the Chaldæan, had

Babylonia Swept with Fire and Sword emerged from the marshes at the head of the Persian Gulf, and with his Aramæan fol-lowers had made himself master of Babylon. When the fortune of war began to set against the nations of the north he did his best to prepare for the coming storm. Alliance was made with Elam on the east, and ambassadors were sent to Palestine in the west to stir up disaffection there and form a league against the common oppressor. All, however, was in vain. Before the confederates were ready, Sargon had struck his blow. His tartan, or commander-in-chief, took the Philis-tine town of Ashdod by storm, while he himself swept Babylonia with fire and sword. Merodach-baladan was driven back to his ancestral marshes and the Assyrian conqueror crowned king at Babylon B.C. 709. Five years later he was murdered and succeeded by his son Sennacherib on the 12th of Ab, or July, B.C. 705. Brought up in the purple, Sennacherib had neither the ability nor the tact of his father. His reign was to a large extent a failure. From the first, Babylonia was in constant revolt, and the vassal kings he appointed over it were dethroned either by their subjects or by the Elamites as soon as the Assyrian

garrisons were away. Elam, after so many centuries of seclusion thus once more entered the political world of Western Asia. With its help Babylonia continued to resist the Assyrian domina-tion, and though Assyria was apparently successful its strength was drained in the contest and Babylonia triumphed in

Sennacherib at Jerusalem the end. What Elam was to Babylonia, Egypt was to Pales-tine. Ethiopian princes had conquered the valley of the Nile and put fresh blood into the old kingdom of the Pharaohs. Lavish in their promises of help they induced the nations on either side of the Jordan to rise against the Assyrian. Hezekiah of Judah put himself at the head of the confederacy, secure in the strong walls of Jerusalem and the expectation of Egyptian aid.

In B.C. 701 a huge army marched out of Nineveh under the command of the king himself. Tyre, indeed, remained untaken, but Sidon was captured along with the other towns of the Phœnician coast. Judah was ravaged up to the gates of its capital, but it was in vain that Sennacherib called upon the Jewish king to submit. At Eltekeh a drawn battle was fought with the Egyptian forces, and when pestilence soon afterwards descended upon the invading army, Sennacherib had no resource left but to return to Assyria. The rebellious vassal at Jerusalem re-mained unpunished, like Greece after the retreat of Xerxes.

For the next few years Sennacherib had more than enough to occupy him in Babylonia and Elam. The great battle of Khalulê in B.C. 689 brought matters to a crisis. According to the Assyrian annals the chariot of Sennacherib waded through pools of blood and rode over heaps of slain. Countless numbers of Babylonians and Elamites strewed the ground, and the Assyrian victory was complete. But the Babylonian records tell a different

The Sack of Babylon story, and claim the victory for Bel of Babylon. As a matter of fact, the battle would seem to have been a drawn one, with the advantage on the side of the Assyrians. In the following year, when they appeared before Babylon, there was no force to resist them, and the holy city of Western Asia was taken and razed to the ground. Its temples and palaces were destroyed, and its ruins choked the canals. The act of sacrilege and brutality made a profound impression upon the civilised world, and more than a century afterwards Babylonian historians held up the name of Sennacherib to execration. His right to rule was never legitimised, for it was never acknowledged by the Babylonian priesthood. When he was murdered by his two sons on the 20th Tebet, or December, B.C. 681, his death **Heaven-sent Vengeance on Sennacherib** was regarded as the righteous vengeance of heaven. Another son, Esarhaddon, was at the time commanding the Assyrian army on the frontiers of Armenia. For forty-two days the conspirators held Nineveh; then they fled with their followers to the Armenian camp, and a decisive battle took place in Cappadocia, on the 12th of Iyyar or April. The Assyrian veterans gained the day, and at the close of it saluted Esarhaddon as king. At once he set out for Nineveh, which had no choice but to confirm the decision of the soldiery.

Esarhaddon, however, proved to be one of the best of the Assyrian kings. At once he entered on a policy of conciliation. One of his first acts was to go in person to Babylonia and there set about the restoration of Babylon. The temple of Bel-Merodach rose again from its ruins, the priests were recalled from exile, and Esarhaddon was acknowledged king of Babylon as well as king of Assyria. Babylon became the second city of the empire, where the king held court during part of the year.

But an unexpected danger threatened both Assyria and the whole fabric of Asiatic civilisation. One of Sennacherib's acts of folly had been to destroy the kingdom of Ellip, which formed a " buffer-state " between Assyria and the wild tribes of the east. Cimmerians or Scyths from Southern Russia crossed the Caucasus and settled in the devastated land, where they allied themselves with the Median tribes. Esarhaddon now found **World-rule of Assyria** himself confronted by the northerners, who had overrun Armenia and attacked the border cities of the empire. Public prayers were ordered to avert the danger, and finally a battle in Cilicia drove the invaders to the Greek and Lydian settlements on the coast of Asia Minor.

The supremacy of Assyrian trade was the next object of Esarhaddon's concern. All attempts at rivalry on the part of Phœnicia were suppressed for the future

by the destruction of Sidon, and the building of a new Sidon, which was filled with Assyrian colonists; while the tranquil acquiescence of Palestine in Assyrian rule was secured by the invasion of Egypt. In B.C. 674 Egypt was conquered and divided into twenty satrapies, each of which was placed under an Assyrian governor. Of all the kingdoms of the civilised Oriental world Elam alone remained independent.

The Bedouins of Northern Arabia had been coerced into order by a punitive expedition which penetrated through the trackless and waterless desert into the very heart of the peninsula. The expedition was an amazing one, and is a remarkable proof of Esarhaddon's military capacities, and the excellence of the Assyrian commissariat.

The Egyptians, however, did not submit to Assyrian rule with equanimity. A revolt broke out, and while on the march to suppress it Esarhaddon died on the 12th of Marchesvan, or October, B.C. 667. His empire was divided between his two sons, Shamash-shum-ukin receiving Babylonia, and Ashurbanipal the rest. At first **Ashurbanipal's Literary Ambitions** the arrangement seemed to work well, the Babylonians being flattered by this acknowledgment of their equality with Nineveh. But after a time Shamash-shum-ukin became more Babylonian than his subjects, and indulged in the dream of restoring the ancient empire of Hammurabi, while, on the other side, Ashurbanipal's claim to be his suzerain became more and more articulate. With a restless Elam behind Babylonia, sooner or later a conflict was inevitable.

Ashurbanipal, however, was no lover of war. He was fond of ease and luxury; his desire was to be a patron of art and literature, and to be known as the founder of the greatest library in the world. The copy of an old book was the most precious spoil that could be sent to him from a conquered city, and his scribes were busily employed in re-editing the ancient literature of the country and compiling works for the use of students. If war broke out, he sent his generals to fight for him while he feasted—or fasted—at home.

Moreover, the earlier years of Ashurbanipal's reign were fully occupied in repressing the attempts of Egypt to recover its freedom. Time after time the Assyrian garrisons were withdrawn, only to be immediately recalled to put down another revolt. Eventually, Thebes, the centre of disaffection, was utterly destroyed; for days the Assyrian soldiers were employed in hewing in pieces its temple-fortresses; two of its obelisks were carried to Nineveh as trophies of victory, and the former capital of Egypt was reduced to a collection of mud-built villages. The city never recovered from the blow.

The Cimmerian hordes, taught by the lesson they had received in Cilicia, still respected Assyrian territory. But Armenia and Lydia were each suffering at their hands, and each accordingly applied for help to "the great king." The unwonted sight was seen at Nineveh of ambassadors from the Lydian Gyges and Sarduris III. of Van, for whom an interpreter was difficult to find. Assyria seemed to have reached the zenith of its power; the whole civilised world lay at its feet, and the will of its monarch was as the will of a god.

But the feet of the colossus were of clay. Suddenly Babylonia burst into revolt, with the armies of Elam behind it, and the other provinces of the empire in its train. For long the issue trembled in the balance. But the disciplined veterans of Nineveh and the wealth of its merchants finally prevailed. Syria and Palestine returned to their allegiance, Babylon was invested by the Assyrian army and at last starved into surrender. The Elamite forces were driven back into their mountains, and Shamash-shum-ukin burned himself amid the ruins of his palace.

A Colossus with Feet of Clay

Egypt, however, was lost for ever. With the mercenaries he had hired from Gyges of Lydia, Psammetichus had succeeded in shaking off the Assyrian yoke and founding the twenty-sixth dynasty in B.C. 660. It was the St. Luke's summer of Egyptian history. An antiquarian revival dreamed of restoring both the art and the political power of the past, and for a while the imitation seemed successful. The ruined temples were rebuilt, the masterpieces of ancient sculpture were closely copied, and the land once more enjoyed peace and prosperity. The later Pharaohs of the dynasty even grasped at the Asiatic empire of the past; Necho made Palestine again the tributary of Egypt, and, like Thothmes, so many centuries before, fixed the boundaries of his dominions at the Euphrates.

But the Egyptian revival was evanescent. It was effected with the help of Greek mercenaries, and the wealth which filled the coffers of the Pharaoh was derived in part from the Greek traders of Naukratis. The European had entered the land, not again to quit it; the valley of the Nile was ceasing to be either African or Asiatic, and was about to become European. The decline of Assyria had allowed Egypt thus to claim once more its old position as a world power. The Elamite wars had ended in a barren victory for Ashurbanipal; Susa, the Elamite capital, was indeed levelled with the ground, the tombs of its kings had been desecrated, and the Elamite monarchy had ceased to exist. But the struggle had left Assyria in a state of collapse. Its treasury was empty, and the bare mountains and ravaged fields of Elam were unable to replenish it; while its fighting-men had perished in the Babylonian revolt and the Elamite wars, and none were left to fill their places. When the Scythian hordes once more crossed the Assyrian frontiers there was none to resist them. Resistlessly they poured over the rich plains and cities of the empire, and penetrated as far south as the borders of Egypt, where they were bought off by a bribe. Calah, the suburb of Nineveh, was taken and sacked. Nineveh was saved only by the strength of its walls. When Ashurbanipal died his empire and with it the kingdom of Assyria itself were tottering to their fall.

Europeans in Egypt in B.C. 650

The end came in B.C. 606. Sin-sariskun, the last Assyrian king, had vainly sought to check the growing power of his satrap in Babylonia, Nabopolassar. Cyaxares of Media led his legions against the doomed city; after a protracted siege Nineveh was taken, its ruler slain, its people carried into captivity, its palaces and temples burnt with fire. Assyria and its empire had passed for ever from the stage of history. Babylonia and Media divided the relics of its empire between them. In 605 B.C. Nebuchadnezzar, the son of Nabopolassar, overthrew the Egyptian forces at Carchemish, and put an end to the dream of an Egyptian empire in Asia. The death of his father shortly afterwards placed the Babylonian crown upon his head, and Babylon again became the capital of the Oriental world. Great architectural

Assyria Passes for Ever

works were undertaken to make it a worthy successor of Nineveh, and it was surrounded by fortifications which made it well-nigh impregnable. Nebuchadnezzar showed himself as able in the arts of peace as he was in war, a patron of architecture and learning as well as a pious worshipper of the gods. When he died, after a reign of forty-three years, the sceptre dropped into feebler hands. The priestly party intrigued against the sovereign, and eventually the throne was usurped by Nabonidus, who seems to have represented the mercantile class. The heart of Nabonidus was in antiquarian pursuits rather than in the government of his kingdom, and the army was entrusted to his son Belshazzar, while no heed was paid to the growing disaffection in the country due to his attempt to centralise religious worship in Babylon.

The Rise of Persia

But a new power was rising in the East. In the closing days of the Assyrian empire the Aryan clan of Persians had settled in deserted Elam, and had there revived the ancient kingdom of Ansan. They yielded a nominal obedience to the Median king, but for all practical purposes were independent. Their princes intermarried with the native Elamites, and one of them, Cyrus II., proved to be a military genius of the first order. By his overthrow of the Median monarchy, in 549 B.C., he became the master of an empire which rivalled that of Nabonidus. The conquest of the Median empire was followed by that of Lydia, which placed Asia Minor at his feet, and for the first time brought Asia into direct collision with Greece.

Then, in 538 B.C., came the invasion of Babylonia. The Babylonian army was defeated near Opis, and Babylon shortly afterwards opened its gates to the conqueror. Nabonidus surrendered, and the death of Belshazzar removed all further opposition to the invaders. They had, in fact, been welcomed by an influential party in Babylonia itself. Cyrus was regarded by the priests as the instrument of Bel-Merodach's vengeance on the godless Nabonidus, and Cyrus was not slack in posing as the orthodox worshipper of the Babylonian god and the rightful successor of Nebuchadnezzar. The exiles from Judah and other countries equally welcomed the conqueror, in whom they saw a deliverer from their Babylonian masters. The later years of Cyrus were employed in bringing the

Babylon Passes Under

lands eastward of Persia under his sway. When he fell in battle against the Scythians, his son Cambyses pursued his father's career of conquest and added Egypt to the empire. The twenty-sixth dynasty ended in Psammetichus II., and Egyptian independence was no more.

But the Nile cast a spell upon its conqueror. He lingered in its warmth and sunshine while revolt was beginning at home. The Magian clan seized the supreme power, and placed one of themselves, Gomates by name, upon the deserted throne. On his way back from Egypt Cambyses died by accident or design, and the line of Cyrus was extinct. An avenger was found, however, in Darius, the son of Hystaspes, who, like Cyrus, claimed descent from the Achæmenian Teispes. Gomates was murdered, and Darius chosen king in 521 B.C. The earlier years of his reign were occupied in fighting against rivals and pretenders in various parts of the empire. But at last Darius prevailed and his rivals were overthrown.

Darius ascribed his victories to Ahuramazda, or Ormazd, the Aryan god. And it was indeed the Aryans and their god to whom the empire of Cyrus had now passed. Its reconquest by Darius made it the Persian empire, the complete organisation of which filled the latter years of his life. The new empire touched the borders of Europe, and Greek colonies sent tribute to Susa. At first the struggle lay between the Aryans in Asia and the Aryans in Europe, beween the Persians and the Greeks of Europe, who were destined to turn a fresh page in the history of the world. The struggle closed with the defeat of Asia. The heritage of the old civilisations, which Darius had united into a single whole, passed to Alexander the Macedonian, and Greek kings sat on the thrones of Hammurabi and the Pharaohs. The foundation of Alexandria was the mark and seal of the new order in human history ; East and West, Asia, Africa, and Europe, all alike met and commingled there, but the founder came from Europe, and though the elements of its culture went back to the dawn of Oriental antiquity, the form which they received, the stamp which they bore, was that of Europe. In Alexandria the old civilisations of the Euphrates and Nile were reborn and became European.

Alexandria a Birthplace of Civilisation

ARCHIBALD H. SAYCE

THE NEAR EAST DIVISION OF THE HARMSWORTH HISTORY OF THE WORLD

Our geographical plan brings us, in this division, to the countries of Western Asia—Persia, Arabia, Syria, Armenia, Asia Minor, and Turkey in Asia. The inset map indicates the great ancient empires of Nearer Asia, whose history is here treated of, including Babylonia, Assyria, Elam, the Hittite Empire, Phœnicia, Israel and Judah, ancient Armenia, ancient Asia Minor, Media, Persia, and the Græco-Bactrian Empire.

ANCIENT EMPIRES OF WESTERN ASIA

BY DR. HUGO WINCKLER & LEONARD W. KING, M.A.

BABYLONIA AND ITS PEOPLES

OF the two civilisations developed in the two great river-basins of the Nile and of the Euphrates and Tigris, the Babylonian civilisation has unquestionably exercised the greater influence on the moulding of the conditions in Nearer Asia, though Greek civilisation, and in consequence thereof our own, has been less influenced by the latter than the former. It is not yet possible to discover all the threads that were woven indirectly between Babylon and Greece, and the paths are still unknown by which some of the ideas and thoughts of the earliest Babylonians reached the civilised nations, European as well as others, dwelling outside the immediate sphere of Babylonian culture. In order to characterise the connection of Greece with Babylonian civilisation, it is enough to point to the one Babylonian word borrowed by the Greeks, μνᾶ, mina. As to the other aspect of the influence of the civilisation along the Euphrates, let us call

Our Babylonian Watches attention to one of its products, which we still carry with us in our pockets—the watch, with its twelve divisions, corresponding to the ancient Babylonian division of the day into twelve double hours. The paths on which the Oriental world, lying apparently so far from us, established these connections with Europe are up to the present still shrouded in complete obscurity. Thus, to take a single example,

it is still a matter for investigation to what extent and by what channels the laws embodied in the Code of Hammurabi may have influenced later systems of legislation. But in one striking instance the mythology of Babylon has survived in European beliefs, and the track of

Babylon and the Bible this connection may be followed; for it is now generally admitted that the biblical accounts of the Creation and the Deluge were in great part derived from a Babylonian source.

The decipherment of the cuneiform writing and of the Egyptian hieroglyphs has practically doubled the space of time which our historical knowledge covers—that is to say, the period we can survey by means of written documents in comparison with that which was regarded as history for the districts of Western civilisation. It is true that excavations on early Greek sites have yielded abundant remains of the Mycenæan and of pre-Mycenæan cultures, while recent discoveries in Crete have included hundreds of clay tablets inscribed in the writing and language of an early Mediterranean people. Further, through periods of pre-Minoan culture, the civilisation of the Mediterranean races may now be traced back to the Neolithic Age. But in a more restricted sense of the term it may be said that the history of Greece can be followed back to the seventh or eighth century B.C.; while the oldest written records of Babylon and Egypt go back to the fourth millennium B.C. The interval which divides their first founders from the Dorian migration and the beginnings of Rome is therefore as great as that which lies between our own days and those of the beginnings of Hellenic history.

Widespread Influence of Babylon The regions influenced by the civilisation and history of Babylon stretch far beyond the countries watered by the two rivers. States which had reached so high a stage of civilisation as those of ancient Babylonia could not exist without laying under tribute the neighbouring countries, and bestowing on them in return their own achievements. Thus we see in remote antiquity that Babylonia encroached on Palestine, Armenia, Elam, even Arabia; trading, conquering, and depositing there her superfluous population and the products of her civilisation, but also exposed to the attacks of her barbarian neighbours, by whom she was often worsted. The history, therefore, of the other states and nations of Nearer Asia, taken all in all, is grouped round that of Babylonia. It is not mere accident that we possess few or no accounts of these except the Babylonian, in consequence of which their history seems to us influenced by Babylonia; for all the surrounding nations looked and were drawn toward the seat of that civilisation, whether they were under its supremacy, or they imposed their own rule upon it. This is most clearly demonstrated by the widespread use of the cuneiform writing, the most conspicuous achievement of the Babylonian intellect, the development of which has already been traced and illustrated on page 265 by Professor Petrie. It was the vehicle of intellectual intercourse in all Nearer Asia. Everywhere, so far as our view at present extends, we meet it: in Elam, in

Cuneiform the French of the East Armenia, and even in the heart of Asia Minor. In Palestine men wrote in cuneiform letters, and must accordingly have been acquainted with the Babylonian language and the Babylonian world of thought. Even in Egypt itself we shall find that the Babylonian writing and language were the means of intercourse with the countries of Western Asia. In fact, in the fifteenth and fourteenth centuries B.C. Babylonian

was the language of diplomacy and commerce, and its employment at this period throughout the Nearer East resembled very nearly the use of French at the present day.

If a study of the development of Babylonia implies in itself a history of almost all Western Asia, the task will be still more complex when we consider that the history, comprising more than 3,000 years, of a civilised world surrounded by barbarians must show the most varied succession of nationalities. It is not *one* people that meets us in Babylonia as the bearer of the "Babylonian" civilisation; it is a long series of most heterogeneous nations belonging to various races, which one after the other advanced into the great plain between the rivers, and lived out the rest of their existence under the dominion of that civilisation. The same holds good of the adjoining countries which were subject to its civilising influence, although, from want of information, we cannot trace the fact so clearly there.

Just as the great civilisations of antiquity have been developed **Sources of Babylonian Immigrants** on great rivers, the natural highways of communication, so natural migrations take their origin in wide regions of steppes, which supply nomadic man with food for the animals by means of which he lives. For, owing to the vast districts required by a nomadic life, these extensive plains can contain and support comparatively few inhabitants. Thus the overgrowth of the population, which is periodically felt, compels the wandering tribes to seek more productive lands, whither the simple but sturdy son of Nature is invited by the alluring splendours of civilisation, and by the prospects of an easy victory over more effeminate and civilised races.

Three such cradles of the human race have to be considered in connection with the region of Babylonian civilisation— the European steppes, from which the peoples migrated over the Caucasus or round the Caspian Sea, and in the other direction through Asia Minor; the Inner Asiatic steppes on the north-east; and Arabia on the south and south-west. Of these, the first district may be almost excluded from our inquiry, since the approach on this side is the most difficult; more important is the Inner Asiatic

CUNEIFORM, THE MOST CONSPICUOUS BABYLONIAN ACHIEVEMENT

These reproductions of Babylonian tablets illustrate the development of cuneiform writing. The first shows the Sumerian picture writing with archaic cuneiform equivalents; the third is a memorial tablet of a governor of Lagash, inscribed about B.C. 4500; while the second is an inscription of Xerxes, about B.C. 470, in the most modern form.

region. With regard to this and the European district, it must be noted that each of the waves of peoples coming from that quarter first beat against the states that were posted in front of Babylonia and were subject to her civilising influence—namely, those of Asia Minor, Armenia, Elam and Syria. Babylonia thus presented against invaders from these directions a natural bulwark of buffer states, and could not, therefore, be so easily overrun by them directly.

On the other hand, the third district, Arabia, with its extensive steppes, from earliest times the home of robber nomads, immediately adjoins the territory of Babylon itself. The only natural boundary here is the Euphrates; and the nomads could roam unhindered up to the towns built upon the right bank, even when a strong power attempted to prevent their crossing into the pasture grounds lying east of the river. It is a long stretch of frontier, running in places through wide steppes, which the Babylonian forces had to guard, and they were seldom able to defend the passage of the river against the nomads who pressed onward from Arabia. It was from this quarter that Babylonia was exposed to the most frequent and most lasting immigrations, and the nations who came from that side

The Semites' Entrance to Babylonia

took possession successively of the plain between the Euphrates and the Tigris. But Arabia, so far as our knowledge reaches, was the home of the nations which, according to a linguistic classification, we designate as Semites.

The history of Babylonia itself is in great part Semitic; that of the adjoining nations, so far as they are subject to its influence, is also largely Semitic, or supplied in the manner stated from the two other storehouses of mankind. The Semites, in fact, attained their highest civilisation in Babylonia. It is true that in its origin much of this civilisation was non-Semitic. Not only their method of writing, but much of their art and many of their religious beliefs, to say nothing of less important elements of culture, were derived from the Sumerians, who at a very early period occupied the whole of Southern Babylonia. But the Sumerian culture was adopted by the Semitic population to meet their own needs, and they brought to its development all that their natural gifts could produce. Even in the earliest times of which we have knowledge we may trace results of Semitic influence, and during the later historical periods it gradually became the preponderating element in Babylonian culture.

Babylonian Civilisation is Semitic

So far back as we can survey the history of Babylonia, its actors were largely composed of Semites. Accordingly, the distinct Semitic character of the population comes out in the language, however much other elements of population were mixed with the Semites. It is, however, obvious that our historical knowledge

The Lack of Babylonian Prehistory cannot reach the beginning of the Babylonian culture. The growth of the means to hand down history, the introduction of a written language, must indeed presuppose a long course of development in culture. It is a long cry from the picture-writing of savages to the written reports of campaigns and of the building of temples, such as the earliest Babylonian inscriptions give us, and to the official records drawn up according to set forms belonging to the same period ; and it may be that the nations which reached that stage of development worked longer at perfecting their inventions than the three thousand or more years during which we know that cuneiform writing was employed.

We shall see that the oldest records with which we are yet acquainted come both from Sumerians and Semites. These records show very clearly the influence of both the peoples who had settled in the valley of the Tigris and Euphrates. On the one hand, the inscriptions of the earliest Sumerian rulers which have been recovered show linguistically numerous traces of Semitic influence. On the other hand, the earliest Semitic rulers of whom we have knowledge employ not only the Sumerian method of writing, but also in great part the Sumerian language, for their inscriptions. Of a time when there were no Semites or no Sumerians in Babylonia we have as yet no knowledge, and it is still a matter for conjecture which of these two races was first settled in the country. All that we

Sumerians and Semites can say with certainty is that Southern Babylonia was the centre of Sumerian influence, while it is in Northern Babylonia that the Semites were first settled.

It has recently been suggested that the Semites may have been the earlier of the two races to inhabit the country, and that they succeeded in establishing themselves in Northern Babylonia, and possibly also in the south, where they lived a primitive and agricultural life in an undeveloped state of civilisation. According to this theory the Sumerians were the conquering race, who, before their invasion of the country, had already attained a high level of culture, and brought with them into Babylonia not only the art of writing, but also the method of fighting in close battalions of heavily armed men ; and that, in virtue of their better weapons, they imposed their own higher civilisation upon the Semitic peasant population, whom they found in possession of the country. Their conquest of Babylonia might, on this theory, be compared to the Dorian invasion in Greece or the Norman conquest in England. On the other hand, it is possible that the Sumerians preceded the Semites in their occupation of Babylonia, and in that case the conquering race was the less civilised of the two. Pressing into the country in overwhelming numbers, they would gradually have gained the upper hand in the northern districts, and have absorbed the higher civilisation of the conquered race. At present we have not sufficient evidence available for deciding definitely between

The Latin of Babylonia these conflicting views. The earliest remains that have yet been recovered exhibit the Sumerians settled chiefly in the south, while in the north we find a Semitic population preponderating, and borrowing for their written records both the script and language of their southern neighbours.

The first records which we possess are composed in the non-Semitic Sumerian language. This language is one of the principal characteristics of the creators of the Babylonian civilisation, the inventors of the cuneiform characters. It is also the most valuable testimony to their racial importance. For, long after men ceased to speak Sumerian ; when the most heterogeneous nationalities had occupied Babylonia, and had gone the same way as the ancient Sumerians themselves ; when the various Semitic peoples in the valley of the Euphrates had played their part ; when Persians, Macedonians, or Parthians ruled there, down to the age immediately preceding the Christian era—Sumerian was still used in Babylonia as a sacred religious language. It played, therefore, a similar part to Latin, which has been the language of the learned world and of the Church in the Middle Ages and modern

TRIUMPHS OF THE EARLY BABYLONIAN ART

Some of these beautiful objects, found at Tello, and now in the Louvre, were executed over 6,000 years ago. The earliest are the copper votive figures (5 and 7) dating from the reign of the first Babylonian king, before B.C. 4500. The beautiful vase (10) is of silver, richly chased and engraved (11 and 12), and was made in the time of King Entemena, about B.C. 4500. Somewhat later are the copper figures of an early Chaldæan god (2) and a bull (6), the decoration for a sculptured vase of Gudea (8), and two gods in terra-cotta (3 and 9). These are all about B.C. 2500. The other objects are a finely-sculptured woman's head from Tello (1) and a Chaldæan bull in stone (4).

times; only, its survival in this form extended over a period nearly twice as long.

For considerable periods of their history the Sumerians speak to us in inscriptions of their own, and thus the past of this remarkable people, from the close of whose era the tradition of civilisation descends **A Language** in an unbroken line to our **that Lasted** own times, has been in some **3,000 Years** degree revealed. Moreover, by the preservation of the language, inscriptions and religious texts in the Sumerian tongue are in our hands, extending over a period which comprises more than three thousand years. The most ancient of the native Sumerian records are the inscriptions of the kings of Lagash, and Sumerian continued to be used as a living language under the later kings of Sumer and Akkad.

With the rise of Babylon under the Western Semitic kings of the first dynasty a great impetus was given to the increased employment of the Semitic tongue in the inscriptions of the period, and Sumerian gradually dropped out of general use. It can easily be imagined that in the succeeding ages the language, which was now only artificially preserved, must have gone through stages like those of Latin in the Middle Ages; for a revival in the spirit of classicism, like that of Latin by the Renaissance, was quite foreign to the Oriental character. Sumerian became, therefore, more and more corrupt when used by later ages. The texts are filled with Semiticisms: the later the period, the more the texts give the impression that they were composed of words merely adapted and declined according to Sumerian; that is to say, the originally quite distinct syntax had been given up. This Sumerian exhibits the same features not merely as the monkish Latin, but even as the Macaronic burlesques; **Sumerian** only, what was merely jesting **Pronunciation** in the latter was seriously **Unknown** intended in the former. If we add the fact that the more ancient the inscriptions are, the more ideographic they are—that is, each separate word is written with a special hieroglyph—we shall realise that our information as to the pronunciation of the old Sumerian is still very unsatisfactory. We know the meaning of the old inscriptions indeed from the signs which are familiar to us

from their significance in Semitic texts, but we learn the Sumerian pronunciation of the words only from the statements of later centuries.

Notwithstanding the numerous texts that have been recovered, we can therefore arrive at no certain conclusion as to many features of the language; but we may establish enough to show roughly the character of Sumerian, one of the oldest civilised languages of the world. It is an agglutinative language, whose construction is not dissimilar to that of the Turkish languages, and therefore completely different from that of the Semitic tongues. Let the following construction serve as an example: egal Ur-Engur lugal Uri galu e-Anna in-ru-a-ka-ta = palace + Ur-Engur + king + Ur + man + e-Anna + he built + genitive particle + in = in the palace of Ur-Engur, the king of Ur, the builder of the (temple) e-Anna. The connecting genitive, which in Semitic, as in English, stands between palace and Ur-Engur, goes to the end of the whole expression, which therefore composes a connected whole, something like a German **Construction** compound word. In the same **of Sumerian** way that which is the most **Language** important word, and therefore placed at the beginning of our sentences, the designation of place " in " (= ta) comes at the end. We must notice also the periphrasis of a Semitic participle by galu....in-ru-a, man.... + he built.

All attempts to establish an affinity with any language of the ancient world, even with the various languages of the neighbouring nations or of those still living, are precarious. Phonetically, Sumerian had already become to some extent corrupt, even as exhibited in the earliest inscriptions that have been recovered. Most words show only simple syllables of vowel and consonant, or consonant-vowel-consonant, the last of which has usually been lost; and a great number of originally distinct words are again phonetically assimilated. Sumerian has thus been worn smooth in the same way as Chinese.

We know nothing of the history of Babylonia before we already find Sumerians and Semites both settled in the country, and both split up into groups of independent city-states. One conclusion, however, can be drawn with perfect certainty from the analogy of similar relations and of later times. The development of civilisation was not possible in an idyllic and peaceful twilight on the fertile banks of the Euphrates. The same relations of hostility and friendship which we find later between the populations of different districts, and which exist between all civilised peoples not separated by insuperable difficulties of communication, must have existed even in the still dark ages of Babylonian history. Even then there must have been trade between the different places; the kings of separate cities must have exchanged communications, and have made war on one another.

Where the dark veil is lifted by means of historical documents—that is, by inscriptions to be reckoned among the most ancient monuments of mankind which speak to us in words—Semites meet us as rulers of the northern districts in the plain of the Euphrates and Tigris. By the term Semites, we designate, in accordance with the table of nations in Genesis, chapter x., the group of races which spoke the same tongue as the Hebrews, there included in the posterity of Shem. It may be noted that since the intro-

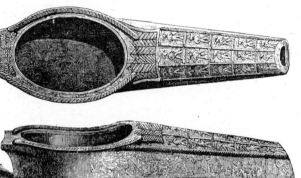

SEPULTURE OF EARLY BABYLONIA

Glazed clay coffins discovered in the ruins of Warka, the ancient Erech, where they were found in amazing abundance. They were covered with elevated ridges forming panels containing embossed and sculptured figures, and were finished with a thick glazing of rich green enamel.

duction of this term the fact has been established that some of the nations there classed among the descendants of Shem did not speak Semitic; however, the designation is now universally accepted.

We may regard Arabia as the home of the Semites; indeed, on geographical grounds, no other land can be taken into consideration. Arabia is, up to the present day, the land where Semites have kept their purity of race, and where they live under the same conditions and in the same stage of civilisation as their kinsmen who, in the fourth millennium before the Christian era, attained the object after which their descendants sigh; they won the rich civilised lands, which were certainly richer and better cultivated then than they are now. The only roads on

Arabia the Home of the Semites

which nomadic nations could migrate from Arabia led to Syria and Palestine. On the other sides the country is surrounded by the sea, and a migration westward or eastward presupposes that the people possessed ships, and had therefore passed from the stage of nomadism on the steppe to that of a settled life, or at least had taken up fishing, although this industry can support only a small people No emigration on a large scale took place then from the south of Arabia; but when the kingdom of Saba and the nations in alliance with it had produced a sort of civilisation, there was emigration to Africa and Abyssinia. The real tide, however, of Semitic migration set toward the north.

The Tide of Semitic Migration

We are in a position to determine roughly the course and the date of the later migrations, for we can fix their beginning and end with tolerable accuracy; for those of the first we depend to a great extent upon conjecture. They result as a natural consequence of the over-population of the country, and must, if the state of civilisation and conditions of life remain similar, be repeated at a similar interval of time. We can distinguish altogether three, and possibly four, great Semitic migrations toward the north. The last, to begin with that one which is traceable in the full light of history, is the Arabian. This culminated in the conquests of Islam. It begins somewhere in the seventh or eighth century B.C., when the advance of the Arabs into Syria is demonstrable. This is preceded by the Aramæan, and we can again roughly determine its beginnings. From the fifteenth to the thirteenth centuries B.C. we find Mesopotamia already flooded by Aramæan nomads. The advance of these tribes must have therefore begun somewhat earlier. The Canaanite-Hebraic migration precedes this, and, as

1589

BABYLON AS IT APPEARED AFTER TWO THOUSAND YEARS
This picture of ruin and the uttermost desolation, reproduced by permission from "The Struggle of the Nations" (S.P.C.K.), shows the ruins of Babylon in the first half of the nineteenth century, before they were disturbed by excavations.

a result, we find that shortly before 2000 B.C., a population, to be described as West Semitic, or Canaanitic, was in possession of Babylonia. Lastly, at the very dawn of Babylonian history as revealed to us by the remains that have been recovered, we find Semites settled in Northern Babylonia, and engaged in acquiring the elements of Sumerian civilisation from their southern neighbours. It is not unlikely that the original home of these Semitic Babylonians was also Arabia, and that their settlement on the banks of the Euphrates was due to a migration similar to those which took place at later times. But, for fixing the date at which this earliest migration may possibly have taken place, the excavations in Babylonia have as yet furnished no evidence.

These are the four great groups of Semitic peoples who have in succession produced great effects upon

the history of the Nearer East. It must be noted, however, that any calculation as to dates can give only approximate results, and that obviously a sharply defined division of the several migrations is impossible. In the migration of races, one wave pushes another before it, and the last portions of a great group of nations may be still in movement when the vanguard of the next is already drawing near. As an example, we may cite the case of the Hebrews and Aramæans about the middle of the second millennium B.C. The immigrating Western Semites of the second migration found existing in Babylonia a highly developed civilisation, which they adopted, like every barbarous people in similar circumstances, and its institutions were valid for them.

Wherever our records speak to us, we find in Babylonia a number of towns whose divine cult was

ALL THAT REMAINS OF NIPPUR, THE CITY OF ENLIL
Nippur was the principal religious centre of the whole of Babylonia.

in high reputation, and whose importance as the centre of high-roads, and the focus of intercourse and civilisation, was maintained throughout all history. We shall mention here the most important, following the Euphrates upward from the south: Eridu, or Abu Shahrain, the seat of the Ea cult; Ur, or Mukayyar, the town devoted to moon-worship in Southern Babylonia; Lagash, also called Shir-pur-la, with phonetic reading of the ideographic style of writing, marked by the mounds of Tello, and known to us by the excavations of the French consul, De Sarzec, and a town not far from Tello, on

known to have been the principal religious centre of the whole of Babylonia. In Northern Babylonia the most important towns are Babylon, the city of Marduk, which did not assume the chief rôle until later; Kish and Opio, in the neighbourhood of the later city of Seleucia; and Kutha, or Tell Ibrahim, the city of Nergal; and more to the north Sippar, or Abu-Habba, the Sun-town of Northern Babylonia; and Dur-ilu, with the cult of Anu, probably marked by the mound of Der. Further to the north begins the steppe of Mesopotamia, and we now meet on the banks of

RUINS OF THE FAMOUS BIBLICAL CITY, "UR OF THE CHALDEES"
Ur was an important city-state of Southern Babylonia, and, like others in the Mesopotamian valley, a town of the most ancient past when first it appears in history. It was the seat of the worship of Sin, the moon-god.

the other bank of the Shatt el-Hai, whose name is expressed by the signs Gish-khu, but was probably pronounced as Umma. The rulers of this city waged a constant warfare with the early kings of Lagash, and their history is typical of that of the early Babylonian city-states. Further, Isin, which was later the seat of a Babylonian dynasty; Larsa, or Senkereh, where the South Babylonian sun-cult had its seat; Erech, Uruk, or Warka, the seat of Nanâ-Ishtar; Nippur, or Niffer, the city of Enlil, which has been examined by American excavators, and is now

the Tigris, going up stream, the important towns of Ashur, or Kala Shergat, Calah Kalkhi, or Nimrud, and Nineveh, at a much later period of the greatest importance as capitals of the kingdom of Assyria. More easterly, toward Media, lies Arbaïl, or Arbela, now Erbil, which commands the East Assyrian country, the district between the Upper and the Lower Zab. Here the roads to Media and the places on Lake Urumiya converge. Returning to the district between the rivers, we find the Sinjar range of hills, certainly once occupied by towns, even if nothing has hitherto been definitely settled on the point. The great steppe of Mesopotamia becomes again suitable for considerable settlements in the two valleys of the Khabur and Belikh. Here there are a number of hitherto unexplored "tells"—that is, sites of towns now covered by earth, and rising in the form of rounded mounds above the surrounding plain. Harran, the moon-city in the upper valley of the Belikh, was the most important, and flourished until a late period.

Babylonia's Dense Population

These are by no means all the chief towns of the region of Babylonian civilisation. On the contrary, we cannot picture to ourselves the density of the settlements with which all the districts that come under our notice—if we omit the parts of the steppe where water was deficient—were then covered. Babylonia, at the time of her prosperity, was, like Egypt, cultivated in a manner which resembles gardening more than our notions of agriculture, and was proportionately covered with settlements. The towns which we have named are only those which have played a particularly prominent rôle through their political and religious importance, or of which we have considerable knowledge in consequence of excavations on their sites. There are besides countless other " tells " which are still awaiting the spade of the excavator.

On the assumption that the Sumerians first occupied the whole of Babylonia, their displacement by the Semites may be described as follows. We may suppose that the Semitic immigrants occupied the country in the same way as at a later period their kinsmen who followed them, the Chaldæans and the Hebrews, can be shown historically to have taken possession of Babylonia and Canaan. They pressed into the open country, where they maintained their position, half on sufferance, half by force, and gradually gained possession of the towns; and thus their supremacy over the whole country was secured. Instead of nomads they were then settled townsfolk, who adopted the civilisation of the country unconditionally. Politically, an important change was thus effected in them. The free nomads, under the headship of a sheikh, became the subjects of a king; for their leader turned the existing institutions to his own advantage more quickly than his " brothers " who followed him. We must, then, assume that there were gradually formed a series of separate city-states corresponding to the old Sumerian centres of civilisation in the districts which were occupied by the several invading tribes. They had scarcely taken possession of these when their kings—just like the separate tribes in the nomadic era, so far as they were not connected by "blood relationship"—became natural rivals; and the struggle between them necessarily began and continued until it ended in the subjugation of the one by the other, and in the gradual formation of one or more great empires.

Sumerians Displaced by Semites

THE KHABUR, A HISTORIC RIVER OF MESOPOTAMIA
A tributary of the Tigris, at Arban, the site of Shadikanna, which was the capital of an Aramæan prince.

EARLY STATES OF BABYLONIA

WE should naturally expect to find as the earliest monuments of Babylonia inscriptions of kings of the various great towns which were at war with one another. This expectation has been fulfilled by the most recent discoveries. Small as they are in comparison with what may still be won from the soil, they are amply sufficient to give a picture of the political conditions of the period.

The earliest inscriptions hitherto known are those of kings of Lagash in Southern Babylonia, of Kish, and of the city of Gish-khu, or Umma, whose rulers we find at war with each other and alternately gaining the upper hand. There is no object in following them minutely, or in attempting to arrange in chronological order all the names of rulers that have been recovered. But a sketch may here be given of the principal facts that have been established.

The Early Priest-Kings The result of these wars is the development of larger kingdoms; for the king of the victorious town is reckoned the lord of the subjugated princes, who call themselves "Patesi," or priest-kings. In the earliest period we know that Lugal-shag-engur, patesi of Shirpurla, or Lagash, was the contemporary of Me-silim, king of Kish, for a mace-head has been discovered at Tello, bearing an inscription of the latter king, which records his rebuilding of the temple of Ningirsu at Lagash at the time Lugal-shag-engur was patesi of that city. We may see in this fact evidence that Me-silim exercised suzerainty over Southern Babylonia, and it was in consequence of his position as over-lord that he was called in as arbitrator in a dispute between the cities of Lagash and Gish-khu, or Umma.

The history of the rivalry which existed at this period between these two neighbouring cities may be summarised, as it is typical of the relations existing between the early city-states. After a treaty of delimitation between their respective territories had been drawn up under the direction of Me-silim, a stele was set up to commemorate the fixing of the boundary, and peace ensued between the two cities for several generations. But at length an ambitious patesi of Gish-khu, named Ush, removed the stele and invaded the plain of Lagash, where he succeeded in conquering and holding a fertile district named Gu-edin. But he was defeated by the men of Lagash,

Rivalry of the City-States and his successor, a patesi named Enakalli, concluded with Eannatum, patesi of Lagash, a solemn treaty concerning the boundary between their cities, which is still preserved upon the famous " Stele of Vultures " in the Louvre, of which an illustration is given on page 262 of this work. A deep boundary ditch was dug, the old stele was restored and a new one set up beside it, and Enakalli agreed to pay heavy tribute in grain for the supply of the great temples in Lagash. Again there was a period of peace, but on Eannatum's death, Urlumma, the successor of Enakalli, broke the treaty by destroying the frontier ditches and breaking the steles in pieces; but he appears to have been defeated and kept in check by Eannatum I., the reigning patesi of Lagash. In the reign of Entemena, the son and successor of Eannatum, fresh trouble arose in consequence of raids on the part of the men of Gish-khu, and

Beginnings of Empire peace was restored only after a pitched battle and the capture of the latter city by Entemena, who henceforth ruled Gish-khu through a governor and administrative officers appointed by himself.

The history of Gish-khu and Lagash illustrates the independent position enjoyed by the separate cities of Babylonia at this early period, and it also enables us to watch the process by means of which the more powerful of two neighbouring cities in process of time succeeded in gaining the ascendancy. But the temporary character of these political combinations is also well illustrated by the sequel; for in the reign of Urukagina, who styled himself King of Lagash, Lugal-zaggisi, the patesi of

Gish-khu, succeeded in capturing Lagash, which he laid waste, destroying its temples and putting its inhabitants to the sword. In consequence of this victory and of his successes against other cities in Southern Babylonia, he claimed the title of " King of the land." Other rulers of this early time, whose period cannot be exactly stated, are Lugal-kigub-nidudu and Lugal-kisalsi, kings of Erech and of Ur ; Enshag-kushana, a king of Southern Babylonia ; and Urumush and Manishtusu, who reigned in Kish at a time when that city was at the height of its power.

The earliest empire in the proper sense of the term was formed with its capital in the city of Agade, under whose kings the Semitic inhabitants of Northern Babylonia for the first time succeeded in enforcing their authority over the whole country. At this time the South Babylonian patesis were subject to the sovereignty of the North Babylonian kings, of whom Shargani-shar-ali, usually called Sargon, and his son Naram-Sin are known to us by a number of inscriptions. The first of the two styles himself King of Agade, in North Babylonia, and had therefore conquered the south from there ; and accounts of his reign and that of his son prove that they extended their victorious career over Nearer Asia, so far as it ever came under the influence of Babylonian culture. They ruled not merely Babylonia and Mesopotamia, but Syria and Palestine. Sargon, indeed, is said, in a late copy of an inscription, to have sailed out into the Mediterranean, and an attempt has been made to prove that in Cyprus are to be found traces of the influence of Babylonia from the most ancient times. But, although this theory is now disproved by recent discoveries, it is certain that he extended his conquests to the Syrian coast. Wars with the northern barbarians necessarily followed, as well as expeditions to the south. In this way a great Semitic-Babylonian empire was founded, embracing the whole of Nearer Asia. The names

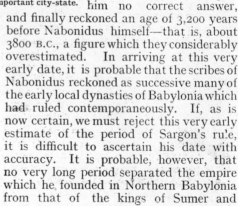

AN EARLY KING OF LAGASH
The statue of a Sumerian royal person-age of Lagash, an important city-state.

of Sargon and Naram-Sin mark, therefore, the zenith of the power attained by the earlier Semitic inhabitants of Babylonia. This is shown by purely external evidence, for their inscriptions are, in distinction from those of Southern Babylonia, composed in Semitic.

Of the later patesis of Lagash, Gudea [see illustration on page 270 of this work] may be specially mentioned, owing to the number and length of his inscriptions, which bear witness that the dominion of Babylonian civilisation was as wide as all accounts make out. He had the materials for his buildings brought from distant countries : cedar from Amanus, stone for his statues from Arabia or Sinai. This is a proof of the extent of peaceable intercourse at that time. It is noteworthy that Gudea did not assume the title of king, so that we may probably regard him and his immediate predecessors as still acknowledging the suzerainty of the northern kingdom founded by Sargon of Agade. The fame of Sargon and his political achievements was handed down to the latest times, even when men were not altogether clearly informed about him. Sargon of Agade became a legendary hero, and when the last king of Babylon, Nabonidus, found an inscription of his son Naram-Sin, and asked his learned men for information as to its date, they could give him no correct answer, and finally reckoned an age of 3,200 years before Nabonidus himself—that is, about 3800 B.C., a figure which they considerably overestimated. In arriving at this very early date, it is probable that the scribes of Nabonidus reckoned as successive many of the early local dynasties of Babylonia which had ruled contemporaneously. If, as is now certain, we must reject this very early estimate of the period of Sargon's rule, it is difficult to ascertain his date with accuracy. It is probable, however, that no very long period separated the empire which he founded in Northern Babylonia from that of the kings of Sumer and

Akkad; in these circumstances we may conclude that he did not live at a period earlier than 2800 B.C. or 2700 B.C.

Within the sphere of the Babylonian civilisation, at one time fighting with the rulers of Babylonia, at another submitting to them, as can be best realised by the testimony of the Assyrian era, there were then Elam, with its border state of Ernutbal, and the tribes inhabiting the mountainous districts extending from Media to Cappadocia. To the north-east of it lived the barbarians of the Umman - Manda, the Manda hordes, the Babylonian "Scythians," and the inhabitants of Gutium, or the district of the "Kuti." We possess an inscription of one of the kings of the last-named country, in the language and style of the Naram-Sin period, about a votive offering in Babylonia, probably in Sippar, similar to the dedications of foreigners to the Greek oracles. Toward Asia Minor, beginning in Cappadocia, lies the district of the "Khatti" and "Hittites," who were soon to make themselves felt in Babylonia, and were to change the course of Babylonian history by bringing the powerful dynasty of Hammurabi to an end. Northern Palestine meets us as "the western

UR NINA, KING OF LAGASH
This bas-relief from Tello, now in the Louvre, shows the king, about B.C. 4500, performing a religious ceremony in the temple of Ningirsu.

NINGIRSU
The divinity of the city-state of Lagash. From a sculptured fragment in the Louvre.

land," and formed an integral part of the empire founded by Sargon of Agade. Arabia may have been more accessible to the earlier Babylonians than later to the Assyrians or even to us. In the south there must have been navigation on the Persian Gulf, for Dilmun, the island of Bahrein, was situated within the sphere of Babylonian interests, and has left monuments in cuneiform characters. It is also hardly imaginable that Gudea obtained his stone from Magan except by sea.

The numerous monuments of this period display a high technical perfection. The first inscriptions and monuments of the kings of Lagash are indeed very rude, but later a stage is reached which is comparable to that of the old empire in Egypt. The inscriptions of Sargon and Naram-Sin, written in a peculiar ornamental script, and the statues of Gudea display great skill. Countless documents concerning the management of temples and estates dating from this period have been discovered on the site of

RUINS OF AKKAD, PERHAPS A SUMERIAN CITY
The kings of Sumer and Akkad gained the supremacy in Babylonia about B.C. 2500.

Lagash. Such is Babylonia, its range and its civilisation, in the third millennium B.C., when it reached, perhaps, a higher stage in the development of art and culture than was attained for many centuries later.

The last inscriptions of the patesis of Lagash known to us, the direct descendants of Gudea, partly contain dedications to new kings, of whom many inscriptions are extant from towns in Southern and Northern Babylonia. These rulers term themselves " Kings of Sumer and Akkad," and their inscriptions, at least the South Babylonian, like those of Lagash, are composed in Sumerian. We have therefore to notice a great alteration since the preceding era : North Babylonia has yielded the supremacy to South Babylonia. The kings of Ur rule Babylonia in the place of those of Agade ; for even the north belongs to them, as inscriptions found there prove clearly enough.

The Kings of Sumer and Akkad

We have in this kingdom of " Sumer and Akkad " to distinguish generally between three dynasties. The first, of which the kings Ur-Engur and his son Dungi are best known to us, was termed the Dynasty of Ur, after the title and seat of government. The numerous inscriptions of the two kings tell us only about the erection of temples in all the important towns of Babylonia, but do not contain information as to their political activity and power. It follows, however, from the dispossession of the Semitic sovereigns of Northern Babylonia that they must have largely encroached upon their territory, and a recently-discovered chronicle definitely proves that such was indeed the case. We learn from this document that Dungi, who succeeded his father, Ur-Engur, the founder of the dynasty, undertook active operations against the north and finally broke the power of the Semitic rulers, who had inherited the empire built up by Sargon of Agade and his son, Naram-Sin. We learn that he succeeded in capturing and sacking the city of Babylon, and he is recorded to have laid hands upon the treasures which had been accumulated in Esagila, the temple of Marduk, the city-god of Babylon. Moreover, it is related that Dungi cared greatly for the city of Eridu, which is described in the chronicle as having still stood at this period " upon the shore of the sea "—that is to say, upon the Persian

Dynasty of " Ur of the Chaldees "

Gulf, whose waters had not yet receded owing to the detritus carried down by the Euphrates and deposited at its mouth.

In Dungi's care for Eridu to the detriment of Babylon, we may see evidence of the Sumerian reaction inaugurated by the dynasty of Ur in Southern Babylonia against the Semitic supremacy of the north. This new record proves that Esagila, the temple of Babylon, had already begun to rival the more ancient shrine of Nippur, the seat of Enlil, as the most sacred temple of Babylonia. The Semitic rulers of Sargon's dynasty had doubtless lavished their offerings at the shrine of Marduk, which had consequently gained in prestige and importance, and had acquired the sanctity and influence of a national shrine. The blow which Dungi struck at its very existence was thus the outcome of a consistent policy, for, by sacking Babylon, and carrying off the treasures of its temple, he demolished the existing symbol and sanction of northern rule. The revolution which Ur-Engur and Dungi carried out was thus not only political, but was also based upon a racial and religious movement.

Moreover, Dungi did not confine himself to a destructive policy, for he at once set about the task of substituting a national shrine, which should furnish a counterweight to the former influence of Babylon, and by its position and associations should assist the transference of power to the Sumerian districts of the south. For this purpose he selected Eridu, the oldest and most sacred shrine of the Sumerians, which was situated in the extreme south of Babylonia. Here we may conjecture he deposited the temple treasures from Esagila, and, by reviving the splendour of the ancient Temple of Enki, he furnished Southern Babylonia with a shrine which he hoped would rival the fame previously enjoyed by that at Babylon.

A Rival to Babylon

The building inscriptions of Ur-Engur and of Dungi which have been recovered are evidence of the extent of the empire founded by these two earliest kings of Sumer and Akkad, for they prove that their influence was not confined to Southern and Northern Babylonia, but extended also to Elam. Moreover, the date-formulæ which have been recovered upon tablets and date-lists of the period prove that Dungi undertook other military expeditions, after his subjugation

of Northern Babylonia, in the effort to extend the boundaries of his kingdom. The fragment of a dynastic chronicle, which has recently been identified among the tablets from Nippur, proves that the dynasty of Ur lasted for 117 years, and, in addition to Ur-Engur and Dungi, comprised the reigns of Bur-Sin, Gimil-Sin, and Ibi-Sin, these five rulers following one another in direct succession.

The dynasty of Ur was directly succeeded by that of Isin, which took its name from the city forming its capital. The new dynastic chronicle states concisely that " the supremacy of Ur was overthrown, and that Isin took its kingdom." We may therefore infer that Isin obtained the hegemony among the Babylonian cities as the result of a war with Ur, in which Ibi-Sin was overthrown by Ishbi-Ura, who founded the dynasty of Isin, and reigned for thirty-two years. He was followed in direct succession by Gimil-ilishu, Idin-Dagan, Ishme-Dagan, and Libit-Ishtar. We possess short inscriptions of the two last kings named in the above list, but they throw no light upon the history of the period. From the fact that Libit-Ishtar was succeeded by Ur-Ninib, who is not stated in the chronicle to have been his son or brother, we may possibly infer that the latter usurped the throne. About this period we know that another son of Ishme-Dagan, named Eannatum, held the office of high-priest in the temple of the moon-god at Ur, which was then under the protection of a certain Gungunu, king of Ur, who also claimed the titles of " King of Larsa " and " King of Sumer and Akkad." It has therefore been suggested that at the end of Libit-Ishtar's reign an invasion of Babylonia took place, possibly from Elam, which

GUDEA, THE PRIEST-KING
Gudea was the most famous patesi of Lagash, and under his rule early Babylonian art reached its zenith.

overthrew the direct line of Isin. Eannatum, who would naturally have succeeded his brother in the event of the latter dying without issue, may have sought refuge with Gungunu, who had taken advantage of the political disturbance to set up an independent kingdom in Ur and Larsa. However this may be, it is clear from the chronicle that Ur-Ninib occupied the throne of Isin, and after a reign of twenty-eight years was succeeded by his son Bur-Sin II., and his grandsons, Iter-Kasha, and a brother whose name has not been recovered. Of the five succeeding rulers, the name of one only, Enlil-bani, is known with certainty, and since none of these rulers are recorded in the chronicle to have been related, it is possible that each was a usurper, and that a period of trouble and unrest followed the reign of Ur-Ninib's last descendant.

Enlil-bani reigned for twenty-four years, but his predecessor ruled only for six months; and the reigns of his three successors lasted altogether for only twelve years, facts which may be cited in favour of the view that it was a period marked by palace revolutions and political unrest. The last two kings of the dynasty were Sin-magir and his son Damik-ilishu, who reigned for eleven and twenty-three years respectively. In an inscription of the former, which has been recovered, the king claims dominion over the whole of Babylonia, so that we may conclude that he succeeded in establishing his throne upon a firm basis. Thus the dynasty of Isin endured for 225 years and six months, and comprised no fewer than sixteen kings. During this period it is probable that the hegemony of Isin was disputed by other great cities of Babylonia. We have already noted the

appearance of Gungunu, an independent ruler of Ur, soon after the reign of Ishme-Dagan, and we may probably assign to the same period another king of Ur, Sumu-ilu, whose name has been found upon a votive model of a dog which was offered to the goddess Nin-Isin, " the Lady of Isin," on behalf of Sumu-ilu, by a high official of Lagash. Two

The Last King of Sumer rulers of Erech, named Sin-gashid and Sin-gamil, are also to be set in this period, or in that of the dynasty of Larsa, the city which probably succeeded Isin in obtaining the lead among the great cities of the land.

We thus come to the third and last independent dynasty of the kings of Sumer and Akkad, which had its seat in Larsa, the town of the Sun-god Shamash. From the times of these kings—up to the present are known Nur-Adad, Sin-idin-nam, Arad-Sin and Rim-Sin, who probably followed each other—as of their predecessors, we have a great number of records of business life, the dates of which are mostly fixed by great events, and thus supply us with much information as to wars and other important under-takings. There are absolutely no royal inscriptions with historical announce-ments ; only the usual inscriptions as to buildings and dedications. The last two kings of the dynasty, Arad-Sin and Rim-Sin, were not Babylonians, but Elamites. They expressly style them-selves in their inscriptions sons of the Elamite Kudur-Mabuk, who seems to have conquered a considerable portion of Southern Babylonia, and established his son Arad-Sin in the cities of Larsa and Ur. We learn from the accounts of the earlier times that Elam was the mightiest opponent of Babylonia. A vigorous blow must at this time have been struck which made Southern Babylonia a dependency of Elam for a time. Arad-Sin was suc-ceeded by his brother Rim-Sin,

Elam in Babylonia who was the last of the " Kings of Sumer and Akkad." The wars which he carried on with Hammurabi, the most famous king of the first dynasty of Babylon, and his final defeat and death at the hands of Samsu-iluna, Hammurabi's son, will best be narrated when we have described the rise of Babylon to power under the West-Semitic kings of its first dynasty.

Coincidentally with the South Baby-lonian kings of Larsa, and partly with their predecessors, the dynasty of Isin, there reigned in Northern Babylonia, in the city of Babylon, a succession of princes which, in accordance with the lists of Babylonian kings, we designate the First Dynasty of Babylon. We have seen that after the days of Sargon and Naram-Sin, when the north had the supreme power, kings were again ruling in the south, in the dynasty of Ur, who styled themselves kings of Northern Babylonia. But now in the numerous business documents of that time and region the rulers of Northern Babylonia, up to the subjection of the south, which we shall soon mention, are not called " kings," although in point of fact they conducted the government. The conclusion may be drawn that we have to deal with the vassal kings of those South Babylonians. The South Baby-lonian kings of Isin accordingly had vassal kings in Babylon who exercised indepen-dent government within their own district. The same conditions continued under the several kings of the house of Larsa. The last king of this dynasty, Rim-Sin, the Elamite, was signally defeated by the fifth of these kings, after the relation of vassal had long been merely formal, and

First Dynasty of Babylon his power was finally broken by his successor. It has hither-to been assumed that when once the Elamites were driven from the cities of Southern Babylonia the independence of the south was ended for ever. We shall see, however, that a new foe was to arise, who succeeded in forming another independent kingdom in the south. But, in spite of the rise of this new kingdom on the shores of the Persian Gulf, it may truly be said that Babylonian history from this time becomes really a history of Babylon.

The dynasty under which the sove-reignty was for ever transferred to the city, and which, in consequence, gave the name to the country, and thus to the whole civilisation, was not "Babylonian-Semitic," but West Semitic or Canaanite, for mean-while the second of the great Semitic migra-tions mentioned above had been completed. This migration flooded Babylonia also. The advancing nomads forced their way from the open country into the towns, and Babylonia received another ruling population in place of that which had lived its day, and this in turn assimilated the Babylonian civilisation.

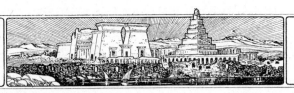
THE RISE OF BABYLON

THE HAMMURABI AND KASSITE DYNASTIES

THE founder of the First Dynasty of Babylon, named Su-abu or Sumu-abu, came to the throne shortly before 2000 B.C., and a recently-discovered chronicle proves that he waged war, not with Southern Babylonia as we might expect, but with Assyria, whose existence as a kingdom is thus proved to have been far older than has hitherto been supposed. Su-abu's opponent in Assyria was Ilu-shuma, one of the earliest priest-kings of Ashur whose names have been recovered, and it is not unlikely that he seized the opportunity of a change of dynasty at Babylon to make a bid for his country's independence. Of the result of this early conflict between Babylon and Assyria we know nothing, and our information is equally scanty with regard to the foreign relations of Babylon under Su-abu's four successors, Sumu-la-ilu, Zabum, Apil-Sin, and Sin-muballit, for the date-formulæ of the period record building operations and the like, and do not reflect the history of the period. Under Sin-muballit's son, Hammurabi [see illustration on page 266 of this work], a change took place, for by signally defeating Rim-Sin, he expelled the Elamites from Babylonia, and extended the authority of Babylon over the southern portion of the country. He thus succeeded in welding together a mighty empire with its capital at Babylon. It is true that Rim-Sin was not finally defeated until the first years of the reign of Samsu-iluna, Hammurabi's son. But it was Hammurabi who practically put an end to the empire of the southern kings of Sumer and Akkad, and raised Babylon to the position of the principal city in the land. So far as her external influence was concerned, we may conclude that Babylonia kept at this period also the supremacy over the West. The Nearer East is still Babylonian, and the conception that we have to form of the importance of Babylonia for the rest of Western Asia at that time corresponds in

Hammurabi's Empire Welding

all main points with the earlier period. The East, which was in the possession of the "Canaanites," resembles on the whole that of the "Semitic Babylonians."

Upon the social condition of Babylonia during the period of the first dynasty of Babylon considerable light has been thrown by the discovery of Hammurabi's famous Code of Laws. This invaluable inscription is engraved upon a huge block of black diorite, which was discovered by De Morgan during excavations carried out in the "tell," or mound, of the acropolis at Susa in the winter of 1901–2. The laws, together with introductory and concluding texts, were engraved upon the monolith in forty-nine long columns of writing, of which forty-four are still preserved ; and at the head of the stone is a sculptured representation of Hammurabi receiving the laws from Shamash, the Sun-god.

Hammurabi's Code of Laws

It would be out of place in the present work to attempt any discussion of the question as to how far the laws of Babylonia, as embodied in this document, have influenced other ancient legal codes, and in particular the Mosaic legislation. We are here concerned only with Hammurabi's code, as an important and recently discovered source of information concerning early Babylonian life and custom. It was drawn up and published by the king for the guidance of his people, and it regulates their duties and their relations to one another in all the pursuits and occupations of their daily life. It defines the responsibilities and privileges of the various classes of the population, and, since it formed an exhaustive set of regulations, it enables us to construct a fairly complete picture of Babylonian society during this early period.

The numerous contracts and letters of the time of the first dynasty of Babylon which have come down to us, and in particular the series of royal despatches of Hammurabi himself, which are preserved in the British Museum, abundantly prove that the code was no dead letter, but was actively enforced under the personal supervision of the king. It may thus be employed as a trustworthy and accurate witness to the conditions which existed in Babylonia during the period at which it was drawn up.

From the code we learn that the population of Babylonia was composed of three **Babylonian** principal classes, each of which **Society in** occupied a separate and well-**B.C. 2000** defined position in the social community. The lowest of these three classes were the slaves, who must have formed a considerable proportion of the population. The class next above them in the social scale consisted of free men, who were possessed of some property of their own, but were poor and humble people, as was implied in the name they bore—mushkenu. The highest, or upper class in the community, comprised the owners of large estates and landed property, the higher officials and servants of the State, and all the officers and ministers of the Court. The privileges and responsibilities which the two classes of free men in the Babylonian community respectively enjoyed are well illustrated in the code by the scale of payments as compensation for injury which they were obliged to make or were entitled to receive.

The penalties enforced upon a member of the upper class were far heavier than those his humbler free neighbour had to pay, but the latter's privileges in this respect were counter-balanced by a corresponding diminution of the value at which his injuries were assessed. Slaves could be owned by both classes of free men, though they were naturally more numerous in the households and on the estates of members of the upper class. The slave was the absolute property of his owner, and could be bought **Rights** and sold, and deposited as **of** security for a debt; but on the **Slaves** whole his life was not a hard one, for he was a recognised member of his master's household, and was a valuable piece of property, which it was to the owner's advantage to keep in good condition. Moreover, the slave had rights and privileges of his own which the code explicitly sets forth. Thus, under certain conditions, it was possible for a slave to acquire property of his own, and by so doing he was entitled, if he obtained his master's consent, to purchase his own

freedom. Marriage between a male slave and a free woman was also possible, and the children of such a union were free, and did not become the property of the slave's master; while if the owner of a female slave had begotten children by her he could not use her in payment for a debt. Thus it will be seen that the law afforded protection even to the humblest members of the community.

The code also supplies considerable information concerning the family life of the early Babylonians. We here have detailed regulations concerning marriage and divorce, the giving of marriage portions, the rights of widows, the laws of inheritance, and those which regulated the adoption and maintenance of children. It is unnecessary to describe or discuss these regulations in detail, but one striking fact which they emphasise may here be pointed out—the recognised status occupied by the wife in the Babylonian household. Evidence of the extremely independent position enjoyed by women at the time of the first dynasty of Babylon may also be seen in the existence of a special class **Independence** of women, who followed the **of** profession of religious votaries, **Women** though their duties were not strictly sacerdotal. Most women of this class, who are mentioned in the contract-tablets of the period, were attached to the temple of the sun-god at Sippar or to that of Marduk at Babylon, but it may be inferred that all the important temples in the country had similar classes of female votaries in their service. The duties of these women do not appear to have resembled in any way those of the sacred prostitutes in the service of the goddess Ishtar, at Erech. On the contrary, they occupied a position of considerable influence and independence. While they generally lived together in a special building, or convent, attached to the temple, they were free to leave it and to contract marriage. Their vows, however, entailed the obligation to remain virgins, and though a married votary was thus precluded from bearing children herself, she could provide her husband with a concubine for this purpose, while she still retained her position as the permanent head of the household.

Even when unmarried, however, the votary enjoyed the status of a married woman, and was protected from slander by special regulations. In return for these privileges, she was obliged, under severe penalties, to maintain a high standard of moral conduct and was precluded from any occupation or act which was derogatory to her high position. She could possess property of her own, and on taking vows was provided with a portion by her father which, on her death, did not pass to the temple, but returned to her own family, unless her father had assigned her the privilege of be-queathing it. The social prestige enjoyed by the votaries is attested by the fact that they included within their body many women of good family, and even members of the royal house; while the rules of the order and the high repute which it en-joyed may be taken to indicate a very enlight-ened conception of the position of women at this early period.

The large body of regu-lations which deal with the duties of debtors and creditors are evidence of the extent to which the early Babylonians en-gaged in commercial pur-suits and undertakings, and we learn that an active interchange of com-modities was carried on between distant cities. Thus, a wealthy merchant would extend his business and obtain large profits by trading with other towns, and for this pur-pose he would employ agents, who may thus be regarded as the fore-runners of the modern commercial traveller. The agent received from the merchant the money, grain, wool, oil, or whatever sort of goods he had to deal in, and he gave to his employer a properly attested receipt for the same. So far as his trading was concerned, he acted inde-pendently, and on his return he would pay to the merchant a fixed share of his profits, retaining the remainder as payment for

THE CODE OF HAMMURABI

Hammurabi, B.C. 2200, was one of the ablest of the world's rulers. He drew up the Code of Laws engraved on the block of diorite illustrated above, which is now in the Louvre. The king is shown receiving the laws from the Sun-god.

Mansell

his own services and the dangers he had incurred.

In the event of the caravan with which the agent travelled being attacked by robbers or by enemies in a foreign country, the loss of the goods was borne by the merchant at home; the code, however, regulates the procedure to be followed in such circum-stances, while at the same time it attempts to pro-tect the agent from any risk of being defrauded by his employer. Im-mense profits were ob-tained by merchants and agents who engaged in this foreign commerce, and we may conclude that at the period of the first dynasty, and for many centuries earlier, the great trade routes of the East were even more crowded with caravans than they are at the present day.

Water-transport was, however, usually em-ployed for the carriage of grain, wood, and other bulky or heavy materials, wherever it was avail-able, and the code con-tains detailed directions concerning the fees to be paid to boatmen engaged in the carrying trade upon the rivers and large canals of Babylonia. Other regulations sought to ensure good work on the part of boat-builders by fixing on them the responsibility for faulty or unsound work, while the boatmen were respon-sible for the loss or damage incurred through their own carelessness to goods entrusted to their charge. A still more important function of the rivers and canals in Babylonia was the irrigation of the cultivated lands, and the code contains detailed regulations for the repair of the channels and dykes and the right to the use of the water. A large body of legislation deals, in fact, with the agricultural life of the early Babylonians, and regulates all cases of dispute which were likely to arise between owners of land and their farming tenants, owners and hirers of cattle and asses, or between shepherds and herdsmen and their employers ; while fines were levied in cases of damage or injury arising through carelessness in looking after cattle.

It is of interest to note that Hammurabi's code attempted to protect the

Penalties for Careless Doctors public from carelessness on the part of two important classes of the community—doctors and builders, and it was singularly just that death or injury arising from bad work on the part of either was held to merit punishment in kind. Thus, if a doctor through unskilful treatment caused the death of a member of the upper class, or inflicted a serious injury upon him, such as the loss of an eye, the doctor was liable to have both his hands amputated—a drastic, but certainly an effective method of preventing other unsuccessful operations on his part. Similarly, if his unfortunate patient had been the slave of a member of the middle class—of poor free men—and had died under his hands, he had to give the owner a new slave, or, in the event of his patient merely losing an eye, he had to pay the owner half the slave's value.

The penalties attaching to jerry-building were even more severe. For if a builder built a house for a man, and his work was so unsound that the house fell and killed the owner, the builder himself was put to death ; and if the owner's son was killed by the fall of the house, the builder's son was put to death. If one or more of the owner's slaves were killed, the builder had to restore him slave for slave, and besides compensating the owner for any damage to his goods, he had to rebuild the house

Death to the Jerry-builder anew, or such part of it as had fallen. These interesting survivals of the law of an eye for an eye and a tooth for a tooth prove that in the medical profession and the building trade, as practised by the early Babylonians, the payment of compensation alone had not been a sufficiently strong deterrent to prevent bad work.

From the brief discussion that has been attempted of some of the most striking enactments of Hammurabi's code, an idea will have been formed of the extent to which the administration of law and justice had been developed in Babylonia

at the time of the first dynasty of Babylon. The laws, however, were not the invention of Hammurabi himself, who merely codified them. They were based upon centuries of tradition, and were the result of innumerable judgments drawn up upon tablets and carefully preserved in the legal archives of the State. In discussing the enactments of the code therefore, we have not been dealing with a temporary phase in the life of ancient Babylonia. On the contrary, its enactments reflect the spirit in which justice had been administered in Babylonia for a long period anterior to the rise of Babylon under her West-Semitic kings, and we may conclude that it continued to influence the administration of the country during its subsequent domination by successive dynasties of foreign origin.

In the native list of kings the first Babylonian dynasty is followed by a second, consisting also of eleven kings. Their Sumerian names, many of which are ingeniously interpreted, and the lengths of their reigns are preserved for us by the lists. Until quite recently we knew nothing

Second Dynasty of Babylon more, since other information about this period was strangely deficient. Its total duration was 368 years, according to the list, but of the events which took place at this time we knew absolutely nothing. It seemed strange that so long a period of Babylonian history should have left no trace behind it on the sites of the ancient Babylonian cities which had been already excavated. If a dynasty of kings had occupied the throne of Babylon during this protracted period, how did it happen that among the many thousands of contract tablets which had been recovered, none had been found dated in the reigns of these eleven kings ?

The answer to this question has recently been supplied by a newly-discovered chronicle which is preserved in the British Museum. From this invaluable document we now learn that the second dynasty of the list of the kings never in reality occupied the Babylonian throne. In fact, the eleven kings of which the dynasty was composed ruled only in a district of limited extent in the extreme south of Babylonia on the shores of the Persian Gulf. This district was known as the *mat tamti*, or " Country of the Sea," taking its name from its position on the littoral of the gulf, to which the

Babylonians gave the name of "The Sea in the East," or the Eastern Sea. From the newly-discovered chronicle we learn that the territory of the eleven kings, who formed the so-called "Second Dynasty," was confined to this strip of coast, and was never extended so as to include the northern and central districts of Babylonia proper. We further learn from the chronicle that the rulers of this little state did not live in the period between the first dynasty of Babylon and the Kassites, as has hitherto been assumed on the evidence of the kings list; but that their reigns were contemporaneous with those of the later kings of the first dynasty of Babylon, and of the earlier Kassite rulers.

The exact date at which Iluma-ilu, the founder of this kingdom on the shores of the Persian Gulf, declared his independence

Under the reigns of Ammi-ditana and Ammi-zaduga, the successors of Abeshu upon the Babylonian throne, we know little of the foreign policy of Babylon, with the exception of the fact that Ammi-zaduga inflicted a defeat upon the Elamites. It may be inferred, however, that Babylon had trouble upon her eastern border from the Kassites, who already in Samsu-iluna's reign had begun to make raids on Babylonian territory, and from the kings of the Country of the Sea in the south. When, therefore, under Samsu-ditana, the last king of the dynasty, Hittite tribes from Cappadocia and Northern Syria descended the Euphrates and attacked Northern Babylonia, the capital fell an easy prey to their onslaught. The great temple of Marduk, the city god, was destroyed, and the statue of the god himself was carried back by the Hittite

A BABYLONIAN SEAL CYLINDER AND ITS METHOD OF USE

A reproduction of an early Babylonian seal, showing the River-god, Sun-god, Ishtar, and other deities. Impressions of the seal were obtained by passing the cylinder, seen on the left, over soft clay, which was then baked.

is not certain, but we know that he waged successful wars with Samsu-iluna, the son of Hammurabi, and Abeshu, his grandson, who succeeded Samsu-iluna upon the Babylonian throne. From the narrative of the new chronicle it would seem that Samsu-iluna took the initiative in Babylon's struggle with the Country of the Sea. In his first expedition he succeeded in reaching the Persian Gulf, but he was defeated, and in a second campaign he met with no better success. His son Abeshu, after his accession to the throne, again attempted to conquer or curb the state upon his southern borders, but Iluma-ilu succeeded in eluding him. In fact, from this time forward the southern portion of Babylonia passed into the possession of the kings of the Country of the Sea.

invaders in triumph to their own country. In this manner we now know that the powerful dynasty of Hammurabi came to an end. How long a period elapsed between the Hittite conquest and the occupation of Babylon by the Kassites we cannot at present determine, but it is unlikely that they would have long delayed their descent upon the city when once its defences had been reduced and it lay at the mercy of an invader.

The Kassites, who now occupied Babylon as the dominant race, and whose rulers are reckoned as the third dynasty upon the list of kings, at first occupied only Northern Babylonia. They formed, in fact, the vanguard of an advancing tide, and they left many of their own tribes behind them in the mountains of Elam. Even in later times, under Sennacherib, traces of them are to be found in the Zagros Mountains. We are compelled to account for their appearance by a great racial movement which poured itself from the east and north-east over the civilised countries, just as the Turks and Mongols did some thousands of years later. We know very little about the past of that tide of nations which flowed on to Babylonia. Later discoveries will, perhaps, some day explain more clearly the form of its connection with Elam and the other neighbouring countries. The migration of these barbarians assumed in any case great dimensions. The mixture of races in Babylonia thus received a new component, and in the Babel-like confusion of tongues we hear the sound of Kassite, which is known to us only by a list of words and proper names. The scheme of the dynasties of Babylon reckons as Kassite its third house of thirty-six kings, a period of 576 years, extending from about 1700 to the eleventh century. We know most of these kings by name, and have information as to the events of that time from inscriptions, royal and otherwise, although there are here also considerable gaps in the tradition.

Appearance of the Kassites

An insight into the order of things at the beginning of this period is afforded us by the inscription of one of the early princes in this dynasty, the seventh, by name, Agum II. He styles himself " King of the Kashshu and Akkadians, King of the wide dominion of Babylon, who settled with numerous inhabitants the land of Umliash, the border land to Elam, King of Padan and Alman—frontier territories to Media—King of Gutium, the king who rules the four countries of the world." The whole enumeration of titles, different from that of the Babylonian monarchs, and the precedence given to the Kassites, show that the Babylonians did not quickly absorb their new conquerors ; a later king, Karaindash, bears the usual Babylonian titles, and only adds at the end " King of the Kashshu," which his successors actually omit. These barbarians thus only gradually adapted themselves to civilisation, and became Babylonians. It is interesting to note that the inscription of Agum II., from which his titles above enumerated are taken, commemorates the recovery from Khani in Northern Syria of the statue of Marduk, which had been

Barbarians Become Babylonian

carried off by the Hittites on their capture of Babylon in Samsu-ditana's reign. Thence Agum brought it back to Babylon.

A fact of considerable importance with regard to the Kassite occupation of Babylonia has recently been demonstrated, to the effect that their conquest of the whole country did not take place at one time. There were, in fact, two Kassite conquests. The first occurred shortly after the Hittite invasion, and was confined to Northern Babylonia, to which the empire of the earlier Kassite kings was limited. During this period the kingdom of the Country of the Sea continued its independent existence on the shores of the Persian Gulf. But we may infer that the Kassites, who had remained behind in the mountains of Elam, continued to harass Southern Babylonia, and it was probably to put an end to trouble from this quarter that Ea-gamil, the last king of the dynasty founded by Iluma-ilu, invaded Elam.

But his temerity was the signal for a fresh advance of the Kassite hordes, who, under the leadership of one of their chieftains named Ulam-Buriash, drove him from the country, and, following him into Southern Babylonia, signally defeated him, and brought his dynasty to an end. The chronicle from which we learn these facts states that Ulam-Buriash exercised dominion over the Country of the Sea, and that fresh conquests were made there by his nephew Agum. It is therefore probable that from this time forward the Kassites occupied the whole of Babylonia, but it is not clear whether the two halves of the country were at once united under one administration with its centre at Babylon. It is probable that the unification of the kingdom was only gradually achieved, and that during the process the country underwent more than one convulsion. The result of these several invasions and the racial conflicts which ensued was naturally to exhaust the resources of the land, and render its rulers incapable of adopting an aggressive foreign policy.

Kassites Conquer the South

The feebleness of Babylonia and the exhaustion of the population are clearly visible in two further occurrences of this time. The third Semitic migration, the Aramæan, makes its mark in the age of the Kassites (1700–1100 B.C.), and the dominion of Babylonia over the west is disputed and finally destroyed by a new power, which now develops itself from a "town kingship" and seeks aggrandisement—namely, Assyria. The future belongs to these two. The Kassites, the temporary lords of Babylonia, shared the fate of their kingdom, which was forced to resign its suzerainty. As the sovereignty had moved up stream from the south to Babylon, so it moved further to Assyria. The history of Nearer Asia after the encroachment of Assyria, which begins at this period (about the sixteenth century B.C.), is changed essentially by this fact.

The struggle between Assyria and Babylonia for supremacy began under the Kassite dynasty, and, owing to the abundant sources of information now open to us, we can follow its vicissitudes more accurately than the events of the earlier age. This struggle and its result constitute the most important subject for subsequent political history. The history of Babylon and that of Assyria concern us, therefore, in the first place, in so far as they touch each other and are interconnected. Thus we are confronted by two streams of development flowing side by side, the course of which we can best indicate in a combined account. On the other hand, Babylon almost always asserted her independence, and after she had been for a time subdued, she emerged at the end once more the conqueror. At the beginning of this war Babylon was the predominant power, and never ceased, even when under the influence of Assyria, to have a separate history and development. If, therefore, we wish to do more than merely chronicle the wars between Ashur and Babylon, if we wish to do justice to the importance of Babylon as the principal seat of the ancient civilisation, which even Assyria acknowledged, we must follow up separately the history of this independent state.

Assyria Becomes a Power

We have seen, in the first place, what districts were claimed by Agum II., the ruler of Babylonia; his power no longer extended to Mesopotamia and the west. The next known inscription, the one already mentioned of King Karaindash, claimed only the sovereignty over Babylonia. We shall see that attempts to recover Mesopotamia were not made until the power of Assyria, which had its seat there, was expelled. The dominion of Babylonia in Palestine had been replaced by that of Egypt. It seems as if Karain-

dash may have been the head of a new family within the Kassite dynasty; his successors, at least, speak of him in their letters in a way which suggests this idea. We must place him about 1500. All that we know of him, besides the above-mentioned inscription, is that he concluded a treaty with Assyria and engaged in a correspondence with the king of Egypt. This last fact is proved to us in a document which one of his successors, Burnaburiash, sent some fifty to seventy years later to Amenophis IV., and for the knowledge of which we are indebted certainly to one of the most surprising of all the discoveries made in the soil of the ancient East. In the winter of 1887–1888, at Tell el-Amarna, in Middle Egypt, which marks the place of residence of Amenophis IV., over three hundred clay tablets inscribed in the cuneiform character were discovered. One of these tablets is reproduced by photography on page 274 of this History. They represent a small part of the State archives, and contain the letters which kings of Nearer Asia and vassal kings from Syria and Palestine addressed to Amenophis III. and IV. There are in the first group letters of the kings of Babylon, Ashur, Mitani, or Mesopotamia, the king of the Khatti, and of others. It is obvious that these letters give most valuable information as to the history of the Nearer East, and we shall therefore frequently have to refer to them in what follows. The Babylonian letters, which concern us first, tell us little of Babylon's greatness and power; but the existence of the collection is in itself evidence of the extent of Babylonian influence. The letters are written in cuneiform characters, and, with few exceptions, in Babylonian Semitic. And, what is still more significant, there are two letters among them of the Pharaoh, the one to the king of Babylon, the other to a vassal of Northern Palestine, which are also composed in that language. Cuneiform writing and Babylonian language were, therefore, the means of intercommunication throughout the whole of the Nearer East. A knowledge of Babylonian literature was the necessary preliminary to mastering them. This is evident from tablets found there containing a Babylonian myth, written in

Letters of Nearer Asia to Egypt

Egyptian Letters in Cuneiform

1605

Babylon and apparently used in Egypt for teaching purposes.

The two kings, from whom we have recovered eleven letters addressed to the two Pharaohs, were called Kadashman-Bel and Burnaburiash. The former wrote in the last years of Amenophis III., the latter to his successor. The letters generally mention no great State events. They deal principally with marriages between the two royal houses. The Pharaohs received Babylonian princesses into their harem, but were not so liberal with their own flesh and blood to their Babylonian friends—these did not at least receive princesses. What Pharaoh sends in gifts is generally stated to be

AN EARLY BABYLONIAN TOMB
A flat-roofed tomb constructed of baked brick from Ur.

too little ; the money is carefully confided to the purifying agency of the furnace and found unduly alloyed, and better metal and more of it is always demanded.

More important for history are the relations between these two regions of civilisation, exhibited in the fact that Babylonia and Mitani send as presents productions of their industries, among them the much-admired lapis lazuli, skilfully worked in Babylon.

Relations with Egypt Egypt, on the contrary, sends primarily gold. It almost appears as if diplomatic negotiations were left to verbal intercourse and to the cleverness of corrupt court officials, for political questions are seldom discussed. One letter vividly pictures the manners of the age. Some Babylonian merchants, travelling for the king—the kings engaged in business, and enjoyed, it would appear, immunity from taxation—were arrested in Akko, where they apparently wished

to take ship for Egypt, by a prince of Palestine, and were in some way badly used, although no reasons are assigned for this treatment. The Babylonian now demands from Pharaoh the release of the prisoners and compensation, since Akko was subject to his suzerainty. A political controversy is only once discussed. The Assyrian king, Ashur-uballit, had found encouragement at the Egyptian court in his schemes of aggrandisement at the cost of Babylonia. Burnaburiash pointed out the inadmissibility of such action, since Assyria was his vassal state, and no direct negotiations could therefore be carried on with it. He referred also to the correct attitude of his father, Kurigalzu, who, when once asked to join cause with the Canaanites, the subjects of Egypt, had refused to countenance such an act of treachery towards Egypt. That such loyalty was not so free from suspicion as these assurances of friendship would make it appear, and that in Egypt no very implicit confidence was placed in the warm friend of Egyptian gold, is proved by the fact that when one of the Phœnician princes wishes to blacken the character of another at court, he accuses him of being a secret adherent of the king of Mitani, of the Khatti, or of Kash—that is, of the Kassites of Babylon.

Political Machinations in Egypt

INTERIOR OF EARLY BABYLONIAN TOMB
Interior of the Ur grave. Jars and dishes containing daily fare for the dead man were left with the body.

We can, indeed, assign to a somewhat later date an attempt of Babylonia to win back the West, when disorders broke out in Egypt after the death of Amenophis IV. Burnaburiash, notwithstanding the anxiety displayed in his letter to Amenophis IV. about the encroachments of Assyria, and although wars between him and the Assyrians are proved to have taken place, had given his son Kara-khardash a daughter of the energetic

Ashur-uballit as his chief wife; and her son, Kadashman-kharbe, became the successor to the throne—a sign of the Assyrian influence. We are acquainted with the attempt, just mentioned, made by this Babylonian king to regain a firm footing in the west.

Assyria, indeed, was at this time encroaching on Mesopotamia, and Babylonia had nothing left but the road diagonally through the Syrian desert. Kadashman-kharbe tried to secure this road by punishing the nomads, the Suti, who roamed those parts, and by digging wells and building fortresses and towns, which he settled with Babylonians. By this means he hoped to transform it into a commercial highway, which should facilitate communication with the coast and make the detour by Mesopotamia unnecessary. It is possible that his plan was suggested by a route already in existence; but in any case he had recognised that it was better policy to satisfy his rival with districts which had first to be conquered, and meanwhile to deprive those districts of their greatest value by diverting from them the traffic so important for Babylonia. That would, indeed, have been a solution of the dispute, then urgent, as to the possession of Mesopotamia. Perhaps Kadashman-kharbe arrived at a peaceful arrangement with Assyria about this plan. If he had carried it out he would, at any rate, have shown himself to be a man who could support his power by more effective means than arms, especially when Babylon, an industrial state, was confronted by the military power of Assyria.

Kadashman-kharbe cannot have reigned long. He was murdered, and in fact fell the victim of an insurrection stirred up by the Kassites. We are not told what the immediate incentive to the deed was. We may perhaps trace the reason to the fact that the kings and the ruling classes of the Kassites had meanwhile, after 1400,

become "Babylonised"—that is, that they felt, and affected to feel themselves, Babylonians. Those of the Kassites who had gone away empty-handed at the division of the spoil, or had lost their share, as often happens in the commercial life of communities engaged in industries and trade, may have formed a party of malcontents, who longed for the good old times when the Kassite was lord and the Babylonian the spoiled. The insurgents therefore raised to the throne a man of low birth, whom the two chronicles which record the fact call Shuzigash and Nazibugash—a "son of nobody." This was a

CONTEMPORARY RECORD OF BURIAL OF THE DEAD
From a stele in the Louvre, showing how the Sumerian and Chaldæan dead were piled up after battle. The priests are heaping up earth to form a mound.

welcome opportunity for the grandfather, Ashur-uballit, who was still living and had been restlessly active in extending his kingdom, to secure the supremacy for Assyria. He appeared in Babylon as the avenger of his grandson and the restorer of order, suppressed the revolt, and had Kurigalzu, the infant son of his murdered grandson, crowned as king.

But the force of circumstances is stronger than blood relationships and gratitude for benefits of doubtful intention. So long as Ashur-uballit lived, and under his son, Assyria was occupied with the conquest of Mesopotamia. But when Adad-nirari I. drove the Mitani thence, Babylon, having no doubt lost the route which Kadashman-kharbe had attempted to open up, had no other course but to secure Mesopotamia for herself, and with it the communications with the west. Since, however, Assyria possessed this country, war ensued be-

Contest for Mesopotamia tween it and Babylon. Under Kurigalzu and Adad-nirari I. the contest for Mesopotamia began between the two states. We have an interesting account of a war of the Babylonian king, Kurigalzu, against Khurbatila, king of Elam, in which he defeated him and took him prisoner on Babylonian soil—that is, in one of the attacks of Elam on Babylon. He must have followed up his victory, for on the back of an inscription which a dependent of King Dungi, of the old dynasty of Ur, had consecrated to the goddess Nana of Uruk stands the words, " Kurigalzu, king of Karduniash [the designation of the Kassite kings of Babylonia] hath captured the palace of the town Shasha [Susa, formerly Shushan] in Elam, and hath presented this tablet to Ninlil of Nippur in gratitude for the preservation of his life."

The tablet was, therefore, carried off from Uruk in a former raid of the Elamites, was then discovered, on a victorious campaign of Kurigalzu's against Elam, in a temple—if in Susa, then probably in the temple of the goddess Shushinak, mentioned in the case of Ashurbanipal—and was deposited by the king in the temple of Nippur more than nine hundred years after its completion. Finally, rediscovered during the American excavations, it has been brought to Constantinople. Not only have books their destinies ! These wars prove to us that the conditions were then present

Conquests of Assyria and Elam which we find continually during the succeeding period. Babylonia lay as a coveted prize between Assyria and Elam. For a time it was able to face the two on equal terms, and, even if occasionally vanquished, it regained the superiority. The struggle fills up the succeeding centuries until the end of the Assyrian empire. In the last period we shall then find Babylonia as a vassal of one of these two states.

Even now the same ebb and flow of events is noticeable. Soon after Kurigalzu, as we shall see in dealing with Assyrian history, Babylonia and Babylon came into the power of Tukulti-Ninib I. of Assyria. Shortly after, under Bel-nadin-shun, who reigned for only one year and a half, Kidin-khutrutash, king of Elam, invaded Babylonia, pillaged Dur-ilu, and conquered Nippur, the favourite resort of the Kassite kings, where they often held their court. Other expeditions, with similar incidents, were made by the Elamites in the reign of Kadashman-kharbe II. and Adad-shum-iddina, when the city of Isin especially suffered. Several songs of lamentation have come down to us, which bewail, in the form of penitential psalms, the devastation of the country, and especially of the city named. In the many centuries of Babylonian history similar circumstances often recurred, but these psalms suit this period admirably, and, even if they did not originate in it, they may have been adapted from similar songs of an earlier

End of the Kassites time, and sung at this period in the temples of Babylonia. We shall see under " Elam " that Babylonia, for the rest of this dynasty, was probably subject to Elamite supremacy.

It will be seen that we are once more at the end of a period. The Kassites had long succumbed to Babylonian influence and had played out their part, and the Kassite dynasty is drawing to a close. It can reckon but four kings more ; among them Marduk-aplu-iddina. Merodach-bala-dan I. alone seems to have offered success-ful resistance to Assyria and to have retained Mesopotamia. The change of dynasties presents, as always, a period of disturbance and weakness, and brings a line of kings to the throne whose task was to resist Assyria and to renew the struggle for Mesopotamia. We shall see that there is good reason to believe that the earlier rulers of this new dynasty succeeded in establishing themselves as independent kings in Isin during the rule of the later kings of the Kassite dynasty in Babylon, and that the rule of the latter was brought to an end by the powerful king Nebuchad-nezzar I., who also freed the country from the yoke of Elam.

BABYLONIAN EMPIRE IN ECLIPSE
THE PREY OF ELAMITES AND ASSYRIANS

THE new dynasty is called in the list of kings the dynasty of Isin, from the Babylonian city of this name. It thus forms the second dynasty of Isin. It is probable that the first two or three kings of the dynasty were contemporaneous with the last rulers of the Kassite dynasty upon the throne of Babylon, because a boundary-stone has recently been discovered at Nippur inscribed with a text of the reign of Nebuchadnezzar I., the third or fourth king of the dynasty of Isin, which would make it appear that this monarch was the first of his dynasty to secure control over the whole of Babylonia. In this new inscription, which is dated in the sixteenth year of Nebuchadnezzar's reign, it is stated that Enlil "broke the weapon of his [*i.e.*, Nebuchadnezzar's] enemy, and placed the sceptre of his enemy in his own hand, that he might pasture Sumer and Akkad, and rebuild the sanctuaries of the City of Mankind, and regulate the tithes of Ekur and Nippur." It is not clear from **Dynasty of Isin** the context of this passage who "the enemy" is whose weapon was broken by the god Enlil, and it might be urged that the passage refers to a defeat of the Elamites, from whose supremacy Nebuchadnezzar certainly freed his country. But upon another inscription of his reign Nebuchadnezzar bears the title of "plunderer of the Kassites," so that we may infer that it was the Kassites he defeated, and, further, that it was the sceptre of the Kassite kings of Babylon which Enlil placed within his hand. We may conclude, therefore, with some probability, that Nebuchadnezzar's immediate predecessors were merely kings of the city of Isin at a time when the last Kassite kings were still in possession of the throne of Babylon.

In addition to his achievements against the Kassites, Nebuchadnezzar I. comes before us as conqueror in wars with Elam, and lord of Mesopotamia and also of the "western land"; he therefore, for the last time indeed, extended the suzerainty of Babylon right down to the Mediterranean. His wars with Elam prove that, under his predecessors, the misery which the invasions of Kidin-khutrutash had already caused had become still more acute. Babylon itself had been captured, **Babylon Captured by Elam** and the statue of Marduk carried away to Elam. Such a rape of the god signified the loss of national independence and a degradation of the country to a state of vassaldom. Just as Marduk served in the temple of the stranger god, so the ruler of Babylon was no king, but a servant of the Elamite. So long as the image of the god was not in Babylon, Nebuchadnezzar did not style himself king, but governor, of Babylon. He did not assume the title of "king of Babylon" until he had brought back the statue of Marduk, which he could only do after a decisive victory over Elam. Songs have been preserved to us which bewail the absence of Marduk from Babylon and commemorate his return. By Nebuchadnezzar's successes some limit appears to have been set to the advance of the Elamite, for a time at least. We shall see, when we come to describe the history of Assyria, that the victories of Nebuchadnezzar had great subsequent effects, and that a successful attack by Assyria, which led to the capture of Babylon under Tiglath-pileser I., produced no permanent results.

Not many facts are known of the reigns of the immediate successors of Nebuchadnezzar I. Marduk-nadin-akhe, who succeeded Bel-nadin-apli upon the throne, fought with Tiglath-pileser I. and won **Babylon's God Carried off** back Mesopotamia from him. He was succeeded by Marduk-shapik-zer-mati, who appears to have extended the borders of Babylonia, and to have ruled a confederacy of a large number of petty kings, or princes, over whom he had forced his suzerainty by conquest. He established friendly relations with Ashur-bel-kala, king of Assyria, and on his return after visiting Assyria took up his residence at Sippar in preference to Babylon. He was succeeded by a usurper, Adad-aplu-iddina, in whose reign a disaster overwhelmed the country. This was the invasion of **Aramæans Ravage the Land** the Sutu, tribes of Aramæan origin, who overran both Northern and Southern Babylonia, and ravaged the country from end to end. We know that the great temple of the sun-god at Sippar was destroyed by them, and for many years the effect of this invasion must have been felt. Not even the full names of Adad-aplu-iddina's three successors are known, but we may infer that they occupied themselves in rallying the resources of Babylon and in making good the havoc wrought by the hordes of the Sutu.

The dynasty which succeeded that of Isin upon the Babylonian throne came from the " Country of the Sea," from which it took its name. Two of the three kings of which it was composed bear Kassite names, and were probably descendants of the Kassite rulers of Southern Babylonia. That the dynasty occupied Northern Babylonia and ruled at Babylon may be inferred from the fact that its founder, Simmash-shipak, was buried in the palace of Sargon. During his reign he partly rebuilt the temple of the sun-god at Sippar, which the Sutu had destroyed in Adad-aplu-iddina's reign. Simmash-shipak was succeeded by Ea-mukin-zer, who reigned for only a few months. The last king of the dynasty was Kashshu-nadin-akhe, in whose short reign of three years the temple at Sippar experienced fresh misfortunes.

Another short dynasty of three kings succeeded that of the Country of the Sea. It is termed in the kings list the dynasty of Bazi, and in it we may probably see another line of foreigners who occupied the Babylonian throne. The three rulers were termed Eul-mash-shakin-shum, Ninib-kudurri-usur, and Shilanum-shukamuna, and the total length of their reigns was little more than twenty years. They were succeeded by an Elamite, whom the native chronographers reckon as having formed a dynasty by himself. His name has recently been recovered as

Aa-aplu-usur, but beyond the fact that he ruled for six years, nothing else is known of his reign.

We see, therefore, that Babylonia was completely powerless and the prey of every foreign invader, of the Elamites above all, if they were not dislodged by the Assyrians. The period of these three dynasties embraces about the years 1000–960, and at its expiry we shall find Assyria, which had been hitherto powerless, once more bent on advance.

We do not know who overthrew the Elamites, or what other causes brought a new dynasty into power. The list of kings from this point is mutilated, and we have until about 750 practically no accounts except the Assyrian. From these latter we can learn quite clearly what was the distinctive feature of this period, even if we cannot give an account of the **Babylonia Completely Powerless** separate reigns. Babylonia, the prize for which the two great states of Assyria and Elam were disputing, was at this time flooded by a migration similar to those of the Semites, who had settled there, and had thoroughly adopted Babylonian customs. From this

INVADERS CARRYING OFF THE NATION'S GODS
After every invasion the Assyrians, or Elamites, carried away the Babylonian gods, thereby reducing the country to vassaldom.

migration we can picture to ourselves the constant ebb and flow of such a method of occupation; a similar instance is afforded by the circumstances attending the seizure of Palestine by the Hebrews. The Chaldæans thenceforth pressed into Babylonia, inhabited the open country, and tried to gain possession of the towns.

However prominent the Chaldæans may be in the subsequent history, and however many details we have recovered of their relations to Babylonia, we cannot yet form for ourselves any satisfactory picture of their national characteristics. All the Chaldæans, indeed, who are mentioned bear thoroughly Babylonian names. No new element in the language can be ascertained to have been introduced by their invasion of Babylonia, so that we can obtain no clue to their original race. Since they evidently advanced from the south and first occupied the districts on the Persian Gulf, they may possibly be regarded as Semites, who immigrated from Eastern Arabia, while the previous migrations, starting more from the west, went first toward Mesopotamia and Northern Babylonia. According to this theory, the Chaldæan migration would have taken place between the Aramæan and the Arabian, and the Chaldæans would have their nearest kinsmen in these two groups of nations, or would be identified with one of them. If they were **Who were the Chaldæans?** Semites, their rapid assimilation of the conditions existing in Babylonia is explained, for other stocks akin to them in language were already settled there, and Aramæan tribes had, as we shall see, already spread over Babylonia. The scanty facts that we can collect at present for a characterisation of the Chaldæans accord well with this view. The designation of Ur, the City of the Moon, as Kamarinē is traced to Berossus. That may be explained from Arabic, in which *qamar* signifies the moon. The

"Struggle of the Nations," S.P.C.K.
MARDUK-NADIN-AKHE
This successor of Nebuchadnezzar regained Mesopotamia from Assyria.

chieftains of the Chaldæans are termed *ra'sani :* that is the Arabic pronunciation of the word for chieftain (Hebrew, *ro'sh*). The only god whose cult may perhaps be reckoned to have been introduced by the Chaldæans is the war god—designated as, or identified with, Girra, whom Nabopolassar, Nebuchadnezzar, and Neriglissar bring into prominence.

Thus we find henceforth by the side of a series of Aramæan tribes of Babylonia a number of Chaldæan principalities or stocks, which are designated by Babylonians and Assyrians as a "house," or tribe, of their princely family. For example, Bit-Iakin, a district in the "Country of the Sea," from which these rulers had shortly before this time occupied the throne of Babylon, Bit-Sa'alli, Bit-Shilani, Bit-Amukkani, Bit-Adini, Bit-Dakuri, in the immediate vicinity of Babylon and Borsippa, and others. The one aim of each of their princes naturally was to gain possession of the adjacent large towns, and, as a culminating triumph, to become king of Babylon. The Chaldæan was the third candidate for the royal throne of Babylon who appeared at this time by the side of Ashur and Elam, and the Babylonian population was less and less able to assert its independence. With such a state of affairs no continuity of development was possible. On the whole, the Chaldæans and Elamites joined cause, while the Assyrian kings endeavoured to appear as the protectors of the national independence, or what they chose to regard as such. The course of the struggle displays a continual fluctuation, until **Chaldæans Rule in Babylon** the Chaldæans attained their object with the fall of Assyria, and Babylon, under a Chaldæan dynasty, once more assumed a place among the great powers. The facts we can collect from the period when Assyria had not as yet regained the supremacy in Babylonia are very few, and hardly go beyond accounts

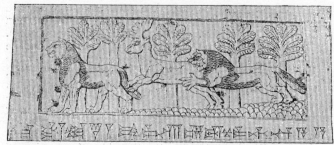

WILD ANIMALS AS TRIBUTE FROM THE PRINCE OF SUKHI
Sukhi, one of the chief Aramæan Euphrates states, was under Babylonian influence, but was subjugated by Ashurnasirpal, king of Assyria.

Nabu-aplu-iddina reigned at least thirty-one years, and died in 854. He was an opponent of Ashurnasirpal and Shalmaneser, and during the reign of the former tried to force his way along the Euphrates into Mesopotamia. In the year 879 B.C. he supported the prince of Sukhi on the Euphrates, who was under Babylonian influence, against Assyria; but Ashurnasirpal defeated the Babylonian forces. The manner in which he speaks of this victory suggests that Nabu-aplu-iddina was a Chaldæan; and this is borne out by the eagerness with which, in an inscription of his own, commemorating the restoration of the temple of Sippar, he represents himself as a good Babylonian.

of wars with Assyria. The first king of the dynasty, who was probably Nabu-mukin-apli, reigned for thirty-six years. It seems as if in a record dating from his time the dominion over Mesopotamia was still ascribed to him, about 960 B.C. He must have been the last Babylonian king who could pride himself on the possession of that district; for about this very time the Assyrian kings also bear, without further interruption, the title in question. The list of kings assigns to his successor, whose name is broken off, a reign of eight months;

THE PROUD ASSYRIAN HUMILIATING HIS CAPTIVE
A bas-relief from Nineveh, showing an Assyrian king placing his foot on the neck of a captive king, and apparently about to strike him with his spear.

Under his reign Assyria did not venture to encroach on Babylon itself; Ashurnasirpal contented himself with Mesopotamia, and seems later to have extended his power toward Northern Babylonia.

Nabu-aplu-iddina's death, in 854 B.C., was, as usually happens in the East, the signal for disputes about the succession between his two sons Marduk-shum-iddina and Marduk-bel-usati. In accordance with the directions of the deceased monarch, they had divided Babylonia

after that there is a great gap until Nabonassar, who came to the throne in 747 B.C.

Some of the names of the kings in this period we cannot determine conclusively. We know Shamash-mudammiq from his war with Assyria under Adad-nirari III. He died during this war, and Nabu-shum-ishkun became king with Assyrian help. He was, therefore, certainly a Babylonian; his predecessor, a Chaldæan. This is in accordance with the fact that a successor, who showed hostility to Assyria, was apparently in turn a Chaldæan. Then follows, possibly, an unknown king. After this,

TRIBUTE OF IVORY AND WOOD FROM SUKHI TO ASSYRIA

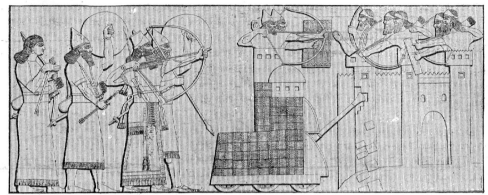

ASHURNASIRPAL ON ONE OF HIS CAMPAIGNS AGAINST BABYLONIA

During the days of Babylonia's weakness the Assyrians repeatedly invaded the country, besieging and sacking the cities. This bas-relief shows the king himself in the fight, and also illustrates the use of the battering-ram.

between them, so that the former received Northern Babylonia with Babylon, the latter Southern Babylonia, and with it the original home of the Chaldæans. The war between the Chaldæan prince and the Babylonian king naturally broke out at once, and the Chaldæan forces displayed their invariable superiority to the Babylonian. The Babylonian Marduk-shum-iddina summoned the Assyrian king, Shalmaneser II., to his aid, and in return he consented to hold his crown from him as a vassal; the Assyrian king did not neglect such a favourable opportunity of realising the object of Assyrian policy, the practical sovereignty of Babylonia. The "Chaldæan peasants" of Marduk-bel-usati fled before his veteran troops back into their swamps. Shalmaneser marched into the towns of Babylonia, offered the sacrifices as supreme lord of the country, and received the homage of the

Chaldæan princes, while Marduk-shum-iddina reigned under Assyrian protection. Shalmaneser naturally possessed from the first the north of Babylonia, which, from the time of Ashurnasirpal was under the immediate government of Assyria. It seems, indeed, that at the close of his reign, when the revolt of his son Ashur-danin-apli drove him out of Assyria, he relied on this part of his kingdom, and that his son Shamshi-Adad made it and Mesopotamia the base of his operations for the subjugation of Assyria.

The impossibility of interfering effectively in Babylonia at this time could not fail to present to the ever watchful Chaldæans another welcome opportunity of attack. So soon, therefore, as Shamshi-Adad was free from some of his most pressing enemies he turned his attention to Babylon, where, after the death—or the expulsion—of Marduk-shum-iddina, in

ASHURNASIRPAL IN HIS CHARIOT BEFORE A BESIEGED CITY   Mansell

A spirited Assyrian bas-relief from Nineveh. Note the emblem of Ashur, the Assyrian god, in the top left-hand corner, assisting the besiegers by shooting an arrow. This bas-relief is now in the British Museum.

823 B.C., we now find Marduk-balatsu-iqbi as king, a Chaldæan prince, who was supported by the Kaldi, Babylonian-Aramæan tribes, and Elam. He was thus another of the Chaldæan chiefs who by Elamite aid—standing thus in the same relation to Elam as Marduk-shum-iddina to Assyria—mounted the throne of Babylon. We see, therefore, for the first time, a condition of things which we shall find repeatedly—Ashur or Elam as the suzerain of the reigning king in Babylon.

No early success of Shamshi-Adad against the Babylonians is mentioned in his inscription; on the other hand, campaigns against Chaldæa and Babylon in 813 and 812 are recorded. The first presupposes a defeat of the Chaldæan king by Assyria, and with it the establishment of the Assyrian supremacy. The second coincides with the year of the accession of Adad-nirari IV. Perhaps the Chaldæans, who were not thoroughly subdued, on the accession of the new king, returned to the attack. Ba'u-akhi-iddina seems at this time to have been king of Babylon. He was conquered and captured by the Assyrians; and Adad-nirari, just as Shaimaneser previously, now sacrificed in the towns as supreme sovereign. It is not certain whether all this happened in 812, or only on the expeditions of 796 and 795 against Northern Babylonia, and of 791 against Chaldæa, about which we know nothing. This much is certain in any case, that this age is marked by attempts of the Chaldæan princes to gain the Babylonian throne under Elamite protection and supremacy, varied by periods during which Assyria asserted her supremacy, as long as other claims were not made on her. On every change of monarch, or when Assyria is otherwise engaged, fresh attempts are made to shake off her yoke. The same spectacle we find elsewhere, and to it the prophets testify most clearly in the case of Judah and Israel — namely, two great parties in the country, who rely on two different great powers, with a continual shifting and changing from one to the other.

We are not told whom Adad-nirari set up as king in Babylon, and we possess little information about the ensuing period, since after Adad-nirari the Assyrian power once more diminished and its influence over Babylonia waned. But Assyria did not abandon her supremacy without a struggle, for many expeditions against Chaldæa are recorded. Thus, there was one immediately on the new monarch's accession in 783 and 782 under Shalmaneser III., and under the same king in 777; also, under his successor, Ashur-dan III., immediately on his accession in 771, there was an expedition to Northern Babylonia, and in 769 one to Chaldæa. The explanation is afforded by the former condition of things, and we can imagine the course of events from the expeditions of Shalmaneser and Adad-nirari. Since we possess no inscriptions of the Assyrian kings recording these events, and have only the brief notices in the chronicles concerning them, we do not know the names of the Babylonian kings against whom the expeditions were directed.

Assyrian influence must have been completely destroyed in the succeeding revolts between 763 and 746, and Babylonia was thus left at the mercy of the Chaldæans. The first fact we learn is the name—from the Babylonian list of kings—of King Nabu-shum-ishkun II., who reigned until 748. We possess a record concerning him, from which we may picture the condition of Babylonia at this time. Nabu-shum-imbi, the governor of Borsippa, the sister town of Babylon, makes a report concerning certain building operations in the temple of Nebo, and says: "Then in Borsippa, the town of law and order, there arose sedition, havoc, uproar, and revolution; under the rule of the king Nabu-shum-ishkun, of Bit-Dakuri, the Babylonians, men of Borsippa and Dushulti from the bank of the Euphrates, all Chaldæans, Aramæans, Dilbateans, turned for a long season their arms against each other, and defeated each other, and waged war with the men of Borsippa about their boundary. And Nabu-shum-iddina (a high official of the temple of Nebo), instigated on his own responsibility a revolt against

THE GOD NEBO Mansell
In whose temple at Borsippa there arose revolt against the Chaldæans

Nabu-shum-imbi, the governor of Borsippa. In the night, like a thief, he collected foes and bandits, and led them into the temple of Nebo. . . . . They raised an uproar. But the men of Borsippa and others, who came to the rescue, surrounded the house of the governor and protected it with bows and with arrows." Thus we find what we should expect: the king of Babylon is a Chaldæan of the stock of Dakuri, and the Chaldæans and Aramæans take possession of the territory of the towns which are divided by internal feuds. It is not surprising that under such conditions the wealthy classes hailed the appearance of an Assyrian king as their salvation, and the same phenomenon will meet us again in the subsequent history. The Chaldæan dominion signified anarchy for Babylonia; for a strong Chaldæan prince and a stable government were hardly compatible with the want of cohesion among the Chaldæans themselves, and with the natural opposition between the greedy invaders and the wealthy, timid population of the towns.

The next king is Nabu-nasir, or, in the form under which the Ptolemaic canon has preserved the name, Nabonassar; he reigned from 747 to 734 B.C. The circumstances just mentioned continued under his rule, and disturbances in Borsippa such as those described by Nabu-shum-imbi led to an attempt on the part of that city to shake off his yoke, which the king took strong measures to suppress. There are scarcely any actions of Nabonassar himself to relate. Berossus, the historian of Babylon under the Seleucids, states that he issued some enactments—it is not yet certain what their nature was—relative to establishing an era. As a matter of fact, the Ptolemaic canon, which has brought Nabonassar's name into prominence, as well as a Babylonian chronicle, which was written under Darius, begin with reference to his reign in the year 747. In the third year of Nabonassar, 745 B.C., was inaugurated a new era for Assyria with the accession of Tiglath-pileser IV.; and Babylonia was immediately aware of the changed order of things. The object of the first expedition of the new king was Babylonia, where he chastised the Aramæans and the most northerly Chaldæan tribes, and placed Nabonassar under his protection. We may conclude from this that he was not a Chaldæan, but a Babylonian. Tiglath-pileser, who henceforth styled himself king of Sumer and Akkad and king of the four quarters of the world, came on his expedition as far as Nippur. Presumably the Chaldæans submitted, and he could not pursue his object further, owing to disturbances threatening from Armenia and Syria. Nabonassar, therefore, reigned under Assyrian protection. If a revolt at Borsippa shows that his power did not extend beyond the city boundaries of Babylon, it was not, on the one hand, to the interest of Assyria to spare Nabonassar his little difficulties; on the other hand, Tiglath-pileser was really for the moment too much occupied to trouble himself more about Babylon than was urgently necessary. It says, however, much for Nabonassar's reputation that for fourteen years no Chaldæan made an effort to make himself master of Babylon.

Nabonassar died in the year 734 B.C., and was succeeded by his son Nabunadin-zer, abbreviated to Nadinu, so that the name appears as Nadios in the Ptolemaic canon. He reigned two years, 734 and 733, when one of the rebellions, which might be expected, broke out. The king was deposed by a governor of a province, Nabu-shum-ukin, a Babylonian therefore, and consequently a leader of the anti-Assyrian party. The latter enjoyed less than two months of royal sovereignty, when he had to give way to the Chaldæan Ukin-zir, or Chinzer in the Ptolemaic canon, the prince of

A KING'S HISTORY Mansell
This clay prism is inscribed with accounts of eight campaigns of Sennacherib.

Bit-Amukani from 732 to 730. Assyria was thus forced again to interfere; for a Chaldæan on the throne of Babylon could have no other object than to win for himself the whole of Babylonia, which Tiglath-pileser had until then possessed. So soon, therefore, as the latter had arranged affairs in Syria, and had captured Damascus, where the siege alone had secured three years of uninterrupted rule to Ukin-zir, he turned against Babylonia, occupied Bit-Amukani, the home of Ukin-zir, as well as other Chaldæan provinces, and took Ukin-zir himself prisoner. In order to put an end to the endless disorders, he resolved, in spite of the troublesome character of the obligation, to be present annually at the New Year's festival in Babylon, to reside there as much as possible, and to assume in person the crown of the kingdom of Bel; and for the remaining two years of his life he commanded that he should be proclaimed as king of Babylon Further, the rights of the Babylonians were to be guaranteed. He, like other Assyrian kings who adopted a similar policy, bore as king of Babylon another name: thus Shalmaneser IV. was known in Babylon as Ululai, and Ashurbanipal as Kandalanu. Tiglath-pileser is entered in the Babylonian lists as Pulu, a name by which he is mentioned in the Old Testament.

Tranquillity prevailed then during these two years, 729 and 728, and during the reign of his successor, Shalmaneser, who from 727 to 722 also had himself crowned king of Babylon. So soon, however, as the great revolution in Assyria began, which, on his death, brought Sargon to the throne, a Chaldæan prince, Marduk-aplu-iddina II., or, as we usually call him with the pronunciation given in the text of the Old Testament, Merodach-baladan, king of the "Country of the Sea," used the opportunity to wrest to

himself the Babylonian crown, having come
to an agreement with Khumbanigash of
Elam. Sargon, it is true, quickly tried
to expel him, but his Elamite protector
was also on the spot. A battle was fought
near Dur-ilu, in which Sargon claimed
the victory for himself, and the Babylonians for Khumbanigash. In any case,
Sargon was compelled to relinquish the
attempt to expel Merodach-baladan from
Babylon. He had, however, retained a
portion of Northern Babylonia, and with
it Dur-ilu. Merodach-baladan calls himself king of Babylon, king of Sumer and
Akkad. He reigned as Merodach-baladan
II. under Elamite protection from 721 to
710, so long as Sargon, precisely like Tiglath-pileser IV., was distracted by the
affairs of Syria, Palestine and Armenia.

Sargon, after ending his wars in these
countries, turned his attention to Babylon,
and drove out Merodach-baladan, who,
after the loss of his capital in the sea
country, Dur-Iakin, sought refuge in the
court of Susa. Sargon was received in
Babylon by his own party, and, above
all, by the priests, as the saviour of the
city and the restorer of order. He assumed the title of "Governor of Babylon"
—that is, he represented a king, though no
one reigned as such by name. From 709
to 705 he held Babylon and the whole of

MERODACH-BALADAN OF BABYLON
A Chaldæan king who was twice driven from his
throne, by Sargon and Sennacherib of Assyria. The
sculptor, following the custom, makes the king appear
taller than the vassal whom he is investing with a fief.

Babylonia on these peculiar
terms until his death.

Under the rule of Senna-
cherib, Babylon enjoyed tranquillity for two years more;
then a revolt broke out, which
brought a Babylonian, Marduk-
zakir-shum, to the throne for a
month. Merodach-baladan then
seized the opportunity to occupy
Babylon once more, with the
help of Elam. His sovereignty
did not, however, last long this
time, for Sennacherib was not
so taken up by other wars as
Sargon had been during his previous occupation of the throne,
and he appeared before Babylon nine months after Merodach-baladan's return. The
latter was defeated at Kish,
together with his Elamite
auxiliaries, and fled, to Elam
probably, where he awaited a
fresh opportunity to make a
descent upon Babylon. Sennacherib treated Babylon merci-

Mansell
CONQUESTS OF TIGLATH-PILESER IN BABYLONIA
Tiglath-pileser IV., an Assyrian king, ruled in Babylon as Pulu after
besieging and taking the principal Chaldæan cities. From a bas-relief.

E   24   G   1617

fully, for it was not the Babylonians who had revolted, and only the property of Merodach-baladan and his followers was confiscated. The Chaldæans were again driven back to their country, and the districts occupied by them were restored to the towns. Even the Aramæan tribes were again kept within their own borders.

Sennacherib installed as king in Babylon Bel-ibni, probably a Babylonian prince, who had been brought up at the court of Nineveh (702 to 700). In the following year, 702, two other provinces were secured on the frontier toward Elam. Bel-ibni may have had the best intentions of remaining loyal to Assyria, but circumstances were too strong for him. Perhaps Sennacherib's ambition to make Nineveh the first city of the East was already recognised. In any case, Bel-ibni was forced, while Sennacherib was occupied with Palestine, to break off with him, and—he can hardly have acted voluntarily—to enter into an alliance with Merodach-baladan, that is to say, with his own rival, with another prince of the Chaldæans, Mushezib-Marduk, and with Elam. In Sennacherib's absence he submitted. But just as the people of Palestine had taken up arms too late, so a miscalculation was made in Babylonia and Elam on the present occasion. Sennacherib raised the siege of Jerusalem, after he had already occupied the whole country, and, turning against his more formidable opponents, quickly broke up the alliance. Merodach-baladan fled from the sea-country to Elam, taking his gods with him; the Chaldæan Mushezib-Marduk withdrew into his swamps; and Bel-ibni was forced to return with his followers to the place whence he had come —namely, to the court of Nineveh. We see from this treatment of him that he had joined Elam and the Chaldæans only under compulsion, otherwise assuredly a severer penalty would have been meted out to him. At Babylon, Assur-nadin-shum, a son of Sennacherib, was installed as king, and reigned from 699 to 694 B.C.

Merodach-baladan must have died soon afterwards, for he is never mentioned again. Disturbances occurred in Elam, and thus Babylonia enjoyed quiet for five years. In the year 694 Sennacherib made an expedition in order to drive out that part of the population of the sea-country which had

SENNACHERIB'S NAVY ON THE PERSIAN GULF
An expedition sent by Sennacherib to disperse the Chaldæans, who constituted a danger which continually menaced Babylonia. From an Assyrian bas-relief.

fled at one time with Merodach-baladan to Elam, and had settled in some towns on the coast, and thus to do away with a danger which continually menaced Babylonia. He describes in detail how he built ships for the purpose, which were brought on the Tigris up to Opis, thence to the Euphrates, and so down to the Persian Gulf. He himself cautiously kept far away from the dangerous element, but ordered his army to be transported by sea to Elam. His forces marched some way up the Karun, devastated the provinces on the coast of Elam, and dispersed or captured the Chaldæans who were settled there.

While the Assyrian army was stationed in Elam, Khalludush, king of Elam, did not remain idle. He entered Babylonia near Dur-ilu on the ordinary military road, captured Sippar, took Assur-nadin-shum prisoner, and carried him back with him to Elam. He appointed Nergal-ushezib, a Babylonian, king in Babylon. Sennacherib tells us only of the heroic courage with which he had faced the raging sea and of his success in Elam. We hear of the Elamite counter-move from the Babylonian chronicles alone. Nothing more transpires as to Assur-nadin-shum, the deposed son of Sennacherib.

The new king possessed at first only the north of Babylonia; he tried now **An Elamite King in Babylon** to drive the Assyrians out of the south also, and captured Nippur. But Uruk, which seems to have joined his side, was recaptured by the Assyrians, and soon afterwards the latter appeared in front of Nippur. Nergal-ushezib met them in the open field, but was defeated and taken prisoner. He had reigned only a year and a half—694 to 693 B.C. While Sennacherib in this same year undertook a punitive expedition against Elam, the above-mentioned Chaldæan, Mushezib-Marduk, seized the opportunity to establish himself firmly in Babylon, and reigned from 692 to 698. He allied himself closely with Elam, and actually sacrificed the temple treasures of Marduk in order to pay to the Elamite, Umman-menanu, his " presents," or what was, in reality, his tribute. This shows that once more the sacerdotal

FIGHTING IN THE CHALDÆAN MARSHES
An Assyrian representation of a skirmish in Sennacherib's campaign against Merodach-baladan and his Elamite auxiliaries.

party supported Assyria. It was not so easy a task this time for Sennacherib to drive out Elam—for that was the real issue at stake. In the year 691 a battle was fought at Khalule, in Northern Babylonia, with Umman-menanu, his vassal, Mushezib-Marduk, the son of Merodach-baladan, and the other Chaldæans. Sennacherib gives a very magnificent account of the battle, in which he naturally claims the victory. The Babylonian chronicle makes Umman-menanu the victor, and is correct in so far as Sennacherib gained no success, for Babylon remained under Elamite protection. In the year 689 Umman-menanu was struck down by apoplexy.

In the same year Babylon fell into Sennacherib's hands, and Mushezib-Marduk was carried prisoner to Assyria. We must assume that in this revolt there was no strong pro-Assyrian party in **Babylon Destroyed by Sennacherib** Babylon, for it is clear that Sennacherib's policy aimed at the ruin of Babylon. The alliance with the Chaldæans had been, therefore, a struggle of desperation, and Sennacherib now lost no time in reaching his goal by the shortest road. Babylon was completely destroyed and its gods taken to Assyria. It has hitherto been supposed that during the years which followed its destruction by Sennacherib the city of Babylon ceased to exist as a centre of political activity. The Babylonian chronicle states that an interregnum of eight years now took place, while the list of kings assigns these eight years to Sennacherib. But a chronicle that has recently been discovered allows us to form a picture of what took place during a portion of this troubled period. It has hitherto been conjectured that no attempt was made to rebuild the capital until the reversal of Sennacherib's policy by his son Esarhaddon, upon the latter's accession to the throne. But we now know that the Babylonians themselves did not remain inactive, and that at least

The City Laid Waste

learn from the new chronicle that they were not left for long in undisturbed possession, for a certain man named Erba-Marduk, the son of Marduk-shakin-shum, "smote them with the sword and defeated them, and he took the fields and the gardens from them and gave them unto the men of Babylon and Borsippa." It is also recorded that in the same year Erba-Marduk set up the throne of Marduk in Esagila, and the chronicle implies that he rebuilt that temple, and also the temple of Ezida in Borsippa. It is therefore certain that Erba-Marduk made good to some extent the damage done to the city of Sennacherib, though the resources at his disposal did not enable him to attempt the rebuilding of Babylon on the lavish scale inaugurated a few years later by Esarhaddon. Moreover,

ASHURBANIPAL OVERCOMES THE ELAMITES

Ashurbanipal's successes against Elam deprived that country of power of making encroachments on Babylonia. This bas-relief shows his soldiers carrying off Elamite spoil and captives, and scribes taking count of the heads of the slain.

one native king occupied the Babylonian throne during this period. It is probable that during the year following the withdrawal of the Assyrian army, and the deportation of Mushezib-Marduk, Babylon did lie desolate and in part deserted by its inhabitants.

It needed the appearance of another foe to call forth a leader, who should rally the citizens and attempt to restore order and organised government. The necessary impetus was soon given by the descent of Aramæans, who saw in the destruction of the defences of Babylon a favourable opportunity for seizing the fertile plain in the neighbourhood of the capital. Their raid was at first successful, for they seized and occupied the cultivated lands and gardens in the neighbourhood of Babylon and of Borsippa. But we

we may see evidence of a shrewd policy on his part in the rebuilding of the temples, for by re-establishing the worship of Marduk and Nabu, he strengthened his own claims to the throne. He had already secured the gratitude of the Babylonians by the recovery and restoration of their lands; his subsequent revival of the national religion, and his performance of the coronation ceremony, which consisted of grasping the hands of the national god, raised him from the position of a popular leader, and set him upon the Babylonian throne. It is thus clear that he was recognised as king by the official priesthood, but how long he succeeded in retaining his position it is not possible at present to determine. That other external foes beside the Aramæans hoped

Babylon Rebuilt by Assyria

to profit by the comparatively defenceless state of Babylon is clear from the fact that Esarhaddon, before rebuilding the city, had first to expel Chaldæan settlers who had succeeded in gaining a foothold in the district.

After the murder of Sennacherib, the first act of his son Esarhaddon after his accession was to give commands for the complete rebuilding of the town and the temple of Marduk. While Sennacherib had been the representative of a purely Assyrian, and therefore strongly military policy, Esarhaddon, like Sargon, had to rely upon the priests. The rebuilding of Babylon thus entirely came within the scope of their efforts. The other party, however, was not dissolved upon the death of Sennacherib; it was indeed deeply rooted in Assyrian polity. The two parties seem to have found leaders in the two princes, Ashurbanipal and Shamash-shum-ukin. We shall see in treating of Assyrian history how, just when Babylon was ready, and the question at issue was a reoccupation of the throne of Babylon, the military party forced Esarhaddon to allow its head, Ashurbanipal, to be crowned king of Assyria, and thereby to ensure its power. His father could only secure Babylon for Shamash-shum-ukin, and perhaps Southern Babylonia. In the year 668 the statue of Marduk was brought back to Babylon, and the two princes were proclaimed kings of their respective realms during their father's lifetime. The existing condition was, however, the same as the old : Babylon was the protectorate of Assyria, and the new king of Assyria

sacrificed in Babylon, Sippar, and Kutha to the Babylonian gods as their protector.

The old feud was thus revived, and an outbreak of hostilities was only a matter of time. After a series of years full of prosperity and brotherly love had been recorded in the inscriptions of both kings, the struggle began anew. Shamash-shum-ukin sought alliances in whatever countries he could find enemies of Assyria, and that was practically wherever the Assyrian power was felt or feared. Elam, the Arabs, the western countries, Palestine and Gutium (the northern countries), armed against Assyria. In the war which now broke out the question was once more to be decided whether Assyria or Babylon was to rule the East. The war really began toward the "fifties" of the seventh century B.C. by the refusal of Shamash-shum-ukin to allow his brother Ashurbanipal to offer the sacrifices, to which he was entitled as protector, in the Babylonian towns. It ended with terrible sieges of Sippar, Kutha, and Babylon, and the death of Shamash-shum-ukin in the flames into which, according to Ashurbanipal's account, his despairing subjects cast him. The war ended in 648 ; and Babylonia had suffered so much during its progress that it remained quiet for some time. The Assyrian king Ashurbanipal wore the royal crown of Babylon from 647 to 626 B.C. under the name of Kandalanu. His successes against Elam deprived that country of the power of making further encroachments on Babylonia. The land thus enjoyed rest until his death.

BABYLONIAN GODS TAKEN BY THE ASSYRIANS TO SERVE IN ASSYRIAN TEMPLES
In the year 689 B.C., after the expulsion of the Elamites, Babylon fell into the hands of Sennacherib. He completely destroyed the city and carried off its gods, as represented above, to serve Assyrian gods in Assyrian temples.

BABYLON, THE METROPOLIS OF THE ANCIENT CIVILISED ASIATIC WORLD, IN THE DAYS OF ITS SPLENDOUR AND POWER

THE NEW BABYLONIAN EMPIRE
ITS LAST BRIEF ERA OF SPLENDOUR

AT the death of Ashurbanipal we find on the throne of Babylon a Chaldæan, Nabopolassar. We do not know which of the petty Chaldæan principalities was his native country. It is very probable that at first he wore the crown of Bel, with the approbation, or at least with the consent, of Assyria. During the first period he avoided any open rupture with Ashur-etil-ilani—that is to say, he recognised his protectorate. At first he possessed only Babylon ; the rest of Babylonia remained Assyrian. We have no information as to the separate stages in his advancement to power. All that is certain is that Babylon did not venture on any action against Assyria on her own resources, but concealed her plans until the alliance with Media was formed. As the royal house of Assyria was related by marriage with that of the Ashkuza, Nabopolassar's son was obliged to marry a Median princess. We

Alliance with the Medes have seen that Nabopolassar after 609 B.C. was in possession of Mesopotamia, and that the downfall of Assyria was chiefly the work of the Medes. When matters had come to this pitch, he was already old or sick ; his son Nebuchadnezzar II. was already holding the reins of government. He was assigned, therefore, the duty of subjugating the western provinces, a task which in itself would have presented little difficulty, since the Assyrian governors, after the fall of Nineveh, failed to hold their own in the provinces where the Assyrian rule was universally detested. It was therefore to be expected of these that they would submit to their new ruler, and any attempts by isolated states to assert their independence were from the first hopeless.

In the meanwhile, however, it had become necessary to recover these provinces from another power than Assyria. Necho II. of Egypt rightly judged that the opportune moment was come to win back the provinces which had been lost since the days of Thothmes and Amenophis. While the Medes were encamped before Nineveh and Nabopolassar occupied Mesopotamia, he advanced into Palestine, where he met with only isolated cases of resistance—for example, that of Josiah at Migdol, 609 or

Nebuchad-nezzar Gains the West 608 B.C.—and gradually, without great difficulty, he occupied all Palestine and Syria.

He had his chief camp for some time at Ribla, in the north of Bekaa, and from that position directed affairs in Jerusalem. In the year 605 he advanced as far as Carchemish, and was on the point of crossing the Euphrates, the boundary of the district, which, since the fall of Nineveh in the interval, was already occupied by Babylonia. Here Nebuchadnezzar, as leader of the Babylonian army, met him and defeated him, so that Necho was forced to relinquish any attempt to establish himself in Syria or Palestine, and retired before the advancing Babylonian army into Egypt. Nebuchadnezzar met with little opposition, and, receiving the homage of governors and princes, occupied the territory as far as the Egyptian frontier. Thus this king, the last among the Babylonian monarchs who met with success in his military operations, accomplished on his first appearance what had been vainly attempted for so many centuries. The West was once more subject to Babylon, as in the palmy days of Babylonian power and civilisation.

This result had not been obtained by any new awakening of the national strength of Babylonia. Babylon, even now, as for

Chaldæan Rules in Babylon centuries past, was in the hands of conquerors who availed themselves of the old fame of the metropolis of culture in order to adorn their power with its historical title. After centuries of struggle between Assyrians and Chaldæans for the crown of Bel, the advantage had in the end rested with the often repulsed, but still indefatigable, intruders. Nebuchadnezzar, before

A MEMORIAL OF NEBUCHADNEZZAR
This vast marble slab, found among the ruins of Babylon, is believed to represent Nebuchadnezzar giving instructions to his generals. He was the last successful Babylonian king.

himself king of Babylon. He held the power from 604 to 562 B.C. His name has become famous from the mere fact that he put an end to the independence of Judah, but his long reign really signified a last spell of prosperity and power for Babylonia.

An outward proof of this may be seen in the immense building operations, about which his numerous inscriptions tell us. The whole of Babylon was rebuilt by him, partly in continuation of works begun by his father, Nabopolassar, and fortified on a scale which excited the wonder of his age. He it was who erected the " Median wall," a line of defence which ran from the Euphrates near Sippar to the Tigris, somewhere by Opis, near the site of the later city of Seleucia ; this was intended to dam up the water, in order, should need occur, to transform the country higher up into a swamp, and thus to render it impossible for an army to advance in the district between the two rivers. A similar construction, starting from the Euphrates in the neighbourhood of Babylon and reaching the Tigris at a point not far from the eastern end of the other dam, completed the work of defence. Nebuchadnezzar was also the constructor of the celebrated terraces, the " hanging gardens of Semiramis " [see page 226 of this History], and he rebuilt the famous temples in all the larger towns.

Contrary to the custom of the Assyrian kings, who relate at length their own campaigns as a preface to any report of

whom even Palestine now trembled, was a Chaldæan. For this reason the representatives of the last Babylonian dynasty are called in the contemporary accounts of the Bible by the name of Chaldæans.

Towards the end of 605, when Nebuchadnezzar was still occupied in Palestine, he received the news of Nabopolassar's death and of the outbreak of riots which were intended to bring a Babylonian to the throne. With rapid decision he made forced marches by the shortest road through the desert to Babylon, and entered it at the right moment to conduct the procession of Bel on the New Year's festival in the method prescribed by immemorial custom, and thus to proclaim

THE LION GOD, SYMBOL OF BABYLONIAN POWER
Before going to war, the army of Nebuchadnezzar defiled before this massive monument, and each soldier bowed low to the symbol of his monarch's power.

their building operations, the Chaldæan kings of Babylon, and notably Nebuchadnezzar, omit from their building inscriptions any record of their achievements in war. It follows, therefore, that we have practically no accounts by Nebuchadnezzar of his campaigns. Besides the expeditions in Palestine, we know only of his thirteen years' ineffectual siege of Tyre, and one or two wars with Egypt. A small fragment of a chronicle refers to one such war in 568 B.C., but too little of the text is preserved to enable us to recover any details of the campaign. We do not yet know whether Nebuchadnezzar ever really invaded Egypt, as Ezekiel prophesied. He did not, in any case,

WHAT REMAINS TO-DAY OF NEBUCHADNEZZAR'S PALACE

This remarkable photograph shows part of the ruined palace of Nebuchadnezzar, the door being bricked up to within a quarter of the top. Many treasures of the great king were found inside. It also illustrates how completely the sands of centuries have embedded the palace, and the manner in which they have had to be dug away to disclose the building.

permanently subdue the country, and it is unlikely that he achieved victories like those of Esarhaddon and Ashurbanipal.

The west was the only field for expansion which Babylonia could still command. The east and north, where of old the kings of Assyria fought, are out of the question : Elam and Urartu do not exist. There the one great Median empire rules from Elam to the Halys, the boundary of Lydia. The existence of Babylonia depends on its relations with this barbarian empire, which now really sways the destinies of Nearer Asia. Babylon stands in the same relation to it as Italy did to the German Empire of the Middle Ages. So long as Nebuchadnezzar lived the relations between the powers appear to have been friendly. The Medes had in reality by the overthrow

of Assyria brought the dynasty of Nabopolassar for the first time into power in its own country. It was due in a large degree to the good will of Cyaxares that they handed over these districts to it ; and it would almost seem as if the marriage alliance with this barbarian royal house had been of greater importance to Nebuchadnezzar than such marriages usually are when diplomacy is more highly developed. Herodotus tells us of Nebuchadnezzar's intervention in Median affairs on an occasion when there was war between Media and Lydia, the third great power of this period ; and it may be noted that in the course of this war the eclipse of the sun occurred which Thales predicted. Nebuchadnezzar is said to have acted as mediator between the powers, together with a certain Syennesis of Cilicia, by whom he was probably advised.

But the young dynasty, which had won its fame in the person of Nebuchadnezzar, practically disappeared with him. After his death his son, Amel-Marduk—

The Last Kings of Babylon the Evil-Merodach of the Bible —became king; he reigned only two years—561 and 560 B.C.— when he was deposed because "he was unjust and ruled tyrannically." Since this verdict is given by the historian Berossus, a priest of Bel, writing in the Seleucid era, and in almost identical words by Nabonidus, we must see in it a verdict of the priestly class, whose claims Nebuchadnezzar, with all his temple building, had never quite satisfied. We know nothing else of Amel-Marduk, except that he treated with kindness Jehoiachin of Judah, who had been brought to Babylon by Nebuchadnezzar. He was murdered, and his brother-in-law, Nergal-shar-usur, or Neriglissar, was raised to the throne, which he held from 559 to 554 B.C. No attempt was yet made to go outside the Chaldæan royal family. It is not clear whether Neriglissar himself was a Chaldæan. Of him, too, we know very little; but good service in the defence of the country is ascribed to him by Nabonidus. Did the Medes now interfere in favour of the dethroned royal house? His successor was his son Labashi-Marduk, a minor; he was deposed after a reign of but nine months, because, as the above-mentioned sources both agree in reporting, "he displayed evil tendencies." The real cause is apparent in the choice of the successor, a Babylonian, who approved himself a man after the priests' hearts, for he was indefatigable in building temples and endowing them.

Nabonidus, this last king of Babylon, who ruled from 555 to 538 B.C., is a strange figure. He looked on unperturbed while the land was occupied first by the Medes, and then by the Persians, being fully engrossed in the excavation of old sites of temples and in the arrangement of the

CYRUS, KING OF PERSIA
Who subjugated all Mesopotamia and Lydia, and put an end for all time to native Babylonian development.

chronology of their founders. Reports as to his discovery of old inscriptions are very valuable for us, but neither they nor his eagerly prosecuted restorations of the temples were of any use to his tottering throne. The Medes do not seem to have looked on passively at the overthrow of the dynasty, which was allied to them by marriage and friendship. Perhaps Neriglissar had already been obliged to act on the defensive; but now, when the rupture with Babylon was complete, they invaded Mesopotamia. Even then, at the outset of his reign, Nabonidus showed himself in his true colours. While Harran, the old city of Sin, in the heart of Mesopotamia, was being invested by the Medes, he did nothing but dream that the gods would set Harran free. And indeed, they granted him his wish, for Astyages was overthrown by Cyrus, and Mesopotamia had peace for some years. But the conqueror of the Medes soon proved to be a far more formidable opponent. Meantime, however, Nabonidus hastened to rebuild the temple of Sin at Harran with grateful heart; for this end he tithed and taxed his subjects "from Gaza, the border of Egypt, the Mediterranean, and Syria, up to the Persian Sea."

Meanwhile the Persian Cyrus secured the foundations of his power. He subjugated the Lydian empire, in addition to the countries already possessed by the Medes, so that the only great nation which could have lent any support to Babylonia was now powerless to do so. Then Cyrus proceeded against Babylonia, which was hemmed in on all sides. Nabonidus himself did not move, but lived in retirement,

Cyrus the Persian in Babylonia or was kept prisoner by a hostile party in his palace. His son, Bel-shar-usur, or Belshazzar, was regent and commander-in-chief; the Bible makes him the last king of Babylon.

Cyrus first occupied Mesopotamia, having crossed the Tigris from Arbela, south of the ruins of Calah. In the next year, 546, he advanced from Elam into

South Babylonia. Nabonidus ordered the gods of the great towns Ur, Erech, etc., to be brought into Babylon, and felt himself secure under their protection. We have no accounts of the next five years, but in the year 539 B.C. we find Babylonia surrounded on every side. The respite may perhaps be explained by the effectiveness of the defence by inundation, for which purpose the Median wall of Nebuchadnezzar and the supplementary works, starting from the neighbourhood of Babylon, were constructed. All this time Cyrus was unable to advance into the region of Babylon either from Mesopotamia or from Southern Babylonia. The surrounding country, therefore, like Holland under similar circumstances in later times, had been changed into a swamp, within which the " kingdom of Babylon " lay, large enough to maintain itself so long as an army did not invade it.

A reminiscence of this is preserved in Herodotus' account that Cyrus was occupied for two years in diverting the course of the Diyala, in order to make his army familiar with the process of draining canals, a knowledge which was of good service to him at the siege of Babylon,

BRONZES FOUND IN NEBUCHADNEZZAR'S PALACE
Figures of a lion and lioness dating from 1800 B.C.—that is, from the first Babylonian empire.

when he changed the channel of the Euphrates. The real object was probably not that suggested by Herodotus, but the construction of a passage for crossing into the district protected by the inundations; for the mouth of the Diyala is near Opis, where the Median wall ends. This theory is confirmed by the fact that the Babylonian army under Belshazzar met him there, between Opis and Sippar, after the passage had been effected; it was defeated in 539, and no more opposition was offered. Babylon sur-

Five-years Siege of Babylonia rendered to the vanguard of an army under Ugbaru, or Gobryas, the governor of Gutium; the great fortifications of Nebuchadnezzar were not defended; the Persians were received as preservers. Cyrus was proclaimed king when he entered four months later; and one of the first acts of his reign

was to conciliate the priesthoods of Babylonia by sending back the gods from Babylon to their own towns.

This concludes Babylonian history. Babylon had become a Persian province.

Babylonian History Ends The ancient glory, indeed, which so shortly before its setting had shone forth unexpectedly, was not yet entirely forgotten. Several attempts were made to recover her independence, but these revolts were always quickly put down. Nabonidus was merely supplanted by Cyrus, and in Southern Babylonia, which had been abandoned by Nabonidus, and from which he had actually taken away the gods, the people certainly looked upon Cyrus as a sort of saviour. The latter was also shrewd enough to hold the reins of government more loosely in the provinces. He not only restored to the Babylonian towns their gods, but showed the same favour to many provinces which had long been confiscated, at the same time giving them self-government; for example, Judah, and possibly Sidon also. Those provinces, therefore, could not fail to see in Cyrus a liberator from the yoke of Babylon.

A new era in the history of Eastern civilisation now opens. Persia, before the capture of Babylon, had already occupied Asia Minor, and had thus come into touch with Greek civilisation. The Persian empire, it is true, as heir of Babylon, still possesses to a certain degree a comparatively high state of culture. But this civilisation is tottering with age, because it is no longer supported by fresh national life. It is easily outstripped by the vigorous vitality of the Greek spirit, which is soon destined to extend its sway over and beyond the regions where Babylonian culture has for so long predominated.

AN IMAGINATIVE REPRESENTATION OF THE SACK AND PILLAGE OF BABYLON

From the painting by John Martin

ANCILLARY
ANCIENT
EMPIRES OF
WESTERN
ASIA

BABYLONIA
VI

THE MESOPOTAMIAN CIVILISATION
ITS LONG VITALITY AND FINAL DECAY

OUR knowledge of the Ancient East is still very young. All that has been learnt of it from the exploration of the ancient monuments dates from the middle of the last century; and much of this knowledge must be discounted, so long as science has to work with insufficient means. We are still very far from being in a condition to speak of any systematic examination of the soil of these old homes of civilisation; all that we possess in monuments and antiquities, and therefore all sources for the history of these countries, form only an infinitely small fraction of that which a more fortunate age may expect to recover. Every attempt to present a connected picture of the course of the development of the ancient nations of the East must therefore prove inadequate. We can at most learn something of those periods, for which chance has placed ampler sources of information in our hands, and we can seek to trace the forces which have determined the course of events. Of other periods we know little as yet, and all that we can do for them is to supply the names of a few kings or rulers of whom little else has been recorded.

How Little we Know

An essential feature of the sources hitherto accessible is that they furnish us with more information about political occurrences than about the nature and extent of the forces at work in the inner life of the people. The inscriptions of the Assyrian kings were the first to become known, and a considerable number of them have been recovered; thus the section of history based on them is that which is known in greatest detail up to the present time. But these inscriptions record almost exclusively wars, sieges, victories, and lists of spoil. What we would gladly know of the social and political life of the people can be gathered only from scattered allusions throughout the texts.

Our survey of the history of civilisation in the Ancient East must, therefore, to some extent prove defective and unsatisfactory, owing to the want of materials for study. Our sources of information are more detailed for isolated periods, such as the era of the first dynasty of Babylon, for Assyrian history from Tiglath-pileser onwards, and again for that part of Babylon from Nebuchadnezzar down to the Persian era. For thousands of records of these periods are in our possession which belong to the business life of the people—namely, contracts, legal decisions, receipts, commercial transactions of every sort, and private letters. These indeed supply a motley of isolated facts as to the private life of the times in question, but in the bewildering crowd of details we can scarcely recognise with certainty the broad principles, the typical cases which have to be considered in the development of national history. Before these great materials can be thoroughly worked, before the numerous records of different periods are thoroughly assimilated, much work and study are required. And it will probably be long before those periods, which are separated from each other by hundreds of years, can be connected together by filling up the gaps through the discovery of new records.

Material Largely Unworked

But, even if science had already succeeded in making full use of these countless records, yet they would reveal only one aspect of the popular life in Babylonia and Assyria— namely, the commercial life, and that, indeed, principally from the private side. So far as they concern the life and the development of the entire people and the state—that is, in their bearing on political economy—very little light is thrown upon the subject for considerable periods; and about much else which we in modern times recognise to be

Economic Life Unknown

important in the life of a nation we must be content for the present to know little or nothing. Trading relations and commercial life in all its aspects, the conditions of the **The Lateness of our Knowledge** tenure of real property in its bearing on the welfare of the state, the rules of administration, etc.—these are matters of which royal inscriptions can tell us hardly anything, and which naturally do not find expression in a commercial or legal contract. To our general want of information on these subjects during long periods of Babylonian history, two periods, however, now present striking exceptions. The famous code of laws drawn up by Hammurabi has furnished material for sketching a picture of the social life of the Babylonians during the period of the West Semitic kings of the first dynasty. The other period is the succeeding one of the Kassite kings, whose numerous deeds and charters illustrate the system of land tenure during the period at which they were drawn up.

But we know little as yet about the beginnings of civilisation in Babylonia. The long periods when men were settled in the valley of the Euphrates before the time when our present knowledge begins are still hidden in the mists of antiquity. We may be compelled for a long time yet to forego any attempt to determine from contemporary sources, or even merely from the products of civilisation, how the first settlers in the valley of the Euphrates, adapting themselves to the needs of the soil, raised themselves gradually from a state of savagery to a higher stage of civilisation. How and under what conditions men arrived at that intellectual result so important for the historian—the development of writing—is a question for which as yet no sources of information are forthcoming. It is clear that the most remote antiquity to which we can go back was already acquainted with a perfected system of writing.

A BABYLONIAN LAND-CHARTER
There exist deeds of the Kassite kings which explain the Babylonian land tenure system. The essential clauses of these were often inscribed on sculptured boundary stones like the "Michaux" stone here illustrated, which is now in the Louvre.

The valley of the Euphrates, now to a large extent desolate and marshy, was one of the most fruitful tracts in the world. The fertility of the soil is described as marvellous at all periods, of which we have some, though unfortunately very scanty, accounts. The Euphrates and the Nile are two rivers the deposits of which give the tiller of the soil the richest reward for small exertions. In the almost rainless climate of Egypt and Southern Babylonia these river-valleys were the only places which enabled an agriculture still in its infancy to work the soil profitably. On the other hand, the distress in times of drought compelled the Bedouins from the scantily watered steppes to seek pasture there for their numerous herds, and, by growing crops for fodder, to supplement the voluntary gifts of Nature in preparation for the dry season of the year. The complete transition from nomadic to settled life in these plains can thus be explained by the nature of the land.

The step from an agricultural life in the open country to the building of fortified towns is not so great, and must have been taken very early in a land which was exposed on all sides to the inroads of the nomads. But even the gradual stages leading to such conditions are, in point of time, far anterior to the date when our knowledge of the Euphrates district begins. The old seats of civilisation, such as Kish, Agade, Nippur, Lagash, Ur, Erech, Larsa, and Eridu, were towns with a most ancient past at the time when they, for the first time, appear in the light of history. They had already been **Oldest Cities of the World** long developed into that which they continued to be for 3,000 years of the most varying political phases, seats of ancient sanctuaries, sacred since immemorial ages, and towns with a purely urban population engaged in trade and industries.

We may assume that even then the conditions of the tenure of real property and professional activity existed in much the same form as that in which they were maintained throughout the later periods of Babylonian civilisation. In distinction to the Western forms of culture, the growth of which we can follow from their beginnings, we here meet with an already systematised form of national life, such as corresponds to the stage of development of European civilisation which was concluded in the Middle Ages; this form endured for 3,000 years, though exposed to the most varied upheavals. Each new migration which spread over the country quickly adopted the existing civilisation, and was subjected to its influence. It is certain that even the less successful among the conquerors must have had their share in the booty; but no fresh distribution of the land among a peasant class ever resulted on a considerable scale, so that we can never follow the course of the national life from the beginning. The leaders of the different conquests always took the place of the old kings. If they did not wish to destroy the whole civilisation, they were obliged to adopt it with its temples and towns, its settled ownership of the soil, and its social classes. This is the principal reason why the individual nationalities so soon die out: they do not start their development from the very beginning, but mount with a sudden leap to a higher stage, beyond which they cannot go. Another reason which no doubt hastened the absorption of the conquering races was intermarriage with the inhabitants whom they found settled in the country. We find, therefore, from the time when our knowledge begins, that the constitution of the land was one of feudal tenure under the domination of the priesthood. The lord of the country is the divinity. He entrusts it to the priesthood

Babylonia Absorbed all Invaders

Mansell

A BABYLONIAN BOUNDARY STONE

This fine boundary stone, like the one on the opposite page, has sculptured upon it representations of Babylonian deities, whose curses were called down upon the person who should remove the stone or alter the boundary which it marked.

and the king; there is therefore temple property and State property. The king has the disposal, above all, of the open country, which he grants to his vassals in fee. His authority does not extend to the territory which falls under the dominion of the god; this belongs to the town in which the god dwells, and, naturally, together with that reserved for the temple, to the patricians in the town. The ground is cultivated by small farmers, who have to pay as rent their share of the profits to the owner — temple, king, noble, or citizen. This system has never been favourable to the prosperity of the peasant class. Even if, after a conquest, confiscated land were divided among the masses of the immigrating people, these could not long maintain their position by the side of the great proprietors, but would be forced to sell the land and become tenants. The small farmer is, usually, personally free—as free as a man can be who retains from the proceeds of what has been wrung from the soil in the sweat of his brow as much as suffices for a thrifty Oriental livelihood. War, indeed, supplied with its prisoners the necessary demand for non-free labourers, the use of whom we have to imagine to ourselves as more common in the industrial operations of the town than in the cultivation of the soil. Out of these is formed the numerous class of freedmen who meet us often in business life.

Land Tenure System

We must, on the whole, picture to ourselves the land as parcelled out into small farms which are cultivated by the tenant for the owner. With the simple means and implements required for farming on a small scale, but with all the grim industry applied to every patch of earth which this system enforces, it was horticulture rather

"Dawn of Civilisation," S.P.C.K.

CHALDÆAN FARM OXEN
The Chaldæans kept considerable flocks of domestic animals, including oxen, asses, sheep, and goats, which were pastured on waste land, where they were liable to the ravages of lions and other wild beasts.

ditions. He is forced to keep the surplus against the times of drought, and he is naturally driven to control the conditions of the water supply.

The country then, from the beginning of our knowledge of it, and as a preliminary condition of cultivation on an extended scale, was intersected by a network of canals, intended to receive the flood-water and to convey it from the districts threatened with inundation to the arid parts where it irrigates the soil in the dry season. These canals in some places lie higher than the surrounding country, so that the required water can be let in through sluices. In other places they are lower; then the water,

than agriculture. The most important condition for a productive cultivation of the soil in the climate of the East, with its rainless summer, is a regular supply of

"Dawn of Civilisation," S.P.C.K.

AGRICULTURAL LIFE IN CHALDÆA, ILLUSTRATED BY ARTISTS OF THE TIME
A seal-cylinder picturing the pastoral life of early Babylonia. On the right is the goatherd driving forth his flock from the goat-house with the crack of his whip. The rest of the lower part of the tablet shows the flock scattered to pasture.

water, and it is the task of the agriculturist to irrigate as large an area as possible. On the other hand, the immense streams of the Euphrates and Tigris, when the mountain snows melt, bring down with them such a volume of water that they flood the most fertile parts of the country, block up the watercourses with their mud, and turn the fields into swamps, as is now the case with great tracts which were once thriving. Thus want of rain, on the one side, and floods on the other compel the dweller in the Euphrates valley to modify these con-

precisely as in the valley of the Nile, is raised to the land by well-wheels, or, if less is required, by buckets which a single man sets into movement. Moreover, the lands lying in the immediate neighbourhood of the Euphrates and the Tigris were irrigated

A MESOPOTAMIAN METHOD OF IRRIGATION
A bas-relief representation of the shaddufs by means of which water was raised, through successive levels, from the rivers to the fields. They are still in use on the Nile.

SWAMPS ON THE TIGRIS WHERE ONCE WERE THRIVING FIELDS

Want of rain at one time, and disastrous floods, caused by the overflowing of the Euphrates and Tigris with the melting of the mountain snows, at another period of the year, compelled the Mesopotamians to control the water supply.

by contrivances similar to those employed by the peasants at the present day. Since the banks of the Euphrates are lower than those of the Tigris, a primitive form of water-wheel is employed for raising the water from the level of the stream to that of the surrounding country. The wheel is formed of rough boughs and branches nailed together with spokes joining the outer rims to a roughly-shaped axle. Around the rim are tied a number of clay bottles or cups for picking up the water, and the wheel is kept in motion by the current, which hits a few rough paddles fixed to the wheel in such a way that they project beyond the rim. The wheel is set up at a spot where there is a drop in the river-bed, and the water runs swiftly over the shallows. Its axle is supported on pillars of rough masonry, and as it is turned by the current, the cups or bottles empty themselves into a trough made from half the trunk of a date-palm, hollowed out; and the water flows thence through a small aqueduct to the irrigation channel on the bank. This is the most advantageous method of raising the water,

A CHALDÆAN KITCHEN
From a terra-cotta tablet showing Chaldæan farm hands preparing a meal. One makes dough into round cakes, and another tends a pot boiling on the hearth, while two others indulge in a quarrel.

for, so long as the wheel is in order and the stream is high enough to turn it, a constant supply of water is assured without the labour of man or beast ; and the water can be cut off at any moment by the simple expedient of blocking the wheel or tying it up.

The higher banks of the Tigris render the use of water-wheels impracticable, and here the water has to be raised by other means than that of the current of the stream. The method employed at the present day is to raise it in skins, which are drawn up to the level of the bank by cattle, horses, or donkeys. A well-like recess is cut into the banks, and over its mouth a wooden spindle is supported upon struts. The skin is raised or lowered in the recess by means of a rope, which passes over the spindle, while the funnel end of the skin is held up by a second rope running over a lower spindle, until its mouth is raised to a level with the trough into which the water is poured. The skin, when full of water, is raised by the beasts fastened to the rope, and they obtain a good purchase for hauling up the heavy weight by being driven down an inclined plane dug out at the top of the bank. Two separate skins and sets of beasts are often employed, and as one is let down the other is pulled up, so that a constant flow of water is kept up in the irrigation channel. There is little doubt that the ancient Babylonians employed both these primitive methods of **Babylonian Irrigators Now in Use** raising the water from the rivers and canals to the higher level of the fields, while representations have been found upon Assyrian bas-reliefs of the "shadduf" in operation, which is more commonly seen in Egypt at the present day than in Mesopotamia. This contrivance consists of a beam, supported in the centre, while at one end is a bucket for receiving the water, and at the other end a stone is fixed as a counter-weight. By using two or more shaddufs, one above the other, water can be raised, through successive levels, to a considerable height.

While the adoption of these smaller contrivances was within the means of the individual owner of the land, the construction of large canals was the work of the State. We find, indeed, among the scanty information which we possess as to the kings' activity at home, records of the cutting of canals, thus showing that the importance of this duty was fully realised. In the older times, when dates were not yet fixed by the reigns of the kings but by the important events of the respective years, we find under the descriptions of the years by the side of " In the year when this or that war was waged," also,

" When the king dug this or that canal." After the conquest of South Babylonia Hammurabi says, for example : " When Anu and Enlil had granted me the land of Sumer and Akkad to rule, and entrusted their sceptre to my hands, then I dug out the canal, named ' Hammurabi is the blessing of the people,' which bringeth abundance of water into the land of Sumer and Akkad. Both the banks thereof I changed to fields for cultivation, and I garnered piles of grain, and I procured unfailing water for the land of Sumer and Akkad for ever." Nabopolassar and Nebuchadnezzar make similar reports of irrigation works. These constructions were sometimes **Babylon's Canal System** used, as in Holland, for the protection of the country, as we find shown in the later days of Babylonia, when Nebuchadnezzar built the " Median wall," and Nabonidus with its help changed his whole " kingdom of Babylon " into an island. Famous canals, which ran through Babylonia, are the Palakuttu and Nahr-sharri, the " canal of the king," and we meet their names even in the Hellenistic era. The former mainly follows the course of the Euphrates on the south side; the latter effects a connection between the Euphrates and Tigris in an oblique line.

We must thus imagine the whole country between the rivers intersected by a network of canals of every size down to simple irrigation ditches. It was only through the efficiency of this system that the whole low-lying district was habitable.

A BABYLONIAN TYPE OF WATER-WHEEL IN USE TO-DAY   Frith

For irrigation the Babylonians used a water-wheel made of rough boughs nailed together, with clay bottles on the rim for picking up the water. The wheel was turned by the current, or by animals, and the bottles emptied themselves into a trough on the bank of the river. The photograph shows a modern Persian wheel of similar construction.

Accordingly, until the ruin of those countries by the Mongols, the superintendence of the irrigation works formed one of the first duties of the government. The destruction of the canals changed a great part of the land into marshes ; and the first task, on an attempt to make this most fruitful of all districts once more valuable to mankind, would be to restore the old watercourses, the beds of which are still visible in many places.

These works, which are restricted in size and extent by the nature of the Babylonian lowlands, are neither possible nor necessary in the higher districts, especially in Assyria, with its hills and neighbouring mountains, and a climate closely resembling that of Central Europe. On the other hand, we find instances of water being brought from a long distance for the supply of the towns. As instances, we may cite the aqueduct of Bavian, by means of which Sennacherib brought the water from the mountain streams to Nineveh, or the tunnel of Negub, through which Esarhaddon conveyed the water of the Zab to Calah in place of earlier works of Ashurnasirpal.

In architecture the inventive faculties of man are greatly dependent on the material at his disposal. Babylonia possesses

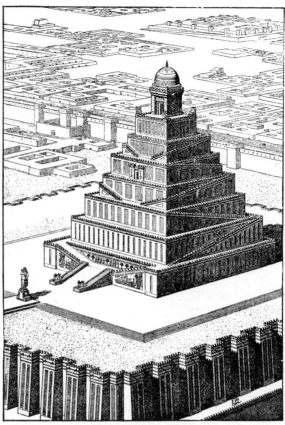

A BABYLONIAN TEMPLE

This reconstruction by Chipiez exhibits the characteristic of Babylonian brick architecture, the terraced tower called a zikkurat. Their summits were thought to be the dwelling places of the god. Hence, probably, the story of the Tower of Babel.

neither stone nor suitable building timber. While the Egyptians found in the upper valley of the Nile the stone necessary for their great buildings, and the river brought it down to the plains, the Babylonians had to fetch even the stone for their statues from a distance, and usually by land ; Gudea, for instance, obtained the material for his statues from Magan on the Sinaitic peninsula. We do not therefore find in Babylonia colossal statues like those of the Egyptians, and their buildings were constructed from clay, the material which the land supplied them in abundance. Babylonia is the land of brick buildings, and the influence of its civilisation on the East is most strikingly illustrated by the fact that the art of building in brick was imitated in places where stone was available, such as Elam, Assyria, and even Syria. The want of

Babylonia the Land of Brick

timber and stone columns led to the invention of a pillar made of bricks. But, so far as we can see, this was seldom employed. The kings preferred to obtain cedar trunks from Amanus, and, when those forests failed, from Lebanon, for the necessary wooden columns and supports, but at no time were they extensively employed. In this respect Assyria followed in the steps of Babylon. The ordinary brick was dried in the sun. It was burnt when additional strength was required, and for the decoration of the walls it was enamelled with bright patterns and designs. The land supplied abundance of asphalt as cement for the burnt bricks, and these were employed in foundations, for pavements, and for strengthening the walls of unburnt brick.

Importance of the Temples

A characteristic product of Babylonian brick architecture is their " terraced

1	$\mathbf{Y}$	11	$\mathbf{\langle Y}$	100	$\mathbf{Y\ Y}$
2	$\mathbf{YY}$	12	$\mathbf{\langle YY}$	200	$\mathbf{YY\ Y}$
3	$\mathbf{YYY}$	20	$\mathbf{\langle\langle}$	300	$\mathbf{YYY\ Y}$
4	$\mathbf{\forall}$	30	$\mathbf{\langle\langle\langle}$	400	$\mathbf{\forall\ Y}$
5	$\mathbf{YYY\ YY}$	40	$\mathbf{\langle\langle}$	500	$\mathbf{YYY\ Y}$
6	$\mathbf{YYY\ YYY}$	50	$\mathbf{Y}$	600	$\mathbf{YYY\ Y}$
7	$\mathbf{YYY\ Y}$	60	$\mathbf{YY}$	700	$\mathbf{YYY\ Y}$
8	$\mathbf{YYY\ YY}$	70	$\mathbf{Y\langle\langle}$	800	$\mathbf{YYY\ Y}$
9	$\mathbf{YYY\ YYY}$	80	$\mathbf{Y\langle\langle\langle}$	900	$\mathbf{YYY\ Y}$
10	$\mathbf{\langle}$	90	$\mathbf{Y\langle\langle}$	1,000	$\mathbf{Y\ \langle Y}$

CHALDÆAN SYSTEM OF NUMERALS

The Babylonians were keen mathematicians and compiled numerous mathematical tables to assist them in the calculations which their astronomical investigations required. Their simple system of notation, adopted in the days of the first monarchy, is illustrated above.

towers " called by the Babylonians *zik-kurratu.* These were pyramidal erections built in several storeys ; they formed an important feature of the great temples, and their summits were thought to be the dwelling-places of the god. The story of the Tower of Babel was probably connected with these buildings.

The temples are by far the most conspicuous works of Babylonian architecture. To a higher degree than even the churches and convents of the Middle Ages they united in themselves all the intellectual and material products of Babylonian civilisation. We have already noted that a great portion of the country belonged to them, and we may see in them the centre of the intellectual life of the people. The priesthood not only exercised an influence through religion, but was entrusted with the care of science and of the technical arts. Each great temple formed a town with a government of its own, and we have ample evidence as to how it managed its affairs. Countless clay tablets from Tello furnish information as to the administration of the temple lands in Southern Babylonia, and the documents of the Kassite period

which have been found at Nippur throw a flood of light upon the organisation of this important religious centre.

Any survey of the intellectual influence exerted by the temples is, from the nature of our sources of information, more difficult. It is obvious that the duty of giving instruction and fostering learning fell upon the priesthood. The art of writing could be thoroughly learned only from them ; they were thus the guardians and patrons of all literature, whether religious or secular, and of the sciences, even those which entered closely into the sphere of practical life. Among the Babylonian priests there were keen mathematicians, and numerous tables have been recovered which were compiled to assist them in their calculations. These comprise multiplication tables, division tables, tables of squares, tables of square roots, geometrical progressions, and the like. Metrological texts have also come down to us, and recent research has shown that the Babylonians could not only ascertain the area of a square or a rectangle by calculation, but could also calculate the area of a right-angled triangle from the length of its two legs, of a rectangle from its base and altitude, and of a trapezoid from its two bases and altitude. From these facts it may be inferred that the Babylonian priests had acquired considerable proficiency in mathematical study, and their

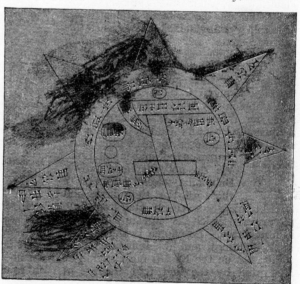

"Dawn of Civilisation," S.P.C.K.

CHALDÆAN MAP OF THE WORLD

The early Babylonian idea of the earth was a disc surrounded by the sea in the form of a stream. Chaldæa occupied the greater part of the map.

THE
WORLD AS
CONCEIVED BY THE
CHALDÆANS

"Dawn of Civilisation," S.P.C.K.

Like the Egyptians, the Chaldæans took the world to be an enclosed chamber floating on the waters or the universe. The earth was the floor, rising at the centre to the mountain source of the Euphrates. The heavens were a dome resting on a wall surrounding the earth, with the oceans collected in the ditch between.

progress in this branch of knowledge was doubtless of considerable assistance to them in making astronomical calculations.

We have abundant proofs that the priests from the earliest periods occupied themselves with the study of the sidereal heavens. Babylonia is the home of astronomy and of astrology, which is in-separable from it in the Eastern mind, and the Chaldæans were reputed to be masters of these sciences even in Græco-Roman times. The movements of the stars were accurately observed and noted. Omens were derived from them, and every possible constellation was consulted. An eclipse is an event which is recorded in the Assyrian eponym canon in a similar way to a war. If the ability of a Thales to foretell an eclipse for the year 585 excited the astonishment of the Greek world, he had obtained his wisdom from the Babylonians, as, indeed, Pythagoras must also have borrowed the suggestions for his symbolism of numbers from the East, with which he is said to have become acquainted as an Assyrian mercenary. A large number of observations of the heavens and the stars are extant, and an even greater number of omens of the most

Babylon the Home of Astronomy

ordinary augural type, which we would gladly exchange for other information.

Closely connected with the observation of the revolution of the stars is the settle-ment of the chronology. The Baby-lonians were the teachers of classical anti-quity with regard to the system of the calendar. We still retain their divisions of years, months, and weeks. The desig-nation of the seven days of the week after the gods, which correspond to the two great stars and the five planets known to them, has come down to our times, as well as the division of the day into twelve double-hours, which we still find upon the dial of our watch. The numerical system was closely connected with these divisions. It is a sexagesimal system with the divi-sional quantities five and twelve, apparently based on astronomical observations and calculations. By the side of it, and combined with it, the decimal notation was employed. Our sources of informa-tion do not yet enable us to trace the origin of either system to its source, or to determine which is the more ancient of the two. The system of weights and measures was based on the same method of com-putation.

Calendar System due to Babylon

WORSHIP OF SIN, THE MOON-GOD   Mansell

The Babylonian gods were personifications of natural forces, and at first each god was worshipped in his own city. Thus Ur was the seat of the moon-cult. This scene is taken from a Babylonian seal, B.C. 2500.

We are faced with a perplexing problem when we are called upon to give an account of the exact duties of the temples and the priesthood, and to explain in detail the observance of cults and the progress of religious development. The phases and forms of men's ideas on this subject during three thousand years furnish matter for a special and comprehensive inquiry, and yet our sources of information on this head are more defective than in the field of political history. Yet a study of the religious and historical inscriptions which have come down to us enables us to gain some insight into the characters of the gods themselves, as they were conceived to exist in the minds of their worshippers.

The gods of the Babylonians present as complex a character as the race by whom they were worshipped, and in giving a summary of the principal facts concerning them it is necessary to bear in mind that the religious system of the later Babylonians was the product of a long period of gradual development. Speaking generally of the pantheon as it existed during the later periods, we may explain the greater gods as personifications of natural forces. Babylonian religion may thus be regarded as a worship of Nature, and the gods themselves may be to a great extent classified as personifications of various natural powers. Thus at the head of the company of the gods, as they were conceived by the later Semitic Babylonians,

stood the great triad of deities—Anu, Enlil, and Ea—whose general spheres of influence embraced the entire universe. Anu was regarded as the god of heaven; Enlil, the god of the earth and of mankind; and Ea, the god of the abyss of water beneath the earth. Under the Sumerians we even find these three deities mentioned in close connection with each other. Other gods who personified great natural forces were Sin, the Sumerian Enzu, the moon-god, and Shamash, the Sumerian Babbar, the sun-god. Other gods personified the storm and atmospheric conditions, pestilence, fire, vegetation, and the like; while others again were connected specially with battle and the underworld; and, as the result of a later development, the separate planets were associated with the greater gods in the same way as special deities had from the earliest times been associated with the sun and moon. The goddesses, with one exception, were not very sharply defined or differentiated from one another, being to a great extent the female counterparts of their respective husbands. Thus it is possible, with the help of the altar inscriptions, to recover the outlines of a very complete pantheon of Babylonian deities.

In tracing the growth of this elaborate system of Nature-worship we are met with a difficulty which has not yet been satisfactorily explained. We have already noted that during the earliest periods of

SHAMASH, THE SUN-GOD   Mansell

A scene from a sculptured tablet showing the worship of the sun-god in his temple at Sippara. His emblem is shown on the altar in front of the god.

MARDUK, THE CHIEF OF THE GODS, DESTROYING TIAMAT, OR CHAOS

Marduk, or Bel-Merodach, the city-god of Babylon, was, after the rise of Babylon, made chief of the gods. His destruction of Tiamat, the representation of chaos, is the central episode of the great Babylonian epic of the Creation. After destroying the monster, Marduk created the universe in the form shown on page 1637, out of the two halves of her body.

history Babylonia was split up into a series of independent city-states, and it was only after many centuries of separate existence that a permanent fusion was effected between them. Yet we can trace the existence of many of the great Babylonian gods back into this remote past. At this time each is worshipped by the people of his own city, and the fortune of the god is bound up with that of his worshippers. Taken in the aggregate, the worship of all these city-gods under their later attributes presents a consistent picture of Nature-worship in its various departments ; but it is not clear how the local distribution of the great natural gods among a number of cities, originally independent, is to be explained. In the present state of our knowledge it is scarcely possible to trace the process by which a local city-god became associated with one of the great powers of nature; and it is also in many cases difficult to decide whether the worship of any

particular deity was of Sumerian or Semitic origin. What is certain, however, is that the great cities were from the earliest periods associated with the worship of special deities. Ur was connected with the moon-god ; Larsa, with the worship of the sun ; Uruk, with seat of Nana, or Ishtar, the female principle ; Nippur, with the temple of Bel. But each of these, together with many other still unknown seats of civilisation, had developed in its temple a special mythology during the centuries and tens of centuries of its existence. Thus was produced a confused medley of different systems in the effort to bring a conception of the particular divinity, based on the nature of things, into harmony or rivalry with the doctrines of the other centres of culture.

In addition to this the various foreign nations which in turn conquered and colonised Babylonia brought their own beliefs with them, and then an adjustment had to be made

RAMMAN, THE STORM-GOD

The worship of this god is an example of the adjustment of the Babylonian beliefs and those of their Western conquerors.

between the newly introduced ideas and those which had been long established in the land. We may cite as an example the introduction of the cult of the storm-god Adad, or Ramman, by the Western Semites. Even when the religious texts recovered up to the present have been published and translated it will be a gigantic task to disentangle the threads that run through the different temple traditions, and to trace them back to their original sources. It may be noted, however, that the farther we go northward, the purer is the Semitic element which meets us in the earlier periods of history ; and, further, the repetition of the cults proves that the country was distinct from Southern Babylonia. Just as there was a South Babylonian sun-god of Larsa, so there was a North Babylonian sun-god of Sippar ; the Ishtar of Uruk was matched by Ishtar of Agade in the north. We know less of the north in the earlier times than of the south. In the later periods other towns became prominent, such as Kutha with the cult of Nergal, god of the lower world. The moon cult, which had its chief seat in Ur, was of inferior importance in Northern Babylonia ; but we hear of its most famous shrine at Harran in Mesopotamia.

A Medley of Worships

We do not yet find any mention of Babylon in the inscriptions of the earliest period, and it owes its importance to political occurrences of a comparatively late period, though recently discovered evidence tends to prove that already under the first kings of Ur its rank as a religious centre was considerable. It appears to have become the chief city of Babylonia under the first Babylonian dynasty. Its elevation to the position of capital of the Babylonian empire and its consequent supremacy in the domain of politics were accompanied, in conformity with Eastern ideas, by the development of a justification of this pre-eminence in the religious beliefs of its inhabitants. Precisely as Athens, having attained the hegemony, tried to prove her antiquity in mythology and history, so the wise men of Babylon took pains to prove that Babylon was the seat of the most ancient civilisation and the centre of the world.

Comparative Lateness of Babylon

The former city-god, Marduk—in biblical pronunciation Merodach—becomes the god round whom the whole creation of the world turns. We have now recovered the greater part of the creation myth of Babylon, in which Marduk plays the chief rôle, and we may conjecture with some probability that similar works of more ancient origin, reproducing the events of the time when their cities flourished, were taught in the temples of Southern Babylonia. The epic of creation expresses the supremacy of Babylon, which was founded by the dynasty of Hammurabi. It is Marduk who fights the war of worlds for the sovereignty of the Dii Superi, who are threatened by Tiamat (Chaos), and it is he who, after cleaving the monster, imagined under the form of a snake or a dragon, creates the universe out of the two halves of her body.

Until recently only fragments of the great Babylonian epic of the Creation had been recovered, the portion of the text which was best preserved relating the battle waged by Marduk against Tiamat on behalf of the gods. But at the beginning of this century many additional tablets and fragments of the great poem were discovered, and these enable us to fill in completely the outlines of the story, and at the same time to separate the older elements which have been incorporated in the epic along with the later additions in honour of Marduk, the city-god of Babylon. We now know that in its later form the epic was divided into seven great sections, or Tablets, and that Marduk's fight with Tiamat was only the culminating episode in a longer story of antagonism between the forces of order and disorder in the universe. We gather that the Babylonian account of the creation of the gods was similar to that given in Damascius, and that it was Apsu, the male representative of primeval chaos, and not Tiamat, his consort, who began the revolt against the gods.

Babylonian Epic of the Creation

Moreover, the defeat of Apsu, which preceded that of Tiamat, was not the work of Marduk, but that of his father, Ea, and Ea continues to play an important part in the narrative. One of the newly discovered fragments of the poem is of peculiar interest, since it contains an account of the creation of man, with which the acts of creation culminated ; and we gather that the Babylonian legend closely corresponds with that given by Berossus, Marduk getting another god, probably Ea, to cut off his—Marduk's—head, that he might use his own blood for the creation of mankind. To summarise briefly the composite character of the Creation epic, it may be stated that the recently recovered texts enable us to separate the legend into five principal strands ; these consist of the birth of the gods, the legend of Ea and Apsu, the Dragon-Myth, the actual account of Creation, and the Hymn to Marduk under his fifty titles of honour. Since the poem in its present form is a glorification of Marduk, and an explanation of how the god of Babylon secured the position of the greatest of the gods, it is but natural that prominence was given to those episodes in which Marduk is the hero, while those in which he plays

of the legend, in each of which the city-god figured as the hero who slew the monster. In accordance with this theory the priests of Babylon ascribed the conquest of the dragon to their own local god, and made the death of Tiamat a preliminary to his creation of the universe. Moreover, other Creation legends existed in which the creation of the world was not connected with the death of a dragon, and although in one of these Marduk figures as the creator, in others Anu, Enlil, and Ea are described as creating the sun and moon, or the gods generally are referred to as having created the heavens and the earth, the cattle and the beasts

Varieties of the Creation Legend

of the field. But there is no doubt that the version of the Creation story which originated in Babylon represents the belief most generally held in Babylonia and Assyria in the periods subsequent to the rise of Babylon to a position of pre-eminence under the West-Semitic kings of the first dynasty.

The briefest comparison of the Biblical accounts of the Creation with that which was current at Babylon suffices to show the close connection existing between them. In each account the existence of a watery chaos preceded the

Mansell

THE SEVEN TABLETS OF THE CREATION OF THE WORLD
The great Babylonian epic of the Creation was divided into seven great sections, or tablets, one fragment from each being illustrated here. It comprised (1) a description of a state of chaos ; (2) the war of the gods ; (3) defeat of Tiamat by Marduk ; (4) Marduk as chief of the gods ; (5) creation of heavenly bodies ; (6) creation of animals and man ; and (7) the hymn to Marduk under his fifty titles of honour.

no part are assigned a subsidiary and unimportant place in the narrative.

The central episode in the poem is thus the fight between Marduk and Tiamat, but we have evidence that this legend existed in other forms than that under which we find it here set out. For another legend which has been recovered ascribes the conquest of the dragon to some other god than Marduk, and the fight is recorded to have taken place, not before the Creation, but at a time when men already existed and cities had been built. Thus the Dragon-Myth existed in more than one form in Babylonian mythology, and it is not improbable that many of the great cities in Babylonia possessed local versions

creation of the universe, and the Hebrew word *tehom*, rendered as " the deep " in the Book of Genesis, is the equivalent of the Babylonian *Tiamat*, the name of the female monster of the deep personifying chaos and confusion. In the details of the Creation there is also a close

Connection with Bible Accounts

resemblance between the two narratives ; we may cite the creation, or existence, of light preceding that of the heavenly bodies, the creation of a firmament to divide the upper from the lower waters, and the separate acts of creation connected with the earth and vegetation, the heavenly bodies, animals, and, finally, man. It is even possible that the connection of the Sabbath with the biblical story of the Creation was suggested by the mystical number of tablets upon which the Babylonian poem was inscribed. Such points of resemblance demonstrate a close connection between the Hebrew and the Babylonian narratives, and the local Babylonian colouring of the stories, and the great age to which they can be traced back, definitely prove that they originated in Babylonia, and were not inherited independently by the Babylonians and Hebrews from a common Semitic ancestor. We may therefore conclude that Babylonian tenets had become naturalised in Palestine even before the conquest of that country by the Israelites. Many such Palestinian versions of Babylonian beliefs the Israelites no doubt absorbed on their occupation of the country, and during the subsequent periods of their history they were subject to the direct influence of Assyria and Babylon. It is clear, therefore, that at the time of their exile the Jews did not come across Babylonian religious conceptions for the first time, but recognised in them many beliefs differing from their own in some essential respects, but presenting an equally striking resemblance on many points of detail. It was doubtless, however, in the period of the exile that the

Babylonia a Spiritual Teacher strongest influence was exerted by the religion of Babylon upon that of the Jews. The Babylonian myths of the Creation are thus recognised as the prototypes after which the biblical myths were formed. How, then, did Babylonia become the teacher of the spiritual life of Nearer Asia ? We have at present hardly any other evidence of this beyond the remains of Assyro-Babylonian literature hitherto won from the soil, and the records of Jewish spiritual life preserved for us in

THE BABYLONIAN HERCULES
Gilgamesh was the hero of the national epic of Babylonia, which exercised even greater influence on the Babylonians than the epic of the Creation of the World.

the canonical books of the Bible. But so long as we have no more material for study, we must try to form our conception of the influence exerted by Babylonian religion from these remains.

Religion has indisputably played a part in the civilised life of these nations which we moderns are prone to underrate. The priesthood is the nursery of knowledge ; therefore all teaching, every attempt to investigate the nature of things, every proof and justification of the existing order, and every attempt to introduce change is referred back to the primitive doctrines of the beginning of things, and by this authority is either approved or discountenanced. To the direct intervention of the priesthood we may therefore trace many of the beliefs which were current both among the Babylonians and the Jews, and the close resemblance in their development of thought explains the ease with which the latter submitted to the influence of their more powerful neighbour. Even monotheism in its perfected form cannot be claimed as exclusively a product of the Jewish mind, though in certain respects it met with singular favour in Judæa. The polytheism of Babylonia finds its historical explanation in the circumstances of times long past in the march of civilisation. If the Babylonian or Assyrian prayed to his god, he did so with the same words as the Jew : his contrition, his submission to the divine will, his trust in his god, were precisely similar—

Parallels to Judaism only that the former people had found an expression for such feelings and thoughts, while the Jew learnt much of it from them. Even if the Babylonian prayed to Marduk or the Assyrian to Ashur, there was little difference between his thought and that of the Jew of the eighth century or so, who supplicated Jahve, or Jehovah. The Jew did not dispute the god of those who dwelt outside the dominion of his Jahve. If it was a false god, it was only so in the sense that every Babylonian saw the true lord of the world in the temple of his own city.

The mental activity of man is manifested in the development of mythology, which comes next to the doctrines of religion and is closely connected with them. So far as this is a doctrine of divinities and temples, we have already realised how limited the range of our knowledge is. We must raise the same lament over the remains of anthropomorphic mythology, the hero legends, which form the first theme of the non-religious poetry of a people. A quantity of fragments testify to the former ex-

Babylonian Hero Mythology istence of a whole series of epics; but of only a few of them have we sufficient remains to be able partially to restore or to guess their contents. The best known is the Epic of Gilgamesh. In it the deeds of the Babylonian Hercules are glorified, and it has given Hellenism the attributes with which to endow the legendary form of Alexander in the so-called Alexander romances. The work received the form in which it is preserved for us at Erech; it reflects the condition to which the old Ishtar-Nana town, considered to have been founded by Gilgamesh, had been reduced by the oppression of Elam.

National Epic of Babylonia This epic exercised an even greater influence on the Babylonians themselves than that of the Creation, for the hero Gilgamesh and his companion Ea-bani appear in countless representations in Babylonian art, and the legend was peculiarly the national epic of the Babylonians. In its latest form it was written upon twelve tablets of equal length, and all are concerned with the heroic deeds of Gilgamesh. They recount his early exploits, the creation of Ea-bani by the goddess Aruru; their expedition against Khumbaba of Elam; the passion exhibited for Gilgamesh by the goddess Ishtar; the fight of Gilgamesh with the bull from heaven; the grief of Gilgamesh at Ea-bani's death; and his journey to his ancestor Tsitnapishtim, who relates to him the story of the Flood. The Babylonian account of the Deluge, which is thus introduced into the national epic, with which it has no organic connection, presents the closest parallel to the Biblical narrative of the same event, and is, indeed, the basis of that account. In this case the parallelisms are so striking that we may set the date of borrowing at a comparatively late period. In addition to the Epic of Gilgamesh we have also recovered fragments of myths and stories connected with the heroes and mythological beings of antiquity. A large number of unpublished fragments, which are still unintelligible on account of their small size, is here, as in the case of all similar literary productions, only further evidence of the information which we may hope to gain some time in the future.

Mansell

THE BABYLONIAN ACCOUNT OF THE DELUGE

This account of the Flood, which presents the closest parallel to the Biblical narrative, is a section in the great epic of Gilgamesh, who visits Tsitnapishtim, a god who dwelt in an ark, and has related to him the story of the Flood inscribed on these tablets.

It would be a most important task to describe the extent of the industries and trade in Babylonia. For this, however, almost all data are wanting, apart from the fact that in the course of 3,000 years there must have been as many vicissitudes in the industrial as in the political life of the people. We may safely assume that

What was Babylonia's Commerce? Babylonia, and—since it is the admitted capital in the period best known to us—above all, Babylon, owed their importance and power to their industries and their trade. During the entire period in which we can follow the power of Assyria, Babylon was impotent as a political community. It was compelled to buy its independence from the Assyrians, just as, on the other hand, it obtained by its gold assistance from the Elamites against Assyria. It probably had not men enough to wage war on its own resources ; indeed, the conditions under which its land was held precluded any such idea. This fact alone is sufficient to give the country its predominantly industrial character.

We can draw conclusions as to the extent of Babylonian commerce in the earlier periods from the inscriptions of Gudea ; he obtained the blocks of stone and the timber for his buildings from Phœnicia, Syria, and Sinai. Some slight information about Babylonian industries is given us by the Tell el-Amarna letters. The Babylonian, like the Mitanian prince, required gold from the Egyptians ; in return they supplied industrial products, especially lapis lazuli, or an imitation of it, which was highly valued by the Egyptians, and was a staple of Babylonian export. The Egyptians obtained weapons and war chariots from Mitani and even from Assyria. If, at the same time, the Babylonian ordered inlaid work of ebony and ivory, it was from a desire for fashionable objects in the Egyptian style, such as have been found in Nineveh ; they have

Sumeria a Naval State no more significance than Chinese porcelain or Japanese lacquer-work with us. The question of the navigation on the Persian Gulf is still shrouded in obscurity, as well as that of the early use of the trade route to India. It is extremely probable that the Sumerians engaged in navigation on the " Sea of the East." The most ancient inscriptions, from the nature of their contents, do not mention anything of such matters ; and thus we must, probably for a long time yet, be content merely to speculate upon the subject. In the later period the road to the sea was barred by the Chaldæans. The centuries of prosperity of a state called " the Country of the Sea," and its obstinate resistance both to Babylon and to Assyria, are partly explained by the wealth won by trade relations with the East. Merodach-baladan possessed ships, in which he escaped to Elam over the " bitter water," the great bay at the embouchure of the two streams ; there was then no fleet in Babylonia, so that Sennacherib was forced to have ships built by Phœnician workmen in Assyria and brought down stream to the coast. Any Babylonian trade with the East is thus inconceivable. Elam, too, must have had much to do with the traffic on the Persian Gulf, and we may expect to obtain much valuable information on this point as a result of the excavations which are being carried on at the present time at Susa.

Hardly any products of Babylonian industries have as yet come down to us. Even the arts of architecture and sculpture,

Art of Babylon comparatively familiar to us in Assyria, are represented to us in the very home of such culture by few and comparatively insignificant monuments. All that is left to us on a large scale are the ruins of Tello, which have supplied us with a considerable number of statues and sculptures of the kings and patesis of Lagash. While the statues of the earliest kings were but rude attempts, rapid progress was made, and those of Gudea and his time [see pages 1587 and 1597] show the highest perfection of execution. The careful and delicate work on the monument of Merodach-baladan [see page 1617] is one of the few productions of a later period of art which are known to us.

In the same way we possess hardly any notices of the order and form of the constitution, of the internal administration, and the military system in Babylonia, though the letters of Hammurabi throw considerable light upon these problems during the period of the first dynasty of Babylon. Anything, therefore, that we can suggest on these points is more clearly explained by the better attested Assyrian institutions, which, since they grew out of similar conditions, exhibit in the main results which must have closely resembled those of Babylonia.

ASSYRIA IN THE MAKING

WE have already seen that the advance of Assyria falls within a period which lies in the full light of history, or can be illuminated without difficulty by the results of excavations. We have further observed that its first natural expansion took place towards Mesopotamia, and that this became its undisputed property, from the possession of which it grew to be a great power, as extensive and as important as Babylonia itself. The history of Assyria itself must therefore be preceded by an attempt to throw light on the conditions of Mesopotamia at this early period.

We have suggested as a probable hypothesis that the great Semitic immigrations reached Babylonia from the north. Mesopotamia would therefore have been first reached by them ; the Semites, who meet us in Southern Babylonia, may thus **Mesopotamia at the Rise of Assyria** have formed settlements there before they pressed southwards along the Euphrates and the Tigris. Any attempt to reconstitute the early history of this region must depend largely upon conjecture, since systematic excavation has not as yet been extended into that region of Western Asia.

Any early kingdom which may have been formed in Mesopotamia probably had its capital at Harran, one of the most ancient seats of the worship of Sin, the moon-god ; and this conjecture appears to be supported by various indications in the subsequent period. However this may be, we can safely assume that Mesopotamia not only stood under the direct influence of Babylonian civilisation, but had a special share in shaping the development of the countries on the Euphrates—a fact that continually finds expression in the high reverence paid to the great sanctuary at Harran. The origin of the cult at Hebron, which the immigrating " Hebrew " tribes may have found there and adopted, is traced by the biblical legend, according to the older tradition, from the seat of the Sin cult in Mesopotamia, while only a later application of the myth claims for it Ur, **A Seat of the Worship of Ba'al** the South Babylonian seat of the moon-god. The adoration of Ba'al Harran, the god of Harran, is found also in Senjirli, in Northern Syria.

In the earliest accounts which we possess, Mesopotamia appears under a foreign dominion. Our sources of information are the Tell el-Amarna letters of King Tushratta of Mitani to Amenophis III. and Amenophis IV. The picture that they afford us of the intercourse between the two countries holds good for the predecessors of the two Pharaohs, so far as they advanced into Asia. They virtually designate Mesopotamia and Syria as Naharina. In this connection it is a matter of indifference to us how much gold Tushratta begged for himself from Egypt, and how many letters he wrote in order to fool his " brother " and son-in-law in Egypt. The point which concerns us is that in these kings of Mitani we may see representatives of a migration of barbarians who possessed themselves of Mesopotamia. We shall learn later that we may possibly assign them to the group **Hittite Rulers of Mesopotamia** of nations which we designate Hittite. As rulers of this country, they play the same rôle which the Kassites, coincidently with them, play in Babylonia.

It does not appear from their letters where the kings of Mitani resided ; but we must look for the country, which is known as Mitani from the letters, somewhere in the region north of Harran, where we may set the centre of their kingdom. We can define its extent, as given in the words "an heir to the old kingdom of Mesopotamia." In the direction of Babylonia it included Nineveh, which, at the time of Tushratta, about 1430 B.C., was in the power of the Mitani. Obviously, all Mesopotamia belonged to it, and on the right bank of the Euphrates, Melitene, or Khanigalbat, and the district called by the Assyrians Musri, and by the Egyptians Sanqara—in a Tell el-Amarna letter from Alashia, Shankhar—a part of Cappadocia abutting on it as far as the Taurus, and possibly across it into Cilicia. Westward and northward of this part of the kingdom were settled the Kheta, or Khatti, the rivals and kinsmen of the Mitani, with whom they were at war, as we learn from a letter of Tushratta to Amenophis. The Kheta must either have forced their way in through the territory of the Mitani when we find them in Syria, or have skirted the real territory of the Mitani kings, by entering Cilicia through the Cilician Gates.

What was true of the friendship of the Babylonians with Egypt is true also of that of Mitani, so verbosely emphasised in the Tell el-Amarna letters. Even the kings of Mitani are referred to by Egyptian vassals in Phœnicia as natural enemies of a true servant of the Pharaoh.

This kingdom must have already existed for a considerable period, for Tushratta, the writer of the letters, mentions his father, Sutarna, who had sent his daughter, Gilukhipa, as attested by an

A ROYAL TYPE
From an Assyrian bas-relief.

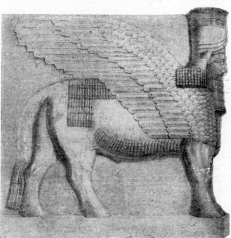
THE HUMAN-HEADED ASSYRIAN BULL
One of the most characteristic features of Assyrian architecture, these statues were set to guard the gateways to palaces and temples, and were of gigantic size.

TYPE OF A EUNUCH
From an Assyrian bas-relief.

Egyptian inscription, into the harem of Amenophis III., and his grandfather, Artatama, who had maintained relations with Thothmes IV., and had concluded a similar bargain—for the chief matter of discussion was the dowry. The writer himself had been at the court of Amenophis III.; he was perhaps educated there as a sort of hostage when his father died. In a letter to the Pharaoh he describes how an insurrection broke out, to which his brother Artashumara fell a victim, and how, on his return, he had suppressed the revolt. The same letter contains an account of the above-mentioned war with the Kheta, who had evidently seized this favourable opportunity for attempting an invasion of the country.

Among all the haggling for presents there is one letter which is of greater interest, as it contains more important news. Tushratta requests Amenophis III. to send back the statue of the goddess Ishtar of Nineveh, which shortly before had been sent to Egypt, as it had already been sent in the lifetime of his father, and had on that occasion been honourably returned. The meaning of this journey of Ishtar is not quite evident. It may probably be explained by supposing that Tushratta, like his father, had conquered Nineveh, and did not take the captured divinity as a badge of victory back home with him, but had sent it to the Egyptian king, whose right of protector was thus acknowledged. The "tribute" of the Egyptian inscriptions would tally well with this theory. The question then

BAS-RELIEF SHOWING AN ASSYRIAN KING HUNTING THE KING OF BEASTS

remains, from whom did Tushratta take Nineveh ? We may conjecture that it was from the Assyrians, who by this time must have thrown off their allegiance to Babylon. More important for us is the fact thus proved that Tushratta was master of Nineveh, for we are thus able to settle approximately the date of Assyria's advance. Tushratta's reign corresponds with the close of the glory of his people. Eighty or a hundred years later, Assyria is in occupation of Mesopotamia, and is defending its new possession against Babylon

A WONDER OF ASSYRIAN SCULPTURE

This colossal stone sculpture of a man-headed lion from the Kuyunjik Palace, Nineveh, is seen in something like its huge proportions by contrast with the figure at its side. The bull opposite is of a similar size.

after the Mitani had been driven out. The rule of the kings of Mitani who are known to us is to be set at the end of the period which had seen this group of nations advance beyond the Euphrates. In its first vigour this advance perhaps extended as far as Babylonia, which we now know was invaded by the Hittites towards the close of the first dynasty of Babylon. The fact that in the Tell el-Amarna period the Kassites of Babylonia and the Mitani of Mesopotamia were enemies may be cited in support of this conjecture.

PORTION OF A BEAUTIFUL ASSYRIAN BAS-RELIEF SHOWING THE HORSES OF A KING

ASSYRIAN STONE-SLINGERS
From a Nineveh bas-relief.

We may picture the "land of Ashur" in its primitive form, just as was the case with the kingdom of Babylon, as being little more than the territory of the city of Ashur, the modern Kala Shergat. It lies, indeed, almost outside the district which later constitutes the true country of Assyria, the land, namely, which is bounded by a line drawn from Nineveh to the mountains, and by the lower Zab and the Tigris. It is possible that Ashur, from its position, which was too far south to form the centre of this district, and from its site on the right bank of the Tigris, may not have been from the first the capital of the subsequent country of Ashur; it clearly has more affinities with the south and Babylonia than with the north and west, in which direction the northern kingdom first expanded. If we also consider that Ashur was only a town, like many others in the Euphrates valley, we shall be inclined to suppose that its patesis, or

SAPPERS OF THE ASSYRIAN ARMY
Portion of a sculpture illustrating the siege of a city.

1648

priest-kings, were subject to the supremacy of Babylonia, and on occasion to that of Mesopotamia also.

It can be proved that in historical times it was not the capital of any considerable kingdom, and, in fact, was governed only by patesis, and the date of the rise of this new power can be fixed with tolerable accuracy. Tiglath-pileser announces, about 1100 B.C., that part of a temple restored by him in Ashur had been constructed 641 years before the time of his grandfather, who himself had added to it sixty years earlier, by Shamshi-Adad, patesi of Ashur, son of Ishme-Dagan, patesi of Ashur. We have, therefore, about 1800 B.C., patesis

ASSYRIAN ARCHERS WITH SHIELD-BEARER
From a bas-relief almost life-size found at Nineveh.

of Ashur who must have been subject to Babylonia or Mesopotamia. Such was the earliest point to which, until recently, we could trace back the history of Assyria. But the recent excavations at Shergat and the publication of a new chronicle in the British Museum now enable us to trace back the history of Assyria beyond the rise of the first dynasty of Babylon. With the exception of that of Ilu-shuma, who we know was the contemporary of the founder of the first dynasty, the periods of the earliest rulers of Assyria can be only approximately determined. The first king of Ashur, whose date we can fix more accurately, is Assur-bel-nishishu, the contemporary of Karaindash. Ashur, therefore, permanently secured her independence between 1800 and 1500 B.C. Its patesis called themselves kings, and, possibly under the influence of a new immigration, began to expand their power.

The cause of this expansion, and the conditions under which it was possible, were similar to those which gave Babylonia to the Kassites and Mesopotamia to the Mitani. The disorders of the time offered to energetic rulers a favourable opportunity to found a kingdom of their own. On the other hand, the two spheres of civilisation, which hitherto had been connected, were parted by subjection to different foreign sovereignties, and so allowed the country that lay between to found a power of its own. Before, however, we come to the history of the new kingdom, it will be necessary to consider to what causes it was due that, while the Semitic world was now everywhere breaking up, the Semites of Ashur preserved that firm attitude and strength which thenceforth ensured victory for their arms ; we will, in fact, ascertain the characteristics of these future lords of the East.

The Assyrian type is totally distinct

which we call the "Jewish" type. Our conception is erroneous, in so far as this type is completely distinct from the Arabian, in which we should expect to find in greatest purity the Semitic type ; on the other hand, in certain points a

SPEARMEN OF THE ASSYRIAN ARMY

correspondence may be traced with that of the modern Armenians, who speak an Indo-European language. It is not our present task to explain this. We have to study the history of the nations, and in doing so have laid down the principle of linguistic classification as a suitable scheme of grouping. The physical characteristics of the nations constitute a principle of classification to be carefully distinguished from the former, for physical mixture of race and development of language follow quite different paths. It hardly comes within the province of history to consider how the Assyrians reached this type, and to which of the larger groups the race belongs. It is sufficient for our immediate purpose to point out the existence of this distinctive Assyrian type.

We are then met by the question, in what did the extraordinary superiority of this people over the other peoples of Nearer Asia consist ?

HUNTING IN THE MESOPOTAMIAN FORESTS
A fine bas-relief from Nineveh, showing huntsmen with a gazelle and a hare.

from the Babylonian, which we have seen to be the result of a great mixture of races. The numerous Assyrian portraits show us clearly marked features, precisely those which we ordinarily regard as Semitic ; in many details they are those

The inquiry will resolve itself into the consideration of two subjects in particular—the political organisation of the state, and the economic condition of the population. The "land of Ashur," down to the times when its superiority over Babylonia was undisputed—that is, down to Shalmaneser II.

and Adad-nirari IV.—must have possessed a free peasantry of its own; while the older and more highly-developed civilisation of Babylonia had only a system of feudal and "ecclesiastical" tenure, with a population completely dependent upon it. This was the source of the weakness of Babylonia, which had no large body of native troops at its disposal; while its defenders consisted of "allies" whose intentions were only too clear. Shalmaneser still called out the militia of "the land" when a bold enterprise was planned. Tiglath-pileser, as we shall see, tried to free this peasantry from the fetters of the feudal system of great estates which had meanwhile grown up in Assyria also, and a later reaction began under Sargon. The power of Assyria in the interval

ignored. Just as David with a trustworthy band was able in the general disorder to seize the throne of a realm comprising various tribes, so the patesis of Ashur did the same on a larger scale.

The strength of Assyria in opposition to the countries of the Euphrates valley, with their high industrial development, was based on the possession of an army; through this alone could it rise into importance or assert its position. A country with a peasantry could supply the men. When this peasantry disappeared at a later period, and even Tiglath-pileser could not save it, recourse was had to armies of mercenaries, who were recruited in all countries, both subject and barbarian. It was with these that

BAS-RELIEF SHOWING ARCHERS, THE MAINSTAY OF ASSYRIA'S ARMY, ON THE MARCH

had reached its zenith—this prosperous period was inaugurated by Tiglath-pileser himself—but had not then shown real development. Its short-lived success without permanent results is due to the other side of its constitutional organisation, which is explained by the formation of the kingdom.

The expansion of the dominion of a patesi into a kingdom, such as the rise of Assyria shows, was possible only if at the time of expansion its princes had a body of efficient soldiers at their disposal. How far that was connected with the immigration of a new population into Ashur and Assyria is beyond our knowledge, though the possibility that such was the case must not be

Sargon and his successors carried on their wars. With such troops, so long as pay and booty were abundant, it was possible to keep the East in subjection; but after a great defeat, and when money was exhausted, a new levy was impossible. The strength of Assyria therefore rested on its army and its population; and, as they changed, so there was a complete alteration in its fundamental constitution. While Assyria could always recover from earlier disasters, in its later condition, as a state completely under Babylonian influence, with a ruling military and sacerdotal caste relying upon a mercenary army, and without the support of a national population, it was destined to disappear and leave no trace.

The first accounts of the "kingdom" of Assyria, which was founded on conquests, show us the new constitution. A king of Babylon, whose name is not preserved, calls down in an inscription the usual curses upon every successor who refuses him the credit due for a building erected by him. Then he adds, as a sign of the times : " The treasures of Babylon shall come to Suri and Assyria, the King of Babylon shall bring to the Prince of Ashur the treasures of his palace, his goods to the (town of Ashur ?)." The prince, not yet the king, of Ashur is the avenging enemy, and the curse was often enough fulfilled in later times.

At how early a period Assyria did come into conflict with Babylon we learn from the fact that Ilu-shuma, one of the earliest known patesis of Assyria, waged war with Su-abu, the founder of the first dynasty of Babylon. The result of the war is not known, but its cause we may probably trace to an early attempt on the part of Assyria to throw off her dependence The change of dynasty in Babylon, brought about by the incursion of the Western Semites, undoubtedly furnished her with a favourable opportunity to make the

SECRETARIES OF ASSYRIAN KING
A bas-relief, now in the Louvre, showing the highly Semitised Assyrian type. The clean-shaven figure is a eunuch.

attempt. That it was not permanently successful we may infer from the fact that Ilu-shuma himself, and his successors upon the throne of Ashur, do not claim the title of king, but merely that of patesi. Moreover, Hammurabi included Assyria within his empire, and from one of his letters we may infer that he stationed regular garrisons in the country.

Thus, for a long period after Ilu-shuma's attempt to cast off the yoke of Babylon, Assyria acknowledged her suzerainty, and her rulers termed themselves patesi. The earliest rulers of the country, such as Ushpia, to whom later tradition ascribed the foundation of the temple of the god Ashur, in the city of Ashur, bore the title " priest of Ashur," and this title was also retained by the later patesis. The exact period at which Assyria succeeded in freeing herself permanently from Babylonian tutelage is uncertain, but we may place it with considerable probability in the early Kassite period, when the powerful dynasty of Hammurabi had been brought to an end by the Hittite invasion, and the Kassites themselves were occupied with the conquest and settlement of Northern Babylonia.

EUNUCH SERVANTS OF ASSYRIAN KING

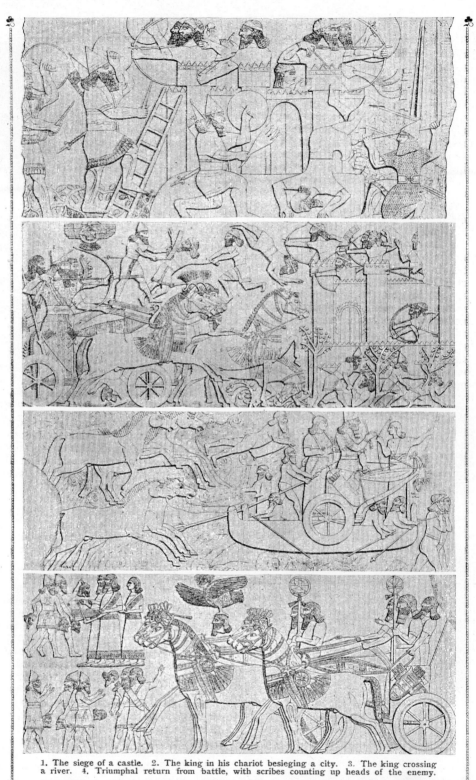

1. The siege of a castle. 2. The king in his chariot besieging a city. 3. The king crossing a river. 4. Triumphal return from battle, with scribes counting up heads of the enemy.

ASSYRIAN WAR SCENES FROM THE MONUMENTS OF NINEVEH

THE OLD EMPIRE OF ASSYRIA

THE natural aim of Assyria. at the period of her rise was freedom from the tutelage of Babylonia. We are fortunate enough to possess a record which enables us to follow the development of her relations with Babylon from an early period. When the mutual relations were arranged under Adad-nirari IV., all the former treaties and wars between Babylon and Assyria were enumerated. This record is what it is usually, though otherwise inappropriately, designated—a synchronistic history of the relations of the two states, The first lines of the tablet, belonging to the library of Ashurbanipal, on which the document is recorded, have been broken away ; its text begins with the treaty between Karaindash and Ashur-bel-nishishu, in the fifteenth century B.C. The details of the treaty are not recounted : it is merely recorded that both states concluded treaties and mutually fixed the boundaries of their territory.

Relations with Babylon We may conclude from this that the contents of the treaty were no longer ascertainable by the archivists of Adad - nirari ; there was probably no information on the point beyond the notices upon the royal steles. The same is true of a treaty between Puzur-Ashur, the next king of Assyria referred to, and Burnaburiash I., by means of which we approach the years immediately preceding the Tell el-Amarna period.

The Amarna period includes Ashur-uballit, from whom we possess a letter to Amenophis IV. We have also recovered other facts about him, and can by their help follow his line of action. He complains in his letter that preference was shown to the king of Mitani, whose territory, as we have already seen, was coveted by the Assyrians. He alludes also to letters which his father, Ashur-nadin-akhi, had already addressed to Amenophis III. A communication of Burnaburiash to Amenophis IV. demands at the same time that the Assyrian offers to enter into

relations should be declined, since Assyria was his vassal. Adad-nirari I., the great-grandson of Ashur-uballit, is able to announce that the royal greeting of his grandfather had been recognised in distant countries ; that is to say, his diplomatic attempts at forming alliances had met with success, notwithstanding

Egypt Recognises Assyria letters of protest by the Babylonians, and he was recognised by Egypt as an independent king. He was also succcessful against the kings of Mitani. A victory over them by him is recorded, and Nineveh, which was in Tushratta's possession, must have been regained by Ashur-uballit. At Nineveh he added to the temple of Ishtar, the goddess who had formerly been sent to Egypt. As regards Babylonia, he followed, under Burnaburiash, or his successor, Karakhardash, the policy of extension of territory by marriage. Karakhardash married his daughter, and their son was Kadashman-kharbe, whose policy and relations to Assyria have been already referred to. We have also seen how the murder of Kadashman-kharbe gave a welcome opportunity to Ashur-uballit of interfering in the affairs of Babylonia. It may fairly be assumed that for the rest of his long life he really governed for his infant great-grandson, Kurigalzu.

This Assyrian guardianship could not but lead to friction so soon as the young king of Babylon was grown up and could inaugurate a policy of his own. Ashur-uballit's successor, Bel-nirari is recorded

Assyrian Guardianship of Babylon to have waged a war with Kurigalzu, in which Babylonia was worsted. The arrangement of the frontier concerned the district " from the borders of Mitani (Shubari) as far as Babylonia." Arik-den-ilu, the next king of Assyria, fought only against northern nations, the Suti, the Bedouins of the plains, and kept in check the invading hordes of Aramæans. His son was Adad-nirari I., about 1300–

1653

1270. Assyria under him reaped the fruits of the preceding wars. He overthrew the kingdom of Mitani and took possession of Mesopotamia. Babylonia could not quietly stand by and see this. The conflict with Mitani she had relinquished, it is true, to Assyria, but the possession of the country, on account of its importance for communications with the north and west she was compelled to try and win for herself. War was declared under Kurigalzu's son, Nazimaruttash, and Assyria was victorious. The frontier between the two countries was fixed by a line which ran roughly from the Sinjar Mountains over the Tigris eastward to the range of Lulumi ; that is, Assyria was assigned the upper, Babylonia the lower, river territory.

Assyria again Victorious

Shalmaneser I., about 1270, completed his father's work. He conquered, in addition, the provinces of Mitani, Khanigalbat, and Musri, lying westward from the Euphrates, and secured Mesopotamia, since he subdued the Aramæans, who were continually expanding in this direction. He then advanced in the region between the two streams towards Armenia, and took measures to provide an advance guard in this district by founding Assyrian colonies. We may conclude that Assyria still had a vigorous surplus population, which sought some outlet ; it was still a land with a peasantry. The settlements of Shalmaneser proved to be full of vitality. Although they received no subsequent support from the mother country, they continued to exist even after these districts had twice been lost by Assyria—in the periods after Tukulti-Ninib I. and after Tiglath-pileser I. When Ashurnasirpal again advanced in the direction of Armenia, about 860 B.C., he found these colonies still there, although the Assyrian settlers had suffered greatly. A further testimony to the strength of the Assyrian powers of expansion is furnished by the cuneiform texts from Cappadocia with the numerous Assyrian names, which, as we have already seen, are to be assigned to a still earlier period.

Assyrians as Colonists

Ashur, the old capital, was now no longer suited to be the seat of government of the newly expanded kingdom. Shalmaneser therefore removed his court farther up stream to a position on the left bank of the Tigris, which more adequately met the requirements of the new régime. Kalkhi, or Nimrud, in the angle of the Tigris and the Upper Zab, became the new capital. The importance of this place as the capital of Assyria while in possession of Mesopotamia is proved by the fact that on the decay of the Assyrian power Ashur became the capital once more, until, after the fresh rise of the kingdom under Ashurnasirpal, Kalkhi was again selected as the seat of government.

So soon as the Mitani difficulty was settled and the possession of Mesopotamia secured, it was merely a question of choice whether Assyria would wait to be attacked by Babylonia or would take the initiative herself. Assyria was always ready to play the part of the aggressor. Under Shalmaneser war had been already declared, and hostilities were continued under his successor, Tukulti-Ninib. In the reign of Bitiliash, Tukulti-Ninib conquered Babylon, and thus became ruler of the whole of Babylonia. From an inscription of his that has recently been discovered we learn that he carried Bitiliash, the Babylonian king, as a captive to Assyria, and then proceeded to appoint his own officers in Babylon, and establish there his own system of administration. He also despoiled Babylon of her treasures, and carried away to Assyria the statue of Marduk from Esagila. Among the booty which he acquired in Babylon was a seal of the earlier Kassite king, Shagarakti-Shuriash, and on this he added an inscription of his own. The seal was afterwards restored to Babylon, when it was recaptured by Sennacherib during one of his conquests of the city. Sennacherib in turn added an inscription of his own, and, though the seal has not come down to us, we possess a copy of the inscriptions upon it, from which we learn that 600 years separated Tukulti-Ninib's period from that of Sennacherib, a welcome help to us in determining the chronology. In his newly-discovered memorial tablet, Tukulti-Ninib bears, in addition to the title " King of Assyria," those of " King of Karduniash, King of Sumer and Akkad," proving that he actually ascended the Babylonian throne.

Babylon Once More Despoiled

This state of things lasted seven years. Then the nobles of Babylonia rose, drove out the Assyrians and placed Adad-shum-usur on the throne. If we compare the similar position of affairs at Sennacherib's death and the rebellion at the end of Esarhaddon's time, we have the key to the meaning of what the chronicle, from which we derive these facts, tells us in this connection. "Ashurnasirpal his son, and the lords of Assyria rebelled, and dethroned him. They besieged him in a house at Kar-Tukulti-Ninib, and slew him with the sword." Accordingly we must assume that Tukulti-Ninib, like the later Assyrian kings in a similar position, had allowed his own policy to be affected by Babylonian influence. This must have caused dissatisfaction in Assyria, because there was the fear that the more cultured Babylonians would assert their superiority and acquire the chief administrative positions. It was therefore an Assyrian military rebellion

successors, Ashur-narara and Nabu-dan, two brothers who reigned concurrently, had during the reign of the Babylonian king, Adad-shum-usur, reduced Assyria to the position it held before its expansion under Ashur-uballit. The tone of a letter from the Babylonian king to the former shows a great departure from the previous terms of courtesy. The pair are not addressed as the " brothers " of the writer, but are sharply reprimanded as subjects. In contrast to this, Adad-shum-usur is described as " king of hosts." Thus Assyria was once more restricted to the " land of Ashur."

There were several attempts of Assyria to recover Mesopotamia. Bel-kudur-usur, who probably succeeded a king named Tukulti-Ashur, fell in battle with Adad-nadin-akhi, king of Babylon. His son,

THE MOUNDS OF KALKHI, OR NIMRUD
Shalmaneser II. found the position of the old capital of Ashur unsuited to his extended kingdom, and moved his court to Kalkhi, the remains of which are seen here. The pointed mound was the zikkurat of the temple.

against the threatening predominance of Babylonia. Probably the Assyrian revolutionary party had come to an understanding with the Babylonians themselves, and Tukulti-Ninib, when expelled from Babylon, found that everything in Assyria was already in the hands of his son. He threw himself, therefore, into his favourite city, built, as we learn from his memorial tablet, by himself after his capture of Babylon, and there he met his death.

If the object of the revolution was a severance from Babylonia, it was very thoroughly realised ; for now the struggle could begin afresh, and Mesopotamia, in particular, would be protected against the once more powerful opponent. We know nothing further of this Ashurnasirpal. It appears, however, that he and his

Ninib-apil-Eshara, led the army back to Assyria. There he seems to have withstood a siege of the Babylonians, who afterwards returned to their own land.

Babylonia continued to maintain the supremacy under the son of Melishipak, Merodach-baladan I., for he boasts of a victory over Assyria, under Ninib-apil-Eshara or his son Ashur-dan. His successor, Zamana-shum-iddina, however, received a reverse at the hands of Ashur-dan on Babylonian soil, to the left of the Lower Zab, about 1200 B.C. But Assyria did not win back Mesopotamia by this victory, for, as we have already seen, the successors to the Kassites upon the throne of Babylon still held it. In particular, Nebuchadnezzar I. once again advanced into Palestine. Ashur-dan was succeeded by Mutakkil-Nusku. His son was Ashur-resh-ishi I, the contemporary and rival of Nebuchadnezzar I. After repeated wars the Assyrian king, according to the " Synchronistic History," is said to have been the victor. He occupied Mesopotamia once more. One of his inscriptions records another check to the hordes of Aramæans in Mesopotamia as well as successes against the Lulumi, and against the Kuti, the peoples of the north.

Wars of Tiglath-pileser I.

If Ashur-resh-ishi's activity on this new rise of Assyria corresponds to that exhibited by Adad-nirari I. on an earlier occasion, the reign of his successor, Tiglath-piles r I., about 1100 B.C., presents a repetition of the successes and of the downfall of Assyria under Shalmaneser I. and Tukulti-N nib. Once more the first object was to secure Mesopotamia by renewed expeditions northward, and by the reconquest of Khanigalbat and Musri westward of the Euphrates. We shall endeavour to throw light on the incursions of the tribes, which here come into prominence, when we treat of the Hitti e movement.

We have an inscription of Tiglath-pileser which deals with his wars in these regions during the first five years of his reign. He first cleared the district north of Mesopotamia by driving back or subduing the encroaching tribes, and advanced toward Armenia, in the district between the two rivers. He thus endeavoured to secure the very territory which Shalmaneser had once occupied with Assyrian colonists. He further subjugated the " Nairi country," the district south of Lake Van—that is to say, the highlands between Armenia and Mesopotamia. On one of these campaigns, at the head of the Subnat, or Sebene-Su, one of the sources of the Tigris, he carved his image in the rock near the exit of a natural tunnel through which the stream flows. This image is still preserved, together with a short inscription mentioning three such expeditions into the Nairi country. He then, like Shalmaneser, checked the Aramæan hordes which had spread over the steppes of Mesopotamia, and drove a part of them over the Euphrates into the territory of Carchemish. He succeeded in crossing the river and took six castles occupied by them in " the territory of the Bishri

Campaigns in Armenia

mountains." This is the identical district which appears under Shalmaneser II. as the part of Bit-Adini lying to the right of the Euphrates, together with the town of Til-Basheri. It is interesting to note that at the time of the Crusades it was made the fief of Joscelin of Tell-Bashir, the feudal tenant of Edessa. In this district Tiglath-pileser also occupied Pitru, in the angle between the Euphrates and Sagur, the Pethor of the Bible, and occupied it with Assyrian colonists. Then, still following the example of Shalmaneser I., he subdued Melitene, or Khanigalbat and afterwards Musri, which was in the hands of the Kumani, and by these victories restored the old Mesopotamian kingdom in its former extent.

An expedition thence brought him actually to Phœnicia. At Arvad he went out to sea in order, as a mighty hunter, to be present at the capture of monsters of the deep. He mentions on this occasion an exchange of presents with the king of Egypt, who sent among other things a crocodile. We do not yet know who this Pharaoh was. But we see that intercourse between the two countries was not yet broken off, and that the Egyptian kings still had their eyes on Palestine, where Saul and David were forming a kingdom, even if they did not actually interfere with its internal politics. The correspondence between the two kings is not extant. But if it is borne in mind that, only a few years before, these northern districts of Phœnicia had been held by Nebuchadnezzar, it may be imagined that besides the exchange of presents weightier issues were at stake, and that the question of fixing their sphere of interest in Palestine had been discussed by the two powers.

Ebb of the Assyrian Tide

Now that the west had been secured, it was naturally the turn of the east to be considered. We thus come to that period of the reign of Tiglath-pileser which recalls the part played by Tukulti-Ninib. The " Synchronistic History " tells us of two successful wars against Marduk-nadin-akhe, of Babylon, in which the North Babylonian towns, together with Babylon, had been captured ; and a small fragment of Tiglath-pileser's annals relates his entry into Babylon itself. But the rapid rise was followed by an equally rapid fall. Sennacherib found on his capture of Babylon, in the year 689 B.C., statues of gods, which Marduk-nadin-akhe had carried away from Assyria " four hundred and eighteen years before, in the time of Tiglath-pileser ; " and this same Marduk-nadin-akhe bears in one of his inscriptions the title " king of Sumer and Akkad " and " king of hosts." He therefore possessed all Babylonia, and may not improbably have won back Mesopotamia as well. Tiglath-pileser accordingly must have lost everything which had been gained in the earlier years of his reign and in that of his father. The extent of Assyria is again what it was after the fall of Tukulti-Ninib I.

After Tiglath-pileser, his sons Ashur-bel-kala and Shamshi-Adad reigned. We must now consider Mesopotamia as under Babylonian supremacy, although this cannot have been very strictly asserted, as is clear from the successful invasion of the Sutu in the reign of Adad-aplu-iddina,

From this period onwards there was until recently a gap in our knowledge of almost one hundred years, during which we had no trustworthy information as to Assyria or Babylon. From inscriptions recently recovered at Shergat it is, however, now possible to trace with some fulness the succession of Assyrian kings at this time, though **Assyria** the data are conflicting as to **Without an** the exact order of the earlier **Empire** rulers. But concerning the history of the period information is still lacking. We learn from later accounts of Shalmaneser II. that at this time Ashur-irbi must have been king of Assyria. He seems to have made an effort to regain what had been lost, for Shalmaneser mentions that he erected a statue on the shore of the sea. This can have been only Lake Van or the Mediterranean ; from the context, probably the latter. According to this view, Ashur-irbi, like Tiglath-pileser I., must have reached Phœnicia on an expedition. It must remain undecided whether his statue was among those at Nahr-el-kelb, north of Beirut, or whether the place was still more to the north. Another account states that Pitru, which was occupied by Tiglath-pileser, was, during his reign, seized by the Ara-

THE SOURCE OF THE RIVER TIGRIS
Assyrian kings on war expeditions seem to have made a practice of cutting inscriptions or representations of themselves at particular spots. Shalmaneser II. and others chose a rock at the source of the Tigris, one of the great rivers of Mesopotamia.

and the later encroachments of the Aramæans. Assyria once more possessed only the " land of Ashur," and was forced for the third time to begin the reconstruction of her empire. Babylonia itself was indeed no powerful rival at this period, and both countries for the time maintained peace. Ashur-bel-kala and Marduk-shapik-zer-mati concluded a treaty with one another, the Babylonian king going to Assyria for this purpose, as we learn from recently discovered chronicles. When the Babylonian king died, and Adad-aplu-iddina came to the throne, the Assyrian king married his daughter, and received, according to the " Synchronistic History," a rich dowry. Ashur-bel-kala was succeeded by his brother Shamshi-Adad.

mæans. This brings us to the movement which has left its mark upon this period.

In addition to the migrations of the Hittites from the north-west, and of the Kassites from the east, Mesopotamia and Babylonia were at this time the object of the third of the Semitic migrations which **The Third** we have distinguished, namely, **Semitic** the Aramæan. We have **Migration** already seen several times that Assyrian kings—for example, Arik-den-ilu, Shalmaneser I., Ashur-resh-ishi and Tiglath-pileser I.—tried to keep in check the " Aramæan hordes " which held Mesopotamia, and to drive them back over the river. The country, therefore, as early as 1300 B.C., had been overrun by these Aramæans, who were still nomads, for

Tiglath-pileser 1. expressly describes them as such.

Mesopotamia with its great steppes was the first object of their invasion, and thence they encroached on Babylonia. They thus came from the north, like the "Canaanites" and "Babylonian Semites." We have already seen that they waged successful wars against the Babylonian king, Nabu-mukin-apli, at a period probably soon after their capture of Pitru from the Assyrians, and we have met references to them as "Aramæan tribes" at the time of the Assyrian supremacy in Babylon under Tiglath-pileser IV. and his successors. The advance of the Chaldæans from the south checked their further progress. Besides this, it can be clearly

Thus even in the eighth and the early part of the seventh century the sequence of the Sutu and Aramæans in Babylonia is clearly recognisable. Just as these tribes first came into the country at the time when the Kassites were able to establish their power owing to the weakness of Babylonia, so, after 1100, when neither Assyria nor Babylonia could offer any vigorous resistance to them, their expansion was all the easier. This period covers the above-mentioned devastation of Babylonia by the Sutu ; and we must also include the advance into Babylonia of the Aramæan tribes which afterward settled there.

At the same time they occupied Mesopotamia, which lay still more open to them. As soon as our sources of information upon

ON THE EUPHRATES, ONE OF THE TWO GREAT RIVERS OF MESOPOTAMIA

traced how the tribes which pushed on before them, and were certainly closely akin to them, hindered their expansion in these districts. These are the Sutu, whom we have found under Ashur-uballit and Kadashman-kharbe still in possession of the Syrian desert. They were forced by the Aramæans toward Babylonia, which we now know they overran and ravaged in the reign of Adad-aplu-iddina, the contemporary of Ashur-bel-kala. They were afterwards driven to the left bank of the Tigris, up to the mountains in the west of Elam, where they still remained at the time of Sargon. Still later, after the destruction of Babylon by Sennacherib, in 689 B.C., we find them raiding Babylonia.

the history of Assyria are again available, we find Aramæan settlements there and a predominantly Aramæan population. The language of the land of Suri then became Aramaic, and the terms "Syrians" and "Aramæans," originally completely distinct, became gradually synonymous. We must picture to ourselves that the century after Tiglath-pileser was filled by numerous settlements of this class in Mesopotamia. The Assyrian kings must have offered some opposition to the Aramæan occupation. On the whole, we may conclude that the fortunes of war fluctuated greatly in the struggle, and that its course may be compared to the typical case of the Chaldæans in Babylonia.

THE MIDDLE ASSYRIAN EMPIRE

ALTHOUGH Babylon and Assyria were not in a position to protect Mesopotamia against the Aramæan migration, they could still dispute its possession. We have seen that Babylon, after the reign of Tiglath-pileser, was superior to Assyria; and this relation appears to have lasted up to the beginning of the "Chaldæan dynasty." So soon as we again have Assyrian records, this question has already been settled once for all; from this time onward every Assyrian king, to the end of the Assyrian empire, probably included Mesopotamia within the limits of his dominions.

The names of the next kings, whose succession is now unbroken, are: Tiglath-pileser III., about 950; Ashurdan II., about 930; and Adad-nirari III. With the reign of the last-named, the "Eponym Canon"—the *limu* list—begins; this document gives a list of the Assyrian Eponyms, *limu*, by which the separate years were dated. Henceforth, to nearly the end of the kingdom, each year of Assyrian history can be verified by its *limu*.

At this period, Mesopotamia has become an integral part of the Assyrian empire, and Harran and Ashur are the capitals of the two divisions of the country. The one **Mesopotamia Becomes Assyrian** division is completely occupied by an Aramæan population, which, even in the old towns, must have caused the same annoyance to the old population as the Chaldæans did to the Babylonians; it also included a number of Aramæan states, the princes of which used every opportunity to assert their independence or to win the sovereignty for themselves. Thus near Harran is an Aramæan state, Bit-Adini, a counterpart to the Edessa of the Crusaders; similarly,

near Babylon is the Chaldæan Bit-Dakuri, and we shall learn of others in the time of Ashurnasirpal. The subjugation of these settlements and tribes formed, therefore, the immediate task of Assyria, which did not intend to be at the mercy of any ambitious prince.

Adad-nirari III. was succeeded by his son Tukulti-Ninib II., who reigned from 890 to 885. The latter, on an expedition to the "Nairi country" had an inscription carved by the side of that of Tiglath-pileser I. at the natural tunnel on the Subnat. The same thing was also done by Ashurnasirpal and Shalmaneser II., his son **Campaigns of Ashurnasirpal** and his grandson. Tukulti-Ninib was afterwards solicitous to secure the districts of Assyria which had been colonised by Shalmaneser and won back by Tiglath-pileser. Under Ashurnasirpal their possession was secured.

With Ashurnasirpal, or Ashur-nasir-apli II., who ruled from 885 to 860, our sources of information once more become abundant. We possess several very long inscriptions, which describe his campaigns in detail. He it was who reduced Mesopotamia to order, and put an end to the independence of the Aramæan princes. He abolished the feudal system, and carried out the principle of provincial administration. His accounts of these achievements give us an insight into the conditions of the country.

COLOSSAL LION FROM THE PALACE OF ASHURNASIRPAL AT KALKHI

In 884 B.C., his first full year of sovereignty, an insurrection broke out in the Aramæan state Bit-Khadippi, or Bit-Khalupi, on the Lower Khabur. There the prince, who was an adherent of Assyria, and had therefore been conquered at some earlier period, had been killed, and a prince had been summoned from the adjoining Bit-Adini, near Harran, who was a sworn enemy of Assyria. Ashurnasirpal was on the Euphrates in Kummukh, and he hastened to Bit-Khadippi. While he was on his way the Aramæan princes

A UNIQUE STATUE OF ASHURNASIRPAL
This fine statue of one of Assyria's most famous kings is of interest because it is the only statue carved in the round which has been found out of many hundred sculptures.

of Shadikanna, or Gardikanna, and Shuna hastened to show their submission by payment of tribute. On his arrival, Sura, the capital of Bit-Khadippi, submitted, and surrendered its prince, Akhiiababa, but did not escape severe punishment.

The course of this insurrection is typical of most of the struggles of Assyria with these Aramæans, as with other tribes in a similar position. If a favourable opportunity presented itself, they sought alliance with others, and suspended the payment of tribute, but they seldom offered resistance to an Assyrian army. On the right bank of the Euphrates, beginning with Syria, and extending as far as Babylonia, Ashurnasirpal was acquainted with three such semi-nomadic peoples as a result of the Aramæan immigration—namely,

the peoples of Laki, Khindanu (around the lower reaches of the Knabur), and Sukhi. They were subjugated in various campaigns. We have already seen that Babylonia interfered in the war with Sukhi. Generally speaking, none of these insurrections were undertaken recklessly, but in reliance upon the powerful aid afforded by Babylonia. Babylon was trying thus to regain her influence over Mesopotamia, and abandoned the attempt only when the whole country was subject to Assyria.

The most formidable opponent was the prince Akhuni of Bit-Adini, the Aramæan state which abutted on the territory of Harran and commanded Northern Mesopotamia. Most of the rebellions of the small states on the Khabur were the result of his instigation. Ashurnasirpal, as soon as he had restored tranquillity on the Khabur and on the Euphrates, turned his arms against him in 878 B.C. Akhuni submitted, as also his ally, Khabini of Til-abnaia. These districts were again traversed in the Syrian campaign of the following year, and tribute was enforced; Akhuni was compelled even to supply

ASHURNASIRPAL AND SERVITORS
From a beautiful painted tile from the king's palace at Kalkhi. It retains all its colours, even after 2,700 years.

troops. At that time Aramæan princes on the other side of the Euphrates, from the most northerly part of Syria, paid tribute. The Aramæan expeditions were not difficult or costly wars, for the restless Bedouins had already become peaceable

Ashurnasirpal's reign of twenty-five years was almost one long record of wars. These scenes are from Nineveh bas-reliefs. The one at the top shows the Assyrian army crossing a river, the horses swimming and men in boats or on inflated skins, which they blow out themselves. The next three show the king receiving prisoners, returning triumphant from battle, and directing the operations of a siege from his chariot.

THE CAMPAIGNS OF ASHURNASIRPAL FROM NINEVEH'S MONUMENTS

peasants and readily submitted to any large army sent against them.

Ashurnasirpal had conducted most of his campaigns in the north against the Nairi country, where his object was to recover and to secure the old possessions of Assyria. In the districts west and south of Mons Masius, the Assyrian **Expedition to Phœnicia** colonists who had been ill-treated by the surrounding population, and had fled to the mountains, were brought back, and the province of Tushkha was once more secured. In the same part, Tela, which was inhabited by Assyrians and had revolted, was punished with barbarous severity ; a like fate befell the disloyal governor Khulai, who had wished to occupy Damdamusa. Some other expeditions were led over the Tigris still farther into the Nairi country. He also advanced on the other side of Arbela toward Lake Urumiya, where the most important countries subdued were Khubushkia, Zamua, and Gilzan.

When, like Tiglath-pileser I., he had attained his immediate object, he undertook an expedition into Phœnicia in 877 B.C. Starting from Bit-Adini, which had been subdued, the king crossed the Euphrates on rafts of inflated sheepskins, a method still employed at the present day, and marched on the left bank down stream to Carchemish, " the capital of the Khatti country." Sangara, " king of the Khatti country," paid tribute and furnished his contingent for the army. The Syrian state of Patini, now occupied by Aramæans, which comprised the district north of the lake of Antioch, the so-called Amq, and stretched farther south to the Orontes, adjoined the district of Carchemish on the west. Khazazi was first conquered, and when the Assyrian army, after crossing the Afrin, advanced to Kunulua, the capital, the king, Lubarna, or Liburna, submitted, paid tribute, and furnished troops for

the rest of the campaign. Gusi, prince of the Aramæan state Iakhani, near Arpad did the same.

The march was continued from Kunulua over the western stream of the Amq, the Kara-su, and then southward, the Orontes being crossed below the lake. Here, in the most northerly hinterland of the Phœnician coast, which had belonged to Patini and was called "Lukhuti," Ashurnasirpal founded an Assyrian colony, following the example of Shalmaneser I. in Nairi. He then marched farther south along the sea, where a sacrifice was offered to the gods. The spot was probably near the mouth of the Nahr el-Kelb, where one of the weather-worn Assyrian reliefs which may still be seen there may perhaps represent the monument erected by Ashurnasirpal to commemorate his victory. Arvad, Gebal, Sidon, Tyre, and the Amorites in the hinterland sent tribute.

Assyrian Triumphs in Phœnicia Another division had been sent northward to the Amanus, in order to fell cedar-trees there for buildings in Nineveh. Tyre is the most southern state of which mention is made. The Omri dynasty was then reigning in Israel, and the movements of the Assyrian army must have been watched and carefully followed by it. Ashurnasirpal did not, however, venture to penetrate further, for the more southern districts either paid tribute to Damascus or were under its protectorate. Ashurnasirpal did not venture on a quarrel with this powerful state. Since he feared it, he makes no allusion to it in his inscriptions ; and he demanded tribute only from such towns and cities as were not subject to the influence of its king. In other respects the expedition of Ashurnasirpal was nearly a repetition of that of Tiglath-pileser I., which he evidently took as his model.

We must regard the steps taken to secure Mesopotamia as the most valuable result of his reign. As Shalmaneser I. had done before

AN ENTRANCE TO ASHURNASIRPAL'S PALACE
Colossal human-headed winged lions or bulls were set at entrances to Assyrian palaces or temples to guard against evil-working deities.

him, so he, in accordance with the altered conditions, removed his capital from Ashur once more to Kalkhi, where his palace, the "North-west palace," has been excavated by Layard; he also constructed an aqueduct from the Zab, which brought water to the city.

His successor, Shalmaneser II., who reigned from 860 to 825 B.C., continued the work of his father from the point where the latter left off. His success in Babylonia has been already described. In Mesopotamia he confiscated most of the fiefs of the conquered Aramæan princes and placed them under Assyrian administration; in the north he subjugated the same districts as his father, and made fresh conquests; finally, in Syria he ventured to attack Damascus, a step which his father had so carefully avoided.

The first years of the reign of Shalmaneser II. were devoted to the affairs of Mesopotamia. In three campaigns, between 859 and 857 B.C., Akhuni of Bit-Adini, who had again rebelled, was defeated, and his territory was forfeited and made a province, and partly colonised by Assyrians. A similar fate **Shalmaneser** befell another Aramæan prince, **Invades** Giammu, in the Belikh valley **Syria** in 854 B.C. Thus, all independent government of the Aramæans in Mesopotamia ceased; they became Assyrian subjects.

For Shalmaneser, as for Ashurnasirpal, the next step after the conquest of Mesopotamia was naturally the occupation of Syria, and, if possible, of Palestine. His father had subjugated the northern part, Patini; it now remained to conquer the state which the former had avoided, and which ruled all Cœle-Syria and Palestine. In 854 Shalmaneser crossed the Euphrates near Til-Barsip, which had recently been Akhuni's capital, and was then the seat of an Assyrian governor, and marched in a southerly direction towards Pitru, which had also been retaken from the Aramæans and placed under Assyrian government. There he received the tribute of the Syrian princes, who had voluntarily submitted or had already been reduced to

submission. They were Sangar of Carchemish, who in 877 had done homage to Ashurnasirpal; Kundaspi of Kummukh; Arame of Gusi; Lalli of Melitene—also already tributary to Ashurnasirpal; Khaiani of Gabar-Sam'al; and Kalparunda of Patini and Gurgum—the two latter, in the district of Senjirli, princes of parts of what was formerly

AN OBJECTIVE IN ASSYRIA'S PHŒNICIAN EXPEDITIONS
Assyrian kings invading Phœnicia came to the mouth of this river, the Nahr-el-Kelb, and carved on the rocks here inscriptions or bas-reliefs of themselves.

Patini. Thence the expedition advanced to Aleppo, which offered no resistance, and Shalmaneser sacrificed to Hadad, the god of the city.

Thence marching in a southerly direction, he reached the sphere of influence of Damascus, the borders of Hamath, where Irkhulini, the prince, was allied **Attack** with King Bir-idri of Damascus, **on** or paid him tribute. Bir-idri **Damascus** with his army met him near Karkar in the vicinity of Hamath. Among the vassals who had to obey the call to arms are mentioned: Irkhulini of Hamath, Ahab of Israel, the princes of Kue or Cilicia, Musri, Irqana, Matin-baal of Arvad, and the princes of Usana, Siana, the North Phœnicians, Gindibu of the Arabians, who are first mentioned here, and Ba'sa of Ammon. Shalmaneser, of course, claimed a splendid victory; but the result of the battle was his withdrawal to Assyria and a continuation of the power of Damascus in its full extent. Since in 852-1 Babylonian affairs prevented any immediate renewal of hostilities, no action was taken until the year 849 B.C., when the results were equally trifling. Shalmaneser fared no better in the succeeding year, 848, when he invaded Hamath from the Amanus—

that is to say, from the tributary country of Patini—won a similar "victory," and was obliged to return to Assyria once more without having achieved any real results. Damascus had thus proved to be a well-matched rival; the Assyrian army had to fight against a thoroughly disciplined force, and not against the levies of an uncivilised tribe. Shalmaneser, however, was only incited to greater efforts to overthrow this rival, whose defeat would secure him all Syria and Palestine. Three years later he undertook another expedition, having this time raised levies "of the land"—that is to say, he recruited his force among the hardy peasant population of Assyria. But his rival placed an unusually strong force in the field; and the "victory" of Shalmaneser was of the same character as the earlier ones which his inscriptions record.

He first gained a definite success when there was a change of sovereigns at Damascus, and he was thus able to win the vassals partly over to his side. Biridri was dead, and Hazael had become king of Damascus; meanwhile in Israel a revolution had set Jehu on the throne, and he looked to Assyria for support. Damascus now stood entirely alone. We have frequently noticed how the death of a king is the signal for a universal defection of his vassals. Hazael was dependent, therefore, on his own resources. Shalmaneser advanced from the north along the coast, in order to attack Damascus from the side of Beirut, where he had an image of himself cut in the face of the rock near the mouth of the Nahr el-Kelb.

Elephant and apes from Musri or Bactria.

Shawls and vessels from Kalparunda of Patini.

Ambassadors of Jehu, king of Israel.

Shalmaneser and ambassadors from Gilzan.
TRIBUTE TO SHALMANESER IV.
Above are represented scenes from the famous Black Obelisk set up by Shalmaneser IV. at Kalkhi, or Nimrud

Hazael tried to bar his passage between Hermon and the Antilebanon, but failed to check him, and was forced to retire behind the walls of Damascus. Shalmaneser besieged the city for some time, but obtained no success. It was not the mud walls of an ordinary provincial town which resisted his battering-rams. He had to be content with laying waste the open country as far as the Hauran, and then to withdraw homeward with the indemnity which Tyre and Sidon always paid, and the homage of Jehu. Even a sixth attempt, in 839 B.C., met with no better results, and Damascus preserved her independence. The state thus continued to exist which blocked Assyria's road to Palestine. The whole course of Israelitish history was determined by this fact. For the next hundred years Israel and Judah remained under the influence of Damascus; and when finally Damascus fell, in 731 B.C., the fate of Israel also was sealed.

Shalmaneser made no further attack on Damascus after 839; Israel and the rest of Palestine were, therefore, left to themselves to deal with Damascus. Although Cœle-Syria and Palestine had temporarily escaped the Assyrian power, a further conquest of Northern Syria and a wider expansion towards Asia Minor remained to be effected. Melitene, Patini, and Amq had acknowledged the Assyrian supremacy; but now Shalmaneser advanced over the Amanus and into the district of the Taurus. Kue, or Cilicia, had been at first tributary to Damascus; it was now, in 840, 835, and 834, subjugated, and at Tarsus Kirri was made king in the

Mansell

USE OF THE HORSE IN ASSYRIAN WARFARE

Before the time of Ashurnasirpal the Assyrian army consisted only of the archers, slingers, spearmen, sappers, and charioteers, who have been illustrated in earlier pages. In his campaigns he introduced the horsed archers, shown in the bas-relief from which the top picture is reproduced. A very typical horsed chariot, with driver, archer, and shield-bearers is shown in the middle, while the third represents chariots and cavalry in action in one of Ashurnasirpal's many battles. The vigorous movement which the Assyrian sculptor has suggested in this sculpture is very striking.

room of his brother Kate. To the north of the Taurus tribute was demanded from the Tabul, who were governed by their own chiefs, and thus the circle of Assyrian vassal states from Cilicia over the Taurus as far as Melitene was completed.

Wars Against Urartu The district of Malatia (Khanigalbat) formed part of the Armenian highlands, and was, therefore, the next object of attack by a power advancing in that direction. It had been secured for Assyria under Shalmaneser, Tiglath-pileser, and Ashurnasirpal, who had already conducted campaigns up to Lake Van. Since in the north of this country some approximation to a united state had been achieved in Urartu, with its capital on Lake Van, Shalmaneser made war upon its kings. By 857 he had once more marched through the districts south of the Upper Euphrates, namely, Alzi, Zamani, and Anzitene, and on the other side of the Arsanias Sukhme and Daiaeni, which had been subject to his predecessors, Shalmaneser I. and Tiglath-pileser. He invaded the territory of Urartu from this point, and King Arame withdrew into the interior. A statue of Shalmaneser was erected near Lake Van, and the march continued through the eastern passes past Gilzan and Khubushkia to Arbael. New expeditions were undertaken in 850 and 845 B.C.; and during these latter the inscriptions of Shalmaneser at the tunnel on the Subnat were probably carved.

Meanwhile, that change of monarchy in Armenia must have occurred which brought to the throne the powerful dynasty that had its seat at Turushpa on Lake Van—the modern Van—and from that centre founded the mighty kingdom of Urartu. This state caused much trouble to the kings of Assyria in the succeeding years, and contested with them the supremacy in Syria. The defection **Armenian Influence in Syria** of Lalla of Malatia in the year 837 is certainly to be traced to the efforts of these kings. Four years later an Assyrian army was sent to the Arsanias in order, it would seem, to reoccupy the districts of Sukhme and Daiaeni, which are situated on its right bank; Sarduri I., the new king of Urartu, was therefore clearly advancing. In 829 a new expedition, this time from the other side, was attempted through the passes of Gilzan and Khu-

bushkia. Musasir, a state to the south-west of Lake Urumiya, was sacked, and a part of Urartu met the same fate. But the Assyrians did not obtain any decisive results here; on the contrary, the power of the new state grew continually during subsequent years, and from the time of Adad-nirari onward Assyria was ousted more and more from these regions. The kings of Urartu encroached on Mesopotamia and Syria, until they were driven back to their highlands under Tiglath-pileser IV.

While Ashurnasirpal's frontier on the east and south-east had been the Zab, Shalmaneser advanced against the districts between Lake Urumiya and the plain of the Tigris, which had often in earlier times been subject to the Assyrian supremacy, but were now more influenced by Babylon. In 860 B.C. an expedition was made into the passes of Holvan, and in 844 a similar one to Namri, the south-western districts of Media. An advance was made in 836 against the prince of Bit-Khamban, who had been installed there; then the march was continued farther northward to Parsua, on the east of Lake Urumiya. Here chiefs of the Medes, who are mentioned **Extending the Eastern Frontiers** for the first time in this connection, brought their tribute, when the advance was continued in a southerly direction to Karkar, east of Holvan. The districts of Kirkhi and Khubushkia, which lay to the south of Lakes Van and Urumiya, and had been already traversed by Ashurnasirpal, were also subjugated, and the Mannai, on the western shore, as well as Gilzan, to the north of Lake Urumiya, were punished.

Shalmaneser's successes in Babylonia have been spoken of in the section on Babylonian history. The close connection with Babylonia and the growth of its influence caused the great rebellion which broke out toward the end of his reign. The peasant class of Assyria must have suffered by the wars, while Babylonia, as the seat of the hierarchy, was able to exert a strong influence upon the priestly and religious classes. Almost the whole of Assyria and the Assyrian provinces, headed by the former capital, Ashur, which had naturally lost much by the change of royal residence, now revolted. Of the important towns, only the capital, Kalkhi, and Harran, the chief city of Mesopotamia, where Shalmaneser had built the temple of Sin, remained loyal;

and it would appear that Shalmaneser found a refuge in Northern Babylonia, which indeed belonged to him. The leader of the rebellion was Ashur-danin-apli, Shalmaneser's son, who maintained his position for at least six years (829–824), and at this time probably bore the title " King of Assyria," since he was in possession of the ancient capital.

Shalmaneser died in 825 B.C., and his son, Shamshi-Adad IV., who at first only possessed Mesopotamia, at length succeeded in subduing Assyria between 825 and 812. An inscription of his, which has been recovered, furnishes an account of his career to his fourth campaign, which was directed against Babylonia. The first expedition he records was to Nairi, and in connection with it he refers to the homage offered him by the entire Assyrian empire from its northern to its southern frontiers, and from the eastern frontier as far as the Euphrates. The second campaign was directed against the Nairi country, through the district between Lakes Van and Urumiya, in the course of which a part of Urartu was laid waste. The third expedition advanced in the same direction, and then was led further to the territory of the Mannai, and round Lake Urumiya up to Parsua ; thence it went in a south-easterly direction through Media, probably to Holvan. A large number of Median districts are enumerated in the account of this campaign. The fourth campaign was that against Babylon ; the narrative breaks off after recording Shamshi-Adad's victory over Marduk-balatsu-iqbi.

The Eponym Chronicle

From the reign of Shamshi-Adad onward, we possess a new source of information which serves as an invaluable guide for the following period : a fragment of it actually deals with the beginning and the end of the reign of Shalmaneser II. This is the Eponym Chronicle, a Limu list, to which short notes are added recording the most important event of each year, usually a campaign ; it is especially valuable for the ensuing period down to Tiglath-pileser IV., from which we have few other inscriptions. We possess some short inscriptions by Adad-nirari IV., between 812 and 783 B.C., which give a general survey of his campaigns, and are supplemented by the accounts of the Eponym Chronicle. On the whole, they represent him as continuing the conquests of his predecessors, or of winning back territories which had become rebellious. He made hardly any important conquests. Among countries in the east which were subject to him he mentions Ellipi (bordering on Elam), also Karkar and Araziash up to Parsua, known from the time of Shalmaneser, and Andia, adjacent to Parsua, on the north-east. He also received tribute from Median chiefs. Three expeditions to Khubushkia and the Nairi country are enumerated, and two to the territory of the Mannai. He did not, however, venture on a further advance against Urartu, which continued to develop its power. He met with some successes in Syria. In 806 and 805 expeditions to Arpad and Azaz are mentioned, and in 797 another to a Syrian town, Mansuate. We may connect with these expeditions the notice that Mari, king of Damascus, paid tribute ; perhaps the accession of a new king at Damascus was the cause. Adad-nirari also mentions among tributary states, Tyre and Sidon, Israel, which thus still held to Assyria, and Edom and Philistia, which last were recent additions to the empire. This list points to a preponderant Assyrian influence in Palestine, and thus to a decay of the power of Damascus. As long as Damascus remained independent, it was always a bulwark for all districts lying south of it. Adad-nirari's relations to Babylonia have been already described in an earlier section.

Tributes to Assyria's Power

For the following period we have no more royal inscriptions, and are, therefore, entirely dependent on the accounts of the Eponym Chronicle. The lack of inscriptions in itself points to a period of weakness, and this is confirmed by the facts which we are able to establish. On the whole, for the next forty years, the kings of Assyria were fully occupied with the task of retaining the territory that had been won. Indeed, in this they were not always successful, for we shall see that in the revival of prosperity under Tiglath-pileser much had first to be won back again. This is especially true of the territories which lay within the sphere of influence of the new kingdom of Urartu. Assyria, when once she ceased to attack, was herself attacked ; hence the changed attitude of Armenia, where the kings, especially Menuas, extended their power toward the south, and deprived Assyria of the Nairi country as well as the districts

A Period of Weakness

of Northern Assyria. Shalmaneser III., who reigned between 783 and 773 B.C., was obliged to wage defensive wars, principally against Urartu ; no fewer than six of his ten campaigns were directed against the incessant encroachments of this rival. There does not seem to have been so much lost toward the east, on the borders of **Aggression of Armenia** Media, for there he had to deal mostly with barbarian states without a firm organisation. Expeditions are recorded to Namri in 749 and 748, and one in 766 against the Medes.

The next king was Ashur-dan III., from 773 to 755 B.C., who conducted several campaigns in Syria ; the first in 773, against Damascus, the second against Khatarikka, to the north of it. He twice marched into Babylonia, in 771 and 767 ; and we may therefore conclude that he attempted to oppose the Chaldæans there. In the second half of his reign his kingdom was convulsed by a shock which was destined to destroy the fabric of tributary states so laboriously reared. A rebellion broke out in the year 763 B.C., which in succeeding years continued to spread from place to place, and must gradually have affected a large portion of the empire. The Eponym Chronicle puts before this year—the year when the chronicle records the solar eclipse, which forms a fixed point in ancient chronology—a mark of division, as at the beginning of a new reign ; for, since the rebellion broke out in Ashur, a rival king was probably proclaimed there.

What the actual cause of the revolt may have been is not stated, but it is not difficult to conjecture, since the rebellion started in the ancient capital of the empire. If we reflect how Tiglath-pileser chose Kalkhi again as a residence, and Sargon, on the contrary, restored the privileges of Ashur, we may conclude that the movement originated with the priesthood, whose privileges were infringed by the removal of the royal residence. The rebellion was suppressed, it is true ; but the next king, Ashur-nirari, from 754 to 746 B.C., seems to have been subject to the influence of its promoters, for the first act of his reign was the removal of the court back to Ashur in 754, if this change had not already taken place in the reign of Ashur-dan himself. The act signified a victory of the hierarchy over the source of Assyria's strength, the army. The monarchy, by ignoring the wishes of the latter, the only support of its power in Assyria, voluntarily weakened its position in 754 B.C.

Ashur-nirari reigned eight years, to **Priesthood Destroy the Empire** each of which (with one exception) the note "in the land" is appended in the Eponym Chronicle—that is to say, the king remained in Assyria and no expedition was undertaken in that year. However, for the last year, 746 B.C., the chronicle records, " rebellion in Kalkhi " ; and in the course of the following year Tiglath-pileser IV. mounted the throne. We possess inscriptions of his which show that he resided in Kalkhi, and was not of the royal stock. We may therefore conclude that he was placed upon the throne by a military rebellion in Kalkhi. Ashur-nirari, who resided at Ashur under the influence of the priesthood, was the last king of his house.

SCULPTURED HINGES OF THE GATES OF SHALMANESER'S PALACE
Two of the gates to the palace of Shalmaneser IV., at Balawat, had broad hinges of bronze, the bands of which ran across the gates. They were embossed and engraved with scenes from the many campaigns of the king.

NINEVEH IN THE DAYS OF ASSYRIA'S ASCENDENCY OVER THE NATIONS OF THE NEAR EAST
A restoration of the Nimroud palaces of Nineveh, prepared under the direction of Sir A. H. Layard for his "Monuments of Nineveh"

THE NEW EMPIRE OF ASSYRIA

WITH Tiglath-pileser IV., who ruled from 745 to 728 B.C., a fresh epoch of Assyrian history opens, a new era of prosperity which raised Assyria to the supremacy in Nearer Asia. He really laid the foundations of the glory of Assyria. This is the age when Assyria subdued Damascus and Palestine, and thus interfered in the history of that small people whose sacred books preserved the name of Assyria for two thousand years, when other records of its history lay buried in the earth, and no one even knew what language had been spoken by these lords of Nearer Asia.

We must distinguish three theatres of war in the reign of Tiglath-pileser : Babylonia, where his successes have been already described ; the North, where he had to fight with the now powerful Urartu ; and Syria-Palestine, where Damascus, far from being crushed, had, on the contrary, been able in **Beginnings of Assyria's Glory** the interval of Assyria's weakness to regain its strength, and had since the last war in 773 discontinued the payment of tribute.

After the Babylonian campaign in his first year, 745 B.C., and another in Western Media in the following year, war was begun in 742 against Sarduri II. of Armenia. The latter had, in the meantime, made continual advances, had subdued Melitene and Kummukh, or Commagene, and even Gurgumi, the northern part of the former Patini, and had compelled their kings to pay tribute to him and not to Assyria. He had then entered into friendly relations with Mati-il of Agusi, who had either already occupied Arpad—an expedition had been sent there in 754—or wished to do so, in order to found a kingdom there for himself. According to the Eponym Chronicle, Tiglath-pileser was actually near Arpad, and was therefore marching against Mati-il, when an Armenian army under Sarduri invaded Mesopotamia. It was defeated in the country of Kummukh. Sarduri was pursued to " the bridge of the Euphrates, the boundary of his land," and

thus a check was put, for a time, on his advance towards Mesopotamia ; further operations against him had to be deferred until a later occasion. The three following years were filled up by expeditions " to Arpad." Mati-il must, therefore, have shown a vigorous resistance. After his fall most of the Syrian princes paid **Syria under Tribute** tribute — namely, Kustaspi of Kummukh and Tarkhulara of Gurgumi, who thus seceded from Urartu, Rasunnu of Damascus, Hiram of Tyre, the prince of Kue, and Pisiris of Carchemish. Assyria's supremacy in Syria was therefore restored in these three years, while the influence of Urartu was destroyed. Only a part of Patini, Unqi—that is, Amq—together with the capital Kinalia, or Kunulua, offered resistance ; its prince, Tutammu, lost his throne, and this part of the country became an Assyrian province.

The next year saw an expedition to Ulluba, one of the Nairi countries ; it also was placed under an Assyrian governor. The object of this movement was naturally to strike a blow at Armenia, from which this territory had been taken. On the side of Armenia the country was secured by fortresses against attack. In 738 B.C. another expedition was made to one of the districts of Patini. Azriau, prince of Iaudi, close by Senjirli, had revolted ; his town, Kullani, was taken. This event threw its shadow as far as Israel and Judah, where Isaiah held up the conquest of " Kalno " as a warning to the Jews. A number of North Phœnician districts — the same region **Assyria in Phœnicia** where once Ashurnasirpal had founded his Assyrian colony Aribua, and which now belonged to Hamath—had joined Azriau, and incurred the penalty of being annexed. The Assyrian province of Simarra was constituted out of them, and stretched from the Orontes to the district of Gebal, but did not include that city or Arvad, which remained independent. This new Phœnician province, which received fresh additions in the year 733, was assigned to Shalmaneser, son of Tiglath-pileser. In this way part of the " foreland " of Damascus became Assyrian. Damascus itself, as well as the remaining Syrian and Phœnician states, Kummukh, Carchemish, Samal, Gurgumi in Amq, Hamath, Kue, Gebal, Tyre, and Menahem of Israel, paid

Tribute from Arabia tribute; the last, as may be assumed from the biblical narrative, did so only when a part of his dominions had been taken away from him. The wider circle of the tributary states which had once been bound to Shalmaneser—namely, Melitene, Kasku, Tabal, and the principalities of Cappadocia and Cilicia—paid tribute once more. The Assyrian king, as the feudal lord of Damascus, received presents from Zabibi, queen of the Arabians.

In the years 737 and 736 B.C. expeditions were led to Media and Nairi, with the object of completely crushing the influence of Urartu ; and in the ensuing year this great rival was finally attacked in his own country. Urartu was traversed. Tiglathpileser besieged the citadel of Turushpa, or Van, but without success, and had to be contented with

TIGLATH-PILESER IV. IN HIS CHARIOT
His reign opened a new era of prosperity, which raised Assyria to the supremacy in Western Asia and laid the foundations of its glory.

erecting a royal statue there in view of the besieged. He annexed the southern part of Urartu, and united it to the province of Nairi. He thus struck an undeniably heavy blow at Urartu, and placed a strong obstacle in the way of any renewed advance by fortifying the frontier provinces. Urartu's dominion over Syria and Nairi was thus ended. But the country did not entirely relinquish its schemes of conquest until its power was broken up by Sargon, and at the same time a dangerous antagonist appeared on the other side in the Cimmerians.

Damascus had continued to pay tribute. But it is always noticeable that the position of tributary to Assyria was never permanent. On the one hand, the sums exacted were so large that only force could wring them from the feudal princes ;

on the other hand, the conditions formed a constant incentive to revolt as soon as there appeared to be any prospect of success. Very often also there may have been an intention on the part of Assyria to force tributary states into revolt, in order to have a pretext to annex them as provinces ; we may compare the policy of the Romans toward their *socii*. The year 734 saw an expedition to Philistia, where Ascalon was brought under Assyrian rule. We have already noted that all Palestine was obliged to follow the destinies of Damascus. Soon afterwards, however, Damascus seems to have shaken off the yoke. The pretext for interference was given by the appeal for help of Ahaz of Judah, whom Rassunu, or Resin, and his vassal Pekah were besieging in Jerusalem, in order to force him to join an alliance aimed against Assyria. Tyre was also privy to it, and there seem to have been hopes of help from Egypt. In the year 733 B.C. Tiglath-pileser arrived before Damascus. In Israel, Pekah, on the approach of the Assyrians, fell a victim to a revolt of the Assyrian party, and in his place Hoshea, the leader of this party, was appointed king. This opportune outbreak deprived Tiglath-pileser of an excuse for annexing the country, and thus a respite of ten or twelve years was purchased, after which this destiny was to be fulfilled. Damascus, as on previous occasions, offered a stout resistance ; but it fell at last, and became an Assyrian province in 732 B.C. Israel,

Israel Bounded by Assyria whose territory even before this had been much curtailed, was now directly bounded by an Assyrian province : the state which had hitherto dominated it in the sphere of politics, and had been its leader in the development of culture, was administered by an Assyrian governor. Tyre also, which had joined in the cause, made peace on the approach of an Assyrian army ; a rich trading town, it was well able to pay tribute.

TIGLATH - PILESER REMOVING SPOIL FROM A CAPTURED CITY Mansell
The seventeen years' reign of Tiglath-pileser IV. was almost entirely taken up with his three series of campaigns in Babylonia, Armenia, and in Syria and Palestine, in all of which he was successful. Bas-relief in British Museum.

The next years were devoted to the conquest of Babylonia and Babylon, which has already been described. Tiglath-pileser reigned for two years as king of Babylon ; in the year 728 he died, and was succeeded by his son Shalmaneser IV., who reigned from 727 to 722 B.C. His reign is merely a continuation of that of Tiglath-pileser, whose policy he seems to have followed consistently. We do not possess any detailed inscriptions of his time. Samaria, in his reign, found itself compelled once more to suspend payment of tribute ; but the expected help from Egypt was not forthcoming, and after a three years' siege the town was captured and made the seat of an Assyrian governor. The Assyrian frontier now ran a little north of Jerusalem.

Shalmaneser died before the fall of Samaria, so that its capture was effected by his successor, Sargon. Sargon, like Tiglath-pileser IV., was the founder of a new

dynasty ; he had been made king by a reaction against that movement which had brought the former to the throne. His account of the measures of his predecessors, which he superseded, throws light upon the nature of this movement, of which we have already found traces in the revolutions of Ashur-danin-apli and of the year 763 B.C.

Tiglath-pileser had, according to this account, endeavoured to restrict the excessive influence of the priesthood and the favoured position of the great cities. These had possessed the most extensive privileges and had enjoyed immunity from almost every burden. If we consider the fact that the greater part of the land belonged to them, we shall realise that the national revenue must have diminished more and more ; and we shall understand why the Assyrian kingdom, in the end, became so impotent. Even the attitude

Source of Assyria's Weakness

EVACUATION OF A CITY CAPTURED BY TIGLATH - PILESER Mansell
An interesting bas-relief, now in the British Museum, showing Assyrian scribes taking account of the spoil, and women and children being removed in bullock-carts. Note the disused battering-ram against the wall at the left.

1671

of the Assyrian kings towards Babylonia was regulated by their views upon this subject. Tiglath-pileser, Shalmaneser, Sennacherib and Ashurbanipal acted energetically; Sargon and Esarhaddon favoured Babylon, where the system of privileged priests and towns flourished, to which this weakness was due. Tiglath-pileser and Shalmaneser tried to put an end to it, and in so doing they must have relied to some extent upon the peasant class, or what was left of it. Obviously we need not for that reason regard them as benefactors of the "small man;" they were concerned only in having subjects that could pay their taxes and perform their duties. They understood, however, that a monarchy which was propped upon the towns and the priesthood could maintain its existence only so long as it had advantages to offer them.

Town versus Country

Henceforward we can trace how the two parties in Assyria worked against each other. Evidence of the struggle may be seen in the series of forcible depositions of the reigning king. It is obvious that a *rapprochement* of the privileged towns and temples was in reality no benefit to the country population. The real point at issue was indeed the contrast between country and town; but the country was mainly represented by the nobility, who to some extent had the army at their disposal. Tiglath-pileser and Shalmaneser were thus under their influence. Sargon, elevated to the throne by a reaction, favoured the towns and temples, to which he restored their privileges. Sennacherib, again, represented the interests of the nobility and army, as is shown by his attitude towards Babylon. He was murdered, and the Babylonian hierarchical party won the day with Esarhaddon. A revolution broke out when Esarhaddon wished to secure the power to his son Shamash-shum-ukin, who held the same views as himself; and with Ashurbanipal the Assyrian nobility were again victorious. These were the two currents which henceforth determined the course of Assyrian history; on Tiglath-pileser's accession they had produced a sharply defined and conscious opposition.

Nobility and the Hierarchy

Thus, in the year 722 B.C., when Shalmaneser died, we suddenly find Sargon on the throne. He was unable to point to any royal ancestors; but he became the progenitor of the royal house under which Assyria reached the zenith of her power, and then rapidly sank. In domestic affairs his reign was the counterpart to that of Tiglath-pileser, while his foreign policy was dictated by the desire to continue the operations of the latter and to execute the schemes which he had been compelled to leave unfinished. We have already seen that his instrument for carrying out these operations differed from that of his predecessors; henceforth the Assyrian army consists of mercenaries collected from every country and province —completely at the disposal of the king so long as he can provide them with pay and booty, but immediately refusing to fight if these are not forthcoming. From Sargon's time onward the "royal" army is the instrument by which Assyria keeps the East in subjection. The sovereign power in Assyria has therefore devolved on the administration—which, according to Oriental custom, is equivalent to the extortion—of the nobility and priesthood; an Assyrian people, to whom Shalmaneser I. and Ashurnasirpal had assigned land in the conquered provinces, no longer exist. If the king now wishes to occupy a conquered province with new settlers, he must meet the difficulty by exchanging the populations of two provinces situated at different ends of the empire. The peasant class in Assyria was extinct; there were only the great landed estates of the nobility or of the temples, cultivated by slaves or paupers.

Peasant Class Extinct

The military operations of Sargon, since they were in continuation of his predecessor's plans, were carried out in the same regions; we have once more to do with wars in Babylonia against Chaldæa and Elam, or in Urartu for the possession of the northern districts, or in Palestine, where he sought to extend his dominion.

We have already described Sargon's successes in Babylonia. In Palestine, as we have just noted, the annexation of Samaria and the "carrying away of the Ten Tribes," which make the name of Sargon of interest to readers of the Bible, were merely results of the siege under Shalmaneser. Hamath, north of Damascus, in Syria, had hitherto avoided this fate by the regular payment of its tribute. But it became acquainted with the "good will" of Assyria in 738, when the revolted towns of Hamath were not given back, but were added to the province of Simirra. Great hopes had been centred on the change of the king in Assyria ; thus we now find, in 720, in place of the pliant king Eni-il, a "peasant," Iaubidi, on the throne and in open hostility to Assyria. He was allied with Hanno of Gaza, who must have submitted to Tiglath-pileser. Both clearly rested their hopes on Egypt. The newly constructed provinces of Arpad, Simirra, Damascus, and Samaria jo ned the cause. The greater part, therefore, of Syria and Palestine tried to free themselves from the burden of tribute or of service under the Assyrian yoke. But the al ies could not decide on combined action, a usua' defect in such confederations of petty states. Hamath was conquered and constituted a province. Hanno, who sought to capture Gaza, was defeated near Raphia, on the southern frontier of the territory of Gaza. The revolted provinces were reduced without difficulty, and tranquillity was again restored in Syria and Palestine.

SARGON WITH HIS VIZIER AND ATTENDANT
Sargon was a king of Assyria, of non-royal descent, who reached the throne as the result of a revolt of the priestly reactionaries.

Sargon could now turn his attention to his third remaining opponent, Urartu. Rusas I. was again active, and attempted to extend his influence to Northern Syria, and in the east to the Median frontier states, and he apparently found ready listeners. Thus Sargon's next task, like that of Tiglath-pileser in his day, was the subjugation of these disloyal vassals.

In 719 B.C. two towns of the Mannai, on the western shore of Lake Urumiya, whose king supported Assyria against Urartu, were punished because they had gone over to the tribe of the Zigirtu, which was fr endly to Urartu ; the same lot befell other towns which had seceded to Urartu. In 718 B.C. one of the princes of Tabal, Kiakki of Shinukhtu, was carried prisoner to Cappadocia, and his dominions given to a loyal neighbour, Matti of Atun.

In 717 B.C. Carchemish fell, which had regularly paid its tribute since the days of Ashurnasirpal. The annoyances of Assyria must have exhausted the patience of this wealthy town and driven it to a war of desperation. It had vainly looked for help to the ruler of the former territory of the Khatti in Asia Minor—Mita of Muski, as Sargon calls him—that is to say, Midas of Phrygia. Pisir's was the last king of Carchemish, and the last relic of the Khatti rule in Syria became thenceforth an Assyrian province.

The years 716 B.C. and 715 brought wars in the east of Urartu, where Rusas meanwhile had made especial efforts to gain Mannai for himself by force ; he had thus abandoned Syria and had turned more to the east. There he succeeded, by stirring up disputes about the throne, in obtaining the sceptre for Ullusunu, a prince favourable to him. But before the party of Urartu had won a firm footing, Sargon appeared and forced the king to do homage, and his example was followed by the Prince of Nairi and other chiefs of those regions. In 714 war was made against Urartu itself. Sargon advanced from Mannai past Musasir, the conquest of which he has represented in his palace, towards Lake Van, while he devastated the country along his line of march. According to Sargon's account, Rusas committed suicide, but, in an inscription of Rusas himself at Topsana, in the district of Rowanduz in Kurdistan, it is recorded that he restored the deposed king of Musasir, and afterwards led his armies as far as the mountains of Assyria.

It would thus seem that Sargon's conquest of Urartu was not so complete as he would make it appear. However, from this time onward the power of Urartu was broken, for it had now to fight for its existence with a new enemy on its northern frontier, whom we have already mentioned—the Cimmerians.

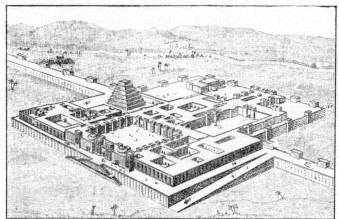

THE GREAT PALACE OF SARGON AT KHORSABAD
A reconstruction of the great palace erected by Sargon at Khorsabad, north of
Nineveh. It was built on an artificial eminence of brick and overlooked the city.

Cyprus, who sought assistance from Assyria in their efforts to expel the Phœnicians of Tyre from the eastern part of the island.

In Southern Palestine an isolated case of refusal to pay tribute was that of Ashdod. This incident is noteworthy from the allusion to it in Isaiah, chapter xx. We can imagine with what hopes and fears men in Judah had followed this rebellion in their immediate vicinity. Indeed, Judah, according to Sargon's account, took part in it with Moab and Edom, without letting matters go so far as open resistance, when an Assyrian army conquered Ashdod and founded an Assyrian colony there.

In the east, Elam, after the expulsion of Merodach-baladan, had not been able to assert her influence in Babylonia. The quarrel between the two rival states showed itself in a dispute as to the throne, which occurred in the borderland of Ellipi, where two hostile brothers sought support, the one from Elam, the other from Sargon. After the former, Nibi, had driven out his brother Ispabara with Elamite assistance, Sargon was obliged to restore the latter to the throne.

Toward the end of Sargon's reign his great palace, which he had caused to be built to the north of Nineveh at the foot of the mountains, was finished and solemnly taken possession of. The royal residence was thus removed from Kalkhi.

Assyria had, it is true, got rid of a rival, but by so doing she had weakened the bulwark which formed her natural protection against the danger now threatening from the migration of Aryan peoples. Henceforth the Assyrian generals in the northern frontier provinces carefully watched the struggles of Urartu with the Cimmerians and other allied tribes, and under Esarhaddon these already began to menace Assyrian territory.

Many districts of the former Patini in Syria had already been annexed; and, under Sargon, Gurgumi with its capital Marqasi, or Marash, shared the same fate. Even Kue and some Cappadocian districts, among them Kammanu, corresponding to the former Musri, as well as Meltene and Kummukh, became Assyrian provinces after unsuccessful attempts at rebellion by their princes. This marked the greatest extension of Assyria in the north-west. Toward the end of Sargon's reign the Governor of Kue actually undertook an expedition over the Taurus in order to check Mita of Muski, or Midas of Phrygia, who was attempting to advance against Assyria in that region and on the Halys.

When Sargon had seized Babylon, he received the presents of seven Greek " kings " of Cyprian towns. This is the first ascertainable contact with " Ionians." Those who paid homage on this occasion were the princes of the western part of

MAIN ENTRANCE TO SARGON'S PALACE
This fine gate, which can be seen in the bird's eye view of the whole palace given above, suggests the magnificence of an Assyrian palace.

But Sargon had been raised to the throne by the party which formerly had their headquarters in Ashur. Since, however, Ashur itself was not adapted from its position to be the seat of government, Sargon founded a new capital of his own, Dur-Sharrukin, the " castle of Sargon," or Khorsabad, on the model of his legendary prototype, Sargon of Agade, whose name he, indeed, adopted on his accession : " Sargon the second " he was called by his loyal scribes. The inscriptions and sculptures from the palace of Dur-Sharrukin — excavated by Botta in the years 1842-1845 —are the chief authorities for the history of his reign. Sargon's death took place in the year 705. We have no particulars concerning it, though it appears from a reference to it by Sennacherib that he met with a violent end and " was not buried in his house," that is to say, no proper burial was accorded to him. This can only mean that he fell fighting with barbarians, as Cyrus did. Such barbarians were almost exclusively to be found on the northern frontier of his empire, among the Indo - Germanic tribes, the Cimmerians and " Scythians." It may, therefore, have been in a war with one of these peoples that Sargon met his death. The song in Isaiah, chapter xiv, 4-21, referred in later times to the death of a king of Babylon, may have been originally composed on Sargon's unexpected death. The hopes therein expressed were, to some extent, realised, for Palestine and Phœnicia attempted a great rebellion.

Sanherib, or Sennacherib, who reigned from 704 to 681 B.C., was first occupied in Babylonia and with an expedition to the

Bricks from the gate of the palace enamelled with coloured representations of winged Assyrian deities.

DECORATIONS OF SARGON'S PALACE

A favourite decoration with the Assyrians, and practically the only decoration used by the Babylonians, were bricks enamelled with bright colours, so lasting that they are now still vivid and clear.

Zagros in 702 ; there he chastised the Kashshu, a remnant of the old Kassites which had preserved their independence and the Iasubigalla. Then, in 701, he turned to Palestine.

Two princes in particular were the soul of the revolt there—Luli of Tyre and Hezekiah of Judah. The former was " king of the Sidonians." He possessed Tyre and Sidon, with a territory which began south of Beirut and extended to Philistia ; in addition, the east of Cyprus belonged to him, with the most important town, Kition. We have already seen that the west of the island was in the possession of " Ionians," and joined Assyria through enmity to the Phœnicians. Hopes had also been entertained of Merodach - baladan, but he had been quickly driven out ; and promises of support had also been received from Egypt. Hezekiah was leader of the revolt here owing to the fact that the anti - Assyrian party in Ekron, a town of Philistia, deposed King Padi, who favoured Assyria, and gave him up to Hezekiah. Such was the state of affairs which had arisen between 705 and 702.

When Sennacherib set out in the year 701 and marched along the coast of Phœnicia it again appeared that each of the confederated states had counted on an annihilation of the dreaded tyrant by the others : there was no combined resistance. The Phœnician states, Arvad and Gebal, paid tribute ; the same thing was done by the southern states of Philistia, as well as by the neighbours of Judah—Ammon, Moab, and Edom. Luli surrendered Sidon and fled to Cyprus, where he died soon afterwards. The only resistance was offered by Tyre, which Sennacherib besieged in vain, and by Hezekiah. Sennacherib installed a new king, Ithobal, at Sidon, so that the "Sidonian" kingdom was again broken up into its two component parts. Then he marched southward to Judah, where Hezekiah, trusting to the approaching Egyptian help, was persevering in his resistance. He conquered Ekron, defeated the relieving army, which consisted of troops of the "princes of Musri, or Egypt, and the king of Melukha," and gradually took forty-six fortified places in Judah. He then appeared before the capital and closely invested it. But the besieged held out, trusting to the disorders which were expected to break out in Babylonia ; in the end, Sennacherib had to withdraw without capturing Jerusalem itself. The independence of Judah was saved for the time being. Hezekiah, however, forfeited the greater part of his territory, for the conquered towns were divided among his neighbours, and he himself lost no time in again offering his submission.

Siege of Jerusalem

After the destruction of Babylon in 689, Sennacherib was able to turn once more to the west. Some petty wars had meanwhile occurred in Cappadocia, or Khilakku, and the province of Kammanu, constituted by Sargon. Some attempts of "Ionians" to land in Cilicia are also said to have been repulsed. No further conquests of importance were made there, and there was no expansion of territory by the formation of new provinces. Tyre had successfully stood a siege in 701 and maintained its independence. The reinforcements from Egypt who marched to Hezekiah's aid had been repulsed, it is true, but Sennacherib had not ventured to chastise them. He now undertook an expedition against Egypt. Jerusalem, too, feared his chastisement, but once more fortune was favourable. The Assyrian army did not enter the country ; on the march thither it was destroyed, probably by a pestilence. Certainly the expedition was disastrous. Sennacherib had to return to Nineveh with the loss of his army. There he was carried off by the fate of so many Oriental kings : he was murdered during a rebellion headed by his sons.

Assyrian Army Destroyed

The reign of Sennacherib had been nowhere successful. He had attempted to solve the Babylonian problem by force, and apparently had accomplished his purpose ; but even in Babylonia he

ASSYRIANS CARRYING A CONQUERED PEOPLE AWAY INTO CAPTIVITY
The Jewish people were taken into Assyrian captivity at least three times. Sargon and Sennacherib both deported the population of Samaria—the "Ten Tribes"—and Nebuchadnezzar took away the remnant of Judah to Babylon.

CAPTIVES OF THE ASSYRIAN HOSTS ON THE MARCH TO THE CAPITAL

This is a continuation of the Assyrian bas-relief of which part is produced on the opposite page, showing a people carried away into captivity with their household goods and cattle. Probably it is a representation of the Jewish captivity.

received from Elam at least as many defeats as he inflicted. Thus, in the year 694 B.C., while his army was plundering in Elam, the Elamites laid waste Northern Babylonia, and took his son Ashur-nadin-shum prisoner. In the west, if we compare him with Tiglath-pileser and Sargon, he distinctly failed, since he was unable to take either Tyre or Jerusalem. He did not win any provinces of importance either in the east toward Media, or in the west in Asia Minor, where his predecessors had made their most valuable conquests. We notice especially the absence of any attempt to face the menacing danger in the north ; the Aryan tribes were spreading more and more widely in the regions of Urartu and the Mannai.

Sennacherib's failures explain his end. He had come to the throne as the candidate of the " Assyrian " military party.
Sennacherib's Reign a Failure and when he lost his army he fell a victim to the opposition, the " Babylonian " party. There must, however, have been separate sections within the latter. Its real and natural leader was obviously Esarhaddon, who administered Babylon. But one of his brothers must have attempted to forestall him in Assyria ; and he was probably the leader of the rebellion in which Sennacherib was murdered " as he was worshipping in the temple of his god," according to the Biblical account.

Esarhaddon turned against him and defeated the army of the insurgents in Melitene, to which country it had retreated, relying on the help of Armenia, the deadly enemy of Assyria. Esarhaddon thus became king of Assyria and Babylonia.

We know that he pursued a home policy quite opposed to that of his father ; the
Esarhaddon a Civilised King most lasting work of his reign was the rebuilding of Babylon. The effects of this policy were such as they could not fail to be ; the civilisation of Babylonia and Mesopotamia once more flourished, and the supremacy over Nearer Asia was secured. It proved to be a momentous change for Assyria, which was the ruling power of the period. In other respects Esarhaddon is one of the figures in Assyrian history which harmonise most with modern conceptions. We read less frequently of cruel punishments inflicted on rebels. And, above all, at his court a taste for literary activity must have prevailed, which was certainly connected with his preference for Babylon. Ashurbanipal boasts of the literary education which was given him, and to it we are indebted for the collection of his celebrated library.

The Assyrian empire under Esarhaddon, as under Sennacherib and even later, obtained no considerable additions apart from the valueless conquest of Egypt.

1677

SENNACHERIB, AN ASSYRIAN KING WHOSE REIGN WAS A FAILURE

Sennacherib was put on the throne by the military party in Assyrian politics, but his wars were everywhere failures, and he was murdered in a rebellion of the pro-Babylonian party, headed by his own son, Esarhaddon. He is here shown in a bas-relief, now in the British Museum, on his throne before the Jewish city of Lachish.

Esarhaddon's wars were, on the whole, merely directed to the maintenance and complete protection of the territory already subjugated. There were attempts at revolt by the Chaldæans in Babylonia during his reign, but matters stopped short at revolts, and did not go so far as the setting up of a rival prince. In the " Country of the Sea " a grandson of Merodach-baladan, Nabu-zer-napishti-ushteshir, made an attempt to seize Southern Babylonia and advanced to Ur, but he was forced on the approach of an Assyrian army to fly to Elam. There, however, contrary to the old tradition, he found no asylum, and was murdered. His brother Naid-Marduk considered it, therefore, more prudent to leave this place of refuge and walk into the very jaws of the lion ; he was pardoned by Esarhaddon and installed as ruler in the " Country of the Sea."

The affairs in connection with Bit-Dakuri serve to illustrate the conditions which the destruction of Babylon had produced, and to characterise the Chaldæans generally. We have already described how on Sennacherib's departure certain Aramæan tribes had descended

upon the district of Babylon and Borsippa ; and how they had been defeated and driven off by Erba-Marduk, who, in return for his services, was recognised as king of Babylon. The Chaldæans appear to have been more successful than the Aramæans, and to have established themselves firmly in the province of Babylon, and the adjoining territory of Borsippa. The restoration of Babylon necessitated the recovery of what had been unlawfully appropriated, and this could not be done without force. Their " king," Shamash-ibni, was deposed in favour of Nabu-ushallim, a member of a different family. In the negotiations which subsequently took place under Shamash-shum-ukin as to the conditions of the tenure and the rights of some villages situated in the district of Bit-Dakuri, the latter came forward as superior lord. The district of Babylon and Borsippa was evidently retaken from the Chaldæans.

Khumbakhaldash of Elam, as we have already seen, had not received the fugitive grandson of Merodach-baladan. Nevertheless, in the year 674 he raided Northern Babylonia as far as Sippar, which consequently suffered great loss. Esarhaddon was no better able than Sargon or Senna-cherib to seek out this dangerous enemy in his own inaccessible country. He was content to secure the loyalty of the tribe of the Gambuli, settled on the Elamite frontier near the mouth of the Tigris, and to entrust their chief, in his fortress of Shapi-Bel, which was strengthened for the purpose, with the protection of the fron-tiers ; a policy adopted at all times by Oriental states. Esarhaddon established friendly relations with Urtaki, the brother and successor of Khumbakhaldash. Urtaki sent back the images which had been carried off from Sippar in the preceding year, even obtaining assistance from

still bore the name of Sidon—and became the seat of an Assyrian governor. Sidon then remained a province, and did not again have kings of its own until the Persian era ; the town of Esarhaddon became the nucleus of the later Sidon. Sanduarri of Kundi—perhaps Kyinda, the old name of the fortress of the later Anchiale—and Sizu, a Cilician prince, had been allied with Abd-milkot. After a three years' resistance his castles fell into the hands of the Assyrians, and Sanduarri's head was brought to Nineveh almost at the same time as that of Abd-milkot.

Tyre offered a more obstinate resistance. The " island " of Sidon must have been

NORTH-EASTERN FACADE AND GRAND ENTRANCE TO SENNACHERIB'S PALACE

It was the ambition of every Assyrian monarch to build himself a new palace, exceeding in grandeur and splendour those of his predecessors. The above is a restoration, by Sir A. H. Layard, of Sennacherib's great palace.

Esarhaddon on the occasion of a famine in Elam, and this worked for peace.

In the west, Tyre, after 701, persevered in its resistance, and after 694 or so found a supporter in Egypt under the Ethiopian king, Tirhakah, who was eager for victory. Sidon also, which had been severed from Tyre by Sennacherib, now revolted in 678 under the new king, Abd-milkot, or Abdi-milkutti, the successor of Ithobal. It was captured, and the old town, which, like Tyre and Arvad, lay on an island, together with the national objects of worship, was destroyed. A new town was built on the mainland, which received the name of Kar-Ashur-akhu-iddina, " the Castle of Esarhaddon "—in reality, of course, it

situated close to the mainland. The island of Tyre was more difficult to capture, and was taken for the first time by Alexander by means of his famous mole, which then connected Tyre permanently with the mainland. When Esarhaddon marched against Egypt, he was compelled to at-tempt the capture of Tyre, and besieged it by land, occupying Ushu, which is situated there, and cutting off the inhabi-tants of the island from all access to the land by means of counter-walls. But the island, which was supplied with provisions from the sea, held out until the news came from Egypt of the expulsion of Tirhakah, in 670. King Ba'al then considered further resistance useless, and offered to pay

1679

tribute. His submission was accepted under the usual condition that he retained only what he actually then possessed—that is, he kept nothing but the island city of Tyre itself, while an Assyrian province was constructed out of the territory held by the Assyrians on the mainland.

In this year, 670 B.C., the stele of Senjirli was set up, which shows us Tirhakah and Ba'al as subject kings before Esarhaddon. The representation on it was finished, and the inscription was about to be engraved when Tirhakah suddenly returned to Egypt, and Ba'al, who indeed had hardly anything left to lose, once more revolted. The end of the inscription, in which it had been intended to give an account of Ba'al's submission, was therefore intentionally omitted. When Tirhakah had been driven out for the second time, in 668, and Tyre had been besieged for five years in all, from 673 to 668—the Assyrian blockading lines had practically remained effective throughout the period—then Ba'al once more submitted. Tyre, this time also unconquered, retained its independence, but its authority was restricted to the small island. Its territory on the mainland was not given back, but remained under Assyrian government.

The possession of all the trading towns on the Syrian coast, especially Gaza, the terminus of the caravan route as well as of Edom, through which the route ran, brought Assyria into contact with the Arabian tribes who were engaged in the overland trade. Sennacherib had tried to subjugate the Arabians of the plains, and had undertaken an expedition by which he overthrew the " kingdom " of Aribi which existed there, took the capital, and brought the queen, together with the gods, to Assyria. Esarhaddon now sent these back on receiving assurances of obedience. On the borders of Cilicia and Cappadocia there were constant disturbances. Esarhaddon tells us of an inroad into the district of the Dua in the Taurus, adjoining Tabal. The Assyrian historical inscriptions tell us nothing of the fact that Melid, or Malatia, had been

ESARHADDON Mansell
From the famous stele of Senjirli, showing the kings of Egypt and Tyre subject before Esarhaddon.

conquered by Mukallu, probably the chief of a Tabal or similar tribe, and that the latter, in alliance with Ishkallu of Tabal, had become dangerous to the Assyrian claims. We learn of this fact from questions upon the subject asked of the oracle in the temple of Shamash, the sun-god. We may conclude that the Assyrian possessions in the direction of Asia Minor had grown less.

These same tablets of oracles afford us the best account of the great Aryan movement in the north, in Armenia. The governors of the frontier provinces no longer, as under Sennacherib, report the reverses which Urartu has sustained from the Cimmerians ; they now anxiously inquire of the sun-god whether the threatening enemies, the Cimmerians, Saparda, Ashkuza, or the Medes, who were already devastating adjoining districts, would spare the Assyrian provinces ; they ask if the Assyrian troops will succeed in relieving beleaguered towns or in recovering those already taken. That is quite a different story from Sargon's announcements of victories. And when Esarhaddon tells of victories over Cimmerians and Ashkuza, he cannot report any results gained by them. We may, therefore, conclude that such victories at the best were won only over roving bands, if they did not actually consist in a retreat. On the whole, it is evident that Assyria's power was waning. Negotiations were now begun with the barbarians on a basis of equality. Esarhaddon looked round for allies against the threatening Cimmerians, and found them in their neighbours on the east, the Ashkuza, whose king, Bartatua, actually received a daughter of the king to wife. We shall again meet these Ashkuza as allies of Assyria in its last days.

The expedition to Media, where, after the disappearance of the Namri and Parsua, the Aryan element became increasingly prominent, are of no real importance. It was certainly an easy task for a disciplined Assyrian army to subjugate isolated tribes and bring booty and prisoners home with them. But the expeditions as far as the " Salt Desert " to the south-east of the Caspian Sea and up to the Demavend had no lasting results ; new tribes immediately pressed forward, and where one wave of this flood of nations exhausted itself, others kept rolling on. Here the destiny of the old Oriental civilisation, in spite of the victories claimed in the inscriptions, was inevitably fulfilling itself. Still, no blame can be attached to the Assyrian king if he did not recognise the full extent of the danger and tried to derive new revenues from the conquest of other lands.

Esarhaddon can re-cord one success which had not yet fallen to any Assyrian king : he conquered Egypt. In so doing he certainly took into consideration the necessity of con-quest for Assyria, to provide employment and booty for the mer-cenary army on whose spears the existence of the empire depended. He was further influ-enced by considerations of state policy.

Egypt was as much dependent on Palestine as the countries lying on the Euphrates. If these latter required the ports on the Mediter-ranean, Palestine was for Egypt the nearest and most promising country, if it ever wished to expand. As long, therefore, as we can trace back the

ASHURBANIPAL

Son of Esarhaddon, whom he rebelled against, assuming the crown before his father's death.

history of these countries, Egypt is either in possession of Palestine, or is trying to win it back. It interfered, therefore, in all revolts against Assyria, but usually failed to render the promised help. " The broken reed which pierces the hand of him who leans on it " was the phrase already coined by Isaiah for the false Egyptian promises of assistance. The continual unrest in Palestine made it prudent to prevent the disturber of the peace from doing further damage ; Sen-nacherib had already tried to do this on his last expedition when he lost his army.

Esarhaddon renewed the attempt ; all the more because Egypt had again become united under the Ethiopian Tirhakah, against whom Sennacherib's expedition was directed, and who was a bolder spirit than the last Pharaohs. We have seen that he was implicated in the revolt of Tyre, which broke out in 673. The Baby-lonian chronicle records in this same year a defeat of the Assyrians in Egypt ; the first attempt to attack Tirhakah in his own country had miscarried. In 671, however, a new army advanced against Egypt, and Tirkakah could not withstand it. The Assyrians advanced irresistibly from Iskhupri, where the first battle took place, as far as Memphis in fifteen days. Tirha-kah five times offered resistance, and was him-self wounded in battle ; he then fled to Thebes. Memphis was taken in the advance " in a half day." The family of Tirhakah and rich trea-sures fell there into the hands of the Assyrians ; fifty-five statues of kings were brought to Nineveh. Tirhakah seems to have been unable to remain in Thebes. His army was scattered, and as a foreigner he found no support in Egypt. He thus fled back to "Kush " —that is, Nubia—and evacuated Thebes.

The Assyrian king placed twenty-two " kings," or governors, over the separate dis-tricts of Egypt, who are all enumerated for us by his son Ashur-banipal. But each of them received an Assyrian official as overseer, with a large body of Assyrian officials at his side. The most southern district named is Thebes. This fact shows within what narrow limits the Assyrian sovereignty was recognised. Esarhaddon therefore uses extravagant language when he styles himself after this success, " King of the kings of Musur, or Lower Egypt, Paturisi, or Upper Egypt, and Kush." Even the Senjirli stele, which, like a memorial carved at the mouth of the Nahr el-Kelb, near Beirut, glorifies this victory, expresses rather the wish than the accomplished fact when it represents Tirhakah as a prisoner, a ring through his lips, imploring mercy on his knees before Esarhaddon. This supremacy lasted only a few months, when Tirhakah came once more upon the scene. The Ethiopian

Son Rebels Against Father

was in fact no Egyptian ; and we see that he had " fled " only in order to bring up a new army. Meanwhile Esarhaddon was again in Assyria, where he had to cope with a rebellion, at the bottom of which was his son Ashurbanipal ; Tirhakah had naturally been privy to this. Then an " express messenger " came to Nineveh and announced that Tirhakah had occupied the whole country once more, and was again ruling as king in Memphis, having driven out or crushed the Assyrians who were in the land. The Egyptians must have looked on at this " restoration of settled order " with the calmness with which this people, accustomed for thousands of years to oppression, have acquiesced in their numerous masters before and since.

After the internal affairs in Assyria had been arranged, and Ashurbanipal and his brother Shamash-shum-ukin had been crowned in 668, the army was once more available for Egypt. Esarhaddon himself started thither ; he had become superfluous at home, and was certainly sufficiently acquainted with the nature of an Oriental throne to see that there was little left for him but to die. He actually died on the march in 668. The campaign was therefore brought to an end in the reign of Ashurbanipal, as he himself records.

The causes which had led to the coronation of Ashurbanipal have already been mentioned in their place. When Esarhaddon wished to put the coping-stone to his work, and to have himself or Shamash-shum-ukin, his son by a Babylonian

Displaced by his Sons

woman, proclaimed king in the rebuilt city of Babylon, the time had come for the Assyrian party to take action. In 669 B.C., so the Babylonian chronicle announces, " the king put to death many nobles in Assyria ; " yet Ashurbanipal reports that when he was proclaimed successor to the throne and co-regent at the beginning of 668 he had " interceded " for them. Esarhaddon had clearly intended that Shamash-shum-ukin should

be at once crowned king of Babylon, in order that the power might be secured to him on his own death. This scheme was now frustrated. With Ashurbanipal the Assyrian military and aristocratic party gained the day over the Babylonian priests and citizens. Under Ashurbanipal's long reign, from 668 to 626 B.C., the Assyrian military system, with its army of mercenaries, a strange medley from the lands of every ruler, achieved its final triumphs.

The success of the Egyptian campaign, in the course of which Esarhaddon died, was rapid and complete. The army with which Tirhakah attempted to defend Lower Egypt was defeated near Karbaniti, the Egyptian city of Qarbana ; he abandoned Memphis to its fate and withdrew to Thebes. In " one month and ten days " the Assyrian army advanced thither. Tirhakah, who could not repose any confidence in the population of the capital, preferred to evacuate this town, and entrenched himself higher up stream on both banks of the Nile, obviously in order to bar the passage of the river plain. The Assyrian army did not advance

Temporary Conquest of Egypt

beyond Thebes, and Ashurbanipal, like his father, could impose kings only in the districts up to this point. In the same year, or soon afterwards, Tirhakah died while holding his entrenchments. His successor in Napata was Tanut-Ammon, his sister's son, who at once assumed the aggressive. The Assyrian army must have already left Thebes, and the nephew of Tirhakah had no difficulty in seizing the rest of Egypt. The Assyrian garrison in Memphis alone offered resistance. Tanut-Ammon invested it and took up a strong position at On, or Heliopolis, to the north of it. Once more an express messenger reached Nineveh with the tidings, and the Assyrian army started by forced marches to the relief of the besieged. Tanut-Ammon thereupon abandoned the siege and evacuated the country as far as Thebes, where he tried to hold his own. But the town was captured in 667 or 666, and the Ethiopians were forced to abandon Egypt. Ashurbanipal was able once more to install his provincial princes. But this state of affairs did not last long. The Assyrian supremacy naturally enabled the Egyptian princes to get rid of the Kushites. When that object was attained, they had only to devise a way of ridding themselves of their not less troublesome ally. Within two years

Psammetichus, son of Necho, to whom Ashurbanipal had given the districts of Memphis and Sais, declared himself independent. The Assyrian army was occupied elsewhere, and thus Egyptian diplomacy proved successful in its plan. It had driven the Kushites out of the country with the help of Assyria, and now seized the right moment for robbing their helper of his reward. Ashurbanipal complained of similarly base ingratitude from Gyges of Lydia. The Cimmerians, at the very time of his accession, had made aggressive movements towards Lydia, and had crossed the Halys. Since Assyria had aided the Ashkuza against the Cimmerians, Gyges asked help from Ashurbanipal, whose Cili-

according to Ashurbanipal's account, in answer to his fervent prayer : Gyges failed to ward off a fresh attack of the Cimmerians. He fell in battle, and Lydia was overrun by barbarians. Gyges' son, whose name is not mentioned by Ashurbanipal, but whom Herodotus calls Ardys, offered his submission. But Ashurbanipal still refrained from sending any effective aid ; the Lydians were forced to help themselves. The attack of the Cimmerians did not break up until it reached Cilicia, on the Assyrian frontier, although its defeat hardly seems to have been due to any efforts on the part of Assyria. This all took place in 668 B.C. and the succeeding years.

ASHURBANIPAL DEFEATS TEUMMAN, KING OF ELAM   Mansell
About 660 B.C., the Elamites descended on Babylonia. This resulted in a succession of wars between the Assyrian and Elamite kings, which finally led to the capture of Susa, the capital, and the annihilation of Elam, thus destroying a " buffer state " which could guard Assyria from the advancing Aryan tribes of barbarians.

cian and Cappadocian possessions, as they adjoined Lydian territory, were equally threatened. Ashurbanipal helped him, indeed, by offering prayers to Ashur, which proved so effective that in the end Gyges conquered the dreaded enemy. He sent two chiefs from among the prisoners in chains to Nineveh, where the strange-looking barbarians, " whose language was understood by no interpreter," caused great astonishment. The thankless Lydian thought that by doing this he had shown sufficient gratitude. He sent no more embassies or " presents," and actually supported the revolt of Psammetichus, not by prayers, but by auxiliaries. This outrageous conduct soon met with punishment,

In 668 also, after Tirhakah had evacuated Thebes for the second time, Ba'al of Tyre finally submitted. He was compelled to be content with retaining only his island city. The king of Arvad, Iakinlu, who had certainly reposed hopes in Tirhakah, now paid tribute again and sent his sons as hostages and pages to the Assyrian court. Another expedition against the rebellious Mannai on Lake Urumiya, in which district the Ashkuza, allies to Assyria, were expanding their power, falls within the first years of Ashurbanipal's reign. It is not difficult to imagine the reasons which induced King Akhsheri to suspend payment of tribute. With the Ashkuza in the country, who were still allied with the suzerain, the revenues would be in a sorry condition. But when the Assyrian army advanced, Akhsheri fell a victim to a rebellion, and his son Ualli submitted to the Assyrians.

About the same time there were expeditions against some Median chiefs.

War with Elam Ashurbanipal did not advance in this direction so far as Esarhaddon and Sargon; this region had already been flooded by the great stream of nations.

War with Elam broke out afresh in 660 B.C. or somewhat later; and once more the Elamites were the aggressors. For the last few years, since Esarhaddon's time, there had been peace with Urtaki. Now, having made an agreement with the chiefs of Babylonian tribes, especially those of the Gambuli, he tried to establish himself firmly in Babylonia, and for this purpose despatched an army thither. Ashurbanipal does not appear to have had his army ready; it was only when the Elamites appeared before Babylon itself that he interposed and drove them back over the frontier. He did not venture farther. Assyria thus, after the one attack led by Sennacherib, which was accompanied by such disastrous consequences, always remained on the defensive against Elam. Urtaki died soon after. The complications following on the change of kings led to war with Teumman, who advanced on Northern Babylonia, but was forced to return after reaching Dur-ilu. An Assyrian army now marched for the first time through the passes of the Zagros to Elam and up to the walls of Susa itself. The successes of Kurigalzu and Nebuchadnezzar I. were thus repeated. This war concludes the operations during the first half of Ashurbanipal's reign.

All the succeeding wars of Ashurbanipal are connected with the great rebellion of Shamash-shum-ukin, which broke out **Rebellion of a Brother** openly in 652 B.C. The Assyrian army asserted its superiority in the suppression of it; but the sympathy which Shamash-shum-ukin had found everywhere, the hopes which had been raised by his efforts in every part of the realm, showed at the same time that the empire was held together only by force, and that it would infallibly fall to pieces if the help of its army of mercenaries should be withdrawn. Ashurbanipal did not, indeed, treat Baby-

lon as Sennacherib did, but, as a representative of the "Assyrian" policy, he acted like Tiglath-pileser and Shalmaneser. This is shown very clearly from the fact that he himself, precisely as they did, assumed the crown of Babylon, and reigned there under the name of Kandalanu from 647 to 626 B.C.

Once more Babylon had received from Elam the strongest support during the rebellion. The result of this was a succession of wars, which finally led to the capture of Susa and the complete annihilation of Elam. Assyria, however, which made no effort to retain the conquered territory, gained only one result: she placed the neighbouring country at the mercy of the advancing Aryan tribes. Just as in Urartu, so here she had destroyed the "buffer state" which could guard her from this enemy. The progress of the annihilation itself, during which we see that Elam suffered from continual disturbances, will be better treated in the history of Elam. In Babylonia itself, as **Elam completely Destroyed** was naturally to be expected, the different tribes had been equally won over by Shamash-shum-ukin; the Gambuli and Puqudu, as well as some Chaldæan states, were chastised for it. The overthrow of Merodach-baladan's grandson in the "Country of the Sea" was connected with this campaign, and contributed its share to the complications with Elam.

In Phœnicia, at this time, Ushu, the town on the mainland facing Tyre, and Akko were punished. The "province of Tyre" had, therefore, attempted a rebellion; this seems to have been the only practical result which the appeal of Shamash-shum-ukin effected in the west.

The king of Urartu, Sarduri III., now voluntarily courted the suzerainty of Assyria, and in 644 B.C. sent an embassy to Ashurbanipal; the invasions of the Aryan tribes forced him to take this step. This is the last event which Ashurbanipal himself records of his reign.

We have no records for the last years of Ashurbanipal's reign: this is a rather long gap, ten or fifteen years, perhaps. We may assume generally from his victories that he upheld the prestige of Assyria. The fact that he remained king of Babylon up to his death is also in favour of this assumption. The rapid downfall which followed shows how this prestige was due to one man and his army.

THE LAST KING OF ASSYRIA DIES IN HIS PALACE

Braun, Clement et Cie.

When Nineveh fell, in 607 B.C., its last king, Sin-shar-ishkun, set fire to his palace and perished in the flames. Legend also records this fate for Sardanapalus, the famous Ashurbanipal, and the celebrated picture by the French artist, L. Chalon, from which the above illustration is reproduced, is known as "The Death of Sardanapalus."

Ashurbanipal's renown in the modern world rests rather upon his patronage of literature than upon his victories, which, however, made his name, under the form " Sardanapalus," celebrated even in classical legend. He founded in his palace at Nineveh a library of cuneiform tablets, which contained copies of all the Babylonian literary productions and old inscriptions which his emissaries were able to discover during a prolonged search through the ancient cities and temples of the land. We owe to the remains of this great library, which have now been recovered and are preserved in the British Museum, almost all our knowledge of Babylonian literature and of many valuable documents, of which the originals are lost. Ashurbanipal's victories do not stand alone in Assyria, but he is unique among Assyrian kings in that he found pleasure in obtaining copies of the ancient records and in reading them himself. Without the wealth of tablets which have come down to us from his royal library at Nineveh we should have no conception of the high level of literary achievement to which the Babylonians and Assyrians attained.

Sardanapalus, Patron of Literature

Assyria had at least two kings after Ashurbanipal, Ashur-itil-ilani and Sin-shar-ishkun. Little is known of their reigns. Babylon was lost upon the death of Ashurbanipal, but not the whole of Babylonia, of which some parts were kept until the end. We are not informed how long either of them reigned, nor are we certain that the throne was not occupied by other rulers in addition to them.

We have at present only some slight accounts of the end of the Assyrian empire. The Chaldæan Nabopolassar could no longer support himself on Elam, as his Chaldæan predecessors on the throne of Babylon had done, for Elam existed no longer. But he found instead a more powerful ally in the successor to Elam, the Medes. Assyria, on her side, had, since the time of Esarhaddon, been allied with the Ashkuza, who, as neighbours of the Medes, were their natural foes. In 609 we find Nabopolassar in possession of Mesopotamia. He boasts of his victory over Shubari, using the ancient designation of Mesopotamia. The power of Assyria must thus have been already broken, for soon afterwards we find the Mede Cyaxares in

Last Kings of Assyria

front of Nineveh. An auxiliary army of the Ashkuza, under Madyas, son of the Bartatua who had married Esarhaddon's daughter, advanced, but was defeated by Cyaxares. This sealed the fate of Nineveh, which fell about the year 607. The last king, Sin-shar-ishkun, is said to have set fire to his palace, and to have perished in the flames—the fate which legend records of Sardanapalus. The Median bands attended to the business of plundering and laying waste far more thoroughly than their ally liked ; for not only Nineveh, but all the towns of Assyria, and even those of Babylonia which had remained loyal to Assyria, were ruthlessly sacked. Nineveh never again rose from her ruins ; a fortunate circumstance for us, for, buried beneath the soil, the remains have been preserved for us which otherwise might have served as building materials for a later age.

Nabopolassar looked with very little satisfaction upon the conduct of his allies, for they were, after all, devastating his own lands. But it is noteworthy that the barbarians seem really to have kept their agreement ; they evacuated the conquered country, and observed the treaty by which the Tigris was to be the boundary of their respective provinces. A new condition of things was thus created. Media possessed all the country to the north of the river district of Elam as far as Asia Minor. Babylon kept Babylonia, Mesopotamia — Assyria would have remained Median — Syria, and Palestine, about 605 B.C.

Assyria Disappears from History

Thus the " Assyrian Empire " disappeared from history. We have already suggested more than once why it was impossible for any attempts at revolt to be made. The " empire " was supported merely by an army of mercenaries and a host of officials. It was long since there had been an Assyrian people in the true sense of the term. In the provinces it was a matter of indifference whether the governor extorted money in the name of the king of Ashur or the king of Babylon. The only feeling excited was the wish for a new master, fostered by the vain hope of an amelioration of their lot. The provinces—Syria and Palestine—had long been incapable of action. Only in some isolated places, such as Judah, was any resistance offered, and this naturally could not withstand a large army.

THE FALL OF NINEVEH: THE DISAPPEARANCE OF THE ASSYRIAN EMPIRE FROM HISTORY
Nineveh fell, never to rise again, in 607 B.C., on the attack of the Median hordes under Cyaxares, who sacked ruthlessly not only Nineveh, but all the towns of Assyria.

SPECIMENS OF THE APPLIED ART OF ASSYRIA

In its principal achievements Assyrian art exhibits little foreign influence beyond that of Babylonia. Carved ivories, such as those shown above (1, 2 and 3), have, however, been recovered from the remains of Nineveh which show traces of Egyptian influence. The bronze lion weight (9) is distinctly Phœnician. Other examples on this page are more purely Assyrian. Such are the pottery, glazed (12 and 13) and unglazed (4, 8 and 6), and the painted bricks and tiles from the palace at Kalkhi (7, 10 and 11), which show the surprising antiquity of some of the designs in modern use. The gem of the collection is the bronze plate (5).

ASSYRIAN CHARACTERISTICS

RETROSPECT OF ASSYRO-MESOPOTAMIAN CULTURE

THE region farther up the rivers—namely, Mesopotamia and Assyria—has a distinctly different character from Babylonia with its hot climate. The vicinity of the mountains tempers the heat of the great plains ; and a more ample rainfall, with some snow in winter, **Climate of Assyria** make its climatic conditions similar to those of the warmer countries of Europe. The two great rivers are here far apart, and flow mostly between rocky banks, so that any idea of the construction of canals on the scale of the Babylonian system is out of the question. Smaller streams, especially the Khabur and Belikh in Mesopotamia, intersect the plains and produce wide stretches of corn-land ; between them lie vast steppes which have at all times furnished the nomads with a welcome home, whence they pressed on toward the cultivated land studded with flourishing towns.

Until some considerable discoveries going back to the pre-Assyrian epoch are made on Mesopotamian soil, we must abandon any attempt to settle the peculiar character of Mesopotamian civilisation in its variations from the Babylonian. The necessary information cannot be extracted from the existing records. All that we can ascertain with certainty is the nature and condition of Assyrian rule.

The country on the left bank of the Euphrates above the Lower Zab did not develop an independent civilisation ; it is in every respect an extension of the sphere of Babylonian civilisation. The sovereignty which it exercised towards the end of the period when that **Assyrian Culture is Babylonian** civilisation held a preponderating influence in Western Asia was purely political and won by force. Our first duty is to ascertain the nature of that sovereignty.

We must assume that Assyria at the time of her first expansion in the fourteenth and thirteenth centuries B.C. still possessed an active and vigorous popula-

tion ; this condition presupposes a numerous peasant class. We do not know how that class came into being, but that it had long been in existence is probable since she was able to send out colonies, and this can best be done when a thriving and multiplying peasantry exists. On the other hand, there are indications that the conditions attending the ownership of the soil were no longer satisfactory, that " over-population " was a growing evil; or, more correctly expressed, the distribution of the soil no longer conformed to the conditions necessary for a peaceful and progressive development of the agricultural classes.

The later Assyria of Ashurnasirpal and Shalmaneser II. had a quite different population, influenced in some degree by the Aramæan immigration. It is true that Ashurnasirpal was still able to lead colonies into the reconquered or newly acquired lands. But we may **Extinction of Assyrian People** hardly assume that the colonists were drawn from surplus masses of the people ; they were really parts of a population which had become indigent through faulty economic policy. We have seen that it is only once recorded, and then under special circumstances, that Shalmaneser II. had " summoned the country to arms." The wars of aggrandisement were waged by Assyria with a standing army—that is, with mercenaries. This points to a complete change of the basis of Assyrian power. Henceforth there is no Assyrian nation which expands by conquest, but only an armed predatory state, which, by the use of troops recruited from every country, crushes the nations, and wrings from them the means for keeping them dependent. The Assyrian people, so far as one existed at all, sank into insignificance before the priesthood, which had obtained the supremacy on the one side, and before the monarchy, with its feudal adherents, on the other. We saw in the policy of Tiglath-pileser IV. an attempt to put the state once more upon a broader basis; but the attempt was unsuccessful, and the powerful reaction under Sargon restored the character of Assyria and sealed her fate.

The power of Assyria lay then in its army. This was an army of mercenaries, **Assyria's Army of Mercenaries** composed of heterogeneous elements, which the king was obliged to support and to provide with pay. The maintenance of the army furnished a motive for incessant expeditions of conquest and plunder. Such an army clamoured for employment and booty, and experience showed that in the East there were no means to support it unless they were wrung from conquered lands. The country was mostly in the possession of the temple-lords and feudal owners; even the larger towns enjoyed freedom from taxation, and the insignificant and oppressed peasant class was naturally unable to furnish the required supplies. Thus a perpetual incentive to new military expeditions was given by the very basis of the constitution. This in itself would have forced Assyria forward on the path of conquest, even if richer or weaker neighbours had offered no tempting prey.

Ashurnasirpal's reign and the beginning of the age of Shalmaneser II. saw the overthrow of the newly formed Aramæan state of Mesopotamia. This ancient sphere of civilisation was thus mainly brought under Assyrian government, and became an essential part of the empire. The Aramæan population, so far as it consisted of the priesthood and feudal lords, was put on an equality with the Assyrian. Assyria, therefore, in the widest sense, comprised the countries extending up to the Euphrates as its western boundary. The perfecting of the system of government was the chief work of the second period of Assyrian history. **Constitution of the Empire** The result thus obtained lasted until the overthrow of the empire and the destruction of its constitution.

The advance beyond the Euphrates marked a new stage of development, which had already begun under Shalmaneser II. and his successors, but did not lead to permanent results until the rise of the new Assyrian empire after Tiglath-pileser IV. Under this latter king, the greater number of the countries

west of the Euphrates for the first time lost their own government and were constituted Assyrian provinces. But no definite successes were attained here; for the new provinces consisted of states which, in spite of everything they owed to the common mother civilisation, possessed a peculiar population and culture of their own. They were thus never assimilated by Assyria. Here also the other sphere of civilisation, that of Asia Minor, exercised its influence and raised a wall of partition, which, in spite of arbitrary political arrangements, was never entirely thrown down, between the civilisations on the right and left banks of the Euphrates.

The policy of the Assyrians toward subject states was that which similar powers—the most recent example in the world's history is the Turkish Empire—have always adopted. The ceaseless unrest caused in the civilised country by nomads eager for booty and land made it necessary to reduce them to some form of subjection in order to be protected from their inroads. The first stage of this sub-**Assyria's Turkish Policy** mission was the duty of paying tribute, since a complete subjugation and the institution of a local government were impossible with such tribes. A similar policy would then be adopted toward neighbouring civilised states. The king is called upon to pay tribute; if he consents to pay it, he retains, as the vassal of Assyria, the absolutely free administration of his own land. Besides the payment of tribute, he is also bound to furnish troops. His suzerain does not as yet interfere with the internal government of his country.

This, indeed, especially in cases where the taxes imposed were considerable and the land incapable of paying them, often meant little more than that the prince filled the office of an Assyrian tax-collector, on whom the responsibility for the punctual payment of the imposts rested. The great king did not consider himself in any way bound to render it possible for the vassal to perform his obligations by guaranteeing him complete protection against enemies. If the vassal, through the offers or the oppression of a neighbouring state, allowed himself to be seduced from his allegiance to Assyria, and accepted the suzerainty of the new oppressor, then an Assyrian army appeared in order to call to account the "rebel," who had probably submitted only to compulsion. The vassal princes therefore usually stood between two or three fires. They were responsible to the great king; on the other hand, the people, who had to supply the taxes, were discontented. Thus parties were formed, each of which sought the advancement of its respective interests in an adhesion to Assyria or another great power. We have contemporary testimony to the existence of such parties in the utterances of the Israelitish prophets. We see how at the time of Amos the question stands in Israel and Judah: adhesion to Assyria, such as Ahaz represents, or to Damascus and Egypt against which Amos utters warning. After the fall of Damascus Hosea knows only of Assyria and Egypt, just as Isaiah does; and again after the appearance of Tirhakah, an Egyptian party continues to oppose the Assyrian. The king stands between the two, usually in a very precarious position, since he can save himself only by joining the stronger power. We can thus trace Hezekiah's vacillation, and recognise from the activity of Jeremiah the pitiful position of the last kings of Judah, who, faced by the choice between Nebuchadnezzar and the Pharaohs, are in the end overtaken by their destiny.

It is in the nature of things that such relations, which merely imposed burdensome obligations upon the vassal, were broken off so soon as any favourable prospect of revolt presented itself—that is, if there was no immediate fear of an invasion by the Assyrian army.

Hard Case of the Vassal But if the army appeared, the fate of the rebellious state was virtually sealed, owing to the military superiority of the Assyrians.

If a state had been completely conquered by force of arms, it was confiscated; it lost its independence, and became an Assyrian province. So long as this process was applied to the districts of Mesopo-

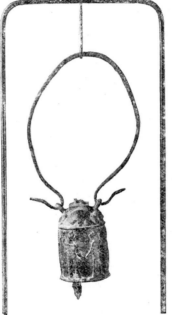

AN ASSYRIAN BELL
From the Royal Museum of Berlin.

tamia, it caused, as we have seen, little difficulty, owing to the affinity of the population and the homogeneousness of the country. But when an advance was made into countries of different character, it was found impossible to force an Assyrian

Reason of the Captivities government on a foreign population, which had shown the vitality of its peculiar customs and institutions by recent rebellion. Such a course would have been tantamount to abandoning the handful of Assyrian officials to certain death on the next recrudescence of discontent. And a deportation of the majority of the population as slaves would have destroyed in great measure the productivity of the new province.

After the time of Tiglathpileser IV., when Assyria itself could supply no more colonists, an attempt was made to remedy these difficulties by transplanting the population, and interchanging the inhabitants of newly-conquered provinces lying at opposite ends of the empire. The Bible has made us familiar with the carrying away of the population of Samaria to Mesopotamia and Media, with that of the Jews to Babylonia, and with the replenishment of the population of Samaria by inhabitants of Babylonian towns under Ashurbanipal after the overthrow of Shamash-shum-ukin. Such exchanges and resettlements are mentioned as matters of course in the inscriptions of Tiglath-pileser and Sargon. The districts were not only re-populated in this way, but the new settlers were naturally less able to trouble the Assyrian government. Torn from their native soil, themselves made up of different elements, and not yet blended with the remnants of the old population with whom they had no affinity, the new settlers found no firm support except in the Assyrian officials. The tribal organisation and class system which had bound them together in their home, and had enabled them to resist the oppression of the powers, was thus dissolved, and they were rendered incapable of offering opposition to the new authorities.

Thus an administration, really capable of civilising and developing, would certainly have found in these products of the two great organisers of Assyria ample material from which a new population might have been formed, whose interests would have been inseparably connected with the continuance of the Assyrian empire.

Short-sighted Foreign Policy

But the administrative arts of a predatory state, based on militarism and a wealthy priesthood, are not adapted to the production of lasting works of civilisation. Assyria wished only to derive advantage from the new provinces, and could give them nothing in return. The ultimate object of Assyrian administration was the enrichment of the government officials, from the lowest tax-collector to the governor himself; each paid tribute to his superior; the governor finally had to pay it to the court. What a province " received," if anything at all, bore no proportion to that which was taken from it. The inevitable end of this was widespread destitution and desolation. When the mother country, as a result of an unwise distribution of the ownership of the soil, had no more vitality, but lived on the impoverishment of its subject states, the transference of its own system of administration to them could have only the same consequences.

If Assyria granted to her vassal states no compensatory advantages for the burdens imposed upon them, she conceived her obligations towards her newly-acquired provinces in an equally short-sighted spirit. The governor, or *shaknu*, who ruled a province was much the same as the former prince of the country, only the administration, which had formerly been in the hands of fellow-countrymen of the subject people, was now in the hands of Assyrian officials.

Rule of the Provinces

The material position of the people was not essentially affected by this change. We need not assume that the Assyrian lords extorted more from their subjects than the former native princes ; at least, that was hardly possible where the greater civilised states were concerned. The governor, who had taken the place of the feudal prince, assumed his entire rights and responsibilities. His administration offered more

security to the great king's interests, because he, in a land which was still strange to him, had to rely on the support which Assyria gave him ; whereas the native prince, on the other hand, was adverse from Assyria, both from tradition and from national feeling. In other respects the position was unchanged. The *shaknu* was obliged to meet the requirements of his province out of its revenues, and to fulfil his obligations toward the court. He had to furnish for campaigns a detachment of troops, which he was compelled to keep out of the resources of his province ; but for the security of his own territory, unless its loss seriously threatened the empire, he had, out of his own personal resources, to provide money and men. The king had his own army, " the royal army," for the support of which he was responsible, and he was therefore at pains to let this duty devolve, if possible, upon his officials ; the governor also had his own troops, whose duty it was to guard the safety of his province, and to furnish a contingent for the royal army in the event of war. The position of the governor was therefore very independent.

Independence of the Governors

He was an imperial officer, and at the same time a reigning prince. It is obvious that he must have had many temptations to push his fortunes elsewhere than in Assyria by joining a new conqueror, or by declaring his own independence in the time of her defeat, for there was no organic tie between empire and province.

If, therefore, the Assyrian " Empire," which had no united population, and by its administration promoted in no degree the cohesion of its separate divisions, disappeared after the fall of Nineveh without leaving a trace, and without inspiring an attempt at its reconstruction, we can feel no surprise. All that held it together was an army of mercenaries and an official class ; when these were destroyed the empire also perished. We can easily comprehend that no one came forward to revive the two institutions. which had served only to impoverish the subject classes of the population.

Assyria subdued the Nearer East with an army of mercenaries, and there was necessarily little selection of recruits ; any were taken who could be found. We may assume without further remark that the adjoining barbarian countries furnished

ASHURBANIPAL FEASTING WITH HIS QUEEN IN A GARDEN BOWER

Mansell

Assyrian monuments do not display the pleasure felt by the Egyptians in scenes from domestic life, and this bas-relief showing the monarch feasting with his consort is an exception. It is an example of the skill of the latest period.

the supply of men in the first instance, just as the Germanic tribes did for later Rome, the Normans and English for Byzantium, etc. When a state was conquered, the king as a rule drafted part of the conquered army into his troops.

Among the various sections of the army the war-chariot was the heaviest, the most dreaded, and the most honourable engine of war; the king in battle is always represented in a war-chariot. It is familiar from sculptured representations, in which it appears drawn by two horses, and holding a driver and a fighting man [see page 1652]. It is still uncertain where this method of fighting had its origin. We know little as yet as to the military system in Babylonia during the earliest period, except what the "Stele of the Vultures" teaches us; this seems to show that in the time of the kings of Lagash a closed phalanx with shield and lance formed the chief method of attack. This subject is closely connected with the question as to the time when men became familiar with the horse and where its original home was. In the Babylonia of 3000 B.C. there is no discovered trace of it; the chariot of Eannatum was doubtless drawn by asses. In the Kassite period horses and war-chariots played a prominent part, as in contemporary Egypt. Had they been

introduced by the "Canaanitic" immigration, or from the north through "Hittite" and similar conquests? At any rate, the Greek epic teaches us that in Asia Minor, at a time which corresponds approximately to the last period of the Assyrian empire, war-chariots were in general use.

The cavalry was unimportant in comparison. The nobles drove to battle in their war-chariots, but the cavalry, never very numerous, seem, at the time with which we are more intimately acquainted, to have been a disparaged arm of the service; they were apparently used only for skirmishes and pursuit. Riding without proper saddle and without stirrups prevented their development into an effective body of troops. The chief strength of the army lay in the heavily armed battalions, who carried lances and short swords, and were protected by shields, armour, and helmets. The archers stood by their side as the light-armed troops [see illustrations on pages 1648 and 1650].

The siege methods were developed proportionately to the numerous wars. Ordinary fortifications did not as a rule long resist the Assyrian attack. A mound —the Roman "agger"—was built up to the walls of the town, on which heavy battering-rams could be brought into position, and brick buildings could not long resist their shock. This device failed against stronger masonry. Damascus, with its walls of stone, defied Shalmaneser II., and we do not yet know whether Tiglath-pileser took it by storm. At the siege of Tyre, which Alexander was the first to capture, an attempt was made to **Ancient** isolate the town by constructing **Siege** an earthwork; but no result **Methods** was accomplished, owing to want of a sufficient naval force. The arming of the troops was naturally the concern of the person who retained them—namely, the king or governor. The building of a palace, which was the consummation of an Assyrian reign, included the erection of an arsenal, which must be stocked with weapons. The maintenance of the army does not seem to have been provided for by a payment in money raised by a definite tax, or out of the total revenues of the king; traces of the nature of its origin may still be detected in the inscriptions.

Originally the duty to bear arms depended on possession of of real property. This duty may have still applied to the noble vassal, but it had been replaced, after the decay of the peasant class, and owing to its inability to perform military duties, by a tax, or military impost, which the small owner had to pay instead of tendering his services. This was assigned to the mercenaries, and, indeed, an attempt has been made to prove that the individual mercenary was assigned a peasant who had to pay him his taxes. The king, when he could not provide sufficiently for the army, tried to place the burden of supporting bodies of troops on high officials, who, naturally, were unwilling to pay the king's troops in addition to their own; thus there were abundant occasions for conflicts and disturbances to **Payment** arise. Even in the period of **of the** prosperity indications can be **Mercenaries** found which show on a small scale the result which had inevitably to follow when once Ashur, which was closely surrounded and limited in its natural resources, had no longer any provinces to impoverish and plunder.

The most complete and productive excavations up to the present time have been carried out in Assyria, and we are

therefore better informed on many subjects there than in Babylonia. The first place may be given to our knowledge of architecture and sculpture, of which important examples have been discovered in the palaces of Nimrud, or Kalkhi, and Kuyunjik, or Nineveh. These familiarise us with the art of the builders and sculptors of the ninth century B.C., with Ashurnasirpal in Kalkhi, and of those of the eighth century—Tiglath-pileser IV. in Kalkhi, Sargon in Dur-Sharrukin, Sennacherib and Ashurbanipal in Nineveh, Esarhaddon in Kalkhi. The recent excavations at Shergat, the site of Ashur, the earliest Assyrian capital, have also furnished information concerning the ground plans and construction of private

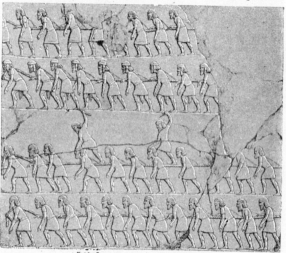

ASSYRIAN SLAVE LABOUR
A continuation of the bas-relief on the opposite page.

and royal buildings, temples, fortifications and river-side quays, built for the most part in the earlier period.

It is a constantly recurring phenomenon in the East that a powerful and wealthy monarch finds a satisfaction to his pride in the erection of colossal buildings, and above all in rearing a palace destined for his own use and enjoyment. This ambition is no doubt dictated in the main by the desire for a splendid abode which may outwardly express his grandeur. Political reasons also combine to influence the change of the royal residences; and, finally, the king may wish to have a worthy place of sepulchre for himself and his family, for it was necessary to remain after death beneath the protection of the household gods if the shade of the dead man was not to wander about restless and homeless. With very few exceptions, the monuments of Assyrian art which have come down to us belong to the later historical periods. But, even so, its Babylonian origin is unmistakable; the material of the vast buildings is the same brick which ancient Babylonia employed. Assyria, too, was unacquainted with blocks and columns of stone, although the vicinity of the mountains would have furnished ample materials for them. The Assyrians built with clay bricks after the Babylonian model, and employed as supports cedar trunks fetched from the Amanus and Lebanon. The country was more favourably situated as regards stone for sculpture than Babylonia, where Gudea was obliged

the colossal bulls of Assyria, and were believed to guard the buildings on the walls of which they were set up.

The ample store of material which was available for facing the brick walls, and the ease with which the soft alabaster could be worked, gave Assyrian buildings their peculiar characteristics. While we have to imagine to ourselves in Babylonia the walls of a temple or palace covered with a plain lime-wash, or, at best, decorated with enamelled tiles, here the walls of the palace are covered by slabs of alabaster, bearing inscriptions and sculptured representations of the achievements of its founder. One or two rows of bas-reliefs and the commemorative inscriptions of the king in question usually

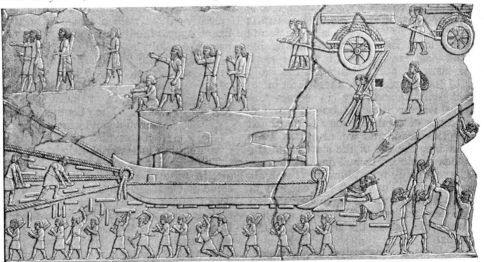

HOW THE COLOSSAL BULLS WERE MOVED GREAT DISTANCES
One of the few bas-reliefs giving an insight into the employment of slaves in building operations. A huge stone figure is being dragged by gangs of slaves, others carrying slips of wood for the sledge to slide on.

to obtain the slabs for his statues from Sinai and Palestine. The mountains to the north of Nineveh supplied alabaster and limestone with which the brick buildings could be faced, and the colossal figure of Arban shows that a pre-Assyrian age was acquainted with the gigantic bulls which guarded the palace doors and city gates. Babylonia has not yet furnished such products of art, for stone was not available for their construction. But the recent excavations at Babylon have proved that brick was employed there for the construction of reliefs on a large scale. In many cases the representations are formed of coloured tiles, and the dragons and other monsters thus depicted undoubtedly served the same purpose as

run round the walls. These inscriptions form one of the chief sources of our information for the history of certain periods. The sculptures are, as yet, the only available commentary on the bare record, and they furnish us with details which cannot be gathered from the inscriptions themselves.

These monuments do not show the pleasure felt by the Egyptian in scenes from domestic life—it must be admitted that we have not any sculptured tombs or decorated buildings of non-royal personages; the sculptures as yet recovered represent only incidents worthy of a king of Ashur. Nine-tenths of them are devoted to the glories of campaigns or hunting expeditions, and the rest to the buildings of the king, for a king of Ashur was interested in little else. It was only the highly developed skill of the latest period under Ashurbanipal which attempted anything of a different character; but pictures like that of the monarch feasting with his consort are exceptions in the long series of battle scenes. There we see the king driving out in his war-chariot, the camp life, the battle, the pursuit of the enemy, the capture of towns. The splendid exploits of the king in building are also duly commemorated. We see how the terraces on which the palaces stand were raised by the employment of enormous numbers of men, how the colossal stone figures, in crates, drawn by ropes, were moved upon rollers by means of levers, and were thus transported from the rafts upon the Tigris to the palace platform; but we learn little of the domestic life of the Assyrians. We do at the same time learn isolated details of the daily life of the people, but these are introduced only incidentally in scenes depicting war or building operations. A few scenes of camp life may be reckoned under this head, and we also gain some insight into the life of the slaves and the methods employed in building operations. We have already noted how great weights were moved. The earth is carried in baskets on the backs of long rows of slaves; an overseer walks here and there and lets his whip fall across the shoulders of the laggards.

The Latest Art Period

Art shows a progressive development, especially in the execution of details. It is possible to trace accurately the progress from the sculptures in the palace of Ashurnasirpal to those of the New Assyrian Empire. While the former still exhibit figures that are comparatively stiff and notably fail to represent large masses of men in battle, a far greater freedom and variety in conception and execution is traceable in the latter. The scenes from the wars of Ashurbanipal show the climax of Assyrian skill. This royal Assyrian art—we know nothing of any other—grows in exact proportion to the power and the wealth which was acquired. We cannot decide whether art was practised by wider sections of the native population, and whether this latter had any large share in the development already noted. If mercenaries fought the Assyrian battles

Development of Assyrian Art

and Phœnician shipwrights built their fleet, artists and sculptors were also probably collected from every country. Carved ivories and examples of metalwork have, indeed, been recovered upon Assyrian sites which show unmistakable traces of Egyptian and Phœnician influence. But in its principal achievements Assyrian art exhibits little foreign influence, except in so far as it was a development of the earlier art of Babylonia. A comparison of Assyrian art with that of the early Babylonians and Sumerians proves that it made no advance upon the high level of excellence attained by these earlier peoples. The stele of Naram-Sin, for example, is unrivalled by any artistic product of the later periods. The first vague efforts to attain an ideal of beauty were abandoned in favour of a stereotyped art, which aimed only at an exact copy of outward forms. We may more certainly regard it as a result of Semitic art, since the same spirit is evident in all we know of Semitic life. It is the complete want of the imagination which dreams of a more beautiful world. The Semite has remained a child whose imagination sees bliss in the limitless accumulation of material delights.

Superiority of Babylon's Art

The reason why the Assyro-Babylonian art, in spite of all delicacy of technique, could not advance to an idealisation has been thought to lie in the fact that it never took as its subject the nude human figure. In the first place, that is not quite correct; we actually possess small Babylonian statuettes of Ishtar, or Venus, and the torso of a large female statue from the time of the Assyrian king, Ashur-bel-kala. It is true, on the other hand, that the Semitic spirit regards the nude human form as something mean. That again is a practical proof of an undeveloped and childish spirit, to which the Semite, even in theory, has never risen superior. The glory of this world finds outward expression in trappings of costly stuffs; therefore he represents his ideal of beauty by infinitely delicate reproduction of costly apparel [see page 269]. In this way we may explain the decline which characterises Assyrian art when compared to the products of the earlier periods in Babylonia. Moreover, the genius of Assyria exhibited itself in war and in political administration rather than in art. In the latter realm she learnt from Babylon, and she did not improve upon her teacher.

THE EMPIRE OF THE ELAMITES

THROUGHOUT the whole of Babylonian history we have been able to trace a struggle with Elam, the neighbouring state on the east, which has often led to the dominion of the Elamites over Babylonia, and temporarily even to the subjugation of wider districts, until the power of Elam was finally broken by Ashurbanipal. But just as Babylonia, which had become Chaldæan, finally triumphed again over Assyria, so Elam in the end became the seat of the power which ruled the whole Nearer East; but then it was no longer Elamite, but had been conquered by the Aryan Persians. As Nebuchadnezzar once again restored the old sphere of Babylonian power, at least towards the west, so Elam under the Persians became the seat of sovereignty for all the countries which had once been subject to the most successful Elamite conquerors, and for a still wider circle.

The real Elam is the region, with Susa for its centre, which in the north is separated from Media by the chain of **The Seat of Persian Power** the Zagros, and is watered by the Kerkha and the Karun. In the south the Persian Gulf forms the natural boundary; in antiquity it extended far more to the north-east than it does at present, and into it the Euphrates, Tigris, and Karun flowed by separate channels. The head of the gulf has been filled up by the alluvial deposit carried down by the rivers, and it now forms the marshy country on the edge of which Basra lies. It was called by the Assyrians Nâr-marrati, "the bitter water." On its northern shore lay Dur-Iakin, the capital of Merodach-baladan, the prince of the "Country of the Sea," which surrounded the shores of the gulf, and, from its perpetual contact with Elam, has already frequently occupied our attention. In the direction of Babylonia, the further natural boundary is the mountain range on the Median borders which **Boundaries of Ancient Elam** shuts off the river valley, the Jebel Hamrin, with its eastern spurs. Toward the east we cannot fix a frontier for the pre-Persian Elam, with which we are now concerned, as the newly discovered inscriptions from Susa do not throw much light upon the expansion of Elam on the east, while from those of Babylonia and Assyria we can, in the nature of things, obtain information only as to her relations with the west.

The district of Susiana stretched in Persian times almost up to the Shapur; a line drawn thence in a northerly direction to the Zagros represents, roughly, the extent of this Persian province. This may, perhaps, have been regarded by the Elamite kings also as their peculiar territory. But precisely as Babylonia considered the country of Mesopotamia to belong to it, so the district which was most closely connected with Elam extended still further; for, even in the seaport of Bushire, Elamite kings raised buildings, and inscriptions by them have been found. We may reasonably assume that kings whose armies had perhaps penetrated as far as the Mediterranean Sea would not have stopped at the frontiers of their native land in an easterly direction; Elamite armies, in times when the empire flourished, may have traversed countries which on this side correspond to the extent of the later Persian empire.

The position of Elam in relation to the sphere of Babylonian civilisation is thus decided from the first. As the first firmly organised state against which the influx of nations pressing westward from the great steppes of Central and Eastern Asia must have struck, it was for the civilised region of the Euphrates the **Elam the Buffer State** "buffer state" which warded off the barbarians from it, or, if conquered itself, it received them and civilised them first before they extended their conquests further to the west. We may, perhaps, discover some traces of this last rôle in the different Elamite conquests.

Down to the year 1898 the only Elamite inscriptions that had been recovered were the bricks of some kings of Susa, and a few scarcely more important inscriptions on stone, also from Susa, which Loftus discovered, some bricks with similar inscriptions from Bushire, excavated by F. C. Andreas, and two longer royal

long series of inscriptions of the native kings and princes. They have, moreover, resulted in finds of the first importance with regard to the history and development of Elamite art. The inscriptions confirm what we must deduce from the course of history—that we meet in Elam a civilisation developed under Babylonian influence, and borrowed from Babylonia, which, however, for its part had impressed its character to a large extent on what it borrowed. The native inscriptions are written in a character modelled on the Babylonian, and, what is more significant, they are composed in the Elamite language. This language, into the structure of which we thus gain an insight, is not closely allied to any of those otherwise known to us, if we except the language of the second column of the inscriptions of the Achæmenidæ. The capital of the country

THE PLAIN OF SUSA AND THE MOUNTAINS OF ELAM
A view from the great tumulus of Susa. The mosque in the centre is said to be the tomb of the prophet Daniel

inscriptions which were found by Layard at Mal-Amir and Kul Fira'un in the Zagros on the upper course of the Karun. Loftus, and more recently Dieulafoy, had excavated at Susa, the extensive works of the latter having mainly brought Persian remains to light. But in the winter of 1897–98 those French excavations at Susa, under the direction of De Morgan, were begun which have resulted in the recovery of a series of unique monuments throwing a flood of light upon the history of Elam and the position which she occupied among the early races of the Nearer East.

It is true that the most valuable of the finds made by the French mission consist of Babylonian monuments which had been carried off to Susa as spoil. But, apart from these foreign importations, the diggings have yielded a

was at all times, so far as we can see, Susa, or Shushan, which is to be regarded as the centre of Elam, properly so called, the heart of the empire. Here was the sanctuary of Shushinak, the national god of Susa, and the city must have been the common centre for the different provinces and tribes. The kings of Elam resided in Susa, which was, therefore, for the empire in question, what Ashur and Nineveh had been for the Assyrian empire. Elam, **Susa the Heart of the Empire** too, must have owed its rise as a state to the subjugation of many towns and tribes, one of which, the Hapirti, was governed by separate kings. The numerous cities, called by the Assyrians "royal cities," are difficult to locate. For information as to these, and as to the political division of Elam, we are indebted to the accounts by Ashurbanipal of his own wars. We can distinguish three or four parts of Elam with their chief towns : Madaktu in the west, then Susa in the district of Bara'she ; further on, Bubilu in the east, and finally, adjoining the Persian Gulf, in a northern situation in the Zagros, Khidalu, which is expressly described as a mountain province. The general Semitic name for the whole country was Elam ; while Anshan, or Anzan, was the general native name for the greater part of it.

The language in which the native inscriptions are composed was probably much the same as that spoken by the first Elamite conquerors of Babylonia ; for the names which they contain are the same, and belong to the same language, as those of the first conquerors, and of the last kings of Elam. This proves that

classify its language under a larger group. The relation of Elamite to Kassite still remains undecided, in view of the fact that only a few words of the latter have as yet been recovered. On the whole, distant affinities are possible, and, in fact, may be assumed. A large **Elamite** number of clay tablets have **Cuneiform** recently been discovered at **Writing** Susa. They are inscribed in what we may term the proto-Elamite writing, in all probability a pre-Semitic system; most of the signs and characters impressed upon them are very different from those of the Sumerians and early Babylonian Semites. Although these texts cannot be fully deciphered at present, it is certain that they contain lists of figures and accounts. Some of the ideographs, such as that for

THE MOUND THAT COVERS THE REMAINS OF THE CAPITAL OF ELAM
This view, looking towards the tumulus, is taken from a point exactly opposite to that shown on page 1698.

the " Elamites " have been of as great importance in the history of the state of Elam as the Semitic Babylonians in that of Babylonia. Obviously, in the period of two thousand years for which these names are authenticated, Elam, not less than Babylonia, had been inundated by other peoples of various ethnic affinities. The fact that, notwithstanding this, the language was preserved points to the same conclusion as the corresponding phenomenon in Babylonia. It was **Original** this people which imprinted its **Language** own intellectual stamp on a **Preserved** previously existing civilisation, and, under the influence of Babylon, created the Elamite civilisation and the organisation of a great state, which afterwards became dangerous to Babylon itself.

We have a difficult task to find the ethnic affinity of this people, and to

" tablet," with which many of the texts begin, resemble those of Babylonia, but the majority are entirely different and are developed upon a system of their own. We have, in fact, in these lately discovered tablets a new class of cuneiform in an early stage of its development when the pictorial origin and hieroglyphic character of the signs can still be recognised.

On the Semitic invasion of Elam in the third millennium B.C., it is probable that this proto-Elamite system of writing was the one generally employed throughout the country. But the invaders brought with them the system which they themselves had adopted from the Sumerians, and in the subsequent period we have the strange spectacle of native Elamite princes employing the Semitic character and language for their own inscriptions. The native proto-Elamite character indeed continued to be employed for the common purposes of life, and we even possess an inscription of the age of Karibu-sha-shushinak written in Semitic Babylonian, to which an addition has been made in proto-Elamite. In course of time a modification of the Babylonian system was adopted by the Elamites for writing their own language phonctically, but for a considerable period Semitic Babylonian was largely employed. This fact, which is amply proved by recent finds at Susa, is a striking proof of the intercourse which took place at this early period between Elam and the Mesopotamian plain. There was only one road by which communication could be made between Babylonia and Elam, since the region round the head of the Persian Gulf was entirely impassable owing to the swamps caused by the water from the rivers—namely, through the passes of the mountain chain of Media and Elam, which led to the plain of Northern Babylonia. We have noticed that Dur-ilu was the town where the Elamites entered Babylonian territory, and that Northern Babylonia was the first object of their invasions. Of large towns at a greater distance, Nippur usually was exposed to their attack, and Uruk, or Erech, if they penetrated farther toward the south.

Intercourse with Mesopotamia

Erech, known at the period of the early city-states as the seat of a separate kingdom, was the centre of a particular sovereignty certainly down to the times of the "kingdom of Sumer and Akkad"; for we have inscriptions of "kings of Uruk" who belong approximately to the same period as the dynasties of Isin and Larsa. Later hymns tell of great distress in Nippur, and in this very Erech, caused by the Elamites; and one of the first historically authenticated accounts relates to a conquest of Erech by the Elamites. These conditions are reproduced in a Babylonian hero-legend. Gilgamesh, the chief figure of the great Babylonian epic, of which the Babylonian story of the Flood forms an episode, is the hero of Erech, the "builder" of the town, and its liberator from the yoke of Khumbaba, king of Elam.

This legend, no doubt, is based upon episodes in early Elamite and Babylonian history, and, though Khumbaba may not have been an actual historical ruler, he may be taken to personify the power of Elam in its early relations with Babylonia.

In the earliest historical inscriptions which have yet been recovered we find the princes of Elam owning allegiance to suzerains in Babylonia, for they bear the title of patesi, or priest-king, proving that they did not enjoy complete political independence. One of the earliest of these native rulers, to judge from the archaic forms of the characters employed on an inscription of his that has been recovered, was Ur-ilim. Of the suzerains to whom these early priest-kings owed allegiance we have evidence from the Babylonian side. Sargon of Agade, and his son, Naram-Sin, both held sway in Elam; and the latter conquered the Elamite district of Apirak. Another early conqueror of Elam was Alu-usharshid, or Urumush, king of the city of Kish, a number of whose inscriptions have been found near those of Sargon at Nippur, proving that he subdued Elam and Para'se, the district in which Susa was probably situated. Victories over the hosts of Anshan, the western boundary of Elam, and the district of Para'se, are also recorded in an inscription of Mutabil, an early governor of Dur-ilu; and Gudea, the famous patesi of Lagash, also boasts of victorious wars against Anshan. But, as neither Mutabil nor Gudea enjoyed the position of independent kings, we must assume that their conquests were undertaken on behalf of their own suzerains in Babylonia. The kings of the Dynasty of Ur appear to have exercised a more enduring influence over Elam, for bricks have been found at Susa proving that Dungi, and his three successors, Bur-Sin I., Gimil-Sin, and Ibi-Sin, all included Elam within the limits of their

Babylonian Sway in Elam

ASSYRIAN PLAN OF SUSA
This plan is taken from an Assyrian bas-relief, now in the British Museum, representing an attack on Susa. The river is the Shawur, on the east bank of which the capital of Elam lay.

empire. The excavations of De Morgan have furnished us with numbers of inscribed bricks, cones, steles, and statues, bearing inscriptions of a number of native Elamite rulers who are to be assigned to this early period. The records consist chiefly of building inscriptions and foundation memorials, commemorating the construction or repair of temples, the cutting of canals, and the like. We do not, therefore, gather from them much information for settling the problems connected with the external history of Elam at this time, but they enable us to form a true conception of the internal administration of the country. By their help we may picture the Elamites of this period as a nation without ambition to extend its boundaries, and content to own allegiance to foreign suzerains. The native princes are not engaged in warlike operations or in the conduct of campaigns, but devote their energies to the worship of the gods and the beautifying of their temples. It is to this period that we may probably assign Karibu-sha-Shushinak, Khutran-tepti, and his descendant Idadu I., who was followed

A Nation Without Ambition in direct succession by Kal-Rukhuratir and Idadu II. Names of other priest-kings are known, of whom we may mention Beli-arugal, and Urkium, both of whom were probably contemporaneous with the later kings of the Dynasty of Ur.

The first authenticated account of the succeeding period deals with a conquest of Babylonia by the Elamitic king Kuturnakhundi. Ashurbanipal, to whom we owe it, states that the latter, sixteen hundred and thirty-five years before his time, therefore about 2280, had carried away the image of Nana, the goddess of Erech, from her temple to Elam. Kuturnakhundi had pillaged Babylonia and oppressed it in every way. We have here to do with a time similar to that described in the Gilgamesh epic, although it was not the first of such epochs in Elam. We have already referred in Babylonian history to the tablet carried away from Erech and rediscovered by Kurigalzu in Susa; this may have been taken away by Kuturnakhundi on that occasion. The account of Ashurbanipal refers us to an earlier age than that of the " First Dynasty of Babylon " in Northern Babylonia, and of the dynasty of Larsa in the South; but Kuturnakhundi's invasion may well have been one of these earlier episodes in the Elamite

wars carried on by the kings of the " First Dynasty." In that case we must conclude that the figures given by the scribes of Ashurbanipal are unreliable, having been based on an exaggerated estimate of the period separating Ashurbanipal's conquest of Susa from the age of Kuturnakhundi. If Ashurbanipal's figures be accepted, we **Elamite Conquests in Babylonia** must set Kuturnakhundi's invasion and his conquest of Erech some two or three hundred years before the rise of Babylon to a position of pre-eminence in Babylonia. In favour of retaining Ashurbanipal's estimate of the period at which Kuturnakhundi's invasion of Babylonia and conquest of Erech took place, we find that the inscriptions recently discovered at Susa furnish us with the names of many rulers who are probably to be set within this period of Elamite conquest and expansion, which was brought to an end by Hammurabi and his son Samsu-iluna. The change in the political condition of Elam appears to have been reflected in the change of title, and the native princes discarded their former designation of patesi, or " priest-king," in favour of a title which may have carried with it the implication of suzerainty over a portion of Babylonia. However this may be, we find that, like their predecessors, they continued to reside at Susa, and carried on their work of temple building. To this period we may probably assign the rulers Shirukdu, Temti-agun, his nephew, Temti-khisha-khanesh, the son of Temti-agun, and Simebelar-khuppak, a descendant of Shirukdu. Another allied group of rulers who probably came to the throne rather later are Shilkhakha, and his brother-in-law Lankuku, whose son was Kuk-Kirmesh, and Attapakshu, Kurigugu, Temti-khalki, Kal-Uli, and Kuk-Nashur, all of whom were descendants of Shilkhakha.

Under the earlier kings of the First Dynasty of Babylon Elam was still the **Suzerain of South Babylonia** suzerain of Southern Babylonia. This state of affairs meets us in a clear and distinctly attested form during the reign of Rim-Sin, the last king of Larsa and of Sumer and Akkad. He had been appointed king by his father, Kutur-Mabuk, as the successor of his brother, Arad-Sin, upon the throne of Larsa, and he reigned in his father's name. In dealing with the history of Babylonia we have already described the defeat of Rim-Sin by Hammurabi, and his death at Samsu-iluna's hands. With his death Elam relinquished her claims to Babylonian territory.

In the period of Elamite expansion before the downfall of Rim-Sin must be set the series of events referred to in the fourteenth chapter of Genesis, with its noteworthy narrative of a campaign by

Expedition Against Palestine the kings of Elam, Babylon, and other countries against Palestine, and of the wonderful rescue of Lot by Abraham. It is permissible for us to conjecture that we here have before us an account which has been derived from Babylonian chronicles or legends. It is there stated that, at the time of the kings Amraphel, or Hammurabi, of Babylon, Eri-Aku of Larsa, and Tidal of Goïm, the king of Elam, Kutur-Lagamar, or Chedorlaomer— he was in the original account the only one who conducted the campaign—undertook an expedition to the west. The connection of this account with the legend of the destruction of Sodom and with the story of Abraham brings the narrative into conformity with that of the Babylonian chronicles. Kutur-Lagamar might have been the king of Elam at the time when Kutur-Mabuk, father of Rim-Sin, was king of the Elamite district Iamutbal, which adjoins Babylonia, and was therefore a vassal of Elam.

These are the principal facts at present known to us of this expansion of the power of Elam, which was brought to an end by Hammurabi and Samsu-iluna. We may perhaps regard it as a precursor, upon a smaller scale, of the Persian power which ruled the east from Susa ; accordingly the Elamite kings, who fought with Assyria for the possession of Babylonia, undertook no unprecedented task, but could appeal to a tradition of former power.

The succeeding period, that of the early Kassite supremacy, is obscure for Babylonia, and still more so for Elam. We may

The Kassite Control of Babylonia avail ourselves of this interruption to enumerate here the more important kings known from Elamite inscriptions, who, it has been suggested, may be assigned to this period. But we will first trace the steps by which, according to our recent information, the Kassites, who were settled in Elam, obtained control over Babylonia. Towards the close of the first dynasty of Babylon we have evidence that an Elamite king named Sadi, or

Taki, was defeated by Ammizaduga, the last king but one of the dynasty ; but in the subsequent period it is certain that the empire founded by Hammurabi quickly crumbled before the onslaught of more vigorous and less civilised invaders.

In dealing with the history of Babylonia we have seen how Iluma-ilu succeeded in founding an independent kingdom in Southern Babylonia on the shores of the Persian Gulf, whose kings must have harassed and weakened the later Semitic rulers of the first dynasty. Moreover, as early as the ninth year of Samsu-iluma the Kassite tribes which were settled in the western mountains of Elam began to make raids upon the Babylonian plain. It is clear that they were repulsed for a time, but, when the first dynasty had been brought to an end by the Hittite invasion, and Babylon lay defenceless and with her great temple and her palaces in ruins, the Kassite hordes poured down from their mountain fastnesses, and probably met with small resistance in their occupation of the city. Large numbers of the Kassite tribes remained behind

Kassites of Elam in Elam at this period, and the Kassite conquest of Babylon represented the advance of what was merely the vanguard of their host. For a considerable period Northern Babylonia only was in their hands, and the kings of the " Country of the Sea " succeeded in retaining their hold upon Southern Babylonia.

The Kassites of Elam must have harassed the " Country of the Sea " in the same manner as their predecessors had harassed Babylon, and it was probably to put an end to such raids that Ea-gamil, the last king of Iluma-ilu's dynasty, invaded Elam. But he had underestimated the number and vigour of his opponents, for Ulam-Buriash, the brother of Bitiliash, the principal Kassite chief in Elam at this period, not only succeeded in driving him from Elamite territory, but followed him into Southern Babylonia, and conquered and occupied the " Country of the Sea." By this conquest the whole of Babylonia became Kassite, and it is probable that a new and extensive migration took place by which fresh Kassite tribes advanced from the Elamite mountains into the Southern Babylonian plain.

The next question is that of the relation of the Kassites to Elam. Since the

Kassites migrated into Babylonia over the mountains of the Median border—that is to say, since they came through the passes by which the Elamites themselves made their inroads, they also may have left permanent traces in Elam. We may, indeed, assume that they were a later group of the same family of peoples to which the Elamites themselves belonged. There is no evidence one way or the other as to the affinity of their language with the Elamite. The remnants of the Kashshu, who did not advance to the conquest of Babylon or to that of Southern Babylonia and of the "Country of the Sea," remained behind in the mountains, where they were attacked by Nebuchadnezzar I., and again by Sennacherib; and in Alexander's time they are mentioned as Kossæans. A tribe of the Kissians is also mentioned as dwelling in Elam, near Susa; it is possible that they were descendants of the Kassites who had settled in Elam, but this cannot, of course, be proved. It is difficult to imagine that Elam did not experience a Kassite conquest, which must have fol-

Kassite Conquerors of Elam

lowed its own course, apart from those of Babylonia; but hitherto we have found no trace of it in the inscriptions. Such victories would be more difficult to prove, since a Kassite name is easily distinguishable from a Babylonian; whereas Elamite names bear a stamp resembling those of the Kassites—a fact which points to the affinity of the two races.

There are two imaginable theories. It is possible that the Kassites who settled in Elam exercised authority over the whole of the country, and in that case such a ruler as Bitiliash, the brother of Ulam-Buriash, must be regarded not merely as a Kassite mountain chief, but as a genuine king of Elam. The other alternative is, that the Elamites proved themselves capable of offering adequate resistance, and thus the conquest of Elam by the Kassites did not lead to a definitely established Kassite supremacy. In any case no lasting union with Babylonia, under Kassite kings, was effected. Agum II. does not mention Elam, and under the later Kassites we find Elam at war with Babylonia. In accordance with this latter alternative, which on the evidence at present available appears the more probable of the two, we may imagine that while the Kassites occupied portions of Elamite territory, particularly the mountainous districts in the west, there was a regular monarchy established at Susa.

In that case it is possible to assign to this period of Elamite history such Elamite rulers as Pakhir-ishshan, the son of Iri-khalki, and Attar-kittakh, his brother; Khumban-ummena,

Early Kings of Elam

and his son Untash-gal, who married Napir-asu, and was an enthusiastic patron of the arts, as the very beautiful bronze statue of his wife, which we have recovered, testifies; and Untakhash-gal and Kidin-Khutran, both sons of a ruler, Pakhir-ishshan, probably the second of that name. During this period we can trace no point of contact between Elam and Babylonia, and they do not appear to have come into direct contact until well on in the Kassite dynasty, when we find that Kurigalzu, the great-grandson of Ashur-uballit, waged war with Elam. It is evident from the accounts that Elam was once again the aggressor; at the beginning she oppressed Babylonia, but she was afterwards driven from Babylonian soil, and from an inscription that has been recovered we may infer that Kurigalzu invaded Elam and besieged and captured Susa. Khurbatila was king of Elam, according to the account of the Babylonian chronicle, to which we are indebted for information as to this war. We learn that, after being defeated at Dur-Dungi, he was taken prisoner by Kurigalzu, but he was afterwards released in return for the cession to Babylon of a considerable tract of Elamite territory.

For the next record of Elamite history we are also indebted to the same Babylonian chronicle. During the reign of Bel-nadin-shum I., king of Babylon, Kidin-khutrutash, king of Elam, invaded Babylonia, captured Nippur and Dur-ilu,

Babylonia the Prey of Elam

devastated the open country, and carried away the inhabitants as prisoners; this was the time when Tukulti-Ninib conquered Babylonia. We thus have the scene presented to us which is so familiar from the later Assyrian age—that is, Babylonia the prey of Elam or of Ashur. Kidin-khutrutash, like Tukulti-Ninib, must have considered himself the protector of Babylon. The invasion was soon afterwards renewed "after that Adad-shum-iddina was returned," as the chronicle says. We may imagine that Adad-shum-iddina, who maintained friendly relations with Assyria, and, perhaps, governed under the suzerainty of Tuk-ulti-Ninib, was attacked by Kidin-khutrutash and dethroned, and that the Assyrian could not help him because a rebellion broke out in Assyria at the same time ; that is the same series of events which we see later under Sennacherib and Ashur-nadin-shum. Babylonia had once more to suffer grievously during this invasion. Once again the country was laid waste, and this time in particular Isin was pillaged ; and it is noteworthy that this ancient royal city is mentioned, together with Nippur, in hymns of lamentation and penitential psalms as being sacked by Elam.

Royal Cities Pillaged

A king of Elam who followed Kidin-khutrutash, after no long interval, upon the throne was Khallutush-in-Shushinak. Little is known of him beyond the fact that he was the father of Shutruk-nakhundi, who succeeded him upon the throne and proved himself a dangerous enemy of Babylonia. For he invaded the country, and defeated and slew Zamama-shum-iddina, the last king but one of the Kassite dynasty. With the assistance of his son, Kuturnakhundi, he sacked the city of Sippar, and carried a rich booty back with him to Elam, including the stele of Naram-Sin and the famous stele inscribed with Hammurabi's code of laws, both of which documents have recently been recovered by the French mission at Susa. He also defeated the king of Ashnunnak, and from the city of Kish in Northern Babylonia he carried away the Obelisk of Manishtusu, which is now in the Louvre. His booty also included numerous Kassite "boundary stones." Though many of these were hammered to pieces by the Assyrians at the sack of Susa in the reign of Ashurbanipal, those that have been recovered during the recent excavations have thrown considerable light upon our knowledge of the Babylonian system of land tenure during

"Struggle of the Nations," S.P.C.K.

AN ANCIENT NEGRITIC SUSIAN

The most important race inhabiting ancient Elam was the negritic type illustrated here, of short stature, with brown skins, and black hair and eyes.

the Kassite period. Shutruk-nakhundi had three sons, two of whom, Kuturnak-hundi and Shilkhak-in-Shushinak, occupied the throne in turn. Numberless remains of the latter's activity as a great builder of temples to the gods have been recovered at Susa. Remains of numerous steles have also been found dating from his reign, from which we may infer that he conferred great benefits upon his land and preserved peace and prosperity within the borders of his kingdom. He had nine children, of whom Khute-ludush-in-Shushinak, the eldest, and Shilkhina-khamru-Lagamar, each in turn occupied the throne. The interference of Elam in Babylonian affairs, which took place towards the close of the Kassite dynasty was brought to an end under the most powerful king of the succeeding dynasty, Nebuchadnezzar I., with whose reign there begins a new independence of Babylonia, which once more proved herself superior to Assyria ; this was the last era of Babylonian prosperity. The statue of Marduk had been carried to Elam in the reign of one of Nebuchadnezzar's predecessors, probably Bel-nadin-akhi, whom he mentions, and we may conjecture with considerable probability that it was Shutruk-nakhundi who carried it off. Babylonia was, therefore, without the lord of the land, who alone could confer the crown upon the king.

After his successes in the west, Nebuchadnezzar proceeded to break down the supremacy of Elam, and, if possible, win back his god. We have fragments of numerous songs written on these wars, as well as two records of enfeoffment, one of which expressly mentions the recovery of Marduk from Susa ; the other describes the war with Elam, and records that during it the king of Elam, whose name is not given, died. The recovery of the statue would, in the first place, presuppose a capture of Susa. It is, however, conceivable that on the change of sovereign the new king lost no time in concluding peace,

Elam's Supremacy Lost

and surrendered the statue. In any case Nebuchadnezzar had shown himself an independent and well-matched opponent of Elam, and by the recovery of his god he had destroyed the outward token of his vassalage. He now could once more style himself with all right and justice king of Babylon.

The success of Assyria after Nebuchadnezzar, under Tiglath-pileser I. was only temporary. Babylonia remained for some time still in possession of Mesopotamia, and was, therefore, probably able to free herself from Elamite tutelage. We are entirely without inscriptions referring to the relations existing between the two countries at this period. We saw that among the successors of the second dynasty of Isin a king of Elamite origin was reckoned by himself as forming a distinct dynasty; we may, therefore, fix a new advance on the part of Elam at that time—about 1000 B.C.— when Babylonia and Mesopotamia were exposed to every kind of devastation, and even Assyria could not protect herself against the plundering hordes of the Aramæans and the Sutu.

If we judge by the events of later times we may reasonably suppose that in the ensuing period, when Chaldæan princes for the most part sat upon the throne of Babylon—Nabu-shum-ishkun and others—Elam also exercised an important influence. It does not seem indeed to have been able at first to interfere actively in Babylonian affairs. We cannot ascertain the cause, whether internal disorders or an invasion from the east, or both; but it is a noteworthy fact that Shalmaneser II., when he entered Babylonia, found no resistance offered by Elam. His successor, Shamshi-Adad IV., regards Elam in a manner which does not correspond to its earlier or its later position as a great power. After this we hear nothing more of Elamite affairs. A period of weakness is also implied by the fact that Shalmaneser, as protector of Babylon, received presents from Bactria, especially Bactrian camels and Indian elephants. We may, perhaps, gather from this that attempts had been

made by this country, which had been long cut off from Babylonia by the power of Elam, to come into renewed touch with the lord of Babylonia. A fresh access of power by Elam nipped these attempts in the bud.

Thus the Far East remained outside the horizon of the Western peoples until in the Persian age Elam became involved with the Persians against

A MODERN NEGRITIC SUSIAN

A descendant of one of the original Elamite races, showing a remarkable resemblance to his forefather, illustrated on the opposite page.

the West, and Alexander once more restored communication by his victories over Persia and her allies. When Tiglath-pileser IV. appeared upon the scene the power of Elam had revived; Bactria was again under Elamite dominion, and the Chaldæans thenceforth found support in the Elamite kings of Susa, who alternated with the Assyrians in being the patrons or feudal lords of Babylonia. It is only a momentary gleam which is thrown on the relations to the east by the Bactrian embassy ; but it is sufficient to make us recognise that Elam, in consequence of her position and civilisation, was really the connecting link between the civilised countries of Nearer and Further Asia, and the predecessor of the eastern half of the Persian empire. The Middle Assyrian empire did not come into contact with Elamite territory before Tiglath-pileser IV. ; the nearest approach was made by Adad-nirari IV., who reckoned Ellipi among his tributary states. We may conclude in any case that Elam in the ninth and the first half of the eighth century B.C. had not yet encroached upon the west. After the accession of Nabonassar, in 747 B.C., and Tiglath-pileser IV., in 745, we have continuous records of Elamite history. The Babylonian chronicle, which begins with this period, describes very clearly, in its condensed and abbreviated style, the actual conditions in Babylonia ; and it continuously refers to the kings of Elam and of Assyria and their relations to Babylonia. It notes only facts, and never draws the slightest general inference from them. But the conclusion which results from the frequent occurrence of these notices has been already drawn in dealing with the history of Assyria ; the ensuing period is taken up with a struggle between Elam and Assyria for Babylonia. There are two parties—an Assyrian, which sees the patron of Babylon in the king of Ashur, and a Chaldæan-Elamite party, which sees him in the king of Elam ; and the chronicle takes account of both by recording the reigns of kings in both countries.

A Connection with the Far East

In 743 B.C. it is recorded that Ummani-gash, or Khumbanigash, became king of Elam ; his father, according to the account by Ashurbanipal, was called Umbadara, and had also been his predecessor on the throne. He reigned until 717, when his death is related to have taken place. Tiglath-pileser, who exercised his rights as protector over Babylon after 745, does not allude to him, even when, in 729, he drove out the Chaldæan Ukin-zir. We may, perhaps, assume that Khumbanigash had at least favoured the latter, although he was not in a position to interfere vigorously in his behalf. Even under

Struggle for Babylonia

Shalmaneser, who indeed reigned in Babylon unopposed, nothing transpires about him. On the other hand, on Shalmaneser's death he entered the lists in support of his protégé Merodach-baladan, who under his suzerainty became king of Babylon ; and when Sargon tried at once to eject him, Khumbanigash advanced into Babylonia and compelled Sargon at Dur-ilu to abandon the territory of Babylon and Southern Babylonia.

In 717–699 followed Ishtar-khundu, as the chronicle has transformed his name, or Shutur-nakhundi, as Sargon more correctly calls him. When Sargon, in 710, once more attacked Merodach-baladan, he began by separating the two confederates. He first turned against Elam, conquered the countries on the Lower Uknu, took the border fortresses erected there by Shutur-nakhundi, and occupied the border countries of Lakhiri, Pillatu, etc. Merodach-baladan hastily sent presents to Elam, and advanced with his army to the province of Iatbur on the Uknu, adjacent to the districts occupied by Sargon ; but the Emalite "accepted his present, yet forbade him to advance farther," or to enter Elamite territory. This is a strange situation. Did he really abandon his vassal in order that war might not reach his own land, or had Merodach-baladan perhaps tried previously to set himself free from him ? In any case he did not venture to advance into Babylonia, and avoided the contest with Assyria. Sargon was able to secure the frontier districts which he had occupied, and to place them partly under Assyrian administration. Soon afterwards, in the disputes for the throne of Ellipi, when Nibe, one of the two brothers, sought help from Shutur-nakhundi, and the latter had installed him in Elam, he did not venture to take any steps in support of his protégé when Sargon brought back his own candidate, Ispabara. The battle at Dur-ilu must have taught Elam a severe lesson, and the army of Sargon became as formidable as that of Tiglath-pileser.

Sargon Attacks Elam

Merodach-baladan, after his expulsion from Bit-Iakin, had in his flight an asylum in Elam, and he was again welcome there, now that he had no army. When Sargon was dead he was brought back to Babylon by an Elamite army in 703, but was immediately expelled by Sennacherib. In the battle of Kish it was the Elamite troops especially who fought for him. Once more he found refuge in Elam, and he again found assistance there when he advanced from Bit-Iakin to Babylon and forced Bel-ibni to join him and thus to recognise the protectorate of Elam. They were once again driven out by Sennacherib in 700. These failures of Shutur-nakhundi possibly contributed to a transference of power into the hands of his brother Khalludush, or Khallushu, who rebelled in the following year, took his brother prisoner, and mounted the throne himself in 699, and ruled for six years. His reign at least produced a more vigorous action against Assyria, and he achieved successes in Babylonia, which balanced those of Sennacherib. In 694 the latter made a descent on the Elamite provinces situated on the great lagoon of the Euphrates and colonised by fugitive Chaldæans from the " Country of the Sea," while at the same time Khalludush invaded Northern Babylonia, capturing and plundering Nippur. Sennacherib's son, Ashur-nadin-shum, was brought as a prisoner to Elam, and Nergal-ushezib was placed upon the throne of Babylon. Elam had thus become liege lord of Northern Babylonia, while the South was still in the hands of Assyria. Nergal-ushezib maintained his power in Babylon as long as his protector reigned. The latter must have found it difficult during the next year and a half to interfere again on his behalf, for the Assyrians invaded his territory from Southern Babylonia and took him prisoner, without any Elamite army coming to his assistance. An explanation may possibly be found in the statement of the Babylonian chronicle, that almost simultaneously a rebellion broke out in Elam in which Khalludush experienced the treatment which he himself had shown to his brother. Kutur-nakhundi, the third of the name known to us, was raised to the throne as head of the rebellion in 692, but did not retain the position for more than ten months. He had been only a short time on the throne when the Assyrians invaded Elam by land —that is, from Northern Babylonia. Kuturnakhundi was in Madaktu, the town which commands the western part of Elam, but he ventured on no resistance and withdrew to Khidalu, the province and town in the Zagros. Since he thus abandoned Susa, we must suppose that

Lordship Over Babylon

he was not acknowledged there. He may have been prince of Madaktu in the same way as there were independent princes of Khidalu, and was therefore forced to relinquish any attempts at occupying Susa, the capital of the empire. It is thus explained why, although he had just proclaimed himself king by means of a rebellion, he had been unable to raise an army with which to face the Assyrians. These ravaged the western provinces, and retook some border districts which had once been held by Sargon and had subsequently been recovered by Elam under Khalludush.

Rebellion Follows Rebellion

This failure could not have served to strengthen the power of the new king. He thus fell a victim, only three months after his flight from Madaktu, in another rebellion, by which Umman-menanu was raised to the throne. His reign marks a new era of success for Elam, and thus of insecurity for the Assyrian possessions in Babylonia. Even while the Assyrian army was in Elam, Mushezib-Marduk had usurped the sovereignty in Babylon, and hastened to make sure of the protection of Elam. Northern Babylonia was once again, as under Khalludush, lost to Assyria. Sennacherib, in 691, attempted to win it back, but Umman-menanu was strong enough to perform his promises made to Babylon. He appeared in Northern Babylonia, and in the battle of Khalule victory was at least so far on his side that Sennacherib was forced to retire to Assyria. It is also important in estimating the situation to notice that the fall of Babylon did not take place until 689 B.C., when Umman-menanu had been struck down by apoplexy and was, therefore, incapacitated from marching to the defence of Babylonia. The Babylonian chronicle in its laconic style leaves this fact to be inferred, by placing the notice of the capture of Babylon between the announcement of the illness and death of Umman-menanu, thus : " On the 15th Nisan (689 B.C.) Umman-menanu, King of Elam, was struck down by apoplexy ; his mouth was affected and he was incapable of speech. On the 1st Kislev the city (Babylon) was taken. On the 17th Adar Umman-menanu died."

Death of Babylon's Protector

His successor was Khumbakhaldash I., who reigned from 689 to 681 B.C. He reigned during the last eight years of

Sennacherib, when, according to the expression of the chronicle, "there was no king" in Babylon, though, according to another chronicle, recently discovered, Erba-Marduk was, for a portion of that period, recognised as king in Babylon and in Borsippa. In fact, after its destruction Babylon was abandoned alike by Assyria and Elam, and she had to rely upon her own weakened resources to defeat the plundering expeditions of Aramæan and Chaldæan tribes. We have already seen that it was in consequence of his success against the Aramæans that Erba-Marduk secured the throne. In the absence of help from Assyria or Elam, the Chaldæan invasion was at least partially successful, and it was not until the reign of Esarhaddon that the immigrants were driven from Babylonian territory. We have no accounts of Sennacherib at this time, and the Babylonian chronicle states merely that a few months before his murder, in 681 B.C., Khumbakhaldash died of fever.

Babylon Neglected by Elam

He was followed by Khumbakhaldash II., who ruled from 681 to 676 B.C., and whose reign falls in the first six years of Esarhaddon. Nothing is at first said of complications with Assyria ; indeed, in the attitude adopted toward Nabu-zir-kitti-lishir, king of the "Country of the Sea," we may well see an effort to establish friendly relations with Assyria and an express repudiation of any claims on Babylonia. This may, perhaps, be the explanation of a statement in the Babylonian chronicle that in 680 B.C. the gods of Dur-ilu and of the Babylonian Dur-sharrukin—not to be confused with Sargon's capital—had come back into their own cities. This can hardly refer to anything else—especially since Dur-ilu is mentioned—than the statues of the gods which had been brought to Elam, presumably by Khalludush, and were now sent back by Khumbak-haldash. But friendly relations did not last for long. Only six years afterwards, in 674 B.C., the chronicle announces as laconically as ever, "the king of Elam invaded Sippar and caused a massacre." No details are told us. Esarhaddon is naturally as silent as Sennacherib was over a similar disaster eighteen years before. We thus know nothing of any relations having been entered into with

Babylon's Gods Restored

Babylonian rebels. Soon afterwards Khumbakhaldash died "without being sick, in his own palace." In this way Assyria was again freed of a dangerous rival.

Urtaki, the brother and successor of the deceased, seems from the very first to have been equally anxious for a good understanding with Esarhaddon, who was certainly glad, for his part, to have in Elam a peaceful neighbour. The Babylonian chronicle reports during the year the arrival of the statues of the gods of Agade, the sister city to Sippar, from Elam. This plainly refers to those which had been carried away by Khumbakhaldash in the preceding year, and were now surrendered to cement the friendship. The famine reported by Ashurbanipal, during which permission was granted by Assyria that distressed Elamites should seek a refuge on Assyrian soil in order to send back this " property," is the only other event which we know of this period. The institution of the frontier guard, which Esarhaddon attempted to form by winning over the Gambuli, is a proof that he did not trust merely to the good will of Elam, but was anxious to secure peace effectually by other means. The peace lasted during Esarhaddon's lifetime. By the reconstruction of the kingdom of Babylon, a most favourable opportunity was presented to the Elamites of once more realising their old ambitions in Babylonia. Urtaki advanced into Northern Babylonia, in order that, in concert with the sheikh of the Gambuli, who was dissatisfied with the rôle assigned to him, and with a Babylonian prince, he might march on Babylon itself. Nothing is said of any measures of defence undertaken by Shamash-shum-ukin. Ashurbanipal, as protector of Babylon, acted as the Elamites Khumbanigash and Umman-menanu had done ; he advanced against Urtaki, and compelled him to evacuate Babylonia. He did not march against Elam, from which we may argue that the border districts once occupied by Sargon and Sennacherib had long since been abandoned.

Peace with Assyria

Urtaki died soon afterward—certainly before 665 B.C. His death furnished Assyria with a motive for interfering in Elamite affairs. This was the beginning of the series of wars which were destined to lead to the destruction of Elam.

Urtaki did not die a natural death; Ashurbanipal's inscriptions are full of expressions about the misery of his violent death, but they do not state the method of it. He was deposed by his brother Teumman; and the latter was bound to act like other Oriental rulers in the same position—to kill all the sons of his brothers in order not to experience the same fate some day at their hands. "He placed himself like a fiend upon the throne," Ashurbanipal writes. The sons of his two brothers and predecessors, Khumbakhaldash and Urtaki, with sixty other members of the royal house and an escort of adherents, successfully made their escape to Assyria, where they implored Ashurbanipal to protect them and to restore them to their home. Teumman demanded the surrender of the fugitives, and, when this was refused, became more peremptory, sending every month insolent letters—a serious breach of the laws of diplomatic courtesy between rival courts—

Teumman Invades Assyria and continued his preparations for an invasion of Babylonia. He appears at this time to have had an epileptic attack, which seemed to Ashurbanipal a divine warning; but it did not deter the Elamite from carrying out his threats and from marching against Assyrian territory. It is not clear how far he advanced. Ashurbanipal himself was now compelled to take serious measures. Judging by the display of indignation, omens, and prayers which he exhibited on this occasion, we feel that it was a very difficult task for

Elam Defeated at Susa him to put an army into the field against Elam. But at last there was no other alternative, and he hastily occupied Dur-ilu in order thus to bar the road into Babylonia.

Teumman does not appear to have calculated on any opposition, for now he did not venture to defend his frontier, but retreated before the Assyrian army to Susa. Ashurbanipal advanced as far as the Ulai, as the Karun and its tributaries were called by the Assyrians—the river in question is the Shawur, on the eastern bank of which Susa lay—and defeated the Elamite army, which here met him in the open field at Tullis before the walls of Susa; Teumman fell in the battle.

Ashurbanipal was now able to install in Susa one of the fugitive princes, a son of Urtaki, named Ummanigash, as the Assyrian reproduction of the name Khumbanigash (II.) runs. Ishtar-nakhundi—that is, Shutruk-nakhundi—who had reigned in Khidalu as an independent king, and in whom we may probably see a son of Teumman, also met his death in the battle. Tammaritu, another son of Urtaki, was appointed in his stead by Ashurbanipal, to whom such a state of affairs could not

URTAKI, COUSIN OF TEUMMAN, SURRENDERING TO THE ASSYRIANS IN BATTLE

THE BATTLE WHICH DESTROYED ELAM'S POWER

An Assyrian bas-relief representing the battle of Tullis, before the walls of Susa, in which Elam was finally defeated by the Assyrian forces under Ashurbanipal. Teumman, the king, is seen under an inscribed tablet being decapitated.

but be welcome, according to the principle "divide et impera." But the same relation existed between himself and his brother in Babylonia. Elam was thus subject to Assyrian influence, a success which Assyria had never hitherto

Assyria's Unwonted Supremacy attained, and was now by no means secure, since the new king must have been anxious to shake off the yoke. When, therefore, Shamash-shum-ukin, who revolted from his brother, began to secure allies and sent "presents" to Khumbanigash—that is, besought and acknowledged his protectorship — the latter was prepared to become a protector instead of a "protected," and to restore the influence of Elam in Babylonia. Ashurbanipal vainly demanded the surrender of the agents of Shamash-shum-ukin; the Elamite granted the help requested and marched to Babylonia. But at the right moment for Ashurbanipal a rebellion broke out in the rear of the army. Tammaritu, the son of Khumbanigash, a fourth brother of Khumbakhaldash II., Urtaki,

and Teumman, proclaimed himself king, and Khumbanigash met the fate of his predecessors; he was murdered together with his family. Ashurbanipal secured however, no further advantage from this at the time; for even Tammaritu, according to Elamite tradition, considered that to be ruler of Babylon was far more desirable than to be ruled by Assyria. He, too, sent an army to the aid of Shamash-shum-ukin, and began, as we shall see, to form alliances in Southern Babylonia. His army was already menacing Nippur, and the tribe of the Puqudu was on the point of joining him, when the same fate happened to him as to his

Assyrian Machinations in Elam predecessor. He, too, fell a victim to a rebellion, the opportune outbreak of which suggests the thought that Ashurbanipal did not rely solely on the prayers to his gods, which were prominent on this occasion, but had taken the precaution of securing help by other means. Tammaritu was, however, more fortunate than his predecessors;

he made good his escape. He fled to Ashurbanipal, and was actually welcomed by him.

The new king, Indabigash, who reigned from 648 to 647 B.C., was not a member of the royal family. He immediately set about establishing friendly relations with Assyria, and refrained from interfering in Babylonian affairs. He merely looked on when Shamash-shum-ukin prematurely met his fate in 648 B.C. It was, however, impossible to avoid complications for any long period, and this time, as so often before, the " Country of the Sea " was the determining cause. Ashurbanipal had despatched an army thither to prevent the advance of an Elamite army, which Khumbanigash had despatched during his reign. The reigning king, Nabu-bel-shumate, a grandson of Merodach-baladan, had to submit with the best grace he could to these " protectors," and was forced to join his troops with them. He succeeded, however, in thus getting the power into his own hands. He compelled the governor of Ur to join him, and delivered the Assyrian troops, probably under Tammaritu, into the hands of the Elamites. All this took place about 651–649 B.C.

Friendship with Assyria

After the taking of Babylon, Nabu-bel-shumate, when the Assyrians once more occupied the south, fled, according to the tradition of his house, to Elam, where in the interval Indabigash had become king. The latter had sent back to Assyria the Assyrian troops which had been handed over to his predecessor, but he refused to surrender Nabu-bel-shumate. Ashurbanipal thereupon threatened war, and the result was a rebellion by which Ummanaldash, or Khumbakhaldash III., son of an otherwise obscure Attametu, was raised to the throne in the stead of Indabigash. But he also refused the surrender of Nabu-bel-shumate and the abandonment of the Elamite claims to the " Country of the Sea." Again there was a rebellion under an Ummanigash, or Khumbanigash, son of an otherwise unknown Amedirra. But this time the prayers of Ashurbanipal were not so effective as on the three previous occasions, and Ummanigash maintained his position. There was no course left for Ashurbanipal if he wished to secure Southern Babylonia but to abandon prayers and intrigue, and

Assyria Abandons Intrigue

to declare war ; he advanced into Elam, and occupied the frontier fortress Bit-Imbi. Ummanaldash had hardly yet been able to set his own home affairs in order, and was not, therefore, able to hold the west and Madaktu ; he withdrew " into the mountains "—that is, to Khidalu.

It seems as if an attack had also been made upon Elam from the side of the " Country of the Sea." A king of Bubilu, the eastern part of Elam, by name Umbakhabua, who had made himself independent there during the preceding disturbances—an analogous case to what we have seen in Khidalu—abandoned his country and capital and retired to an island, where he was safe, at any rate from the Assyrians.

Thus the country was in the power of the Assyrians, and Ashurbanipal once more installed there the fugitive Tammaritu as his vassal. But hardly was that done and the Assyrian army on its return, when Tammaritu, who saw his throne in jeopardy, found himself forced to draw the sword against his " benefactors." Ashurbanipal, it is true, speaks of a second subjugation of Tammaritu and of a plundering and laying waste of Elam ; but, if we may judge by the usual style and method of Assyrian accounts of wars, this is nothing but a plausible periphrasis for a forced retreat. In this way Assyrian diplomacy was for a time outwitted by that of Elam.

Elam Outwits Assyria

Ashurbanipal's accounts of the succeeding years are vague. He says that Tammaritu had been deposed ; clearly that happened only after the withdrawal of the Assyrians, not before : the new king was put on the throne by Ashurbanipal. He was Ummanaldash, or Khumbakhaldash II. The latter had returned from Khidalu for the second time, and had either himself driven out Tammaritu or had commanded his followers to do so. In any case Tammaritu fled to Assyria, where he was detained in dishonourable captivity at the court of Ashurbanipal.

Ummanaldash, when he had established himself firmly on the throne, drove out the Assyrian garrison from Bit-Imbi ; this left Ashurbanipal no alternative but to take up arms once more. He occupied Bit-Imbi and the border province of Rashi. Ummanaldash abandoned the west with Madaktu, and entrenched himself behind the Idide, the Ab-i-Diz, near Susa. The

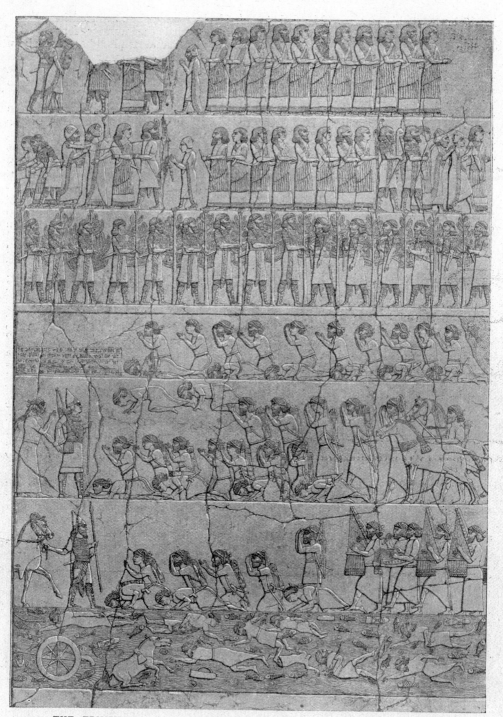

THE TRIUMPH OF THE ASSYRIANS AFTER THE BATTLE OF TULLIS

From a relief in the British Museum, showing the Assyrians' triumph. After the battle the victors were met by a throng of people from Susa, which opened its gates to the Assyrians, with priests, singers and harpers, to welcome the new king, Khumbanigash II., appointed by Ashurbanipal. He is seen at the beginning of the second row from the bottom. Note how the river Shawur is choked with corpses of men and horses and battle débris.

Assyrian army long hesitated to attack this strong position, and contented itself at first with scouring the defenceless country and occupying the fortresses. Finally, after much questioning of the soothsayers, the Assyrians ventured on an attack, and met with no resistance. The cause of this is not revealed. Ummanaldash had once more withdrawn to Khidalu, and abandoned Susa as before. The old capital was sacked and pillaged, the sacred grove desecrated, the temple and royal castle plundered and destroyed. Twenty statues of gods and thirty-six statues of kings were carried away to Assyria, and the tombs of the Elamite kings were violated. The statue of Nana, which, according to Ashurbanipal's account, had been carried away from Erech by Kutur-nakhundi 1,635 years before—a record which we have already discussed—was then brought back to Erech. An oracle was found which Nana had presumably given on her removal from Erech to the effect that " Ashurbanipal will bring me back from the hostile land of Elam." Nana had thus predicted the reign of her liberator, an interesting contribution to the history of oracles.

Sack of Susa The excavations conducted by the French mission at Susa have revealed numerous traces of the havoc wrought by the Assyrian soldiers on their capture of the city. The damage they wrought is much to be regretted, as it destroyed many memorials of the old centre of civilisation, which often dominated a wider world than Babylon itself.

The task of the Assyrian army was thus fulfilled. No attempt was made to form an Assyrian province, for that would have given rise to endless insurrections. The army was withdrawn. Ummanaldash was able to occupy his devastated country afresh and to return to Madaktu. But his power of effective resistance was broken. When the surrender of Nabu-bel-shumate was again demanded, he assented to it. But the descendant of Merodach-baladan freed him from the necessity of surrender, since he and his armour-bearer died together by their own hands. Thus Ummanaldash could send only his embalmed body to Nineveh. There Ashurbanipal outraged his dead enemy with the insults he would have offered to the living man. Ummanaldash had by this act declared his submission. For this reason he secured Assyrian support against an opponent who clearly had been pitted against him by the anti-Assyrian party. This was Pa'e, who held his own for a time, but could not in the end resist the threats of Assyria and the attack of Ummanaldash, and, like Tammaritu, made his way to Nineveh.

Ummanaldash himself could not long submit to be a vassal of Assyria. He **End of Elam** incurred the fate which befell all kings in his position : he stood between two parties, one of which urged defection from Assyria, and the other, with the help of Assyria, frustrated the results of any such defection. So soon then as his loyalty toward Ashurbanipal began to cool, the usual rebellion of the Assyrian party broke out at the "command of the Assyrian gods"— that is to say, at Assyrian instigation. Ummanaldash had to seek refuge from this party on a mountain, which was probably in the vicinity of the Assyrian frontier ; there he was taken prisoner by Assyrian troops and led to Nineveh. Here there were now the three rivals together—Tammaritu, Pa'e, and Ummanaldash—and they were employed by Ashurbanipal to enhance, as his servants, the magnificence of his triumphal processions.

This happened somewhere about 635 B.C. We learn nothing more of Elam. Ashurbanipal does not name the successor whom the rebellious subjects had proclaimed king. We are inclined to conclude from this that Elam, through this rebellion, had slipped out of his hands. We have, besides, approached the time when Elam again came forward as an opponent ; after the year 626 B.C. Babylon was once more in the hands of the Chaldæans.

The old game would certainly have begun again had not another force appeared upon the scene. It is no longer with the help of Elam that Nabopolassar tries to assert his power in Babylon and acts against Assyria, but with that of the Medes. This is indeed a great change, and yet it is only the continuation **Elamites Displaced by Medes** of the old policy : the Medes have simply taken the place of the Elamites. We can at most insert a period of twenty years between the time when Ummanaldash was brought to Nineveh and that when Nabopolassar entered into an agreement with the Medes, if indeed he had not been supported by them from the very first. If we take this fact into consideration, the question involuntarily suggests itself whether

Ummanigash after all was not the last king of Elam, and whether Ashurbanipal's noteworthy silence over the subsequent conditions in Elam is not to be explained from the fact that the land had then fallen into the hands of the invading Aryan tribes. If we reflect that Esarhaddon had already shown some anxiety in his attitude towards them, that he was not ashamed to enter into alliances with one of these new peoples, the Ashkuza, against the other two, the Cimmerians and Medes, it is a probable supposition that Ashurbanipal himself may very soon have understood the case; he had himself placed the country at the mercy of these dangerous antagonists, whose power he had only succeeded in checking. The result of deposing Ummanigash was that he suddenly found fresh enemies in Elam, who soon adopted the policy of their predecessors, and helped their protégé in Babylon against Assyria. Just as in Urartu,

A Buffer State Destroyed

so now in Elam, Assyria had herself abolished the natural " buffer-state." Elam, therefore, according to our theory, fell into the hands of the Medes soon after, and was occupied by an Aryan population. It did not play any prominent part during the Median rule. But it was once more raised by Cyrus to be the seat of empire, and Susa became the capital of the East. We shall treat this subject more fully in dealing with the history of the Medes and Persians.

The French excavations at Susa have yielded material remains of Elamite activity ranging from prehistoric times down to the period of the Achæmenian kings. The influence of the early Semitic inhabitants of Babylonia upon the artistic and social development of Elam was so great that it undoubtedly furnished the mould in which Elamite civilisation was cast. On its artistic side this Babylonian influence can be traced in a remarkably complete degree.

Civilisation of Elam

THE ELAMITE SCULPTURES OF MAL-AMIR
Elamite sculptures, though artistically inferior, show distinct evidences of Babylonian influence. The bas-relief illustrated here is one of three hundred in the valley of Mal-Amir, portraying princes of local Elamite dynasties.

On the whole, we may regard many of the attainments of the Elamites as imitated or borrowed from Babylonian civilisation; this is shown by the script, as well as in works of art, the style and technique of which correspond in many particulars to the art of the Babylonians. If it were not for some details of dress, the sculptures of Mal-Amir, for example, might well be taken for Babylonian. But in spite of the strong Babylonian element in Elamite art, the Elamites themselves added something of their own which serves to differentiate their productions from those of contemporary artists in Babylonia. In their work in bronzes, ivory, and the precious metals, the Elamites attained to a high level of design and technical perfection, and it is now possible to talk of Elamite art as quite distinct from that of Babylonia and Assyria.

The large number of votive and building inscriptions that have been recovered throw some light upon the number and names of the great temples and other sacred buildings in Susa, while the sumptuous foundation deposit found in the temple of Shushinak is of the **The Art of Elam** greatest interest from the nature of the offerings which it comprised. But for the character of the Elamite religion as a whole, and of the details of the ritual, we are still to a great degree dependent on conjecture.

The Elamite inscriptions and Ashurbanipal give us a series of Elamite names of deities, but they still remain little more than names for us. An exception may be made, perhaps, of the principal "Susan" goddess, who was identified by the Elamites and Babylonians with the Nana, or Ishtar, of Erech. It is inevitable, with the multifarious conquests and relations of Elam with Erech, that legends of one shrine should have been interwoven with those of another, and that a dispute as to the antiquity of the two should have been decided empirically by making the statues accrue as spoil to the victors.

There is little doubt that Susa was the principal city of Elam from the earliest times throughout the whole course of her history. But we are still without information with regard to the relations of the capital to other great cities in the land. Ashurbanipal designates all important places—that is to say, all fortified towns—as royal towns, thus departing from the custom in other countries where only the capital is so called. Were all fortified places, in contrast to the Babylonian and Assyrian usage, the property of the king, and were there thus no municipal rights emanating from that ownership of the land by god and temple, which is so characteristic of the Semitic idea? This would point to a great diminution, as **Priesthood Influence Diminished** compared with the Semitic civilised countries, in the influence of the priesthood, which, with its large possessions, formed a prominent factor in the development of the Semitic peoples and states.

That the Elamites were great warriors is fully proved by the history of their battles with Babylon and Assyria. When the Assyrians speak of Elamite spoil the baggage waggon plays a prominent part in it. The Assyrian is acquainted only with the chariot as an offensive weapon of war. The Elamite has carts drawn by mules, on which he carried his baggage. The principal weapon of the Elamites is not the spear or sword, but the bow. It is obvious, however, that Babylonian civilisation influenced their mode of warfare. Still the bow must have been the original weapon, and for the noble Elamite it was the badge of the warrior.

If the geographical position of Elam makes us fix our attention on countries and peoples of another kind than those which determined the fortunes of the Nearer East, we might expect information from this quarter as to the migrations and extension of Babylonian civilisation to the East. It is only under the Persians, Alexander the Great, and the Caliphs, that history shows us events which must have been foreshadowed even in the times of the real prosperity of the East. If the trade with India and Eastern Asia is one of the most important factors in the history of the world, Elam must also, in the days of her power, have **Importance of Elam in History** interfered in the decision of points at issue, obstructing if unable to assist, but always having an important word in the matter. Her position on the borderland of Western Asia thus endowed her with a strategic and commercial importance, which explains the prominent rôle she played among the civilised races of the ancient world.

HUGO WINCKLER
LEONARD W. KING

PASS THROUGH THE MOUNTAINS DEFENDING THE HITTITE CAPITAL

THE PLAIN AND MODERN VILLAGE OF BOGHAZ KÖI

SANCTUARY OF THE TEMPLE: ALL THAT REMAINS OF THE ANCIENT CITY

BOGHAZ KÖI, THE GREAT CAPITAL OF THE MYSTERIOUS HITTITE EMPIRE

EARLY NATIONS OF WESTERN ASIA

BY DR. HUGO WINCKLER, L. W. KING, M.A.,
DR. K. G. BRANDIS & H. R. HALL, M.A.

SYRIA AND THE HITTITE EMPIRE

THE tract between the Euphrates, the Armenian mountains, the Taurus, and southward as far as the end of the Lebanon—that is, as far as Hermon—is roughly what is designated *Syria*. The name has an historical development, and is, therefore, applied here with some freedom, in a way, perhaps, more suitable to later ages. Its origin is now known. The Babylonians termed the land which runs northward of Mesopotamia to the mountains and westward to Cappadocia, Subartu, or, as the characters in the original ideograph for the name may very probably be read, Suri ; the latter name survives even in classical times in that of the Leuco-Syrians in Cappadocia. When Assyria and the southern part of Syria became Aramæan the name was then extended to the more southern countries, since Aramæan and Syrian became to a certain extent synonymous terms.

Syria, in our sense of the term, had no uniform history. Situated between the civilisations of Babylonia and **Syria's** Egypt, it was exposed to their **Varying** influence, and its history is **History** completely dominated by them. But yet a third civilisation had great power here ; one which for the least obscure part of its history had this region for its scene, so that Syria appeared until quite recently to be the country where we were best informed as to an otherwise unsolved riddle of the East. But recent discoveries have shown that it is to

Cappadocia we may look for further enlightenment upon the subject. We call this civilisation the " Hittite," after the people, the Khatti, who are the most clearly recognisable representatives of it. Khatti is the title of this people among the Assyrians ; in Egyptian, Kheta. The reader must, however, understand that in **The** what follows we designate by **Hittite** this name only this one people, **Peoples** while by this term Hittite a complete ethnic group is meant, to which the Khatti belonged. According to our present knowledge, they appear to us to be the most important people of the group, for the recent discoveries at Boghaz Köi in Cappadocia prove that on that site stood the ancient capital of the Hittite empire, which bore the name of Khatti and gave its title to the Hittite people. Here, as we shall see, was the original centre of the great Hittite empire, and it is probable that the city from the earliest times played a prominent part in the history of the race.

We know nothing of the Syria which was contemporary with the Old Babylonian empires. Since, however, Phœnicia was subject to their influence, Syria must also have received its share of the " Semitic Babylonian " and " Canaanite " immigrations. What sort of nations invaded or tried to invade simultaneously from the north, whence the " Hittites " were advancing, is a question about which we know little as yet, though the Hittite invasion of Babylonia at the close of the first dynasty of Babylon is proof of the early date of the Hittite southward movement. We do obtain further information at the time of the eighteenth Egyptian dynasty, when Egyptian accounts and the letters from Tell el-Amarna and the despatches recovered

Coming of the Hittites from the native Hittite archives at Boghaz Köi afford us some insight into the conditions. We see from them that in the meantime a non-Semitic population had forced its way forward, and that other portions of the same race were pressing on behind, and from this period we can form at least a rough idea of Syrian history.

This is the population which we call Hittite, and its characteristics may probably be traced in a number of monuments which give representations of early dwellers in Asia Minor, or are covered with inscriptions in hieroglyphic writing. The Hittite type differs considerably from the Semitic : race, dress, finally technique, show that we have to do with representatives of a peculiar civilisation distinct from the two great Oriental forms. In dress we find a characteristic feature in the Hittite cue and the shoes, usually with points bending upward. The writing is also characteristic : a clearly defined hieroglyphic script employing pictures, which has no affinity with the Egyptian or the Babylonian script [see page 1729]. We possess a number of these hieroglyphic inscriptions ; but hitherto no one has succeeded in deciphering them and in making the language or languages of those who engraved them speak to us in their own form. But since the Mitani population and the " Urartæans " probably belong to the same group, we have in them two languages of "Hittite" peoples, although not of that section which employed this picture-writing. The native inscriptions,

Languages of the Hittites written in Babylonian characters upon clay tablets, which have been found at Boghaz Köi furnish numerous examples of the principal Hittite language employed during the period of the empire ; and it is probable that we shall be able to recover the linguistic outlines of other Hittite dialects. Moreover, when the new material is published and made available for study, it will be possible to form a more definite opinion on the disputed question of

the Hittite origin of the hieroglyphic inscriptions.

The Hittite civilisation was brought to Syria from outside by the conquerors, especially by the Khatti. The question arises, whence ? The Khatti were settled, before their invasion, in Cappadocia—that is to say, in North-east Asia Minor. There we possess in the rock sculptures of Boghaz Köi conspicuous monuments of " Hittite " art, and it is on this site, as already stated, that recent excavation has brought to light a wealth of tablets inscribed not only in Babylonian, the early language of diplomacy, but also in the native tongue. Similar monuments are found over the whole region of Asia Minor as far as the west coast, where the " Sesostris " sculptures in the vicinity of Smyrna are the best known. We conclude, therefore, that Asia Minor was the home of Hittite civilisation. Future research will, perhaps, throw light on the relation of the Hittites in question to the pre-Aryan populations of the West, and render it possible to compare them with Etruscans, Iberians, and other

Whence Came the Hittites ? types which loom in the mists of primitive history. We cannot, at present, do much more than conjecture that the population of Asia Minor in the second millennium, and even earlier, was Hittite, and that we must look there for the centre of this civilisation, which here concerns us only in so far as it spread over the Taurus. Here, again, it is impossible at present to establish proof of the mutual connections and affinities of the separate nationalities, but it is unreasonable to suppose that in an organised and united movement of nations different races took part promiscuously. When, therefore, the problem of the "Hittite" hieroglyphic writing is solved, we may, perhaps, find different dialects represented in the inscriptions of the different countries, inscriptions having been found in Syria, especially at Hamath, Aleppo, Carchemish, Marash, and Cilicia.

The Hittites, at the epoch when our information begins, had already forced their way into Syria, Mesopotamia, and even Northern Babylonia, for our earliest mention of them is in a recently discovered chronicle in the British Museum, which proves that they succeeded in capturing and sacking Babylon at the end of the first dynasty of Babylon before the Kassite conquest. Later on, in the fifteenth century, Mitani possessed the supremacy in Mesopotamia and Northern Syria, especially Khanigalbat, or Melitene, and in Musri, the tract which lies south of it, reaching away to the Anti-Taurus and the Taurus. This is the most ancient Hittite people with whom we are acquainted by means of their own inscriptions; it is, however, to be conjectured that they formed by no means the first detachment of the race which penetrated to Syria and across the Euphrates. In the Tell el-Amarna letters we find many indications of a Hittite population even in the southern district of Syria; the name of a prince, whose town we must look for in the territory of the Phœnicians, is undoubtedly Hittite. It cannot be ascertained at present to what extent we must look for Hittite names among the many which have not a Canaanite sound, especially in Syrian towns. This much, however, is clear— that the Hittites by that time had penetrated far into Syria.

By the side of these early Hittite tribes the empire of the Khatti, or Kheta, must have already existed, being called so uninterruptedly after the time of Thothmes III. We can now accurately determine from its own records and from the letters of Tushratta that it still had its capital in Cappadocia. We do not yet know how far it extended to the west, but we can trace both in the Tell el-Amarna letters, and in recently found documents at Boghaz Köi its later advance toward Syria. Tushratta himself was attacked by the Khatti, and before the end of the reign of Amenophis IV. the kingdom of Mitani had been brought to an end by the victorious advance of the Hittite king Shubbiluliuma and his successors, Murshili and Muttallu. In Phœnicia it was known how to make their menacing inroads not less alarming to the Pharaoh than the plans of the Babylonians. Aziri, the Amorite, in particular based his attacks against Nukhashshe, in the district of Aleppo, on the invasion of the Khattian king, from whom he professed to wish to rescue the land for the Pharaoh. As it turned out, Sapalul had already invaded Nukhashshe—that is to say, had advanced south of the territory of Mitani. Some fragments of the correspondence between him and the Pharaoh are extant. They testify to a strained position. Matters

had gone to the extent of a refusal to show respect, since in the correspondence the king of the Khatti placed his name in front of that of the Pharaoh instead of after it, the position which is demanded by courtesy. This furnishes the subject of a special letter of the Pharaoh.

The advance of the Khatti, which is thus attested, was favoured in the next period by the impotence of Egypt. Accordingly, Assyria and the Khatti were natural rivals in Syria. So long as Adad-nirari I., Shalmaneser I., and Tukulti-Ninib

A HITTITE SCULPTURE FROM WESTERN ASIA

Hittite sculptures are found over the whole of Asia Minor as far as the west coast. This is one of the " Sesostris " sculptures, near Smyrna, showing the pointed cap and turned-up boots.

asserted their power and kept possession of Mesopotamia, their advance must have still been blocked; indeed, under Shalmaneser, Assyria advanced as far as the borders of the Khattian empire itself. However, by the precipitate downfall of the Assyrian power, owing to the death of Tukulti-Ninib, about 1270 B.C., they obtained a free hand in Syria.

We now find them, on the renewed advance of Egypt in the twelfth century B.C., in possession of almost all Syria, and it is to this period that the large and important find of tablets at Boghaz Köi mostly belongs. It was already known from the Egyptian inscriptions that under Rameses II. friendship existed between the kings of the Khatti, Sapalul, and Mautenra —that is, that Egypt had tolerated their advance. Seti I. records wars against the king of the Khatti, when he begins to **Egypt's** reconquer the Asiatic provinces; **Hittite** but it is improbable that he had **Wars** already won victories over him. Ramses II., on his further advance into Palestine, had been forced to fight several battles with the Khatti, and boasts, in particular, of a great victory at Kadesh, on the Orontes, one of the towns which even in the Tell el-Amarna period had a prince with a name that is probably non-Semitic. The battle is more important from its description than from its results. Sixteen years afterwards a solemn treaty was concluded between the two powers, in virtue of which both states mutually acknowledged their respective rights, and pledged themselves to guard their common interests. The king of the Khatti was Khetasar—or, as we now read the name in his own inscriptions, Khattu-shili. While Egypt, by this agreement, claimed Pales-

tine roughly as far as Mount Carmel, Syria was completely conceded to the Khatti, and belonged to them as absolutely as it did, for example, to the Assyrians in the eighth to the seventh centuries. Henceforth the term "land of the Khatti" was adopted by the Assyrians to designate Syria; and the title remained, and was even extended further to the south in times when the Khatti had long since disappeared, or only the small remnant of their former greatness, the kingdom of Carchemish, still existed.

It is interesting to note that among the tablets recently found at Boghaz Köi one of the most important of the diplomatic communications as yet deciphered is **Treaty** a version in the Babylonian **with** language of the treaty drawn **Egypt** up between Khattu-shili and Ramses II., which was previously known to us only from the Egyptian copy upon the walls of the temple of Karnak. The tablets, and fragments of tablets, found upon this site during the excavations carried out since the summer of 1905 number several thousands, and it is probable that the site is still far from exhausted. They are all

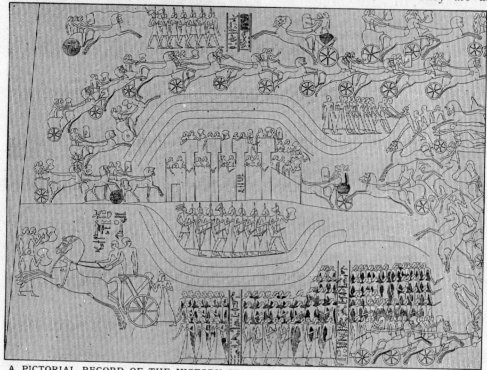

A PICTORIAL RECORD OF THE VICTORY OF RAMSES OVER THE HITTITES AT KADESH
From a sculpture in an Egyptian temple commemorating the victory of Khatusaru

HITTITE SPIES CAUGHT BY THE EGYPTIANS

From a picture in an Egyptian temple, illustrating an incident before Ramses' battle with the Hittites at Kadesh. The spies, being beaten, disclosed the secret of a Hittite ambush, thereby contributing to the Hittite defeat.

written in the cuneiform character of Babylonia ; but while some are composed in the Babylonian language, the majority are written in the native language of the country. Those in the former category, like the Tell el-Amarna letters, are composed in Babylonian, since that was the language of diplomacy throughout the East. Of these several represent diplomatic communications which passed between Ramses II. and the Hittite king Khattu-shili, the most important being the Babylonian text of the treaty already referred to. From these documents we learn that the native name of Khattu-shili's wife was Padu-khipa, and that among his predecessors upon the Hittite throne were Shubbiluliuma, Murshili and Muttallu, under whom the Hittite advance into Northern Syria took place. As might be expected, the tablets also begin to furnish information concerning the kingdom of Mitani, and the names of other members of the family of Tushratta who occupied the throne have recently been recovered. We may note that **Hittite Egyptian Letters** in Khattu-shili's correspondence the full name of Ramses II. is given as Uashmuaria Shate-puaria Riamashesha mai-Amana, which gives the appropriate pronunciation, doubtless slightly altered in a foreign tongue and writing, of the Egyptian name which we conventionally read as Usermaa(t)ra setepenra Ramses meri-Amen. We thus see, as in the Egyptian names which occur in the Tell el-Amarna

letters, that no modern transliteration of ancient Egyptian represents accurately the true pronunciation of the characters. It is natural that of the documents discovered, those in the Babylonian language should be the first to be deciphered. When the whole " find " has been made available for study we shall be able to **Babylonian Hittite History** trace in considerable detail the history of the Hittite empire at the period of its greatest prosperity. A preliminary examination of the documents composed in the native tongue seems to indicate that this was employed for communications to vassal states, for matters of internal administration, and for local and commercial intercourse. The decipherment of this class of tablets is facilitated by the fact that the language is written upon them in the Babylonian character, which was thus employed by the Hittites of this period in much the same way as the Arabic character by the Persians and the Turks. The language itself, it is already noted, is very similar to that of Arzawa, in which two of the letters found at Tell el-Amarna are written, and it is not improbable that the tablets will furnish us with examples of other native languages and dialects. These documents, both Babylonian and Hittite, are already yielding the names of a large number of provinces and cities of the Hittites themselves, and of the races with whom they were in contact, and when they have been completely deciphered

CARCHEMISH, A LANDMARK OF THE VANISHED HITTITE POWER IN SYRIA
This mound at Jerabis, on the Euphrates, probably covers the remains of the Hittite state of Carchemish.

and translated, there is little doubt that they will reveal an entirely new chapter in the ancient history of the Nearer East.

The supremacy of the Khatti in Syria did not last long ; they were not driven out by Assyria, which did not stand in the way of their advance, but when Tiglath-pileser again invaded Syria their empire had already lost its power. It had been overthrown by peoples of its own race, those which followed the very same road as the Mitani in former times. We find these people in 1100 B.C. in the extreme north of Mesopotamia and on the borders of Asia Minor in conflict with Tiglath-pileser. They may have destroyed the empire of the Khatti in Northern Asia Minor, and occupied the most northerly part of Syria as well as the adjacent districts of Asia Minor, invading them from the north. The sole remnant of the Khattian empire was the state of Carchemish, on the Euphrates, which may at first have also possessed part of Syria. After this time this state is termed Khattian by the Assyrians, and this is the cause of the transference of the term "land of the Khatti" to Syria proper. But soon, being hard pressed on the south by the Aramæans, it lost its importance, and after the time of Shal-

maneser II. it meets us as an insignificant tributary state of Assyria, or of the other great powers which dominated Syria, such as Urartu, before 745 B.C., and was then annexed by Sargon under its last king, Pisiris.

The newly immigrated peoples which thus took the place of the Khatti, and were, according to the theory referred to above, Hittites also, were especially the Kummukhi, or Kumani, who had been settled for some time in the district south of Armenia on both banks of the Euphrates when Tiglath-pileser mentions them for the first time. They remained permanently settled there, and their name (Commagene) was retained for the district on the right bank up to Hellenistic times. In the Assyrian era they were governed by kings of their own, but, like Carchemish, they were gradually brought under the yoke of Assyria, or had to obey the existing rulers of Syria. During the wars of the Assyrians with Urartu, the princes of Kummukhi, being situated exactly between the two powers, naturally vacillated from one to the other. The Hittite population here, as throughout Armenia, was first driven back by the immigrating Indo-Aryans. Besides this older stratum of the Kummukhi, the Kaski are mentioned, who

KHATUSARU, PRINCE OF THE KHATTI
From an Egyptian sculpture of the Hittite prince and his daughter.
The above is reproduced from "The Struggle of the Nations," S.P.C.K.

dwelt towards Northern Asia Minor—roughly speaking, Armenia Minor—and soon disappeared from the Assyrian horizon; it is possible that their name is identical with that of the Colchians. Tiglath-pileser mentions together with these, for the first time, the people of the Muski, some of whose levies tried in his time to conquer the territory on the left bank of the Euphrates, which had already been occupied by the Kummukhi. They were repulsed, and likewise disappeared from view, until their name meets us 400 years later, when Mita of Muski, as sovereign of a powerful kingdom in Asia Minor, waged war with Sargon on the Halys and in Cilicia, and was solicited by Carchemish for help against the Assyrian. The fact that the last representative of the Hittite power in Syria did this proves that the Muski were regarded by him as the successors of the Khatti, who once dominated

TYPES OF HITTITE SOLDIERS

"Struggle of the Nations," S.P.C.K.

A PRINCE OF THE KHATTI HITTITES

under an over-lord, which amounted to a regular Tabal kingdom. Thus Sargon actually gave his daughter in marriage to Ambaridi, the "king" of the Tabal, and ceded to him, as a dowry, a portion of Cappadocia. He evidently intended by this favour to secure for himself a sort of "buffer state" against Midas, and thus to bring the Tabal—who had never been subjugated—if not under Assyria, at least under a native yoke. These were considerable nations, which had preserved the bond of national homogeneity, and in the highlands, a district more remote from the influence of Babylonian civilisation, were better able to retain their characteristics as well as the organisation of their tribal life. These immigrations also left some trace in the Syrian towns. We can clearly distinguish in them down to the Syrian age a non-Semitic as compared with an Aramæan population. But in them, just as in Carchemish, we should, on the whole, see not component parts of this new wave, but rather remains of the conquest by the Khatti, or of the "Hittite" immigrations which preceded them. At least, no definite people is here named by the Assyrians, but the accounts speak of princes who had long been in possession of the land, bearing both Semitic and non-Semitic, that is, Hittite, names.

Asia Minor. They must, therefore, have replaced these in the supremacy of the Halys, and further westward; for Mita of Muski is none other than the Midas of Phrygia, who, soon after 700, met his death in the wars with the Cimmerians.

Melitene itself was also a separate state under princes of its own. The inhabitants were closely akin to the Tabal, who adjoined them on the south, and were settled mainly in Cappadocia as far as the Taurus, which separated them from Cilicia. They were split up generally into a number of cantons, which were governed by their own princes; their neighbours in Melitene were occasionally included among them, although sometimes we hear of a union

We must equally reckon among the Hittites the population of Cilicia, called by the Assyrians Kue; and here hieroglyphic rock-inscriptions have been found right up to the Taurus. We may see in this population a wave of the great stream which flowed thither from the Tabal. We ascertain from the Tell el-Amarna letters that the Lukki, also mentioned in Egyptian inscriptions, engaged in piracy on the coast of Asia Minor and proceeded as far as Cyprus ; this was the people which gave Lycia its name, and from which Lycaonia also derived its title. If we add to this the

Western Group of Hittites Leuco-Syrians, who naturally are not "white Syrians," as the popular Greek etymology signifies, but are the Lukki from Suri, or Cappadocia, we thus have another branch of the Hittite migration which we may probably bracket with the Khatti. We might include in it the Hittite inhabitants of Cilicia. They would thus form a broader stratum than the Kummukhi, Muski, and Tabal, and would have entered the country almost contemporaneously with the Khatti.

If we consider these and the Tabal to compose a western group as compared with the eastern, which is represented by the Mitani and the Urartu nations—the Kummuki also belong more to this group—we can find authority for this division in a fact which, in the lack of other evidence, rivets our attention. The eastern group worshipped as their chief divinity Teisbes, or Teshub, who was identified with the Semitic Hadad, or Ramman. In classical times we find him still represented as Jupiter of Doliche in Commagene, with thunderbolt or lightning and the Hittite double axe. The chief deity of the western group, on the contrary, is Tarkhu, or Tarku, whose name meets us in the composition of many proper names. The hieroglyphic rock-inscriptions which we possess from Syria and Cilicia probably date from a period before Assyria was supreme there, or, indeed, had appeared upon the scene, and they may belong to the period of the earliest Hittite migration. The most ancient Hittite sculptures on Syrian soil have been brought to light by

Most Ancient Hittite Sculptures the excavations at Senjirli Amq. They belong to the pre-Assyrian age, the most ancient of them probably to the second millennium B.C. ; in Senjirli we assume at all events only an old Hittite population, springing at latest from the Khatti ; Aramæans forced their way there later.

The result of this development is that Syrians and Aramæans are treated as synonymous, although this is true only in later times. In reality the Aramæans did not immigrate into Syria first, but became predominant there only after they had already spread over Babylonia and Mesopotamia. The reason of this is not far to seek ; the Hittite migrations had been able to advance only so long as no state powerful enough to offer a vigorous resistance was formed in the valley of the Euphrates. Mitani and the Kassites had advanced from two sides of the civilised country ; the earliest waves of the Hittites had equally profited by the weakness of Babylonia and Assyria. Contemporaneously with this stream, the flood of the Aramæan migration spread from the south over the Euphrates valley and Syria, meeting with no resistance from the Kassites who had settled on the river banks but forced to fight in Syria with the Khatti and their successors. Thus districts which appear to us at a subsequent period as completely Aramæan can have been occupied by Aramæans only at a comparatively late date. Damascus, Aleppo, and the towns of Northern Syria thus became Aramæan last of all, when Mesopotamia and Babylonia had long since been inun-

Limits of Aramæan Influence dated by Aramæans. A town such as Pethor on the Euphrates, until then Hittite like Carchemish, was occupied only by Aramæans under Ashur-irbi ; Carchemish had always resisted them, and the more notherly districts of " Suri," like Commagene, had never been conquered at all by Aramæans, but had remained, until the annexation by Assyria, under the government of Hittite princes and tribes—a state of things which does not exclude the possibility of an advance by sections of the Aramæan population.

The picture which Syria presents to us of the Aramæan migration about 1500 B.C. is as folllows : The old Canaanite population was driven out or subjugated by the Hittites, and now the Aramæans were advancing against these latter. Since Hittites still possessed in the twelfth century Cœle-Syria as far as Kadesh, the advance of the Aramæans into Syria was not, like that of the Arabians, immediately connected with the Syrian hinterland—that is, with the occupation of the countries of Damascus, Hamath, and Aleppo. They first went in a more easterly direction along the Euphrates, and, having seized Mesopotamia, they crossed the Euphrates and advanced towards the west—that is, toward Central Syria. Tiglath-pileser I.

ENTRANCE TO PALACE OR TEMPLE AT OYUK, GUARDED BY TWO SPHINXES

BAS-RELIEF AT FRAKTIN, REPRESENTING SACRIFICES TO HITTITE GODS

FACADE OF SCULPTURED STONES AND ENTRANCE TO BUILDINGS AT OYUK

HITTITE ART AND ARCHITECTURE IN CAPPADOCIA

drove the Aramæans at Carchemish over the river, where they occupied places of retreat on the right bank. The Hittite towns of Syria, with the exception of Damascus, were not occupied by them until later. It was only, therefore, in the Assyrian time that Aramaic supplanted the old Canaanite language. In the inscriptions of Senjirli from the time of Tiglath-pileser IV. we have perhaps the first attempts at Aramaic writing in these districts. Further to the north the Aramæan migration came into contact with the last wave of the Hittites, the Kummukhi, etc., and was thus hindered from any further advance. On their side they again prevented the advance of these latter into the regions once occupied by the Khatti as far down as Cœle-Syria. The action of Assyria after Ashurnasirpal prevented the Aramæans from occupying the larger cities and thus completing the subjugation of the countries already overrun by them. When that happened, the power of the Hittites to resist had certainly been broken, as is shown, for example, by the above-mentioned occupation of Pethor by Aramæans. But now everything was subdued by the Assyrians; the supremacy rested with them, and in a few districts with the Hittites. The failure to gain the political control is no proof indeed that the population was not becoming Aramæan; this tendency indeed would increase, unhindered, by peaceful methods.

Growth of Aramaic Language

The interference of Assyria explains the fact that we do not meet Aramæan states —that is, states where Aramæans ruled, a point which is almost clearly shown in our authorities by the names of the princes— in the old seats of civilisation of Central Syria; we may disregard those settled in the open country, since they could have had little influence on history. The only considerable Aramæan state which had for its home one of the centres of civilisation was Damascus; this, the farthest from Assyria of all those which we have mentioned, was the last to be attacked by the Assyrians.

Damascus Ruled by Aramæans

When Ashurnasirpal undertook his Phœnician expedition in 877 B.C., Amq, the tableland extending north of the lake of Antioch as far as the spurs of the Taurus, was united under one government, the kingdom of Patini. This is called in the Bible Padan-Aram, and is therefore regarded as Aramæan, the document which so calls it being the late Priestly Code. Nothing more need be inferred from this than that the population here at a later period was Aramæan. It does not seem probable that Aramæan princes ruled here in the time of Ashurnasirpal, and that the kingdom was therefore Aramæan; the names of the princes are indeed non-Semitic, therefore Hittite probably, so that we may see in this state a product of the Hittite conquest. We can determine from the Assyrian inscriptions the names of several kings; these are, Lubarna or Liburna, in the time of Ashurnasirpal; then Sapalulme, Kalparunda, Lubarna II., who died in 833 B.C., under Shalmaneser II.; Surri in 832 B.C., and Sasi after 832 B.C. The centre of the state is Amq, with its capital, Kinalia. The whole state had, like all these products of the Hittite time, a feudal constitution based on the system of cantons and tribes, the separate princes of which were independent or subject, according to the power of the suzerain. When, therefore, subsequently, Tiglath-pileser appeared upon the scene, the princes of the separate districts acted independently, and the kingdom of Patini apparently ended. We find, therefore, in its place the following separate states: Marqasi, the present Marash; Gurgum, Unki, or Amq, the former capital of the kingdom; Sam'al, and Ia'udi; and they were gradually annexed by Assyria.

Break-up of the Kingdom of Patini

The inhabitants of these countries, whose kings were, as compared with the Assyrian kings, merely large landowners, became in the meantime strongly tinged by Aramæan influences, although this does not prove that the Aramæans were rulers. Indeed, the names of the princes, such as Panammu and Karal, are hardly Semitic; and the only Semitic name, Azriia'u of Ia'udi, is probably not Aramæan, but Canaanite, and therefore belongs to the pre-Hittite stratum; the former have actual analogies in Cilician proper names, and may therefore be Hittite. On the other hand, the spread of the Aramæan language is noticeable, and the use of Aramaic and of alphabetic writing begins. It is also illustrative of the composition of the population, and of the persistence of an old Canaanite strain, that even now Canaanite was written in the "Phœnician" style, as is proved by a small fragment found a mile or two west of Senjirli.

The traces of the Aramæan script and language of this period were derived from excavations carried out in Senjirli at Amq, the capital of the small country Sam'al. These documents were drawn up by Barrekab, the vassal of Tiglath-pileser IV., the son of the Panammu mentioned by Tiglath-pileser, who died, according to his son's inscription, in 732 or 731 B.C., in the camp of Damascus, to which place he had followed the army. A somewhat older monument comes from Gerjin, a place five miles east of Senjirli, and was erected by Panammu the elder, "king" of the neighbouring district Ia'udi. The inscriptions are the most ancient texts in Aramaic which we at present possess, and they show by an unskilled employment of the language, and the want of any uniform orthography, that we have here the first attempts made in these regions at writing Aramaic. It follows from this that Aramaic was now spoken here, and that Aramæans had established a dominion by peaceful measures such as they could not have founded by force.

To the east of this district lies Aleppo, which is not mentioned in the Assyrian inscriptions as the seat of a separate state. When Shalmaneser II. came there on his first expedition against Damascus, in 854 B.C., he sacrificed to Hadad, but he tells us nothing as to the political position of the town ; we might suppose that it then had its own government, and was therefore a relic of the Canaanite-Hittite power. In the Tell el-Amarna period we find in this country the state of Nukhashshe, which had a constitution similar to that of Patini. Its suzerain writes to Amenophis III. that his grandfather had been appointed by Thothmes III. ; he himself was being hard pressed by the Khatti. Aziri, the Amorite, speaks of kings of Nukhashshe ; the land was governed, therefore, by various cantonal princes.

Aleppo a Separate State

To the south of this, Hamath commands the country between the territories of Aleppo and of Damascus. In the Tell el-Amarna letters the towns Ni, Katana, and Kadesh are named in its place. We may see in the first two the most important towns of the country, Apamea and Hœms, or Emesa, or their predecessors. They were occupied by a Canaanite and Hittite population ; we have already become familiar with Kadesh as the home of the

Khatti in the twelfth century. Here, too, the Aramæans were unable to make conquests. We therefore find in the kingdom of Hamath, which soon afterwards comprised the whole country, a state with a mixed population of Canaanites and Hittites. When Shalmaneser, in 854 B.C., marched against Damascus, among his "allies," in reality his vassals, were Biridri and Irkhulini, king of Hamath. Like the other vassals, he broke away from Damascus on the change of dynasty under Hazael, and appears to have joined Assyria, since after that time no more is heard of Hamath. We meet Hamath again, under Tiglath-pileser IV., as an Assyrian vassal state, but under Sargon in the rebellion of Ia'ubidi it lost its independence.

Hamath a Vassal Kingdom

The territory of Damascus, the last great city toward the desert, adjoined that of Hamath on the south. At the period of the Tell el-Amarna letters it plays no more important part than Hamath, although it is mentioned as still subject to the Egyptians. It then suddenly appears, contemporaneously with the kingdom of David, as the seat of another kingdom, which had arisen during the impotence of the greater nations. From the very first it was in the possession of Aramæans, for the kings of Damascus were Aramæans, and this state is always expressly designated as Aramæan. This is the only instance in which the Aramæans, generally speaking, were ever rulers of a considerable state, based on an old centre of civilisation, and in which we can speak of any encroachment of the Aramæans on the political field of world history.

Damascus owed this advantage to its situation, which long protected it from the attacks of Assyria. On the other hand, it lay the nearest of all the centres of civilisation to the plains ; and its importance consisted then, as now, in its peculiar position as the starting point of the caravan route through the Syrian desert. Damascus was thus the emporium of the Arabian and Babylonian trade with Syria and Palestine. It was therefore the great city in Syria which was first exposed to the attacks of the Aramæans invading from the plains, and it thus first fell into their hands. Even among the Tell el-Amarna letters a short despatch to the Egyptian court speaks of a menacing advance of Aramæan hordes ; it is not clear

Damascus Syria's Greatest City

from what place they came, but the writers must have been settled somewhere in Syrian territory. The advance of the Aramæans and their successes in this district are further proofs of the fact that to the south of Damascus in the time of Saul and David there was a small Aramæan state in Soba, and also,

Scene of Absalom's Banishment stretching right up to Israelitish territory, the state of Geshur, where Absalom lived in banishment. But these states attained no position of importance, nor did they endure for long. It is indeed a probable conjecture to associate the rise of Damascus under such circumstances with its occupation by the Aramæans. According to this view the empire of Damascus would rank from first to last as a creation of the Aramæans, and may, from the standpoint of political development, be regarded as the focus of Aramæan history.

The first references to the empire are found in the Bible. According to these, in the time of Solomon, Rezon, son of El-yada, threw off the yoke of his lord Hadad-ezer, king of Zobah, seized Damascus, and thence, like David from Hebron, increased his power. Zobah must thus have been a centre of the Aramæans, who had pressed on against Syria. The occupation of Damascus would accordingly be the next stage in their advance, as well as their greatest success in this region. Rezon is said to have been continually at war with Solomon. Galilee and the district east of Jordan are henceforth a constant object of contention between Damascus and Israel. The Bible mentions other kings of Damascus ; the tradition is uncertain, however, and the names are corrupt. It is most probable that we have in them the next two kings, the first of whom is called by the Bible Hezion, and may well have been named Hazael ; he was followed by Tab-Rimmon, or

The Rise of Damascus Tab-el, but nothing beyond their names is known. In the period after their successor Bir-idri, the Ben-hadad of the Biblical narrative, our accounts are more copious. Damascus under him, about 885–844 B.C., comes into prominence as the leading state in Syria. In the year 854 B.C. Bir-idri was attacked by Shalmaneser II. On this occasion the latter enumerates the states dependent on Damascus, which had been forced to supply troops, as follows :

Hamath, Israel—under Ahab, Moab and Judah are included as being dependent on Israel, and Edom, in its turn, dependent on Judah—the North Phœnician states to the north of Gebal, Ammon, and Kue, or Cilicia, in fact a list of vassals which represents an empire such as cannot be shown to have ever existed there before. The battle at Karkar did not result in any success for Shalmaneser. Equally fruitless were the attempts in his next expeditions to defeat this vanguard of Syria. So long as Damascus was not subdued, Assyria could not get a firm footing there. While this was the case, it was impossible for any states in those regions to side with Assyria, even if they wished to, for they were always exposed to the attack of Damascus so soon as the Assyrian army was withdrawn. We can trace this fact in the history of Israel. The issue now always turns on the question whether Assyria or Damascus should be supported ; and this question continued to influence the policy of the smaller states until Damascus was taken by Tiglath-pileser.

We must regard the increased power of Damascus, which we now first notice, as

Powerful Kings of Damascus due to Bir-idri. Even in later years he and his successor Hazael were taken by the Israelites as types of the greatness of Damascus. Amos (i. 4) mentions the palaces of Ben-hadad as signs of the flourishing power of the state, which then for the last time was interfering in the history of Israel. Damascus is not alluded to before Shalmaneser. But we may, perhaps, gather from the silence of Ashurnasirpal on his way to Patini, and from the road which he then took, that the empire of Bir-idri already existed at that time, and that the Assyrians avoided any collision with it. For this reason he did not extend his movements beyond Patini, and did not march further southward into Phœnicia ; with the exception of Arvad he mentions no tributary Phœnician states, beyond a few which Shalmaneser does not enumerate as vassals of Damascus. It is possible that here also a critical state of affairs may have existed. In any case he avoided an attack on the hinterland or even a demand for tribute from it ; this may account also for his silence as to Israel—then, perhaps, under Omri— which was tributary to Damascus, while Tyre, for example, pays tribute to Assyria. The Bible tells us—in 2 Kings viii.—

of the death of Bir-idri in one of the narratives of the prophet Elisha, but in a way which does not make it clear what part his successor Hazael played in the matter. This change of monarchy is clearly connected with the fall of the house of Omri —that is, of the great Yahve movement in Israel and Judah, which had brought Jehu to the throne. Since Jehu quickly submitted to Assyria, it may be concluded that Assyria had a hand in the revolution, which she fostered in the hope of weakening an enemy

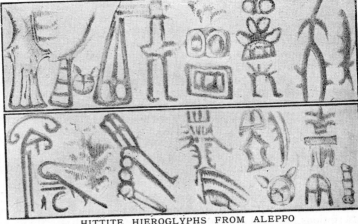

HITTITE HIEROGLYPHS FROM ALEPPO
An untranslated inscription representing a distinct Hittite dialect.

AN UNSOLVED PROBLEM IN HIEROGLYPHS
This Carchemish inscription, like all other Hittite inscriptions, has not been deciphered.

she could not subdue in the field. Hazael may also, perhaps, have courted Assyria in order to secure his throne, but, so soon as he was king of Damascus his interests demanded resistance to Assyria and an attempt to recover his old power. We therefore find him at once, in 842 B.C., at war with Shalmaneser. But a vast difference is now perceptible, which shows how Assyrian diplomacy had carried out its task. While under Bir-idri the vassal princes were always mentioned,

Hazael now stands alone; and while the Assyrians had always hitherto been repulsed, they advanced this time right into the territory of Damascus itself, and Hazael was forced to defend himself in the capital. The other strong places were naturally not captured; Shalmaneser was obliged to content himself with laying waste the open country in the true Assyrian fashion. The expedition of 839 B.C. met with equally small success, and after that Assyria renounced for the time any further efforts to reach her goal. A disastrous time now dawned for the

HITTITE INSCRIPTION IN HIGH RELIEF FROM CARCHEMISH

M   24   G

states—Israel among the number—which meanwhile had joined Assyria, for Hazael began to subjugate them once more. Their position was the more unenviable, since a renewal of submission to their old lord implied a defection from the new lord, whose vengeance was then to be dreaded. They were thus placed between two fires. Israelite history shows us the distress to which this state was reduced, and the Bible has preserved the recollection of it when it makes Elisha bewail the evil which Hazael would bring upon Israel.

Israel Between Two Fires

The successor of Hazael must have been Mari, who is familiar to us from the inscriptions of Adad-nirari III. ; the Bible in 2 Kings xiii. 25, appears to mention him also under the name Benhadad. He had been again attacked by Assyria, and had submitted after a siege of Damascus. Through this the other vassals of Assyria at least enjoyed peace, among them Israel. The decadence of the Assyrian power after Adad-nirari had once more given Damascus a free hand. In 773 we have evidence of a new expedition under Shalmaneser III. ; then nothing more transpires as to Damascus until Tiglath-pileser IV. appears to resume and to conclude the struggle.

We must see the successor of Mari in Tab-el, whom the Bible, in Isaiah vii. 6, names as the father of Rezon ; nothing further is known of him. With his son and successor, Rezon, we have once more additional sources of information. We find him, in 738 B.C., on the first appearance of Tiglath-pileser IV., still among the tribute payers. But soon afterwards he revolted, and at the same time, by contriving the rebellion in Samaria, which caused the fall of Pekahiah, the son of Manahem, who was loyal to Assyria, he raised his partisan Pekah to the throne. We then find the two together in 735 B.C. before the gates of Jerusalem (Isa. vii.) attempting to overthrow Ahaz, who adhered to Assyria, and hoped with its aid to gain Israel. But in the very next year Tiglath-pileser appeared in Palestine, subjugated Philistia, overthrew Pekah in Samaria in 733 B.C., and besieged and captured Damascus in 732 B.C. Rezon lost his throne and his life, and Damascus became an Assyrian province. This virtually completed the subjuga-

Final Subjugation of Syria

tion of Syria, since no further resistance of a serious nature was possible. The rebellion of Ia'ubidi of Hamath, which had hitherto supported Assyria, was easily suppressed by Sargon. Syria after that time was ruled by Assyrian governors, or feudal lords, who were unable to follow out any independent policy of their own.

There never was a Syrian civilisation in the sense in which we speak of a Babylonian or Egyptian culture. History has shown us how Syria, lying between the two great zones of civilisation, was almost always subject to their influence. Such investigations, as was the case with the political history, present far greater difficulties than in the region of the Euphratean empires, since a system of petty states has always prevailed in Syria, which renders it hard for the historian to adopt a comprehensive view, even if he were sufficiently acquainted with the necessary details. Here, therefore, we must content ourselves for the present with ascertaining isolated facts of which chance has informed us. At the same time we possess in the monuments on Syrian soil the productions of a civilisation the history of which is only beginning to be revealed to us. The explorer looks with longing eyes at the so-called " Hittite " hieroglyphs, in which an increasing number of inscriptions are being found. The materials are as yet, comparatively speaking, insufficient to furnish a key to their decipherment, which a more copious supply of specimens or the discovery of a lengthy bilingual inscription may reveal in the future. We can demonstrate that the system of writing employs the same fundamental notions as the cuneiform characters and the hieroglyphs, the main principle being the employment of separate signs for the syllable and for ordinary ideas ; but a simple conjecture might have deduced that from the mere number of the written characters. Only their outward forms, therefore, are clear to us as yet, and these show, apart from their shape, a fundamental distinction from those of Egypt and Babylonia. While the Egyptians or Babylonians scratch or cut the writing into the material, the greater number of the Hittite inscriptions which we at present possess are executed in high relief upon the stone. It is idle to speculate as to the origin of this custom from the

Civilisation That is Still Obscure

comparatively late documents which have been found on a foreign soil ; but, since the incised cuneiform writing is the reproduction of what was originally scratched or impressed on clay, the reverse usage must point to a different origin. It is, indeed, a point to be considered that we have as yet to do only with monuments engraved with this hieroglyphic character ; simple documents, corresponding to the Babylonian clay tablets and our written papers, with which the writing originated, are wanting, for the tablets found at Boghaz Köi, including the native Hittite texts, without exception employ the Babylonian syllabary. It is worthy of note that the style of the older Aramæan inscriptions on Syrian soil meets us in those of the eighth century, while, on the other hand, the oldest inscription found on Canaanite soil—the stele of King Mesha, of Moab, the contemporary of Omri—is scratched upon the stone. If we are to recognise in the latter the influence of Babylonia and Assyria, it is clear that the Hittite custom continued to operate in a district once occupied by the Kheta. As we have already stated, the tablets discovered at Boghaz Köi will probably furnish us with evidence on which we may decide the disputed question as to the origin and date of these hieroglyphic inscriptions, which are usually regarded as products of the Hittite civilisation.

Granted that the Hittite culture exercised an influence which for a time matched that of the other bank of the Euphrates, this will have shown itself in many achievements of civilised life which are as yet unknown to us. We possess perhaps an important testimony of this in the *mina* of Carchemish, which was distinguished by

THE MOABITE STONE
This stele of Mesha, king of Moab, is the oldest inscription found on Canaanite soil. It is cut in the stone, while Hittite inscriptions are in high relief.

the Assyrians from their national one. It is not, indeed, established whether that was a weight adopted from the Hittites. But if such was the case, this alone would indicate a far-reaching influence of the Hittite spirit upon trade and business transactions ; and indeed even on the conditions of the tenure of the soil. From this it would result that not only a dominant section of the Syrian population represented the Hittite strain, but that in reality a population had developed which preserved its national characteristics, and under the changed conditions of life in their new home continued to develop independently. If an art, which existed there only for the powerful and ruling classes, and was fostered for them alone, had comparatively little to do with the subordinate sections of the people, the universal adoption and recognition even by the later Assyrian rulers of the Hittite weights and measures show that the population of Syria in all its classes must have been Hittite, or permeated with Hittite customs. This would, besides, tally in every respect with what we are as yet able to ascertain as to the religious conditions. We have not regarded the conquest by the Khatti as the first appearance of "Hittite" peoples in Syria, and we may assume that, both with them and after them, other kindred nations settled there. The conquest of Syria, evidence of which we begin to see in the Tell el-Amarna letters, was one undertaken by a great state, which had its seat and the central point of its civilisation and power in Asia Minor. It thus differed little from the Assyrian conquest two centuries later ; just as this did not give Syria an Assyrian population, so that of the Kheta, or Khatti, did not make the country "Khattian" down to the plain of the Orontes. The actual result was only a military occupation of the country and its impoverishment by officials. If, therefore, we may conclude that the population even of the ninth and later centuries B.C. contained an admixture of the earlier Hittite elements, we must equally see in it the result of occurrences which preceded and followed the conquest. Out of **Hittite Influence in Syria** the countless waves of this great immigration that of the Khatti represents only one, possibly the most far-reaching in its effects, but not for that reason the most lasting. Similar migrations of homogeneous tribes which inundated the empire of the Khatti in its original home, and gave it a new population, must have also affected the Syrian conquests of the Khatti. So soon as a foreign power ceased to hold in subjection the separate countries which were ruled by their native princes or governors, the result immediately followed that these hitherto dependent countries constituted so many small " kingdoms " which waged war with each other. The result of the Khatti conquest was a " Hitticising " of the country in so far as the country was open to the advancing tribes.

The same conditions prevailed when the Aramæans a little later advanced from the south. The result of this contest between the two great movements which here crossed each other's path was a population mainly Aramæan in the south, a mixed population in the centre, and a predominantly Hittite one in the north. It was organised in separate petty states, which remained independent until conquered by Assyria, a power as strong as that of the Khatti.

Such conditions could not develop any true Syro-Hittite culture. The state of things was too precarious, and revolutions followed too rapidly to allow anything peculiar to the Syrian soil to be formed which might be compared with the

Babylonian civilisation. All, therefore, that we possess of the productions of " Hittite " art is very rude. Of course, an unimportant provincial town like Sam'al, or Senjirli, to which we owe the oldest sculptures, cannot be regarded as determining the extent of Hittite achievements on Syrian soil.

We may expect to find a genuine Syro-Hittite art in Carchemish, which remained for the longest period the most flourishing seat of the Hittites. Indeed, a large number of monuments have been discovered there, but not sufficient to enable us to pass a final judgment upon Hittite art. Those brought to Europe are for the most part fragments on which all that is preserved is the inscription ; other sculptured slabs were not removed from the mound during the excavations on this site, and they are still to be seen above the soil. They include representations of two Hittite gods, the figure **Products of Aramæan Skill** of a Hittite goddess, and the like. We can summarise briefly the productions of Aramæan skill. The only specimens, indeed, to be considered are the sculptures of the last period of Sam'al-Senjirli, the statue of the god Hadad, the statue of Panammu, and the reliefs of the palace erected by his son Bar-sur. Just as the execution of the writing in high relief imitates that of the Hittites, here again hardly anything original is to be found. If it were not that Aramaic inscriptions are cut on them they would be included with the rest as merely Hittite. We have little else that is Aramæan ; nothing actually from a soil which was more purely Aramæan than the Sam'al of the eighth century. The Aramæans display but small capacity to produce independent results in culture and intellectual achievements. Just as the Arab lived on the powers of Byzantium and Persia, so they lived

HITTITE KING AND A WARRIOR
From the remains of Senjirli, Northern Syria

A HITTITE CASTLE IN ANCIENT SYRIA
A reconstruction, from remains at Senjirli, Northern Syria, of a brick castle of the Syro-Hittites.

on those of the Babylonians, Assyrians and Hittites.

Senjirli, the only ruined place in Syria which has hitherto been thoroughly excavated, has given us information as to the architecture, since it has transmitted to us the form of a midgal, or castle. This, from being the centre and place of refuge of an originally open settlement, became later the nucleus of a walled city. The influence of Babylon is noticeable in the choice of brick as the building material. It would be premature to form from this one building any opinion of the construction of the rich and powerful Syrian towns, the different centres of civilisation: Carchemish or Hierapolis, Aleppo, Hamath, Damascus, etc.

It would be still more rash to attempt to formulate the Aramæan ideas of faith and religion. A few names of deities in later tradition comprise nearly all that could serve as a basis for such speculation. The Aramæan characteristics are most strongly marked in Southern Syria, owing to the comparatively weaker influence of the Hittites, which the old Canaanite life of the second Semitic migration had successfully resisted. The ideas of Canaanites and Aramæans may, indeed,

be assumed with some probability to have been originally identical, and the question is mainly one of different names for similar religious conceptions. Thus, in view of the traditions of a time which had no longer any comprehension of the old stratification of the peoples and their different characteristics, we are hardly in a position to single out anything as peculiarly Aramæan. If, even at the period of the eighth century B.C., traces of the Canaanite language can be proved to have existed in the district of Senjirli, we must also regard the few names of gods in the inscriptions found there as a Canaanite, and therefore pre-Aramæan, inheritance which was not affected by the intermediate rule of the Hittites. At the same time, it is of course to be remembered that foreign influence must have made itself felt in great centres of culture sooner than in remote provincial towns. Thus the divine name El is clearly common to Canaanites and Aramæans. Rekab is originally Canaanite, and is found in Southern Judah. Only Hadad, whose cult is proved to have been the most important in Damascus, may be Aramæan; his Canaanite name was Ramman. or Rimmon, the god of weather and fertility.

VIEW OF MODERN SIDON SHOWING CONNECTION WITH MAINLAND

SIDON FROM THE NORTH SHOWING THE FORTIFICATIONS

THE ISLAND CITY LOOKING TOWARDS THE LEBANON MOUNTAINS

SIDON, THE ANCIENT SEAT OF PHŒNICIA'S RELIGIOUS CULT

PHŒNICIA AND CANAAN

THE strip of land which is bounded by the Syrian desert and the chain of Antilebanus on the east, and by the Mediterranean on the west, has never been the home of a great unified kingdom. Being chiefly mountainous and intersected by the two streams which rise in the centre and are of no importance for communication, the Orontes from south to north, and the Jordan from north to south, it was never able to advance far beyond the cantonal system natural to highlands, and was always hindered by the system of petty states. The sea, indeed, afforded a natural high-road of commerce for the towns on the coast ; but these lacked the hinterland, which would have offered the requisite territory for a larger population bent on developing a higher civilisation. They were thus prompted from the first to extend their power beyond the sea, and the more so since they were hard pressed in the **The Need of Oversea Expansion** rear by a succession of new and still uncivilised nations. The country, in consequence of its situation between the two great civilised states on the Euphrates and the Nile, must have been a natural goal for the efforts at expansion made by both nations long before we have any record of it. The history of these regions varies according to the power, whether Babylonian-Assyrian or Egyptian, to which they were subject. The ever-recurring spectacle, which has continued from the Hellenistic period through the Middle Ages down to our own time, is due to the position of the country and its configuration, which prevents the formation of a large state.

Accordingly in the millennia of the development and full expansion of the Sumerian and of the contemporary Egyptian civilisations a population was settled there which was probably of mixed origin. That there was a pre-Semitic element is certain. We cannot say that the pre-Semitic Palestinians were connected by kinship with the Sumerians. It is most improbable that the Sumerian race ever extended itself west of the Mesopotamian valley. And the pre-Semitic elements in Palestine are quite different from the pre-Semitic elements in Mesopotamia. There are elements in the Semitic cultures of both Palestine and Mesopotamia which must be put down to the pre-Semitic inhabitants of these lands, but **Nature of Pre-Semitic Influences** whereas in Mesopotamia these elements are evidently of Sumerian origin, in Palestine they are to be ascribed to the older inhabitants of the Mediterranean basin, whose race is to be found in Spain, in Italy, in Greece, and probably also in the Egyptian delta and the Northern African littoral : the short, dark, dolichocephalic race, which is collectively known to us now as " Mediterranean." It is to this race that the distinctively " Canaanitish " elements in the Semitic culture of Palestine must be ascribed ; in Palestine, as in Crete, sacred stones and groves were venerated, and modern British archæological labour has made it very probable that these elements of religion are in Crete of pre-Hellenic, in Palestine of pre-Semitic, origin. This is but a cursory reference to a revolutionary theory, which considerations of space forbid us to elaborate further here.

Eventually, the Semites, whom we find in the earliest ages of Egyptian history settled in the Sinaitic peninsula and possibly also in the highlands of Southern Palestine, pressed northwards, and supplanted in Palestine and Mesopotamia the older inhabitants. Henceforward Semitised Canaan, connected by kinship with the ruling people in Babylonia, was subject to its **Semitic Migrations to Palestine** influence and acknowledged its sovereignty alternately with that of Egypt. Just as all subsequent Semitic migrations probably brought to Palestine a new stratum of population, so the first of them, the Semitic Babylonians, may have discharged there some portion of its tribes. Even if this stratum of the population is more tangible for us, since it is historical in Babylonia at least, and if we can therefore see traces of it later in Phœnicia, in much that strikes us as Babylonian, yet we know nothing of any tribes which pushed on from the north toward Phœnicia; we are still without detailed accounts of the civilisation of Asia Minor at this early period.

The real history of Canaan and Palestine begins for us with the immigration of the **The Canaanite Group** new inhabitants. These nations really developed themselves there, and on the soil of that land sustained the part they played in the world's history. Since during this time Canaan in its peculiar way was comparatively independent, we term this group, which alone has given a certain importance to the country, the Canaanite. We have assumed that this migration led also to the occupation of other countries—of Babylonia, and thus of the whole Euphrates valley—and not impossibly influenced early Egypt. In Canaan and Palestine we can distinguish two sections of this immigration—an older one, which, already settled at the time when our sources of information are more copious, had long been in possession of the towns, especially of the seaports; and a younger one, which at this very time was on the point of conquering the country. The former is called the Phœnician, after its chief representatives; the second, in conformity with the Bible and the Tell el-Amarna letters, the Hebraic group. While therefore we understand by the former almost all the tribes which immigrated first, and accordingly settled in the towns and on the sea coast, the latter comprises the section which the documents at our disposal distinguish as still migrating and conquering, and thus opposed to and at war with the former. The best known of these are the tribes which the Israelite national confederation comprised, the Moabites, Ammonites, and Edomites.

Israel's National Confederation They spoke, on the whole, the same language; but the distinction between the two main groups is noticeable by differences of dialect. It is not improbable that the red-headed Amorites were not of true Semitic origin, but were Berbers, or Libyans, from Africa, possibly ultimately, like some of the Egyptians, of "proto-Semitic" affinities. They then represent a third element in the land—the Libyan or Kabyle—as distinct both from that of the Mediterranean and the Semitic.

Our present task is to treat the elder of the two Semitic groups, the settled group, according to our accounts. This contains, first and foremost, the inhabitants of the towns on the coast, the Phœnicians, as they were called by the Greeks. They immigrated into Canaan probably before the middle of the third millennium, B.C., and overran the country at first, until, pushed on by the masses following after them, they established themselves in the maritime district. The kindred tribes which pressed on after them are the Canaanites of the Bible, whom we then find, at the time of the Hebrews, in the towns of the interior, and of whom we hear nothing except their struggle with the "Hebrews."

The immigrating "Phœnicians" were naturally not a people under a uniform government and rule, but tribes which usually pressed forward independently, swept on by the general stream, pushing and being pushed, until the surviving fragment of them finally found in some place rest and settlements. There they distributed themselves among the various fortified towns, or the districts **Phœnicians a Settled People** lying under their protection. Thus they were not the founders of these towns, but took over what had been already achieved by the earlier population. Their destinies were those of settled nations. They entered into alliances with each other when their method of life brought them together; they separated when it kept them aloof. The Phœnicians proper are a settled people, and, as such, a product of the conditions which had forced them to settle permanently. Their individual groups did not migrate as compact units, and it was not until the new homes were reached that these combinations were formed.

We can distinguish some of these groups, taking them from north to south, which correspond in their main features to the important towns. The most northerly of the Phœnician states proper is Arvad. The towns lying to the north certainly belonged to it. Its exact site is known, and to the present day retains its name, Ruad. The town was situated on an island, as are Sidon and Tyre. As we go further towards the south, we come on Gebal, or Byblos, the modern Jebeil, built on the mainland, with the cult and temple of the "Ba'alat of Gebal." This town already existed before 2000 B.C., when it was known to the Egyptians at the beginning of the twelfth dynasty as Kapuna, a name which it preserved always in Egyptian. South of this comes Beirut, a separate kingdom at the Tell el-Amarna period, afterwards usually joined to Gebal ; it is never mentioned by the Assyrians. Then comes Sidon, also originally situated on an island. Its chief cult was that of Astarte, and it contained the acknowledged national sanctuary of the Phœnician tribes. Finally, the most southern state, Tyre, possessed the sanctuary of Melkart, Melek-kiryat, "King of the city," who was afterwards imported by the Tyrians into Greece as Melikertes of Corinth. More of the coast was also originally in the possession of kindred tribes ; these, however, either did not, or could not, join the Phœnician tribal league. Even in the Tell el-Amarna period we find independent princes there, whom we must call, according to the Biblical designation, "Canaanites." But then these towns, so far as they did not belong to Tyre, like Akko, Dor, and Jaffa, were occupied by the Philistines, who were not of Semitic race at all, but **Regime of Independent Princes** European immigrants from the Ægean. Their connection with the Phœnician league was thus once for all frustrated. To these larger states belonged the separate small towns. These, in part originally occupied by portions of the tribes which conquered the chief towns, in part subdued in the natural course of affairs or by force, had been compelled to join them. Many of these may occasionally have had their "king," or some other form of self-government, though they never attained any importance.

Of the four states of Arvad, Gebal, Sidon, and Tyre, not one ever extended its dominion beyond its own coast territory ; thus their position was quite small, or even insignificant. The most influential of the four were Tyre and Sidon, and they were consequently always rivals. This rivalry led for a long period to the subjection of the one by the other—the kingdom of the "Sidonians," with its capital, Tyre. A union of all the Phœnicians, or even the subjugation of the hinterland, was never accomplished. There never was an empire of all Phœnicia.

Only Sidon and Tyre attained any importance in the world's history, while the two northern states sank more and more into the background. We must not over-estimate, however, the importance of the former ; it was their reputation which made them prominent in comparison with the other two, rather than a conspicuously powerful position. They owe this reputation to the fact that precisely at the time when they appear on the horizon of the west—that is, when they came **Eminence of Sidon and Tyre** into touch with the Greeks— the Sidonian empire of Tyre was in existence, which was in reality somewhat superior to the others. Thus the name of the Sidonians and Tyrians is prominent after the ninth and eighth centuries. Two or three centuries previously there was not the slightest trace to be observed of it. In the Tell el-Amarna letters in the fifteenth century they are all equally petty, Sidon and Tyre perhaps more so than Gebal, and all alike threatened by the Amorites, who had then already occupied Arvad.

Sidon must, however, have occupied a peculiar position. The "Phœnicians" were designated by the neighbouring peoples, as by the Israelites, by the collective name of Sidonians, and it is proved that they must have so called themselves, since the same appellation is found among the Greeks of the oldest period in Homer, and the kings of the united kingdom of Tyre and Sidon bore the title "King of the Sidonians." This does not imply merely the inhabitants of Sidon, but the entire people, so far as it was then a coherent whole. That designation shows that Sidon must have assumed a commanding position, which, in conformity with these conditions, can have been only that of a universally acknowledged federal sanctuary. This position is clearly demonstrated in the veneration which was shown to the sanctuary of Sidon, the famous temple of Astarte ; it was for the Phœnicians somewhat the same as Delos or Dodona was for Greek races. This did not lead to any political supremacy any more **The Famous Sanctuary of Sidon** than in Greece the common devotion of certain states to a certain deity meant the recognition by them all of any political supremacy of the state in whose territory the common sanctuary lay. On the contrary, the only case of a permanent subjugation of a considerable tract of the coast, which we shall have to notice, originated with Tyre.

The accounts of the earliest times are more than scanty. The traditions

ALL THAT REMAINS TO-DAY OF ARVAD, ONE OF THE PHŒNICIAN STATES
The most northerly of the four Phœnician states was Arvad, now known as Ruad. It was situated on an island.

concerning Sargon of Agade and his western conquests at the beginning of the third millennium, though they have come down to us in documents of a late date, are probably trustworthy so far as they record his conquest of the Palestinian coast, and are evidence of Babylonian influence in that region. We have merely a few statements of the Sumerian patesi Gudea as to the intercourse of his country with the West. We require to realise the significance of this influence not less than that of the succeeding period, and must not judge it by the paucity of such records. Even then it is possible that ships put out to sea from the settlements which afterwards the Phœnicians occupied, and were the medium of intercourse with the West. The nameless inhabitants of this coast may even then have distributed the products of Babylonian civilisation to the rising peoples of the eastern Mediterranean.

A change in the situation was later produced by the immigration, which made the Phœnicians and their congeners lords of the land. It may have been this same immigration that brought Babylonia and

Egypt also into the hands of Semitic "Canaanites," in Egypt called the "Hyksos." Thus during this period the bond of union with the great civilised country on the Euphrates had been drawn closer ; on the other hand, intercourse was maintained with their kinsfolk in Egypt. It is thus intelligible how the influence of this connection meets us later in the civilising effects of the Tell el-Amarna period, and how the Palestinian chiefs, when subject to Egyptian rule, exchanged

PHŒNICIAN TOMB OF EGYPTIAN DESIGN
A Phœnician adaptation at Arvad of tombs at Memphis. It contained several stories, with chambers for the bodies. From a reconstruction by Ernest Renan.

with the Pharaoh letters written in cuneiform characters.

While the " Canaanite " rule in Babylonia was being ended by the Kassites, Egypt was in revolt against the barbarian Hyksos ; and the revival of prosperity induced the Pharaohs to turn their attention to Palestine, which the Kassites, who met the opposition of the bands pressing forward from Asia Minor, had been obliged to leave to its fate. There now begins the period of the Egyptian rule which was founded by the kings of the eighteenth dynasty, notably Thothmes III., and lasted for a long time.

Under his successors, Amenophis III.

attitude towards Egypt. There are letters from all the places thence as far as the southern frontier of the country. All these letters are written in cuneiform, and composed in a language which may be described as Babylonian adapted to Phœnician, a lingua franca which employed the Babylonian vocabulary, but often modelled it on the laws of Phœnician, and constructed new forms, particularly in the conjugation of the verb, which is very distinct from the Babylonian.

We are now concerned chiefly with those states only—among the number represented in the letters—which lie to the west of Lebanon and further to the south in the

PHŒNICIAN TOMBS AT ARVAD AFTER CHALDÆAN MODELS

Two chapel-tombs in the Phœnician cemetery at Arvad, with the Chaldæan round tower and cupola. Like the pictures on opposite page, the above was obtained by the official French mission to Phœnicia under Ernest Renan in 1862.

and IV., we have in the Tell el-Amarna letters the most trustworthy documents as to the condition of Palestine under the Egyptian rule, and we can by their aid picture to ourselves the state of the country in the second millennium, the era into which the immigration of the second, or Hebrew, group of the Canaanite population falls. We possess some 300 of such letters, which were sent by princes of Syria and Palestine to the Pharaoh or his officials. All countries, so far as they acknowledged the Egyptian suzerainty, are represented in the collection. The most northern country, corresponding to the district of Aleppo, is Nukhashshi, which maintained a very independent

territory of the subsequent kingdom of Israel. We will begin with the most important, the Phœnician. These states, like the whole land, were governed by their own native princes, under the sanction of the Pharaoh. No actual Egyptian administrators on the model of the Assyrian provinces were appointed. We may best call the established system an Egyptian " protectorate," as that will serve to give a picture of the local independence controlled by Egyptian residents and subject to state service which prevailed under the Pharaohs in the outlying lands of their empire.

The most northerly Phœnician town, Arvad, precisely at this time fell into the hands of a prince named Aziru, advancing from the hinterland. He is described as an Amorite. His rise determined the entire policy in Northern Phœnicia ; for, being dissatisfied with Arvad, he advanced further toward the south, where the nearest state was Gebal—then the only one of any considerable extent—and conquered in the hinterland towns of the Beka'a, such as Tunip, perhaps Heliopolis-Baalbek, and, further to the north, Ni. He extended his territory northward as far as that of Nukhashshi. His career proves that we have to do with all the phenomena of a feudal state, and one without a strong superior lord. The Pharaoh indeed does not admit any obligation to secure tranquillity in the country. His vassals have the right of declaring war, and only when they declare themselves independent, or throw themselves into the arms of another great power, or are suspected of so doing, is there any excuse for taking active measures against them. Accordingly we find continual wars waged by one neighbouring prince against another, and each one tries to make the court consider his opponent disloyal. Suspicions thrown on the loyalty of others, and assurances of their own fidelity, with protests against the accusations of the others and requests for support against them—such matters compose the contents of the letters.

Aziru was a prince of tribes which first conquered the land, and so belonged to the later stratum of the great Canaanite immigration, and thus stood in natural opposition to the inhabitants already permanently settled. These latter we described as Phœnician, from their oldest and most powerful representatives ; the former, as Hebrew, for, as in the Old Testament, " Hebrews " is the designation of the first tribes who immigrated, living in the open country and aspiring to the possession of the towns. That the Hebrews are the same as the tribes called in the letters of the Egyptian national archives " Khabiri " is doubtful, since the initial guttural is quite distinct in the two words, but is by no means impossible.

Aziru, advancing southward from Arvad, and conquering two or three small towns,

ASTARTE
The goddess of Sidon.

among them Arka, ruled by princes of their own, which lay on his route, reduced to great straits the territory of Gebal, whence the prince, Rib-Adda, sent letter after letter to the Egyptian court asking for help. Sumur, or Simyra, a town on the coast north of Gebal and belonging to it, was captured, and Aziru invested Gebal itself without the Pharaoh's intervention. Rib-Adda went to Beirut to obtain assistance, and thus lost his throne to his brother, who did not relinquish it again. Aziru then advanced still further ; he was indeed the ultimate cause of all the disorders in that country. At last, however, he was forced to appear at the court to answer for himself, and was kept under arrest. We possess a letter of condolence sent to him in Egypt by one of his loyal followers, which must have been intercepted by the Egyptians, since it was put among the records and preserved in the State archives. The Amorites, nevertheless, advanced still further. The oldest of the written documents of the Old Testament describes the original inhabitants of the Israelitish territory as Amorites.

Going southward from Gebal we come to Beirut, where Rib-Adda sought refuge with the king Ammunira, who seems to have been anxious not to quarrel either with Rib-Adda, who really had reposed trust in Egypt, or with his dangerous opponent. Zimrida, king of Sidon, gives little sign. We gather from the complaints of his neighbour, and thus his natural enemy, Abimilki or Abimelech of Tyre, that he made common cause with Aziru, and thus attempted to gain an advantage over his neighbour in Tyre. Things went very badly with the latter. He was besieged on his island and cut off from the mainland by Zimrida, who had secured the support of Aziru, so that he could not even draw water on the land. He tried to propitiate the Pharaoh by communicating all sorts of news from the country. Neither he nor Zimrida had any considerable territory, and there is no idea of the supremacy of the one or the other.

Further to the south, Akko had a prince of its own ; it is often mentioned as a port for travellers to Egypt. Jaffa and Gaza, further on, were under one prince, and

VIEW FROM THE MAINLAND SHOWING THE ARTIFICIAL ISTHMUS

RUINS OF OLD SEA WALL: ALL THAT REMAINS OF ANCIENT TYRE

FROM THE MAINLAND SHOWING RUINS OF AQUEDUCT TO THE ISLAND

REMAINS OF THE ISLAND CITY AND KINGDOM OF ANCIENT TYRE

Askalon, between the two, under another We cannot decide whether these were already Philistines, immigrants from Crete; but their names do not look like those of Phœnicians and Canaanites, and the Greek tribe of the Danuna, or Danaans, are already mentioned as settled on the coast. The only one of the numerous princes of the hinter-

Abdkhiba King of Jerusalem land that interests us is Abd-khiba, king of Jerusalem, not an hereditary prince, but one appointed by the Pharaoh. He is hard pressed by his neighbours Tagi, Milki-el, and the sons of Lapaia, and cannot find words to express the certainty that, if help is not brought to him, the country, which otherwise would be secured to the king, will inevitably fall into the hands of the Khabiri. A detailed description of the letters would take too long; a large number of well-known Biblical localities are specially mentioned as objects of these wars. The princes from a whole series of towns merely announce in short formal letters their readiness to submit to the royal commands and to put their troops at the disposal of the Egyptian general.

A remarkable document has been found in Tell Hesy, the ruined site of Lachish. Closely resembling the Tell el-Amarna letters in writing and appearance, it is a letter addressed to an Egyptian general, which announces the defection of two princes. The one of them is called Zim-rida, like the Sidonian prince, and he is known to us, both by one of his letters from Tell el-Amarna and by his accounts of Abd-khiba, as king of Lachish. By a remarkable coincidence this isolated tablet was found in the excavations at Tell Hesy almost at the same time as the great discovery of archives in Egypt was made known. The discovery at Tell Hesy can be explained only on the ground that the letter of Zimrida had been intercepted.

The letters from Tell el-Amarna cover only a few years of the last period of Amenophis

Rivalries of Petty Princes III. and of the beginning of the reign of his successor. All accounts lead us to conclude that the Egyptian power was not firmly established. It rested really more on the impotence and the discord of the innumerable petty princes than on the strength of Egypt. Rib-Adda, then, tries to traduce his rival Aziru, who is, he says, conspiring with the kings of Babylonia, Mitani, and the Kheta, and if he seizes the country, will hold it as a fief from them.

In the disorders which ensued on the death of King Amenophis IV., Egyptian influence, especially in the north, was destroyed, and the land became dependent on the Kheta, whose advance we can ascertain even from the Tell el-Amarna letters. Shubbululiuma their king, and his successors, Murshili and Muttalu, were bent upon the extension of their power over the whole of Northern Syria, and were only checked by the defeat of Khattushili by Ramses II. at Kadesh a century later. Babylonia could not extend her power to the west. She had in Assyria a perpetual opponent which diverted her attention. The kingdom of Mitani, which bulks so large in the Tell el-Amarna letters, was destroyed by Shubbiluliuma before the end of the reign of Amenophis IV. The Egyptian rule was therefore once more established in the thirteenth century B.C. by the repulse of the Kheta and the treaty made with them under Ramses II., who left a monument of his presence in Phœnicia in the shape of the stele of the Nahr el-Kelb. The picture presented by the land at this time thus presents

Ramses the Great in Phœnicia the closest resemblance to that which was noticeable two centuries before, only that the bearers of other names played the parts of Rib-Adda, Aziru, Abd-khiba, etc. At that very time the tribes of Israel may have conquered their homes, and have combined into a tribal federation. In the north the Egyptian supremacy had once more been shaken off, and even in the south the princes turned to the Pharaoh only as a last resource, when they could not hold their position with their own forces. The eleventh century sees the conquests of the Philistines, immigrant from Crete and the Ægean, and the rise of the monarchies of Saul and David; the new millennium sees the kingdom of Damascus, when neither Egypt nor Assyria, which in the interval had come to the front, was powerful in Palestine. In the south merely banished princes like Hadad of Edom, or unsuccessful pretenders, like Jeroboam, sought an asylum, and sometimes saw their wishes realised by the arrival of an Egyptian army, as Jeroboam did.

The four Phœnician states were still less affected by these circumstances than the countries in the interior, for the sea always gave them more independence, and the wealth which their trade procured them lent them the strength to resist the Egyptian armies, or the means of securing their freedom by payments. Arvad had received a new population from the Amorite conquest, and we left Gebal when Aziru was on the point of subduing it. The Amorites by their further advance, as the subsequent dialect shows, apparently succeeded in winning this also. The two did not appreciably change their character in consequence ; they remained maritime and commercial cities as before ; but they were certainly detached from the old confederation of the Phœnicians or Sidonians. There is the additional fact that Egypt's power here in the north was less strong, so that these towns were forced to submit sooner

without any hindrance. So the kingdoms of David and of Tyre and Sidon grew up. In the time of David and Solomon, Tyre had already assumed the lead ng place. Its princes styled themselves " kings of the Sidonians " ; they dominated Sidon as well as the whole coast, so far as it still belonged to the confederation of the "Sidonians"—that is to say, all except the northern states. If the term " Empire of the Phœnicians " can ever be used, it is applicable at this period. We really do not know much beyond the little which the Bible tells us of the relations of Solomon to Hiram. We know that Hiram and his father Abi-baal did the most for the extension of their " kingdom." If a reading in Josephus is correctly restored,

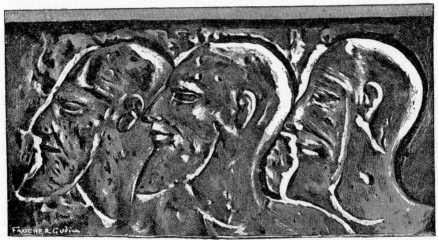

CONTEMPORARY PORTRAITS OF THE RED-HEADED AMORITES OF CANAAN
The Phœnicians, Hebrews and Amorites were the principal immigrants into Canaan. It is not unlikely that the Amorites were not Semites, but Berbers or Libyans. From " The Struggle of the Nations," S.P.C.K.

than Tyre and Sidon to the powers pressing on from Syria. They will thus have been tributaries to the Kheta, or Hittites, at a time when Sidon and Tyre must have still remained loyal to the Pharaoh. When Tiglath-pileser was in Arvad, which had therefore acknowledged his suzerainty, the Pharaoh sent him presents, and thus maintained neighbourly relations with him as the lord of the southern country. We may assume a similar state of things quite soon afterwards between Egypt and Nebuchadnezzar I., when the latter, before his defeat by Ashur-resh-ishi, had occupied Palestine.

The eleventh century B.C., which shows the least traces of any encroachments on the part of Assyria and Egypt, was the period when large states might arise in Phœnicia

Hiram founded Kition in Cyprus, which means that he captured the town with its inhabitants, and installed a Tyrian governor there. Kition is, however, mentioned by the Egyptians, with other Cyprian cities, as early as the time of Ramses III. (1150 B.C.), who speaks of the countries of Salames-ki, or Salamis, Katian, or Kition, Aimare, or Marion, Sali, or Soloi, and Ital, or Idalion, together. The *ki* at the end of the name of Salamis may be accounted for on the supposition that the Egyptian scribe was transliterating from a cuneiform original, and had inadvertently transliterated the city-sign *ki* after the name Salames. These names are all in very much their Greek form : were Aryan-speaking Greeks already settled in Cyprus as early as the twelfth century ?

In the Tell el-Amarna period (1400 B.C.) Cyprus was the seat of a kingdom of Alashia, the king of which conducted a correspondence with Amenophis III. and Amenophis IV., and even then was supplying them with copper. He also wrote in " Babylonian," and used cuneiform characters. Nothing is certain as to his nationality, but that he was

Cyprus Before the Phœnicians
"Greek" is highly improbable, though he may have been "Minoan"; no Phœnician name appears among the few mentioned. Indeed, it does not seem as if a Phœnician population had by that time assumed a commanding position in the island. Its seizure by Hiram three hundred years later would, therefore, mark the first foundation of Phœnician influence there. As is usual in such cases, the captured town Kition was "refounded," as the Assyrian expression is, and received a new name, in this case Kartikhadasti, or " New Town," the same, therefore, as the " New Town," or Carthage, in Africa. The island of Cyprus, which now became subject to the kingdom of Tyre and Sidon, was thenceforth administered partly as a Tyrian province under governors, partly by tributary kings of the separate towns. This must have been the most important possession of the Tyro-Sidonian kingdom; we can hardly entertain the idea that any of the African colonies were dependent. The splendour of the new kingdom found expression in Oriental fashion by the erection of new and magnificent buildings on the island of Tyre.

We are indebted to an abstract by Josephus from the Annals of Menander, the Greek-writing historian of the Phœnicians, from whom these accounts are also taken, for the record of the most valuable facts about the reigns of the subsequent kings; being extracted from the Tyrian archives they have a claim to be reproduced in spite of their vagueness. According to them, after

From the Archives of Tyre
Hiram his son Baal-azar reigned seven or seventeen years, about 970–953 B.C., and then his son Abd-ashtoreth for nine years. He was murdered by the " four sons of his nurse," one of whom, Methu-ashtoreth, became king and reigned twelve years. He was followed by his brother Asterymus for nine years; the latter was murdered by his brother Phelles, who held the power for eight months. Nothing is said as to the

motive for the rebellion of the brothers, nor does it appear what revolution was signified by their accession to power.

Phelles was overthrown by Ithobal, the " Priest of Ashtoreth," who reigned thirty-two years, about 900 B.C. Even in this instance it is not known how the internal conditions affected this change, especially how far any antagonism between the two capitals, Tyre and Sidon, may have contributed to it. Ithobal is also mentioned in the Bible; Jezebel, the wife of Ahab, was his daughter. Then followed his descendants, Baal-azar, six years, Metten, nine years, and Pygmalion, forty-seven years — until about 800 B.C. Josephus draws up his list so far after Menander, since Carthage is said to have been " founded " under Pygmalion, and he makes a point of settling this date at the place in question. In any case it is certain that the dynasty of Ithobal held the power for a long period. The story of Dido and the foundation of Carthage have been connected with the revolution in which Pygmalion killed the husband of his sister, the priest of Ashtoreth.

Priesthood Against Monarchy
Since there is no need to doubt the historical nucleus of the story, we may well assume that the high-priest, connected by marriage with the king and probably otherwise related, had attempted to seize the throne, but had been defeated in the attempt. Thus it was a struggle of the priesthood against the monarchy, an incident common in the East and observable at this same period in Israel and Judah.

We can extract very little from the notices of Josephus, derived from Menander, as to the relations existing between Tyre and Sidon. With the rise to power of Abi-baal, Tyre becomes the ruling city, while Sidon, the seat of the universally acknowledged cult, and thus enjoying a religious prestige, is in reality the subject city. It is conjectured that in the two revolutions just mentioned this position was to some extent affected. Our accounts do not inform us whether the " Empire " still continued to exist under these circumstances, or whether a fresh separation of the two states resulted. At any rate, the Assyrian accounts from the period after Ithobal speak of the two towns as separate. Shalmaneser II., both in 842 and 839 B.C., mentions the Sidonians and the Tyrians (under Pygmalion therefore) as paying tribute separately. As, then, Ithobal in the Bible is still termed " King of the Sidonians," a separation must have taken place in the interval between 900 and 800 B.C.

Adad-nirari III. speaks of Tyre and Sidon as two states ; his expedition towards the west must have taken place soon after Pygmalion's death. Assyria, perhaps, had favoured and brought about a separation of the two states on the principle " divide et impera." Tradition places the "foundation of Carthage" about 845 B.C.—namely, at the time when Shalmaneser, after 854 B.C., waged war in the west with Damascus ; in 842 B.C. Sidon, Tyre, and Jehu of Israel paid him tribute. On the basis of similar circumstances it may be supposed that the intrigues in Tyre between Pygmalion and his brother-in-law had been carried on with the support of Assyria. Sidon would thus have probably acquired its independence as regards Tyre through the support of Assyria, and would have lost it when help was not forthcoming ; at least, that happened again in 701 B.C. At the time when Assyria could not interfere in the west the old conditions had been restored. When Tiglath - pileser again appeared here in 738 B.C., he recognised only a king of Tyre, and none of Sidon, which accordingly must have been once more subject to Tyrian supremacy.

Sidon Subject to Tyre

The territory of the empire was, however, restricted then by the Assyrian province created by Tiglath-pileser in 732 B.C., which, comprising several of the northern Phœnician towns, Simirra, Arka, and the district of Lebanon, had been entrusted to his son and acknowledged successor, Shalmaneser. Hiram II., then king, always paid his tribute and avoided any misunderstanding with Assyria. Metten II. must have succeeded him about the year 730 B.C. He let things go so far as a war with Assyria, but was soon brought to reason by an Assyrian army in the year 729 B.C., and had to dip deeply into his well-filled coffers in order to purchase peace.

Metten had not a long reign, and possibly his submission to Assyria led to his fall. In the year 727 B.C., that is, shortly after the death of Tiglath-pileser, Elulæus, as the account of Menander preserved by Josephus calls him, or Luli, as Sennacherib afterwards calls him, suspended the payment of tribute. Shalmaneser is said to have marched towards Tyre, but consented to conclude peace ; this is equivalent to saying that Luli declared his readiness to resume payment of tribute. We then have a further, but not very clear, account by Sargon, who says briefly that " he had hauled the Yavna (Ionians) like fish out of the midst of the sea, and had thereby procured peace for Tyre and Kue, or Cilicia." This obviously refers to a repression by the Phœnicians under Assyrian leadership of the piratical attacks of the Greek Ionians, now in the heyday of their " young, light-hearted " mastery of the waves, and spreading colonies along all the shores of the Mediterranean.

Rise of Grecian Sea Power

When the West rose after the death of Sargon, Luli in Phœnicia and Hezekiah in the hinterland were the leaders round whom the insurgents rallied. But then, as usual, there was no organised resistance, and all the towns, with the exception of Tyre, surrendered to the Assyrians without more ado. Sennacherib enumerates on this occasion the kings of Phœnicia, and thus affords us a welcome insight into the existing conditions. There were Menathem of Shams-maron, an otherwise unknown and unimportant Phœnician town, Abd-le'at of Arvad, and Uru-melek of Gebal. All the towns of the kingdom of Tyre and Sidon were seized without difficulty. Sennacherib mentions Great Sidon, Little Sidon, Bet-Zaiit, Sarepta, Makhalliba, Ushu, opposite the island of Tyre, Ekdippa, or Akhzib, and Akko. Tyre itself was unsuccessfully besieged, a fact about which Sennacherib naturally is silent ; but we know of it from Menander, who tells us that even the Phœnician ships of Sennacherib were destroyed by the Tyrians. Luli himself fled to Cyprus, that is, to Kition, in order to wait there for a favourable opportunity of returning to Tyre, which still held out. He must, however, have died soon after, whether in Kition or after a return to Tyre, we do not know. Sennacherib is very reticent on these events. In his record of the year 700 B.C., the account of Luli's death is still missing, but occurs in the next record of 691 B.C. The most probable explanation would be that Luli came back quietly after the withdrawal of the Assyrians, and took steps to regain his lost territory.

Tyre Besieged by Assyrians

Sennacherib had meanwhile taken advantage of the enmity between Sidon and Tyre to secure his own influence. He set up Thubaal, or Ithobal II., as "King of the Sidonians" in Sidon, who received the whole maritime district of the empire of Sidon and Tyre, with the exception of the unconquered island of Tyre. This

Enmity Between Tyre and Sidon was of course tantamount to a declaration of war between the two cities or states, and Assyria secured the part of arbitrator. At first, indeed, Sennacherib was still occupied elsewhere, and he died while engaged on the task, so that he did not even chastise Jerusalem. Besides that, the advance of Tirhakah in Egypt brought a new opponent into the field, from whom Tyre and Sidon could find support.

The precise details of the events at this time are not clear. Contrary, however, to what might have been expected, we find Sidon rebelling against Assyria at the beginning of Esarhaddon's reign in 680 B.C. Abd-milkot, in all probability the successor of Ithobal II., who had been set on the throne in 701 B.C., was forced to abandon the town, and met his death two years later with his confederate Sanduarri. Sidon itself was completely destroyed. From Esarhaddon's account we gather that hitherto it had been situated on an island ; this island is the part of the modern town which juts out into the sea, and thus at that time must have been separated from the mainland by a narrow strip of water. Esarhaddon ordered the town to be absolutely demolished, and a new city to be built as the capital of the newly constituted province of Sidon, according to the usual custom, in "another place"—that is, on the mainland opposite. This Assyrian town, of course, was called by the inhabitants Sidon, and became the nucleus of the later Sidon. But the destruction of the city was of grave moment for

Sidon Falls to Assyria the Phoenicians, since their national sanctuary was obliterated and Sidon ceased to be the seat of the ruling religion. According to a tradition, which probably refers to this event, the gods were then carried off in safety to Tyre. Thus Tyre, from being the political centre, now became the religious centre of the Sidonians, while their old federal city was destroyed, and its name was borne by the capital of an Assyrian province, where

sacrifices were offered to Ashur and not to Ashtoreth, or Eshmun. It was only under the Persian rule that Sidon, like Jerusalem, regained its independence. After that there were again kings of Sidon. But during these and later times there are proofs, both from names and in other ways, that the worship of the Assyrian gods obtained there. The new Sidon presented the same features as Samaria, a town of Babylonian "Cuthæan" inhabitants with their native cults. Just as Samaria was a rival to Jerusalem, so Sidon afterwards disputed with Tyre the precedence belonging to the highest antiquity ; that is, according to the ideas of the time, it disputed which of the cities could claim the honour of sheltering the gods, to whom the land of the "Sidonians" belonged.

After the territory of Sidon had become an Assyrian province, Phoenician history is limited to the kingdom of Tyre. The fact that such a kingdom existed, and that it still possessed territory to lose proves that in the meantime Luli, or a successor, operating from Tyre, must have

Sidon Lost to Phœnicia recovered the territory on the mainland which belonged to the town. Whether Kition was lost in the interval or not is doubtful, for Esarhaddon and Ashurbanipal mention a special king of Kartikhadasti, Dumusi. It can hardly, therefore, be assumed that the whole island had meanwhile come into the hands of Greeks, for Dumusi is not a Greek name. But all the other kings of Cyprus at this time were Greeks. Ten kings tendered their homage to Esarhaddon ; besides the Semite Dumusi they are Aigisthos (in Assyrian "Ekishtusu") of Idalion, Pythagoras (Pilagura) of Chytroi, Keisos, or Kissos (Kesu), of Salamis, Etewandros (Etuandar) of Paphos, Heraios (Eresu) of Soli, Damasos (Damasu) of Kurion, Admetos (Admezu) of Tamassos, Onesagoras (Unasagusu) of Ledra, and Pytheas (Putsuzu) of Nure.

At Tyre, King Ba'al, presumably Luli's successor, was at first loyal to Esarhaddon and actually accompanied him on his first Egyptian expedition. But then he allied himself with Tirhakah evidently in the hope of gaining by this the territory of Sidon. Esarhaddon, therefore, during the campaign in 673 B.C., sent a detachment of his army against Tyre ; this force occupied Ushu on the mainland, and constructed moles opposite the island, which cut off all communication with the land, while the harbour was blockaded from the sea. The island of Tyre itself held out until the news of Tirhakah's expulsion. Ba'al then tendered his submission, but was allowed to retain only his island. On the news of the return of Tirhakah he rejoined him at once, so that the siege by the Assyrians was hardly interrupted. When, in 688 B.C.—now under Ashurbanipal—Tirhakah was again driven out, he submitted as before and had finally to consent to see his " kingdom " limited to his own small island. But opposite it, on the mainland in Ushu, was the seat of the Assyrian governor of the province Tyre, which comprised the territory of Tyre. Thus there was even less left of Hiram's empire than of Solomon's. There, at any rate, in addition to Jerusalem, there were two or three country towns, but here a man could walk round the whole " empire " in half an hour ; in fact, it was not possible to fetch water without the sanction of the Assyrian governor. This

The Tiny " Empire " of Tyre was a state of things which must have perpetually fostered the wish for an insurrection. Just as in Jerusalem, so here there was a party, which was always urging defection, and made the king, who for good or for evil was forced to incur the odium attaching to a loyal subject of Assyria, feel his petty crown uneasy and full of thorns. The promises of Shamash-shum-ukin certainly found some response in Tyre, and in the " forties " of the seventh century B.C. a rebellion in the province actually broke out ; it was, however, easily suppressed by Ashurbanipal and ended with the severe chastisement of Ushu and Akko.

Thus, the aspirations to regain the old power were not realised, so long as the power of Assyria lasted. Then came the great downfall, and with it the attempt by Necho of Egypt to build up his power out of the ruins. At Tyre advantage was taken of this opportunity to gain a footing once more on the mainland. The attempt met with little success, and when Necho was vanquished it was seen that Nebuchadnezzar was not dispoed to concede favourable terms to the conquered. Another revolt followed under Ithobal III., the next king of Tyre, with whose name we are already acquainted.

According to the account given by Josephus, Tyre was besieged for thirteen years, from 598 to 585 B.C., without any result. No doubt, hopes were entertained of Egyptian help, but as vainly as at Jerusalem. But even this time there was no capture of the city, although it was confidently expected ; a fact to which the

Island Independence Maintained well-known hymn in Ezekiel xxvii. gives expression ; Tyre by its position could defy the siege tactics of the Assyrians and Babylonians. It was thus once more saved from the fate of Jerusalem, and the island retained its own government. Its commerce enabled the city to pay the tribute punctually.

The records of the ensuing period are as follow : Ba'al II. succeeded Ithobal, reigning ten years ; then came five Judges, each for a few months only, and a king, Balatorus, between them. Clearly we must assume a period of disorders, and various attempts by pretenders to usurp the power. Finally, a petition was sent to Neriglissar that Merbaal, obviously a member of the royal family, who lived, like so many other princes' sons, as a hostage at the court of Babylon, should be appointed king ; the request was granted. He reigned four years ; after him, at a similar request, his brother Hiram III. was nominated king, and reigned for twenty years. In the fourteenth year of his reign Babylon fell, and Tyre had a new suzerain.

Cyrus of Persia abandoned the Assyrian policy of provincial government by officials ; he left to the towns and states the management of their home affairs, and made them subject only to the supreme authority of the satraps. Accordingly, in cases where a confiscation had already begun, but all possibility of the restoration of a national constitution had not disappeared, he restored the old régime. The most familiar example is Jerusalem ; another is Sidon. Even Tyre

New Life for Tyre and Sidon must have derived a certain degree of benefit from the new policy, since it was allowed to recover its territory on the mainland.

Thus there was once more the two states of Tyre and Sidon as close neighbours. The events of the intervening period had meanwhile obliterated the antagonism between " Sidonians " proper and North Phœnicians. The northern states, which had never ventured on a revolt, had suffered less severely; Tyre and Sidon, which had been forced to pay so dear a price for their efforts at independence, were now like these, completely dependent on the Great King, although enjoying their own government. In addition to this, the differences between the component parts of the population **Phœnicia** had in the course of centuries **Under** been mitigated. Thus the **Persia** similarity of their positions might well contribute toward their reappearance as a united people. Now, under the Persian rule, there existed once again the condition which we were able to assume only during a prehistoric age, one people from Arvad to Akko, which was regarded as united, and considered itself to a certain degree also as homogeneous. They are the "Phœnicians" in opposition to the old "Sidonians." The remaining history of Phœnicia occupies so brief a space that we may conveniently give it here, instead of deferring it in accordance with our chronological plan.

Now, as before, there were the four kingdoms of Arvad, Gebal, Sidon, and Tyre, as well as occasionally some smaller ones with which we have also already become acquainted. Gebal was less prominent. As the representative of the Northern Phœnicians, we find Arvad. This fact is supported by the otherwise not very trustworthy story about Tripolis, which was said to have been the federal metropolis of the three ruling states—Tyre, Sidon, and Arvad. Sidon and Tyre, as the nearest neighbours, and living on recollections of the past, continued their old rivalry. This opposition finds a sentimental expression in the dispute between the two as to the greater antiquity, which carried with it the honour of being the capital. Under the new conditions there is no longer any idea of a Phœnician "kingdom," even on the scale of Hiram's **End of** kingdom. The separate states **Phœnician** were now only what it suited **Kingdom** Persian policy to make them. Persia could have no interest in leaving them more freedom and unity than was necessary in order to gain wealthy tribute-payers. On the other hand, the efforts of the separate states were naturally directed towards the acquisition of the greatest possible degree of independence; and their self-government afforded them more opportunities of exercising an inde-

pendent policy than would have been the case under the provincial administration. Still they had to coin money according to the Persian standard, with a figure of the Great King in his chariot on the coins, and often a little figure of an Egyptian king walking in humility after him—a visible reminder to the Phœnicians not to put their trust in Egypt, itself now a Persian province. The Persian supremacy, however, was not a very satisfactory guarantee that their territorial rights would be protected. They had to defend themselves against the attacks of neighbours in two ways—by warding them off with their own forces, or by gaining their cause at court. This latter procedure was

THE WORLD'S FIRST ALPHABET
To the Phœnician intellect is due the evolution of the first alphabet, illustrated above. Arabic equivalents are given on the left in the order of the Greek alphabet.

costly, for intercession at court, as we know from the Tell el-Amarna time onward, entailed lavish presents even in Susa. Persian help was given in return, as Assyrian help had been given before, for the recovery of Cyprus, which was effected through the treachery of the Greek king Stasanor, in 497 B.C. A peculiar rôle, which was indistinctly conducive to their independent position, was assigned to the Phœnicians under the Persian supremacy as previously under the Assyrian. They had to furnish the fleets with which Persia enforced her oversea policy, and which the Persians themselves were as incapable as the Assyrians of constructing. Thus Phœnician ships formed a large part of the Persian armadas at Lade and Salamis.

Sidon seems soon to have risen to its former prosperity. It made overtures to Athens and concluded treaties of amity with her. A large Sidonian colony was settled in the Piræus ; some of the rare Phœnician inscriptions are known to us from this source. Sidon suffered a severe blow in the year 351 B.C., when it was chastised by Artaxerxes Ochus as a penalty for the part taken by it in the Egyptian revolt. By this event Tyre regained the ascendency. Shortly before it had been distinctly retrograding ; indeed, that very Tyre which once had dominated Cyprus had actually become tributary to King Euagoras of Cyprus. We thus find Tyre, thirty years later, the only Phœnician town which offered resistance to Alexander, while Sidon, "from hatred of the Persians," gladly welcomed him.

There must have been peculiar circumstances attending this resistance of Tyre to Alexander the Great, who for the first time conquered and destroyed the city. Tyre did not imperil its existence from any loyalty to Persia. The reason is not far to seek. Sidon had from the outset gained over the new lord, and Tyre was destined to lose some of its independence. Alexander had indeed wished to offer the sacrifices in the temple of Melkarth. This request was refused ; for by so doing he would have been declared king of Tyre. Was Tyre in any way deprived of its self-government, possibly in favour of Sidon ? The course and the end of the siege are familiar. It left perhaps a permanent result, for the mole which Alexander ordered to be built is said to have connected Tyre for all time with the mainland, since the sea silted up more and more land on each side. From the new state of things Sidon in fact at first derived advantage. Some inscriptions of kings of Sidon, dating from the period of the early Ptolemies, inform us how at that time Tyre had taken the lead.

Alexander Destroys Tyre

With Alexander we have come to a time when ancient Nearer Asia has played out its part. After this it was subject to the dominion of Græco-Roman civilisation. The Phœnician states, at no time politically important, continued to exist on the old footing, prosecuting their commerce in the midst of petty jealousies. Their history runs precisely in the same grooves, so long as anything at all remained of the Ancient East.

The Phœnicians, or "Sidonians," were the Semitic people with whom the Greeks in their competition for the Mediterranean trade first came into close contact. They must have appropriated from them many achievements of Oriental culture. Since in their eyes the owners and the founders of towns were the same, the possessors of the sea-ports, which commanded the routes into the interior, seemed to them a people of an importance ; which might flatter the conceit of the Phœnicians, it is true, but can hardly be substantiated in the light of history. We have become acquainted with Phœnicia as a narrow strip of coast, insufficient to allow a people to develop any constitutional greatness. This also excludes any possibility that a national civilisation can ever have been evolved here by the side of the civilisation of the other great states. The merchant facilitates the exchange of the productions of civilisation ; in his home, as the focus of intercourse, much may also be produced which assumes a peculiar character as a result of the different forms of mental and industrial activity known there. But if a civilisation is to grow up with a natural development and is to reflect the character of people and country, it is necessary that this civilisation be indigenous, or at any rate, in harmony with racial feeling. And Phœnician culture bore no very national and characteristic impress. Its art was composed chiefly of Egyptian and Babylonian elements tastelessly mingled together ; even the gods were represented as half Egyptian, half Assyrian. This art was transplanted to Cyprus, and mingled there with Greek elements, which resulted in an extraordinary mixture. Left to themselves, as at Carthage, the Punic race produced a miserable art, without character or distinction.

Culture of Phœnicia

In the case of the Phœnicians also, we must raise our often repeated lament that up to the present so little is known which can afford us any real insight into their life at the time of their true development. The mere absence of excavation may be in other instances to blame, but on Phœnician soil this prospect holds out little promise. It almost seems as if the continuously inhabited places, where Phœnician magnificence flourished, had retained less evidences of the antiquity

Phœnician Soil Unexcavated

with which we are now concerned than those of other centuries, where the piled-up heaps of débris have loyally preserved their treasures for the explorer's spade. No large building and no site of a town of the Phœnician time are known to us in their former condition; no lengthy inscription or other document speaks to us as yet in the words with which a Phœnician of the year 1000 B.C. composed it in his own language and style. The "invention"—or rather it should be called "evolution"—of alphabetic writing, which through the Greek alphabet has become the mother of all European writing, is generally regarded as the peculiar property of the Phœnician intellect. We might conceivably look in Babylonia for the home of an alphabetical writing, the phonetics and principles of which were used for a Semitic language. In fact a number of peculiarities in the alphabet show that it must have been influenced considerably by Babylonian philology. But that the alphabet is of Babylonian origin is not probable. Probably the alphabet first developed in Phœnicia, and passed thence on one side to Greece, on the other to the Aramæans and Mesopotamia. The real basis of the Phœnician alphabet would seem to be one of the many systems of linear signs that were current from early times in the Mediterranean basin; we find them in Egypt very often. It is quite conceivable that the Phœnicians had inherited some such system from their non-Semitic predecessors, and that though for a time they used the cuneiform script, at some period about 1000 B.C. the old "signary" came into general use for commercial purposes as being less cumbrous than the foreign system of wedge-writing. But naturally the use of cuneiform had its effect on the development of the alphabet. The Phœnicians were probably the inventors of alphabetic writing, just as the commercial towns of our era are the leaders of the intellectual and technical development of modern times.

Invention of the Alphabet

Purple of Phœnicia

It is impossible to ascertain accurately the significance of the manufacture of purple by the Phœnicians. Tradition never differentiates between the inventor and the supplier; and it is uncertain what is the meaning of the Phœnician production of purple. We do not yet possess any notices of this valuable commodity from the times of Ancient Babylonia. The Assyrians allude to it under the same name as the Phœnicians, *argamannu* for scarlet, *takiltu* for dark purple; but whether the names and thus the idea are originally "Phœnician," must remain a moot point. A very definitely adverse verdict must be given with regard to the other invention attributed to them, that of glass; this attribution is a mere piece of later ignorance. Glass was an invention of the Egyptians, which passed from them to the Phœnicians, who probably made the glass found at Nineveh. Later on, the invention passed to Greece and Italy.

The celebrated Phœnician towns, Tyre and Sidon at the head, were indeed, according to our notions, absurdly small places. Tyre and Sidon on their islands were restricted to an incredibly narrow space, not larger than that of a good-sized public garden in the middle of our large cities. The size of the harbours in both these places of world-commerce quite confirms this view. An ordinary modern three-master would not be able to turn in them, even if it actually sailed in; the small basins with the narrow inlet were intended to receive only vessels which we should term boats. Yet these were the famous ships of Tyre, Sidon, and Tharshish, which navigated the Mediterranean in all directions.

The Tiny Navy of Phœnicia

It is satisfactorily proved that Phœnician trade nevertheless had the same importance for the civilised world of Nearer Asia as the present emporia in the west have for the commerce that includes our own world. We have demonstrated, as in Etruria from excavations, the traces of this trade in countries which it embraced. The evidences for it are based on direct observation, and therefore give us a trustworthy representation of the significance of these seaports for their civilised world. We find in Isaiah songs about Sidon—chapter xxiii., where originally Sidon was meant and only at a later period Tyre was understood by it—and in Ezekiel xxvii. one about Tyre. The sumptuous products which the trade of that time to the coasts of the Mediterranean and with Arabia are recorded to have supplied, always found a ready market; the inland dwellers of the Nearer East and the Semitic barbarian of the hinterlands of those coasts willingly gave what they had for such marvels. We know that already in the time of the eighteenth and nineteenth dynasties in Egypt trade between the Nileland and Greece, as well as Phœnicia, was carried by sea in Phœnician bottoms ; the Egyptians were no sailors, and the Greeks of that period seem to have been warriors rather than traders. Later on, when the "Mycenæan" culture of Greece proper, succeeding the civilisation of "Minoan" Crete, had in its turn been overthrown, and Greece returned temporarily to barbarism, the Phœnicians had taken advantage of the opening thus afforded for their commerce in the Ægean. There, however, their commercial predominance was of short duration. The Ionian Greeks began, after no long interval, to bestir themselves, and by the eighth century B.C. the Phœnicians seem already to have been ousted by the Greeks from the northern coasts of the Mediterranean.

Anything else that is recorded of their valiant

A VESSEL OF THE FAMOUS PHŒNICIAN NAVY
Phœnicia was essentially a maritime state, and her famous navies, composed of tiny vessels we should call boats, navigated the Mediterranean in all directions and were used by Egypt and other ancient nations.

exploits at sea is untrustworthy. Their ships may have penetrated as far as the Cassiterides in order to bring back tin. But in the first place we can never know what part the "West Phœnicians," the Pœni, or Carthaginians, had in this ; and secondly, the regular trade-communications never went far beyond the Straits of Gibraltar. Many bold enterprises ascribed to them, such as the circumnavigation of Africa, starting from the Red Sea, which is said to have been undertaken at the instance of Necho, must have been carried out by Phœnician merchants. But the sphere where the Phœnicians commanded the trade was only a part of the Mediterranean, and in this connection we must always make an allowance for the share of the Carthaginians, who formed a distinct nation.

The few data that we have for our knowledge of Phœnician culture tell us but little. The country offered splendid material for magnificent buildings in the alabaster of Lebanon, which the Assyrians fetched from Nineveh. The Phœnicians, however, conforming to Egyptian architecture, employed granite and syenite. The numerous pillars found on Phœnician soil are of this material, which, it is clear, must have been laboriously procured from Egypt.

Almost all the productions of an early period—between 1500–1000 B.C.—which we have from Phœnicia, are purely Egyptian ; so long then as Egypt was supreme, the Phœnicians appear merely to have adopted the technique of the ruling country. Some later products of the sculptor's art display, indeed, a "Phœnician" style; whether this, however, was a peculiarity of the Phœnicians, or whether it ought not rather to be described as Canaanite and placed on a level with the Aramæan, is one of those questions that are best left unanswered.

The dependence on Egypt during the early period, and the formation of an Egyptian style, are perhaps visible in the architecture, in the more lavish use of the pillar, which in the Euphrates country was rarely, if ever, found. The Assyrian kings after Tiglath-pileser IV. always mention that they had adorned their palaces with an edifice, which was called in the language of the Phœnicians Bit-khilani, "Khilani-house," after the model of a "Khatti-palace" (Phœnicia is included under the term Khatti, or Kheta, country). This Bit-khilani was a gateway decorated with pillars, which served as a place for all the public business of the king ; it was the royal yamên, the "sublime porte." A representation of the temple of Baalat of Gebal on coins of the Roman Imperial era

THE "SUBLIME PORTE" OF PHŒNICIA

Phœnician and Syrian palaces were adorned with a gateway, called a Bit-khilani, decorated with pillars,
which served as a place for the king's public business. This shows the foundations of one at Senjirli.

shows a similar gateway. The culture of the Phœnician towns, so far as it was not the inheritance of a period still withdrawn from our knowledge and subject to the supremacy of Babylon, or did not consist in an imitation of Egyptian productions, can, after all that we have proved as to its political unimportance, lay no claim to an independent evolution. The hinterland, which came into less direct contact with the two predominating civilised countries, Egypt and Babylonia, was naturally still less subject to the influence of those civilisations, however little Egyptian life may have penetrated into the Phœnician towns. This is most clearly expressed in the religion. The conceptions of the Phœnicians as a group of the "Canaanite immigration" are distinguishable in no respect from those of the other Canaanites, as we know them from the Old Testament and other scattered accounts. Here, again, anything which can be put down to the previously existing institutions of an earlier "Semitic Babylonian" population is problematical, and for the present insufficiently proved. If we compare the Babylonian cults before and after the Canaanite immigration, we find that the worship of the stars—that is, the special reverence for the sun and moon, which we observed in the valley of the Euphrates—was less general in Canaan and Phœnicia. We can at least conjecture that this was a Sumerian inheritance in Babylonia, and was therefore unknown in Palestine originally. If we find in the place-names of Canaan such as Bet-Shemesh, "House of the Sun," traces of such a cult, its origin may be looked for in the Babylonian period, or it may be of Egyptian origin; at any rate, the sidereal bodies played no part as ruling powers comparable to that of Sin and Shamash in the sphere of Babylonian civilisation.

The characteristic of the Canaanite religion is a Dualism, which distinguished the two sexes, represented by the male Baal and the female Baalat. Of these the female divinity meets us mostly under the name of Ashtoreth, or Astarte, the Babylonian Ishtar. The male divinity, originally distinct in different tribes and nations, appears under special names. Ramman, Rimmon, or Haddad, who must have been peculiar to a tribal group, which preponderated in Mesopotamia and Babylonia, and, to judge by its early appearance was one of the first, is among the most celebrated. Dagon, who was much venerated on the Palestinian coast, was a foreign Philistine god, akin to the ἅλιος γέρων ("Old Man of the Sea") of the Greeks.

The chief deity of the Semitised Canaanites was "the lord" Baal, the male principle of nature. Each separate tribe retained his name for the original Baal-conception and established his worship when they seized a stronghold. The Baal of the wandering tribe thus became the lord of a settled place and country, the *genius loci*, lord of the city. Such Baalim are Melkarth in Tyre; the female principle

Ashtoreth in Sidon; the same, under the name of the female principle, Baalat, in Gebal; and all the countless Baals, which were worshipped in every stronghold if it formed a tribal centre. It lies in the nature of things that these separate Baalim, who bore different names according to their respective tribe and place, and whose importance grew or sank with that of their worshippers, developed special attributes so soon as they once assumed a personal character, and thus became separate divinities. The whole creative power of nature, which appears as the male principle, is seen in hot countries first in the fruit-bringing rain and in the storm accompanied with thunder and lightning. Ramman, therefore, was pre-eminently the storm-god. In a town without agriculture the natural side of the divine agency is neglected; in Tyre, Baal becomes a Melkart or Melek-kiryat, a " king of the town." But the evolution of the various conceptions of the divinities always recurs to the two original embodiments of the sexual principle. It is in this form that the true meaning of Semitic religious

it; no god of a tribe, or of any larger national group ever bore this name. If it occasionally appears also as a personal divinity—in Southern Arabia and Senjirli —that is evidently a later personification of the originally abstract idea. A similar explanation is necessary when an Elat is mentioned by the side of an El; this is nothing more than the conception of the female divinity, which was added to that of El on the analogy of Baal-Baalat.

The higher civilisation, with its literary training, tried to explain in its own fashion the cults as they had been evolved from existing and introduced elements in the different tribal and local sanctuaries during the historical progress of the peoples, and to form out of the different aspects of the original fundamental thought a pantheon, the members of which, according to their various characters, were explained to be the creators and rulers of the universe.

In the different states, which were equally possessors of a revered sanctuary, these cosmologies and theologies were distinct, since, naturally, each system was anxious to make its own sanctuary the central one. We have summarised what is as yet known of such matters in Babylonia. For Phœnicia a mere extract from such doctrines only is available, and that in a very garbled form, dating, too, from later times. It is the mythology of Gebal, or Byblos, which a certain Philo of Byblos composed under Nero, and, according to the custom of the time, published as a translation of the work of a very early priest, San-

CHARACTERISTIC PIECES OF PHŒNICIAN GLASS-WARE
The invention of glass was supposed to be one of the great achievements of the Phœnician civilisation, but it is now known to be due to Egypt; later it passed to Greece and Italy.

conceptions can be most clearly recognised.

" El," meaning God, seems to be a pure abstraction of the conception of the Deity; it meets us among the Canaanite, Aramæan, and Arabian peoples. The personal character of Baal originally diverged from

choniathon, who lived " before the Trojan War." It can, at most, furnish in isolated points explanations of the nature and growth of Phœnician religion, since in it the spurious wisdom of various centuries of culture are inextricably blended together.

THE PEOPLE OF JUDAH CARRIED AWAY INTO BABYLONIAN CAPTIVITY BY NEBUCHADNEZZAR
From the painting by E. Bendemann in the Berlin National Gallery by permission of the Berlin Photographic Co.

ANCIENT
NATIONS OF
WESTERN ASIA

III
THE HEBREW
PEOPLES

THE HEBREW PEOPLES
THE MAKING OF THE TWO NATIONS

BY far the best known of all Oriental peoples are the tribes which form the last components of the second great Semitic migration of the Nearer East. These are the Hebrew tribes, whose home, the farthest toward the desert, would in itself indicate that they came as the last of the great "Canaanite" migration, driven on by the precursors of the next, the Aramæan. These are the tribes which combined themselves into the people of Israel, and their neighbours who dwelt still further toward the desert, the Edomites, Moabites, and Ammonites.

The Tell el-Amarna letters prove the advance of Hebrew tribes in the land as early as the fifteenth century B.C.; one nation in particular comes prominently forward, which expanded from the north—namely, the Amorites. These appear to the Israelites, in the writing which presents the oldest form of their tradition, as the inhabitants from whom they **The Coming** must wrest the land; when **of the** the Israelites marched in, the **Israelites** former had already become occupants instead of immigrants. We may thus regard the Israelites as the next stratum after the Amorites, and may place their immigration somewhat ater. The earliest mention of Israel is contained in an inscription of the Pharaoh Meneptah II., about 1200 B.C. Whether that is, however, the tribal federation which we understand by this name, or some forgotten tribe, of which no record is left in Biblical tradition except the name of the collection of tribes banding round it and its sanctuary, must remain at present an unsolved question.

Within recent years much progress has been made in the true understanding and interpretation of the books of the Bible which have come down to us, and it has been demonstrated that the Biblical narrative is of a more composite character than had formerly been supposed, and embodies traditions of widely different origin and value. Historical criticism assumes that the Biblical narratives are to be treated as human documents, and are to be submitted to the same critical tests **Historic** which are applicable to all other **Value of** records of antiquity. It will, of **the Bible** course, on the other hand, be maintained that such methods are invalid when applied to the sacred narrative, and that any conclusions reached thereby must be rejected. From that point of view any historic account that deviates from the Biblical narrative will be repudiated.

The historical, or, as they should rather be termed, narrative books of the Bible, in the form in which they are now extant, are the work of a late period. The peculiar nature of the use made in antiquity of separate documents allows us to dissect the books into their component parts, so that we are in a position to distinguish the different authorities with some confidence, and to weigh the evidence of one against another.

The result of this division of sources, which is most apparent in the Pentateuch, is as follows. Two ancient documentary writings, designated, according to the name used for God by their respective **Elohist** writers, as Elohist and Jehovist, **and** had been combined in very **Jehovist** early times. The writing of the Elohist is indeed the more ancient, because it alone still preserves recollections of the actual conditions of remote antiquity. For instance, it represents that the Land of Promise must be won from the Amorites; whereas the Jehovist usually speaks of Canaanites—that is, it applies to the older inhabitants a general designation taken from the name of the country. The Elohist retains in its traditions traces of a post-Israelite immigration of Edom, Moab, and Ammon; while the Jehovist, which judges from the standpoint of later times, regards these tribes as already settled in their homes at the time of the immigration of Israel. Both

The Prophetic Code

writings were probably intended as introductions for annals, each of which was brought down to the time of its author. Of the strictly historical parts of these "Annals" only inconsiderable fragments have been preserved for us, which deal especially with the later period of the kings, and are easily distinguishable by their scanty form; other portions have been replaced in the revisions of later times mainly by accounts of the Prophets, of which the nature is best represented by the stories of Elijah and Elisha. This "Prophetic Code" is based on the point of view prevalent in the period about 600 B.C., after the introduction of Deuteronomy, although it is still imbued with the spirit of the older period.

The Deuteronomic code, on which the hierarchical constitution was based, was introduced by Josiah. Its contents are preserved for us in the legislative portions of Deuteronomy, the Fifth Book of Moses. This law acquired its true importance only during the exile in Babylonia, when the people, having become a religious body, saw in it the guide for all conduct. A priest, then, during the banishment, tested the whole history of Israel by these regulations, many of which exhibit the influence of the ancient laws of Babylonia. His direct work survives in the present form of the books, which extend from "Joshua" to "Kings." He has taken the older documents, but has extracted still more carefully the annalistic

elements from them, and in addition has briefly expressed his own views as to the separate sections, especially the reigns, in conformity with the Deuteronomic legislation. His work is, therefore, a review of Israelite history in the light of the divine origin of this law. The "Deuteronomist" explains the history of the people by their neglect or observance of this "Law of Moses"; he is a writer with a declared purpose, and his own additions are not hard to distinguish. Their nature is most easily and clearly seen in the summarised verdicts on the reigns of the various kings, thus: "He walked in the ways of Jeroboam and did that which was displeasing to God," or vice versa. To him also is due the settlement of the chronological scheme of the Bible, which, historically, is not of vital importance, since it represents an artificial calculation of dates, based on late information obtained during the period of the exile.

The further development of the religious community, which is henceforth represented by Judaism, led to the building up of a hierarchical constitution in the most pronounced sense of the term. This constitution was committed to writing in the so-called Priestly Code, either a work of the exile, or a product of the attitude of mind then prevalent. The code describes the whole development of the people of Israel from the creation of the world, and was intended to serve as a brief introduction to the giving of the law on Mount Sinai, which contains the new law. This work, originally standing by itself and reckoned as a post-exile code, was afterwards incorporated into the work which the "Deuteronomist" had adapted from the earlier records. It is easily recognised by its language; to it belong the account of the Creation in the first chapter of Genesis, and

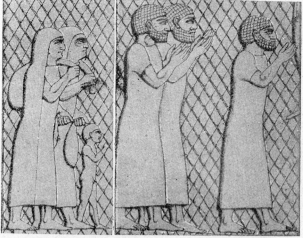

JUDÆANS IN THE TIME OF SENNACHERIB
An Assyrian representation of men, women and children of Judah about 700 B.C. From a bas-relief of Sennacherib now in the British Museum.

more especially the dry lists of genealogies referring to the patriarchal age. There is reason for congratulation that the author of the Priestly Code did not go further than the giving of the law on Mount Sinai. If he had treated the rest of the history from his point of view it would have been barely possible to use any portion of the narrative for historical purposes ; for, in contrast to the "Deuteronomist," he has made a clear field for himself, and has removed everything which did not agree with his own system. While the former gave us patchwork, and thus preserved many fragments of old tradition, the latter in an independent treatment has uniformly represented everything in accordance with his own view, and is thus of no help as an authority for history, or, as regards the early legends, for literary history. An example of this class of editing is presented by the Books of Chronicles, a long, post-exile account of Jewish history in the spirit of the Priestly Code. As their source of information, use has been made principally of the Books of Kings, although in a more detailed form than we possess them.

Ancient Editing of the Bible As documents of secular history they are, apart from some isolated facts, of comparatively slight importance in the construction of an actual chronicle of the people of Israel. But even the older accounts, contained in the work of the "Deuteronomist," would not furnish any historical picture if we had not a standard in the results obtained by ethnology and other investigations of the history of the Ancient East, by which to separate the earlier traditions from the accretions of a later age. Moreover, the evidence of inscriptions, especially those of Assyria and Babylonia, often furnishes us with information by means of which it is possible to compare and supplement the Biblical accounts.

As might be expected, the ideas of Israel as to its origin and early history are, like those of every people, clothed in the form of hero-legends ; the later hierarchical form of the tradition has subsequently given them a special colouring of its own. Historical records could not have existed until comparatively settled conditions had been established in the kingdom of Saul and then of David. All that goes back to the period anterior to historical records was naturally little more than a scanty local tradition. But even the oldest historical period was certain sooner or later to appear in the light of legend. Moreover, the priestly tradition preferred the legendary to the historical ; and the reason is clear, since for its purpose facts were often less advantageous than their legendary counterparts. Thus it is that so little authenticated history of the earliest period of the kings has been preserved.

Emigration from Egypt Tradition begins its account of the history of Israel with the emigration from Egypt and the entry into the "Promised Land." Modern historians, however, are of one mind in thinking that any emigration of a considerable tribal federation, a march through the countries of kindred tribes living under the same conditions of social economy, would have necessarily ended in the rapid dissolution of that federation, since alliances would have been made with the tribes of the countries traversed or annexed. Unification can, in the first place, result only after settled homes have been obtained, and necessarily presupposes a previous sojourn in the country. The Israelite tribal federation—that is, the people of Israel—did not receive its organisation until it was already settled in the country. Its individual tribes, therefore, did not previously stand in closer relation to each other than to their neighbours the Edomites, the Moabites, and many others which had disappeared as tribal organisations ; it was only the acquisition of fixed settlements of a certain uniformity that brought them nearer together and separated them more from the others. This evolution is the result of the interval between the Tell el-Amarna period and the first appearance of the "people of Israel."

It would be out of place in the present work to discuss at length the rival theories as to the Biblical account of the Exodus. It is generally acknowledged that bodies of Hebrew nomad tribes may well have pastured their flocks in **At the Time of the Exodus** the Wadi Tumilat, and in this way may have come into direct contact with Egypt, and have been subject to Egyptian authority. It is clear, however, from the reference to the people of Israel upon the slate of Meneptah, that other kindred tribes were already settled in Canaan at the time when Hebrew nomads were presumably in the Eastern Delta. In fact, the exodus must be regarded as an episode in the general migratory movement towards Canaan, later tradition having magnified its importance by representing the whole body of the later tribal divisions as having taken part in it. We have no means for determining accurately the date of the earliest inroads into Canaan or the length of the period during which the movement lasted;

Migration into Canaan
and any account of the conquest of Canaan by the Israelites must necessarily depend mainly upon conjecture. We can, however, picture to ourselves the conquest of the country on the model of well-known migrations—as, for instance, that of Britain by Jutes, Angles, and Saxons, and we may assume that the individual tribes, out of which the people of Israel was afterwards formed, conquered their homes, perhaps in combination with other vanished tribes, and were welded into a large federation in the country under the stress of circumstances. It is also probable that other tribal elements did not belong to them originally, but became attached to them only in later times. The true Israelite tribes had their homes " in the desert." Of the period when the tribes were not closely united, and a common cause of action was not yet generally, if at all, possible, we have reminiscences handed down by tradition, under the heading of the " Period of the Judges," which clearly exhibit tendencies to the formation of separate tribal principalities, and thus infer the distinct existence of the individual tribes. Such are the narratives of Jephtha in Gilead and of Gideon in Manasseh, the latter greatly disguised by additions. In both it can still be seen that we have to do with tribal traditions, and that no commonwealth of Israel is presupposed. It is only subsequent revision that has introduced at the end of the story the picture of a united Israel. The natural course of events leads to the

Judges of Israel
result that the sheikh, the head of a tribe, who conquers a country, derives the chief advantages from this conquest and obtains more ample means of power, which exalt him above his fellow-tribesmen. Settled life in a town and the adjacent localities dissolves the tribal organisation based on equality of rights, and leads to lordship and monarchy; the voluntarily acknowledged sheikh becomes an absolute monarch. This

development must have taken place more readily where the immigrants found such conditions already in existence, and where the conquest of a royal city actually implied that the conqueror adopted the institutions found therein. While, therefore, in the two examples of " judges " already referred to we can recognise the representatives of a country population, the next stage in the development, the tendency toward monarchy, is visible where an " Israelite " tribe is found in possession of a town. It was the tribal monarchy, which Abimelech founded for himself in Shechem. Notwithstanding that it soon ended, and left no permanent effects, it may be reckoned as typical of many similar phenomena of the time when the Israelite tribes obtained possession of the towns, and became acquainted with the unwelcome conditions that accompanied the coveted treasures of civilisation. This represents one form of the growth of the monarchy. It anticipates the natural development of tribes or clans into nations and states in so far as it effects a complete breach

Growth of the Monarchy
with its own tribe and thus strips itself of the aids by which it had just become prosperous and great. Such a tyranny, arising from no true development of the existing form of government, had no permanence. A monarchy, originating in the conditions of the further growth of the tribal life and its new needs, which was based on the members of the nation proper, alone had any lasting results.

We have only one piece of evidence as to any combined action of the Israelite tribal-federation, which would seem to be that mentioned by Meneptah—namely, the so-called Song of Deborah, one of the most ancient Hebrew poems that has come down to us. This composition, which, in consequence of mistakes in the tradition, is hardly yet intelligible in all its details, extols the triumph of the Israelite tribes in war. Almost all the Israelite tribes are named in it. The mention of Benjamin is, however, an interpolation, probably due to the need subsequently felt of seeing no tribe omitted from the list.

The advance of the Philistines in the twelfth century B.C. brought the Israelites under their power. Two alternatives were thus possible; either the newly immigrated tribes possessed the power to drive

JEPHTHAH, JUDGE OF ISRAEL, BEFORE THE SACRIFICE OF HIS DAUGHTER

The narrative of Jephthah in Gilead, from the "Period of the Judges," is taken to be evidence of the time before Israel became a commonwealth. This picture by Sir J. E. Millais is reproduced by permission of Lord Armstrong.

out the new rulers, or they would lose their nationality and become Philistine subjects. The first is what happened. It was the struggle against the new enemy that stimulated a closer unification and thus enabled the people to show a bolder front. War can be waged with permanent success only under a single command. A condition of ceaseless conflict must finally establish the power of a successful leader, who first, by the expulsion of the enemy and the reputation thereby acquired, gains a commanding position within his own tribe—that is, he becomes king—and then proceeds to set himself up as the liberator, and at the same time the lord, of the remaining tribes.

This explains the rôle of Saul, the leader of Benjamin, in the war against the Philistines. There is no clear proof that Benjamin belonged to the league of the northern ' Ten Tribes '' ; on the contrary, the subsequent intimate connection of Benjamin with Judah on the overthrow of David's kingdom supports the view that this tribe was opposed to

the northern tribes, which were already united. Here, in the country of the tribe, which was settled between Philistia proper and the territory of the Israelite tribes, a competent soldier might succeed in making himself lord of his own tribal country during a victorious war against the foreign domination, and then he might proceed to wrest from the Philistines the Israelite territory, which thus fell to him as to its natural lord. We must form for ourselves some such picture of the growth of the monarchy in Israel.

Saul has always remained in tradition a romantic personality. It is noteworthy that the story of David, the recorders of which had certainly no cause to cherish Saul's memory, never succeeded in obliterating it. We gather from the narrative that he kept his kingdom in hand so long as he lived, and that even David did not venture on any action against him. On the death of Saul, his kingdom of Israel lapsed to David ; but even the admirers of the latter have been obliged to spare Saul's memory. We know very little of him historically. One motif runs through all accounts of him—the struggle against the Philistines by which he founded his kingdom, which occupied all his life, and in which he met his death on the battlefield. **Wars of Saul** A fragment of old tradition—1 Sam. xiv. 47, modified in its present form — has left us one more short account of his other wars : " He fought against all his enemies on every side, against Moab and against the children of Ammon, against Aram and against the king of Zobah, south of Damascus, and against the Philistines." Our accounts, so far as they are historical, tell us nothing of Saul's relations to David; as we shall presently see, they cannot have known anything of the original opposition between Judah and Israel.

By the side of the kingdom of Saul, in the country of the kindred tribes inhabiting the less civilised district further to the south, on the fringe of the desert, a separate kingdom had meanwhile been formed in the same way as that of Saul, only starting from a still lower stage of development. This was the kingdom of David, of which Judah appears in tradition as the chief tribe. To David, as to so many conspicuous figures in history, all kinds of stories—heroic legends, even popular jests,

and the like—have been assigned, which were told of the man who represented the greatest power of the kingdom of Israel and Judah. His period appeared to posterity as a golden age, something in the way in which popular story has made Alfred the hero of English history. But along with this we have to distinguish another tradition of quite definite political tendency, the object of which is to describe David as the representative of an originally united people of Israel, to which Judah also belonged. This is the claim which, in modern phraseology, was put forward by David's historians and supporters in order to work in his interests and to win the people over to his house. Almost everything which we possess from Israelite sources was written from this point of view.

To this legend, modern research would seem to indicate, belongs almost everything which was intended to prove a union of **Rise of David** Israel and Judah, and, above all, that which is narrated of the origin of David, of his youth, and his relations to Saul. But in the legend are incorporated sundry details which are in clear contradiction of it, and are far more likely to correspond to the actual facts. According to these his rise was closely connected with the growth of the " Tribe of Judah." As the

LOUS, THE ANCIENT SHECHEM, ONE OF THE OLDEST CITIES OF PALESTINE

h founded the first Israelite tribal monarchy in Shechem. It was afterwards the principal city and metropolis of the Samaritans, and was colonised by Shalmaneser and Esarhaddon with Babylonians.

THE YOUTHFUL DAVID PLAYING ON HIS HARP BEFORE KING SAUL
From the picture by Mr. Ernest Normand, by whose permission it is here reproduced.

connection of Benjamin with Israel and the creation of a "Kingdom of Israel" must be called the work of Saul, so the formation of a "tribe" and kingdom of Judah was the work of David.

In the course of Oriental history again and again some leader of a tribe or band assumes the title of king and finally succeeds in ruling a large realm. David, even according to the tradition, was leader of some such band in Ziklag, far away to the south in the desert, situated in Edomite territory. He thus held his own for a time as the lord of a stronghold, and gradually gathered round him a devoted band of followers, with whose help it was not difficult to subdue the less mobile

David's Band of Followers — tribes, which had no leader. Whether, as the tradition assumes, he recognised the suzerainty of a Philistine king —Achish of Gath—must remain uncertain; but it is possible that such was the case.

The natural path of David's conquests led northward. He subjugated several tribes, which appear later as component parts of "Judah," and he became a prince whose power could no longer be ignored by the subjugation of the tribe of Caleb, with its centre at Hebron. The tradition preserves these conquests in the form of

David's Royal City — the story of Nabal (1 Sam. xxv.) but it is more clearly expressed in the fact that David's first royal residence was Hebron, the chief town of Caleb. Henceforward he was reckoned a king or a prince. Some reminiscence of this origin of his real power was preserved in an obscure passage —2 Sam. iii., 8 — where Abner later speaks contemptuously of him as "the prince of Caleb." Abner means to say : " Am I a rival of such as thou, David, that thou shouldst think I wish, by marriage with a wife of Saul, to gain some claim to the crown ?"

Caleb was bordered on the north by the territory of the " Hebrew " tribe Judah. This had not hitherto been closely allied with Israel. David now subjugated it, and thus united it with Caleb and the other subject tribes. The most important town of this district was Jerusalem, situated almost on the northern frontier towards Benjamin and Israel. We hear of it in the Tell el-Amarna letters as already the seat of a prince who governed these districts. Israelite tradition recognises that before it was conquered by David it did not belong to the "Hebrew" Judah but was still under kings of its own, who were "Canaanite"—that is to say, they had long been settled there. These "Jebusites" need not, however, for that reason have been much older than Judah itself. The mere fact that they were in possession of a town soon made them distinct from the inhabitants of the open country; and such, indeed, constitutes the difference between "Hebrews" and "Canaanites." Accord-

DAVID, KING OF JUDAH
From the statue by Michael Angelo

ing to the tradition David made Jerusalem his capital only after the sub-jugation of the whole of Israel. This is hardly probable, and the reason for making the statement is obvious—Jerusalem was to be reckoned the capital of the united kingdom. Originally, indeed, it had been intended for the capital of only the

newly conquered territory, and David removed his court there, since it was the richest portion of his land, and nearer the frontier of the country which was then the next object of his conquest—namely, Israel, the kingdom of Saul.

David had hitherto kept on good terms with the Philistines; if we reflect on the political movements disclosed in the Tell el-Amarna let-ters, it is more probable that the Philistines and David were in league against their common and dreaded opponent than that David was in league with the king of the northern tribes. Later tradition had every ground to disguise this enmity to Saul, who was not for-gotten in Northern Israel, and to substitute for it a friendship with the son of Saul. David was favoured by for-tune. Saul fell in the war with the Philistines, and, according to the story, to the great sorrow of David. But it is equally possible that the hero David had contributed his share to Saul's overthrow. The fate of the northern kingdom was thus sealed. The cause of the house of

A MODERN VIEW OF HEBRON, KING DAVID'S FIRST ROYAL TOWN
Hebron was the principal town of the tribe of Caleb, whom David subjugated, becoming their prince.

Saul, in spite of the brave defence by Abner, became more and more desperate. There is naturally no likelihood that the Israelite tribes voluntarily did homage to David, as tradition assumes : there was actually an attempt made to secure the sovereignty for Benjamin by the revolt of Sheba, the sheikh of the Benjamite canton Bichri, who at last tried to hold his own in the north of Israel, in Abel-beth-Maachah (2 Sam. xx.). Since this revolt was incompatible with the traditional account of the voluntary acknowledgment of David, it was transferred to the later years of David's reign; but the fact that, in the struggle against Sheba, only Judah from its southern frontier as far as Jerusalem stood on David's side, speaks too significantly, in the judgment of modern criticism. It probably took place immediately upon Saul's death, when David threatened to seize the territory of Israel. He cannot have brooked delay in the matter, and a rapid success must have crowned his efforts. It was impossible for Abner to secure for Eshbaal, Saul's son, more than the district east of the Jordan. Israel properly so-called thus fell into the hands of David without any further resistance than that of Sheba. Abner held the land east of Jordan for Eshbaal, according to tradition, for some time longer. Then he was murdered in Hebron, when anxious to negotiate with David in order to surrender to him the land east of Jordan. The account assigns vengeance for Joab as the motive, and repudiates any complicity on the part of David. At all events he reaped the advantage. Eshbaal also was murdered.

David could thus occupy the land west of Jordan without difficulty, and so became king of Judah and Israel. He had thus conquered almost the whole of his kingdom. Descended from a foreign stock, and having subjugated the peoples which obeyed him, in the first place by force, he himself, according to the story, maintained his sovereignty only by the help of his army. It is easy to see why policy should elaborate a tradition ascribing to him a high Hebrew ancestry, analogous to the Hellenic pedigree of the

royal house of Macedonia. Caleb seems to have been his home, and Judah the canton from which he sprang in a wider sense ; for his capital he chose Jerusalem on account of its favourable position for his purpose, since it was situated exactly between the two great divisions of his kingdom.

According to the ideas of Oriental nations the real lord of a country was the god, the Baal, according to his Semitic name. The king reigned in his name, and by him was called to

KING DAVID PLAYING UPON HIS HARP
Reproduced from the picture by Domenichino now in the Louvre.

power, as the Babylonians and Assyrians were never weary of emphasising. If a conquered country was only made tributary, it retained its own government and its king, and remained the property of its god. If, on the other hand, it became a province, it was absorbed into the conquering state, and thus forfeited everything, and its god was deposed, just as much as its king. The god was carried away, and brought into the temple of the victorious god, where he now " stood before his face "—that is, he served him, just as the vanquished king stood before his victor. The victorious god took possession of the land in his place; a temple was built for him there, and a cult established; in this way the new province was incorporated into the conquering state. That which had one god was one people; and every people possessed a god of their own. Thus, when David subdued new lands and added them to his territory, he completed the acquisition of his new possessions by installing the worship of God in the place of the old pagan cults. God was called Yahve or Jahve, for Jehovah, though familiar to us, is a false vocalisation of the Divine name, never in later times pronounced by the Jews, who assigned to the consonants of the name Yahve the vowels of Adonai, signifying "my lord," which, in a spirit of reverence, was read in place of the original name.

The god Serving other gods

Whether the gods previously worshipped by the several tribes were ejected in favour of Jehovah, or were identified now with the new religion, or there had already been a common cult, the supremacy of the house of David was intimately associated with the God of David, proclaimed as the God of the ancestral Hebrew stock. Later, at any rate, it was claimed as the unique and primeval characteristic distinguishing the religion that the God of Israel was not to be worshipped under or represented by any image or symbol. But the Bible narrative itself proves with sufficient clearness that the worship of local gods under other rites was irrepressible.

It is certainly a proof of the importance of David that the vigorous vitality of his policy was able to exert so marked an influence on the tradition of subsequent times. It is not wonderful that the people in later times lent a willing ear when the exploits of David's kingdom were appealed to. In fact, David's reign was the only one under which Israel as a united kingdom could have taken a position by the side of the other powers in Palestine and Syria. David's time thus appeared as the good old days when Israel was powerful; its dark side, and the resistance which was shown by the people, were soon forgotten.

Golden Days of David

The power of David extended far beyond the borders of Judah and Israel. He subjugated Edom; this union lasted longer than that with Israel. Israel first burst the bond, while Edom long remained

THE SO CALLED "TOMB," OR PILLAR, OF ABSALOM, SON OF DAVID, NEAR JERUSALEM

THE VISIT OF THE QUEEN OF SHEBA TO SOLOMON, FROM THE PAINTING BY LE SEUR

Hanfstaengl

united with Judah. David further subdued Moab, which remained subject long
after the severance of the kingdom ; it
belonged, however, naturally to Israel.
He also fought with Ammon, but his
wars led to no permanent conquest. He
did not penetrate beyond
Extent Israelite territory in a northern
of David's direction, as later tradition
Kingdom would imply. On the north of
Gilead the small Aramæan states of Soba
and Geshur adjoin and run up into
Israelite territory. With these he had
both friendly and inimical relations
without permanently subjugating them.
Damascus, soon the rival of Israel, lay
too far away, and had not yet acquired
strength. During his reign the Philistines
were finally restricted to their territory
on the coast ; they made no further serious
attempt to advance against Israel.

The rebellion of Absalom must be
placed quite at the end of David's life.
Tradition does not give us a clear account
of the matter. Yet one thing is apparent :
David's sympathies were with the rebel ;
he was a mere helpless puppet in the
hands of Joab and the military party.

It is not said for whom Joab wished to
secure the throne ; probably even then
for Adonijah. When Absalom fell, slain
by Joab in defiance of David's command,
David lamented for him. But Joab
upbraided him insolently, and gave him
plainly to understand that his sovereignty
was at an end if he did not change his
attitude. It is worthy of further remark,
as regards the whole rebellion, that David,
as formerly Eshbaal, the son of Saul, also
sought and found an asylum in the country
east of Jordan. There is a detailed
description of the intrigues by which un-
wearying efforts were made to induce
David, now completely worn out, to pro-
nounce in favour of Solomon's accession
to the throne. The factions at court are
now clearly recorded. Solomon
Intrigues is the candidate of the
Against priesthood, while a military
David party, represented by Joab,
wishes to elevate Adonijah to the throne.
The tradition in its simplicity makes no
disguise of the means by which the priestly
party conquered. The result is clear.
Solomon succeeded in securing the throne
for himself, and a pretext was soon found

1765

to remove out of his path his rival Adonijah with his partisan Joab, in spite of the immunity which had been promised them.

Solomon was placed on the throne by the priestly party. The party, therefore, upon which the new king relied, rather

Solomon on the Throne
than on the devoted bodyguard of his father, had thus become the interpreter of the will of God, whom David had accepted as Lord over Israel. The tradition chose Solomon for its favourite hero, notwithstanding the fact that it had greater trouble in creating out of him a morally noble personality than out of David, who, in spite of his human failings, was acknowledged to possess the one sterling quality of having won by his own merits all that he possessed. David had proved himself superior to all the adventurers and robber chieftains who had fought with one another for the possession of the land. In order to form a just estimate of him we must judge him by the standard of Bedouin ethics—and Bedouins have the ethics of nomads.

The older records tell us little about Solomon. The candidate of the priestly party was credited with the building of the Temple as his greatest achievement, in which we may see confirmation of his good understanding with his adherents. Otherwise we have only a few disconnected accounts of his reign. The records of an extension of his power as far as the Euphrates date from post-exile times, their object being to glorify the favourite hero of legend from whom the development started which culminated in Judaism. To the same source is to be assigned the legend of the "wisdom" of Solomon. There was little in his history which could be eulogised except his "wisdom," of which, indeed, he gave striking proof when he relied upon

SOLOMON, LAST KING OF JUDAH AND ISRAEL
From the picture by Van Ghent in the Palazzo Barberini.
Anderson

the priesthood instead of the army. His reign in other respects was of the usual Oriental type. He tried to display before men's eyes the external magnificence of a mighty king by raising immense buildings and keeping up an imposing court ceremonial. In order to defray the cost of his buildings, he is said to have ceded territory to Hiram of Tyre. In this, as well as in a notice of his maritime trading operations on the Red Sea, we realise the fact that the half-nomadic, fighting tribe with which David had conquered his territory had been driven back by the influence of the already more civilised northern tribes; civilisation, represented by Israel, had gained the superiority. The conquered civilisation here, as everywhere, eventually overcame the barbarian conqueror.

A single record of a small acquisition of territory by Solomon is valuable. He is said to have taken in marriage a daughter of the Pharaoh—this would naturally mean only a daughter of one of the women of the harem—and to have received as a dowry the city of Gezer, which had hitherto been independent. Light may be thrown on this notice by the conditions represented in the Tell-el-Amarna letters. Solomon may have openly written to the Pharaoh in the spirit of Rib-Adda, Abi-Milki, and Abd-khiba, his predecessors on the throne of Jerusalem, and may have enforced his claims on Gezer. He may

Solomon and the Pharaoh
have represented himself as the "loyal servant of his lord," and by diplomatic means have obtained the town from the prince of Gezer.

It would follow from this that the whole previous development was actually accomplished under the suzerainty of Egypt, feeble though it was at times,

At the top is a picture of Jerusalem as it appeared in the time of David and Solomon, and underneath it a photograph of an American model of the temple built by Solomon. At the bottom are shown the three immense reservoirs constructed by kings of Judah, probably by Solomon, to supply Jerusalem with water. Inset is Mount Moriah, on which Solomon's temple was built.

VIEWS IN AND AROUND SOLOMON'S ROYAL CITY OF JERUSALEM

Such was the reign of the great and "wise" Solomon, of whose wisdom tradition has told all sorts of stories. But we notice also in the accounts the voice of the historian of the prophets, which dates from the period of hostility between the prophets and the ruling party; and we may see its classical expression in the hostility of Samuel to the monarchy. The blame for the disruption of the kingdom is, indeed, quite openly ascribed to the policy of Solomon's reign. As a matter of fact, the state of affairs appears to have been that the more developed districts in the north were subject to the rule of the less developed. Solomon had, therefore, absorbed the former. His ancestral domain must have derived benefit from the fact that it now came into closer touch with civilisation. This result may have been very agreeable to the ruling parties in Jerusalem, but less so to the subject parties in the north. There is the additional fact to be noted that even the disadvantages of civilisation now made themselves felt in Jerusalem. The barbarous but warlike Caleb was replaced by a Jerusalem which had been assimilated to the civilised north. But by this very fact the foundation of David's superiority over Israel was undermined. Judah no longer found support in the rude strength and rapacity of the Bedouins; it had become a civilised state, and now learned the weakening influence of culture. Thus when there was again a struggle upon equal terms, the south no longer prevailed. The northern tribes were superior in civilisation, and they conquered Judah. This finds its expression first in the separation, but soon in the domination of Judah by Israel.

THE KINGDOMS OF ISRAEL AND JUDAH

THE severance of Israel from Judah was not merely a struggle which the two halves of the kingdom waged with each other, as tradition represents. The Egyptian inscriptions show clearly enough that the conquest of Jerusalem by the Pharaoh Sheshonk was connected with it. What had been Rehoboam's attitude toward the latter, and what induced him to appear as a disloyal servant of Egypt, **Egypt Conquers Israel** we do not know. But this much is clear—that the Pharaoh took most of the towns of Northern Israel from Rehoboam and gave them to Jeroboam; there is also a tradition of his residence in Egypt. The record of it is at variance with the legend, and must be regarded in the light of the Tell el-Amarna letters. Jeroboam succeeded in forwarding his plans at court better than Rehoboam; the Northern Israelite had more of the sinews of war, by which the disputes of the civilised world were fought out, than the king of Jerusalem, and these he placed at the disposal of his advocates at court.

We have no evidence which would enable us to decide whether Rehoboam trusted to some other source of help in his resistance to the Pharaoh, though it is conceivable that he calculated on Damascus, which was now coming into prominence. In any case Damascus, owing to the ceaseless struggles between the now separate halves of the kingdom, very soon became the supreme arbitrator in the affairs of Palestine, since Egypt after the last attack of Sheshonk does not seem to have interfered again decisively, and Assyria had not yet appeared upon the scene.

From the first the most powerful of the two states was Israel, which very soon showed its superiority. The Books of Kings do not contain detailed records of the war which was "always between Rehoboam and Jeroboam" (1 Kings xiv. 30). But they have preserved for us a very valuable notice. It proves that Jeroboam had done that which we might have expected of him from the first. He was bound to make the people aware that he did not agree with Judah, and it was to his interest to oppose the idea of the justification of David's power. He was **Jeroboam Revives Baalim** induced, therefore, to attempt to abolish the religion of David and to revive in its place the ancient national sanctuaries. He was, for this reason, solicitous that the two ancient sanctuaries of Bethel and Dan should be once more brought into vogue. It must be borne in mind that the great festivals, which were celebrated in such places, did not acquire their main significance from their religious side as festivals, but that they exercised a far wider economic influence; they were the fairs which the whole nation held, under the protection of the peace of the sanctuary. For this reason a king of Israel must have been still more anxious to keep visitors away from the sanctuary in Jerusalem, and to deprive the other capital of the advantages accruing from such traffic. Since in this way the greater part of the revenue of the splendid new temple was lost, the priests had every reason to regard Jeroboam as the type of an impious king.

According to our accounts, Jeroboam was followed by his son Nadab, who reigned only two years, roughly about 910 B.C. He is said to have been murdered during the siege of the Philistine Gibbethon by Baasha, of the tribe of Issachar. The new dynasty did not, therefore, last long ; and the disturbances, which are typical of the kingdom of the Ten Tribes, did not delay their appearance. Baasha became king, and reigned, according to the accounts, from about 910 to 886 B.C. He greatly harassed Judah. In order to render any communications with Jerusalem impossible, he fortified a place, Rama, a little north of Jerusalem. Asa was thus compelled to throw himself into the arms of Damascus and to implore its protection and suzerainty. Bir-idri naturally welcomed the proposal. He invaded Northern Israel, and thus forced Baasha to evacuate the frontier of Judah. The fortress of Rama was again razed to the ground ; but Judah had become a vassal of Damascus, and Baasha, too, had no alternative but to bow to him,

Judah a Vassal of Damascus as his predecessors had to Egypt. Baasha's son, Elah, is said also to have reigned for only two years, and to have been murdered by the commander of the army, Zimri, who, from Gibbethon, where the army lay, attacked him in his palace at Tirzah.

The tradition, therefore, assumes that the two first dynasties of Israel consisted of two kings each, the second king

REHOBOAM, KING OF JUDAH

S.P.C.K.

From an Egyptian cartouche. He was probably carried away to Egypt after Pharaoh Sheshonk took Jerusalem.

in each case being murdered after a reign of only two years, and in both murders the army, which lay before Gibbethon, had a part. Exception has been taken to this by the critics, and it has been suggested that the tradition may be incorrect. Zimri was unable to hold his own.

Rule of the Army The army did not support him, but took the side of Omri, the commander-in-chief, who advanced at the head of the "whole people"— a national army is still presupposed at this time—up to Tirzah, where Zimri sought his death in the flames of the king's palace. In the meantime Omri had not been acknowledged king without further difficulty, "for half of the people followed Tibni, the son of Ginath." This latter seems to have held his own for a considerable time as a rival king, until he was vanquished by Omri. Parties, therefore, existed in Israel ; these may have corresponded to the different conditions of life existing in the population, which had advanced from the state of peasants to a higher civilisation. In the ceaseless disturbances which such feuds must have produced from time to time, vigorous measures could be taken only with the indispensable support of a strong monarchy, a trustworthy army. This was the policy which Omri and his house pursued, following the example of David. In home affairs the policy of encouraging traffic was adopted, and attempts were made to establish favourable relations with foreign countries, especially with Tyre ; Omri's son, Ahab, married a Tyrian princess, Jezebel. Omri's position towards Damascus is not recorded ; probably, however, he recognised its suzerainty, and secured his throne only by doing so. He again subjugated Moab, which, on the separation, had taken up an uncertain attitude towards Israel ; and, doubtless, it was he also who brought Judah under his own suzerainty ; this position is attested under Ahab. He made Samaria the capital of the empire in place of Tirzah. Omri's policy both at home and abroad was continued by his son Ahab. He was a vassal of Damascus, had a strong army under his orders, tried to promote intercourse with foreign countries, and therefore showed friendliness to all strangers. By this action he excited the opposition

Ahab of Israel

of the peasant population ; tradition attests this fact in recording the zeal displayed by the prophets against the Baalim, the gods of the strangers. The natural opposition to the dominating classes by the agricultural population, which suffered under the development of trade and the encroachment of the military feudal system, found vent in the opposition of Elijah and Elisha. Judah was now subject to Ahab, and its king, Jehoshaphat, was compelled to take the field with him. The relations to Damascus are clearly seen in the first notice of Israelite history, which is chronologically certain. In the year 854 B.C. Shalmaneser II., at the battle of Karkar, saw in the army of Bir-idri of Damascus an actual contingent from Ahab of Israel, which the latter had furnished as vassal of Damascus ; Judah, as subject to Israel, is naturally not named. The attacks of Assyria on Damascus would naturally have incited Ahab to shake off the yoke. But Shalmaneser was always repulsed by Bir-idri ; and Ahab met his death in one of the fights, in which he tried to hold his own against Bir-idri, at Ramoth-Gilead. This seems to have taken place soon after the battle at Karkar, therefore about 853 B.C.

His son, Ahaziah, was probably obliged to acknowledge the suzerainty of Damascus, and equally so his brother Joram, who followed him on the throne, presumably only two years afterwards. He would thus have been forced to take the field with Bir-idri in the subsequent campaigns of Shalmaneser. But he also did not fail to make attempts to liberate himself, and is said to have been wounded in a battle which he had to fight near Ramoth-Gilead against Bir-idri, or, now, Hazael. While attempting to return home, in order to recover from his wounds, he fell a victim to the revolution of Jehu.

Judah was from the very first at a disadvantage compared with the northern

Judah and Egypt

kingdom. The latter owed its freedom to the intervention or the approval of the Pharaoh, and Rehoboam had to suffer severely from Sheshonk's chastisement and the enforced contributions. It is a proof of the permanence of David's measures that Edom remained loyal to Judah, notwithstanding that an attempt had been made by a descendant of the old royal house—Hadad, according to the tradition—presumably under Solomon

RAMA, ONE OF THE MOST BEAUTIFUL CITIES OF ANCIENT PALESTINE
Rama, a few miles north of Jerusalem, was fortified by Baasha, king of Israel, about 900 B.C., to prevent communication with Jerusalem from the north. It lies in a fertile plain, and is now remarkable for its olive groves and fruit gardens.

(I Kings xi.), to gain its independence by the support of Egypt.

Neither Rehoboam nor his son Abijah can have had long reigns. Asa, the successor of the latter, realised the supremacy of Israel under Baasha, and was forced to solicit the suzerainty of Damascus in order to protect himself from the former.

Judah Subject to Israel The "Deuteronomist" in the Books of Kings commends him; the priesthood must therefore have flourished under him. Jehoshaphat also is said to have been a pious man. Judah was now no longer directly dependent on Damascus, but was subject to the suzerainty of Israel; for Jehoshaphat took the field with Ahab, both when he fought at Karkar for Damascus and when he fought against his feudal lord in Gilead. It is further recorded that he also made an attempt to resume the navigation of the Red Sea inaugurated by Solomon.

His son Joram meets us also as a loyal supporter of the northern kingdom under Ahaziah and his brother Joram. It is clear that he was completely under the influence of his wife Athaliah. This fact proves that the house of Omri understood how to secure their power, which they had founded through the instrumentality of a strong army, by other means as well. Athaliah was the daughter of Ahab, and sister of Joram of Israel. The part which she played proves that in reality the influence of the house of Omri was already absolute in Judah. But they never realised their object of restoring the empire of David by the amalgamation of the two dynasties, this time starting from Israel and under Israel's supremacy.

Edom shook off its yoke under Joram. An attempt to reconquer it seems to have turned out very disastrously for the king of Judah. He was followed by his own and Athaliah's son, Ahaziah, **Rebellion of Jehu's Party** for whom his mother had contrived to secure the succession. The house of Omri seems almost to have reached its goal when the opposite party aimed their blow and exterminated the proud dynasty. Ahaziah accompanied his feudal overlord and uncle, Joram of Israel, to battle in Gilead, where both fell victims to Jehu's rebellion.

Jehu, the head of the rebellion, was, like Omri, a military commander. He won over the army while he was in the field at Gilead and Joram had gone home to recover from his wounds. The army now turned the scale; as often happens, that which had been the support of a strong monarchy became its most dangerous enemy. The cause of the rebellion is stated to have been the murder of Joram and his vassal Ahaziah of Judah. The blow was clearly enough aimed at the whole house of Omri and its partisans, that is, the son of the princess of the house of Omri in Judah. But the energetic Athaliah in Judah was able to hold her own by means of the army, the constant support of her house. It is well known that she ordered all the male descendants of her deceased husband to be murdered. This seems at first sight an incomprehensible act of cruelty, but it finds its motive in the simple fact that the murdered Ahaziah had been her only son; while Joram's other sons were by different wives. On the death of her son the sovereignty would thus legally have fallen to one of the other sons, who had no blood of Omri in his veins. Nothing was left for her but to follow the tactics of her rival if she did not wish to abandon the policy of her house. Thus the complete success of the rebellion was frustrated by her bold action. It was only in Israel that the house of Omri was

Athaliah Queen of Judah

exterminated and Jehu became king. But what were the deeper-lying causes of the rebellion? The prophets had been favourably disposed to the dynasty of Omri. They expressed the views and wishes of the people, especially of the people of the south with their inferior economic development, as opposed to the policy of Omri and his descendants, who had brought Judah also under their sway. It was the resistance of the nomads and peasants to the development of a civilisation which was prejudicial to them. It was the revolt, too, of the spirit of nationality, whose ideal expression, after David, was centred in the national worship of the God of Israel, against the policy of the ruling dynasty, which favoured connections with foreign countries, and appeared as a worshipper of strange Baalim. It is plainly evident in the course of the insurrection that this resistance, if not originating with Judah, was at any rate strongly supported by it. Its leaders are expressly said to have been a tribe, Rechab, which lived in the south of Judah on the fringe of the desert, in the simple conditions of agriculturists who had not yet altogether abandoned the ideas of a nomadic life, and who are said to have been believers in Israel's God. If we also take into account the support of the Hebrew prophets, expressly proved by the legend of Elisha

Revolt of National Spirit

A MODERN VIEW OF SAMARIA, THE CAPITAL OF THE ISRAELITE KINGDOM

MICAIAH BEFORE AHAB, KING OF ISRAEL, AND JEHOSHAPHAT, KING OF JUDAH
Judah was subjugated by Ahab, and Jehoshaphat the king was compelled, against his own will and policy, to take the field with him. This picture shows the prophet Micaiah warning Ahab before the battle of Ramoth-Gilead.

to have been given to Jehu, we see what claims had been put forward by the revolutionists. We have not here to do with a mere military revolt, but with the shock of two opposing classes of the population.

It is one thing to offer promises to discontented followers, and another thing to execute them. From the moment when Jehu became king, he had perforce to follow in the main the same line of policy as his predecessors. His scheme had miscarried in Judah owing to Athaliah's intervention. The kingdom of David, for which the co-religionists of David, who supported him, had fought, could not be restored; Jehu was restricted to Israel. He was compelled, therefore, to renounce the religion of the southern kingdom, which he had adopted so far to serve his ends, since he, as king of Israel, now stood in natural opposition to the religion of Judah, which was in the hands of Athaliah. He therefore renounced the religion of David, and served henceforward the old gods of his people, although he had started his revolution in the name of the God of Israel.

External circumstances also soon compelled him to abandon the idea of nationality, which must have helped to bring him to the throne. He was forced, in order to secure his sovereignty, to obtain the acknowledgment of the great powers, and he clearly from the first took into account the existing political conditions. His rebellion must be placed in the year 843, or perhaps 842 B.C. In this year Shalmaneser appeared on his expedition against Hazael before Damascus. He mentions Jehu as a tributary king. The latter had therefore lost no time in obtaining support from the new power instead of Damascus, which had hitherto been supreme. This step was perhaps taken in conformity with the immediate wish of the national party; in reality, it was bound to end at the point to which the policy of the house of Omri was directed. After Shalmaneser had once more vainly tried—839 B.C.—to subdue Hazael, he abandoned his attempts at conquest in the west. Jehu was now in a difficulty, for Hazael naturally proceeded to attack him. Whether Jehu continued to pay tribute as before to Assyria, we are not informed; but he did not submit to Hazael. He offered resistance to him, and lost in the struggle the territory east of Jordan. Judah, which had eluded him owing to Athaliah, does not appear, even

1773

after her fall, to have again been subject to him.

Jehu's reign, therefore, which ought to have seen the restoration of David's kingdom, implies a downfall of Israel from the height previously attained, especially under the house of Omri. It receded also under his son Jehoahaz.

Downfall of Israel Israel was more and more oppressed by Hazael, since Assyrian help was not forthcoming; we are told in 2 Kings xiii. 3, that Israel was completely in his power. Then "the Lord gave Israel a saviour." The account does not mention this "saviour" by name; it was Assyria. About 800 B.C. Adad-nirari subdued Mari of Damascus. Even his son and successor, Joash, continued in the position of a vassal of Assyria, and was thus enabled to recover from Damascus certain lost territory, presumably east of Jordan. Judah itself was probably conquered once more; Amaziah of Judah vainly tried to shake off the yoke. Jeroboam II., in whose period occurs the expedition of Shalmaneser III. against Damascus in 773 B.C., was equally successful through Assyrian help; it is recorded of him that he reconquered the districts of Northern Israel. During his reign, which is said to have been long, Israel enjoyed for the last time a period of comparative peace.

Soon after his death the new rise of Damascus under Rezon, and the encroachments of Tiglath-pileser, which were connected with it, herald a period of continuous revolutions down to the end of the kingdom. If Israel had fallen from its former position under Jehu, we are now witnesses of its death agony. Zachariah, son of Jeroboam II., was the first of the series of kings who were deposed by violence in rapid succession. He is said to have been slain by a certain Shallum, after a reign of only six months. This latter could hold his own only for one month against **Assyrian Supremacy Acknowledged** Menahem, son of Gadi (2 Kings xv. 14). The date of Menahem is accurately fixed by the notice of Tiglath-pileser IV., that he paid tribute to him in the year 738 B.C. Thus he acknowledged the Assyrian supremacy, evidently under compulsion, for Tiglath-pileser took from him the northern part of his territory. Menahem must have died soon afterwards, probably in 737 B.C. His son, Pekahiah, is said to have reigned

two years, 736 and 735 B.C. He seems to have remained loyal to Assyria, for he was overthrown by Pekah, the son of Remaliah, whose revolt was supported by Damascus. After the appearance of Tiglath-pileser, the cry of the two opposite parties was once more "Damascus or Assyria." Pekah, as vassal of Rezon, marched with him in 735 or 734 B.C. against Ahaz, who in Jerusalem was consistently loyal to Assyria. The attempt to defeat him was unsuccessful. In the following year Tiglath-pileser appeared and invested Damascus. Pekah lost his northern territory, or, as Tiglath-pileser expresses it, only Samaria was left. This gave the Assyrian party in Samaria the upper hand; they overthrew Pekah, and proclaimed Hoshea king, and his election was ratified by Tiglath-pileser. Soon afterwards Damascus fell, and became a province of Assyria in 731 B.C.

The state of affairs was thus completely changed. Now Assyria proceeded to take every opportunity of systematically draining the resources of the subject people, that is, of creating out of them Assyrian **Israel an Assyrian Province** provinces. Ever since 738 B.C. the territory of Israel had touched the province of Simirra, which had been created there; and a considerable part of Israelite territory was now assigned to this province. Damascus, too, was now Assyrian. The annexation of Samaria was necessarily the next step. There were only two possible ways of retaining their self-government, and these were either to pay the tribute or to obtain help from another power. The tribute was too exorbitant to be permanently endured, and the king, through inability to pay, was usually soon driven to suspend the payments—that is, to declare his revolt. Help from outside was now sought in Egypt, which had never ceased to cast her eyes on Palestine.

It was not, indeed, long before Hoshea was compelled to suspend his payments of tribute, trusting to Egyptian aid. The prophet Hosea, whose activity coincides with the period subsequent to the fall of Damascus, describes to us the conditions of vacillation between Egypt and Assyria. In the year 724 B.C. an Assyrian army advanced in order to annex Samaria. The town is said to have resisted for three years; it finally fell when Shalmaneser IV. had just died and Sargon had mounted the throne in 722 B.C. King Hoshea was carried

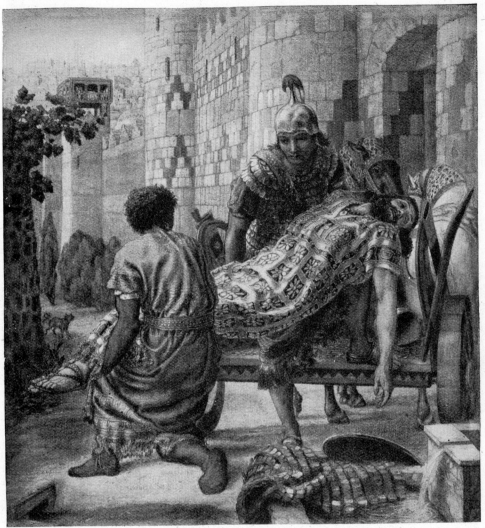

THE DEATH OF AHAB AFTER THE BATTLE OF RAMOTH-GILEAD
From the picture by T. M. Rooke, in the possession of Mr. M. Russell Cotes, by whose permission it is reproduced.

away into captivity, and with him the larger portion of the inhabitants, 27,290 souls in all, as Sargon accurately records. They were settled in Mesopotamia, in the vicinity of Harran, and on the Khabur and in the Median Highlands. The loss of the population was replaced in the usual fashion by settlers from other parts of the empire; Babylonian citizens from Cuthah in particular were settled in Samaria.

The capital of Israel had thus become an Assyro-Babylonian city. Samaria, henceforward the seat of an Assyrian governor, may be compared with the Sidon of Esarhaddon. The inhabitants

were afterward actually termed Cuthæans, from the predominance of the Cuthæan element in the population.

It is generally believed that this "carrying away of the Ten Tribes" signifies a dissolution of the people of Israel, which is regarded as having formed a part of Judah, and as having shared the same views. Starting from this standpoint, certain writers have attempted to trace remnants of the "Ten Tribes" in every imaginable place on earth, being influenced by the account which represents the two peoples of Israel and Judah as one nation. The 27,290 souls whom Sargon enumerates were not, however, "the people of Israel";

1775

they were only the larger portion of the population of Samaria and of its immediate vicinity which alone at the last formed the "kingdom" of Israel, since the northern districts had been captured still earlier. But, apart from this, there was in the territory of the Ten Tribes an absence of the bond which afterwards kept the

Captivity of the "Ten Tribes" Jews together in Babylonia; that is, a common cult, to say nothing of a more highly developed religious conception and a closely organised priesthood. Since the severance, the God of Israel had ceased to be the centre of a national worship, and any traces of such worship, which had been retained in the north from the time of David, were quite insignificant. Tradition has not preserved the names of the gods of Bethel, Dan, and the other national sanctuaries. In reality the Ten Tribes were not differentiated, as regards their religious conceptions, in the slightest degree from the other nations dwelling round about them. They were not, therefore, "Jews." The want of a national bond caused even those who remained in their old homes to retain but little recollection of the "kingdom of Israel."

The province of Samaria, two years after its conquest, in combination with its companions in misfortune, Damascus and Simirra, or Northern Phœnicia, and in concert with Hamath, made a renewed attempt to shake off the Assyrian yoke. But Iaubidi of Hamath was defeated by Sargon. Thus all hope of Syrian independence was destroyed. Samaria after this remained an Assyrian province. It repeatedly received new strata of population, for instance in the reign of Ashurbanipal after the subjugation of the Babylonian revolt of the Cuthæans. At a later period, as Judaism grew stronger, it became the home of the sect of the Samaritans, of which the last remains disappeared only in modern times.

The Power of the Priesthood During the revolution of Jehu, Athaliah had succeeded in holding her own by means of the army. If Jehu was thus forced to fail in his promises to his helpers, still the revolution, notwithstanding this momentary reverse, meant in the end the victory of the party that still followed the God of David, which was unfriendly to the foreign dynasty of Omri and its policy. The priesthood in Judah, which had gained strength since

Solomon, was clearly the real soul of the resistance. It is obvious that, so long as there was any opposition, people and priesthood formed one composite party. It was only after the victory that the conflicting interests of the two parties were felt, as is usual in revolutions. Athaliah is said to have held her own for six years longer. Then the priestly party succeeded in overthrowing her and in wreaking vengeance upon her; they had won over the "Pretorian guard," the support of Athaliah. The only surviving son of Joram, who, when his brothers were murdered, had been sheltered as a child in the Temple, was raised to the throne. It matters little whether he was really the last scion of David's house or was put forward in this character; the important point was that he had been "educated by the high-priest," and placed by him upon the throne.

A schism was now formed between priesthood and people. The two no longer stood as the ruled and oppressed class in opposition to the monarchy, for the

The Priests versus the People sovereignty was now actually in the hands of the priests. These, together with the king, who was dependent on them, were now held responsible by the people for all grievances. If, therefore, the spokesmen of the people had hitherto been opponents of the monarchy, they were now equally opposed to the governing priesthood. But, in accordance with the stage of culture which Judah had attained, truth and justice were represented by an appeal to God.

Thus, if any one of the people accused the priests of crimes or mistakes in home or foreign policy, he appealed to God as the representative of justice and right. These spokesmen were the prophets. From the time of the governing priesthood dates the feud between prophets and priests, between the God of the prophets and that of the priests, who was not distinguishable from the Baalim, against whom both had before been united. This then was the origin of the Prophetic Order, properly so called, such as we see it in its chief representatives, Amos and Hosea.

Not much else is known of the state of Judah under Joash. When Jehu, in 842 B.C., paid tribute to Assyria, Judah is not mentioned, probably for the reason that Shalmaneser's influence did not reach so far to the south. It must, however, very soon afterwards have become subject once more to Jehoahaz and Joash, for Amaziah made fruitless attempts to shake off the yoke ; Israel, through Assyria's help, was still the stronger. Joash fell a victim to a palace revolt. Since the conspiracy started with officials, we may perhaps conclude that it formed an attempt to check the supremacy of the priesthood. His son and successor, Amaziah, was equally subject to priestly influence. He made unsuccessful attempts to reconquer Edom, and was unfortunate in the war by which he intended to make himself independent of Israel. We do not know

permanent successes were achieved. Edom asserted its independence after it had once secured its freedom. Since Azariah was a leper, the government was principally carried on by his son Jotham. No events of importance are recorded of the independent reign of the latter from about 752 to 736 B.C. Since in 738 B.C. Judah is not mentioned among the states tributary to Tiglath-pileser, we may assume that it was still dependent on Israel.

Ahaz, the son of Jotham, who succeeded to the crown about the same time as Pekah secured the throne in Samaria, used this opportunity to liberate himself from Israel by acknowledging the Assyrian

DEATH OF JOASH, KING OF JUDAH
After the death of Joram of Judah and the revolt of Jehu, all his sons except Joash were murdered, and his wife Athaliah ruled as regent for several years. Joash was secreted in the Temple and raised to the throne on the assassination of his mother. He attempted to become independent of Israel, but fell a victim to a palace revolt.

how far he had reckoned on aid from Damascus. In any case, Joash of Israel, the vassal of Assyria, proved the stronger, and defeated him at Beth-Shemesh. Amaziah himself was taken prisoner, and was able to purchase his freedom only by the payment of a heavy ransom. He was also compelled to raze to the ground a part of the fortifications of Jerusalem. He, too, fell a victim to a conspiracy, and was murdered at Lachish ; we cannot, however, clearly understand the circumstances which attended his death.

His son Azariah is said to have continued the wars with Edom, but no

supremacy. The immediate result was the siege of Jerusalem by Rezon and Pekah in 735, or at latest 734 B.C. Ahaz had not miscalculated when he built his hopes on Tiglath-pileser ; the latter appeared in 734 and 733 B.C., and he put an end to the splendour of Damascus. But in his other calculations Ahaz had deceived himself. He had clearly hoped to receive from Tiglath-pileser the northern kingdom as a reward for his loyalty, and in this way to restore once more the kingdom of David. But Tiglath-pileser considered it more prudent to secure for himself the power of turning the scale at any time by means of the old disunion, and he consequently installed Hoshea. The internal policy of Ahaz was equally directed toward his goal, the possession of Israel. He turned against the now too powerful priesthood. In so doing he was forced to seek the support of the people, and to promise them redress for

Ahaz and the Priesthood the extortions of the priests and the officials. He had to adopt a friendly attitude towards foreigners, a policy which drew upon him the hatred of the priestly caste, but could no longer damage him in the eyes of the people, since they had ceased to trust to the leadership of the priests.

A prophet thus furthered the cause of Ahaz when he reproached the powerful priests with grasping and excess, and spoke in the northern kingdom of Judah as the representative of right and equity, thus seeking to create a feeling in favour of the conquest of Israel by Ahaz. This prophet was Amos. His activity coincides with the period when the question was to be decided, whether a treaty should be made with Assyria or Damascus.

All hopes of the reunion of the kingdom must have been abandoned for ever when Samaria was captured by Sargon. Ahaz seems to have died shortly afterwards, probably in 720 B.C. His son Hezekiah found a state of things very different from the former conditions. Damascus had fallen, and a suzerainty of Israel was no more to be dreaded. Thus at first only one course was left open to him—to pay tribute and to wait until a great power equal in strength to Assyria came to his help. There was no lack of offers ; at the very outset of his reign envoys appeared from Merodach-baladan, in order to incite him to revolt from Sargon. But Babylonia had too long kept aloof from

Babylon Interferes in Israel the western scene of operations : and Hezekiah appears to have accepted Isaiah's warning, while the envoys found a more willing audience in Philistia. Some years afterwards, however, in 713 B.C., he shared in the revolt of Ashdod. The revolt was suppressed ; but Hezekiah emerged without great loss, since once again he made timely submission. With the overthrow of Merodach-baladan, in 710 B.C., his hopes became fainter. But when

Sargon, in 705 B.C., met a violent death, the whole West thought that the hour was come when the hated yoke of Assyria might be thrown off. The hymn of triumph over the tyrant's death, which has come down to us in the prophecy of Isaiah (Isa. xiv. 4-20), represents the feeling of the time. But the joy was short lived. In 701 B.C. Sennacherib advanced, and on the withdrawal of the army, Hezekiah, happy at having escaped vengeance through the outbreak of the Babylonian rebellion, was compelled once more to submit.

Thus, Hezekiah had won nothing by his revolt, but had lost the greater portion of his territory ; for all the towns, which Sennacherib had taken by force, were divided among his neighbours. When, therefore, Egypt, under Tirhakah, undertook a new expedition and attempted to win Palestine for itself, there were willing ears in Jerusalem. Moreover, it seems as if after Hezekiah's death the young Manasseh was already king. Sennacherib advanced against Egypt, and now in Jerusalem men trembled at the appear-

Sennacherib Before Jerusalem ance of the Assyrians before the gates. But Isaiah's words were fulfilled. Sennacherib's army was destroyed, and he himself soon afterwards met his death in his own country. Jerusalem had once again escaped the fate which menaced her. Ahaz had trusted to Assyria and had tried to break the power of the sacerdotal party ; this, in its hostility to the monarchy, sought support from Egypt.

Thus, it was a natural consequence that the sacerdotal party almost always advocated relations with the latter, while the kings, estimating more correctly the actual conditions, held to Assyria and afterwards to Babylonia. Hezekiah wavered between the two. Prudence advised him not to break with Assyria, and an honest counsellor like Isaiah solemnly warned him against it. But after he had once been driven to rebel, and had twice, contrary to his own expectation, escaped the vengeance of Assyria, the priestly caste had the situation in their own hands. He could no longer withdraw himself from their influence, and was obliged to concede their most far-reaching demands. He finally granted their request that he should acknowledge the Temple of Jerusalem as the only true place for the worship of God, and should abolish the

AN IMAGINATIVE REPRESENTATION OF THE FALL OF JERUSALEM
In the sixth century B.C. Judah was subject to Babylon, but owing to the impossibility of paying the tribute exacted revolt was inevitable. Nebuchadnezzar, king of Babylon, captured and destroyed the city in 586 B.C.

sanctuaries in the country. By this the influence of the priestly caste at Jerusalem was immensely increased. There were now no rivals left who would diminish their power. They became the only recognised interpreters of the will of God, and the foundation stone of the hierarchy was thus laid. God was now thought of as a Spirit dwelling in the Temple of Jerusalem on

Rise of the Hierarchy Mount Zion—according to the conception of the priesthood, which was enforced only after further long struggles. God for Isaiah still lived "on the mountains." Hezekiah may have been influenced also by the loss of territory, to which he had been forced to submit in 701 B.C. If a large number of his towns had been given to neighbouring states, little more was left to him than Jerusalem, and he, therefore, had material reasons for centralising the worship of God in Jerusalem.

During his reign further fights with the Philistines are recorded (2 Kings xviii. 8). An episode in them is also referred to in the cuneiform inscriptions. Padi of Ekron had not joined the rebellion in 701 B.C. Taken prisoner by the Judaic party in his town, he was handed over to Hezekiah, but was reinstated by Sennacherib, after the latter had conquered Ekron and had secured the surrender of Padi by Hezekiah.

Hezekiah died, at the latest computation, shortly after Sennacherib, and therefore about 680 B.C. Soon afterwards, under Esarhaddon, Manasseh is mentioned as king of Judah. The unfavourable judgment passed on him by the "Deuteronomist" shows that he was opposed to the priestly party. His continued acknowledgment of the Assyrian supremacy is in keeping with this. He is called a persecutor of the prophets, who were at this period partisans of the priestly caste, not men like Amos and Isaiah. When Shamash-shum-ukin tried to win over the west, hopes must have been entertained in Judah also. It is possible that the prophetic denunciation of Nineveh, which bears Nahum's name, and gave expression to the wishes of the party which was inciting revolt, dates from this time. Manasseh did not offer actual resistance, even if the notice of the chronicle is trustworthy that he was taken a prisoner to Babylon; if such was the case it was probably to undergo a trial, conducted before Ashurbanipal, in which he was fortunate enough to justify himself or to receive pardon. Manasseh reigned long, and, as we may infer, happily, in spite of the hatred of the priestly class. His son Amon was murdered, after a reign of only two years, in 642 B.C., evidently at

Manasseh King of Judah

1779

the instigation of the priesthood, since he followed the policy of his father. " But the people of the land slew all them that had conspired against King Amon " ; a proof that the people differed from the sacerdotal party in their ideas with regard to these " persecutors of the prophets." A boy of eight years was raised to the throne—a repetition of the policy followed with Joash. The government under this boy, Josiah, brought the party of the priests within site of their goal ; under him the hierarchy was constitutionally established by the introduction of " Deuteronomy " as the legal code. This code, which comprises the greater part of the fifth book of the Pentateuch in the form in which it has come down to us, is said to have been promulgated in the year 623 B.C. ; the spirit that animates it is best seen in the provision that the punishment for " false prophets " shall be death. False prophets were men who opposed the ruling sacerdotal party ; the enactment meant death for political opponents.

A Boy on the Throne

Josiah is said to have made attempts to enlarge his territory ; among other acts he destroyed the sanctuary in Bethel. This is conceivable at the time when the empire of Assyria was drawing near its end. When Necho advanced into Palestine Josiah fell in battle against him at Migdol. The later account, such as the chronicle gives, has attempted to trace some faults in this ideal king of the " Deuteronomist " in order to explain his end. His government appears to have pleased the priesthood more than the people, which now, just as it had slain the murderers of Amon, raised to the throne Jehoahaz, the son of Josiah, who was by no means acceptable to the priesthood (2 Kings xxiii. 30). This latter is said, after three months, to have been deposed and kept in captivity by Necho, who meanwhile had moved into his headquarters at Ribla in the Beka'a. He seems, therefore, not to have tendered his submission at the right moment, or we may see in his deposition the influence of the priests, who always stood by Egypt. In Jehoahaz's place his brother Eliakim, who now assumed the name of Jehoiakim, was raised to the throne by Necho about 608 or 607 B.C. He was from the first compelled to raise the taxes considerably in order to pay the sums exacted by Necho.

The Priests Against the King

When Necho, in 605 B.C., was driven back to Egypt by Nebuchadnezzar, Jehoiakim submitted to the new lord and is said to have remained loyal to him for three years,

THE BLIND ZEDEKIAH, LAST KING OF JUDAH, BEFORE NEBUCHADNEZZAR OF BABYLON
Nebuchadnezzar destroyed Jerusalem in 580 B.C., and punished Zedekiah, the rebel king, with whom the kingdom ceased to exist, by putting out his eyes, slaying his sons and taking him away captive to Babylon with the people of Judah.

from about 605 to 603. He then rebelled, in vain expectation of help from Egypt, and in spite of the advice of Jeremiah that he should hold fast to the Chaldæan monarchy. A Chaldæan army did not long delay its appearance. Jehoiakim had, however, died in the meantime, and thus the fate intended for him befell his son, Jehoiachin, who was forced to surrender after a three months' siege in 597 B.C. Jerusalem once more retained its independence, for Nebuchadnezzar had consideration for the strong Chaldæan party. A large number of the chief men were even then carried off into exile, among them the prophet Ezekiel, whose speeches form a commentary upon the succeeding events at home. Nebuchadnezzar appointed as king a third son of Josiah, Mattaniah, who now took the name of Zedekiah. But, as Jehoiakim, by the excessive amount of tribute, had been forced into rebellion, so in the end Zedekiah, in spite of all resistance, and the dissuasion of Jeremiah, was compelled to yield to the pressure of his "patriots" and priests. He had hopes also from the new Pharaoh, Hophra. The hopes were vain. Nebuchadnezzar captured and destroyed Jerusalem in 586 B.C. Zedekiah was cruelly punished by the loss of his eyes, his sons were slain, and a large part of the population was carried away. Judah became a Babylonian province, and the people of Judah ceased to exist.

JUDAISM AND ITS DEVELOPMENT

JUDAH and Israel, regarded from the standpoint of political history, were insignificant states, of no greater importance for the history of the Ancient East than the local history of the Highlands of Scotland for the empire of Great Britain. This remarkable people has attained its importance for mankind not through its political

Babylonian Growth of Judaism history, but through the religion which had its sanctuary and its birthplace in Jerusalem. We cannot, however, entirely accept the view which sees in the Jewish religion, with its further developments, a creation of the Jewish spirit. Precisely as Christianity did not grow in its strength and in its spiritual ideas in Judah itself, but on the soil of the whole Hellenistic world, so Judaism was not evolved in Judah, but could have attained its development and its expansion only on the soil of the wide civilisation of the Ancient East. The details of this subject are as obscure or even more obscure than the beginnings of Christianity. This much is, however, clear—it was in Babylonia that Judaism first became that which it was and still is ; and it could never have reached this stage unless it had come into close contact with the highest civilisation of Western Asia.

Nevertheless, the people of Judah contributed their share to its development, and were its first embodiment. If, therefore, historical investigators cannot accept the story of the "Chosen People," yet this story, in virtue of its wide acceptance, has still a claim to careful consideration, as also the nation which was its embodiment. In contrast to the traditions which we have for the rest of the East, we notice in the history of Israel strong accentuation of religious ideas and of all that is connected with them. As popular ideas on this subject rest mainly on the Biblical narrative it is interesting, as well as instructive, to sketch them briefly for ourselves in the light of the universal laws of human progress.

It is probable that Israel and Judah had originally little to do with each other ; the proof of unity, the common worship of one God, can have been given them only by the man who united them—that is, by David. The God who represents the thought of fraternal association with Judah is Yahve, or Jehovah ; even in the conception of historical times He was still identified as the God of the old home of David, the south of Judah. Jehovah was recognised in Israel only as the God of the victorious David for a sign of his dominion. He had never previously been the God universally worshipped by the northern tribes. The rapidly ensuing division of the kingdom induced the kings of Israel to deny Him. Israel, therefore, had little to do with the development of Judaism. As historical students we must

Distinction Between Judah and Israel therefore modify the conception, according to which Judah would appear to be far more nearly akin to Israel than, for instance, Edom, Moab, and Ammon; and undue regard must not be paid to the picture of a homogeneous nation under David and Solomon. This view can be best expressed in the phrase, which may sound paradoxical but yet aptly characterises the true relationship of the two peoples : " The Israelites were not Jews."

Thus the investigation of the development of the idea of God and the Hebrew religion is, from the first, restricted to Judah, as the original, and before long the only, home of the worship of God. We may omit certain attempts to encroach on the territory **The God of David** of Israel, the motive for which was always the realisation of a political supremacy. In the view of pure historical investigation, it is urged that the worship of God, whom David worshipped in his home and afterwards as prince of Caleb in Hebron—which can, however, hardly have been the original seat of the religion—was introduced into the newly-acquired parts of the kingdom as the area of conquest widened; it was thus a sign of sovereignty. There were, however, pagan deities still worshipped in different parts of Judah, as elsewhere; but these Baalim had really no more than a local significance.

The very fact of its being introduced into other places shows that the religion was not originally confined to Jerusalem, though it had indeed been first introduced there. But it followed quite as a matter of course that the splendid sanctuary in Jerusalem, which was situated in the focus of traffic, should have eclipsed the other seats of worship in the country round. Moreover, the part must be considered which the priesthood in Jerusalem began to play after Solomon's reign; it thus gained a superiority over its colleagues in the other sanctuaries, which corresponded to the superiority of the capital over the provincial towns. The real representation and development of the Hebrew religion, or the worship of the only true God, so far as it was of political significance, rested with the priesthood of Jerusalem. After Solomon the priests possessed the ascendency in Jerusalem and knew how to keep the kings amenable to their wishes. This state of affairs received a rude shock through the domination of the

ISAIAH THE STATESMAN-PROPHET
From a frieze by Michael Angelo in the Sistine Chapel

house of Omri. The religion of David had not been the national religion in Israel since Jeroboam. Israel now encroached upon Judah, and Omri and his successors, who had taken care to connect the kingdom of Judah with their family, thus became dangerous to the religion as the standard of a sacerdotal domination. But this very danger united their natural antagonists in Judah. The priesthood of Jerusalem had, as the ruling party, already become antagonistic to the other priesthoods in the country, and above all to the people itself, for their natural aims could never be those of the people. But so soon as there was a common enemy, all sections of the people, provided that the parties were not so sharply separated that the people as a whole had little vigour left, would soon regard the question from a common standpoint. This popular standpoint was, in the present case, the opposition to the foreign dominion of the house of Omri, which was destined to make Judah, formerly the ruling state, dependent on Israel, while the priesthood acted in opposition to the strange gods which the dynasty of Omri worshipped. We must also consider the fact that Judah was now threatened with the same fate which Israel had formerly incurred—namely, that, when defeated, it would have been forced to accept the gods of Israel, just as Israel had once received the God of David. Schooled by necessity, the priests of Jerusalem bethought themselves **Prophets Denounce Abuses** of a truer worship of their God than the leading of a luxurious life. We therefore find all worshippers of the supreme God, the priesthood and the rough worshippers from the desert—the Rechabites—united against the foreign domination; and in Judah, as well as in Israel, prophets denounced in the name of Jehovah the abuses of the kingdom. Elijah and Elisha are such figures. Their followers were able to win over Jehu in the northern empire, and with him the army, to its side ; and the rebellion of Jehu was organised in the name of God for the restoration of the empire of David. But it failed, as we have seen, in the very place where it originated.

Why Jehu Failed The restoration of David's empire came to nothing, and the encroachment of the religion upon the territory of Israel miscarried, Jehu being compelled to abandon the attempt.

The absolute power of the priesthood begins with Joash. Once more we see the feud between the people and the priesthood, which now more and more became the ruling party ; at the same time the priesthood abandoned the true God, the one God to whom men appealed as the protector of their rights, in favour of Baal worship—that is to say, they sacrificed everything to forms of ritual, since these were the source of large revenues, which the people had to pay. The good resolutions formed during the period of opposition were forgotten. Henceforth, therefore, the prophets strenuously attacked the priests, although in the rebellion of Jehu both had gone hand in hand.

We see this most clearly defined in Amos, the first prophet of whom copious utterances are extant. His date is fixed by the allusion to Assyria, of which little could have been known there before 738 B.C. Amos prophesied under Ahaz and in his favour, since he tried to create a feeling in the northern kingdom in favour of the re-establishment of David's empire. Once more, therefore, the name of God was used as the rallying-cry of a policy which sought to unite Judah and Israel. Amos would hear nothing of the God of the priesthood ; he was a man of the people, and he reproached the ruling classes with their sins in burning and passionate words which the reformers of the Middle Ages gladly employed.

The same thing holds good of Hosea whose mission falls not much later, although certainly after the annexation of Damascus by Tiglath-pileser—that is, after 731 B.C.—since he does not refer to the state which up to that time had played so important a part in Palestinian affairs. He does not indeed inveigh against the ruling classes with the bitterness of Amos, although he sees the cause of the calamity in their sins. This is partly due to the fact that Amos, as he distinctly averred, was no " professional prophet "—that is to say, not one of those men who, being quasi-dervishes, devoted their lives to religious meditation and public oratory, but a herdsman and countryman, who had been induced by the prevailing distress to proclaim his message throughout the land. He therefore laid more stress on the cause of the miseries, which he had experienced in his own person.

Isaiah, the next prophet, stands on a higher plain. He was a well-educated man ; he lived at Jerusalem near the king's person, was familiar with all the knowledge of that day, well versed in literature — his songs show that he was acquainted with Babylonian literature—and he surveyed the whole

THE PROPHET JEREMIAH
From a Michael Angelo frieze in the Sistine Chapel.

political movement of the time. In brief, he was a statesman who had reached the highest pinnacle of his age. For this very reason he belongs to neither of the ruling parties, whether priestly or royal, although doubtless he was a member of one of them by birth. He stood above them. His political insight forced him to

Isaiah the Statesman take his place as counsellor by the king's side, and to warn him against rash enterprises. But when the storm of disasters once burst upon the country, he exhorts the nation to hold out ; and the result proved that he rightly estimated the political situation. He opposed the arrogant claims of the priestly party, and thus laid stress on the miseries of the people ;

but he was not a true man of the people, since he was not in any sense a partisan.

The next period contains no prophet of importance ; for Nahum's denunciation of Nineveh, if we are indeed to place him under Manasseh, and one or two utterances which pass under Isaiah's name and may also belong to this age, concern

Jeremiah the Last Prophet only foreign policy. It is expressly stated in 2 Kings xxi. 16, that Manasseh took stringent measures against the opposition ; but we may assume that the passage refers to prophets who spoke in favour of the priesthood, which had been deprived of its influence, and not to men of the people preaching in the spirit of Amos. On the contrary, the people were probably well satisfied with the rule of Manasseh.

A striking personality appears at the close of the history of Judah in Jeremiah. We may compare his attitude on foreign policy with that of Isaiah. He was, however, a pronounced supporter of the Chaldæan party, a point which cannot be asserted of Isaiah as regards Assyria. History has shown that he was undoubtedly right when he uttered warnings against a breach with Nebuchadnezzar. He was antagonistic to the priestly party, with its Egyptian traditions, and had in consequence to suffer during the siege ; whether justly so, from the point of view of his opponents, we will not attempt to discuss. It would be in keeping with the views of his day if he had maintained relations with the Chaldæans ; the treatment which he received after the conquest of Jerusalem makes us suspect some such conduct on his part. A completely different spirit from that of the earlier prophets is revealed in the utterances of Jeremiah. Amos and Hosea are demagogues, and even Isaiah, with the eye of a statesman standing above the parties, has a clear opinion as to the true causes of the national calamity, which cannot be

Non-worldly Spirit of Jeremiah relieved by joining either Egypt or Assyria. All three wish to probe deeper, and expect the evil to be cured only when the national life is more healthy. They express this belief in the spirit of their age by an appeal to the will of God, but in a formula which really suits the connection of events : " Do that which is right, according to the will of God, and you will be healed." In Jeremiah, on the other hand, we find, in contrast to this

practical standpoint, a prevalence of the religious, non-worldly spirit, which has found its most distinct expression in the tenet of Christianity : " Seek first the kingdom of God, and all this will come to you of itself." It is a confusion between cause and effect that has made Jeremiah as a thinker inferior to his predecessors, but has also made him the favourite prophet of a religious development which seeks its salvation in another world. The ideal world of seclusion, which offers escape from the world of flesh, finds its expression in the prophecy of Jeremiah.

The introduction of Deuteronomy as the legal code implied the victory of the hierarchical party ; it was the codification of priestly rule. Such legislation, which was too diametrically opposed to the demands of the real life of the people, was of course certain to meet with many hindrances in practice, and contributed largely to the destruction of the state ; moreover, its original promoters, the priests, forced the king to revolt from Babylonia. But this code could have come into prominence only at a time when

The Deuteronomic Code the people no longer formed a nation but rather a religious sect, which was ready to recognise it as their guiding principle. That which in the turmoil of national life must have led to the ruin of the people could, in the security afforded by the protection of a powerful state, be further developed, and, through the feeling of homogeneity with which it filled those who professed it, might become a factor in their economic progress. The component parts of the people of Judah, which had been led away into captivity in Babylonia, were precisely those which were anti-Chaldæan ; that is to say, the priestly party, those who were active supporters of Deuteronomy. The rest, indeed, had remained behind in the country. In this way we may explain the fact that the Jewish community, in contrast to so many others which had been transplanted by Assyrians or Babylonians, held together and preserved a distinct individuality. They were from the first a religious community, and as such they were further developed, since by their new environment they were thrown more together and brought into intimate relation one with the other. " Judaism " was developed in Babylon, a closely united religious body in the midst of a great, heterogeneous, and, as they regarded it, foreign population.

On the other hand, it was quite inevitable that Judaism should have adopted much of the Babylonian culture in the atmosphere of which it lived. Precisely as a Jew living in a modern country shares in its intellectual and economic growth, and is affected by its influence, so it was the case in Babylonia. Our material still remains incomplete for ascertaining in any detail how far the sphere of Jewish religious thought had been influenced by that of Babylonia. Certain evidence that we do possess makes it very apparent that we cannot estimate this influence too highly ; some day, probably, many of the institutions of Judaism which seem to be " Jewish " will be shown to be Babylonian in the sense that much of the Mosaic code of legislation is now proved, by the discovery of Hammurabi's Code of Laws, to have been directly derived from Babylonia. What, again, is more characteristic of the spirit of this civilised Judaism, humiliated in a manner so strongly contrasted with its pride, than the penitential psalms, in which it implores forgiveness from its God ? They were composed during the exile, and were copies of similar productions of the Babylonian intellect.

Debts to Babylon

Just as Judaism at a later age eagerly took part in Hellenistic culture, and then in the Arabian, mediæval, and modern intellectual movements, so it tried at this time to turn to its own use the treasures of Babylonian wisdom. A striking instance of this is afforded by the author of the Book of Kings, who wrote during the exile. He found in Babylon a perfected system of records and a laboriously exact chronology. The chronological scheme, for which he found in his own documents an insufficient basis, was elaborated on the Babylonian model, and was thus the result of calculations prepared by the aid of Babylonian science. The Jew who lived in Babylon appropriated the stores of Babylonian knowledge ; he even studied the cuneiform documents, and searched them for information about his own people. The same spirit, which meets us in the explanation of Biblical accounts by the later Jewish commentators, was also characteristic of the Jews of the exile in elaborating the history of their ancestors. They employed chronological calculations, prepared in the same spirit as those of the Christian chronographers, Julius Africanus, Eusebius, etc. But we meet at the same time the characteristic spirit of Judaism, which makes itself so prominent in Josephus. There is always the recurring effort to prove Judah to be the Chosen People, both from history and from the accounts of other nations. Modern authorities are persuaded that not only the Jewish religion, but all the traditions of Judaism were developed in Babylonia during the exile.

History Written in Exile

From this time forward there was never a people of Judah. We possess few historical facts as to the time of the exile ; but, from what we have already ascertained, it follows that we must picture to ourselves the rôle of Judaism during this period as having been the same as in later times. Even then it must have begun to expand, otherwise we can hardly explain its development in the following centuries ; for such an expansion would hardly have been possible except for the intellectual stimulus provided by the new environment in Babylon. On the other hand, the closely compacted community, spiritually united through the rigid organisation given it by the priesthood which was deported to Babylonia, naturally saw its home in Jerusalem and the true seat of the Most High in the temple on Mount Zion. In this connection we notice the survival of the idea of the old national God, who could dwell only in the land of his own people, and who, since the time of Hezekiah, had chosen Jerusalem itself for His dwelling-place.

With the captivity began also the intense longing for a return. Since this was out of the question under a Chaldæan supremacy, the Jews of Babylon waited longingly for the saviour who was destined to bring them freedom from the hated yoke. In the second part of Isaiah are expressed the hopes, so often disappointed, with which men followed the vicissitudes of Babylonian history. The liberator came at last, and there were real grounds for rejoicing that the dominion of Bel and Nebo was broken. Cyrus occupied Babylon, and Judaism was now quite certain of its champion.

Champion of Judaism

ARMENIA BEFORE THE ARMENIANS

OF the highlands in which the Euphrates and Tigris have their source, and which rise to the north of Mesopotamia and its outlying mountains, we know little at the time when Babylonia still dominated the whole Euphrates country and Assyria did not exist as an independent kingdom. But the state of things which meets us in later times, when the country received its culture from Assyria, and the latter was forced to subdue the mountain tribes unless it wished to become their prey, must have already existed in the preceding ages. Indeed, if we must assume that the territory of the later Median empire had been the seat of an organised administration even in the earlier Babylonian epoch, we may surmise that Armenia also had then become united in a certain degree, and had already abandoned its primitive tribal organisation under the influence of Babylonian civilisation. Armenia probably stood at that time in far closer relation **Armenia and Babylon** to the Babylonian sphere of culture than Urartu later to Assyria, and was apparently on a higher stage of civilisation than two thousand years afterwards. We do not know what nations or what races then inhabited the mountains on which the Babylonian represents the ark of Khasisadra, his Noah, to have rested. But we may conjecture that the prosperity of Mesopotamian civilisation in its widest extent dates from a very early period, and that the last millennium, with which we are better acquainted, already marks a great decadence as compared with the height to which it attained in earlier times.

The first definite information as to the history of these countries is derived from the inscriptions of the kings of Assyria, from Tiglath-pileser I. onward. Shalmaneser I. had already made an advance into the country between the Euphrates and Tigris towards the highlands, and by planting Assyrian colonies there had formed a secure frontier for Mesopotamia. We may regard the nations which he subjugated there as " Hittites," as this whole

advance was but a continuation of the expulsion of the Mitani. The struggle was, therefore, between Assyrian and Hittite nationalities.

The country to the east of this—that is, the region south of Lake Van—was called by the Assyrians the Nairi country. Tiglath-pileser had conducted three expeditions against it, making Mesopotamia his starting point, and advanced as far as the sources of the Tigris, where he carved his effigy and engraved an inscription at the natural tunnel near the source of the present Sebene-Su. The southern portion of the Nairi country, bounded on the south by the Tigris, was called Kirkhi. Khubushkia adjoins it on the east. We may include its inhabitants in the eastern Medo-Elamite group of nations, and may conjecture that the Hittites did not encroach on the district south of Lake Urumiya.   The assumption that their migration as a whole took place from Europe is supported by their settlement to the south and west of Lake Van. A group advanced also to the east of the lake. The petty state of Musasir, which we find mentioned from the eighth to the ninth century, seems to have had a population of the " Urartean " Hittite group.

So far as we can trace the history of the countries now under consideration, they meet us first in a condition such as we might expect after a recent migration of uncivilised tribes. There were no large states ; if any such had previously existed, they had been destroyed by these or earlier immigrations. In the period after Tiglath-**Assyrian Colonies in Armenia** pileser I. the tribes which had advanced into these districts from the north naturally expanded, and destroyed the advantages, in any case not very important, which the Assyrians had gained. The districts which Shalmaneser I. had colonised were again seized by the advancing barbarian tribes. Ashurbanipal was therefore obliged to secure for Assyria this district, which was roughly bounded in the south by a line drawn from Amid to Malatia, and to reinforce the old Assyrian colonies. In the ninth century Shalmaneser II., when he advanced on Armenia, and, starting from the Nairi country, which had been subjugated by Ashurbanipal, marched towards the north, struck the territory of King Arame of Urartu, whose dominion comprised mainly the district north of Lake Van. He was attacked by Assyria on the west and south-east of the lake, on the southern frontier of his country, somewhere on the Arsanias in the year 857 B.C.

For some time very little is heard of Urartu, until, in 883 B.C., towards the end of Shalmaneser's reign, a new expedition to that country is mentioned, in which Siduri, king of Urartu, after crossing the Arsanias, is said to have been defeated. Two inscriptions of this Siduri have been found at the foot of 'he fortress of Van which record the erection of buildings by him. He styles himself in them Sarduri, son of Lutipri, king of Nairi. The inscriptions are composed in Assyrian, and even the titles of the king are copied from the contemporary Assyrian formulæ. Neither he nor any one of his successors styles himself king of Urartu — that **Kingdom** was perhaps merely the designa-**of** tion adopted by the Assyrians **Urartu** from the name of the mother country. We may conclude from this state of things that the sovereignty of this Sarduri (I.) followed a revolution in Urartu. Since the royal title is not given to his father, and, on the other hand, another king is recorded to have preceded him in Urartu, his reign may imply the rise of a new tribe among the large number of newly immigrated peoples which were still living in Urartu under their tribal constitution. Sarduri is the ancestor of the royal family, under which an important empire was developed, the most recent of all the empires of Hittite origin In it for the last time Hittites opposed the Assyrian empire with success.

The seat of this empire of Urartu was the district along Lake Van. With the exception of the southern shore, it stretched in an easterly direction as far as Musasir, the small state south-west of Lake Urumiya, and in a north-easterly direction right up to Lake Gok-cha, and was therefore watered by the Araxes. We can trace from Sarduri onward the succession of its kings, chiefly from their own inscriptions, up to the Aryan immigration. Urartu, the natural opponent

of Assyria, thus came into contact with Babylonian culture. Assyrian influence strikes us at once in the character in which the kings of Urartu had their inscriptions written. While Sarduri I. had them written in Assyrian, his successors employed the vernacular, but in an alphabet which had been adapted, not **Imitation** from the Babylonian, but from **of** the Assyrian form of writing. **Assyria** They were imitators of the Assyrians even in their titles. We know little of the new royal family or of its place of origin. We find in after times Tuspa, or Turuspa, in the district of Biaina, the modern Van, the capital of the empire. It does not appear to have been the original home of the royal family. A somewhat mutilated inscription seems to record that Biaina had a king of its own even under Ispuinis ; in any case, we may regard him as an under-king or feudal lord of a district. We may conclude that the empire was formed by the subjugation of separate chiefs and princes, and that the kings were supported in the process by a strong dynastic, central power. By the annexation of the district of Biaina they came into possession of Tuspa. This district cannot have been subdued for the first time by Ispuinis. Sarduri I. had already built at Van.

The successor of Sarduri was Ispuinis, a contemporary of Shamshi-Adad, whose general, Mutarris-Ashur, encountered him on an expedition to Nairi. Thence the new empire was extended further towards the south—that is, into the regions which the Assyrians had traversed or seized. Ispuinis adopted his son Menuas as co-regent. Owing to this fact, most of the inscriptions of this time bear the names of both these rulers. As an example we may cite the inscription in the pass of Kelishin, a sort of boundary stone set up in the district taken from Assyria, recording **Extensions** the acquisition of the Biaina **into** district and of Tuspa, which **Assyria** henceforth served as the capital. The successor of Menuas was Argistis I., who did most for the extension of the empire. He was contemporary with Shalmaneser III. and Ashur-dan in Assyria, and the numerous campaigns against Urartu under the former, in combination with the condition of the country at a later time, show that Assyria was obliged to act on the defensive against the attacks

1787

of Argistis. Records of victories by Argistis' were recorded in eight large panels upon the rocks of the fortress at Van—the longest Urartean inscription which we possess. They contain a report of successes against Assyria, and of a conquest of those regions which the Assyrians designated as the Nairi country.

Urartu Supports the Rebels There is a further mention of places as far distant as Melitene—that is, of districts which had already stood in the fixed relation of vassals to Assyria. During the period anterior to Tiglath-pileser IV., Sarduri II., the son of Argistis, who encroached further towards Syria, was the support of all the states in the east and west which attempted to revolt from Assyria. While he extended his influence as far as Arpad, he drove Urartu out of Syria and finally attacked that country itself. Even if this denotes an actual decline of the political power of Urartu and of all the kindred nations which leant upon it, yet, regarded from an ethnological standpoint, the result of the Urartean advance must be noted as an expansion of the kindred tribes and a retrogression of the Semitic population in the countries farthest to the north. The districts between the Upper Tigris and the Euphrates, which Shalmaneser I. had occupied with Assyrian colonists, were once more lost, and their Assyrian population was dispersed, until under Esarhaddon we find that a final attempt was made to reoccupy them with Assyrians.

In Sargon's reign, his successor, Rusas I., attempted a new attempt on Assyria, where the revolution and the change of kings in 722 B.C. seemed to furnish him with a favourable opportunity. But he, too, failed, and in despair he committed suicide in 714 B.C. The power of Urartu was broken by his overthrow. At the same time, under Argistis II., an attack was made from the north by Aryans.

Urartu's Power Broken The reports of Assyrian governors on the northern frontier in the period between 710 and 705 B.C. announce that heavy defeats were inflicted on Urartu by the Aryan tribes. These wild incomers lived for a time on the borders of Urartu and within its territory until, pushed forward by their neighbours on the east, the Ashkuza, and by other tribes which were pressing on, they moved further westward and overran the whole of Asia Minor. This took place between 670 and 660 B.C., under one of the successors of Argistis II. ; that is to say, under Rusas II., Erimenas, or Rusas III.

Only one episode in the period of Rusas III., the contemporary of Esarhaddon and Ashurbanipal, is recorded in detail. In the year 674 B.C. Esarhaddon records an expedition which he undertook against the country of Shupria in order to subdue a chief, without doubt of Urartean stock. The latter, calculating already on the confusion caused by the advance of the Cimmerians, had attempted in the universal disorder to found an independent state of his own. He was aided by fugitives both from Assyria and Urartu, whom he assiduously attracted to his country. All the demands of Esarhaddon and of Rusas that he should surrender their subjects were rejected, so that Esarhaddon finally found himself compelled to take measures against him. Once more the fortresses of the country were occupied by Assyrian colonists, in order to form an Assyrian province. We must no longer regard these colonists as

Urartu Joins Assyria forming an actual Assyrian population, but rather as consisting of foreigners who were transplanted thither from other conquered districts. A very few years afterwards, in 668 or 667 B.C., the same chief —or another of the same country—in conjunction with the Cimmerians, attempted a sudden attack on the new province, but was killed in doing so. It is noteworthy throughout the whole affair how Assyria and Urartu were for once brought together by a common peril.

The last king of Urartu was probably Sarduri III., who voluntarily submitted to Ashurbanipal in order to obtain assistance from him against the Aryan tribes.

We do not know whether before this an Aryan chief had raised himself to the throne of the Urartean empire, or whether the empire was only ended by the Medes. If we reflect, however, on the development of the power of the Ashkuza in the interval, we can hardly assume that these allies of Assyria had not already established themselves firmly in this region. The whole population began to blend with the Aryan immigrants, and the Armenian people thus came into existence.

HUGO WINCKLER
LEONARD W. KING

ANCIENT ASIA MINOR

ITS HISTORY BEFORE THE PERSIAN CONQUEST

THE great peninsula projecting from the Asiatic continent towards the west has been called Asia Minor (ἡ μικρὰ Ἀσία) since ancient times. It is divided from Syria and Mesopotamia on the south and the south-east by the Taurus range and its north-western continuation, the Antitaurus. On the north-east the range of the Paryadres, which follows the south shore of the Black Sea, and on the east the whole Armenian highlands along the upper course of the Euphrates, separate it from the Caucasus region. On the north the boundary is the Black Sea, on the west the Ægean. For the most part, Asia Minor consists of a large elevated plateau, stretching from the Taurus Mountains to the mountains running along the southern coast of the Black Sea. Only in the west there extend fertile, well-watered plains between the deeply-indented seaboard, **Features of the Country** full of bays and harbours, and the various ranges on the coast, which form, as it were, the passage to the tableland. In the north the coast of Asia Minor approaches within a few miles of Europe, from which it is separated only by the narrow straits of the Bosphorus and the Hellespont, while further southward the numerous islands of every size form a sort of bridge across to Hellas. In fact, from one point of view, the Ægean coast and islands of Asia Minor really form part of Hellas, from which they nowise differ in geographical features or in population. Thus Asia Minor forms a connecting-link between Asia and Europe, and is influenced by both in its historical development; but as geographically it does not form a perfect unit, it has never attained political or national independence.

We meet here from the very first a large number of different tribes. The Mæonians and Lydians dwelt in the country watered by the Hermus; they were bounded on the south first by the Carians and then by the Lycians. In the gorges and valleys of the western Taurus and its spurs lived the Milyæ, Solymi, and especially the Pisidians and Isaurians. The Cilicians possessed the main range of these mountains with the southern ridges, while **The Asia Minor Peoples** Cappadocians and Lycaonians had occupied the tableland northward of the Taurus. Notwithstanding our extremely scanty knowledge of the earliest times, we can notice some shifting of population in this medley of peoples. Thus the name of the Cappadocians and Cappadocia occurs first in the Persian era; before that time these regions as far as the Taurus were held by Tibareni and Moschi, whom we rediscover later as small tribes in the mountains on the coast of Pontus, and still earlier the Kheta, or Hittites, had descended hence into Northern Syria. But, taken all in all, these nations always inhabited the same territory and stand out in sharp contrast to the Thracian and Greek tribes, who are known to have been immigrants. They must therefore be reckoned as autochthonous. The close relationship between the tribes is proved most conclusively by similarity in language. In the whole district inhabited by them there are very numerous names of places ending in " ssos " and " nda "—Termessos, Sagalassos; Œnoanda, Laranda—and many names of persons agreeing in roots and endings.

Formerly attempts were made to assign the nations in Asia Minor partly to the **Non-Semitic and Non-Aryan** Semitic and partly to the Aryan stock, but the conviction has gradually gained ground that in dealing with the inhabitants of Asia Minor we have to deal with a distinct race. The peoples of Inner Asia Minor were probably distinct in race and language from the inhabitants of the west and south coasts, who were no doubt of the dolichocephalic

"Mediterranean" type of Sergi, like the earliest Greeks, Italians, and Egyptians, while the peoples of the inner highlands seem to have been brachycephalic, like the modern Kurds. As these "autochthonous" inhabitants were peculiar in race, so also their religious ideas bear a characteristic stamp of their own.

Characteristic of many tribes in Asia Minor is the worship of the great Mother of the Gods, Ma, or Ammas, a nature goddess, who has her seat on the mountain-tops and takes many titles from them, such as Dindymene Idaia, Sipylene, Cybele; from her proceed all growth and decay in nature, as well as all civilisation. She is the protectress of city walls and gates, and wears, therefore, the mural crown. In her honour feasts were celebrated with wild revelry, with dance and crashing music, and in her service priests gashed their bodies, and maidens prostituted themselves. In the great centres of the worship of the Mother of the Gods there were numerous priests and an equal number of sacred slaves.

Peculiar also to this entire district are the colossal rock-hewn reliefs, which agree in style, as well as in the fact that the figures thereon represented wear mostly the same costume—namely, a high-peaked cap, short tunic, and high-pointed boots. They are found spread over a region extending from the north slopes of the Taurus and the Pisidian lakes to the Halys on the one side and as far as the Ægean Sea on the other side. The figure carved in the living rock near Smyrna, representing a warrior with spear and bow, was famous even in antiquity, and was ascribed to Sesostris [see page 1719]. At the present day in Boghaz-Köi and the neighbouring Öyuk, on the right bank of the Halys, directly

THE MOTHER GODDESS OF ASIA MINOR
The worship of Ma, the Mother of the Gods, was characteristic of many of the tribes of ancient Asia Minor. This picture is from a rock-hewn relief in Cappadocia.

south of Sinope, and east of Ancyra, in a district called Pteria in antiquity, the remains of old city walls and the foundations of large palaces have been discovered, clearly the centre of an ancient civilisation [see page 1725]. In Boghaz-Köi, outside the walls, an almost rectangular courtyard was cut in the rocks, the walls of which are covered with reliefs. In one place a long procession of men is on the march; in another place our attention is fixed on a group of seven gods, who stand not on the ground, but on beasts or the tops of mountains, or, in one case, on the necks of two men. The costume which we described above belongs to these figures, too; but, unfortunately, up till now the hieroglyphic signs accompanying the figures have not been deciphered. It has long been recognised that these monuments, both in style and in the manner of inscription, are very closely connected with those which have been discovered in North Syria; and we are now justified in regarding them as relics of a Hittite domination.

In contrast to Hittite peoples, which may be called the peoples of Asia Minor in the proper sense, since as far as our knowledge goes we find in the north-west and on the entire west coast such tribes as evidently were not indigenous to Asia Minor. To these belong, in the first place, the Aryan Thracian tribes, who crossed from their European mother country over the Bosphorus and Hellespont and pressed on from the regions which skirt these straits gradually eastward. This immigration did not certainly take place at any one time; in the course of a long period new bands kept coming into Asia Minor from Thrace, driven either by the scarcity of food, resulting from over-population, or by the onward pressure of tribes from the north and west.

The Thracians, Phrygians, and Mysians seem to have been racially Slavs. The name of the Phrygian supreme god Bagaios—also called Papas, or "father"—is nothing but the Slav *bogu*, "god." The Thracian Zalmoxis or Zamolxis, mentioned by Herodotus, is an earth-god whose name is the same as the Slav word *zemlya*, "earth," which again occurs in the name of the Thracian goddess Semelé. Men, the moon-god, is Aryan enough also, and so, no doubt, is Osogo, another Phrygian deity.

The worship of Sabazius was universal among the Thracians of Europe and Asia

We may also venture to point out that the method of burial in large earthen mounds, or barrows, seems to have been customary on both shores of the Propontis. From the exploration of such barrows the astonishing fact has been brought to light that their construction is identical. They consist of several layers—beds of ashes and burnt earth, containing earthen vessels, animal bones and sherds alternating with thick strata of earth and broken stone. This method of interment agrees with that which Herodotus describes as Thracian.

The later Trojans, who inhabited the country along the Propontis on the north slopes of the Ida range, belong to this

"Passing of the Empires," S.P.C.K.

A CENTRE OF CIVILISATION IN ANCIENT ASIA MINOR
Remains of the city of Pteria, in Cappadocia. The ruins of the city walls and palace foundations can be clearly seen.

Minor. He is familiar to us in the Greek form of Dionysus, a divinity who rules all animate nature. He was represented as awake in summer and asleep in winter: and, accordingly, the awakening of life in spring was celebrated with orgiastic feasts, while the death of Nature was deplored with wild grief. Many ill-directed speculations have credited this deity with Semitic characteristics, and he is supposed often to have been of Phœnician origin. As a matter of fact, however, there is nothing whatever that is Semitic about Dionysus; and it is very evident that he was an Aryan deity of Nature, of Nature's gift of grapes and wine, and of the divine drunkenness which results from its consumption.

Phrygo-Thracian group. If the different layers or towns discovered by Schliemann at Troy really belong to one and the same population, they must have immigrated at a very early epoch, probably as early as 3000 B.C. But it is more probable that the Trojans of the first six cities of Troy were of the ancient "Mediterranean" stock of the Ægean, like the Minoan Cretans. The Trojans, though they hardly appear elsewhere in history, are familiar to everyone through the Homeric poems, in which their long war with the Greeks and the final destruction of their city are told. Even if the fact itself cannot be disputed that a splendid capital was destroyed by Agamemnon, king of Mycenæ, and his followers, yet it is an isolated event, which can hardly be brought into a strict historical connection; except in so far as the Egyptian records show us that during the "Mycenæan" period the tribes of the Ægean were in a state of great restlessness, and that tribes of Mysians, Lycians, and Achaians even crossed the sea to attack Egypt.

Siege of Troy The legend of the siege of Troy may well enshrine some real expedition of this kind undertaken by a Mycenæan confederacy against the people of Troy.

According as the main body of the Greek emigrants came from Northern, Central, or Southern Greece, the more northern or the more southern regions of the coast of Asia Minor were their goal. Gradually, after centuries of struggles, the land was won from the aboriginal inhabitants. At last flourishing and powerful communities were formed out of what were certainly small settlements at first.

The process of colonisation probably had begun even in the Mycenæan period. The name Yevanna has been supposed to be given on the Egyptian monuments to some auxiliaries of the Kheta (the Egyptian name for the Hittites); and it has been concluded that this name is identical with that of the Ionians. But there is no proof that real Greeks existed in Greece in the thirteenth century B.C., so that we should hardly expect to find Ionians mentioned then; but Ionian art shows so strongly a survival of Mycenæan tradition that we may well place the Ionian immigration at the end of that period, about the eleventh century B.C. The chief goal of the emigrants from Northern Greece was the island of Lesbos, from which the Teuthranian and Lydian coast was colonised. Pitane, Elaia, Grynion, Myrina, Kyme, Aigai, Temnos, and Smyrna on the southern, and Magnesia on the northern, foot of Mount Sipylos are Greek towns.

Immigrants from Greece The inhabitants of all this district regarded themselves as belonging to one stock, and called themselves Æolians. Different races from Central Greece occupied the Lydian and Carian coast from the mouth of the Hermus to the peninsula of Miletus, and here the name "Ionians" was fixed upon the Greek settlers, who entered into a close alliance, and became a united state with its religious centre at Panionion,

where Poseidon was worshipped. The most advanced post towards the west was Magnesia on the Mæander. Later in point of time was the settlement of the Dorians, who pressed forward from Crete and the Southern Cyclades, which they had previously occupied, to the two great island outposts of Asia Minor, Cos and Rhodes, and then to the widely jutting promontories of the mainland itself, Cnidos and Halicarnassus. The league of these Dorian towns had its religious centre in the sanctuary of the Triopian Apollo.

The oldest historical information as to Asia Minor is to be found in the Egyptian monuments, and dates back to the time of the twelfth dynasty, about 2000 B.C., when we find the first mention of the Kheta, or Hittites. Then we hear of an invasion of Mesopotamia by the Khatti, who are the same people. They took Babylon in the reign of Samsuditana, and probably it was by their agency that the dynasty of Hammurabi came to an end. This was, however, merely a raid. In Egyptian monuments of the eighteenth

Egyptian History of Asia Minor dynasty we find various mentions of the coasts and peoples of Asia Minor. Then, in the Tell el-Amarna period, about 1400 B.C., we discover in the country afterwards called Commagene or Cappadocia the Kheta, who pressed victoriously southward and planted themselves firmly in North Syria. Ramses II., king of Egypt, waged a long and bitterly contested war against them, and in the end the kingdom of the Kheta won recognition as a sovereign power. But this kingdom, which held its own against the Pharaohs, and extended northward and southward into the upper valley of the Orontes, soon broke up into many small states, several of which were traceable in North Syria as late as the eighth century, and were subjugated only by the Assyrians. When the Kheta fought against Ramses II. they were allied with the "Princes of all Lands," who marched to their aid with troops : thus we come to hear of the nations of the Lukki, Dardeni, Masa, Ariunna, Pidasa, and Kalakisha, of whom we may take the Lukki to be Lycians; the Dardeni, Dardani; Ariunna, Oroanda; the Kalakisha, probably Cilicians; the Masa, Mysians; and the Pidasa, either Pisidians or Leleges—whose capital was Pedasa. Under the Pharaoh Meneptah, soon after 1250 B.C., there appeared on the west frontier of Pharaoh's kingdom, together with the Libyans, certain " nations from the countries of the Sea," and these were annihilated in a bloody battle there. Besides the Lukki, who are already known to us, the Akaiwasha or Achaians, the Turusha or Tyrrhenes of Asia Minor or Tylissians of Crete (?), the Shardana or Sardinians from the island of Sardinia (?), and Shakalesha, or Sagalassians, took part in this expedition. It is to be noted that Professor Petrie's theory, according to which these tribes were not Greeks or Heliens but Kabyles from the north coast of Africa, is not generally accepted. Under Ramses III., about 1200 B.C., the like incidents recurred. Partly in large, open rowing-boats

the name of the city of Axos, and that of the Zakkara quite possibly still survives in that of the modern village of Zakro. The peculiar terminations, -sha and -na, of many of their names are no bar to these identifications ; they have been satisfactorily explained as ethnic terminations, -äzi and -ñna in Lycian. It is thus evident that most of these names, whether belonging to peoples of Asia Minor or not, came to the Egyptians through the medium of a language of Asia Minor which was known to them, probably Hittite. The felt helmet, adorned with feathers, which was worn by some of them—a dress which Herodotus ascribes to the Lycians— proves not only their intimate connection with each other, but also their connection with the peoples of South-west Asia Minor.

"Passing of the Empires," S.P.C.K.

THE RUDE ART OF THE EARLY PEOPLES OF ASIA MINOR
A rock-hewn relief in a ravine in Pteria, showing a procession of priests and votaries.

by sea, partly in ox-waggons overland through Syria, came an expedition of the Pulesti, Zakkara, Shakalesha, Danona, and Uashasha, who were likewise annihilated cn land and sea. Of the two last-mentioned groups, the Akaiwasha, Danona, and possibly the Shardana, were not natives of Asia Minor ; of the others, the Lukki, Lycians, and the Shakalesha certainly were such, and so, possibly, were the Turusha, while the Pulesti, who are the Philistines of the Bible, the Uashasha, and the Zakkara were probably Cretans.

All tradition points to the Cretan origin of the Philistines, whose first settlement in Palestine probably occurred at this time ; while the name of the Uashasha was probably preserved in

The enterprise of the Hittites in making conquests outside the borders of the peninsula and founding a kingdom there, gave the example to the people of Asia Minor. All the kingdoms which were established on this model were restricted to the more or less limited confines of the peninsula itself. It was only Mithradates the Great who united with his ancestral kingdom a great part of the north coast of the Black Sea. The attacks made by the " maritime nations," the Lukki and their allies, on Egypt were almost typical of the whole south-west coast of Asia Minor, where Carians. Pisidians, and Cilicians were for centuries notorious for piracy and privateering, even though we hear nothing further of the

THE DESTRUCTION OF TROY BY AGAMEMNON OF MYCENÆ

Though the Trojans are familiar through the Homeric poems they do not play an important part in history, and the account of the siege of Troy is a legend based on a Mycenæan tribal expedition. From the picture by Pierre Cornelius at Munich.

great allied expeditions against Egypt, which the threatened land resisted effectively only by calling out all its forces.

In earlier times no country on the peninsula of Asia Minor played so prominent a part as Lydia, though it is true that in the legends Phrygia and her kings also enjoyed a certain prominence. In Phrygia a Midas

Midas of Phrygia and a Gordius reigned alternately, agriculture was early practised, and ants are said to have carried grains of wheat into the mouth of the child Midas, and thus to have foretold his future wealth; and, consequently, his wealth is represented as the fruit of tillage. This close connection of the Phrygian kings with agriculture finds its expression in the story that the deity of the country, Lityerses, who competes with the reapers and scourges the idlers, is given to Midas as a son; Midas is said also to have discovered the flutes used in the worship of the Mother of Gods, whose introduction into Phrygia is referred back to him, since the Phrygians, like all Thracians, particularly loved and eagerly practised music. But real historical knowledge of them is absolutely non-existent. It is only after the rise of the Lydian kingdom that the sources begin to well up more copiously and more clearly; then first we stand on more or less certain historical ground.

Like the Phrygians, the ruling race, at any rate in Lydia, was of Thracian, and so of Aryan origin. The first royal house ruling over Lydia, the Atyadæ, is quite

mythical. Then follow kings of the race of the Heraclidæ, and of these we know little more than that they are supposed to have reigned 505 years. During the century immediately preceding their fall the names of five or six kings have come down to us—that is, Alyattes, Kadys, Ardys, Meles, Myrsos, and Kandaules. The last name meant in Lydian, or Mæonian, "Dog-strangler."

More important than these names and the stories of the murder of the one and of the succession of the other, is the fact that Lydia at this time, as also later, was a feudal state, and that under the sovereigns numerous lords ruled in the country, who were the owners of the soil to whom the country population stood in the position of serfs. And since it is expressly told us that one of these lords was conceded immunity from taxation for his district as a reward for his co-operation in raising Ardys to the throne, we may reasonably conclude from this that the other lords had to pay tribute. Besides this, they had

Lydia a Feudal State not all the same rank; one of them stood next to the king and was also regent in case of the death or disability of the king, and usually held an office like that of the Frankish mayor of the palace, while some others composed a sort of court under the official title of " Friends of the King."

In the highly-coloured romances of Lydian history which have come down to us through the Greeks, traders often appear, together with innkeepers; and the Lydians are spoken of as the first people who coined money and who were retail merchants and pedlars. Since they were cut off from the coast by the Greek towns, their trade was an overland trade. From Sardis the wares of the East reached the sea, passing through the hands of the Greeks. An important industry grew up in Lydia at an early date. Skilfully-wrought fabrics and brilliantly-coloured garments were made on the looms of the weavers and in the dyers' shops, and all sorts of ornaments were found in the workshops of the goldsmiths and silversmiths. In Sardis, and even in the other towns, which were of small importance as compared with the capital, there resided a trading and manufacturing population about whose political rights we have no special information. They could be summoned by the king, under exceptional circumstances, to a popular assembly and be asked for their opinion.

It is worthy of notice that King Ardys is renowned for the care he devoted to the army. He is said to have raised his cavalry forces to 30,000 men, and in later times the Lydian cavalry proved formidable to their foes. A new era in the history of Lydia opens with Gyges.

TUMULUS OF ALYATTES, KING OF LYDIA
Illustrating the ancient method of burial in large mounds made up of layers of ashes, earth, and stone. Alyattes was one of the greatest kings of Lydia, and freed Asia Minor from the Cimmerians.

According to the legends handed down from antiquity, Gyges was originally either a royal spearman, like Artaxerxes, the first Sassanid, or a shepherd, like King David; this thoroughly corresponds to the ideas of the Eastern nations, who like to raise the ancestors of the kingly families from the dust to the highest human power.

In reality he sprang from the lordly race of the Mermnadæ, a powerful family in the country. His father, Daskylos, lived in voluntary exile at Sinope. Thence Gyges, at the age of eighteen, was recalled to the court at Sardis, and soon, as the recognised favourite of the king, was nominated his mayor of the palace. By a

THE SUPPOSED TOMB OF MIDAS, KING OF PHRYGIA
A striking monument associated with the name of a king whose history is largely mythical. The "tomb" is cut in the solid rock and is about 25 feet high.

court revolution, in which the last Kandaules met his death, Gyges won the hand of the royal widow, and with it the crown, and defended it successfully in battle in 687 B.C. With Gyges begins a new policy of the Lydian kings—a policy of conquests, of which the Greek coast towns were the ultimate object. While the towns of Æolis, with the exception of Mitylene, were agricultural towns and had attained no importance, the Ionian towns, thanks to the fertility of their territory, the excellence of their position, and the activity of their citizens, had developed into important centres of trade and industry. Through their close trade connection with the Phœnicians and the Lydians, who, as we have seen, were in control of the overland trade with the East, they became emporiums for Oriental wares, which they sent on further west, together with the products of their own labour. Gyges now attacked these Ionian towns. While Miletus and Smyrna warded off his attack, and the spearmen of Smyrna actually overcame the Lydian cavalry, Colophon, which was renowned for its great riches, was subdued. Even the

RUINS OF SARDIS, THE CAPITAL OF ANCIENT LYDIA

In early times no country played so prominent a part in Asia Minor as the kingdom of Lydia.

King Mita, dreading their approach, killed himself, the legend says, by drinking bull's blood. Sinope was next assailed. In a little time the territories conquered marched with the territories of the Assyrian king, who had advanced his frontiers to the Halys. On the banks of the Halys was fought the great battle which turned back the tide of Cimmerian invasion from the borders of Assyria. In this contest against the "Gimirrai," as the Assyrians called them, King Esarhaddon won a complete victory and secured the safety of his dominions from the barbarian onset in 679 B.C. The invaders, repulsed from the east, then turned on Lydia. Gyges in terror implored the aid of the Assyrians. The aid was promised on condition that Gyges would do homage to the Assyrian monarch and acknowledge his suzerainty. The Cimmerians and Thracians were repulsed, the Assyrians having abstained from lending any other aid

Troad came under Lydian domination. Gyges showed his successors the way, but he did not himself proceed to further attempts in this direction.

When the great tide of Scythian invasion swept from Asia over the great Russian plain, it bore down upon the northern shores of the Black Sea, where the people known as the Cimmerians dwelt. These people were closely allied to the Thracians. To Thrace naturally they turned their steps, flying from the terrible Scythian invaders. Their kinsmen in Thrace made common cause with them. The allied forces crossed to Asia, as many Thracian tribes had previously done, and the descendants of these Thracian Tribes in Asia Minor joined them and shared their conquests. In Bithynia and in the Troad these Asiatic Thracians had settled. The united forces of Cimmerians and Thracians marched on Phrygia. King Midas, who is mentioned by the Assyrians as

Cimmerian Invasion of Lydia

MYTELENE, OR LESBOS, CHIEF CENTRE OF THE GREEK IMMIGRANTS

than their prayers, so Gyges repudiated the suzerainty in 660 B.C. He was then abandoned to his fate by his former allies. Psammetichus of Egypt, to whom he had sent help to throw off the yoke of Assyria, could not assist him. The **Cimmerians Overrun Lydia** storm soon burst upon his kingdom. This time the barbarians met with little opposition. Gyges fell in battle. His capital, Sardis, surrendered. The hordes of invaders were let loose upon the Greek settlements. Ionia was overrun, Magnesia was destroyed, and the temple of Artemis at Ephesus was burnt, while towns on all sides were given up to plunder and devastation. " It was a raid and not a subjugation of the towns," says Herodotus, and his words are true in so far as they apply to the conduct of the invaders after the conquest of Lydia ; but the Lydian war itself was in no way a

as such history knows them no more. Nor was this great work the only service which Lydia owed to Alyattes. The son and the grandson of Gyges, Ardys and Sadyattes, had now and then turned their arms against the Ionian towns, and in turn had besieged Miletus in vain. But Alyattes went to war in grim earnest. For years a struggle went on between the sea city and the military kingdom, until at last, wearied of the strife, both parties willingly made peace and sealed it with a treaty of alliance. The Lydians now destroyed Smyrna and held the coast at three important points. Eastward the course of Alyattes was barred. Assyrian influence reached up to the Halys until the Medes and Babylonians divided between them the great empire of Nineveh, which had fallen asunder.

IONIAN CARVING, SHOWING CIMMERIAN HORSE AND FOOT SOLDIERS
In the seventh century B.C. Cimmerians overran Lydia, and occupied it for two reigns, until Alyattes freed all Asia Minor from their bondage. This is reproduced from " The Passing of the Empires," S.P.C.K.

raid, but a regular struggle between organised powers. Besides, the occupation of the northern and eastern territories of Lydia was permanent. King followed king, no doubt, on the Lydian throne. To Gyges succeeded his son Ardys ; to him in turn his son Sadyattes. But the Cimmerians held firm hold of their conquests through these two reigns. It was only during the reign of Alyattes, the successor of Sadyattes, that Lydia finally expelled the Cimmerians.

Alyattes freed Lydia and all Asia Minor from the bondage which the barbarians had imposed. Whether the Cimmerians wandered back to their old homes or sank into servitude in Lydia or were allowed to blend with the inhabitants no one can now say. But with the liberation of Lydia by Alyattes their career as a conquering nation closes, and

Eastern Asia Minor then fell to the Medes. Their power grew, and, under Cyaxares, threatened Lydia. War broke out and lasted for many years. Peace came in a very remarkable manner. On May 28th, 585 B.C., while a battle was actually raging there took place a total eclipse of the sun, which Thales of Miletus had foretold. Struck with religious alarm, both sides sued for peace. The rulers of Babylon and Cilicia were appealed to as mediators. The son of Cyaxares and the **A Peace Due to an Eclipse** daughter of Alyattes were united in marriage, and all danger from the Medes was now averted from Lydia. Freed from all anxiety on the eastern borders, Alyattes was able to devote his attention in part to the internal organisation of his kingdom and to preparation for wars of aggression, which seemed to him inevitable wars of self-defence, for between the Ionian cities and the Lydian kingdom durable peace was, he believed, impossible. Accordingly Alyattes made up his mind to determine once and for all which power would be supreme in Asia Minor. In the result Lydia emerged victorious and Alyattes was able to hand on to his son the sceptre of a great and flourishing kingdom. Under Crœsus, who succeeded Alyattes, Lydia reached the most splendid and powerful position. He conquered Ephesus, imposed tribute upon the remaining Greek cities which had not been subjugated by his predecessors, incorporated Phrygia, after the death of the last king, Gordius, into his kingdom, and exercised the supremacy over Bithynia. All too soon misfortunes burst on him. In the year 553 the Persian, Cyrus, revolted against the Median king, Astyages, and made himself Great King in his place. Partly to avenge the fall of his brother-in-law, partly to prevent the dangers threatening him from Persian ambition, Crœsus negotiated an alliance with Nabonidus, king of Babylon, and the Pharaoh Amasis. He invaded Cappadocia with a strong army, but was compelled by Cyrus to retreat across the Halys, completely defeated in the valley of the Hermus and besieged in the acropolis of Sardis. This last place of refuge was taken by treachery, and Crœsus fell into the hands of the victor in 546 B.C., henceforward to occupy the post of Mentor at his court. Thus Lydia became Persian.

Crœsus, King of Lydia

The greater number of Greek cities in Asia Minor had been first brought under the Lydian supremacy by Crœsus, but in spite of their being dependent and tributary, they had been kindly treated by the king, who was a friend to the Greeks. Miletus still enjoyed benefits of the treaty of friendship and alliance concluded with Alyattes. Taken all in all, this was a time of great prosperity. The Ionian cities now begin to send out colonies and found factories. Miletus founded Abydos and Cyzicus on the Hellespont, stages for the journeys to the Black Sea, on the shores of which Milesian colonies soon sprang up everywhere. The grain of the South Russian coast and the hinterland, and the costly skins of wild beasts, the timber and precious metals from the southern coasts of the Black Sea—

The Greek Cities

of all these precious commodities the Milesians knew how to obtain control in order to establish a prosperous trade.

By the side of Miletus the other towns sink into insignificance. Yet Phokaia is worthy of mention, because in the founding of Lampsacus it was actuated by the importance of the passage of the Bosphorus for trade. Towards the south also brisk trade relations with Egypt existed at this time. King Amasis actually conceded the town of Naukratis as an emporium to the Greeks, and allowed them to live there with their own civic rights. This activity in trade was paralleled by a lively activity in the intellectual sphere. Marble was here first worked artistically and the foundation laid for the great development of Greek sculpture. Bronze was first artistically worked again in Samos, and it was in Ionia that the first Greek vases of the early Renascence, after the downfall of Mycenæan culture, were painted. Lyric poetry was perfected, and here arose the first philosophers, who systematised the result of their speculations. But there was a dark side also to this bright picture. The artistic development and the great wealth of the Ionians led to the practice of an unbridled luxury, which was a by-word among the continental Greeks, who tell us of the haughty Ionians, trailing their long and gorgeous robes on the ground as they walked, and priding themselves on their long hair, which they wore braided up on their heads with gold, like women. And the Ionians were as quarrelsome as they were proud. The many struggles and wars between separate cities had their counterpart in long and violent party struggles in the communities. The original form of government, a monarchy, had been changed to an oligarchy, composed of the nobility. The citizens, becoming conscious of their power through industry and prosperity, began to struggle for political equality and for a share in the municipal government. These struggles did not, indeed, always lead to the establishment of a democracy, and often an individual forced his way into power. Such men, whom we come across in many cities of Asia Minor, were called by the Greeks Tyrants.

Ionian Art and Culture

The same spectacle was repeated when the Persian danger threatened. The

THE ART AND CULTURE OF ANCIENT ASIA MINOR ILLUSTRATED

The Lydians were, perhaps, the first coiners of money. Of those illustrated 6 and 7 are the earliest known coins in the world; these and 2, 3, and 5 are of electrum, 4 is gold. The pottery is Lycian (1) and Carian (8). The bas-relief (9) shows Lydian horsemen. Beneath this are specimens of early jeweller's work, a serpentine mould (10) and trinkets of a more advanced period (11 and 12). The worship of Cybele, the nature goddess of Lydia, is shown in 13.

Æolians and Ionians, it is true, united at first in order to submit to Cyrus on the same conditions as formerly they submitted to the Lydian kings. But Miletus had stood aloof and had been able by timely measures to maintain the privileged position which she had formerly held under the Mermnadæ. Cyrus rejected the proffered terms. The Greek cities turned in a body to Sparta for help and prepared to offer a determined resistance. Sparta declined to help them, and we hear nothing further of common action and common resistance. After Priene and Magnesia on the Mæander, which had rendered help in the ill-starred revolt of the Lydians under Paktyas, had been conquered and severely punished, the remaining states were subdued one by one. Thus the whole Greek coast—the Dorian cities surrendered mostly without resistance—became subject to Persia, and was forced not only to pay tribute, but to furnish soldiers and obey the Tyrants appointed by the great king. When Caria and Lydia had been conquered the whole of Asia Minor belonged to the Persian kingdom. Of the islands, Chios and Lesbos submitted; Samos, where the famous Polykrates was tyrant, was to be conquered later. Cilicia retained its own rulers, but owned the suzerainty of Persia.

K. G. BRANDIS
H. R. HALL

PALACE OF DARIUS AT SUSA, THE FIRST CAPITAL OF THE PERSIAN EMPIRE

The famous palace of Darius at Susa is illustrated here from the beautiful reconstruction in the Louvre. The top picture shows the audience-hall, or Apadana, of Darius, and is noteworthy for the free use of pillars, the distinctive feature of Persian buildings. The capital and base of one of these columns are shown at the bottom from the actual originals. The beautiful workmanship of the enamelled tiles which covered the walls of the palace is well shown in the reproduction in the middle of the page. The remaining picture is of the pavilion of the throne-room of Darius's palace.

MEDIA AND THE PERSIANS

THE MEDES BEFORE THE PERSIANS

THE old Babylonian inscriptions furnish as little information for the most ancient periods of Median history as they did for that of Armenia. The earliest name for the country appears, from the inscriptions, to have been Anzan. The rulers of Lagash record wars with Anzan, and a governor of Dur-ilu announces a victory over the hordes of Anzan. It is not possible to ascertain its eastern frontier, while on the north we may make it extend round Elam. Inscriptions in the old Babylonian language in the Zagros indicate that Babylonian influence prevailed there in the country of the Lulumæans in the very earliest times ; and incidental allusions by the Assyrian kings prove that Babylonia once exercised, even politically, a more widely extended influence there than ever Assyria did in later times. Towns are incidentally mentioned as old Babylonian foundations. The Assyrians had a province of Arpakh, in the district watered by the tributaries of the Adhem, and it is possible that some traditions point to the former existence of an empire of the same name, but no certain conclusion can be arrived at on this point.

The population is clearly connected with that of Elam. This Medo-Elamite group, the eastern branches of which are lost in the darkness of Central Asia, encountered to the south of Lake Urumiya the Urartu-Hittite group, whose most westerly representatives we found in Khubushkia. We do not find that any **Medo-Elamite Group** considerable states were formed here in the Assyrian period, of which we are tolerably well informed. We meet everywhere petty states, such as Parsua, on the eastern shore of Lake Urumiya. Towards the north-east the country is bounded by the " salt desert." Thence poured in the hordes of Central Asia, for whom the Babylonians had the collective name of Umman-manda, or Manda hordes. This term, of course, does not convey the idea of a definite race, but merely that of their uncivilised condition. There were certainly among the Umman-manda, who are referred to during widely different periods of Babylonian history, representatives of heterogeneous races, amongst them the very peoples whom we find in possession of Media. Thus at a later **Media Pioneer of Persia** period the Aryan Medes and Persians bore this designation. Since no great states were formed here, or rather, since no facts have yet been ascertained as to the existence of such, we may leave this welter of nations to itself with the scanty notices of its collisions with Babylonia during the most ancient period. The most important of the Assyrian attempts at subjugation were described when dealing with the history of Assyria. Media interests us chiefly as the land where was developed the empire which has always been recognised as the pioneer and precursor of the Persian world-empire.

The Medes are among the first Aryans whose appearance we can definitely trace in that part of the Nearer East now under consideration, although recent discoveries would seem to show that further to the west, in Mesopotamia, the Mitani represent a still earlier wave of the same migration. These, as the Medes, became the ruling race in a large empire, which afterwards, under the Persians, dominated the East as far as Babylonian culture extended, and perhaps more widely still. Median history is thus a prelude to that of Persia.

The Medes, or the Madai, appear for the first time in Assyrian inscriptions under Shalmaneser II., who, in the year 836 B.C., on an expedition against Media, mentions the Amadai between Namri and Parsua towards the interior of Media—that is, where later on the centre of their dominion lay. Henceforth they are repeatedly named by Tiglath-pileser, Sargon, Sennacherib, and Esarhaddon, each of whom prides himself on having received tribute from their chiefs. Each of them also regularly asserts that no one of his predecessors had entered the territory of these dangerous foes—the title " dangerous " Medes being given them as an *epitheton ornans*. The Assyrians never really occupied their country ; and Assyria soon trembled before the Medes. We see

Assyria and Media
from the accounts that the country was divided into separate cantons — Sargon enumerates a large number of them—which were governed by chiefs, never kings, and were obliged to pay tribute whenever an Assyrian army was in the vicinity. In other respects they did not trouble themselves about the Assyrians. There was no sign as yet of a Median empire.

Before we can point to the appearance of a comprehensive imperial power among the Medes we must trace the history of

asks whether Bartatua, king of the Ashkuza, ought to be given the daughter of Esarhaddon in marriage, as he requests. The policy of the succeeding period shows that his wish must have been granted. Esarhaddon, therefore, just as Sargon formerly in Zabal, was anxious to form a bond of union between himself and the barbarian princely house, and thus to turn the enemy into a guard for his frontier. Bartatua's son, Madyas, is mentioned by Herodotus as king of the " Scythians," who advanced to the relief of Nineveh when besieged by Cyaxares. After that time Assyria was allied with the Ashkuza. But the people which Herodotus, or his authority, terms Scythians, and which became dangerous to the Cimmerians, were the Ashkuza in question ; they had driven the Cimmerians, the enemies of Assyria, towards the west. Esarhaddon himself claims to have defeated the Cimmerians ; but the victory

CONTEMPORARY SCULPTURES OF ANCIENT PERSIANS
The first figure of this group, from the Persepolis sculptures, wears the Median robe of honour, and the group probably represents part of the triumphal procession of Cyrus described by Xenophon.

the other Aryan nations who appeared around Lakes Van and Urumiya. As early as the closing years of Sargon's reign, the Cimmerians were pressing hard on Urartu and were overrunning the empire, whose power had been already broken by Assyria. We conjectured that the violent death which Sargon met in some unknown place was perhaps the result of the signal defeat inflicted on an Assyrian army by the Cimmerians. This disaster re-echoed throughout the whole East, and is referred to in a hymn of victory which has been preserved in the book of Isaiah (xiv. 4–21). We can realise the movement of the nations in Armenia through the questions put by Esarhaddon to the oracle of the Sun-god, which show that Assyria was afraid of the intruders, and with difficulty guarded her frontiers against her new antagonists. One of the questions put to the oracle

was insignificant, since from the first the objective of the Cimmerian advance was Asia Minor more than Assyria.

This was the beginning of the great Cimmerian movement which partly obliterated the states of Asia Minor, or Phrygia, and partly inundated them. Lydia was overrun, and only the citadel of Sardis was able to hold out. We now understand why Gyges, who was attacked by

Cimmerian Raids in Asia Minor
the Cimmerians somewhere on the Halys, sought an alliance with Assyria, the provinces of which, both there and in Cilicia, did not lie far from his frontier. The Cimmerians then devastated Asia Minor for a time, until their power broke up and gave way before the newly rallied forces of the civilised nations. One of their leaders, Dygdamis, is known to us from classical history. The Ionian towns had also to suffer from the wild

hordes, and the destruction of Magnesia finds an echo in the poems of Archilochus. This Dygdamis, mentioned in an inscription of Ashurbanipal, met his death, according to the classical account, in Cilicia—possibly Homer's Cilicia in the Troad; he was succeeded by his son Sandakshatra. The Cimmerian onslaught gradually spent itself in distant regions, and the remains of it were dispersed by the Lydians.

Classical tradition tells us of the Treri, a people not yet identified in the inscriptions, which accompanied the Cimmerians on their expedition. The Saparda, who have been already mentioned with them on Lake Van, must have also advanced

expeditions reached the Egyptian frontier, where Psammetichus bought them off. They then withdrew and destroyed Ascalon. The " power of the Scythians " was, according to Herodotus, broken by the Medes when they besieged Nineveh and Cyaxares became master of the territory conquered by the " Scythians "—that is, the countries from Lake Urumiya down to **Ashkuza Power Broken** the river Halys, which is the boundary of Lydia. The empire of the Ashkuza was thus a precursor of the Median sovereignty, and served to pave the way for their supremacy in " Upper Asia."

The Medes had hitherto inhabited the Median tableland and the regions east of

SOLDIERS OF THE BODYGUARD OF CYRUS, BY ARTISTS OF THE TIME
The two soldiers on either side were members of the personal bodyguard of Cyrus. The centre figure is clothed in the royal Median robe, while the other two wear the Persian costume. From the sculptures at Persepolis.

into Asia Minor in conjunction with the Cimmerians, or following in their steps. From this time onward we find Saparda occurring in the Bible just as in the inscriptions of the Perso-Seleucid age, as the name of Central Asia Minor—Phrygia **Ashkuza Conquer the Medes** and the adjoining countries. The Ashkuza, by the departure of the Cimmerians and the treaty with Assyria, became masters of the situation in Armenia ; in Herodotus they appear as the " Scythians " who drove out the Cimmerians. Of these he tells us that, after a conquest of the Medes, which is to be mentioned immediately, they ruled " Upper Asia " for twenty-eight years, and in their

Lake Urumiya in separate districts and tribes, without ever having been really subjugated by the Assyrians. The questions asked of the oracle by Esarhaddon show us this people playing precisely the same part as the Cimmerians and Ashkuza—threatening the Assyrian frontiers and occasionally occupying isolated tracts. They distinctly figure as a third group by the side of the other two. Assyria, by winning over the Ashkuza, had obtained a defence not only against the Cimmerians settled to the west, but also in the east against the Medes. These thus became the natural antagonists of the Ashkuza. The constant war against this state, strengthened by the support of

Assyria, could not fail to furnish the Medes with a motive for unification, in order that they might not meet the same fate as the Cimmerians.

Herodotus's narrative connects the first unification of Media with the name of Deioces. One of the authorities for Median history which Herodotus used **First King of Media** has recently been proved to be trustworthy, so that it is conceivable that the royal house of Media actually called its original ancestor Deioces. All else that is told of him bears the stamp of a naïve conception of the evolution of monarchy, and is unhistorical. The fact that Ecbatana was later the capital of the Median empire leads to the conclusion that we must trace the concentration of the separate tribes to this district.

His successor, according to the same tradition, was Phraortes. The subjugation of the Persians is attributed to him. The new Median empire would have accordingly stretched from Persis, including also Elam and Susa, as far as the borders of Ashkuza. Phraortes is said to have undertaken an attack upon Assyria, which would probably have taken place during the reign of one of Ashurbanipal's successors. Herodotus says that Assyria on that occasion was deserted by her " allies," and it is possible that the Ashkuza are meant, who then certainly plundered Assyrian provinces. Phraortes is said to have fallen during this expedition.

The son and successor of Phraortes was Cyaxares. With him we at last stand on demonstrably certain and historical ground. It was he who destroyed Nineveh, and by the subjugation of the Ashkuza became the real founder of the Median empire. His war with Assyria shows that Media had entered into a treaty with Babylon, which had once more become independent under Nabopolassar, and had supported the latter in his resistance to Assyria. We find, therefore, the two nations from this time onward as allies, and the Median and the Babylonian dynasties connected by a marriage between Nebuchadnezzar and the daughter of Cyaxares.

Thus Nabopolassar and Cyaxares had a mutual understanding when they both attacked Assyria in 608 or 607 B.C. Mesopotamia was occupied by an expedition from Babylonia, but Nineveh itself was invested only by Cyaxares, who " wished to avenge his father," as Herodotus says. Madyas, the king of the Ashkuza, then advanced to its aid, but was utterly defeated with his army. Cyaxares was thus master of the countries as far as the Halys, and Assyria was stripped of her last resource. The victory of the Medo-Babylonian alliance was assured. Cyaxares received the country north of the Tigris, and his empire now stretched as far as the Halys.

States like that of the Medes must, so long as they are full of strength and vitality, continue their victorious career. Friendly relations to Lydia under Alyattes, their newly acquired neighbour on the Halys, were therefore not maintained for long. The war, according to Herodotus, was carried on for five years with varying success until, after a battle, when **Alliance with Lydia** the well-known eclipse which Thales predicted occurred in 585 B.C., an armistice, and afterwards a peace, were concluded as a result of the intervention of Nebuchadnezzar and King Syennesis of Cilicia. Here also friendly relations were cemented by a matrimonial alliance, and Astyages received to wife the daughter of Alyattes.

THE RISE OF THE PERSIAN EMPIRE

WESTERN ASIA was thus divided among three masters. According to the customary course of events, it was now a question which of the three would put an end to the other two. Strange to say, however, all three, or more correctly the Medes, who as conquerors are alone to be considered, preserved peace with the other two until the man appeared who took the three for himself. It would be inconsistent with the spirit of the ancient East, and with the policy of the civilised states, if the Median barbarians had really observed their treaties with Babylonia and Lydia, and had remained loyal to the friendship sealed by marriages. But their relations to Babylonia did not alter until the family of Nabopolassar was dethroned there, and a Babylonian came to the throne. Astyages, who meanwhile had succeeded Cyaxares, immediately after the accession of Nabonidus, in 555 B.C., advanced into Mesopotamia and besieged Harran. The dreaming

Nabonidus could hardly have saved Babylonia; but rebellion in Media gave him a short respite. Astyages was attacked at home and overthrown by his "vassal" Cyrus; thus the dominion over the Median empire passed to the Persians. Although we can picture to ourselves the general causes which produced this change, we are unable to obtain from the extant accounts any clear view as to the details of the persons and peoples who brought it about. The narrative of Herodotus assumes that Phraortes conquered the Persians, and that they, under Cyrus, overthrew the Median dynasty. We know that Medes and Persians were of kindred stocks, and the equality of both nations in the Persian empire is proved by the circumstance that the Median rule was acknowledged by the new conquerors; only the dynasty was put aside, and the nobles of both nations made common cause with each other. Darius was certainly a Persian; that is, he was descended from the nobility of the Aryan people, which at the time of the formation of the Median empire had made its home in Persis, east of Elam. The difficulty consists in obtaining any definite information as to the personality of Cyrus. It appears that the Achæmenian account, as well as that of Herodotus, which is based upon it, must have intentionally lied when it represents Cyrus as related to the Achæmenians. The object of such an invention is clear; by this means a legitimate claim to the throne could be established, and Cyrus and Cambyses were thus considered the rightful kings of Persia. **Who was Cyrus?** Monuments erected later, with the inscription "I am King Cyrus, the Achæmenian," had of course the same object. Undoubtedly we ought not to regard Cyrus as a prince of the old population, but as a member of the newly immigrated Aryan nobility; whether he was Persian or Mede must remain a disputed point, but this was immaterial when he once became a prince. It is still uncertain to

which country he belonged and how great his territory was. Nabonidus terms him a "petty" vassal of the great Mede; that, however, may only express the contrast between him and the Great King. The Babylonian chronicle, which deals with the events of this period, **First King of Persia** calls him, up to the capture of Ecbatana and the overthrow of Astyages, "king of Anzan," but afterwards "king of Parsu (Persia)." Cyrus had in fact, as the tradition puts it, made use of the Persians for his own purposes, and had therefore been recognised by them as their leader. Whether the Persians at an earlier period, as Herodotus implies, were already subject to the Median kings, or now for the first time really took

THE TOMB OF CYRUS, FIRST KING OF PERSIA
Cyrus was an obscure vassal of the Median emperor Astyages. With the help of the Persians he created an empire which ruled the entire East

an active part in the internal struggles of Media, Cyrus in any case knew how to avail himself of their help against the sovereign whom he wished to dethrone.

We can at least take it for proved that Cyrus—whether himself a Persian or not—was able to overthrow the Median royal house only by the help of the Persians. The revolution has no further significance. Since the Medes themselves had taken part in the conspiracy, their position remained untouched, and they were for the future the governing people by the side of the Persians. No difference existed between Median and Persian nobles; the difference between the two peoples was indeed only that between two independent tribes. It is not surprising that Cyrus now designated himself king of the Persians, since he was bound to give the honour and preference to the people who built up his power and supported his claims. But he was soon destined to be more than this, and he made the Persians and Medes the ruling people of the entire East. After Astyages, in the year 550 B.C., had been taken prisoner by Cyrus, **Empire of Cyrus** the latter's empire extended as far as the Lydian frontier. The question suggests itself, what town then became the royal capital of the new empire in place of Ecbatana ? If we consider how the Achæmenians represented themselves as the lawful successors of Cyrus, Susa must have been the capital from the very first. In this way Cyrus would have put himself forward as heir to the old Elamite claims to the sovereignty of the East.

As ruler of the new Medo-Persian empire he found in the realm of foreign politics the conditions existing which had been produced by the treaty between Alyattes and Media. Persia had to share the sovereignty of the Nearer East with Lydia and Babylonia. But while Nabonidus dug for old records and built temples the Lydian Crœsus recognised the altered state of affairs and the danger which had become threatening ; he exerted himself to arm the East against the new enemy. He received abundance of promises, but no efficient support, and was defeated before his allies, especially Egypt, had roused themselves to make an effort in 547 or 546 B.C. Even the Greeks of Asia Minor shared the fate of their rulers.

Cyrus was thus master of Asia Minor also, and could now turn his attention to Nabonidus, who expected more help from his elaborate system of fortifications than from his power of action. In the year 539 B.C. the Babylonian empire also ceased to exist. Cyrus was thus master of the whole Nearer East, for the provinces had then no more power of resistance than on the fall of Assyria.

We are familiar with the story of Cyrus' death, which is said to have taken place in the year 530 B.C. in battle with savage tribes on the eastern frontier of his territory, on the other side of the Jaxartes, in the zone of the " Turkish peoples," occupied by other non-Aryan tribes.

He was succeeded by his son Cambyses, who after the capture of Babylon had already governed there as viceroy. We have still less information about him than about his father. The Greek accounts, so far as he is concerned, are entirely influenced by the distorting Achæmenian legend which meets us in the Behistun **Cambyses the Scoffer** inscription of Darius. Of the events of his reign Herodotus relates only the occupation of Egypt in 525 B.C., by which he revived the conquests of Esarhaddon. The account may naturally be traced to Egyptian sources. Cambyses, in fact, from his natural disposition, had incurred the bitter enmity of the native priesthood by constantly scoffing at their religious ideas ; while, on his return from his unsuccessful campaign in Nubia, he even killed a newly-found Apis bull. According to this story, he must have been an excitable prince who, contrary to the habits and notions of the civilised peoples ruled by him, exhibited the simple intolerance of the primitive man in place of the stately dignity of the Oriental despot, and often vented his caprice on what seemed to him foolish. While on Egyptian

RUINS OF ECBATANA, THE CAPITAL CITY OF MEDIA

territory Cambyses received the tidings of the rebellion of the pseudo-Bardia, presumably a "Magus," named Gaumata. We can at present follow only the Achæmenian account of him. Was he really only a pretender, and not, after all, a true brother of Cambyses? However this may be, Bardia was acknowledged in Persia, Media, and elsewhere. We can fix the date of his reign, 522 B.C., from a number of dated documents from Babylonia. Cambyses had nothing more than his army with which to oppose him. He set out immediately, but, as Darius records, committed suicide on the way. The reasons and motive for his action are obscure; the deed may have been due to mental derangement.

We do not know the proper meaning of the term "Magi," and we cannot therefore make use of the untrustworthy Achæmenian account to decide what the relations of this monarch were to the people and to the now extinct house of Cyrus. This much is clear, that his sovereignty was everywhere acknowledged, even by Persians and Medes, and found a strong body of supporters among the people. It represented, therefore, a resistance offered by the mass of the people to the development of affairs, necessitated by the conquest of the great civilised countries, through which the nations, hitherto free, came under the dominion of a king and a nobility. It is expressly stated that Bardia granted a remission of taxation and took measures to check the pretensions of the priesthood, which had been favoured by Cyrus. Darius and six confederates surprised Gaumata in a castle near Ecbatana and murdered him. Darius was then proclaimed king and succeeded in holding his own. He claims, indeed, to have put down the revolts in the scattered provinces of the empire in the course of a single year. His cause must, therefore, from the first have found support in other quarters. Atossa, the sister and wife of Cambyses, whom Bardia had tried to put out of his path, was on his side. She became the wife of Darius, and is the first of the Persian queens who played an important rôle in state affairs.

Darius Gains the Throne

Darius was not related to Cyrus and his family. The reason, however, why he asserted his Achæmenian descent is clear. He wished to be reckoned the lawful heir

TOMB OF CAMBYSES, SON OF CYRUS

of the old royal house, and he required, in addition to the support afforded by the nobility, whose interests were bound up with his own, a tradition which might win him the reverence of the people.

Whether Cyrus was a Persian or not, he in any case felt himself to be king of the civilised countries of the Nearer East, and showed himself in that character. He adopted to a large extent the existing conditions, and provided only his own people with unencumbered estates, so that a nobility, devoted to him, arose, which must soon have gained further influence in the same way as the conquerors of earlier times. But the nobles of the eastern parts of the empire, especially Persis, which, more remote from civilisation, were still the recruiting grounds of the real strength of the people, were threatened with a loss of their share in the great prizes. Owing to the preponderance of power which their compeers in the western parts of the empire received from the treasures of civilisation, they were faced by the danger of being reduced to a position which would only too soon make them members of the ruled instead of the ruling class. It was this nobility which used the

East Against West

opportunity offered them by the attempt on the part of the Magi to seize the sovereignty. Their attempt was a rising of the uncivilised East against the West and its predominant class, already reverting to the culture of the ancient East.

It was by the exploit of the Seven that the new empire came under a really Aryan rule. The protest of the Aryan spirit, or the Persian, as we may call it after this victory against the policy of Cyrus, now finds an outward expression in the employment of the Persian language for official inscriptions. It is further expressed in the promotion of Persepolis to be the royal city by the side of Susa, which Cyrus had selected as the capital of his empire, so closely bound up with old tradition. The protest is finally exhibited in the stress laid on the Aryan Ahuramazda, or Ormuzd, cult as the religion of the ruling people, and as the religion of the empire, in opposition to the policy of a Cyrus, who had allowed the religious ideas and institutions of the western half of the empire to remain in the ascendant. The East, which had thus conquered the West, is still shrouded in darkness. All that we know of it is learnt only at the close of the Persian empire, on Alexander's expedition. It is the proper home of the Aryans—that is, the country where the tribes with whom we are here concerned found their widest expansion and still further developed their characteristics. The valley of the Indus on the east, and more to the north the ranges which shut off Central Asia, form its natural boundary.

The spiritual side of these Aryan stocks is rendered to some extent familiar to us by the Avesta. The book, which is extant under this name, was not reduced

DARIUS, FOUNDER OF THE PERSIAN EMPIRE
These two representations of the king are from Persepolis, the second showing him like the god Ormuzd overcoming a winged lion.

to its present form until the rise of the Sassanids, and was only then promoted to be the code of a rigid national religion. From its form, which contains old elements, especially the Gathas, or ancient songs, and from its advancement to a canon, it may be compared with the Bible in its relation to Judaism. All that remains to us is only a portion of a lost and larger work, which was for the Aryan nations something similar to what the Vedas were for their Indian kinsmen.

The Avesta is the sacred book of the Ahuramazda religion, the official religion of the Persian kings, which naturally did not yet possess the high culture in which the code of the Sassanids knew it. The Achæmenids showed themselves the representatives of the East, as opposed to the West, which accepted the ancient cults, by the fact that they continued in the religion of their fathers, to which they assigned the first place. They and the Persians prayed to Ahuramazda, and the inscriptions of Darius and his successors mention no other gods. In this way they were at one with the Aryan peoples of the East, and felt the contrast with the governed West. But if the Avesta, in its present form, bears somewhat the same relation to its earlier form that the Hebrew priestly code bears to the Jehovist narrative, or Malachi to Amos, a distinction must be drawn between the home of the Avesta and the old Persia, which had the same religion as that to which the basis of the later development in the Avesta is traced. The Avesta has come to us in a dialect which is indeed closely allied with that of the old Persian inscriptions, but is still of another country; so for its home we must look further

PERSEPOLIS, THE SECOND CAPITAL OF THE PERSIAN EMPIRE

At the top is given a reconstruction of the entrance to the great palace of Darius, while the picture at the bottom conveys an idea of the scale and situation of the palace. Above this, on the left, is a picture of the ruins in modern times. The other illustrations show one of the tiles of the palace and two Persian bulls, copied from Assyrian models.

towards the East. The historical events, which explain its importance, are obscure; but the splendour of the Persian empire, where an Aryan people ruled, may not have been without some effect upon it. The Iranian legend expresses this when it invents an old Bactrian realm which waged incessant wars for many centuries with the peoples of the East, the Turanians. There, under a king "Vistaspa," Zarathustra was the prophet of Ahuramazda. The name Vistaspa is, by a hardly fortuitous coincidence, the same as that of Darius's father, Hystaspes. It is certainly significant of the reflected glory and fame of the Persian empire in the Far East that the father of the head of the Persian dynasty was represented as ruling in the country where the origin of the Avesta was certainly known. This is how the Oriental legend expresses itself when it wishes to state that the region where the religion and its code have been developed was also the home of the people which dominated the Orient.

The Persian empire was a creation of Cyrus; the rule of the Persians— that is, of the nobility of the East—still uninfluenced by civilisation, was founded in this empire by Darius—in Persian, *Darayavaush*. The new sovereignty was not yet secure, in spite of the first success against Gaumata. Rebellions broke out in all the larger countries, which had to be suppressed before the new lord with his fellow-conspirators could enjoy his success. The insurgents everywhere appealed to the ancient empires which had existed in the countries concerned, and tried to prove themselves genuine descendants of the former dynasties. Darius records these insurrections and their suppression in his great Behistun inscription. At Susa a certain Atrina appeared, who attempted to gain support from the old Elamite population, and attempted to revive the ancient empire of Elam. He was quickly crushed by a Persian army. Nidintu-Bel asserted himself for a rather longer period; he was acknowledged in Babylon under the title

ORMUZD, THE GOD OF PERSIA
From an ancient Persian sculpture at Persepolis showing Ormuzd fighting the spirit of darkness.

of Nebuchadnezzar III., and documents dated during his reign have been preserved. A second revolt in Susiana, under Martia, who called himself Ummanish, king of Susa, was stifled at the outset. The most dangerous was the opposition in Media, where Phraortes, probably an actual scion of the old royal house, proclaimed himself king, and was also recognised by the Hyrcanians living to the east of Media and the Parthians. He was taken prisoner by Darius himself, after the Persian armies had fought several times against him without success. Almost at the same time insurrections broke out in Babylon under a second pseudo-Nebuchadnezzar, in Armenia, in Margiana, or Merv, in the Far East, where a new pseudo-Bardia arose, and among the Sagarians. These last insurrections must have expressed the opposition of the Aryan peoples to the newly founded dominion of the Persian nobility, since they were now in almost the same position under the dominion of Darius as, shortly before, the latter and his partisans had been under the power of the house of Cyrus.

While the empire was exposed to these shocks, the provincial governors in the west were tempted to repudiate the new rule and make themselves independent. Oroctes, the satrap of Sardis, made such an attempt, but Darius got rid of him by murder. Aryandes, the equally suspected satrap of Egypt, who had, however, been appointed by Cambyses, was soon afterwards removed. A demand for submission seems to have been also sent to Carthage, but without result, although the interests of Carthage in the hostility against the Greek world, which was now showing itself, forced it to adopt in a certain degree the same policy as Persia.

Herodotus, in whose narrative the official statements of the Persian government find expression, represents Darius as the creator of a completely new and organised administration for the new empire—as though, like Charlemagne, he had been a law-maker on his own initiative—in contradistinction to a fickle despotism which was supposed to have existed hitherto. Up to this time merely " presents " had been made to the king; thenceforward a fixed tribute was paid. In point of fact, the Persians merely took over the administration of the Babylonians, and they that of the Assyrians. The tribute was of course strictly regulated at all times, and Darius made no sweeping alterations in the terms and incidents of dependence. Any reforms, however, that he made in the method of administration may probably be traced to the fact that he filled the more important posts with his own noble adherents, to give them their promised share in the prizes won by their common efforts. The difference between the earlier system and that of the Persians consisted mainly in the fact that large satrapies were now insti-

From this point onward we have no native accounts of Persian history, but only the Greek narrative, so that we are informed merely of incidents on the Mediterranean—that is to say, of the wars with Greeks and Egyptians—and of other affairs only in so far as they affected them. We are not in a position to ascertain the general facts which modified the history of Persia, and we can, on the whole, see matters only in the light in which they appeared to the Greek observer, and not as they revealed themselves in Susa.

The empire of Darius, according to our view, differed from its predecessors merely in the fact that Persians actually governed it. So long as it was vigorous it sought to conquer, and when it could no longer conquer, it approached its fall. It existed for two centuries in all, and therefore not so long as many other similar powers which rose and fell.

DARIUS'S RECORD AND MONUMENT OF HIS TRIUMPH AND ROYAL DESCENT
On a great rock about 1,700 feet high, at Behistun, Darius had carved in cuneiform an account of his victories and Achæmenian descent. The rock also bears the sculpture reproduced here showing Darius receiving captives.

tuted, while Cyrus had retained the smaller Assyrian provinces. This change only, and the execution of the requisite measures to carry it out, were due to Darius. Herodotus, however, has an obvious excuse for attributing the creation of the organisation to Darius. Cyrus and Cambyses had not extended the Babylonian system to Asia Minor, which was first brought under that form of administration by Darius.

It is improbable that the position of the population of the empire generally underwent any radical change. The process of extortion was left indeed by preference to the native authorities, who were responsible for the collection of the taxes. A Persian administration existed only for the affairs of the satrapy, as under the Assyrians, while the administration of the different communities was left in the hands of the old locally regulated organisations.

Darius had hardly secured himself in the old seat of power when, in conformity with the nature of his empire, he planned new conquests. At first an advance was made towards the east. In the Behistun inscription " India " is not yet mentioned as a province, although it certainly is in a later one from Persepolis, and in the inscription on Darius's tomb at Naqsh-i-Rustam. This obviously can refer only to the country round the Indus.

The next undertaking was the Scythian expedition, about 515 B.C. It must have ended without definite results, like almost every campaign conducted against nomads. Herodotus informs us of the course of the expedition. The fleet was furnished by the Asiatic Greeks. The Bosphorus was crossed, presumably by a bridge; so, too, was the Danube. There were no victories to be won over an enemy which would not face a battle.

So, in the end, Darius, after heavy losses through hunger, thirst, and sickness, had to return. It is known that he was saved by Histiæus of Miletus and the other Greek tyrants, who had resisted the proposal of Miltiades that the bridge should be broken down because the overthrow of Darius would mean the end of the power of the tyrants.

Even if the expedition into the regions north of the Danube resulted in no tangible success, still the frontiers of the empire had been secured and extended, for Thrace and the district south of the Danube were permanently subjugated. The king of Macedonia also submitted, and the islands of Lemnos and Imbros were conquered. Thus the Greeks in Europe, surrounded on every side that was strategically important, were the next object of Persian conquest. The complications which led to the outbreak of hostilities bear, from the Persian point of view, precisely the same character as those which have often met us in the relations of Oriental empires to their neighbours. An opportunity for intervention is found in the appeal of a banished tyrant —Hippias—for assistance, coupled with the intervention of Athens herself in a revolt of the Great King's Greek subjects within the Persian dominions in Asia Minor. Before we turn to the account of that struggle, we will dismiss certain other events contemporaneous with its earlier stages. Egypt had remained tranquil under Darius, since he, in contrast to Cambyses,

THE ROCK TOMB OF DARIUS
One of the finest pieces of sculpture at Naqsh-i-Rustam is this tomb of Darius, the founder of the Persian Empire.

appears to have understood how to conciliate the priests. Something was even done by him for the improvement of the country. An inscription of his, which was found during the construction of the Suez Canal, proves that he had constructed or repaired a canal from the Nile to the Red Sea. In the year 486 B.C. events gave rise to a revolt, during which a certain Khabbash styled himself king of Egypt. Darius died in 485 B.C., during the revolt which was suppressed in 484 B.C. According to Herodotus, Egypt was after this more heavily burdened, a fact which is thoroughly in keeping with the customs of Oriental policy. Achæmenes, brother of the new king, became satrap.

Under Xerxes, who reigned from 485 to 465 B.C., a revolution broke out at Babylon, which still regretted the loss of its former independence. The name of Shamashirba, who was then proclaimed "King of Babylon," is recorded in inscriptions. The city must have been captured by storm, so that we may connect with this the long siege, to which Herodotus has attached the legend of Zopyrus, which meets us so frequently throughout the East. The capture must have occurred after the return of Xerxes from Greece. It is expressly recorded that he then destroyed the great terraced tower of the Temple of Marduk. The privileged position of Babylon had hitherto been respected by the Persian kings. It had voluntarily surrendered to Cyrus, and Darius had, in spite of various rebellions,

THE REMARKABLE ROCK TOMBS OF NAQSH-I-RUSTAM
One of the features of the Persepolis remains is the series of tombs cut in the living rock, including that of Darius

left its old constitution intact. He had, according to Herodotus, wished to carry off the statue of Marduk, but had not ventured so far. Xerxes was the first to do so. This signifies, as we know, the refusal to recognise any claim on the part of Babylon to form a distinct kingdom; and in this connection we may note the fact that Xerxes and his successors no longer styled themselves "King of Babylon," while Darius had continued to use this title.

The burdens which the Great King laid on Asia Minor could not have been very heavy. Apart from the revolt of the Ionians, we hear of no risings. The insurrections against the satraps in the fourth century B.C. originated with ambitious governors desirous of independent rule, not with a people struggling to throw off an oppressive yoke. On the other hand, it must be emphasised that the institutions attributed to Darius, the son of Hystaspes, were beneficial to Asia Minor. Of the twenty satrapies into which his empire was divided, four or five were in Asia Minor. Thus, Ionia with Caria, Lycia, and Pamphylia formed one, Mysia and Lydia the second, the Hellespont, Phrygia and Bithynia the third, and Cilicia alone the fourth.

This division was especially important for the levying of troops and the raising of taxes, to which each satrapy had to

XERXES
From a coin
of his reign.

contribute a fixed sum. This amounted, in the case of Ionia, Caria, and Lycia to 400 talents of silver; Mysia and Lydia paid 500; the Hellespont and Phrygia only 360. But to this must necessarily be added the expenses, which had to be separately defrayed, of feeding the troops which were permanently stationed there as well as those temporarily marching through the country, and the cost of keeping up the governor's court. It was, however, surely a boon for the subjects that their taxes to the Great King were definitely assessed, since formerly, under the name of presents, irregular imposts had been exacted. The establishment of the royal post-road was bound to benefit Asia Minor. It is true that from the earliest times a caravan route ran from Sardis across the Halys, skirting the north of the Lycaonian salt desert to the Euphrates, and thence further to the east; but Darius placed everywhere at fixed intervals along this road stations with inns, and placed watch-towers at river fords, mountain passes, or where else such might be necessary. By this means the security of travellers was considerably increased; and even if his first thought was for the royal service and for a rapid and certain communication between Sardis and Susa, the greater security which he thus ensured must have redounded to the good of his subjects.

1813

At the same time Darius established a uniform coinage throughout the empire, adopting, like the Greeks, this invention of the Lydians; but while the striking of gold coins was made a royal monopoly, rulers and cities, especially the Greek cities, were allowed to strike silver coins of any standard and with their own **First Persian Coins** legend. The royal coins were of gold and silver after the Lydian system, and according to Babylonian weights. For the numerous inhabitants of Asia Minor who traded directly with the East this was a beneficial institution.

But a state of affairs which nations accustomed to absolute monarchy considered endurable, perhaps even pleasant, produced discontent at first and soon open disaffection among the freedom-loving Greeks. It is true they could realise the advantages of a uniform currency and of a safe royal highway, and they had already paid tribute under Crœsus; but the levies of troops and ships which they had been forced to furnish to Cyrus for the subjugation of Lycia, and in larger numbers to Darius for the expedition against the Scythians, were especially resented by them. There was the additional circumstance that men who were friendly to Persia had been placed by the Great King as tyrants in their midst. Owing to this, the active corporate life which had flourished, in Ionia especially, must have been seriously checked; for the authority of these tyrants depended on Persia, and their anxiety to win the favour and good graces of the Great King must have been greater than their eagerness to rule to the satisfaction of their fellow-citizens.

The discontent that was fermenting among the Greeks at that time is shown by isolated facts that have come down to us about the progress of Darius's Scythian campaign, already mentioned. Byzantium **Discontent Among the Greeks** and Chalcedon revolted when the tidings of the disastrous result of the expedition reached them. The people of Chalcedon broke down the bridge thrown over the Bosphorus, so that Darius had to cross from Sestos to Asia by ship. Yet the fragments of the army which the king had rescued from the Scythians were still so large that the insurgent cities were reconquered and punished in 513 B.C. Soon after, however, events occurred

which were destined to show more clearly the prevalent feeling among the Greeks. In the year 500 B.C. aristocrats from Naxos, who had been exiled by the people, came to Miletus, where, in the absence of Histiæus, who was staying at the court of Susa, Aristagoras, his son-in-law, was conducting the government. He received the Naxians and promised to reinstate them. He laid a suitable plan before Artaphernes, the satrap of Sardis, offered to bear the cost himself, and asked for approval of his scheme. The cities then were ordered by Artaphernes to send ships and foot-soldiers, but Megabates, and not Aristagoras, as he had hoped, was appointed commander of the fleet and of the army against Miletus. The expedition failed completely; the Naxian people successfully defended themselves for four months against all attacks, so that at last Megabates withdrew without effecting anything.

Aristagoras could not make good the expenses of the war, as he had promised, and feared that he would be deposed from his office on account of a quarrel with Megabates, a near relation **Revolt of Miletus** of the king. In this difficult position he received a message from his father-in-law, Histiæus, urging him to revolt from the king. Aristagoras, therefore, determined on revolt, and found at Miletus support for the scheme. The fleet, too, which was still assembled after the disastrous result of the Naxos expedition, joined in the revolt. Many cities expelled their tyrants and made common cause with Miletus; each chose *strategoi*, or generals, as supreme officials to constitute a supreme council of war.

At first the common cause seemed to meet with success. Eretria sent five ships, Athens twenty, to their assistance. In the spring of 499 B.C. the allies advanced to Sardis, took the city, without, however, being able to capture the citadel, held by Artaphernes, and burnt the greater part of it. In this conflagration the temple of Cybele, the great goddess of the country, was destroyed; this so embittered the inhabitants that they rose themselves against the Greeks and forced them to withdraw. In the meantime, the Persian generals had assembled; they came up with the army of the allies at Ephesus as it was retiring from Sardis, and inflicted on them a crushing defeat. On the other hand, the fleet of the allies ruled the sea and induced the Greek towns on the Hellespont and Caria to revolt. Such successes, however, were not lasting, as the Persian commanders with superior forces soon reconquered the towns on the Hellespont and defeated the Carians at Labranda. Aristagoras, who had at first been the soul of the enterprise, became so discouraged that, seeking safety for his person, he fled to Thrace, where he was murdered by the Edonians. "He was not a magnanimous man," Herodotus says; and clearly when he fanned the flame of revolt and made himself its leader, he had let himself be swayed by selfish motives. When, therefore, the fleet of the allies with its 350 sail was annihilated by the Persians at Lade in 497 B.C., the united resistance of the Greeks was crushed. Each town was reconquered separately. Miletus alone held out against

had miscarried. The great Greek campaign was the outcome of a scheme already planned by Darius in revenge for Marathon. Having no Persian accounts, we are not able to take up a standpoint which will be fair to the Persians. The triumph of the Greeks was so overwhelming and so unexpected that their accounts of it are not judicial. In fact, they are obviously exaggerated in two different directions, by the desire to magnify the odds against which they fought, and to pour contempt on their adversary. Thus the mere impossibility of providing commissariat for a million of men must compel us to reduce the number of the invading host; while, on the other hand, we may credit that host with being largely formed of the tolerably disciplined and practised troops which Xerxes undoubtedly possessed. But the fact which there is no sort of reason to dispute is that the Persian armaments, both by land and by sea, enormously outnumbered those of the Greeks, and that they were irremediably shattered. The victory of the Greeks on land is explained by the superior attacking power of the Greek heavy-armed soldiers when opposed to the Oriental

SPECIMENS OF THE COINS OF DARIUS

Darius, adopting the Lydian invention and system of coins, established a uniform coinage in gold and silver throughout his empire. These coins all show the figure of the Great King.

siege and assault until it, too, had to surrender after an heroic resistance, in 494 B.C. By this the Persian domination was everywhere re-established, and the hated tyrants ruled in every Greek city as representatives of the Great King.

After the suppression of the revolt (about 495 B.C.) and the destruction of Miletus, Mardonius, the Persian commander, attempted to advance against Greece itself, and actually subdued the north-western archipelago, but was checked in his advance by a disaster to his fleet off Mount Athos. A second and a larger fleet was sent two years later under Datis and Artaphernes. This conquered Naxos, destroyed Eretria in Eubœa, which also had supported the Ionian revolt, and landed in Attica, where the army was defeated at Marathon by the Athenians under Miltiades in 490 B.C. The attempt to reinstate Hippias as tyrant in Athens

method of fighting and equipment, which was not adapted to a regular hand-to-hand battle. At sea it was due to the superior tactical methods of the Greek sailors, very much as with the overthrow of the Spanish Armada by the English two thousand years later. The Persian ships were furnished entirely by tributary states, the Phœnicians, and the maritime states of Asia Minor, to whom no competent commander-in-chief from headquarters could be assigned; and the manning the ships with land troops could not fail to give the experienced Greek sailors the advantage from the first.

This war was destined to free the settlements of Asia Minor eventually from the Persian yoke. Marathon, Thermopylæ, Salamis, Platæa will ever remain as the greatest deeds of heroism in this Greek struggle. And just as at Platæa the Persian army was annihilated and the Persian camp stormed, so, at the same time, perhaps on the same day, the Persian fleet was shattered at Mykale on the coast of Asia Minor by the confederates. This was the signal for the small Greek towns of Asia Minor to make common cause with the mother country and to revolt from the Persian king. The confederacy of Delos

League Against Persia was then formed with Athens as the chosen head; its place of meeting was at first Delos, afterwards Athens, and its members pledged themselves, while completely retaining their autonomy, to provide ships and crews and to furnish money contributions in order to found a war treasury.

The members of the new league prosecuted the war against Persia, and under the protection of this aspiring and rapidly powerful league, the small Greek towns of Asia Minor were secure from Persian attacks and from Persian vengeance for their revolt. The war continued for many years. The Persian garrisons were driven out of the towns of the Hellespont and from the Thracian coast. A large Persian fleet, which had sought protection from the advancing fleet of the confederates in the mouth of the Eurymedon, a river in Pamphylia, with the object also of effecting a junction with the Persian army, was annihilated, together with the army, by the bold attack of Cimon, in 467, or in the summer of 465 B.C., and the camp of the Persians was stormed. Elsewhere, too, where the Asiatics met the Greeks, they were worsted. Whether or no a regular peace was concluded, from about 449 B.C. hostilities ceased on both sides. In fact, the Greek towns in Asia Minor enjoyed liberty and governed themselves.

The end of the Greek expedition marks the turning point in the history of Persia. States built up on conquest must advance, or they recede. With the year 479 B.C. the retrogression of the Persian empire

Persia's Turning Point begins. It must always be remembered in this connection that we have no information as to occurrences on the other borders of the empire; we may, however, reasonably assume that under Cyrus and Darius the Persian supremacy in the Far East was more securely established than we find it in the time of Alexander. Victorious Greece at once crossed over to the attack. The islands and the Thracian coast were now almost entirely recovered from the Persians. Henceforth Persia never made any serious attack on Greece; and it had, indeed, to defend itself against the aggression of the latter, until it finally succumbed to Hellenism.

Xerxes was murdered about this time— 465 B.C. This was the result of a private palace intrigue, and the accounts, as usual, do not enable us to be clear about the deeper causes which underlay it. Artaxerxes, the youngest of the sons of Xerxes, was raised to the throne, his elder brother Darius being put out of the way at the time. The king-maker was Artabanus, the captain of the bodyguard, who was soon afterwards himself removed by Artaxerxes.

Artaxerxes, known by his Latinised surname as Longemanus, or "Longhand," reigned from 465 to 424 B.C. From this point onward we no longer have a tolerably connected account of Persian history even from the Greek standpoint, and are dependent chiefly on records of isolated occurrences. During this reign Themistocles came to the court of Persia, and knew how to pose before the king as the man

Artaxerxes Reigns by whose help Greece might be subjugated. Soon after the beginning of this reign the second rebellion in Egypt broke out under Inarus, the son of Psammetichus, a Libyan prince, who called in the help of the Athenians about 460 B.C. These had undertaken a renewed attack on Cyprus, whence they sailed to Egypt, drove back the Persians with their partisans into the citadel of Memphis and besieged them there. Persia tried, in the first place by diplomatic negotiations with Sparta, to compel the Athenians to withdraw. When that method proved ineffectual, a strong army was sent out under Megabyzus, and Egypt was conquered. The Athenian auxiliaries were annihilated, and a similar fate befell a subsequent detachment of fifty ships. Inarus fell into the hands of the Persians, and was crucified; his son, however, was taken into favour, and received back the province of his father. Amyrtæus, who had also called in the Athenians, and had obtained a detachment of sixty ships from Cimon in Cyprus, maintained his position in the swamps of the Delta. The siege of Citium was raised in consequence of the death of Cimon, but another victory, both by sea and land, was won in 449 B.C., after which hostilities ceased. It is a moot point whether this "peace of Cimon" was really solemnly ratified, or whether the war had gradually died out. Athens, at any rate, renounced her claims on Egypt and Cyprus. On the other hand, the coast of Asia Minor and the Greek towns on the Black Sea were set free. In the empire itself Megabyzus, the conqueror of Egypt, revolted against Artaxerxes in Syria; but in the end this rebellion also was quelled by peaceful means. The accounts now begin to record the political interference of the ladies of the palace; but not much reliance can be placed on the gossip of Ctesias, the Greek physician at the court of Artaxerxes Mnemon. Xerxes II., son of Artaxerxes, was murdered in 424 B.C. by one of his half-brothers after a reign of only a month

Intrigues of Court Ladies

PERSIAN FIRE ALTARS

These two fine altars were set up in the valley near Naqsh-i-Rustam. They probably represent an early form of Persian nature-worship.

and a half, and this latter in his turn was ousted after six months by his brother Ochus, satrap of Hyrcania. Ochus assumed the name of Darius II., and was surnamed Nothus, since he was the son of Artaxerxes by a concubine; he reigned from 424 to 405 B.C. Ctesias marks out from the very beginning his sister and wife, Parysatis, as the chief promoter of all intrigues. His brother Arsites and a son of Megabyzus in Syria rose against Darius. Arsites was taken prisoner owing to the corruption of his Greek mercenaries, and was put to death at the instigation of Parysatis. The third Egyptian revolt broke out in 410 B.C. By this effort Egypt was freed for more than sixty years from the Persian supremacy. The satrap Pissuthnes revolted in Sardis; he was crushed by Tissaphernes. His son Amorges, sup-

ported by the Athenians, held his own in Caria.

After the disaster to the Athenians in Sicily in 413 B.C. a favourable opportunity was presented to Tissaphernes to reconquer the Ionian towns. He, as well as his rival, Pharnabazus, the satrap of Northern Asia Minor, or Phrygia, jointly called in the Spartans in order to deprive the Athenians of the towns on the coast. But the interests of the Persians and Spartans were far too distinct to render possible any energetic course of combined action. The Athenians finally left off with so distinct an advantage that Pharnabazus was compelled to renounce his readiness to escort Athenian envoys to the court in order to negotiate a treaty there.

At this same time, however, a revolution occurred. Tissaphernes was removed from his satrapy, and retained only the towns on the coast. In his place Cyrus, the younger son of Darius Nothus, was appointed to be satrap of Lydia, Greater Phrygia, and Cappadocia, and he carried out a vigorous anti-Athenian policy and strongly supported the Spartans. At the same time, Lysander received the supreme command for Sparta; and while his policy established Spartan ascendency, it led later to a rupture with the Persians.

We are told of an insurrection of the Medes in the heart of the empire during the year 410 B.C. Ctesias also records a revolt of Terituches, whose sister Stateira was married to Arsikas, the eldest son of the king. After his fall, enmity rankled between the queen-mother Parysatis and Stateira. In the year 405 B.C., Darius Nothus died, and his son Arsikas mounted the throne as Artaxerxes II. Mnemon. Cyrus, summoned by his mother, whose favourite he was, came too late. He was arrested on the advice of Tissaphernes, but released at the instance of Parysatis and sent back to his satrapy, in order to make the preparations that were to be anticipated. Cyrus's first move was to seize the towns of his opponent, Tissaphernes, a war of one satrap against another. He then collected an army of Greek mercenaries, and, in 401 B.C., marched with it, secretly supported by the Spartans, into the heart of the empire in order to depose

Satrap against Satrap

his brother. This is the "March of the Ten Thousand Greeks" described by Xenophon. The inability of the empire to resist a Greek army was now plainly revealed. The 13,000 Greek mercenaries defeated the immense army of the king at Cunaxa, in the province of Babylon. But Cyrus fell in the battle, and the throne of Arta-

March of the Ten Thousand xerxes was saved. On former occasions the Greeks in the employ of Persia would have then imparted fresh strength to the helpless colossus, but now they had detected the real nature of the dreaded foe, and were completely disillusioned. They knew now that in the heart of the empire whole districts and tribes, especially in the mountains, did not acknowledge the Persian suzerainty. The open quarrels of the satraps showed plainly enough the dissolution that was already beginning, and offered welcome opportunities to the advance of the restless Greeks.

The intrigues at court were only intensified by the death of Cyrus, since Parysatis could not be reconciled to the loss of her beloved son, and contrived gradually to remove out of her path all those concerned in it, among them the momentarily triumphant Stateira, who was poisoned. Artaxerxes II., it is true, then banished his mother, but soon called her back again. The satrapies of Cyrus were given to his rival, Tissaphernes, who had conducted the defence during the great rebellion. Sparta, the supporter of Cyrus, was already hostile to him; so when he demanded the fulfilment of the conditions on which help had been furnished by Persia in the shape of a surrender of the Greek towns of Asia Minor, the result was war in 401 B.C., which Sparta carried on in Asia Minor, especially with the help of the survivors of the Ten Thousand. It was conducted after 396 B.C. under the supreme command of the Spartan king, Agesilaus,

Sparta Defeats Persia who won a great victory at Sardis in 394 B.C., although no decisive results were obtained from it. In the meanwhile Parysatis had succeeded in bringing the hated Tissaphernes into disfavour at court; he was replaced by Tithraustes and afterwards executed. The struggle was prolonged by the wiles of the two satraps and by negotiations, until Agesilaus was recalled to Europe. In the meanwhile the tide had changed

to the disadvantage of Sparta. The Athenian, Conon, had fled to Euagoras in Cyprus after the defeat at Ægospotami, and had induced Pharnabazus to fit out a fleet for him in order to be able to carry on war against Sparta by sea. At first, being hindered by remissness in payment of the subsidies, he went himself to the court, secured the supreme command of the fleet for Pharnabazus, which meant for himself in reality, and defeated the Spartans at Cnidus in 394. The result of the victory was the overthrow of the Spartan naval power and the restoration of the Athenian under the protection of Pharnabazus. Athens held her own by the help of Persia, and Persia could not play any part on the sea without Athenian guidance. On land Sparta continued for a long time to be the chief military power. During the never-ending plots and schemes at the Persian court, Tiribazus, the satrap of Sardis, who adopted the policy of Tissaphernes, was able once more to come to the front and to bring Conon into disfavour. The latter again fled to Euagoras, where

Peace at Last he soon afterwards died. But Struthas, who again supported Athens, was finally appointed satrap in Sardis. Thus there were incessant disputes, intrigues, and counter intrigues, until at last it was settled by the "peace of Antalcidas," in 387 B.C., that the Asiatic towns belonged to Persia, but that the island and all other Greek states should be autonomous.

Cyprus was expressly acknowledged in the treaty to be Persian territory. In reality it was practically independent, since Euagoras had united the Greek elements throughout the island in a common war against the Phœnicians, and was king of the island. His loyalty to the supreme feudal lord must soon have appeared doubtful. An attack was therefore made on him in 390 B.C. He offered a stout resistance, being openly aided by Athens, until, after the peace of Antalcidas, Persia took more rigorous measures to bring him to submission, as he was daily becoming more dangerous, commanded the sea as far as Egypt, and had succeeded in firmly establishing himself at Tyre. He was defeated, but was able to obtain favourable terms of peace. Not long after he was murdered. Cyprus, under his successors, broke up again into different small states. In the expedition of Artaxerxes against the Kadusi, a nation of mountaineers south-west of the Caspian Sea, his large army met a reverse which was like that of Salamis ; he was surrounded and had to pay ransom. Egypt, really independent, still resisted Persian attempts at subjugation. A more vigorous attack was made when Pharnabazus, in 376 B.C., was placed at the head of a larger army. He did not, however, accomplish much in the end, since regard for the continual change of feeling at court rendered any vigorous conduct of the campaign impossible. The results of the instability of Artaxerxes were seen towards the end of his reign in a series of revolts, of which that of Ariobarzanes in the Hellespontine satrapy and that of Datames in Cappadocia were the most formidable. Mausolus also, the prince of Caria, maintained a loyalty which was not always above suspicion. At last even Tachus, the king of Egypt, assumed the aggressive, since he adopted the old policy of the Pharaohs and attempted the conquest of Syria. He advanced as far as Phœnicia, being supported by an army of Greek mercenaries under Chabrias, and by the Spartans under the veteran Agesilaus. But when his nephew Nectanebus had himself been proclaimed king in Egypt he was forced to take refuge with the Persians ; and he became utterly powerless and inactive.

Invasion by Egypt

When Artaxerxes' death was imminent his son Ochus, favoured by Atossa, whom, though his own sister, Artaxerxes had married at the instance of Parysatis—for instances of marriage with a sister, daughter, and even mother can be found in the history of the royal house of Persia— had contrived to remove his brothers out of his path and to secure the throne for himself in 359 B.C. The reign of this energetic Artaxerxes III., Ochus (358–338 B.C.), marks a last rally on the part of Persia. His actions show that he did not hesitate to carry out his ends after the methods of a true Oriental monarch by unscrupulous bloodshed and merciless wars.

He had first to deal with the revolts in the empire. Our accounts of them are vague and incomplete, but it is so far clear that the king was more successful than his predecessor. Artabazus, the satrap of the Hellespontine province, and Orontes on the coast of Asia Minor, could not hold their own, notwithstanding occasional help given by the Greeks. In Greece there appears to have been alarm at the energy of the Great King from the very first, and it was debated whether the aggressive ought not to be assumed against him. Demosthenes was compelled to warn the Greeks against breaking with him without good cause. In Egypt, at first, even under his rule no success was gained, and the revolt, as formerly was the case under Tachus, spread once more to Palestine. We have very little information about the causes of the movement, but the revolt of Sidon and of the nine kings of Cyprus, as well as an allusion to a chastisement of Jerusalem, prove that we here meet with phenomena similar to those presented by the revolts of Palestine against Assyria, which were supported by Egyptian help. Sidon was especially conspicuous this time. Ochus finally took over the chief command himself, and advanced into Syria with a powerful army, in which some ten thousand Greek mercenaries were included.

Spread of Revolt

Sidon received aid from Rhodes under Mentor, but when the Persian marched against them, Mentor and Tennes, king of Sidon, entered into negotiations. The details are obscure. Sidon was surrendered and a terrible punishment inflicted on it. The remaining Phœnicians then submitted. There must also have been wars in Judæa. Egypt finally, after having resisted for so long, was subjugated and became once more a Persian province in 344 B.C. Very severe measures were adopted towards it, and Ochus seems to have outraged Egyptian sentiments in the brutal fashion of a Cambyses. Cyprus also was again subjugated under the command of Idrieus, the prince of Caria.

The power, however, was already dawning which was fated to crush Persia. It was seen in Susa that Philip of Macedon must become dangerous so soon as he had effected the conquest of Greece. An alliance was, therefore, made with Athens in order to take measures against him. The capture of Perinthus by Philip was prevented by the joint action of Athens and Persia. But the battle of Chæronea, in 338 B.C., coincided almost exactly with the death of Artaxerxes. This made Philip master of Greece, and created conditions by which the

Alliance against Macedon

Greek world and Hellenism were impelled to attack Persia in Asia.

Artaxerxes is said to have been murdered by Bagoas, who placed Arses, the youngest of the king's sons, upon the throne, only to slay him in turn when he seemed to be contemplating action against his minister in 336 B.C. In the mean-

Persian King Maker while a Macedonian army had advanced into Asia Minor, but its further progress was checked by the murder of Philip. After the death of Arses, Bagoas placed a distant relation of the murdered man, Codomannus, a great-grandson of Darius Nothus, on the throne. He reigned from 336 to 330 B.C. under the title of Darius III. Codomannus. But this time the king-maker did not escape his doom ; he was soon put out of the way by Darius. Darius was the last king of Persia. We cannot form any notion of his character from the available records ; but we may at any rate conclude that he was not in a position to do anything to prevent the fall of the empire. The great empire became the booty of Hellenism. The disruption had begun, as we have seen, soon after the defeat at Salamis ; a proof, indeed, of the nature of the much-lauded "organisation" by the first Darius. The

Ten Thousand of Xenophon would in themselves have been enough to overthrow the Persian monarchy, if they had had a competent general ; now, when at last a powerful antagonist, with a definite aim before him, appeared upon the scene, the booty fell without trouble into his hands. It was a great success which Alexander enjoyed, but it was not a great exploit to overthrow an empire already tottering to its fall. The history of the ancient East has shown us numerous examples of similar conquests. The many revolutions, which have brought to the East its various populations are on a level with the Hellenistic conquests, although the glory of their leaders is not sung so loudly as that of the representative of the foremost civilised people in the western world.

End of Persian Empire The result of this conquest was not then decisive ; the East was indeed conquered by the arms of the Greeks, but it resisted its civilisation, and it finally drove out the conquerors once more.

The narrative of the conquests of Alexander the Great belongs to the Greek portion of our history of Persia. All that we are here concerned with is that the establishment of Alexander's empire terminates that of the Persians. The

VICTORY OF ALEXANDER AT THE BATTLE OF THE GRANICUS
One of the fights in Alexander's conquest of Persia, where Darius III. was defeated. From the picture by Le Brun.

THE DEFEAT OF DARIUS III. AT THE BATTLE OF ISSUS

A reproduction of a mosaic from Pompeii, showing Darius III. in his chariot at the battle of Issus in 333 B.C. against Alexander. The Persian stategy is said to have consisted chiefly of running away.

immediate disruption of the new empire and the vicissitudes of its various portions are the subject of the ensuing chapters; but when Persia appears as a political entity, it will be a different Persia, not the Achæmenid empire.

The Persian empire from its wars with the Greek world stood in the full light of history. The Achæmenian empire appears before us in the brilliance which it displayed to the Greek historian. But looked at from East instead of from West, it appears in a completely different aspect. That which seemed to the Greek the irresistibly powerful heir to a civilised world, shrouded in mysterious darkness and possessing inexhaustible riches, lies clear before us in its evolution. We know that it was neither the first, nor the most lasting, nor the most powerful, although perhaps the most extensive phenomenon of its kind. Many a conquest of a similar character has been seen and absorbed by the old civilised world of the East. Even

Correct View of Persia the Persian régime was not able to change its character fundamentally, and did not exert more influence upon it than any other of the well-known conquests. The sharp division which we were able partially to recognise in the evolution of a western and an eastern Persia, a result of the conquest of highly civilised countries by peoples which were still in the early stages of society, and, further, the reconciliation of the Persian families who

were at the head of affairs with the Medes and the ruling powers of the subjugated provinces, all clearly show that the dominant power claimed nothing beyond a purely political conquest of the vanquished countries. Some Persian nobles supplanted refractory rulers of the old population, and one or two Persian officials governed the provinces.

Conquests Without Changes But substantially nothing was changed. A Persian or other Aryan migration, which might have introduced a new population into the old civilised countries, was kept back, after the great flood of nations had once been checked through the organisation of a Persian empire by Cyrus. The fact that Darius, although he had at first taken advantage of successful efforts in this direction, could no longer submit to them when king, is only one of those innumerable phenomena in history where circumstances are more powerful than men, even when they have had the very best intentions.

Thus only that portion of the empire had become Persian or Aryan which had been struck by the wave of migrating Aryan hordes before they had yet formed a firm union; that is to say, while they had not yet become aware of the power of the civilisation which they wished to conquer. These countries were precisely those which had not possessed a superior civilisation of their own— namely, the eastern districts. When,

1821

however, the Aryans had come within the mystic circle of Babylonian culture, into Media and Elam, they submitted to it. Media had long been removed from Assyro-Babylonian influences, and Elam's power had been broken by Ashurbanipal; therefore both lands offered suitable conditions for receiving an Aryan immigration with-out obliterating or absorbing its race and character. The popula-tion of both lands, indeed, them-selves received an Aryan tinge. The incomers, on the other hand, fell under the spell of that culture whose very cradle they had violently seized.

Invading Aryans Civilised

After the subjugation of the western civilised countries that process ceased, by virtue of which, through an immigration of nomadic hordes, a new social life had grown up out of the blending of influences, all tending to evolve a vigorous civilisa-tion. In place of this, political conquest, resting on force, was now made the object of rulers. There could thus be no further prospect of an independent evolution of the Aryan spirit. In the place of a Per-sian nation, which would have worked itself upward from stage to stage to a higher civilisation and so to dominion over the East, there was now a Persian administration, like an Assyrian, which drained the strength of the civilised lands, and thus became dependent upon them. Not the Persian people, nor a Persian state, but the Persian empire, represented by the army and officials, now held the reins of power in Nearer Asia.

This new empire, in its fundamental principles merely a repetition of the As-syrian empire during the eighth and seventh centuries, shows the same charac-ter in all its phenomena. In the admini-strative sphere the Persian satrap was merely the Assyrian shaknu, although his province was, as a rule, disproportionately larger. Like him, too, he was in fact only a Persian viceroy, who had been placed in the position of the old native ruler. He possessed within his province all rights of a sovereign. Above all, he maintained an army at his own cost, pursued to some extent an independent policy, and thus usually reached the point where the thought of revolt must involuntarily have suggested itself, whenever the intrigues of the courtiers threatened to become danger-ous to him. The constitution of the later satrapies is traceable to Darius. Cyrus had

The Persian Satrap

in the west simply adopted the old insti-tutions. The accounts of him and his son speak of 127 provinces, which extended from India to Ethiopia. Accordingly the east must have been divided up some-what after the model of the west. Darius, who went hand in hand with the eastern nobility, instituted the larger satrapies, and the Persians, who administered them, became rulers over separate countries.

After the flood of immigration had abated, and the conquerors had become owners, who on their part had to ward off the hordes that were pressing on after them, wars had to be waged with troops supplied by the civilised states. These proved to be useless material to a great extent. Those of the immigrants who were marked out by landed possessions to be the nobility, and thus the backbone of every army, could do no more than form the backbone of a royal army. The satraps, who were in the first place responsible for the defence and mainten-ance of their provinces, could not avail themselves of this resource. Every satrap, therefore, had to keep an army of his own, soon composed, especi-ally in the western provinces, of mercenaries, and those chiefly foreign. The overplus of capable soldiers which the vigorous development of the Greek people produced always found there a ready acceptance. In this way the satraps of the western provinces were soon in possession of armaments which might become a menace to the Great King.

Persian Army System

The royal Persian army, in contradis-tinction, seems to have been constituted on the basis of a feudal state, such as corresponds to the organisation of a newly immigrated people. Any man who had received a grant of land was liable to perform military duties corresponding to his share of the soil. There must, indeed, have been a very motley mixture of nationalities in the army, especially if the same system obtained in the provinces, where civilisation had long passed this stage, and in the western provinces par-ticularly. It is not certain how matters were arranged there; but the " barbarian army," which Cyrus the younger led against Artaxerxes, in addition to his ten thousand Greek mercenaries, can hardly have been collected on another system. Such armies were distinct in armament and customs, even if we are

ALEXANDER BEFORE THE DEAD BODY OF DARIUS III., THE LAST KING OF PERSIA
Darius fled to Media in 331 B.C. and was murdered just before Alexander overtook him.

not required to accept Herodotus's description of the army of Xerxes as accurate in all its details.

In other respects the administration, apart from the satraps and the highest officials, was in the provinces the old national one. Even the Assyrian substitute for the now impracticable colonisation of conquered countries—namely, the plan of new settlements with a population ingeniously formed into Assyrians, and of the transplantation of prisoners of war to different parts of the empire—was entirely abandoned. The treatment of

Sidon, which had been made Assyrian by Esarhaddon, and the permission accorded to the Jews to return to Palestine, are two striking instances in point. How far in the latter case any alliance of Cyrus with the Jewish element, so powerful in Babylon, may have played a part must remain an undecided question. The first instance, however, and the general abandonment of this procedure prove that the Assyrian policy had been deliberately reversed. It was clearly seen that institutions, established by force, could never attain the same prosperity as economic structures which are built upon the soil and rise from national development. Thus, the Persian empire made no attempt to interfere with the old-established institutions in the various provinces. In spite of the Persian supremacy, the inhabitants of Babylonia thus remained Babylonian, and those of Ionia Greek.

Persia's Derived Civilisation The picture of the effectiveness of the Persian sovereignty in the eastern provinces is quite otherwise. Here from the first the conditions were different. While the centre of the empire, Susiana and Persis, received culture from the west, it must have transmitted it in turn to the east. So far it became important for the conditions which were developed later by the Parthian and Bactrian empires. Western ideas in this way reached India, and finally the Sassanid empire determined the course of the civilisation of Islam. So that in truth we cannot speak of a Persian civilisation in the west. That portion of it which developed in its original home possesses a still smaller value for the evolution of mankind. If Elam, during almost as many millennia as the Persian empire lasted centuries, had already borrowed from Babylonia the fundamental principle upon which its power rested, that will also hold good of its heir. A glance enables us to recognise in the pictures from Persian royal palaces, or in the glorification of the victories of a Darius on the cliffs of Behistun, an intellectual kinship with the Assyrians, the same object of glorification, the same conception, the same technique. The beautiful workmanship of the enamelled tiles which covered the walls of Persian palaces [see page 1800] is also largely due to Babylonian influence.

Doubtless the active and gifted people of the Greeks, which after the eighth century B.C. entered into intimate relations with the Asiatic empires, assisting **Greek Art in Susa** Cyrus in his Persian wars and participating in his victories, that people which had supplied mercenaries to the Assyrian and Chaldæan armies, and furnished whole armies, as we saw, to the Persians, also sent artists to the court of Susa. It would, however, be an idle task to attempt to trace the influence of Greek art in purely Persian productions. The Persian king was a successor of the old Oriental kings. Just as he, full of

dignity, discharged his time-honoured duties with wig and long, flowing robe, so there remained for the art which served to glorify him no other path except that marked out by millennia of veneration. The Persian buildings have one feature distinct from the Assyrian ones known to us, and that is the ample employment of pillars. It is, perhaps, a permissible conjecture that Greek influence may be seen in this. But it is also conceivable that Egyptian influence, through the medium of Phœnicia, may have travelled through the Euphrates valley as far as Susa and Persepolis. Yet, granted the case that Hellenic architects and artists had helped in building the palaces of Xerxes, their Hellenic spirit could evince itself at most in secondary details. What they created must always have been Oriental, copied from the old models, as the Oriental love of tradition demanded.

A production similar to this royal art, which in some degree had abandoned the national spirit, is the Persian cuneiform script. It was adapted from the Baby- **Persian Cuneiform Script** lonian, or more correctly the Elamite, in order to provide an alphabet for the language of the new sovereign people. This was not suited to the grammatical scheme of the old civilised languages, and therefore could not be written with the old hieroglyphic and syllabic script which had closely followed the structure of the Sumerian and later the Semitic. In further pursuance of the principle already traceable in Elamite, a specially simplified syllabic writing was invented—actually invented in this case at the royal command—in order to be able to carve the inscriptions of the kings in the Persian language also. A written language in the sense of Babylonian was never developed from this, so far as our present knowledge goes. Even the Persians made use of Aramaic as the imperial language of intercourse, so far as the Babylonian language and its cuneiform script did not maintain their rights. The Persian cuneiform script, evidently first introduced by Darius in order to emphasise his national policy as contrasted with that of Cyrus and Cambyses, has had no history and exerted no influence on the development of civilisation ; the Avesta was written in a literal alphabet derived from the Aramaic.   HUGO WINCKLER
LEONARD W. KING

WESTERN ASIA FROM THE RISE OF PERSIA TO MAHOMET

BY DR. HUGO WINCKLER, DR. K. G. BRANDIS, LEONARD W. KING, M.A., AND H. R. HALL, M.A.

ASIA MINOR AFTER ALEXANDER

AT the death of Alexander, in 323 B.C., the empire which his conquests had created extended over all Western Asia and into the Punjab, besides Hellas and Egypt. Its continuance seemed secured at first by the selection of his stepbrother, Arrhidæus, as king under the title of Philip, by the birth of a son and heir, and by the appointment of Perdiccas as regent of the empire. But the foremost generals became governors of the provinces into which it was divided, and at the same time commanders of the troops stationed or about to be levied in their administrative districts. Every governor bestirred himself immediately to raise a trustworthy army, by which he might make himself as independent as possible of the imperial power and might carry out his own ambitious designs without regard for the welfare and prosperity of the whole. This naturally furnished the ground of many disputes. The scene of these wars of the Diadochi, or "Successors," was Asia Minor.

Wars of the Diadochi Antigonus was sent thither from Babylon as governor of Greater Phrygia, Leonnatus went to Hellespontine Phrygia, Eumenes to Cappadocia, Cassander to Caria, Menander to Lydia, and Philotas to Cilicia. While the others all went to provinces long since subdued, Eumenes had first to conquer his province. The Cappadocians, whose land had hardly been touched by Alexander himself, had never reconciled themselves to the Macedonian rulers placed over them, and had actually set a native noble—probably of Persian origin—by name Ariarathes, at the head of affairs. He being a clever,

Conquest of Cappadocia enterprising man, had extended his rule over the whole of Cappadocia, to which Pontus then belonged, and maintained it with the help of a strong army of 15,000 horsemen and 30,000 foot-soldiers. According to the commands of the regent of the empire, Antigonus and Leonnatus were to help Eumenes in expelling Ariarathes; but neither obeyed orders. Perdiccas, therefore, was obliged to march against Cappadocia with the imperial army. Ariarathes was defeated, taken prisoner, and crucified, and Eumenes received the country as his province. The nephew of Ariarathes, his namesake, saved his life by flight into Armenia, whence, at a later period, he came back to influence the destinies of his fatherland.

Leonnatus had in the interval aided Antipater, governor of Macedonia, in his struggle against the Hellenes, and had lost his life in the campaign. Antigonus, instead of answering the summons to explain his refusal to obey the regent's orders, fled to Antipater in Europe, and effected there an alliance against Perdiccas, in which Ptolemy, the governor of Egypt, joined. War followed; Perdiccas was murdered in Egypt, and Antipater became regent of the empire in his stead. Antigonus received back the province of Greater Phrygia, from which he had fled, and was given the supreme command of

Fall of the Regency the imperial army, with the task of carrying on the war against Eumenes, who had been on the side of Perdiccas, and had successfully held his own against Antipater and Craterus. Eumenes was defeated in the open field, but successfully defended himself in the steep mountain fortress of Nora against Antigonus, escaped, and in a short time assembled a new army, with which he conquered Cilicia and Phœnicia and finally crossed the Euphrates, in order to bring the governors of the eastern provinces over to his side. At last, in the year 316 B.C., after many battles, he fell, through the treachery of his picked troops, into the hands of Antigonus, who had him put to death. Previously to this, and in 319 B.C., immediately after the death of Antipater, who had appointed Polyperchon as his successor and regent of the empire, Antigonus had renounced obedience to the new regent, had driven out the governors of Hellespontine Phrygia and Lydia, who were on the side of Polyperchon, and had given their satrapies to men of his own party. Now, after the death of Eumenes, he was ruler of all Asia, from the upper provinces of which he returned to Asia Minor with enormous treasure.

But the great power and ascendency of Antigonus produced a hostile coalition of the other governors. These were Cassander, the son of Antipater, who meantime had driven Polyperchon out of Macedonia; Ptolemy; Lysimachus, who in the year 323 had received Thrace as a province, and after subduing the warlike, freedom-loving mountain tribes, had founded for himself an important state; and, lastly, Seleucus, who, driven from his satrapy of Babylon by Antigonus, had fled to Ptolemy in Egypt. Antigonus refused their request to divide the satrapies equally; so wars resulted, which dragged on with changing fortunes and some

interruptions from 315 to 301. In these the last members of the royal family—Alexander's posthumous son, who was called after him, and his illegitimate son Heracles—met their death. The rulers, therefore, proceeded to assume the title of kings in 306 B.C. Antigonus retained his power, and Asia Minor remained his choicest possession until he succumbed to the last mighty onslaught of his enemies, and was killed at the battle of Ipsus in Phrygia in 301 B.C. There is no sign of lasting institutions or of a government bringing blessings to its subjects in this disturbed period of new and constantly-growing armaments. Only the Greek cities of Asia Minor enjoyed peculiar consideration and retained their self-government and immunity from taxation.

After the death of Antigonus there were four kingdoms in existence—Egypt, under Ptolemy; Thrace, under Lysimachus; Macedonia and Greece, under Cassander; and Syria, under Seleucus. Asia Minor was divided between Lysimachus and Seleucus, who had taken the most important share in the overthrow of Antigonus. Both remained in possession of the portion that fell to them, notwithstanding that Demetrius Poliorcetes, "the Besieger," the son of Antigonus, made numerous attempts to reconquer his father's realm. Lysimachus was defeated and killed in 281 B.C., in a battle against Seleucus, to whom, as victor, Asia Minor justly fell. During the immediately succeeding period the line of Seleucus is in the ascendant, and possess, indeed, the greatest power as far as extent of territory goes; but the Seleucidæ are no longer sole rulers, as once Antigonus was.

PHILETÆRUS
Founder of the kingdom of Pergamus about 280 B.C.

In the confusion in which Asia Minor was involved after the death of Alexander

Last of the Separate States new states had gradually been developed there, which, growing into greater power, stamped their mark on the whole subsequent period. Once more we find on the soil of Asia Minor for the first, and indeed for the last time since the dissolution of the Lydian dominion, states with a separate history and a separate policy, in complete independence of any great political power whose capital and centre of gravity lay outside the peninsula.

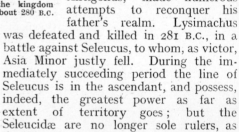

Ariarathes, the nephew and adopted son of that Ariarathes whom Perdiccas had crucified at the time when Antigonus was waging his disastrous war against the allied kings, had returned to Cappadocia from Armenia, and, supported by the good will of the population, which had never grown accustomed to the Macedonian rule, entered upon the heritage of his father. His attempt was favoured by events in the immediate neighbourhood Mithradates, the grandson of Ariobarzanes, a former satrap on the Hellespont, who had been in the service of Antigonus, warned by Demetrius Poliorcetes that his life was in danger, fled to Paphlagonia. There he was able to occupy the town of Kimiata in the gorges of the Olgassys, which he surrounded with strong walls, and now, in concert with Ariarathes, he summoned the Paphlagonians and the inhabitants of the north coast to arms. The lieutenant of Antigonus had to give way to the two; and when, after the **Birth of New States** battle of Ipsus, the two victors, Lysimachus and Seleucus, turned their attention to the subjugation of these outlying districts, it was too late. An army of Seleucus was totally defeated in Cappadocia, and Mithradates was able to hold his own in the north. Later, after the death of Lysimachus and the invasion of the Gauls, and during the continuous wars of the Seleucidæ, both within and outside Asia Minor, no more thought was entertained of their subjugation. Thus Ariarathes created an independent kingdom in Cappadocia, with which he united Cataonia; and Mithradates, who received the name of Ctistes—the Founder— founded a kingdom in the valleys of the Amnias and Iris, which, situated on the Pontus Euxinus, or Black Sea, came gradually for brevity to be called Pontus. The rulers of both territories naturally styled themselves kings.

In the north-west new states grew up. Bithynia had been ruled in Persian times by princes of its own, who recognised the suzerainty of the Great King and were subject to his satraps, even though they often enough disobeyed them. Alexander

LYSIMACHUS AND POLIORCETES
After the death of Antigonus and despite the efforts of his son, Demetrius Poliorcetes, Lysimachus, king of Thrace, and Seleucus of Syria shared Asia Minor.

freed Bithynia from the Persian domination, but apparently left the princely families in possession of their hereditary power; the Macedonian governor of Hellespontine Phrygia, Calas, was appointed to complete their subjection. But the Bithynian prince, Bas, repelled his attack in the open field, and his son Zipoites succeeded during the wars of the "Successors" in maintaining and even in extending his hereditary position. Zipoites is the first who styled himself king; this must have happened in 297 B.C. after a victory over Lysimachus, since the era of the Bithynian kings begins with the autumn of 297. He also maintained his position against the successor of Antiochus, Seleucus, who had sent his general, Patrocles, to force Bithynia to submission. In any case, after this Bithynia finally entered the ranks of independent states. Zipoites was able to bequeath to his son Nicomedes a realm which towards the east included the Greek towns of **Founding of Pergamus** Teion and Cieros. About this time there arose an independent state in the valley of the Caïcus, on the borders of Bithynia. At the outbreak of the war with Seleucus, Philetærus had abandoned Lysimachus, whose citadel and treasures he was guarding at Pergamus, and had gone over to Seleucus. When the latter was soon afterwards murdered he won the gratitude of Antiochus by sending him the body of his father, held Pergamus, and succeeded in bringing the whole valley of the Caïcus as far as the sea under his dominion, and thus laid the foundations of the kingdom of Pergamus.

Once more a race of invaders became prominent in Asia Minor and exercised an important influence on the conditions of the country. Just as previously, at the time of the Mermnadæ, Cimmerians, combined with Thracian hordes, had crossed over into Asia Minor and had long scoured the land, plundering and robbing, so now the Gauls appeared. They had before this made inroads into Thrace and Macedonia; now in 277 B.C., Nicomedes, who was contesting his inheritance with his brothers,

NICOMEDES
Son of Zipoites, first king of Bithynia. From a coin.

took a Gallic army under Leonnorius into his pay and by their aid subdued Bithynia. At the same time a second Gallic force, under Lutarius, crossed the Hellespont, joined the force under Leonnorius, which now was again free, and, both combined, raided the fields of Asia Minor and burned the towns. Antiochus, in order to protect, at any rate, his own part of Asia Minor from the Gallic pillagers, marched across the Taurus. A pitched battle was fought between him and the Gauls. In overwhelming force—so ran the account of the fight—the "Galatians" confronted the king in a dense phalanx, twenty-four ranks deep, with 10,000 horsemen on each wing. From the centre of the line of battle eighty four-horse chariots, armed with scythes, and twice as many two-horse war chariots were to charge. It may easily be conceived that the king's courage almost failed him at the sight of this formidable multitude, especially since the greater part of his inferior army consisted of slingers and other light-armed troops. He even wished to make terms; but one of his generals encouraged him and devised a plan of battle for him. The sixteen elephants which the king had with him were driven headlong against the enemy; the enemy's horses, which had never seen an elephant, took fright, galloped in wild rout back on the ranks, and caused universal confusion. The overthrow of the Gauls was complete.

Antiochus Fights the Gauls

This victory checked the wandering of the Gauls, in so far that they were driven back to the eastern part of Phrygia on both sides of the Halys and restricted to a region to which they gave their name permanently. Here in Galatia they founded their capital, Ancyra, which attained later great prosperity, and at the present day, as Angora, is the chief town of Central Asia Minor. Here they grad-

ually obtained secure settlements and lived, mixed with the natives, without abandoning their language, habits, or constitution, under twelve tetrarchs, each of whom belonged to one of the four cantons of their three tribes—Trocmeri, Tolistoboii, and Tectosagi—and under a council consisting of three hundred members. Often enough, starting from here as mercenaries of the rival princes, they helped to decide the destinies of the peninsula. For, unfortunately, there was no prosperous development in Asia Minor even after the defeat of the Gauls by Antiochus. In the many wars between Egypt and Syria, which led to the occupation of the coast of Caria and Lycia by the Ptolemies, then in the long, bloody war between the brothers Seleucus Callinicus and Antiochus Hierax, sons of Antiochus Theos, the whole west coast and the central and southern districts, Caria, Phrygia, Lycia, and Cilicia, were at one time in the hands of Callinicus, at another of Hierax. No wonder that the Gauls, too, reappeared in this confusion, and, after inflicting a crushing blow on Callinicus in the interest of Hierax, once more assumed a position which threatened danger. Once more they laid waste the fields; and their neighbours, to secure peace from them, were forced to pay tribute. Even Antiochus Hierax could not secure immunity in any other way.

The Gauls Reappear

The credit of averting the new danger of the Gauls belongs to the princes of Pergamus. After Eumenes I., the successor of Philetaerus, had defeated Antiochus I. at Sardis in 262 B.C., the permanence of their rule was secured. The disturbed times gave an opportunity for strengthening and extending it. Attalus I. (241–197 B.C.), the son and successor of Eumenes, had brought his name into history by an

THE STRENGTH OF THE ARMY OF ANTIOCHUS
A terra-cotta statue of an elephant seizing a Gaul, reproduced from "Passing of the Empires," S.P.C.K. In the battle between Antiochus of Asia Minor and the Gauls the Galatian army, which included 20,000 horsemen, was routed by sixteen elephants.

action which conferred on him lasting fame in the eyes of his contemporaries and of posterity. He refused to pay to the Gauls the customary tribute, and faced their consequent invasion in a battle, where he completely defeated them. By this means he greatly contributed towards ending their raids and confining them to their own territory. On account of this splendid achievement Attalus was honoured by the towns and princes who were saved by him from the Gallic danger, and assumed the royal diadem. Eumenes II. dedicated to him an imposing monument, an altar to Zeus standing on a massive pedestal, round the sides of which ran reliefs, which glorified for all time the victory of Attalus over the Gauls under the representation of the battle of the gods with the giants. Pergamene art, as shown us by these reliefs, marks in some ways the highest point reached by the Greek art of the later style. The statues of Pergamus were regarded as triumphs of art by the Romans, and the various figures of " Dying Gauls "—erroneously called " Dying Gladiators "—in our museums were copied from Pergamene originals.

Attalus I. not only permanently secured his realm, but extended it also by a war **Kingdom of Attalus** with Antiochus Hierax, who, after long disputes with his brother Seleucus Callinicus, had finally withdrawn and held Asia Minor north of the Taurus, so far as it was distinctly Seleucid. Hierax was defeated at Coloë, in the neighbourhood of Sardis, and compelled to fly from Asia Minor; Seleucid Asia Minor fell into the hands of Attalus. But the Seleucidæ were destined once more to establish their power in the peninsula, and, as it seemed, more firmly than ever. Achæus, the general of Seleucus, retook from Attalus the territory he had recently conquered, but could not resist the temptation of founding a separate state and of placing the kingly diadem on his own head during

the confusion which prevailed in Syria after the death of Seleucus. This kingdom, severed from the main Seleucid state, lasted some years, until Antiochus III., who had restored his authority in his own kingdom by a successful war against

RUINS OF THE ANCIENT METROPOLIS OF PERGAMUS
In the second century B.C. the city of Pergamus became the most important kingdom in Asia Minor and a centre of civilisation. These ruins are all that remain to-day.

insurgent satraps, felt himself sufficiently strong to deprive Achæus also of his sovereignty. Achæus, being beaten, shut himself up in Sardis and held out a considerable time, but was eventually murdered by traitors. Thus Antiochus III. reunited a large part of Asia Minor to his own main territory in 214 B.C.

A letter of the king preserved for us in an inscription gives us a slight glimpse into the internal administration. The Seleucid kingdom, like the Persian, was divided into satrapies : we do not **Worship of King and Queen** know how many of these were included in Asia Minor. By the side of the worship of the native gods, which naturally remained fixed, a similar worship of the king and the queen was introduced ; for both there was in each satrapy one high-priest, and sacrifices were offered to both, just as, two hundred years later, in the provinces high-priests were appointed for the Roman emperor.

But Antiochus III. did not rest content with these acquisitions. It was not enough that he had brought even Greek towns on the western coast of Asia Minor into his power; he aimed at Europe also and laid claims to Thrace on the ground that it was by right a possession of the

Seleucidæ, owing to the defeat of Lysimachus by Seleucus. He had already become master of the town of Sestus, and had made Lysimacheia, which he restored, the headquarters of his army and the capital of a province of Thrace that was still to be conquered, when he became involved in a war with Rome.

Seleucidæ Confined to Cilicia In the revolt, the dominion of the Seleucidæ in Asia Minor on this side of the Taurus was ended for ever. They kept only the territory on the far side of the Taurus—that is, practically, Cilicia—and did not venture to cross the sea with war-ships to the west of the mouth of the Kalykadnos. Rhodes and Pergamus, which had taken the part of Rome, were both splendidly rewarded for their loyalty. The former received the country of Lycia and Caria as far as the Mæander ; Pergamus, which had withstood a siege from Antiochus, and whose territory had been ravaged, received Hellespontine Phrygia, Greater Phrygia, Lydia with Sardis and Ephesus (which had been occupied by Antiochus and had not soon enough gone over from him to the Romans), and the part of Caria which lay north of the Mæander. The Greek towns of Asia Minor, which had sided with the Romans on the day of the battle of Magnesia, where Antiochus had met with his overthrow, were conceded self-government and also immunity from tribute. By the despatch of Manlius Volso against the Galatians, who were defeated by him in two battles, the Romans deserved well of Asia Minor ; for even after the defeat inflicted on the Galatians by Attalus many towns had still been obliged to pay tribute to them to secure protection from their marauding invasions. The Galatian scourge was now destroyed once for all.

The results of the battle of Magnesia are of the most far-reaching importance. Rome, without appropriating a foot's breadth of land, becomes from this time the foremost power in Asia Minor. It is clear on the face of it that Pergamus and Rhodes, which had long been allies of Rome, would seek to further their prosperity and power by this connection ; but the longer the other states, Bithynia, Cappadocia, and Pontus itself, resisted, the less they could avoid the influences of Rome. The power of the Macedonian, Syrian, and Egyptian monarchies over

Rome the Mistress of Asia Minor

Asia Minor was broken from that day. For at least a century the peninsula enjoyed peace, in which it had had no share since Alexander's death. What conception Rome had of its rights as the leading power is clearly shown by the political changes which were introduced into Asia Minor thirty years after the battle of Magnesia. After the third Macedonian war Rome, being dissatisfied with the conduct of the free city of Rhodes and its unwelcome intrusion into the course of this war, deprived it of its possessions on the peninsula of Asia Minor and declared Caria and Lycia to be " free." The Rhodian garrisons had to be withdrawn from these countries, and the considerable tribute which till then had flowed into the Rhodian treasury from that source was stopped. Thus the power of Rhodes suffered a heavy loss. The trade of Rhodes was bound to fall off, since the Romans had established the free harbour of Delos and had blocked the main artery of the Rhodian exports and imports on the coast of Macedonia, which had now become Roman.

Lycian City League In Lycia the towns, of which there were many of various sizes, formed themselves into a close organisation, the Lycian league. They had always unwillingly submitted to the Rhodian rule, and knew how to make good use of the freedom now conceded to them for the welfare of the country. The beginnings of this Lycian city-league may have been older, especially as far as the common worship of the Lycian tribal deity is concerned ; but now other duties fell upon the league : the representation of the country in foreign lands, negotiations with strange powers, the maintenance of the common interests, as well as the establishment of systematic and assured conditions at home. Though such a city-league in itself presented no novelty, the fundamental thought on which the Lycian league rested was new and excellent. Every member of the league had a different number of votes, according to its size, distributed in such a way that the largest towns gave three, the intermediate towns two, and the small towns one vote, respectively, at the meeting of the league, which was held in turn in each of the communities. At the head of the league was placed a president, chosen similarly in turn from the towns which were members, and elected annually. The

ONE OF THE TRIUMPHS OF THE ART OF PERGAMUS: AN ALTAR TO ZEUS

This imposing altar to Zeus was erected in honour of Attalus I., who completely routed an invasion of the Gauls. The reliefs round the sides of the altar mark in some ways the highest point reached by the Greek art of the later style.

towns exercised their right of voting through representatives. A similarly organised league, the Chrysaorian, existed in Caria, where there were comparatively few towns, but many large village communities.

The most splendid picture at this time is presented by Pergamus, which, through the courage and statecraft of its kings, had become an important kingdom. From the struggle against Bithynia, which broke out immediately after the war with Antiochus III., Eumenes II. emerged as victor. Prusias of Bithynia had occupied some territory in Mysia, which in the peace with Antiochus had been conceded to Eumenes. On this ground a quarrel began between the two, which has the greater interest for us because Hannibal for the last time played a part in it, and for the last time, uselessly, it is true, tried to form a powerful coalition against Rome. Despite some successes of Hannibal,

Eumenes was not only able to maintain his position, but also to incorporate into his own kingdom the territory conquered by Prusias on the Sangarius. Prusias did not venture to shelter Hannibal when the Romans demanded his surrender; and the great Carthaginian, being abandoned, put an end to his life at Libussa, on a height above the Gulf of Nicomedia. The princes of Pergamus, distinguished as they were for their cleverness and statecraft, were not less renowned for their warm interest in art and science. We have already mentioned the altar to Zeus. On the acropolis, which towers above the city, they reared a rich group of buildings, which, rising in terraces one above the other, crown the summit of the royal citadel. And in the middle of it, among palaces and temples and public buildings, was the library, which was also a museum, where, besides a rich collection of books, originals, as well as copies of prominent works of the older Greek art, were preserved. In this manner Pergamus became an important centre of civilisation, and will be always mentioned with honour by the side of Alexandria.

By the side of Pergamus, Bithynia fell into the background; its princes had gradually subdued the whole territory from **Extent of Bithynia** the Rhyndacus and the Mysian Olympus to Heracleia, and southward from Heracleia over the Sangarius up to the Paphlagonian frontier. Hellenism early made an entrance here; and an increasing number of Greek towns sprang up. But none of them can be compared with Pergamus in glory and importance.

Up to this time Rome had had no possessions of her own in Asia Minor. But when Attalus III. of Pergamus died in the year 133 B.C. and made Rome his heir, the Romans accepted the inheritance. Here begins a new phase in the historical development of Asia Minor. It is true that Aristonicus, a scion of the princely house of Pergamus, disputed the inheritance with the Romans, raised an army, found adherents, and went against them, sword in hand. But it was impossible for him to hold out long. In the year 129 B.C. the revolt was crushed and its leader murdered. The consul, Manius Aquillius, created the Roman province, Asia, co-extensive with the kingdom of Pergamus. In addition, there was Caria, which had taken part in the revolt of Aristonicus. The latter had been besieged and captured in Stratonicæa. Aquillius, having been bribed, had given Greater Phrygia to Mithradates Euergetes of Pontus; Bithynia raised a protest. The proceedings in the senate on this point were prolonged interminably, until at last Rome appropriated the country herself. From that time, 116 B.C., all Greater Phrygia, Hellespontine Phrygia, Mysia, Lydia, and Caria, were included in the new Roman province. Of the Greek towns, free up till now, those that had supported Aristonicus were deprived of their liberty and made provincial towns; but the others were recognised as free and autonomous.

At first, indeed, Rome had magnanimously relinquished all claim to taxes, which had long been raised by the kings of Pergamus; but soon some of them were

MITHRADATES
The Great, king of Pontus,
from a coin of his realm.

restored. They introduced a tax of one-tenth on the produce of the soil, a tax on pasture land, and duties on imports and exports; the collection of revenue was made over to a company of Roman knights, who farmed all these taxes at Rome. This method of taxation was the plague and ruin of the provincials. The Asiatics, exposed to the tyranny and caprice of these companies, who considered only their own profit, and never the welfare of the taxpayers, and who naturally wished not only to get back the sums paid at Rome for farming these taxes but to enrich themselves greatly by it, were shamelessly plundered by them, and could never hope for success if they ventured on a judicial complaint at Rome; for the very knights who composed these companies for farming the taxes were the judges.

A Roman governor, who changed yearly, stood at the head of the province. Even if some of them, such as Mucius Scævola, were very honourable and worthy men, who really had the welfare of the province at heart, the majority of them brought with them only a mass of debts from the capital; and the province was reckoned by them and their compeers to be the most suitable sphere for getting rid of their debts and acquiring new wealth. There were, indeed, opportunities enough for the governor to wring out money for himself, especially since the province had to provide all expenses for him and his suite. The amount, however, which had to be expended for him depended on his own discretion, since he could impose taxes for a definite object, such as for the building of ships to resist the bold attacks of pirates, or generally for the protection of the land; and it rested with him alone to determine the **Romans Plunder Asia Minor** rate of taxation, while no one controlled its proper application. Again, he alone distributed the garrisons among the towns, and many towns were only too glad to be quit of these unwelcome guests by a money payment to the governor. It was not, in any case, difficult for the Roman officials to plunder thoroughly the province entrusted to them. And, unfortunately, the number of the selfish governors at this time was greater than that of the honourable. Besides this, the suite of the governor was large, and consisted mostly of young aristocrats, to whom the opportunity for acquiring wealth was not unwelcome.

In short, the maladministration of the Romans was appalling. And in Rome itself the senate usually turned a deaf ear when complaints against its members were raised. Such misgovernment must have greatly excited the anger and dissatisfaction of the provincials. Only a spark was needed to kindle a terrible conflagration, and the man was soon found who knew how to deal with these conditions. We saw earlier that the house of Mithradates in Pontus had founded a dynasty.

Appalling Misgovernment of Rome

In the course of time the frontiers of this kingdom were widened. The Greek towns on this coast, Amastris, Amisos, and, above all, Sinope, with its own colonies of Trapezûs and Cerasus, had been conquered and Sinope made the capital of the kingdom of Pontus. On the other hand, the various attempts of the Pontic princes to bring Galatia and Greater Phrygia under their rule were frustrated, either by a coalition of the other kings in Asia Minor or by the intervention of Rome. Mithradates Euergetes, who had fought in the war of Aristonicus on the side of the Romans, and then thought he had claims on Greater Phrygia, was murdered, at his own wife's instigation, before the transactions with Greater Phrygia were completed. He left a son of tender age, who, young as he was, fled from the plots of his mother and

FAMOUS BRONZE FROM PERGAMUS
The statues of Pergamus were regarded by the Romans as triumphs of art. This group is "The Gaul and his Wife."

remained for many years hiding in the lonely mountains. Mithradates Eupator reappeared at Sinope as a young man of twenty, and the people hailed him as their king. His mother was obliged to resign the government to him. Filled with ambition and energy, his first and foremost thought was the aggrandisement of his kingdom; but that required means money, and soldiers, of which he had not sufficient at his disposal. A happy chance helped him. In the Tauric Chersonese, the modern Crimea, the Scythians of the great South Russian steppe were pressing hard the free town of Chersonesus and the kingdom of Bosporus, now Kertch; Mithradates, being asked for aid, sent over his general, Diophantus, with an army. He

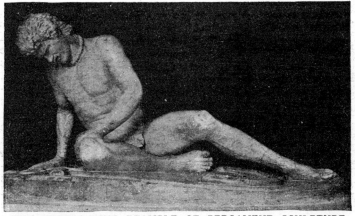

THE OUTSTANDING EXAMPLE OF PERGAMENE SCULPTURE
The familiar figures of "Dying Gauls" in the museums, erroneously called "Dying Gladiators," are Roman copies of Pergamene originals. The above is from an original.

defeated the Scythians, drove them back from the peninsula, and admitted the Chersonese, as well as the kingdom of Bosporus, which had submitted to his master, into the union of the subject states.

Perhaps more important than the increase in territory was the replenishment of the Pontic treasury by the taxes which flowed in from the Crimea.

Training the Army of Pontus Mithradates strengthened his army and increased its efficiency by continual training. He had already conquered Paphlagonia and Galatia in combination with Nicomedes of Bithynia, had partitioned them with his ally, and had secured his influence in Cappadocia, when the protests of Rome forced both of them to relinquish their conquests. Mithradates bowed this time to the dictates of Rome, since he did not yet feel himself strong enough for defiance; but the wish to wreak vengeance on Rome for having prevented first his father and then himself from realising the ardently desired scheme of conquest was cherished from this moment.

The disputes about the succession in Bithynia between Nicomedes III. and Socrates, who held possession of the throne by the help of Mithradates until Nicomedes, supported by the Romans, expelled him, and finally the invasion of the territory of Pontus by Nicomedes, led to the outbreak of the war between Rome and Mithradates. This so-called First Mithradatic War broke out in 88 B.C., at a time when the Romans were still fully occupied in Italy itself. The Roman legate, Manius Aquillius, levied, indeed, some troops in Asia; but he, as well as the remaining Roman commanders in the province of Asia, were defeated by Mithradates or repulsed without attempting serious resistance.

The king marched by way of Apamea and Laodicea into the Roman provinces. Isolated towns, such as Magnesia, near **Slaughter of 80,000 Italians** the Sipylus, and Stratonicæa in Caria, resisted for some time the attacks of the king, and had to be conquered by him; but these were exceptions. Mithradates was received with open arms and hailed as a liberator from the universally hated yoke. In a very short time the province joined him. At his orders on one day 80,000 Italians were murdered. These had gradually become numerous, as more and more people had poured into the

incalculably rich land of Asia for the sake of gain and commerce. Greece also was affected. Athens first of all espoused the cause of Mithradates; the Bœotians, Achæans, and Lacedæmonians declared for him. His general, Archelaus, was in Greece with 100,000 men, and had his headquarters at Athens. At Rome itself there was civil war. Not until the beginning of the year 87 B.C. was the great Sulla able to start with an army for Greece. His mere appearance brought many Greeks back to their allegiance. Only Athens resisted and remained loyal to Mithradates, and was conquered on March 1, 86 B.C. after a long siege; a few days later the Piræus also was stormed and given to the flames. The first great success was followed by others. Sulla defeated Archelaus at Chæronea, and Dorylaus, who had come up with considerable reinforcements, at Orchomenos.

In Asia Minor also the situation was not as favourable for Mithradates as at first. Rhodes had refused submission to the king, and Lycia did likewise. The siege of Rhodes, like that of Patara in Lycia, **Peace with Rome** had been a waste of time, for on both occasions Mithradates had been forced to withdraw without effecting any result. Again, the cruel and tyrannical government of the liberator began soon to prove intolerable. At Ephesus, Tralles, and other places the king's governors were murdered or expelled, and the towns put into a state of defence. Lucullus, Sulla's general, had assembled a fleet in Syria and Egypt, with which he took Cos, Cnidos, Chios, and other towns from Mithradates. Pressed on every side, the king resolved to enter into negotiations for peace with Sulla. By the terms of peace Mithradates was obliged to evacuate the Roman province, give up his conquests in Bithynia, Paphlagonia, and Cappadocia, and to restrict himself to his Pontic territory; he was also to surrender 70 warships and pay 2,000 talents as war indemnity.

Thus ended the First Mithradatic War, and the Province of Asia was once more Roman. Sulla reorganised it. Rhodes was rewarded for its heroic resistance by a gift of Caunia and other districts on the Carian coast; the towns which had remained loyal were declared free; while those that had revolted were punished and a heavy fine was imposed upon them. This penalty weighed heavily upon the towns ; and since it had to be met by loans, it materially retarded their prosperity, already seriously impaired. Ten years afterwards we see Lucullus endeavouring by wise measures to discharge the debts of many of the towns, and vigorously combating the pernicious system by which unpaid interest was regarded

The Work of a Wise Financier as bearing interest in turn. He reduced the rate of interest, wiped out the interest which had run up above the amount of the original capital, and appropriated the fourth part of the income of the debtor for the satisfaction of the creditor.

The Second Mithradatic War, from 83 to 81 B.C., was in reality nothing more than a marauding expedition of Muræna, the governor of Asia, into the Pontic territory.

Towards the end of the year 74 B.C. Nicomedes III. of Bithynia died and bequeathed his kingdom to the Romans. That gave Mithradates a welcome opportunity to invade Bithynia in the spring of 73 B.C., and to bring the whole land under his rule. Lucullus and Cotta were immediately sent from Rome to Bithynia, and the Third Mithradatic War began. Cotta, to whom the supreme command of the fleet had been given, was to defend Bithynia. He withdrew to Chalcedon, while Lucullus advanced from Cilicia and Asia with the legions which had been collected there. Cotta offered battle under the walls of Chalcedon, and was defeated ; at the same time Mithradates' fleet forced an entrance into the harbour and captured sixty Roman warships. After this success Mithradates began the siege of the rich, free town of Cyzicus, which was loyal to the Romans and defended itself bravely. Lucullus advanced to its relief. Mithradates, taken on two sides, and no longer besieger, but besieged, with his mighty army crippled by hunger and disease, was compelled at last to abandon his attempt and to fall back hastily on Pontus, saving

The Last War of Mithradates what he could. Even his fleet was by degrees driven out of the Ægean Sea. Lucullus, on his part, now marched through Bithynia and Paphlagonia into the king's territory, defeated him at Cabeira, and compelled him to fly to his son-in-law, Tigranes, King of Armenia. After the conquest of the towns of Amisus and Sinope, Lucullus advanced into Armenia, defeated Tigranes at Tigranocerta in 69 B.C., and after a second victory at Artaxata, was making preparations to subdue all Armenia, when his soldiers mutinied and forced their general to retreat. As even the enormous booty captured on this retreat did not alter the soldiers' purpose, Lucullus was forced to abandon Armenia.

Meantime, Mithradates had escaped and collected a new army, with which he advanced to reconquer his kingdom. The hostility of the equestrian class in Rome to Lucullus was so strong that he was recalled, and Pompey was entrusted with the conduct of the Mithradatic War in his place.

Pompey had just ended the War with the Pirates. After the Seleucid and Egyptian fleet had lost the mastery of the Ægean Sea, piracy became rampant. Pompey deserves the credit of having at last energetically checked this plague. Covered with glory in this war against the pirates, he appeared the most competent general to end the Mithradatic War. He therefore started in the year 66 B.C. for the new theatre of war, and so completely crushed Mithradates at Dasteria, which he

Pontus Falls to Rome himself afterwards named Nicopolis or City of Victory, that the king of Pontus could save himself only by precipitate flight through Colchis to the Bosphorus. In the midst of mighty preparations and great plans—he intended to lead against Italy a large army of Scythians, Thracians, and Celts, and to attack Rome itself—he was betrayed by his son Pharnaces and the army, and died by his own hand. Thus Pontus, the kingdom of Mithradates, fell to Rome ; Bosporus was left to his son and betrayer, Pharnaces. Pompey organised Pontus as a province, founded eleven townships in it, and united it with Bithynia under one jurisdiction. Rome was now mistress of all Asia Minor, except Cappadocia, Galatia, and Lycia. By 25 B.C. Galatia too was a province. Cappadocia was absorbed after the death of its last king, and Lycia in the middle of the first century A.D.

Asia Minor had no separate history in the time of the Roman emperors, just as later under Byzantine and at present under Turkish rule. It has been a part of world-empires, and only as such has it had a share in the events of world-history. The age when its independent states played a part in the history of the world passed away with the early years of the empire.

REMAINS OF SYRIAN TOWNS FOUNDED BY SELEUCUS

The first picture shows the remains of the port of Seleucia, on the Mediterranean, built by Seleucus Nicator near the mouth of the Orontes. The second illustrates the actual ruins and some of the Seleucid sepulchres cut in the rock. The third is a picture of the walls on the west side of Antioch, built by Seleucus when he founded the city.

THE EMPIRE OF THE SELEUCIDÆ

FROM Asia Minor, after the death of Alexander, we turn to follow the fortunes of another portion of his empire: the eastern countries extending between Asia Minor and Egypt from the Phœnician coast to the Jaxartes and from the slopes of the Taurus to the Indus. The death of the great king brought no great immediate changes to these districts; Babylon remained the capital of the empire, and the provinces continued, for the most part, under their previous governors, excepting Media. At the partition of satrapies at Babylon, Media fell to Peithon, son of Craterus, while its former possessor, the Persian, Atropates, was restricted to the north-western part of Media, the province later called Atropatene after him. Syria was given to Laomedon of Mytelene.

A great change in the affairs of the East took place at the death of Perdiccas in 321 B.C. Babylon ceased to be the capital.

Seleucus Governor of Babylon — The new partition of satrapies at Triparadisus, arranged by the new regent, Antipater, affected the East much more than the former partition. Laomedon, indeed, retained Syria; Peucestas, Persia; and Peithon, Media; but Parthia received a new governor in Philip, as did Bactria and Sogdiana in Stasanor, Mesopotamia in Amphimachus, Susiana in Antigenes, and, what is most important for the ensuing period, Babylon in Seleucus.

Seleucus was born about 356 B.C. A member of the Macedonian nobility, he, like all his companions, entered early into the army and followed Alexander into Asia. He owed it not merely to his birth, but also to his courage and capabilities, that he belonged to the more intimate circle around the king. We are told, as an instance of his great strength and his courage, that one day in the presence of Alexander he brought a raging bull to the ground. He distinguished himself in the Indian campaign and in the battle against Porus. After Alexander's death he assumed the command of the household cavalry in place

of Perdiccas, who became regent of the empire; Alexander had attached peculiar distinction to this post, and the holder of it, who was then called Chiliarch, filled, according to Persian precedent, at the same time one of the highest places at court. In this office he made the campaigns of Perdiccas against the insubordinate governors, first against **The Rise of Seleucus** Antigonus, and later against Ptolemy of Egypt. When the Egyptian campaign failed, he was among those generals who abandoned their commander; and it is to him and Antigenes of Susiana that the murder of the regent is ascribed. He was appointed governor of the province of Babylonia, giving up the Chiliarchy and the command of the household cavalry. It therefore became his first concern immediately to create an army for himself. Alexander's principle that no satrap should keep an army had been disregarded directly after his death. Seleucus was very soon drawn into the whirlpool of events. Eumenes, who had sided with Perdiccas, had been declared an enemy to the empire at Triparadisus; Antigonus had been appointed strategus, or captain-general, and entrusted with the conduct of the war against Eumenes. This war took a new turn when Eumenes, after the death of Antipater, had been appointed strategus in Asia by the regent, Polyperchon, and by Olympias, mother of Alexander, and had been amply provided with funds. The theatre of war was shifted to the east, where he at once found support from **Alexander's Empire Breaks up** the governors of the eastern provinces. These were still with their troops in Media, where they had expelled Peithon, who had killed Philip, satrap of Parthia, had placed his own brother in his place, and had thus roused the suspicions of other satraps.

But Seleucus neither took part in the combination against Peithon nor did he then join the side of Eumenes. He expressly declared that he could not make common cause with the enemy of the empire. On the contrary, he joined Antigonus, who came to the East in order there to prosecute the war against Eumenes. Fortune, indeed, seemed to smile on Seleucus at first. He received the province of Susiana, the former governor of which, Antigenes, fought on the enemy's side ; but fortune proved fickle.

Seleucus Flees to Egypt When Antigonus had put to death Eumenes, betrayed by his own troops, and handed over to his enemy, he behaved as an absolute despot and arbitrarily appointed and deposed governors. When he was in Babylon he required from Seleucus, from whom he had already taken away Susiana, an account of his administration ; Seleucus refused, and, feeling himself no longer safe, fled from Babylon to Egypt and the court of Ptolemy.

The great power of Antigonus, as well as his despotic behaviour, led to an alliance of Ptolemy, Lysimachus, and Cassander, to the consummation of which Seleucus contributed his share. Wars then ensued, which continued almost without cessation from 315 to 301. Here we are concerned only with the struggle for Syria and Phœnicia, with which the first war began. Ptolemy had occupied these countries ; Antigonus drove him out, and when he himself went back over the Taurus, in order to be near the scene of war in Asia Minor, he left behind his son Demetrius there. The decisive defeat of the latter at Gaza and the reconquest of Syria by Ptolemy allowed Seleucus to return - to Babylon in 312 B.C. Seleucus had undertaken the march with only 800 infantry and 200 cavalry ; but the population, whose love he had known how to win previously, welcomed him back. As most of the garrisons, too, went over to him, he was able without great trouble to re-enter on the possession of his province. When Seleucus, together with Lysimachus of Thrace, appeared in Asia Minor

Founding the New Empire for the last decisive passage of arms with his old opponent, Antigonus, he had extended his power far over the borders of Babylonia, and created for himself an empire which went from the Euphrates eastward to the Jaxartes and comprised all the so-called upper satrapies. It would be interesting to be able to follow the distinct steps of this expansion of his power, but our sources fail here.

We hear only that Seleucus unexpectedly by night attacked Nicanor, who had been placed in command by Antigonus in Media and the upper satrapies, and had advanced upon the news of Seleucus' return to Babylon. In this night attack many distinguished leaders fell, among them the satrap of Persia ; and the greater part of the troops went over to Seleucus. Nicanor was forced to fly. Susiana, Media, and Persia fell to Seleucus, who thus won a powerful position. The feeling of the upper satrapies was not favourable to Antigonus, which was to Seleucus' advantage. The governors of those parts either voluntarily submitted or, as in Bactria, were forced into submission. Similarly he tried to make the Macedonian power once more felt in India, where it had been destroyed since the establishment of a strong native empire by Chandragupta. Seleucus crossed the Indus to fight him, but concluded a peace on favourable terms for the Indian prince. In return for a tribute of 500 elephants he confirmed Chandragupta in his former dominions, and

Tribute from India a subsequent alliance by marriage established permanent friendly relations between the two empires. Seleucus had thus in a few years founded an empire and grown strong enough to interfere in the West. Like his neighbour, he assumed the royal diadem in 306 B.C. The advance of Demetrius Poliorcetes in Hellas, and his pressure on Cassander, induced the latter immediately to turn to Antigonus, in order to make his peace with him. Antigonus demanded complete submission, and thus unequivocally asserted his claims to the overlordship. Lysimachus, Ptolemy, and Seleucus, to whom Cassander communicated this answer, saw the common danger—all four kings concluded a new treaty of alliance and began the war against Antigonus. But only Lysimachus and Seleucus took active part in it. When the former marched across the Hellespont to Asia Minor, Seleucus went to join him with his army in Phrygia, and in conjunction with Lysimachus offered Antigonus battle at Ipsus in 301 B.C., where Antigonus was defeated and slain.

The allies divided the spoils. The chief share in it, as was fair, fell to the two actual conquerors. Lysimachus received north-western Asia Minor— Caria, Lydia, Ionia and Hellespontine

Phrygia; Seleucus had Greater Phrygia and Syria. Ptolemy, who as a member of the alliance against Antigonus had invaded Syria, but had again evacuated the land on the false news of a victory and further advance of Antigonus, was forced to waive his claim on Syria, for the possession of which he had long striven. The expedition of Demetrius Poliorcetes—who had lost Macedonia— into Asia in 286 B.C. was without noteworthy influence on the affairs of Asia Minor, for he soon fell into the power of Seleucus and died a prisoner in 282 B.C. But once again Seleucus had to take the field. Lysimachus had caused his son and successor, Agathocles, to be killed on the malicious accusation of his wife, Arsinoe, and her brother, Ptolemy Ceraunos, who had fled from Egypt to Macedonia because his younger brother had been appointed successor. Lysandra, widow of Agathocles, fled with her children to Seleucus in Syria. Thither also resorted Ceraunos, who no longer felt himself secure in Macedonia, and another son of Lysimachus, by name Alexander.

Thrace and Asia Minor Gained Seleucus received them all with friendly hospitality. Hence a war broke out in 281 B.C. between Lysimachus and Seleucus. Lysimachus was killed in battle, and Seleucus entered on his inheritance in Asia Minor and Europe.

Seleucus appointed his son Antiochus, who had for a long time administered the upper satrapies, regent of Asia, desiring himself to reside in Macedonia, in order to end his days in the land of his birth; while he intended Thrace for the children of the murdered Agathocles. He had already landed in Europe when, in 281 B.C., he fell beneath the dagger of Ceraunos, the very man who had shortly before fled to him, beseeching help. The murderer made himself master of Macedonia and Thrace.

In a long life Seleucus had, indeed, learnt the uncertainty of all things, but towards the end had enjoyed permanent prosperity and had attained greatness. Shortly before he died the greater part of Alexander's empire was in his hands. But he was not merely a fortunate conqueror, who forced large tracts of land to his own rule, and might with justice style himself Nicator, or Conqueror, but he resembled Alexander the Great in having done all that lay in his power to

disseminate Hellenic culture, while he promoted trade and traffic in his own dominions and opened new sources of prosperity. He continued on a magnificent scale the policy of colonisation begun by Alexander. The founding of seventy-five towns is ascribed to him, including Seleucia on the Tigris, which, rapidly flourishing, contained soon after **Founder of Seventy-five Towns** the Christian era 600,000 inhabitants; Antioch on the Orontes, which flourished even in later antiquity; Seleucia Pieria, the port of Antioch; Seleucia on the Calycadnus in Cilicia; Laodicea in the Lebanon, and Apamea on the Orontes. In the east also numerous towns were founded on the Greek model, with a senate and a popular assembly; and these soon became centres of culture and growing prosperity.

When Seleucus I., Nicator, died, the empire established by him had attained its greatest expansion. The power of the Seleucidæ—the name usually given in honour of its creator and founder to the dynasty which, through Seleucus, became lords of these dominions—stretched then from the Bosphorus and the western coast of Asia Minor to the Indus and from Syria to the Jaxartes and the Pamir. Those who wish to designate the empire of Seleucus no longer by the reigning dynasty, but by a geographical term, are accustomed to call it, in accordance with the true position and the real fulcrum of the power of its rulers, the Syrian empire; this designation is, indeed, less appropriate for the period of Seleucus and his immediate successors than for the later Seleucidæ.

But this empire was merely a conglomeration of countries, inhabited by the most heterogeneous nations. In this lay its weakness. Seleucus at first resided in Babylon, at about the centre of his empire. He afterwards removed his residence to Antioch on the Orontes—that is to say, **Antioch the Capital** almost to the western border. This shifting of the centre of gravity of the empire from its central point to the circumference was clearly due to the fact that Seleucus had entrusted his son, Antiochus, with the administration of the upper satrapies; but Antioch remained the capital even after his death. The choice of the royal residence was a very important matter for the empire, which, badly defined and devoid of natural coherence in all respects, as it was, found its ideal unity only in the person of its monarch. Although the Seleucidæ obviously did not renounce any claim on the eastern satrapies by this arrangement, these became, in fact, far removed from the heart of the empire and withdrew more and more from the influence of the central authority. The

The Love of Antiochus first successor of Seleucus was his son, Antiochus, surnamed Soter, who even in his father's lifetime had administered as co-regent the countries lying east of the Euphrates. He had taken to wife Stratonice, daughter of Demetrius Poliorcetes. Stratonice was originally married to his father, but had been voluntarily surrendered by the latter to the son, who was wasting away with love for her, an occurrence which soon became a fertile subject for the Greek writers of romances. He followed his father's example, and nominated his two sons as regents ; first the elder, Seleucus, and after his murder, the younger, Antiochus.

The history of the next two generations, which are taken up by the reigns of Antiochus I., Soter (281–261), Antiochus II., Theos (261–246), and Seleucus II., Callinicus (246–226), is marked by the relations of Syria to Egypt and by the wars which the Seleucidæ had to wage with the neighbour states. The position of Syria as regards the states of Asia Minor was not less important. In addition, there was the defection of the countries on the Oxus and Jaxartes ; for now began the subjugation of the Parthian province by the neighbouring inhabitants of the steppes and the formation of the new Parthian empire.

Complications with Egypt began directly after the death of Seleucus. The first question at issue was that of the possession of Phœnicia and Cœle-Syria, countries to which Ptolemy Soter laid claim on the ground that he had conquered them

Wars with the Ptolemies in 318 B.C., had lost them through Antigonus, but had demanded them once more on the occasion of the last alliance of the kings against Antigonus as a prize of victory for his share in the war. Since, however, the battle at Ipsus had been fought without Ptolemy's assistance, Syria had been awarded to Seleucus in the distribution. For this reason Ptolemy's son and successor, Ptolemy Philadelphus, soon after the death of Seleucus, began the

First Syrian War. We know little of its course. Philadelphus conquered Cœle-Syria, the southern part of Syria, and by means of his fleet brought strips of the coast of Asia Minor under his rule, so that Egypt firmly established herself on the coasts of Cilicia, Pamphylia, Lycia, Caria, and Ionia.

But besides the Ptolemies, other foes to the Seleucidæ had arisen in Asia Minor. In the north-western corner lay Bithynia, which had been able under native princes to preserve its independence throughout the whole of their period. Even the attempt made by Antiochus, immediately after his accession, to subdue Bithynia had failed. To the south-west of it, in the valley of the Caïcus, lay Pergamus, a strong fortress, the commander of which, Philetærus, revolted from his new masters, the Seleucidæ, after Lysimachus' death, and, being amply provided with funds, was able to lay skilfully the foundations of an important dominion. In addition, the Galatians had come into Asia Minor as a new power. They had been invited in

Coming of the Gauls 277 B.C. by Nicomedes of Bithynia to come over from Thrace, and had remained here. They occupied the country on the upper Sangarius and middle Halys, and as far as political influence went, greatly contributed to the disintegration of Asia Minor. Against them also Antiochus had to fight to protect his territory. It is recorded that he defeated the Galatians. This victory helped to confine them to the district called, after them, Galatia, but it did not effect their subjugation. Antiochus was still more unlucky in the war against Eumenes of Pergamus, in which he was defeated at Sardis. Soon afterwards he died, in 261 B.C.

His son and successor, Antiochus II., surnamed Theos, who reigned from 261 to 246 B.C., was not in a position to alter the state of affairs in Asia Minor and to win back the districts torn from his kingdom. With Egypt he waged the Second Syrian War. We know nothing more of it than that its objects, the recovery of Cœle-Syria and the driving out of the Egyptians from the coast of Asia Minor, were not realised. The status quo was recognised in the subsequent peace ; and to seal and confirm it, Ptolemy Philadelphus gave his daughter Berenice to Antiochus in marriage. Antiochus' first wife, Laodice, who was disgraced and divorced for the sake of the Egyptian princess, in revenge poisoned her husband and instigated her eldest son, the new king, Seleucus II., surnamed Callinicus, to the murder of his stepmother. To avenge this crime, Ptolemy Euergetes, who in 246 B.C. had followed Philadelphus on the Egyptian throne, began the Third Syrian War. While Euergetes marched to Syria at the head of his troops his fleet sailed from Cyprus to Cilicia, where his many Seleucid officials, as well as many Cilician towns, voluntarily joined the Egyptians; the officials devoted to their old lord, had

Only Seleucia and the Cilician coast remained in the Egyptian power.

The reign of Seleucus II. was extremely stormy and disturbed; and its records lack coherence. His brother Antiochus, surnamed Hierax, disputed with him the dominion over Asia Minor and rose against him, relying on the independent states of the Bithynians, Cappadocians, and Galatians. But in the war of the two brothers against each other and in that with Attalus, Prince of Pergamus, who conquered and routed Hierax, the country as far as the Taurus was lost to the Seleucidæ. Hierax was murdered in

THE LOVE OF ANTIOCHUS FOR HIS STEP-MOTHER STRATONICE

Stratonice, daughter of Demetrius Poliorcetes, was married to Seleucus I., who voluntarily surrendered her to his son Antiochus because the latter was wasting away with love for her. From the picture by De Lairesse.

to fly, and the towns who favoured him were besieged. The fleet then sailed for North Syria. Seleucia, the important coast town, and later Antioch, the capital, which lies a short distance from it, were occupied. Euergetes himself crossed the Euphrates with an army, made himself master of the upper satrapies, and brought back the treasures and relics which the Persians had in earlier times carried off from the Egyptians. In spite of such astounding successes, the Egyptian king suddenly concluded peace, because, it was said, uproar and revolt in his own country summoned him back.

his flight by robbers about 227 B.C. Even in the east the dominion of the Seleucidæ fared badly. In the time of Antiochus Theos the Bactrian governor, Diodotus, had revolted. He proclaimed himself king of Bactria, and was recognised in Sogdiana and Margiana in 250 B.C. About the same time the brothers Arsaces and Tiridates, chiefs of the nomadic tribe of the Parni, whose pasturing-grounds were on Bactrian territory, had moved further west and had occupied the Seleucid territory of Astabene. Arsaces was immediately proclaimed king there. Thence they invaded Parthia, and, after defeating the governor, made themselves masters of the country. The attempt of Seleucus Callinicus to expel Arsaces failed, and the Parthian empire of the Arsacidæ became established more firmly; it disappeared only in 226 A.D., after a duration of 480 years. When Callinicus died, in 226 B.C., the Seleucid empire comprised only Northern Syria, without the important seaport Seleucia Pieria; Cilicia, with the exception of the coast; and the land eastward from the Euphrates as far as Media, Susiana, and Persia. Asia Minor this side of the Taurus and all the land east of Media was in the hands of the enemy: Cœle-Syria and Phœnicia, for which battles had so often been fought, belonged now, as formerly, to the Egyptians.

The Reduced Empire

Seleucus III., surnamed Soter, eldest son of Callinicus, reigned only a short time—226–223 B.C. He was assassinated while on a campaign over the Taurus against Attalus of Pergamus. He was followed by his brother, Antiochus III. (223–187 B.C.), aged twenty, to whom the surname Megas, or the Great, has been given. At first he was a pliant tool in the hand of his first Minister, Hermeias, an intriguing Carian. The settlement of affairs in Asia Minor, where, after 227, Attalus had extended his territory up to the Taurus, and the war with Pergamus, were entrusted by him to his cousin, Achæus. He himself planned a war against Egypt, in order to bring once for all under his power the long-disputed Cœle-Syria. And in this plan he still held firmly to the counsel of Hermeias, when, in 222 B.C., news was brought him of the revolt of the Median satrap Molon, and his brother Alexander, who governed Persia. Antiochus did not himself march until Molon had conquered several of his generals, placed the diadem on his head, and, starting from Apolloniatis after the capture of Seleucia on the Tigris, had actually taken Babylonia. In 220 B.C. Antiochus crossed the Tigris and pushed into Apolloniatis, in order to cut off his enemy's retreat into Media. A battle was fought, Molon was defeated, and died by his own hand. As a warning example his corpse was crucified and displayed on the highest point of the Zagros Mountains, over which the road from the West into Media led. Antiochus settled affairs with leniency and moderation.

Wars of Antiochus the Great

Seleucia alone was severely punished. He then invaded Atropatene. Here the prince, Artabazanes, who had taken Molon's side, was terrified by the sudden invasion and made a treaty favourable to Antiochus. Hermeias, the powerful Minister, was afterwards murdered.

Antiochus on his return to Syria began extensive preparations for the Egyptian war. The campaign of the year 219 B.C. opened favourably. Seleucia Pieria, the port of Antioch, which had been Egyptian since the time of Ptolemy Euergetes, was taken. The Egyptian governor of Cœle-Syria, Theodotus, an Ætolian, went over to Antiochus and delivered up the seaports of Ptolemais and Tyre. Other towns also surrendered to him. But what was universally expected did not happen. Instead of attacking Egypt, which was ill-prepared for war, the king marched back from the Phœnician coast to Seleucia. Now began negotiations by Ptolemy's Ministers, Agatholes and Sosibus, while they were busily arming; and in the winter of 219-218 B.C. the conclusion of a four months' truce was actually obtained.

A Truce After Victory

In the summer of 218 Antiochus was again in Cœle-Syria and defeated the Egyptians; but when Ptolemy, in 217 B.C., after mighty preparations, took the field in person, Antiochus was beaten at Raphia on the borders of Syria and Egypt and was forced to relinquish the conquered districts. Ptolemy made no further use of his victory.

Meantime, in Asia Minor, Achæus had revolted from Antiochus and had been proclaimed king. Antiochus took up the war, and in 216 marched over the Taurus, forced the enemy back to Sardis, and after a siege of two years took the town by a stratagem. Achæus was delivered into the hands of Antiochus, who caused him to be executed.

There now followed a series of successful operations. In 209 B.C. Antiochus undertook a campaign of several years' duration in the East. He first invaded the territory of the Parthians, where the Arsacid dynasty was compelled to recognise the supremacy of Syria. He then marched to Bactria. Euthydemus encountered him on the Areios, but had to retreat after a gallant fight. Bactria, the capital, was besieged; and Euthydemus, reduced to great straits, threatened

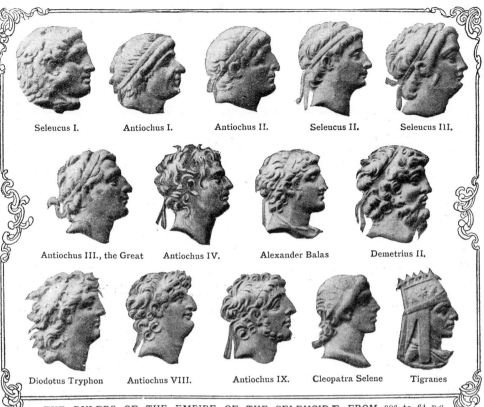

| Seleucus I. | Antiochus I. | Antiochus II. | Seleucus II. | Seleucus III. |

| Antiochus III., the Great | Antiochus IV. | Alexander Balas | Demetrius II. |

| Diodotus Tryphon | Antiochus VIII. | Antiochus IX. | Cleopatra Selene | Tigranes |

THE RULERS OF THE EMPIRE OF THE SELEUCIDÆ FROM 306 to 64 B.C.

The dynasty and empire of the Seleucidæ was founded by Seleucus I. about 306 B.C. Under the rule of his three successors, Antiochus I. and II. and Seleucus II., who waged the three Syrian Wars, the realm fared badly. Seleucus III. reigned for three stormy years, but his brother, Antiochus III., the Great, restored the empire to its original importance. Both he and his son, Antiochus IV., however, had to submit to Rome. Alexander Balas, an upstart king encouraged by Rome, was driven out by Demetrius II., and he, in turn, by Diodotus Tryphon. Antiochus VIII. and IX. and the latter's son all married, in turn, Cleopatra Selene. Tigranes, king of Armenia, conquered Syria before the final supremacy of Rome. The portraits are from coins in the British Museum.

to call the nomads into the country and to give up the Greek civilisation to their mercy. The Seleucid, whose house had disseminated Greek culture everywhere, did not refuse to listen to such arguments. The parties then concluded an offensive and defensive alliance in 206 B.C. Antiochus now went over the Hindu-Kush into the valley of Kabul and renewed with the Indian king, Subhagasena, the friendship which Seleucus Nicator had formed with Chandragupta. Subhagasena also gave him elephants and furnished his army with provisions. He began his return through Arachosia and Drangiana and wintered in Carmania, or Kerman. From there he made a digression towards the opposite Arabian coast to the rich trading nation of the Gerrhæi.

Thence the king returned to Seleucia. This campaign brought the Seleucid name once more into honour in the East, and won for the king among his contemporaries the surname of "the Great."

In the meanwhile, the young Ptolemy Epiphanes had come to the throne in Egypt in 205 B.C. The kings Antiochus of Syria and Philip V. of Macedonia concluded therefore a treaty, with the avowed object of seizing the Egyptian possessions and of dividing them among themselves. Philip crossed into Asia Minor, but was there entangled in a war with Pergamus, Rhodes, and lastly with Rome herself. Antiochus sought to realise his former intentions against Cœle-Syria and Phœnicia. The diplomatic interference of Rome in favour of her ward, Epiphanes, was not able to check the king in his project, successfully begun, of subjugating Cœle-Syria, which was completed by the defeat of the Egyptians under the Ætolian mercenary, Scopas, on Mount Paneum, near the sources of the Jordan, in 198 B.C. Cœle-Syria and Phœnicia thus became once more Syrian.

Marriage With Egypt As Antiochus wished to have a free hand for Asia Minor and Europe, he concluded peace with Egypt and sealed it by the betrothal of his daughter Cleopatra to Ptolemy Epiphanes.

In 196 B.C. Antiochus crossed over to Europe, occupied the Chersonese, rebuilt Lysimacheia, made this town his arsenal, and set about the conquest of Thrace, as if all belonged to him which his great ancestor, Nicator, would have ruled if he had not been suddenly murdered. The strained relations with Rome were intensified when Antiochus hospitably received Hannibal, Rome's greatest foe. After diplomatic negotiations, war with Rome finally broke out, when Antiochus, at the instigation of the Ætolians, crossed to Greece in 192 B.C. and began to subdue Hellenic towns and provinces. Contemptuously ignorant of Roman power, he landed with ten thousand infantry and five hundred cavalry. He attempted to bar the advance of the Roman army at Thermopylæ, but was eluded and defeated. With few followers he fled to Asia Minor in 191 B.C. The Syrian fleet also had been defeated at sea : first in 191 B.C. by C. Livius at Corycus, between Chios and Ephesus, then in 190 B.C. by Æmilius at Myonnesus. The king's consternation at this reverse was so great that he evacuated Lysimacheia, his fortified arsenal on the Thracian coast, and thus left the road to the Hellespont free to Cornelius Scipio. The decisive battle took place at Magnesia on Mount Sipylos ; Antiochus was completely defeated in 190 B.C. By the terms **Expensive Peace With Rome** of the peace he had to cede Asia Minor as far as the Taurus, to surrender his elephants and his fleet, except ten ships, and to pay a war indemnity of 15,000 Euboic talents (£4,800,000), of which 3,000 were to be paid at once, and 12,000 in the course of the next twelve years. Soon afterwards Antiochus was killed by the Elymæi, or Elamites, on an expedition to the East, where he wished to plunder the

temple of Belus, in order to fill his empty coffers in 187 B.C.

Antiochus was succeeded by his sons, Seleucus IV., surnamed Philopator (187–175 B.C.), and Antiochus IV., surnamed Epiphanes (175–164 B.C.). Seleucus, who had to struggle with the financial distress caused by the payments to Rome, was murdered by his minister, Heliodorus. The latter attempted to usurp the throne, but could not hold it. Antiochus came to the throne, supported by Pergamus. He was immediately entangled in a war with Egypt. His sister, Cleopatra, had married Ptolemy Epiphanes in 193 B.C. and had received as a bridal gift the assignment of the taxes from several towns in Cœle-Syria. Cleopatra died in 173 B.C. and disputes arose over her dowry. The Egyptians claimed the towns, and demanded the continuance of the payments even after the death of the queen. Antiochus declined, since the Syrian claim of supremacy had never been relinquished there. Very shortly, war resulted. A victory at Pelusium delivered that important town into **Antiochus Conquers Egypt** the hands of Antiochus, and made his road to Egypt open. The king, Ptolemy Philometor, fell into the hands of the enemy, and at the wish of the people his brother, Physcon, undertook the government in Egypt. Epiphanes was repulsed, but kept Pelusium. Philometor, having regained his freedom, came to an agreement with his brother. Epiphanes now attacked Egypt afresh and besieged Alexandria.

At this juncture C. Popillius Lænas appeared in the camp of the king at Alexandria with an order from the Roman senate, bidding Antiochus leave Egypt at once. He marched out of Egypt, and gave up Pelusium, but kept Cœle-Syria and Phœnicia in 168 B.C. The peremptory command of Rome had been enough. Enlightened by his father's disaster, and feeling himself not strong enough to wage a war with Rome, he was compelled to recognise the domineering foreign power in distant Italy, and submit himself to it. In the course of a generation, then, Syria had fallen for ever from the position of a world-power, which it held under Antiochus III.

We have just seen how Armenia had formed itself into two independent kingdoms. The next campaign of Epiphanes was directed thither in 166 B.C. He penetrated far into the land, took King

Artaxias prisoner, but replaced him in his kingdom, just as once his father, notwithstanding successful campaigns, had in the end recognised the kings of Parthia and Bactria. Armenia must certainly at this time have recognised the supremacy of Syria, but it did not again become a Syrian province. From Armenia, Epiphanes turned to the Persian Gulf, where he rebuilt a town founded by Alexander at the mouth of the Tigris, which had fallen to ruins, and called it Antioch. The new Antioch at the mouth of the Tigris having been again destroyed by the floods, was rebuilt afresh by the satrap, Hyspaosines, secured by strong dams, and called Charax. It soon afterwards became a flourishing commercial town and capital of a small kingdom. On the way to Persia to suppress a revolt, Antiochus IV. died at Tabæ, in 164 B.C., of consumption. The story of his relations with Judæa and the Maccabees is related in a following section.

After the short reign of Antiochus V. Eupator (164–162 B.C.), Demetrius I. Soter came to the throne (162–150 B.C.). He was the son of Seleucus IV., and had **Under Roman Tutelage** been at Rome as a hostage when his father was murdered and his uncle, Epiphanes, became king. From the outset he had to contend with the hatred of Roman tutelage. Timarchus, satrap of Media, revolted from Demetrius, and with the assent of the Roman senate assumed the diadem. In alliance with Artaxias of Armenia he soon subdued the neighbouring lands, and became master of Babylonia; but when Demetrius took the field against him, was defeated and slain in 160 B.C. Thus Media and Babylonia were again saved; and the grateful Babylonians, who hated Timarchus, gave to Demetrius the title of Soter, "the Saviour."

But Rome, irritated at the destruction of her protégé, created fresh difficulties for Demetrius and formed an alliance of the neighbouring countries against him, in accordance with which a certain Alexander Balas, who was given out to be the son of Antiochus Epiphanes, set up as a rival king, and invaded Syria. Demetrius fell in the war against him in 150 B.C. The new king, who styled himself Alexander Theopator Euergetes, was, however, totally incapable. Ptolemy Philometor of Egypt, who had joined in supporting him, soon put forward Demetrius, son of Demetrius I., against him. After long struggles, in which

Alexander Balas was worsted, Demetrius II. became king in 145 B.C. But against him also a certain Diodotus rose as a rival under the name of Tryphon, and succeeded in driving Demetrius out of the greater part of Syria. The effect of these calamitous civil wars was soon apparent. The rich and fertile provinces of Media and **Victories of the Parthians** Babylonia were now lost and passed into the power of the Parthians. Seleucia, on the Tigris, the proud creation of the first Seleucidæ, was taken by them, and Demetrius II. himself was defeated by the Parthians and taken prisoner in 138 B.C.

His brother, Antiochus VII. Sidetes, who took his place in Syria, succeeded in ending the civil dissensions, after removing Tryphon, and in re-establishing the royal power. In 130 B.C. he undertook a campaign against the Parthians. The latter, being defeated on the Lycus, now released his brother Demetrius from captivity, probably in the hope that he would begin afresh the civil war and thus draw off Antiochus from Parthia. But before that happened the Parthians once more confronted Antiochus, and this time he was defeated and slain in 129 B.C. Thenceforth the dominion of the Seleucidæ was limited to the countries west of the Euphrates.

When Demetrius returned to his home under Parthian auspices, he began a war immediately with Egypt. The Syrian towns, especially the capital Antioch, and Apamea, sick of incessant war and misgovernment, and contemptuous of a Parthian protégé, revolted; and Ptolemy of Egypt set up against him in Syria Zabinas, the son of a merchant, who received the name of Alexander, and was passed off for an adopted son of the fallen Antiochus. He succeeded in defeating Demetrius, and the unpopular Demetrius went to Tyre, where he was killed as he disembarked from his ship in 125 B.C. **Antiochus "Long Nose"** Demetrius II. had two sons by his marriage with Cleopatra. Of these, Seleucus was killed by his own mother soon after the father's death, because he had assumed the diadem without her consent; the other, however, mounted the throne. A disturbed reign was the lot of this Antiochus VIII. Grypus, or "Long Nose," as it had been that of his father. A breach between Ptolemy and the rival king, Alexander Zabinas, led to closer relations between the Egyptian and Grypus, in consequence of which the latter received not only ample assistance from Egypt, but also the hand of the Egyptian princess, Tryphaena. This open help from Egypt brought many Syrian towns to the side of Grypus, who thus, being supported on all sides, could confront his rival. Alexander

War of the Brothers Zabinas was worsted in the battle; a fugitive, he was seized by robbers, and was brought to Grypus and killed. Thus Grypus was lord and ruler of his father's realm. He did not, however, long enjoy the sole rule. His stepbrother, Antiochus IX. Cyzicenus, opposed him. The war between the brothers led eventually to a partition of the realm. Grypus obtained Syria proper and Cilicia; Cyzicenus had Cœle-Syria and Phœnicia. In the year 96 B.C. Grypus was murdered. His son, Seleucus VI., repulsed, indeed, the attack of Cyzicenus, but had to fight with his four brothers. In Cœle-Syria and Phœnicia, after the death of Cyzicenus, his son, Antiochus X. Eusebes, " the Pious," reigned. He married—an event which throws light on the morality of family relations at that time — his own mother, Cleopatra Selene, who had been the wife of Grypus and then of Cyzicenus, after having been previously wedded to Ptolemy Lathyrus of Egypt.

A greatly diminished empire, torn by fraternal wars and civil dissension, whose history teemed with murder and horrors of every kind—that is the unedifying picture of the conditions of the Seleucid dynasty about 100 B.C. There was no longer any thought of accomplishing the great task pointed out by Seleucus, that of making the powerful empire into a state which should spread the blessings of civilisation and should find its most honourable work in the dissemination of Hellenism.

Antiochus III. had ultimately given back to the empire for a brief moment the position which it had held under the first Seleucidæ, although none of the successors had ruled an empire as wide as that which Seleucus had bequeathed to them. Antiochus Epiphanes and Antiochus Sidetes had striven earnestly to re-establish the former power, but all they created or founded soon fell to pieces again.

Under their successors the empire was abandoned to the influence of the neighbouring powers. The intervention of Rome or Egypt in Syrian affairs proved too often fateful and calamitous to the house of the Seleucidæ.

In this helpless condition of the empire King Tigranes of Armenia was able to conquer first Syria proper in 83 B.C. and then the greater part of Phœnicia with Ptolemais in 74 B.C. The Roman, Lucullus, prepared the death blow to his supremacy in these regions. Shortly after, in the year 64 B.C., Pompey appeared in Syria and put an end to the Seleucid rule. Henceforth Syria ceases to have any history of its own. It flourished under the strong arm of the Roman emperors, for Rome carefully continued all that the Seleucidæ had accomplished by the extension of Hellenic culture. The land passed from the Romans to the Byzantines, and from them to the Arabs.

K. G. Brandis
H. R. Hall

GREEK INFLUENCE ON INDIAN ART
The wonderful Buddhist art of Gandhara, the modern district of Peshawar, of which the above is an example, was based on the tradition of classical art brought to Bactria and India by Greeks.

WESTERN
ASIA TO THE
TIME OF
MAHOMET

III
BACTRIA

BACTRIA : A GREEK CENTRE IN THE EAST

NORTH of the Hindu-Kush, west of the Pamirs, and east of Iran there stretches towards the Caspian Sea and the Sea of Aral a wide region, through which two streams, the Oxus and the Jaxartes flow. In antiquity the country on the upper course of the Oxus was called Bactria, on which Sogdiana bordered in the direction of the Jaxartes, towards the north, while the country on the lower courses of these two rivers, which stretched to the Caspian and the Sea of Aral, was usually called Chorasmia or Khwarezm.

The Bactrian kingdom, the rulers of which are said to have fought for many centuries against the Turanians—that is, against the nomads—and to have won great victories, was of immense antiquity. But the kings in the accounts handed down are mere mythical figures.

The Bactrian kings ended when Cyrus on his great expedition to the East subdued Bactria and gave the administration of the **Bactria Under Persia** land to his brother, Bardias. The supremacy of Persia over the Iranic East was maintained until Alexander the Great, as heir of the Persian empire, which had been destroyed by him, subdued Bactria and Sogdiana in the course of his conquests. He sought, by founding towns —among them Alexandria Eschate on the Jaxartes—to ensure the obedience of the conquered country and to win it over to Greek civilisation. He settled Macedonian and Greek soldiers here ; and these, doubtless, were joined soon by merchants and enterprising persons of all sorts, since the country, through which of old the wares of India were brought to the Black Sea, promised rich profits.

On the tidings of Alexander's death, the Greeks settled by him in the military colonies, consisting of 20,000 foot-soldiers and 3,000 horsemen, marched out, wishing to force their way to their old home ; but, at the orders of the regent, Perdiccas, Peithon, governor of Media, went against them, defeated them through the treachery of one of their leaders, and his victorious troops put them and their generals to the sword, in order to seize their property. Notwithstanding this, the Macedonian supremacy remained unshaken here.

When Seleucus became governor of Babylonia and founded round it a great empire for himself, Bactria and Sogdiana **Settling a Greek Colony** formed part of it. The first Seleucidæ spared no precautions to secure these Eastern dominions. Alexandria Eschate was strengthened, and a new town, Antioch, founded in the same district, and others were restored or strengthened. These countries remained provinces of the Seleucid empire until, in the year 250 B.C., the governor, Diodotus, revolted and caused himself to be proclaimed king. Margiana and Sogdiana belonged from the first to the new kingdom. The times had been peculiarly favourable for the revolt. The successors of Seleucus Nicator had been so occupied in Asia Minor and by the wars with Egypt that their attention had been completely diverted from the Far East. The Bactrian empire was able, in the meanwhile, to strengthen itself. The treaty that Diodotus II., the son and successor of the first king, made with Tiridates of Parthia against Callinicus shows that both rulers recognised their common danger. Diodotus might enjoy his possession undisturbed so long as the Parthian empire lay between him and his former masters.

But the dynasty of Diodotus was soon dethroned by a Greek from Magnesia, in Asia Minor, named Euthydemus. When Antiochus III. had brought the Parthians at least to recognise the Seleucid supremacy and marched against Bactria in 208 B.C., Euthydemus ruled there. The campaign ended with the recognition of **Greek Rule in Bactria** Euthydemus as king, and with the betrothal of his son Demetrius to Antiochus' daughter in consequence of the Bactrian ruler's threat of calling the nomads into the country and giving up Hellenic civilisation to their mercy. The treaty shows the importance attached both by Euthydemus and Antiochus to Bactria as a barrier against the " Scythian " barbarians.

The same Demetrius, to whom Antiochus III. had betrothed his daughter while his father still lived, crossed the Hindu-Kush and extended the Bactrian rule as far as the Indus and the Punjab. Thus, the valley of Kabul and the Punjab, which Alexander had once possessed, were won back to Hellenism. The old town **Bactrian Conquests in India** of Sangala, henceforth called Euthydemia, was made the capital of the Indian possessions. About the same time Arachosia, where the city of Demetrias, so called after Demetrius, was founded, and probably also Aria and Drangiana were made subject to the Bactrian supremacy. This is the period of Bactria's greatest power. Demetrius succeeded his father, Euthydemus, in the government, but was fated to see Eucratidas successfully contest the rule with him. Eucratidas also fought against the tribes inhabiting Aria, Drangiana, Sogdiana, and Arachosia. We have no details about these internal wars,

and culture from them. At any rate, these conditions greatly simplified the conquest of Bactria by the barbarians.

When, about 140 B.C., the Yue-tshi, nomads akin to the Tibetans, driven by the Turkish people of the Hiungnu from their abodes, appeared on the Bactrian frontiers, in order to seek new homes for themselves there, they found no opposition. The land as far as the Oxus fell to them. This sealed the fate of Greek culture north of the Hindu-Kush. South of the Hindu-Kush the Greeks maintained themselves a century longer. Among the numerous kings, handed down to us on coins, who seem to belong to this era and this country, only Menander is known from other sources also. He extended his dominion over the Punjab up to the middle course of the Ganges, but ruled also down to the mouth of the Indus and east of it in Syrastene, the present Gujerat. He is said to have been a Buddhist, and was renowned for his

| Diodotus | Euthydemus I. | Demetrius | Eucratidas | Euthydemus II. |

CONTEMPORARY PORTRAITS OF RULERS OF BACTRIA FROM THEIR COINAGE
Diodotus proclaimed himself king in 250 B.C. His dynasty was overthrown by the Greek Euthydemus, who was followed by his son Demetrius. Eucratidas, in turn, overthrew him. Euthydemus II. was one of the later kings.

but only hear that the Parthians, under Mithradates, at this time became masters of Aria, or Herat, and that Eucratidas, on his return from an expedition to India, was murdered by his son.

But in addition to him there were other kings. The civil war had thus had ruinous consequences. Numerous royal names have been handed down to us on the coins, and the empire was clearly broken up into separate portions, the respective kings of which were at war with each other. But however little we are able to give with certainty the order of succession among the recorded kings, or the period of their reign, or the country where this or that king ruled, still it is very certain that this empire, weakened by intestine wars and manifold divisions, must have continually become more alienated from its chief task—namely, that of keeping the barbarians far from its frontiers and in protecting civilisation

justice. This Greek dominion in India was ended by a chief called by the Chinese Kieu-tsieu-Kio, or Kadphises in the Greek legend on the coins, the prince of Kushang, one of the five tribes into which the Yue-tshi were broken up. After he had united all these nomads into one aggregate, he conquered Kabul and Kophene south of the Hindu-Kush. His son, Kadaphes, added part of India to his dominions. This Scytho-Indian **Greek Art in India** empire lasted to the end of the fourth century A.D. Its central point was the territory of Gandhara, the modern district of Peshawar. Here developed in the first century B.C. the wonderful Buddhist art which was based on the tradition of classical art brought to Bactria and India by the Greeks [see the statue of Buddha reproduced on page 1846]. The influence of Greek art on that of Gandhara is obvious.

THE JEWS AFTER THE CAPTIVITY

WITH the Persian conquest of Babylonia, the "Babylonian captivity" of the Jews was brought to an end. Cyrus, who on the whole followed the policy of granting self-government to small communities, had nothing to say against the desire of the fervent Jews to sacrifice to God in His own dwelling place. He granted permission for the return. From this point we have as authorities only the Books of Ezra and Nehemiah. From the post-exile narratives, such as the Chronicles furnish, it is impossible to gather even such facts as can be established from the Books of the Kings. Ezra and Nehemiah write in the spirit of the Chronicles—namely, from the standpoint of the hierarchical party. Although we are unable, in the absence of other sources of information, to compare their statements with secular narratives or evidences, historians may make use of them by recognising the **Return From Exile** bias which underlies their narrative. Soon after the occupation of Babylon by Cyrus, in 539 B.C., a caravan of Jews—stated to consist of 40,000 persons—started for the Promised Land under the leadership of Zerubbabel, a descendant of David and of the priest Jeshua. In Zerubbabel's descent we may see evidence of the belief that the house of David and the priesthood must govern together the promised Jewish kingdom. The newcomers fared like all enthusiasts. They found everything very different from what their spiritual Utopia had made them expect. They could not be prominent in the midst of a population which cared little about the Jewish people, and the kingdom of David soon proved to be still a thing of the future, like the ideal states of so many a Utopian undertaking of later times. On the other hand, the temporal and spiritual powers, the prince of David's lineage and the high-priest, soon fell out. Cambyses then forbade the completion of the Temple.

A new stimulus, or rather, subsidy, was given to the undertaking, in the year 520 B.C., under Darius, at the urgent request of the new community, which found expression in the prophecies of Haggai and Zechariah. The rich body of Jews in Babylonia and elsewhere in the **Help From Darius** empire went out of their way and exerted all their influence to effect the completion of the Temple. At the same time the quarrel between the prince and the high-priest was decided in favour of the latter. The high-priest was recognised as possessing equal privileges. It must, however, have been apparent that the returned exiles had already begun to show themselves ordinary mortals in place of religious sectaries. Many, including the leaders themselves, had abandoned their strict isolation and had begun to seek contact with the heathen world. It was seen from the very first of what spirit "this return from exile" was the offspring. It was an attempt to realise the hierarchical ideals of Judaism, with the aid of its supporters throughout the world. The situation was precisely the same as would be created if the Jewish plutocrats of the present day founded a new Jewish Jerusalem. There never was a state which has been independently developed on the basis of the Jewish code, and there never can be one, for this code is the organisation of a religious body. It arose as such, and as such it was employed; but a state **No Political History** obeys the universal laws of the development of mankind, and these are different from those of a religious body, which lives under their protection. There has never been any political history of Judaism, and least of all can the history of the period we are now examining be regarded as political. A history of Judaism belongs to the internal history of the development of all civilised countries—in fact, of all nations lying within the region of Western civilisation, from the Persian era to the present day. The branch of Judaism, which hoped to attain its ideals in the Promised Land, was far from playing the most prominent part in this development, and it has little or no bearing on the history of the world. Even Chris-

Judaism in Persia tianity did not grow up in the narrow sphere of this Jewish hierarchy, but in the wider domain of the civilised East, flooded by Judaism, as well as in the countries of Hellenistic culture over which it also spread. Judaism, which was a power in the Persian empire and at the court, was forced therefore to make a fresh advance if it did not wish to acknowledge the ideals of its religion to be impracticable. It was powerful and sufficiently imbued with its faith to undertake even costly political attempts. Ezra, described as a Jewish scholar from Babylonia and of priestly descent, received in the year 514 B.C. permission from Darius—tradition erroneously makes him out to be Artaxerxes Longimanus—to head the second great migration to Jerusalem, in order to realise the ideal state of the Jewish hierarchy. The undertaking was carried out with the fullest sanction and support of the state. Judaism accordingly was in a position to obtain a hearing for its wishes at court. But Ezra and his trusted followers soon experienced the stern realities of life to the detriment of their ideals. Ezra met at once with opposition from the most influential part of the population already settled in the land, which was by no means willing to submit to his demands. There was especial opposition to the stringent regulation that non-Jewish wives should be put away, and mixed marriages avoided. Even strict Jewish discipline had to give way before the force of the requirements of daily life.

Rebuilding of Jerusalem Our accounts are vague, and give no actual facts for the ensuing period of his activity until thirteen years had passed. The hierarchical party, in order to secure for themselves the possession of Jerusalem, took steps to rebuild the walls of the city. The secular party, as we may term them, who saw in this the consummation of the rule of the intolerant priesthood, strained every effort in order to hinder the undertaking, through the Persian

officials and the neighbouring princes—Tobiah the Ammonite, Geshem the Arabian—with whom they entered into close relations. But strictly enforced orthodoxy had long been the firm bond of Judaism throughout the empire, and thus the party of the priests won the day. The influence of the Jewish element which listened to them was stronger at court than that of the government officials; and Nehemiah, a Jew holding, it is said, the high post of cupbearer, was enthusiastic enough to devote his powers to the service of the holy cause. The Persian government, meanwhile, came to the conclusion that the purely hierarchical organisation was not a success. Nehemiah was therefore nominated Persian governor, and given full authority, which placed him above the secularised high-priest. Armed with all constitutional authority, which the influence of the great Jewish party procured for him, he started for Jerusalem, and in the face of all the difficulties which his antagonists, supported and incited by the secular party, placed in his path, he carried

Nehemiah Governor of Jerusalem out his purpose of fortifying Jerusalem with a wall. He thus offered to the hierarchy the means by which to exclude the influence of their neighbours, and to control those sections of the population in the city which were in league with them.

Nehemiah is said to have governed in Jerusalem for twelve years, and then to have retired to the court of Susa. But he had hardly turned his back, when the ascendency of the orthodox party was again threatened; he was compelled to return if he was not to abandon the realisation of the ideal religious state. Once more he exerted all the power which the influence of his sect conferred on him in order to exercise compulsion on the refractory; and he converted them by force to an acknowledgment of the strict demands of their religion. Even the family of the high-priest was bound to admit that Israel endured no attack upon its institutions. The Ammonite Tobiah, who was related to the high-priest El-ashib, was expelled from the Temple precincts; and a grandson of the high-priest, who had married a daughter of Sin-uballit, or Sanballat, probably the prince of Moab—not as usually assumed, Samaria — was driven from Jerusalem. Strictest orthodoxy reigned.

EZRA, LEADER OF THE SECOND MIGRATION TO JERUSALEM, READING THE BOOK OF THE LAW

Ezra received permission from Darius to head the second migration from Babylon to Jerusalem, and, with Nehemiah, legalised the experimental state by the publication of the book of the law, which event is here pictured.

The new order of things, such as Ezra and Nehemiah wished to introduce into the experimental state, received its legal confirmation by the publication of the book of the law, which comprised the institutions of Judaism, the priestly code. The account given of the outward ceremonial which attended its solemn publication by Ezra is unimportant; as might be expected, he tells us only of the rejoicings and enthusiasm of the people. The record of the difficulties which had been surmounted enables the historian to form a correct idea of the matter. The law was not the work of Ezra and Nehemiah, nor did they raise it to be the effective law of Judaism. It had long been the standard round which Judaism in the empire rallied; and its introduc-

The Book of The Law

tion into Jerusalem signified only the obligation of the ideal state, restored with the help of Judaism, to observe the law which it had been founded to fulfil. The real development of Judaism was not perfected on the soil of Palestine. The law was not the product of a political community, but of a religious body, and it was not the result of a national struggle for existence. The spirit of the law itself, which had thus been long in force for Judaism throughout the empire, is tolerably familiar. It is the spirit which since then has prevailed and has become only more rigid—the spirit which Judaism has observed down to the present day.

Vague and scanty as are the accounts for this period of the vigorous activity shown by the new Jewish spirit

The Priestly State

in the process of its development, they are still more so during the ensuing period of the Persian rule. We can, however, reconcile ourselves to this lack of information. The hierarchy which was here established presents in no respect a momentous event in the history of mankind. It was not even a unique phenomenon in the history of antiquity. Similar constitutions were possible even in the sphere of pagan religions, as is shown, for example, by the priestly state in Comana, in Cappadocia. In the Persian period the development of the hierarchy continued to advance. Although Ezra and Nehemiah exercised a sort of secular power, conferred on them by the court, and were to some extent governors, and although from the first there had been the wish to uphold the royal dignity of David, yet power was gradually concentrated in the hands of the high-priest. The Persian court looked on quietly at this growth, which threatened no danger to the maintenance of order and was fostered by the influential body of Jews. As punishment for an attempt to take part in the Syrian insurrection against Artaxerxes Ochus, the Jews had to submit to the deportation of part of their population into Hyrcania; the satrap Bagoas is said then to have shown that Persia would not tolerate any contumacy. Dissensions, which are reported to have been rife at this period in the family of the high-priest and to have led to the murder by the high-priest of his own brother, were certainly connected with the hostility of the rival parties, but are, after all, of no great importance.

Growth of the Priesthood

When Persia broke up, the Jews are said from the very first to have secured for themselves the favour of Alexander by adroit compliance. From this point onward we possess accounts which are influenced, even more than those of the Persian period, by Jewish self-complacency. Flavius Josephus is an untrustworthy and, from his conceit, irritating authority.

The disputes among the Diadochi severed Egypt from Babylonia. Syria was the apple of discord, but soon came under Egyptian influence. During the prosperity of Egypt under the Ptolemies we see Judaism also powerful and prosperous and affording welcome assistance to the government in all matters of trade and of administration.

Judaism undoubtedly did not then come to the front in Egypt for the first time. Just as one part of the hierarchical party had been brought by Nebuchadnezzar to Babylonia, so another had taken refuge in Egypt. During a later attempt at insurrection, Jeremiah and others had been carried there by force. With the further spread of Judaism these fugitives and newcomers had there, as elsewhere in the empire, gained in importance and had played a prominent part. It is, however, quite plain that the real strength of Judaism lay with the ruling power of the East—that is, in Persia and Babylonia. The East was now divided, and we see at once two centres of Judaism—in Babylonia-Syria and in Egypt. This is again an indication that the evolution of Judaism did not have Palestine for its

Judaism in Egypt

scene. A Hellenic. Judaism now comes into prominence at the court of the Ptolemies, which was able rapidly to appropriate the results of the ripening Hellenic spirit ingrafted on the East, and adroitly adapt them to its own requirements. It was more through this transference of the centre of the power of Judaism from Persia and Babylonia to Egypt than through political conformity to the rule of the Ptolemies that the Jewish state fell under the influence of Egyptian Hellenism. A production of Egyptian Judaism is the Septuagint Version, intended in the first instance for the use of those who could no longer read the Holy Scriptures in the original language.

Towards the end of the third century, in the struggle between the Seleucidæ and the Ptolemies, the former gained the upper hand and Judah became subject to Syrian supremacy. Antiochus III. was received by the Jews with open arms. Assistance was even given in the siege of the Egyptian garrison in the Akra, the citadel of Jerusalem. Antiochus is said to have shown himself correspondingly gracious at first and in particular to have sanctioned a remission of taxation, which was certainly calculated to win men's hearts, since their own compatriots had already proved themselves very active tax-collectors in the service of the Ptolemies. But when the power of Antiochus was afterwards broken by the battle of Magnesia, in 190 B.C., the greater advantage seemed once more to rest in an alliance with Egypt. Antiochus, in order to pay the war indemnity, was certainly forced to wring from his subjects all that he possibly could; on the other hand, the influence of the Egyptian Jews, in whose support hopes were now centred, must have been powerful.

Antiochus in Jerusalem

How far the ever restless spirit of enterprise had already ventured to cross from the land of the Pharaohs to the latter's powerful protectress on the Tiber we do not know, but we can hardly place the beginnings of a Jewish colony in Rome at a much later date. In short, the influential and wealthy members of the Jewish body must now be looked for more and more in Egypt and the west rather than in the east, which at this time under the Parthian rule was quite severed from civilisation. Accordingly, Judah, which was thrown upon the support of those

JUDAS MACCABÆUS, THE HERO OF THE JEWS, ADDRESSING HIS TROOPS

The famous rebellion of the Maccabees against the rule of the Seleucidæ was begun by Mattathias Maccabæus, and waged most successfully by his son Judas, who defeated the Syrians. From the engraving by Gustave Doré.

who held the same faith, was forced in its policy to incline more to the west than to the empire of the Seleucidæ, now approaching its end.

In conformity with old tradition, it was once more the orthodox party that leaned towards Egypt. The Seleucidæ attempted, with the support of the elements in Jerusalem which were inclined to Hellenism, to secure Judah for themselves. Jason, the brother of the high-priest Onias, was favoured by Antiochus IV. For a time everything in Jerusalem followed the Athenian mode, and the theatre and the palæstra attracted the Jewish youth, who were eager to ape their Greek models. The domestic quarrels of the family of the high-priest with the Tobiadæ, the chief representatives of philhellenism, are of no importance here. The accounts do not tell us how, after

Jerusalem Becomes Hellenic the failure of the philhellenic pro-Seleucid party, an open breach with Antiochus IV. was brought about ; but Israel is represented as having been an innocent victim. We may see the reason for the intervention of Antiochus in the fact that the orthodox party really had the upper hand and was in sympathy with Egypt and Rome. When Antiochus, in 168 B.C.,

returned from the expedition to Egypt, which had begun triumphantly and had been so suddenly interrupted by Rome, he called the Jews sternly to account ; they must have known the reason well. Jerusalem was stormed, sacked, and de-

Antiochus Sacks Jerusalem vastated, the walls razed to the ground, the inhabitants massacred and dispersed. Only the " renegades " remained behind and were reinforced by pagan settlers ; all that could escape fled to Egypt.

But the destruction of Jerusalem was not enough. Antiochus knew perfectly well that the power of Judaism did not depend on the existence of the city. He took measures against the entire body of Jews in his dominions, and he must have had deeper motives for his action than his philhellenism. He did not wish to extirpate the Jewish religion, as tradition represents, but to disperse the subject community which had the seat of its power in the enemy's country, and must therefore naturally be in favour of a union with it. His fury was not really directed against the Hebrew religion and its unaccustomed manifestations, and he was no ardent supporter of Zeus. Antiochus did not attack the Jewish religion, but the Jews,

1853

who in his empire courted Egypt and had in their religion a bond which kept them together. It was no accident that the orthodox and the philhellenic parties in the Jewish body collapsed.

Antiochus with his forcible intervention now met the resistance which brutal violence always provokes when opposed to a living ideal, especially that of **Rebellion of the Maccabees** stubborn Judaism. The Books of the Maccabees tell us of those who sealed their faith with their blood, many of whom have had their deeds extolled in verse down to our days. The more violent the measures taken by Antiochus, the more stubborn became the resistance, which finally found its expression, after the characteristic method of the country, in the formation of a band of men, which grew from small beginnings among the mountains into a force that at last could not be easily suppressed. The famous rebellion of the Maccabees has been assumed to be a glorious monument of Jewish heroism, owing to the method of description adopted by our authorities ; but it was nothing extraordinary, and has its parallels by the score in the history of Oriental as well as of other peoples.

The course of the rebellion, according to the account given us by the First Book of the Maccabees, was as follows : In Modin, a place between Jerusalem and the sea, a priest, Mattathias, of the family of the Hasmonæans, resisted the violent Hellenising measures of the Syrians, and gradually collected a band, which was joined by the pious, and succeeded in holding its own among the mountains. On his death soon afterwards, in 166 B.C., his son, Judas Maccabæus, took over the command, and defeated the detachments of Syrian troops sent against him. Antiochus, meanwhile, had started on his Parthian expedition, in the course of which he died. In the place of Philippus, the intended guardian of his son, Antiochus V. Eupator, Lysias usurped **Victories of Judas Maccabæus** the regency of the empire. This latter now sent a larger army against Judas, to help Gorgias, the commander of the troops in Philistia ; but Judas was able by a sudden attack to defeat it also in 165 B.C. When Lysias himself advanced against him in the same year, he had no better success. Judas was now able to reoccupy the pillaged capital, Jerusalem, with the exception of the Akra, which was held by a Syrian garrison. The Temple and divine worship were restored, and in the name of the true God vengeance could now be taken on the " renegades," the adherents of Syria. But we have no particulars of their martyrdom.

For two years Lysias desisted from operations, and Judas ruled with unlimited power as the head of the orthodox party. The country, as may be easily imagined, does not seem to have found this system of administration an unmixed blessing. Numerous attempts at resistance—which our accounts naturally term contemptible raids—were made against the dominance of the minority. It is clear from the records that the country was still far from being Jewish, and that the " liberation " by Judas was in fact a despotism maintained by force of arms, though it championed the cause of right.

It was a fortunate occurence for Judas that Antiochus IV. died on his expedition in 164 B.C., and that Lysias's attention was thus occupied with the arrangement of affairs. Judas proceeded to lay siege to the Akra, which had hitherto been a refuge for the partisans of Syria. The question **Jerusalem Falls to Lysias** of active interference was now urgent for the government. Lysias therefore started with a nominally large army, accompanied by his ward, the young king Antio chus V., and marched against Jerusalem from the south. He defeated Judas in the field near Beth-Zachariah, captured Beth-sura, and besieged Jerusalem where the temple hill had been fortified. After a long resistance, negotiations were begun which Lysias accepted, since he wished to turn his arms against Philippus, who in the interval had raised claims to the crown in Syria. The contents of the treaty are not known ; but since Lysias ordered the execution of Menelaus, the candidate for the high-priesthood who had been previously recognised by him, we may fairly assume that the orthodox party had offered guarantees of their loyalty, and that the trustworthiness of Menelaus had been questioned.

Soon after this, Lysias and Antiochus V. were deposed by Demetrius I., who seems on the whole to have given the Jews in Jerusalem a free hand. He had every reason to avoid a breach with Rome ; however, even then the power of the ubiquitous Judaism was making itself felt. His appointment of Alcimus, of the family of the high-priests, as " Ethnarch," proves

BURIAL OF JONATHAN MACCABÆUS, A HERO OF THE MACCABÆAN REBELLION

At the death of Judas Maccabæus, his brother Jonathan held out against the Syrians, and eventually succeeded in founding the Hasmonæan dynasty, which lasted in Jerusalem from 145 to 63 B.C. From an engraving by Gustave Doré.

1855

that the power of Judas had, as a matter of fact, been restricted by Lysias. Alcimus, ushered in by an army under Bacchides, was accepted without resistance ; since, however, he was a representative of the Syrian Hellenistic party, it would have been strange indeed if he had not very soon aroused the dissatisfaction of the orthodox. Naturally, according to the version in our account, Alcimus was the peace-breaker ; but we may perhaps find a cause for the revolt among the Maccabæans also, who, on his appointment, had certainly been forced to leave Jerusalem. So soon, therefore, as the Syrian army had withdrawn the orthodox party revolted, and Alcimus had once more to fly. He was brought back by an army under Nicanor, and the two were received with acclamations in Jerusalem. The Maccabæans, however, defeated Nicanor at Adasa, in the vicinity of Beth-Horon, in 161 B.C. The country was forced once more to recognise in Judas the " liberator," until Bacchides himself with an army, reputed to have been very large, advanced against him and totally defeated Judas, whose whole following amounted only to 800 men. We may estimate from this his relative importance to the "nation." After a gallant resistance near Elasa, Judas himself was slain. The Hasmonæans thus lost their warlike leader, who had confidence both in himself and his righteous cause.

The Syrian party was once more quit of the blessings conferred by the orthodox, and Alcimus was reinstated in Jerusalem. No sort of restrictions were placed on the exercise of religion. Bacchides restored order in the country and cleared it of the unsettled bands of Maccabæans. A part of them still held out under the leadership of Jonathan, a younger brother of Judas, and lived as nomads in the desert of Thekoa. To these circumstances—namely,

How Ecclesiastes was Written the struggle between the religious zealots and the fruitless efforts of an enlightened party to Hellenise the Jews—the most remarkable book which the biblical canon has accepted, Ecclesiastes, owes its origin. The work gives expression to the pessimism of a well-meaning man who, while holding the post of ruler, was anxious to guide his people aright, but at the end

in despair lets his hands fall feebly by his side. The suggestion is forced upon us that Alcimus the high-priest was himself the author, and that the book may have been published after his death, with some additions in the same spirit. Owing to its

The Work of the High-priest reception into the canon, which could not have been refused to the work of a high-priest, it was afterwards furnished with qualifying rejoinders in the spirit of devout orthodoxy.

Alcimus died in 159 B.C. When Bacchides soon afterwards withdrew, the Maccabæans once more caused trouble. A message was therefore sent from Jerusalem to Bacchides imploring help. But since a sudden attack on the castle of Jonathan failed, Bacchides concluded peace with him and acknowledged him as high-priest. Jonathan was probably no longer a zealot for the faith and the interests of Egyptian and international Judaism, but he fought for the establishment of a Hasmonæan dynasty. To attain this end, he ceased to be a " Jew " and made his peace with the Seleucidæ. Jonathan, in the wars between Demetrius I. and Alexander Balas, and under Demetrius II. from 145 to 138 B.C., held his own ; and finally, notwithstanding his action against the Syrian party, obtained acknowledgment from Demetrius II. He then joined cause with Tryphon. He at last went to the length of setting aside the influence of the Syrian party with the help of his orthodox followers, and seems to have had the sanction of the court in doing so. At least the influence of Judaism over Tryphon seems to have ceased ; and the latter advanced with an army into Palestine. Jonathan now presented himself at Akko to render an account of his actions, and was arrested.

In his place Simon Maccabæus took over the management of affairs. When Tryphon attempted to interfere, the former was skilful enough to frustrate all the designs of the Greek army, including an attempt to relieve the Akra, and he contrived to free the land from it. By means of giving the required hostages in the shape of his brother's sons, he at the same time got rid of any rivals to himself. When the Syrians had left the country, and the walls of Jerusalem had been rebuilt,

COINS OF SIMON MACCABÆUS
Simon Maccabæus struck money in his own name, dating it from his accession in 142 B.C. as the year 1.

he could securely regard himself as prince of Judah. With him the princedom of the hierarchy of Judah—that is, the high-priesthood—was transferred to the Hasmonæans. Simon struck money in his own name, and dated it after his accession the year 1 (142 B.C.).

Reign of Simon the Maccabee The Syrian party was thus overthrown, and orthodoxy could benefit the people in its own way. The records speak only of tranquillity and happiness in the land.

Simon was murdered in 135 B.C. by his son-in-law, who aspired to power ; but his son, John Hyrcanus, succeeded in securing Jerusalem and the crown for himself. The rapidly advancing downfall of the Seleucid empire was favourable for him, for he could thus assert his independence. When he had successfully concluded an alliance with the Romans he proceeded to demonstrate the splendour of the new realm and to realise the ideal of his religion—namely, the restoration of the kingdom of David. His comparatively small territory was enlarged by a successful subjugation of Sichem, of Samaria—thanks to Roman intervention—and of Edom.

Hyrcanus was succeeded by his son, Judas Aristobulus, who secured his authority, according to Oriental custom, by the murder of his relations. He died after one year. His widow, Salome, by marriage procured the sovereignty for his eldest brother, who had been kept in captivity by him, Jannæus (Jonathan) Alexander, who held the power from 104 to 78 B.C. The latter first secured his position by the removal of one of his two brothers, and proceeded to complete the conquest of Palestine. As he was besieging Akko he was hindered in the further prosecution of his plans by the intervention of Egypt, and he was saved from the direr consequences of his ambition only by the efforts of the Jewish influence with Cleopatra, mother of Ptolemy Lathurus, in 100 B.C. He then conquered Raphia and Gaza, and secured to himself the country east of Jordan.

Revolt of the Pharisees But Jannæus here came into collision with an enemy stronger than himself, the North Arabian empire of the Nabatæans ; and he was defeated by their king, Oboda, in Gilead. When he returned to Jerusalem without an army an insurrection broke out among the orthodox party, the Pharisees, which, after many changes of fortune,

ended in the victory of Demetrius Euchærus, who had been called in by the insurgents, over Jannæus in 88 B.C. But the indefatigable Hasmonæan was able to collect a new force around him in the mountains, and, after the withdrawal of Demetrius, to reoccupy Jerusalem. He wreaked his vengeance there, as only Orientals can, in the course of party struggles in 87 B.C. After Jannæus had thus firmly re-established his power, he renewed the war with the Nabatæan king, Oboda ; but as the latter had meantime won for himself Coele-Syria, Jannæus was worsted and was forced to make peace. He then strengthened his power once more in the territory east of Jordan, and died there on an expedition. He, like his father, had extended the Jewish dominion, although he did not gain possession of the whole of Palestine. The map of this country, so adapted for petty states, presented even under h m a very chequered appearance.

Jannæus always relied on the support of the now powerful party of Sadducees, which tried to harmonise in some degree

Rise of the Sadducees the unendurable bonds of Judaism with the demands of ordinary life. This led insensibly to a closer sympathy with Hellenism, and the Hellenic culture which dominated even the East. The house of the Hasmonæans, which had formerly entered the war on behalf of religion, thus became a purely Oriental dynasty, which adapted itself to the requirements of religion only so far as was necessary to serve its purposes. Now the state had only been founded to realise this very ideal of a hierarchy in the sense of the " law," and not in order to call into existence a kingdom, on the model of so many others, with a Jewish religion. So long as the state existed, it was constantly brought back to the path which it wished to desert, until such attempts were brought to an end by Titus and Hadrian.

On the death of Jannæus a reaction followed. His wife, Salome Alexandra, took over the government, which had been nominally conferred on her by Jannæus on his deathbed. Her son, Hyrcanus II., a feeble character, who was completely under her control, was appointed high-priest, while his capable brother, Aristobulus, was passed over. This state of things lasted for nine years, from 78 to 69 B.C.

Meanwhile, the Pharisees governed after their own heart and laid no restraint upon themselves.

The country, however, could not possibly tolerate the Pharisaic rule for long, and **Intolerable Rule of the Pharisees** Aristobulus gained more and more adherents. After the death of Salome there could be no more doubt to whom the kingdom belonged. The Pharisees had no sort of following in the country. They attempted a resistance and led Hyrcanus, with the mercenary army, against Aristobulus. But at Jericho, where the battle was fought, their troops went over to Aristobulus, and he was able without great difficulty to occupy Jerusalem. He was acknowledged as high-priest and king, and Hyrcanus retired into private life.

Tranquillity, however, did not last long. Jannæus had appointed as governor in Idumæa a native convert to Judaism, Antipater, the father of Herod. This man himself cast longing eyes on the throne of Judah. He followed a policy of his own and induced Hareth III., king of the Nabatæans, to make an expedition in 65 B.C. against Aristobulus, who defended himself in the Temple. The protracted siege was ended by Roman intervention.

The Arabians were forced to withdraw from Jerusalem, and Aristobulus momentarily triumphed over Hyrcanus, although the latter had part of the country on his side. When, then, in 63 B.C., Pompey came in person to Palestine, after many prevarications on both sides, he finally decided against Aristobulus. The latter was taken prisoner ; his adherents threw themselves into the Temple and gallantly defended themselves against the onslaught of the Romans, until they finally succumbed, and the Temple was taken by storm. This brought the rule of the Hasmonæans to an end, and Judæa became a component part of the province of Syria. Pompey granted the Jews liberty of religion and confirmed Hyrcanus in his office of high-priest. The orthodox party loudly sang the praises of the great Roman ; they preferred that Judæa should be tributary rather than non-Pharisaic. The new **Judæa a Roman Province** province, and with it Judæa, received four pro-consuls, until the overthrow of Pompey made Cæsar master of the East and West. Cæsar allowed the Jews religious liberty, and appointed as procurator Antipater, the Idumæan, who was clever enough to make himself indispensable.

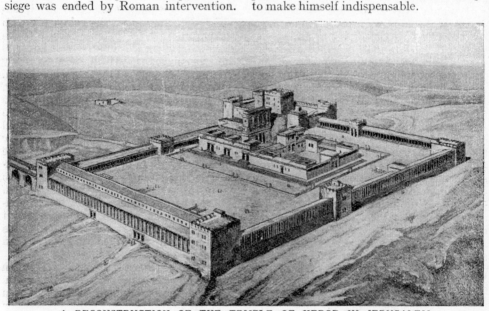

A RECONSTRUCTION OF THE TEMPLE OF HEROD IN JERUSALEM

Under the Romans the religious influence of the Jews greatly increased throughout the empire, and although Herod, the Roman king of Judæa, spent much in building the Temple, he never succeeded in winning his subjects' affection.

THE DESTRUCTION OF JERUSALEM BY THE ROMANS

From the painting by Francesco Hayez in the Royal Academy of Venice

TO FACE PAGE 1859

THE ROMAN EMPIRE IN ASIA

AFTER the final campaign of Pompey, Western Asia lost its political independence. Nevertheless, the part it played in history during the first six centuries of the Christian era was not insignificant.

The chief of the Roman possessions in Western Asia, Asia Minor and Syria, were retained by Rome throughout their whole extent until the Arabian conquest, and to them were added, during favourable times, portions of Mesopotamia, Armenia, and the South Caucasian districts. Asia Minor was the most tranquil, the best protected, and the most uniformly organised of the Roman Asiatic provinces. Scarcely a trace remained of political independence; but in many of the country districts and towns a certain form of self-government, such as the Romans were in the habit of allowing to their dependencies, still existed. The larger of the settlements in the peninsula were, as a rule, of Hellenic origin.

Greek Influence in Asia Minor Thickly distributed along the western coast and in the river valleys, more sparsely on the elevated plateaus and among the mountains of the interior, they formed the centres of the Greek influence which had penetrated into the peninsula during an earlier period, encouraged by the Attalidæ, and in later times had been allowed to continue undisturbed by the Romans.

When Rome first took possession of the peninsula, entire provinces exhibited hardly a trace of Greek influence; others, such as Lycia and Pamphylia, had developed an independent civilisation on a Hellenic foundation. In the very centre of the land were settled a Celtic people, the Galatians, who had preserved both their language and their martial spirit, and during the times of the emperors furnished the majority of the recruits from Asia Minor. But gradually these local peculiarities grew less and less apparent, the language and civilisation of the Greeks, slightly Latinised, it is true, became diffused over the entire peninsula; and, finally, even rustic Cappadocia sent to Athens its bands of students, whose rude dialect must, indeed, have caused the cultured professors to wring their hands in despair.

The few politically independent provinces and small states that had survived the period of Roman conquest, as well **Last Independent States** as a number of unimportant principalities which had once belonged to the empire of Mithradates and were allowed a provisional existence by the Romans, disappeared during the first period of the emperors. The kingdom of the Galatians was transformed into a Roman dependency as early as 25 B.C. Shortly after his accession in 17 A.D., Tiberius put an end to the independence of Cappadocia. The territory of the Lycian league of cities was annexed in the year 43 A.D., and the provinces of Pontus were added to the Roman Empire in 63 A.D. The wildest, least civilised districts of Roman Asia Minor were the Taurus provinces, Isauria and Cilicia. The Cilicians were practically unconquerable so long as they remained in their native surroundings. The thickly wooded mountains that sloped down to the sea oon became the favourite haunt of the dissatisfied spirits and criminals of the Roman Empire, who, together with the native inhabitants of the coast, soon gave themselves up to piracy, which became in time their habitual occupation. Neither the republic nor the empire was able to put a stop to the deeds of robbery by sea and by land, or to subdue the inhabitants of the mountains, among whom several tribes of the Pisidians are also to be reckoned. But in Asia Minor also, with the gradual opening up of the country, customs became **Pirates of the Taurus** less rude; and the mountain dwellers were compelled to cease their warfare, although even a short period of political disorganisation was sufficient to cause them all to return to their o'd manner of life. In fact, the Cilicians and Isaurians constantly made their appearance as robbers and pirates, until the sturdiest of the wild rabble attained the honour of forming the bodyguard of the Eastern Roman Emperor ; and finally two of them, Zeno and Leo III., succeeded to the imperial dignity itself.

The remainder of Asia Minor became under the Roman emperors a flourishing land with a dense and highly civilised population. The province was governed **Asia** by the Senate, and was divided **Minor** into four districts, of which only **Flourishes** two—Asia Minor proper, and Pontus together with Bithynia —were situated on the mainland. Cyprus and Crete, to which Cyrene in Africa was added, were accounted parts of the peninsula for purposes of administration. In later times this division was frequently altered ; and during the period of Byzantine rule, owing to the constant danger of invasion, the province was separated into a great number of districts and governed according to military law. The inroads of hostile nations began at the time of the Persian wars. In the year 609 A.D. the Iranians first appeared in Cappadocia, and during the following decade they marched through the peninsula several times, finally threatening Constantinople itself. The invasion of the Persians was only the first of many blows dealt to the civilisation of Asia Minor.

The condition of Syria was totally different from that of Asia Minor. Only the eastern boundary of the latter was a frontier of the Roman Empire, and was, moreover, protected by the buffer states Armenia and Iberia. Syria, on the other hand, was directly adjacent not only to that portion of Mesopotamia, for the possession of which continual war was being waged between Romans and Persians, but also to the boundless Arabian desert, over whose anarchic Bedouin tribes a permanent government was never to be established by the Romans. The province itself, however, was exceptionally favoured by its racial and political peculiarities ; **Syria** then, as to-day, it was a har- **Open to** bour of refuge for an immense **Invasion** number of different peoples and adherents of various creeds. Two of the most remarkable states known to history, the Phœnician league of cities, which occupied a narrow strip of Mediterranean coast, and the kingdom of the Israelites in the mountains of Palestine, arose during an early period on Syrian soil. The prosperity of both had faded when Syria became a Roman province ; in fact, Phœnician freedom, if not Phœnician civilisation, so far as commerce and industry were concerned had long ceased to exist. There were still flourishing settlements scattered along the coast, and commerce was actively carried on ; but the civilisation of Phœnicia was that of the Greeks. Hellenism had expanded in all directions from the city of Antioch as a centre during the period of the Seleucidæ ; and as for the northern districts of Syria, however undisturbed the native population had been allowed to remain, and however little influenced by Greek culture, they formed at the time of the Romans practically a Greek province. It is true that the infusion of Oriental luxury and effeminacy was of the greatest injury to the Greek spirit ; and Antioch as a city of sensuality and pleasure stood in sharp contrast to Alexandria, which had developed under the influence of the Greeks on Egyptian soil. The shiftless inhabitants of the Syrian metropolis contributed little enough to the development of morals ; but for all that, Syria long remained the centre of the Eastern Roman Empire. As a **Syria the** result of the dominion of the **Centre of** Seleucidæ and the subse- **the East** quent process of Hellenisation, Northern Syria fell into the hands of the Romans as a tolerably well-organised province, which even during later periods developed no very marked characteristics, and of which the administration presented no great difficulty. Southern Syria, on the other hand, consisted of a multitude of small mutually antagonistic states. There were some more or less independent principalities in Lebanon, which had ever been a land of promise for the dispersed and conquered races. On the borders of the desert lay the kingdom of the Nabatæans, and Arab tribes were constantly appearing on the steppes and along the Mesopotamian frontier.

The greatest confusion of all, however, was to be found in Palestine. At first the Romans found it to their own interest to increase the number of minor states in order to avoid the risk of united resistance. Many different races and parties were clamouring for a settlement of their political, national, and religious claims. The Jewish ecclesiastical state of Jerusalem, constantly striving for freedom, and yet not strong enough to

ART AND CIVILISATION OF LYCIA AND PAMPHYLIA UNDER ROME

When Rome took possession of Asia Minor most of the provinces and settlements were centres of Greek culture, but a few, such as Lycia and Pamphylia, had developed an independent civilisation on a Hellenic foundation. The outstanding examples of their art are their tombs. The top picture on the right is of a Pamphylian tomb among the mountains. That on the left is a Lycian tomb at Xanthus, some of its sculptures being shown at the bottom right. The remaining illustration shows one of the remarkable rock-tombs at Myra, which occur throughout Lycia

maintain the independence it so greatly desired, could not be treated as a helpless minor province. Indeed, in dealing with the Israelites of Palestine the Romans had to reckon with the entire Jewish people, already widely diffused throughout the empire and in many districts dangerously numerous, who could not have regarded

Rome and the Jews a violation of their ancient sanctuary as other than an attack on their very existence. Moreover, the religious influence of the Jews was increasing, for the unsettled state of religious thought led numerous proselytes to join their ranks. It even appeared for a time as if Judaism would succeed in overthrowing the belief in the deities of the Greeks. The rise of Christianity, however, turned this phase of development into another channel.

In spite of all the caution exercised by the Romans in their administration of Palestine, the antagonism between the claims of political life and the rigid ritual of the priesthood remained a constant source of complication. In the year 47 B.C. Julius Cæsar appointed Antipater the Idumæan procurator and successor of the Maccabees, and he could scarcely have made a better choice. Nevertheless the numerous champions of the Jewish national spirit were not in the least satisfied ; and after the invasion of the Parthians, during which the new dynasty was temporarily compelled to take flight, Herod, the son and heir of Antipater, was obliged to resort to force in order to subdue his rebellious subjects. Herod passed through the period of the great struggle between Cæsar Augustus and Marcus Antonius with singular good fortune ; but he was unable to win the affection of the Jewish people. The ruthless manner in which he put to death the members of his own family injured him, however, far less in the eyes of his subjects than his foreign origin and leaning to Hellenism.

Division of Herod's Kingdom After the death of Herod, in the year 4 A.D., his kingdom, which had been considerably enlarged by the annexation of minor principalities, thanks to the benevolence of Cæsar Augustus, was divided between his three sons : Galilee and Peræa fell to the share of Herod Antipas, the region south of Damascus to Philippus, and Judæa, Samaria, and Idumæa to Archelaus. The two northern kingdoms continued in existence for many years ; they were

united into one state by Agrippa II., a great-grandson of Herod, and remained intact until the time of Trajan. In the south, however, insurrections soon broke out among the Jews. Archelaus proved incapable of government, and it was not long before Cæsar Augustus found it necessary to transform Palestine into a Roman province with Cæsarea as its capital. It is obvious that this time also the Romans desired to spare the feelings of the Jews as much as possible ; but a true reconciliation with the subjects of the Jewish ecclesiastical state, whose demands increased rather than diminished with the growing hopelessness of their cause, was impossible. Christianity provided a means for escape from the bigotry that must finally have led to destruction, although it received but little support from the true Jews, among whom the national spirit was at first strongly at work. In general, the Christian religion cannot be said to have played other than a subordinate part in the political history of Palestine.

The hostility between the Roman emperors and the Jews of Palestine gradually

First Anti-Semite Riots increased. The Jews who had emigrated to various parts of the empire also received but little sympathy, as was proved by the terrible riots that broke out in Alexandria during the reign of Caligula—the first manifestation of anti-Semitism in the Roman world. It was unfortunate that the imperial government had not from the very first taken such precautions as would have rendered a rebellion in Palestine an impossibility ; instead of ruling with a firm hand, it carelessly allowed events to take their own course. Bands of rebels were in constant activity as early as the year 44 A.D. ; Roman soldiers and officials were murdered more and more frequently ; and a spirit of sullen hostility gradually spread over the entire province. In the year 66 A.D. an insurrection broke out in Cæsarea ; another soon followed in Jerusalem, where frightful scenes of carnage took place ; and soon the whole of Judæa was in a state of civil war. Vespasian, the imperial legate, conquered the land anew in a difficult campaign which lasted for several years. The confusion that reigned in the Roman Empire until Vespasian himself ascended the throne in 69 A.D. was of great assistance to the Jews, although a final victory

PETRA, THE ROCK-CAPITAL OF THE NABAT/EAN KINGDOM

Nabatæa lay between the Red Sea and the Jordan and even included at one time Damascus. Petra, its capital, situated on a rocky plateau, perhaps flourished most under Roman rule. At the top are shown some of the remarkable cliff structures above the city, and below on the right the most beautiful of the relics, probably a tomb. On the left is the ravine by which the city is entered at the east, and at the bottom a view of the plateau from the theatre.

of the Hebrews was out of the question owing to their fanaticism and lack of unity. In the year 70 A.D., Titus, son of Vespasian, entered Jerusalem, destroyed the Temple, and put an end to all hopes of Jewish independence.

Jerusalem lay in ruins until the time of Hadrian. The Jews of Palestine had **The Last Effort of the Jews** but little share in the great rebellion which broke out during the reign of Trajan ; and it is a significant fact that the last great insurrection of the Jews in the Holy Land came about owing to the well-meant design of Hadrian to establish a new city on the ruins of Jerusalem. At that time the Jews arose in final despairing revolt under the leadership of Eleazar the priest and the bandit Bar-Kokhba, with the result that their country was completely devastated and lost even its name of Judæa, henceforth being known as Syria Palæstina.

A quiet neighbour, and in later times a dependency of the Roman Empire, was the kingdom of the Nabatæans, which during its period of widest expansion embraced the greater part of the region north of the Red Sea and east of the river Jordan, at one time even including Damascus. The original Nabatæan people in all probability were descended from a mixture of Arabian and Hamitic, or, at least, Syrian elements. A part of their kingdom lay on the north-eastern coast of the Red Sea, and was at the same time a natural junction of many caravan roads ; the Nabatæans had thus from the earliest times devoted themselves to commerce, thereby acquiring a culture that rendered them far more capable of developing a permanent state than the Bedouins of the neighbouring steppes, for all their love of freedom and courage in battle. The capital of the kingdom of the Nabatæans and the residence of the sovereigns was Petra, situated on the rocky plateau that lay **Kingdom of Nabatæa** between the Dead Sea and the Gulf of Akaba. Nabatæa submitted to Cæsar Augustus, and in spite of various small misunderstandings remained undisturbed until the time of Trajan, when, together with the bulk of the minor Syrian states, it was transformed into a Roman province. In the year 106 A.D., Damascus was annexed to Syria, and the remainder of the kingdom, henceforth known as the " Province of Arabia," was placed under

Roman rule—by no means to its disadvantage, as the ruins of its once flourishing cities testify. Roman Nabatæa included only a portion of the northern border of the Arabian desert, and was environed by a number of semi-independent Bedouin states, of which the influence and extent greatly increased when the power of the empire began to weaken.

Remarkable for sudden changes of fortune was Palmyra, a kingdom of the Syrian-Arabian borderland. In early times, before the occupation of Syria by the Romans, a flourishing community arose in an oasis of the great Syrian desert that had long served as a convenient halting place for caravans travelling between Phœnicia and the middle Euphrates. The city was made a dependency of the Roman Empire during the first period of the emperors ; but owing to its important frontier situation between Parthian and Roman territory, it retained a certain amount of freedom, and at the same time became possessed of considerable power. The necessity of protecting the caravan routes led to the formation of **Growth of the Power of Palmyra** a well-organised army ; and constant feuds with the Bedouins, which, as a rule, terminated in the victory of the Palmyrans, resulted in continual accessions of territory, so that Palmyra finally embraced the greater part of the region between the Euphrates and the Syrian border.

The language of the Palmyrans was not the Arabic of the Bedouins, but the Syrian of the agricultural and town-dwelling classes. Originally the city may have been organised as a republic ; but the Romans, who were accustomed to choose a ruler from among the native inhabitants of their provinces, created a monarchical form of government that finally became hereditary. No small amount of power lay in the hands of a Palmyran sovereign, who possessed a well-trained army of veterans who had taken part in numerous struggles with Arab tribes, and the hoarded wealth of a strongly fortified city—a city, moreover, that was in addition protected by the desert. Thus it is not surprising that before many years passed an ambitious ruler came to the throne, who resolved to take part in the border wars between Rome and Persia, to seize the balance of power, and to establish a new empire at the expense of both the contending parties.

RUINS OF PALMYRA, THE "MIRAGE" KINGDOM OF THE SYRIAN DESERT

Palmyra arose, before the Roman occupation, in an oasis on the Parthian frontier, and became supreme over Syria. It fell as suddenly as it rose. The ruins of its magnificent city are now one of the sights of Syria. The principal remains are shown at the top and bottom of the page, and in the centre are a temple to Diana and specimens of Palmyran sculptures.

The opportunity for such an undertaking was never more favourable than during the reign of the Sassanian Shapur I. The Roman emperor Valerian was a prisoner in the hands of his enemies. Antioch had been captured, and the whole of Syria, with the exception of a few unimportant strongholds, lay open to the

Palmyra Supreme in the East

Persians, who, eager for plunder, marched about hither and thither in disorganised companies. As soon as Shapur began to withdraw his forces, the Palmyran cavalry sallied forth, dispersed whole divisions of the scattered Persian army, and returned to their desert city with untold spoils. Odenathus, king of Palmyra, made the most of the prestige won by this daring stroke by immediately espousing the cause of Gallienus, son of Valerian, whose opponents in the struggle for the succession had gained the upper hand in the east. As a result, when Gallienus finally triumphed over his enemies and ascended the throne, Odenathus was rewarded with the title of Augustus, and became practically supreme in Syria. He soon restored affairs to order, strengthened his troops by the addition of the remains of the Roman legions, and marched against the Persians. After clearing Roman Mesopotamia of the enemy, and raising the siege of Edessa, he appeared twice before the walls of Ctesiphon.

On the death of Odenathus, his wife Zenobia, or Bat Zabbai, seized the reins of government in the name of her son, who was not yet of age. Her energy was quite equal to that of her husband, but she was lacking in the diplomatic skill which had enabled the latter to preserve at least the appearance of being a vassal of Rome, and thus successfully to maintain his difficult position. As "Regent of the East" she laid claim to both Asia and Egypt, invaded the valley of the Nile, and advanced into Asia Minor—sufficient

Fall of Zenobia's Empire

cause for a declaration of war on the part of Aurelian, the new emperor, who realised that unless a decisive step were taken it would not be long before the last trace of Roman power would disappear in the East. Egypt was reoccupied by the Romans in the year 270 A.D., after a severe struggle; and in the next year Aurelian himself appeared in Syria at the head of a powerful army. The forces of Zenobia were defeated at Antioch and

at Emesa; but Palmyra, difficult to approach and still more difficult to besiege, still remained in her hands. However, when Aurelian made it clear that he intended to march on the capital, she lost courage; under cover of night she fled towards the Euphrates in order to escape into Persian territory. It may have been that she also hoped to relieve the city with the aid of a Persian army; but she was immediately pursued and taken prisoner by Roman cavalry. Thereupon Palmyra opened its gates to the Romans, and the empire of Zenobia fell. A riot of the citizens in the year 273 A.D. ended with the complete destruction of the city, which never again arose from its ruins. Like a mirage of the desert, this strange empire suddenly arose on the eastern horizon of the Roman world, and as suddenly disappeared.

In Armenia, the rugged mountainous country from which the Euphrates and Tigris flow down into the Mesopotamian plain, a warlike, freedom-loving people had developed from a mixture of ancient Caucasian and Iranian elements. The

Expansion of Armenian Empire

original Armenian race must have been very heterogeneous. The presence of numerous small feudal demesnes and strongholds scattered over a land of ravines and forests caused their country to be from the earliest times a theatre of private warfare and a home for robbers and fugitives of all nationalities. As time passed, the influence of Iranian culture and religion smoothed over the roughness of the native population. The example of the Persian emperors fired the ambition of Armenian rulers, and at the same time aroused the national spirit to the development of unexpected power.

For a time it appeared as if the Armenians were destined to become the most representative of all the Iranian peoples. Under the rule of Tigranes the Armenian empire expanded with surprising rapidity and power. But the mutual jealousy of the various sovereigns of Western Asia bore bitter fruit. Tigranes did not make the slightest attempt to assist his great western neighbour, Mithradates, king of Pontus, in his hopeless struggle with Rome; and with the same composure the Parthian emperors rejoiced when Tigranes, cast down from his high estate, knelt before Pompey and placed his crown in the hands of the Roman consul.

THE CAPTURE OF ZENOBIA, QUEEN OF PALMYRA, BY THE ROMANS

After the death of Odenathus his wife, Zenobia, reigned. She did not maintain the fiction of vassalage to Rome, and the emperor Aurelian marched on her capital, from which she fled, but was captured by his cavalry.

After the overthrow of Tigranes, there was no longer any hope of Armenian supremacy. Several times Armenia was separated into a western and an eastern province, temporarily, as early as the days of the Seleucidæ, and again during a later period, when the Eastern Roman Empire and the Persians agreed as to the division of their spheres of influence. Moreover, the country was usually a patchwork of dominions of minor princes, who seldom refused to accept foreign aid against their own sovereign.

It is scarcely worth while to give a detailed account of all the varying phases of the wars between Rome and Parthia, or to enumerate the constant changes that took place in the dominion of the Romans and Parthians in Armenia. It is, however, important to remember that throughout this troubled period, in spite of all confusion that reigned in political affairs, the Armenian consciousness of nationality constantly increased, and finally produced a spiritually independent people ; and that this people, by developing a purely Armenian civilisation, ultimately succeeded in defeating the attempt of the Iranians to acquire a position of intellectual supremacy.

The decay of these world powers, largely brought about by their own fierce rivalry, prepared the way for the advance of Islam. The process of disintegration, which marks the period between the close of the Alexandrian epoch and the earliest of the Arabian conquests, rendered the task of the Mohammedan generals easier than it would otherwise have been, but it does not in itself explain their success. The empire founded by the Arabs after the death of Mahomet was the result of an influx of new blood, brought by the nomads, who once more were pressing forward from the Arabian peninsula, and were beginning to flood and overwhelm the more highly civilised but decaying races of Western Asia. Signs of this expansion had not been wanting in the previous period, as we shall see when we turn later to Arabia itself in order to trace in greater detail the earlier periods of her history, and to define the events which preceded and led up to the victory of Islam.

THE EMPIRE OF PARTHIA

AS a result of the wars of Alexander the Great, the Persian nation was suddenly cast down from its position of supremacy, and placed under Greek rule. The dominion of the Seleucidæ also rested upon a Greek foundation, and found its most powerful support in the Hellenised cities of Syria and Mesopotamia; within Persia, strangely enough, the civilisation of the Greeks took firmer root in the eastern mountain districts and in Bactria than in the western and more ancient provinces of Iran. But the Seleucidæ soon recognised the impossibility of holding their vast empire together, and decided to move the centre of government to the west, and we have seen that a new Power arose in the east, which, unlike the Seleucid empire, was never brought within the Roman dominion.

The New Power in the East

Even during the most gloomy periods, the old civilisation and religion of Iran had not been wanting in a place of refuge. Atropatene, a small Persian state, had all the while preserved its existence in the mountainous country of the north-west, in the neighbourhood of Lake Urumiya. This district was either overlooked or intentionally spared during the stormy period of Alexander; for, according to all appearances, it was the seat of no temporal power, but a region sacred to the priestly class of Persia, a sort of Iranian ecclesiastical state which Alexander did not venture to destroy.

The origin of that religion itself, and the history of its founder, Zoroaster, or Zarathustra, are obscure. It would seem to have been the outcome of an effort to spiritualise the Hindu doctrines at an early stage. Its fundamental tenet is the dualism which sets in opposition, in eternal war, the spirit of Good, Ormuzd, and the spirit of Evil, Ahriman; and undoubtedly influenced later Western conceptions of Satan. Fire and, by consequence, the Sun are the visible manifestations of the good spirit, the emblem of purification. Hence arose the prohibition against burning the bodies of the dead, extended first in the case of the priesthood to prohibition of burial. The Zoroastrians have their representatives at the present day in the Parsees of India, who "bury" their dead on a high tower where the corpses are consumed by birds of prey.

It is significant that the foundations of the Parthian nation do not seem to have been laid by a man of Iranian blood, but by a Turanian, a member of one of the nomadic tribes, of which many had already won for themselves a secure position in the steppe lands of Central Persia. But the Turanian ruling house that gained the position of supremacy in Iran had already become conversant with Persian customs and culture before its advance to power; indeed, it consciously trod in the footsteps of its great Persian forerunners, tracing its origin back to Artaxerxes III., the Achæmenian.

The early history of the Parthian empire was so devoid of interest that the contemporary Greek chroniclers hardly mentioned the affairs of Persia, and have left us little more than a few bare statements concerning them. Moreover, since all Parthian kings were known by the name Arsaces on their accession to the throne, many changes in the succession must have taken place, of which we now possess little or no knowledge. It is probable that Arsaces I., the founder of the dynasty, reigned but a short time. In the year 248 B.C. he made way for his brother and successor Arsaces II., or Tiridates I., who, profiting by the neglect into which the eastern provinces of Syria had fallen, greatly enlarged his dominions at the expense of the Seleucidæ. Unfortunately, the extent of the territory originally occupied by the Parthians is no longer known with certainty. There can be no doubt that it was situated in the north-eastern part of Persia; and that it must have consisted largely of steppes may be inferred

Territory of Parthian Empire

from the fact that the bulk of the Parthian army was made up of cavalry. Although the Parthians were not of pure Iranian descent, both the language and civilisation of the empire were Persian.

Tiridates I. also added to his empire the province of Hyrcania ; this included the greater portion of the Khorassan of to-day, of which the inhabitants were especially nearly related to the Parthians. The rulers of the neighbouring kingdom of Bactria, that remarkable Greek state on Iranian soil, were, naturally enough, at first unfriendly to the new empire. With the assistance of the Bactrian king, Diodotus I., Seleucus Callinicus expelled Tiridates from his kingdom in the year 238 B.C. ; but Diodotus II. reversed the policy of his predecessors, joined forces with Tiridates, and compelled Callinicus to withdraw. At the end of these wars the Parthian empire may be looked upon as firmly established.

The mountainous country in the west was also conquered by the Parthians, with the old Median capital, Ecbatana. The ecclesiastical state of Atropatene entered into a close relationship with the new empire, without, however, becoming merged in it. In later periods it even happened that this curious nation of priests at times assumed a position of decided hostility to the Persian rulers, who were never looked upon as true Iranians, and allied itself with the Romans. That Antiochus the Great planned a campaign against Atropatene after crushing the rebellion of the Median governor Mo'on from 222 to 220 B.C. proves only how dangerous this little state had become now that the Iranians had entered into a conflict with Hellenism and the religious influence of the priesthood was beginning to transform itself into a political agency. Artavasdes, the governor then in office, escaped the storm through timely submission in 220 B.C. The third Parthian Arsaces, Artabanus I. (214–196), was also compelled to acknowledge the

A Nation of Priests

ZOROASTER
From a Persian rock sculpture.

supremacy of the Seleucidæ when Antiochus advanced with a powerful army into Iran and penetrated as far as India in 209 B.C. ; but this acknowledgment was little more than an empty form, and the campaign of Antiochus remained for a long time the last attempt made by the Seleucidæ to maintain their prestige in the east. The vigorous efforts towards expansion made by Antiochus the Great in the west, and the rise of the Bactrian kingdom in the east, were great obstacles to the development of the Parthian state. Not until the accession of Arsaces VI., (or Mithradates I.), who came to the throne in the year 174 B.C., did circumstances become more favourable to Parthia. While the empire of the Seleucidæ was in a state of hopeless confusion, Mithradates invaded the western provinces of Iran at the head of his multitudes of horsemen, and advanced into Media and Persis. He next broke through the mountain passes, subdued the Elimaei, who inhabited the south-western slope of the Iranian mountains, and finally appeared on the broad plain of Mesopotamia—a region that was destined long to remain a field of action for the hordes of mounted Parthians.

Seleucid Supremacy in Parthia

In the east, also, the decay of Bactrian power furnished an opportunity for engaging in a successful war, as the result of which Bactria lost several provinces, and finally acknowledged the sovereignty of the Parthian king. An attempt to reconquer Western Iran, made by Demetrius II., Nicator, terminated in the capture of the Syrian king in 139 B.C. Mithradates gave Demetrius the hand of his daughter in marriage, and then endeavoured to place him upon the throne of the Seleucidæ as a vassal of the Parthians. Although this effort to extend the influence of Parthia failed, the Seleucidæ were unsuccessful in winning back their lost provinces. The vast army which Antiochus VII. assembled in the year 130 B.C. was attacked, and the greater part of it destroyed at its winter quarters in Mesopotamia, almost without assistance from the Parthians, by the non-military inhabitants of Western Iran. With this event the period of wars between the Seleucidæ and the Parthians ended.

Turks Against Parthia The former contented themselves with their western provinces until they were overcome by the Romans ; the latter were soon obliged to defend themselves against new enemies.

Phraates II., the successor of Mithradates, for the conclusion of the struggle with Syria obtained the aid of troops of " Scythian " horsemen ; not Aryan Scythians, but probably Turks The Turks, however, arrived too late upon the scene, and were told that they would have to return to their Turanian home without receiving either pay or plunder. Thereupon they attacked the Parthians, who sought to strengthen their army by enrolling among their ranks the prisoners captured during the campaign against Antiochus. These recruits went over to the side of the Scythians. The Parthians took to flight, and King Phraates was slain on the field of battle in 127 B.C. The Turkoman Scythians, laden with booty, now returned to their native steppes ; but their disappearance was followed by a new and still more serious invasion of the nomads.

Another great movement had taken place among the Central Asian races—a movement similar to the many that were constantly recurring in this boundless region. The nomadic tribes of the Yue-tshi, a mixed Turkish-Mongolian race, driven from their homes in the north of China by the Hiung-nu at the beginning of the second century B.C., had thrown themselves upon the regions lying to the south, but were again dislodged and driven still farther southward by the Usun, a race that had likewise been disturbed by the Hiung-nu. After marching through the plains of Turkestan, the Yuetshi finally descended upon the eastern provinces of Iran, and took possession of the kingdom of Bactria,

Mongols in Bactria about the year 126 B.C. Thus the Parthian empire also was threatened by a formidable enemy upon its very borders. This danger was not to be warded off so cheaply. The Yue-tshi soon succeeded in establishing their power, and by conquering the northern valley of the Indus as well as a portion of Turkestan, secured

for their ends the control of populous territories. Mithradates II., perhaps the most able of all the Parthian kings, was all his life engaged in endeavouring to subdue the Yue-tshi, and also to force back the Scythians, who had again attempted to take possession of the western provinces of Iran. In the west the activities of Mithradates were necessarily limited ; but it speaks volumes for his political sagacity that he sought to extend the influence of Parthia over the rising nation of Armenia.

On the death of Mithradates II., in the year 76 B.C., it soon became apparent that the wars in the east had not only weakened the Parthian empire, but had also endangered its position in the west. The kings of Armenia, in pursuance of their newly-instituted policy of expansion, took possession of Northern Mesopotamia, and even of the sacred state of Atropatene ; and with the latter they also obtained a certain political influence over the whole of Iran. Tigranes, king of Armenia, at that time considered his power sufficiently great to warrant the assumption

Tigranes, " King of Kings " tion of the title "King of Kings," which, as a highly-valued inheritance of Achæmenid times, had descended to the Parthian Arascidæ ; in other words, Armenia made preparations for supplanting the Parthians in their leadership of the Iranian race. Tigranes, however, soon became entangled in the wars of Mithradates, king of Pontus, against Rome and lost his kingdom. When Pompey took control of the affairs of Roman Western Asia there were repeated disputes with Phraates III. (Arsaces XII.), king of Parthia, who laid claim to the Euphrates as the western boundary of his dominions ; but the moderation of the Romans and the internal disorders that followed the assassination of Phraates by his son Mithradates III., Orodes, prevented the outbreak of a serious conflict. The attempts of the Parthians to regain possession of the provinces that had also been torn from them by Armenia led to no open warfare. In the year 54 B.C. the civil war in Parthia came to an end ; and Orodes, now sole ruler, was in a position to enter into the first great struggle with the Roman Empire.

That Rome was unable to gain any permanent success in this war, and that the Roman legions failed to make their way to India across the mountainous frontiers of Western Iran, following in the footsteps of Alexander, are facts of vast historical significance. The civilisation of the western world, which had once been carried by Alexander as far as the Indus, was destined for more than a thousand years to be cut off from all contact with the world of the east; for the small flame of Greek culture that shed its feeble rays over Bactria counted for little and was soon extinguished.

When the Parthian empire first made its preparations for war with the Romans no one would have ventured to prophesy that the power of Rome would be unable to penetrate beyond the Tigris, or that the Euphrates was destined to become the eastern boundary of Latin influence. The land ruled by the kings of Parthia was great and populous, it is true; but it was possessed of small unity, being rather a conglomerate of small and more

sovereignty of the Parthian emperor. As in China, the native population, owing to the superiority of its civilisation, despoiled their conquerors not only of their national character, but also of their dominion.

United Parthia Defies Rome Thus it finally became an easy matter for the Parthians to overthrow the feeble government of the foreigners, and through the installation of a branch of the house of the Arsacidæ, once more to unite the eastern provinces to Western Iran. Hence the Parthian kings were enabled to oppose the Romans with the undivided strength of their empire.

There was also another small kingdom of Arsacid origin in Persia; but of this our knowledge is very indefinite. It appears that on their accession to power the family of the Arsacidæ came to an understanding as to the division of the spoils. One branch obtained the imperial dignity, and the others were granted semi-

Mithradates I.   Phraates III.   Orodes I.   Tiridates II.

SOME OF THE RULERS OF THE PARTHIAN EMPIRE

Mithradates I. (174 B.C.) extended the Parthian dominion to Western Iran and Mesopotamia. Phraates III. claimed the Euphrates as his western boundary. He was assassinated by his son Orodes I. Tiridates II. reigned from 33–32 B.C.

or less independent kingdoms. Everywhere, especially in the mountainous districts, small dynasties had been preserved, and retained their independence throughout the storms of the Alexandrian period. These princes played an important rôle in the struggle between the Seleucidæ and the Parthians for the possession of the mountain regions of Western Iran. In the wars with the Romans, however, they took a less prominent part, because the scene of conflict lay further to the west in the Mesopotamian plain.

The most distinguished of the minor dynasties—one, moreover, that was frequently independent of Persia—was the Armenian. Here the **Armenia Subject to Parthia** Arsacidæ had succeeded in placing one of their own family upon the throne. It is worthy of note that in Eastern Persia also, after the government had been overthrown by the Yue-tshi, Arsacid dynasties soon came to the front again, and acknowledged the

independent dominions, most of which were situated in the northern part of Persia. Certain hereditary offices also seem to have been given to members of the imperial family—for example, the Suraship, a bearer of which title commanded the forces sent against Crassus in the year 53 B.C. The Sura was also possessed of other important functions, and his title seems to have signified both an office and a family name, somewhat in the way that the name Arsaces was adopted by all the emperors as a title as well as a surname.

The Parthian empire being thus loosely constructed, its military system remained badly organised and thoroughly inefficient. On the outbreak of a conflict each of the separate nations of the empire were called upon to furnish its quota of irregular horsemen. These assembled in helpless masses, differing greatly from one another in armament as well as in methods of battle, and ever ready to scatter in wild flight on the death of their leader. There is also but little to be said in favour of the Iranian infantry. The strength of the army lay in the mercenary cavalry, mainly Turanian, before whom the Roman legions, for all their uniform equipment, and their magnificent tactics and discipline, were constantly compelled to retreat. Archers, who overwhelmed the opposing forces with a hail of arrows, formed the bulk of the Parthian cavalry, and behind them rode heavily armed lancers, ready at any moment to break through the weakened ranks of the enemy.

It was fortunate for the Parthians that the decisive battles against Rome were fought on the plains of Mesopotamia, where

A ZOROASTRIAN TOWER OF THE DEAD
Zoroastrians are forbidden to bury or burn their dead, but, like the Parsees of India, expose the corpses on high towers where they are consumed by birds of prey.

the hordes of Iranian cavalry found a field well adapted to their peculiar methods of fighting. The effects of the heavy blows dealt by the well-tried Roman legions were completely lost on the endless plain, and the clumsy pilum and short sword were useless against the scattered Parthian squadrons. The latter, fleeing before the legions, poured back upon them a storm of lances and arrows, and returning from all sides, surged over the awkward masses of Roman infantry as storm-tossed waves dash over a sinking ship. The hot sun that beat down upon the arid plain was the best ally of the Parthians, for it placed

many a body of hostile troops almost defenceless in their hands, and proved but a small obstacle to the movements of their desert-bred horses. Thus, it was with true nomadic weapons that the Parthians fought and conquered in a region thoroughly adapted to their national methods of warfare. However, the Romans were not **The Limit** completely lacking in allies. **of Western** There were still remains of **Culture** former civilisation and abundance to be seen in Mesopotamia along the banks of the rivers. After the conquest of Alexander a number of towns and cities were founded there by the Greeks, the inhabitants of which in later times were by no means inclined to acknowledge the supremacy of the Parthian emperors. As long as the Seleucidæ ruled over Mesopotamia these cities had been the firmest support of their power—indeed it seemed then that the whole land would be Hellenised and permanently united to the culture of the West. After the downfall of the Seleucidæ the Romans became the representatives of the western world. It is true that they were less sympathetic to the Greeks than the Seleucidæ had been; nevertheless, they were far more acceptable to them than the hated Iranian races. That the Romans were able to establish themselves at least in the northern provinces of Mesopotamia was due in a large measure to the influence of the Greek cities.

As soon as Romans and Parthians had become close neighbours, a conflict was only a question of time. Julius Cæsar himself looked upon war as inevitable. Nevertheless, the outbreak of the first struggle was due entirely to minor considerations. M. Licinius Crassus was elected consul for the second time in the year 55 B.C., and received from the senate a commission to restore order in the eastern provinces. This important **Rome** but comparatively humble task **Against** promised as little gratification **Parthia** to his ambition as did the plunder to his greed for possessions. Moreover, his being sent to Asia was little more than a compensation granted him by his allies, Cæsar and Pompey, in return for the pitiful part he had already played elsewhere. However, he now resolved to make the most of his opportunities. The deeds of Lucullus, who had returned from Asia with boundless treasure, awakened in the vain man a spirit of rivalry, and it was not long before his lively imagination presented to his eyes the vista of a campaign even greater than that of Alexander.

Affairs were not entirely unfavourable to Crassus when he first arrived in Western Asia. The struggle for the Parthian succession between Arsaces XIII. and Arsaces XIV. had just been brought to an end by the assassination of the former, and the new emperor had had as yet scarcely time to seat himself firmly on the throne. King Artabanus I., or Artavazd, of Armenia, voluntarily allied himself with the Romans ; and the Mesopotamian cities welcomed Crassus as a liberator. But the consul was unable to take advantage of his position. To

shot into the closely formed legions from all sides, as they toiled painfully onward under the hot rays of the sun. After a contest that lasted for two days the remnants of the Roman army took refuge behind the walls of Charran. Crassus was treacherously put to death while negotiating **10,000 Captive Romans** with the Parthian general, and his troops were soon forced to lay down their arms on June 9th, 53 B.C. This unlucky campaign cost the Romans more than 30,000 of their best soldiers, of whom about 10,000 were taken prisoners by the Parthians, and sent to the eastern provinces of Iran. But the Parthians did not follow up the victory, and so lost their natural rewards, Mesopotamia alone falling into their hands. They also failed to

A GROUP OF MODERN ZOROASTRIANS IN PERSIA OF TO-DAY

be sure he crossed the Euphrates in the year 53 B.C. without making a very careful search for a pretext, won several victories over the Parthians, whom he surprised, and occupied a number of cities which offered but little opposition ; but in the autumn he recrossed the river in order to seek more comfortable winter quarters, **Parthian Defeat of the Romans** and left the conquered cities under the protection of disproportionately feeble garrisons. The Parthians took advantage of this laxity, and, collecting their forces, marched against the Romans.

The two armies met not far from the city of Charran, on the river Belikh. The Romans were able to effect little or nothing with their short swords in face of the showers of arrows that were

reap any advantage from the wars between Cæsar and Pompey, although the latter had prevailed upon them to become his allies. Cæsar's plan to invade Iran was shattered only by his assassination in the year 44 B.C. On the whole, the Parthian successes amounted to very little indeed ; everywhere they had been foiled by the stubborn valour of the Romans.

Yet Antony's expedition in 35 B.C. was entirely unsuccessful. He intended to avoid a battle on the Mesopotamian plain, and by invading the mountainous districts of Iran thought to avail himself of the superiority of his infantry. But he neglected to make proper arrangements for provisioning his vast army. When he had advanced as far as Atropatene, he began to lay siege to the city of Phraspa with insufficient war materials at his disposal, and was soon obliged to retreat and to seek refuge in Armenia, after suffering severe losses. The faithlessness of the Armenians, who did not send the promised reinforcements, contributed not a little to the defeat of the Romans,

Retreat of Antony who soon afterwards—in 30 B.C. —led away the Armenian king, Artavasdes, a prisoner to Alexandria. Shortly after the retreat of Antony, the king of Media and Phraates IV. quarrelled, and as a result the repulse of the Romans led to no further Parthian successes. Antony was even able to form an alliance with the Medes.

During the following years Phraates IV. was fully occupied in maintaining his position on the throne, and consequently he treated the Romans with great deference. In the year 20 B.C. Cæsar Augustus received back from the Parthians the captured insignia and the prisoners of war, to the general satisfaction of the Roman people. Neither Phraates nor his incapable successor took any important part in the Armenian-Roman wars. Several Parthian princes were educated in Rome, not, however, to their advantage, for when one of them, Vonones I., became emperor, his preference for Latin institutions made him so unpopular that he was soon forced to abdicate in favour of a rival, Artabanus III. (Arsaces XIX.), in the year 16 A.D. Artabanus was scarcely more successful than his predecessor; his endeavours to reconquer Armenia failed. A powerful party of his own subjects rose against him with the assistance of the Romans, and finally drove him into the eastern provinces. On his return he concluded a treaty with the Emperor Caligula, was once more obliged to flee, but nevertheless died as emperor in 40 A.D. The civil war continued under his successors also, and disturbances in

Parthian Sovereignty in Armenia Armenia and in the East caused the empire to tremble to its very foundations. In the years 58–60 A.D. the Romans and Parthians were once more on such good terms that they finally succeeded in bringing the Armenian question to a peaceful issue. As a result of this the Parthian prince Tiridates went to Rome in 62 A.D., and was there ceremoniously invested with the sovereignty of Armenia, as a dependency of the Roman Empire.

The decay of the Parthian empire proceeded apace during the years immediately following. The Parthian people became less and less energetic, and the Iranian provinces and principalities gradually gained in independence; indeed, at one time the empire seems to have been divided into several independent states. For many years the Roman emperors showed no inclination to take advantage of the disturbances in the Parthian empire. Trajan was the first to resume the policy of conquest which characterised the age of the Cæsars, and the affairs of Armenia once more furnished a pretext. The great weakness of the Parthian empire was shown by the feeble resistance offered by the Arsaces of the period, Khosru I.; little opposition was encountered except that of the minor princes of the frontiers. Trajan, after the conquest of Northern Mesopotamia, crossed the Tigris, and, with the aid of a rapidly-constructed flotilla, advanced as far south as Ctesiphon, captured the golden throne of the Parthian emperors, and even penetrated as far as the Per-

Trajan Invades Parthia sian Gulf in the year 116 A.D. Serious disturbances in the newly-conquered region rendered it necessary for the victorious emperor to withdraw his forces after having ceremoniously—but, of course, fruitlessly—appointed a Parthian prince as ruler in his stead.

The death of Trajan, in 117 A.D., brought his unsuccessful undertaking to an end. Hadrian, his successor, hastened to recall the Roman troops from Armenia and from beyond the Euphrates, and thus re-established the old boundary line. Hadrian realised that the days of great conquests were past. Not until the time of Marcus Aurelius was Mesopotamia permanently occupied, and the boundary of the Roman Empire pushed forward to the Upper Tigris. The wretched condition of the Parthian empire finally enticed Caracalla also to seek easily-won laurels through a treacherous attack on Emperor Arsaces XXXI. in 216 A.D. Artabanus V., Macrinus, the next Parthian emperor, was obliged to content himself with the possession of Mesopotamia. Shortly afterwards a complete change took place in the affairs of the Iranian empire, when the dynasty of the Arsacidæ was supplanted by the house of the Sassanidæ.

THE NEW PERSIAN DOMINION

UNFORTUNATELY we have no certain knowledge of the more immediate causes of the change of rulers in Parthia, to which the old name of Persia is restored. The new dynasty of the Sassanidæ was beyond all doubt—as indeed became evident in later times—a more genuine representative of the Iranian race than the Turanian Arsacidæ, who must always have appeared as foreigners to the Aryan Iranians. That the downfall of the Arsacidæ betokened a more or less conscious return to the ancient Iranian spirit was shown by the great importance attached by the Sassanian rulers to questions of religion and unity of belief. The religion of Zoroaster was an exclusively Iranian creation. The early Parthian emperors had never shown the slightest inclination towards religious propaganda ; on the other hand, the Sassanidæ were fanatical defenders of their faith. The **Defenders of the Faith** fact that the Iranian people became more and more enthusiastic in regard to their ancient religion proved only that they too were unable to escape the general tendency of the times. Questions of faith were not only becoming more and more prominent, but were also gradually being transformed into elements of political power. It was during this period that Christianity was beginning to shake the spiritual life of the ancient world to its very foundations ; and the waves of this movement had already begun to flow over the frontiers of Iran. If the new religion had struck firm root in Persia, if it had finally won the victory over the worship of fire, then there would have been an end to the isolation of Persia. Iran would have become a member of the western civilised world, just as in later days it became a portion of the Mohammedan empire. The Jewish religion had already penetrated into Persia. There were large colonies of Hebrews in Babylon ; and about the year 57 B.C. the king of Adiabene, a dependency of Parthia, within

which was included a portion of ancient Assyria, became a convert to the Jewish faith. Toward the end of the first century Christianity had begun to spread over Mesopotamia, and the first Christian **Iran Rejects Christianity** missionaries must also have appeared at that time in the highlands of Iran. The priests of Zoroaster were inflamed with anger when they beheld the advance of the new doctrine which diminished their sphere of power in the west, while in the east Buddhism had been at work for centuries in undermining the pillars of their faith. The downfall of the Parthian princes, who had looked upon matters of religion with indifference, may perhaps have come about indirectly owing to the influence of the priests ; certainly there is no doubt but that the dynastic change was most welcome to the latter. The very first of the Sassanian rulers appears in history as a religious fanatic, whose accession was especially dreaded by the Jews. Almost immediately after coming to the throne he issued several edicts commanding the suppression of the Hebrew faith. During the following years the Zoroastrian religion became one of the chief means for attaining imperial unity. Its diffusion was the highest duty of the ruler ; and the sacred fire remained a symbol of the exclusive and isolated Iranian nationality until it was finally quenched by the waves of Mohammedan conquest. The founder of the Sassanian dynasty, Ardishir Babekan, or Artaxerxes, son of Babek, was born in Persis, the centre of ancient Iran ; his family claimed descent from **Founder of the Sassanidæ** a mythical ancestor, Sasan, and for that reason possessed a hereditary right of priesthood. His father, Babek, seems to have founded a small kingdom in Persis and to have seized the territories of various minor rulers. Although Ardishir vigorously continued his father's policy of territorial expansion, Artabanus V., who died in 224 A.D., permitted him to pursue his way in peace. When it was too late the "King of Kings" took hostile measures against his unruly vassal. Ardishir conquered and put to death Volagases V., the

ARDISHIR, THE FIRST OF THE SASSANID KINGS OF PERSIA
Ardishir Babekan extended his power from the small kingdom of Persis until he conquered the last of the rulers of Parthia and formed the Sassanid empire of Persia. From a rock-sculpture showing the king receiving the sacred symbol from Ormuzd.

last of the Arsacidæ, on the plain of Hormujan in the year 227 A.D.

It was not long before Ardishir was acknowledged as King of Kings by the western provinces of Iran as well as by Armenia ; and the east also soon became subject to his rule, the surviving Arsacid princes taking refuge in India. Other branches of the family of the Arsacidæ became reconciled to the new emperor and retained their provinces. A new feature entered Persian history with the appearance of the first of the Sassanidæ. The ancient traditions of the Achæmenian period were brought into prominence once more, and the consciousness of national unity greatly developed. Ardishir had scarcely founded his empire when he hastened to send a pretentious embassy to the Romans, and demanded that they should cede to him the whole of Western Asia. Soon afterwards he sought to regain the lost provinces in Mesopotamia by force of arms. This was in the year 230 A.D. War with the Persians, as the Iranians were once more called in the west, now that the ancient ruling nation had again risen to power, became inevitable—

whether welcome or otherwise to the Emperor Alexander Severus. The first campaign, fought in the year 231 A.D., was indecisive. In the interior of Persia, however, the culture of Iran was awakened to fresh life and received the full support of the triumphant priesthood. New towns were founded, schools and temples arose on all sides, the judicial system and the army were thoroughly reformed. Everywhere there appeared evidences of a new development of the true Iranian spirit, and before long the nation deemed itself sufficiently strong once more to enforce its old claims to the sovereignty of Western Asia.

The period of the Persian-Roman wars began with the accession of Shapur I., or Sapor, who came to the throne on the death of his father, Artaxerxes I., in the year 241 A.D. The first campaign opened in the following year ; Shapur advanced as far as Antioch, and after several severe engagements had

SHAPUR I. TRIUMPHANT OVER VALERIAN
Shapur I. began the period of the Persian-Roman wars ; in his second campaign he invaded Syria and took the Roman emperor prisoner.

been fought, was forced back to the river Tigris. The Emperor Gordian ceded Armenia and Mesopotamia to the Persians in order to avoid further conflict with a dangerous opponent during a time when serious disturbances were taking place in

Rome. The two empires remained at peace with one another until 258 A.D., when the Persian king again invaded Syria, took the Emperor Valerian prisoner together with his army in 260 A.D., captured Antioch, and returned triumphantly to his country with an immense quantity of plunder. The rising power of the Palmyran king, Odenathus, who declared war on Persia and advanced as far as the gates of Ctesiphon, saved Syria from further invasion; for Shapur was no longer in a position to make war on Rome.

The general state of affairs in his own country may also have diverted the attention of Shapur—an enthusiastic believer in the religion of Zoroaster—from matters of foreign policy. As with all the great religions of the world, imitations and degenerate cults were constantly cropping up among the Zoroastrians. An attempt was made to combine the Iranian faith with Christian and Hebrew elements, and thus to create a new and uniform belief. The leader of the new movement was Manes, the founder of the Manichæan sect, whose first appearance probably took place in the year 238 A.D. Various accounts have been preserved of his relations to Shapur. It is probable that the emperor, who died in 272 A.D., although at first disposed to treat the Manichæans

or Bahram, and his followers were dispersed. Thus the danger of a split in the national religion of Persia was avoided. Iran preserved its own character, but became isolated from all other nations, and in the future was obliged to depend entirely on its

THE SASSANID KING NARSES
In the successful Roman campaign in Persia, Narses was defeated by Diocletian, who obtained a favourable peace.

own resources. There is little to be said about the immediate successors of Shapur, many of whom remained but a short time upon the throne. The war begun by the Emperor Carus in the year 283 A.D., simply because the disturbances in the kingdom of the Sassanidæ seemed to present a favourable opportunity for an invasion, came to an end on the sudden death of the Roman emperor, after his army had advanced as far as Ctesiphon. The campaign of Diocletian in the year 297 A.D. was more successful; after being defeated in one battle the Romans won a brilliant victory over the Sassanian king Narses. A peace favourable to Rome followed. Armenia became a Roman dependency, and several districts beyond the

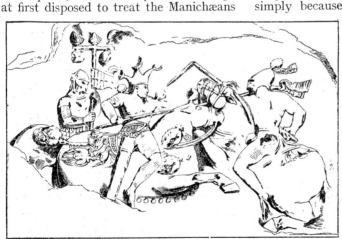

BAHRAM V. FIGHTING THE TARTAR PRINCE
In the reign of Bahram V. the frontier of Persia was pushed out into Transoxania, the country of the nomads. Tradition alleges a personal conflict with the Emperor of China, which is probably represented in this sculpture from Naqsh-i-Rustam.

with tolerance, was finally induced by the orthodox priesthood to take steps toward suppressing the sect. Manes fled to the east, and on his return to Persia in the year 274 A.D., was seized and executed by the son of Shapur, Varanes I.

Tigris were surrendered to the victors. The confusion in Persia did not come to an end until the accession of Shapur II., who ruled from 309 to 380 A.D. His was a truly Oriental government with a born leader of armies at the head of the state.

The wars with Rome, now under Constantine, continued, but with little positive result; the first period ended with a futile siege of Nisibis, or Mygdonia, the Roman stronghold of Eastern Mesopotamia, in the year 350 A.D. When the struggle broke out anew in 359 A.D., Shapur captured the strongly fortified town of Amida after a long and severe contest. The death of Constantine was followed by the accession of Julian the Apostate, who also resolved to walk in the footsteps of Alexander the Great. He set out from Antioch with a well-tried army, and without encountering any great difficulties arrived before Ctesiphon in the year 363 A.D.; but owing to a lack of supplies, he had to fall back pursued by the main body of Shapur's cavalry. Soon after Julian was mortally wounded in a battle, and his successor, Jovian, whom the soldiers had elected from their midst, was compelled to make peace on humiliating terms, in order to save his army from annihilation. Shapur recovered Eastern Mesopotamia, together with Mygdonia, and, thus in possession of a favourable strategic position, was enabled once more to turn to Armenia.

Shapur Defeats the Romans

Armenia was the chief scene of the religious - political struggle that was then taking place along the entire western frontier of the Persian empire; it was a struggle between Christianity and fire-worship, Roman influence against Persian. When, on the accession of Constantine the Great, victory was assured to the Christians in the Roman Empire, the rulers of Armenia and Iberia hastened openly to adopt the Christian faith. They naturally encountered opposition from the adherents of the older religion, who immediately endeavoured to win the support of the Persians, while the Christians looked to Rome for protection.

Even the influence of Julian the Apostate was insufficient to prevent the struggle between Persia and Rome from becoming more and more of a religious war; and, as a result, it followed that until its downfall the Persian empire, in spite of many brilliant successes, was always on the defensive, never once appearing as a conquering nation.

The sweeping victory of Christianity in the west rendered it impossible for the Iranian faith permanently to keep pace with the Persian dominion in Armenia and Mesopotamia. The Iranian emperors had to content themselves with the persecutions of the Christians, begun by Shapur II., and thus at least to ward off the danger from their own territories in the east. The diffusion of Christianity in the west was, therefore, the fundamental reason why the victorious expeditions of the Persians into Roman territory remained so unfruitful; in effect they were little more than sorties from a besieged fortress, or invasions of robbers on a large scale; they were certainly not wars of conquest. After a struggle that kept him actively employed all his days, Shapur succeeded in establishing Persian rule in Armenia; but he was unable to do away with the Christian religion. Under his successors it was in 388 A.D. finally agreed that Armenia should be divided into two parts, one Roman and the other Persian, each of which was to be ruled by a native prince. We have little definite knowledge of the war in which Shapur was engaged on the north-eastern frontier of his kingdom. It is certain, however, that the Persians had to keep a sharp look-out on the nomads of Central Asia, whose frequent migrations were a constant source of danger.

Why Persia Made no Conquests

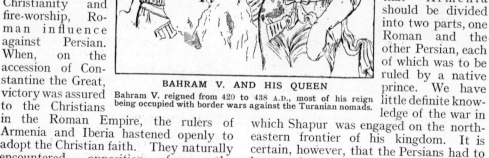

BAHRAM V. AND HIS QUEEN
Bahram V. reigned from 420 to 438 A.D., most of his reign being occupied with border wars against the Turanian nomads.

Of the immediate successors of Shapur, the most distinguished was Yesdigerd I.

(399–420 A.D.), called by his subjects "the Bad," who at first seemed to lean towards the Christian faith, but during his later years became an orthodox believer in the religion of Zoroaster, and a fanatical persecutor of the Christians. In consequence of Yesdigerd's barbarity, war was declared by the Romans, and continued through the second year of the reign of his successor, Bahram V. (420–438 A.D.). On the other hand, the Oriental accounts of an alleged conflict of Bahram with the Emperor of China are wholly without foundation, and were, no doubt, derived from an exaggerated report of one of the frequent border wars against Turanian nomads. It is almost certain that during this period the north-eastern boundary of the Persian empire was pushed out further and further into Transoxania, and that the Persians were actively engaged in diffusing their culture and religion among the Turanians, endeavouring to subdue them by the same method that was employed with such marked success by China on her nomadic neighbours. During the Arabian con-

Wars With the Turanians quest a small nation of Zoroastrians was discovered in the Bokhara of to-day; it bravely resisted the advance of the Moslems, and must at one time have been an advanced post of Persian civilisation in the land of the Mongols.

The Persian emperors were soon compelled to turn their attention to the passes of the Caucasus also ; troops of Huns and "Scythians" had already broken through into Iran, for the inhabitants of Caucasia either could not or would not check their advance. The most important event of the reign of Yesdigerd II. (442–459 A.D.) was the occupation and fortification of the passes of Derbent, near the Caspian Sea. Unfortunately the emperor also permitted himself to be drawn into an attempt to crush the Christians in Armenia, which led only to ruinous wars and remained without permanent result. The Persian kings were well aware of the importance of maintaining their position in the Caucasus ; the Emperor Peroses even requested contributions from the Byzantines for the support of the mountain garrisons, on the ground that the closing of the passes was to the interest of Persians and Romans alike. Peroses successfully made war on the nomads, who advanced from the west of the Caspian Sea ; but

he encountered great difficulty in subduing the Cushans and the Hephtalitæ, who had established a kingdom in Turania, losing his life during the struggle in the year 484 A.D.

The period of Kobad I., who occupied the throne from 488 to 531 A.D., was remarkable in many respects. During his **Reform of the Priesthood** reign there developed a new reforming sect of the fire-worshippers, who were at first favoured by him, but who subsequently involved the empire in serious complications. Although a change in the orthodox belief had been avoided through the suppression of the Manichæans, nevertheless the practical lesson taught by the development of Christianity had produced an effect which was only the more powerful because concealed. The orthodox priesthood became more and more unpopular as time passed ; and, as is almost invariably the case in popular revolutionary movements, extreme political and social opinions were united with ideas of religious reform ; finally both tendencies found their most definite expression in the doctrines of Mazdak. The religious principles of the reformer, which were in the main a continuation of Manichæan ideals, were far less radical than his plans for a social revolution, of which the fundamental idea, a community of goods—even of wives—was received with the utmost enthusiasm by the people. For a time Kobad seems to have regarded the new doctrines as an excellent means for combating the feudalism into which his empire had fallen, and the overwhelming influence of the priesthood. It was not until later that he learned to his sorrow that communism is not precisely the best foundation upon which to build up an Oriental despotism. Mazdak no doubt meant well ; but his methods of improvement were adapted only to the capacities of model citizens, and deteriorated greatly **An Early Persian Communist** in the hands of his followers. The enemies of reform took advantage of the first opportunity offered them for bringing about a successful reactionary movement. Kobad himself was imprisoned, and for several years deprived of all share in the government. Finally, with the assistance of a tribe of nomads, he succeeded in recovering his crown, but was obliged to repeal all laws which had been framed in accordance with the views of Mazdak.

Kobad's second period of rule was occupied chiefly with wars with the Romans, in which he found a good means for diverting the attention of his people from domestic affairs. For the first war the refusal of Rome to pay the customary contributions toward fortifying the passes of the Caucasus furnished a satisfactory

Renewed Wars With Rome pretext. After this quarrel was settled, a second soon followed. During the very last days of his life Kobad was compelled once more to lead an army to the west, this time in order to maintain the influence of Persia over Lasistan, an important South Caucasian kingdom, whose prince had become a convert to Christianity and an ally of the Byzantine empire.

After the death of Kobad the usual quarrels as to the succession arose, and finally ended in 531 A.D. with the accession of Khosru I., or Anushirvan, whom Kobad had looked upon as the most capable of his sons. Khosru was a champion of the ancient Persian spirit, a friend of the priestly class, and an irreconcilable enemy of the reformers of the school of Mazdak, who had chosen one of his numerous brothers as their imperial candidate. During his reign the Persian empire attained to the height of its splendour; indeed, the government of Khosru I., " the Just," was both equitable and powerful. But it must not be forgotten that it also signified the final victory of reaction and the cessation of all development. Nor did the brilliant feats of arms accomplished by Khosru alter this fact, of which the results were, one hundred years later, suddenly to become manifest, with most disastrous effects.

One of Khosru's first acts was to make peace with the Romans, who agreed to pay a large contribution towards the fortification of the Caucasian passes, which the Persian emperor began anew on a great

Khosru, a Splendid Reactionary scale; the Byzantines, however, retained Lasistan. In addition to strengthening the Caucasus, Khosru also sought to fortify the north-eastern frontier of his empire by constructing a great wall after the Chinese model, at the same time substantiating by force of arms his old claims to a portion of North-western India. But he soon turned his attention again to the west; for during the reign of Justinian I. the Byzantine empire had

suddenly awakened to new life, overthrowing the dominion of the Vandals in Africa and annihilating the Goths in Italy. The impression made by these events on the Christian inhabitants of his kingdom was alone sufficient to cause Khosru to take measures of defence; and of all defensive measures, the very best, according to the opinion of the Persians, was a sudden campaign of aggression. Consequently, war against the Romans followed in the spring of 540 A.D., without being preceded by the conventional declaration. The Romans had no army with which to fight the Persians, and Khosru, who did not entertain any thoughts of permanent conquest, plundered as many Syrian towns as possible during a short campaign, and exacted from others exorbitant ransoms. He also captured Antioch, which was very badly defended, and refused to return to his own dominions until a large sum of money had been paid him by the Byzantines, and an annual tribute promised. During the next few years he

Raids on Byzantine Dominions met with less success, and in 545 A.D. a peace was concluded. In Lasistan, however, the war with the Romans still continued; for Khosru was most anxious to acquire possession of this country, which extended as far as the Black Sea, and he even formed a scheme for building a fleet there, in order to attack Constantinople by water. On the other hand, the Romans considered themselves to be the natural allies of the Christian inhabitants of Lasistan, and looked upon the province itself as a bulwark of defence against the encroachments of the tribes of the Caucasus, as well as of the Scythians and Huns, who were ever lying in wait beyond the mountain wall. The struggle ended disastrously for the Persians, and Lasistan was surrendered to the Byzantines in the year 556 A.D. During the last few years of this war the attention of Khosru had been directed chiefly to Central Asia, where affairs had once more assumed a threatening aspect. The kingdom of the Hephtalitæ had fallen before the attack of the Turks, who burst forth from Eastern Turkestan in 555 A.D., and founded a powerful empire in Transoxania. Owing to the skilful diplomacy of Khosru, Persia escaped the consequences of this storm, and was itself able to take part in the sharing of the plunder. During the following years there were no further military operations on the western frontier; but the spiritual war between Christianity and fire-worship still continued. That Khosru was greatly interested in the religious life of Western Asia was proved by his interference in the affairs of Yemen, whither Christianity had penetrated through the agency of the Abyssinians. With the help of a Persian army the latter were driven out of Arabia in 575 A.D., and a Persian protectorate, which lasted until the time of Mahomet, was established in the south-western part of the peninsula. Towards the end of the reign of Khosru war broke out anew with Rome; Persian troops advanced as far as Antioch, and a number of indecisive battles were fought in Armenia.

Under Khosru's successor, Hormuzd IV. (573–590 A.D.), the boundary dispute continued. One of the results of this constant state of war was that the Persians dethroned their emperor, who was most unpopular and apparently of disordered intellect. His son, Khosru II., was installed in his place, but was straightway compelled to flee the country by Bahram, a general who had risen in revolt. With the help of the Byzantines —who were, of course, well paid for their good offices—Khosru II. finally succeeded in expelling the usurper from his provinces. But the friendly relations with Byzantium were not of long duration; in fact, an insurrection that broke out in Constantinople

Plunder of Syria and Mesopotamia

gave Khosru, or Aparvez, "the Victorious," a welcome pretext for declaring himself in favour of the losing side, that he might set out on a plundering expedition through Syria and Mesopotamia. Although these campaigns of robbery, which began in the year 604 A.D., and constantly increased in radius of action, were of little benefit to the Persians and cost them dearly in troops, they had a marked effect in preparing the way for

the Mohammedan conquest. It was owing to these same expeditions of Khosru that the power of Roman Syria and Mesopotamia was broken. The Arabs of the steppes, however, who assisted both Persians and Romans, according to the whim of the moment, became trained in war and pillage, and

Preparing the Way for Islam

were constantly being stirred up to the highest pitch of excitement, until finally the hand of Mahomet welded their various tribal elements into a power that Western Asia was totally unable to resist.

Persia arrived at the height of her military glory during the years 614–622 A.D. Damascus was captured and plundered in 614 A.D.; Jerusalem, together with the whole of Palestine, yielded in 615 A.D.; Egypt was conquered in 616 A.D. The armies of Persia then advanced into Asia Minor; and finally Persian troops encamped on the shores of the Bosphorus, within sight of Constantinople, at the very same time that a Scythian army was threatening the city from the European side. Heraclius, the Roman emperor, resolved to avert

KHOSRU II. RECEIVING THE ROYAL DIADEM
Khosru II., one of the last Sassanid kings of Persia, was surnamed Aparvez, "the Victorious." He broke the power of Roman Syria and Mesopotamia and thus prepared the way for the Mohammedan conquest.

the danger by making a counter attack on Persia. His plan was wholly successful; he advanced through Armenia to Atropatene, destroyed the temple of the Zoroastrians, and compelled Khosru to return to Persia in 623 A.D. During the following years, also, he held the Persians in check, threatened Ctesiphon in 627 A.D., and finally brought matters to such a pass that Khosru was deserted by his own subjects, who had become thoroughly embittered, owing to the excessively heavy burdens of war. The army, which until this time had been encamped opposite Constantinople, retreated in disorder to Persia, and found that Khosru had already been dethroned and put to death in the spring of 628 A.D. The fact that it finally became necessary to enrol even women in the ranks of the Persian forces is a proof of the terrible loss of life occasioned by the ambition and insatiable greed of the king.

Khosru was succeeded by Kobad II., who reigned seven months only—from February to September, 628 A.D.—and made peace with Heraclius. The reigns of Kobad's successors also were short. Among them were two daughters of Khosru, who came to the throne on account of the lack of male princes, and the grandson of Khosru, Yesdigerd III. (632–651 A.D.), the last of the Sassanidæ. The wars with the Arabs broke out during the first years of Yesdigerd's reign, and at the same time the gradual dissolution of the empire began.

Lack of Male Soldiers and Princes

It has already been mentioned that the exhaustion of the Persian empire—a result of the incessant wars with the Byzantines—contributed greatly to the victory of the Arabs; but that the Persians were so swiftly and thoroughly conquered by the Moslems was due almost entirely to the isolation into which both people and prince had fallen, and to the stubbornness with which they held fast to their obsolete religion and culture. All that was pro-gressive in the teachings of Manes and Mazdak had been forcibly suppressed; and while the most profound religious conceptions were developing in other lands the faith of Zoroaster became utterly ossified.

Practically nothing had been accomplished in either science or art; and when Khosru II. determined to build a city that should surpass Antioch in splendour, the result was little more than a grotesque imitation of Roman models. The pagan philosophers, who sought refuge and sympathy at the Persian court, returned bitterly disappointed to Roman territory. That Persia proved incapable of becoming an active member of the western civilised world, but obstinately preserved its own worst characteristics, only to be compelled finally to exchange them for an even less efficient religion and culture, was one of the greatest misfortunes in the history of Western Asia. How far Christianity would have continued in its victorious course had it not been for the barrier of Iran is hard to determine; at any rate, the great success attained by the one Christian sect that was tolerated by the Persian emperors, the Nestorians, proves that it would have made great progress.

Persia's Lack of Culture

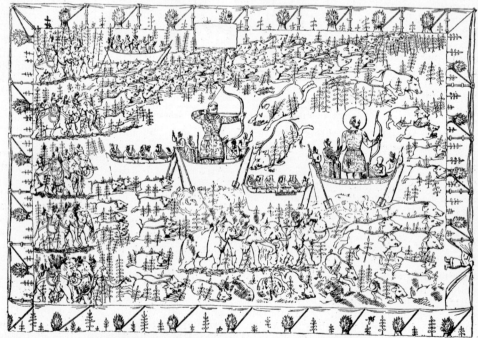

BAS-RELIEFS FROM THE PALACE OF KHOSRU II.

Khosru II., "the Victorious," determined to build a city which should surpass Antioch in its splendour, but the result was little more than a grotesque imitation of Roman models, and this relief from his palace seems to bear out the view.

ARABIA BEFORE ISLAM

THE name Arabia or Aribi did not originally belong to the whole peninsula, but, in the Assyrian inscriptions where it first meets us, designated only the north-western portion, substantially the Syrian desert and the adjoining districts ; that is to say, the region occupied by the nomads who came into contact with the inhabitants of the countries on the Euphrates and of Syria. There, after 1000 B.C., the fourth great migration settled, that of the Arabs themselves, after whom the land henceforth was called.

The Syrian desert stretches along the hinterland of Northern Palestine in its widest extent towards the north. Here to the east and the south of the district of Damascus was one of the most suitable points of attack for Arabian tribes. Here, then, we find Arabs mentioned for the first time. In the great army which Bir-idri of Damascus put into the field against Shalmaneser II., the Arab " Gindibu "— the name is quite regular in the Arabian form, Jundub or Gundub—was also forced to furnish his contingent. We must regard him as an Arab sheikh, who lived within the sphere of Bir-idri's power, and stood in a dependent relation to him, a position which we shall repeatedly find after this time. The mention of this fact signifies the beginning of the Arabian immigration into those parts ; that is to say, the beginning of the same great movement which culminated in the spread of Islam.

Beginning of Arabian Immigration

Our next notice is that Tiglath-pileser IV. made expeditions to Arabia and forced various Arabian tribes, whom he enumerates, to pay tribute. He was acquainted with a " kingdom " of Aribi in the north, in the Syrian steppe, which was ruled by queens—for instance, Zabibi and Samsi—who paid tribute and acknowledged the suzerainty of Assyria, as he definitely records, in 738 and 733 B.C. The subject condition of Aribi or Arabi, occasionally enforced by fresh chastisements, is recorded under Sargon, Sennacherib, and Esarhaddon.

Further to the west, in the land which adjoins the district of Southern Philistia and comprises the borderland of Egypt, or Musri, Tiglath-pileser IV. appointed a Bedouin sheikh as Assyrian " overseer." The district, which hitherto had been subject to Egypt, thus became an outlying Assyrian state under native princes, appointed by Assyria. A theory, according to which there were two " Musris," the one being Egypt, the other an unknown country in Northern Arabia, has lately been put forward. It is sufficient to say that the case made out for this view is wholly inadequate. The Musri over which Tiglath-pileser appointed the Arab sheikh Idibi'ilu as warden of the marches is the borderland of Egypt, not a hypothetical country in Northern Arabia. Idibi'ilu did not hold his own for long ; for under Sargon we find that the governor of Musri, who is no longer appointed by Assyria, but is dependent on the " king of Melukhkha," is no other than Pharaoh, king of Egypt, or Pir'u of Musri. The king of Melukhkha is, without question, the Ethiopian monarch with whom Egypt was allied, probably Kashta.

Arabia Under Assyria

Until the year 670 B.C. only the kingdom of Aribi was kept in strict subjection to Assyria. Esarhaddon then, in continuance of his Egyptian policy, attempted to bring additional parts of Arabia under his dominion. The discord between Assyria and Babylonia, which was accentuated by the victory of the military party and the accession of Ashurbanipal, destroyed all these successes won in the spirit of Babylonian influence. Shamash-shum-ukin sought help against Assyria where he could, and summoned into the land the Bedouins, who had been so long kept in check on the frontiers. Other tribes and peoples under their " kings " now meet us as allies of the Babylonians. Besides the kingdom of Aribi, which played a less aggressive part, there were in particular the Kedar, nominally a vassal people of Aribi, and west of these the Nebaioth of the Bible, or Nabaiati of the cuneiform inscriptions. The Nabaiati possessed the Syrian desert up to the borders of the Assyrian province ; they harassed the vassal states, Moab and Edom,

Raids of the Arabs situated on the border of the steppe and roamed northward as far as Damascus. They were, it is true, chastised by Ashurbanipal's expeditions, and driven out of the region of civilisation; but it lies in the nature of the circumstances that they would be kept back only as long as they continued to fear a power which at once anticipated every encroachment. When, therefore, with the death of Ashurbanipal and Nabopolassar's declaration of independence, the beginning of the end drew near, the Arabs had a splendid opportunity. Naturally they immediately advanced once more. According to a notice in the book of the prophet Jeremiah, which may perhaps be traced to the annals of the kings of Judah, Nebuchadnezzar undertook an expedition against the Kedar and punished them by destroying their stronghold Hazor.

The want of native accounts from the Persian era deprives us also of any notices as to the relations of Persia with Arabia. The few materials, however, that we possess are at least sufficient to corroborate the idea which we should naturally form from the preceding and the subsequent periods. So long as the Persian empire was firmly consolidated and adopted a strong foreign policy, even the Arabs had to curb their eager passions. At a later period they were restrained more by concessions and payments. When Cambyses marched against Egypt they were compelled to supply him with the means for his march through the desert, more particularly the camels.

Persia and Arabia Darius mentions North Arabia — the Assyrian Aribi — among the countries subject to him ; but since it is uncertain whether some other names of subject peoples refer to Central and Eastern Arabia, we do not know how far his sovereignty extended. In any case the advance of the Kedar against Palestine, begun under Ashurbanipal and Nebuchadnezzar, assumed wider importance. In Yemen the kingdom of the Sabæans was now flourishing ; in the

north political organisations, like those of the Aribi, Kedar, and Nabaiati, were the medium of trade. We do not know when these peoples were replaced by others ; and after all it does not signify what the names of the sheikhs were who maintained relations with the Persian officials. The rule over the wild sons of the desert certainly was secured to them by this alliance, and yet they remained in all their sympathies and ideas no less Bedouins than their countrymen. They cannot indeed be compared with the Bedouin sheikh, who is distinguishable from his poor fellow-tribesman, his " brother," only by a larger share of cattle ; they had by this time thoroughly well civilised themselves, so far as it was a matter of filling their purses.

An inscription from Teima, which belongs to the Persian or the New Babylo-Assyrian time, gives us a picture of the life and organisation of the North Arabian towns and states with their sanctuaries. This resembles far more the picture which some of the towns of Palestine and Israel present during the time of the kings

Life in Early Arabia than that which the later Islamitic tradition has given of the conditions of the pre-Islamitic time. There is a city sanctuary with a specified domain, which is reserved for the maintenance of the cult and its priests. The hierarchy, at all times ready to open the doors of the temple to new divinities, was bound then to take measures for their support. The necessary means were derived partly from the temple income, partly from the royal revenues ; even the king, therefore, had his " fiscal " domain. The language of the inscription is not Arabic, which was not written until Mahomet, but Aramaic. This result of civilisation was therefore borrowed from Assyria or Babylonia, where Aramaic was the written and spoken language of commerce ; the portrait of the high-priest Salm-ushezib shows Assyrian finish, and he himself bears a name constructed on Babylonian analogy. With the written language were borrowed also the political and fiscal terminology.

The fall of the Persian empire would have been a welcome opportunity for the Arabs to invade the civilised countries had not more energetic opponents soon arisen in the Hellenistic states. In addition to this, civilisation had already taken a somewhat firmer hold of these countries. The beginnings, traces of which may be seen in the kingdoms of Aribi, with the inscription of Teima, developed during the Hellenistic era into the kingdom of the Nabatæans, which now exists for some three centuries as a marvellous creation of the mixed civilisation of North Arabia, thoroughly preserving its national Arabian character, on the borders of a civilisation which was once Oriental but now impregnated afresh with Hellenism. Of this kingdom an account has already been given.

The annexation of Nabatæa by the Romans resulted in the prosperity of a new Arabian commercial state—namely, Palmyra, for which also we may here refer our readers to a previous section.

With the fall of the restraining state of Palmyra (273 A.D.) the Saracens, a name by which the Arabs inhabiting the steppes were usually designated by the Romans, found the civilised country open to them whenever the Roman power was unable to protect the frontiers with a firm hand. In the wars of the Romans, Byzantines, and Sassanidæ, they played **Rise of the Saracens** an important part as lords of the desert, and as valuable allies in the struggle for the broad districts on the Euphrates so easily traversed by them.

Both Byzantium and the court of the Sassanidæ were unable to extend their frontiers further than the region of civilisation, and were compelled, like the Assyrians and Persians, to allow the Saracens to retain their territory. As usual, it was thought to be enough if the sheikhs of the adjoining tribal districts were won over and brought into loyal relations with the empire. Just as Idibi'ilu was appointed by Tiglath-pileser to rule over the frontier district of Egypt, and the Nabatæans were the allies of the Romans, so now the Byzantines and Persians favoured the formation of Arab states on their frontiers, the " kings " of which, by their support from the Great Power, and with titles conferred on them by it, ruled over the sons of the desert. With an organisation superior to the Bedouins, they formed a protection both for the Persians and Byzantines against the advance of subsequent tribes. In this way both the princely house of the Ghassanidæ, on the Byzantine frontiers in Syria, and the Lachmidæ, on the

Babylonian frontiers, ruled under Persian supremacy as the connecting link and barrier between civilised country and steppe. They discharged this function, perpetually warring against each other, both on their own initiative and in the service of their liege lords, with ceaseless skirmishes and raids, which the earliest **Last Semitic Migration** Arabian poets known to us have sung. Finally, the pent-up power of the tide of nations in the heart of the country broke away through, and, under the flag of Islam, once more flooded the countries of civilisation, helping the " Arabian migration " to force its victorious way, and at the same time rolling on the last wave of the Semites which the history of the world knows. In the ninth century B.C. we found the first Arabs on the frontiers of civilisation pressing on after the Aramæans ; in the seventh century A.D., 1,600 years later, the Islamitic movement inundated the East. Since then 1,200 years have elapsed, and we cannot perceive any new movement in the cradle of the Semitic nations, which is, to a great extent, depopulated.

We now turn to Eastern Arabia, with the coast districts on the Persian Gulf, and their mysterious centre, Yemama. The Chaldæans, or Kasdim, whom we meet in the civilised zone first in South Babylonia, probably came hence into the light of history. So far as they became Babylonians, they no longer concern us here. But as the western districts, already occupied by " Arabs," present, even in the time of Ashurbanipal, distinct traces of their earlier Aramæan inhabitants, we may equally conjecture that remains also of the Kasdim were left in Arabia itself, until they were absorbed by the onward movement of the Arabs. The Bible is acquainted with Arabian Kasdim, who are to be found in the East—that is to say, toward Yemama ; in these may fairly be seen the first stratum of the great **Chaldæans in East Arabia** migration. Later they are regarded in the introduction to the Book of Job on the basis of ancient tradition as being, with the Sabæans, the rulers of Central Arabia.

A part of the Kasdim must have occupied the Arabian maritime districts of the Persian Sea. As the Chaldæans of the South Babylonian " sea country " were masters of all that was still left of Babylonian navigation and commerce on the Persian

Sea, so these Chaldæans also must have occupied the island of Dilmun, or Bahrein, which in ancient times was in close connection with Babylonia. Under Sargon, their king Uperi, after the capture of Babylon, entered into the same relations with the Assyrians which he had hitherto kept up with Merodach-baladan, the

Yemama Invaded by Assyria king of the "sea country" and of Babylon. Whether this king was an Arab, or still a Chaldæan, must remain uncertain. Esarhaddon records his expedition into the interior of Eastern Arabia, called by him Bazu, the biblical Buz ; it can hardly be looked for elsewhere than in Yemama. Eight " kings " and queens are enumerated whose " towns " had been captured. If ever information should reach us from this still unexplored corner of the earth, we may become acquainted even there with the traces of a culture of which notices are found in Arabian writers.

Strabo, following old accounts, can speak of Chaldæans on the sea, whose capital and seaport, Gerrha, formed the emporium for the trade with the interior. Antiochus the Great, after the rebellion of Molon, once more secured the eastern provinces of his empire and resumed friendly relations with the Indan kings. Further, on an expedition undertaken against the maritime districts of the Persian Sea, in return for a very considerable " present," he confirmed, in 205 B.C., the independence of the Gerrhæans, who were all-important for the commerce on the Persian Sea and with the interior of Arabia.

Under the dominion of the Parthians, who did not trouble themselves about such trifles as the command of the sea and trade, a successor of the former Chaldæan " sea country " arose in the shape of Messene. This was a state which, about the beginning of the Christian era, ruled the delta of the Euphrates and Tigris,

State of Messene as well as the adjoining coast districts, and thus controlled the trade with Babylonia, so far as it yet existed on the Persian Sea, and did not go through Yemen. From some notices of classical writers and from coins, we are acquainted with a series of kings of Messene, who were subject to the influence of Hellenism and Parthia, and had a preponderance of Aramæan subjects, but nevertheless are certainly to be claimed as Arabs. Possibly, the head of

the dynasty was a certain Adad-nadin-akh, whose inscription has been found upon bricks in a late addition to the palace at Tello, the town of the old Babylonian kings and patesis of Lagash ; he had, therefore, built his palace there. The inscription is bilingual, being written in Aramaic and Greek.

The most important part, as the seat of a peculiar civilisation, was played in antiquity by the south, or rather the south-west corner of Arabia, the so-called Arabia Felix. This name was, perhaps, originally given, owing to a misapprehension, which took the Arabian meaning of Yemen, the land lying to the right of the Arab looking toward the east, in the sense of the augur, to whom the right side was the propitious quarter. The country, a lofty mountain plateau, with isolated higher elevations and better watered than the north, although only by mountain streams, was always carefully cultivated in the times to which the inscriptions refer. Here also the rivers forced the inhabitants to take measures to dam up the precious water in times of

Civilisation of Arabia Felix brimming streams, and to store it against the dry seasons. The dam of Mareb, the ruins of which are still standing, appeared to the Arabs of the desert as something marvellous.

Numerous ruined sites have been already discovered, the old names of which are mentioned in inscriptions still visible ; but little has been done towards furnishing science with what is on the surface, to say nothing of all that is hidden in the earth, to which these remains bear witness. Where only copies of the inscriptions themselves, hastily made by an intrepid traveller at the risk of his life, are forthcoming, it is impossible to form any idea of the remaining ruins ; and the temples and buildings to which the inscriptions refer, and the site of which they record, exist for us only in name. These do not enable us to draw a connected picture of the political development.

The most ancient inscriptions which we possess belong to an age which ends in the eighth and seventh centuries. A proof that a connection already existed with the great civilised countries is shown by the character of the script. This alphabetical writing, which has been developed from the general Semitic alphabet, with the invention of some additional symbols for the greater variety of sounds in this South Arabian Ma'initic or Minæan language, may perhaps be taken to represent in the perfection of its form a completely independent effort, as compared with the North Semitic alphabet of the Aramæans and Canaanites. Alphabetical writing was invented in Phœnicia. There the Canaanites and Aramæans became acquainted with it ; and thence it made its way to Yemen. It is evident that the same, or perhaps a still brisker intercourse was then maintained with the regions of civilisation from the Euphrates to the Mediterranean than in the times on which light is gradually being cast by inscriptions. We found indications of this intercourse in the ancient Babylonian inscriptions of Gudea and Naram-Sin. The very same streams of nations, which can be traced from the south of the peninsula so far as the civilised countries of the Mediterranean during the Islamitic age, were flowing at the time when the " Canaanites," and later the Aramæans, flooded the East. The tribe of the

Sabæans Masters of Yemen Sabæans, which submitted to Assyria, is mentioned as early as the reigns of Tiglath-pileser and Sargon. Of all the Arabian tribes then mentioned, it is the one which dwelt farthest to the south. Later on, the Assyrians were no longer able to re ain their hold upon the country. In the north, therefore, " Arabs " became masters of the country. At the same time, in the south also, inscriptions mention attacks of " Arabs." These inscriptions, however, are not composed in the language of the Minæans, but in a dialectic variety. The new masters of the south are the same people whom we have recognised as allies of the Assyrians—namely, the Sabæans. Approximately about Esarhaddon's time the Sabæans became masters of the country in place of the Minæans. For a half century, therefore, we now meet with " kings of Saba " as masters of Yemen and its civilisation.

The "treasures of Arabia," henceforth, according to Oriental ideas, belong to the Sabæans ; Sabæans now meet us in the Hebrew inscriptions, in place of the Minæans, and the intercourse with the south is now maintained by the Kedar. It is seen that Assyria had once more to her own advantage separated the masses

of nations in Arabia. The position of the great Minæan nation, which had dominated the south, was now taken by two peoples of different stock—the Kedar are " Arabs," but not the Sabæans—who, being enemies, acted as a counterpoise to each other and rendered it easier for Assyria to rule. Esarhaddon had shown

Assyrian Policy in Arabia himself here, in continuation of his Egyptian policy, to be one of the acutest of Oriental statesmen. If finally the " Assyrian policy " had not prevailed over the " Babylonian," the trade of Arabia would have been carried on under the control of Assyria. The struggle between Assyria and Babylon destroyed all this ; for although the Kedar could be chastised, any influence over the south was lost. The Sabæans were able to withdraw from this Assyrian guardianship and to assert their independence. The realm of Saba had its most important towns situated south of the Jof country of the Minæans. The capital is Mareb, as it appears up to the Himyaritic conquest. The kingdom remained purely Sabæan for several centuries. Then other nations obtained the supremacy, and their rulers styled themselves " kings of Saba."

The period of Ma'in and Saba, down till about 300 B.C., was that of Yemen's greatest prosperity ; and for a considerable time it commanded the trade with India. Babylonia was then cut off from the Persian Sea by the Chaldæans. Egypt was not in a position to hold the Red Sea, and thus it was a prosperous time for the intermediate trade, which went through Arabia from Yemen by land northward to the Philistine towns, or from the ports of Western Arabia to the harbours of Egypt. On the caravan route which led from Kuser, or Leukos Limen, on the Red Sea to Thebes and Koptos, the main line of communication of the Thebaid to the sea, Minæo-Sabæan inscriptions, besides numerous Egyptian ones, have been cut on

Greatness of South Arabia the face of the rocks, testifying to the former commercial greatness of South Arabia. While the Sabæans were dependent for their intercourse with Palestine and the Euphratean countries on the services of the North Arabian Kedar, and afterwards of the Nabatæans, through whose land they passed, the Minæans had reached those districts directly ; in Warka, or Uruk, in South Babylonia, a monument of these relations has been found in a

Minæan inscription. When once more the Orient came under a dominion which embraced the old seat of culture in Babylonia, and at the same time was able to revive the Babylonian ideas in place of the Persian feudal economy, the conditions were then altered to the disadvantage of South Arabia. Sabæan **Sabæan Commerce Ruined** interests must have been greatly prejudiced when the Ptolemies really set free the sea route round Arabia, and actually utilised it for trade, while the Seleucidæ reckoned with the Nabatæans and Gerrhæans as middlemen. Ptolemy II., Philadelphus, in his wars with the Seleucidæ circumnavigated Arabia and made an attack on the Seleucid possessions on the Persian Gulf. He and his successor founded on the western coast of the Red Sea, as far as the straits of Babel-Mandeb, Egyptian colonies, which sapped the vitality of the Sabæan commerce with Abyssinia and Egypt. These colonies undoubtedly formed stations for a direct Indian trade. In Adulis, or Zulla, where the communications between Saba and Habesh, or Abyssinia, crossed, Ptolemy III., Euergetes, erected an inscription commemorating one of his victories. Thus it was not a revived Babylon of Alexander that became mistress of the Indian trade and the ruin of Saba, but Alexandria.

We must place in the third or second century B.C. the internal commotions to which the realm of Saba was exposed. These brought another people into power, the Himyarites, who had settled originally in the south-west corner of the peninsula and occupied the capital at this time. Their kings, just like their predecessors, style themselves " kings of Saba," but add to this title " and of Raidan," the name of their Himyarite ancestral fortress. Thus, then, no longer Sabæans but Himyarites rule in Saba.

At the same time, or soon afterwards, **Extension of Abyssinia** the lords of Abyssinia, whither formerly the Sabæans had sent colonies, began, as the Egyptian power dwindled, to extend their dominion beyond the seas. Starting from the reoccupied Adulis, where one of their kings, Zoskales, son of Alizanes, had his inscription cut by the side of that of Ptolemy Euergetes, they crossed to Arabia and first gained a firm footing on the coast. There they had possessions as early as the first century B.C. ; that is, the sea, or

at least intercourse with Abyssinia, was barred for the rulers of Saba, who were exposed to continual attacks from the Abyssinian governors. The same king, who perpetuated his name as Adulis by the side of Ptolemy's, then subjugated the whole Arabian coast to Leuke Kome, the former seaport of the Nabatæans, and Yemen, so far as the Sabæan royal title, which became gradually wider, laid claim to it. From that time, from the second or third centuries A.D., Sabæa is subject to the suzerainty of Abyssinia.

This sovereignty did not escape opposition ; the South Arabian Himyarites made many, and occasionally successful, attempts to eject the Abyssinians from the country. They succeeded, indeed, for a considerable time in once more winning their independence under the standard of Judaism, which in the last centuries before the Christian era conquered Arabia and led to a revival of power in the old state of Yemen. Our information does not go so far as to enable us to recognise the political parties and currents from which the new prosperity **Judaism in Yemen** was developed ; from the nature of things, however, the general condition of affairs may be approximately ascertained. Judaism was a power to be reckoned with in all the great empires of civilisation, played a foremost part in the kingdom of the Nabatæans, and was especially prominent in Egyptian business life. In its still eager desire to proselytise it was spread by commercial connections into South-west Arabia, whither the civilised empires could not go with their armies, although they had long cherished a desire for the land, the possession of which would have put the Indian trade into the hands of its masters. The prevailing religion there was that of the old Sabæans. The shrewd Jewish men of business were opposed to this heathenism. While the ruling nobles who owned the land clung to the old religion, the missionaries of Judaism found receptive hearers, where it was possible for men to appreciate in their own persons the value of their promises of happiness—namely, among that section of the population which was engaged in trade and industries. In contradistinction to the nobility, it must have been the town population which received Judaism. By its connection with Judaism this population acquired new trength ; the land-owning nobility lost nore and more in influence before the ncreasing wealth and power of the commercial class. Finally the kingdom saw tself compelled, as, for example, in Adiabene also, either by peaceful or by violent changes to side with the merchant class rather than with the nobility, and to accept Judaism ; that is to say, the organisation of the feudal state formed by the Himyarite conquest had been transformed nto that of a mercantile community. This reorganisation put Yemen in a position to expel the Abyssinians from the country. For some centuries now Jewish rulers held the dominion as " kings of Saba."

Such independence did not benefit Rome. The Roman attempts under Augustus to obtain possession of Yemen had been made in a period when the Himyarites were weak, and yet they had failed. Judaism had led to a recovery of strength ; then the spiritual power could be opposed only by another spiritual power, and this was found in Christianity. Even the dominion of Judaism in Yemen had its dark side and could not but meet with a period of decline. Christianity, the religion of the poor, which followed on its track, here found its path made easy. Just as Judaism had once formed the standard under which the vigorous components of the people rallied against a ruling class which was no longer competent to discharge its duties, so all who were excluded from the government joined forces under the sign of the Cross.

Jewish Kings in Yemen

The legends of the Christian saints recount terrible sacrifices of human life, which the movement against the ruling class entailed. Despite all the zeal of the Christians in the lands of civilisation, they could not win an unaided victory. The attempt had to be made indirectly. After about the fourth century Abyssinia was won for Christianity from Egypt. The relations maintained with the Ptolemies were once more resumed, and were kept up by the Church, for Abyssinia always received bishops from the patriarch in Alexandria. Since Egypt was Byzantine, the kings of Abyssinia were on friendly terms with the court of Byzantium, and both shared in the common desire for the treasures of Yemen. But at Byzantium the lesson once taught to Augustus had not been forgotten, and it was recognised that the desired goal could only be reached by the former conquerors, who had been driven out by Judaism ; an attempt was therefore made to incite these to a new attack. In the year 525 A.D. the Jew sh-Sabæan empire fell, after a valiant resistance by the last Jewish king, Joseph dhu Nuas, who is represented in the martyrologies as a monster, but is better appreciated in the otherwise obscure Islamitic tradition. Yemen became more Abyssinian and was governed by an Abyssinian viceroy, who was very independent. Tradition tells of four rulers, the reign of one of whom is recorded in inscriptions. This state of things lasted some seven hundred years.

Fall of the Jewish Kingdom

The Jewish monarchy fell, but the old nobility was not yet destroyed ; the latter was forced naturally to place its hopes on the opponents of the Byzantines, the Persians. A descendant of the noble families went first to Babylonia and then to the Persian court in order to obtain help from that quarter. Khosru Anushirwan crossed over to Arabia and drove out the Abyssinians about 575 A.D. Yemen became first a vassal state of Persia, then a province under Persian governors. Christianity and Byzantine influence were thus overthrown. The old nobility and paganism once more enjoyed a brief renaissance until, some fifty years later, the great union of all Arabia under Islam was completed.

In the rise of the power of Mahomet also the opposing forces which were at work are recognisable ; the threads which ran to Byzantium and the Sassanian court can be taken up in Mecca. The nobles of Mecca, who commanded the trade of the important caravan station, were closely connected with Yemen. Mahomet, however, having failed to find help from Judaism, looked for support against the Meccan nobility, strengthened by the paganism of Yemen, from the Abyssinians who, even then, had possessions on the Arabian coast. But the old forces and contrasts of civilisation outlasted the conqueror and his bandits. The party of the nobility reached the throne, and the contrast between Northern and Southern Arabia is continually reappearing in the history of the following centuries.

The Rise of Mahomet

HUGO WINCKLER
LEONARD W. KING

MECCA, THE HOLY CITY OF THE MOHAMMEDAN WORLD, SHOWING THE PILGRIMS AT THE KAABA

Mecca was the religious centre of the old pagan tribes of Arabia. It grew up around the Kaaba, a square temple, in the wall of which was inserted the famous Black Stone. Although Mecca was hostile to Mahomet in his early days and had to be conquered by him he preserved the sacred character of the holy city.

WESTERN ASIA FROM THE TIME OF MAHOMET

BY DR. HEINRICH SCHURTZ & LEONARD W. KING, M.A.

THE HEROIC AGE OF ISLAM

THE inhabitants of Arabia are separated into two distinct classes as a result of differences of occupation and manner of life. Even during the period of temporary union at the time of the Mohammedan conquests, the cleft caused by these differences was but superficially bridged over. The free Bedouin nomads who dwell in tents on the pasturages of the steppes, whose possessions are their flocks and herds, look down with hatred and contempt upon the agriculturists, who cultivate the scanty fertile regions— "dragging the plough with their own hands like slaves"—and crowd together, with labourers and menials, in the villages and towns. On the other hand, the agricultural classes, superior to the Bedouins both in numbers and in education, return the predatory nomads of the desert their dislike in full measure. Nevertheless, the Arabians never succeeded in making a mark in history until both elements forgot their differences, and were welded into temporary unity by a higher power. No unifying force can emanate from the Bedouins, for their whole endeavour is towards disintegration; moreover, the poverty of their land is in itself an insurmountable obstacle to their joining together in large bodies. The tribal sentiment, which transcends all other instincts and emotions, excludes the conception of nationality; and constant feuds only increase antagonisms, and hinder all mutual understanding. Even the possibility of the scattered races being forced into union by the sword of an ambitious ruler is small; for every attempt of this nature has first to reckon not only with the independent character of the Bedouins, to whom servile obedience is unknown, but also with the all-powerful clan interests, before which the very idea of individuality vanishes. Before the time of Mahomet, however, the thought had never occurred to any Bedouin that he might make use of religious fanaticism as a means for union; few races of Western Asia are so completely devoid of the religious emotions as are the inhabitants of the Arabian steppes. In this respect the Arabs stand in sharp contrast to their Semitic relatives, the Jews of Palestine, as well as to the ancient Semites of Babylonia, whose ability, first to extend their influence over the lands of Sumerian culture, and finally to attain a position of supremacy, seems to have been due almost entirely to their advanced religious development. There was no such thing as a perfected mythology in Arabia. Nothing more than a cult of rude images—which originated, no doubt, in the worship of ancestors—and a veneration of certain stars and trees, together with an indefinite belief in a supreme being, Allah, was exhibited by the Arab of early times. Even to-day the true Bedouin has but little interest in matters of belief, and is far enough from being a fanatic ; to h m the prohibitions and dogmas of the Koran seem scarcely to be in existence. This scanty develop-

Bedouins' Scanty Religion ment of religion and insuperable indifference to matters of faith is an outcome of the poverty of imagination of the Arabian people, a characteristic which has also left unmistakable traces in the later civilisation of the peninsula. Glowing passion, a tendency toward romantic unrestraint, and finally the gift of brilliant oratory, easily conceal in the Arabs their lack of creative genius. Herein lies the most profound difference between East and West.

Europe is a continent of discoveries and of unlimited progress, a land of nations that constantly endeavour to extend their influence and power ; on the other hand, the Mohammedan East, imperturbable in its self-sufficiency and composure, is a region that recognises neither labour nor war as other than a means for obtaining sensual enjoyment and undisturbed pleasure of life. Thus the Oriental and, above all, the Arab of the steppes conceal behind the veil of romance a spiritual inactivity which they are never able to overcome. The only art that is cultivated in the desert, the poetry of the Arabians, is very different from the poetry of Europe. The Arabs have never succeeded in the free and imaginative forms of composition that seem to be the peculiar gift of Aryan Indians and Persians, as well as of Europeans—he is fettered to the actual ; to present facts in bold comparisons and images is his greatest glory, and dexterity in the manipulation of metre and rhyme is to him an indispensable require-

Poetry the Art of the Desert ment. The Arabian mind is distinguished chiefly by its mastery of dialectic ; and, naturally, this feature is also reflected in Arabian verse. The poet is a warrior in the world of intellect ; with biting metaphor and satirical play on words he falls upon the enemy of his clan. He proclaims in triumph the glory of his tribe, and with mingled praise and scorn spurs on the soldier to heroic deeds. In this sense, at the time of Mahomet, poetry was almost a common

possession of the Arabs, and the ability to make verses was even more necessary to the success of a leader than his sword and lance. The development of Bedouin poetry played an important part in the unification of the Arabian tribes, and had its beginnings about a hundred years before the birth of Mahomet.

Before the birth of the Prophet it seemed impossible that a vast, passionate, spiritual movement, capable of bearing an entire people along with it, could arise in such a race, yet nothing short of such a movement could have rendered the inhabitants of the Arabian peninsula a danger to the neighbouring world. And it was at the very centre of the Arabian world that precisely such a movement arose— at first of a religious nature, but later national — which gave to the people of Arabia a dominion over Western Asia that was to last for centuries. This movement began in Mecca, and its leader was Mahomet.

The rise of Mohammedanism was closely connected with the character and history of two cities, Mecca and Medina, both of

The Holy Cities which are situated in the steppe lands of Western Arabia, the former not far from the coast, the latter further inland, and close to the elevated plateau. The two cities differed from one another in every respect, and seemed to have been predestined to rivalry from their very origin. The doctrines of Mahomet could have arisen only in Mecca, and it was simply the hostility between Meccans and Medinans that saved them from destruction.

Mecca was the Rome of Arabia, the central point of the feeble religious life of the old pagan tribes. In a barren, desolate valley, that was but seldom exposed to the ravages of sudden rain-floods, was situated a very ancient sanctuary, the Kaaba, a square temple built of unhewn stones, in the wall of which was inserted the famous " black stone "—a meteorite, believed once to have been white, and to have descended from Paradise. According to a later legend, accepted by Mahomet, the temple was known as the oldest house of God ; and was supposed to have been built by Adam and restored by Abraham. For a long time the Kaaba, like so many other Arabian sanctuaries, may have been only occasionally visited by the Bedouins who dwelt in the neighbourhood, until finally a small settlement

CARAVAN GUIDE

BEJA ARABS

A MOUNTAINEER

GROUP OF BEDOUIN HORSEMEN ARMED WITH THEIR LONG LANCES

BEDOUIN TRIBESMAN

A GROUP FROM PETRA

BEDOUIN SHEIKH

TYPES OF THE NOMAD BEDOUIN RACE OF ARABS

Photos Underwood & Underwood

1893

arose, the existence of which in the midst of the desert was rendered possible probably through the discovery of a spring called Zemzem. The water of this spring, which in later times became one of the most venerated objects in the Mohammedan world, is at the present day drinkable, indeed, but strongly impregnated with **The Sacred** mineral salts. Perhaps the **Zemzem** water was originally valued on **Spring** account of its medicinal properties; it is possible, however, that the presence of foreign elements may also have been due to the bad drainage of the city that gradually grew up about the spring.

In the middle of the fifth century A.D., under the leadership of Kuzai, the Qurais forcibly obtained the custody of the sanctuary and settled down about the Kaaba, which at that time had long been an object of pilgrimage. The restless, predatory Bedouin tribe soon found a rich means of livelihood in sheltering the pilgrims and in supplying them with food and water, and was thus led to exchange its old nomadic pursuits for commerce. In a short time the favourable location must have greatly furthered the prosperity of the city. The pilgrimages to the Kaaba—in which no fewer than 360 tribes placed their clan deities under the protection of the black stone—had during early times led to the custom of looking upon certain of the months of the year, the first, seventh, eleventh, and twelfth, as sacred, during which every feud must cease, and the pilgrims be permitted to travel undisturbed to the places of worship; at the same time a way was opened up for inland trade and intellectual communication between the isolated Arab tribes. Long before the city of Mecca was founded, the pilgrims had been in the habit of assembling at certain places during the holy months for the purpose of holding fairs, where they exchanged not only material wares, but **Founding** also products of the intellect. **of** The most celebrated market **Mecca** was at Okaz. Even when the rise of Mecca caused a falling off in the commercial prosperity of this city, as late as the time of Mahomet, the boldest and most eloquent men of the tribes of Arabia assembled there in order to recite poems, competing with one another in singing the praise of their clans and celebrating the deeds of their countrymen, or striving to win the prize offered for the

best love songs. The sheikhs of the tribes under the presidency of a " king of the poets," were the judges in the competition, which took place during the months of peace, and of which the result was awaited with intense interest throughout entire Arabia.

Thus during the months of the pilgrimages the attention of the whole peninsula was directed towards the sanctuaries, of which there were several in addition to the Kaaba. But as soon as the inhabitants of Mecca began to take advantage of their opportunities for commerce, their city became the centre of Arabian life, the single point at which a union of the scattered tribes could take place. There are many indications leading to the conjecture that in the course of time a monotheistic belief, either the Jewish or the Christian, would gradually have taken possession of the sanctuaries and have filled the pilgrimages with an entirely new spirit, had it not been for the fact that a strange religion displaced both; a religion that, although it arose from external sources, became essentially Arabian in nature, having its deve- **Medina,** lopment in Mecca, while **the Prophet's** through it the politically un- **Refuge** important land of Arabia was suddenly assured dominion over a boundless empire. In contrast to Mecca, a settlement of Bedouin nomads of the Mahadite race, who are not townsfolk at all in the ordinary sense of the word, Medina was inhabited by various tribes of the hostile group of stationary Arabs, called Yemenites, after the most important of their provinces. Medina is situated in an oasis on the innermost terrace of the elevated plateau, copiously watered by springs that flow down from the neighbouring mountains. At the time of Mahomet's birth the people of Medina were industrious peasants, who guided the plough with their own hands and irrigated their own date groves, but showed little interest in either cattle-raising or commerce.

There was a further ground of difference. Several of the stationary tribes dwelling round Medina had turned to the Hebrew religion; and although the bulk of the population of the city remained faithful to the old animistic belief and joined in the pilgrimages to Mecca, nevertheless the inhabitants of Mecca, ever watchful of their own interests, looked upon the Medinans with increasing apprehension,

ARAB MERCHANTS OF THE HOLY CITY OF MECCA

AN EXAMPLE OF ARAB DIGNITY　　　　　YOUNG ARAB WOMAN

MOHAMMEDAN WOMEN OF ARABIA WITH THEIR CHILDREN

TYPES OF THE ARABS WHO ARE SETTLED IN TOWNS AND VILLAGES

1895

inasmuch as they had discovered signs of Jewish propaganda in their own city. The Medinans certainly showed themselves to be true Arabs; there were constant feuds between the two chief tribes of the city, and thus all united action was rendered impossible. Not until Mahomet arose did these dissensions end. The

Rivalry of the Cities religious - military movement that began after the appearance of Mahomet was at first limited for the most part to a severe struggle between the two cities, the true Bedouins of the desert appearing on the scene only as predatory spectators, or as auxiliaries; never once did they have the decision of an important battle in their hands. Owing to their closer concentration, the town dwellers possessed a vast superiority over the scattered Bedouin hordes. Judging from the size of the army that fought under the flag of Mahomet at the time of his attack on Mecca, the population of Medina and its immediate neighbourhood could not have exceeded 16,000 souls. Even to-day, in spite of the advantage of processions of pilgrims and consequent traffic, the number of inhabitants of the same territory can scarcely amount to over 20,000. Mecca, on the other hand, had been exceptionally favoured from the very beginning, and apparently possessed a somewhat denser population. Of the other towns of the Hedjaz, Tayef, to the south-east of Mecca, alone seems to have been of any importance. In fact, Mahomet had first looked to Tayef as a place of refuge instead of Medina; but his plans fell through because of the determined hostility of its inhabitants.

The conjectured date of Mahomet's birth is April 20th, 570 A.D. His family, although old and distinguished, had become impoverished at the time of the Prophet's birth, and had fallen into the background. Mahomet's father, Abdallah,

The Prophet's Family who died two months after his son was born, left to his heirs a very modest fortune; and when Amina, the mother of the future Prophet, died a few years after, the boy was thrown mainly upon the charity of relatives, one of whom, his uncle, Abu Talib, although himself poor, treated him with the greatest kindness. For a long time Mahomet was unable to better his condition; he was compelled to hire himself out as a shepherd, and even, later,

when he first entered the service of Kadija, the widow of a rich merchant, he seems to have accepted a very humble post. Although opinions are divided as to whether or not Mahomet made various commercial journeys to Syria and Southern Arabia with his uncle, it is beyond doubt that after his twenty-fifth year he several times accompanied the caravans of Kadija, and was thus brought into closer touch with the adherents of more developed religious beliefs. In the meanwhile the chief sources of inspiration for his doctrines were to be found in Mecca itself, where there was no lack of proselytes to Judaism, and whither germs of Christianity—to be sure in a very garbled form—had been brought by traders and slaves from Southern Arabia and Ethiopia. Mahomet, who was decidedly unpractical by nature, seems not to have been a success as a merchant, but was suddenly freed from his material cares by an unexpected event. Kadija, although considerable older than he, chose him for her husband, and married him in spite of the opposition of her relatives. Until his fortieth year

Mahomet's Early Life the Prophet lived the life of a quiet citizen in Mecca; and how little he thought of an attack on Arabian polytheism during these years was shown by the fact that he named one of his sons Abd Manaf—that is to say, servant of the deity Manaf. It may be remarked here that of the numerous children Mahomet had by his several wives, all, with the exception of a daughter, died before him and consequently do not figure in the history of Islam.

Finally, Mahomet, whose inquiring mind had eagerly absorbed ideas from both the Hebrew and Christian religions, became convinced that he was called upon by Allah to do away with the polytheistic worship of the Arabians, to transform the Kaaba—to which as a true citizen of Mecca he held fast with unshakable faith—into a temple of the One God, and to construct from the fragments of Christian and Hebrew doctrines, with which he had happened to become acquainted, a new and purely monotheistic form of belief. His activity was, therefore, confined to the simplification and re-establishment of that which was already in existence rather than to creative reconstruction, for which as an Arab he lacked the necessary intellectual

AN ENCAMPMENT OF NOMAD BEDOUINS ON THE PLAINS

ARAB POSTMAN RESTING WITH HIS CAMEL IN THE DESERT

SCENES IN THE DESERT LIFE OF ARABIA TO-DAY

Photos Underwood & Underwood

1897

qualifications. The imaginative descriptions that appear in the Koran concerning either the delights of Paradise or the terrors of Hell, are nothing more than confused echoes of the folk-tales and myths of other races which were employed

Code of the Koran

by the Prophet chiefly in order to supply a historical foundation for his doctrines, such as is possessed by the Old Testament. The scoffing assertion of unbelieving Meccans, who claimed that many of the sayings of Mahomet were clumsy imitations of those fabulous Persian stories which in later times formed the nucleus of the "Thousand and One Nights," and had just then penetrated to Arabia, was significant enough. In general, the revelations of the Prophet concerned matters of practical life and civil morality—in fact, the simple ethical code of the Koran is the best and the

most powerful portion of the Mohammedan faith.

When, in the fortieth year of his life, Mahomet experienced the vision in which he alleged that the archangel Gabriel revealed to him his mission, a portion of the inhabitants of Mecca had already received a certain preparation for a reform in their belief through their intercourse with Jews and Christians. However, the personality of the new prophet aroused at first but little confidence. His family, the most important factor in the life of an Arab, had a good name to be sure, but nevertheless was impoverished. Mahomet himself, although distinguished in appearance and of benevolent nature, did not possess such characteristics as were likely to make the greatest impression upon Arabs. He was a bad poet, and the smallness of his right to boast of warlike virtues became more

MAHOMET'S ARRIVAL AT MEDINA
Mahomet's migration to Medina, in 622, was the first step toward the unification of Arabia, for it meant the triumph of religious over tribal sentiment. From that time the Arabian empire began, Mohammedans reckoning time from that year.

and more evident as time went on. "Couldn't God have found a better prophet than you?" was the cry that greeted him on his first appearance in Tayef. He had the mystical qualities of his nature to thank for his final victory; and although these very characteristics were ultimately to be traced back to an epileptic complaint, they were always looked upon by him as a gift from heaven, and announced as such with evident sincerity.

He himself was the first convert to the visions and dreams in which his constant meditations on the true faith became plastically embodied. He learned how to heighten his states of ecstasy through fasting and long hours of prayer, and gradually succeeded in developing the tenacity of purpose and undaunted confidence which rendered his personality irresistible, and were a constant attraction to new adherents. At first he had no thought whatever of deception; but as time went on, the inner voice frequently showed a

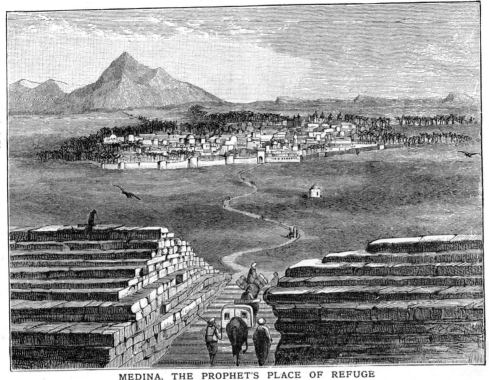

MEDINA, THE PROPHET'S PLACE OF REFUGE

Medina, the second city of Arabia, is situated in an oasis on an elevated plateau. When the hostility of the orthodox drove Mahomet from Mecca he sought refuge there, and made it his centre until he conquered Mecca.

most remarkable docility in respect to the Prophet's personal affairs and intentions.

Nevertheless, the Mahomet of later years was no mere impostor. No longer a prophet, he was then the ruler of a vast and constantly growing empire; and it was the necessity that arose from his position which forced him into a half involuntary combination of sincerity and dissimulation, a characteristic that finally becomes a second nature to all leaders of multitudes. In later years, also, his visions were associated with serious attacks of an epileptic character, which he could scarcely have simulated. Personally the Prophet was modest in his requirements, setting aside the sensuality which constantly led him to increase the number of his wives, and prepared for him many a mortification. Fortunately for him the Arabians, like most Oriental peoples, are very lenient in regard to this point. Simplicity in food and drink undoubtedly appealed to him; but in sexual matters his sympathies were by no means with the ascetics.

Simplicity of the Prophet

It was with no finished dogmatic system that Mahomet first appeared. For a long time his position in respect both to Christianity and Judaism, neither of which he thoroughly understood, was undecided; in fact he even displayed a passing inclination to recognise, as a matter of policy, the chief gods of the Meccans, at least in the form of intermediary spiritual beings; though he soon hastened to withdraw that concession. The germ of his teaching was from the very beginning a pure monotheism bound up with a simple but impressive doctrine of immortality. Beyond doubt, the minute descriptions of heaven and hell produced a deeper impression on the pagan Arabs, whose conceptions in regard to the life beyond were extremely meagre, than did any other portion of his doctrines.

By thus combining the visionary accounts of what was to take place in the future with his easily understood ethical teachings and the indispensable prescriptions of ritual, Mahomet succeeded in creating a religion that was throughout adapted, by reason of its simplicity and directness, not only to awaken the interest of a half-civilised people, but also in a certain measure to subject them to discipline. The Koran, which gradually arose as a firm pillar of the religious edifice, was not written by Mahomet himself—indeed, it is doubtful whether the Prophet knew how to write at all ; it

Mahomet's First Disciples was not until after his death that the fragments of his revelations and sayings were united into a book. Owing to his innate bashfulness, it was long before Mahomet could summon up enough courage to appear in public. His first disciples were the members of his own family. The prophet's wife Kadija, his daughter, his nephew Ali, later his slave Zaid, and finally a friend, the honest Abu Bekr, were the earliest converts, to whom as time passed other adherents, such as Othman, who later became caliph, and, above all, Omar, the true representative of the Mohammedan policy of aggression, joined themselves.

Not until the fourth or fifth year after his first revelation did Mahomet resolve to preach to his fellow-tribesmen ; and his first efforts were attended with very small success. All the while his family protected him after the Arabian custom, at least from the ill-usage with which the innovator who attacked the worship of the gods, and therewith the commercial prosperity of Mecca, was constantly threatened. The greater portion of his disciples, many of whom were members of the lower classes or slaves, and who, through their defiant behaviour had aroused the anger of the citizens of Mecca, fared far worse than he, and in all probability were the cause of the at first cool, not to say hostile, attitude of the higher ranks of society. For a time a number of the converted turned to the Christian Abyssinians—an incident that was perhaps not without its influence on the later doctrines and views of the Prophet. Mahomet himself, although safe from

Mahomet Driven from Mecca bodily harm, was in a most disagreeable situation. Especially unpleasant were the jeers of scoffers who demanded miracles or benevolently offered to send for a celebrated physician to cure him of his lunacy. After the death of Kadija and of his uncle Abu Talib, his position finally became unbearable. He was compelled to look about for a place of refuge where men were not unalterably hostile to his teachings.

After having been driven from Tayef, where he had sought assistance, Mahomet's choice fell upon Yathrib, the jealous rival of Mecca, which he afterward named Medina. Pilgrims were in the habit of making annual journeys to the Kaaba from Yathrib, as from almost all other parts of Arabia. The Prophet, who possessed relatives in Medina on his mother's side, had established connections with some of these Medinan pilgrims, and was favourably heard by them, for they had already become partly estranged from the worship of a plurality of gods, owing to Jewish influence ; moreover, unlike the inhabitants of Mecca, they were not prejudiced against his doctrines by apprehensions for their material interests. A Mohammedan community arose in Medina, which soon far exceeded the settlement at Mecca in number ; and finally the Prophet himself determined to emigrate thither with his followers, although at first he, as well as every other true Meccan, was an object of hatred and of suspicion to the people of the rival town. Thus was the first great step taken toward the unification

Arabian Unification Begun tion of Arabia. Religion was victorious over tribal sentiment ; and from the very moment that Mahadites and Yemenites joined together under the banner of the Prophet the period of Arabian empire began. It is not without reason that Mohammedans reckon time from this year of the Hegira, or "the Flight," A.D. 622.

The number of emigrants capable of bearing arms who gradually arrived from Mecca could scarcely have been over one hundred ; but the accession of the greater part of the inhabitants of Medina, who placed themselves under Mahomet's orders as *ansâr*, or "helpers of the Prophet," furnished him with an army at one stroke, and rendered his final triumph certain. The Prophet met scarcely a single irreconcilable opponent in Medina ; but, on the other hand, he had the greatest difficulty in establishing even a moderate amount of unity in the loosely banded community that practically acknowledged no chief ; and he was at first obliged to be content with reconciling so far as was possible the two principal tribes into which the population was divided. This he accomplished by means of his great influence, and through the erection of a mosque, the first centre of the Mohammedan faith. However, all his attempts to convert the Jewish inhabitants of the region, in whom he had placed great hopes, failed; even the concession first granted to the Jews, permitting men in prayer to turn toward Jerusalem instead of toward Mecca, remained without effect, until finally the favour of the Prophet turned to hatred, and he resolved on the destruction of the Jewish tribes.

Mahomet was soon entirely absorbed by the quarrel with Mecca. He saw the absolute necessity of subduing the inhabitants of the spiritual centre of Arabia if he ever expected to gain any great influence over the widely scattered tribes which forgot their disputes only during the months of pilgrimage to the Kaaba. The fact that Mecca, as an artificial settlement, was dependent upon its traffic and the importation of food products opened to Mahomet the possibility of worrying and injuring his unbelieving countrymen by watching the roads and making sudden descents on caravans in the usual fashion of Arabian private warfare. He had but little success at first; but on one occasion, having missed a caravan to Mecca, which he had determined to attack, his band encountered an armed force that had been sent out from Mecca for the protection of the threatened caravan; and thus the first pitched battle took place—at the wells of Bedr.

Mahomet's First Battle

Although greatly outnumbered, the Moslems won; and Mahomet, who had viewed the struggle from a distance, sent rich spoils and triumphant news of victory to Medina. This was in the year 624.

The wealth and distinction obtained by Mahomet through the victory at Bedr enabled him to establish still more firmly his position in Medina, and above all to come to a settlement with the irreconcilable Jewish Bedouin tribes of the neighbourhood. First of all the Benu Kainukah, who were able to put 700 armed men into the field, and possessed a strong fortress not far distant from Medina, felt the weight of the Prophet's wrath. They called in vain for assistance from one of the chief clans of Medina, with whom they had been once allied. Only a safe conduct to Syria was granted to them; their possessions fell to the Moslems.

Bedouin Jews Expelled

In the autumn of 624 the believers finally succeeded in capturing a Meccan caravan on the road to Babylon. But in the spring of the next year the grave tidings reached Medina that an army of Qurais, strengthened by the addition of several Bedouin tribes, and numbering some 3,000 warriors, was advancing against the city under the command of Abu Sufiyan, a sheikh of Mecca, tacitly chosen to be leader, who was now determined to wash away the ignominy of the defeat at Bedr in the blood of the Moslems. Mahomet would gladly have awaited the attack within the walls of Medina, but the impatience of his companions, who saw that their fields were being laid waste, soon necessitated his setting out against the Meccans at the head of about 1,000 fighting men.

The Prophet met the enemy near Mount Ohod, and was immediately deserted by

MAHOMET, THE PROPHET OF ALLAH

Mahomet was born in 570 A.D., and it was not until he was forty that he started the destruction of Arabian polytheism which ended in the unification of the Arabian race and their subjugation of the Near East.

300 of his followers, who fled at the very sight of the enemy. The battle ended in the rout of the Moslems, and the Prophet, who wore a coat of double chain mail and an iron helmet, and this time had himself taken part in the struggle, escaped being made prisoner by a mere chance. The battle resulted in the loss of some seventy

Rout of the Prophet of the faithful, and of about twenty of the Qurais, and in spite of its insignificance was a severe blow to the reputation of the Prophet. The Meccans, delighted with their triumph, straightway marched back to their native city.

Mahomet then sought to awaken fresh courage in his followers by an attack on the Jewish tribe Nadir, and succeeded in compelling them to emigrate to Syria. Thus the Prophet was now in a position to reward his faithful disciples with possessions of land ; and all had time to settle themselves in their new homes, an expedition that had been planned against Mecca falling through owing to the unusual dryness of the next few years.

This delay gave the indefatigable Abu Sufiyan an opportunity to form a league against Medina, which was joined even by tribes of Central Arabian Bedouins, who had been roused to action by the Jews, and were also well aware how greatly their liberty was threatened by the growth of Moslem power. The religious influence of Mecca was in this instance of the greatest assistance to the Qurais. The Quraidhah, the last Jewish tribe that had been permitted to remain in Medina, were also concerned in the alliance.

This time Mohammed's plan of remaining on the defensive met with no opposition ; a deep ditch was dug for the protection of the single vulnerable side of Medina, on the advice of a Persian freedman, and behind it the Prophet and the 3,000 armed men then at his disposal took their position. This primitive fortification, the

Siege of Medina first defensive work ever seen in Central Arabia, was completely successful in preventing the hostile army, three times as large as that of the defenders, from undertaking any serious operations; and the approach of winter finally rendered it necessary for Abu Sufiyan to withdraw his forces. The Qurais had no sooner disappeared than Mahomet marched forth and fell upon the Jewish Quraidhah ; the men to the number of 700 were beheaded,

and the women and children were sold to the Bedouins.

All the while Mahomet was, and remained at heart, a Meccan. While he was resolved to win the victory for monotheism, he saw that it would be better for his cause not to destroy the beginnings of a common Arabian cult, such as existed in the sanctuary at Mecca, but rather to adapt the latter to the requirements of his own faith. His attachment to Mecca sufficiently explains the fact that he had always retained in view the object, first, of becoming master of the sacred city without any unnecessary bloodshed, and secondly of obtaining the right to take part in the general pilgrimage of Arab tribes to the Kaaba at the head of his Moslem followers. Early in the year 628, during one of the sacred months, the Prophet appeared with a small force before his hostile birthplace ; but it was in vain that he demanded entrance to the sanctuary. Nevertheless the expedition was a decided success. The Meccans, weary of the constant injury suffered by their trade concluded a ten years' truce with the

Peaceful Conquest of Mecca Prophet, and on his promising to withdraw this time, granted him permission to visit the Kaaba with his followers the next year. Thus was the first step taken toward the peaceful conquest of Mecca ; the Qurais yielded the very point they had been most anxious to defend.

During the truce Mahomet was not idle in extending his power. The oasis of Kheyber, about sixty miles north of Medina, into which a portion of the expelled Jews had retired, was conquered. The land was divided among his followers, who now united with the Islamites who had previously emigrated to Abyssinia. The number of believers constantly increased ; the Prophet's growing sense of importance found expression in his sending letters to the sovereigns of neighbouring regions, in which he demanded that they should submit to his rule and embrace his doctrines. These messages were not, as a rule, received in a way likely to arouse any sanguine hopes of success.

More important was the pilgrimage to Mecca that took place in 629. The Qurais retired from the city for several days in order that there might be no cause for trouble with the Moslems while the latter were fulfilling their mission. It became more and more apparent that there was no

MOUNT ARAFAT, WHERE MAHOMET PREACHED HIS LAST SERMON

In 632 Mahomet took his last pilgrimage to Mecca, and the ceremonies then employed became a model for all time. After-wards he delivered an address from Mount Arafat summarising and establishing in their final form the moral laws of Islam.

one in Arabia capable of withstanding for any length of time the steadily increasing power of the Mohammedans. One after another the Bedouin tribes surrendered, and soon the Prophet turned his eyes to-ward Syria, where the Arabs, having received a smattering of higher culture owing to the proximity of the Byzantine empire, had here and there united into small states. An army sent out against one of the minor Arabian rulers of the region to the south of the Dead Sea was severely defeated at Muta. The time for conquests beyond the borders of Arabia had not yet come.

On the other hand, Mecca fell into the hands of the Prophet without a struggle. A trifling dispute furnished him with a **Mecca Falls to Mahomet** pretext for suddenly putting an end to the truce with the Qurais; he immediately sum-moned his adherents in full force, and appeared before the astonished city in January, 630. Resistance was not to be thought of ; soon the most distin-guished Meccans stood before the victor imploring grace and repeating the custom-ary Mohammedan confession of faith.

Reason and love for his home led the Prophet to impose mild conditions of peace upon his humbled foes. He angrily took away the banner of a Medinan sheikh, who had announced in triumph that the day of reckoning had come, and that no **The Idols Destroyed** one would be spared, and he commanded that pardon should be granted to all Qurais, with the exception of a few oppo-nents for whom he cherished especial hatred. The Kaaba now stood open to the conqueror, who knocked the idols to pieces with his staff and permitted the black stone alone to remain in its place as a symbol of the One God. The Meccans came forward in crowds to repeat their confessions of belief, and thus to take their places among the ranks of the Prophet's adherents. It was now recognised by all that Mahomet had no intention of destroying the holy city, but was striving rather to exalt it.

The work of Mahomet as a prophet was crowned by the act of taking posses-sion of and purifying the Kaaba. The permanence of his doctrines was now assured, at least in Arabia, inasmuch as he had succeeded in transforming the centre of the old religious life into a sanctuary of the new belief. It was also evident that sooner or later all the tribes of his race would be compelled to recognise his teaching, and that even his death could not check the progress of Islam. Immediately after the fall of Mecca, the Prophet, assisted by a levy of Meccans, set about reducing the neighbouring regions to subjection. During a fight with the Bedouin tribe of Havayins, the result of which hung in the balance for many hours, the Qurais acted in a decidedly suspicious manner ; indeed, a true conversion could not yet be looked for from the greater portion of the Meccans ; but Mahomet once more put his old tribesmen to shame by his magnanimity, allotting to them a larger share of the plunder than was received by his own Medinan followers.

Permanence of Islam Assured

The inhabitants of Tayef, who had more than once insulted the Prophet during his earlier years, again bravely withstood the Moslems, and refused all proposals for capitulation. Not until many months had passed were they forced to come to terms, owing to the complete isolation of their city after the conversion of the tribes that dwelt in their neighbourhood. Their ambassadors naturally sought to obtain the most favourable conditions from Mahomet, and expressed, moreover, the remarkable desire that they might be permitted to worship their favourite goddess, Allat, for another year. The Prophet would have agreed to these conditions had it not been for the influence of Omar, the most energetic and fiery of his adherents. The Tayefites were ordered to surrender unconditionally, and Allat was destroyed amid the woeful howls and lamentations of the women and children. During his long career, Mahomet had to contend against the satirical rhymes of the poets of his enemies. How greatly embittered he was by these attacks was shown unmistakably at the capture of Mecca, when he went to the length of sentencing to death a woman named Sara, who had delighted the Qurais with her derisive verses on the new prophet. It actually happened that the conversion of a certain tribe came about through a poetical competition—Mahomet, who possessed neither voice for song nor the gift of making verses, choosing the best poet among his adherents to be his representative. This extraordinary event took place in the year 630. The envoys of the Beni Tamina assembled before the house of the Prophet and sent in a formal challenge ; the singers of Mahomet capped the climax of their opponents' blustering with a still greater display of bombast, and fairly shouted them down. The challengers thereupon owned, with great mortification, that the Moslem public speakers and poets were better than theirs, and that their voices, too, were much louder ; and forthwith made their confession of faith. Gradually all the poets of Arabia united their voices in praise of Mahomet, and it was only from the tents of distant Bedouin tribes that now and then a poisoned dart of song was launched against him.

Conversion by Poetic Contest

MAHOMET'S TRANSLATION TO HEAVEN
From a Persian MS. representing the Prophet's ascent to heaven, his face being covered with a veil to hide his glory.

The increasing feebleness of the Prophet, who had again taken up his residence in Medina, allowed him to participate only in one more warlike expedition against Southern Syria, the region by which the Arabian Peninsula is connected with the rest of Western Asia. The campaign began in the year 630, and was attended with no decided success, apart from the subjection of a few frontier tribes. The pilgrimage to Mecca in 631, although not led by Mahomet, but by Abu Bekr, nevertheless signified a further step in the conversion of Arabia to Islam. The Prophet commanded it to be announced in the Kaaba that from this time forth unbelievers would no longer be permitted to take part in the pilgrimages, and that all men who desired to approach the sanctuary must first make a confession of faith. This showed how certain Mahomet was of the final success of his cause. In fact, at that time the whole of Arabia, with the exception of some of the most distant regions, formally acknowledged the supremacy of the Prophet. The minor princes of Arabia Felix and the Persian governors, who, after the expulsion of the Abyssinians by a Persian army, ruled a portion of Yemen, also gave notice of their submission, and so did numerous chieftains of the Syrian frontier.

Mahomet's last pilgrimage to Mecca, the ceremonies of which became a model for all time, took place in the year 632. The Prophet solemnly walked round

BLINDED AFTER SEEING THE SACRED PROPHET'S TOMB
After praying at Mecca it was not unusual for pilgrims to destroy their sight by gazing at white-hot bricks, so that they might never look on earthly objects again.

the Kaaba at the head of countless believers, performed the rites with scrupulous care, and delivered an address to the assembled multitude from Mount Arafat, in which he summarised and established in their final form the moral laws of Islam. The words with which he recommended to his followers his cousin and favourite, Ali, against whom various complaints had arisen, played an important part in the later history of Islam : " He who loves me will choose Ali for a friend (*maula*). May God be with them who protect him, and desert those who are his enemies." Since the word " maula " may signify either friend or ruler, the claims of the sectarian Shiites, who recognised Ali as the lawful successor of the Prophet, rested above all on this statement.

Three months after his return from Mecca, Mahomet fell ill with a fever. The damp, malarial climate of Medina, which had caused the death of many a Meccan fugitive, also proved injurious to the health of the Prophet, already enfeebled by the constant exertions and excitement of the last twenty-four years of his life. The sick man was able to withstand the disease but a short time ; on July 8th, 632, the twelfth day of the third month in the year 11 of the Hegira, Mahomet, who had been looked upon by his followers as immortal, and who himself had not opposed this belief, died in the apartment of his favourite wife, Ayesha.

The faithful were filled with confusion, and a great uproar immediately arose ; but the work of the Prophet had been accomplished, and was no longer to be destroyed. The Arabian nation arose in the place of the visionary, and countries in which no man had ever heard of Mahomet during his lifetime soon became subject to the dominion of his heirs.

The new religion derived its firmest support from the sayings of the Prophet, **The Sacred Koran** which had been written down by his most trusted followers, at first circulated merely in fragmentary transcripts, but later collected and arranged by scribes at the command of Abu Bekr, the first Caliph. The 114 chapters, or " suras," of the Koran when chronologically arranged fall into two groups, the Meccan and the Medinan. Owing to the fact that in many cases these chapters were closely connected with the life and adventures of the Prophet—who frequently endeavoured to obviate difficulties among his adherents by means of well-timed revelations— and also by reason of their numerous contradictions and repetitions, they form a remarkable commentary on Mahomet's chequered career and final triumph.

The style and substance of these revelations underwent a striking change as time passed : the earlier, composed in short rhymed lines in the vague, obscure language of the Prophet, occasionally display true poetic power, and bear witness to the genuine inspiration of their author ; the later suras are more prolix and tedious, and were obviously intended to produce a shrewdly calculated effect. The reason for this is very plain. During his life in Mecca, Mahomet attacked the polytheistic belief of the Arabs with clear and powerful arguments in favour of the unity of the Divine Being—such arguments as immediately presented themselves to his simple and ill-trained, but ardent and ingenious mind. In Medina, the Prophet's time was largely taken up with polemical utterances delivered against the Jews and **Doctrines of Mahomet** Christians ; moreover, it was also necessary for him to exercise all his powers of intellect in order to govern and control the unruly, warlike community by which he was surrounded. It was entirely owing to the already mentioned necessity of governing his followers that Mahomet's most lasting work—his moral and legislative doctrines, which, together with the ritual, the prayers, ablutions, and fastings form the skeleton or framework

of the Mohammedan religion—arose. Th simple, in no wise profound, but neve theless admirable moral code of Islam the most valuable gift which the followe of Mahomet brought with them to le civilised peoples. In the main the doctrines rest upon a foundation of o Arabic custom, refined, however, throug the influence of Jewish-Christian pre cepts. Many a fundamental princip was a result of the personal inclinatior of the Prophet ; for example, the ur favourable position that he assigned t woman was not in reality in harmon with the true Arabian spirit, but orig nated in Mahomet's own sensual, jealou nature. His attitude in regard to th deeply-rooted Bedouin custom of infant cide, which he immediately prohibited was more deserving of praise. Moreover on grounds of mere national econom he was wise in his action. The positio of the Prophet at Medina gave rise to new religious impulse. Mahomet soo found it necessary to harmonise hi doctrines of immortality with the injunctio to wage a religious war, as well as with th **The Religious War** doctrine of fatalism, which under different circumstances he would scarcely have made so prominent in his teachings Although the glowing descriptions of th delights of Paradise promised to th champions of the faith did not preven Islamite armies from taking flight upon occasion, they proved to be an excellen means for awakening fanaticism in simpl minds. And this was all the more im portant, for, owing to their small numbers the Arabs were soon obliged to draw upon all men capable of bearing arms who dwel in the conquered regions.

Thus the Koran gradually became the nucleus of Moslem power, and the centre of the spiritual life of all nations that subjected themselves to its law. Its effects were not immediately shown. The more Islamite scholars devoted themselves to the study of the sacred book the greater became the differences of opinion in regard to doubtful passages and obvious contradictions ; and a separation of the believers into numerous sects was an inevitable consequence. Indeed, there were other considerations besides these which in very early times contributed to the division of the Mohammedans—above all the question, who was to be the legitimate successor of the Prophet.

THE COMPANIONS OF THE PROPHET
AND THE BEGINNINGS OF CONQUEST

MAHOMET'S one surviving child was his daughter Fatima, the wife of Ali, who as cousin and perhaps earliest disciple had always enjoyed the especial affection of the Prophet ; and it was to Ali that a more or less obscure declaration of Mahomet in regard to his successor seemed to apply. Had this claimant triumphed, a hereditary monarchy would have been established. The coveted position, however, was obtained by another ; with the result that the Mohammedan government became an elective sovereignty, which was more in harmony with the democratic spirit of the Arabian people. The affairs of the time were favourable to Ali, but unfortunately he was not the man to take advantage on them. During the course of his life Ali had constantly shown that, for all his courage in battle, he possessed a weak character and inferior intelligence. He

Ali the Unready was invariably put aside by others, even when he believed himself to have been the determining factor. This time also he neglected to make the best of his opportunites, wasting his time in useless occupations, and entirely losing sight of his political goal—the attainment of which he believed to be absolutely certain.

Since the choice of a caliph was intimately connected with the general condition of affairs that had arisen in Arabia on the death of the Prophet, a certain insight into these conditions is indispensable to a correct understanding of the history of the period. Although Mecca had once more come into favour, its temple being recognised as a sanctuary, and although the majority of the Arabs had at least externally adopted the new faith, it was nevertheless certain that Medina was the centre of Mohammedan power, and consequently the place where the election of a successor should be held. The class differences that had caused the people of Arabia to be divided into sects and parties on this occasion had but

small influence on the decision in regard to the caliph, for the choice lay in the hands of the original and most faithful adherents of the Prophet. These " Defenders " nevertheless proved themselves to be true Arabs, inasmuch as it was

Electors of the Caliphs not long before they gave the elements of discord that existed between the separate groups, and had been but superficially effaced by Mahomet's personal influence, an opportunity for reasserting themselves with renewed power.

The eyes of the Prophet had scarcely closed when the party of Meccans who had left their native city and the inhabitants of Medina independently made up their minds each to choose a successor, in order thus to obtain political ascendency. Ali, on whom both parties might have agreed, was not present at either election. The Meccans chose Abu Bekr, the old friend of Mahomet and father of Ayesha, his favourite wife, to be their candidate ; while the Medinans selected for the position their influential leader Zaid.

The prudence and foresight of Abu Bekr, who knew well how to turn the old enmity that existed between the two chief tribes of Medina to his own advantage, obviated the risk of any serious rivalry between himself and Zaid ; and this in the very nick of time, for the news of the illness of the Prophet alone had been sufficient to cause rebellions to break out in various parts of the peninsula, and as soon as Mahomet's death became known, the whole of Arabia revolted, threatening utterly to

Whole of Arabia in Revolt destroy the life-work of the Prophet. The faithful who had been installed as commanders of troops and governors of provinces fled to Medina from all sides ; and to make matters worse, there was no army at the disposal of the Moslems ; for, in fulfilment of one of Mahomet's last commands, and perhaps to rid himself of the presence of the discontented Medinan tribes, Abu Bekr had, immediately after his election, despatched all the available fighting men to the Syrian border.

The insurrections in Arabia were a demonstration of the profound impression which the appearance of Mahomet had made upon his countrymen.

Rise of New Prophets
It was no longer a land of pagans that arose against the caliph. The most dangerous of the rebels were under the leadership of new prophets, who sought to imitate or to excel their prototype. Even before the death of the founder of Islam, tidings were brought to Medina that in Yemen Abhala the Black had assembled a powerful army and brought almost the entire region under his dominion. Soon afterward Musailima, another prophet, raised aloft the banner of insurrection in Yemama; and in Nejd the discontented tribes collected about a leader of their own race, called Tuleiha. In the neighbourhood of Medina such serious disturbances had taken place that an attack on the city itself was feared; for here also, although no " prophet " had made his appearance, the dissatisfaction with the new political conditions, and, above all, with the taxes that, at Mahomet's command, had been imposed on all believers, was sufficient to occasion a revolt.

Abu Bekr's most striking characteristic was an unshakeable belief in the future of Islam. He was a man who had never once lost faith in the Prophet; and for this very reason during these times of trouble, when even the boldest of his adherents despaired, he was the one leader most fitted for the situation. Fortune also aided him. The most dangerous of his enemies, the prophet in Yemen, was murdered by his followers, who then acknowledged the sovereignty of the caliph; and a small campaign against the revolted tribes of the neighbourhood of Medina met with decided success. The

Wars of the First Caliph
army returned from the Syrian frontier; the caliph was in a position once more to begin the subjugation of Arabia. Khalid, a man of vast energy but of doubtful character, to whom Mahomet himself had given the name " the sword of God " (Saifallah), was appointed commander-in-chief of the Moslem forces, and directed his first campaign against Tuleiha, the prophet of Nejd. After a severe

struggle Khalid routed the army of h[is] opponent, and killed the prisoners an[d] wounded with the utmost brutality.

Khalid then turned to the district [of] Yemama, in the southern part of Nej[d] where a still greater army of rebels ha[d] collected about the standard of Musailim[a] after having defeated two bodies of M[o]hammedan troops. Their resistance wa[s] stubborn in the extreme, and the positio[n] of Khalid would indeed have been de[s]perate had he not succeeded in separatin[g] Musailima from the main body of hi[s] troops, compelling him to retreat to [a] walled estate; there, after the gate ha[d] been burst open, he caused the entire garr[i]son to be murdered in cold blood. Neve[r] before had so many Arabs fallen in battl[e]. The Moslems also lost such a great numbe[r] of men that Abu Bekr is said to hav[e] immediately resolved upon the collectio[n] of the scattered fragments of the Kora[n] before any more of the old companions [of] the Prophet, who had stored up his saying[s] in their memories, had lost their lives.

While Khalid was engaged in subjugat[ing] the interior plateau of the peninsul[a]

Terror of Islam
other divisions of the caliph'[s] army succeeded in enforcin[g] obedience from the district[s] bordering on the Persian Gulf[,] Bahrein, and Oman, and in once mor[e] establishing the supremacy of the M[o]hammedans in Yemen and Hadramau[t]. Neither the wounded nor the defenceles[s] were spared; entire tribes were anni[hi]lated, until finally the whole of Arabi[a] fell into a palsy of terror. The victory o[f] Islam was complete. But no sooner ha[d] Abu Bekr the entire peninsula once mor[e] under his control than he again took u[p] the plan that Mahomet had alread[y] sought to follow during the last years o[f] his life—namely, the dissemination of th[e] Mohammedan religion, and the establish[ment] of Moslem rule over all countrie[s] bordering on the peninsula of Arabia.

During the following period of expan[sion] sion forces and influences that had appar[ently] ently been hidden or conciliated durin[g] the lifetime of Mahomet again asserte[d] themselves. Mahomet had indeed tem[porarily] porarily succeeded in stifling the ancien[t] feuds and disagreements between th[e] Arabian tribes; but he had not been abl[e] entirely to destroy them. The single clan[s] still preserved their prejudices and mutua[l] hatred. The great chasm separating agri[culturists] culturists from shepherds and Yemenite[s] rom Mahadites, which appeared to have been bridged over by the affiliation of the fugitives from Mecca with the agricultural people of Medina, soon showed itself again with effects even more far reaching than before. Mahomet himself had with difficulty suppressed his inborn dislike for cultivators of the soil, and while still in Medina he once permitted himself to be so far overcome by his feelings on seeing a plough as to utter the words : "Never does such an implement come into a house without bringing disgrace."

To these old prejudices new ones were soon added. The ancient tribal nobles of the Arabian race were suddenly confronted with a new aristocracy set above them, which laid claim to political supremacy, and had now succeeded in overcoming all opposition. This aristocracy was composed of the faithful friends of the Prophet, the "Defenders" and the "Emigrants," the flower of the devout, who we may be sure were not wanting in intellectual pride and ambition, though by no means united among themselves.

Naturally, the warlike devotees were looked upon with but little favour by the freedom-loving Bedouins. But the inhabitants of Mecca, the Qurais, **Danger from Mecca** who, as guardians of the Kaaba, exercised an immense influence over the whole of Arabia, soon showed themselves to be the most dangerous enemies of the new régime as soon as they had begun to recover from the effects of the humiliation that had been inflicted upon them by Mahomet. Ever since they had ceased to oppose Islam they had been endeavouring to place themselves once more at the head of the religious movement. The importance of the sacred city and the old influence of the Meccan nobles, now under the leadership of the Omayyad family, proved irresistible, however much the first Caliph strove to suppress their aspirations and to exclude them from participation in the government of the empire. It was not long before men who during Mahomet's lifetime had overwhelmed the Prophet with hatred and scorn stood at the head of Moslem armies and provinces. The nobles of Mecca, who were not too scrupulous as to the fulfilment of the precepts of their religion, and who ever held aloft the ideals of old Arabian life, were far more sympathetic to the common people than were the gloomy fanatics of Medina ; and all the while that

the faithful were stretching forth their hands toward world dominion a storm was gathering over their heads, and the blessings of the Prophet proved to them finally a curse. But, at the outset, an endless vista of victory and plunder opened itself to the comrades of Mahomet. The armies of Abu Bekr departed from Arabia— **War Against the West** finally subdued after unspeakable horrors had taken place— in order to throw themselves upon the rich possessions of the Persians and Byzantines. The exhaustion of the Eastern Romans and the Persians did not of itself occasion the triumph of the disciples of Mahomet. Had it rested, indeed, only with tribes of Arabia proper, small in numbers and recently weakened by the losses sustained in the conflicts following the death of the Prophet, to achieve the aggressive expansion of the new faith, the victory of Islam would have been a matter of great doubt. But the area occupied by Arabs had long ceased to be limited to the peninsula of Arabia.

Although the Bedouin tribes had n ver combined into a united people, they had extended their habitat from Sinai to the Tigris ; had fought, as pleased their fancy, for Rome or for Parthia ; had occasionally established a kingdom such as that of the Nabatæans or of Palmyra ; and had learned the practices of organised warfare. It was on this expanded Arabia that Islam was to rest its power. The moment the champions of Islam succeeded in awakening enthusiasm for the new religion among their compatriots in Syria, Irak (ancient Babylonia), and Mesopotamia, they had at their disposal a numerous and in part well-trained and armed body of fighting men, whose onset the inhabitants of the towns and cultivated districts were totally unable to withstand. Mahomet himself had been well aware of all this, as was **Mahomet's Last Project** shown by the remarkable persistency with which he sent army after army into the Dead Sea region, the central province of the Nabatæan kingdom, even planning a new expedition during the very last days of his life.

After Abu Bekr had quelled the disturbances in Arabia, he immediately made preparations for continuing Mahomet's policy of conquest. That he resolved to direct the first blow, not against Syria, but against Persia, was natural enough. Mahomet's range of political vision had in the main been limited to Western Arabia. Syria was the only foreign country with the affairs of which he was to some degree familiar. On the other **Islam** hand, Abu Bekr was at this **Against** time well acquainted with the **Persia** political situation, not only in Arabia, but also in the surrounding nations. There was no possibility of his failing to recognise that the unusually dense Arabian population in Irak, who had naturally followed the course of events in Arabia with great interest, would be far more favourable subjects for the propaganda than the inhabitants of the Syrian frontier. In spite of the fact that, by reason of their inaccessible position, the Arabs of Irak

himself at the head of a hastily assembled army. On receiving the command of Khalid to accept the Mohammedan faith, Hormuz forthwith replied with a challenge to a duel ; and when Khalid succeeded in overcoming his opponent in sight of both armies, the Persians, true to their ancient Oriental custom, immediately dispersed in all directions. Other armies were subsequently sent out under various Persian commanders, without either order or method, only to meet with a fate similar to that of the forces of Hormuz. The fortified towns also offered but little opposition. Hira, in the neighbourhood of the Hillah of to-day, and other cities were captured, and the region west of the Euphrates cleared of Persians. Khalid had not yet ventured to cross that river, when in the next year he was recalled and

SEAT OF AN EARLY MOHAMMEDAN STATE NEAR ANCIENT BABYLON
Hira, on the Euphrates, now Hillah, near the site of Babylon, was one of the earliest states formed by the Arabs.

had suffered much less than other peoples during the Persian-Roman wars, they had, nevertheless, long been thoroughly weary of Persian oppression. Their land, still fertile, and constantly enriched through commerce with India, had been for many years a favourite source of revenue to Persia, and the demands of the Persian rulers had become more and more exorbitant ever since the king of Hira had been superseded by a Persian satrap. Only a slight impetus was necessary in order to destroy completely the sovereignty of Persia in these regions.

In March, 633, the Mohammedan general Khalid advanced with his army of veterans from the interior of Arabia against Persia. The Arabians, whose number soon increased to 18,000, at first encountered Hormuz, the military commander of Obollah, in Irak, who had placed

transferred to the command of the Syrian army.

Khalid arrived in Syria at the very time he was most needed. As soon as he had been able to form a new army out of the soldiers who were returning from the various scenes of civil war in Arabia, Abu Bekr had immediately commanded an attack on the frontiers of Palestine, and by sending out several reinforcing divisions he increased the number of Syrian troops **Conquest** to 36,000. But the opposi- **of** tion everywhere encountered **Palestine** by the Arabs was unexpectedly great ; and the spirit of discord that had arisen between the commanders, who had already divided the conquered districts among themselves, and were no longer to be moved to common action, proved a complete bar to the success of the campaign. Khalid, however, succeeded in putting an end to all discord, and also in defeating a Byzantine army greatly superior in numbers after an exceptionally severe struggle on the Yarmuk, not far from the Lake of Gennesareth.

The messengers despatched from the field of battle with trophies and tidings of victory were received by a new caliph on arriving in Mecca. The old friend and most faithful disciple of the Prophet, to whom the dominion of Arabia had fallen as a result of the incapacity and dissensions of the followers of Ali and the Medinan party, had lived to fill his difficult office only for the short space of two years (632–634). During this time Abu Bekr had remained what he had always been, a simple, kindly man of exemplary piety, a model of what a true Islamite should be, according to the opinion of Mahomet, and a blind reverer of all the sayings and commands of the Prophet. His whole course of action during his short period of rule was nothing more than a continuation of what Mahomet had begun. Through him the spirit of the Prophet still cast its shadow upon the

THE MOSQUE OF OMAR AT JERUSALEM

world of the living. Much more important than any of Abu Bekr's personal deeds was the fact that through his election the adherents of Ali, who had striven for a hereditary monarchy, received a blow from which they never recovered. Under Abu's immediate successors the caliphate remained an elective monarchy, with all the merits and defects of the system.

For some years the merits preponderated. Before his death Abu Bekr succeeded in bringing about an agreement to the effect that Omar, the most energetic of the old disciples of Mahomet, a man peculiarly adapted for the leadership of a conquering people, should be his successor. Opposition was at first encountered; but as soon as Omar had laid firm hand on the government, resistance was out of the question. Even Ali, who was indeed quite conscious of his own incapacity, accepted the new sovereign with good grace as soon as his own party had ceased to goad him to further resistance.

In truth, Omar now did little more than openly assume the leadership, which he had

THE MONUMENT OF THE ARABIAN CONQUEST OF JERUSALEM

After the conquest of Persia the victorious troops of Omar broke the power of the Byzantines in Syria, all the strongholds of Palestine, including Jerusalem, where the mosque named after the caliph was erected, falling before them.

already held during the days of Mahomet and Abu Bekr. The warlike policy of the Prophet had been in the main his work, and a large number of the laws and "sayings" could be traced back to his influence. Nothing could be more characteristic than the words with which he addressed the assembled people on entering into his new duties : "By Allah, the weakest among you shall be in my sight as the strongest, until I have obtained for him his rights. But him that is strongest will I treat as the weakest, until he submits unto the law."

Omar the Great

Omar proved that his inaugural address had been spoken in earnest ; for, in spite of all the authority he possessed as sole ruler, he never denied the tendency towards equality which, received by the first followers of Mahomet as a heritage from the Bedouins, had also been one of the prime secrets of Moslem success. To his love of justice Omar added great abilities in organising the military power of Arabia. A fifth part of all the spoils that fell to the share of the caliph was set aside as a nucleus for a public treasury. It was not mere fanaticism that caused Omar to order all Christians and Jews dwelling in Arabia either to become converts to Islam or leave the country. The command sprang rather from a desire to transform the peninsula of Arabia into an absolutely secure base of operations.

The next step was to reinforce as largely as possible the Arabian troops in Persia, who were now encountering stubborn opposition. Recruiting was by no means an easy task ; the older provinces of Arabia neither would nor could place an unlimited number of warriors in the field. During the first year of his reign, for three days Omar had stood in the pulpit at Medina exhorting men to enroll themselves as volunteers for the Persian war, and not until the fourth day did his efforts meet with the slightest success.

Omar Recruits His Army

All considerations of orthodoxy had to be laid aside ; even the faithless, the tribes that had been subdued by Abu Bekr, and all the former adherents of false prophets, whom Abu Bekr had sternly excluded, were now embodied in the army.

Omar, however, took good care that, in spite of the accession of troops less firm in faith, his army should not deteriorate in religious fervour ; for he added to the ranks of each command a large number of priests, whose office was to recite the sayings of the Prophet amid the tumult of battle, and thus arouse the enthusiasm of the warriors. Omar also allowed the army to retain the form of organisation which had long existed in conformity with the quotas supplied by the various tribes, each tribe having its own leader ; the caliph appointed only the commanders of the larger divisions. An alteration of this earlier form of organisation, proved by experience to be thoroughly adapted to the Arabian national character, would have been neither desirable nor possible.

For a long time the war with the Persians occupied the whole of Omar's attention. After the withdrawal of Khalid, his successor, Motanna, was obliged to act solely on the defensive ; for in the meanwhile the disturbances which had been taking place in the interior of Persia, to the great benefit of the invading Arabs, had come to an end ; moreover, Rustum, an able field-marshal of the empire, had been placed at the head of the Persian forces. It is true that after the arrival of Abu Obaid with reinforcements the Arabs succeeded in defeating two armies of Persians.

Persian Victory over Arabia

But when, intoxicated with their victory, they crossed the Euphrates and offered battle with the river at their backs, they were completely defeated, Abu Obaid together with a large portion of the army losing their lives. However, the struggle for the Persian succession in Ctesiphon prevented the Iranians from following up their victory. Motanna maintained his position on the Euphrates, annihilated a Persian army in 634, and even undertook minor campaigns in the region that lay between the two rivers. But when Yesdigerd III. ascended the throne, and with the help of Rustum assembled all the forces of his kingdom, the Arabs were compelled to retreat to the borders of the desert. Messenger after messenger appeared in Medina imploring aid ; it appeared as if all the advantages won by the previous victories had now been lost.

But Omar, in the meanwhile, had exerted every effort to collect new troops of believers, and to arouse them to the highest pitch of enthusiasm. He had at first taken the supreme command himself, but finally decided to appoint Zaid, an old companion of the Prophet, commander-in-chief. This time, in 636, the struggle took place at Kadesia, on the right bank of the Euphrates, in the neighbourhood of the Bagdad of to-day. For three days the battle continued ; it was a confusion of hand-to-hand conflicts, accompanied by an incessant advancing and retreating of the engaged forces ; even during the fourth night Arab and Persian troops were still here and there engaged in desultory combat. A single incident—the death of Rustum, the Persian general—decided the day in favour of the Moslems, who had also been greatly assisted by the wind, that drove stinging sand into the faces of the Persian soldiers, unused to desert warfare. This victory brought the region west of the Tigris into the hands of the Mohammedans, who immediately proceeded to build the city of Basra, on the Shatt-el-Arab, and thereby shut off the Persians from all traffic on the River Euphrates and trade with India.

The next year Yesdigerd III. evacuated Ctesiphon, which was already surrounded take refuge in Shuster, and in taking him prisoner, after a siege of six months.

The Persian army arrived too late to derive any benefit from the resistance that had been offered in Chusistan ; for two months it remained encamped in the mountain country to the south of Hamadan, near Nehavend, facing the Arabian forces, until finally a strategic blunder on the part of Firuz, the Iranian commander, led to an engagement followed by a total defeat. Thus, in the year 641, the dominion of the Sassanidæ came to an end. Nevertheless, a struggle of several years' duration had yet to be fought before the single provinces were completely subjugated. Yesdigerd, " the Hapless," escaped to Khorassan, where he hoped to form a new army out of Turkish mercenaries. But fortune had deserted the cause of the Sassanidæ, and in the year 651 the last of the Persian emperors met his

End of the Sassanidæ

RUINS OF TARAKHUN, A DESERTED CITY OF SEISTAN

Tarakhun, said to have been founded about 1000 B.C., and deserted since 1060 A.D., was the birthplace of Rustum, the Hercules of Persia, and almost the only Persian general who succeeded in combating the Arabian advance.

by Arabian cavalry, and withdrew to his second line of defence, the mountain region of Medo-Persia, not, however, without suffering severe losses during his retreat. Unfortunately, he had no army capable of defending the passes ; and the Arabs at once succeeded in taking possession of the most important of the mountain roads, as well as of a portion of Chusistan. At Yesdigerd's call for aid, once more the Iranian forces assembled in Media, ready to engage in a final struggle for their ancient religion and nationality. Chusistan and Farsistan, the two southern provinces that had been cut off from the rest of Persia by the advancing Arabian army, likewise continued their opposition. Hormuz, the governor of Chusistan, threatened the new city of Basra ; and not until many difficulties had been overcome did the Arabs succeed in compelling him to

The Final Iranian Struggle

death at the hands of an assassin. In the meanwhile the power of the Byzantines in Syria and Mesopotamia had also been broken. After the flight of the Syrian militia, at the battle of Yarmuk, resistance was offered by the larger towns alone, and they, too, were soon forced to capitulate. The fact that immediately after his accession Omar, the Mohammedan puritan, recalled the victorious Khalid, who was, to be sure, the " sword of Islam," but at the same time an accomplished rake, had practically no influence on the course of the Syrian war. Damascus capitulated in the year 635. The withdrawal of some Arabian troops to reinforce the army in Persia gave Heraclius, who had hastened to Jerusalem, a short respite, during which, however, he only became convinced that it would be impossible to check the advance of the enemy with the means at the disposal of his exhausted province ; for a new Syrian army was not to be thought of. When, in the year 636, the emperor left the country, he took with him from Jerusalem the most sacred relic of the Christians, the true cross : a plain indication of the desperate straits into which his land and his creed had fallen. Still, some years passed before the re-

Syria Abandoned By Rome sistance of the Syrian cities was finally overcome. Several of the centres of Christian Hellenism defended themselves to the uttermost, but the Aramaic inhabitants of the land looked upon the struggle with stolid indifference. The cities of the north, Emesa, Haleb, and Antioch, were the first to fall ; then followed the strongholds of Palestine. The conquest of Jerusalem was no easy task for the Moslems ; but the city finally opened its gates to the caliph, who had been by no means loth to arrive in time for a triumphant entry. The seaport Cæsarea was defended with still greater bravery, but it, too, finally fell in 640. In the meantime Northern Mesopotamia had been conquered, and Edessa captured. Not until the Arabian forces had penetrated as far as the mountains of Armenia and the Taurus did their victorious advance come to an end.

To these extraordinarily rapid successes a newer and still greater conquest was added. Egypt's feeble powers of defence had already been exhibited when the country was plundered by a Persian army in 616. The native population, who had never been friendly to the customs of the Greeks, and who had also become completely estranged from their political masters owing to the formation of numerous Christian sects, had then been of no assistance whatever to the Byzantine generals in resisting the enemies of the empire. The danger of an Arabian invasion had long been appreciated, and the Egyptian governors were the only rulers who had

Sectarian Curse in Egypt replied to Mahomet's messages with even a semblance of courtesy. Nowhere had sectarianism, the curse of the Eastern Roman people, struck such firm root and become so intimately united with national antipathies as in the Nile valley. In vain had Heraclius endeavoured to reconcile the " monophysitical " Egyptians with the " monotheletic " Greeks through the introduction of a conciliatory formula of belief : the burning national hatred,

which merely hid itself beneath a cloak of religion, rendered all his well-meant efforts abortive.

The kings of Persia had already intentionally shown favour to both Monophysites and Nestorians, and during their wars with the Byzantines had obtained great benefit from this policy ; Omar adopted the same course, and brought the conquest of Egypt to a successful issue, even before the last battle had been fought in Persia and Syria. Amr ibn As, the caliph's field-marshal, invaded the valley of the Nile with a force of but 4,000 men. After several engagements had been fought the Arabs obtained possession of the right bank of the river, and the arrival of reinforcements made it possible for them to cross the stream ; still, the Christians in reality lost but little ground until their army was weakened by the wholesale desertion of the native Monophysites. The result was a brilliant victory for Amr and for the policy of Arabia.

All the troops that the Greek generals were able to collect from the various Egyptian fortresses were placed in the field

Arabian Conquest of Egypt against the Arabs ; but the Byzantines soon found themselves driven to take shelter behind the walls of Alexandria, the centre of Hellenic influence. The dying Heraclius had done all that he could to strengthen the last bulwark of Byzantine power from the sea, and at first it seemed as if the Arabian army would bleed to death before the walls of the strongly fortified city. In the meanwhile, however, a wretched dynastic quarrel broke out on the death of Heraclius. The imperial court of Byzantium was filled with confusion ; and the longed-for ships bearing provisions and reinforcements to Alexandria did not arrive until the siege had lasted fourteen months, and the defenders were completely exhausted. The wealthiest of the inhabitants left the unfortunate city by sea ; the remainder of the population surrendered to the Arabian general in December, 641.

As usual, the conquered were treated with comparative leniency ; it is true there were scenes of disorder, but the alleged systematic crusade of the Arabs against the treasures of science and art has been proved to have been purely mythical. Alexandria was not chosen to be the capital of the country by the Arabs as it had been by the Greeks ; but a new city,

Fostat, the Cairo of later times, was built on the right bank of the Nile, not far from the Delta, in the neighbourhood of ancient Memphis. From this it became quite evident that the new rulers of Egypt intended to make use of the land in an entirely different manner from that of either the Greeks or the Romans, who had looked upon the country merely as a source of wealth.

The conquest of the Nile valley was not enough for the Arabs, who, as true children of the desert, were but little impeded in their advance by the sterile regions of North Africa. Amr swiftly marched upon and captured the Pentapolis, and even Tripolis was surrendered by its surprised garrison.

During these many wars Omar had remained at home in Medina. Such an energetic man as he must have chafed greatly under his self-imposed restraint; but he could have adopted no policy better suited to the state of affairs of the time. Its results were of the greatest value to the future of Islam, for during the storm and stress period of Mohammedanism nothing was more necessary to the success of the Arabian cause than a secure and powerful base of operations. Instead of going into the field himself, Omar was content to take upon his shoulders the more modest task of making preparations for war, collecting reinforcements, and replenishing the national treasury with money that had been captured in battle, and with the tribute of the conquered lands. Furthermore, he organised the newly acquired dependencies, especially Irak, where he commanded the city of Kufa to be built on the borders of the desert in the neighbourhood of the right bank of the Euphrates, as a centre for the Arabian population, while the already semi-Arabian Damascus

MOHAMMEDAN MOSQUE AT CÆSAREA
Cæsarea, the Roman capital of Judæa, was one of the last strongholds to fall in the extraordinarily rapid conquest of Palestine by the victorious Mohammedans.

was made the capital of Syria. Omar did not favour the settlement of the conquered territories by Arabian troops; for he looked upon a ceaseless continuation of the religious war until both Pagans and Christians were completely overthrown as the labour of his life, and held the camp to be the true home of his companions in faith.

During the last years of his life Omar adopted extraordinary measures for the benefit of the State treasury, as we have learned from his remarkable correspondence with Amr, whose consignments of money from Egypt did not come up to the caliph's expectations. Omar was neither just nor courteous to his general, who deserved all praise; and in his treatment of the conquered his avarice showed itself in a most unpleasant light. In fact, this smallness in his nature was the indirect cause of his death by the hand of an assassin. A Christian artisan of Kufa, who had journeyed in vain to Medina in order to beg that his relatively inordinate taxes might be decreased, struck down the caliph in the mosque in November, 644, just as the latter was about to begin his morning prayer. Omar still possessed strength enough to name a successor; but as Abd ur-Rahman, whom he had chosen, absolutely declined to accept the difficult office, he called upon the six oldest companions of Mahomet to choose a new caliph from among themselves—a method of escaping the difficulty which led to evil results.

Once more Ali, who, together with Othman, Abd ur-Rahman, Zubeir, Talkha, and Zaid ibn Wakaz, had been called upon by Omar to elect a new caliph, stood at the head of the list of candidates, and again he experienced a bitter disappointment.

Zubeir, Talkha, and Ali contested the position ; the other aspirants stepped into the background. Mutual jealousy prevented all reasonable agreement, and the upshot of the affair was that the choice finally fell on Othman, who of all the candidates was least fitted for the position. He was a good-natured old

A Caliph of Seventy man of seventy years, and had been one of the very earliest companions of the Prophet ; but personally he was a complete nonentity. On his first attempt to address the assembled people after his election, he made a pitiable exhibition of himself, since, after a painful pause he could only murmur the words, " The beginning of all things is difficult," and then descend from the pulpit with a sigh. Othman was not the man to curb the violent efforts which the various parties were making in order to increase their power ; the strong hand of Omar had long held them in check, but now they burst forth again, threatening to bring confusion to the entire Mohammedan world. He was also totally unable to effect a reconciliation between the quarrelling and deeply embittered tribal groups of the Arabian people. During his reign the personal influence of a sovereign was replaced by the ineradicable antagonisms of tribes and provinces, which were only increased by new enmities and rivalries that had developed during the period of conquest ; and all Mohammedan leaders who lived in the time of Othman were compelled either to make allowance for these elements of disturbance, or—often without being conscious of it themselves—to be moved and guided by them.

The old comrades of Mahomet still remained the most powerful of the political parties. Generals and governors of provinces were selected from their ranks, and a large amount of the treasure

The Old Comrades of Mahomet that had been won in war found its way into their strong-boxes. They knew well that they were not popular ; but so long as they were able successfully to claim the election of the caliph as their right, it was a difficult matter to thrust them down from their position of supremacy. Now, however, the lack of unity in their leaders, which had enabled the feeble Othman to come to the head of the state, had opened up the way to their destruction.

Othman was, indeed, one of the companions of the Prophet, an " emigrant " from Mecca ; but he had been far too weak and good-natured to break completely with the past, and to join himself without reserve to the new community of fanatical believers that had formed itself about Mahomet. He was much too favourably inclined toward his old Meccan relatives ; already during the Prophet's lifetime he had come forward in their defence, and at the capture of Mecca several of the most deeply compromised of Mahomet's enemies owed their lives to his intercession. Now that he had become caliph, he was soon surrounded by the neglected aristocracy of Mecca as by a swarm of hungry locusts ; first one and then another managed to persuade him to hand over a post as governor, a position as commander, or this or that well-paid office. With increasing anger the eailier believers beheld the success of these intruders, whose fathers had not only fought against the Prophet with weapons in their hands, but had also wounded him with the poisoned darts of satire—these Meccans

The Meccans' Opportunity whose religious faith and manner of life were more than suspicious. Their angry looks were soon directed even against the caliph ; they clung all the closer to Ali, whose time seemed at last to have come. But even now he was unable to bring the members of his party into harmony with one another.

The rivalry between Medinans and Meccans was not the only rift that extended across the Arabian world. The ancient enmity between nomads and agriculturists, Mahadites and Yemenites, still smouldered beneath the ashes, only again to burst forth into flame in later times ; but at the present moment the antagonisms that had been called forth by differences of geographical situation—a result of Omar's conquests—were of greater importance. To Omar Arabia had still been the heart of the Mohammedan empire ; all his measures had for their object the strengthening of the peninsula and the development of the Arabian military forces. But as soon as the great neighbouring lands of Syria and Irak had been subdued by Islam this policy could not be continued. The new territories were far more populous than desert Arabia, and the greater culture of their inhabitants gained for them, slowly but surely, a preponderance of power. In fact, it may be remarked in anticipation that Arabia had already fallen from its supreme position at an early period in the history of Islam, and had now become little more than an insignificant appendage of Western Asia.

Hence, Irak and Syria, the two chief centres of Mohammedanism, soon entered the lists in hostile competition for the leadership. Their inhabitants were not on friendly terms with one another. The serious, determined Bedouins of Syria looked upon the effeminate, restless inhabitants of Irak with hatred and contempt. They particularly despised the people of Kufa, in whom all the evil characteristics of an over-refined race seemed to have been united—true dwellers of great cities were they, lions at home, lambs in the field. Whoever gained the friendship of one of these rivals made sure of the hostility of

to the safety of Byzantium. The wars were successfully continued in Northern Africa, the Greeks losing Carthage; in the east, the Omayyad Muaviya, to whom Othman had entrusted the command of an army, spread desolation in Asia Minor.

Carthage Lost to Islam Thus, so far as the Arabian policy of conquest was concerned, Othman was a by no means unworthy successor of the victorious Omar. As a matter of course, these successes in arms were insufficient to reconcile the angry early adherents of the Prophet, who beheld with increasing bitterness Muaviya, whose mother had been a deadly enemy of Mahomet, winning victory after victory and rich spoils in Asia Minor. To his great misfortune, Othman finally placed just such a weapon in the hands of the " companions " as was required by those models of piety; he undertook a revision

TOMBS OF THE CALIPHS AT CAIRO, THE ARABIAN CAPITAL OF EGYPT

To extraordinary successes in Syria the armies of the great caliph Omar added the conquest of Egypt, a new city, Fostat, which afterwards became Cairo, being built on the Nile in the neighbourhood of the ancient Memphis.

the other. Owing to the fact that the Omayyads looked to the Syrians for aid during the civil wars, they won the victory over Ali and his companions, who turned to the fickle inhabitants of Irak for support.

In the meanwhile, however, under Othman's government the new Mohammedan empire became more powerful and increased in area. An attempt of the Greeks, who had managed to recapture Alexandria, to extend their power once **Extension of the Empire** more over Egypt failed completely; Alexandria was severely punished, and in like manner various insurrections were crushed in Persia. It was also during Othman's reign that a Mohammedan fleet of warships was constructed with astonishing rapidity on the Phœnician coast with the object of conquering Cyprus; this same fleet also became a serious menace

of the Koran on his own authority and endeavoured to enforce its acceptance by the old believers. But, instead of calling forth a melancholy wail of lost influence from the " emigrants and defenders," he was assailed on all sides by the enraged cries of men who insisted that he had falsified the words of the Prophet. Ali resolved this time to act in earnest, and despatched his emissaries into the various provinces. The gold pieces which the nephew of the Prophet had managed to heap up in abundance as a consoling indemnity for his political failures were scattered in all directions; and everywhere, as a result of the extraordinary expenditure, Ali was extolled as the single true champion of the traditions of Islam. But, in spite of all, the idol of the hated devotionalist party was not popular, and the revolts that broke out here and there did not lead to the wished-for results.

Then bands of suspicious characters appeared in the narrow streets of Medina, Bedouins, whose services were to be had for a trifling payment; these assembled about the house of Othman, and with savage threats demanded his retirement. This time the feeble old man offered a determined resistance, but they finally stormed his house and assassinated him in the year 656. The Meccan nobility, who had endeavoured to defend Othman, fled from the city; and the Medinans, not one of whom had lifted his hand in the defence of the caliph, readily accepted Ali as his successor. Thus at last Ali was able to throw the imperial mantle about his shoulders; but the garment was soiled and blood-stained. A spirit of revolt and abhorrence spread over the entire Mohammedan world. There was an immediate cleavage among the conspirators at whose instigation the murder of Othman had been accomplished; for Zubeir and Talkha soon came forward with their claims, assisted by the powerful support of Ayesha, the favourite wife of the Prophet, an ambitious and intriguing woman, who had long been one of Ali's most deadly enemies.

Ali Gains the Caliphate

It soon became obvious that an appeal to the sword alone could decide between these two hostile groups of old believers. At first neither party could look to the provinces for assistance; Syria especially was hostile to both. Nothing was left to Ali but to fall back once more upon the assistance of the people of Irak, whom he won over to his cause. The rebels, who had no more to hope for from Syria than had Ali, turned to Irak and occupied Basra. Later, when Ali advanced on them from Kufa with a superior force, they entered into negotiations with him; but, owing to a misunderstanding, a battle was fought that ended with the deaths of Zubeir and Talkha and the capture of Ayesha. Ali was now master of all Irak. Arabia was also on his side, and he was at least formally recognised in Egypt; but the "Battle of the Camels" had cost him the lives of many of his ablest adherents. In Syria, Muaviya, the Meccan, who now openly laid claim to the caliphate, made preparations for a final conflict.

The Battle of the Camels

Muaviya was the typical champion of the nobility of Mecca, courteous, of knightly bravery, and a born leader of the people, whom he guided with both courage and wisdom; he was also ambitious, and inspired with an undying hatred for the bigoted followers of the Prophet, who returned his hatred in full measure.

Ali was now assured of the aid of the people of Irak also, since his quarrel was with the Syrians. For many years only a pretext had been wanting to bring the two races into open conflict with one another. But, in spite of all this, the morale of the army that Muaviya raised in Syria was vastly superior to that of the regiments of effeminate Irakans; and Ali was not a man likely to fill his adherents with any great amount of enthusiasm. Accustomed always to be led by others, and almost completely lacking in self-dependence, Ali became the chosen victim of various ambitious spirits who had resolved to sell their services to him as dearly as possible, and were already prepared eagerly to stretch out their hands for the gold of Muaviya.

Thus the battle that after long negotiations and many skirmishes finally took place at Siffin, in 657 A.D., on the right bank of the Euphrates, had an end rather amusing than tragic. While his cavalry were in the very act of pursuing the retreating Syrians with loud shouts of victory, open rebellion broke out in Ali's tent. The party which was in secret understanding with Muaviya compelled the hapless caliph first to recall his troops, and then to appear before a court of arbiters, the members of which were obviously enough entirely opposed to his claims. The nucleus of his forces, the old believers, renounced their allegiance and elected a new caliph: and on January 21st, 661, Ali met his death from a dagger-thrust by one of these same fanatics.

The End of Ali

On the death of Ali, the cause of the old believers broke down completely. Since Ali had been one of the champions of the hereditary caliphate, his claims naturally descended to his son Hassan. But Hassan, a cowardly voluptuary, was unable to accomplish anything with the army that had been placed at his disposal; and, in order to rid himself of all responsibility, he finally sent his most ardent adherents, under the leadership of Kais, against the Syrians. On their return after a severe defeat he made peace with Muaviya.

THE RULE OF THE MECCA CALIPHS

THE power and influence of the old adherents of the Prophet had completely come to an end when the proudest of the noble families of Mecca, the Omayyads, took possession of the caliphate as a hereditary dignity. At the time that the new dynasty made its appearance the Syrians also were rejoicing in their victories. The hated Irakans had been completely defeated, and, to the great chagrin of the ambitious inhabitants of Kufa, Damascus had now become the capital of the Mohammedan world-empire.

But still the empire continued in a state of war and rebellion. While the old antagonisms had been temporarily forced into the background by the decisive victory of the one party, a new political sect arose. Its adherents were filled with the wildest spirit of fanaticism, and had already displayed their activity in the **Democratic Party of Islam** assassination of Ali, as well as in a contemporaneous attack on Muaviya. The party was one that in view of the general state of affairs of the time arose almost of necessity ; in it was incorporated the democracy of Islam, which, under the cloak of religious zeal, came forward to oppose the aristocracy.

The true Bedouin of the desert in reality recognised neither the government of nobles nor the rule of a sovereign. He was indeed a slave to his own tribal traditions, but he was not accustomed to bow before any individual who laid claim to unconditional obedience. The recent developments of the Mohammedan movement had been a mockery of the Bedouin spirit of liberty. With arbitrary despotism the oligarchy of Medina had chosen a caliph from their midst, without even going through the form of submitting their choice to the approval of the great mass of believers ; and when, on the appearance of Muaviya, the unpopular government of the old believers fell, it was only that a new nobility might come forward in its place. From the standpoint of religion,

too, the more democratic of the Moslems had grounds for complaint when they compared the increasing luxury and love of splendour of their present leaders with the simple manner of life and definite precepts of the Prophet.

Thus the sect that was formed during the struggle between Ali and Muaviya, **Demands of the Democrats** which elected a new caliph in opposition to Ali, and was, at least, the indirect cause of the attacks on both Ali and Muaviya may be called the democratic-puritanical party ; and the most serious demand which it made upon those in power was that every Arab should not only have a voice in the election of the caliph but should also himself be eligible as a candidate. Basra was the headquarters of this new puritan party ; and its most powerful members were the Bedouin veterans— perhaps the most correct and virtuous of all Moslems. These fanatics, ever eager for self-sacrifice, were yet to be a source of great trouble to the Omayyad caliphs.

But Muaviya had also to keep a sharp look-out in another direction. Ali, who had always been too late during his life, proved after death a dangerous enemy. As long as he had stood at the head of the party of old believers, his obstinate and weak character had only led his followers to their ruin ; now, however, that he lived only in their remembrance, his name became the war-cry of the older party as well as of the people of Irak, and his tragic end an unlimited source of fanaticism. The **Ali Becomes A Hero** Arabian habit of enveloping their heroes in a cloud of legend soon caused the honest but mentally inferior Ali to appear as a most illustrious personage, upon whose purity, uprightness, and nobility of character no doubts were to be cast. And although the hero himself was dead, a son who appeared to be a worthy successor was still living. This was Husain, brother of the cowardly Hassan ; to him, as their last hope, the old believers and the Irakans turned. In the meanwhile Muaviya had found a lieutenant in the person of his half-brother, Ziyad, who was capable of putting an end to all trouble with Irak and with the inhabitants of Kufa. Ziyad had not long occupied the position of governor of the dissatisfied province before the boldest of

Irak Chastened and Subdued his enemies scarcely ventured even to grumble, and all ironies and satires against the dominion of the Omayyads were stifled on their very first appearance. And after the death of Ziyad, whom Muaviya had apparently chosen as his successor, the Irakans were still in such a state of terror that the appearance of Husain failed to awaken any genuine enthusiasm among them. Nevertheless the hereditary caliphate of the Omayyads was as yet by no means on a secure footing. Muaviya experienced extraordinary difficulty in obtaining recognition for his son Yezid as his legitimate successor ; and the easily led, thoughtless character of the latter was a cause of many complications and misgivings. It was only owing to the fact that the Syrians had the utmost enthusiasm for him that Yezid was enabled to retain his position.

In spite of all domestic disturbances, the religious war of conquests, although now possessed of less significance than formerly, was carried on vigorously during the reign of Muaviya. Great progress was made in the east, where the Arabian forces crossed the Oxus, advanced into the valley of the Indus, and for the first time came into contact with the Turkish races that were in later times to play such an important part in the history of Islam. In Africa, also, the policy of conquest was continued, and the city of Kairuan was founded on the site of ancient Carthage as a centre of Mohammedan influence. After the death of Ali the Byzantines were assailed both by sea and by land ; a por-

The Religious War tion of Asia Minor was devastated, and Arabian war vessels sailed as far as Constantinople, without, however, engaging in any decisive combat. Still, these struggles were of great advantage to the Omayyads, since they increased the popularity of Yezid, who had taken part in them at the desire of his father.

When Muaviya died in 680, the Omayyads were in a position easily to crush opposition. The chief rebellious spirits were the old

comrades of Mahomet, now for the most part of great age, but surrounded by numerous ambitious descendants who held fast to the claim that a new caliph must be chosen from their ranks. The old believers could not look upon Yezid, who was not of a particularly serious disposition and troubled himself little about the precepts of the Koran, as other than an impudent pretender. In Mecca, another band of dissatisfied Arabs, rich in distinguished names but poor in followings, assembled about the banner of Husain. The latter joyfully received a long petition from the people of Kufa, in which they invited him to their city and offered him the dignity of caliph.

Once more, then, the old alliance between the companions of the Prophet and Irak threatened to become dangerous to the Omayyads ; but before Husain arrived in Kufa, Yezid had already sent out a new governor, Obaidallah, a son of the terror-inspiring Ziyad, who, with his father's example before him, well understood how to deal with the rebellious Kufites. As a result, when Husain ap-

Fall of a Pretender proached the gates of the city, not a hand was raised in his favour. The troops of Obaidallah advanced to meet him, and since he was unwilling to submit without a struggle, a battle followed, in which his weak forces were routed and he himself, together with most of his companions, put to death on October 10th, 680 A.D.

The fall of Husain revealed that ancient Arabia, although externally faithful to Islam, was in arms against the orthodox. The sacred cities alone appeared to offer a secure place of refuge to the faithful. Before their gates the storm of opposition abated, and it was thought that the original religious empire might perhaps once more be established from them as centres. In Mecca, Abdallah, eldest son of Zubeir, formerly candidate for the caliphate, laid claim to the supreme office and defied the ambassador of Yezid from behind the sacred walls of the Kaaba, at Mecca ; on the return from Yezid's court of envoys who had beheld with horror the frivolity of the caliph and his comrades, and reported with passionate emphasis what they had seen, a terrific uproar arose in the city. But the Medinans refused to admit the claims of Abdallah ibn Zubeir, and established a

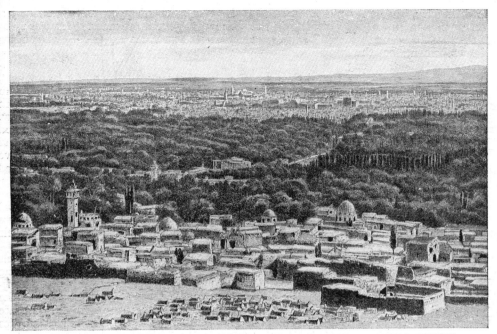

DAMASCUS, ONCE THE CAPITAL OF THE MOHAMMEDAN WORLD-EMPIRE
When the Omayyad dynasty of Mecca succeeded the companions of the Prophet in the caliphate, the Mohammedan capital was removed from Kufa to Damascus, and Syria became the heart of the empire in place of Arabia.

provisional government in order to avoid an immediate outbreak of dissension. Further progress was to follow as time passed; but that Yezid would take hostile measures against the old comrades of the Prophet and advance against the sacred cities no one would believe, in spite of the general abhorrence that had been called forth by his god-lessness. Nevertheless, the old believers were doomed to disappointment. A Syrian army marched into Western Arabia under the command of a man who could not have been better chosen as avenger of the various sanguinary campaigns by means of which the Prophet and his followers had compelled the sons of the desert to accept the new faith. Moslim, Yezid's general, was a superstitious pagan, uneducated, rude, furiously energetic, a true Bedouin of the old school, without a glimmer of reverence for the sacred memories of the Prophet. As a relative of the murdered Caliph Othman, he was fully bent on vengeance. What was to be expected from the barbarous Syrian nomads under his command, who had accepted the Mohammedan faith superficially only, who were in the eyes of the pious Medinans little better than heathens, and who returned the contempt

The Old Believers Attacked

of the old believers with a most cordial hatred?

The comrades of the Prophet anticipated the fate that was in store for them when the Syrian army appeared before the walls of their city. Scarcely ever before in the history of Arabia had a battle been fought in which such blind, fanatical fury was displayed as at this time before the gates of Medina, and is known as "the day of Harra." The standard bearer of the Syrians had already fallen, and the army began to waver, when, on August 26th, 683, a troop of Syrians were admitted to the city by traitors, and thus enabled to fall upon the unprotected rear of the old believers. The fate of the defeated was terrible; all men capable of bearing arms were ruthlessly slaughtered, the women were violated, the city plundered. The blood of the comrades of Mahomet flowed down the steps of the mosque from which the Prophet had so often addressed his followers, and its sacred courts served the barbaric Syrians as a stable for their horses.

Holy City Sacked

From Medina, where Moslim died of a severe illness, the Syrian army turned toward Mecca. Catapults were already engaged in hurling great masses of stone into the city, and firebrands had already been thrown upon the roof of the Kaaba, setting the sacred edifice in flames, when, for the time being, the defenders of the city were rescued, owing to the confusion that broke out in Syria on the death of Yezid. But, for Medina, the temporary change in

Prophet's Companions in Spain
affairs had come too late. The survivors sought refuge in Africa, the greater part of them joining the army that conquered Spain under the command of Musa ; and in later times Spain became the last asylum of the companions of the Prophet and their descendants, for whom there was no longer a home in their native land.

Matters had come to a serious pass for the Mohammedan religion. Even yet it was not firmly rooted in the hearts of the Arabians ; the bulk of the Bedouins so far understood little more than the rudiments of Mahomet's doctrines, and it must already have appeared problematical whether or not the work of the Prophet would disappear amid the conflicts of parties and sects. The venerable men who had once assembled about the Prophet were now either dead or wanderers without a home ; the sacred Kaaba, and the mosque at Medina, were shattered and polluted ; the people were split up into hostile groups. And finally there was a caliph at the head of affairs who did not even preserve the appearance of obeying the laws of Mahomet, but seemed rather to pride himself on his profligacy. Everywhere it seemed that Islamism was falling into decay. But never in the history of the world has the power of spirit and of thought shown itself to be more irresistible than during the first century of the Mohammedan religion. Like a moonbeam upon the sea a ray of idealism and religious sentiment rested upon the dark waves of war and politics. However

The Secret of Islam's Power
meagre in comparison with the greater religions of the world, Islam yet represented an idea, and therewith a power that no earthly weapon could destroy. The sudden death of Yezid, in November, 683, rescued Mecca and Abdallah ; but at the same time it plunged the empire into the utmost confusion. Muaviya, son of Yezid, died a few months later, and cannot be said to have in reality succeeded to the supreme office ; but at

h's death the Omayyad party was for the moment without a leader. This was sufficient to cause the old tribal antagonisms to come to the surface once more among the Syrian Arabs. They had been suppressed during the period of conquest, and Muaviya I. had understood how to render them harmless, even to cause them to be of service to the empire. Now, however, Yemenites and Mahadites stood face to face, armed to the teeth ; and candidates for the caliphate must have known that the office was to be procured only through the assistance of one or the other party. Instead of seeking to take advantage of the quarrel of the rival parties in Syria, the people of Irak were content to limit their activities to their own province.

In Irak, the place of tribal feuds was taken by the dissensions of sects, among which the puritan democrats, or Kharijites, were no less distinguished than the followers of Ali. Owing to the influence of Iranian elements the various parties gradually became less and less Arabian in character. Nowhere, however, were

Abdallah the Pretender
there any signs of unity. Still, a powerful movement arose in all districts against the Syrian governors and officials, who, like the companions of the Prophet of earlier days, conducted themselves as high and mighty lords and masters, arousing a spirit of hostility wherever they appeared.

The inhabitants of Irak finally chose for their leader Abdallah ibn Zubeir, the pretender of Mecca and last representative of the party of old believers, who, although he had shown himself to be both a hypocrite and babbler, must at least have been more acceptable to the members of the various quarrelling parties than a man selected from among their inveterate enemies, the Syrians. Had Abdallah been an able man and of strong will and character, it is probable that this time he would have succeeded in making good his claims to the caliphate. The tidings of the death of Yezid had scarcely reached the camp of the Syrian army before Mecca, when Husain, the Syrian commander, sought to make peace with Abdallah. The Mahadite tribes of Syria in their hatred of the Yemenites also placed themselves on his side. Egypt declared ·for him ; and he was certain of the support of a powerful party in Irak. But his very first political action proved that he was incapable of taking advantage of the favourable situation, inasmuch as he refused to grant Husain and his army amnesty for the destruction of Medina. Thus, to ingratiate himself with the feeble party of the old believers, he threw away the opportunity of advancing into Syria at the head of a powerful force and of winning an important victory.

Husain thereupon returned to Syria without Abdallah, and found there an Omayyad chieftain, Mervan, who was ready to defend the seriously endangered rights of his family with decision and courage, and also to assume the position of caliph. Since the Mahadites, or Kaisites, as they were generally called after their most important Syrian branch, had first decided in favour of Abdallah, and had afterward chosen Dhakhak, the governor of Damascus, to be their leader, Mervan was obliged to turn to the Yemenites, or Kelbites, who after long hesitation decided to give him their support, provided he would promise to fulfil the various conditions which they imposed. Mervan and his Kelbite allies defeated the Kaisites on the meadow Rahit near **Kaisites Against Kelbites** Damascus in 684. Dhakhak fled to Abdallah, whom he now recognised as caliph ; and the Kaisites retreated to the north-east of Syria. One of the conditions imposed upon Mervan by the Kelbites was that he should marry the mother of Khalid, another Omayyad who had first been chosen by them to be their candidate for the caliphate, and should name her son as his successor ; but he broke his word after the battle, and appointed his own son Abdelmelik to be his heir, with the result that he met his death at the hand of the revengeful woman in April, 685.

The murder of Mervan was followed by sporadic revolts, of which the most serious was that of the democratic Kharijites. Goaded on by persecution, they rose during the period of confusion that followed the death of Muaviya ; and their former torturers soon learned that they, too, understood how to wage war and to devastate no less than they had formerly known how to die. In their extremity the orthodox inhabitants of Irak declared for the cause of Abdallah ; but the governor whom he sent out was soon killed in a battle with the infuriated sectarians. The terror inspired by the Kharijites was so great that at one time two thousand Irakans took to flight before a troop of forty of these redoubtable sectaries ; in fact, it seemed as if the ardent enthusiasm and contempt of death that Mahomet had once infused into his comrades had revived in these dauntless zealots. The struggle was chiefly confined to the city of Basra, which was constantly threatened by the revolutionaries and preserved from destruction only by the heroic defence of Mohallab, the Irakan general. At the same time that the Basrans were trembling before the Kharijites, the Kufans were in a state of no less terror because of the adherents of Ali—the Shiites or sectarians, from the Arabic *shi'a*, a sectary. The appearance of this sect was remarkable in many ways ; here the reviving spirit of the Iranian people made its appearance for the first time. The Persians had at first shown their inclination to shake off the Arabian yoke, together with the new religion that had been imposed upon them, only through occasional minor revolts. Now, however, as adherents of Ali and of Husain, and as champions of a schismatic tendency in Islam, they sought to adapt the new doctrines to their national character and to establish an Iranian form of the Mohammedan faith.

Forty Fanatics Rout Two Thousand

True to their old preferences, the Shiites, in contrast to the Kharijites, with whom they have often been confused, were partisans of unlimited despotism. And just as they had once set the highest value on the descent of their Arsacid and Sassanid sovereigns from a mythical, deified paternal ancestor, demanding pure blood in a sovereign as a condition of their loyalty, so at this time they claimed that the hereditary caliph should be a descendant of Mahomet, declaring that Ali, the nephew and son-in-law of the Prophet, had been the first legitimate caliph, and that the Omayyads, together with the Meccan caliphs were nothing more or less than usurpers. But these religious and political claims were merely a cloak to the true national spirit of the Shiitic movement, which found its most ardent adherents in Persian freedmen and slaves, and struck deep root in the land of Iran.

Persian Form of Islam

Under the leadership of a crafty and ambitious Arab, Mokhtar, the Shiites took possession of Kufa, and began a rule of terror. Owing to their desperate resistance and to the treachery of the imperial auxiliaries, Abdelmelik's first attempt to recapture Kufa was a failure. However, Mozab, brother of the caliph Abdallah, succeeded in putting the leader of the Shiites to death and in occupying Kufa in the name of Abdallah in 687. But in truth Mozab had only opened up the way for the Syrian caliph. Abdelmelik, who in the meanwhile had made peace with the Kaisites, led a new army into the province, and in a surprisingly short time defeated the Irakans in spite of constant treachery on the part of the Kaisite leaders. Mozab fell in the battle ; and Kufa opened its gates without resistance, as did also Basra, where Mohallab, the Irakan general, in spite of his great courage, demonstrated that he was as inconstant as the rest of his countrymen. Thus the most important province of the empire was lost by the Meccan caliph, who on his part was scoundrel enough secretly to rejoice at the death of his heroic brother, and, instead of taking decisive measures for the recovery of Irak, contented himself with delivering a well-turned funeral oration over the fallen in battle.

Contest of the Caliphs

Although the importance of Arabia had greatly decreased, so far as the temporal power of the caliphate was concerned, the moral influence which Abdallah as master of the sacred cities was still able to exert upon the numerous pilgrims who journeyed thither must not be underrated. For this reason alone Abdelmelik resolved to destroy his rival. Hadjaj, the general whom he sent out against Mecca, was a worthy successor to the dreaded Moslim, whose troops had sacked Medina. In November, 691, Hadjaj arrived before the city, and began a bambardment with his catapults. The Meccans held out for months, but finally fled, seeing that there was no help to be expected from without. The caliph Abdallah ended his life in a nobler manner than he had lived, for with his most faithful companions he made a sortie upon the besiegers, meeting death bravely at the head of his troops.

Siege of Mecca

The death of the last caliph of the old believers was an event of but small importance to the Mohammedan world. In the furthest north-east only, in Khorassan, was resistance offered by one of the

governors who had been appointed by Abdallah. In the year 693 the entire empire of the caliphs was subject to the Omayyad dynasty ; nevertheless, as yet there were no signs of peace and quiet. Unrest boiled and bubbled as in a geyser tube throughout Irak and Persia, and furious outbursts of the hidden resentment that flamed in the hearts of the people were visible from time to time. Even the rule of brute force instituted by Hadjaj, to whom the caliph had entrusted the governorship of the eternally restless province of Irak, failed to put an end to the rebellions that broke out again and again amid the confusion of races in that country of an old and fallen civilisation. Kelbites and Kaisites troubled Syria with their feuds and petty wars.

At the death of Abdelmelik, in October, 705, the influence of the Kaisites preponderated, and Velid, the new caliph, found in them his firmest support. Although Abdelmelik had been occupied almost constantly with domestic affairs, and had even been obliged to conclude a humiliating treaty with the Byzantines during the early part of his reign, Velid was now able to reassume the policy of conquest, which was far more in harmony with the original nature of the caliphate. There was no lack of soldiers, especially in Irak and Persia, and from these provinces men flocked to the banner of the caliph that they might win fame and plunder in the foreign wars.

A Period of Magnificence

For these reasons the reign of Velid was more brilliant than that of any other Omayyad caliph. Under his rule the Mohammedan empire attained to its greatest extent and magnificence. Kuteiba commanded the Arabian forces in the war fought on the north-eastern frontier of Persia, which had for its object the conquest of Transoxania and the subjection of its Iranian and Turkish races. After a severe struggle the city of Bokhara was captured in 709. Three years later Samarkand was taken, but in the year 715 the Mohammedan army was suddenly recalled while on the road to Kashgar, owing to the death of Velid. Contemporaneously with the Transoxanian campaign an attack was made on India. Under the command of Mohammed ibn Kasim, a Syrian army advanced into the valley of the Indus, and took possession of the city of Multan, after a long siege. However, the Moslems were unable to follow up their success. The Arabian general was even compelled to admit to the Hindus that their religion, like those of the Christians and the Jews, was entitled to be looked upon with tolerance by Mohammedans.

All the while that victories were being won in the east, the Byzantines were hard pushed by the armies of the caliph. A quarrel about the succession had again broken out in Constantinople, paralysing the powers of the state, which was already in an exhausted condition owing to the wars with the Bulgarians. Thus it is not surprising that Arabian troops marched unopposed through Asia Minor, and finally appeared before Constantinople, while at the same time the fleets of the caliph sailed into the Sea of Marmora. But if for this reason Velid was led to believe that the end of the Eastern Roman Empire was at hand, he deceived himself as to the tenacity of the Byzantines, who even in later days proved themselves to be possessed of an almost inexhaustible vital power. Decisive victories were won in Northern Africa,

An Exciting Chapter of History where Musa was engaged in a hard struggle with the Berber tribes, who had at first supported the Arabians in their war with the Byzantines, but were now fighting for their own freedom. Musa occupied the whole of the northern coast of the Atlantic Ocean, and from the African side of the Straits of Gibraltar cast longing looks toward the peninsula of Spain. How Tarik defeated the king of the Goths, how Musa himself followed on with fresh troops, and how in a surprisingly short time all Spain was made subject to the caliphs, the Arabian forces crossing the Pyrenees and penetrating far into France, is one of history's most exciting chapters. At that time all Europe trembled before the apparently irresistible advance of the enemies of Christendom, who were knocking at the gates of Constantinople and watering their horses in the Loire at the same moment that their fleets were threatening the islands of the Mediterranean. But it was also apparent that the Moslem bow had been bent to the point of breaking. The movement of expansion soon came to a halt, and the fall of the gigantic empire became only a question of time.

The character of Velid was such as is rarely to be found in a despotic ruler.

The caliph distinguished himself rather through a wise employment of talented subordinates than through his own personal abilities. He also possessed the capacity of securing the respect as well as the loyalty of all men with whom he came into touch. His son and successor, Suleiman (715–717), a weak, mistrustful crea-

Suleiman the Ungrateful ture, did not possess this gift, and however pitiable a spectacle he made of himself in his gross ingratitude to the great soldiers and statesmen of his father's reign, it must at least be admitted in his favour that he could not do otherwise than cast aside tools which he was incapable of using. Hadjaj, the ablest of Velid's councillors, had long forseeen what the future would bring to pass, and it had been his one desire to die before his master. That he was granted this piece of good fortune saved him from an ignominious end. The generals, some of whom were still at the head of their armies on the death of Velid, found a still more evil fate awaiting them. Musa was accused of misappropriating public money, compelled to pay an exorbitant fine by way of restitution, and ended his life as a pauper. Mohammed, the conqueror of the Punjab, was dragged to Damascus in chains, and tortured to death in prison. Kuteisa, who was well aware that a similar lot awaited him, sought in vain to arouse his troops to rebellion, and was soon put to death by the adherents of the new caliph, who sent his head to Damascus.

In spite of the wretchedness of his character, the deeds of horror perpetrated by Suleiman would scarcely be comprehensible were it not that at the time of his accession a complete change had taken place in the relations of the Arabian tribal groups. The Kaisites, who had enjoyed a golden age during the days of Velid, ruined themselves through an unsuccessful attempt to place a prince

A War of Revenge of their own choice upon the throne. Since Suleiman was in consequence compelled to look to the Kelbites or Yemenites for support, he was likewise obliged to yield to their desire for revenge upon their old rivals. Yezid, a son of the Irakan general Mohallab, the deadly enemy of Hadjaj, stood at the head of the Yemenite party; he attained almost unlimited power, and waged a successful war against the last defenders of Iranian independence, who dwelt in the mountainous south-eastern coast of the Caspian Sea, but had brought themselves into disrepute owing to their excessive ostentation and greed.

The foreign undertakings of Suleiman were attended by no great success. The Byzantines, who had provided themselves with a most effective means of defence in **Defeated by the Byzantines** the shape of their celebrated Greek fire, were now, in 717, under a very capable leader, Emperor Leo the Isaurian. An Arabian army which laid siege to Constantinople met with total defeat. The caliph's fleet of some four hundred vessels was also destroyed, and for a time Asia Minor remained in the possession of the Byzantines. Suleiman did not survive these reverses. But his successor, Omar II., a simple, upright Arab of the old school, was in turn unable to retrieve the fortunes of the empire; he reigned for too short a time—717-720—to be able to accomplish anything of importance, or even to put his favourite scheme of increasing the number of Mohammedans, through a systematic conversion of the inhabitants of the various lands subject to the caliphate, into execution. It was greatly to the credit of Omar II. that he espoused the cause neither of Kaisites nor of Kelbites, but endeavoured to keep away from all factions and parties.

During the reign of his successor, Yezid II., who belonged body and soul to the Kelbites, the domestic feuds once more came into prominence. A name-sake of Yezid, the son of Mohallab, entrenched himself in Basra, and called upon the Irakans, who had not forgotten their old hatred for the Syrians, in spite of the various tribal feuds, to revolt against the caliph. He was, however, defeated. At the same time a rebellion broke out in Africa, and it also became evident that the Moors intended to establish an independent kingdom in **Decline of the Caliphate** Spain. The short reign of Yezid II, — 720 to 724 — was marked by a decided falling off in the imperial power and supremacy of the caliphate. Nor did this retrograde movement cease completely during the reign of the next caliph, Hisham, although he was an abler ruler, and thoroughly aware of the course events were taking. Hisham displayed great wisdom in assuming a position of neutrality between Kelbites and

Kaisites. Since Kaisite and Yemenite leaders and statesmen alternately obtained the leadership, a certain amount of political sagacity developed, so that men soon were able to foretell with a reason-able degree of correctness the principles according to which the one or the other party would administer its offices. The Kaisites were of the school of Hadjaj, the conqueror of Irak; a tight hold on the reins of government, an overwhelming burden of taxation, exclusive favour shown to Arabs, and disregard for the newly converted of other races, were the fundamental principles of their policy. It became almost proverbial that no man could equal a Kaisite governor in obtain-ing vast sums in taxes from a province. In contrast to the Kaisites, the Kelbites, or Yemenites, were of more liberal opinions, placing more value in diplomatic methods and in a policy of leniency towards the conquered. Moreover, they did not endeavour, as did the Kaisites, to extort the poll-tax exclusively from the newly converted; in short, their policy was one of conciliation, in contrast to the **Politics in the Caliphate** Kaisite policy of brute force. The two political systems were not yet founded on firm and consistent principles; it was usually quite sufficient for a true Kelbite to see a Kaisite perform an action, in order himself immediately to endeavour to effect the contrary.

Hisham, who was filled with an insati-able greed for wealth, soon discovered that the Kaisites were the party best adapted for executing his wishes; therefore the Kelbite governors, who had at first been in favour, were now everywhere replaced by the tyrannical Kaisites. The Spanish Arabs, who were almost exclusively com-posed of Yemenites, were now for the first time placed under the rule of a Kaisite; and in Africa, Obeida, and after him Obeidallah, extorted tremendous sums in taxes from the province.

The result was a vast upheaval of the population of Northern Africa, in whom the Kharijite missionaries of the period had at last found a people after their own hearts; so that here also those who arose in revolt against the insufferable burden of taxation became imbued with religious-democratic ideas and displayed the highest degree of fanaticism. The Berbers have never accomplished much under leaders of their own race; but under the

THE DEFEAT OF THE MOHAMMEDAN FLEET BLOCKADING CONSTANTINOPLE
In the glorious reign of Caliph Velid an Arabian army appeared before Constantinople, the fleets of the Caliph sailed into the Sea of Marmora, and all Europe trembled before the Mohammedan advance; but the tenacity of the Byzantines, and their Greek fire, saved the city, and in the next reign the Caliph's army and fleet were destroyed

intellectual guidance of alien spirits they have exhibited a remarkable eagerness for self-sacrifice and great courage. In the year 740 the district of Tangier revolted. Khalid, the general sent out by Obeidallah, was killed, and with an exceedingly large number of Arab chieftains. The caliph was now obliged to throw his beloved treasure chests wide open, and to form an army of picked Syrian warriors for service in Africa. The troops were sent out under the command of Koltum and Baldsh, and were joined in Egypt by a levy of Arabs. Nevertheless, the battle with the Berbers ended in another defeat for the caliph; his infantry was for the most part annihilated, and Koltum fell. Baldsh managed to escape with the cavalry to Tangier; and thence, after many adventures, he arrived in Spain, where he was still to play a great rôle in history, recorded in another part of this work. Hisham did not live to see the end of the rebellion in Africa.

Successful Revolt in Tangier

In Irak also, after many months of peace under a Yemenite governor, an insurrection broke out on the appointment of a Kaisite to the office. The government was in a still worse plight in Khorassan, where Kelbites and Kaisites openly declared war on one another, as well as in the neighbouring province of Transoxania, where the native population was decidedly unwilling to accept the usual fate of the conquered. Since the Kaisite rulers were in the habit of beginning their terms of office with the imprisonment and exploitation of their Yemenite predecessor, the arrival of a Kaisite governor in Khorassan was sufficient to drive the Kelbites into open revolt and to cause them to form an alliance with the Turks; and it was not until a Kelbite governor arrived and general amnesty was granted that quiet was again restored in this important frontier province. Khorassan included at that time the whole of North-eastern Iran as well as Transoxania, and was of great importance from a military point of view as a barrier against the nomadic tribes of Central Asia. In like manner the mountain countries to the south of the Caucasus, which commanded the entrance to the passes, became military provinces in which incessant fighting took place with Armenians, Scythians, and Iberians, and sometimes with the Tartar hordes that strove to make their way into the plain of Mesopotamia.

Fighting in the Caucasus

The war with the Byzantines was continued with varying success. The Arabians still hoped to win a final victory by striking a blow at the heart of the empire; Asia Minor was repeatedly laid waste, until a brilliant victory of the emperor Leo finally set a limit to the incursions of the Moslem forces.

Hisham died in 743, leaving to his nephew and successor, Velid II., an empire that, in spite of the unsuppressed revolt in Northern Africa, was still possessed of abundant vital power, thanks to the frugal financial policy of the caliph and to his skilful management of the two great political groups. Nevertheless, the antagonisms of sects and parties were by no means reconciled. There were, indeed, men who looked upon loyalty to the caliph alone as their chief virtue, and who thus formed the nucleus of a purely dynastic party. The tribe Rabia, which for many years had assumed a position of neutrality in the quarrels between Maha-dites and Yemenites, and of which the members had for that reason frequently been chosen to fill difficult diplomatic offices, served as a point of departure for further development. But the jealousy between the Arabs of Syria and the Irakans, who were under the influence of Persia, was too deeply rooted to disappear easily. Indeed, the more influence the Persians obtained, the more decided was the tendency of the Irakans to turn away from the Syrians. Finally, it became evident that the Mohammedan Iranians would eventually gain the upper hand by force of numbers alone.

Persians Come to the Front

In this lay the greatest danger to which the Omayyad dynasty was exposed. Lifted to the throne by the Syrians, the Omayyads prospered, and finally fell with their most faithful adherents. As soon as the centre of the empire was removed to Irak, the days of the Damascus caliphate came to an end. The position of the Omayyads was undermined by the natural course of events; the stagnation of Syria, the Arabian inhabitants of which had fought the battles of the caliph, and had therefore fallen off rather than increased in numbers, and the growing multitude and wealth of the Irakans, were the chief causes of the decline of the Omayyad dynasty. Already during the reign of Hisham, the continuation of Omayyad rule had become dependent on whether or not his family could win the favour of the Irakans and the other inhabitants

Beginning of the End

of the eastern provinces. It is hardly necessary to say that in this case also movements which were national were a cloak of religion. However much men continued to disagree as to whether the first of the caliphs had been justly entitled to the dignity, whether Abu Bekr or Ali had been the legitimate successor of the Prophet, one thing at least was certain—all the sectarians were united in the belief that the Omayyads were usurpers. But the question who should succeed them was not to be decided so easily. The descendants of Ali, who turned up from time to time and always found supporters in Irak, seemed without exception to have inherited the incapacity and misfortunes of their paternal ancestor; the few who remained of the old comrades of the Prophet had retired to the farthest west, to Africa, and Spain. Thus it came about that a noble family of Mecca, the Abbas-sides, who had long been known as the hereditary custodians of the spring Zem-zem, and who were more nearly related to the Prophet than the Omayyads, succeeded in becoming the leaders of the dissatisfied sects. Already during the reign of Hisham their secret designs had assumed a serious aspect; under his feeble successors they arose in open revolt. Velid II. did his best to scatter the treasures of his predecessor, leading a life of careless debauchery; but in spite of his lavishness he succeeded in winning few true friends, and aroused the hostility of the other Omayyad princes by appointing his younger son to be his successor. In the year after his accession he was dethroned and put to death by Yezid III., the champion of the Yemenite party. Disturbances immedi-ately followed in Irak and Khorassan. Mervan, the Omayyad governor of Armenia and Azerbijan, advanced on Damascus, defeated the Yemenites, and compelled the Syrian Arabs to accept him as regent during the minority of the son of Velid II. But the power of the Omayyads was rapidly declining, and Mervan, although a man of great ability, was unable to ward off the impending destruction. Embittered by their losses, the Yemenites had become his enemies, and thus the Syrian Arabs were once more divided at the very moment when unity was most needed. Already the descendants of Ali had raised the banner of rebellion in Persia; and in Irak the Kharijites were once more in revolt. No

Rise of the Abbassides

help was to be expected from the western provinces. In Africa the Berber troubles were not yet ended ; and in Spain a civil war was raging between Kaisites and Kelbites, who even in this distant land had not been able to forget their ancient tribal hatred.

The first blow was dealt in Khorassan. Here, in the year 747, Abu Muslim unfurled the black flag of the Abbassides, and drove out Nasir, the Omayyad governor. Nasir vainly endeavoured to make a stand in Western Persia, and this province also was lost by the Omayyads. In the summer of 750, on the Abbassid troops appearing before Kufa, the gates were immediately opened to the revolutionists. It had been of no advantage to Mervan that he had seized and put to death Ibrahim, the intriguing head of the Abbassid family, for the place of the latter was taken by his sons ; and the movement itself, which was not in reality founded on the ambition of the Abbassides, but on the excessive hatred of Irakans and Iranians for the Syrians, pursued its course without interruption.

Last of the Omayyads
Mervan assembled a powerful army on the southern frontier of his old province, not far from Mossul ; and here on the Great Zab the Abbassides encountered the superior forces of the caliph, on January 25th, 750. Even at this decisive moment the tribal hatred of the Bedouins did not lessen in intensity ; just as the battle had practically been won by the Syrians, Mervan's entire Yemenite following deserted him. The result was a complete rout. After vainly seeking refuge in Damascus, the caliph escaped to Egypt, where he lost his life in a fruitless attempt to organise resistance. The banner of the Abbassides now waved triumphantly over the walls of Damascus ; and thus the people of Irak finally gained the victory over their hated Syrian neighbours, the East over the West.

With the victory of the Abbassides a period of short splendour, followed by gradual decay, began for the empire of the caliphs. Many changes which had for years been developing in comparative seclusion now made their way to the light ; and many features that had formerly been all-important to the welfare of the Omayyad dynasty were lost. Thus the moment has come for us to cast a backward glance over the domestic affairs of the Mohammedan empire, which arose out of nothing with such marvellous rapidity, and finally extended from the Pyrenees and the shores of the Atlantic Ocean to the Indus and the Jaxartes.

The Bedouins, who marched forth from the interior of Arabia, brought to the peoples of Western Asia a simplicity of life and a homely greatness of spirit and deed hitherto unknown to those more refined and effeminate races. In the Bedouins, the luxurious Syrians and Persians once more beheld men who looked upon mere sensual enjoyments with contempt, and were capable of fighting to the death for a principle. For the first time for many years a manly, often a heroic, spirit was infused into the history of Western Asia. The love of freedom of the Bedouins dissipated for the time being the suffocating atmosphere of gloomy, indolent despotism that arose like a poisonous mist from the rich plains of Mesopotamia and Persia. It was no lasting inheritance that Arabia presented to its neighbour countries. Never in history has a victorious race been able permanently to alter the character of the conquered territories and the spirit of their inhabitants ; the conquerors themselves must finally succumb to this same character and spirit. None the less, the infusion of foreign blood is often sufficient to arouse the exhausted soil to new fruitfulness, to awaken a fresh development of national life.

Greatness of the Bedouin

Still, it would be incorrect to look upon the Arabians of the time of the Prophet as merely rude, uncultured Bedouins, however large a proportion of the population was composed of that class ; the industrious agriculturists of Medina and the far-travelled merchants of Mecca stood upon a vastly higher plane of civilisation than the simple tribes of the desert. In Yemen remains were still preserved of a former period of flourishing commerce and advanced moral development ; and the Arabs who led a semi-stationary existence on the frontiers of the Roman and Persian empires had not remained uninfluenced by the civilisation of their neighbours. From these various elements were recruited the populations of the towns that shortly became the centres of Mohammedan civilisation in the various provinces. The true Bedouin took but a small part in the intellectual life of these central groups ; his passionate love for

Arabs of the Towns

an unfettered life on the steppes was unconquerable. No one has expressed this sentiment more convincingly than the mother of Yezid I., who prevailed upon her husband to allow her to return to her tribe in the desert : " A tent swayed by the wind is dearer to me than a lofty castle. . . . A piece of bread in the corner of my desert home tastes **Love** better than the daintiest sweet-**of the** meat. I long for my home ; **Desert** no palace may take its place." It is obvious that the immediate effect of the wars of conquest waged by the caliphs could not have been favourable to civilisation ; but the destruction and loss of life inflicted in the countries that were first attacked and quickly subdued were comparatively insignificant, despite the fact that these were religious wars, which, as experience has shown, are the most merciless of all struggles. Mahomet's humane treatment of both Christians and Jews, the ease with which conversion to Islam could take place—through the mere repetition of a formula—as well as regard to the finances of the state, were the chief preventives of general massacres.

Commerce very soon became one of the chief sources of the power and splendour of the Mohammedan empire. The most important trade routes from east to west fell at one blow into the hands of the followers of the Prophet ; not a grain of Indian spice could reach the western world without first passing the customs depôts of the Arabians ; and the amounts of the tolls assessed lay entirely at the discretion of the caliph. In earlier times trade had favoured sometimes one, sometimes another route, according to circumstances ; an exorbitant duty in Egypt driving commerce from the Red Sea, the route through the Persian Gulf and the valley of the Euphrates to Syria became popular. The merchant was enabled to avoid the risk of transportation of goods by sea by **Arabian** sending his caravans overland **Control of** through Persia and Mesopo-**Commerce** tamia. It was not long before wares from the Farthest East, Chinese silk in particular, were sent through Iran, sometimes through Transoxania and across the Caspian Sea to South Russia, often by ship from China to Ceylon, there to connect with the trade routes from India to the West. The gates of commerce were in the hands of a single people ; and the profits of all the customs depôts, from

Basra and Alexandria to Bokhara and Multan, flowed into the imperial treasury.

With the growth of material prosperity there was a corresponding increase of intellectual activity, which, however, did not reach its zenith until the times of the Abbassides. So long as the Syrian Arabs governed the empire, the ancient Arabian spirit reigned triumphant ; and, as a result, poetry and romance were more popular than science.

The army organisation had remained under the Omayyads just what it had been during the first days of the caliphate. There was practically no standing army ; and the caliph's bodyguard was of no special importance until the Abbassid dynasty came into power. The conquered countries were rendered secure by means of military colonies ; for, as a rule, the armies that won provinces for Islam immediately settled down in the new territories and continued in the service of the governor. The natural result of this wholesale emigration was a surprisingly rapid increase in the political significance of **The** Arabia during the days of the **Army** first caliphs. The military **Organisation** organisation, however well adapted to the simple conditions of life of the Arabs, was incapable of development, and the Abbassides were compelled to form their bodyguards and standing armies out of foreign mercenaries, who finally became the rulers of the empire

The celebrity of the Arabians as breeders of horses might easily lead to the incorrect idea that the troops of the first caliphs consisted exclusively of cavalry ; in truth, however, the number of serviceable horses in Arabia was never very large, and the Arabian armies were chiefly made up of infantry, and camel riders who usually fought dismounted. The backbone of the army was indeed composed of horsemen, well armed with steel helmet and chain mail, bearing lance and sabre ; but the bulk of the soldiers were, at least during the early days of the caliphate, very badly off for arms,

The surprisingly rapid development of Mohammedan sea-power—the navy was constructed with the assistance of impressed inhabitants of the Syrian coast—has already been mentioned. It was fortunate for the Christian Occident that the dreaded " Greek fire " was discovered in time. It perhaps saved Constantinople from a premature fall.

THE GREAT DAYS OF BAGDAD

IT was not love for a brave general or for the followers of the Prophet, whose claims to the caliphate were much more valid than those of the rulers in Damascus, but hatred that caused Irakans and Persians to unite against the Syrians. There was no lack of candidates for the empty throne; once more the numerous descendants of Ali stood in the front rank. They had never ceased to labour for the downfall of the Omayyad dynasty, and in all probability the bulk of the soldiers who fought for Irak and defeated Mervan at the Great Zab believed that they were also fighting for the house of Ali. But the curse that seemed to accompany this family of pretenders continued with undiminished power: into the place of the descendants of Ali, the diplomatic, crafty grandchildren of Abbas thrust themselves, and as soon as they dared to lay aside the

Usurpers of the Caliphate mask, held fast with iron grasp to the longed-for office. Abbas was an uncle of the Prophet, a distinguished man, but of doubtful character, who had opposed his nephew until finally the scales turned in favour of the latter. He then enthusiastically welcomed Mahomet as the messenger of God. Through this ancestor—whose spirit had descended upon his children—the Abbassides based their claims to the caliphate, not without foundation according to Arabian law, for among the Omayyads also, not the son but the brother of a prince was looked upon as the legitimate successor. Besides, Mahomet had left behind him no male descendants, but only a daughter, the maternal ancestor of the Ali branch. The success of the one family or the other depended entirely upon the personalities of their leaders, and so far as this was concerned the Abbassides were greatly superior to the descendants of Ali, who never yet had succeeded in pursuing a definite policy.

Abdallah Abul-Abbas, with the honourable nickname of Al-Saffah (the man of blood), perhaps invented by himself, was of all the family the man most capable of assisting the cause of the Abbassides to victory both by trickery and force. By him the new period of Mohammedan history was ushered in in a manner characteristic of the whole age. When the Hashimids, the name given to the opponents of the Omayyads and supporters of the true descendants of Mahomet, had taken possession of Kufa, Abdallah was at hand immediately

Reign of the "Man of Blood" and succeeded in winning over their general to his cause. The commander of the Khorassan rebels, Abu Muslim, had always been inclined to favour the Abbassides, and others, whose loyalty seemed doubtful, were put out of the way either by open force or secret assassination. Arriving in Syria, Abdallah hastened to massacre all members of the Omayyad family upon whom he could lay hands, and caused the graves of the Omayyad caliphs to be opened and their bodies mutilated. It was in vain that the followers of Ali rebelled in Irak, and the adherents of the Omayyads in Syria. When, after a reign of four years, the "man of blood" died, the entire empire, with the exception of Spain, which then broke off for all time from the rulers of the East, was in the hands of the Abbassides.

The true founder of the Abbassid dynasty was Abu Muslim, who had first caused Khorassan to revolt, and now governed this important province with its military colonies and warlike inhabitants—a man who, owing to the intolerance and bigotry in which he had been educated, had become a bloodthirsty fanatic. Not until shortly before his death did he appreciate and regret the evil

A Fanatic Who Repented results of his blind religious zeal, as is shown in a remarkable letter written by his hand. It was inevitable that such a powerful, independent personage as he should have awakened the suspicions of the caliph, who made several attempts to cause him to be assassinated. When, after the death of Abdallah, a struggle for the succession broke out between his brothers, Abu Muslim hastened up, and with the aid of his army decided the victory in favour of Abu Jafar Mansur. But it was fated that Muslim should never return to his province. As soon as he felt his position to be secure enough, the new caliph lost no time in putting into practice the political tendencies which he had inherited from his father. Abu Muslim was enticed to court, and there cut down before the caliph's eyes. After his death a rebellion in favour of the descendants of Ali broke out in Khorassan, and at the same time the contemporary head of the family, Mohammed, incited the Medinans to revolt; but Arabia was no longer the land from which a new dynasty could arise. Mohammed fell in battle, and the rebellion in Khorassan was easily crushed.

Founder of the Abbassides Murdered

During Mansur's reign the effects of the fall of the Omayyads and the termination of Syrian supremacy came fully into the light. Abdallah had already chosen Irak for his residence. Mansur, however, did not choose the frontier town of Kufa to be the capital of his great empire, but built the city of Bagdad in the heart of Persia, on the banks of the Tigris, at a point where it is separated from the Euphrates by less than thirty miles. At first it had not been his intention to establish the capital here. He had desired to found a military town, or, more correctly, a fortified camp as a headquarters for the mercenaries, with whose aid he expected to hold the restless Irakans in subjection. But Mansur could not shake himself free from the latter, among whom he enjoyed great popularity. Kufa, fallen into disfavour, was deserted; and after a few years had passed the walls of Bagdad became too narrow for the inhabitants who came streaming in from all directions. On the left bank of the Tigris a new and splendid quarter of the town sprang up; in short, whether he would or not, the caliph beheld a metropolis arising about his residence, a city which seemed to be a reflection of the Nineveh and Babylon of ancient days. The attempt to found a military camp in the land which was now elevated by the Abbassid caliphs into the centre of the Mohammedan empire, was of itself sufficient to prove that a change had begun to take place in the relations between the rulers and their subjects. The Omayyads had dwelt in Damascus, in the midst of

Bagdad Grew by Chance

a population of pure-blooded Arabs, who were loyal to the dynasty and dangerous to the caliph only when they became divided among themselves on account of tribal prejudice and hatred. Equal loyalty was not to be expected from the inhabitants of Irak, a mixed population of which the various elements were constantly in a state of war with one another; and the Arabs of Irak were no longer to be depended upon, for they had long before become enfeebled and degenerate.

Thus it became necessary for Mansur to substitute for the small bodyguard that had proved sufficient for the Omayyads a larger force, of which the nucleus was composed neither of Syrians nor of Irakans but of border troops from Khorassan, and Turkish mercenaries. For the first time in the history of Western Asia the barbarous sons of the north-east strutted about the streets of Bagdad in the brilliant uniform of the life-guard, and cast longing looks on the vast treasures of the "capital of the world." Tidings of the fabulous splendour of Bagdad soon reached the Turkestan steppes; and the warlike nomads, seated about their camp-fires, eagerly listened to stories of the luxury of the metropolis and the cowardice and lack of unity of its inhabitants told by their returned companions. There was no longer any need for the caliph to impress or to entice Turkish mercenaries into his service; already more than enough had volunteered.

Turks Covet Bagdad

The removal of the centre of the empire to the east was a result chiefly of the growing power of the Persians, who were now completely reconciled to the Mohammedan religion. During the days of the Omayyads it had been almost impossible for a Persian to attain a position of influence in the state; but under the Abbassides the number of Iranians occupying high offices constantly increased. With them a new spirit, foreign and hostile to the old Arabian character, became supreme at the caliph's court. The mixture of aristocracy and democracy, peculiar to the Arabs as a natural result of their nomadic manner of life, with clans and chiefs was entirely unknown to the Persians, who had always shown that a despotic form of government was better adapted to their national character. The Arabs of the old school

GRASS BOATS USED AT BAGDAD

A MOSQUE IN OLD BAGDAD

GENERAL VIEW OF THE CITY OF ORIENTAL ROMANCE AND SPLENDOUR

ANOTHER SCENE IN THE CITY ON THE BANKS OF THE TIGRIS

ON THE TIGRIS, SHOWING THE BRIDGE OF BOATS IN THE DISTANCE

BAGDAD, THE GREATEST CAPITAL OF THE MOHAMMEDAN EMPIRE

Photos Underwood & Underwood, London

had not the least comprehension for that blind idolisation of a ruler which the Persians had exhibited from the earliest times. Far from endeavouring to oppose this tendency, the Abbassides became less and less accessible to the people, and entirely gave up the immediate, almost comrade-like relation of ruler to subject

Creation of the Vizirate in which the Omayyads had stood to their faithful Syrians. It soon became necessary for Mansur to create a new official, a vizir, who occupied the position of intermediary between the more or less deified caliph and the common people. It is obvious that the vizirate cannot well be compared with the chancellorship of a European state, inasmuch as the vizir was not the adviser of the caliph, but his agent in matters pertaining to external affairs. His duty was merely to execute the commands of his master, whose profound wisdom and infallible judgment decided upon all questions of administration, but who was far too august to take a personal share in the actual details of administration. Thus the vizirate was one of those positions of which the significance depended entirely upon the character of the incumbent, or of the prince whom he served. Some vizirs were mere lay figures ; others were friends and advisers of the sovereign ; in some cases, indeed, they were the true rulers of the nation, and in their hands the caliphs were little more than puppets.

Although the Abbassides were willing to accede to the demands of the Iranian spirit in the matter of the vizirate, it was necessary for them to exercise the utmost caution in regard to another trait of Persian character somewhat similar to that which has already been described. The movement which enabled the Abbassides to place themselves at the head of the Mohammedan empire was in the main a result of Persian activity, and had for

Policy of Ali's Descendants its immediate object nothing further than the destruction of the Omayyad dynasty in order that the true heirs and descendants of Mahomet might occupy the throne. It is obvious, however, that the Abbassides attained their position of supremacy owing rather to their superior diplomacy and cunning than to a general recognition of their rights. Inflamed with anger, but not in the least discouraged, the descendants of Ali still awaited an

opportunity for putting forth their claims. The Abbassides themselves knew only too well that the grandchildren of the deified son-in-law and nephew of the Prophet possessed in reality far more adherents among the inhabitants of the empire than did the house of Abbas ; and even had they not realised it, the revolts that were constantly breaking out in favour of the Ali branch would soon have taught them the obvious truth. However much the Abbassides were indebted to the various sectarians who assisted them to the caliphate, and however enthusiastic they may have been as Shiites during the years preceding their elevation to the throne, upon attaining the position of supremacy they were obliged to renounce their sect and to ingratiate themselves with the orthodox party, to which the bulk of the Arabian population belonged. The first step taken in this direction by the caliph Mansur may not have been easy ; in fact, its immediate effect was to endanger his throne. But the permanent result of an understanding between the despotic monarchy and the State Church

Caliphs Heads of the Church could not have been otherwise than beneficial to the future of the dynasty. Their position in regard to the orthodox party was of the highest importance to the Abbassides. As caliphs they were not only the rulers of a vast empire, but also the spiritual guides of all Mohammedans, defenders of the faith as well as of the realm. During the time of the Omayyads the two offices had united into one ; in all regions through which the new doctrines were disseminated the temporal supremacy of the caliph was also recognised. Although the Abbassides soon perceived that they would not be able to retain their double position in all parts of their exceptionally extensive empire, they recognised at the same time that the religious influence which they possessed was also a means for preserving the state from dissolution, and that at least their spiritual authority could be maintained in regions where the power of their arms was no longer feared. On the other hand, dissenters had the choice either of entirely severing their connection with Bagdad through the election of a new caliph, or of taking a middle course by refusing to recognise the temporal supremacy of the caliphate while subjecting themselves to its spiritual authority. Thus, under these conditions, it must have been a matter of great importance for the Abbassides to win the friendship of the orthodox party as well as of the Arabian tribes, which, notwithstanding all removals of the centre of power, still retained the political leadership of the Mohammedan world.

Nevertheless, in spite of Mansur's wise policy, the unity of the empire was not preserved entire during his reign. At the same time that the centre of the empire was transferred to the east, Spain, the farthest western province, was lost to the caliphs; not only the temporal but the spiritual bonds of connection were completely severed. It was in vain that Abdallah, "the man of blood," had endeavoured to annihilate the Omayyad family. A member of the fallen house, Abd ur Rahman, escaped to Africa after manifold adventures, and finally reached Spain, where after long struggles between Kaisites and Kelbites, the Kaisite leader, Yusuf, had obtained control of the government and driven out the Abbassid emissaries. Shortly after his landing, Abd ur Rahman succeeded in deposing Yusuf with the assistance of the Kelbites. He then established an independent government, and, as a descendant of the unjustly deposed Omayyad dynasty, took upon himself the title of caliph, in 756.

All Mansur's attempts to destroy his rival were without effect. In general, his reign was so disturbed at home by revolts of the followers of Ali and other parties that foreign undertakings were out of the question. The caliph was forced to content himself with maintaining the frontiers of the empire, here and there perhaps succeeding in advancing them a trifle. At all events, Mansur was successful in rendering secure the throne of the Abbassides.

HARUN AL RASHID THE GREAT CALIPH
Harun al Rashid, "the Just," came to the throne in 768 A.D. in the golden days of the Mohammedan civilisation, and before the decay of Bagdad and the caliphate.

It may have been that a cold, calculating, faithless character such as his was needed at this time with the assistance of the Irakans to maintain the supremacy of the Abbassides.

The golden age of the Abbasside dynasty did not begin until after the death of Mansur, in 775, when his son Mahdi succeeded to the caliphate—much against the will of his uncle, who, as brother of the late caliph, had first claim to the throne according to Arabian custom. But the constantly recurring inclination of reigning caliphs to abrogate the usual form of succession in favour of their own descendants in this case led to no serious conflict. Mahdi was the very opposite of his father both in character and disposition, but none the less just such a ruler as the Irakans most valued. Under his government Bagdad began to develop into the city with which we have become acquainted through legend and tale as the most brilliant and joyful capital of the world, and at the same time the centre of Eastern literature and science.

That in spite of Mahdi's mild rule there was no peace in Irak, and that the old struggles of sects and parties broke out anew, now here, now there, is self-evident from the character of the people. In like manner the warlike inhabitants of Khorassan, although they had assisted the Abbassides to the throne, nevertheless looked upon the departure of the latter from the Shiite doctrines with great displeasure. The tremendous revolt headed by the prophet Al Mukanna (the Veiled One) in Transoxania was not completely quelled until the year 780. Just as if there were not enough sects and parties already in existence, Arabian revolutionaries arose in Irak and preached a republican form of Mohammedanism.

Their principles may perhaps be considered to be the sharpest protest put forth by the Arabian national spirit against the Iranian despotism of the Abbassides. Among the Persians the old communism of the followers of Mazdak, who had embittered the life of the last of the Sassanidæ, appeared once more in a Mohammedan garb. The Iranian adherents of Ali finally arrived at the summit of absurdity in the deification of their idol. They had ever been ready to recognise the Abbassid caliphs also as divine beings on account of their connection with the Prophet, until the departure of the Abbassides from the orthodox faith transformed this overwhelming veneration into hatred. There is no doubt that the majority of the sects emanated from the Persians, and that they were, in a way, the outward evidences of the severe spiritual conflict occasioned by the conversion of the Iranians to Mohammedanism and the blending of the Persian and Arabian conceptions of life. Acquaintance with the religions of India, especially with the doctrine of the transmigration of souls, which found many converts in Khorassan, contributed not a little to the general confusion.

In spite of the domestic disturbances, Mahdi was able to undertake several successful expeditions against the Byzantines, without, however, firmly establishing his position in Asia Minor. An army to invade Spain was annihilated by the Omayyad caliph. The latter had already formed a plan of attacking Syria in order to arouse the old followers of his house to battle with the Abbassides, when, fortunately for Mahdi, Charlemagne began his wars against the Moors in Spain.

Rule of the Caliph's Wife During the last years of his life the policy of Mahdi was guided almost entirely by his ambitious wife Khizuran, who had also managed to cause her sons Musa and Harun to be named his successors. But when, in the year 785, Musa ascended the throne, taking the title of Hadi, her ambition encountered a sudden check, since he advised her with great emphasis

to busy herself with the duties of a woman, and to spend more of her time reading the Koran. However, Hadi's attempt to exclude her favourite Harun from the succession in favour of his own children led to his assassination in the next year.

Harun al Rashid, the Just Harun al Rashid came to the throne without opposition, reigning from 786–809. He had always enjoyed great popularity, his generosity and kindliness contributing no less to the affection in which he was held by his subjects than the warlike deeds he had performed during his father's lifetime against the Byzantines. Still, he had inherited the evil characteristics of his Abbassid ancestors in full measure, showing himself on more than one occasion to be both treacherous and cruel. The high praise which tradition has accorded to his celebrated justness, perpetuated in his surname Al Rashid, "the Upright," must be accepted with restrictions. However, he has now become a favourite name of legend ; and Bagdad, his residence, which attained its greatest prosperity during his days, now stands for that epitome of fabulous splendour which the traveller in the Orient often seeks but never finds. Harun's name is connected the more closely with Bagdad

TOMB OF HARUN'S QUEEN
A striking monument on the plains, near Bagdad, to Zobiede, queen of Harun al Rashid.

for the reason that its decay set in almost immediately after his death, and with the magnificence of the city the glory of the caliphate itself became less and less, until finally it too vanished. On the whole, however, it may be said that the period of Harun's reign was one of domestic prosperity and of successful foreign wars. The ruinous effects of the Abbassid system of government were not felt to any great extent during his lifetime. But complete domestic tranquillity was not to be thought of. It was impossible for the Irakan and Persian sects to renounce their favourite pastime of quarrelling ; again and again they sought to take up arms, and in Syria, Kelbites and Kaisites fell upon one another with undiminished fury. The ever-restless inhabitants of Khorassan were no less inclined to revolt now than they had always been. In Africa things came to such a pass that the authority of the caliph was no longer recognised in the western provinces; and a dynasty of the house of Ali arose, refusing to be subject either to the temporal or to the spiritual influence of the Abbassides.

The campaigns of Harun against the Byzantines, although temporarily successful, were attended by no **Destruction of the Barmecides** permanent results. Constantinople was harassed to the uttermost by the Bulgarians, and repulsed the armies of the caliph with the greatest difficulty; more than once the city was compelled to pay tribute to Harun. The expeditions often led by Harun himself into Asia Minor were little more than predatory raids, for the empire of the caliph was already too decayed and tattered to permit of the permanent acquisition and Mohammedanising of new provinces; in fact, soon after Harun's death the Byzantines themselves took the offensive. The most noteworthy event of Harun's life was the destruction of the Barmecides. Had it been only the murder of over-ambitious generals or governors, or merely one of the scenes of carnage that occur in endless succession throughout the history of Oriental empires, the incident would scarcely be worthy of notice. But in reality the deed itself, together with the events that led up to it, may be taken as a characteristic prelude to later conditions; through it the authority of the office of mayor of the palace, which was in later times called into existence by the weakening despotism as an executive and support, was for the time being abolished. Already, under the predecessors of Harun, the Barmecide family had attained to great authority; and its influence became almost unlimited when one of its members, Yahya, by timely interference succeeded in securing the throne for Harun on the death of Hadi. And when

Jafar, a son of Yahya, obtained as a result of his wisdom and charm of personality the highest favour of the caliph, and held the office of vizir with almost boundless power it seemed indeed as if a new ruling house had arisen with the Abbassides. Already the whims of Jafar were looked upon as of greater importance than those of the caliph; already measureless wealth had fallen to the share of the favoured family; when, in 803, a sudden catastrophe destroyed its hopes of further distinction and influence, and at the same time led to the annihilation of the all-powerful favourite. Had it been insight into the threatening danger that led Harun to take extreme measures much might be said in his defence; but it was in reality nothing more than an ordinary harem affair through which Jafar and his family came to their ruin. The affair was certainly not greatly to the credit of the caliph, and the deed awakened extreme dissatisfaction among the people of Bagdad. Grumbling and embittered, the ageing Harun left the city, and resided during the last years of his life in Rakka in Mesopotamia, assiduously but vainly engaged in an attempt to obviate later quarrels as to the succession.

During the reign of Harun the Abbassid empire reached the zenith of its external power and domestic culture. The foundations of prosperity were, on the whole, the same as they had been during the Omayyad period, but internal conditions had changed. The removal of the centre of the empire from Damascus to Bagdad exerted a tremendous influence on the life and morals of the Mohammedan races. Transported from the dry, strong desert air of Damascus and placed in the hot, damp plain of Irak, the civilisation of the caliphate developed more rapidly, but also more artificially, under the new conditions.

Inasmuch as the residence of the caliph was removed to the richest and most

Underwood & Underwood

HARUN AL RASHID'S PALACE
All that remains of the splendid palace of the Great and Just Caliph at his ancient capital of Bagdad.

densely-populated province of the empire, it followed that the caliphate itself gained new lustre, and at the same time became further estranged from its old Arabian simplicity. In order that the caliph might maintain the splendour and dignity of his supreme position among the countless rich merchants of Bagdad, in the midst of a **Splendour** population given over to pre-**of Bagdad's** tension and display, it became **Court** necessary for him to arrange his court in a manner entirely different from that which had previously been the custom under the majority of the Omayyad rulers. Magnificent palaces, bridges, mosques, artistically laid out gardens, water conduits, and public fountains aroused the wonder of his subjects no less than did the splendour of the arms and uniforms displayed by caliph and court on holidays, or the plenitude of treasures accumulated in the palace of the ruler, and the lavish way in which money was freely distributed to beggars and the unemployed. A luxurious spirit of good cheer pervaded the entire city; and, as once in the Rome of the emperors, not only the gold of the provinces, but also the native products of the various quarters of the globe were brought by commerce to the markets of Bagdad, where the silks of China and the furs of Siberia were heaped together with the spices of India and Arabia and the coloured leather wares of Cordova. At that time Bagdad was the centre of the world's commercial routes, which led from China to the West, from India to Byzantium and to Western Europe.

Although there were still dangers and difficulties to be overcome, it was a golden age of commerce; the majority of the roads were in excellent condition, provided with milestones and caravanseries, and protected by garrisons in the less-frequented regions. The great annual pilgrimages to Mecca, which united devotion and trade in a most profitable manner, **The Golden** contributed not a little to the **Age of** increase of traffic, although the **Commerce** Arab merchant, as a rule, was quick enough to follow in the track of the warlike Mohammedan propaganda, sometimes indeed preceding it and appearing in the rôle both of missionary and trader. The onset of the religious wars had thrown down all the barriers which had previously encircled the lands of Western Asia like Chinese walls; the Mohammedan merchant now found in all

regions countrymen and tribal relatives who were ready to give him shelter and protection and all the assistance in their power.

Nor was the sea closed to him. Commerce on the Indian Ocean had long been in the hands of the Arabians, who penetrated as far as the Southern Chinese ports, and through their superior industry had practically ruined the once flourishing shipping trade of China. In the Eastern Mediterranean the warships of the caliph had forced back the Byzantines; in the year 826 the conquest of Crete provided Mohammedan commerce and piracy with a base that for more than a hundred years defied every attack of the Eastern Roman emperors.

The desert was as little an obstacle as the sea to the Mohammedan merchant, who was well acquainted with its dangers, and knew by what means they could be overcome. Northern Africa had scarcely been conquered before commerce with the Sudan, hitherto merely a small, unprofitable trade, began to flourish; vast caravans traversed the desert of Sahara and **Trade** brought the products of Arabian, **in the** Persian, and Egyptian industry **Desert** to the blacks, returning home with gold-dust, ostrich feathers, and negro slaves. In all regions into which the Arab merchant penetrated arose those small settlements and colonies which even to-day exist on the Eastern African coast as precursors of Arabian civilisation and Mohammedanism.

The intellectual movement that was brought about through the extension of trade, and the consequent furtherance of the unity of the empire, were of still greater importance, still more wide-reaching in their results. Already under the Omayyads this process had begun, but not until the caliphate had been removed to Irak, where there was so great an intermingling of races, did it attain to its full extent.

Even before the invasion of the Arabs the population of Irak had been a remarkable mixture. The ancient Babylonian race still formed the nucleus of the stationary inhabitants and the peasant class; in the cities there was a large amount of Greek blood, and finally Semites had immigrated in such numbers that during the period of the Sassanidæ bands of Jews had succeeded in keeping the land in a state of terror for months at a time. The long-

A MOHAMMEDAN TRADING CARAVAN AND PILGRIMAGE FROM CAIRO TO MECCA
The desert was as little an obstacle as the sea to the Mohammedan merchant, and vast caravans traversed the deserts, while the great annual pilgrimages to Mecca united devotion and trade in a most profitable manner.

continued supremacy of the Parthians and the Sassanidæ had very naturally led to an extensive immigration of Iranians, who had now—also in an ethnographic sense—become the leading race, as was abundantly proved by the close connection in which Irakans and Persians appeared in later times, especially in the various revolts and rebellions.

It has already been described how the Arabians, who had dwelt in the steppe regions since the earliest times, destroyed the Iranian power at the beginning of the Mohammedan movement, increased in numbers, and founded a new state. With the establishment of the Islamite world-empire the way was opened for an unlimited blending of races; and when Bagdad became the centre of the empire as well as of commerce there was not a race-element of the Arabian empire and its bordering lands unrepresented, no civilisation that had not exerted its influence on the medley of peoples in the world-city. Here, on a soil that had known culture

from the earliest ages, arts and sciences could not fail to flourish; and for a time Bagdad was the centre of learning of the world of its day. Scholars and poets needed but the invitation of such a sovereign as Harun to flock to his court from all quarters of the empire.

In view of the present condition of Islam and the intellectual paralysis into which its followers have fallen, it is difficult to believe that such a broad and free scientific and literary life really existed during the first period of the Abbassides. But convention had not yet imposed the practically exclusive and consequently sterilising study of the Koran on all scholars. During the age of the Abbassides the Koran had not yet become the absolute guide of life; its laws were not yet so infallible, its believers not yet so fanatically credulous as they are to-day. Without scruple the caliph and his confidants gave themselves over to the full enjoyment of wine, that was so hateful to the Prophet, scarcely even troubling to veil their scandalous conduct from the public eye. With the same freedom Harun patronised scholars and philosophers whose views would have made the hair of every orthodox Moslem stand on end. Nor could he very well have done otherwise. Irak had ever been the classic ground of sects. The caliph would have been compelled to annihilate at least two-thirds of his most intellectual subjects had he desired the orthodox belief to obtain full play. Moreover, the fact that the Abbassides had originally been adherents of the Shiite heresy, and were always suspected of a relapse, was as well known in Bagdad as elsewhere. It would not have been advisable to provoke the sectarians too much; for, as it was, they were constantly on the verge of revolt.

Only against the communists—the Zendikists—were laws enacted, and a formal court of inquisition established for the destruction of these stragglers of the old Mazdakite persuasion. Through this the caliph ensured himself the applause of the wealthy classes, who at this time, as always, were far more apprehensive of the evil effects of a raid on their purses than of any number of heretical attacks on the sacred paragraphs of the Koran.

However much economic development was impeded by the constant tumult and rebellions caused by the various sects, their existence was nevertheless of the greatest advantage to intellectual progress, owing to the large degree of tolerance which the caliph was obliged to exhibit on their account. Every new idea, however daring it might be, could hope to find approbation and adherents, not only among the well-educated higher classes of Bagdad, but even among the people and at court. Doubters and sceptics were permitted publicly to expound their views by the side of the unyielding orthodox; and the numerous Christians and Jews took an active part in the labour of civilisation—according to their own methods.

In most cases, however, the various sects and religions were nothing more than the intellectual expression of the differences of race, which indeed were the true foundation of the rapid development of Irakan civilisation. The characteristics of the different peoples who came together in Bagdad supplemented each other in a marvellous way: the sharp, somewhat matter-of-fact intellect of the Arabs became united at a most favourable moment with the unbridled creative imagination of the Iranian, and conceptions of the harmony of early Greek life, as well as of the mystic depths of Hindu thought, were awakened by the representatives of these two opposite poles of Aryan culture.

Hellenism, represented by the immortal works of its greatest age, was the basis of all scientific activity; and the writings of Aristotle, at a time when they were forgotten in Western Europe, became the oracle of the Mohammedan world. Nevertheless the products of Greek intellectual life did not achieve popularity as rapidly as one might have expected. Direct translations of Greek texts were not made until the reign of the caliph Mamun (813–833); until this time Persian translations as old as the

THE ARCHITECTURE OF THE ARABS
A beautiful Arabian fountain in Jerusalem.

THE DECORATIVE BEAUTY OF MOHAMMEDAN ART

The preference for a superfluity of detailed ornament shown in Mohammedan art, of which some fine examples are given here, is a result of Mahomet's injunction against pictures and images, which forced the artists to express themselves in decoration. The panel of tiles at the top is from a Damascus mosque. Below, in the middle, is shown an Arabian marble mosaic, while on each side is a carved arabesque from a Cairo pulpit door.

days of the Sassanidæ had been found sufficient for all purposes. Thus, in this respect, at least, the period of Harun al Rashid was not the highest point of development.

The chief branches of learning patronised by the caliph were naturally such as were especially congenial to the Arabian spirit—that is to say, those requiring intellectual penetration rather than powers of invention; for example, philology and grammar, logic and rhetoric, religious dogmatics and jurisprudence. It is scarcely necessary to mention that mathematics also were extremely popular among the Arabs. Another peculiarity of the Arabs, their delight in tribal traditions and in endless genealogies of families, required only the influence of Greek models in order to become transformed into history; knowledge of geography also developed as a result of historical investigation as well as of the great commercial activity of the period. It is characteristic that of these two branches of science the latter developed more freely and in greater tranquillity; history was never able to emancipate itself from the bonds of partiality for particular princes and sects. Chemistry was rarely pursued independently for its own sake, being looked upon for the most part as a means for the artificial production of gold; nevertheless, some of the best work of the period was done by the Arabians in this branch of natural science. Finally, medicine, furthered by the translation of Greek handbooks, attained perhaps not to a completely free development, but at least to a very advanced state of progress.

The idea that attention should not be devoted exclusively to a single branch of knowledge, but that men should endeavour to obtain a more general education **Height of Arabian Culture** through the study of several sciences, was not unknown to the Mohammedan world of the eighth and ninth centuries. Already during the reign of Mansur a school had been established in Bagdad in which the Arabian language, the art of poetry and astronomy were taught. The effort to attain distinction in science on the foundation of an all-round intellectual training was not confined to Bagdad alone. Focuses of learning arose at the courts of governors and in the prosperous commercial centres ; the activity of trade in material goods aided the exchange of intellectual products. A large number of the scholars and writers of the day were in the habit of wandering from city to city, from court to court ; the world was open to them, and they were always certain of being received everywhere with enthusiasm. Not until last century did the Western world, as a result of vastly improved methods of communication, acquire a unity analogous to that of the Arabian empire under the Abbassides ; nevertheless, the possession of a universally understood written and spoken language rendered the culture of the Abbassid state in many ways superior to that of modern Europe.

Among the arts music was zealously cultivated, although none of the great Mohammedan races have attained to more than mediocrity in a province that seems to be the peculiar property of the Western Aryans. Whatever talent existed for the plastic arts was restricted, in view of **Sculpture and Painting Forbidden** the mandate of Mahomet forbidding pictures and images, to architecture and to the various handicrafts ; and perhaps the latter were pursued only the more industriously since the way was closed to the highest endeavours of sculptor or painter. The preference for a superfluity of detailed ornament is one of the results of this command of the Prophet—an injunction that could have been uttered only by a typical representative of the matter-of-fact, logical, unimaginative Arabian race.

Literature alone was permitted to develop in complete freedom in the empire of the caliphs, and even that was unhampered only in so far as the airy creations of poetic genius could not easily be gagged and checked ; satire still continued to be one of the most dreaded weapons employed in the struggle of parties and sects. But the old unconstrained spirit of Arabian poetry had ceased to exist at the time of Harun, although during his reign verse-writing had become a mania and the poet an indispensable court functionary.

In spite of many weaknesses, the civilisation of the Mohammedans during the caliphate—at a period when Europe was first beginning to recover from the general destruction that followed the Teutonic migrations—cannot be looked upon as other than the guardian of the traditions of better days. It was due to Moslem culture alone that the progress of civilisation was not wholly interrupted at a time when the energy of the Southern European nations had slackened and the **Bagdad a Reflection of Babylon** northern barbarians awkwardly and with difficulty, although with fresh powers, were beginning to restore the institutions which they themselves had destroyed but a few years before. The prosperity of Bagdad was a fleeting but by no means unworthy reflection of those earlier days, when for centuries the only civilisation of the world was that which flourished on the banks of the Euphrates and the Tigris.

The culture of the Arabians was not without its influence on Europe ; the young nations of the Middle Ages did not remain long unacquainted with the splendour and polish of the caliph's empire. It was the conquest of the Pyrenean Peninsula that led to a close relationship between the most powerful rulers of the West, the Frankish kings, and the Abbassides. Inasmuch as the Omayyad caliphs in Spain were the rivals of the Abbassid princes in Bagdad, it was natural that the Christian states of Europe should become the allies of the latter. Embassies were exchanged as early as the time of Pepin. The negotiations of Charlemagne with Harun al Rashid made an especially deep impression on the Occidental world, although followed by no practical results.

THE PASSING OF BAGDAD
AND PERSIA IN THE LATER MIDDLE AGES

HARUN may have foreseen that the loss of Spain was a sure sign of approaching decay; and it was perhaps with a conscious intention of making the best of an unavoidable situation that shortly before his death, in 809 A.D. he resolved to divide the temporal power of the empire among his three sons, Emin, Mamun, and Kasim, placing the ecclesiastical sovereignty, however, in the hands of the eldest alone, thus to gird the whole with an indivisible spiritual bond. In accordance with this plan, Emin was promised the caliphate, together with the provinces of Irak, Southern Syria, Arabia, and Africa; Mamun, the entire east; and Kasim, Mesopotamia and Northern Syria. But almost immediately after Harun's death, at Tus during an expedition to Khorassan, his plans regarding Emin were rendered abortive, for the latter hastened back to Bagdad at the head of the army and laid claim to absolute dominion over the whole empire.

Struggle of the Brothers His brother Mamun, at first in secrecy, later openly, renounced allegiance to him, and took up a strong position in Khorassan. In truth, behind this apparently dynastic struggle were concealed the racial antipathies which sooner or later were to destroy the unity of the Mohammedan empire. Emin's vizir, who represented the power behind the throne, was a champion of the orthodox Arabian party; Mamun's vizir was a Persian, and a believer in the mystical doctrines of the Shiites.

The result of the struggle was apparent from the very beginning. As an Abbasside, Emin could look for no assistance from the Syrians; the latter indeed, revolted on their own account. Thus he found support only in the untrustworthy Irakans and in the state troops, unfortunately chiefly composed of mercenary Khorassanians and Turks, who already, by reason of their increasing consciousness of independence, were more of a danger to

him than to his enemies. Defeated by Tahir, Mamun's general, they returned to Bagdad full of resentment, and it was only by an increase in pay that they could be induced to remain faithful to the cause of Emin; but in the long run these undisciplined guards proved as little able as the cowardly Irakans to withstand the advance of the warlike inhabitants of Khorassan. After a war that lasted

Unreliability of the Mercenaries four years Emin was finally besieged in his capital and reduced to the utmost straits by Mamun's Persian generals, Tahir and Hortuma. He finally surrendered to the latter, but before he could be brought to a place of safety was attacked and killed by the command of Tahir in 813.

In the meantime Mamun had remained quietly in Merv, and even now showed no intention of marching to Bagdad, however much his presence was needed there. Indeed, the general state of confusion seemed to have increased rather than diminished on the death of Emin. The Arabian party still continued to offer a stubborn resistance to the Khorassanians, and the followers of Ali once more endeavoured to make good their claims by taking possession of Kufa and Mecca. Finally, the inhabitants of Bagdad revolted, embittered because of the losses sustained by trade owing to the absence of the court.

At length, on the advice of Fazl, Mamun made a tardy attempt to restore order through an alliance of the Abbassides with the descendants of Ali, and married his daughter to one of the latter, whom he

Revolt and Rebellion named as his successor. But their mutual hatred remained deeply rooted in both parties; the Abbassid family, greatly offended at the elevation of one of their most deadly enemies, chose another of their race to be caliph in place of Mamun. The latter finally hastened to Bagdad and experienced little difficulty in conquering the rebels, but was compelled to give up his attempt to reconcile the two families ; the green banner of the Ali family, which had already waved triumphantly at the head of his army, was once more replaced by the black flag of the Abbassides. Thus Mamun freed himself from his Persian advisers, and at the same time won back the confidence of the Irakans,

Caliph's Double-dealing only again to give free rein to his preference for the Persians. But the national differences and antagonisms had already become too acute to be smothered by any double-dealing on the part of the caliph. The inhabitants of Khorassan were loyal to Mamun so long as he remained in their midst and adhered to the principles of the Shiites ; but after his return to Bagdad they lost all interest in him. Tahir, to whom was given the control of Khorassan, his native province, succeeded without difficulty in establishing an almost independent government. During the same period an insurrection led by Babek, the sectarian, broke out in Northern Persia; it was fundamentally a reaction of the Iranians against the Arabians and the orthodox, and doubly dangerous for the reason that Babek succeeded in forming an alliance with Byzantium.

All the while that the eastern provinces were breaking away from the empire, the state of affairs in the west had gone from bad to worse. Harun al Rashid himself had been able to retain only a nominal supremacy over the northern coast of Africa, and had been powerless to prevent the governor of Tunis, Ibrahim ibn al Aglab, from becoming practically independent and establishing the hereditary monarchy of the Aglabites in 800. Even earlier, in the year 790, a dynasty of the descendants of Ali, the Edrisites, had arisen in Morocco. A revolt now followed in Egypt ; and it was with the utmost difficulty that Mamun succeeded, by

Revolts in Africa and Egypt personal interference, in temporarily restoring order. The incipient decay of the empire of the caliphs had no immediate ill effects on the diffusion of Mohammedanism, for the Aglabites conquered Sicily during the reign of Mamun, and at about the same time Crete fell into the hands of Andalusian corsairs. After the separation from the caliphate, Spain may be said to have arrived at the summit of her prosperity under the Omayyads.

The reign of Mamun was, on the whole, favourable to the development of Mohammedan civilisation. An admirer of the progressive doctrines of the Shiites, he was also interested in the serious discussion of scientific questions ; and owing to his influence a large number of Greek works were translated into Arabic. He seems especially to have valued the earlier literature of Persia.

Although Mamun was not lacking in the evil traits of character peculiar to his family, he was nevertheless beyond doubt intellectually the ablest of the Abbassides, and in religion as well as in science the champion of a movement that sought to open up the road to free development. His endeavours were frustrated, owing to the opposition of the old believers, whose views could not be brought into harmony with the Persian-Shiite conception of life, as well as to the profound antagonism that ever exists between despotism and independent investigation. From the time of Mamun the spiritual power as well as the temporal power of the caliphate steadily decreased.

Decay of the Empire After Mamun's death, in 833, Mutassim, his successor, made a despairing attempt to keep his unruly subjects in check by means of an army of mercenaries of foreign extraction, in spite of the fact that on his accession he had only with the greatest difficulty succeeded in crushing a military revolt. The number of mercenaries was gradually increased to 70,000. The caliph soon felt his position in Bagdad to be no longer secure, and removed his residence to Samarra, a few hours north of Bagdad; the foundations of the empire became weaker and weaker.

The further history of the decline of the Mohammedan empire was little more than a barren, monotonous succession of sectarian revolts, military rebellions, and ecclesiastical quarrels, interspersed with vain attempts to restore order on the part of the caliphs.

The latter became more and more the creatures of their vizirs ; province after province awakened to independent life, and one governor after another founded a new hereditary dynasty; though an occasional caliph succeeded in turning the tide of temporal and spiritual power in his own favour, winning back something that had been lost, or in temporarily checking the course of decay.

In regard to this struggle of the caliphs against fate it was significant that Mutavakkil (847-861) forsook the doctrines of the Shiites, turned from the followers of Ali, and joined forces with the orthodox party, the Sunnites, as they were then called. The Sunna, or supplement to the Koran, composed of authentic traditions, was compiled during the first half of the ninth century, and soon became the palladium of the orthodox believers ; it was entirely discredited by the Shiites, whose allegorical mystic interpretation of the sacred book was naturally not to be brought into harmony with the belief of the orthodox. In favouring the orthodox party, Mutavakkil returned to the original policy of the Abassides ; indeed, he went further, inasmuch as he revived the severe measures of Omar against the Jews and Christians. With this change of religious front was naturally combined an attempt once more to reign with the assistance of the Arabs and to dispense with the services of the mercenaries.

But the unfortunate division of the Arabian people into two parties again led to disastrous results ; the Yemenites preferred to join forces with the Persians, and the Kaisites with the Turks, rather than work together for the re-establishment of the lost influence of their race. Thus the power of the mercenaries constantly increased ; and the Turks became only the more dangerous as the empire diminished in area and in wealth.

Nevertheless, a few years of prosperity were still left to the empire. During the reign of Mutamid (870-892), whose office was in reality administered by his more capable brother Muvaffak, the caliphate

Last Years of the Empire

once more returned to power and regained several of the lost provinces. This advance in general welfare continued until the death of the caliph Muktafi, in 908, when a new period of confusion set in. Already at that time events of greater importance took place in the various independent or semi-independent provinces than in the capital of the empire. It

THE CALIPH MUTAVAKKIL
Who ruled during the last years of Bagdad, forsook the intellectual party and became orthodox, attempting to reign without the assistance of the Turks.

finally became apparent that the strength of the central government could be increased only through an alliance with, or, indeed, through subjection to, a foreign power. The desire for independence developed earliest in Persia. Gradually

The East Becomes Independent

the east became wholly independent, or, at the most, nominally recognised the spiritual supremacy of the caliph. In the year 876 affairs had already come to such a pass that the Saffaride Yakub ibn Laith made war on the caliph and advanced to within a few miles of Bagdad. The bravery, however, of the more loyal of the Samanides ensured, at least for the time being, the safety of the capital.

At the same time that the Saffarides were menacing Bagdad the whole of Egypt was in uproar. Here the governor Ahmed ibn Tulun had declared his independence ; and to all appearance it seemed that the dynasty of the Tulunides would become a permanent institution. Tulun, whom we must credit with a thorough knowledge of the political situation, took possession of Syria and the line of the Euphrates ; in fact, he even made an attempt to extend his influence over the caliph himself, in order to procure for his followers the most important positions at court, and thus indirectly to become the head of the empire. But his plans were defeated by the interference of Muvaffak. After Ahmed's death Syria was regained, and in the year 904 the Abbassides managed once more to take possession of Egypt, which they retained until the appearance of the Fatemides.

The authority of the caliph was badly shaken, even in the provinces which were situated in the immediate neighbourhood of the capital. The democratic-religious party of the Kharijites, who displayed an almost indestructible vitality, established an independent state in Northern Mesopotamia, where the Arabian element preponderated, and where the Abbassides had never been popular, with Mossul as its centre. When, in the year 894, the caliph succeeded in becoming to a certain degree master of these rebels, it was only to be confronted by a new danger : the family of the Hamdanides were given the governorship of Mesopotamia, and managed not only to secure the dignity as a hereditary right, but took possession of a portion of Northern Syria in addition. It was fortunate for the caliphs that the Hamdanides did not immediately strive for absolute independence, but sought to avoid a complete break with the central power, to which in time of necessity they were obliged to turn for assistance, inasmuch as their province was situated on the frontier, and constantly exposed to the attacks of the Byzantines. In spite of all, however, hostilities twice—in 913 and again in 935—arose between the Hamdanides and the caliphs.

Hamdanide Dynasty in Mossul

The Hamdanides arrived at their period of greatest prosperity during the second half of the tenth century, when Saif ed-Dauleh (Sword of the Empire) occupied Haleb and made war on the Byzantines, while his brother Hasan, or Nasir ed-Dauleh, resided in Mossul. Saif was an ideal Arab—or Saracen, as the Christians now began to call the Moslems—a man of great courage and munificence, possessed of considerable poetic gifts, an enthusiastic patron of the arts and sciences, but also inspired by the ardent desire for power, and capable of ruthless barbarity. The Arabians of Syria, who looked upon the Irakans and their caliph with the utmost contempt, found in him a new champion and guide. But the Hamdanides were unable permanently to maintain their precarious position between Byzantines, Irakans, and the Fatemides, who were now steadily advancing from the south.

The Fatemide conquest of Egypt, which took place during the course of the tenth century, was only a part, although perhaps the most important part, of a great religious-political sectarian movement that spread rapidly during these times of confusion, in opposition to the caliphs, who had once more joined the orthodox party. The Ismailians, a sect named after a great-grandson of Ali, were in reality nothing more than a branch of the Shiitic group, and, like the Shiites, arose among the Persian Mohammedans. The Ismailians consciously endeavoured, through the blending of Islamite, Zoroastrian, and Christian doctrines to create a new world-religion, and in a certain measure strove

A New World Religion

to revive the great work of Manes ; thus they were ensured a prominent position and countless adherents during a time when the orthodox form of Mohammed-anism seemed to have lost all its powers of obtaining new converts, as well as to have forfeited the confidence of the masses, owing to its alliance with the unpopular Abbassid caliphs. The allegorical inter-pretation of the Koran, already received with great enthusiasm by the Shiites; the promotion of mystic arts, and the assertion that the true spiritual head of the faithful dwelt concealed from the eyes of men and communicated with the people only through his messengers, led the most varied elements of the Mohammedan population to embrace new doctrines of which the political tendency was naturally directed against the Abbassides. The great danger to which the caliphate was exposed by this movement lay in the fact that owing to the wide diffusion of its doctrines the dissatisfied of all sects and parties assembled under the Ismailian banner ; nor was its propaganda confined to the Iranians alone, as was that of the true Shiites. Serious rebellions of the Ismailians occurred first in Irak and in Arabia, where the rebels were usually called Karmates, after their earliest leader. Several times the sacred cities of Arabia were in their possession ; Bahrein and Yemama were conquered, and from the last-named province emissaries were sent to Africa in order to spread the new doctrines among the Berbers. In the year 906 the Karmatic disturbances were at least temporarily quelled ; but the spark of insurrection had blown over to Africa, and, although it appeared at first to have been extinguished, it soon enkindled there the flame of destruction. In the year 900 the Aglabites had found it necessary to oppose the Ismailians by force of arms, for after many failures the sectarians had finally succeeded in gaining over enthusiastic adherents among the Berbers, led by the Karmatic emissary Abu Abdallah. Not long afterwards the rule of the Aglabites, weakened by internal dissensions, came to an end, and in the year 908 the capital, Kairuan, surrendered.

Growth of the Ismailians

Obeid Allah, a descendant of Ali, now arose as prophet or Mahdi, and was placed at the head of the newly established empire. Abu Abdallah may have hoped that the spiritual and temporal ruler

THE MOUND OF ANCIENT NINEVEH AS SEEN FROM THE MODERN CITY OF MOSSUL

appointed by him would be contented with the rôle of puppet; but in this he was disappointed. Obeid Allah seized the reins of government with powerful hand, defeated all who opposed him, and enlarged his kingdom by the conquest of Morocco. On his death, in the year 934, the new dynasty of the Fatemides was firmly established. His successor took possession of Egypt in 968, where already, in 933, the family of the Ikshidites had become almost entirely independent of the caliph. Subsequently a prince of the orthodox party, who recognised neither the Abbassides in Bagdad nor the Omayyads in Cordova, resided as spiritual head at Cairo, or Fostat. In the meanwhile new rebellions had been aroused by the Karmates in Arabia, Irak, and Syria, through which the caliphate became greatly weakened; and although the rebels were constantly defeated, they held themselves

—at least in Bahrein and Yemama—in constant readiness to take up arms again. Not one of the various provinces of the Mohammedan empire was now in the immediate possession of the caliph; the loyalty even of the portions of Irak adjacent to the capital was questionable; and the former executive and administrative powers of the supreme ruler were now in the hands of the vizirs and Turkish generals. Thus it came about that the Abbassides were finally compelled to throw themselves upon the protection of a newly-established Persian dynasty, being thereby enabled to prolong their existence, although at the cost of the remainder of their independence. This dynasty was that of the Buides, who originally came from Tabaristan, and claimed descent from the Sassanid emperors. The Buides had taken advantage of the confusion in Persia, and had occupied Farsistan,

MOSSUL, THE MOHAMMEDAN CITY, FROM NINEVEH, THE ASSYRIAN CAPITAL

During the days of Bagdad's decline the Kharijites, a democratic-puritanical sect, who had always been a menace to the caliphate, established an independent state in Mesopotamia with Mossul, where Nineveh stood, as its centre.

the centre of ancient Iran ; soon afterward, in 934, they took possession of Chusistan, thus approaching dangerously near to Bagdad. However, during the years immediately following, Bagdad was left to its own troubles ; the chief question seemed to be, whether the leaders of the mercenaries, the Hamdanides, or the

Persians Rule in Bagdad Ikshidites, should finally succeed in becoming the " protectors " of the caliph, and thereby obtain for themselves the position of supreme authority over the empire. The Buides, then under the command of Mo'izz ed-Daulat, made the most of their opportunities for conquest; for while the Ikshidites and Hamdanides were quarrelling with one another, and Bagdad was the scene of insurrections which even the Turkish guards were unable to overcome, a Buidian army advanced on the capital. The vizir of the caliph Mustakfi fled, and Mo'izz installed himself as temporal ruler at the side of the caliph, to whom only his spiritual supremacy now remained.

The most prosperous period of Buidian rule was the reign of 'Adhud ed-Daulat, who took possession of the greater part of Persia and the lands of the Hamdanides in Mesopotamia and Syria. But on his death, in 982, decay set in and was hastened by family disputes. The unfortunate custom of dividing the property of the reigning house led to constant struggles for the throne. It thus came about that Mahmud of Ghazni (998–1050) managed to rob the Buides of their possessions in Iran, that the Fatemides occupied Syria, that independent rulers arose in Northern Mesopotamia, even in the midst of Irak, and that finally Buides and Abbassides descended together to the same low estate into which the caliphate had already fallen when first assailed by Mo'izz ed-Daulat. In Bagdad the Shiitic adherents of the Buides and the Sunnitic-Turkish

Persia in the Later Middle Ages mercenaries fought with one another continually in the streets, causing the utmost confusion and tumult. Finally the Seljuks destroyed the last remains of Buidian authority, and took into their own hands the government of the empire. Here we must turn to the developments which had been taking place beyond the Tigris, since Persia was never fully assimilated by the Arab conquerors. It had been a severe blow to the Persian

people when their state, and at the same time their ancient religion, fell before the lances of the Arabians and the doctrines of a visionary Bedouin. The blow was only the more severe because entirely unexpected, inflicted by a race that had before scarcely been deemed worthy of consideration—that had even been despised because of its lack of political unity and its poverty. " We have always looked upon you as of no account," said the unlucky Yesdigerd III. to the ambassadors of Omar ; " until to-day Arabs were known in Persia only as merchants and beggars." Soon afterward these merchants and beggars were the masters of Iran ; the bulk of the Persian people were forced to accept the new religion ; and a small minority, who for many years still continued here and there to offer a desperate resistance, succeeded only in causing many regions to become almost desolate, and in still further reducing the vitality of the Iranian race. Farsistan, the ancient land of the Achæmenidæ and Sassanidæ, suffered most during the struggle ; nor did the Mohammedans succeed in establishing

Guarding the Asian Frontier their religion there. The most stubborn opposition, however, was that of the rude mountain folk who dwelt along the southern coast of the Caspian Sea in the districts known as Deilem and Tabaristan. One of the most difficult tasks of the Persians had been that of guarding the mountain passes which led into Central Asia, in order to dam back the flood of nomads that constantly threatened to inundate the plains of the south-west. The empire of the caliphs had now to take this labour upon its own shoulders ; and, in truth, the Arabian rulers were conscious of their duty from the very first. They found the frontier country of Khorassan already in a highly developed state of military organisation, and sought, by substituting military service for tribute among the dwellers of the borders, to render the frontier troops still more efficient. In addition, entire Arabian tribes were transplanted to Khorassan, where they have in part maintained themselves to the present time, free from all admixture of foreign blood. Moreover, there was always the possibility of forming new divisions of troops out of nomadic mercenaries, with the help of whom other nomadic races could be kept in check and even pursued into their desert strongholds. The military

BEDOUIN SHEPHERDS OF PALMYRA

BEDOUIN SHEIKHS OF JUDÆA

CROSSING THE ARABIAN DESERT

ARAB'S HOME ON THE CAMEL

BEDOUIN ON HIS DROMEDARY

A BEDOUIN HORSEMAN

THE DESERT RANGERS OF ARABIA

forces at the disposal of the governor of Khorassan corresponded to the area of his province, which, although it did not always remain the same, included the greater part of Eastern Iran, together with Transoxania. In no other province of the empire were so many attempts made by ambitious governors to establish an independent dynasty as in Kho-

Struggle of the Iranian Spirit rassan. It was due chiefly to the influence of the Arabian military colonies that for a long time the many movements which began here were not, as a rule, directed against the caliphate and the Arabian nation. But this influence became less and less the more the Iranian national spirit arose, and the Iranian people prospered under the beneficent effects of Arabian legislation and domestic policy. Although the Iranians were defeated in the political field, and for a long time rendered powerless as foes in arms, they nevertheless engaged in a spiritual conflict with the Mohammedan doctrines which had been forced upon them ; no longer openly, it is true, but by adjusting Islam to their own requirements they sought to transform it into a new belief, corresponding more nearly to the Persian national character. The abstinence and simplicity taught by Islam and its Prophet found no more favour among the imaginative Persians, who had long been acquainted with the philosophies of Greece and India, as well as with the lofty thoughts of Manes and Mazdak, than it had previously gained among the true Arabs, to whose semi-democratic tribal form of society and independent spirit it was little adapted. Nevertheless, we find that at a very early period the Persians were the adherents of all parties that sought to place the true descendants of the Prophet on the throne, at first as enthusiastic followers of Ali, later as the true victors in the struggle that ended in the supremacy of the Abbassides.

The Koran a Book of Mysteries At the same time, however, the religious differences became more and more apparent. While the Arabs were engaged in compiling the Sunna, the Koran itself became, in the hands of the Persian theologians, more and more a book of mysteries, of which the elucidation was possible only to especially favoured persons, and in the secret depths of which evidence was sought for the strangest of doctrines. Complete harmony between the various Iranian

sects that thus arose was naturally out of the question ; and many of them developed a remarkable power for winning converts. The Ismailians, the far-reaching effects of whose doctrines were felt even in Egypt, where a dynasty was placed on the throne through their influence, shook the caliphate at Bagdad to its very foundations, and their last branch developed into the terrible Assassins (1100-1256), whose name was derived from *hashishin*, " eater of hashish."

The rise of religious differences was followed by an increase of political disunion—not a sudden rupture, but a gradual modification of existing conditions—leading in time to a complete change of tendency. When, after the death of Harun al Rashid, Mamun dethroned his brother Emin with the help of Khorassanian and Persian generals, and after long hesitation decided to remove his residence from Merv to Bagdad, it was well known that only the presence of the caliph could preserve Khorassan to the empire, and that chiefly for this reason he had remained for so long a time on the eastern frontier. By hand-

How Khorassan Was Lost ing over the province, together with Pushang, the capital, to his most deserving general, Tahir, and by permitting the latter to establish a semi-independent dynasty, Mamun chose the best way open to him for escape from a difficult position ; the Tahirides continued to acknowledge at least the spiritual supremacy of the caliph, and for a long time prevented the rise of disloyal houses.

Division of possessions and family quarrels gradually undermined the power of the Tahirides ; finally, when Yakub ben Laith arose in Seistan, first as a robber chieftain, later as a ruler of the province, and at last as a conqueror, the descendants of Tahir were compelled to submit to their fate, and were succeeded by this upstart son of a tinman, who had raised himself to the position of an independent sovereign, founding the Saffarid dynasty in 872. The new ruler was a serious menace to the caliphate, and apparently resolved to put an end to the Abbassid government. The caliph Mutamid endeavoured in vain to avert the threatening danger. That he freely offered Yakub the governorship of Khorassan was of as little avail as was the solemn cursing of the rebels from all the pulpits of the empire, which made no impression upon them at all ; and when the army entrusted with the defence of Bagdad met with a complete defeat, it seemed that the fate of Mutamid was sealed. However, the Abbassid ruler was saved by the sudden death of Yakub in 878. Yakub's successor, Amru, acknowledged the supremacy of the caliph and led his army back into Khorassan, thereby missing an opportunity most favourable to the fortunes of his family.

In the meantime the Samanides, a new ruling house of Turkish descent, arose in Transoxania ; and it was necessary for Mutamid only to ally himself with them in order to bring about the fall of the Saffarides in Khorassan. In the year 900 Amru lost a battle and at the same time his province to the Samanide leader Ismail, who succeeded him as governor, without coming into conflict with the caliphate. On the death of Ismail, in 907, the caliph acknowledged his son Ahmed II. as legitimate successor to the governorship. Ahmed managed to drive the rest of the Saffarides out of Seistan, as well as to take possession of the lands of a dynasty of the house of Ali, which had settled down in Tabaristan.

The Buide Regents of the Caliph At about this time the already mentioned house of the Buides, or Dailemites, arose to power. Samanides and Dailemites together ruled the greater part of Persia for the space of a century, although there was obviously no lack of minor independent states in the neighbourhood. The loyalty at first shown to the caliph by the Samanides did not prevent them from making war upon him subsequently ; the Buides, however, remained faithful, and finally succeeded in insinuating themselves into the court at Bagdad as temporal regents at the side of the caliph. The fall of the house of the Samanides soon gave them control of Khorassan also.

The whole of Eastern Iran did not fall immediately into the hands of the Buides. During the days of the Samanide dynasty a small state arose at Ghazni in Afghanistan under the rule of a Turkish house which at once made preparations for enforcing its claims on the heritage of the Samanides. The warlike Sultan Mahmud, who ascended the throne at Ghazni in 998, experienced small difficulty in overthrowing the Buidian government in Khorassan and Rai, so that finally nothing remained to the Buides but Irak, Farsistan, and Kerman. Mahmud did not follow up his campaign against the west, but found it more advantageous to inaugurate a series of invasions of India, and there to extend the power of Islam at the sword's point. For this reason Mahmud of Ghazni occupies a very important position in the history of the diffusion of the Moslem faith, while his reign also marks a period of reawakening of the Iranian national spirit.

Mahmud of Ghazni in India With his accession a new phase of Persian culture began. During the reigns of the first Abbassid emperors the Mohammedan possessions in India, none of which extended very far beyond the eastern banks of the Indus, were tolerably closely united to the empire. The influence of the caliph was supreme in both Multan and Mansurah, the two chief commercial towns, while the remainder of the region belonging to the Mohammedans was governed by princes who paid tribute to the caliphate.

Even before the days of Mahmud, his father, Nasir ed-din Sabuktegin, defeated the most powerful of the Punjab princes, who at that time also occupied the Iranian passes and the valley of Kabul, descended into the valley of the Indus, and laid waste the whole region in his march. Immediately after his accession, in 998, Mahmud began to extend these conquests. His victorious campaigns extended as far east as the Jumna and southward to Somnath and Surat, and were of the utmost importance to the later history of India, inasmuch as the sultan looked upon the conversion to Islam of all subjected provinces as his chief duty.

From another point of view, Mahmud's attitude in regard to religion and politics laid the foundations for many a later historical development. His was a great and simple nature, such as is not unfrequently found among the dwellers of the steppes. Clearly he was no friend to that fantastic, mystical, allegoric faith into which the doctrines of Mahomet had been transformed by the Iranian priesthood, and he was nothing **Orthodoxy of Mahmud** less than a declared enemy to the remains of the ancient Zoroastrian religion, of which there were still many champions in his state. Mahmud showed himself throughout to be an enthusiastic adherent of the orthodox faith, a Sunnite of the purest water. Hence he was a friend of the caliphate, the spiritual supremacy of which he willingly acknowledged, without, however, feeling dependent upon it in regard to temporal affairs. He prevented the Shiites from establishing a separate Iranian Church, brought the Eastern Iranians back to the banner of orthodoxy for all time, and laid the foundations for that division of the Persian people into two religious sects which still exists to the present day. Neither the glory

A Great Patron of Literature accorded to Mahmud by the Mohammedan world for his zealous adherence to the orthodox faith, nor the celebrity of his sanguinary wars can be compared to the services which, in spite of his love of conflict and his Turkish-Sunnitic inclinations, he rendered to civilisation through his furtherance of the intellectual life of Iran. Under his protection the first fruits of Persian literature were harvested, and it was he who uttered the call that awakened the ancient Iranian epic from its slumber.

When the power of the Arabian conquerors began to fail in the East, their language, too, fell more and more into disuse ; and the speech of the subjected Persians once more made its appearance, and even won friends at the courts of governors and princes. The more the East developed in independence, the prouder the folk of Iran became of their ancient celebrity, the louder and freer resounded the Aryan tongue. Inasmuch as the rulers began to seek for popular support, and to adapt themselves to the peculiarities of the Iranian people,they soon became aware of the magnificent store of legend which had been faithfully transmitted from father to son by the simple dwellers of the mountains and steppes.

But although the poets of Iran now undertook with reawakened powers the renovation of their ancient but shapeless literature, they were compelled to admit that the school of the Arabians had not been without value to them, that the union of harmony and force which caused

Poetry of Iran Revived their work to be celebrated throughout the Eastern world resulted from the combination of Iranian imagination with Arabian clearness and insight. Mahmud of Ghazni, however, who had taken possession of the lands of his predecessors by force of arms, also inherited from them a desire to foster and protect the germs of native literature ; he rewarded the poets with a generous hand, and invited the best authors and scholars

of the country to his court. No sovereign has ever surpassed or even equalled him as a patron of literature. The number of poets by whom he was surrounded at Ghazni did not fall short of 400 ; and inasmuch as Mahmud selected one from their midst to be laureate, appointing him judge of the poems submitted in competitions for prizes, he succeeded in creating a centre of artistic life.

Many great works were produced at the court of Mahmud ; but the greatest of all was certainly the reconstruction of the ancient Iranian hero epics. The Saffarides and Samanides had already laid the foundations for such a work; and by means of large rewards, as well as by dint of his own unsparing effort, Mahmud was able to add largely to the store already in existence.

Finally the thought occurred to Mahmud that it would be well to collect all the fragments of epics, the myths, and semi-historical traditions, and recast them into one huge work. The language chosen was necessarily the Persian, which had already supplanted Arabic even in the law-courts and government offices. None of the

Persian National Epic numerous attempts made at first were satisfactory to the sultan ; finally, good fortune led him to an author under whose hand the fragmentary raw material developed into an imperishable memorial of the ancient heroic spirit of Iran. This was Abul Kasim Mansur, generally known as Firdusi.

Firdusi was the first as well as the most brilliant representative of the reawakened Iranian spirit ; he was acquainted with the Arabian language no less thoroughly than with the Persian, and since his earliest youth had been an enthusiastic admirer of the heroic age of Iran and its traditions. After twelve years' labour Firdusi completed the " Shahnameh," the Book of Kings, in the seventy-first year of his life, 1011.

In Firdusi's works the spirit of the Iranian people, which had vanished at Cadesia, once more arose ; an intellectual unity of race was again created, and therewith, as it appears, the way was prepared for political unity also. But when Mahmud died, in 1030, the prosperity of his dynasty abruptly ended. The first blow that fate directed against the throne of the Ghaznavides, as the dynasty is entitled, caused the entire Iranian division of the Mohammedan empire to crumble into dust.

WESTERN ASIA UNDER THE SELJUKS
THE EMPIRE OF THE NOMAD TURKS

FOR many years fresh swarms of Turks had been following their countrymen into Persia from the plateaus of Tartary and Turkestan; and soon it was no longer as bands of mercenaries or slaves that they crossed the borders of Khorassan, for entire tribes now joined in the movement, pushed forward by the masses in their rear, ready at a moment's notice to fight for new pasturages, either as the allies of princes or as independent units. With the greatest difficulty the powerful hand of Mahmud had temporarily succeeded in damming back the stream of immigration; but now that Persia was given over to the quarrels of his feeble successors, the flood burst through the barriers that had been erected by the labour of centuries, and the first great wave of Turks burst upon the plains of Iran. Transoxania, a land cultivated and civilised by the Iranian race after years of increasing effort, had long **The Turks' Attack on Iran** been the defensive wall of Khorassan; and as late as the period of the Abbassides its farmers and town-dwellers were still able to keep the Turks in check. But on the decay of the Samanide dynasty troops of nomads from Eastern Turkestan not only found a foothold in Transoxania, but practically completed its conquest; Ilek Khan of Kashgar occupied Bokhara, the capital, while Mahmud was engaged on his Indian campaigns, and a short time later several minor Turkish states arose in the neighbourhood.

Soon afterwards the Turkish tribes dwelling to the north on the steppes surrounding the Aral Sea were set in motion. A chieftain, called Seljuk, led his clan towards the region of Bokhara, at the very time when the last of the Samanides were looking about for friends to assist them against the advancing Ilek Khan. As an ally of the Samanides, Seljuk regained a district in Bokhara, and strengthened his forces by the incorporation of other Turkish tribes.

Under the successors of Seljuk the power and number of the Turkish tribes constantly increased; the Seljuks themselves, however, hard pressed by their countrymen in Bokhara and Khiva, advanced toward the pastures of Khorassan. On the death of Mahmud the vanguard of the nomads appeared at Merv, and from this city as a centre **Rise of the Seljuks** began their conquest of the Persian frontier province. In 1030 the eldest son of Mahmud blinded and imprisoned his brother Mohammed, who had succeeded to the throne; he then marched against the Seljuks, who were already engaged in laying siege to Merv. None of his undertakings, however, were successful; and when he finally set out, in 1039, on an expedition to recapture Merv, which had fallen in the meanwhile, he met with a terrible defeat. During the retreat his troops mutinied and restored the throne to the blind Mohammed. It was fortunate for the Ghaznavides, whose power was now completely broken, that the Seljuks did not take immediate advantage of their position in Khorassan, through which the way to the east as well as to the west had been opened up to them, but, instead of invading Eastern Iran and India, turned toward the west. The dynasty, however, ceased to be an effective force, and even its Indian dominions were shortly afterwards wrested from it by the house of Ghori. After the downfall of the Ghaznavides and the conquest of Khorassan, Toghril-Beg (1037-1063) and Jaghri-Beg, who died in 1060, two brothers who ruled the Seljuks during **The Turks Attack the Caliphate** the days of Mahmud, turned their attention to the empire of the caliphs, which, in spite of the protection of the Buides, had sunk once more into the depths of decay. First, however, the brothers protected their rear by overthrowing the Khivan princes. The Turkish troops for the time being spared Southern Iran and marched into North-western Persia, from there setting out on campaigns of devastation against the Christian Armenians and Iberians. The Byzantines came to the assistance of their allies, but were defeated by Toghril-Beg ; and the entire Mohammedan world rejoiced at the spectacle of a Roman emperor once more being compelled to pay tribute to a champion of Islam.

Rome Pays Tribute to Islam It was, however, with great anxiety that the quarrelling sects and parties in Bagdad beheld the rise of Seljuk influence ; nor did the leaders of the nomads hesitate to make the most of their exceptionally favourable position.

After the death of the caliph Kadir, in 1031, the government fell into the hands of his son Kaim, a man of feeble character, who was unable to restore order even in the capital of the empire. At his side the Buidan sultan Jelal ed-Daulet Abu Tahir, one of whose relatives had taken possession of the Buidan provinces in Persia, led an existence scarcely less miserable than his own. In the streets of Bagdad the Sunnitic Turkish mercenaries of the caliph brawled unpunished with the Shiitic Dailemites, the bodyguard of the Buides, once, indeed, driving Jelal himself out of the city. There was comparative quiet for a few years after the death of Jelal, in 1043 ; but it was not long before fresh struggles arose between Sunnites and Shiites. The caliph and his Buidan sultan were mere puppets in the hands of their viziers ; the unhappy ruler of the faithful was not secure from attack even in his own palace.

It is scarcely surprising that in these circumstances the caliph should have looked to the Seljuk chieftains for aid ; indeed, the orthodox caliphs had always been certain of greater loyalty from the Sunnitic Turks than from the heretical Buides. Thus, in 1055, Toghril-Beg, who went on a pilgrimage to Mecca, succeeded in occupying Bagdad almost without resistance as well as in taking prisoner the Buidan sultan Malik Rahim. It is true that on the Seljuks being called back to Persia in order to put down rebellions the Buidan vizir recaptured the city, replaced the Abbassid caliph by the contemporary Fatemid governor of Egypt, and compelled Kaim to fly for his life ; but on the return of Toghril, in 1059, all opposition came to an end. From the reinstalled Abbassid caliph, Toghril

The Turks Rule in Bagdad

received the title " King of the East and West," as well as the hand of the princess Zaidah Khatun, daughter of Kaim ; but he died soon after.

Thus the caliphate was once more restored to artificial life ; but dominion had passed to the Turks, now at one stroke under a ruler of their own race. The Persians, who had seemed to be in the act of attaining to supremacy in the Mohammedan world, and of whom the Buides may be looked upon as the pioneers, suddenly found themselves once more cast down from high estate, overpowered in their own country by the nomads of the steppes.

At first the influence of the Seljuks, who had once more taken the caliph under their protection, was followed by the best results for the conquered territories, especially for the city of Bagdad. Order—at least, as understood by the Turks—so long desired in vain, was soon restored to all the useful and active provinces of the empire. Arts and manufactures, freed from the oppressive burden of insecurity, arose once more in the towns ;

Turks Encourage Culture the caravans of merchants again made their way along the public roads, and the agriculturist returned to his neglected fields. In the streets of the capital the brawls of Sunnites and Shiites ceased ; and after the expulsion of the Buides the scuffles of Turkish soldiers and Dailemites came to an end. Both literature and science flourished during the rule of the Seljuks, who espoused the cause of intellectual pursuits with an enthusiasm scarcely conceivable in the chieftains of a semi-civilised nomad folk. Whatever they may have lacked in culture was replaced by a generosity and nobility of character that, in spite of all original barbarity, caused them to stand on very much the same plane as the Arabs of the deserts and steppes. The period of the Seljuk dynasty was indeed to a certain degree a reflection of that earlier century during which the Arabs first became diffused over the lands of Western Asia.

Toghril's successor as " King of the East and West " was his nephew Alp-Arslan, who reigned from 1063 to 1072, under whose government the Seljuks attained to the zenith of their power. He captured Haleb and all Syria and Palestine from the Fatemides, and was successful in a war with the Byzantines, who, after having already lost Syria and their African provinces to the Moslems, now beheld Asia Minor, their last Asiatic dependency, gradually receding from their grasp. The emperor Romanus IV. Diogenes vainly endeavoured to retrieve his fallen fortunes by advancing into Syria in 1068; in 1071 he invaded Armenia in order to support the princes there subject to his empire, but met with a crushing defeat and was taken prisoner. Henceforth the Byzantine lands were no longer disturbed by mere incursions of robbers; entire tribes of the Seljuks now penetrated into the interior of Asia Minor, and settled down on the steppes of Iconium. It was in vain that the Eastern Roman Empire made one despairing attempt after another to dislodge the intruders.

Hitherto, despite the spread of Islam, Asia Minor had remained an integral portion of the Byzantine empire. The passes of the Taurus proved a secure line of defence, and though the Arabs occasionally forced a passage, permanent conquest had been impossible. When **Byzantine Aggression in Syria** the power of the caliphate began to weaken, it was Byzantium that took the offensive, recovered territories beyond the Taurus, and advanced even to Tyre and Damascus. The caliphs and their Buidan protectors and masters were able to offer but small opposition to the Byzantines in Syria and Asia Minor after the decay of the powerful Hamdanide dynasty.

In Asia Minor the population increased and civilisation flourished. Although the ancient splendour of the Greek cities of the coasts had vanished, the interior of the country became more and more homogeneously organised and settled, and the unity of government was rendered more secure. The careful attention paid to the garrisoning of strong positions, as well as the endeavour of the wealthy families of the towns to invest their riches in extensive estates, led to the creation of a feudalised system of landed property, with its unfailing evil consequences.

The feudal nobility became a danger to the state, while the native-born peasant population sank to the position of serfs; the inhabitants who had been killed or led away captive by the Moslems were replaced by slaves, who, when fortune once more favoured the arms of the Byzantines, were obtained in especially large numbers from Mohammedan Syria and Mesopotamia.

In spite of the attempts to suppress them made by various emperors — but without support from the Church, which looked for a share in the spoils, and from officials whose interests ran counter to those of the feudatories—the power of the **Decay of Byzantine Empire** nobility steadily increased; and when the Seljuks finally took possession of the steppe districts of Central Asia Minor the destruction of the already undermined Byzantine empire followed with surprising rapidity.

It is a fact of great historical significance that the Seljuk invaders did not attack the passes of the Taurus, but marched through Armenia, and that as a result of these incursions not only Christian Armenia but even portions of Iberia were laid waste. Both provinces had been, if not entirely trustworthy, at least indispensable supports of the Byzantine frontier, and at the same time favourite recruiting grounds for the imperial armies. In spite of their fallen fortunes and apparent loss of warlike virtues, the Armenians still maintained their reputation for courage and strength no less than their faithful adherence to the Christian religion. But neither in Armenia nor in Georgia was there any sign of political unity; at the end of the tenth century as many as nine different dynasties were reigning in Armenia, while Georgia was divided into five more or less independent minor states.

Thus the Seljuks succeeded in entering Asia Minor at the Armenian boundary, while the bulwarks of the empire still remained intact in the south; nevertheless the defences of the southern frontier were in a constant state of siege, and had long been in grave danger. The Armenians emigrated from their desolated homes and concentrated in Cilicia, where they energetically set about defending the land **Seljuks and Saracens in Armenia** from the attacks of Seljuks and Saracens. However, on discovering that they were cut off from all assistance from the Byzantines they dissolved even their nominal connection with the Eastern Roman Empire, and established the kingdom of Lesser Armenia, of which the first ruler was Rhupen, or Reuben, who ascended the throne in 1080. With the accession of this king the last remnant of the old line of defence to the east of Cilicia was lost to the Byzantines, despite the fact that Antioch managed to hold out for a few years longer.

The establishment of an organised government in Asia Minor by the Seljuks **Great Days of the Seljuks** did not take place during the lifetime of Alp-Arslan, who met his death in 1072, stabbed to the heart by a revolutionist whom he had condemned to death. His son Melekshah assumed the role of protector of the caliph Kaim as well as of Muktadi, who succeeded the latter in 1075; and he became, in fact, the ruler of all the Seljuk dominion. Melekshah equalled his father in ability, and succeeded not only in restoring order, but also in furthering the material prosperity of his extensive dominions. Above all, he put an end to the system of local customs, duties, and tolls, the curse of minor states, which had developed to an alarming extent during the times of the Buides. The flourishing financial condition of his sultanate rendered it possible for him to be a patron of science and art ; poets and scholars once more enjoyed a golden age.

Nevertheless, signs of decay began to appear. Melekshah decided no longer personally to command his troops in Asia Minor, or to employ the main army of the empire in the war of conquest, but entrusted the task to his cousin Suleiman, granting him permission to establish a semi-independent kingdom in the steppe lands of the peninsula. Thus the new Seljuk kingdom of Rum, or Iconium, that arose in the years following 1073 under Suleiman cannot be looked upon as an integral part of the Seljuk-Abbassid empire. In like manner, without troubling himself very much as to the wishes of the sultan, another Seljuk leader, Ansiz, took possession of Palestine, and pursued the retreating army of the Fatemides as far as Egypt in 1077. Not until Ansiz found himself in difficulties, and called upon Melekshah for assistance, did the sultan succeed in removing this all too independent general, by sending out his brother Tutush, who brought Syria and Palestine under the immediate control of the Seljuk government.

The kingdom of Suleiman in Asia Minor was soon firmly established, chiefly **Division of the Land** through the abolition of the ownership of large estates and the division of the land among the people — after the old custom of Islamite conquerors—a large, prosperous, and consequently loyal, peasant class being thereby created, while the Seljuks themselves continued their old nomadic methods of life.

THE BEILAN PASS IN THE TAURUS : A DEFENCE AGAINST THE ADVANCE OF ISLAM

THE TAURUS MOUNTAINS: A BYZANTINE BARRIER TO ISLAM

The Taurus Mountains were a secure line of defence to the Asia Minor portion of the Byzantine empire against the Arabs, who, though they occasionally forced a passage, found permanent conquest impossible.

But, however willing the peasants may have been to enjoy the advantages of the new régime, and notwithstanding that here and there the cultivation of the soil was pursued with great profit, none the less the presence of the Seljuks in the interior of the **A Victory of Nomadism** peninsula betokened only a new step toward the desolation of Western Asia, a fresh victory of nomadism over agriculture, of the steppe over the ploughed field. The more violent the efforts made by the Byzantines, and soon afterwards by their allies, the Crusaders, to regain possession of the lost territory, and the more wildly war raged in its fury over the elevated plains of Asia Minor, the more rapidly did the stationary population diminish, the sooner were fertile districts abandoned and transformed into the steppe pastures from which they had once been reclaimed with a vast expenditure of labour, and the more free were the nomads and their herds to expand over the desolated fields. Thus the Seljuks may be looked upon as having prepared the way for the work of devastation finally completed by the Ottomans and Mongols.

The remarkable freedom granted by Melekshah to his vassals in the west was of itself a sufficient proof that the centre of the Seljuk empire lay at that time in the east. In fact, the sultan was anxious to secure as well as to widen his eastern provinces, which after the subjection of the prince of Kashgar extended as far as the Chinese frontier. But the unity of the empire was not long preserved even in Iran. Immediately after the death of Melekshah, 1092, a violent struggle for the succession broke out, which dragged along for years, and paved the way for the final dissolution of Seljuk power. Not until the year 1104 was peace restored for a short time under the victorious pretender Mohammed. But again and again, just as in former days under the early Abbassides, attacks were made upon the reigning sultan in Bagdad from Khorassan, where the Seljuks were most firmly established and could levy efficient troops of auxiliaries among the warlike native population.

During the first decades of the twelfth century one insurrection followed another, **An Arab Revival** in which Dubais, the feudal lord of Hillah in Irak, especially distinguished himself as an implacable enemy of the reigning Seljuk sultan Mahmud (1118–1132). In Dubais the powers of resistance of the Irakan Arabs once more awoke to life; and he might, indeed, have succeeded in restoring the supremacy of his race had he formed an alliance with Mustarshid, the caliph of the time, who was likewise endeavouring to free himself from the burdensome rule of the Turks. Unfortunately, however, these champions of the Arabian race hated each other bitterly in true Bedouin fashion. But from this time forth the decline of Seljuk power was continuous. A transformation was taking place in Syrian affairs : the Europeans had not only once more seized upon Palestine, but had founded a number of feudal states which were not to be overcome and finally annihilated by the champions of Islam until many a desperate battle had been fought. In this war, however, it was neither the Bagdad caliphs nor the Seljuk sultans that represented Islam; the contest was entered and the prize borne away by other Powers. Irak and Persia were torn asunder by the struggles for succession among the Seljuk princes, and consequently Egypt was given an opportunity for assuming the leadership of the Mohammedan world in its wars against the Crusaders, when the powers of the Syrians failed. A fundamental change thus took place in the conditions of the western part of the Mohammedan empire ; and this necessitates a backward look over the affairs of Syria.

Decline of Seljuk Power

When, during the days of the early caliphs, the Arabs of Syria had raised the Omayyads to power the native Syrians were not concerned in the struggle, since most of them were only gradually converted to Islam, while many held fast to the Christian faith with the greatest pertinacity. The caliphs, as a rule, did not care to convert the highly taxed Christians into free Islamites, for the sake of their own incomes ; moreover, conversion to Islam was attended by greater difficulties in Syria than in any other province, owing to the trade with the West, which had never been entirely suppressed, and to the constant pilgrimages of Christians to Jerusalem. With the accession of the Abbassid caliphs, the political significance of Syria still continued to diminish, inasmuch as the discordant elements of the population showed no signs of developing the idea of political unity. The heterogeneous character of the geographical formation of the country has at all times prevented it from forming a really homogeneous state.

Syria's Importance Diminishes

Thus so early as the ninth century the southern portion of Syria had become involved in the various Egyptian struggles. The rebellious governor Ahmed Ibn Tulun advanced as far as the Mesopotamian frontier ; under the leadership of his son, Egyptian armies penetrated beyond the Euphrates. Then the Abbassides recovered their supremacy in Egypt, and by consequence in Syria; and then once more the decline of the caliphate awakened a desire for independence on the part of the Egyptian governors, as a result of which Syria also suffered. Mohammed of Ferghana founded the dynasty of the Ikshidites, seized Southern Syria, and finally, in the year 940, compelled the caliph to recognise his right to the newly conquered territory, while the northern part of the land, as has already been mentioned, after many vicissitudes fell for the greater part into the hands of the Hamdanides, the dynasty whose possessions lay chiefly in Northern Mesopotamia. However, this courageous race was unable permanently to withstand the constant attacks of Ikshidites, Byzantines, and Buides. When the struggle between the Ikshidites and Fatemides broke out for the possession of Egypt, the Hamdanides allied themselves with the former ; but of this the only result was, that after the triumph of the Fatemides the Hamdanides found in their victors a still more hostile frontier neighbour.

Syria Suffers with Egypt

The ultra-Shiitic movement in Iran, and its branches—Karmates on the one side and Fatemides on the other—have already been described. Their tendency was naturally in opposition to the caliphate and its allies ; and after the Fatemides had struck firm root in Egypt as a political power, they remained in close union with the Shiites of the east who belonged to the Ismailian sect. The Karmates, who owed their development to the same sources, and who succeeded in taking possession of the greater part of the Arabian peninsula, did not show the slightest inclination to humble themselves before the Fatemides ; on the contrary, they disputed with the latter their supremacy in Syria. The Fatemides, however, succeeded later in organising the Persian Ismailians as well as in setting the dreaded sect of the Assassins as outposts of the Fatemid-Ismailian

THE VALLEY OF THE JORDAN FROM THE MOUNTAINS OF JERICHO

A SCENE IN MOUNT LEBANON

THE DEAD SEA FROM ENGEDI

ISOLATED VILLAGES AMONG THE FASTNESSES OF THE LEBANON MOUNTAINS

THE HETEROGENEOUS CHARACTER OF SYRIA'S GEOGRAPHY

movement in the rear of their opponents. From the year 974 onward the struggle for Syria continued; in addition to the Karmates, the Fatemides were opposed by the Byzantines, and by a Turkish general who endeavoured to found an independent state in the north. The Hamdanides also took up arms in the defence of the remainder of their possessions. The Fatemides nevertheless maintained their position in Syria, except in the extreme north. Although during the reign of the Fatemid caliph Hakim (996-1021) in Egypt there was no lack of isolated rebellions of governors, the dominion of his house over Syria remained unshaken, and his realm even included Haleb, owing to the voluntary submission of the Hamdanides. Hakim's successor, Mustanzir, tried to drive out his Abbassid colleagues; but he succeeded only in drawing on himself wars and insurrections. Syria and Palestine fell bit by bit into the hands of the Seljuks. Acre alone held out. After its governor, Bedr, had betaken himself to Egypt and had restored order with the help of his troops on the call of the caliph, the Fatemides succeeded in recapturing Palestine from the Seljuks, although the latter had already ventured on one campaign into Egypt.

Syria Fails to the Seljuks

This, then, was the condition of affairs when the first Crusade was preached in Europe, at the end of the eleventh century: Jerusalem was no longer in the possession of the Seljuks, whose unfriendly treatment of the Christian pilgrims, although not the direct cause, had nevertheless furnished a pretext for an expedition of vengeance on the part of the European nations. The defence of the Holy Land fell to the Egyptians, while the Seljuks at Damascus and Bagdad remained inactive, and beheld the developing drama with undisguised satisfaction. It was not the orthodox caliph of the Mohammedan world, but his Shiite rival, who led forth his troops against the Christian armies. The true ruler in Cairo at the time when the army of the Crusaders was marching through Asia Minor against Syria was not the Fatemide, but his vizir Alafdhal, the son of Bedr. The Seljuks of Asia Minor were the first to withstand the attack of the mail-clad Europeans, and paid for their resistance

Crusaders' First Attacks

with a severe defeat, from which, however, they soon recovered, for the Christian forces immediately continued their march. The ruler of Lesser Armenia stood on very good terms with his Western co-religionists; and the Christians were also able to count upon the sympathy of the much-contested Northern Syrian boundary provinces, which had been torn from the Byzantines a few decades before, and contained a large Christian population.

Thus the principality of Edessa arose in the region of the old Roman military frontier; and on the coast Antioch, followed by Tripolis, also became the centres of small Christian kingdoms. All these were possessions of Seljuks which now fell into the hands of the Christians. But the unsettled state of political affairs in the Mohammedan empire prevented the rulers at Bagdad from coming to the rescue of the semi-independent governors in the north-west of Syria, especially after the main body of the Christians had advanced into Palestine proper, the possession of the hated Fatemides. The negotiations between the Christians and the latter were without result. While the Egyptian vizir Alafdhal was still engaged in fitting out his army, the Europeans besieged and stormed Jerusalem, at that time the chief stronghold of Palestine. Almost all the Mohammedan and Jewish inhabitants were massacred by the victors, and the city opened its gates to a new population of native Christians. When Alafdhal's army finally advanced, it received an annihilating defeat in August, 1099. The Christian kingdom of Jerusalem now arose amid the ruins of the Fatemid power in Palestine.

Christian Conquest of Jerusalem

It has already been mentioned that the Fatemides possessed a terrible weapon in their struggle against the caliphate and the nations of Christendom in the Ismailian sect of Assassins—a weapon, however, soon lost to the Egyptian rulers. We have related how the Ismailians developed out of a mixture of Mohammedanism and various other beliefs, of which perhaps the most important were the communistic doctrines of the Mazdakites; and how from the Ismailians grew the Karmates, and finally the caliphate of the Fatemides. The doctrines of the Ismailians themselves were gradually transformed into an esoteric system of belief, which, in the hands of the most intellectual of its adherents, approached pure nihilism—the conception that all things are indifferent, and hence all actions are permissible—while the bulk of the believers lived in a state of mystic respect for their still more mystic superiors and leaders. An academy in which the Ismailian doctrines were taught was founded in Cairo, and thence emissaries were sent forth into the lands of the Abassides in order to prepare the way for the supremacy of the Fatemides over the entire Mohammedan world. At the same time the Ismailians of Persia looked to Egypt for their political and religious salvation.

was to be its basis and security. The first lurking-place chosen by Hassan was the mountainous region south-west of the Caspian Sea, of which the inhabitants had been looked upon by orthodox Mohammedans, even as late as the Abbassid period, as incarnations of **Origin** heathen obduracy, and where **of the** the mountain fastnesses and **Assassins** castles had for centuries been the homes of the most desperate revolutionists. In the year 1090 the powerful fortress of Alamut, in the district Rudbar, north-west of Kaswin, fell through treachery into the hands of Hassan and his followers. With this began the political activities of the sect, who were in the

THE SYRIAN CITY OF ACRE, FAMOUS IN THE CRUSADES AND ONCE A CHRISTIAN KINGDOM
Acre, one of the most important cities of Syria, has always been a prey of war. It was stormed by the Saracens and Crusaders at least five times; became, in the twelfth century, a Christian state, and, in the sixteenth, fell to the Turks.

Thus it came to pass that an ambitious sectarian, Hassan-i Sabbah—born at Rai, in Northern Persia—after a vain attempt to acquire influence at the court of Melekshah in Bagdad, betook himself to the palace of the Fatemid ruler in Egypt, and there formed the plan of establishing **Planning** an Ismailian rule of terror in the **a Rule** East, quite in accordance with **of Terror** the unscrupulousness of his party. The power of the movement was not to be derived from extensive possessions of territory or great armies, but from the unconditional devotion and fanatical contempt of death of its adherents, who had at their disposal several impregnable fortresses as places of refuge; not open war, but assassination

habit of working themselves up into a high pitch of bloodthirsty excitement by taking hashish and other narcotics, and hence became known as Hashishins, or, in the tongue of the Crusaders, Assassins.

Two years later, the first victim of importance, Nizam el Mulk, the vizir of the first Seljuk sultan, and a friend and companion of Hassan's youth, fell under the dagger-thrusts of the Assassins. He was the first of a long series of unfortunates who paid with their lives for the attempt to suppress the sect. The blind submission of the sectarians to their superiors was almost incredible. The fact that mothers were overcome by despair because their sons returned from successful forays without having lost their lives, thus failing to die for their faith, and that Assassin sentinels cast themselves down from high towers and cliffs at a signal from their commander merely in order to prove their absolute obedience abundantly explains why the Powers of Western Asia and Egypt trembled before the daggers of the fanatics, and negotiated with the chief of the sect as with the sovereign of a mighty empire. After the capture of the fortress of Alamut, Hassan-i Sabbah remained within its walls for the rest of his days ; indeed, it is said that he left his room only twice. As the "Old Man of the Mountain," he lived in mysterious retirement, directing the activities of his adherents and extending his power, ever faithful to the traditions of the Ismailians. About the year 1100 the Assassins succeeded in capturing several additional strongholds in Iran. At the same time as the Crusaders, their first emissaries arrived in Palestine, and, favoured by the Seljuk prince Ridhouan, established themselves in the mountains of Syria. Although on the death of Ridhouan they were exposed to frightful persecutions, they were no longer to be driven away. Their daggers were kept actively employed and brought terror to their opponents.

Old Man of the Mountain

The death of Hassan, in August, 1124, did not hinder the expansion of the Assassins, for Kia Buzurg-umid, his successor, proceeded with his work with equal craft and energy. Banias, in Syria, was captured in 1128, and twelve years later Maziat, which from this time forth became the centre of Assassin power in the west. The sectarians had then long been free from the influence of the Fatemides ; and not only the Abbassid caliphs, Mustarshid and Rashid, but also one of the Fatemid rulers fell under their daggers. The practices of the sect made a profound impression on the Christians of the Holy Land. The Europeans in general did not look upon them as unconditional enemies ; it seems indubitable that the Order of Knights Templars was not closed to the influence of the Assassins, and, in fact, that many of its characteristics were adopted in imitation of the secret Mohammedan association. Thus, curiously enough, the attacks of the Assassins became involved in a strange manner in the desperate struggle fought for the possession of the Holy Land between the Crusaders and the rulers of Egypt.

Power of the Assassins

The Seljuks took a relatively small part in the struggle between the West and the East at the time of the Crusades. At the most, only a few frontier princes interfered in the affairs of Palestine, and were hostile to the small Christian states which had been established in Northern Syria. Not until the year 1111, when disturbances arose in Bagdad itself, did the sultan Mohammed deem it necessary to despatch an army to Syria. In 1113 Baldwin I., king of Jerusalem, was defeated at Tiberias. But shortly afterward the leader of the Seljuk army was murdered by the Assassins ; the result was a long series of quarrels between the Seljuk governors and princes, which effectively hindered all further action. Not until Zenki was appointed Atabeg of Syria and Mesopotamia in 1127, and was entrusted with the leadership in the war against the Christians, did fortune again follow the Seljuk banners, although Zenki had to contend not only with the Christians but with other Seljuk rulers. Until the day of his death, in 1146, he was the most formidable of all the enemies of the Crusaders. His son Nur-ed-din continued the war, and in 1153 took possession of Damascus, which Zenki had vainly endeavoured to capture from Anaz, a member of his own race. The successes of Zenki and his son aroused the entire Mohammedan world to a high pitch of enthusiasm, which was of great significance to the continuation of the struggle, and, as a result, even the most unfavourably disposed of the princes were compelled to support Nur-ed-din with both money and troops. Nevertheless, Nur-ed-din did not arrive at the height of his power until he succeeded through a lucky chance in destroying the Fatemid supremacy in Egypt, and was thus enabled to add the rich valley of the Nile to his possessions. At that time two vizirs were quarrelling in Cairo over the position of adviser to the weak caliph Aladhid. One of them, Shawer, fled to Nur-ed-din, and by making many promises contrived that an army should be placed at his disposal under the capable Seljuk general Shirku. But since after attaining his object he did not keep his promises, and called upon the king of Jerusalem to assist him against Shirku, he became involved in a war with Nur-ed-din, which, after many vicissitudes, finally ended in his being driven away ; with the consent of Nur-ed-din Shirku was installed

Successes Against the Crusaders

MEETING BETWEEN SALADIN, THE CHAMPION OF ISLAM, AND RICHARD CŒUR DE LION
Saladin, or Salah ed-din, who combined in himself all the good qualities of the Turkish character, was firmly resolved to put an end to Western rule in the East. He captured Jerusalem and won a series of other brilliant victories over the Crusaders.

in Shawer's place, and after his death, in 1168, his nephew, Salah ed-din Yusuf, or Saladin, became vizir of the Fatemid caliphate.

The Seljuk Saladin (1137–1193) soon made himself supreme over all Egypt, although he permitted the Fatemid caliph to occupy the throne until 1171, probably because the existence of this lay figure guaranteed him greater independence so far as Nur-ed-din was concerned. All the good qualities of the Turkish character, bravery, generosity and decision, were united with a highly-developed mind in Saladin, who felt that he had been chosen by fate to be the champion of Islam against Christendom. Nur-ed-din soon perceived that he would find in him no pliant implement for the furtherance of his own plans, and was already engaged in making preparations for war against his insubordinate vassal when his sudden death turned the danger from Saladin, and, in fact, enabled him to wrest the Syrian provinces of this truly great ruler

from his feeble successors. Disputes between Salih, the son of Nur-ed-din, and his cousin Saif ed-din of Mossul, as well as the quarrels of various court officials who laid claim to the vizirate, or, more correctly, the governance of the young Salih, caused Saladin to advance into Syria and occupy Damascus. After a long struggle with Salih, who had allied himself with Saif ed-din and various Christian princes, not despising even the help of the Assassins, Saladin succeeded in taking possession of his dominions as far east as Haleb, and in the year 1176 assumed the dignity of Sultan. After the death of Salih, in 1183, Saladin captured Haleb, and extended his empire as far as Mesopotamia and the Lesser Armenian frontier.

Thus a tremendous power encompassing the Christian possessions in Palestine was now united in the hands of a man who had firmly resolved to put an end to the rule of the Occidental nations in the East. The fate of the kingdom of

Jerusalem was soon settled. In 1187 the Christian army was defeated by Saladin at Hittin, not far from Tiberias. The king himself was made captive. A few months later all Palestine, including Jerusalem, was in the possession of the sultan; only a few Syrian coast towns still held out, together with Tripolis **Palestine** and Antioch. The arrival of new **Lost to** crusading armies, commanded **the West** by Philip the Fair and Richard Cœur de Lion, resulted in the recapture of Acre in 1191, in spite of most desperate resistance on the part of Saladin; however, he was at least able to hold Jerusalem. Shortly before his death Saladin, in 1192, concluded a treaty according to which the Christians were permitted to occupy the coast of Tyre as far as Jaffa, and some strips of territory in the interior; but he maintained possession of the interior of Palestine together with Jerusalem.

However brilliant the victories won by Saladin over the Christians, and notwithstanding the inclination of Western historians to judge him in the light of these deeds alone, the fact remains that these wars comprised but a part, and, so far as the history of Western Asia is concerned, perhaps not even the chief part, of his activities. The Christian kingdoms in Palestine were and remained an artificial product, kept alive only by the constant importation of fresh settlers. They were at no time a serious menace to Islam; with the Turkish conquest of the old Christian land of Asia Minor, which thenceforth became a Mohammedan possession, and the establishment of a new and yet more powerful Mohammedan empire in the interior of Syria, the fate of the Christian kingdoms was sealed. And this was Saladin's achievement, however much his work may have been furthered by the previous conquests of Zenki and Nur-ed-din. The fall of the **Egypt** Shiite caliphs of Egypt is also **Falls to** one of the most important **Saladin** events in the history of Islam. Their place was taken by Saladin's descendants, the Ayubides, as they were usually called after Saladin's father, Nejm ed-din Ayub. With this the victory was won by the Sunnitic orthodoxy in the west. Saladin himself took good care that his empire should not become a menace to the caliphate; for, following the bad custom

of the Seljuks, shortly before his death he divided his kingdom between his three sons, in addition presenting single towns and districts to his numerous relatives. The result was a succession of wars, which finally ended when Saladin's brother Aladil united the bulk of the possessions of the family under his rule in 1200.

The empire soon fell to pieces again after Aladil's death, when confusion once more broke forth, in 1218, on an invasion of Egypt by the Crusaders. Alkamil, who succeeded to the thrones of Egypt and Palestine, concluded a treaty with Frederick II., under which Jerusalem was restored to the Christians in 1228. During the next ten years constant wars took place in Syria, an attempt being made in the north to form an independent state with Damascus as its capital, while the Egyptian Ayubides continued their desperate efforts, with the assistance of the Christians and all other allies whom occasion offered, to maintain their supremacy over the entire empire of Saladin. In 1250 a change of the occu- **Beginnings** pancy of the throne of Egypt **of the** took place, with the result that **Mamelukes** the throne of the Ayubides fell into the hands of the leader of the mercenary bodyguards. With this began the period of Mameluke supremacy, which, in spite of various interruptions, continued until the days of Mehemet Ali in the early nineteenth century.

The affairs in Syria and Egypt developed during the eleventh and twelfth centuries in comparative independence of the events which had been taking place in the eastern part of the empire of the caliphs. But here too the power of the Seljuks was in process of decay. In Irak, Mesopotamia, and Iran an entire series of minor Seljukian states — Farsistan, Luristan, Azerbijan—had been formed; not to speak of the feudal provinces already in existence, which now became more independent than ever. The bulk of these states were ruled by princes called Atabegs, who—like Nur-ed-din—recognised merely as a matter of form the supremacy of the caliph and the sultan. Moreover, the throne of the sultan at Bagdad was a constant cause of violent disputes. Thus it came about that even the caliphs regained a portion of their old political influence, and here and there ventured to take up arms against their Seljuk "protectors," or the minor princes of the neighbourhood of Bagdad. The power of the Seljuk sultans was now concentrated in Persia; but here also they were threatened by new dangers. It had indeed been an easy task to deal with the decaying Ghaznavides; and the Ghori dynasty was more interested in the affairs of India than of Iran; but the frontier provinces of the Central Asian steppes were once more in a state of the utmost tumult and confusion.

Transoxania had been lost to Turkish tribes, while at Khiva a new and powerful state had developed, whose ruler soon set out toward Persia on a campaign of conquest. Sinjar, sultan at Bagdad since 1132, had already engaged in a severe struggle with these opponents, who were threatening the same gates of his empire through which the Seljuks had broken many years before; and at his death, in 1157, a portion of Persia fell into the hands of the Khivans. A period of confusion followed: the caliphs at Bagdad endeavoured to arouse further dissensions among the Seljuks in order to free themselves from their burdensome guardianship; the Seljuks, on the other hand, fought among themselves for the sultanship, and the Khivan princes battled against each other for the rich inheritance of their house. When, finally, Caliph Nasir, the last energetic Abbasside, came to the throne in 1180, he was already in a position to extend his dominions, owing to the wars which had been carried on between Seljuks and Khivans; nevertheless in the end he was obliged to grant to the victorious Khivan, Tekesh Khan, the rôle of protector, which had so long been enjoyed by the Buides and Seljuks. After the death of Tekesh, in 1199, Nasir attempted to assume a position of independence, and opposed Tekesh's successor, Mohammed. But Mohammed, who shortly after his accession had annihilated the Ghorides in Eastern Iran and had extended his dominion as far as the Indus, resolved not only to restore Khivan influence but to do away with the Abbassides entirely, replacing them in Bagdad by a caliph chosen from the descendants of Ali. However, the early approach of winter rescued the Abbassid caliph for the time being. Before Mohammed could collect his forces for a new move, the troops of the Mongolian conqueror Genghis Khan, who had been called upon for aid by Nasir, appeared in his rear; and with this a new act began in the tragic history of Western Asia.

BALDWIN IV., KING OF JERUSALEM, DEFEATING THE SARACENS AT ASCALON IN 1177

IN THE GRIP OF THE MONGOLS

LACK of enthusiasm in Iran for the cause of the Khivan princes contributed not a little to the victory of the Mongols—perhaps more even than the original appeal of Nasir to Genghis Khan for assistance against his enemies. Upon the Khivan Mohammed, who reigned from 1199 to 1220, devolved the defence of Western Asia when the Mongol armies advanced on Transoxania; but when he assembled his troops for the rescue of Iranian culture he had not even the support of the Persians, not to speak of the other Western Asian nations. Besides this, to his great misfortune, he appeared to be ignorant of the value of his strong defensive position in Transoxania, and boldly marched out to meet the enemy on their own steppes. The result was that he received a crushing defeat in the year 1219.

Advance of the Mongols

All Transoxania was occupied by the Mongols during the next few years; the province was lost not only politically to Persia but to civilisation. Mohammed, whose native country Khiva was also invaded by the Mongols, entirely lost courage. He retreated from his second line of defence in Khorassan without a struggle, and retired to Azerbijan, from which he was soon driven by squadrons of Mongol cavalry, which advanced as far as Georgia; finally he took refuge on a small island in the Caspian Sea, where he soon died in misery and want. His son, Jelal ed-din, who had escaped into Afghanistan, was compelled to retreat to India before the victorious standards of Genghis Khan. His cause was ruined by the hatred of the Iranians for the Khivans, which was not forgotten even during this time of extremity. New Mongol forces streaming in through the open gates of Khorassan finally annihilated the last vestiges of his power in August, 1231.

Where resistance was offered to Ghenghis Khan he wrought fearful devastation; judicious submission was frequently rewarded by clemency. The Iranian civilisation was not overwhelmed. In fact, the rise of Persian literature was so little affected by political changes that its zenith was not attained until after the Mongol invasion. But gradually the results of the war became more and more visible, and it was soon evident that the ancient civilisation of Iran was beginning to deteriorate with the constant additions of foreign elements.

After the death of Genghis Khan, in August, 1226, Persia fell to the share of his fourth son, Tuli, who also died in a short time. Tuli was succeeded by Hulagu, after Mangu had been elected emperor of the Mongols. In 1256 Hulagu invaded Iran at the head of a vast army and re-established the authority of the conquerors; for after the death of Genghis Khan the Mongols had made but little progress in Persian territory. Hulagu could not have chosen as an object for his campaign one better calculated to win for him the sympathy of all Western Asiatics than the destruction of the Assassins. The wasp's nest of Ismailians still hung fast to the cliffs of Alamut, and the daggers of the fanatics continued to threaten all men who awakened their mistrust or anger. The Mongol ruler turned against these scourges of Western Asia; his summons to princes of Iran, bidding them assist with auxiliaries, did not meet with a single refusal. The caliph in Bagdad alone was unwilling to comply with the request, and

Scourges of Western Asia

this furnished Hulagu with a welcome pretext for making war on him soon after, and for putting an end to the sovereignty of the Abbassides. Thus, without desiring it, but in entire harmony with the spirit of their faith, the Assassins, even while in the throes of death, were indirectly responsible for the destruction of Bagdad and the murder of the last orthodox Abbassid caliph by the sabres of the Mongols.

The first half of the thirteenth century had not been without its effects on the Assassins also. Without altering its principles to any appreciable extent, the sect had passed through several external changes, the Syrian branch having won for itself an almost completely independent position. The esoteric doctrines of the Assassins had been known only to the higher orders of the sect; the rest were kept in a state of blind submission by the aid of a mystic and complicated formula of belief. But such a system was no more capable of permanent existence in the case of the Assassins than in that of any other sect. The secret doctrines gradually became known to the lower orders; and the higher authorities took no pains to avoid the inevitable; in fact, were all the more willing that it should be so, inasmuch as the unscrupulousness and contempt for death of their disciples were increased rather than diminished by the general spread of nihilistic opinions.

Until their mysteries were disclosed, the representatives of the order had always been able to preserve the appearance of being upright adherents of Islam, even better Mohammedans than the orthodox caliphs. The veil of deception, however, became more and more transparent, and the answer to the now openly confessed principles of the Assassins was an outburst of wrath from the entire Mohammedan world. Now, indeed, it might be said of the Ismailians, as of their Ishmaelite namesakes, that the hand of every man was against them as their hands were against every man. It was impossible for them to offer permanent resistance—their enemies were far too numerous; a fundamental change in their principles was unavoidable. Thus the Assassins, together with their grand master Jelal ed-din, suddenly began to embrace the orthodox faith. The "Old Man of the Mountain" burnt a mass of writings, alleged to contain the godless esoteric doctrines of the Assassins, in the presence of several orthodox Mohammedans, who had been invited to Alamut as witnesses; he sent off his wife on a pilgrimage to Mecca, where she outshone even the most princely of her fellow-

pilgrims through her lavish almsgiving and other good works; and finally he sought to connect the neighbouring feudal rulers of Azerbijan and Tabaristan with his house by marriage.

In fact, the Ismailian rulers were developing a dominion which required to rest on something more than systematic murder. Instead of bands of Assassins, Ismailian troops now appeared in the field, and in the year 1214 an army was despatched by Jelal ed-din to Irak in

THE MOSQUE AT MESHED, THE HOLY CITY OF KHORASSAN

order to assist the caliph in subduing an insubordinate governor.

Nevertheless, when Jelal ed-din died from poison in November, 1221, and was succeeded by his nine-year-old son Ala ed-din, the sect lost no time in openly reverting to its old principles. Ala ed-din, who remained weak in intellect throughout his life, was not the man to face the dangers that soon arose as a result of this latest development. When, after his murder in 1255, his son Rokn ed-din assumed the leadership of the order the Mongol hordes bent on the destruction of the Assassins were already approaching.

However bold and unscrupulous the Ismailians had been until this moment, their fall was mute and inglorious. Only a single one of their fortresses held out for any length of time ; the others surrendered immediately. At first it appeared as if timely submission would save them from the worst ; but Hulagu waited only until the last sign of resistance had disappeared. Then he gave the signal for a general massacre. Almost all the Ismailians of Iran were slaughtered in cold blood, and with them the last grand master of the order, on November 19th, 1256. The Syrian branch of the sect continued to exist for some years, until Beibar, sultan of Egypt, drove the dispirited sectaries out of their strongholds in 1271. However, the order was not completely annihilated either in Syria or in Persia. In the fourteenth century, unscrupulous princes frequently employed Ismailian murderers from Syria ; and even now some harmless remains of the sect are to be found in Lebanon and in the mountainous regions south of the Caspian Sea.

The Doom of the Assassins

The destruction of the Assassins was soon followed by the fall of the Abbassides. Hulagu aimed at the subjection of all Western Asia. He was, no doubt, well pleased that the infatuated caliph had refused to supply him troops for the campaign against the Assassins, thereby furnishing the Mongols with an excuse for next turning their arms against him ; and no time more favourable than the middle of the thirteenth century could have been chosen for an attack on the spiritual centre of the Islamite world. The decay of the Seljuks had deprived the caliphate of its natural protectors, the caliphs themselves contributing not a little towards bringing about this state of affairs, for they had once more begun to adopt policies of their own, extending their possessions and increasing their authority in Irak and Western Iran by the employment of mercenaries. So long as they had to do only with vassal princes and atabegs, they were more or less successful in their efforts to augment their own political importance ; it would even have been possible for an energetic and clever caliph to have transformed the

Mongols Attack the Caliphate

spiritual supremacy of the caliphate into a far-reaching temporal dominion.

But, unfortunately, the successors of Nasir, who had always set before himself a fixed policy and had laid the foundations for further successes in reorganising the financial system and army of the caliphate, were men of small abilities. Mustanzir scattered the money that had been saved by Nasir, by erecting splendid edifices and establishing various religious foundations. His successor, Mustazim, who came to the throne in 1242, went to the opposite extreme, and reduced his single means of defence, the mercenary army, in order to save expenses. Thus, having robbed himself of his own power, he was helpless at the time of the greatest danger, and, in the usual manner of weaklings, refused to acknowledge that his position was endangered till it was too late.

First Mustazim attacked the Mongols with insufficient forces ; then he entered into feeble negotiations with them ; thus he allowed the last chances of escape to slip by. The city of Bagdad still remained to him ; and its excellent strategic position, on both banks of the Tigris in a district cut through by canals, rendered a siege extremely difficult. Nor did the Mohammedan rulers of the western provinces, once an integral part of the empire, leave their spiritual head entirely in the lurch ; but when a Mongol army crossed the Tigris near Mossul, and threatened the western side of the city, the caliph lost all hope, and repaired to the camp of Hulagu. His life was spared long enough for him to disclose the places where he had hidden his treasures ; on March 21st, 1258, he was executed.

Sack of Bagdad

The inhabitants of Bagdad were led out in crowds and massacred in cold blood ; the Mongols plundered and brawled in the streets for forty days. The greater part of the city, together with the priceless library of the caliphs and many of the finest buildings, were destroyed by fire. Single quarters, indeed, were spared. The splendid situation of the city enticed new settlers thither, and to this day Bagdad has in a large measure retained its importance. The success of Hulagu, however, had a ruinous effect on Mohammedan civilisation. Bagdad was the connecting link between the western provinces of Islam and Persia ; within its walls the learned men of Syria, Egypt, and Andalusia

Edwards

SULTANABAD, ONE OF THE LARGEST TOWNS IN THE PERSIAN PROVINCE OF KHORASSAN
Khorassan, in the north-east of Persia, is the largest province, and includes a large portion of the desert land of Persia. It constituted a Persian line of defence against the Mongols, and was the first district to be overrun by them. It has, from its military position, always played an important part in Persian history.

had united in common pursuits with the scholars of Persia and Transoxania, so that the city was indeed the centre of the intellectual as well as of the ecclesiastical power of the Mohammedan people. But the murderous thrusts dealt by the Mongols struck Oriental civilisation to the very heart. Never since has it arisen to its former lustre; it has lived during the last six hundred years only in the reflection of its former achievements. The poetry of Persia, indeed, continued to flourish for a couple of centuries, but it no longer found an echo in the west; and finally it, too, died away in its loneliness.

After the capture of Bagdad, Hulagu continued his campaign of conquest in the west, first declaring war upon Northern Syria. He stormed Haleb in 1260, compelled Nasir ed-din, the Ayubide, to flee from Damascus, marched through Palestine, and threatened Egypt; but on being severely defeated by Kotuz, the Mameluke regent of the empire, at Ain Jalut, not far from Shechem, he was obliged to withdraw his forces from the west. The small Ayubide dynasties in Northern Syria were soon forced to take

one side or the other, and were for the most part annihilated in the repeated conflicts between Mongols and Egyptians. Just as Western Asia became more and more desolate as a result of these devastating struggles, so the political history of the land became less interesting and more cheerless as time went on.

For a long time the history of Western Asia was occupied with the antagonism of two great powers, the Mongol dynasty of the Ilkhans in Persia and Irak, and the Mameluke sultans in Egypt and Syria. The leaden cloud of hopeless stagnation soon settled over the land, though occasionally lighted up by flames of burning villages and homesteads. The work that had been begun by Katur was completed by his successor and murderer, Beibar: Syria, together with its Ayubide princes, was brought under Egyptian influence, the power of the Assassins broken, and that of the Christians shaken. The princes of Iconium and Lesser Armenia, who had allied themselves with the Mongols, defended themselves with difficulty against the attacks of the Egyptians. Since the greater part of

Arabia and Mesopotamia also recognised the supremacy of Beibar, Egypt was, in 1277, on the death of this none too scrupulous but energetic sultan, the centre of a powerful empire, which, in spite of all quarrels as to the succession and its constant state of confusion, successfully barred the west to the Mongols. The

Vitality of Iranian Culture Mongol chieftains who had taken possession of Persia were soon affected by the influence of Iranian culture no less than by the religious belief of their new environment, and the intellectual life of Iran did not at first suffer to any great extent under the new political conditions ; the burning of the centres of learning in Transoxania and the desolation which had been brought to Bagdad had in reality only destroyed the outworks of Iranianism, which still remained sound at the core.

Above all, Farsistan, the heart of Iran, had scarcely been touched by the ruin and havoc of war ; its ruling dynasty still remained on the throne, and in Asia Minor an offshoot of Iranian culture flourished at the court in Iconium. The great mystic poet Jelal ed-din Rumi found a secure refuge in Iconium ; and his great contemporary Sa'di ended his days in peace at Shiraz in Farsistan. It was not long before the Mongol rulers became quite as distinguished as patrons of literature and science as the native dynasties had been in former times.

After Hulagu's death, in 1265, Abaka succeeded to the throne. The decay of the Mongol empire, which now set in, leading to bitter struggles between the various princes and to violent onslaughts of fresh tribes from Central Asia, hindered the expansion of the power of the Mongols towards the west. Under the followers of Abaka—who died in 1281—the Iranian-Mongol empire was torn in pieces by quarrels as to the succession as well as by other feuds, until, in the year 1295,

End of Mongol Expansion Ghazan ascended the throne, who adopted Mohammedanism as his religion. Even more important than his conversion to Islam was Ghazan's capacity as a legislator ; his code served as a model for all the later conquerors of Western Asia—above all, for the Osmans, or Ottomans—and in truth was exceedingly well adapted to the mutual requirements of a warlike nomadic people and the stationary agricultural inhabitants

of the conquered territories. From a perusal of these laws, which were indeed sadly needed, we are able to gather much information as to the miserable condition into which Persia had fallen during the Mongol period. The wealthiest district of Farsistan paid in taxes at the time of Ghazan but the eighth part of the sum which it had paid with ease during the Seljuk period.

The burden of taxation had been greatly increased by the evil system of farming out the taxes—a system which Ghazan himself did not abolish—and soon became unbearable. Broad tracts of fertile ground lay bare and deserted ; such of the inhabitants as had escaped the sabres of the conquerors, or of the troops of Mongol robbers who rode plundering through the province, fled before the inexorable tax officials, or were driven from their homes, hopelessly in debt to Mongol usurers. The tenth part of all produce of the land, which was set apart for the support of the Mongol warriors, was collected over and over again in a most unsystematic manner, until

Misery of the Taxpayers finally Ghazan succeeded in restoring a small degree of order by allotting certain fixed districts to certain bodies of troops. No good was expected from the increasing dissatisfaction of the Iranian people, as was shown by Ghazan's order commanding the disarmament of the native inhabitants of Farsistan. The general misery had been increased by one of Ghazan's predecessors, who had unsuccessfully endeavoured to replace specie by paper money after the Chinese method. Ghazan himself rendered an undoubted service to his subjects by reforming the currency, introducing coins worth their face value and of fixed fineness and weight.

Whether or not the new laws would have produced a fundamental change for the better in Iranian affairs, we cannot say. At any rate, the confusion that followed the death of Ghazan and continued until the end of the supremacy of the Ilkhan Mongols prevented any true recovery of the enfeebled Persian people. After the expedition of Genghis Khan into Syria during the years 1300–1303, which ended in failure, nothing more was done in the way of conquest by the Mongol princes of Iran ; and in 1323 Bu Zaid, the last Ilkhan who was able to maintain the integrity of his empire, concluded peace with Egypt. Soon afterwards the Mongol empire was divided, at first into two parts, Irak and Persia. At the same time the family of the Mozaffarides obtained for themselves greater independence in Farsistan, their first sultan being Mobariz ed-din, 1313–1358, and the Turkomans founded an independent state in Kurdistan. The increasing power of Farsistan showed that the Iranian element was once more regaining strength and preparing for a fresh attack on the Mongols, whose powers were declining rapidly. Perhaps a Persian national state would again have been founded had not a new and still more frightful storm of conquest burst over the land of Iran, destroying all Persian hopes. The victories of Timur completely re-established the waning power of the Mongols.

At the time when Tamerlane's troops were pouring in upon Western Asia and India a complete transformation had taken place in the affairs of Asia Minor, where a new monarchy was developing in the place of the decaying Byzantine empire and the sultanate of Iconium.

Timur's Storm of Conquest The Byzantines, who had so long been successful in holding Asia Minor against the Mohammedans, were no longer able to drive the Turks out of their territories ; and the Crusaders also, of whom so much had been expected in Constantinople, had likewise succeeded in obtaining temporary victories only over the Seljuks in Asia Minor. It is true that the most serious dangers had been averted with the assistance of the Western Europeans ; Nicæa had been recaptured, and the western half of Asia Minor cleared of the Turks. But the hordes of nomads, constantly reinforced by new bands of Turkish immigrants, were no longer to be driven from the steppe lands of the interior of the peninsula.

Had it been possible to strengthen Armenia once more, after the old Roman military frontier had been again established through the rise of the Lesser Armenian state in Cilicia and the Christian kingdoms of Edessa and Antioch, then perhaps the Byzantines might have succeeded in surrounding, and finally in assimilating, the masses of foreigners within their boundaries. But Armenia as well as Georgia was utterly helpless, and formed only the open door through which the hordes of Turkomans streamed in from the East. The Seljuk empire of Iconium, or Rum, which was only once united under the rule of a capable monarch, Izz ed-din Kilij Arslan (1152–1190), who died in 1192, suffered in general under those evil conditions of disintegration and quarrels between brothers as to the succession which were the usual characteristic of Seljuk states. Nevertheless, the people of Asia Minor were to all appearances better off under the government of the Seljuks than under the Byzantine bureaucracy, for the smaller the Eastern Roman Empire grew the heavier became the taxes. It was a source of great anxiety to the Byzantines that from certain of the imperial provinces of Asia Minor the inhabitants emigrated en masse into the Seljuk principalities.

Armenia the Gateway of the Mongols

When, in the year 1204, the Byzantine empire was overthrown by the Latins, and feudalism regained the upper hand, the stationary population of Asia Minor had no longer any reason for hoping that they would derive the slightest advantage by offering resistance to the increasing power of the Turks. On the other hand, the Seljuks, who had continued their old manner of life, wandering about with their flocks and herds, and at the same time always prepared for war, patronised the agriculturists, who had become indispensable to them, and whose interests in no wise conflicted with their own.

The growing power of the Turks was still more increased when Persian-Arabian civilisation began to awaken in the towns, for at the beginning of the Mongol wars scholars from Persia and Arabia sought and found refuge in Asia Minor, where they were gladly received by the Seljuk princes. Thus Ala ed-din Kai Kobad (1219–1236) did all that lay in his power to further the intellectual development of his people. But the Turks of Asia Minor did not entirely escape the Mongol storm ; they were now compelled to atone for having left the iron gates of Armenia and Georgia open behind them. Genghis Khan took the same route along which so many Turks had already passed, marching from Azerbijan to the peninsula ; and only the timely submission of the Seljuks whom he encountered saved them from a far greater evil. For a long time the

The Turks Give Place to Mongols

Seljuks of Asia Minor were the most faithful vassals of the Mongols, and, as such, the natural enemies of the Egyptians, whose sultan, Beibar, wrought havoc in the Turkish kingdom of Iconium, advancing far into the interior of the peninsula in 1277. The discipline of the Egyptians was fairly good ; but the Mongols who came later under Abagha could not deny themselves the satisfaction of either massacring or enslaving the inhabitants of Iconium. Thus it seems that it stood written in the book of destiny that in Asia Minor also the Mongols should destroy all that the Turks had spared.

End of the Seljuk Dominion

The destruction of the Seljuk dominion in Asia Minor was the natural result of the Mongol invasions ; but the Turks were already too firmly rooted in the peninsula for the Greek empire, temporarily restored in 1261, to derive any benefit from the fall of the Seljuks. Another Turkish race immediately came forward in place of the latter. During the Mongol wars a horde of Turkomans from Transoxania had marched toward the west under the leadership of Suleiman. A portion of this horde, of which the command was taken over after Suleiman's death by his son, Ertogrul, emigrated to Asia Minor. The Seljuk prince Kai Kobad allotted pasturages in the neighbourhood of Angora to the new arrivals, and was not displeased to see that they soon began to increase their lands at the expense of the Byzantines. Ertogrul's successor, Osman, or Othman, who came to the throne in 1288, continued the conquests, strengthening his forces by the addition of other Turkish tribes, and finally freed himself entirely from the suzerainty of the Seljuk rulers. In honour of Osman, their first independent sovereign, his subjects, consisting of many different tribes, took the name of Osmanli, or Ottomans.

Beginnings of the Ottomans

Shortly before Osman's death, in 1326, Brussa was captured, and a few years later was selected to be the capital of the new empire by his successor, Orchan. This new state, in which the entire military and destructive power of the nomadic Turks once more found a firm support, and which had succeeded to the civilised kingdom of the Seljuks, was naturally a serious menace to the culture of Asia Minor. It was only with the assistance of Persian civilisation that the Seljuks had been tamed, but at this time whatever culture there may have been left succumbed completely to the blows dealt by the Ottomans. With this the victory of nomadism was assured for centuries. During the reigns of Orchan and his successors a number of the small Turkish principalities in Asia Minor were overthrown, and the European possessions of the Byzantines were also attacked. Murad I. captured Adrianople in Europe, as well as Angora, Kutahiah, and various other towns in Asia Minor. His successor, Bajazet I., conquered the whole of Asia Minor with the exception of the principality of Kastamuni and the imperial state Trebizond, and was on the point of continuing his victorious campaign to Constantinople when the invasion of Timur began, hindering for the time being the rise of the Ottoman empire.

A great change, too, had taken place in the balance of power in Western Asia, which for the last century had been determined by the mutual antagonism of the Mongol empire in Persia and the kingdom of the Mamelukes in Egypt. The empire of the Mongols had fallen ; in North-western Iran only was a portion of its old power retained, and after the downfall of the Seljuk states and the victorious invasion of the Ottomans, the influence of the Mongols had naturally come to an end in Asia Minor also.

Fall of the Mongol Empire

It was not long before things came to such a pass in Egypt and Western Asia that all development of power was confined exclusively to the newly arrived hordes of barbarians, while the original native populations, the old representatives of civilisation and industry, sank to a position of feebleness and decay. Again a wave of semi-barbarous nomads swept over the unfortunate land ; and, to make matters worse, the appearance of the new conqueror was preceded by the plague, or black death, which spread over Western Asia and Europe, and raged longest in the hot valley of the Nile.

The invasions of Timur were nowhere so destructive as in Western Asia, in the provinces that were just beginning to recover from the effects of the first Mongol storm. In the year 1380 Timur appeared at the head of his army in Khorassan, after he had conquered Transoxania and Khiva. He marched along the old Mongol and Turkish routes south of the Elburz Mountains to Azerbijan, Armenia, and Georgia. Farsistan—still ruled by the Mozaffarides—was conquered, Ispahan stormed, and a pyramid of 70,000 skulls erected, an example of what Timur's conquests meant for Western Asia. After the national dynasty of Farsistan had ended on the death of Shah Mansur, in 1392, the Ilkhan, Ahmed ibn Owais, who had maintained his position in Irak after the loss of Azerbijan, was driven out of Bagdad.

The defence of the threatened provinces of the west fell to the Ottomans and the Egyptians, who were unfortunately unable to agree with one another or to engage in common undertakings. The Ottoman sultan Bajazet II. was, however, at least able to support the Armenians and Georgians, and assist the Ilkhan in Bagdad. On the other hand, Berkuk, sultan of Egypt, who had more reason to tremble before his own Mamelukes than before the Mongols, evacuated Syria after much boasting and little fighting, and left his
Timur Devastates Asia Minor Syrian subjects to be the helpless victims of Mongol fury in 1400. In the year 1401 Timur invaded Asia Minor and totally defeated Bajazet, taking him captive. Asia Minor had already suffered greatly from the Ottomans ; now it was once more plundered and its inhabitants massacred. Even the last of the wealthy seaports, Smyrna, which had not yet fallen into the hands of the Turks, was completely destroyed. The Ottoman empire became a Mongol province, and Egypt itself was saved from the sword of Timur only by the immediate submission of its ruler.

The death of the dreaded conqueror, in 1405, was not only followed by a halt in the advance of the Mongols, but was the
Timur's Empire Breaks up signal for the dissolution of Timur's empire. In Irak, the Ilkhan, Ahmed, who died in 1410, returned to the seat of government ; in Kurdistan, Kara Yusuf, the ruler of the Turkomans of the Black Ram, captured Bagdad and put an end to the old Mongol dynasty, which dated back to Genghis Khan ; the Egyptians reasserted their influence in Syria, and the Ottomans were restored to their independence in Asia Minor.

Persia alone remained to Shah Roch, the successor of Timur, who carried on successful wars with the hordes of Turkomans of the Black and the White Ram in Kurdistan. His efforts to restore his devastated country to prosperity, and to assemble about his throne the few remaining scholars and poets of Iran, were a pleasing contrast to the rule of blood of Timur. But the intellectual no less than the economic power of the country was in a hopeless state of decline. The barren spirit of the Turkish people finally became supreme, the literature of Iran being replaced by bombast, while mechanical verses in the form of epistles supplanted the true poetry of former times.

BRUSSA, THE CAPITAL OF THE TURKISH EMPIRE IN ASIA MINOR

A DRUSE   A SHEIKH OF LEBANON   ARMENIAN WOMAN

ARMENIANS ARMED FOR DEFENCE AGAINST THE TURKS AND KURDS

DRUSE WOMEN OF LEBANON   NESTORIAN TEACHERS OF ARMENIA

TYPES OF THE VARIED PEOPLES OF TURKEY IN ASIA

THE TURKS IN WESTERN ASIA
FOUR CENTURIES OF OTTOMAN SUPREMACY

ALTHOUGH some small signs of progress were still visible in Persia and in Asia Minor, Syria and Mesopotamia had reached the lowest ebb of wretchedness—the one suffering under the miserable government of the Egyptian Mameluke emirs, and the other filled with hordes of nomads, who, after their old custom, looked upon a civilised country as existing only for plunder. These Turkoman nomads were divided into two main clans : the Kara Koinlo, or the Black Ram, and the Ak Koinlo, or the White Ram, so called after their war standards. They had gradually succeeded in taking possession of a large part of Armenia, Kurdistan, Mesopotamia, Azerbijan, and Eastern Asia Minor. All the lawless and unsettled hordes of Western Asia assembled under the banner of the Turkoman chieftains, united only in the hope of obtaining spoils ; and when Kara Yusuf, the leader of the Kara Koinlo, prepared for war against

The Lost Leader of the Nomads Shah Roch, he was joined by innumerable bands of predatory nomads, all eager for an opportunity of advancing into the rich land of Persia.

Kara Yusuf died suddenly while on the march, and on the same day his vast army dispersed in all directions. The corpse of the leader, naked and despoiled, the ears cut off for the sake of their golden pendants, lay unburied on the trodden soil of the deserted camp. It was fortunate for Western Asia that the black horde soon became the deadly enemies of the Ak Koinlo, and that the two clans began to destroy one another ; but before the desired end was attained the circle of devastation had increased to an alarming extent. The Kara Koinlo conquered Mesopotamia, and even took possession of Bagdad, but were finally defeated by the Ak Koinlo under Uzun Hassan, who temporarily ruled over the greater part of Persia, and destroyed the last remains of Timur's empire in 1467. Persia remained in the hands of Uzun Hassan and his successors for about twenty years, until at last, after a long period of servitude, the Iranian people began once more to develop a national spirit, and a domestic dynasty arose to power.

Since Egypt was able to maintain itself through the exploitation of merchants, in spite of its abominable government by the Mamelukes, and since the feeble empire of Trebizond in northern Asia Minor managed to cling tenaciously to life— only for the reason that a small portion of Asiatic trade found its way to the Black Sea through Northern Persia and Armenia—it was at least to be hoped that, after order had been somewhat restored in Western Asia, the celebrated ancient commercial route from the Persian Gulf through Basra and Bagdad to Syria would again come into use ; that, as a result of this, agriculture and manufactures would also begin to reawaken in Irak ; and, finally, that new life would be infused from the natural centre and heart of Western Asia into the other provinces. But Bagdad's former splendour did not return. The city still remained the greatest in the region of marshes that to-day, as before the beginning of ancient Babylonian civilisation, extends between the Euphrates and the Tigris. It still harboured many merchants and contained numerous bazaars, but richly laden caravans no longer made their way thither from India ; no ships brought the wares of the Farthest East to the former emporium of Western Asia, and no long trains of merchants journeyed from Bagdad to the west, distributing their wares among the peoples of Europe. The caravans of Persian pilgrims that each year crossed the Tigris near Bagdad were the only sources of mercantile life remaining to the city. The final blow to the sinking prosperity of Western Asia was dealt by the nations of Europe, whose early navigators had discovered the new ocean route to India, thus leaving the overland roads through Persia in hopeless desolation.

Twilight of Bagdad's Splendour

Europe Deals the Final Blow

During the time when the sultans of Egypt were filling their treasuries with tolls extorted from merchants of all nations, and endeavouring to satisfy the constant demands of their Mamelukes with gold obtained from new monopolies and taxes,

Discovery of the Route to India the pioneers of Portuguese maritime trade were cautiously feeling their way along the coast of Africa, until finally the Cape of Good Hope was discovered, and the ships of Vasco da Gama sailed into the ports of India. The warlike merchants of Portugal took good care that their discovery should be rewarded by a monopoly of the Eastern trade. Their men-of-war blocked up the commercial route through the Red Sea in the year 1507; and soon afterwards Ormuz, the most important intermediate trading station on the Persian Gulf, fell into the hands of the Portuguese Albuquerque. Ten years later the Mamelukes of Egypt, deprived of their artificial means of support, succumbed to the attacks of the Ottomans.

That warlike people did not immediately recover from the crushing defeat inflicted on them by Timur near Angora; moreover, the empire was torn asunder by struggles as to the succession. The attention of the Ottoman rulers was chiefly directed to European affairs, and thus for the time being the Turkish principalities, still existing in Asia Minor, were enabled to retain almost complete independence. Not until the year 1424, during the reign of the sultan Murad, did the Ottomans reassert their influence throughout the peninsula. At this time the military organisation of the Ottomans had reached a very high state of perfection; the Turkish cavalry was supplemented, after the Egyptian example, by enslaved or impressed Christians, who received a thorough military training and were incorporated into the standing army of infantry, the Janissary guard. In later years this army became as great a menace to the safety of the sultan as the Mamelukes had been to the ruler of Egypt; but for the time with which we are dealing they answered every purpose. A new era began for the Ottomans when the last remains of the Byzantine empire disappeared with the capture of Constantinople in 1453; and the Turks succeeded to the inheritance of this vast empire as well as to the claim to supremacy secured to them by the possession of the gigantic city on the Bosphorus.

That the Ottoman sultans invaded even Apulia because it had once formed a part of the Byzantine empire, and was therefore looked upon by them as theirs by right of conquest, was a certain proof that it would not be long before their covetous eyes would be turned toward the kingdom of the Mamelukes in Egypt. The two nations had been hostile to one another as early as the time when the hordes

Ottoman Advance in Asia Minor of Timur were threatening without discrimination the whole of Western Asia; and as years passed the feeling of enmity increased rather than diminished. The Egyptian sultans clearly recognised that the small Turkish states in Asia Minor, which had hitherto withstood the Ottomans, formed their best wall of defence against the danger that was threatening them from the north. Especially important was the kingdom of Karaman, in the southern part of the peninsula, for which Ottomans, Egyptians, and Turkomans of the White Ram had long struggled, sometimes resorting to diplomatic deceit, sometimes to the sword. When the Ottoman sultan Mohammed finally succeeded in driving Uzun Hassan, the Turkoman ruler of Persia, out of Asia Minor, in 1473, Karaman fell to the share of the Turks, no attempt being made by Egypt to dispute the possession of the land with them; in

THE CITADEL OF ORMUZ IN THE 16TH CENTURY
After the discovery of the ocean route to India, the Portuguese gained, in 1507, Ormuz, the most important trading station on the Persian Gulf.

MOUNT ARARAT, THE MOST FAMOUS OF ARMENIA'S MANY MOUNTAINS

fact, Kait Bey, then sultan of Egypt, instead of taking an active part in the struggle, did nothing, and was content to imagine that the power of the Ottomans was being weakened by their wars with the Turkomans.

In later times also the Egyptians were unable to support the small states of Asia Minor. In the meanwhile the **The Final** Ottomans had engaged in a **Contest** successful struggle with the **with Egypt** newly-awakened kingdom of Persia, in order to render secure their eastern frontier. The final contest with Egypt now became only a question of time, inasmuch as there was no lack of excuses for a war in view of the troubles over the boundary question in south-eastern Asia Minor. The wretched financial condition of Egypt had not only prevented the sultan Kansuveh Alguri, who ascended the throne in 1501, from entering into an alliance with Persia, but had put a stop to all proper preparations for meeting the threatening danger. When Kansuveh finally succeeded in concentrating his forces in the North of Syria, the Ottoman sultan, Selim I., had already assembled a superior army on the frontier ; deceiving the Egyptians by pretending to enter into serious negotiations with them,

he crossed the Cilician passes unhindered in 1516. The decisive battle was fought on the plain of Dabik to the north of Haleb, and, in spite of the bravery of the Mamelukes, the Egyptians were utterly defeated. Kansuveh fell, and the remnants of his troops retreated to Egypt. Syria fell into the hands of the Ottomans almost without a struggle ; indeed, Selim was welcomed with joy in many provinces as a liberator from the Mameluke yoke.

During the following years Egypt also was conquered, an end soon being put to the courageous but hopeless resistance of Tuman Bey, the newly-chosen Mameluke sultan ; Syria and Egypt henceforth became provinces of the Ottoman empire. **Ottoman** Selim also carried the Abbassid **Supremacy** caliph off with him to Con- **Achieved** stantinople. The latter was the last representative of a long line of spiritual governors, who, although possessed of only the shadow of temporal power, had led a very comfortable life of contemplation and ease in the valley of the Nile. The Ottoman sultans kept up the farce of having an Abbassid caliph for some years, until they finally did away with this unnecessary arrangement and took the dignity upon themselves. They had all the more right to do this, because, together with Egypt, the sacred cities of Arabia had also fallen into their power. The sceptre of the caliphs regained its old authority in the hands of the dreaded Ottoman rulers ; the Persians alone were able to shield themselves from the consequences of this event by openly declaring for the Shiite doctrines. Syria had neither gained nor lost by becoming a part of the Ottoman empire ; but Egypt, already reduced by the turn taken in commercial affairs, not to speak of the fact that the greater part of her diminished income was now sent to Constantinople, became more and more desolate. The interests of the Ottoman sultans thereafter remained bound up chiefly in European affairs ; at first they succeeded in forcing back the defenders of Occidental civilisation, but in later times they were desperately engaged in defending themselves from the counter-assaults of the Christian nations. As time passed, also, war became the main interest of the Ottomans ; the idea of endeavouring to alleviate the misery of the conquered races of their vast empire scarcely entered their minds. It was only in respect to the art of warfare that they learned anything from the Europeans : for example, their artillery was admirably organised after European methods at a very early period. But in other respects the unimaginative, barren mind of the Ottoman held fast to old customs and conceptions of life with indomitable tenacity ; every attempt towards improvement or progress was crushed. Thus, Turkish Western Asia continued to remain in the same hopeless condition into which it had been plunged years before by Timur's campaigns. Wherever a sign of prosperity became visible the Turkish system of government took good care that poverty and misery should be restored as soon as possible.

Evils of Ottoman Misrule Unnoticed and avoided, untouched by the world's commerce, and unable to arouse themselves to new life without external aid, the Ottoman provinces of Western Asia continued to exist only as arid, hopeless wastes.

Evil enough has been the destiny of Armenia, the western neighbour of Persia. Never, since the short-lived efforts of Tigranes to establish a great empire, has Armenia been either independent or united. It is true that the mountainous character of the country has to a certain extent protected it from attacks from without ; but it has also favoured the division of the land into small and defiant tribal kingdoms, whose constant feuds have presented foreign Powers with welcome opportunities for interfering with Armenian affairs.

The conversion of the inhabitants to Christianity, and the remarkable tenacity with which they held fast to their belief, converted Armenia into a bulwark of the Byzantine empire, and at the same time a favourite object for all attacks made with the object of weakening the Eastern Roman Empire and the power of the Christians. As long as the Byzantines were able to hold the line of the Taurus Mountains it was necessary for the Armenians and Georgians to defend a portion of their frontiers only ; and at that time the Armenians, who were still a warlike race, had little difficulty in maintaining their position in spite of their lack of unity. Not until the downfall of the Abbassid caliphs, followed by the invasion of Azerbijan and the lower country of the Kur by the Turks, who not only constantly harassed the Armenians but opened up through their country a way to Asia Minor, did the days of complete destruction begin. Azerbijan now became the favourite headquarters of the nomads and Armenia their chief plundering ground and highway to the west. The Seljuks were followed by the Mongols under Hulagu, and the latter by the armies of Timur. In later times the unfortunate land was torn by the struggles between Turkomans, Ottomans, and Persians.

Already during the time of the Seljuks multitudes of Armenians had emigrated southward to Cilicia. After the victories of the Byzantine emperor Nicephorus Phocas, Cilicia was evacuated by the Mohammedans ; its rough mountain valleys and ravines offered a welcome place of refuge to the feudal nobility of Armenia. But this state of "Lesser Armenia," an independent principality subsequent to 1080, and a kingdom under Christian rulers after 1198, was in itself a land of roads to the west, for the possession of which many a sanguinary contest was fought. Sometimes the Byzantines or the Crusaders, and again the Egyptians, the Mongols, or the sultan of Iconium sought to render their influence supreme. Finally, in 1350, the Egyptian Mamelukes conquered Armenia, then in close union with the Christian kingdom of Cyprus, and put an end to the Lesser Armenian state. The emigration from Armenia itself still continued, however, when, after the Mongol period, the Turkomans of the Black and the White Ram founded their kingdom in the Armenian-Kurdish mountain country ; and the place of the retreating population was soon taken by Kurds and Turkish tribes. The Persian-Ottoman wars, of which the bulk of the expenses was paid by the Christian Armenians and Georgians, completed the evil ; scarcely 1,000,000 of the original inhabitants were now left in their native country. The majority had become

serious attempt to improve the condition of its inhabitants. And this is also true of the rest of Turkish Western Asia, of which the history for the last 400 years has been on the whole a period of complete stagnation. Nor could it well have been otherwise, according to the principles of Ottoman administration. Asia Minor, however, has always been better off than **Four Centuries of Stagnation** the other Western Asian provinces. It is true that, with the exception of a few remnants left in the cities of the coast, the ancient Roman-Byzantine civilisation wholly disappeared ; but as an offset to this a healthy peasant and soldier population speaking the Turkish language developed in the heart of the peninsula. With this population, thanks to the years of Seljuk rule, the greater portion of the

ERZEROUM, THE CAPITAL OF TURKISH ARMENIA

The mountainous character of the Armenian country, while protecting it from external attacks, has also favoured its division into tribal kingdoms, and it has never, since the days of Tigranes, been independent or united.

scattered over the provinces of Western Asia, some indeed penetrating as far as Eastern Europe.

During this period of trial and misfortune the character of the Armenian people underwent a fundamental change. Once warlike and lovers of liberty, feared on account of their exceptional bravery, they now became merchants and money-dealers ; and it was with **Change of Armenian Character** dissimulation and deceit, the weapons of the oppressed, that they struggled for their existence. But the part lately occupied by Armenia in the " Eastern Question " of to-day belongs properly to European history, and is dealt with in another volume.

The Ottoman government was not only unable to prevent the decay of Armenia, but, moreover, never made any really

original inhabitants have amalgamated. The old Phrygians and Cappadocians, Bithynians and Galatians, now appear in history as " Turks," however small the infusion of Turkish blood may often be ; to this very day it is from Asia Minor that the Ottomans derive most of their power, and here will they be able longest to withstand the advance of European civilisation.

An entirely different picture is presented by Syria, only temporarily awakened from her lethargy by the conquest of Selim I. Here an extensive immigration of Turks did not take place ; and the Mohammedans who had dwelt there before the advance of the Ottomans were confronted by a large population of other confessions, especially Christians, who were a serious menace to the Turkish government, inasmuch as the nations of Europe had taken a certain interest in the affairs of Syria ever since the Crusades, and had ever striven to protect the Christians who dwelt there. Far from the centre of the empire, encompassed by hostile neighbours, and entrusted with the welfare of the unstable inhabitants of their own provinces, the governors of Syria and Mesopotamia led a practically independent existence, although it is true that the Damoclian sword of imperial disfavour was always suspended above them. They sometimes even went so far as to make war on their own initiative; and such of them as had powerful friends at the court in Constantinople, and were ready to offer bribes at the right moment, were able not only to retain their positions, but often to pursue their own policy unmolested. The pashas of the smaller districts, however, possessed far less authority, especially in Syria, where neither the mountain tribes of Lebanon nor the Arabs of the steppes were willing to submit to the Turkish yoke. The jealousy between the pashas of Egypt and Damascus formed an absurd epilogue to the old struggles between the Egyptians and the Western Asian peoples for the possession of Syria.

Syria's Independent Governors

MUSCAT, AN INDEPENDENT SULTANATE OF ARABIA
On the old overland route between India and Mesopotamia there arose, after the Ottoman conquest, the independent sultanate of Muscat in South-eastern Arabia.

For a time it seemed as if the mountain tribe of the Druses would succeed in establishing an independent kingdom in Northern Syria. The Druses were one of those remarkable races of refugees that are formed out of various elements in almost all lands of high mountains, and originally developed from a colony of Ismailian immigrants who wandered into the ravines of Lebanon about the year 1020 during the period of confusion that followed the death of the caliph Hakim. In the course of time they were joined by the persecuted of various other nations. The Druses were distinguished from the other mountain tribes, especially from the Christian Maronites, the descendants of monotheistic refugees who had long been their neighbours, by their peculiar religion — a combination of

The Druses of Lebanon

Ismailite, Christian, and Zoroastrian doctrines. They had no relation whatsoever to the remnants of the Assassins.

Towards the end of the sixteenth century the Druses greatly increased in number and influence; and it was only their division into two hostile groups, the Yemenites and the Kases, or Kaisites, after the manner of the ancient Arabians, that enabled the Turks once more to reassert their influence in the mountains of Lebanon. An Ottoman army was despatched against them in 1585; but, in spite of fire and sword and all possible atrocities, the success of the Turks was temporary only.

In 1599 Fakhr ed-din, a man of great ability, assumed the leadership of the Kases, subjected or expelled the Yemenites, and took possession of a portion of the Syrian coast. Interest was aroused in Europe, and Ferdinand I. of Tuscany entered into an alliance with Fakhr ed-din and planned a great league between the Pope, Spain, Tuscany and the Druses for the reconquest of Jerusalem. But the Druses could not exist without constant support from Europe and the bribing of influential personages at the Ottoman court, who were able to prevent any active steps being taken against them; as soon as they were deprived of these two pillars of support their kingdom came to an abrupt end. In 1633 a Turkish fleet blockaded the coast, and an army advanced into the mountains; the next year Fakhr ed-din surrendered, and soon afterward was beheaded in Constantinople. In comparison with this attempt to establish a national government, the numerous rebellions of Turkish pashas, of which the recent history of Syria is chiefly composed, scarcely deserve mention. Mehemet Ali, who sought to renew the ancient claims of Egypt upon Syria,

No Syrian National Spirit accomplished but little of permanent good during his temporary period of rule, which lasted from 1833 to 1840. The fate of Syria continued to be unfortunate until the present day; the influence of European civilisation has finally begun to reach the districts of the Mediterranean coast, and progress is now noticeable, especially in the economic conditions of Palestine. But the rise of a national spirit is not to be thought of. In the middle of the nineteenth century, from May to October, 1860, the Druses began to massacre the Maronites, and thereby gave the French occasion to renew their old claims to the protection of the Syrian Christians. During the most recent times the majority of the Druses have migrated to the Hauran, where they live still more independently of the Turkish pashas.

Irak and Arabia, once centres of the Mohammedan world, have continued to sink lower and lower, until to-day little remains to either of its former prosperity and importance. Irak had always been a semi-artificial state, chiefly dependent on a vast system of canals and the commercial route from India and Persia to the west for its wealth and power. But the constantly recurring invasions of hostile races, combined with the change in the routes taken by the world's commerce, transformed the ancient plain of Babylon once more into a desolate, poisonous land of swamps and marshes, which the Turkish pashas, of all men, least understood how to restore to welfare.

Modern Insignificance of Arabia Arabia sank to an insignificance that was in truth wholly consistent with its small population and low plane of culture. It was left to itself; and its degeneration into small, mutually hostile emirates was not hindered by the caliphs. Only in Mecca and Medina the Abbassides, the Fatemides, and all other powers who laid claim to the leadership of the Mohammedan religious world sought to retain their influence. The pilgrimages, in consequence, were often warlike expeditions.

Not long after 966, when the Egyptian Fatemides obtained the place of honour in the sacred cities, an Alidic family succeeded in putting an end to the republican-anarchic state of affairs in the city of pilgrims, and established the Grand Sherifat of Mecca, which from this time forth possessed sometimes more, sometimes less power in Western Arabia. The ablest of the Grand Sherifs was Oatadah (1200), whose descendants reigned over their little kingdom until the time of the Wahabis in the eighteenth century. Various influences were at all times centred in Mecca; even from Yemen claims were constantly being made to the sovereignty of the city. When the Ottomans conquered Egypt, Yemen could be subdued only by force of arms. The old commercial significance of Yemen was lost after the country was conquered by the Ottomans. As an offset to this, the independent sultanate of Muscat arose in South-eastern Arabia on the ancient commercial route between India and Irak, and, after the

Reform By Fire and Sword Portuguese had been driven out, developed into a firmly constituted state, setting firm foot in Persia and finally also in Zanzibar. But in the central provinces of Arabia a storm arose in the middle of the eighteenth century that calls to mind the early warlike period of Mohammedanism. The reforming sect of the Wahabis, founded by Mohammed abd-el Wahab, about 1745, expressed their views with all due emphasis of fire and sword, and finally succeeded in conquering Mecca itself in 1803. A striking parallel to Mahomet was presented by this reformer. The doctrines of the Wahabis were a protest on the part of the old Arabs against the caricature of the original belief which had gradually developed out of the simple teachings of Mahomet as well as against the degeneracy and luxury of the inhabitants of Mecca. That city did not remain long in the possession of the Wahabis; for in the year 1818 the Egyptian Viceroy, Mehemet Ali, took advantage of the confusion that reigned in Arabia and occupied Hedjaz. However, the plans of this ambitious prince eventually came to nothing, and Western Arabia was once more placed under the direct government of the Turks.

Abbas the Great

Aga Mohammed

Kerim Khan

Tamasp

Hosain

Futti Ali Shah

Nadir Shah

SOME OF PERSIA'S RULERS, FROM NATIVE PAINTINGS

Tamasp, son of the founder of the Sefid dynasty, who reigned from 1524 to 1576, abandoned part of his empire to the Turks, but Abbas I., the Great, brought the empire to great prosperity. Hosain, the last of the Sefids, abdicated in 1722. Nadir Shah, a Turk, gained great victories in India, and was followed by Kerim Khan (1751-1779), an anti-Turk. Aga Mohammed Khan, a monster of cruelty, founded, in 1794, the dynasty which still rules. He was followed by Futti Ali Shah.

WESTERN ASIA
FROM THE
TIME OF
MAHOMET

IX
MODERN
PERSIA

PERSIA IN MODERN TIMES

THE SURVIVAL OF AN ANCIENT NATIONALITY

THE fate of Persia was more fortunate than that of Egypt, for the people of Iran showed that in spite of all the misfortunes to which they had been subjected there was at least enough vitality left in them for the formation and maintenance of a national government of their own.

In Azerbijan—that is to say, in a region that, together with the neighbouring provinces of the Elbruz Mountains, held longest and most tenaciously to its Iranian character—arose the national dynasty of the Sefids, who, it must be confessed, were greatly indebted for both their influence and power to the mixture of Turkish blood that ran in their veins ; the Iranians were, indeed, compelled to make the best of the Turkish elements that were now ineradicably fixed in the heart of Persia. At the same time, however—as had now become the rule in Persia—the new dynastic movement centred in a religious question which was very closely connected with the national feeling. The

The Old Religious Question Turks had become orthodox Mohammedans or adherents of the Sunnitic doctrines almost without exception, the simpler Arabian spirit of the Sunnitic teachings appealing far more to their nomadic temperament than the imaginative symbolical treatment of Islam of the Shiites. All things that had to do with the latter originated with the Iranians. The house of Ali always succeeded in finding adherents in Persia ; an Alidic dynasty had long been able to maintain itself even in the mountain valleys of Tabaristan.

Thus Ismail el-Safi, the founder of the Sefid dynasty, "the Sofies," was able to unfurl the banner of the Shiites, together with the national standard, without arousing the enmity of the Turks ; for he was descended on his mother's side from Uzun Hassan, the sultan of the Turkomans of the White Ram, and, indeed, his most faithful followers were Shiitic Turks. Ismail experienced but little difficulty in establishing himself in Ghilan, and in a comparatively short time succeeded not only in depriving the descendants of Hassan of their inheritance, but in extending his dominion from Armenia and Irak as far as Transoxania, in 1507. The new Persian Government at once aroused the hostility of the Ottomans, the more so for

Moslem Sects at War the reason that the doctrines of the Shiites had become the national religion of Iran, and were in open opposition to the Sunnitic confession of the vast majority of the Turks. The Ottoman sultan, Selim, was not slow to follow the time-honoured traditions of his race, inasmuch as he immediately made arrangements for a persecution of the Shiites in his empire on a great scale, cutting down without mercy all he could capture of these natural allies of the Persians. Ismail, who thereupon fell upon the eastern Ottoman provinces, was forced to retreat before the superior forces of Selim, and was thoroughly defeated at Tebriz in 1514 ; the result was the loss of Mesopotamia, Kurdistan, and Western Armenia. Ismail's son, Tamasp, who reigned from 1524 to 1576, was obliged to abandon Irak and Azerbijan to the Ottomans in 1534 ; not until the reign of Shah Abbas I., 1586–1629, was the Persian frontier extended farther to the west.

Although the adoption of Shiitic doctrines played a great part in the reawakening of the Iranian national spirit, it was at the same time an insurmountable obstacle to complete unity. Ever since the time of the Ghaznavides, the Afghans had been fanatical Sunnites, and, as a

Perpetual Division in Iran result, were far more sympathetically inclined towards the Turks than towards their Shiite relatives. The unfortunate state of affairs that had reigned in Iran ever since the fall of the Sassanidæ was still visible in this religious division. However, the Iranian people were well able to control the Turks, at least so long as the latter did not receive fresh additions from the north-east. The Kisilbashes, a tribe of

Turks who had adopted the Shiitic faith together with the Persian language, were the first example of the coming amalgamation. It is true that these Turks considered themselves to be the true masters of the land ; and it was not until Abbas I. had succeeded in surrounding himself with a circle of unconditionally faithful adherents, and in esta-

Nomadic Immigration Stopped blishing a standing army of Persian infantry and cavalry, that the supremacy of the Iranianised Turks was overcome. At all events, the Sefids performed the great service of closing the gates of Khorassan, thereby checking the advance of the Central Asiatic Turks towards Eastern Iran. The military importance of Khorassan again caused this province to play a very independent part in Persian history ; the Sefid, Abbas, reigned there independently for many years, even during the lifetime of his father, the shah of Persia, until finally the rest of Iran fell to him as an inheritance.

During this comparatively prosperous period of Sefid rule, the economic condition of Persia gradually improved. Abbas sought to infuse new life into industry by inducing Armenians to immigrate into his provinces, and to further commerce through the construction of new roads and bridges. The discovery of the ocean route to India had affected the commercial position of Persia no less than that of Egypt. Iran was now scarcely taken into consideration as a commercial route from India to the west ; still, the Persians of the southern coast were able to establish direct commercial relations with the maritime nations of Europe ; while in the north trade began to develop with Russia over the Caucasian passes and the Caspian Sea. Traffic with Russia was also furthered by the bitter hostility between Persia and the Ottoman Empire, which led to the blocking up of all the overland routes to the west.

Persia an Ally against the Turks Persia was the natural ally of the European nations that were threatened by the Turks ; and European envoys appeared more and more frequently in Iran as time went on, Abbas having already endeavoured to form a great confederation of nations against the Ottomans. The English in particular sought aid from the Persians during their attempts to take possession of India and of East Indian trade ; and thus it came

about that Persian troops, in combination with an English fleet, conquered Ormuz, still a flourishing province, drove out the Portuguese, and transformed the land into a wilderness. But the Persians were sadly disappointed in their hopes of a great development of Iranian-English commerce. The port of Bender Abbas, founded by Shah Abbas, never attained to any great importance.

The chief article of export from Persia at that time was silk—no longer the silk of China, carried by caravans along the celebrated routes of Central Asia over Transoxania to Iran, but a product of Persia itself ; as early as the period of Sassanidæan rule the silkworm had been imported from China to Iran and the west. But Persia only temporarily maintained her supremacy in silk-weaving ; as soon as the Byzantines became acquainted with the trade they outstripped all competitors, Greek silk taking the place of Persian. In the dowry of Fatima, daughter of Melekshah (1072–1092), who married the caliph Moktadi Billah in 1077, were included 900 camels laden with Greek silk. But the

Persia's Silk Trade fall of the Byzantine empire, and the decay of its economic prosperity following the capture of Constantinople by the Turks, caused Persian silk once more to become an important article of the world's commerce.

But now that Persia had once more risen to prosperity after centuries of devastation and decay, the land became a tempting goal for nomadic robber expeditions. Shah Abbas attempted to adapt the excellent military system of the Turks to Persian requirements, and to form the nucleus of a national army by the creation of a standing force of infantry ; but his weak successors added nothing in the way of improvement to these insufficient beginnings ; and finally the Sefids submitted almost without a struggle to the attacks of new opponents.

These new enemies were the Afghans, the Eastern Sunnitic branch of the Iranians, who had managed to retain a large amount of independence owing to their geographical situation between Persia and the powerful empire of the Great Mogul and the successors of Timur in India. Finally, it became necessary for the Persians to send an army to Kandahar in order to re-establish the influence of the Shah and to strengthen the Indian frontier.

THE LOT OF REFORMERS: A GROUP OF PERSIAN POLITICAL PRISONERS

A PRINCE OF PERSIA

DERVISH OF THE PERSIAN DESERT

PERSIAN LADY

PERSIAN LADIES TAKING OUTDOOR EXERCISE

A MERCHANT

ONLY PEOPLE OF WESTERN ASIA PRESERVING THEIR ANCIENT NATIONALITY

The unscrupulous conduct of the Persian troops drove the Afghans into rebellion ; and since the latter took up arms also as champions of the Sunnitic faith, numerous Turkish and Kurdish tribes followed their example and rose against the Shiitic rulers of Persia. At the same time another horde of Turks burst into Khorassan.

Afghans Rule Persia Mahmud, the leader of the Afghans, boldly advanced on Ispahan with a small army, defeated the Persians, and after long siege entered the capital in triumph ; Hosain, the last independent ruler of the Sefid dynasty, abdicated in favour of Mahmud in the thirty-second year of his reign (1722).

Apparently the Iranian element had now won a complete victory, and had shaken off the last remains of Turkish influence, which the Sefids had still been obliged to tolerate. Nevertheless, the differences in religion rendered it impossible for a true reconciliation to take place between East and West. When Mahmud, who had at first distinguished himself by showing a great moderation, finally lost his head completely in his endangered position at Ispahan, and endeavoured to render his throne secure by senseless massacres, as well as by filling the ranks of his weak army with semi-barbarous Kurds, all hopes of prosperity under Afghan rule disappeared. Moreover, the kingdom was unprotected from external foes. The Russians, under Peter the Great, occupied the passes of the Caucasus at Derbent without encountering opposition ; and the Turks were prevented from advancing into the interior of Persia only by the heroic resistance of the inhabitants of Tebriz. In fact, a division of Northern and Western Persia between the Russians and Turks had already been agreed upon. Fortunately for Ashraf, the successor of Mahmud, the war against the Sunnitic Afghans was as little popular with the Turkish people and

Ottoman Ascendency in Persia army as was the alliance with the Christian Russians. Ashraf made the most of these circumstances ; and, after winning a small victory near Ispahan, showed a most generous spirit of reconciliation, and consequently was enabled to come to fair terms of peace. The western provinces, however, were lost, and the result of the war was that the Persians were obliged to recognise the spiritual supremacy of the Ottoman sultan.

The new Afghan dynasty did not remain long at the head of affairs. The Sefid prince Tamasp occupied Masenderan, and his troops, commanded by the Kisilbash Turk Nadir, finally routed the Afghans in 1730. It was not the Sefid prince who ascended the throne of Persia, but his general, in whom he had evidently placed too much confidence. It appeared, in fact, that Persia was incapable of an independent existence without the Turks. Nadir, after several successful campaigns against the Ottomans, advanced his frontiers further to the west ; he also completely overthrew the power of the Afghans, and on doing away with the last remains of the Sefids in 1736 felt himself called upon to renounce the doctrines of the Shiites and to become a convert to orthodoxy. The dissatisfaction aroused by this step did not appear immediately ; the energy of the shah, and the brilliance of his victorious campaigns against the descendants of Timur in India, silenced all opposition. Owing to his defeat of the Afghans, Nadir was enabled to occupy the Indian passes ;

A Reign of Prosperity and he well knew how to make use of the advantages gained thereby. The empire of the Moguls under Mohammed Shah (1719–48) was thoroughly plundered in 1738–39, and the Indus became the future Persian boundary ; laden with booty, the army returned home. The large amount of money now in circulation, coupled with a general reduction in the taxes, although a cause of great joy to the common people, was naturally of no lasting benefit to the economic affairs of the land. But at least the army, which had been splendidly trained by Nadir, lost none of its efficiency. The subjugation of the Transoxanian Turks and the Khivans soon proved that Persia was able to hold the gates of Khorassan as well as to undertake expeditions against the nomadic tribes of the north.

Unfortunately, Nadir, like so many of his predecessors in the Orient, became transformed from a clever and energetic ruler into a mistrustful, bloodthirsty despot, who was led to commit unspeakably stupid atrocities out of anxiety for his treasures and suspicion that the Shiites desired to deprive him of his throne. His efforts to increase the national revenues and to enliven commerce were praiseworthy, however unpractical ; for example, he ordered wood for the construction of a fleet on the Persian Gulf to be sent all the way from the Elbruz Mountains. Nevertheless, he showed in all his attempts to improve the economic condition of his state knowledge of what constitutes the true wealth of a land—a knowledge that is rarely found among Oriental rulers.

After the murder of Nadir on June 20th, 1747, a new period of adversity began. The Afghan Ahmed Khan immediately proclaimed his independence in Kandahar, while Persia itself was given over to quarrels as to the succession. At last the successors of Nadir were able to hold Khorassan alone. The confusion continued until Kerim Khan, a member of the nomadic Persian tribe of Zend, took possession of the throne in 1751, and came

descendants of Nadir, was once more conquered, and the unfortunate province of Georgia, which had placed itself under Russian protection, was reduced to the utmost state ot desolation. A Russian army shortly appeared and threatened Azerbijan ; but the death of the Empress Catherine and the accession of her successor Paul averted a conflict that would in all probability have been fatal to the fortunes of Aga Mohammed.

It was then that the first suspicion may have dawned in Persia of what the vast, constantly advancing power of Russia signified for Western Asia. Twice Persia endeavoured to drive back the champions of Western civilisation and Christianity beyond the Caucasus ; but each time her efforts were of no avail. Under the terms

RUINS OF AN ANCIENT ROYAL PALACE OF SHIRAZ, ONCE THE CAPITAL OF PERSIA

forward as a champion of Iran against the Turks.

After his death, in 1779, the land fell once more into complete decay, until, in 1794, Aga Mohammed Khan, the leader of the Shiite Turkish tribes of the Kajars in Masenderan, succeeded after a severe struggle in founding the dynasty which occupies the throne of Persia to-day. The transference of the capital to Teheran was of itself an indication that the kingdom was again ruled by Turks, for Teheran is situated nearer to the pasturages of the Turkish clans of the north-west and north than is either Ispahan or Shiraz [see illustration at the top of page 1989], the residence of Kerim Khan, who characteristically chose the ancient Persis for his seat of government. Khorassan, the headquarters of the

of the peace of October 24th, 1813, the majority of the Persian provinces of the Caucasus fell into Russian hands ; and after a second war, Persian Armenia, together with the capital Erivan, were evacuated by Persia, under a treaty concluded on February 23rd, 1828.

Throughout the later wars carried on by Russia against the tribes of the Caucasus, Persia has remained inactive. During the course of the nineteenth century Russian armies also advanced to the east of the Caspian Sea, and into Transoxania, where one province after another was compelled to acknowledge the supremacy of the conquering Europeans. Finally, the last tribes of free Turkomans of Akhal-tekke and Merv submitted to the superior arms and discipline of their opponents. There is no longer any danger to be expected from the nomads of Central Asia; it is the civilisation of Europe that now knocks for admittance at the gates of Khorassan. Thus, the old conditions are reversed. Culture once flourished in Iran, and again and again overcame the might of the intruding barbarians. To-day Persia herself is in a condition of semi-barbarism; the dangerous task of assuming the manners and

THE NORTH GATE AT TEHERAN
Teheran was made the capital of Persia in 1794, following Ispahan, of which a view is given at the top of page 1989.

customs of the superior races of Europe without being devoured by them during the process now lies before her.

The relations between Persia and Russia began to create a certain interest in Persian affairs in the minds of British Indian statesmen at the opening of the nineteenth century. The alliance between Napoleon and the Tsar at the Treaty of Tilsit called attention to the possibility of an overland invasion of India. Diplomatic relations, first opened in 1801, were renewed; but interest lapsed when the fear of Napoleon disappeared. In India, indeed, the Government has ever viewed the continuous approach of the Russian shadow with apprehension; in Great Britain fits of extreme alarm generally alternate with fits of extreme negligence. No serious effort was made to counteract the pressure of Russia on Persia, which, without British support, found itself driven into the arms of the Slavonic Power.

With surreptitious encouragement from Russia, or at least with a rash expectation of Russian support, Mehemet Shah, in

1836, dreamed of a restored Mohammedan empire extended over Hindustan, and with that ultimate end in view attempted to recover the Persian suzerainty in Afghanistan. Russia, however, had no intention of embroiling herself, and Persia was forced to retire. A similar move, though doubtless with a less ambitious aim, was frustrated in 1856–7, during the reign of Nasir ed-din (1848–1898), the shah whose visits to Europe in 1873 and 1878 excited much public curiosity.

For the last fifty years there has been a continuous rivalry between Russia and Great Britain, the former Power exercising a persistent and the latter an intermittent pressure to obtain commercial and railway concessions and counter-concessions, the dominating fact being the consciousness of both that if ever Russia achieves access to and possession of a naval base in the Persian Gulf, Indian waters will cease in effect to be exclusively British waters. Of recent years, the

THE FAMOUS DIAMOND GATE OF TEHERAN

international position has been somewhat further complicated by signs that the Germans also are taking an interest in Persian railway schemes. Between Russia and Great Britain, however, the antagonism has been at least modified for the time by the Anglo-Russian Agreement of 1907, which has apportioned definite spheres of influence to the two Powers.

HEINRICH SCHURTZ
LEONARD W. KING

WESTERN ASIA IN OUR OWN TIME

BY ANGUS HAMILTON

PRIOR to the arrival of Germany in Asia Minor and Russia in Central Asia Great Britain may be said to have dominated the Middle East. With the intention of preserving Persia from the unfortunate influence of Russia, the British Government in the past had followed on occasion an unusually energetic policy. Britain's operations in respect of Herat, however, had succeeded merely in impressing Persia with a feeling of bitterness against her, equalled only by the dread with which that Power regarded Russia.

Before Germany had begun to sap the position of Great Britain at Constantinople, and Russia to impress the Shah with the power of her sword, the British Government was content to exercise jurisdiction over the Persian Gulf, the coasts of Arabia, and, in fact, the whole of Southern Persia. Mohammera and Bushire, as well as the island of Kharak, were in Britain's possession in 1857. An earlier depôt, serving as a military and naval station, was the island of Kishm, where Britain had settled first in 1820, and on which the Admiralty maintained coal yards.

In the Persian capital British influence was no less assured. Again, at Bagdad, **British Influence in Persia** across the border, Britain had laid the foundations of a position which reached its height in the middle of the last century. From Bagdad, and throughout Mesopotamia to the shores of the Gulf, respect was readily accorded to British authority by the semi-independent, wholly lawless, and usually piratical sheikhs who exercised despotic dominion over the region. Indeed, if the seventeenth and eighteenth centuries witnessed successive conflicts between Portuguese, Dutch, French and British pioneers of East Indian adventure, at the dawn of the nineteenth century the influence and trade of Great Britain were unquestionably pre-eminent because foreign trade was satisfied to rely upon British protection. Although the situation created at Teheran **Landmark in Persia's Evolution** by the troubles on the Afghan frontier in 1885 was most unfortunate, the damaging effects attaching to it were soon eliminated by the personal influence of Sir Ronald Thomson, Britain's progressive and enlightened Minister in the Persian capital. Not only had Sir Ronald Thomson won the entire confidence of the Shah, but he pushed British interests to a foremost place by advocating most strongly the opening of the Karun river, the construction of a road between Teheran and Ahvaz, as well as the provision of a service of steamers on the Karun. Sir Henry Drummond Wolff, who went to Persia in 1887, carried the efforts of his predecessor several stages further, and in 1888 the Karun river was open to international navigation as far as Ahvaz.

The year 1888 became a landmark in the economic evolution of Persia. Not only was the Karun river freed to commerce, but on June 25th the first railway was opened under the auspices of a Belgian company. This little line, with a length of five and a half miles, the first and last of its kind in Persia, ran from the capital to the mosque Shah Ab-dul-Azim. Since 1893 two branches, two and a half miles in length, have been added, but the lines, together with the Teheran tramway, built in 1889, long ago passed into the hands of a Russian company. Although failure was not contemplated by the pioneers in the Persian field of concessions, the Imperial Bank of Persia represents the sole instance of success. Issued on January 30th, 1889, to Baron Julius de Reuter, in exchange for a concession granted in 1872, which leased for seventy years all possible forms of commercial development in Persia, the charter for the formation of a Persian state bank carried with it the exclusive right of issuing bank-notes as well as the control of a variety of mines and mineral deposits. Although the concession of 1872 had not materialised, and Baron de Reuter had paid to the Shah no less than £40,000 deposit, which was lost when the concession was cancelled, Russia was known to be much annoyed at the character of Baron de Reuter's latest concession. Early in the following month, therefore, Prince Dolgorouki, the Russian Minister in Teheran, obtained a pre-emption over all railway concessions in Persia for the following five years, as well as the right to establish a Russian Consul-General at Meshed. Eight months later, on October 23rd, the Imperial Bank of Persia, having bought out for £20,000 the recently established New Oriental Banking Corporation, opened its doors. In November, 1890, however, the Russian Government succeeded in having the terms of its secret railway agreement with Persia extended until the year 1900.

The Gamble of Concessions

Secure in its possession of the rights over the mineral wealth of Persia, the Imperial Bank of Persia ceded to the Persian Bank Mining Rights Corporation, in 1890, its powers in respect of mineral deposits. In the following year, too, the Imperial Tobacco Corporation developed from the concession of a tobacco monopoly which had been granted to British capitalists in 1890. Unhappily, the fates of these two companies were disastrous. The former

Ellis & Walery
NASIR ED-DIN, SHAH OF PERSIA
Nasir ed-din, who was assassinated in 1896, appreciated the value of an understanding with Great Britain, and during his rule Russia obtained no great success at British expense.

went into liquidation in 1894. The latter, on account of local differences and disturbances, which reached a head on January 4th, 1892, suffered the cancellation of its concession in the following April. At the same time it received from the Persian Treasury an indemnity of £500,000, met by a loan of £500,000 at six per cent. on the security of the customs of the Persian Gulf from the Imperial Bank of Persia. Similar misfortune attended a concession for the monopoly of lotteries, which, granted to a Persian subject and ceded to a British syndicate for £40,000, was withdrawn, inflicting a direct loss of the purchase money upon the promoters. With the retirement of Sir Henry Drummond Wolff, for reasons of health, in 1890, and the arrival of his successor, Sir Frank Lascelles, in the autumn of 1891, a new era may be said to have been inaugurated. Save for the activity of the Imperial Bank of Persia in developing a system of carriageable roads, for the next nine years British enterprise stood still. On the other hand, the interests and prestige of Russia increased. Enhanced by the diplomatic skill of the Russian Minister in Teheran and the efforts of the Russian Consul-General at Meshed, a steady development had marked Russian commercial relations with North-east Persia. Russian interests were further promoted in 1895 by the announcement of a tariff, designed for the express purpose of stopping the Indo-Transcaspian trade that made Khorassan its centre of distribution. Unfortunately, the system of rebates offered by Russian railways to goods of Russian manufacture that were destined for the Persian markets, and the granting of subsidies to manufacturers who were interested in the Russo-Persian trade, had already brought about the practical extinction of Indian trade with Khorassan. With a view to meeting Russian competition, therefore, the Indian Government

Disastrous Ends of Monopolies

decided in 1896 to open up a trade route between Quetta and Seistan. The action of Russia in North-east Persia had aroused the attention of the Government of India as early as 1890, but action was impossible since the Amir of Afghanistan occupied a portion of the region through which the suggested route would pass. By the terms of the Durand Agreement of 1893 this obstacle was removed, and between 1894 and 1896 boundary commissions delimitated the Afghan-Baluch and the Perso-Baluch borders, upon completion of which the new route was opened.

While Russia and India were competing for the trade of Khorassan, Nasir ed-din was assassinated on May 1st, 1896. The late Shah appreciated the value of an understanding with Great Britain, and in spite of the political advantages which described the Russian position, Russia had obtained under his rule no very conspicuous success at Britain's expense. With his successor, Muzaffar ed-din, who had been compelled to seek the financial assistance of the Imperial Bank of Persia in order to travel from Tabriz, where he was crowned and where he had resided as Governor-General of Azerbijan, to take his seat on the throne, matters were different, since for many years he had been subject to Russian control.

Among the difficulties confronting the new Shah at his accession was an entire absence of money. A loan was sought, but, although the sum wanted was only a million sterling, the British Government did not follow the advice of Sir Mortimer Durand, then British **British Financial Aid Refused** Minister at Teheran, and guarantee the amount. In the negotiations British capitalists demanded the right of placing their own agents in charge of those custom houses whose receipts were offered as security. Although, in regard to a sum of £50,000 this point was conceded to the Imperial Bank of Persia, it was declined where it

SHAH MUZAFFAR ED-DIN
Muzaffar ed-din, who reigned from 1896 to January, 1907, was subject for many years to the control of Russia, who secured the sole right of issuing loans to the Persian Government.

had reference to the larger sum. As a consequence the proposals fell through, to the bitter disappointment of the Shah, who, abandoning a contemplated visit to Europe, formed a most unfortunate impression of the British Government.

Compelled by stress of financial difficulties to find methods for improving the revenue, the reform of the customs department was decided upon in 1898. The services of a number of custom house officials from Belgium were obtained, and the complete reorganisation of the methods begun. Under the supervision of M. Naus, lately Director-General of Persian customs, the new system was instituted first at Tabriz and Kermanshah in March, 1899, and twelve months later throughout the whole of Persia. Although the total Persian revenue at once appreciated, the Shah himself was still pressed for funds, and in the course of the summer of 1899 negotiations for a loan were opened again with London. Rendered impatient by delays, however, the Shah issued a firman in September which authorised the Russian Banque des Prêts, now called the Banque d'Escompte de Perse, to float a loan, when it became known that British capitalists were willing to advance £1,250,000 at five per cent. to be issued **A British Offer Too Late** at 82. This offer came too late for acceptance, and, on January 30th, 1900, the Russian Government officially announced the issue of a loan for £2,400,000. Secured upon the custom receipts of the whole of Persia, with the exception of those for the Persian Gulf, it was guaranteed, bore interest at five per cent. and was issued at 85.

Although Russia waived the right of control over the Persian customs, upon which British capitalists had insisted, she made it a condition that the balance of the British loan of 1892 should be paid off, and the indebtedness of the Persian Treasury to the Imperial Bank of Persia and the International Bank of Commerce liquidated. It was stipulated, too, that Persia should contract no other loan with a foreign government for ten years. The loan nominally was for £2,400,000, but Persia had so many obligations that she had but little more than a million sterling to her credit when they had been satisfied. Within a few months a further loan was required. On October 27th, 1901, Persia received from the Russian Government a further million and a half sterling, on the understanding that the tariff of the Persian customs should be revised in favour of Russia and that the period during which Persia should contract no further loan from Powers other than Russia should be increased to 1912, while the Railway Agreement was extended to 1905.

Persian Dependence on Russia

While Russia—by means of the secret railway agreement and the loan agreement, and through the advantages accruing to her under the 1901 Russo-Persian tariff revision and from the reorganisation of the Persian customs—established a political, as well as an economic, supremacy over Northern Persia, Germany followed in Asia Minor a policy inspired by an identical purpose. Committed to commercial expansion as an economic necessity, she conceived the plan of developing Asia Minor by an elaborate system of railways which should connect her own commercial centres with new, but none the less profitable, markets. Hitherto, no attempt had been made to exploit the commercial capacity of Turkey-in-Asia. For many years only two railways of importance were in existence : the Smyrna-Aidin Railway, for which a concession had been granted in 1856 to an English company, and the Smyrna-Kassaba Railway, which dated from 1863. In 1871, the Ottoman Government had constructed some fifty-six miles of railway between Haidar Pasha and Ismid, which in 1880 had been leased to an English company for a term of twenty years, subject to compensation if the arrangement were terminated before the expiry of that period. In 1888, ten years before the German Emperor made his dramatic pilgrimage to the Holy Land, Germany secured two Imperial Irades which conveyed to an agent of the Deutsche Bank powers over the Haidar Pasha-Ismid line, and a ninety-nine years' concession for its extension to Angora,

Germany Develops Asia Minor

with a retrospective guarantee of 10,30 francs per kilometre, and a prospective guarantee of 15,000 francs per kilometre

The Ottoman Company of Anatolian Railways, financed by German capital now blossomed into existence, and by 1892 work had been completed. In the following year another Irade granted to the company the right to construct a branch from Eski Shehir to Konia, which was completed in 1896, as well as powers to extend the line from Angora to Kaisariyeh, with authority to carry it via Sivas, Diarbekir, and the Tigris valley to Bagdad. The irritation aroused in Russia by the announcement of a German railway in the northern part of Asia Minor was sufficient to cause the Angora-Bagdad project to be abandoned in favour of the Konia-Bagdad route, in respect of which a preliminary concession was signed in 1899 between the representatives of the Porte and the Anatolian Company. A little later, on January 16th, 1902, an Imperial Irade, approving the final details of the earlier proposals, was issued, but not before the Porte had conceded to Russia, in the terms of the Black Sea Basin Agreement of 1900, priority of rights throughout the Asiatic provinces of Turkey that drain into the Black Sea in respect of the construction of railways.

The Bagdad Railway

With a view to eliciting the co-operation of foreign capital in the development of the powers granted by the conventions of 1899 and 1902 to the Anatolian Railway Company, the Imperial Ottoman Bagdad Railway Company came into existence. Signed on March 5th, 1903, the third and last convention modified in certain aspects the terms of the previous agreements. None the less, it gave to a German corporation a right of way across Asia Minor from the Bosphorus to Basra on the waters of the Persian Gulf. With the intention of making the project an international one, overtures were made in the spring of 1903 to British, as well as to French, capitalists. Although the scheme was regarded quite benevolently by the French, the view held in Great Britain by no means encouraged British participation. Although marked inequality existed between the conditions governing British capital and those put forward on behalf of German capital, financial points were not the only ones over which it became impossible to agree. In detail, the proposals did not appeal to the British Government, to whose guarantee London financial houses were looking before embarking upon so large and so precarious a venture. As a consequence, British assistance was not forthcoming. With the collapse of the negotiations for British co-operation, those with the French group similarly fell through. Germany, left to finance the great concession, has not yet attempted the task, save for the section from Konia to Eregli, a distance of sixty-two kilometres.

Under the influences which had already appeared in the Near East, as in the Middle East, the position of Great Britain in Western Asia was directly challenged by Russia from Central Asia and Northern Persia, by Germany from Asia Minor, and by a combination of France, Russia, and Germany from Southern Persia, the situation thus precipitated necessarily affecting British prestige in the Persian Gulf. Ostensibly there was no connection between the action of Germany in Asia Minor and the action of Russia in Northern Persia, but active wire-pulling from **British** Constantinople and Teheran **Position** caused identical action to be **Challenged** taken by Turkey and Persia under conditions which were a constant source of embarrassment to Great Britain.

Persia and Turkey possess sovereign rights on their respective shores, but expression was seldom given to them prior to the advent of Germany at Constantinople, of France at Muscat, and of Russia at Teheran. At the same time, while true to the traditional policy of maintaining the peace of the region for international interests, Great Britain has persistently encouraged the extension of Persian, as of Turkish, authority over the littoral of the Gulf. By the reiterated statement that she would not permit any but these Powers to exercise territorial rights there, considerable umbrage has been give in Constantinople and Teheran. The attitude, moreover, has run counter to the ambitions of Russia, who has expressed a longing for a naval base in Southern Persia, and to the aspirations of Germany, who, in recent years, earmarked either Basra or Kowyet as a possible terminus for the Bagdad railway.

France, by virtue of a treaty with the Sultan of Muscat, since 1862 had been conceded equality of treatment with Great Britain, and thus occupied a position which it was impossible to oppose. It was not until 1894, however, that the terms of this agreement were brought into force, and then it was more with the intention of assisting the descent of Russia to the Gulf than for her own purposes that France established a consul at Muscat. **Politics** Since that day German and **of the** Russian naval squadrons have **Persian Gulf** visited the ports in the Gulf ; protection has been offered and accepted by certain of the sheikhs, and the Gulf in some degree has ceased to be the exclusive British zone that it was when the Indian Government furnished naval and military expeditions for the purpose of suppressing piracy or the operations of some troublesome chief. Trade, too, in some districts, followed the flag of Germany or that of Russia, while it is safe to say that the plots and counter-plots of which so much has been heard were the work of the political agents, who, under the guise of consuls, began with the close of last century to represent the interests of France, Russia, and Germany in the region of the Persian Gulf, ever a centre of intrigue.

During this period it was not only in Northern and Southern Persia that questions with Russia were arising. After experiencing the advantages to be gained by encroachment upon Khorassan, it was hardly to be expected that the prospect of political difficulties with India would check the development of Russian policy in Eastern Persia. Accordingly, when Russia found that the facilities offered by the Nushki-Nasratabad route offset in great measure the penalties imposed upon Indian trade by the frontier regulations of 1895 and the Russo-Persian tariff of 1901, she contrived, in 1902, with the aid of the Belgian customs, to throw additional obstacles in the way of those caravans from India which entered Persia. Besides **Russia** a bureau of the Belgian cus- **Spoils Indian** toms which was established in **Trade** Seistan a Russian consul was detailed to Nasratabad, their mutual efforts being supported by a quarantine cordon, improperly brought into existence, to check the spread of Indian plague, as well as Indian trade. Under the stress of these devices, Indo-Persian trade was thrown into confusion, which was not materially reduced by the announcement that the Government of India proposed to extend to Nushki the railway then terminating at Quetta.

Remonstrances addressed to Teheran seemed hardly to reach Seistan. For the moment the special measures designed by Russia for the discomfiture of Anglo-Indian interests in a region offering equal conveniences to Russia or India—according to the forward or defensive movements with which it might be concerned—were largely successful. Moreover, affairs in Seistan were already rather unsettled, since a question concerning the waters of the Helmund river had arisen between the Afghans and the Persians. By the early autumn of 1902 the controversy had begun to assume alarming dimensions, when, by the terms of Article 6 of the Anglo-Persian Treaty of 1857, it was submitted to the arbitration of Great Britain. By virtue of this, early in January of 1903, an imposing mission arrived on the scene, where, although experiencing the hostility of the Persians and arousing the indignation of the Russians, it remained for three years, intent upon the demarcation of the Perso-Afghan boundary and the appropriation of the Helmund waters between the respective peoples of the border region. Although a check was placed upon Russian activity in Seistan by the presence of the McMahon mission, the outbreak of war between Russia and Japan in 1904 was no less instrumental in bringing about material depreciation in the gravity of the situation. At the same time due recognition must be paid to the revival of official Indian interest in Persia. Stimulated by Lord Curzon, the Government of India since 1899 had gradually increased the number of consuls and vice-consuls while providing imposing mounted escorts to all consulates. Similarly, military officers were attached to Meshed and Teheran, the Gulf postal and telegraphic services were improved, while the medical officers appointed to the Gulf ports took over the duties of plague inspection.

Walery

THE PRESENT SHAH OF PERSIA

Mohammed Ali Shah, who succeeded in January, 1907, began his reign with a quarrel with his parliament, but has had to yield somewhat to the demands of the Nationalist party.

Under an increasing interest the position of Great Britain regained something of its earlier importance, and, in spite of the nature of the Russian loan agreement, the Shah borrowed, in 1903, from the Government of India. Although the result of the campaign necessarily exercised a modifying influence upon the development of Russian policy in Western Asia, Russia has not ceased to be a power of great importance in Persia. The conclusion of peace with Japan in August of 1905, however, gave rise to a wish for the readjustment of relations with Great Britain, and after many attempts negotiations were set in foot with this end in view. In the meantime changes which had taken place in Russia through the granting of a form of parliamentary liberty by the Tsar to the people had stimulated the imitative zeal of the Persians, who, in the spring of 1906, compelled Muzaffar ed-din to agree to the creation of a Mejlis or national assembly. The constitution was dated January 1st, 1907, but before the Persian Parliament had had time to become accustomed to its existence the Shah died.

With the accession of Mohammed Ali Shah, on January 8th, the influence of the negotiations then in progress between Great Britain and Russia so governed the situation in the Middle East that, in order to facilitate the position of the new ruler, the Russian and British Governments offered him a loan of £400,000 in order to relieve his more pressing necessities. Although the Shah and his responsible Ministers were in favour of accepting the terms, which sought merely the usual lien on the customs, the Mejlis scouted the proposals, thereby inaugurating the quarrel between the monarch and his parliament.

Beginning with the exclusion of the members of the Mejlis from the ceremonies of the coronation, which took place on January 19th, as from the general durbar, which was held on January 20th, Mohammed Ali Shah throughout his reign has treated the Nationalist movement with contempt, although unexpected boldness in the attitude of the Nationalist leaders has compelled him upon occasion to yield with discretion. None the less, the first demands were a little startling, and embraced, in addition to a number of far-reaching reforms, the recall of several important officials from centres of provincial government, where their malpractices had inflamed the neighbouring populations, and the dismissal of M. Naus, the head of the Belgian customs.

Accustomed to an atmosphere of autocratic government the Shah expressed reluctance to conform with these demands, particularly as the reactionaries were able to present the efforts of the reformers in a light that was not conducive to their ultimate success. Accordingly, the Shah became the centre of a number of intrigues, behind some of which could be traced the influence of Russia. Distinct progress was made, however, although the assassination of the Prime Minister, Amin-es-Sultan, in August, 1907, threw back the cause of the reformers, creating an animus against them in the mind of the Shah that gave rise, at the end of 1907, to an attempted coup d'état. The struggle between the people of the capital and their ruler was not the only difficulty against which Persia had to contend at the dawn of 1908. Inspired by sympathy with the plans of the reformers, wide areas in many parts of the kingdom exhibited signs of suppressed revolt, the existence of these disorders encouraging a corresponding spirit among the Kurdish tribes on the Turkish side and the Turkomans on the Russo-Afghan side of the frontier. While the operations of the Turkomans were confined to raids in the vicinity of Meshed, the movement among the Kurds on the western border threatened to be attended by serious complications. Hitherto, unless threatened with extreme measures by the reformers, no attention was paid to their demands, and the Shah rode roughshod over the most delicate situations without any expression of concern.

The continuation of the state of affairs which has distinguished the first twelve months of Mohammed Ali's reign has brought Persia to the edge of revolution. Crisis has succeeded crisis, and while each outburst has threatened to precipitate the

Unrest in Persia

downfall both of the Shah and of his Parliament the situation at best may be said to represent a truce with Fate which, so soon as it is broken, will afford the world the spectacle of a Persian débâcle.

Negotiations for the readjustment of the points of disagreement between Russia and Great Britain in Asia were begun in 1905, and concluded in the autumn of 1907. By the treaty then disclosed, British and Russian interests in Persia were divided by a line which, in the case of the British sphere, ran from the Afghan frontier by way of Gazik, Birjand, Kerman and Bender Abbas ; and, in the case of the Russian sphere, passed from Kasr-i-Shirin through Ispahan, Yezd, and Kakhk to terminate at the intersection of the Russian and Afghan frontiers. In accordance with this arrangement the area allotted to Great Britain and Russia became a neutral zone, open to the commercial activities of any Power.

Persian Débâcle Possible

Although it would be out of place to discuss here the political bearings of so recent an instrument, it may be affirmed that the announcement of its terms came as a surprise. If not in spirit, at least in effect, the region hitherto identified with British interests has been thrown open to international exploitation. As things stand now, therefore, the dual division hitherto existing between Russia and Great Britain may be expected to give way to a tripartite arrangement by which the Power that controls the Persian Gulf terminus of the Bagdad Railway will become the controlling factor in the neutral area.

Moreover, since Germany failed to secure international co-operation in the Bagdad Railway, she has never ceased to recognise the advantages which the construction of such a line by her own unaided efforts would bestow upon her, and Asia Minor, the Persian Gulf, and Western Persia have been steadily exploited by Teuton traders. Further, it has been suggested, since Britain has repeatedly declared the necessity of maintaining the territorial status quo in the Persian Gulf, that she should assume responsibility for the construction of the sections of the Bagdad Railway which give to a German company the right of approach to the Persian Gulf, and to all the important centres in Mesopotamia and Western Persia. ANGUS HAMILTON

German Aims in Western Asia

ESSENTIAL INFORMATION ABOUT NEARER ASIA

Politically, Nearer Asia is divided between the Sultan of Turkey and the Shah of Persia, and may therefore be treated in two sections.

TURKEY IN ASIA

AREA AND POPULATION. The Asiatic portion of the Ottoman Empire has an area of 693,610 square miles and a population of about 17,000,000. It embraces the following provinces :

	Sq. miles	Population
Asia Minor	193,540	9,089,200
Armenia and Kurdistan	71,990	2,470,900
Mesopotamia	143,250	1,398,200
Syria	114,530	2,890,400
Arabia	170,300	1,050,000

The districts are divided in vilayets, or governments, which are split into sanjaks, or provinces, and these in turn into kazas. or districts, and sometimes even into sub-districts. The army of officials hold office under the direct will of the Sultan, and the humblest subject is eligible for the highest office. For general particulars regarding administration, etc., see ESSENTIAL INFORMATION ABOUT TURKEY.

ASIA MINOR. The chief towns are Smyrna (210,000), Brussa (72,000), Kaisariyeh (72,000), Adana (45,000), Konia (44,000), Swas (43,100), and Trebizond (35,000). Agriculture is the chief industry. The chief products are wheat, barley, millet, rice, cotton, opium, tobacco, and fruits, including grapes, figs, oranges, lemons, apples, and pears. The Angora goat is bred for its silky hair. The principal exports are wheat, cotton, figs and raisins, wine, oil, mohair, tobacco, meerschaum, silk, honey, beeswax, and ores of silver, lead, and antimony. Coal and lignite are also mined. More than 50 per cent. of the trade is with Great Britain.

ARMENIA AND KURDISTAN. The chief towns, with their populations, are : Erzerum (39,000), Bitlis (39,000), and Diarbekr (34,000). Much of the country is high plateau and the climate severe. The land is fertile, and yields grain, tobacco, cotton, and grapes. Ores of the base metals are found, but not worked to an appreciable extent. Carpets, rugs, and shawls are manufactured, but the external trade is negligible.

MESOPOTAMIA. The chief towns are Bagdad (150,000) and Mossul (61,000). Agriculture and industry are in a backward condition. The exports consist chiefly of wool, hides, gum, galls, opium, carpets, and dates.

SYRIA. The chief towns are : Damascus (230,000), Aleppo (127,150), Beirut, or Beyrout (118,000), Jerusalem (42,000), and Gaza (40,000), Industry and commerce are similar to Armenia.

ARABIA. The chief towns are the holy cities of Mecca (60,000) and Medina (48,000), and Jeddah (40,000) on the Red Sea. Coffee is the principal article of export.

POSTAGE RATES. Great Britain to Turkey in Asia. Rate for letters : 2½d. per oz. and 1½d per oz. over. Insurance of letters can be effected only to certain places. Commercial papers, 2½d. for 10 oz. or under and ½d. per 2 oz. thereafter. Printed papers, ½d. per 2 oz. Parcel post rates vary according to destination, route, and to the agency of transmission. Lowest rate is 1s. for 3 lb. to Beyrout and Smyrna by British agencies, and the highest 3/- for 3 lb. by the daily service by Ottoman post.

TELEGRAMS from Great Britain to Turkey in Asia, 6½d. per word.

PERSIA

AREA AND POPULATION. The area of Persia is estimated at 628,000 square miles and the population at about 10,000,000. The chief towns are Teheran (280,000), Tabriz (200,000), Ispahan (70,000), Meshed (80,000), Kerman (60,000), Yerd (60,000), and Shiraz (60,000).

GOVERNMENT. The reigning shah is Mohammed Ali Mirza, who succeeded his father in January, 1907. The latter, Shah Muzaffar ed-din, granted a constitution in August, 1906. The National Assembly has 162 representatives, but the peasant and working classes have no votes.

REPRESENTATION IN BRITAIN. H. E. Muhtasham-es-Saltaneh, Cornwall House, Cornwall Gardens, London, S.W.

INDUSTRY. The principal products of Persia are cereals, cotton, gum, dried fruits, opium, silk, and tobacco. The pearl fisheries in the Persian Gulf are important, and turquoises are found. There are deposits of base metal ores, but they are not worked to any extent. An oil-field in Southern Persia has been worked by an English company for some years. The manufacturing industries are domestic, carpet manufacture being the only important one.

COMMERCE. During the year 1905-6 imports were of the value of £6,441,000 and exports of the value of £4,885,700. Great Britain supplied about 32 per cent. of the imports and purchased 9 per cent. of the exports. The chief exports are raw cotton, wool, pearls, opium, rice, fish, carpets, and raw silk. The chief imports are cotton piece-goods, sugar, woollens, silk goods, and tea. The trade with India is important and increasing. The shipping on the Persian Gulf is almost entirely British.

CURRENCY. The unit of money value is the kran, a silver coin, the value of which fluctuates. It was formerly worth a franc (9½d.), but is at present worth only about 4·3d. (£1 = 50 krans). Accounts are calculated in dinars, an imaginary coin, of which 1,000 make 1 kran. The currency is as follows :

1 pul			= 0·12d.
2 pul	= 1 shahi		= 0·24d.
20 shahi	= 1 kran		= 4·80d.

WEIGHTS. The unit of weight is the miskal.

1 gandum			= 0·74 grain
4 gandum	= 1 nakhod	= 2·96 ,,
24 nakhods	= 1 miskal	= 71 grains
16 miskals	= 1 sir	= 2·6 oz.
5 sir	= { 1 abbassi, wakkeh, or kervankeh }	= { 13 oz. (about). }

Most articles are bought and sold by a weight called a man or batman, the most common of which is the Tabriz man, which equals 6·49 lb.

MEASURES. The unit of lineal measure is the zar, or gez, which varies, but is usually between 40 and 45 inches. The most common is 40·95 inches. A farsakh is 6,000 zar of 40·95 inches, and is therefore 3·87 miles. The unit of superficial measurement is the jerib, which contains from 1,000 to 1,066 square zar, or from 1,294 to 1,379 square yards.

POSTAGE RATES. Great Britain to Persia. Letters and papers as for Turkey in Asia [see above]. For parcels the cheapest route is the weekly service viâ Bombay, the time from despatch to delivery being about six weeks, and the rates 2/-, 3/-, and 4/- for 3, 7 and 11 lb. respectively.

TELEGRAMS from Great Britain to Persia. To Bushire 1/9 and to other places 1/6 per word.

HARMSWORTH HISTORY OF THE WORLD

FIFTH GRAND DIVISION

AFRICA

FIFTH GRAND DIVISION

AFRICA

The African Continent forms a geographical region so definite and intelligible that it has been taken by itself as forming our next Grand Division. On the like ground, since it is virtually bisected by the Equator, it has been divided into two main portions—the north and the south.

The northern portion falls into four clearly marked sections: Egypt; the regions bordering on the Mediterranean; the Sahara, with the Sudan (that is, the belt which stretches eastward up to Abyssinia—included in this section—and westward to the Atlantic, inhabited by races only partly negro); and the next belt, almost pure negro, whose southern border is roughly the Equator.

The division of South Africa is less obvious, since, except in the far south, which is not negro but Hottentot, almost the whole land is covered by kindred tribes of Bantu negroes. Here the territorial division is no longer fundamental: its place is taken by the natural division into an account of the native peoples and states, and of the modern development of a European ascendency.

The two first divisions of Northern Africa, Egypt and the Mediterranean littoral, are so closely connected, historically, with the main stream of civilisation from the earliest times, and later with Mohammedanism, that it might have been included with the Near East Division, under the title of the "Semitic Area"; but it was felt that such a division would have been less readily grasped by the average reader than that which has been adopted

PLAN

AFRICA—THE LAND AND ITS PEOPLES
By Dr. Heinrich Schurtz

EGYPT
By Stanley Lane-Poole, H. R. Hall, and Carl Niebuhr

NORTH AFRICA
By Dr. Heinrich Schurtz

SOUTH AFRICA
By Dr. Heinrich Schurtz and Arthur D. Innes

For full contents and page numbers see Index

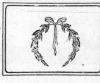

AFRICA: THE LAND

AND THE PEOPLES

THE CHARACTER OF THE CONTINENT
AND ITS NATIVE RACES

BY DR. HEINRICH SCHURTZ

ETHNOLOGICALLY and historically, Africa falls at once into two main divisions ; on the one hand, we have the lands on the north of the Sahara, including Egypt ; on the other hand, we have the main bulk of Africa, which lies to the south of that line of desert. As a matter of convenience only, the portion which lies north of the equator is here treated under the heading of Northern Africa.

The equator almost bisects the continent, and the larger portion of its area lies within the tropic zones, so that Africa is the hottest quarter of the globe. This fact undoubtedly accounts for many peculiarities in the African races. Their dark complexion, so often considered the brand of Cain, is certainly due to the climate and the burning sun, though science may be unable to explain the details of the process. Whether primitive man was fair or dark is an insoluble question. This much, however, is beyond doubt ; as the light complexion of the Aryan points to his origin in the cool regions of the globe, so the dark colour of the negro is evidence for the fact that this family of the human race was developed in the same hot climate which forms its environment at the present day.

The African climate is hot and, generally speaking, dry rather than damp, although exceptions to this rule are by no means rare. Its northern portion contains the greatest desert in the world—a

mighty barrier, forming the boundary which divides tropical Africa from the civilisation of the old world. Arabia is really a portion of this desert, divided from the continent by the waters of the Red Sea gulf. The desert is broken by the Nile valley, which forms a narrow strip of civilisation amid the surrounding desolation ; the river would form a convenient means of communication with the interior of Africa were it not for the rocks which bar its passage in mid career, so that the verdure of its banks disappears in places where the river is forced to pass these obstacles in rapid and cataract. However, the desert itself is passable for the adventurous merchant at several points. It is also inhabited, in spite of its desolation, by peoples who have exercised a considerable influence upon neighbouring civilisations. The history of the Sudan— the belt which stretches from the Upper Nile to the furthest West Coast, south of the great desert—is to be explained only by a knowledge of the Sahara and its peoples.

The hypothesis that the Sahara is merely the bed of a prehistoric sea can no longer be maintained ; it is a district of very diverse characteristics, and its general desolation is due solely to the absence of water. But even this scarcity is not everywhere so terrible as earlier descriptions would lead us to suppose. Upon occasion, rain seems to fall in every part of the desert, and of the total area about 2 per cent. may be oasis and quite 16 per cent. pasture and prairie land; hence we find nomadic races tending their flocks in districts which have been characterised as entirely uninhabitable. The percentage of arable and pasture land is highest upon the west; in proportion as we advance eastward the drought increases and the population diminishes. Thus the Sahara, in spite of its desolation, is the dwelling-place of important peoples, differing one from another in race, although their environment has stamped them ineffaceably with the same marks of character. Its races also show similarity of habits; they are restless nomads, forced by the poverty of their lands not only to wander, but also to be constantly fighting for the pasturage and fruitful lands of the oases. Poor, warlike, and eager for booty, they have never been content merely to subdue and plunder the settled inhabitants of the oases or to rob the merchants travelling through their districts with precious goods; they have also proved a danger to the fruitful frontier lands of the desert. The north, with the snow-crowned Atlas and its hardy mountaineers, has seldom attracted them; Egypt, fortunately for herself, was protected by the Libyan desert; but the negro lands upon the south lay open and defenceless before them. Upon these districts the peoples of the steppes and of the desert have descended again and again, until a zone of conquered states and mixed populations was formed, lying as a broad strip along the south of the desert. This district is the Sudan, of which the Egyptian Sudan, not infrequently referred to in Britain as the Sudan, is only a portion.

Rainfall of the Sahara

The Sudan is distinguished from the rest of Africa both by the character of its inhabitants and by its geographical nature; it again falls into several more or less similar divisions, but these are of no very high importance, as a glance at the geography and the configuration of Central and Southern Africa will show.

Physical Features of Africa

The special characteristic of the whole of this quarter of the globe can be at once made plain in figures. The average height of Africa above the sea-level is probably about 2,000 feet. This is considerably in excess even of the average height of Asia, although Asia has the highest moun-

tains and the most extensive tablelands in the world. The force of this fact becomes plain as soon as we remember that Africa has a very few regular mountain ranges, and cannot display that backbone of lofty peaks which is a special feature in almost every other continent. She does not owe her high average in this respect to the possession of separate mountain systems; instead, the larger part of the whole country forms a tableland, from which particular peaks rise here and there—a tableland which only in places, especially upon its edges, rises into a true mountain range.

The inhospitable and exclusive nature of the continent is the immediate result of its configuration. Behind the scanty harbours of the fever-smitten coast-line tower these highland heights, impassable in many places for the individual, and much more so for the trader's caravan.

In Africa the rivers partake of the hard repellent character of the continent. In the interior they certainly form extensive waterways, which will become of great importance in course of time; but their descent from the highlands to the coast is a succession of rapid falls and whirlpools, so that even when the mariner has entered the river mouth, he cannot pass the coast-line.

Rivers of Africa

But while the configuration of Africa offers no facilities for penetrating the interior, the interior itself is devoid of those natural clearly marked barriers which assist in the formation of separate nationalites. There are no long mountain ranges dividing the country into distinct provinces; no gulfs running into the heart of the land and separating one settlement from another.

This uniformity of configuration has ensured uniformity of population. Peoples have been continually driven in rout, like the dust before the wind, by the onslaught of warlike invaders, and the tribes that have settled again and again upon these broad plains have invariably tended toward a greater uniformity, while the refugees collect in every place which affords some protection, in the inaccessible mountains or in the swamps and islands of the rivers. Thus, in the interior of the continent constant movement and commixture has ever been the history of the black races; the inhabitants of the plains bordering upon the prairie and the

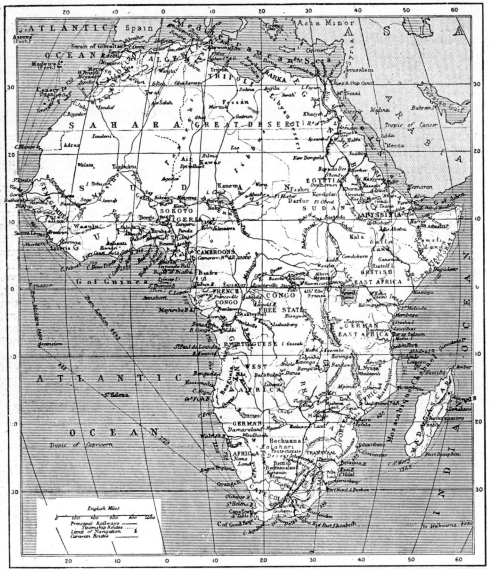

AFRICA: THE FIFTH DIVISION OF THE HARMSWORTH HISTORY OF THE WORLD

Unlike the preceding Grand Divisions of our History, the Fifth is devoted to one entire continent. It sets forth the story of Africa and its peoples from our earliest accounts of the "Dark Continent" down to the present time. Egypt, though geographically only a small part of the great continent, is historically of greater importance than all the other territories of Africa, and is here dealt with, of course, from the historical point of view.

desert succumbed to the attacks of the desert tribes, and states were founded upon this mixture of different nationalities, in which conquerors and conquered gradually coalesced to form new races. But the districts in which individual tribes could escape the levelling influences of migration and commixture are very scattered and very small in extent. Such isolated districts are the cradles of those individual peoples who are content with the natural conditions of their home, and long retain their special characteristics and peculiarities, even after they have found their territory too small and have gone forth on a war of conquest. In Africa, typical swamp-races are to be found, such as the Dinka on the Upper Nile; there are hardy tribes of mountaineers in Kilima-Njaro and on the slopes of the Kamerun Mountains; but all these little tribes are too scanty in numbers to have exercised any definite influence upon the inhabitants of the African plains. Nor has Africa any of those extensive islands which in other parts of the world have been the birth-place of distinguished nationalities, such as England in Europe or Japan in Asia ; Madagascar is the only great island. The sole marked exceptions to the law of assimilation are the sons of the desert ; however long a tribe may have been settled in the

The Mixture of Races Sudan, it preserves, while it maintains its exclusiveness, those characteristics which have been stamped upon it by a nomad life in the thirsty plains—the lean, nervous frame, the lighter complexion, and the flashing eye. But upon admixture with the negro tribes of the Sudan some even of these peculiarities gradually disappear, and, again, a mixed race is formed, in which the negro element preponderates.

In order to comprehend these details some consideration of the several districts of Africa is indispensable. The Mediterranean North may be left aside in view of its special ethnological and historical situation ; let us then begin with the Sudan.

By the Sudan in a general sense we mean all that district bordering upon the south of the Sahara—that is to say, the district of transition which divides the desert from tropical Central Africa, and forms a zone of mixed populations and civilisations. It is impossible to lay down any hard and fast boundary on the north of the Sudan, for on that side the fruitful soil becomes gradually poorer and poorer, until it fades away into steppes and deserts ; similarly upon the south there is no natural line of demarcation between the pure negro districts and the Sudan districts under the influence of Islam.

The entire zone of the Sudan is a unity, not so much by reason of its orographical or hydrographical characteristics, as in virtue of its climatic, and therefore of its ethnological, features. As it is the meeting-point of two climates, so it is also of the

Peoples of the Sudan two peoples belonging to these climates, the light brown Hamite and the dark-skinned negro. The east is the most mountainous portion of Africa, and is at the same time rich in the possession of great lakes. A central highland with mountainous frontiers and wide depressions in which the great lakes have been gathered may be distinguished from the lower steppes of the tablelands lying farther to the east, Somaliland and Gallaland. Farther

southward the mountains fringing the central plateau come down so near to the sea that room remains only for a strip of coast line more or less narrow. Like Somaliland, the tableland of the interior has, in general, but a scanty rainfall. Where the surrounding mountain ranges tower aloft, where isolated volcanic peaks rise from the plateau, or where the steep sides of the depressions catch the cloud-laden breezes from the west, there rain falls more abundantly, and vegetation grows in tropical luxuriance. Hence it is that about the deep inlet opposite Zanzibar, which is chiefly exposed to external influence, a fruitful mountainous country extends behind the coast ; to this succeeds a dreary region of steppes, and finally, about the great lakes the rainfall again becomes more frequent and regular, and agriculture is consequently more extensive. The mountains on the eastern frontier, among which should be considered the volcanic peaks of Kenia and Kilima-Njaro, are higher and more important than those of the west ; in truth, the highland of Abyssinia and its mighty elevations form

Desert, Mountain, & Seaboard merely the northern forerunners of this high range. From this description of the Sudan it becomes obvious that the Atlantic seaboard must not be included in that great zone of mixed populations and Mohammedan politics which we comprehend under the name of the Sudan, but that we have here a district of true negro population, as is proved by anthropological evidence, and by the nature of its civilisation.

In the extreme north of this district, in Senegambia, special circumstances have to be taken into account ; for Senegambia borders immediately upon the desert, and is therefore, to a certain extent, subject to those influences which produced the ethnological conditions of the Sudan ; hence it remains a doubtful point whether or not this country is better included in the Sudan. Another special characteristic of Senegambia is the fact that the two great rivers, the Senegal and the Gambia, make communication possible far into the heart of the country, which consequently loses much of that exclusiveness which is characteristic of the larger portion of the Guinea coast.

The northern boundary of the district is determined by the course of the Senegal and the frontiers of the plateau of the

West Sahara. The southern boundary cannot easily be defined. In Senegambia we have a fairly well-watered country, stretching unusually far northward to the very edge of the desert—a fact to be explained by the existence of the Futa-Jallon mountain system, which collects the moisture of the breezes from the coast and transmits it by numerous rivers, partly to the coast, and partly to the Niger.

The coast line between Senegal and Gambia belongs by origin to the sandy district on the southern border of the Sahara, but has been increased to an extensive plain by the alluvial deposits of the rivers. Further south the mountains run closer down to the sea, and the plains on the coast, which become appreciably narrower towards the south of Senegambia, are further diminished in size about Sierra Leone. The conformation of this plain is, however, totally different from that of the more northerly plains with their boundary of monotonous sandhills; numerous rivers widen into broad estuaries, swampy peninsulas and islands are formed, and at low tide banks and strips of land appear for a moment before they are again covered by the returning sea. Here we have a district eminently fitted to shelter the wrecks of persecuted peoples, and here the influence of the Sudan definitely ceases.

Features of the West Coast

The Grain Coast is not so broken, though the plains are not wide, for the spurs of the highlands run close down to the sea. That coast formation, however, soon begins, which is characteristic of Guinea as far as the Bight of Biafra, known as the Lagoon Coast. Instead of the huge delta-shaped estuaries and the islands lying at their extremities, we have a sandy and generally even strip of land stretching away, upon which the rollers of the Atlantic thunder, and which is broken only at rare intervals. Only here and there, especially in a large part of the Gold Coast, does this kind of coast formation disappear, and the hilly country come down to the sea.

At the Bight of Biafra the Lagoon Coast terminates, and in its stead begins the huge swampy delta, formed by countless river mouths, which the Niger has built up in the sea; further onward the coast takes a southerly turn, and we have a district of broad estuaries, the land of the "Oil Rivers." But just at the point where the coast line bends round, between the mouth of the Calabar and the estuary of the Kamerun rivers, rises a mighty mass of volcanic mountains, the Kamerun, of which Clarence Peak, in the opposite island of Fernando Po, is a continuation. Farther inland rises the tableland of Central Africa in terraces; at this point and farther southward it catches the warm west wind and occasions the growth of the wildest primeval forest, forming a zone of almost impenetrable thickness; in the depths of this forest the remnants of the shy dwarf peoples have found a refuge. Such is the formation of the coast line almost as far as the mouth of the Congo.

In the Region of the Congo

South of the Congo the vegetation of the coast becomes scantier, and almost disappears as we pass on to the steppes of South Africa. The formation of the coast line, behind which the highlands rise in successive terraces, remains in its main features the same as in Upper Guinea, except that the plains upon the coast in the district south of the Congo are considerably narrower than they generally are in the north.

The coast of Lower Guinea is broken by the mouth of a mighty river, the Congo, which is deep enough to admit ships of considerable draught. But the passage is soon barred by a series of rapids and cataracts. For centuries the short navigable distance through the plains upon the coast was the only known part of this great river, until Stanley's expedition informed Europe of the enormous area covered by the Congo river-system with its multitude of navigable tributaries.

About the point where the eastern source of the Congo, the Luapula, first crosses the equator, the river rushes in a number of cataracts, the Stanley Falls, over one of the terraces of the highland of Central Africa. Now begins the central and navigable course of the Congo; it makes a gigantic curve far to the north of the equator, and then sweeps southward again, passing at length over the lower falls already mentioned before entering upon its short course to the sea. The central division of th s broad stream, richly studded with islan s, traverses the immense forests of Central Africa which extended from about the point where the Ubanghi enters the Congo almost to the western sources of the Nile This thickly wooded Congo

The Real Heart of Africa

basin forms the real heart of Africa. Here, until very recently, the true African tribes remained wholly undisturbed by foreign influence ; here the remarkable races of dwarfs have maintained themselves in largest numbers. During its course through this district the Congo receives numerous tributaries, such as the Aruwimi **The Congo's** and the Rubi on the right **Mighty** bank, and the Lomami on the **Tributaries** left. The position, however, of the Congo relative to its mighty tributaries is peculiar, and forms a special feature of the whole district. These secondary rivers run almost parallel to the main stream, receive all the waters which flow down toward it, and then deliver them into the Congo itself. Cases in point are the Ubanghi upon the north, and the Luapa and Lulongo on the south, and especially the Kassaï, which, with its numerous tributaries, absorbs almost all the water south of the Congo valley.

The sources of the Kassaï and of its southern tributaries lie beyond the forest region of Central Africa : at this point begins a savannah district, interrupted here and there by forests, and finally passing into the steppes of South Africa. Geographically this most southerly portion of the Congo valley has certain affinities with the Sudan, and from an ethnological point of view parts of it are not unlike the frontier zone of the Sahara. Within the Congo valley there never was any approach to anything like a uniform native state, whereas in this district important states existed till lately, such as the famous kingdom of Lunda and others to its east and south.

The valley of the Zambesi, the river of the east, is of primary importance as forming a transition district from the well-watered tropics to the deserts of South Africa ; the peoples permanently settled about this river have always been under the influence of the shepherd tribes of **Importance** South Africa. As it descends **of the** from the highlands of the west **Zambesi** coast into the lowlands of the interior and enters the depression which divides the tablelands of East and South Africa, it forms numerous waterfalls and rapids, including the Victoria Falls, the biggest in Africa. It is important, too, as a boundary line— a protecting barrier, behind which peoples might find a domicile and a temporary refuge from the attacks of the warlike

shepherd tribes of the South. But it wa not a barrier which remained permanentl impassable.

In South Africa we have a new zon before us, again the scene of ethnologica convulsion, which, like the Sahara, exer cises a powerful influence not only upo neighbouring districts, but also, mediatel or immediately, upon the far interior of th country.

Those bold and simple features whic characterise the configuration of Afric generally are to be found in their entiret in this southern portion. South Africa is tableland, the edges of which attain th height of mountains, running in some place close down to the coast, and in other leaving room for plains upon the seaboard of varying breadth. On the eastern side these mountains are higher and of mor massive structure than those upon th west. The consequence is that the east which is further benefited by the prevailing winds blowing from that quarter, i much better watered than the west which, with the exception of the southernmost region, possesses only periodica **Features** streams. The Orange River **of South** certainly runs out on the west **Africa** coast, but rises in the eastern mountains, as do all its tributaries. The district with the smallest rainfall, which is therefore the driest and the most desolate, is the interior, the Kalahari desert.

The mode of life and the character of the inhabitants of South Africa correspond to the special peculiarities of each district. In the centre are the wandering Bushmen ; on the west, shepherd tribes of comparatively scanty numbers ; in the east, the numerous warlike Kaffirs, half cattle-breeders, half tillers of the soil, the most important native race of South Africa. Finally, the southern extremity was the home of a race which did not belong to the black peoples, the Hottentots, who were driven forward by successive waves of migration, and finally found a home in the remotest corner of the continent.

On the north-east, the mountains bounding the tableland retire far enough from the coast to leave room for a broad, low-lying plain, through which the Limpopo, the chief river of South-east Africa, runs down to the sea, as also does the Zambesi at a more northerly point. Here the nature of the country and of its inhabitants more nearly resembles that of the tropical districts.

Thus within Africa three main zones may be distinguished—a mighty region of steppes and desert upon the north, a smaller region of steppes in the south, and, lying between these two, tropical Central Africa with its vast forests and rivers. These three great zones correspond to the three main ethnological groups of Africa—the light races in the north, the yellow Hottentots and Bushmen in the south, and in the heart of the continent the black negro type. Each group has conformed to the special nature of its environment. They have grown up influenced by the characteristics of their habitat; and when we have learned the special nature of their country some of the secrets of their mysterious origins stand revealed before us.

As void of vegetation we may note the peaks of certain mountains, and in particular the vast area of the North African desert. We have already seen, however, that the Sahara is not so black as it has been painted. Even in the most barren districts the least drop of moisture will produce one or other of the sturdy desert growths with which the much-enduring camel may satisfy its hunger.

Vegetation is richer in the thirsty valleys, and even becomes luxuriant so soon as a mountain thunderstorm has filled the watercourse with its rapid torrent. Moreover, in the western portion of the Sahara, districts are to be found which for part of the year are covered with green verdure; and in the oases under the groves of date-palms other more delicate nut-bearing plants flourish.

The savannah, with its thick grass and scattered trees, forms the commonest and most characteristic landscape of Africa. This feature of the country, together with the extensive high table-lands, is so widespread that the interior of Africa presents but few obstacles to the fusion of peoples which has constantly taken place; whereas the conformation of the coast line offers almost insurmountable obstacles to penetration into the interior. Hence we may trace one of the special characteristics of African history—constant movement in the interior of the country, but little interchange of influence between the interior and the coast.

The savannahs are connected with the treeless steppes, and the steppes with the desert, by almost imperceptible gradations. Again, the transition from the savannah to the forest is by no means invariably abrupt. In the grass-grown plains the groves become thicker and thicker, the lakes are surrounded with the characteristic "gallery woods," and thus the steppes gradually change into woodland, and the primeval forest begins, broken with open clearings and grassy glades.

The huge primeval forests are the second great feature in the vegetation of Africa, which is of importance for the development of the population. The main portion of this forest growth fills the eastern side of the Congo basin, reaching almost to the western sources of the Nile and, in a westerly direction, nearly to the mouth of the Ubanghi and Lake Leopold; northward, the whole of the forest district does not extend far beyond the valley of

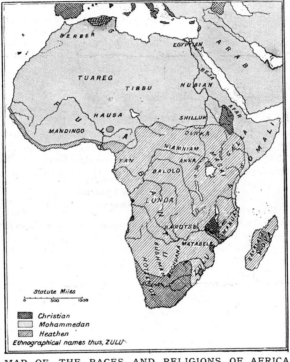

MAP OF THE RACES AND RELIGIONS OF AFRICA
The peoples of Africa may be divided into three groups: the light races of the north, including the Hamite peoples; the black negro type in the centre; and the yellow Hottentots and Bushmen in the south.

the Congo ; southward it passes some-what beyond the valley of the Sankuru. Beyond these limits the savannah country begins, although there is no lack of close forest, especially in the Western Congo Valley. A second forest district begins upon the Upper Nile, and continues up to the ethnographical boundary of this

The Forest Primeval

remarkable district. The forests upon the edge of the African tablelands may also be considered as a third group of primeval forests which rise with the coast line in terraces to the level of the interior, the moisture giving every opportunity for the forests to take root in the declivities. Thus in Guinea, especially in the Kamerun and Gaboon districts, a broad strip of forest divides the interior from the coast ; a similar belt, though not of uniform depth throughout, is a feature upon the East African coast for a considerable distance. Where these woods which border the tablelands have been strongly developed we may consider them as the most important of those obstacles which shut off the interior of Africa from external communication.

The primeval forest is inhospitable alike to the European and to the true negro. Only upon the border line between forest and savannah, where the gloomy shadows of the woods are broken by broad glades, can the negro make his plantations, fell the giant trees to clear fresh spaces, and penetrate this uninhabitable zone more deeply as the pioneer of agriculture. There are, however, peoples who belong to these forests and keep body and soul together within their depths ; dwarf tribes, who wander through the forest lands of the Congo basin and of the interior of the Kamerun and Gaboon district.

Compared with the forest and savannah, those districts in Africa overgrown with scrub are of small importance, though in other countries, especially in Australia,

Africa's Predatory Animals

they are an important feature in the landscape, and may be a serious obstacle to communication. They are most extensive in Somaliland and in South Africa, and may be considered as a special and by no means useful variety of the steppe.

When we turn from the general to the special influences exercised by the natural world upon man, we have, first of all, to consider the " influences of opposition "— that is to say, the dangers with which the existence of harmful animals and plants threaten mankind. In this respect Nature has dealt kindly with Africa, as compared with other countries ; the reason may be found in the fact that the African climate is for the most part dry. At any rate, the number of victims to beasts of prey or to snake bite is far smaller in Africa than in India. Predatory animals naturally exist in largest number in those districts which are richest in game, and therefore especially in the plains of East and South Africa, whereas West Africa, which has but few wild animals, can sustain but few beasts of prey. When the game upon the plains has been driven out or exterminated, and man appears with his flocks and herds, then the war against predatory animals is naturally prosecuted with vigour, and man generally proves victorious in the struggle.

Of much greater importance is the influence exercised by poisonous insects and by those minute organisms to which the spread of epidemic diseases must be ascribed. Even in this respect Africa is

Influence of Epidemic Disease

better off than some districts of Asia, the breeding - place of those devastating plagues which may desolate a whole continent ; and, moreover, the population of Africa is, upon the average, far more tenacious of life than any other of the races of mankind. Contagious diseases have found their way to Africa from other continents ; but they have proved far less destructive than in Polynesia or in South America.

By far the most important of the local diseases of Africa is the swamp fever, or malaria, a defence against invaders, invisible, it is true, but more formidable than any other, for Europeans are especially liable to its attacks, and in most cases succumb sooner or later. It will, perhaps, ensure the black races in the possession of the larger part of tropical Africa. The negro does not, indeed, enjoy complete immunity. Even Africans who have passed from a healthy district into a malarial zone do not escape the attacks of this disease. Thus we have a factor to be reckoned with in the internal history of Africa ; by this influence migration must often have been checked, and the pursuit and extermination of a conquered people hindered. In a country which provides support for so many shepherd peoples as Africa those enemies become highly important which strike at the very basis of man's existence by imperilling the safety of his flocks and herds. The larger beasts of prey are often of relatively small importance compared to the destructive powers of smaller foes. Among these the tsetse fly is known to be one of the most fatal possessions of Africa. Putting all exaggeration aside. it remains perfectly certain that this diminutive winged organism, whose bite is harmless to man but deadly to cattle and horses, makes cattle-breeding impossible in places, and thus restricts the wanderings of the nomadic tribes. The area of its distribution begins nearly upon the northern frontier of the Transvaal, and continues towards German East Africa. The fact that the Transvaal boundary was pushed no further northward and that no Boer states were formed north of the Limpopo, is due chiefly to the destructive agency of this insect, which killed horses and oxen upon every attempt at settlement, and thus checked all advances northward.

Ravages of the Tsetse Fly The tsetse fly is confined merely to certain districts and does not extend its ravages beyond these ; the contrary is true of another destructive insect, the locust, and of a destructive epidemic disease, the rinderpest, probably not indigenous. Political changes can generally be retraced to causes of this nature ; tribes are weakened by the destruction of their sources of support, become incapable of resisting their enemies, and are shattered and destroyed, or forced to give up their land and so seek new and less fertile districts.

At the outset of our enumeration of domestic animals we are confronted by the difficult question of their origin. Some of them are very probably of African origin, in particular the donkey, assuming the supposition to be correct that the wild ass of Eastern Africa is the ancestor of our patient beast of burden, which certainly seems to have been first domesticated in the Nile valley. The African elephant also appears to have been tamed in ancient times by the Egyptians, as also was the dog. The dog is found in every continent as the companion of man, so that only by careful examination into the characteristics of the different breeds could we gain information upon their respective origins. It is noteworthy that the dwarf tribes in the primeval forests of Africa keep a special breed of hunting dogs : other races use the dog for food.

The other domestic animals have certainly been introduced from other continents—as, for instance, the camel, **Historical Importance of the Camel** which seems to have been entirely unknown in Africa before the period of the great migrations in Western Asia, about 2000 B.C. This is a fact of no small historical importance : it is the camel which now makes communication possible between the Sudan and the north coast of Africa ; consequently the want of this " ship of the desert " in earlier times must have hampered communication, and this helps us to explain the absence of relations at that period between Mediterranean North Africa and the negro districts.

The horse is of importance only in the north and in the Sudan ; cavalry is the strongest arm of the service of the Sudanese potentates, and brought destruction upon the heathen negro races who were exposed to its attack upon the open plains. It first reached Northern Africa with the invading Semitic tribes of the Hyksos, who occupied Egypt about 2000 B.C. In South Africa the introduction of the horse by European agency has transformed certain Hottentot races into tribes of mobile riders ; but in this case the tsetse fly has in places prevented the northward advance of the horse and his owner.

In West Africa sheep pasturing has spread among the natives as far as the southernmost point, and also in the Sudan and the north-east of the continent ; the pig, originally brought to the west and south coasts by Europeans, is now to be found far in the interior. Of much greater importance than either pig or sheep is the ox, which was also introduced, though it seems to **Care and Use of the Ox** have been domesticated within the Black Continent from a very early period. It is the chief means of subsistence to many great tribes ; there are even typical nomad peoples to be found in Africa who devote the same tender care to their herds, and make their welfare the motive of their every thought and deed, as did the old Indian Aryans in the case of their " sacred cows." It is the ox that makes the steppes habitable enough to be the cradle of those great tribes whose attacks upon the fortunes of their agricultural neighbours form so large a part of African history. With the exception of a few scattered districts elsewhere, the Congo basin—that is, the forest zone of Central Africa—is the only district where the ox is also entirely unknown.

Meats Prohibited as Food While we are considering how far the possession of cattle and of poultry for food made existence possible we must not forget the fact that everywhere customs universally recognised, or special prohibitions of certain meats, precluded all possibility of using certain animals for food. Thus the pig was excluded from Mohammedan districts ; poultry, which are to be found almost everywhere in Africa, were in many cases not eaten, and even the eggs were despised. Among many nomadic tribes the ox was so highly reverenced that the owners contented themselves with the milk of the cows. Similar prejudices prevent the eating of this or that kind of game, and on a large portion of the East African coast fish are never touched.

Whatever the importance of hunting and cattle-breeding among large portions of the population of Africa, the existence of the negro is based upon the cultivation of certain plants useful to man, agricultural operations being performed in the simplest fashion with the mattock, or hoe. The African is most teachable in this respect : he has adopted a large number of plants from other tropical countries, and has gradually imparted them to races dwelling further inland. Africa itself is not particularly rich in such plants. The most important, and probably the first to be cultivated, are those like *Panicum distichum*, *Holcus sorghum*, and *Eleusine*, from which the negro is able to brew intoxicating liquors. Beside these, there is the maize, which was introduced from **Growth of Exotic Plants** America, and the manioc root, from the same continent. European grain corn, in its several varieties, will grow in the tropics only upon the higher mountain districts, which are in Africa no very prominent feature ; it is cultivated successfully, however, in the sub-tropical districts up to the far interior of the Sudan. Rice, on the other hand, a true tropic plant, is gathered on the east and west of the continent in the better-watered valleys. Earth-nuts and special kinds of beans and peas are probably indigenous. The banana, which is a staple food in places, especially in Eastern Africa, becomes scarce elsewhere, and seems to be sporadically distributed. The date palm, a native of Western Asia, is found only in the deserts of the North and their frontiers ; the coco palm is confined to the coasts. On the West African coast, the trade in palm oil and the fruit of the oil palm is rapidly increasing, and is likely to become a permanent source of income, as it does not usually involve the destruction of its source ; on the other hand, the collecting of indiarubber in the woods upon the coast has lately received a considerable impetus, but is so unsystematically carried on that it will probably decline. It is only quite recently that plantations of any size have been made under European direction, a movement which may revive the trade to some extent.

In consequence of the great uniformity of the African continent, the conditions essential to successful agriculture are rarely **The Negro as a Cultivator** so different in neighbouring districts as to offer any obstacle to the spread of population. Moreover, the number of plants for cultivation is large, so that for every piece of ground, even when offering only moderate possibilities, the proper kind of plant or grain is easily procurable, and the negro, generally speaking, is a cultivator by no means to be despised. The desert peoples, however, upon their invasion of the fruitful Sudanese districts, had to give up their diet of dates ; and this sudden change of habit produced dangers and inconveniences to them, which may be considered as tending in some slight degree to protect the inhabitants of the Sahara frontiers.

We have now to inquire what position is occupied by the negro, the inhabitant of tropical Africa, in a general scheme of the human race as a whole. Physically, he belongs to a separate and special type of humanity, whose characteristics are familiar. It is only in point of language that the race does not form a distinctive unity. The theory that the negro is of Melanesian origin may be dismissed. Although we may readily admit the probable existence, in some remote age, of a connection by land between Africa and the negro districts in the East, the overwhelming presumption is that the negro developed in the tropical regions which are still his principal habitat.

A shade of colour distinguishing the negro from other African races is the colour of the skin, often enables us to recognise the mixture of a fair Hamitic element with indigenous dark-skinned negro races, though in itself colour is not always satisfactory evidence ; for even within the pure African tribes greatly varying shades of colour are to be found, a result undoubtedly due to varying conditions of climate. "Among the dark races colour varies with habitat and mode of life, and the type alone remains constant." Yet, on the other hand, it appears that the dark complexion is the most easily transferable of all the racial characteristics, as is seen in the case of commixtures of negroes and fair races, and no amount of subsequent commixture appears to weaken the depth of colouring. At any rate, a case in point is to be found in the Arab-Nigritic bastards, almost the sole representatives of Araby on the east coast and in the Sudan. In darkness of complexion they are in no degree inferior to the purest negroes, while at the same time their sharp-cut profile betrays their Semitic origin. Still, crossbreeding between negroes and Europeans appears to produce quite different results.

Height and breadth are also important evidences of origin. Thus the small stature of certain Central African races points to the existence of a strain of dwarf blood ; the dwarf peoples themselves must be sharply distinguished from the negroes chiefly on account of their difference in stature. Slightness of build, on the other hand, is a distinguishing feature of the desert tribes, and is often continued long after emigration into fertile districts. In South Africa, among the Hottentots and Bushmen, this slender build is often combined with rugosity of skin, and also with excessive fatness in certain parts of the body—steatopygy, or obesity—a characteristic which is also found among the races on the Upper Nile and on the steppes of North-east Africa.

The formation of the head, which is highly characteristic in the case of the negroes, is invariably an important feature, though too little attention has been paid to it in the past. Investigators have generally contented themselves with skull measurements, and though this is a valuable inquiry, yet it has led to no definite result, as it affords information only upon one part of the head, and that comparatively unimportant. As it is by their physiognomy that the mixed Arab races can be most sharply and definitely distinguished from the pure negroes, so only by examination of those marks which the countenance displays will the investigator be able to discern other fusions of races going back to prehistoric times. Together with the dark complexion, the hair is another racial feature of the African which often enables us to note a strain of negro blood in tribes which are generally considered to belong to other races. On the other hand, if we find negroes with hair diverging from the woolly type, we may presume an earlier commixture with some other nationality. Next to these physical characteristics comes language. Philology teaches us

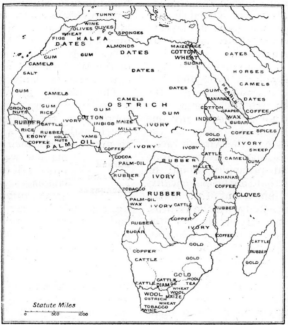

MAP OF THE NATURAL PRODUCTS OF AFRICA
Africa is not remarkably rich in cultivatable plants of native origin, but many plants from other tropical countries are grown. Among the most important are maize, corn, rice, the palms and rubber trees. The mineral wealth of the continent is chiefly confined to the south.

one great fact—that the nigritic populations are connected by the common tie of language. All the races that live south of a certain line—with the exception of the utterly different Hottentots and Bushmen — speak the Bantu languages, which are very closely related to one another, and are to be distinguished

The Tie of Language

by special characteristics from the other great families of languages in the world. This line begins on the Atlantic coast about the old northern boundary of the German Kamerun, then continues in an easterly direction to the Victoria Nyanza, leaving the states of Unyoro and Uganda on the south. In East Africa itself the line has been much broken as the result of recent migrations; however, Bantu peoples are found as far north as Tana.

From the special group of Bantu-speaking races we are obliged to exclude the negroes of the Sudan, and also those of the Guinea coast. Though the languages of these negroes do not belong to any one family, we must consider them as the second great division of the African races. It is thus obvious that a division upon purely philological principles would be erroneous, seeing that, anthropologically, the pure negro of Guinea and of the Sudan is inseparably connected with the Bantus. If this fact is not strongly emphasised, the whole foundation of African pre-history will appear in a false light. None the less, the distribution of the languages of Africa is a matter of high importance for the history of the continent. For the extension of the Bantu languages is undoubtedly the result of a long period of development and of important historical events.

Anyone who examines dispassionately the present condition of such uncivilised races as those, for example, of Australia will recognise that we have to admit the multiplicity of primitive languages as the

Languages in African Antiquity

first step in our investigation; within small and isolated races there is a constant tendency to form separate dialects. Hence we may assume that in African antiquity a large number of different languages were in use. The last stages of this state of affairs are now apparent in the distribution of the languages on the coast of Guinea and in part of the Sudan. Upon the great

tableland to the south a change gradually set in, the process of which is in close connection with long wars, displacements, and fusions of the inhabitants of that district. In course of time, one people imposed its language upon all the others; but who were that people, and how can we picture the whole process to ourselves?

We are helped to the answer to the second of these questions by an important fact, which shows us that those forces which brought about the spread of the Bantu languages are at work elsewhere in Africa at the present day. In the Western Sudan a district of uniform language is being formed, and we can follow the formation very closely. Here it is the Hausa language which is gradually defeating and overpowering the other tongues, so that it is already predominant over a large part of the Western Sudan and is yet further extended as the language of commerce.

The people known as Hausa are a motley mixture sprung from different sources, and their language is the sole tie which makes them a unity and enables them to extend their influence. In like

Spread of Bantu Languages

manner we must conceive the process of extending the Bantu languages, though with one great difference necessitated by the lack of civilisation in Central and Southern Africa; the Bantu dialects must have been spread more by military conquest than by peaceful trading. Such a process must have involved great disturbances. It is not, however, necessary to suppose that the original Bantu-speaking race overran, subdued, and colonised the whole district. The whole process may have been carried out very slowly, lasting through thousands of years; in many cases, peoples may have helped to spread the Bantu languages who had themselves received it from others, and in this way the tongues may have been passed from race to race in the most varied way. From this point of view the linguistic uniformity of Central Africa may be considered as the result of opposition to those seething movements of the outer world which, for a very long period, form the history of Africa, and are a consequence of that lack of obstacles to communication within the interior which is characteristic of the continent. HEINRICH SCHURTZ

EGYPT

AT THE DAWN OF HISTORY

BY H. R. HALL, M.A.

THE archæological excavations of the last ten years in Egypt have given us a totally new idea of the beginnings of Egyptian history. Ten years ago, the name of Sneferu, the last king of the third dynasty, stood alone, a solitary figure on the threshold of Egyptian history. The admirable history of Heinrich Brugsch-Pasha, "Egypt under the Pharaohs," which was for all the text-book of the annals of Ancient Egypt, could tell us of no real historical fact, of no real historical personage, before Sneferu. Carved on the rocks of Sinai, his figure stood, striking down the barbarian Menti, a warrior-king of old, with the possible exceptions of Sargon and Naram-Sin in Babylonia, the oldest historical person known to us. Mena, the founder of the Egyptian monarchy, there was indeed, but he was a purely legendary figure. Tjeser Khet-neter and Send of the third dynasty were known to us, the one as the possible builder of the Step pyramid at Sakkara (*vice* Ata, of the first dynasty, whose claims

Egyptology Ten Years Ago were always most shadowy), the other from the later slab from the tomb of his priest Sheri, which was brought to England by the Aleppo merchant Tradescant in the seventeenth century, and placed in the Ashmolean Museum, of which it still forms one of the oldest possessions. But of none of these three was anything beyond legend known : Sneferu and his contemporaries, Nefermaat, Rahetep and Nefert, whose beautiful statues are perhaps the most valuable possessions of the Cairo Museum, and others, were the most ancient Egyptians whom we knew. Yet a mere glance at the artistic works of Sneferu's time sufficed to show that Egyptian art did not begin with them. It could not be supposed that Egyptian sculpture sprang,

What We Did Not Know perfected, out of nothing, like Pallas, "all armed," from the brain of Zeus ; there must have been a long history of development before these fine works of the Pyramid builders came into being. And the Pyramids themselves, these monstrous stone barrows of perfect mathematical accuracy of form, could hardly be the conceptions of architects who lived a bare half century after Sneferu. Yet of this earlier history of culture-development we knew nothing.

All this is now changed. The excavator, trained and made ready by a decade of work in other and less important fields, turned in the fullness of time to sites which, if hidden records remained, would, it was felt, reveal to us the most ancient age of Egypt. And the brains and money which enabled the work to be done were almost exclusively British and American. The French alone can share the credit of the achievement with us. It was the work of the Anglo-American "Egypt Exploration Fund," directed by Petrie, Mace and Maciver at Abydos and al-'Amra, of the exclusively British "Egyptian Research Account" under Petrie and

Quibell at Koptos, Nagada, Tûkh, and Hierakonpolis; and of the Frenchmen De Morgan and Amélineau at Abydos and in many other ancient necropoles of the earliest period throughout Egypt, that gave us our new knowledge of Archaic Egypt. And recently the American expedition of the University of California, directed by Dr. Reisner, has **British and American Excavation** added new facts to our knowledge. To summarise this new knowledge as succinctly as possible will be the object of this section.

The best general summary of the results of the new excavations that has hitherto appeared is that contained in the first volume of Dr. E. A. Wallis Budge's "History of Egypt," published in 1902. Of course, "much water has flowed under the bridges" since 1902, but nevertheless, if we leave out the inevitable modifications that five years' more work and consideration have rendered necessary, Dr. Budge's description still remains the handiest that we possess of the archaic civilisation of Egypt.

The fact that so good a general description of the new discoveries could be written five years ago shows how swiftly these discoveries were made. One followed immediately upon the other; each season's work provided a mass of new material. In fact, the years 1897–1902 were epoch-making for Egyptologists. Perhaps the new discoveries may really be said to have begun somewhat earlier, with Professor Petrie's work at Koptos in 1894.

Of the French investigators the work of M. Amélineau at Abydos is different in kind from that of the others. His was a private venture, and from circumstances over which, we can well understand, he had little control, the scientific results from Abydos were of small value till Professor Petrie took over the site, and began his yearly publication, under the auspices of the Egypt Exploration Fund, **Oldest Kings of Egypt** of the series of volumes which gave us our first connected idea of the earliest Egyptian dynasties. Previously to Petrie's work at Abydos, that of Mr. Quibell at Hierakonpolis had given us our first conception of the peculiarities of archaic Egyptian art, and our first names of the oldest kings of Upper Egypt. At Abydos Professor Petrie found many more monuments of these and other new kings, and for the first time marshalled the facts in order.

It must be understood that the newly discovered antiquities fall into two main classes: those of the primitive Neolithic Period, and those of the Archaic Period, properly so called, the age of the beginnings of the Egyptian monarchy, from the first to the third dynasties inclusive. Apart from these, we have also the newly identified relics of the Palæolithic Age in Egypt, centuries before the Neolithic Age. Its relics are the worn flint implements which are found upon the surface of the desert plateaus on both sides of the Nile. With the users of these Palæolithic implements, the most ancient human inhabitants of the Nile Valley, our survey begins.

These primitive people were in point of culture contemporaneous with the European man of the Quaternary Period; but whether they were not really later in point of date is not yet settled. The climate of Egypt in their time did not differ radically from that now obtaining in the Nile Valley. The dryness of the atmosphere, due to the existence of the high deserts on each side which is **The Primitive People** nowadays so characteristic of Egypt, and ensures an almost perpetual summer in that favoured land, cannot have been much less in Palæolithic days than it is now. We have to dismiss from our minds all ideas of a heavy rainfall, with watercourses descending to the Nile from forests crossing the mountains and desert, where now not a blade of vegetation is to be seen. We can suppose only that the rainfall was rather heavier than it is now, so that the desert-torrents, which now once in two or three years after rain descend through the stony wadis to the cultivated land, were then far more frequent. That these wadis were originally carved out by the action of torrents is undoubted—they present all the characteristics of dry watercourses.

Then there was, of course, no cultivated land. The valley of the Nile was a marsh. The inhabitants lived on the desert slopes and on the plateaus. On these are now found the relics of their presence in the shape of their flint implements, lying just as they were left thousands of years ago by the Palæolithic flint-knappers who went up on to the desert to make their weapons out of the countless pebbles of flint and chert which cover the surface of the ground. Regular factories of these flints have been found just as they were left, with spoilt fragments, broken as well as perfect weapons, lying around. The flints are of the well-known European types of St. Acheul, Chelles, and Le Moustier. Considerable attention has been devoted to these implements of recent years, and though their Palæolithic character was at first doubted, there is no doubt now that they are the African fellows of the flint implements found in the gravel deposits of England, France and Belgium [see page 238]. Other traces of Palæolithic Man in Egypt there are none.

Ages passed away before the primitive Egyptians gradually passed, like the rest of the world, from the older to the newer age of stone. When we reach the Neolithic Period we see an enormous advance in civilisation. The flint weapons of the Neolithic Egyptians are probably the finest known. None hitherto found in Europe or America can compare with them in accuracy and beauty of finish. They mark the apogee of the art of flint-knapping. Naturally, they must be placed late in the history of the Stone Age in **Beauty of Egyptian Flints** Egypt. For at the time they were made the Egyptians were already preparing to pass into the age of metal, and in the succeeding " Archaic " Period, properly so-called, we find them in the " Chalcolithic " era of human progress, when copper and stone are used indifferently and side by side. Copper is already found sporadically in the later graves of the Neolithic people.

For it must be remembered that our knowledge of the Neolithic Egyptians is derived almost exclusively from their graves. The last resting-places of the Palæolithic people are naturally utterly unknown to us ; perhaps they ate one another, but we know nothing of how they disposed of their dead. It is otherwise with their Neolithic successors. They were buried, usually in the cramped position characteristic of primitive nations, in shallow, oval graves packed closely together, on the lowest desert slopes near the cultivated land. Sometimes they were placed in pots, sometimes they were covered merely with a reed mat. Ready to the hand of the dead man were his flint weapons and tools, his pottery to contain the funeral meats with which the love or fear of the living had provided for his sustenance. With the body were

also buried articles of personal adornment, such as combs, or slate palettes on which to grind face paint. Small dolls or figures of men and women are also found.

From this sketch of the objects found in these graves it will be seen that the Neolithic Egyptians had progressed far **Beginnings of Egyptian Civilisation** beyond the civilisation of Rudyard Kipling's " Ug," in which their Palæolithic predecessors had lived. They were no longer naked savages killing each other and their fellow-beasts, the lions and jackals, with rudely-fashioned lumps of stone. In fact, with them Egyptian civilisation has begun. We have spoken of the excellence of their flint weapons. Not less excellent was their pottery. Made without the aid of the wheel, which was not yet invented, it yet attained a perfection of form which makes the fact that they were built up solely by the hand of the potter almost incredible.

The commonest type of this pottery is a red polished ware with black top, due to its having been baked mouth downwards in a fire, the ashes of which deoxidised the hæmatite burnishing, and so changed the red colour to black. Later in date are red and black wares with rude geometrical incised designs, filled in with white [see page 235]. Later again is a buff ware, either plain or decorated with deep red wavy lines, concentric circles, and elaborate drawings of boats sailing on the Nile, human beings, ostriches, and so forth. With this ware the prehistoric pottery reached its apogee ; thenceforward it degenerated throughout the Archaic Period till, in the time of the fourth dynasty, fine wheel-made pottery of a deep red colour came into use. So enormous have been the finds of prehistoric pottery of late years that these ancient crocks are to be seen in nearly every museum. The dividing line between **Where History Begins** the Neolithic and Archaic Periods is not by any means clear. Roughly we might place it where history begins, with the unification of the whole country under the earliest kings of the first dynasty. Yet this point of division does not coincide with the real division between the two stages of culture. Perhaps it makes rather the central point of the Archaic Period, when the growth of civilisation had progressed so far that a unified " culture-state." could be founded, rather than the division between the older and the more developed civilisation. We can see that the older culture was very different in many ways from the later. Archaic Egypt is, in spite of its archaic character, the Pharaonic Egypt which we know, with king, nobles, and commoners, officials and **Egypt's** artists, priests and scribes, just **Archaic** as we have them in the days **State** of Thothmes and Rameses. Neolithic Egypt has none of these; its people were more like North American Indians than anything else; they were simple hunters and primitive cultivators, and much of the remains of their culture would not necessarily be put down at first sight as Egyptian at all. Yet in them we see the germs of the later Egyptian state. Writing was not known to them, yet individual signs which afterwards became Egyptian hieroglyphs, were; we have one—the oldest hieroglyph known—the symbol of the god Min upon a slate "palette" from al-'Amra.

The use of metal weapons was not known to them till near the approach of the Archaic Period. But we cannot say when they actually passed from the pure Neolithic to the Chalcolithic period of culture any more than when they first began to write in the true sense of the word. The whole elaborate structure of the later Egyptian religion was unknown to them, yet we can see that many of the gods of the later Egyptians had been gods in Neolithic Egypt also—above all, the animal objects of popular worship, the beasts and birds who were afterwards identified with higher deities or became their "sacred animals." We can see that these were the tokens of different Nilotic tribes in Neolithic times, and they are so represented on the early pottery. Yet we cannot say when the Egyptian state-religion, as such, first took the form and shape which we find it **Origin of** has assumed in the Archaic **Egypt's Religion** Period, and which it ever **Unknown** afterwards preserved. In fact, we cannot draw any hard and fast line of division between the two stages of culture. As we examine their relics, we find the primitive culture developing and merging imperceptibly into the Archaic civilisation before the unification of the kingdoms. At al-'Amra, more particularly, we can trace this development best as regards burial customs,

from the simplest pot-burial to small brick chambers, between which and the brick royal tombs of the first dynasty there is but a step. Dr. Reisner's discoveries at Nag 'ed-Dêr, opposite Gîrga, have notably supplemented Maciver's results at al-'Amra.

We can, then, see that the stone-using Egyptians gradually increased in civilisation until their various tribes combined to form larger entities, which eventually coalesced into two chief states—Northern and Southern Egypt—which had capital towns, Buto in the north and Nekhen, the Hierakonpolis of the Greeks, in the south. Of these two, the southern kingdom was the more purely Egyptian. As we shall see in the next chapter, the Delta was probably never so truly Egyptian, nor is it now, as the Sa'îd, or Upper Country. Mediterranean tribes akin probably to the Cretans lived on the shores of the Delta. The Egyptians called them the "Hau of the marshes," the signs of which name, reading Hauhenu, were in later times misread as Ha-nebu, which could be translated as "Lords of the North" or "All **Nile Delta** the Northerners," and early **Not** appears, using another word for **Egyptian** "North," as Meht-nebu. This process may be rather obscure to those who are not familiar with the possibilities of an ideographic mode of writing, but the meaning would be perfectly clear at once to a Chinaman or Japanese. Afterwards this name, Ha-nebu, pronounced something like "Huenim" in later Egyptian, became the regular late-Egyptian word for "Greeks," Oueeienin. The Hau of the marshes were abominated by the developed Egyptian religion, and none of the magical charms of the "Book of the Dead," by the help of which a man, when dead, could force his way past all the unknown dangers of the other world to the fields of the blessed, might be communicated by a pious Egyptian to one of the outcast Hau. Yet ethnology and archæology both combine to tell us that the sea-people of the Egyptian coast, and even their congeners over the sea in Crete, were in all probability not racially very different from the Egyptians.

The many resemblances between the early Ægean civilisation and that of Egypt may prove ultimately to be due far more to a common African origin of the two cultures than to the mutual influence which was exercised in later times by the one over the other. More than this we can hardly say at present.

Other elements which must have modified the Deltaic Egyptians from the earliest times are the Libyan on the west and the Semite on the east. No doubt the Libyans were closely connected with the Nilotes, and so with the Mediterraneans; and in Palestine, where at that time the Semites had probably not yet settled, there no doubt existed a primitive population of Mediterranean origin. In the eastern desert, however, in Sinai, and perhaps also in the Wadi Tumilat, the land of Goshen, true Semites already lived.

Their culture, such as it was, was distinct from that of Nilote or Libyan. Behind them, in the far Mesopotamian basin, lived the peculiar people of the Sumerians, un-Semitic in blood and speech, to whom the Semites owed all that they ever possessed then of culture. It can hardly be doubted, as we shall see later, that this Sumerian culture exercised through the Semites considerable influence over that of the Northern Egyptian kingdom. The original knowledge of the cultivation of cereals may well have come to

Culture from Mesopotamia

Egypt from Mesopotamia, and it is almost certain that brick architecture was directly transmitted to the Egyptians from the Sumerians. Other points of resemblance between the Archaic Egyptian culture and the Sumerian may be noted, such as the common use of the stone cylinder seal and the peculiarly shaped macehead. And, finally, it is probable that the Egyptian script first developed out of a primitive picture-writing under the influence of the Sumerian ideographic system, which afterwards became what we know as " cuneiform." For the Egyptian language, as we find it first developed under the fourth dynasty, has in it a distinctly Semitic element. And long before this, in all probability, Semites had adopted the Sumerian signs for their own use. That the Semites who introduced elements of their tongue into the Nile valley also brought with them perhaps some of the earliest combinations of the Sumerian picture-signs, is by no means improbable.

Yet this Sumerian-Semitic culture-influence must have been very ancient, for the Semitic element in Egyptian might perhaps be more fairly described as " proto-Semitic," and the languages of the Libyans, the Berbers, and the Imosh-

agh, or Tawarek, had and have just as much of this " proto-Semitic " element—to be distinguished from modern corruptions of Arabic—in them as had Egyptian. Are we to assume a very early wave of proto-Semitic conquest of the Delta, passing on to the Libyans beyond ? The theory that Semites did come into Egypt

Likelihood of Semitic Invasion

by the Wadi Tumilat at a very early period has many arguments in its favour; among others, the existence at the Egyptian end of that valley of the sun-sanctuary of On, or Heliopolis. Of sun-worship, which afterwards was so characteristic of the Egyptian religion, we have as yet found no trace among the Neolithic Egyptians, the Nilotes of " Mediterranean " race, whose stone weapons and pottery we have described. Yet it was characteristic of Sumerian-Semitic religion. And in this latter we find no trace of the equally typical Egyptian veneration of birds and beasts, which we have seen was certainly practised by the primitive Nilotes. We believe, then, that sun-worship was introduced into Egypt and grafted on to the ancient animal worship by these invading proto-Semites.

There was in Archaic Egypt, as distinct from Neolithic Egypt, also another sun-god, of southern, however, not of northern origin. He is Horus of Edfu, as distinct from Ra of On. Afterwards the two were combined as Ra Harmachis. It might be supposed that because this sun-god came from the south, therefore he is an indigenous Nilotic deity. This is, however, by no means the case. Of him it was always told in legend that he was a conqueror, and that he advanced down the Nile valley to overthrow the ass-headed god of the north, Set, whom he defeated in a great battle near Dendera. He was accompanied by followers called Mesniu, or Smiths, who were armed with metal weapons. This certainly looks as

The Primeval Tragedy

if we had here a tradition of a foreign race of conquerors, whose metal weapons gained them the victory over the indigenous people of the valley. It is that old story in the dawn of the world's history, the utter overthrow and subjection of the stone-users by the metal-users, the primeval tragedy of the supersession of flint by copper and bronze. That these invaders from the south were Semitic sun-worshippers is very probable. If so, we may see in them a southern Semitic wave from Arabia, which crossed into Africa by the Straits of Bab el-Mandeb, and reached the Nile valley either by way of the Blue Nile or up the coast and thence westwards by the broad Wadi Hamamat. It is curious that at Koptos, almost opposite Dendera, where the legendary

Deity of the Primitive Peoples battle between the Mesniu and the aborigines took place, at the Nile end of the Wadi Hamamat, Professor Petrie discovered some of the most ancient relics of Egyptian civilisation. Among them were statues of the god Min, on which are incised rude sculptures of animals and crioceras shells, which belong to the Red Sea. It may be that these are relics of the invaders. But the god Min seems to belong to the primitive inhabitants rather than to them. However this question may be solved, it may well be that by Horus and his Smiths we are to understand a second Semitic conquest, distinct from the northern Semitic wave which entered by way of the Wadi Tumilat.

In the south, then, we have also Semitic influence, though less marked than in the north. It is possible that to this influence in the south and north is due the development which ended in the rise of the two kingdoms of Hierakonpolis and Buto. Of the pre-dynastic kings of the south and north we know nothing. By chance we have as a monument of the fifth dynasty the " Stele of Palermo " [see page 249], a list of some of the northern kings, whose names are simple and primitive in form—Seka, Desiu, Tiu, Tesh, Nihab, Uatj'antj, Mekha. But we possess no contemporary relics of them or of any of the southern kings before the latter began the wars of conquest which ended in the subjugation of the north and the confiscation of the kingdom. Then, at the beginning of the first dynasty, we first have contem-

The First Dynasties porary monuments. The excavations at Hierakonpolis and Abydos have yielded to us the monuments of the kings whose names appear in altered forms in the later lists as the Pharaohs of the first two dynasties.

The information which, before the new discoveries, we possessed with regard to the Egyptian kings who preceded Sneferu was of a very jejune character. It was derived solely from the lists of their predecessors which the kings of the nineteenth dynasty set up at Abydos, supplemented by another list of the same kind in a private tomb at Sakkara, side by side with the lists handed down to us by the Ptolemaic annalist Manetho. Now we have the actual contemporary monuments of many of these kings, and can see how far we have been rightly guided by the later list-makers.

The royal lists of Abydos were no doubt put up there because it was known that the tombs of the earliest kings were there. We use the word " tombs " here, but, as a matter of fact, it is more probable that these were not all the actual tombs of the kings of the first dynasty. One, Aha, was, we know, really buried elsewhere, at Nagada. But it was often the custom of Egyptian kings to have cenotaphs put up in their memory at Abydos, where every pious Egyptian desired to be commemorated.

The names of the following primeval kings have been found at Hierakonpolis and Abydos. Apart from words such as Ro, Sma, and Ka, which have been

The Primeval Kings supposed by Professor Petrie to be those of kings who lived before the first dynasty, and are therefore assigned by him to a " Dynasty O," but are by no means certainly royal names at all, the list is as follows. The hawk, or Horus name, borne on a banner called the srekh, or cognisance, comes first :

1. Horus Aha (King Men ?).
2. Horus Narmer, or Betjumer.
3. Horus Tjer (afterwards misread Khent).
4. Horus Tja, King Ati.
5. Horus Den (or Udimu ?), King Semti.
6. Horus Atjab, King Merpeba.
7. Horus Semerkha, King Nekht.
8. Horus Qa, King Sen.
9. Horus Khasekhem, or Khasekhemui (King Besh ?).
10. Horus Hetepsekhemui.
11. Horus Raneb.
12. Horus Neneter (or Netrimu ?).
13. Horus Sekhemab, Set Perabsen.

It will be noticed that the last king has a Set name, appropriate to him as king of Lower Egypt, as well as the Horus name as king of Upper Egypt. When the king-name is not given, it is unknown. The queried names are all doubtful. Netrimu and Udimu are given merely because they are forms that have been proposed by German scholars, but they are not very convincing. Besh, as the name of King Khasekhem, is usually accepted ; but it is more probable that Professor Naville's disbelief in it is justified, and that it refers really to the land of Bi—that is, Lower Egypt. The name of the king of Lower Egypt was " biti " ; that of the king of Upper Egypt was " suten," which afterwards became the ordinary word for king, a curious sign of the position of Upper Egypt as the conqueror. Mr. F. Legge has lately shown that the name " Men," which has been supposed to have been read on tablets of Aha, is more doubtful than ever, and no definite identification of Aha with the legendary Menes can be founded on it.

It will be noticed that the above list does not entirely agree with those published by Professor Petrie. This is because it is not based upon Professor Petrie's own writings only, but also on those of the other Egyptologists who have discussed these questions and have criticised his conclusions. For instance, Professor Petrie's king " Merneit " does not appear in it, because there is no positive proof that the name is that of a king. Narmer, too, is assigned to the first dynasty, because, unless this is done, there are too many names for the first dynasty as it stands in the later lists, on the assumption, accepted by Professor Petrie, that Aha is Menes. The certain identification of these contemporary names with those of kings for the first two dynasties given in the lists are these :

A PRIMITIVE GOD
Min was a god of the primitive Egyptians, and his symbol is the oldest hieroglyph

5. Den Semti = Hesepti, Manetho's Ousaphais.
6. Atjab Merpeba = Merbap, Miebis.
7. Semerkha Nekht = Shemsu or Semsem, Semempses.
8. Qa Sen = Qebh, Bienekhes.
9. Khasekhemui = Betjumer (?), Boethos.
12. Neneter = Bineneter, Binothris.

Of these names Professor Sethe was the first authority to point out the chief identifications, those of the names of Semti and Merpeba with Hesepti and Merbap.

Hesepti, then, is the earliest historical king in the lists. Professor Petrie, however, taking Aha to be Menes, goes on to identify Tja Ati with Ateth, which may eventually prove to be correct, Merneit with Ata and Tjer with Teta. The two last are arbitrary identifications, and we have not recognised Merneit as a king at all.

It is very probable that the names Teta, Ateth, and Ata, which are given in the nineteenth dynasty lists as those of the immediate successors of Menes, are really all later inventions, founded on Ati, the personal name of Tja. Tja had become triplicated in legend, while Tjer and Narmer had disappeared from it, for the authorities used by the nineteenth dynasty list-makers must have been largely legendary : Menes was to them much what King Arthur is to us. Perhaps, however, Betjumer Narmer, the powerful king who has left so many relics of his presence at Hierakonpolis, had not disappeared from legend altogether, but was in it rather combined with his predecessors (?) Aha, " the fighter," to form the heroic figure of Mena, or Menes, the traditional founder of the monarchy ; while in the lists his name has got out of place, having been set in the form Betjumer—which is quite possibly more correct than Narmer—at the beginning of the second dynasty, and read by Manetho as Boethos. Professor Naville holds the view that this is his proper place, and that with Khasekhemui, whose monuments were found with his at Hierakonpolis, he should be put at the head of the second dynasty—if, indeed, Khasekhemui, the conqueror of the North, does not rather belong to the first.

But there is no doubt that Narmer's monuments [see pages 247-248] are among the most archaic of those of the earliest kings. Judged by the criterion of style, they are certainly almost contemporary with those of Aha, and antedate those of Tja and Tjer. And Khasekhemui's, judged by the same criterion, are certainly later than those of all the kings of the first dynasty. Therefore we may retain Khasekhemui at the head of the second dynasty, and suppose that because Narmer was also a conqueror of the North, his name was misplaced in the royal lists, as we have shown it in our list above. His contemporaneity with Aha, and the position of both before Tja and Tjer being practically certain, we hold that Professor Petrie is justified in putting him, with Aha, at the beginning of the whole list. But, not recognising Aha as the sole original of Menes, and seeing no reason why we should strive, with Professor Petrie, to place the kings of the first dynasty upon a Procrustes' bed, and lop Narmer off, because, if Aha is above Menes, he does not fit in with the lists of the nineteenth dynasty and of Manetho (in which we believe the names of the first four kings before Hesepti-Ousaphais were purely traditional), we can well conclude that Aha, the great king, who was buried at Nagada, and Narmer, who reigned at Hierakonpolis and conquered the North, were the joint originals of Mena or Menes. The "Scorpion" king, also found at Hierakonpolis, is, on account of the absolute identity of his monuments in style with those of Narmer, to be regarded as identical with him.

Who Were the First Kings?

Archæology has, therefore, discovered the real kings of the beginning of the first dynasty, who were known to the later Egyptians only in legend. It is as if we were to discover the real originals of Agamemnon or Theseus—which, indeed, we may do yet—in Greece on Mycenæan monuments. The earliest king of whom the later Egyptians had real historical knowledge would seem to have been Semti, whose name was misread by them as Hesepti, which form was copied by Manetho as Ousaphais. It is at least significant in this regard that the private list at Sakkara places not the legendary Menes but the successor of Semti (Merpeba), as the first king of Egypt. We may then regard Semti and Merpeba as the first kings who were really known to the later Egyptians. Their successor, Semerkha, is the first of whom a contemporary monument has been discovered apart from the actual royal "graves" at Abydos: this is his stele, or tablet, in the Wadi Maghara, in the Sinaitic peninsula. With these three monarchs, therefore, Egyptian "history," as apart from either legend or archæological probability, may be said to begin. What history there is to be told of this early time may be seen from the

Earliest Known Kings

succeeding chapters, in which the traditions of the later Egyptians are combined with what we know from the contemporary monuments. Here it may be said that it is firstly a record of the conquest of the North by the kings of the South, which was not finally consummated till the reign of Khasekhem, literally, "Power appears," who, however, after the final conquest apparently, changed his name to Khasekhemui, "Two Powers appear," the powers of North and South, not of the South alone. On the commemorative maceheads and state shields (so-called "palettes") of this time, which were dedicated in the temples, we have records of these conquests. On small tablets deposited in the royal cenotaphs at Abydos we have records of the foundation of temples and other buildings, notably one found by Petrie at Abydos, and now in the British Museum, which commemorates the establishment by Den of a temple of himself at Osiris, on the occasion of his Sed festival—the festival "of the end," at which he, like many other Egyptian kings, was deified before his death. On the Palermo stele, already mentioned, we find records of the years of several of the kings of the second dynasty, in which little but the building of palaces or the celebration of festivals is chronicled.

Egypt's Unchanging Civilisation

The story, so far as it is known to us, of the expansion of Egypt at this time, of the occupation of Sinai, and of wars with the Libyans, of the greatness of kings like Tjeser of the third dynasty, the first pyramid-builder, and so forth, will be found in the next chapter.

Here we are concerned chiefly with the general aspect of the oldest civilisation of Egypt, which, though the same as that hitherto known to us, is yet different, inasmuch as it is that civilisation in its infancy, in the making, swiftly developing, till in the times of the fifth dynasty it was stereotyped, so that there is less difference between the Egyptian religion and royalty of the days of Nectanebus (350 B.C.) and Ne-ueser-Ra (3000 B.C.) than between those of Ne-ueser-Ra's day and of Narmer's (4000 or 3500 B.C.). Minor art might change, fashions of dress alter, language decay and be re-cast, but religion and royalty, and the common people, the fellahin, remained the same, like the unchanging Nile valley itself.

It was in the space of but a few centuries that Egyptian civilisation swiftly developed till it came to a stop. With art and handicraft developed political and religious ideas, and when a stable state had been firmly erected, and the goal of progress seemed reached, political and religious cohesion imposed stability, and therewith fossilisation on art, and, to some extent, on thought also. The machine ceased to move of itself, and the only motive power which afterwards ever sent it further along was applied from without by Hyksos or Assyrian or Greek or Arab conquest, or, in modern days, British conquest too. It may, indeed, be argued with some probability that even the initial impulse to the original development of ancient Egyptian civilisation was given, also from without, by the invasions of Semites, which, as we have seen, probably took place before the rise of the kingdoms of Buto and Hierakonpolis, and transformed the Neolithic people of the Negada graves into the archaic Egyptians.

However this may be, the archaic culture certainly seems to owe something to the Sumerian civilisation of Babylonia. The use of the cylinder-seal, the shape of the maceheads, the invention of brick—the original Egyptian building material being wattle and daub—the peculiar crenellated brick architecture which at Abydos and at Nagada, in early tombs as in fortresses, is exactly the same as that of the walls of Gudea's palace at Tello in Babylonia, the introduction of burial at full length even, in place of the older crouched position—all these point to early Babylonian influence. How far the Sumerian script influenced the development of Egyptian writing we do not know ; little real connection between the two sets of picture-signs can be traced even in their beginnings. Their later development was quite other in the two states. This was due to the use of clay tablets in Babylonia on which the signs were impressed with a stilus, while the Egyptians preferred to write with ink on papyrus, pottery, or wood. We find ink used to write even on stone under the first dynasty, so it was invented then. The Babylonians never used it, though the Egyptians sometimes used the stilus on soft bricks. The Cretans wrote both with ink in Egyptian fashion on pottery, and, more usually, with the stilus on clay in Babylonian fashion. Thus, though it is said that the oldest Sumerian name for the god Marduk was Asari, and was written by means of a group of two ideographs which are very like the Egyptian ideographs of the name of the god Asari or Osiris (between whom and Marduk there is little in common, by the way : Osiris would seem to be a primitive Nilotic rather than an imported Sumerian-Semitic deity, and the sun-gods and the goddesses Hathor, Sekhmet, and Bast seem to be the most Semitic of the original Egyptian deities), we cannot say that the connection between the Egyptian and Babylonian picture-writings is yet proved. The original Egyptian pictures were, as we have seen, probably of indigenous Nilotic origin.

Egypt's Debts to Babylon

Hieroglyph and Cuneiform

It is in the development of the writing during the Archaic Period that the great advance of Egyptian civilisation at this period can be recognised even more clearly than in the development of art. In both cases the swiftest development took place at the beginning, under the first dynasty. If the century and a half, or, at most, two centuries of this period saw the advance of art from the crude and clumsy style of Narmer and Aha to the developed, though still archaic style of Khasekhemui, between whose and Ne-ueser-Ra's art in the fifth dynasty there is less difference than between Khasekhemui's and Narmer's, they also saw a far greater advance, the development of the Egyptian script from a mere painful stringing together of rude pictures, analogous to those of the Bushmen or Red Indians, to a writing which could express thought with more or less clearness.

When we reach Sneferu's time we find the complicated hieroglyphic system, with its array of alphabeto-syllabic and syllabic signs—designed to express sound though not necessarily meaning also—as well as of determinative signs, practically developed to the full. The scribes of the Ramessides could easily have read Sneferu's or Tjeser's inscriptions, Khasekhemui's even, without extraordinary difficulty, but those of Den, still more those of Narmer, would have given them almost as much trouble to decipher as they do us. As the development progressed, unsuitable signs were dropped, so that in these archaic inscriptions we often meet with hieroglyphs, the meaning of which

Hieroglyph System Developed

is unknown to us. The Egyptian scribe was inventing his script, and he often abandoned his inventions if they were found to be unserviceable, and invented others in their place.

So did the artist and architect. Brick was introduced, but it was not long before stone, which lay to hand so near in the mountains on either side of the valley, was pressed into service also. We find it first used in the middle of the first dynasty. Buildings increased in size ; the royal tombs became labyrinths of chambers very different from the oval graves of the Neolithic people, and under the third dynasty a great stone pyramid, the first of its kind, was erected over a king's tomb instead of a brick mound. Soon followed the wonders of the world, the pyramids of Gizeh, those mightiest monuments ever erected by the pride and power of man. The mathematical accuracy with which the architects and engineers of Sneferu, Khufu, and Khafra did their work is the best testimony to the mental advance which five centuries had seen. A Bushman or a Red Indian had developed into a designer of Forth Bridges and Eiffel Towers.

The World's Wonders

It was an age of swift change and thrust upward and forward ; an age, too, of cheerful savage energy, like most times when kingdoms and peoples are in the making. When Khasekhemui finally conquered the North, he slew 47,209 "northern enemies." The attitudes of the slain northerners were so greatly admired and sketched by the artists of the time that some of the most picturesque were reproduced on the pedestal of the king's statue, found at Hierakonpolis by M. Quibell, which is now at Oxford. And on the earlier reliefs of Narmer we see the king, accompanied by his page bearing his sandals and a vase like a teapot, containing his favourite drink [see page 248], going out in comfort to inspect the bodies of his enemies, which were tastefully laid out in rows, with their heads severed and their toes artistically turned in, whether to make them look ridiculous or not we cannot tell.

An Age of Savage Energy

From monuments such as these we learn a good deal of the position of the king and of the general state of the Egyptian polity at the beginning of history. We have said that at the time of the fifth dynasty the Egyptian monarchy and religion crystallised, and altered but little thereafter. This statement is, of course, to be taken in a general sense, especially as regards the monarchy. The polity of the fifth dynasty was an absolute monarchy, or, rather, theocracy, in which a god ruled over his court nobles and his slaves, the common people. Under the twelfth dynasty we see a king, always by courtesy called a god, controlling from his palace a number of feudal nobles to whom the people actually owed allegiance ; under the eighteenth dynasty a king, one among other kings, of Babylonia or elsewhere, at the head of a bureaucratic state of very modern type. Yet the general proposition is true : in the eyes of priesthood and people the king was always what he had been, his titles never varied from age to age, all ceremonies connected with him, religious or civil, were conducted just as they had been conducted in the time of the pyramid builders, and, as far as artistic representations are concerned, there is little or no difference between Nectanebus and Ne-ueser-Ra. And, as is natural, there is also not much difference between Ne-ueser-Ra and Narmer. The princes of Hierakonpolis, the sutens of Upper Egypt, were living sun-gods, " Horuses," with their subordinate chiefs around them ; they wore high straw hats covered with white cloth and trailed cow's tails behind them to distinguish them from the vulgar, and were naïvely represented in art as being twice as large as ordinary mortals. This was quite natural in the primitive period, and since the power of the king was already absolutely autocratic, as he was the lord of all, who were his slaves and worshipped him as a god at the beginning of the first dynasty, there was no room for further development of his power, and but for the invention of new titles, such as " Son of the Sun," there is no alteration in the position or description of the king during the Archaic Period. And when his position really altered, after the nobles had learnt that successful rebellion was possible, and they might themselves by that means come to sit on Pharaoh's throne, the description had long before been fixed and remained so for ever, so that the Roman emperor Decius still wears Narmer's high cap and cow's tail on the walls of the temple of Esne.

Deification of the Kings

H. R. HALL

ANCIENT EGYPT

THE LAND OF THE PHARAOHS
BY CARL NIEBUHR AND H. R. HALL, M.A.
TO THE TIME OF THE PYRAMID-BUILDERS

IN "geologic" times the habitable Egypt of to-day formed a long, narrow gulf extending from the Mediterranean to the first cataract. In the course of ages the gulf was filled up by the heavy deposits of silt which the Nile still continues to bring down, every year increasing its delta. The rainfall is of small amount, and but for the regular flooding of the Nile valley every year a country now arable would be at the most a region of arid steppes.

At Assouan—the Suenu of ancient Egypt and the Greek Syene—the Nile leaves Nubia and begins its lower course, first breaking through a granite barrier which has thrust itself between the ridges of red sandstone that extend along the sides of the valley to this point. The fragments of rock in the river bed, large enough at this point to form **The Nile's Cataracts** islands, render the navigation of this first cataract extremely difficult. At a distance of 38 miles below Assouan, at Gebel Silsila, the sandstone formation draws nearer to the course of the Nile, narrowing the river bed to the breadth of 300 yards. When this gorge has been passed, the fall of the river is very gradual, from Assouan to Cairo barely 300 feet, and thence to the coast 32 feet, so that the river is free to extend as it will. The mountain chains to the right and left retreat further and further

from the stream, and at Esne change to a Tertiary limestone formation. At Luxor, the site of ancient Thebes, the arable land of the valley is over five miles in breadth. A short distance further on begins the system of irrigation canals. Here, in the district of Abydos, the arable land is eleven miles in breadth, nine on the west bank, and two on the eastern. This general breadth of the cultivated land is preserved **The Narrow Land of the Nile** till Cairo is reached, broader now on one bank, now on the other, as the cliff-border of the desert now approaches, now recedes from the river, on one side or other. The eastern mountain chain preserves its precipitous character until it joins near Cairo the Mokattam range, which there takes a turn to the west. The rolling hills on the western side permit the passage of the so-called Joseph's Canal, or Bahr Yusuf, the most ancient of all the irrigation streams of any size, which branches off from the river in lat. 27° 5' N., and after flowing parallel to the Nile for a distance of over 450 miles, passes the line of hills and creates the habitable district of Fayyum. In early times this western dependency of Egypt was watered by a great stagnant lake, the "lake Moeris" of the Greeks; in modern times the canal now flows further to the west, into the brackish "lake of horns"—Birket el-Kerun, 130 feet below the sea-level—although its water still continues to fertilise a considerable portion of the Fayyum.

Some twelve miles below Cairo the Nile, which there attains a breadth of over 300 feet, divides into the two branches by which it now reaches the sea—the Rosetta Nile and the Damietta **The Nile Delta** Nile. Here the Delta begins. In remote antiquity this district consisted almost entirely of marsh land; but very early in Egyptian history the work of reclaiming the marshes was begun, and by the fourteenth century B.C. the cultivated land of the Delta was probably as great in extent as it is now. At the present day it has an area of 13,500 square miles, and a coast line of 180 miles in length, and is intersected by a network of streams with a total length of 8,400 miles. The regulation of the Nile floods, a difficult task in this low-lying region, was in modern times first attempted in the nineteenth century by the construction of the barrage, a great dam at the southern extremity of the Delta. Of the seven chief mouths as known to classical antiquity by which the Nile flows into the Mediterranean, the Bolbitine corresponds with the Rosetta Nile; the western arm, the Canopic, was replaced in 1820 by the Mahmudiyah Canal, which flows into the lagoon near Alexandria. To the east of the Bolbitine Nile followed in order the Sebennytic, the Phatnitic, or Damietta, the Mendesian, the Tanitic, and the Pelusian. The Mendesian and Tanitic branches are now represented by canals which enter Lake Manzaleh from the south. The Pelusian branch, which originally reached the sea considerably to the eastward of the modern Port Said and the Suez Canal, has entirely disappeared.

The land which is fertilised by all these channels from Assouan to the borders of the Delta has an area in round numbers **Egypt a Little Country** of 18,500 square miles—that is, a little larger than Belgium. The population, however, is at least a third more numerous. The total area of the country, a large proportion of which consists of the barren districts of the Arabian desert, between the Nile and the Red Sea, and the Libyan desert, which loses itself in the Sahara on the west, is about 640,000 square miles.

The names under which Egypt has been known to neighbouring peoples in the course of history have never yet been satisfactorily explained. The native name for the country was "Kemet," in later forms, "Kemi" and "Khemi," signifying "the Black Land," the land of dark soil; the ancient Egyptians called

MAP OF THE BASIN OF THE RIVER NILE

themselves simply Romitu, "the people." When the priest of Saïs told Herodotus that of the 360 priests who had succeeded each other at Saïs from time immemorial each one was a "*piromis*, and the son of a *piromis*," he meant that each one had been "a man and the son of a man," in Egyptian *pi-romi*, with the definite article *pi*. Modern investigations have made it probable that the name Egypt may have been derived from the native name of the town or the temple precinct of Memphis, Ha-ka-ptah. As early as 1400 B.C. Memphis was known to foreigners under the form of "Hikuptah." The Semitic peoples called the country Misr, or in Hebrew, Misraim. The kings of Egypt at any rate those of the eighteenth dynasty, in their letters to foreign powers generally styled themselves rulers

VIEW OF THE NILE AT THE FIRST CATARACT

of "Misri." The Persians turned this name into "Mudraya." But the origin and the meaning of the word are unknown.

The same uncertainty prevails with regard to the name Neilos, by which the Greeks called the river. The ancient Egyptians called the Nile Hapi; but this, in popular language, was replaced by *Itur*, river, of which the Coptic, the last surviving dialect of ancient Egypt, has preserved the derivative form *Iaro* or *Eioor*. The Israelites called the Nile by the same name, Yeor, the Assyrians, Yaru; and in Syria the Delta region was known about 1380 B.C. as the country of "Yarimuta," of which word the second part still awaits explanation.

Meaning of Egyptian Names

Egyptologists are by no means altogether agreed that ancient Egyptian civilisation originated wholly in the East, and opinions are still divided as to the origin of the earliest inhabitants of the land. Both the negroes and the western neighbours of the Delta, the Libyan nations, have been considered possible progenitors. The first may be ruled out at once; there was negro blood in Egypt in ancient times, as there is now, but the

Egyptians were not, and are not, a negroid race. But that they were closely akin to the Libyans, now represented by the Berbers, Kabyles, and Tuareg of Northern Africa, is very possible; the Egyptian language, though it contained many "proto-Semitic" forms, was not more Semitic in general character than are Berber dialects, which are distantly related to the Semitic tongues. But that in very early times a distinctly Semitic immigration took place from Arabia, bringing with it elements of Mesopotamian culture, seems highly probable. With the exception of the Mediterranean coast, the

VIEW OF THE NILE AT THE SECOND CATARACT

only points at which the invasion of Egypt by a horde or army of any size is at all possible are the former isthmus of Suez, the Libyan border of the Delta on the opposite side, and finally the pass of Assouan in the south. In antiquity the Nile valley was absolutely closed against the advance of large armies, from Cairo upward, on both sides. Oases, it is true, are not entirely wanting, but their situation is not such as to have permitted a direct attack upon the pass into the valley between Assouan and the Fayyum.

In the age of the Ptolemies and the Romans the eastern desert was inhabited by a nomadic race, known to the Egyptians who wrote in Greek as Trogodytes —not Troglodytes, which would mean cave

against witchcraft. Battles occur for the possession of the pasture lands ; the conflict is begun with fists, continued with stones, and should a wound be inflicted with these weapons, arrows and knives are brought into play ; thereupon the women rush between them and reconcile them by their appeals.

The Most Ancient People Their food consists of flesh and bones, which are mingled together and crushed, wrapped in skins and then roasted and prepared in various ways by the cooks, whom they call unclean. Thus they devour not only the flesh, but also the skin and bones ; they also partake of blood mingled with milk. The drink of the great majority is an infusion of buckthorn ; the chiefs, however, drink a kind of mead, for which purpose honey is pressed from a certain flower. . . . They invariably go naked, hung about with a skin and carrying a club. They are not only mutilated, but some of them are also circumcised, like the Egyptians. Some of the Trogodytes bury their dead, fastening the legs of the corpse to the neck with withes of buckthorn ; they then joyfully and with laughter pile stones upon the corpse until it is hidden from view. Then they set

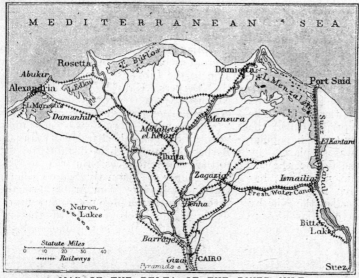

MAP OF THE DELTA OF THE RIVER NILE

dwellers. It was only in the region between the Nile and the Red Sea, where they were secure from any persistent pursuit or expulsion, that the remnants of these most ancient inhabitants of the Nile valley were able to maintain their primitive existence. Artemidorus, about 270 B.C., thus describes the habits of this people : " The Trogodytes lead a nomadic life ; their several tribes are ruled by chiefs of unlimited power. Women and children are held in common ; only the families of chiefs are excepted. Whoever defiles the wife of a chieftain must pay a fine of one sheep. The women take great care in blackening their eyebrows— [which shows that they were not negroes]. Shells are worn round the neck as a charm

up a goat's horn upon the pile and go their way." Similar modes of burial to those here described are to be found far and wide in Central and Southern Africa at the present day. The goat's horn placed above the grave was the " totem " of the deceased, which he wore while alive, suspended from his neck together with the shells. Whether these **Ancient Race of Pygmies** Trogodytes had any connection with the primitive population of Central Africa, who seem to have been pygmies, may be rendered more certain by knowledge of the pygmy races at the sources of the Nile and in the Congo district. The existence of these latter was well known to the ancients, and individual representatives occasionally

A scene on the River Nile, where it broadens in its course, above one of the reservoirs.

Arab trading boats with their familiar lateen sails on the Nile at Luxor.

The banks of the Nile, showing a typical scene on the lower reaches of the river.

SCENES ON THE NILE: THE RIVER TO WHICH EGYPT OWES ITS LIFE
In the course of ages the Nile has filled up with its silt, a black and very fertilising mud, the narrow gulf which extended in geologic times from the Mediterranean to the first cataract, creating in the desert a long, narrow strip of arable country of an average breadth of about eleven miles.

made their way to Egypt, such as the "Deng," who was brought by the traveller Herkhuf to the court of King Merenra, as related below, in the time of the seventh dynasty, and "delighted the heart of his Majesty more than anything." A similar dwarf had been brought from the land of Punt by the Chancellor Baurdad in the time of King Assa. Whether the Nile valley was ever inhabited by pygmies remains uncertain ; there is evidence for their wide ethnographic distribution in ancient times.

Dwarfs at the Court

Only a few years ago, inquiry into the origin of Egypt and its civilisation was founded entirely upon the list of kings drawn up by the priest Manetho about 260 B.C. According to this list, Menes, the first king of the whole country, who was indeed preceded by ten unnamed human rulers, began in his person the "first dynasty," a fixed starting point which had been accepted by learned Egyptian writers long before Manetho. The list given in the "papyrus of kings," in the Turin Museum, dating probably from 1500 B.C., also begins with Menes— Egyptian "Mena "—and names as his predecessors the Shemsu-Hor, that is, the successors of the god Horus. These, then, were demi-gods ; they, also, appear in Manetho's list, under the name of "Nekyes," or "Ghosts," though separated from Menes by the ten human rulers previously mentioned. The chief account of this monarch states that he came from This, the district round Abydos, north of Thebes, and proceeded to Memphis, where he established his capital. Thus, the region considered in historical times as the original settlement lay in the south. This hypothesis, in itself highly probable, has been entirely confirmed by the recent excavations of Flinders Petrie, Quibell, De Morgan, and Amélineau. The list of kings given by Manetho is not only very full, but also begins at the right place, and provides connecting links between a number of figures which emerge dimly from the darkness of a remoter antiquity.

The Earliest Kings

All the excavations referred to above are grouped around the king's tomb at Nagada, the royal "tombs" at Abydos, and the remains of the primitive buildings at Hierakonpolis ; and at Ballas and Tukh. The great tomb of Nagada proved to be an erection of sun-dried bricks, the remains of which now form a buried rubbish heap some 160 feet long and 80 feet wide. The interior was divided into chambers, the largest of which occupied the centre. Here the body of the king, whose name was Aha, was originally laid out upon the bier ; the other chambers, which decreased in size as they approached the outer walls, contained the sacrificial offerings. The vessels holding the latter were for the most part broken into fragments on the occasion of the burial ceremony. The whole building, and the central chamber in particular, was then destroyed by a great fire, which did not perhaps take place before Christian times.

The most salient features of the civilisation of this early period are the facts that the bodies are not mummified—in all probability the art of embalming the dead was then unknown ; further, that this people were in a state of transition from the later Neolithic to the Bronze Age ; and, finally, that the implements of the period already showed a considerable development of artistic skill. Together with numerous beautifully-worked implements of stone, including knives of high quality, bronze utensils, and objects of ivory, linen cloth and gold ornaments have been discovered. The greatest progress, however, is shown in the pottery of the time, although the large vessels of every kind of pattern show no trace of turning on the potter's wheel. Furthermore, it is clear that basket-making was here the parent art of clay-modelling, and therefore one of the earliest acquired of human accomplishments.

Early Artistic Skill

The Egyptians of the Nagada period also gave their pottery the appearance of stone ; their panel ornamentation showed a preference for spirals, wave and N-lines, as well as for rows of triangles, a characteristically African design. Their representations of men and animals show that their art had already reached a high stage of development. The ostrich often appears depicted walking in single file and as often at full speed ; the same bird is also represented in the tomb-paintings found at Hierakonpolis by Green, and by ancient wall-chiselling, or graffiti, at Arb-Assouan, a few miles below the first cataract, the most southerly point at which sculptures of the Nagada period have been discovered. Pictures of the camel or the horse nowhere appear; the cat also seems to be unrepresented, while elephants constantly recur, and are sometimes boldly depicted as balanced on the mountain tops. Antelopes, goats, bulls, asses, and geese, lions, hippopotami, crocodiles, jackals, dogs, scorpions, all kinds of fish, and finally the sparrowhawk, the bird sacred to Horus, are the chief representatives of the animal world in the art of this period. In contrast to the drawing in profile hitherto known as "Egyptian," an attempt is made at foreshortening, movement being indicated by curving the legs, and, in the case of the ostriches, by the oarlike posture of the wings. The measured stride of men and animals characteristic of the later art does not appear in the drawings of this period. Scorpions and crocodiles stretch their legs out sideways with a resultant life-like appearance of crawling which is not to be found in later work. It may also be mentioned that the Nile river-boats are pictured quite as often as one would have expected.

Of particular interest are the tall, sacrificial urns, often four or five feet high, tapering to a point at the bottom, and the slate tablets used as amulets for the dead. The urns differ only in their elongated form from those in use in Egypt at the present day, but the means of stoppering employed is worthy of mention. The narrow orifice was covered with a disc of burnt clay upon which were placed two bell-shaped lids,

Early Traces of Writing also of clay, one fitting over the other, the stopper having thus the appearance of a sugar-loaf. Stamps were printed upon the soft clay stoppers by means of cylinder seals; naturally the impressions upon the innermost lid are generally in the better state of preservation.

The designs most numerous are the Horus names of the kings—indicated by the picture of a sparrow-hawk above the inscription—pictures of animals, and various ornaments. The art of writing, therefore, though but little practised in the early days of the Nagada period, was not unknown; proper names could, at any rate, be inscribed.

The amulets of slate are sometimes called "palettes," because they sometimes show traces of colouring, and are supposed **Amulets of the Dead** to have been palettes for face-paint. Remnants of rouge paint have also been found in the graves which contain bodies buried in a crouching position; in these graves alone have such palettes been discovered. The tablet of slate was laid between the hands and face of the deceased; its use as an amulet is indisputably established. In most cases holes are found drilled in the tablets, whence it may be conjectured that they were worn during the possessor's lifetime. A unique headless figure, discovered in one of the graves at Tukh, bears extraordinary painted or tattooed designs on the trunk and limbs. In the spring of 1898, Mr. J. E. Quibell directed his attention to the temple of Hierakonpolis, situated further to the south; another chambered tomb, surrounded by a wall of bricks, was brought to light, and in this case it was possible to announce a discovery dating within historic times. The structure had been twice renovated, for the first time in the sixth, and again during the twelfth dynasty of Manetho. From this it is concluded, or rather presumed, that the Egyptians of that age, which was a period of literary activity, were acquainted with the affairs and history of the Archaic Period, in contrast to the Egyptians of the New Empire, whose lists of kings display little knowledge of that era. Of these discoveries an account has already been given.

The age of Khasekhemui and Narmer is posterior to the true "Nagada period." As has already been seen in the essay on

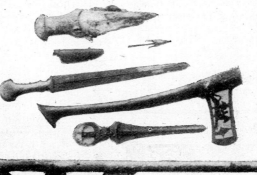

Mansell

THE TRANSITION ART OF EARLY EGYPT
The implements of the Egyptians of the first dynasties, who were in a state of transition from a stone to a bronze age, showed considerable artistic skill, as the flint dagger, knife and arrowhead, and bronze daggers, hatchet and war-axe, shown above, exemplify.

Archaic Egypt, prefixed to this chapter, both Narmer and Aha are in reality to be assigned to the first dynasty of Manetho, as these three principal monarchs are in all probability the originals of the legendary " Mena," who is then to be regarded as a compound figure, typifying the beginnings of the monarchy under those early kings of Hierakonpolis. With them the Nagada period ends, and the civilisation of the first dynasty, as revealed to us by the excavations at Hierakonpolis and Abydos, begins.

Our interest in the hypotheses concerning the origin of the Neolithic Egyptians of the Nagada period requires no justification. The results of grave exploration have made it clear that the fundamental type of this people was closely allied to the Trogodytes in the east, if it was not identical with them. The description

AGRICULTURE IN EARLY EGYPT
This vivid scene in the agricultural life of the early Egyptians is taken from an Egyptian wall-painting reproduced in Sir Gardner Wilkinson's standard work, "The Manners and Customs of the Ancient Egyptians."

given by Artemidorus of the Trogodyte custom of binding together the heads and feet of the dead is a description of the procedure necessary to secure the bodies in the embryonal position of the Nagada graves, where the goats' horns of the Trogodytes find their prototype.

Of capital importance for the decision upon ethnographic grounds of the question whether the Neolithic Egyptians and the Trogodytes were of primitive African origin are the ancient rock graffiti at Hierakonpolis and Arb-Assouan, together with certain vase paintings found at Abydos and Nagada. Mr. R. A. Macalister, who visited the Trogodyte desert from Upper Egypt in December, 1899, speaks of similar drawings on the cliffs at the confluence of the Wadi Munila and the Wadi Shaid. The primitive rock-drawings of the Bushmen of South Africa

irresistibly invite comparison with the primitive productions of the Nagada period ; while the proportions of the skulls found in the southern burying-ground at Nagada often point to a close connection with the Bushmen and Hottentots. Many of the Nagada statuettes exhibit traces of the fatty development peculiar to both of

Bushmen and Trogodytes these South African tribes. The Egyptians, at any rate those of the eighteenth dynasty, are said to have recognised a relationship with the inhabitants of Puenet, or Punt, the land of incense, which lay to the south of the Red Sea. But the statement that the sailors of the Egyptian Queen Hatshepsut worshipped the goddess Hathor as the deity of Punt is in itself insufficient evidence, inasmuch as Hathor was the special goddess of seafarers and vouchsafed the favourable wind without which the journey to Punt was impossible. From the mural decorations in the temple of Der el-Bahari, it may be concluded that about 1500 B.C. Punt was inhabited by brown-coloured races. They dwelt in huts built on piles and entered by ladders, and endeavoured to acquire articles of metal, and weapons in particular, by means of barter. The Puntites, as represented by the Egyptians, are always remarkably like the Egyptians themselves ; and it may well be that these people, who were no doubt of the Galla race, were recognised by Egyptians as akin to themselves. The higher—Asiatic—race of the Archaic Period was no doubt nearly related to the Galla stock, which probably came originally from Arabia.

The condition of political affairs in Egypt at the end of the Nagada period shows that in contrast to earlier times the

First War with the Libyans military power of the land had now to be directed toward the north, where Libyan tribes had occupied the Delta and cut off the Upper Nile from communication. The greatest achievements of Menes, the first traditional king—who is probably a compound of the early monarchs Narmer and Aha, so that the latter's sepulchre at Nagada may perhaps be called the " Tomb of Menes "—were his removal of the royal residence from the

THE STONEWARE OF ANCIENT EGYPT: ALABASTER VASES 5,000 **YEARS OLD** Mansell

south to Memphis, and his defeat of the Libyans. One theory put forward is that the conquerors who founded "dynastic" Egypt were Asiatics who advanced by way of the Isthmus of Suez.

But, as we have seen in the preceding section, it is by no means certain. Another theory would bring these conquerors into Egypt by way of the Wadi Hammamat. In fact, all that can be said is that the most ancient kings appear as southerners, who subdued the north, and thus united the "two lands" under one sceptre. The kings who effected this, and founded the first dynasty, figured in Egyptian tradition as one man, named "Mena," the "firm," who came from This, or Thinis, near Abydos, and founded the city of "Mennefer," or Memphis (Fair Haven) near the apex of the Delta, thus consolidating his conquest of the north. Neither in history nor tradition have we any confirmation of the otherwise very plausible hypothesis of an initial movement of the dynastic Egyptians from north to south.

There is no country in the world that can be compared with Egypt in wealth of antiquities. It is true that the valley of the Euphrates and Tigris is not far behind in respect of the number of discoveries there made, but it can show nothing approaching the variety of objects found in Egypt which illustrate the different departments of human activity. Egypt unfolds before us the daily life of all classes from the highest to the lowest. The methods of manufacture and agriculture, specimens of all articles and utensils of luxury and necessity, from children's dolls and draughtsmen to the valuable gold onaments of royal personages, the carefully

ART IN EARLY EGYPT: A TOMB DECORATION PAINTED 3,500 **YEARS AGO**

preserved bodies of famous conquerors, the songs, myths, and fairy tales that were the delight of young and old, the writing materials with which they were immortalised, the amulet, the sandals, even the wig worn by the scribe—of all these we have examples, and often in abundance. If these fragile remnants have lost something of their freshness in the course of thousands of years, the loss can be supplied by the faithful representations and richly-coloured paintings on the walls of the tombs.

Wealth of Egyptian Antiquities

Invaluable as was the realism of the Egyptian people, it proved unable to stand the test the moment tasks were encountered transcending the tangible and the visible. The vast achievements of early Egyptian art, and its no less imposing course of development, are only too liable to render us blind to the fact that throughout its entire progress it rested upon one and the same foundation—rigid adherence to the material, and consequent intellectual constraint. Again, in literature and in art, each new phase of development seems to have emerged at stated intervals as a completed whole, invariably appearing at the end of long periods of "Egyptian" darkness, these intervals being occupied by reviving fusions of Asiatic influence as a result of political changes. Such a period of darkness was the supremacy of the Hyksos, which continued too long and had too profound an effect upon the Egyptian people to vanish entirely upon its expiration. At the end of this period the "New Empire" begins. One new and unexampled effect of this period was the awakening influence which it exerted upon the previously shadowy

historical sense which the Egyptians possessed. The kings began to draw up lists—of select names only—of such of their predecessors as could be collected, and endeavoured to secure the relation of their own deeds in proper sequence. We have several such "cursory" lists, three of which are in a fair state of preservation: a tablet from the temple at Karnak, or Thebes, upon which Thothmes III. does obeisance to sixty-one ancient kings; another, discovered in the temple of Osiris at Abydos, with seventy-five names; and a third from a tomb near Sakkara, an abridged copy of the preceding, and, like it, belonging to the time of Rameses II. The Turin papyrus professes to contain more than a mere collection of names;

Royal Egyptian Records

but unfortunately the document consists only of fragments of which but a small portion has been pieced together. The list given by this papyrus not only extends from the gods who ruled on earth to the period of the Hyksos, but notes the exact length of each reign in years, months, and days. Even if the transcription be of later date, and to be placed at the beginning of the nineteenth dynasty, the original from which it was compiled undoubtedly belongs to the time immediately following the Hyksos. An obvious imitation of Babylonian lists of kings, the text remains unique by reason of the detailed character of its statements. Compilers, doubtless, were soon wearied by the labour involved in carrying accuracy to such extremes.

Not until the Alexandrine period was the history of Egypt written by a native pen. The high-priest and temple scribe, Manetho of Sebennytos, who had received

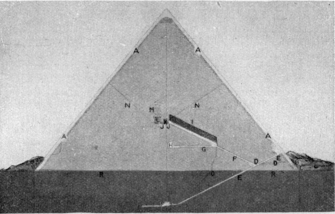

THE INTERIOR OF THE GREAT PYRAMID OF GIZEH

In this section of the pyramid A is the ancient casing of polished granite; B, sand and debris; C, casing now remaining; D, a passage forced by a caliph; E, descending entrance; F, ascending passage; G, passage to the queen's chamber; H, queen's chamber; I, the great gallery; J, passage from the great gallery to the king's chamber; K, ante-chamber; L, king's chamber and sarcophagus; M, chambers used in building; N, ventilating chamber; O, well; P, subterranean chamber; R, the rock base of the pyramid, about 750 feet long.

THE WONDER OF EGYPT: THE GREAT PYRAMID TOMBS OF GIZEH

Built by Khufu, Khafra, Menkaura, and other Pharaohs of the fourth dynasty about 3800 B.C., these tombs are among the oldest and most stupendous edifices known to mankind. The largest was built by Khufu, or Cheops.

a Greek education, composed his work " Ægyptiaca," which remains to us only in the shape of excerpts and quotations. No doubt he had a rich store of material at his disposal, although it is evident that he was unduly influenced by contemporary opinion; he even accepted the popular myth of the world-conqueror Sesostris, unless this and similar matter has been interpolated into the citations which have come down to us. So many false accounts of other matters were foisted upon Manetho in antiquity that only in a few isolated cases can we obtain more than a general idea of his work; however, his chronological system was accepted until modern times. According to him, the Old Empire begins with Menes, and embraces the first to the eleventh dynasties; the Middle Empire extends from the twelfth to the nineteenth dynasties; and the New Empire begins with the twentieth, and continues to the time of Alexander. This system cannot be entirely maintained in the face of the archæological evidence which we possess. It is usual to consider the Middle Empire as having begun with the eleventh dynasty, and as ending with the seventeenth. The Old Empire, however, must be reckoned as ending with the conclusion of the sixth dynasty, where there is a long break in the course of events. The scanty information which we possess concerning dynasties seven to ten is to be considered

First Egyptian Historian

as marking a transition period leading to the Middle Empire, while the New Empire begins with the expulsion of the Hyksos, and continues until the outset of the twenty-sixth dynasty, so that the scheme of Manetho is abandoned from the reign of Psammetichus I. onward. There is no possible doubt that Manetho made use of such records as the Turin papyrus and the lists of kings inscribed on their monuments, but the beginning of the New Empire must be considered as the earliest limit of his sources of information.

The kings of Manetho's first dynasty are as follows: Menes, with a reign of 62 years; Athothis, with 57; Kenkenes, with 31; Uenephes, with 23; Usaphaïs, with 20; Miebis, with 26; Semempses, with 18; and Bienekhes, with 26. The succession invariably passed from father to son. The list of the second dynasty contains nine rulers: Boethos (38 years), Kaiekhos (29), Binothris (47), Tlas (17), Sethenes (41), Khaires (17), Neferkheres (25), Sesokhris (48), Kheneres (30). Both houses were called "Thinites," and hence Manetho assumes their extraction from the district of Abydos, while, according to him, the next dynasty originated in Memphis. Finally, the list of the third dynasty contains nine kings: Nekherophes (28 years), Tosorthros (29), Tyreis (7), Mesokhris (17), Soüphis (16), Tosertasis (19), Asykhes (42), Sephouris (30), and Kerpheres (26). Thus we may be said

The First History Criticised

to have altogether twenty-six kings, who reigned during a period of seven hundred and sixty nine years. Such is Manetho's list of the kings of the first three dynasties. In the main it agrees remarkably well with the evidence of the monuments, as far as the first two dynasties are concerned. Of the third

Early History Upheld we have few monuments but those of the great King Tjeser, who is probably Manetho's Tosorthros. But the earlier kings of the second dynasty and those of the first dynasty in Manetho's list agree very well in number, and often also in name, with the historical rulers of this period, as far back as Miebis and Usaphaïs, whose real names were Merbepa, or Merpeba, and Semti (read " Hesepti " in later times, whence the Manethonian form). Semti, who also bore the name of Den, or Udimu, seems to be the most ancient historical king of Egypt known to Manetho and the ancient annalists from whom he gained his information. The lists of Abydos and Sakkara agree with Manetho as to the number, and in two cases as to the names, of the four kings before Semti or Usaphaïs ; but it is evident that these are merely legendary figures. The historical kings who preceded Semti do not agree with them either in name or number ; even the occurrence of the name " Men " as an appellation of King Aha, which has been supposed to be inscribed on a tablet of this king found at Nagada, is uncertain, and will in the long run probably not be maintained. Setting aside certain names, which—if they are names at all, and this is doubtful—belong to monarchs of the time of the Shemsu-Hor, we have, as we have seen, the following list of historical kings of all Egypt at the beginning of the first dynasty : First, Aha, Narmer or Betjumer, and a monarch called " Scorpion " ; these are

The Historical Kings probably the originals of the legendary Mena : the " Scorpion " may not impossibly be identical with Narmer. Then follow Tja, the " Serpent," who possibly bore the additional name of Ati, which may be the original of the legendary Teta, Ateti, or Ata, perhaps of all three ; " Ateti " is evidently the original of Manetho's " Athothis." As has been said in the preceding chapter, it is hopeless, as well as quite unnecessary, to try to force

the historical names into the cartouches of Mena, Teta, Ateti, and Ata. The lists which give these names agree with Manetho, except as regards the forms of the names " Kenkenes " and " Uenephes " ; but this is only because Manetho was copying these very lists or similar ones, and their knowledge of the kings who united the kingdom was evidently quite legendary and uncertain. It is only with King Semti Den that we reach firm ground. He is the Hesepti of the lists, the Usaphaïs of Manetho. It is probably not a mere chance that his successor Merpeba, the Merbep of the lists and Miebis of Manetho, begins the royal list of Sakkara instead of Mena. At Memphis he was evidently regarded as the first historical king of all Egypt of whom anything definite was known in the time of the nineteenth dynasty. His successor, Nekht, was called in the lists " Semsu," which is the origin of the Manethonian " Semempses." After him came Sen, also called Qa, whose name was misread " Qebh " by the compilers of the lists. He is certainly Manetho's

Founder of the Empire " Bienekhes," but the origin of this form of his name is impossible to divine. The names of these kings are known from their tombs at Abydos.

Manetho's account of the events during this period is purely legendary. Naturally, the account of Menes, the founder of the empire, is richest in detail. In addition to the fact of his removal of the seat of the empire from Thinis to Memphis, where he founded a temple of Ptah, the god of the town—the first temple ever erected in Egypt—it was also said of him that he invented the hieroglyphic system, introduced the worship of the sacred bull Apis and of the crocodile, and taught men the art of luxurious living. He waged wars against Libyan forces, and met his death from a hippopotamus. Obviously, no mention was made of the tomb of Menes in the sources of information open to Manetho.

Athothis is said to have built the king's fortress in Memphis, and to have written an anatomical treatise. As a matter of fact, the Ebers medical papyrus contains the recipe for a hair-wash concocted by Shesh, the mother of Athothis. Finally, during his reign a two-headed crane— that is, a bird sacred to the god Thoth, of which name "Athothis" is a compound—appeared in the land, an event signifying prosperity. The reigns of the successors of Menes seem to be characterised by a preponderance of misfortune ; the reign of Uenephes was made memorable by a famine, that of Semempses by " many wonders " and a great plague.

Manetho's list of events for the second dynasty is equally wonderful. The reign of Boethos is remarkable for the fact that a cleft in the earth opened in the delta at Bubastis, and caused the death of many men ; Kaiekhos, as Manetho relates, introduces the worship of Apis into Memphis, that of Mnevis into Heliopolis, and that of the sacred ram at Mendes ; under the king Neferkheres the Nile flowed with honey instead of water for eleven days ; and, finally, Sesokhris was a " very dangerous man," five cubits and three palms high. The difference between Manetho's Greek transliteration of the kings' names and the hieroglyphic forms of the same words may be clearly seen by the comparison of the first five kings of this dynasty and the list from **The Second Dynasty** Abydos. This list gives the names in accurate order of succession : Betjau, Ka-ka-u, Ba-neter-en, Uatnes, and Sent ; the other four names are missing. On contemporary, or nearly contemporary monuments, we have the names Khasekhemui, Kakau, Neneter, or Netrimu, and Sent. Khasekhemui was the first king of the second dynasty. His successor was Hetepsekhemui. Then came Raneb, who may or may not be identical with Kakau-Kaiekhos, and then Ba Ne-neter, certainly the historical Neneter or Netrimu, who succeeded Raneb. Uatjnes, or Tlas, is not known to the monuments ; but both Sekhemab Perabsen and Sen, who came next, are.

Manetho's account of the third dynasty is exceedingly scanty ; with its last representatives the first glimpse of historical tradition appears. Of the first two kings we are told only that the Libyans revolted in the reign of Necherophes, but fled in horror when the moon suddenly increased in size. Further, Tosorthros, or Tjeser, was a great physician and architect, and improved the script in use ; he built an edifice of hewn stone. The pyramid of Sakkara, built in steps, shows that its builders had not as yet advanced to the art of smoothing the sides, which indeed

THE GALLERY IN THE GREAT PYRAMID
It is very difficult to give a pictorial idea of the great gallery, but this section, from the " Description de l'Egypte" gives as good an impression as it is possible to convey.

was not the original plan. This name occurs in the account of a papyrus among the immediate predecessors of Sneferu, with whom the third dynasty ends. It is probable that Manetho's account of the edifices erected by Tosorthros refers to Tjeser and the pyramid of Sakkara.

Tjeser had another tomb, a great "mastaba" of bricks, at Bet Khallaf, near Abydos. Another king buried there was named Sanekht. A papyrus also contains the observation that King Huni died and Sneferu succeeded him.

Nowhere in the course of history have such vast masses of stone been piled up upon such comparatively small areas by human labour as in Egypt at the command of the pyramid builders. The idea of constructing these gigantic tumuli originated, no doubt, in the natural heaping up of earth or stone in the form of a barrow over the tomb of a dead man. For the pyramids are nothing but tombs. They have no astronomical intention or meaning whatever. The ideas of Piazzi Smyth and others on this point are now known to be mere vain imaginings, based upon insufficient knowledge of Egyptian archæology and love of "the marvellous." There is nothing marvellous about these great tombs except their size and the accuracy of their building. At any rate, the pyramids of the fourth dynasty have become imperishable landmarks of Egypt, and are numbered among the oldest edifices known to mankind. All are situated on the western bank of the Nile, between Gizeh, near Cairo, and the extreme north-eastern corner of the Fayyum. They are divided into groups, named after the Arab settlements near which they rise, hence the terms the Pyramids of Gizeh, Abu-Roash, Abusir, Sakkara, Lisht, Dashur, Medum, Illahun and Hawara. The remains of smaller imitation pyramids, of which two exist in the Fayyum itself, as well as the very late attempts at constructing smaller edifices near Meroe in Ethiopia, need not be further considered. There are in all more than seventy examples within the district of the Pyramids proper ; but the majority of these served as quarries in later years, and have consequently disappeared to their very foundations. Those which still remain are pierced by sloping passages running through the interior and leading to the burial chambers. In other respects there are many differences of plan ; for instance, the great pyramid of Gizeh contains several burial chambers in its centre, one built above the other, whereas others have but one such chamber.

World's Vastest Tombs

The Seventy Pyramids

That these complicated and extensive pyramid buildings were severally designed as the tomb of some one king—Menkaura and Sneferu erected two each for their own use—is proved among other evidence by the fact that the high officials in the old kingdom were accustomed to erect their tombs of different shape, the "mastabas," or "benches," within the shadow of the royal sepulchres. Curiously enough the mastabas are the richer in information upon their dead occupants. That the surfaces of the pyramids were covered with long inscriptions, as is stated in some ancient records, has been doubted, upon strong evidence. We have also reason to believe that the builder of a pyramid permitted the bodies of the members of his family to be deposited in the central chamber with his own. We must first learn those conceptions which gave the impulse to the erection of these tremendous structures. No doubt the safety of the mummies and their rich surroundings were considerations of the first order.

The adoption of a pyramidal form was undoubtedly inspired by natural considerations ; a pile of stones is naturally conical or pyramidal in form. It is possible that the construction of the pyramid was first arrived at by superimposing mastabas of gradually decreasing size upon one another; indeed the mastaba itself somewhat resembled a square platform, with sides sloping outward. Mastabas differed greatly in size, their bases varying in area from about 250 to 12,000 feet square. They contained a chapel, the walls of which were covered with pictures and inscriptions, a separate chimney-like compartment for the stone image of the deceased, and finally an underground sepulchral chamber, void of decoration, where the enswathed mummy lay in a sarcophagus of stone. Our chief knowledge of the life and doings of the Egyptians of the Old Empire is derived from the pictures on the walls of the chapels, which were accessible from without, and were intended as depositories for the sacrificial gifts, for incense offerings —in short, for the soul-worship continued by the descendants of the deceased. In the smallest mastabas, in place of the chapel there is a blind door set into the outer wall, inscribed with prayers and the name of the deceased.

Why the Pyramids Were Built

THE HALL OF COLUMNS IN THE GREAT TEMPLE OF KARNAK

THE PYRAMIDS OF ABUSIR AS THEY APPEARED IN THE TIME OF THEIR BUILDER, KING NE-USER-RA, ABOUT 3600 B.C.

This beautiful reconstruction is the work of Herr Borchardt, the well-known German Egyptologist, and is reproduced by permission of Messrs. Heinrichs, of Leipzig, from his "Grabdenkmal des Königs Ne-user-ra."

THE EARLY DYNASTIES

ACCORDING to Manetho, the fourth dynasty begins with King "Soris," the Shaaru of the monuments. He evidently succeeded Sneferu, Manetho's Sephouris. Until a short time ago, Sneferu was the first Egyptian ruler known to us from his own inscriptions, discovered in this case in Wadi Maghara on the Sinaitic peninsula. In fact, the copper mines in that peninsula, which are now exhausted, were known as the "Mines of Sneferu" as late as the period of the New Empire. It is known, however, that Sneferu was not the first to bring this region into the possession of Egypt; King Nekht Semerkhat of the first dynasty was the first to inscribe his name on the rocks of Sinai, and he was followed there by Tjeser and Sanekht, before Sneferu, whose inscription shows him to have been the conqueror of the Mentiu, the small Bedouin tribes of the peninsula. With the exception of a similar inscription of Khufu, there is no further mention of war during the fourth dynasty. It was only in times of peace that the mass of the population could be employed year by year in the construction of gigantic edifices, or for other useful purposes. Sneferu's two pyramids were at Dashur and Medum. The personages buried in the surrounding mastabas were his subjects, as was Rahetep, the "Great Man of the South," whose lifelike sitting statue, together with its counterpart, a still finer image of his wife Nefert, now adorns the museum at Gizeh. The king was deified immediately after his death, and his worship continued to the time of the Ptolemies.

The Fourth Dynasty

Sneferu was succeeded by Shaaru, and he by Khufu, the Cheops of Herodotus. Of all the names of the fourth dynasty, that of Cheops is the most celebrated. However, of him we know nothing more certainly except that the largest pyramid is his; it measures 480 feet high and 764 feet square at the base. Remains are still visible of the paved causeway along which, according to Herodotus, the building-stones quarried on the other side of the Nile were landed and dragged to the site of the edifice. The short inscription found in Wadi Maghara again refers to a chastisement of the Bedouins. The mastabas that lie behind the pyramid of Cheops provide no information upon the history of the king, though containing the tombs of several royal children. They point to the existence of an exclusive nobility clinging to strict forms and customs in death as well as in life.

Cheops and his Pyramid

The pyramid of Medum is situated at the extreme south of the pyramid district; on the other hand, the pyramid of Khufu lies to the north near Gizeh. They are thus separated from one another by a distance of some thirty-seven miles. It is therefore probable that Khufu resided in Memphis, which was close at hand, and that Sneferu's residence, the full name of which was in all likelihood Ded-Sneferu, must be sought for in the neighbourhood of Medum or Dashur.

Khafra succeeded Khufu, who was probably his father, although Herodotus gives "Chephren" as the name of Cheops's brother. The pyramid of this king is not far distant from the great pyramid, and is only some twenty-seven feet lower. A magnificent diorite statue, a stately and faithful representation of Khafra, has been discovered, together with six smaller images of the same ruler, the latter in a badly damaged condition, in the shaft of the temple of the Sphinx, not far from the pyramid. The lofty throne is surmounted by the sparrow-hawk of Horus, whose beak projects over the low headcloth of the sovereign, the broad ends of which lie folded upon his shoulders. The great Sphinx belongs, however, to a later time, although as early as the New Empire Khafra seems to have been looked upon as its maker. At that time a small temple was constructed between the outstretched feet of the Sphinx; and it appears from contemporary documents that the figure was considered to be an image of the sun-god. It is a matter of doubt, however, whether

The Sphinx and its Temple

this idea is a full explanation of the original purpose of the Sphinx, which during the greater part of its existence has been buried in sand-drifts. Hewn out of the adjacent rock, it is over sixty-five feet in height, and represents a lion couchant with a human head; unfortunately the features have been badly mutilated by fanatical Arabs.

Mystery of the Sphinx

Here and there mention has been found of a king Radadf, likewise of the fourth dynasty; his pyramid is at Abu Roash, but his place in the succession of rulers is uncertain. He is evidently Manetho's " Ratoises," and therefore should come between Khafra and Menkaura. Menkaura, the Mycerinus of Herodotus, stands as the immediate successor of Khafra. His sepulchre is in the third pyramid of Gizeh, which is only 218 feet in height. The last king of the fourth dynasty was Shepseskaf ; it has not been ascertained which of the pyramids is his. Mariette (1821–1881) discovered the tomb of a dignitary called Ptahshepses near Sakkara, who gives us some valuable personal information. He was first adopted by Menkaura and then by Shepseskaf "among the number of royal children" ; the latter gave him the hand of his eldest daughter, Khamaat, in marriage. Ptahshepses was also appointed priest of three obelisks of Ra ; it is here that we first meet with these slender-pointed stone columns erected in honour of the sun-god, the tallest of which, situated at Thebes, measures over 100 feet in height. The inscription of Ptahshepses is now in the British Museum.

The popular tradition of later times represented the pyramid builders as unjust oppressors of Egypt. The character of this

belief may be gathered from Herodotus. Cheops and Chephren are said to have closed the temples and stopped the sacrifices in order to employ the whole strength of their subjects in the construction of their monuments. These two kings are the builders of the largest pyramids. Mycerinus is said to have been the first king to resume the practice of justice towards gods and men. But, continues the myth, in a manner truly typical of the gloomy theory of life entertained by the fellahin in all ages, the gods had no consideration for him ; they cut short the life of Mycerinus, alleging it to be their will that the land should continue still longer unfortunate.

Pyramids at Expense of Justice

Thus this king, although he built a much smaller pyramid than his predecessors, was none the less guilty of disobedience. Further, a myth of great intrinsic interest, which apparently originated in the course of the Middle Empire, relates how the gods turned away from Khufu and his house. The manuscript, which forms a part of the "Westcar papyrus," unfortunately breaks off at the very point where the development of the story begins. Nevertheless, in the portions which are still preserved it is related that King Khufu once summoned a magician, Dedi, to court through the prince Hordadf, who appears in the Book of the Dead as a son of Menkaura. When the enchanter, "who was 110 years old, and devoured 500 loaves of bread, a joint of beef, and 100 jugs of beer on the same day," had given an exhibition of juggling feats before the king, he prophesied that three sons that were to be born to Ruddedit, wife of the priest of Ra at Sakhebu, would one

KHAFRA AND MENKAURA, KINGS 5,800 YEARS AGO
Khafra, whose magnificent diorite statue is shown on the left, was the fourth king of the fourth dynasty, and Menkaura the fifth.

Mansell

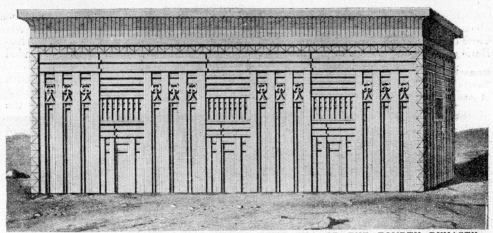

THE RESTORED SARCOPHAGUS OF KING MENKAURA OF THE FOURTH DYNASTY
A fine basalt sarcophagus, eight feet long, dating from about 3840 B.C., which once contained the body of King Menkaura.

day be rulers of Egypt. Khufu was greatly alarmed at this piece of news, and immediately determined to set out for Sakhebu. The birth of the three boys with the assistance of the gods is next related. Isis names them Userkaf, Sahura, and Kaka ; in fact, the three first kings of the fifth dynasty appear in this order in the list of Abydos. The story ends with an account of how a maid-servant attempted to disclose to the king the existence and destiny of the three children, but was prevented from putting her design into execution. Although the scribe with true court politeness handles Khufu with all possible deference, nevertheless the general feeling is obviously against him. He is the representative of an extinct and unpopular line ; the three sons of Ruddedit wield the sceptre, and are therefore " popular."

It is evident that the fifth dynasty did not originate in Elephantine in Upper Egypt, as stated by Manetho, but in Sakhebu on the " Two-fish canal "—in the Delta, according to Petrie. The nine kings of the line were buried in relatively small pyramids ; the situations of four have been determined with probable accuracy, those of Sahura, Ne-ueser-Ra, and Neferari-ka-Ra at Abusir, and Unas, the last representative of the dynasty, at Sakkara. During their period this dynasty is even poorer in historical records than the preceding. Possession was retained of the Sinaitic mines, the kings Sahura, Ne-ueser-Ra—Ra-en-user (Manetho's "Rathouris")—Menkauhor, and Assa being represented there by inscribed tablets.

The Fifth Dynasty

In the reign of Assa, whose first name was Dedka-Ra, the first copy of the Prisse papyrus was written ; the author was Ptah-hotep, a relative of the king and a high dignitary. Our copy is of the period of the Middle Empire, and seems in general to reproduce the formal literary style in vogue at that period. Fragments of other papyri connected with the reign of Assa were discovered by peasants near Sakkara in 1893. The Prisse papyrus contains the meditations and maxims of Ptah-hotep — much like other meditations and maxims. Assa's successor, Unas, whose pyramid, together with portions of his mummy, was discovered in the spring of 1881, ruled for thirty years, according to the Turin papyrus. The epitaph of an official named Senetjem-ab, discovered at Gizeh, is the authority for this order of succession ; but no mention is made of Unas as co-regent during the lifetime of Assa.

Earliest Known Papyrus

The German excavations at Abusir have brought to light remains of temples and bas-reliefs executed during the fifth dynasty, which show that religious art at least arrived at its zenith of development under the fifth dynasty, and was ever afterwards fixed and stereotyped. No change in the hieretic representation of the gods, for instance, is observable after this time. These excavations, carried on by the German Oriental Society by Messrs. von Bissing, Borthardt, and Schaefer, are of great interest, especially the clearing of a remarkable sanctuary of the god Ra near Abusir, built in the reign of Ne-ueser-Ra. In this temple stood a great Sun-obelisk on a pedestal, like those described above, of which Ptahshepses was minister. Close by, also, was found a great imitation Baris or Boat of the Sun, of gigantic size, built in brickwork. In the court of the temple, before the obelisk, stands a huge altar of alabaster blocks, and at the end of the court is a row of great alabaster bowls, to hold the blood of the sacrifices. For here animals were undoubtedly slaughtered in honour of the god. At Abusir the funerary temple of King Ne-ueser-Ra has entirely been cleared, and many interesting conclusions as to the architecture of this early period have been drawn from it. Its lotus-bud columns of granite, and floors and walls of black basalt, were very fine. In the reign of Ne-ueser-Ra lived Thi, whose tomb at Sakkara is so famous for its fine reliefs.

Remarkable Sanctuary of Abusir

From the nature of the inscriptions relating to the last two dynasties, we must conclude that this period was peaceful. This condition of affairs soon changed after the beginning of the sixth dynasty, which originated in Memphis, according to Manetho, and comprised five kings, concluding with a queen. However, the evidence of the lists and monuments gives us at least eight different names of kings. Their pyramids are situated on the edge of the Sakkara district. In 1880–1881 they were investigated, and could be assigned to separate kings, as follows : Teta, his successor Ati, then Pepi I. Merira, Me-renra, whose first name was Mehti-em-saf, and Pepi II. Nefer-ka-Ra. The texts discovered within the pyramid were entirely concerned with religious affairs, and the most interesting discovery was the mummy of Merenra, which had certainly been plundered and unwrapped, but was otherwise in good condition. An examination of the remains showed that the king died young, as he wears the plaited lock of hair or pigtail at one side of the head which Egyptian boys and youths always wore. Therefore, the four years' reign with which the Turin papyrus credits him rested upon a reliable basis of tradition.

KING NE-UESER-RA

Mansell

One of the most famous of the fifth dynasty, about 3500 B.C., who built the wonderful sanctuary of Abusir.

If the papyrus is also correct in the next case, we have for Pepi II. a reign of over ninety years, the longest known to history. Manetho relates that he ascended the throne as a boy of six years old, and continued to rule till the hundredth year of his life. In the spring of 1898 Victor Loret excavated near Memphis the tomb of the king's mother and of the queen Apu-it, which had been restored by one of the Hyksos, and still later by the Ramessides. With the exception of one or two doubtful queens of the first dynasty, she is believed to be the earliest queen of Egypt of whom we have mention, and to have shared the reigns either of Teta or of Pepi I. It is a significant fact in the internal history of the empire, which continued to expand to the south and the east during the sixth dynasty, that the village chiefs and other high officials began under the sixth dynasty to show an inclination to build their tombs in the district where their property was situated. Thus the burial-grounds of mastaba tombs ranged around a royal pyramid slowly go out of fashion ; the court nobility is becoming transformed into a landed aristocracy, and becomes capable of developing a power of its own independently of the king.

Longest Reign in History

In two epitaphs of this period we find expressions of well-marked satisfaction upon the part played in life by the deceased. One from Abydos, the ancient necropolis, relating to Unas, tells how he began his official career as a boy under King Teta, and was honoured with the confidence of Pepi I. The inscription continues : " His Majesty resolved upon war against the Asiatics ; an army of many myriads was assembled from the whole of the south, from Elephantine, from the Northland, &c., from the Negro countries Aartet, Metja, Amam, Wawat, Kaau, and Tataam ; his majesty sent me forth at the head of his army. There stood the princes, the High Treasurers, the nearest friends of the Palace, the country chiefs and prefects of cities of the South and Northland, the

A WALL-PAINTING IN A TOMB OF THE FOURTH DYNASTY

friends, and the superintendents of the gold [perhaps bearers of golden tokens of honour], the chiefs of the prophets and the overseers of the temple property [each one] at the head of a troop of the South or of the Northland, of the cities and districts over which they ruled, and of the negroes of those lands." This account presents us with what is, comparatively speaking, the clearest picture we possess of the political constitution of Egypt and of its unwieldy military system toward the end of the Old Empire. The levies of negro troops, together with the motley array of national militia, were not made without reason. Five or six campaigns were necessary before Unas succeeded in scattering the enemy, who were in all probability the aggressors. Finally, the Egyptian commander went, by sea perhaps, to the coast of Palestine, where " he defeated and slaughtered them all." These Asiatics are called Heriu-sha, literally " Those who are on the sand."

A second and still more valuable inscription from Assouan, relating to Her-khuf, makes mention of campaigns against the countries of Nubia and the western oases. Her-khuf was governor of the Southland, an important post even at that time, under Merenra, the successor of Pepi I. A march of eight months far into the interior of Nubia seems to have been crowned with success. The next campaign is said to have been directed from

Asyut against Tamehu-land, " the west of heaven "—the Libyan oasis El-Khargeh —which had been captured from the Nubian prince of Amam; this undertaking proved successful. Her-khuf was honoured by a royal rescript or personal letter from the young king Merenra, expressing the great satisfaction of the king with a dwarf, or " Deng," whom Her-khuf had brought from Nubia. Her khuf seems to have got as far as Kordofan and Darfur, to judge from the fact that he brought back ivory and ebony to Egypt, as well as this pygmy. The kingdom had exhausted its strength in a constant succession of enterprises, and seems to have sunk into weakness under Pepi II., of whose presumably long reign we hear very little.

According to both Herodotus and Manetho, Menthesuphis, who must be a second Mehti-em-saf, was overthrown by a revolt after a reign of one year. His wife and sister Nitocris (or Neitakert) succeeded to the throne, and revenged herself by inviting the rebels to a feast in a subterranean chamber, into which she turned the waters of the Nile and drowned the entire assembly. Shortly afterward she was able to escape the consequences of this deed only by suicide of an equally desperate nature ; she threw herself into a room filled with glowing ashes. This story, however, has certainly no historical value as an account of the extinction of the dynasty; on the contrary, it has been proved that it was the twelfth dynasty that ended with a queen. The Nitocris legend, after furnishing the Greeks with material for use in all kinds of connections —for instance, in the legend of Rhodopis, afterwards transformed into a Cinderella tale—is still current as a ghost story among the Mohammedans living **An Egyptian Cinderella** in the neighbourhood of the pyramids. Very possibly the name Nitocris is a confusion between that of the real queen of that name who belonged to the twenty-sixth dynasty, shortly before the time of Herodotus, and the name of a king named Neterkara, who reigned at the end of the sixth dynasty.

With the extinction of the sixth dynasty the unity of the Egyptian empire apparently comes to an end for a considerable period, or its restoration upon a permanent basis proved impossible for the moment. The configuration of the country requires, above all things, a central government, which should make the necessities of irrigation as they arise the guiding principles of its policy. These necessities kept the petty princes in a continual state of feud ; a shortage of water in the

A DWELLING IN ANCIENT EGYPT 5,000 YEARS AGO

north immediately occasioned complaints against the owners of canals in the south. It may have happened often enough that an imperial dynasty was overthrown simply because the Nile god, and therefore the other gods also, manifested their anger by denying the necessary floods. A passage in the decree of Canopus clearly shows the connection between the height of the floods and the security of the throne, and makes plain that as late as the Ptolemaic period it was thought desirable in official circles to speak in veiled language of these unpopular occurrences, even of such as had occurred in earlier times.

For the house of Pepi there can be no doubt that war also produced fatal effects. It is but rarely that we catch a

glimpse of any events of real importance throughout the " history " of the Old Empire, which in truth was as yet no empire at all. The chronology of the period is in a similar state of obscurity. The earliest reliable date occurs in the period of the Middle Empire—the beginning of the twelfth dynasty, about 2000 B.C., though even this is uncertain. The period from the beginning of the twelfth to the end of the sixth dynasty may be considered 500 years, so that the latter dynasty lasted from 2700 to 2500 B.C., and the fifth from 2820 to 2700 B.C. On the other hand, the great pyramid builders of the fourth dynasty can hardly have been a burden to the land for more than a century in all. The supposition or tradition that Khufu lived to see the birth of the founder of the succeeding dynasty is perhaps supported by the epitaph of a certain prince Rasekhem-ka, who served five kings of the fifth dynasty. Hence the period occupied by the fourth dynasty may be well limited to the years 2920--2820 B.C. We have no means of ascertaining the duration of the first three dynasties, but the 769 years assigned must be too many. We shall be nearer the truth if we assume that the great kings of the first dynasty ruled about the year 3500 B.C., and that the originals of the traditional " Menes " (Aha and Narmer ?) reigned a century or so earlier. In view of recent discoveries, even earlier dates are by no means improbable. It is, for instance, difficult to reconcile **Kings Who Ruled 5,500 Years Ago** the date of 2000 B.C. for the beginning of the twelfth dynasty with the apparent fact of the long duration of the thirteenth. On the other hand, the estimate of the period between the sixth and twelfth dynasties at 500 years may eventually prove to be too long. We can also say that the pyramids of Gizeh were built at the latest about 3000 B.C.

ONE OF THE COLUMNS IN THE TEMPLE OF HATHOR AT DENDERA
The general effect of a series of these splendid Hathoric columns is illustrated on page 2046.

AN ENTRANCE TO ANCIENT THEBES: THE GATE OF A TEMPLE AT KARNAK

A faithful restoration of the immense gate, sixty-five feet high, of the temple of Khonsu, at Karnak, which stood at the end of a two-mile avenue of ram-headed sphinxes leading from the temple of Luxor. The procession seen in the picture is that of a Pharaoh, with his victorious army, entering Thebes, of which Karnak was a district.

ANOTHER OF THE WONDERFUL TEMPLE GATES OF ANCIENT EGYPT

This magnificent gate gave entrance to the ancient temple of Dendera, on the banks of the Nile, and it is represented by the artist during the festival of the Nile. The plate is reproduced from a work issued under the patronage of Napoleon, "Le Description de l'Egypte," and gives a vivid idea of how these gateways appeared in Egypt's prime.

THE WONDERFUL ROCK TOMBS OF THE KINGS OF EGYPT IN THE MOUNTAIN FASTNESSES OF THEBES

For thousands of years the Pharaohs of the eighteenth to the twenty-second dynasties lay here, in glorious sculptured tombs cut deep in solid rock; until, in our own time this resting-place of the Pharaohs was revealed. The Valley of the Tombs of the Kings has been the scene of the most remarkable discoveries, and the passing of dead Pharaohs, conveyed in state vessels down the Nile to Cairo amid the lamentations of the natives, was one of the most moving spectacles in the modern world.

AN INTERIOR VIEW BY MOONLIGHT OF THE GREAT TEMPLE OF AMON AT KARNAK

A restoration of the largest and finest of the great temples at Karnak, once part of the ancient city of Thebes. Amon, "the Unrevealed," was an Egyptian deity who corresponds to the Greek Zeus, and Thebes, or No-Amon, was the principal seat of his worship. The great pyramidal towers at the entrance served defensive as well as architectural purposes.

THE PORTICO OF THE GREAT TEMPLE OF ISIS AT TENTYRA
This temple, built in the Libyan desert, probably in the time of the early Ptolemies, is remarkable for the richness of its sculptures, a suggestion of which is conveyed in this fine drawing by one of Napoleon's savants.

THE WORSHIP OF THE GODDESS HATHOR IN THE TEMPLE OF DENDERA
This restoration of the portico of this beautiful temple shows a procession of priests entering for worship. Each column of the portico bears at the top the head of Hathor, and scenes of her worship are sculptured on the walls.

INTERIOR OF THE BEAUTIFUL TEMPLE OF PTOLEMY IV. AT DER EL-MEDINEH

A reconstruction of the splendid temple dedicated to Hathor, built by Ptolemy Philopator, a little earlier than 200 B.~., on the site of a more ancient temple built in the reign of Amenhotep III., about 1500 B.C., which had fallen into ruins.

THE COLOSSI OF MEMNON, BUILT BY AMENHOTEP III. AT THEBES, AS SEEN AT THE OVERFLOWING OF THE NILE

GREAT DAYS OF THE OLD EMPIRE
AND THE RULE OF THE SHEPHERD KINGS

A FRAGMENT of the Turin papyrus gives a summary of the reigns of the "Old Kingdom," to the effect that 1,755 years had elapsed since the reign of Menes. This would agree roughly with the estimate already given. Further calculation makes it clear that Manetho computed the period between Menes and the end of the sixth dynasty as about 250 years less than the number above stated. A mere list of the dynasties computed by Manetho is all the information to be obtained from him upon the very obscure period dividing the sixth from the twelfth dynasty. Remarkably enough, the seventh dynasty is said to have had "seventy kings in seventy days." In view of the more independent position of the landed aristocracy under Pepi, it has been thought to recognise in the seventy monarchs of a day a wholly unsuccessful attempt on the part of the aristocracy to replace the monarchy by a government of nobles holding the power in rotation. At an early period an epitomiser read or amended the statement as "five kings in seventy-five years," perhaps in order to avoid lending his support to a tradition of such historical absurdity.

70 Kings in 70 Days

Like the preceding rulers, the 27 kings of the eighth dynasty—146 years—are said to have sprung from Memphis. They were followed by two dynasties from Herakleopolis. Of these the ninth consisted of 17 kings, who reigned 409 years, and a tenth, likewise of 17 kings, reigning 185 years. Their place of origin was Herakleopolis—Khenensu of the Egyptians—in Upper Egypt.

This lack of information is partly met by Manetho's statement, which can also be supported by the evidence of inscriptions, that the founder of the ninth dynasty, Akhthoes, was the most tyrannical ruler that the country had yet known. After committing many evil deeds he went mad, and was finally eaten by a crocodile, which reptile seems in ancient Egypt to have been specially supplied by Providence for such purposes. From this instructive story many deductions have been drawn in modern times. The Herakleopolites are supposed to have been foreign conquerors, who broke into the pyramids and destroyed the mummies.

The Pyramids Ravaged

A number of sculptures found in the Delta, the style of which is certainly foreign, have been supposed to belong to their time. But so small a body of evidence is hardly sufficient basis for such extensive conclusions. The sculptures and their strange style should more probably be ascribed to the later kings of the twelfth dynasty, perhaps to Amenemhat III. Akhthoes is certainly himself an historical character, though the tales of his cruelty may well be apocryphal. His name in the hieroglyphs is conventionally read Kheti, and was probably pronounced Ekhtai. He also bore the name Ab-meri-Ra. Of another Herakleopolite king, named Ka-meri-Ra, we have a monument in the inscriptions of Tefaba, prince of Asyut, which record the wars with Tefaba waged on behalf of Ka-meri-Ra against the princes of Thebes, who were now for the first time aspiring to the sovereignty of all Egypt.

According to Manetho, the eleventh dynasty included 16 kings of Thebes, who ruled 43 years. This is the first appearance in history of the "southern residence" of the kings of Egypt, although it was not till the beginning of the New Empire that Thebes attained its full importance. As early as the Roman period the city had again become nothing more than an area of gigantic ruins interspersed with villages. Four main groups of ruins still indicate the approximate area of the ancient city: on the east of the river, Karnak to the north and Luxor to the south; on the west of the river, Medinet Habu to the south and Kurnah to the north, both named after

Kings of Thebes

neighbouring fellahin villages. On the west the slopes of the hills are honeycombed by numerous tombs, among which those of Shekh Abd el Kurnah and the Assasif, with the terraced temples of Der el-Bahari are the best known. The celebrated " valley of the kings' tombs," Biban el-Muluk, winds far into the chain of hills behind Der el-Bahari.

Tombs of the Kings At Thebes is the Ramesseum, incorrectly called the " Memnonium " by classical authors subsequent to Strabo. Between it and the great temple of Medinet Habu tower the two statues of Memnon. Three miles away, on the opposite bank of the river, rises the great temple of Karnak. The sanctuary of Luxor together with the obelisk is situated close to the river. The " city of the living," once a populous metropolis called Uaset by the Egyptians, extended from Karnak to the mountain range ; the temple precincts of Karnak proper were named " Apet " ; the quays for the river · traffic were at " Southern Apet," or Luxor. On the western bank of the Nile lies the great necropolis, the corresponding " city of the dead." The " dwellings rich in possessions " and the one hundred gates, which are mentioned with admiration in the Iliad—unless these are really, as seems most probable, the great pylons of the temples—even the fortress of the kings, known as " Ka-em-khut "—literally, " high on the horizon " —during the time of Amenophis III., have totally disappeared. The great artificial lake of Tjarukha, where Amenhotep III. (or Amenophis III.) and Queen Tii sailed in their state barge, the " Tehen-Aten " (the Sun-disk glitters), is a mere field surrounded by mounds. Of the huge funerary temple erected by the same king nothing but the mighty twin Colossi remain.

Memphis, or Hikuptah, the northern capital, has also disappeared, together with its more durable pyramids and rows of mastabas. We are unable to

Memphis Rebuilt in Cairo discover even the situation of the chief sanctuary, the temple of Ptah ; the " white fortress " has also vanished. According to Arab testimony the low hill of rubbish near Mit-Rahine, south of Gizeh, was covered with stately ruins about six hundred years ago ; in all probability it served even then as a stone quarry for the growing city of Cairo. The rapid dis-

appearance of the last edifices at Memphis is to be accounted for in the same way.

The time from the beginning of the seventh to the end of the eleventh dynasty according to Manetho's reckoning would amount to far more than the five hundred years allotted to the period of transition. This number, however, is apparently capable of reduction. It has been thought that the twelfth dynasty ruled Egypt from 2000 to 1788 B.C., though the evidence for this is as yet by no means universally accepted as conclusive, and it has long been known that about the year 1580 B.C. the eighteenth dynasty freed the land from the Hyksos. Thus there remains a period of little more than two hundred years in which to place the era of the foreign supremacy of the Hyksos, during which the Egyptian polity and society underwent a steady process of change, although many decades must have elapsed before the complete subjugation of the land by the Hyksos. But when Manetho proceeds to insert into this narrow period his thirteenth, or Theban, dynasty of sixty kings reigning for 453 years, and the fourteenth dynasty, which origi-

Muddle of the Dynasties nated in Xoïs—that is, Sakha, in the centre of the Delta, where apparently no ruins remain— consisting of 76 kings ruling for 484 years, all attempts to satisfy the demands of consistency are baffled. Up to the present time the Turin papyrus has always been considered the chief support of Manetho's account, because the kings of the thirteenth and fourteenth dynasties are there enumerated in full and with much greater detail, comparatively speaking, than in any other account. However, while on the one hand it is possible that the Turin papyrus repeated an erroneous tradition reproduced by Manetho at a later period, on the other hand we have to take into account the condition in which this manuscript was found ; the fragments of the papyrus when first pieced together were arranged in accordance with Manetho's list. Of the lists contained in inscriptions, one only, the chronologically worthless one at Karnak, contributes a series of names of kings which could correctly be assigned to this period. Of the Xoïtes, a provincial dynasty, no monuments have as yet been discovered.

In like manner the various monuments provide no connected account of the period of transition. Two or three names may perhaps be assigned with some certainty to the period between the seventh and tenth dynasties. Among these is King Kherti, who appears upon the monuments and whose deeds of prowess against Syrian enemies are mentioned in a papyrus. Some graves of dignitaries at Sakkara are considered to belong to the Herakleopolites—as, for example, that of Apa-ankhu, who lived under King Merikera, and was " not only of true royal blood, but was indeed the favourite of his master and governor of the lands."

Antef and Mentuhotep are the royal names which occur most frequently in the eleventh dynasty. As provincial governors of the fertile and extensive valley of Thebes, the first members of this house attained to great importance, while the tenth dynasty gradually exhausted itself in

enumerated as being Pharaohs, it is hardly probable that the first ruled the whole country ; the moderate estimate of forty-three years given to the whole line by Manetho is therefore certainly incorrect. Mentuhotep II. alone at least reigned for forty-six years, and was supreme

The Eleventh Dynasty over Egypt from Assouan to the coast. On the other hand, this reign was not able to recover Ethiopia, which had apparently long since been lost to the kingdom. The date of Antef IV. Uahankh is given by the stele erected in his fiftieth year, which forms part of a larger scene, where the ruler is represented surrounded by his four favourite dogs. From a papyrus report of an investigation into the tombs of the Theban kings, which took place about 1130 B.C., we learn of the existence of the pyramid of Antef IV., which " lies to the north of the outer court of the temple of Amenhotep, and before which the stele has been erected. Here is to be seen the figure of the king, with his dog named Behukaa between his feet." King Uahankh Antef is known to belong to the eleventh dynasty, because a twelfth dynasty official traces his descent back to a contemporary of

AN EXAMPLE OF EGYPTIAN SCULPTURE 4,500 YEARS AGO
A fine bas-relief, remarkable for its accuracy of outline, showing the sacred ox

struggles, details of which are unknown to us. This family soon began to expand ; one branch settled in the neighbouring Hermonthis, where an Antef sought to connect himself with the earlier rulers by repairing the ruined pyramid of Nekhtiaker.

The acquisition of Abydos, the religious importance of which town was closely connected with its early political claims, seems to have immediately followed the proclamation of the head of the family as "lord of the upper and the lower land." Probably the future royal residence was also transferred to Abydos. Hence a provincial governor, named Antef, again appears in Thebes with special titles, showing the importance of the city of Amon at that time. This Antef is at the same time warder of the frontier and a " pillar of the south." Of the five or six Antefs and the three Mentuhoteps who are

Uahankh ; but other Antefs, who formerly were considered to belong to this period, are now known to be posterior to the thirteenth dynasty. Seankhkara seems to have been the last ruler of the eleventh dynasty ; he entrusted his official Heru with the fitting out of an expedition to Punt, which advanced eastward through the valley of Hammamat, and then proceeded by sea. Although Henu

Expedition to the Land of Frankincense only accompanied the expedition to the coast of the Red Sea, he caused a remarkably boastful description of the undertaking to be carved at Hammamat, which dates from the eighth year of Seankhkara, and perhaps was not set up until after the king's death. Considerable additions have been made to our knowledge of the eleventh dynasty of recent years. Many new names of kings have been found : a new Antef, who bore the Horus name Nekht-neb-tep-nefer, a Mentuhotep with the Horus name Sankh-ab-tani, and a duplicate of Mentuhotep II., with the prenomen Neb-hapet-Ra, like Mentuhotep II., but spelt in a different manner. This last new king is known

The Latest Excavations to us from the latest excavations (1903-7) at Der el-Bahari, which have revealed to us the funerary temple of Mentuhotep I., to which additions were apparently made by Mentuhotep III. (Neb-hapet-Ra II.). This building, which was known as Akh-asut-Neb-hapet-Ra, "Glorious are the seats of Neb-hapet-Ra," lies to the south of the great temple of Queen Hatshepsu at Der el-Bahari, in the necropolis of Thebes. It consists of a square platform artificially hewn out of the rock, on which stood a small pyramid, surrounded by an ambulatory or colonnade. This was approached from the east by a ramp of ascent, on either side of which is a small colonnade, on the level of the ground. On each side of the platform is a deeply cast court. At the back of the pyramid is the descending dromos of what is either the actual tomb of King Neb-hapet-Ra I. or a cenotaph, an "empty tomb," made not to contain the actual mummy of the king, but the statue of his ka, or double.

A NOMARCH OF ANCIENT EGYPT
The provincial governors introduced by Amenemhat I. about 2700 B.C. were called nomarchs and replaced a landed nobility.

Thus it is rather a sanctuary than a tomb, properly speaking. Of the two views, the latter is considered to be the more probable by the discoverer, Prof. Naville. The gallery of this "tomb-sanctuary" is 400 feet in length ; at the end of it is a chamber, made in all respects like the tomb-chamber of a pyramid, which contains an alabaster shrine, in which, in all probability, once stood an image of the king. (Not far off, in 1898, a great royal tomb was found which contained nothing but the statue of another king, Mentuhotep —this is perhaps the analogous "tomb-sanctuary" of Neb-hapet-Ra II.) At the back of the colonnaded court which contains the dromos, is a hypostyle hall, in which immediately beneath the towering cliffs of Der el-Bahari is a small sanctuary, containing an altar placed before a niche cut in the rock. The whole

of this temple was decorated with painted reliefs of the highest excellence, which have given us a totally new idea of the art of the eleventh dynasty. This building is the only temple of the Middle Empire which is at all well preserved, and is the most ancient building at Thebes.

From the fact that Uahankh Antef was separated in time by less than a century from Senusret I. we see that the eleventh dynasty immediately preceded the twelfth, as has been usually supposed. In order, however, to reconcile the undoubted length of the thirteenth dynasty with the short period of 300 years allowed between the twelfth and eighteenth dynasties, if we accept the Kahun date for Senusret III., it has been proposed to place the thirteenth dynasty before the twelfth. But to intercalate it between the eleventh and twelfth is impossible, and it is equally impossible to place it before the eleventh. For one thing, the scarab designs of the thirteenth dynasty are obviously intermediate between those of the twelfth and those of the eighteenth dynasty. Here is a case in which practical archæology comes forward with definite evidence to correct ill-considered and hasty historical theories. From the inscriptions, too, of Asyut it is quite evident that the Theban kings of the eleventh dynasty rose to power by war against the Herakleopolite princes of the tenth. There is no room for the thirteenth dynasty before the eleventh or twelfth. We have, at any rate, the definite fact that Senusret I. reigned less than a century after Antef IV., so that Seankhkara must have been almost the immediate predecessor of Amenemhat I., the first king of the twelfth dynasty.

Value of Archæology When King Amenemhat I., the founder of the twelfth dynasty, appointed his son Senusret I. co-regent in his old age, he is said to have presented him with a book of profound "instructions." Several long fragments of this work still remain. From them, and from inscriptions on the tomb of a provincial lord, Khnumhotep, at Beni-Hassan, we gather that it was not until after a severe struggle that Amenemhat raised himself to the Egyptian throne, and that the grandfather of Khnumhotep rose to greatness as the result of a general change in the provincial governorship. He became lord of the Nome of the Goat, with a residence at Menat-Khufu, to which was later added the neighbouring Nome of the Gazelle. It was here in Central Egypt that the new dynasty seems to have specially secured its position, for, like the previous line, it undoubtedly originated in Thebes, and apparently removed the seat of power to the Fayyum.

SENUSRET III. Mansell
Part of a black granite portrait statue, now in the British Museum, of one of the most successful kings of the 12th dynasty.

We learn from inscriptions—especially from those in the tombs of the provincial governors at Asyut, Bersheh, and Beni-Hasan—that Amenemhat I. introduced

nobility they became an official class, and were transformed from petty princes into prefects. This change again made a simplification of the government possible as regarded the highest authorities. During the Old Empire the division of the country into "the south" and "the north" formed the basis of the administrative machinery, the king, as "lord of both lands," forming the connecting link. Now, under the twelfth dynasty, the personal tie gives place to a union of political reality. Nevertheless, the historical distinction between north and south, resting as it did upon racial differences, was too deeply rooted to disappear entirely.

Side by side with the king, the high treasurer now appears with authority

THE MODERN VILLAGE OF ABYDOS, ONE OF THE OLDEST SITES OF ANCIENT EGYPT

far-reaching changes into the administration, and that in this respect at least he must be looked upon as a great reformer. He set aside or entirely abolished the old aristocracy of the provincial rulers, and introduced new laws defining the authority of their successors. The new governors, or nomarchs, were placed on an equality with their predecessors, in so far as the landed property vacated by the latter was for the most part handed over to them; thus they still remained the most powerful landed proprietors in any one district, with the exception of the interest represented by the temple property and the royal domains. But from a landed

over the whole of Egypt. Under the Old Empire the importance of this official had steadily increased until he took precedence over all others. Among other titles of this highest official were "greatest of the great, prince, overseer of the human race, who advises the king, and to whom the entire land renders account." His responsibility was appropriately expressed in the title "overseer of all that exists and of all that does not." Next in rank stood the "treasurer of the god," or "chief warden of the silver house," whose chief duty seems to have been to prepare estimates for the general expenditure; while the "chief judge and head of the

FUNERARY PYRAMID OF ABYDOS
A reconstruction of one of the smaller pyramids of the Middle Kingdom, possibly the tomb of a court official, built about 5,000 years ago.

overseers," the vizir of the Old Empire, received the post of prefect of the capital, a position of great splendour but of limited authority. Officials of middle and lower rank now appear in large numbers. They also were chiefly con-

Officials of the Old Empire cerned with the treasury, and looked up with awe to the high treasurer, " who nourishes the people." He also made provision for the sacrifices to the gods and the dead—that is, so far as the customary offerings of the king to the distinguished dead were concerned—and attended to the repair and decoration of the temples.

The Old Empire, with its bewildering profusion of high offices, dignities, and titles of honour, bore the character of an oligarchy of court nobles moderated by the despotism of the king, and in some respects reminds us of the mandarin system ; whereas the state of Amenemhat and Senusret was governed upon principles of administration closely resembling the econo-mic system of the eighteenth century of our era on the continent of Europe — that is, a kind of "modernised" feudalism. The dependence of the temples upon the royal treasury is plainly marked, although the colleges of priests controlled their own incomes, derived from a mortmain possession of lands sufficient to support them.

THE OBELISK OF ON
All that remains of Heliopolis, the ancient city of the Sun.

But the state not only controlled the sacrifices by means of the ingenious edict that the nomarch must receive his appointed share, but the colleges them-selves also found it advantageous to place at their head the chief authority in the nome. It was rarely a matter of great difficulty to make such an authority eligible for inclusion in the legitimate families by means of fabricated gene-alogies.

The salary of such an official, holding at the same time the lucrative position of chief priest and prophet, when added to the revenue of his private estates and official lands, rose to an amount enabling him to support a princely establishment. It is certain, however, that his outgoings and expenses were not small. The govern-ment, in the person of its highest adminis-trator, the high treasurer, was very exacting in its demand that a good profit should be forthcoming from the nome when the accounts were balanced.

The treasury expenditure was not to exceed the income ; on the contrary, the nomarch was to arrange the average imposi-tion of taxes so as to have a credit balance of taxation in reserve which could be drawn upon in bad years. In many nomes this was an easy matter, in others it was more difficult. Possibly, also, the great financial adviser, who stood so close to the king's ear, was none too ready to grant assistance in the time of want. " When years of famine came," writes Ameni, the prefect of the Nome of the Gazelle under Senusret I., " I ploughed the fields of the province to its frontiers on the south and on the north " — a reli-gious rite originally incum-bent upon the king. " I preserved the lives of the inhabitants of the province, and gave them sustenance, so that there were none starving therein. I gave the same portion to the widow as to the married woman, and never preferred the great before the small in granting my assistance. And afterward the river rose high, wheat and barley throve, and there was abundance in the land, but I did not oppress the peasant because of his arrears." Although years of drought were the most severe test of the capacities of a nomarch for administration, yet his current expenses at other times were of very considerable amount. It was necessary to exceed the expectations of the court by paying a carefully calculated surplus in excess of the regular demands. In order to carry on the business of his own little centre, the nom-arch was obliged to keep an office with a

Finances of the Nomarchs comparatively large number of scribes. Should the Pharaoh set out " to make the foreign countries tremble before his majesty," the nomarch was obliged to call out his contingent—Ameni provides 400 to 600 men—and to take the field with his sovereign. The chief treasury officials had also to be conducted to the quarries and mines in the land of the Trogodytes or in the Sinaitic peninsula, or the nomarch himself was despatched upon royal commissions. If successful, he was the recipient of high praise, as well as of material rewards on his return to court.

The nomarch greatly cherished the right of journeying to the quarries on his own account, there to order the stone decorations for his future tomb or to have his statue carved in heroic size. What he valued most, however, was the royal assurance that the governorship of the nome should become the hereditary possession of his house. When this assurance was received, the tomb within the cliffs truly became a place of consolation in view of the period after his death. His family would never be threatened by want, and there would be no interruption to the sacrifices to the ancestors.

The reign of Amenemhat I. began about 2000 B.C., at the very latest — possibly in reality a century or two earlier; ten years later he appointed his son Senusret, or Usertsen I., co-regent, and died on the seventh day of the Egyptian month Phaophi, after a reign of thirty years. Apparently the old king's chief motive in appointing his successor as co-regent at such an early date was, above all things, to secure the crown to his own house; in all other respects he himself remained at the head of affairs. The decade of the co-regency was occupied by foreign wars. A poetical inscription of the twenty-fourth year of Amenemhat's reign, now in the Louvre, refers to wars against

Wars Against the Nubians the Nubians, the Bedouins of the Sinaitic desert, the Trogodytes, and even against Punt. We have an undoubted reference to a campaign in the twenty-ninth year of the reign against the Nubian land Wawat; and when the king died within his palace, Senusret was abroad upon an expedition against one of the northern oases.

NEGRO CAPTIVES OF THE EGYPTIANS

Everything possible had been done to ensure that this change in the government should be carried through without difficulty. A gleam of light is thrown upon the process by a story of adventure, which certainly rests upon a basis of fact.

Romance of a Court Official Sanehat, a near relation and court official of Amenemhat I., who is also said to have been "high in the queen's favour," was at that time in the capital. As soon as "the god had ascended to heaven," and the palace was closed, the chief court dignitary despatched couriers to Senusret I. Sanehat had either committed himself to the support of another claimant to the throne, or he had been on ill terms with Senusret at an earlier period; at any rate, he went out a stage from the town to meet the returning couriers, and was not a little terrified on seeing Senusret approach with a small company of followers. Trembling, he crawled into a bush until the king had passed, and in the conviction that a revolt would break out in the capital he fled southward, crossed the Nile, and finally reached the eastern desert near the Bitter Lakes, after creeping through the frontier entrenchments of the so-called "prince's wall" by night. The Bedouins treated him with great respect. Ultimately he becomes chief of a tribe, wins fame in war, and sees his sons grow up around him. But in his old age a letter of pardon is sent to him by Senusret granting him free return to Egypt. He calls for hymns of praise to be sung, and utters not a word of sorrow at parting from his adopted home. In fact, to a description of the comfort which once again surrounded him at the court he adds the remark: "The filth was left to the desert, the coarse clothing to the sand-dwellers. I was clothed in fine linen and anointed with the oil of the land. I slept in a bed.

Thus I grudge not the sand to those who dwell upon it, nor the oil of the tree to him that hath no better."

Senusret I. reigned forty-four years. He, too, must apparently be included among the great builders. Three stone sculptures of him have been found at Tanis, which must have been for many years the first city of the Delta. At **Senusret a Great Builder** Heliopolis he erected a temple, where one of two obelisks is still standing. The temples of Osiris at Abydos, of Amon at Karnak, and that of Koptos were all repaired by the care of Senusret. The primitive temple at Hierakonpolis, which had already been repaired by the kings of the sixth dynasty, was again restored. Inscriptions of Senusret I. have come to light at Wady Halfa at the second cataract, one of which mentions the eighteenth year of his reign and speaks of victories over Nubian tribes. We have also a narrative of this event

pyramid of Illahun has been identified as the tomb of this king, and an interesting seated statue of his wife, Nefert, wearing a padded wig that falls over her breast in two spiral curls, has been found in Tanis.

The reign of Senusret III., which follows, is characterised by important incidents of another kind. The first third of his reign was occupied chiefly in war : the king directed his main efforts against the Nubian peoples. The southern frontier of the Egyptian kingdom was again pushed forward beyond the second cataract—that is, almost to the limit of the extension which it reached later under the Sebekhotep kings. At Semneh and at Kummeh on the opposite bank of the Nile, about latitude $21°$ N., Senusret III. erected two great barrier forts, the remains of which are still of sufficient size to afford an idea of ancient Egyptian methods of fortification. Even at this early period the device was employed of

THE COMING OF THE SEMITES INTO EGYPT

In the reign of Senusret II., about 1895 B.C., the first tribe of Semites appeared in Egypt, bearing objects of barter and possibly desiring to settle in the land as the family of Jacob did. From a painting in Khnumhotep's tomb.

from Ameni, mentioned above, dating from the king's forty-third year.

Two years before his death Senusret followed his father's example and appointed his son Amenemhat II. co-regent. The monuments erected during the reign of this king seem to have been of less architectural importance than those of his father. We have no mention of war during his reign. With the accession of Amenemhat II. the period begins when the dynasty could enjoy in peace the fruits of the labour of the first two kings. In this reign Khnumhotep succeeded his father as governor of the Nome of the Goat ; and all the other changes in the officials of which we hear seem in like manner to have been directed to secure the succession to this family. According to Manetho, Amenemhat II. lost his life in a palace revolution ; he had appointed his son Senusret II. as co-regent. The

curving back the upper parts of the great brick bastions, in order to prevent the use of scaling-ladders. An inscription set up at Semneh in the eighth year of the king says : " This is the southern boundary. No negro or his cattle may pass north of this line either by land or by water. Should they appear in the land of Aken for purposes of trade, or if they have any business there, nothing shall be done to them ; but their boats may never pass beyond Heh." Nevertheless in the sixteenth and nineteenth years of Senusret's reign fresh campaigns **Further Nubian Wars** became necessary. The first is commemorated by another inscription at Semneh, which contains contemptuous reference to the negroes. The king warns his descendants never to be driven back from this frontier ; any one who should retreat was not to be called his descendant.

There were good reasons for this exhortation. In the Osiris town of Abydos the king's high treasurer, named Ikhernefer, erected a monument to commemorate the completion of an important commission for glorifying and presenting gifts to the god, on which he had been sent by Senusret III.: " The royal order to . . . the nearest friend, the superintendent of the houses of gold and silver, the high treasurer, Ikhernefer. My Majesty commands that thou be guided to Abydos, to erect a memorial to my father Osiris [the king speaks as the incarnation of the god Horus on the earth], the overlord of the West, and to adorn the secret places [the adytum of the temple] with the gold that my Majesty brought forth from Nubia with victory and honour." Thus it is probable that the two fortresses in the Nubian Nile valley defended the entrance to the goldmines of the south.

history of the New Empire were already known, it was possible to calculate by means of the astronomical data thus given that Senusret's seventh year lay between 1876 and 1873 B.C. This discovery would have made an end of the various hypotheses regarding the chronology of the Middle Kingdom, the beginning of which had been variously dated 2130, 2778, or 3315, were

The First Certain Dates it absolutely certain that this date is really correct. But, as a matter of fact, this date has many grave objections to contend against. For one thing, the computers are by no means agreed on this date. Mr. Nicklin places it some fifty or sixty years earlier than 1875 B.C. And even this revised estimate leaves us no more than 300 years for the rest of the twelfth dynasty, the assured long duration of the thirteenth, and the period necessary for the domination of the Hyksos, till we reach the certain date of the beginning

FORERUNNERS OF THE HYKSOS PRESENTED TO THE EGYPTIAN GOVERNOR
Continuation from opposite page of the painting depicting presentation of the Semites to the governor Khnumhotep. About 1800 B.C. the native dynasty was overthrown by the Hyksos, who were probably the Hebrews of the Exodus.

Of great importance, however, to history would be the supposed discovery of the first Egyptian date of real chronological value in this reign, could it be accepted without reserve. The ancient city at the entrance of the Fayyum, now known as Kahun, has yielded a comparatively large number of papyri of the twelfth dynasty. In a kind of diary discovered among the " Kahun " papyri is found a notice to the effect that on the twenty-fifth day of

Fixing Egyptian Dates the seventh month of the seventh year of Senusret III. the superintendent of the temple informed the governor that he proposed to make preparations for the festival for the rise of Sirius, which occurred on the sixteenth day of the following month ; in fact, we find on the day following the date thus stated a list of " the festival offerings for the rise of the star Sirius." As two similar dates in the

of the eighteenth dynasty, about 1580 B.C. To try to simplify matters by transferring the Sebekhotep kings of the thirteenth dynasty to the age before the eleventh dynasty is impossible for archæological reasons. To reduce the duration of the thirteenth dynasty is impossible, for we have certain evidence of many important reigns in that dynasty. To transfer the twelfth dynasty a whole Sothis period, or Sirius cycle (1461 years), back into time is equally against reason. So that we must suspend judgment on the matter for the present.

Under Amenemhat III. the greatness of this powerful dynasty begins to wane. This king had two pyramids. One is at Dahohur, the other rises in the inner border of the Fayyum to the east near Hawara. His solicitude for the worship of the crocodile-god, Sebek, is evidenced by several monuments and by the great temple at Hawara, the fame of which, as one of the wonders of the world, was continued by its name of "Labyrinth." This was evidently the funerary temple attached to the pyramid of Amenemhat. Some statues and busts of Amenemhat III. are remarkable for the obvious pains that have been taken to produce a likeness : the cheek bones are prominent, and the mouth shows a characteristic wrinkle. Accurate portraiture of this kind is characteristic of the art of the twelfth dynasty, and is not confined to statues of this king. At Der el - Bahari has been discovered a series of portrait statues of Senusret III., representing him at various periods of his life from youth to old age. Three of these are in the British Museum, and one is at Cairo. Two other equally good portraits of the same king have been found at Abydos and Karnak. Equally faithful portraits of Senusret I. have been found at Koptos and elsewhere. The heads of Senusret

Accuracy of the Portrait Statues

III. and Amenemhat III. present curiously marked and angular features, like those of the supposed Hyksos statues from Tanis. It has therefore been supposed that the Hyksos blood already existed in Egypt under the twelfth dynasty, and that the later kings of this line had Hyksos, or "Hittite," blood in their veins. But this is a very doubtful speculation, and it is much more probable that the Tanis and Bubastis portraits formerly assigned to the Hyksos or to the Herakleopolites really represent kings of the twelfth dynasty, some of them in a peculiar costume of which we do not know the precise signification. Certain pieces of evidence go to show that Amenemhat III. had peculiar religious ideas, to which these curious figures may owe their origin. Shortly before his death the king

AN ANCIENT EGYPTIAN FORTIFICATION
A reconstruction, by MM. Perrot and Chipiez, of the great barrier fort at Semneh erected by Senusret III. on the Nubian frontier of his kingdom in the early part of the third millennium B.C.

appointed his successor Amenemhat IV. as co-regent. He is said to have reigned nine years in all, six of which can now be verified by evidence. He was succeeded by his wife, who was perhaps his sister, Sebeknofru, who also continued the building operations at Hawara ; but the dynasty came to an end, according to Manetho, with her death four years later. The length of her predecessor's reigns has led to a doubt whether the succession was invariably from father to son or may have been transferred to the son-in-law, that is to say, to the female line.

After Amenemhat III., we are not again on firm ground until we reach a series of kings, most of whom bore the name of Sebekhotep, showing that they energetically maintained the cult of Sebek, the crocodile-god of the Fayyum, which had come into prominence in the later years of the twelfth dynasty. These kings seem, indeed, to have ruled from Crocodilopolis, as the later kings of the twelfth dynasty had ruled, not from Thebes, but from a royal burg called Itht-taui, "Seizing the Two Lands," which was situated somewhere in the neighbourhood of Lisht, on the Nile, a little northward of the Fayyum. The tradition of royal residence in this part of Egypt seems to have been handed down from the Herakleopolite kings.

The Sebekhoteps were powerful monarchs who ruled for a considerable length of time over a united and peaceful country, whose bounds were even more extended than at the present

The Crocodile Kings

day, ranging from the Mediterranean in the north to beyond the third cataract in the south. A statue of a Sebekhotep has been found in the island of Arko, north of Dongola, and it is known that the grey granite quarries of Tombos were worked at this time. That the thirteenth dynasty was a period of peace is evident in spite of the fact that a king, Smenkhkara, of whom two enormous statues of Tombos granite were erected at Tanis in the Delta, calls himself by the resounding title of Mermenfatiu, "General of the Soldiers." The succession of the kings was regulated apparently by descent in the female line : "the blood of Ra" was handed on by the queens, who raised their consorts to the position of Pharaoh. It is noticeable that in the case of private persons female descent is unusually emphasised under the Middle Kingdom. Thus the father of Sebekhotep II. was merely a priest named Mentuhetep, who held quite a subordinate position. Sebekhotep III. and Neferhotep, who were brothers, were the off-

End of the Native Dynasty spring of the marriage of another princess with a certain Haankhf. Neferhotep restored the temple at Abydos in accordance with information regarding the original plan derived from the sacred books. The remaining kings of this line form a long list, but the monuments tell us little or nothing about them; evidently prolonged peace and undisturbed comfortable possession had resulted, as usual, in general slackness and weakness, so that the proud kingdom of the Senusrets fell an easy prey to an invading horde of Asiatics from the north, who are known to us by the name of the Hyksos, or "shepherd kings," not earlier than about 1800 B.C.

"There ruled in our land," relates Manetho (quoted by Josephus), "a king named Timaios. In his time it happened, I do not know why, that a god was angry with us. And from the east there appeared unexpectedly people of low origin who defiantly invaded our land and took forcible possession of it, meeting with no serious resistance. After taking captive the rulers they burnt our cities, destroyed the dwellings of the gods, and inflicted all manner of cruelties upon the inhabitants ; some were massacred, the wives and children of others were enslaved."

This description of the rapid victory of the Asiatics is evidence for the fact that the excellence of military equipment must have fully compensated for the disadvantages of "low origin" ; in all probability they were the first people to acquaint the Egyptians with the use of horses and chariots in battle. Until this time great

Victory of the Asiatics heroes—for example, Senusret I.—were praised for their swiftness of foot, but after the liberation of Egypt the Pharaohs drove out to battle in their chariots.

With the arrival of the foreigners, the so-called Hyksos, the valley of the Nile was overrun by a people who possibly came from Arabia ; whether their appearance in Egypt was connected with the conquest of Babylon by the Kassites, or Kash-shu, which either began or was completed about 1700 B.C., is doubtful. According to Manetho's account it would appear as if the conquest of Egypt at first implied the dependence of the country upon some Asiatic empire. "Finally they made one of their leaders king, who was called Salatis. He went to Memphis and levied tribute from Upper and Lower Egypt. He also placed garrisons at suitable points." His attention was, however, directed chiefly to securing the eastern frontier in view of a possible attack from the growing Assyrian power. The term "Assyrians" is here employed to denote the empire for the time being on the Tigris and Euphrates. It is significant that Salatis, whose name recalls in many respects the Egyptian title "Shallit," which the Joseph of the Bible received from Pharaoh, immediately sought to fortify his kingdom in the direction from which his own nation had come.

"Salatis died after ruling nineteen years. After him another, named Beon or Bnon, reigned forty-four years. He was succeeded by Apakhnas, who reigned thirty-six years and seven months.

EGYPTIAN PORTRAITS OF ASIATICS
Contemporary pictures, from a wall-painting in an Egyptian tomb, of people of Asiatic race. The native fourteenth dynasty was displaced by an invasion of Asiatics known as the Hyksos.

After him came Apophis with a reign of sixty-one years, and Ianias with fifty years and one month. Finally came Assis with a reign of forty-nine years and two months. These six were the first of their rulers, and during their days there was continual war with the Egyptians, whom they endeavoured to annihilate. The people as a whole were called Hyksos, or Shepherd Kings; for 'Hyk' means king in the sacred language and 'Sos' a shepherd, so also in the popular tongue, and hence was 'Hyksos' compounded. By some they were considered to be Arabs. Thus this people is called the shepherd kings; they and their descendants held possession of Egypt for 511 years." Thus far Manetho's very ordinary account, which Josephus probably quotes from the original narrative.

AN EGYPTIAN SOUL HOUSE
A resting-place for the soul of a dead Egyptian, placed above his grave so that his wandering spirit could rest within it.

This Hyksos conquest (Hiku-Shasu, "Princes of the Shasu" = Bedouins) was an irruption on the grand scale, like the Arab invasion under Omar, 2,000 years later. There is no proof that among the Hyksos proper, the leaders of the invaders, there may have been non-Semitic elements from Northern Syria or Asia Minor, of the blood of the Khatti or "Hittites." Still less is there any proof of a racial or cultural connection between the Hyksos and the Minoan Greeks of Crete.

The period of the rule of the Hyksos has been exaggerated in the same manner as were the periods ascribed to the eighth, ninth, and tenth, and in part to the thirteenth dynasty. Instead of five centuries the supremacy of the Hyksos in the Nile valley probably lasted little more than two hundred years. The first six rulers mentioned above form Manetho's fifteenth dynasty. They are followed by the sixteen "other shepherds" without names or dates. Manetho gives a seventeenth dynasty as consisting of forty-three

Theban kings, who ruled contemporaneously with forty-three Hyksos during a period of 151 or 221 years. This is probably correct, for the supremacy of the Hyksos did not always extend much further than their stronghold Avaris, the Egyptian Hauar or Hatuar, in the Wadi Tumilat, though it seems later to have reached into Palestine and to have lost ground in Egypt itself. Wherever the Asiatics retreated and allowed the natives to supplant them, their monuments were also exposed to destruction.

Of the six kings, Apophis alone has left any historic traces behind him in the Delta and in the region of Memphis. From these it has been shown that at least three Hyksos bore his name in the form Apepi. "Ianias," however, may be identified with the king Khian, of whom the base of a stone statue has been discovered in Bubastis, a lion marked with his signet in Bagdad, and an alabastrum-lid bearing his name at Cnossos in Crete. As a statuette of an Egyptian of the Hyksos period, called Abnub, has also been found at Cnossos, we have in these two objects valuable evidence as to connection between Egypt and Greece at this period. The Hyksos kings, ruling in the Delta, naturally came into close contact with the Minoan "Thalassocrats" of Cnossos. The fact that objects bearing the name of Khian

AN EGYPTIAN MODEL BOAT MADE 4,000 YEARS AGO
This fine model of a boat, from a tomb of the Middle Kingdom, is probably an accurate representation of the boats used on the Nile about 2000 B.C.

have been found in places so far apart as Cnossos and Bagdad is an interesting comment on a title borne by Khian : *ank adebu*, " embracing territories," though of course we cannot assume that he exercised any kind of authority over Crete or Babylonia. The names, not only of Khian, but of several other Hyksos kings, are found on signet cylinders and scarabs —reproductions of the sacred dung-beetle in stone or porcelain — bearing these non-Egyptian titles, engraved in a primitive style. Scarabs of a similar primitive style have been found with the inscriptions " Uazed " and " Yapekhar." Khian and the Apepi kings belong to a time when the Hyksos court, and also methods of government, had become entirely Egyptian. Apepi Ra-neb-khepesh even restored the tomb of Queen Apuit of the sixth dynasty at Memphis, thus showing that he professed himself a lineal descendant of the ancient families. Under Apepi Ra-aa-user, who left behind him some short dedicatory inscriptions, a papyrus was written treating of mathematical problems. Finally the name of Apepi Ra - aa - kenen has been found on the well-wrought base of an altar which he set up to the god Set of Hauar. He also appears to have attempted to immortalise his name by inscribing it on several statues of earlier kings—as, for example, on that of Mermenfatiu, where he calls himself "the life-giving son of the sun, Apepi, beloved of Set." On the other hand, Amenhotep III. has replaced this name with his own on another statue. Generally speaking, this custom of appropriating earlier memorials began in the Hyksos period, and increased greatly in later times. The eastern Delta, especially at Tanis, has remained hitherto the chief source for monuments relating to the Hyksos. Examples of unique interest in the history of art are the two standing figures of the " fish sacrificers," a sphinx, a king's head from Bubastis, and the upper part of a statue from Mit-Faris in the Fayyum.

A SO-CALLED "HYKSOS" SPHINX FROM TANIS

If these figures, with their bony, broad-nosed faces and thick hair, are fully representative of the style of portraiture which the Hyksos brought into the country, this people were certainly not a pure Semitic type. These monuments, however, like the Bubastite colossi and the sphinxes of Amenemhat III. at Tanis, which used to be assigned to the Hyksos, may really date from the time of the twelfth dynasty and be connected in some way with the worship of Sebek as lord of the fish-producing province of the Fayyum. Their peculiar facial type, whether it be Egyptian or foreign, is, as we have seen, probably that of the later kings of the twelfth dynasty, not of the Hyksos.

Upper Egypt was undoubtedly for a time subjected to the Hyksos. It would seem that at the end of the thirteenth dynasty a family of kings bearing the name of Sebekemsaf ruled at Thebes in succession to a series of Mentuhoteps. Probably the last Mentuhoteps and the Sebekemsafs were tributary to the Hyksos. Later on, under a family who bore the name of Antef, the people of Upper Egypt seem to have become more or less independent of the Semitic conquerors, though they still paid tribute to them. Finally, under a series of kings who bore the name of Taa, and are reckoned as belonging to the seventeenth dynasty, a regular war of liberation was undertaken, and the Hyksos king and nation were expelled by the Egyptians after a series of desperate conflicts. These Asiatics were not absorbed ; their ruling family was not assimilated to the native race either by marriage or adoption.

The rise of the Theban kings, who were mere nomarchs, or provincial governors, before the coming of the Hyksos, was described by a writer of later years as follows. It happened that Egypt had no lawful rulers. Sekenen-Ra Taa was prince of the south, Apepi was sovereign in Hauar; the latter, however, had control of the land and its rich products. Behold,

Apepi chose Sutekh, that is, Set, for his god. He built him a permanent temple and served none of the other gods of the land. Apepi sent an urgent message to Sekenen-Ra in which the position of Amon-Ra in the Egyptian system of worship was discussed. Sekenen - Ra, however, was seized with great conster-

A Holy War nation. "The prince of the south called his great and wise men about him and told them all the words of the King Apepi. They, however, remained silent in perplexity and found no answer for good or bad. The King Apepi sent——" And here the manuscript breaks off. The struggles of the seventeenth dynasty ostensibly appear as a holy war. Sekenen-Ra is apparently the third of that name. His mummy, together with many others, was discovered in 1881 in a hiding-place in the cliffs near Thebes. When it was unwrapped it was clear that the prince had come to a violent end in the prime of life. The skull had been split by a blow, and the body had been hastily embalmed after putrefaction had already set in. From this discovery we may conclude that Sekenen-Ra fell in a battle or in flight at a date somewhere about 1600 B.C., and that the enemy left his body unburied. His successor is supposed to have been Kames. The war with the Hyksos probably continued, though not uninterruptedly.

About the year 1580 King Aahmes, perhaps the brother of Kames, succeeded to the throne of Thebes, and prepared to put an end to the Hyksos supremacy. An official under this king, also named Aahmes, the son of Baba, caused the story of his life to be inscribed upon his tomb at Nekheb. This is the earliest known attempt made by an Egyptian to inform posterity of the great events of his age ; and though clumsy in style, it furnishes a striking clue to the transformation which had taken place in the

First Historical Inscriptions Egyptian national feeling during the Hyksos period. Aahmes first saw active service as a youth on board the boat "Sacrificial Bull"; after his marriage he served on the ship "North." "And when the king rode forth in his war-chariot— [this is the first notice we have of the use of chariots in Egypt]—I followed him on foot. And we laid siege to the town of Hauar ; I showed bravery under the eyes of his majesty. Then I was appointed to the ship 'Appearing in Memphis'—[a name of importance for the development of affairs, as chronicling a formal coronation of the king in Memphis, after the capture of that city]. We fought on water in the lake Tjedku of Hauar. There I won a hand which was mentioned by the royal scribe, and gained me the golden necklace for bravery."

Hauar was taken apparently about the year 1560, but the Hyksos still retained their Asiatic possessions ; and even after Sharuhen, in the south of Palestine, was also taken the position of King Aahmes was still sufficiently difficult. His efforts in the north had encouraged the Nubian tribes to rise against him.

After a campaign in the south, one "Aata advanced into the upper country; but to his own destruction, for the gods of the south laid hands upon him." The hostile forces met at Tenta-a, and Aata was taken alive by King Aahmes. From the captain Aahmes's mode of expression, it appears probable that this was a Hyksos king from whom the Egyptians thus freed themselves. But

War Against the Hyksos the gallant captain does not tell us whether Aata invaded Egypt from beyond the frontier, or whether it was in the Delta that his rising began. The victories gained for Aahmes not only a number of slaves, but also a considerable increase of his landed property in Nekheb. His supremacy over the empire was definitely assured.

Compared with the account of Aahmes, the narrative given by Josephus, according to Manetho, of the expulsion of the Hyksos displays the Egyptians in a decidedly unfavourable light. "After all these things," he writes, "the kings of the Thebais and other Egyptian nomes rose against the Shepherds, when a long and difficult war broke out between them, until the Shepherds were overcome by a king named Misphragmuthosis, who drove them out of the other parts of Egypt and confined them to a place called Avaris, which has an area of 10,000 arures of land. The Shepherds surrounded this entire district with a strong wall in order that with all their forces they might there protect their property and plunder. However, Thummosis, the son of Misphragmuthosis, attempted to reduce them by siege, and advanced upon the place with 480,000 men. When he was beginning to despair

ISRAEL IN EGYPT UNDER THE PHARAOH WHO KNEW NOT JOSEPH

The oppression of the Hebrews in Egypt probably represents a phase in the Egyptian war of expulsion against the Hyksos, which ended in the exodus, according to Manetho and Josephus, of 240,000 men with their families and possessions through the desert to Syria. From the painting by Sir Edward J. Poynter by permission of the Autotype Co.

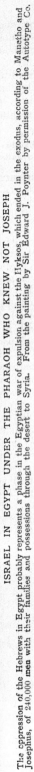

of success, they themselves offered to surrender on condition that they should evacuate Egypt and depart in whatever direction they might choose without let or hindrance. These terms were accepted, and they marched away, no fewer than 240,000 men, with their families and all their possessions, through the desert to Syria. As, however, they feared the Assyrians, who then ruled Asia, they built a city in the land now called Judæa, large enough to accommodate their numbers, and gave it the name of Jerusalem." It is clear that we have here a description of the Biblical Exodus of Israel from Egypt, as seen from another point of view. Criticism is as yet unable to decide whether Manetho related the story as it stands, or is responsible for that part of Josephus's version which identifies the Shasu with the Israelites. Some modern German scholars have come to the conclusion that the Israelites were never in Egypt at all, but in another country of the same name —Musri or Mitsraim—in Northern Arabia. The Musri theory and its pendant, the Jeahmeel theory of Professor Cheyne, have already passed in the minds of the archæologists and historians, if not yet entirely in those of the textual critics of the Old Testament, to the limbo of exploded fallacies. That the Misraim to which the Israelites went was Egypt, the Nile valley, is evident from the Biblical description, and we cannot doubt that the account of the Exodus, though of course written from the Jewish standpoint alone, and therefore open to criticism, also describes an historical event, an exodus from Egypt. Modern opinion seems to be veering most

The Exodus to Judæa

decidedly in the direction of accepting the statement of Manetho as given by Josephus, and regarding the identification of the Hebrews with the Shepherds of Manetho as correct in its main features. This was the conclusion arrived at by the patristic writers in accordance with the general testimony of tradition. It seems highly probable that the Pharaohs who were favourable to Joseph and the Israelites were Hyksos, and that after the expulsion of the latter by Aahmes, the " Pharaoh who knew not Joseph," followed the Oppression and finally the Exodus, probably in the reign of Thothmes I., or Thummosis. The occurrence of the name " Raamses " as one of the store-cities built during the oppression may be ascribed to a later stratum of the story, derived from knowledge of the " land of Goshen " in the time of the nineteenth dynasty B.C. when the Rameses ruled. Israel as a national name has as yet been found only once in an Egyptian inscription, and that belonging to the reign of Meneptah, who was till lately considered by some authorities to be the " Pharaoh of the Exodus." However, as we shall see later, the inscription in question implies that the Israelites were already settled in Palestine during the reign of this king. To assume that they were a branch of the race already in Palestine before the main Exodus is unnecessary if we identify the Exodus with the expulsion of the Hyksos.

Israel in Egypt

With the expulsion of the Hyksos Manetho brings the seventeenth dynasty to an end. According to his table Aahmes figures as the last king of the Middle and the first king of the New Empire.

A CONTEMPORARY MODEL OF A COMPANY OF ANCIENT EGYPTIAN INFANTRY

THE NEW EMPIRE
THE RISE OF EGYPT AS A MILITARY POWER

WHAT the Asiatic inroads and immigrations of earlier ages had failed to accomplish was brought to pass by the Hyksos. After their expulsion the kingdom of Egypt for centuries assumed a military character, which for a time it was able to maintain. Probably the kings of the Middle Empire who extended their supremacy over Nubia and the oases had not hesitated to invade the land of Canaan, nothwithstanding its greater power of resistance. Even during the days of the Old Empire fortresses of that country had been stormed and captured by Egyptian troops. But it was only under exceptionally favourable circumstances that the Egyptians could permanently overawe foreign powers, for their military forces consisted of the nucleus formed by the king's feeble palace guards, the contingents levied by the various nomarchs and the auxiliaries obtained from Nubian subject tribes who had been employed at an earlier period, but could be **The New Soldiery** sent into battle only under the strictest supervision. The contingents of the nomes were never more than armed peasants, whose sole incitement of bravery was the knowledge that if they broke and fled in the midst of a foreign country they would never see their homes again. On the other hand, a hostile army, when once it had crossed the Egyptian frontier, could safely count upon a sudden attack of homesickness among the native militia—an affection which was apt to become uncontrollable at the beginning of a battle. Now, however, about the year 1580, the monarchy of the restored empire possessed a new weapon in the war chariot and a professional soldiery composed of a class, for the moment numerous, who had lost their possessions and their means of livelihood during the long war of liberation ; to these were to be added emancipated slaves who had lost their masters. The stronger, however, the New Empire became, the more rapidly did this last class of soldiers diminish. It was, moreover, impossible to replace them by native recruits, to the extent of maintaining a strong standing army. The agricultural character of the Egyptian state, which in earlier centuries had necessitated recourse to Nubian auxiliaries in time of war, was incompatible with such a system of **Agriculture Versus Militarism** organisation. The tribes of the south of Wadi Halfa, the "Nine bows," were incorporated by Thutmosis III., and soon became the only true regiments of the line. About the year 1400 the soldiers of the Pharaoh were known to the Syrian subjects of the empire simply as "archers," or *pidati*. The *pidati* and war chariots were the king's sole material for any display of force.

If, however, the Pharaoh wished more particularly to spread the terror of his name, he sent out the "Shardana"—apparently the people who gave their name to Sardinia. Possibly their main settlements lay even then on the African coast opposite. They were soldiers of fortune who had been enlisted in detachments under the eighteenth dynasty. The Ramessides made no attempt to conceal the fact at a later period that these mercenaries were really Egypt's best soldiers. This reputation they can be proved to have gained among the Asiatics as early as the reign of Amenhotep III., and probably earlier under Thothmes III., or even before his time. Armed with long swords and great round shields with double handles, heavy coats of mail and large metal helmets, decorated with the crescent of the moon **The Regular Army** and the ball of the sun, sometimes also bearing dagger and javelin, the favourite tactics of the Shardana were to scatter the enemy by charging in close formation. That such an effect could be produced by an infantry attack was, even to a late period, unknown to the tacticians of Oriental armies. Of less reputation during the eighteenth dynasty were the Libyan auxiliaries. It was not until a later period that the Libyan tribes of the Kehak and the Mashawasha entered the service of the Pharaohs in any great number. As long as the New Empire was secure the rulers were cautious about employing the services of these border neighbours. The increased numbers of Libyans in the armies of King Rameses II. is a certain sign of weakness ; in fact, the time was then by no means far distant when Libyan mercenary commanders were to usurp the Egyptian throne. The prisoners of war and their descendants, called " Matjoi," after a Nubian tribe, also deserve mention. The organisation

of the national forces would naturally have continued on a separate basis in war as well as in peace. It is obvious, however, that the formation of combined bodies of troops was frequently ordered in battle to meet a sudden necessity. It may be gathered from the best of the official reports that it was not considered desirable to make mention of victories won by the national militia. Similarly, when the king was present at a victory, there is one chariot only, his own, the advance of which puts the enemy to flight.

The reign of King Aahmes, who lived to be about forty years of age, is, in other

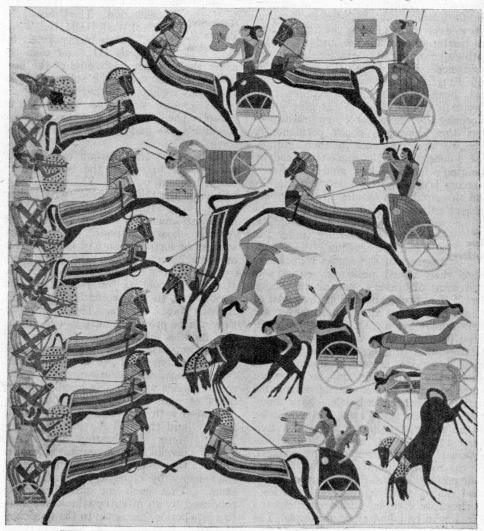

THE CHARGE OF THE CHARIOTS OF WAR IN ANCIENT EGYPT

Until the days of the New Empire Egypt had no army worthy of its importance, but about 1560 B.C. a professional soldiery was organised, and a new and important weapon, the war-chariot, introduced. From a temple painting.

THE MERCENARY SOLDIERS WHO SPREAD THE TERROR OF PHARAOH'S NAME
The most formidable soldiers of the organised army of the New Empire were the Shardana mercenaries, armed with long swords, shields, coats of mail, and metal helmets, sometimes also bearing dagger and javelin.

respects, not very rich in memorials. His mummy was discovered in the shaft of Der el-Bahari. Like that of Seknen-Ra his head was not shaven, as was usual among civilians and priests, but has long curls, as befitted a warrior ; on campaigns the Egyptians seem to have let their hair grow, and professional soldiers no doubt " wore their own hair," in eighteenth century phrase, and not wigs like the civilians.

The relations of Aahmes to the members of his family seem to have differed from those of the other Pharaohs. It appears that in the second half of his reign a change in the succession was introduced to the disadvantage of the king's brothers and sisters and their descendants. This dated from the time when Aahmes shared the throne with the queen Aahmes-Nefertari, when she and her children were shown special preference. The ecclesiastical dignity of a " woman of god " of Amon at Thebes was in all probability created specially for her. Finally, she and her son Amenhotep I. (or Amenophis) became objects of worship, and were practically canonised, as Neb-hapet-Ra Mentahotep had been before ; he with Aahmes Nefertari and her son Amenhotep were regarded as gods of the dead in the Theban necropolis. This, not Ethiopian blood, is the reason why they are often represented in tombs with black or greenish-blue faces, like the god Osiris. Amenhotep I. (also rendered Amenophis), **Early Days of the New Empire** about 1560 B.C., began his reign with a campaign against Kush, " in order to extend the boundaries of Egypt." Of this undertaking we have an account on the walls of the tomb of Aahmes of Nekheb.

Little information has come down to us regarding the life of Amenhotep I. Neither the civilisation nor the traditions of a new empire had attained their coming development in his days. The first attempts were even then being made, starting from the basis of twelfth dynasty civilisation, to develop upon Egyptian lines the new habits and progress introduced by the Hyksos. Perhaps it was his success in this direction which raised the memory of Amenhotep I. to the high honour in which it was **A Pious King** held in later times, an honour really due to his father. He was probably a very pious person like his mother, and assiduous in venerating the gods ; we can well imagine that it was he who founded the fortunes of the mighty priesthood of Amon at Thebes, and received in return the honour of a very special apotheosis after his death. We know that he began the magnificent buildings which have been made the great temple of Amon at Karnak, the wonder of the world. His successor, Thothmes I., has left us two copies, cne supplementing the other, of the formal announcement of his accession, sent to the " Prince of Kush," the Egyptian viceroy of Nubia. It runs as follows : " Royal command to Turo, the prince and governor of the south land. Behold this royal command is brought to thee, telling thee that my Majesty, who lives in happiness and health, is to be crowned king eternal and without equal on the Horus throne of the living. But my names shall be : (1) Horus, the strong bull, beloved of the god [of truth] Maat ; (2) the uniter of both lands [Upper and Lower Egypt], crowned with the royal snake, the powerful one ; (3) the golden Horus, with years of plenty [that is, the future years of his reign] cheering all hearts ; (4) the king of Upper and Lower Egypt, Aakheperkara ; (5) the son of the god Ra, Thothmes [the first], who lives omnipresent and eternal. Now bring offerings to the gods (of Kush), with votive sacrifices for the life, welfare, and health of the king Aakheperkara, the one inspired with life ; let oaths be taken by the name of my Majesty, who lives in happiness and health, born of the royal mother Senseneb, with whom all is well. This is written for thine instruction ; know that the house of the king is prosperous and secure. Given on the twenty-first day of the third winter month in the year 1, on the day of the coronation feast." Of the five names here assumed by the new ruler, Thothmes I., the first three were probably employed only in connection with the ritual ; the fourth is the official fore-name as king used in correspondence with foreign powers ; finally, the fifth is the personal name,which chiefly occurs on the monuments, and has consequently remained the historical designation for this as for all other kings. In cases of identical names, which are rather the rule than the exception, the Egyptians were accustomed to avoid confusion by the addition of the fore-name. The fore-name of Thothmes I., Aakheperkara, was probably pronounced something like "Okhpirkeria." His own name, Thothmes, was probably pronounced "Thutmases," and that of his father, Amenhotep (Greek, Amenothes), "Amanhatpe." That Amenhotep I. had already invaded Asia at the head of an army more than once may be concluded from various historical representations. The presence of Thothmes I. was, however, first demanded in Nubia, where the chiefs refused to take the required oaths. The king then turned upon the enemy in Asia. It seems that the tribute due to Egypt had not been paid. Two short references of King Thothmes III. to this war contain among other things the proof that his predecessor advanced almost to the Euphrates.

It was probably with the Iranian kingdom of Mitani, between Euphrates and Tigris, that the dynasty carried on its struggle for Syria. The blow dealt by Thothmes I. in this region apparently led

An Accession Proclamation

AMENHOTEP THE PIOUS
One of the early kings of the New Empire, who was afterwards worshipped as divine.

to the conclusion of a peace in terms favourable to himself. The Kushites were more obstinate ; before he had reigned three years the king was again forced to set out " to crush the miserable Kush." On this occasion the value of his greater military experience made itself manifest. The measures taken by the great conqueror of the Ethiopians, Senusret III., were resumed, for Thothmes I. not only reinforced the frontier garrisons of Semneh and Kummeh, but also reopened to navigation the canal through the first cataract.

Thothmes I., who, like Amenhotep I., added to the buildings of Karnak and raised on the western side of Thebes the oldest parts of the temple of Medinet Habu, reigned only thirteen years. As if he had had some premonition of his premature death, he made arrangements for the succession which he hoped would satisfy the most varied claims that could be raised. Sethe, Professors Naville, and Breasted have thoroughly investigated the special questions arising out of these regulations. However, the genealogy and order of succession from the death of Amenhotep I. to the beginning of the sole rule of Thothmes III. is still somewhat obscure. In the first place, it is unknown whether Thothmes I. was the son or son-in-law of Amenhotep I. ; in the latter case, his right to the succession was probably derived from his marriage with Queen Aahmes, or Amensat, the heiress to the kingdom. Thothmes I. was succeeded by Thothmes II., whose half-sister Hatshepsut was first co-regent with him during their father's life, then queen-consort, and then again queen-consort with the successor Thothmes III.—who was probably their half-brother, but possibly their son.

Succession of the Thothmes

Our information concerning Thothmes II. is but scanty. If the obscure but boastful testimony of a rock inscription near Assouan can be trusted, he gained brilliant victories over both the Nubian Khentnefer and also over the Asiatics. The fact of a war against the Ethiopian races is indirectly confirmed by our knowledge of improvements made in the fortress at Semneh and elsewhere. The most ancient parts of the temple of Der el-Bahari were also begun by this king. His activities, however, were brought to a close by his premature death. The mummy of Thothmes II. gives the impression that the king had succumbed to a severe illness. Though he was but thirty years of age, the head is almost entirely bald, and the features are strangely sunken. He cannot have reigned longer than ten years (1513 to 1503 B.C.).

Hatshepsut, as sole real ruler, in effect completed the temple of Der el-Bahari— Thothmes III. was a mere boy—where the wall-paintings are of much importance both for the history of the period and for the development of its art. The most interesting of these designs has for its subject the great expedition which Hatshepsut sent out in the ninth year of her reign to Punt. Eight ships sailed through the Red Sea and returned loaded to the yards. The arrival of the treasures of the land of incense, which had been gained by bartering Egyptian metal products, and especially weapons, gave occasion to festivities and military displays at Thebes, at which Thothmes III. modestly appeared as a priest of Amon. The queen, who preferred her portraits drawn with a beard and in male

THOTHMES I.
His campaigns in Nubia, Asia and Ethiopia were most successful. From a wall-painting at Der el-Bahari, by permission of the Egypt Exploration Fund.

THOTHMES II.
From a photograph of the head of his mummy, now 2,400 years old.

costume, showed a decided preference for all public ceremonies calculated to display the greatness of her power.

Under Hatshepsut we also find traces of favouritism. "The grand nurse"—that is, the tutor of the Princess Nefrura, a certain · Senmut—was made "great in both countries" though of humble origin. The queen erected two massive obelisks in Karnak in the sixteenth year of her reign, and died about 1491 B.C. She was originally buried in an extraordinary tomb excavated to a great depth in the cliffs of the Biban el-Muluk. It descends into the mountain in the form of a corkscrew, the excavators having sought in vain to find rock hard enough for a good tomb-chamber to be made. The masonry had disappeared, nothing being found but the sarcophagi of the queen and of Thothmes I. and II. Whether they had originally been buried here with her, and not in their own tombs, is uncertain. The work of excavating this tomb, carried out by Mr. Howard Carter, then chief inspector of antiquities at Thebes, for Mr. Theodore M. Davis, of Newport, R.I., was of the most arduous character, the air, owing to the great depth and confined area of the tunnel, having been very bad. We hear nothing more of the Princess Nefrura, whom she destined for her successor, and Senmut also disappears from history. The names of both Hatshepsut and Senmut were effaced from the monuments by Thothmes III. These measures, however, were unable to hide the fact that the change in the succession had been accompanied by violence. The power of the empire must have declined in the foreign provinces, especially in Syria, and could be restored only by the removal of the queen. The existence of a victorious commander, whether Thothmes or another, would have been a constant menace to her power.

Thothmes III. was one of that rare class of sovereigns whose successes are due to a temperate conception of their duties and to a capacity for energetic action

KUSHITE TRIBUTE TO THE EGYPTIAN CONQUEROR

depended greatly upon the advice of experienced leaders. On the monuments the king is naturally represented as guiding all things by himself alone. But, on the other hand, the Harris papyrus in London, a collection of legends and fairy tales, begins among other tales the story of the general, Thutia, who is said to have captured the city of Jaffa for his king, Thothmes III., in a marvellous manner. He is represented as having made use of the king's magic wand, and

at the proper moment. He had been obliged from his earliest youth to submit in silence to all governmental measures, whether he approved of them or not. His task as a politician, the restoration of Egyptian prestige abroad, was clearly marked out before him ; but a less tenacious character would probably have been well content with the frontiers which were found sufficient by Rameses II. in later years. This little man with the coarse features—as we know them from his mummy—until now the stepchild of his house, may well have been the hope of the military leaders, old and young, who during the last years of Hatshepsut must have counted on his antipathy to the empty splendours of her rule. Nor were they deceived. It is certain that Thothmes III., who at first may have had little or no knowledge of war,

by its spells to have enclosed 200 Egyptian warriors within earthen jars. These were then taken into Jaffa without suspicion and placed in the magazines. The Egyptians left their hiding-place, bound the Syrian garrison with cords, and handed over the place to the king. However, the general, Thutia, was a historical personage, and can be proved to have served under Thothmes III. ; valuable objects from his tomb have been transferred to various museums.

The arms of Egypt were a terror in Asia long after the period of Thothmes III., and Syria at length became convinced that the military power of the Nile countries under the terrible "Manakhpirria" (Men-kheper-Ra Thothmes) was not lightly to be withstood. On the northern wall of the wing added by the king to the temple of Amon at Karnak was set up a

SYRIAN TRIBUTE

During the reign of Thothmes III. the arms of Egypt became a terror in Syria, and at the taking of Megiddo "the princes of the land made prayer for their lives" and "brought forth their tribute."

connected narrative of his campaigns and of the tribute which he levied. This monumental history of the campaigns of Thothmes III. is usually known as his "annals"—an appropriate term, in so far as it is designed or written on the model of the annals of the Babylonian kings. The events of the king's twenty-third year are related in the dry manner of an annalist, but the first campaign forms a connected literary whole, in which the course of events is clearly developed.

It records the advance to Megiddo. In sight of the town order was given for the troops to draw up in line of battle. "His Majesty, in the panoply of war, ascended the chariot of gold and silver. Like was he unto Horus the dispenser of power, and to Month of Thebes [the god of war]; his father Amon gave him strength. The right wing of the army rested on a hill south of the brook Kina ; the left wing extended to the north, west of Megiddo. His Majesty remained in the centre ; at the head of his army he stood high above all. When thus the enemy saw him, they made all speed to fly to Megiddo, and left behind them their horses and their chariots ornamented with silver and gold." An account of the siege of Megiddo follows.

"His Majesty made poclama- tion to the army : ' If ye take Megiddo speedily, I shall be beneficent as Ra ; for therein are the chiefs of all the rebellious towns, and to conquer Megiddo will be to con- quer a thousand towns at once." Finally, " the princes of this land came forth with their followers. They kissed the earth before his Majesty, and made prayer for their lives. They brought forth their tribute [which they had previously refused], and the king

THOTHMES III.
A sovereign of rare capacity and character. From a colossal statue of the king.

ordered the government anew." The military equipment of the Syrians was excellent ; among other spoils 924 chariots and more than 200 shirts of mail of the best workmanship are mentioned.

The description of the terror with which Thothmes III inspired his enemies when he appeared in battle is represent ative of the typical method of conceiving such events in Egyptian art. The capture of Megiddo was a signal success, and must have entirely changed the low esteem in which the power and self-reliance of the Egyptian king had hitherto been held. The king's assertion that the capture of that town, in which the majority of Assyrian rebels were gathered, would cause the fall of thousands of others was not altogether an exaggerated statement. A list of towns in Karnak con- tains several hundred names. The neutral Asiatic princes also came over by degrees. The prince of Assur, or Assyria, then a ruler of no particular importance, was the first to introduce the custom of exchanging gifts with Egypt. The first mention of the Assyrians in an Egyptian document dates to the preceding reign, that of Hatshepsut, when the name of an Assyrian slave was recorded at Der el-Bahari. Fresh campaigns were necessary to convince the districts south of Lebanon of their obligations of obedience to Egypt. In the twenty-ninth year of the king, a date that can be fixed by the Karnak inscrip- tions, it appears that a great war against the Iranian kingdom of Naharina, or Mitani, situated athwart the Euphrates, from the Orontes to the Tigris, was the result of these ex- peditions. The fortress of Tunip, north of Damascus was conquered and

TRIBUTE FROM THE PHŒNICIAN ARVADITES
Thothmes III. made two great campaigns in Syria, and in the second captured Arvad, which, however, rebelled, and had to be reconquered.

dedicated to the sun-god. Subsequently the Phœnician Arvad or Aradus was captured, and treated with such severity that the inhabitants immediately revolted. Consequently, in the following year operations became necessary for the reconquest of Arvad and of Sumur, which was situated to the south of this town. This victory had been preceded by the fall of Kadesh, on the Orontes, which, however, shortly afterward again became a centre of resistance. On this occasion Amenemheb, a young comrade of the king, who became a general at a later period, appears for the first time. On this campaign he made two prisoners, and was decorated in consequence. His tomb in Thebes is ornamented with an abstract of his recollections of war, which, although somewhat confused, contain interesting references to several minor campaigns, of which, however, the dates are unknown. In the course of the next few years Thothmes made only a few short visits to Thebes in order to pay his thanks to Amon, his father's god, for the wealth which flowed to him from the spoils and the tribute of the conquered. Most of his time was spent in long, and not always successful, campaigns, in the prosecution of which he displayed a rare constancy of purpose. In the thirty-third year of his reign the Egyptians advanced to the Euphrates, to the point where Thothmes I. had set up his memorial stone, and erected a new monument in the same place. The city of Nii, situated somewhat to the north of Aleppo, surrendered, after a Phœnician army sent to its relief had been defeated beneath its walls. Thothmes III. made this town his headquarters for a time and erected

"CLEOPATRA'S" NEEDLE

Erected by Thothmes III. at Heliopolis, removed to Alexandria by Cæsar, and finally set up in London on the Thames Embankment.

another inscription. From the names of those countries which sent tribute and presents at the end of the year it can be inferred that an armistice had been entered into by Thothmes and the kingdom of Naharina. The king imposed such conditions upon his conquered enemies that any show of hesitation on the part of the governor of a town or district, no matter how loyal he might seem, might be construed as indicative of double dealing. This vigorous prosecution of operations within his own sphere of interests proved so objectionable to the neighbouring ruler of the Mesopotamian lands that two years later he sent out another army to prevent the capitulation of Araana. But the Egyptians were finally successful, and peace was at last made in the king's fortieth year, about 1460 B.C..

The enemy beyond the Euphrates at once began carefully to consider whether some spark was not to be found which might be fanned into a conflagration. In the forty-second year of his reign Thothmes III. once more, and for the last time, appeared in Asia with an army. First "his Majesty took the way along the coast in order to chastise the town of Irkata," a community in the north of Phœnicia. Tunip also seems to have been in a state of revolt. Kadesh, on the Orontes, however, was the centre of resistance. The siege was interrupted by a battle and a victory over a relief force from Naharina, and ended with the crossing of the moats and storming of the city. The king presented large

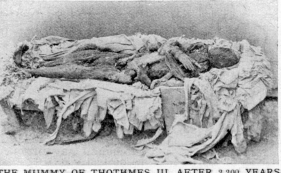

THE MUMMY OF THOTHMES III. AFTER 3,300 YEARS

Thothmes III., a little man of coarse features, as we know from his mummy, was a ruler whose successes were due to a temperate conception of his duties and energetic action at the right moment.

scarabs, bearing inscriptions in his honour as conqueror of Kadesh, to all who were present at the siege or took part in the festival of victory held in Thebes. At this point the Karnak inscriptions come to an end. We know only that Thothmes visited Nubia once again in his fiftieth year and terrified some dissatisfied tribes into submission. An extremely fine monument to commemorate this victory, inscribed with the indispensable poetical formulæ of adulation, was set up in a special position in Karnak. Amon-Ra is here represented as addressing the king : " I give to thee power and victory over all peoples. I set thy spirit and the fear of thee over all countries, and the dread of thee goeth to the four pillars of the heaven. I make thy power great in all bodies. I make thy shout to pursue the people of the nine bows. The great of all lands are joined together in thy hand. I, even I, raise my arm and bind them for thee. I

III.) at Thebes. In these tomb-paintings we see the Minoan chiefs of Crete marching in procession, carrying precious vases as gifts, just as they are represented in their own fresco-paintings in the palace of Cnossos in Crete, excavated by Dr. Arthur Evans. They appear as tall, slim-waisted, dark men with long, wavy black hair hanging below their waists or knotted on the top of their heads, like their successors the " long-haired Achaians," just as they represented themselves on the frescoes of Cnossos, the steatite vases from Agia Triada, or the golden cups of Vaphio. Crete escaped real tribute because the Egyptians had as yet no seagoing fleet ; we have here one of the earliest instances of the " influence of sea-

Influence of Sea-power on History

A LONELY VALLEY OF THE DEAD: THE TOMBS OF THE KINGS AT BIBAN EL-MULUK
Thothmes I. abandoned the use of small pyramids and introduced a new royal sepulchre, causing his tomb to be tunnelled into the cliffs in the desert valley west of Thebes. Similar burial places were constructed there by his successors.

gather together the Ethiopian nomads for thee as living prisoners by tens of thousands and the inhabitants of the north by hundreds of thousands." And so on for ten symmetrical stanzas, which tell us, among other things, how the renown of the king had spread even to the isles of the Mediterranean, which may well have feared lest the attention of the great conqueror should be turned in their direction. But though Cyprus (Yantinay or Yatnan) sent tribute, being too near Palestine to escape wholly, Crete (Kefti) did no more than send complimentary embassies with presents, as it had done in the peaceful days of Hatshepsut. We have representations of these embassies of the Cretan " Keftiu " in the tombs of Senmut (reign of Hatshepsut) and Rekhmara (reign of Thothmes

Tribute from Cyprus

power on history." The land of Asya, or Alasya, sometimes considered to be Cyprus, but more probably on the Cilician coast, sent regular tribute as a subject ally.

Egypt had now for the first time become so nearly a military state that the learned classes were alarmed. It would have been neither wise nor grateful for them to have complained during the lifetime of the great conqueror. The wealth of Asia was distributed with great liberality by Thothmes III., but Amon, the god of Thebes and of the royal house, was favoured above all other recipients. With a premonition of the danger liable to result from such excess of favour, the king turned his attention to the other temples upon the conclusion of his campaigns—as, for instance, at Heliopolis.

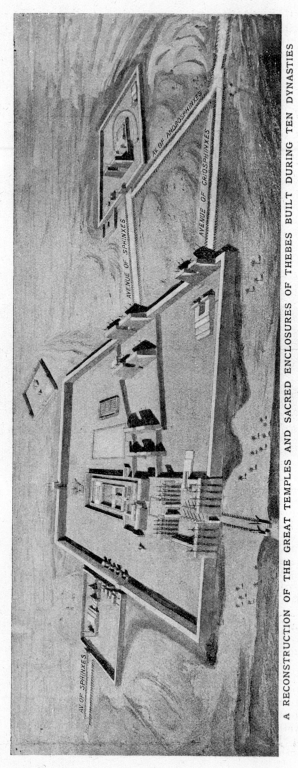

A RECONSTRUCTION OF THE GREAT TEMPLES AND SACRED ENCLOSURES OF THEBES BUILT DURING TEN DYNASTIES

Nevertheless, the dislike of the learned classes of Egypt to their soldier king may have found expression lasting into after years; it seems that the recollection of him as a popular hero was carefully discouraged. At any rate, it can be demonstrated that the priests designedly avoided all mention of the name of Thothmes in later years. When Germanicus visited Karnak, in the year 19 A.D., an aged priest translated the annals to him literally, and named as their author "King Rameses."

Besides caring for Thebes and Heliopolis, Thothmes erected new buildings at Memphis and Dendera, the seat of Hathor. At Elephantine also an extensive sanctuary, the ruins of which were levelled in 1832, was erected or restored by Thothmes III. A few fragmentary inscriptions, rescued in later times, are of chronological importance for the calendar information they contain.

Much was done for Nubia, especially in Amada and Wadi Halfa. The tomb of the conqueror was not discovered until the year 1898, though his mummy had been found fifteen years earlier in its hiding-place at Der el-Bahari. So far as has yet been determined, it seems that Thothmes I. had introduced a new style of royal tomb; abandoning the use of the small detached pyramid with its vestibule, and a tunnel in the rock behind it, leading to the tomb-chamber, he caused his tomb to be tunnelled into the cliffs in the desert valley to the west of the Theban necropolis. Similar sepulchres communicating with the upper world by one door alone, without a pyramid or external chapel, were also constructed there by his successors, so that this lonely valley of the dead still bears the name of the "tombs of the kings" (Biban el-Muluk). Although the neighbouring subterranean tombs of the Ramessides were explored long since, M. Loret discovered, in 1898, at a point then untouched, the shaft, sixty or seventy feet long, which led into the sepulchral chamber of Thothmes III. The walls of the innermost room, in which the sarcophagus stood, were covered with a painted tapestry of texts from the Book of the Dead. The entrance chamber was also ornamented with more than 700 images of the gods.

Very little is known of Aakheperura Amenhotep II., about 1450 to 1425 B.C. From the fragmentary remains of his inscriptions, and the biographical details given by his general, Amenemheb, we can only conclude that, as a warrior, Amenhotep II. ("Okhpruria") was no unworthy successor to the terrible "Manakhpirria." Hardly had he been crowned in Thebes when the news came that several of the Syrian provinces refused to send him the presents betokening their homage. The king suddenly appeared in Galilee, crossed the Orontes, utterly defeated a division of the enemy, and appeared before Nii, the gates of which town were immediately opened to him. At the conclusion of a campaign against the land of Takhisa, Amenhotep sent to Thebes the bodies of seven princes of that district, which were hanged by the legs from the bow of the king's ship, in accordance with the triumphal customs of the period ; six of them were subsequently exposed upon the city walls, and the seventh corpse was sent on to Napata, or Gebel Barkal, in the Sudan.

A movement of the Nubian tribes forced Amenhotep to advance as far south as the modern Khartum. No **Triumph in Syria** trace of Egyptian supremacy at this time has been found further south than Gebel Barkal, where two small figures of stone belonging to this period—Amenhotep is represented as presenting offerings of wine on his knees to the god Khnum—were dedicated. They were actually found much further south, in the Roman-Ethiopian temple of Ben-Naga, south of Shendi, to which

Mansell
AMENHOTEP III., THE LION
Amenhotep III. worshipped himself, choosing the lion as his symbol

they had been removed in later times. The tomb of Amenhotep II. is somewhat poor both in design and elaboration. In it were found the mummies of a man, a child, and a woman bound fast to wooden boats, apparently intended as companions of the king on his journey to **In the Tomb of Amenhotep II.** the nether world — unless they were judicial victims of the privy court of the following king, Thothmes IV. They were placed in the tomb before the process of drying was completed, and one of them received in consequence a deep cleft in the skull, though this may possibly have been inflicted by a thief in later times. The mummy of Amenhotep II. was also found in the tomb, and with it the remains of seven other kings, which were laid in a side chamber about 1100 B.C., that they might escape the raids of plunderers, while the others were deposited in the shaft of Der el-Bahari.

With the accession of Menkheperura Thothmes IV., about 1425 to 1415, the reaction, which the non-military grandees had long desired and prepared, began to make itself felt. The class of "scribes" succeeded in making a change which had certainly not existed under Thothmes III. All the high positions of military command became their monopoly, and indeed were given to officials who were already in occupation of other posts. Thus, at the time of the Ramessides matters had come to such a pass that the "king's first charioteer," who also held the offices of ambassador and "chief of the foreign lands and peoples," proceeds in a poetical letter solemnly to dissuade his young subordinates from entering the "stable of the king" or the infantry. Officers of this type, who quite obviously thought only of the flesh-pots of Egypt in time of war, were certainly never willing to march to Syria, but preferred to open a career to foreign mercenaries on the Nile.

We find a similar phenomenon nowadays in China, where it is the man of books, who has passed the highest examinations in learning, who rules, and though he may possess many military posts in title, in reality leaves the despised soldiering to the "Tartar generals" and the Manchus.

King Thothmes IV., who was not perhaps the chosen successor of his father, on ascending the throne immediately

The Sphinx Uncovered ordered the great sphinx at Gizeh to be cleared of the sand beneath which it had long been buried—the consequence of a dream of this pious monarch : vainly, however, since the monument was immediately covered again with the sand. The priestly class favoured the prince. But the time had not yet come for him to enjoy a peaceful reign. Thothmes IV. was first obliged to subdue the Ethiopian tribes, and also to reduce certain rebellious cities in Phœnicia to obedience ; his campaigns, in fact, are said to have extended as far as Naharina on the north, and to the Nubian land of Kare on the south. Moreover, the generals of the old school of Thothmes III. and Amenhotep II. had not entirely passed away ; to them belonged Menkhepru-Ra Meri-Amon, the "first of the commanders." The mummy of Thothmes IV., which was found in the

tomb of his father, reveals him as a handsome young man, not thirty years old. We cannot divine the reason of his death at so early an age, after a reign of only nine years. His body shows no sign that he was murdered, so that in all probability he fell a victim to some sudden illness, which the Egyptian physicians had no real knowledge how to treat. Life in Oriental countries is often cut very short by ignorance both of sanitation and of therapeutics. Considering the shortness of his reign, many monuments to this king exist, and many scarabs bearing his name are found. His actual sepulchre, from which his body was removed to the tomb of Amenhotep II. in the time of the priest-kings, was

Royal Funeral State discovered by Mr. Theodore M. Davis. The tomb was found to contain many remains of the royal funeral state ; most especially worthy of notice being a chariot-body of embossed leather, decorated with representations of the sphinx trampling down Asiatic enemies ; a piece of tapestry woven in colours, representing the royal cartouche on a ground, in heraldic language, *semée* of lilies and papyrus-flowers, like the fleurs-de-lis on the oriflamme of

THE FAMOUS "SPEAKING STATUES" OF MEMNON AT THEBES

These two colossal statues of Amenhotep III., known as Memnon, were famous in classical days for the vocal sounds they were supposed to emit at sunrise. They were 70 feet high, and were erected as warders of a temple of which not the slightest trace now remains. Another view, during an inundation of the Nile, is given on page 2048.

RUINS OF THE TEMPLE OF AMON, BUILT BY THOTHMES III. AT KARNAK 3,300 YEARS AGO
Thothmes III. spent much of the wealth gained in his Asiatic campaigns on temple building, and Amon of Thebes was favoured above all other gods. He also erected great sanctuaries at Heliopolis, Memphis, Dendera and Elephantine.

ancient France ; and a collection of vases of a most wonderfully brilliant blue glazed faience. An interesting point with regard to this tomb is that it had evidently been violated even in the short time between the reign of its owner and that of Horemheb, probably in the period of anarchy which prevailed at Thebes during the reign of the heretic Akhenaten (Amenhotep IV.), for in one of the chambers is a hieratic inscription recording the repair of the tomb in the eighth year of Horemheb by Maya, superintendent of works in the Tombs of the Kings.

Thothmes IV. inaugurated a practice novel in the house of the Pharaohs. He married a foreign princess, the daughter of Artatama, king of Mitani, the already mentioned Iranian kingdom of Northern Mesopotamia. This princess was the mother, in all probability, of Amenhotep III., who during his reign showed peculiarities probably due to his half-Iranian origin, and handed them on in an exaggerated form to his half-mad son Amenhotep IV., or Akhenaten.

On the fertile soil of the western bank of the Nile, at Thebes, which is overflowed by the river

SCULPTURE OF QUEEN TEIE
The "Great Royal Consort" of Amenhotep III., who was worshipped for centuries as divine.

in autumn, rise the two famous colossal sitting statues, one of which was supposed in the Roman period to give out a ringing sound at sunrise, and was known as the statue of " Memnon," a name which it has retained. The name of " Memnon " is derived from that of the erector of these statues, Amenothes, or Amenhotep III. (about 1415 to 1380), the son and successor of Thothmes IV., who ordered these stone images of himself, each of which is some seventy feet high, to be erected by his high official, Amenhotep, the son of Hapu, as warders of the gates of a new temple, which has now almost vanished. The legends of later times represent the king and his namesake, the wise son of Hapu, who " seemed to have a share in the divine being " by reason of his knowledge, almost as inseparable companions. The " prince and royal scribe," Amenhotep, who was subsequently permitted to build a private temple in the neighbourhood, and edified posterity as the author of magic litanies, was something more than a distinguished member of the circle of priests who assembled about the new king. We know of only one campaign undertaken by Neb-maat-Ra—or "Nibmutria," evidently often pronounced "Nimmuria" or "Nimmuaria"—Amenhotep III. at the outset of his reign of thirty-six years; this was directed against Nubia. He posed as an Asiatic conqueror; probably he did not wish to allow this honourable claim to fall into disuse. The foreign policy of the kingdom was now directed to prevent any outbreak of war by paying over a portion of the money appropriated to military equipment in presents to the independent kings of the neighbouring states. There was, too, the further advantage that the custom enjoined the return of friendly gifts of this nature. Obviously, in times of peace intercourse of this kind between the courts had always existed. It is due only to chance that a large portion of the Egyptian archives recently brought to light, and known as the Tell el-Amarna tablets, should have belonged to the latter part of the reign of Amenhotep III., and to that of his successor. Nevertheless, in these clay tablets, written in cuneiform script and mostly in Babylonian Semitic, the general diplomatic language of that period, allusions have been found indicating the existence of less friendly relations in earlier reigns. King Tushratta of Mitani declares that a daughter of his grandfather, Artatama, had been given to Thothmes IV. only under compulsion, and in like manner his sister, Gilukhipa, had been sent to Amenhotep III. When, however, Tushratta himself gave his daughter, Tadukhipa, with a large dowry, to the ageing Egyptian king, he received a great quantity of gold in

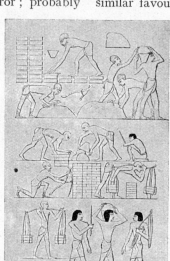

CAPTIVES MAKING BRICKS
From the tomb of the chief architect of Thothmes III., showing foreign slaves making bricks for the temple at Thebes.

THE DIVINE QUEEN TEIE
Teie, the consort of Amenhotep III., was honoured as few queens before her, though, apparently, not of royal birth. Her name was always associated with the king's, and a temple was erected to her in her lifetime.

return, together with the assurance that a sufficiency of Egyptian gold would always be found in Mitani. The general connection shows that this hint was given with the object of obtaining a return of similar favours. However, contemporary letters from Assyria and the kingdom of Alashya prove that the great gifts of gold from Egypt to Mitani aroused the wonder and envy of all other nations. Consequently, Amenhotep III. must have abandoned the previous policy of intimidation in favour of an attempt to establish a community of interests. His mistake, however, soon became apparent. There is no doubt that the kings of Western Asia soon began to distrust one another as a result of their rivalry for the gold of the Pharaoh. Individual sovereigns immediately raised their demands higher and higher, so that toward the end of the reign of Amenhotep III. friendly relations, at any rate with Babylonia, had become somewhat strained. The drain upon the treasury caused by these continual gifts was probably the reason for the diminution in the presents received by the "brother" whose dominions were farthest from Egypt, Kadashman-bel of Babylonia. A pretext for this reduction was provided by his demand that the Egyptian king, who desired a Babylonian princess for his harem, should give one of his own daughters in return. The answer, that never yet had a royal princess of Egypt been given to anybody, quickly put a stop to this scheme of alliance by marriage. But the insulted ruler of Babylonia now demanded to know what had become of his sister who had previously been given in marriage to Amenhotep. The " reassuring " answer of the Pharaoh has been preserved in the original text. It is characterised throughout by a tone of derision and contempt, and no doubt the royal chief scribe at Thebes obtained his master's approval to the terms of his reply.

There are other letters of the time of Amenhotep III. preserved among these archives which came from Tarkhundaraush, king of Cilicia, and from the princes of the Khatti, or Hittites, who were now pressing southwards into Palestine. Tushratta refers to his wars with them when they helped his rebellious brother, Artashumara, against him. In all these letters the Egyptian king is referred to in terms of great deference, for he claimed to be what no Semitic ruler ever was considered—a living deity on earth. The

A LADY'S WIG
Worn about 3,500 years ago, when the Egyptians did not dress their own hair.

also by a scarabæus of frequent occurrence bearing an inscription to the effect that the king had killed 102 lions in the first ten years of his reign. One of the figures at Soleb was named " Amenhotep III., the Strong Lion." Hitherto the bull had been regarded as a symbol of bodily strength. Buildings erected by King Amenhotep III. are numerous also in Egypt. In Memphis he built the oldest part of the Serapeum and entombed therein an Apis bull. Thebes, however, was chiefly benefited by his efforts. He enlarged the temple of Karnak on all sides, and first gave it the massive character it now bears. From the sacred lake Asher, constructed by Thothmes III. near Luxor, for a distance of over three-fourths of a mile northward he erected a series of new edifices connected by alleys of sphinxes. A road of

NECKLACE OF AN EGYPTIAN LADY OF THE TIME OF THOTHMES, 1500 B.C.
A fine example of ancient Egyptian jewellery, made of gold, carnelian, lapis lazuli, and felspar beads.

' good god," as the Pharaohs had long been known to their subjects, made an advance toward deification under Amenhotep III., who began to worship himself, or more correctly his own soul in bodily shape ; indeed, an extremely stately temple at Soleb, in Nubia, was specially devoted to the worship of its builder, who introduced himself in this case as the god of the country of Kush. As his symbol, the king chose the figures of lions couchant ; their majestic expression and the artistic skill displayed in their execution aroused even then such general admiration that they were carried away by the Ethiopian king Amonasru to his residence, Napata. That the imagination of Amenhotep III. ran continually upon lions is shown by his preference for the lion-headed goddess Sekhmet, and

A TOILET TABLE 3,500 YEARS AGO
Containing vases of unguents, eye-paint, a comb, a bronze " shell " on which to mix the unguents, cushions and a pair of sandals.

sphinxes was also laid out from Karnak to Luxor. The main part of the temple of Amon at that spot, with its finely ornamented columns, was also built by this king. In one of the chambers the birth of the god-king is represented as an event which was accomplished only by virtue of the greatest exertions on the part of the gods. The tombs of many officials and private individuals who lived under the long reign of Amenhotep III. have been preserved. They supply no information of value beyond indicating that the art of ancient Egypt entered upon a really flourishing period under the eighteenth dynasty.

Princess Giiukhipa of Mitani, in spite of her royal birth, did not receive the rank of a " great royal consort "—that is, the rank of a reigning queen—and

STOOLS USED AT THE TIME OF THE 18TH DYNASTY
The stool on the left is of ebony inlaid with ivory, while that on the right, with the legs ending in ducks' heads, was a folding stool and had a leather cover. Now in the British Museum.

Mansell

her niece Tadukhipa fared no better at a later time ; both found this position already occupied. Tii, or Teie, the daughter of one entitled Iuaa and his wife Tuyu, had anticipated all competitors, and was moreover honoured as few queens before her. Whenever there was a ceremony to be performed, the king associates the name of Teie with his own. She even shared in the increased divinity of the son of the sun, and a temple was erected to her at Sedeinga, not far from Soleb, in Nubia. The fact that her worship after death was continued under the Ramessides and at a later period, enables us to gain some idea of her popularity during her life. Mr. Theodore N. Davis, of Newport, R.I., has for several years been exploring the valley of the tombs of the kings and has there discovered the tombs of Hatshepsut and Thothmes IV. ; he found also in 1905 the tomb of Iuaa and Tuyu, and in 1907 that of Teie. The queen's body was not found in the tomb, but instead of it the remains of a young man, who is quite possibly Akhenaten, her son, to whom the coffin certainly belonged. Evidently the burials of mother and son had been confused in the hurry of a probably secret removal. But we have compensation for the loss of the queen's body in the beautiful portraits and busts of her which formed the tops of some alabaster "canopic jars" found in the tomb, which show us a very beautiful face. Far different was the condition in which were found the mummies of her parents. The bodies of Iuaa and Tuyu are perfectly preserved, exhibiting very interesting Egyptian types. There is no real proof that Queen Teie and her parents

were of non-Egyptian blood, though it has often been supposed that they were Mitanians. Whatever foreign blood there was in the royal family came, not from Teie, but from Amenhotep III. himself, who was probably half-Iranian in blood.

As in the tomb of Teie, gold was freely used on the objects discovered with the mummies of Iuaa and Tuyu. These consisted chiefly of most magnificent and beautiful examples of Egyptian cabinet-work—chairs, beds, and so forth. Many of the chairs remind us strongly of those of the period of the "First Empire" in France.

Soon after the arrival in Thebes of the young princess Tadukhipa, the king's health began to fail. He sent a request to his old friend Tushratta to send a statue of the goddess Ishtar of Nineveh to Egypt, probably to heal him. The "day of departure" apparently came upon him in the thirty-sixth year of his reign, about 1380 B.C., and his mummy remained for about three hundred years in the silent "valley of the kings."

Mansell

EGYPTIAN CHAIR OF 3,500 YEARS AGO
There is little in modern furniture showing any great advance on this remarkable chair made about 1500 B.C.

EGYPT MAGNIFICENT IN RUIN

The past sacrificed to the present : Temples partly submerged as a result of damming the Nile.

The magnificent Ptolemaic pylones as they appeared before the construction of the Nile Dam.

A TRIUMPH OF PTOLEMAIC ARCHITECTURE: THE TEMPLES OF PHILÆ

Nowhere in the world is there such a wealth of antiquities and well-preserved ruins of great age as in Egypt, owing to the dryness and invariability of the climate. In the following pages the difficult task has been attempted of selecting some of the more striking monuments of Egypt's ancient splendour.

A marvel of the classical world : the "speaking" colossi of Memnon as seen at low Nile.

The great mountain temple at Der-el-Bahari built by Hatepshut, the woman Pharaoh.

THE GREAT COLOSSI AND THE ROCK-BUILT TEMPLES

Colossal sculptures of Rameses' temple at Abu Simbel, cut in the living rock of the mountain side.

An entrance to the temple guarded by colossal statues of Rameses II., the builder.

EGYPT'S GREATEST TEMPLE, BUILT BY RAMESES II. AT ABU SIMBEL

A hall of enormous carved pillars in the Ramesseum, showing the fragments of a colossal statue.

A general view of the ruins of the Ramesseum as seen from the north-west.

THE RAMESSEUM : RAMESES THE GREAT'S MONUMENT AT THEBES

Remains of a magnificent pillared portico guarded by colossi.   An outer view of the same is given below.

The temple from the west as seen during the overflowing of the Nile.

TWO ASPECTS OF THE SPLENDID PILLARED TEMPLE AT LUXOR

An inner corridor of massive sculptured pillars.   Gateway of the temple, built by a Ptolemy.

An interior view of the second court of the temple, showing the proportions of the immense stone pillars.

LATER ARCHITECTURE OF ANCIENT EGYPT: TEMPLE OF MEDINET HABU

The sphinx, partly excavated, showing remains of a temple between its paws, now covered with sand.

The sphinx and the great pyramid of Khafra, showing how the sphinx is again buried in sand.

Ruins of the half-buried temple of the sphinx, built in the reign of Pharaoh Khafra.

THE GREAT SPHINX, ONE OF EGYPT'S MIGHTIEST MONUMENTS

RICHNESS AND VARIETY OF EGYPTIAN ARCHITECTURE

The temple of Edfu (1) is one of the most impressive ruins in Egypt, and hardly less striking is the solitary pylone at Karnak (2), while the view of part of the remarkable Avenue of Sphinxes (3), one mile long, which ran from Luxor to Karnak, gives some idea of ancient Egypt's prodigality of sculpture.

This fine series of photographs is reproduced chiefly from the well-known originals of A. Beato, Luxor, and Bonfils, Beyrut.

THE REIGN OF THE HERETIC KING
WITH AN ACCOUNT OF EGYPT'S RELIGIONS

ON the death of Amenhotep III. the accession of Amenhotep IV., the son of Teie, whose first name was Nefer-khepru-Ra—in the Amarna letters "Napkhuria" or "Napkhururia"—seems to have met with no serious opposition. The successor to his throne had apparently reached the age of manhood, and had long been fully prepared for this event. From the letters of foreign kings of the period it appears that it was not customary to take cognisance of the existence of a crown prince ; hence Amenhotep III. cannot have promoted his son to the co-regency.

Equally scanty mention is made of Teie in previous correspondence with foreign powers. However, the lack of foresight displayed by Tushratta of Mitani in designating his daughter Tadukhipa as " mistress of Egypt " when he sent her to Amenhotep III. was now remedied on the occasion of this succession ; Tushratta addresses Teie by this title, and

A Comedy of Ancient Egypt is careful to recognise the subordinate position of Tadu-khipa, who seems to have been handed on to the new king as a subordinate wife. The ill-will of the queen mother may have been aroused by difficulties in the harem excited by the pretensions of the daughter of the king of Naharina, and her displeasure may have been increased by Tushratta's importunate demands for gold. When this monarch attempted to extort money from the new Pharaoh on the doubtful pretext of an old promise given by the late Amenhotep, he received a refusal couched in unusually blunt terms. The ridiculous manner in which Tushratta subsequently sought to make it appear that nothing had occurred to disturb the relations of himself and his " dear brother " in Egypt forms one of the most entertaining comedies in the world's history. The Tell el-Amarna letters, which contain other amusing material, reached their highest point of literary skill in their references to this incident. Teie was personally requested by Tushratta to mediate in his favour, but seems to have taken no action in the matter, while the replies of Amenhotep IV. became more and more discourteous ; at any rate, the old friendship between the two courts was almost a thing of the past

Quarrels With Babylonia at the date of the last letter which has come down to us. A similar quarrel took place with King Burnaburiash, the successor of Kadashman-Bel in Babylonia. Amenhotep IV. neglected to send his wishes for the recovery of this king, who had been ill for some time.

The Egyptian officials and tributary princes in Canaan also seem to have considered that nothing was to be feared from the Babylonians. They plundered Babylonian embassies and caravans of merchants in the most barefaced manner. Although this in itself was a sufficient ground of complaint, the reception of an Assyrian embassy in Thebes induced the Babylonians to make serious remonstrances. It was represented that the Assyrian prince Assur-uballit was a Babylonian vassal, that his people could have no business in Egypt, and that it would be well for Amenhotep to remember that the father of Burnaburiash had once suppressed the beginnings of a Canaanite revolt against Egypt.

None the less, relations with the Assyrians were continued, although Egypt gained no advantage thereby. The Egyptian envoy Hai appears at the court of Burnaburiash to fetch one of

Exchange of Princesses his daughters or relatives to Egypt, in exchange for whom an Egyptian princess must have been given. A short and unfortunately mutilated letter of the " king's daughter " to " her master," which was delivered by Kidin-Ramman, expresses the hope that the gods of Burnaburiash will protect him on his journey. The manner in which " thy city and thy house " are further spoken of is probably to be explained as a reference to the removal to the new residence of Amenhotep.

The king of the Hittites and his modest neighbour, the petty king of Alashya, soon had reason to be dissatisfied with the change of rulers in Egypt. Shubbiluliuma, the former of these kings, was offended

Viceroy of the Delta

by Amenhotep IV., who addressed him in a manner involving a breach of etiquette, and received as good as he gave. The king of Alashya was obliged to defend himself against the accusation that his subjects had been in alliance with Lycian pirates. It is uncertain whether the Lycians landed in the Delta, or whether they had made a raid upon some Egyptian settlement in Alashya. At any rate, the people of Alashya were probably justified in complaining that the commercial relations between the two countries had been injured by the aggressions of the Egyptian customs officials. Not only the king, but also his chief official, " the Rabisu," issued edicts warning the " Pakeri " not to interfere with merchants, envoys, and ships from Alashya. But anyone who passed through Lower Egypt in order to transact business at the court of Amenhotep IV. found, so to speak, a dragon in his path in the person of the viceroy of the Delta (Yarimuta). From the Amarna letters we learn that, at that time at least, the power of this official was as absolute as that of the " prince of Kush " ; thus Egypt proper was guarded on the south as on the north.

The governor of Syria-Palestine had a wholesome respect for the " Rabisu of the king," who " is in the land of Yarimuta " —that is, the Delta. Two very amiable communications accompanied by gifts were also sent to this personage by the Rabisu of Alashya ; consequently his name Yankhamu was one of the best known in the country. It apparently depended entirely

The Power Behind the Throne

upon the pleasure of this man whether the measures ordered by the Pharaoh should be executed slowly or promptly, sternly or with forbearance, and whether the pretexts or remonstrances of vassals should be seriously considered or be treated as deserving of punishment. Yankhamu accepted backsheesh, but at the same time he was apparently upright enough to act in entire accordance with the orders of his superiors and not to yield to the

counter claims of his own personal inclinations. None the less, the prestige of the Egyptian supremacy in the Asiatic provinces rapidly declined.

In the meantime, events were taking place in Thebes such as the Egyptian people had never before heard of, and, indeed, were never again to hear of, after the period of their occurrence. The king became involved in a quarrel with the priesthood of Amon, which had been steadily increasing in wealth and power. Amon, at first the god only of his own house, had gradually been raised to the head of the Egyptian pantheon. And now Amenhotep became the champion of a new heresy.

It is certain that long before this time a new creed had been formulated by the society of priests connected with the temple of the Sun at Heliopolis, which was extended to exalt above all the hybrid deities of the Nile the visible sun in the sky, " Aten," as the sole creative and preservative deity. This doctrine had probably become more or less fashionable at the court of Amenhotep III., which

The Egyptian Pantheon

prided itself on its intellectual atmosphere and lent a ready ear to any new theory. What, however, was but a pastime to his predecessor, Amenhotep IV. considered as the serious business of his life. For whatever reason, relations between Amon and the new king were strained to breaking point, and an open rupture took place between the fourth and sixth years of his reign. The court left Thebes, and a religious reform on the lines of the Aten doctrine was begun with severity and zeal.

Now the system of the Egyptian pantheon is obscure. The various conquests of a much-conquered country had their usual effect here as elsewhere. The captured territory is considered by the new arrivals as a gift of the gods who accompanied them thither ; and to these the previous possessors, deities as well as men, must first be subjected, and with them ultimately be incorporated. Thus is explained the great antiquity of such of the purely Egyptian conceptions as originated in the configuration of the country. To these belong the divinities of the water and the desert, as well as the simple harvest gods. The first movement recognisable as such among the gods of Egypt begins with the rise of Horus and his struggle to break down the obstinacy of Set. In Nubia, as a rule, the conquering Horus received the offerings of the kings of Egypt, who erected temples and dedicatory inscriptions. But he did not have the field to himself. Under the Ramessides, Amon, Ptah, and Ra also appeared in company with Horus with earlier divinities such as Merula, Didun (the Tithonos of the Greeks), and He.

Min of Coptos, a deity who had fallen into obscurity as early as the period of the Middle Empire, was rediscovered in Nubia by the kings of the eighteenth and nineteenth dynasties, worshipped there with the greatest enthusiasm, and, in consequence, eventually restored to importance in Egypt also. Min, however, was an ideal rustic deity, who must have once been worshipped throughout a wide district, extending far beyond the frontiers of Egypt to the south, and perhaps also to the south-east. As a result, Coptos, the point of junction of several desert roads from the south, continued for a long time to be a secure stronghold for the worship of Min, even after he had been supplanted elsewhere by deities of later **Egypt's** origin. In the god Khem of **Rural** Achmim (north of Coptos), who **Deities** was originally the counterpart of Min, the Greeks immediately recognised their own Pan ; accounts of the primitive rustic character of his festivals have been preserved. But though Horus, who usually intruded upon such occasions under the most extraordinary disguises, was unable to prevail against Min, the ape god Bes, a rival from the southernmost part of Nubia, was more successful. This koboldlike dwarf with his bushy crown of feathers seems to have been closely connected with the goddess Thoueris (Egyptian Ta-ueret), whose image was an erect hippopotamus with the breasts of a woman. She may indeed have accompanied him upon his first arrival from Ethiopia, and have taken the place of the corresponding deity Apet, who was worshipped in Thebes at a comparatively late period. At any rate, Bes and Thoueris played a very important part in the Eygptian pantheon after they had deprived Min and Apet of their important office as patron deities of midwifery.

The subsequent introduction of Bes and Thoueris into the circle of sun divinities and their ritual companions, the gods of the dead, ended their advancement.

However, such an instance of the overthrow of primitive Egyptian deities by gods of yet earlier origin from the south is absolutely unique. As a rule, the ancient Egyptian gods were only in part replaced by deities introduced from the north, who failed to eject them completely. Thus the ancient capital of the first or southernmost nome **Strange** of Upper Egypt was Ombos, **Fusion** on the eastern bank of the **of Myths** Nile, the temple of which was sacred to the crocodile god Sebek. The worshippers of Horus were late in establishing themselves in the nome, and were restricted for a time to the island of Elephantine, which was not consecrated to Horus but to Khunm ; he, as creator of the world in the age preceding the birth of Osiris, and as the father of Horus himself, was a god eminently suitable for a region so exposed, where he bears the title "defender against the Nubians." When, at a later time, Ombos opened its gates to the new cult Horus had become humbler, and contented himself with one half of the Sebek temple. The result was that, together with his neighbour "great Horus," Sebek also assumed the attributes of a sun-god, and from this time forth was known as Sebek-Ra, one of the most extraordinary of the many mythological fusions which took place in Egypt. Unfortunately, little has remained to us of the myths in connection with the temple at Ombos. A fragmentary account from this source indicates that Osiris was there born to Apet, the hippopotamus goddess.

It is certain that Sebek was one of the chief divinities of the Nile valley prior to the Negada period, and also suffered less than any other primitive god from the antagonism of later times. In the age of the Old Empire the crocodile god was generally worshipped, and at the time of the Middle Empire he rose **Worship** to great distinction, and **of the** possessed temples in various **Crocodile** parts of Egypt, though more especially in the Fayyum, until the final disappearance of the native beliefs. Their inalienable characteristics as deities of the water may have proved a valuable support both to him and to the hippopotamus goddesses ; but between the desert god Set and the religion of the historical period a relation of armed neutrality invariably persisted. All, however, that is known about Set is intimately connected with his mythological struggle with Horus.

Horus never lost his traditional character as a champion and conqueror of the land ; his name signified sovereignty, and was assumed by every Pharaoh. The mythic story of the wars fought by Horus

Horus the Champion against Set and his allies throughout the whole of Egypt has been preserved to us in two versions in connection with each other. The earlier of these represents Horus as a son of the beneficent god Osiris, who appeared as a human king and refined the bestial manners of Egyptian life by teaching the duties of cultivating the soil, worshipping the gods, etc. But Osiris was entrapped by his evil brother Set, who enticed him into a great coffer, which he immediately closed and set adrift on the sea. During the despotic rule of Set the adherents of Osiris either left the country or withdrew into hiding-places ; but when the body of Osiris was recovered by his sister and wife Isis in the Phœnician seaport Gebal—first mentioned in the time of the twelfth dynasty—their son Horus arose and conquered Set after a long struggle. During the war with Set, Isis and Horus were assisted by Thoth, the ibis-headed god of wisdom, and Anubis, the jackal-headed deity.

Although we are indebted to no earlier authority than Plutarch for this myth, and although in Plutarch's original the Delta only is represented as the Egyptian scene of action, nevertheless numerous versions of and allusions to the story in ancient Egyptian texts prove not only its genuineness but also the fact that it was equally current in Upper Egypt. A calendarian list, in which horoscopes and rules of conduct for favourable or unlucky days are given, states that on the 17th of Athyr, the day of Osiris's death, the lamentations

Death of Osiris of the goddesses Isis and Nephthys at Saïs could be heard as far as Abydos, the final resting-place of Osiris. The length to which the process of mythological transformation could be carried among the Egyptians is well shown in a later version of the myth, which may have been remodelled during the New Empire, and met with ready acceptance by the priesthood of the temple of Horus at Edfu. In this

2092

adaptation Osiris has entirely disappeared, his place being taken by the sun-god Ra of Heliopolis, whose annihilation was indeed neither possible nor desirable. Consequently Horus appears as the son of the Sun in the form of the winged solar disc. His struggle with Set and his brood of crocodiles is represented as a chastisement inflicted upon conspirators, whose crime consisted simply in their rebellion against Ra. Nevertheless, even from this greatly altered variant of the myth several valuable additions can be obtained which supplement the account of Plutarch. Thus one passage reads : " Hereupon the enemies of Ra went into the river. They metamorphosed themselves into crocodiles and hippopotami. But Ra entered a boat, and when he came within reach of the animals they opened wide their mouths in order to injure the majesty of the god. Then came Horus—that is, the Edfu Horus—and the servants of his train—Shemsu-Hor—bearing weapons of bronze ; each carried a lance of iron and a chain in his hands. Then they smote the

Likeness of Horus and Marduk crocodiles and hippopotami. And they dragged forth 381 enemies and put them to death in sight of the city of Edfu." These words take us back to the period of Negada, which marks the beginning of the bronze age in Egypt, when the Horus people perhaps invaded the land.

Not Ra, but Osiris, was the original deity who opposed Set and assisted Horus to victory. There is some ground for tracing back Osiris and the Babylonian god Marduk to a common origin ; but if this identity ever existed it must have early disappeared, for in the comparatively late period during which we first hear of Babel and its Marduk this deity was a warlike hero, world-creator, and at the same time father of Nabu, the god of wisdom. Osiris, on the other hand, appears as early as the Ancient Empire as the inoperative god of the dead, and his merit must be considered as resting chiefly upon his former sufferings. The resemblance of Horus to Marduk, however, becomes so striking that it is difficult not to believe that this part of the genealogy of the Egyptian deities must once have undergone a fundamental change.

The opposing god, Set, who was represented symbolically in an extraordinary animal form resembling nothing so much

THE PRINCIPAL DEITIES OF THE EGYPTIAN PANTHEON

Osiris (1), the god of the dead, was the chief of the gods, and husband and brother of Isis (8 and 11), the queen of the gods; their son Horus (9) carried on great mythical wars with the evil desert-god Set (4), who had murdered Osiris. In this struggle Horus was assisted by Thoth (2), the ibis-headed god of wisdom, and Anubis (6), the jackal-headed assistant of Osiris in the judgment of the dead. The dwarf ape-god Bes (3 and 7) and the erect hippopotamus goddess Thoueris (5) were two primitive Nubian deities who displaced the native primitive gods Min and Apet They, and Sebek (10), the crocodile god, were admitted to the circle of the sun divinities.

Photos by Mansell

as the okapi, but who was also in the habit of transforming himself into a snake in combat, was recognised quite as much as Horus as a deity of the empire. The kings of Egypt wear the uræus serpent above their foreheads as a badge of dignity, and are the favourites not only of Horus but of Set. Not until the end of the empire was the conclusion drawn from the legend of Osiris that Set, who, as "Sutekh," had begun to assume the attributes of the Phœnician Baal, was an object of worship unworthy of a truly pious Egyptian. Thus the ancient deity finally fell from his high estate, after a sudden and vain attempt to disguise himself as a sun-god at his principal residence in Tanis. Nevertheless, as a local deity at Ombos, and to a still greater extent in the western frontier nome Oxyrynchus, where his worship had been preserved in its greatest purity, he survived all hostility. As a son of Nut, the goddess of heaven and tutelary divinity of the Nile, Set seems to be the most purely Egyptian

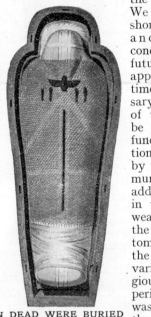

HOW THE EGYPTIAN DEAD WERE BURIED
The Egyptian belief in the resurrection of the body was limited to those bodies that remained intact; thus extraordinary care was taken in embalming and bandaging the body, as may be seen in this mummy and its case.

of the deities who retained their general characteristics during historical times.

No information as to the origin, growth, and development of the Egyptian doctrines of a future life is obtainable from the myths of Osiris. We can only give a short account of ancient Egyptian conceptions of a future life as they appeared in historical times. It was necessary that the bodies of the dead should be preserved. This fundamental condition was satisfied by the process of mummifying. An additional safeguard in the case of the wealthy classes was the construction of tombs of masonry, the forms of which varied with the religious idea of different periods. The mummy was looked upon as the home of the "spiritual parts" of the deceased, which could leave the body at will. There were several of these spiritual parts, chief among which was the Ka, or dream-soul. Even during a man's life his Ka showed a tendency to wander. Whoever made journeys during

A CHAPTER HEADING FROM THE BOOK OF THE DEAD: THE JUDGMENT OF THE SOUL
The Books of the Dead consisted largely of formulæ to plead for the dead in the judgment court of Osiris.

his dreams and experienced good or evil while his body lay in sleep knew that his Ka had been active. The Ka proved its power of free movement still more definitely by appearing as a physical being to others in their dreams whether its unconscious owner were alive or dead. Two further spiritual elements, the Khu—that is, the "shining one"—and the Ba, which had the form of a human-headed bird, seem to have represented one and the same conception—that is, the renown of the deceased. In all probability the same was the case with the Sahu and the Sekhem, which are depicted as wrapped mummies or free figures; the difference of form and name was due to local variation of doctrine. It is strange that the shadow of men was included among the spiritual elements; possibly it was a later parasitic conception, for the kingdom of the dead of Osiris was by no means an abiding place of shadows. Consequently it was entirely opposed to Egyptian piety to supply their departed with shadow pictures of bread, meat, dishes, etc. During the Negada period it appears that the sacrifices—that is to say, the repasts for the dead—were still offered *in natura*. In later times, imitations made of stone, clay, or wood, which were supposed to become permanently endowed with nourishing qualities by the recital of magical formulæ, were employed. Other formulæ of this kind, of which the tedious literature of the "Books of the Dead" is largely composed, were thought to assist the deceased to overcome the difficulties and dangers of the way to the throne of Osiris, to plead for him before the court of judgment in the nether

IMAGES OF THE DEAD
Such realistic statuettes of the deceased were frequently placed in tombs of the ancient Egyptians.

world, and even to influence the turn of the scales in which the gods Thoth and Horus weighed every heart against a feather, the symbol of truth. What happened to those found wanting at this final judgment was an obscure and apparently a forbidden subject, although a vicious-looking female animal resembling a pig, with the head of a crocodile, called the "devourer," always sat before or close to Osiris. But on and after the interment the dead man was called "true to his word," his righteousness and consequent salvation being thus presupposed. Thus blessed, he was straightway sent to Osiris and led by the god to the fields of Aalu, where all was well. There was room for everyone at the richly-decked table of Osiris, and whoever desired more had but to go to the tree of life close at hand, from which the goddess of heaven freely dispensed her gifts to the dead.

The offerings of food, etc., were also intended to secure to the deceased, at least so long as he remained in the tomb, that welfare which he could not have enjoyed in any other way. It is a striking fact that even the kings fully shared the general desire of their subjects to be buried, if possible, in the Osiris city Abydos. They could not, however, well be actually buried there, but commanded their bodies to be interred in Thebes, like those of their great nobles. But probably the popular custom of sending the mummies of the deceased to Abydos, whence they were transported back to the starting point, where their graves awaited them, was considered necessary by the kings. The kings of the first dynasty, some of whom were buried

AN EGYPTIAN FUNERAL SLEDGE
In sledges of this type the bodies were drawn to the tomb.

probably at Negada, others at Hierakon-polis, had a series of imitation tombs, or commemorative "Houses of the Ka," built for them at Abydos. These cenotaphs were provided with all the requisites for the continued life of the Ka in the other world, even including actual slaves, who were killed and buried with the kings. That is to say, the commemorative "Ka-houses" at Abydos were complete tombs, with all the necessary appurtenances, except the corpse. With

Mansell

KING MAKING AN OFFERING TO THE APIS BULL
Memphis was the scene of the worship of the Apis bulls, considered divine, while other animals were merely incarnations of various gods.

the exception of Ra, it is seldom that any information of importance can be extracted respecting the gods of Ancient Egypt. Overladen as they were with changing attributes, their original forms are now unrecognisable; their myths also are still unknown. Ptah, the ancient god of Memphis, is now only to be found—except when he is identified with the god Tatenen—represented as garbed in the swathing of mummies; therefore he must have adopted the character of Osiris, or vice versa Herodotus considered Ptah as the Egyptian Hephæstus; in fact, he was often represented surrounded by dwarf gods, his assistants in the creation of the world. Ptah may have been in some way connected with the Nile god Hapi, who possessed an unusually magnificent temple in Memphis, and was subsequently worshipped in Rome as the classic "father of the waters"; he was also accompanied by gnomes, who, though they signified the proper height of the Nile in ells, resemble the kobolds of Ptah. Memphis was also the scene of worship of the Apis bulls, whose divine attributes had been recog-

EGYPTIAN CARE FOR THE DEAD
On the left is a canopic jar, sets of four of which, containing various organs of the deceased dedicated to particular gods, were always placed in tombs. On the right is a beautifully cast bronze situla, which contained votive offerings on behalf of the departed.

nised as early as the Ancient Empire. A connection between Ptah and Apis can scarcely be proved. During his lifetime the bull seems to have formed a part of the Ra cult, and after his death to have belonged to that of Osiris. Thus it is possible that the soul of the bull was finally transformed into an independent deity, Osiris-Apis, who, after personification under Greek influence, received the name of Serapis, supplanted Osiris, and became associated with Isis as deity of the dead. The great mausoleum of Apis bulls discovered by Mariette at Sakkara still contained the heavy stone sarcophagi in which the mummified remains of the animals had been successively laid from the time of the eighteenth dynasty, in order somewhat parallel to the succession of mummies of the Egyptian kings. Pharaoh and Apis possessed the attributes of personal divinity in death as well as in life. The other sacred animals found in the temples are merely incarnations of the various gods, such as the Suchos-crocodile in the Fayyum, the Mendesian ram, and the bull Mnevis of Heliopolis, whose worship fell into decay at different times. Together with Mnevis, a fabulous creature known as the bird Bennu—the "Phœnix" of the Greeks—had his headquarters at Heliopolis. Perhaps a rare species of heron was bred there. Finally, on arriving at the stone sphinxes—for the most part the heads of kings set upon the bodies of animals, an inversion of the conception of gods with animal heads—we find ourselves within the domain of sculpture and architecture.

THE PASSING OF A PHARAOH : FUNERAL CEREMONIES OF A KING OF ANCIENT EGYPT

At Dendera a temple of the goddess Hathor, inscribed with accounts of the worship as well as with the history of its building, still remains in a good state of preservation. From this we learn that at the beginning of the third summer month this Egyptian Aphrodite was accustomed to set out upon a ceremonial journey to the god Horus in Edfu, which was not far distant. After or within five days she then returned home in her boat "The Greatness of Love." This custom is in complete correspondence with the name of the goddess, which signifies " the house of Horus." Curiously, there was a group of seven Hathors, who presided over births, who in their turn are connected

with Nekhebet, the goddess of births, worshipped in El-Kab ; and they appear also in the form of vultures hovering about the king, protecting him during his lifetime. Hathor herself, on the other hand, is often represented with the head of a cow, and even when pictured as a woman she retains the cow's horns and often the ears. The Greeks identified their own Leto with Buto, the oracle goddess in the Delta town of Buto, and Athene with the goddess Neith, worshipped at Saïs. The symbol of Neith, originally a square shield with two arrows crossed behind it, was transformed into a shuttle, in later times worn as a national token by the Libyans, who appear in Egyptian drawings. This points to a Libyan origin for her; but she, together with Hathor, Buto, the cat-headed Bast of Bubastis, and almost all the female divinities of the ancient Egyptian pantheon, subsequently lost all traces of their original character under the influence of the Isis myth. A closer examination makes it plain that even those divinities which appear to have an individuality of their own are mere variants of Isis, "great in enchantment" (Ueret-hekau). The exception to this rule is Maat, the goddess of truth and justice; for she, as an abstraction, was above all influences of mythological transformation. She is sometimes represented wearing the well-known bandage over her eyes, "for justice decides without regard of persons." Of the god Khuns, or Khonsu, who perhaps represented the new moon and formed a counterpart to Ioh or Aah, the god of the full moon, nothing need here be said, except that he, like so many other divinities, was ultimately merged in the "sun." Under the twentieth dynasty a vain attempt seems to have been made to restore him to his proper dignity. War-gods appear in increasing numbers under the New Empire. The valiant Month (Mentu) was often summoned by the kings from Thebes to inspire them with bravery in battle equal to his own. The worship of Month in the nome of Thebes was perhaps even more ancient than that of Amon, for the chief sanctuaries of both were in local opposition. The goddess Sekhmet, the destroyer of degenerate mankind in the Ra myth, obtained a certain degree of preference from Amenhotep III., and appears in the papyrus literature as the lion-headed spreader of panic who marches in the vanguard of armies. In other respects she belongs to the family of Ptah. In later times, however, it was said of the Isis-Hathor at Philæ that she was "kind as Bast, terrible as Sekhmet," so that this divinity also was deprived of her original characteristics. The Syrian divinities also acquired a

SUN-GOD, RA

AMON-RA
Ra, the Sun-god, was, after Amenhotep III., combined with Amon as Amon-Ra, king of the gods.

certain standing in Egypt, especially under the Ramessides. The chief of these were Baal and Astarte, Reshef and Anath.

The sun-god Ra, as is plain from his myths, had his first centre in Heliopolis as early as the period of the Ancient Empire. None the less he was the youngest of all the greater divinities. This fact is proved by the comprehensiveness of his nature, as compared with the Hades nature of Osiris and the solar conception of the sun offered by Horus. Before Ra came to Egypt he had attained a certain mythological maturity within the imagination of another people, and hence the rapidity of his success. But apart from this, he possessed all the attributes which make for popularity. The new sun-god is the absolute lord of creation; he traverses the entire heaven and the nether world in his narrow boat within twenty-four hours, annihilates all that is evil, or at any rate makes it inoperative so long as he is present, and so compels every other god who is desirous of being termed "good" to enter his company. Thus within a comparatively short time the solar disc of Ra becomes the predominating symbol among the other gods; indeed, this same symbol was unconsciously accepted as the sign of divinity in general, and was ultimately borne even by those gods who, from their very nature, were and remained opponents to Ra. Conversely, the sparrow-hawk of Horus became an emblem of the true sun-gods; Ra himself was represented with a bird's head. He also appropriated to himself many other external marks borrowed from earlier rites and conceptions. However, he clung all the more tenaciously to his main office. He who had been the friend of Ra during life had the right to claim in death a place on his boat when it passed through the heaven during the day. Thus the deceased arrived in the nether world under the auspices of a powerful protector, and far more easily than by the solitary and dangerous way of the Osiris doctrine. When Ra had arrived at his territory in the nether

DEATH IN THE MIDST OF LIFE: PROCESSION OF THE CORPSE AT AN EGYPTIAN FEAST

The care and reverence of the ancient Egyptians for their dead, and the detail and number of their funeral ceremonies, amounted to actual worship; and though there was an unorthodox section which did not accept the doctrines of immortality, the bulk of the people did, and were accustomed to be reminded of the shortness of life by the presence of a corpse at their feasts. This reproduction is made from an engraving of the picture by Edwin Long, by permission of the Fine Art Society, 148, New Bond Street, London.

regions (which implies that Osiris and other deities of darkness had a considerable domain) he disembarked the souls in the fruitful field, where they continued an existence resembling their earthly life. In consequence of the division of Ra's subterranean dominions into twelve sections of one hour's journey each, divided from one another by "doors," the dead under his protection could unfortunately enjoy the sight of the god, the sun, for only one hour, and were left in darkness for the rest of the time. However, during this short period of light the greatest activity prevailed, for the protégés of Ra had also to labour in the land beyond the grave ; they sowed, they ploughed, irrigated their land and gathered their harvest, in order not to suffer the pangs of hunger.

Life Beyond the Grave

It is interesting to remark that members of the wealthy classes made provision for both the Ra and the Osiris theories of the future life. Near the mummies, together with their Book of the Dead, and their supply of food for the next life, on the Osiris theory, are found small figures of wood, called "Shawabti," or Ushabti, that is, answerers, equipped for the most part as slaves or field labourers, and in many cases inscribed with the name of the dead man to whom they belonged, whose duty was to answer for the deceased and to act as his substitutes if he should happen to arrive at the fields of Ra and there be called upon to work.

At what period of the early history of Egypt the sun-god Ra secured the chief position in the popular beliefs cannot be determined with certainty. If the legend concerning the origin of the fifth dynasty can be trusted, the characteristic title of the kings, "sons of Ra," which was invariably emphasised in subsequent times must have originated at that period. This, however, would only roughly indicate the close of the first stage of development. During the long and obscure period of transition from the Ancient to the Middle Empire many a convulsion must have shaken the existing body of religious belief. A result of the conclusion of peace between Horus and Ra was undoubtedly the appearance of the popular mixed deity Ra-Harmachis, which was associated in the legends with the winged solar disc, flanked on each side by a small uræus snake. This token, which was to be

Rise of the Sun-god

seen over the entrance of every temple, possessed the significance of a symbol of union, which was ultimately extended over all the gods of the country. Nevertheless, in the Tell el-Amarna period the letters of the Syrian officials to the Pharaoh almost invariably employ a form of address which represents him only as the son of Ra, while Rib-Adda of Gebal employs another, and perhaps older, set of titles, in which no mention whatever is made of the sun.

In view of the difference of opinion among the Egyptians concerning the life after death, and the increasing confusion in the mythology, together with the slight efficacy of the formulæ of enchantment, a spirit of scepticism could not have failed to arise. Whether traces of a belief that the dead ascended to the stars are to be included among the evidence for this spirit is still a matter of uncertainty ; at any rate, such a conception does not seem to be of Egyptian origin. A stronger piece of evidence is, however, the fact that occasionally, though not on the memorial stones, we seem to find doubts of, at any rate, the happiness of a future life. Side by side with all the priestly doctrines of the adventures which the dead undergo in the next world before fully attaining felicity among the followers of Ra, we meet with the idea that the deceased lay rigid in eternal darkness, yearning for the delights of earthly life. For this reason man was to make the best use of his existence, to seek joy and pleasure, and to cast away all sorrow. Generally popular under the new kingdom was the "Song from the tomb of King Antef," composed by the harper.

A Creed of Cheerful Paganism

This minstrel appeals in turn to ancient sages who taught : "Ruined are the dwellings of ancestors ; they are as if they had never been, and no one returns from the beyond to tell us what has become of them." To the living the advice is given : "Adorn thyself as beautifully as may be, and let not thine heart fail thee so long as thou remainest upon earth. Trouble not thyself until the day of mourning breaks. For he whose heart has ceased to beat hears no lamentation ; he who rests in the grave shares not thy grief. Therefore, let your days be glad, your countenance joyful, and be not idle ; for no man takes his possessions with him, nor does he ever return."

A FUNERAL RITE OF ANCIENT EGYPT: THE TRIAL OF THE DEAD

Before the body of an Egyptian could be borne to the caverns of the dead it had to undergo trial by the judges of the dead, before whom any man might accuse the departed, burial in sacred ground being denied if the charges were proved.

The poetical "dialogue of one weary of life, with his soul," is, as regards its fundamental conception, a precursor of the Book of Job. Moreover, its fate seems to have been similar to that of the Biblical work, in so far as a recapitulation is added establishing a connection with the current religious belief, although the book was doubtless composed with the object of exposing the illogical nature of the orthodox creed.

The "one weary of life," ill and feeble, deceived by the world and abandoned by his relatives and friends, entreats his soul to follow him into death. But at this prospect even this last companion desires to abandon him, and is with great difficulty persuaded to agree to a compromise. In the course of the argument it becomes clear that the Egyptians were not only inclined to scepticism, but also that some of them regarded the useless pyramids and the worship of the dead with mockery and contempt. The soul expresses the opinion in no measured terms that precisely the same prospect awaited the most carefully preserved mummy and the body devoured by fishes of "a weary one who died on the river embankment leaving no posterity."

In all probability this remarkable composition was considered by its readers as belonging to the class of popular productions, the possession of which was not to be proclaimed aloud before the guardians of public morals and manners. The later addition of a short deprecatory hymn to Ra as the giver of happiness was intended to secure a measure of toleration for the work.

Two affecting songs of the man tired of life—a complaint against the world that indefatigably persecutes the tender-hearted but opens its arms to the insolent, and a salutation to death, the deliverer—give the work a high place in the literature of the world, and incline us to regard more charitably many of those features of ancient Egyptian life which we are inclined to consider with aversion. Even the refractory soul makes the admission when the deserted one has shown it that the earth is full of evil-doers: "Death stands before me to-day like the near fulfilment of the longing which a man has for his home after many years of imprisonment."

The soul then promises to accompany him : " Thy body shall return to the earth, and where thou abidest I also will abide ; we two will make our abode together."

Thoughts such as these were certainly of themselves incapable of initiating a reform in the national religion in Egypt. Nevertheless they are evidence that an intellectual movement had be-**Beginnings** gun, and that a small number **of Religious** of educated men had cast away **Reform** their fears of the unknown and their belief in the enchantments and " protections " which were to ensure to them an orthodox heaven ; that they were beginning to direct their more rational praise to the sun-god, as the obvious author of all life and fertility on the living globe. Most of the epitaphs belonging to the decade immediately preceding the reform appealed separately to Osiris, the god of the dead, and Ra, the god of the living, and the hymns addressed to the sun-god increase in fervour. Amon himself comes to be invoked in monotheistic terms as Amon-Ra. The tendency increased under the eighteenth dynasty. Constantly we find worshippers referring to Osiris, Ra, or Amon, as if he was the only deity existing in the universe. The conception of pure divinity is often met with, and this often savours of pure monotheism.

Under Amenhotep IV. (Akhenaten) the worship of Ra, or rather of Harmach, was— in his actual visible form of the Aten— exalted by royal favour into a real monotheistic cult. The symbol of the Aten cult was the simple solar disc pouring down its rays. Each ray was represented as ending in a little hand. Some of these hands are open, while others hold the emblem of life, the well-known ringed cross. Whenever the king, or, as was now customary, the assembled royal family, performed a public ceremony the sun's disc stood immediately above their heads, **Monotheistic** so that, if possible, every **Worship** person might be struck by **of the Sun** one of these emblems at the end of the rays. The " doctrine " itself was formulated in a long hymn, of which one passage must suffice for our quotation : " Thou didst create the seasons for the completion of thy work, the cool winter and the hot summer ; thou alone didst build the vault of heaven, thy lofty path, whence thou surveyest all that thou hast made. Thou

art Aten, the day of the world ; my heart belongs to thee, but no one knoweth thee as doth thy son [the king] Nefer-khepru-Ra. Thou hast revealed to him the knowledge of thy mighty coming and going. On that very day when thou establishedst the world thou didst cause it to be created for thy son, who is the express image of thy glory, even for the king of Egypt, the truly living one, the lord of both lands, Nefer-khepru-Ra, the son of the sun that existeth in verity, Akhenaten, who liveth for ever. And with him the great, the beloved royal spouse, the mistress of both lands, Nefer-neferu-Aten, that is, the immortal and flourishing Nefertiti."

The " doctrine " was thus established as the official religion, as had once been the case with the worship of Amon, only on a more comprehensive scale. The creed was inclined to monotheism in so far as no room is left for the existence of other deities, which indeed were not so much as mentioned, and soon were formally rejected. Thus, whenever the night was spoken of, any reference to the stars was carefully avoided, as it was not desired to refer to the stellar deities, the **Strange** " host of heaven." The day **New** had been generally considered **Doctrines** to begin at sunset, whereas the new doctrine did not preach that the day consisted of " the evening and the morning," but that it began with the rising of the sun. Far from believing in any beneficent influences exerted by the star and moon deities, the sun doctrine hinted rather at the opposite. The wonders of Aten are the marvels of nature and not the result of enchantments. It was argued that if the king, like his predecessors, was a god and a son of the Sun, he must necessarily increase in majesty by the introduction of the new religion ; hence the curious avowal of the natural conclusion that Aten created the world with the knowledge of his son, who reigned upon earth, and indeed for his especial benefit.

Thus it is indisputable that in the Aten worship of Amenhotep IV. we may see the germs of religious conceptions which have hitherto been attributed to a much later period. The king of Egypt who was a god in virtue of his position during his life, who chooses for his father a unique god, the creator of the world, consequently becomes, at least historically, connected with this god as his associate from the very outset.

With Amon and his circle all the other (non-solar) deities were proscribed. The king permitted those who were weak in faith to consider Ra as the equal of Aten. Ptah, Osiris,. Horus, and Isis fell from their high estate. But the various formulæ and rites belonging to the worship of the dead, even those pertaining to Osiris, continued without opposition. The beliefs of the mass of the people with regard to the life after death could not be lightly interfered with. Indeed, upon this delicate question the sun doctrine in general acquiesced in the legend of Ra's—nightly journey. And since Aten was the god of the day and of the living, he had nothing to do with night and the dead, so that the " doctrine " had nothing to say on this subject. Amenhotep and his court were buried in tombs of the usual type, though no representations of the traditional wanderings of the soul in the underworld were inscribed on their walls—the subject was tacitly avoided—but Amon and the other gods were persecuted, and their names were erased from the temples.

Amenhotep IV. probably died at the outset of the seventeenth year of his reign, thus occupying the throne from about 1380 to 1364 B.C. His children by his wife Nerfertiti, who seems to have been without a rival in his affections, were all daughters ; hence the succession devolved upon some future son-in-law. For the moment, however, the attention of Amenhotep IV. was occupied chiefly by the opposition offered to the "doctrine" by the adherents of Amon in his capital at Thebes. Had the Pharaoh merely neglected the orthodox worship of Amon, such lack of piety might have been tolerated ; but that which could not be forgotten or forgiven was his omission of the gifts customary on these occasions. Since the time of Thothmes III. these gifts had been an ever-increasing item, and had become a serious burden to the royal treasury

The Unorthodox Pharaoh

during times of peace. Since the industrial population of Thebes was far more dependent upon the college of Amon than upon the court, the probable effect of the change is obvious. Finding his position in Thebes untenable, the king, who had begun to build a sanctuary of Aten in Thebes itself, decided to found a new sacred city on a more satisfactory spot, to be consecrated to the sole worship of the "solar disc" and of his son. The new residence "Khut-Aten"—that is, the horizon of the disc—was founded almost precisely midway between Memphis and Thebes, on the eastern bank of the river. This spot was then believed to be the centre of the world, and therefore well adapted to the requirements of the new religion.

A New Sacred City

All that remains to us to-day of the city of Khut-Aten is the mass of ruins at Tell el-Amarna. The tombs in the surrounding cliffs, together with their texts, which are of high importance as a source of information for the worship of the solar disc, have long been objects of attention. It was also known that the ground plan of the town could be clearly recognised and the sites of the most important buildings be determined. But it was not until the discovery, in the spring of 1888, of the archives, written in cuneiform characters on clay tablets, treating of the relations between Egypt and Asia that further excavations were undertaken, with the result that both the ruins of the king's palace and of the Aten temple were brought to light. This period was a time of reform in art as well as in religion. It is a remarkable fact that many of the sculptured bas-reliefs discovered in the tombs of Tell el-Amarna deal with the domestic life of Amenhotep IV. Intended primarily as tokens of homage, these scenes show very clearly how naturally the divine son of Aten lived and moved among the children of men. Hitherto there had been no more than half a dozen

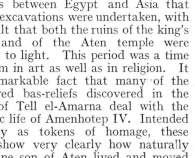

THE PORTRAIT SCULPTURE OF EGYPT
Two very fine examples of ancient Egyptian sculpture. That on the left is the famous wood-carving known as the Sheikh el-Beled, and that on the right an alabaster head of a Pharaoh of Saïs, both obviously likenesses.

poses in which the sculptor or designer was permitted to represent a king ; he might be seated, for example, stiffly on his throne or no less stiffly in his war chariot, making offerings, etc. Now, however, we see him in the company of the queen and his family of little princesses, though always caressed by the hands terminating the rays of Aten, or distributing from a balcony golden decorations to deserving co-religionists. He goes forth in a chariot of gold and silver, with a bodyguard running at his side, or is shown in the act of performing ceremonies. The figures are naturally grouped and motion is naturally indicated. The traditional stiffness is replaced by an effort at correct portraiture, at any rate in the case of the king himself.

Domestic Life in Egypt

The personal appearance of Amenhotep IV. was by no means attractive. His face was disfigured by prominent cheek-bones, a protruding chin, and a wrinkled mouth ; he had also thin legs and a large stomach. However, he insisted that all defects should be faithfully reproduced ; and the whole court, the queen included, were depicted with the same physical peculiarities. One relief, for instance, represents the king with a particularly forbidding expression of countenance in the act of kissing his eldest daughter, with the queen and two other daughters sitting opposite.

The probability that foreign influences had led to the development of a new style of art has been confirmed by the discovery of a richly-painted stucco floor in the palace, representing a marshy landscape filled with animals, as well as by objects made of variously coloured glass and numerous vases and fragments closely resembling those of Mycenæ and Cyprus. A corresponding stucco floor and glazed pottery in the same style have been found in Amenhotep's palace. The stucco floor painting is, of course, purely Egyptian, but the imported foreign pottery is a mark of the extensive connection with lands over sea which is characteristic of the eighteenth dynasty. Traffic by sea with the Greek coast must, however, have begun much earlier, for we find pottery of the middle and early Minoan period—contemporary with the twelfth and sixth dynasties ; and we have already seen that ambassadors from Minoan Crete visited the Egyptian court at the time of the eighteenth dynasty.

Foreign Artistic Influences

The command to build the city of th solar disc must have coincided with th removal of the court from Thebes. Pos sibly the king retired to Memphis pendin the completion of his new residence Nevertheless, the " Horizon of the Sun was occupied before the city was ha constructed. Not until the completion c this work, about the year 1374, did th sovereign feel himself entirely free ; h then discarded the name of Amenhote and chose the title of " Akhenaten "– that is, the spirit of the solar disc. Hi family and adherents followed his example and named themselves after Aten.

This was practically a declaratio of war against Amon. The refractor town of Thebes was finally compelled t submit and to tolerate the authority of governor who believed in the " doctrine. The systematic effacement of the wor " Amon " from inscriptions, even fror those of the tombs, was only to thoroughly carried out. A measure of per secution was also directed against Mu and Khuns, the nearest relatives of Amor King Akhenaten, as he is now stylec obviously desired to obliterat the memory of Amon through out Egypt. As we learn fror the stele of King Tutankhamor recently discovered at Thebes, the pries hood of Amon was dispersed, and th goods of Amon were confiscated to th Aten. Not only at Thebes. but at Helic polis and in the northern capital, Memphi as well as in the " colonial " capitals c Napata in Nubia and Jerusalem (?) i Palestine (Khinatura), temples of the Ate were set up, bearing the same nam Dester-Aten (" Red is Aten ") or Gen Aten (" Found is Aten "), as the heretica shrine at Thebes. This last was probabl never finished, and certainly the ne worship could hardly be carried on fc long safely in the city of Amon, dethrone and dispossessed though her great go might be. We know that for a tim anarchy reigned at Thebes, and the roya sepulchres in the Biban el-Muluk wer abandoned to the depredations of tomb robbers. The temple of Amon was re placed by a magnificent new shrine c the solar disc at Khut-Aten, which wa established as a national sanctuary. Th high-priest bore the same title as the hig priest at Heliopolis. The king neve wearied of the task of celebrating th various festivals of consecration. Th

The Egyptian Reformation

queen-mother Teie did not appear at Khut-Aten until the court had already been settled there; she was then inducted by her son with great display of pomp. In the meanwhile, however, in spite of all the proofs of devotion and piety shown by the Aten worshippers under the eyes of the king, the fact remained that the new belief became more and more unpopular among the people. One of the new boundary stones of the precinct of Khut-Aten was even found one day to have been destroyed.

Akhenaten therefore considered it of all the more importance to strengthen his cause by a conversion of distinguished men. He seems therefore to have considered the conversion of the " divine father," Aï, who had apparently risen to his relatively modest hierarchical dignity in the temple of Amon, as an event of special significance. Aï was already fan-bearer at the king's right hand, chief master of the horse, and the " truly beloved royal scribe," when the king ordered the treasurer to " lay gold on his neck, on his back and on his feet, because

Divine "Father" Converted

he has hearkened unto the doctrine." And when Aï married the " king's nurse," who also bore the name of Teie, the couple became the recipients of still richer gifts of gold. Aï ordered " this beautiful event " to be immortalised in sculpture and described in detail on the walls of his tomb in Tell el-Amarna, which, however, he never occupied.

The opposition between the beliefs of the Egyptians and those of Akhenaten was of itself sufficient to prevent the king from embarking upon such warlike enterprises as had been undertaken by Thothmes III.; the Pharaoh could not venture to leave his country. Nevertheless, at the time of his death the Egyptian possessions in Asia, though internally in a state of complete disruption, seem to have continued to recognise the supremacy of Egypt; they did not, at any rate, break into open revolt before the beginning of the struggles which put an end to the reformed doctrine. Our information concerning the destruction of the heresy and the consequent fall of the eighteenth dynasty is unusually scanty. Akhenaten himself seems to have been the last male representative of his line. Of his six daughters, Mekt-Aten died before her father, and was laid in a splendid tomb

at Tell el-Amarna, which she seems to have shared with her father, the king, whose body must at some time, however, have been removed to Thebes, like that of his mother, Teie, for the mummy of the heretic was found with the other royal bodies in the tomb of Amenhotep II. Since he had been buried in the orthodox

Fall of the Eighteenth Dynasty

way, no formal destruction of the heretical king's body was attempted. Akhenaten was succeeded by Semenkh - ka - Ra, who a short time before had married his eldest daughter, Merit-Aten. Inscribed wine-jugs from the ruins of the palace at Tell el-Amarna show the seventeenth year of Akhenaten to be the earliest possible date for this event. The fact that there were several younger daughters, one of whom, Ankhs-en-pa-Aten, became the wife of a certain Tut-ankh-Aten, was soon turned to advantage by the oppressed Amon party. This latter couple laid claim to the throne on their own account, and recognised the faith of Amon. Both reappear in Thebes as King Tut-ankh-Amon and Queen Ankhs-en-Amon—apparently rival rulers either to Semenkhka-Ra or to a third brother-in-law.

Buildings and restorations to the Theban temples, carried out by Tut-ankh-Amon, as well as a large representation of the reception of tribute from Syria and Ethiopia, discovered in the tomb of one Hui, point to the fact that the orthodox Pharaoh was for a time the absolute ruler of the whole kingdom of Amenhotep; on the other hand, indications of the continuation of the heresy during this period are not wanting. Marriage into the family descendants of Akhenaten probably enabled other ambitious lords to put forward pretexts to the throne. After Tutankhamon, the " divine father," Aï, was able to get possession of the throne. His wife, Teie, who was at most a very

Rule of the " Divine Father "

distant relative of Amenhotep IV., served to give him a claim to the succession. As before, in the days of his patron, Aï was once again able to adapt his views to altered circumstances. He occupied the royal castle at Thebes, abjured his former errors, and added the title of " divine father " to his official name. The length of Aï's reign is a matter of conjecture. He was followed by a more famous ruler from the heretical party. A certain Horemheb had risen to be commander-in-chief of the north under Akhenaten, who, on his tomb at Sakkara, was able to speak of himself as " chief of chiefs, greatest of the great . . . who had been sent forth by the king at the head of an army against the lands of the south and of the north. To him the king had entrusted **A Soldier** the administration of both **Seizes** lands, and he caused them to **the Throne** rejoice, he, the companion of his master, on the day the Bedouins were defeated." The mention of campaigns against the east is of interest in spite of its brevity, for under the successors of Horemheb it appears that the empire had lost a portion of its Asiatic possessions. Aï gave Horemheb his full confidence. But the commander-in-chief was only waiting a fitting opportunity to seize the supremacy of Egypt for himself. It was first necessary to secure the support of the priesthood of Amon at Karnak by means of great promises, which were afterward performed. When the priesthood gave the signal, Horemheb appeared in Thebes at the head of his troops, and perhaps put an end to the government and even to the life of Aï, and received from Amon both the crown and the princess who was heir to it, about 1350 B.C. The princess was called Netjem-Mut. She may have been a sister of Nefertiti, although, as in the case of the younger Teie. there is probably here nothing more than a similarity of names and an intentional transference to the usurper

of the claims necessary to his purpose. Rarely has the policy of a king been so clearly marked out before him as was that of Horemheb. His task was the ruthless persecution of the worshippers of the solar disc, and the destruction, so far as was possible, of all traces of the " doctrine." Wherever the name of Amon had been effaced, it was restored ; but wherever that of Aten appeared upon tombs or elsewhere, there was immediate work for stonecutters and painters.

A new era of prosperity began for Thebes ; the losses suffered by Amon were repaid with usury so far as circumstances permitted ; in Karnak the king undertook the construction of large edifices. Of Horemheb's military operations we hear only by way of allusion. However, it is probable that he retained the approach to the Nubian gold-mines, and despatched marauding expeditions into Asia.

A remarkable inscription in the temple of Karnak complains of the general disorder in the country, and threatens the officials, and especially the troops, with severe corporal punishment **Beginning** unless they cease their rob- **of** bery and embezzlement **Reconstruction** Consequently Horemheb himself was obliged to march through the country in order to enforce his rights, as the indefatigable Thothmes III. had done before him. A period of dilettantism, or religious activity, and of new tendencies in art had been followed by the downfall Now began the slow and difficult process of reconstruction.

SARCOPHAGUS OF AÏ, A "DIVINE FATHER" AND HERETIC PHARAOH OF EGYPT

UNDER THE SPLENDID DYNASTY

WE do not know how the question of the succession was settled on the death of Horemheb ; it seems, however, that the transition to the new dynasty was peacefully effected. The double crown descended to a new family. Rameses, or Ramses, I., the first king of the nineteenth dynasty, was a ruler of no historical importance, and almost immediately appointed his son, Seti I., or Sethos, to the co-regency.

Seti I., about 1320 to 1310 B.C., is chiefly remarkable for his name, which suggests Set, and opposition to the national Osiris-worship, and no doubt points to an origin in Lower Egypt for this dynasty. The predilection of Rameses II. for Tanis, in the Delta, points the same way. The king was alive to the fact that his name might be unpopular, and therefore styled himself " Osiri " in the inscription on his own temple of the dead and magnificent tomb in the necropolis at **Rule of Seti I.** Thebes, in order to avoid the possibility of making an unfavourable impression upon the ruler of the next world by a mention of the name of his enemy Set. In later times, when the god Set became more nearly identical with the devil, the Egyptians attempted to efface the name of Set from all secular memorials.

The comparatively short reign of Seti was distinguished by the erection of many buildings, some of which are of considerable size. Thus, for example, he began the construction of the great hall of columns in the temple at Karnak, the completion of which was left to his successor ; he also undertook extensive restorations in Thebes, which continued to be the royal residence. Buildings were also erected by him in Memphis, and a palace in Heliopolis is said to have been his work. The attention of Seti, however, was chiefly directed to the south. Supported by Amen-en-apt, prince of Kush, he effected so many improvements in Nubia that in a short time the country was but little inferior to Egypt in respect of culture and density of population. His

work was subsequently continued by his son Rameses II. Seti also undertook the systematic boring of wells in the desert of the Trogodytes ; these, together with their handsome temple in the desert east of Redesiya, opened up a trade route by **Improvement of the Desert** which the traffic with the coast of the Red Sea could be guarded and controlled. These desert roads also served as routes for the convoys of gold and emeralds. A very rude papyrus map of the Ethiopian gold-mines at Akita, the Wady Olaki, which is the earliest Egyptian map yet discovered, dates from the reign of Seti.

The body of the king has also been preserved to us. Seti I. was a tall, thin man, with an intelligent countenance and fine teeth, although he had certainly reached the threshold of old age before his death. Of the high officials of this period other than Amen-en-apt we are acquainted with a certain Paser, who stood at the head of the administration of Egypt proper. He must have been a very pious person, for he dedicated memorials of himself almost in every shrine in Egypt.

The campaign in Palestine and Phœnicia undertaken by Seti I. at the beginning of his reign was obviously intended to check the southward expansion of the Hittite kingdom, which had taken advantage of the anarchy into which Akhenaten had allowed the Asiatic dominions of Egypt to fall. From the Tell el-Amarna letters we see that Akhenaten, absorbed in his religious reform, allowed Palestine to fall into complete confusion. **Campaign in Palestine** The letters of Ribadda, governor of Byblos, beseeching the king to send him aid against the revolted sheikhs, are alternately pathetically pleading and indignant in tone. But the philosopher-king did nothing forcible, as is the wont of his kind, in such emergencies, and the wandering Khabiri, or Hebrews, and the Hittites waged war in the land as if Pharaoh was not. The Amorite princes, Abdashista and Aziru, his son, revolted in

Northern Palestine in concert with the Hittites and with Hakama, the Mitanian prince of Kadesh, on the Orontes, in spite of the efforts of Ribadda. In the south, Abdkhiba, the governor of Jerusalem, and Yankhamu, the viceroy of the Delta, were powerless against the Khabiri. The Egyptian general Bikhuru could do nothing : he did not know friend from foe, and his troops sacked Ribadda's city. It was about this time that the kingdom of Mitani came to an end. Shubbiluliuma, the Hittite, had taken from it the lands on the western side of the Euphrates, which since Thothmes III.'s day it had held under the suzerainty of Egypt. Tushratta, the king, was murdered, and his son, Mattinaza, as we learn from the documents lately discovered at Boghaz Köi, placed himself under the protection of Shubbiluliuma.

The pressure of the Hittite advance had already become perceptible on the Egyptian frontiers. The Bedouins, encamped along the eastern outworks, were speedily driven away by the army of Seti when, in his reign, the Egyptians deemed themselves sufficiently reorganised to reconquer their lost dominion ; they also suffered a general defeat at an unknown stronghold in the south of Palestine by Seti I. All serious opposition seems then to have been overcome as far north as Carmel. Even Tyre delivered the customary tribute. While advancing northward in the direction of Galilee, Seti encountered a Hittite army, led by Mursilis, son of Shubbiluliuma, which he attacked and drove back, in the forest region Yenuam. The Pharaoh turned his victory to advantage by procuring a supply of wood for building purposes, which he commanded the petty chiefs of the neighbourhood to cut for him in all

RAMESES I.
From a statue in the Turin Museum.

Mansell
RAMESES II.
Who made himself the most famous of the Ramessides, by appropriating credit for various achievements due to former Pharaohs.

haste. After occupying two fortresses in the Lebanon mountains, and threatening Kadesh, he marched homeward. He was received with great demonstrations of homage by the high officials of Egypt assembled at the fortifications which guarded the entrance to Tjaru, near the modern Suez Canal. He had, in fact, successfully checked the Hittite advance. We also learn that Seti I. and his son began a war with the Libyans.

The sharp contrast between the main characteristics of the Ramessides and those of the eighteenth dynasty first becomes definitely apparent in the son of Seti I. Rameses II. reigned sixty-seven years (about 1310–1243), much longer than any other Egyptian sovereign, if we except the ninety years of Pepi II. The account of his achievements set forth by his numerous and boastful proclamations was subsequently elaborated by legend. He was called by the Greeks, who obviously obtained their information from later Egyptian accounts, the great conqueror of the world, the law-giver and statesman, "Sesostris" by confusion with the Senusrets and Thothmes III., who vanquished the Scythians, Colchis, India, Arabia, and Libya. Rameses II. is now known to us as being nothing more than a ruler of average ability. He in no way deserves the title of "Great" which has been given to him, whereas Thothmes III. as certainly deserves it. Rameses II. was the first king to appropriate on an extensive scale the credit of building the monuments erected by former rulers by erasing their names and substituting his own. In this case the motive was not hate, as with Akhenaten, but petty vanity.

In all other respects Rameses II. pursued the policy of Seti I. The colonisation of

Nubia was continued, and at the end of his long reign there were prosperous towns where now remain only the ruined temples of Beit el-Walli, Wadi es-Sebua, and, above all, the celebrated structure of Abu Simbel. The Sesostris legend was first connected with this architectural wonder of Africa, which, with its numerous colossal statues, its graceful columns, and the perfection of its design and execution, marks the zenith of ancient Egyptian art, as far as rock-sculpture is concerned.

As is usually the case, the period of high achievement was

HEAD OF SETI I.
From a photograph of the mummy of this Pharaoh, who died over 3,200 years ago.

followed by rapid decline. Side by side with edifices in Egypt proper, which in elegance of design are even superior to those of Abu Simbel, we find the remains of composite temples dating from the later years of the reign of Rameses II., which were hastily put together solely to create an effective impression from a distant point of view. The king's architectural zeal is mentioned both in the literature of classical antiquity and in the Old Testament. His activity in Thebes was almost boundless: the Ramesseum, dedicated as a temple of victory to Amon-Ra, and consequently of great value as an historical monument, was perhaps even excelled by the additions to the temple of Karnak, the state sanctuary, as well as by other improvements which the king made in his capital. Tanis and Memphis were equally rich in colossal edifices erected in his honour. Legend has also credited Rameses, and indeed other Egyptian rulers, with the temporary realisation of the old dream of a navigable canal

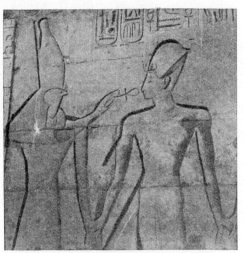

THE GOD HORUS GIVING LIFE TO SETI I.
Seti I., or Sethos, who ruled about ten years from 1310 B.C., was the first of the Ramessides of historical importance.

RAMESES II.
Who claimed to be the creator of everything Egyptian. Reproduced from the actual head of his mummy.

from the Nile to the Red Sea. In short, Rameses II., on his own showing, was actually the sole creator of everything, and the Egypt which he left behind him bore throughout its length and breadth the impress of his usurping signet ring.

It was not unknown, however, even to his contemporaries, that the king had depended largely upon the wisdom of other men during his long reign. What Amenhotep the son of Hapu had been to Amenhotep III., Prince Kha-em-uaset was to his father, Rameses II. As legitimate son of the Pharaoh he occupied a number of high ecclesiastical offices, such as the high-priesthood of Ptah; he assisted his father in ceremonies connected with the ritual, and is said to have discovered sacred books—an impossibility at that time except for clever men—and in later times acquired the reputation of a mighty enchanter. In temporal affairs Setau, the viceroy of Kush, seems to have gained especial celebrity. On the other hand, Prince Meri-Atum, the son of the chief royal spouse Nefertari—called "Naptera" in the Boghaz Köi tablets—was provided with the position of high-priest of Heliopolis. He styles himself a judge over men, whom the king placed before both lands, and whose counsel would be found good. But inasmuch as the mother of Meri-Atum died long before Rameses, at which time Kha-em-uaset, the son of Queen Nefereset, may have risen to the height of his power, we may presume that the counsel of Meri-Atum, the judge over men, was not in every instance found good by Rameses.

On the whole, it is probable that the leading personalities in the household and cabinet of Rameses were occasionally changed, in spite of the fact that they usually were his own sons. In an inscription at Abydos he credited himself with sixty sons, and in Wadi es-Sebua with as many as one hundred and eleven sons, together with thirty daughters. Toward the end of his reign his fourteenth son, Meneptah, was recognised as heir to the throne; no doubt the majority of the older princes had preceded the king to the grave. The mummy of Rameses has been recovered from Der el-Bahari. We are able to compare it with a statue representing him in the prime of life. The characteristic of these faces is the absence of that strained expression which betokens a vigorous intellectual activity in the features of men, for example, those of Seti; in this case we are rather reminded of a proud but kindly "serenissimus." The face of the

ONE OF THE MANY STATUES OF RAMESES II.
Rameses II. was the greatest forger in Egyptian history, for, though a man of but average ability, he acquired the title of "Great" by substituting on many monuments and inscriptions his own name for those of previous rulers.

mummy is that of a highly aristocratic, but not very intelligent, old man. The mummy of the prince-minister Kha-em-uaset was found in the tomb of Amen-hotep II.; and it has not yet been unrolled. There is a statue of him in the British Museum.

What Rameses II. was unable to carry out in person was effected by the foundations which he established. The school for the future officials of state, conducted by the priesthood of the Theban Ramesseum, has left to us a considerable portion of its papyrus note-books, which were known almost one hundred years ago, "Select Papyri," which have now found a resting place in the museums of Europe. Boys who were destined for the higher offices of state were required to familiarise themselves with practical composition, writing, and with exercises in correspondence; hence our knowledge of the working of the state machinery under the Ramessides has

THE GREAT HALL OF COLUMNS IN THE TEMPLE OF KARNAK
The architectural zeal of Rameses II., apart from his dishonest claims to fame, was considerable, and this addition to the state sanctuary excelled perhaps all his other achievements. From a fine restoration by M. Charles Chipiez.

been greatly furthered by these papyri. They present us with the picture of a highly organised bureaucracy with all its corresponding disadvantages. The educated scribe considers himself a lord in the land ; he looks upon the peasants, the sailors, and handicraftsmen as " asses," whom he had been appointed to drive. This overbearing superiority was naturally accompanied by strained relations between the officials themselves ; disputes upon questions of salary are of constant occurrence.

The influence of foreigners steadily increased, and was already making itself felt in the written language, which begins to include words borrowed from the Semitic and other tongues. It was the court that

RAMESES II. STRIKING A NUBIAN CAPTIVE
From a painting in Rameses' temple at Abu Simbel.

or Pentaur, describes how the king himself, in his chariot, begins the attack upon the Hittites with his troops drawn up in line of battle. Just as he had come to close quarters and was looking before him, he beheld 2,500 chariots of the enemy enclosing his own ; but " there was with him no prince and no charioteer, no officer of the footman ; they had abandoned him, and no one was there to fight beside him." Rameses II. escaped from his dangerous position by recalling to his father Amon the long list of his acts of piety toward him. Finally, the god in distant Thebes heard his prayer, and bethought him of the pylons, monuments, gifts, and honours which the pious king had enumerated. " I have called from the end of the land, and my voice has passed through Hermonthis. Ra hearkens

SIEGE OF A MOUNTAIN FORT BY RAMESES II.
Rameses II. carried on many wars which, as in this painting from a Nubian temple, were always recorded as victorious.

set the fashion in language, where the mixed Egyptian of the favourite Syrian slaves of the Pharaoh, and the barbarisms of his foreign satellites, excited interest and were imitated accordingly. For the rest, the Egyptian scribes knew very well that they were only rendering homage to fashion by imitating the language and customs of the " hereditary enemy." Whenever the Pharaoh bent his terrible bow, to the dismay of the miserable Asiatics, the poets on the Nile proceeded to tune their lyres in expectation of the—invariably great—victory. A poem which has come down to us in a copy made by a certain Pentaueret,

RAMESES ON AN ASIATIC CAMPAIGN
Rameses often " bent his bow to the terror of the miserable Asiatics," a group of whom this painting depicts him in the act of striking.

and appears, stretches forth his hand to me and says : ' Thou art not alone, for I am here, thy father ; my hand is with thee. I am to thee more than hundreds of thousands, I the dispenser of victory, who loveth bravery ! ' Then I regained my courage, my heart rejoiced. Like Month I sent my arrows in all directions ;

Amon Rescues Rameses like Baal, like the arrow of the plague, I came down upon them. And I found the 2,500 chariots laid low before my horses." The remainder of the enemy fled with great loss. Rameses long continued to tell the story of this brilliant exploit, and to hold it up before his troops as a shining example.

As a matter of fact, the Hittite struggle, which apparently broke out on his accession and continued with long intermissions until 1297-1296, ended in the practical result that Egypt was obliged to renounce whatever empire she had possessed in Syria. Rameses constantly gathered all his strength to give battle to the Hittites, whose military power was now far superior to his own. The poem above mentioned refers to a battle fought not far from the town of Kadesh in the fifth year of the king. In the previous year the Egyptian army had marched through Phœnicia. Evidence of this fact is an inscription of Rameses II. on the rocky bank of the Nahr el-Kelb, not far from Beirut, to which another was added in later times, perhaps in his tenth year.

The great engagement at Kadesh was probably the conclusion or the chief incident of an advance by which Rameses frustrated an attempt of the Hittites, under Mursitus, to push farther south. The Pharaoh's army was encamped in the south of the city, according to the inscriptions and reliefs in the temple at Luxor and in the Ramesseum ; it was surrðunded by a wall formed of the heavy shields of the infantry. But

The Battle of Kadesh it does not appear to have been very well adapted for defence, owing to the disproportionate size of the baggage train. Amid the ox teams and sumpter asses were the king's tamê lions. The battle ended with the defeat of the enemy's wing, which was driven across the Orontes. Many of the leaders and allies of the Hittite king were drowned or put to death in the flight. The Egyptians also must have suffered severe losses, which they were unable to conceal, and they soon set out on their homeward march.

During the next two campaigns the advantage seems to have been on the side of the Hittites. Not until his eighth year did Rameses succeed in securing his occupation even of Palestine ; he re-conquered Askalon and several other fortified towns south of Lebanon, among them Dapur, situated in the highlands. The attitude of the Phœnician cities varied with the successes or failures of the Egyptians. Previously the Phœnicians had been among the most loyal of the Pharaoh's Asiatic subjects ; however, the long duration of the war, together with the diminishing prospect of an ultimate Egyptian victory, no doubt weakened their fidelity.

When finally the Hittite king Khattusil succeeded to the throne on the death of his brother Mutallu, son of Mursilis, peace was made. Our knowledge of the terms is derived from an inscription upon the south wall of the great Hall of Columns in the Karnak temple. Unfortunately the copy is incomplete, owing

Treaty With the Hittites to the omission of all paragraphs unfavourable to the Egyptians. Consequently we have in this copy not only the earliest instance of a treaty between nations, but also the results of a benevolent censorship, which passed over in silence that which it could not falsify. Numerous allusions are made to previous treaties which had been valid from ancient times until the reign of Mutallu and which Khattusil now renewed. The delimitation of the new frontier in Asia is missing, although the remainder of the agreement contains clauses which treat in detail of future support to be rendered by the contracting powers in the event of an attack upon either, and of the mode of dealing with deserters from both sides. It was also stipulated that in future the encroachments of individuals or communities upon the boundaries of either kingdom should not be permitted. Of her former Asiatic dominions, Egypt succeeded in retaining the cities of Phœnicia and Palestine south of the Lebanon. But the rise of the Palestinian kingdom of Judah deprived her, about a century later, of even this remnant of the conquests of Thothmes III. The last of the Rameside Pharaohs seems to have had no possessions in Asia, except perhaps

A PAGEANT OF ANCIENT EGYPT: RAMESES II., "THE GREAT," AND HIS LIONS IN PROCESSION THROUGH HIS ROYAL CITY

Gaza, beyond the eastern wall at the Bitter Lakes. The only subsequent reference to Egyptian dependencies in Asia is dated in the third year of Meneptah, about 1240 ; it is a short list of travellers who passed the frontier guard, in which mention is made of royal embassies to Tyre and of the work of Egyptian officials in Palestine. This important **Hittite** treaty ushered in a long period **Visit** of peace. Khattusil and the **to Egypt** king of Kode (the North Syrian coast) subsequently paid a formal visit to Egypt, where they were received with great honour by Rameses II. Although Rameses had married Khattusil's daughter, who received the name Urmaa-Neferu-Ra, according to the then existing conceptions of good faith between sovereigns, the king of the Hittites ventured to pay his visit only under the protection of a powerful escort, a portion of which immediately occupied the place of landing, while the remainder accompanied him on his journey inland.

We have a record of the visit of Khattusil even in far Nubia, where Rameses sculptured a record of his coming at Abu Simbel, including the departure of the Hittite guest, who is speeded on his way to his northern home in Cappadocia with the hope that neither snow nor ice will hinder his passage over the mountain passes of the Taurus. Abu Simbel is a curious place in which to find a mention of snow and ice. That the treaty with Rameses was an offensive and defensive alliance is proved by this, no less than by the fact that the goddess of Kadesh was worshipped in Egypt ; that grain was supplied " in order to nourish this Khetaland " ; and finally by a subsequent legend, according to which Rameses II., while engaged in a victorious campaign in Naharina, married " the daughter of the great one of Bekhten, Neferu-Ra." When her sister, Bentresh, **Wonder-** was seized by an illness, he **Working** sent the god Khuns from **Image** Thebes to Bekhten ; there the people insisted on retaining the wonder-working image, until it finally freed itself by a further series of miracles. Bekhten is presumably another name for the Khetaland, Cappadocia, not Bactria, as used to be thought. We have very interesting evidence as to the relations of Rameses II. with the Hittites in the cuneiform tablets which have lately been found by Winckler at Boghaz Köi, the site of the Hittite capital, Khatti, the Greek Pteria, east of the Halys. These are diplomatic despatches of the same kind as those from Tell el-Amarna. Even a duplicate of the famous treaty between Rameses and Khattusil is said to have been found. This will give us the " Hittite text," so that we can see the reverse of the medal ; audiebimus alteram partem ! In these letters the Egyptian king is called " Uashmuariya satepuariya Riyamasesa Maiamana," which gives us approximately the real pronunciation of his name, which we conventionally write " Usermara setepenra Rameses meri-Amon."

Rameses II. died at an advanced age, and was succeeded by his son, Meneptah, himself no longer a youth, who cannot have reigned more than ten years (1243 to 1233). Although far from a military genius, the course of events during his reign involved Egypt in a severe war, which was conducted to a brilliantly successful issue. The Libyans and the Shardana, who probably had always been in the habit of passing through Libya to take **Brilliant** service as mercenaries under **Successes** the Pharaohs, rose in alliance **in War** against Egypt. Marmaiu, the Libyan king, succeeded at the same time in allying himself with a horde of pirates from Greece and Asia Minor, composed of Lycians, " Turisha, Akaivasha, and Shakalusha," who had " constantly made inroads into Egyptian territory, sailing up the river, and remaining for days and months in the land."

They advanced as far as Heliopolis, but the god Ptah appeared to Meneptah in a dream and promised him victory ; in fact, his army succeeded in routing the dreaded allies in a hard-fought battle near the city of Piari. Marmaiu fled before the final attack of the Egyptians, and left his camp, together with vast quantities of plunder, to the victors, who pursued him with a troop of cavalry, the first of which we hear in Egyptian history, until he finally escaped under cover of the night. More than 9,000 prisoners and a like number of dead bore witness to the military strength of the allies. At the same time the Shardana, serving in the Egyptian army, did not hesitate to fight bravely against their countrymen on this occasion. The suffix -sha is an ethnic termination, which occurs in Lycian in the form of -aza or -azi. The Turisha, Akaivasha, and Shakalusha were probably Tyrrhenian, Achaian, and Sagalassian pirates. Meneptah united Nubia more firmly to Egypt by a campaign against the south, and again invaded Palestine with effect, as is proved by a granite stele discovered in Thebes by Petrie in 1896. Here, for the first time in an Egyptian text, mention is made of Israel, as Isiral, directly as a people, definitely settled in Palestine, which they had had plenty of time to become since the days when their ancestors, the Khabiri, had ravished Palestine in the time of Akhenaten. Till lately it was supposed that the exodus of the Israelites took place in the reign of this king Meneptah. There never were, however, any real grounds for this supposition, which is a mere guess. It is far more probable that the Exodus is really the same event as the expulsion of the Hyksos, as Josephus thought.

The warlike deeds of Meneptah were, however, of but small avail to Egypt. On his death the kingdom was seriously endangered by untimely quarrels as to the succession. His son, or, more probably, grandson, judging from the youthful appearance of the best of his excellent portraits, subsequently succeeded him as Seti II. After came his son, Amenmeses, and shortly afterward an ambitious grandee named Bai seized it for his own candidate, Si-Ptah, a brother of Amenmeses who married his sister, Ta-Usert. Bai seems to have administered the kingdom. From a statement of the revenue of Rameses III., drawn up some sixty years later, it appears that Seti II. and the older line of the Ramessides suffered under " years of want." The Nile god withheld his blessings and plunged the kingdom into misery. The nobles, who were already practically independent and continually quarrelling, " put one another to death in their insolence and pride ; they did what they pleased, for they had no ruler."

In the meantime a Syrian sheikh took advantage of the confusion. He invaded the country, overthrew the petty princes, and gradually made the once powerful land tributary to himself. We are

Years of Want

acquainted neither with the name of this Syrian ruler, which was formerly incorrectly held to be " Arsu," nor with the situation and extent of his Asiatic possessions ; apparently we have here to deal only with a temporary supremacy, the creation of which was facilitated by the general disorder in Egypt. Shortly before the year 1200 the Syrian conquerors themselves became destitute and began to plunder the temples ; " they used the gods as they had used men, and ceased to make offerings." This treatment finally spurred the priests to work for the restoration of the kingdom. " And the gods installed Setnakht, their son, who had issued from their members, as lord of the land. He was as the god Set in his anger ; he restored the whole land to order from uproar ; he slew the enemies who dwelt therein." This is practically all that we know of the founder of the twentieth dynasty, the line of the later Ramessides. Setnakht himself was probably a scion of the older line.

Egypt Conquered By Syria

MUMMY OF RAMESES III.
This small, rather hard-looking man was the last great Pharaoh of the New Empire of Ancient Egypt.

The restoration of Egypt, however, was far from complete. The majority of the temples still awaited the fulfilment of the divine promises. Half of the Delta belonged to the Libyans, and the former masters of the country, who had been driven into Syria, could scarcely have resigned themselves to the change when the liberator left the scene of his exploits, the details of which are in any case unknown. Rameses III. (1200–1168), who succeeded him, had already shared his father's government, and during the first four years of his reign enjoyed an interval of comparative peace. The recruiting of Libyans and Shardana for the Egyptian army seems now to have been carried on with great activity. This in itself tended to relieve the tension upon the western frontier. Perhaps the subjugation of " the mighty one, Kush," whose name occurs at the beginning of a later list of defeated opponents, also took place at this time. Thus, although Kush had remained under the government of an Egyptian viceroy, it is evident that subsequently to the reign of Seti II. the first of a series of changes, ending in the independence of Ethiopia, took place. While the kingdom of the Pharaohs was visibly increasing in power, the countries of Syria were busily engaged in defending themselves against new invaders; consequently the Libyans were obliged to make their attempt against Egypt in 1195 unassisted, "but their schemes were broken and turned against them." Before the various tribes were able to unite in full force they were intercepted by a clever disposition of the Egyptian forces and dispersed with great loss. The attacks of the last of the Libyan princes ended in flight before the troops of Rameses III., by which time the enemies' losses amounted collectively to more than 12,500.

The effects of this defeat were still felt by the Libyans when, in the eighth year of the reign, about 1192 B.C., the storm which had long been threatening from Asia approached the eastern frontier of Egypt.

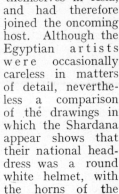

RAMESES III. AND HIS QUEEN NEFRARI
Reproduced from two splendidly coloured portraits copied by M. Champollion, from the walls of a Nubian temple.

in Lycian); and Vashash (Axians from Crete ?), who had come from their distant coasts; and finally the Shardana of the sea, that is to say, robber bands belonging to this western nation, who had been unable to maintain themselves in Asia, and had therefore joined the oncoming host. Although the Egyptian artists were occasionally careless in matters of detail, nevertheless a comparison of the drawings in which the Shardana appear shows that their national headdress was a round white helmet, with the horns of the moon branching from each side; when they entered the service of the Pharaoh, a spike was added to the helmet, terminating in a metal disc, as it were the badge of the sons of the sun. The Turisha and Shakalusha were probably neighbours and relatives of the Lycians, while as early as the time of Amenhotep III. the Shardana and Danuna are mentioned as mercenaries on the shores of Palestine, and also as settlers there. The Pulesti, the Philistines of the Old Testament, and the Zakkar seem to have been Cretan tribes who had settled on the coast of Palestine. This agrees with the old tradition of the Cretan origin of the Philistines. We find Solomon's guards called Cherethim (Cretans) and Pelishtim (Philistines); so that we have the same Cretan tribes acting as the Varangians of the Israelitish kings as they had a century before for the Pharaohs. Under the twenty-first dynasty the Zakkar are still mentioned as pirates on the Palestinian coast.

RAMESES III., THE VICTORIOUS, IN HIS CHARIOT
Rameses III. was almost as great a warrior and conqueror as Thothmes III.; he rescued Egypt from Syria and recalled the glories of the New Empire.

The attack was again made by the Turisha and Shakalusha, now materially strengthened by the addition of new peoples— the Pulesti, or Philistines; the Zakkar, or Cretans of Zakro (Teukrians ?); Danuna, or Danaans (na is also an ethnic suffix

This mixed horde of Cretans and other folk from the Ægean and Asia Minor, after subduing Alashya and Kode (Cilicia), the kingdom of the Hittites, and finally the Amorites, assembled its forces in their territories for an invasion of Egypt by land and sea. Their well-manned fleet, consisting of long, narrow sailing vessels, arrived first, and endeavoured to force an entrance into one of the eastern mouths of the Nile. But the fleet and army of the Pharaoh had concentrated in the threatened district under his personal command, and were in a position to fall upon the enemy at the first favourable opportunity. Driven towards the coast by the Egyptian navy, and there received with showers of

THE LAST OF THE GREAT TEMPLES OF ANCIENT EGYPT
A restoration, by M. Chipiez, of the splendid funerary temple built by Rameses III. at Medinet Habu. It was the last of the great temples of Ancient Egypt.

arrows by the land forces, the enemy suffered a severe defeat, losing many ships. The remainder were in no condition to continue the struggle, and disappeared from Egyptian waters ; this is the first great naval battle known to history. The tactics of King Rameses III. recalled the skill of Thothmes III., the great conqueror, and although the strategy of the former was confined to a smaller compass, it in no way suffers by the com-

made a further bulwark. The battle was won by the Egyptians, chiefly owing to the powers of the Tuhirs, or " mighty men," of the Shardana in Egyptian service, who, like mercenaries all the world over, had no scruples about fighting against their kith and kin. But in spite of the severe losses sustained by the enemy, especially in prisoners, they remained sufficiently numerous to reconquer within a short time the coast of Shephelha, between Gaza and Carmel, which Rameses III. had recently triumphantly defended. In the meanwhile the Pharaoh followed up his momentary success, and turned against the Amorites of Lebanon to punish them for their alliance with the enemy. Tidings now arrived of a threatened movement upon the Libyan frontier, and when Rameses III. withdrew his army in consequence, the last remains of Egyptian supremacy in Syria disappeared. However, the blow delivered by the king against his foes on the west, under their sole prince Mashashar, the son of Kapur, in the eleventh year of his reign, was only the more severe. The Libyans were completely subjugated ; fixed settlements were assigned to their chiefs under the supervision of Egyptian officials.

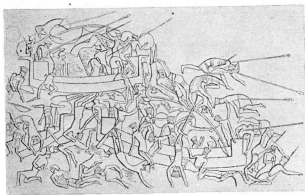

THE FIRST GREAT NAVAL BATTLE
About 1192 B.C. a horde of Asiatics, including Philistines and Cretans, attempted an invasion of Egypt, but were defeated by the Egyptian navy at a mouth of the Nile, in the first great naval battle known to history.

parison. The land forces were immediately despatched to Asia, and overtook the main body of the enemy in Southern Phœnicia, not far from the former frontier of Egypt. The peoples of the north, for the most part armed for hand-to-hand conflict, drew up their ox-waggons, in which they placed their families, after the manner of modern gipsies, into squares, forming a zareba of waggons behind which the shields of the defenders

The last great temple was now built in Thebes, the Ramesseum serving as its model. It is the funerary temple of the king. Its imposing ruins now bear the name of a former Coptic village, Medinet Habu. Our knowledge of the exploits of its royal builder is derived from the rich inscriptions, and especially from the decorations on the walls. These vigorous drawings often illuminate for us the meagre words of the text.

The summary of the reign of Rameses III. concludes with the words : " I made the country to be inhabited by people of all classes and of both sexes. I made

A Reign of Peace and Plenty
green trees to grow and to cast their shadows in all places. I brought it to pass that the women of Egypt could go about freely without molestation from scoundrels. During my reign foot soldiers and chariot warriors lived orderly lives in their towns ; the Shardana could roll about on their backs, drink and be merry. They no longer had to march to the posts ; their wives and children were with them. Every man was filled with loyalty and courage, for I stood there in power to protect them with the terror of my name."

Nevertheless, we learn from the papyrus records of a secret prosecution of conspirators in the palace of Rameses III. that certain members of his court formed a plot to set up a new king, who would then be compelled to bestow wealth and high offices upon other people—that is to say, the conspirators. A harem lady of high rank, Tii, the mother of a prince, was at the head of the conspiracy, which was secretly furthered by the chief eunuch and other persons in authority. Letters from the royal harem to a commander of troops in Ethiopia, who was to march to Thebes and there seize the unsuspecting Rameses, seem to have been delivered to the wrong person ; and thus the restorer of Egypt was saved by chance from a fate unworthy of him. It also appears that even after this timely discovery his most faithful adherents regarded him as a lost man. But the victor in so many dangerous campaigns proved capable of grappling with this hidden danger. The details of the trial are interesting for the history of

A Secret Court Trial
law and of civilisation. All the conspirators of rank were examined under fictitious names before a court chosen by the king from his own retainers, while the official judges belonging to the bureaucracy presided only at the trials of lesser conspirators, slaves, maid-servants, harem guards, etc., who had merely acted as messengers or worked for concealment. The son of Tii, who was probably the candidate for the throne, was forced to commit

suicide ; in other cases the verdict was paraphrased, " He was found guilty and his punishment was carried out "—probably the same penalty elsewhere referred to as " the great punishment of death, of which the gods say, ' Let it be executed upon him.' " Under ordinary circumstances the courts of Ancient Egypt could only pass sentence, and were not allowed to inflict the penalties, the execution of which lay in the hands of the Pharaoh alone ; consequently their extraordinary powers were derived from a verbal authorisation.

Rameses III. died on his throne. When the mummy of this small, well-proportioned, rather hard-looking man was conveyed to the valley of the tombs of the kings the last great Pharaoh of the New Empire had gone to his rest. He was succeeded by no less than nine kings, all bearing his name, none of whom was of any historical importance, and several of whom were his sons. The exhausted dynasty of the later Ramessides was allowed to retain the throne solely in consequence of the deep-rooted conviction that only a legitimate Pharaoh could bring

The Last Great Pharaoh
prosperity to his country. Perhaps the high-priests of Amon, who were already practically independent in the south, hoped to become supreme in the Delta, where an equally independent monarch guarded the frontiers.

The numerous official documents of the period throw some light upon the condition of the working classes at a time when wages and money were unknown. Payments in kind by the state, as well as by the temples, to their numerous bands of workmen were delivered to the labourers collectively, not individually. If the foreman happened to be brutal or knavish, the division of payment was unpunctual, and want, misery, and vexation resulted. Not all labourers were bondsmen ; but probably, on the whole, the freemen were worse off than the slaves.

For the rest, long intervals of cessation from toil were willingly agreed to, and the most remarkable excuses seem to have been readily accepted from individuals who had taken a holiday. Starving workmen were in the habit of enforcing the payment of arrears of wages by noisy demonstrations and insurrections if the scribe persisted in forgetting the time when their claims were due.

ANCLENT
EGYPT
VII

THE LAST
EGYPTIAN
DYNASTIES

DAYS OF THE LAST DYNASTIES

WITH the accession of Smendes, the first of the kings resident at Tanis, begins Manetho's twenty-first or Tanite dynasty, so called from the name of this capital. Our historical knowledge of the Egypt of this period is practically nil. Herihor, who was perhaps a grandson of Rameses VI., and his successors, ruled in Upper Egypt as autocratic high priests, although at the same time they at first recognised the Tanite kings as legitimate Pharaohs and allied themselves to the royal family by marriage. Manetho enumerates seven Tanites: Smendes (Nisbanebded), 26 years; Psusennes I. (Psbukhanu, "the star appearing in the city"), 41 or 46 years; Nephelkheres, 4 years; Amenophtihs (Amenemapet), 19 years; Osokhor, 6 years; Psinakhes, 9 years; and Psusennes (Psbukhanu) II., 14 or 35 years—a list in which some of the names are more correct than the number of years assigned to the several sovereigns.

Rule of the High Priests In Thebes, Herihor was succeeded for a short time as high priest by his son Piankhi. Pinetjem I., however, son of Piankhi, and husband of the Tanite princess Hent-taui, finally assumed the royal insignia. Menkheper-Ra, the son of Pinetjem I., appears first as the high priest of Amon and later as king, at which time the spiritual office devolved upon his brother Masaherta. His reign was a long one. We also hear of princesses who were "women of god" of Amon, and princes who filled lower positions in the service of the same deity. It follows that during the twenty-first dynasty Upper and Lower Egypt were for a time ruled by two Pharaohs and two high priests. Consequently, a great sanctuary of Amon must have then been established in Northern Egypt independent of that at Thebes, in the vicinity of which the Tanites constructed their tombs, although it is not probable that the Tanite high priest could permanently have filled the office side by side with a descendant of Herihor of equal rank. The supposition that there was a

temple of Amon in Lower Egypt helps us to understand how it came about that a sanctuary subsequently famous was established in the Libyan oasis of Siwah.

End of the 21st Dynasty The last ruler of the twenty-first dynasty seems to have made an attempt to restore the authority of Egypt in Asia. According to Hebrew tradition, Solomon married a daughter of the Pharaoh, receiving as a dowry the Canaanite city Gezer, which had been conquered by his father-in-law. Chronology shows that this transaction can be attributed only to the above-named personalities. But that Egypt remained at that time for almost a century and a half at peace with all nations is not probable. All architectural work ceased. About the year 1000, even the outhouses of the Rammeseum had become so dilapidated that their site was used as a burying-ground. The temples of Der el-Bahari were treated in the same way. The Pharaohs of the twenty-first dynasty, in spite of their ecclesiastical veneer, ingloriously gave up the struggle with robbers of the tombs of the ancient kings. Finally the threatened mummies were hidden in the cleft in the rock above Der el-Bahari, which was enlarged for their reception; and here the bodies of Thothmes, Seti, and Rameses lay undisturbed for almost 3,000 years. Finally the secret of the whereabouts of the gallery and sepulchral chamber was obtained from the fellahin, and the contents of this hiding-place were removed to the museum at Bulak.

Mercenaries Come to the Throne For a long time a hereditary commander of mercenaries, descended from a Libyan royal family, had enjoyed great influence in Bubastis. Ever since the Shardana had disappeared from the service of the successors of Rameses III. their Libyan comrades, more especially the warriors of the Mashawasha, not only formed the nucleus of the imperial army, but now prepared to resume possession of the Delta by migration. Nemart, commandant of

Bubastis, "the great of the great," son of a Tanite princess, married a relative of the royal dynasty. A son was born to them, named Sheshonk. He, again, as well as his son Osorkon, married daughters of Psusennes II., and thus looked upon the throne of Egypt as assured to his descendants. Jeroboam had already **Dynasty of the Libyans** found protection at his residence when fleeing from Solomon. But as events moved more rapidly in Palestine than in Egypt, the war between Rehoboam, Solomon's successor, and the adherents of Jeroboam was carried on for some years before the twenty-second dynasty of the Bubastites ascended the throne of Egypt.

King Sheshonk (about 930 B.C.), the Shishak of the Old Testament, began a career of conquest immediately upon his accession. The greater part of a list of cities and provinces in Palestine conquered by him, probably about 930, has been preserved in Karnak. Jerusalem must have stood among the twenty-three names which are to-day illegible, for the Old Testament expressly mentions that Shishak took away the treasures of Solomon. Of the remaining 133 names, many belong to Northern Israel, whence it is to be concluded that the victory of Jeroboam over Judah was chiefly due to Egyptian support. How long the two Israelite states continued to pay tribute to Egypt is unknown; according to the later Jewish view, thirty years.

Although the Libyans of Bubastis as commanders of the Egyptian army had succeeded in making good their claims to the double crown, and had begun their rule of 170 years with a brilliant campaign in Asia, Egypt continued to decay still more rapidly under their government. The kings built temples and monuments in Memphis and the Delta cities, awakened anew the memory of the Ramessides, and occasionally called their younger sons or **Egypt's Decay Unchecked** cousins "royal children of Rameses"; otherwise, the customs of the Tanites were retained. Sheshonk I., whose favourite wife Karama also bore the title of "god's wife," appointed his son Aupuat high-priest of Amon, according to the precedent laid down by Pinetjem. Ethiopia began more directly to menace Upper Egypt. We know practically nothing of Osorkon I. (900 B.C.), and his successors Takeloth I. and Osorkon II.

Takeloth II., who succeeded Sheshonk II., reigned about 850, and spent the first eleven years of his reign struggling with insurrections in all parts of Egypt; subsequently he commanded his son to restore the worship of Amon in Thebes. Apparently the later years of his reign were also disturbed by rebellions.

It is certain that at about this time the various Libyan governors of cities, who were equals of the king, began to look upon themselves as independent. According to the inscriptions in the Apis tombs, which are of great importance to the chronology of this period, Sheshonk III. reigned fifty-two years—that is to say, until about 780. The list of his deeds inscribed in the "Bubastic corner" of the temple of Karnak concludes, however, at his twenty-ninth year. Hence it may be inferred that Thebes fell into the hands of the Ethiopians about the year 800.

The last two kings of the dynasty, Pimai and Sheshonk IV. (750 B.C.), had to fight for the possession of Middle Egypt; and the army of Sheshonk once advanced as far as the island of Sehel at the first cataract. The colonial kingdom in Ethiopia had **Independence of the Colonies** been really independent of Egypt for centuries. The kings of the eighteenth dynasty had founded a sort of priestly colony of Amon-worshippers from Thebes at Napata under the shadow of Gebel Barkal. This always maintained friendly relations with the mother-temples at Thebes; and when the priest kings of the twenty-first dynasty were finally deposed by Sheshonk and the Bubastides, there is no doubt that Napata received members of the dispossessed family, who erected an Ethiopian kingship for themselves there. From these exiles was descended Piankhi, the conqueror of Egypt.

With the aid of the Bubastic dynasty the kingdom fell apart into a number of independent principalities, whose chiefs usually assumed the insignia of pharaohs. At the beginning of the campaign of the Ethiopian king Piankhi against Lower Egypt, about the year 730, the state of the country was somewhat as follows. In Saïs, a king Tefnakht had arisen, who added Memphis to his territory and made preparations for the restoration of the empire of the Pharaohs. Of four other "kings," three were in all probability members of the Bubastic dynasty—Osorkon of Bubastis, Aupuat of Tent-remu, and Nemart of Shmun or Hermopolis Magna. They attached themselves "like dogs"—according to Piankhi—to Tefnakht, while the fourth king, Pefdudubast of Herakleopolis, or Ahnas, favoured the Ethiopians. Fifteen additional adherents of Tefnakht were for the most part mercenary commanders, in possession of the town districts; two called themselves hereditary princes. In Letopolis the high priest of Horus was supreme. This condition of government is termed by Manetho the "twenty-third dynasty," to which he assigns four kings in succession—Petubastis, Osorkho, Psammus, and Zet.

According to a long inscription on Mount Barkal, near Napata, in which the events of his life are set down with an accuracy unknown to Egyptian chroniclers, Piankhi must have advanced in person into Egypt in the twenty-eighth year of his reign; therefore his rule in Egypt dates from about 750. Puarma and Lamersekni, the two Ethiopian military governors installed in Upper Egypt by Piankhi, had been defeated by Nemart, prince of Shmun, while at the same time Tefnakht threatened Herakleopolis. Upon the receipt of this news, Piankhi at once set out in person, celebrated the festival of the new year before Amon in Thebes, and then hastened "to let the lands of Lower Egypt taste the flavour of my finger." After a stubborn defence Nemart was forced to surrender in Hermopolis. The conqueror, who was received with great ceremony on entering the town, did not trouble himself about Nemart's wives and court attendants but immediately examined the plunder, setting aside a portion of it for Amon. "His Majesty then went to the stables and to the foal paddocks. He perceived that these animals must have suffered from hunger, and said [to Nemart]: 'By my oath it seems to me that the most evil of

THE MEMORIAL OF TIRHAKAH
Tirhakah, who gained the throne by force, was the first to struggle seriously with the Assyrians for the possession of Egypt.

thy sins is that of allowing the horses to all starve!'" The fortifications at the entrance of the Fayyum were also unable to hold out. On the other hand, incited by Tefnakht, Memphis, which was surrounded by new walls, resisted until it was stormed from the river side. How Piankhi straightway set a guard over the temple of Ptah and made a pilgrimage to it, and to the temple of Ra at Heliopolis, is described in the inscription with an attention to detail which has proved of great value to the study of religious ceremonial, and also throws considerable light upon the bigotry of Ethiopian pietism. Aupuat and several petty princes had already appeared with tribute before Piankhi in Memphis, and when the conqueror advanced to Athribis a general submission followed. Tefnakht alone insisted that he should be permitted to take the oath of allegiance at home in Saïs before the emissaries of Piankhi.

During the few years of obscurity which followed the personal retirement of Piankhi to Napata, Tefnakht's son, Bocchoris or Bokenranef, regained authority in Lower Egypt, with his capital at Memphis, contemporaneously with the rule of king Kashta, the successor of Piankhi, in the south. Bocchoris was, according to the Greek historians of later times, a wise lawgiver and sagacious judge; others represent him as an avaricious and ungodly weakling. Manetho asserts that he was the sole representative of the twenty-fourth dynasty, and that he was taken captive and burnt alive by Sabako.

Shabaka, or Sabako, the second successor of Piankhi, succeeded in re-subjugating the whole country about 715. Amenerdis, the sister of Sabako, is constantly mentioned in Thebes as the "woman of god" of Amon; she was the daughter of King Kashta, and appears as queen regent and consort of a younger Piankhi, who also seems to have become king. Manetho places Sabako as the founder of the twenty-fifth dynasty, eventually known as " Ethiopian." Circumstances seem to have brought him into collision with Sargon of Assyria, for he appears as the ally of Hanno of Gaza, and as the Seveh of the Bible, on whose help the last king of Northern Israel thought he might rely. Sabako's son and

Supremacy of the Ethiopians successor, Sebichos—in Egyptian, Shabataka—built a small storehouse on the sacred lake at Karnak, where his portrait is still to be seen ornamented with a turban cap and earrings, in the usual Nubian style. Amon-Ra promises to place all foreign countries beneath the sole of his foot, an undertaking not likely to be performed in view of the Assyrian advance in Asia. The victory of Sennacherib at Altaku in the year 701 was gained over a confederacy which had long previously been united for the relief of Jerusalem, and with which the Egyptians can hardly have failed to co-operate. Herodotus relates a pious legend of the " Sethos priest of Hephæstus," the successor of Sabako. Sennacherib is said to have marched against Egypt, which had been left defenceless by a mutiny of her soldiers ; but field mice, sent by the gods, gnawed all the leather work of the weapons and the bow-strings by night in the camp before Pelusium, and Sethos was saved. Mice, and still more rats, usually precede an outbreak of plague, and in these details the story is in harmony with the Biblical account of the saving of Jerusalem from Sennacherib.

Taharka, or Tirhakah, was the first ruler to enter seriously upon the struggle against the Assyrians for the possession of Egypt. He was a son of Piankhi III., and grandson of Kashta. It is probable that he deposed, and probably killed, Shabataka about 693 B.C.—his collision with Esarhaddon, the dissolution of the Ethiopian monarchy north of Assouan, and the

Struggle with Assyria capture of Thebes by the army of Ashurbanipal in 668, was detailed in our history of Assyria. The supremacy of the Sargonide kings of Assyria, from 671, was of no long duration. Ashurbanipal proposed to execute his authority in the Nile valley from so far a distance as Nineveh by means of a numerous body of town governors and nomarchs, twenty of whom were specially created by the great king. These form Herodotus's " Dodekarchy."

When the plunderers of Thebes retreated, Prince Nekau of Saïs and Memphis found success much more nearly within his grasp than had Tefnakht a century before, but he was prevented from seizing his opportunity by death.

His son Psametik—probably pronounced Psamatiko ; Greek, Psammetichos—found very little difficulty in making himself " lord of both lands." He continued to pay tribute to the Assyrians, and possibly rendered other services in view of this special opportunity. In return, he received forthwith the reinforcements which he required to repulse the advance of Tanut-Amen—called by the Assyrians Tandamane—the successor of Taharka, who had been expelled to Nubia by the Assyrians. Shepenapet, an Ethiopian princess and a niece of Amenerdis, continued to rule as " god's wife " in Thebes under Psametik I. ; hence it appears that he was anxious to promote a good understanding with Ethiopia. However, an indispensable preliminary was the acknowledgment of the new king's daughter Nitocris, or Neitakert, as the future

Petty Kings of Egypt successor to the throne. Although the majority of the petty princes of Egypt may have been inclined to support Psametik, the remainder could easily have combined to do him a mischief. The further Ashurbanipal pushed his eastern campaigns, the higher, in the opinion of the confederated petty kings of Egypt, rose the prospects of a restoration of the " balance of power," a primary condition of which was naturally the recall of the Ethiopian kings.

Psametik could expect no help from Libya. That narrow strip of land, having relieved itself of all its superfluous population by over-sea emigration and fruitless attacks on Egypt, had become much weakened ; what is now the territory of Barka had been colonised by Greeks in the eighth century B.C. ; the Greek city of Cyrene now dominated the inhabitants of the interior, who no longer looked to Egypt as an overlord who might demand assistance from them in war. The Cyrenaica was now a Greek state, with the usual Greek city-constitution in Cyrene. During the eighth century B.C., the Nile delta had constantly been visited by the trading ships of the prosperous Greek towns in Asia Minor ; to this fact is due the more accurate knowledge which we possess of the

GIRLS DANCING TO THE PIPE AT A FEAST IN ANCIENT EGYPT

GRAPHIC PICTURE OF A FOWLER SNARING WILD DUCKS IN THE PAPYRUS MARSHES

A DOMESTIC SCENE: GOOSEHERD AND A GROUP OF SERVANTS MAKING OBEISANCE
Photos by Mansell

AN ART REVIVAL IN ANCIENT EGYPT SHOWN IN THE TOMB PAINTINGS OF 1000 B.C.

Ethiopian conquest, of the liberation by means of Asiatic intervention, and of the " rule of the twelve kings " mentioned by Herodotus. At the present moment an alliance with this foreign people was the more attractive, inasmuch as they had been united into a strong kingdom under Gyges. Reinforcements of Ionian and Carian—that is, Lydian—troops soon enabled Psametik to rid himself of the burdensome city governors and nomarchs. The supremacy of Assyria disappeared with their expulsion about 660 B.C.

The Assyrians Expelled

The empire which a favourable conjunction of circumstances in Further Asia enabled Psametik I. of Saïs (664 to 610) to found endured for about 140 years, and bears only a superficial resemblance to the Egypt of the Pharaohs. The influence of Hellenism during this period and under the Persian supremacy made for progress on new lines. These northern foreigners whom Psametik settled at that time in Bubastis and on the Bolbitine mouth of the Nile in the " Milesian camp "—that is, bazaar—proved a valuable support to the new Egyptian dynasty. The old Phœnician-Semitic influence, which had never made for much improvement, was replaced by the far higher and more civilised influence of Greek ideas. At first, indeed, the anti-Semitic reaction took the form of a return to the " good old days," when the Egyptian was an Egyptian, the " golden age " of the pyramid-builders, for inspiration not only in art but also in national life generally. This ultra-nationalism naturally militated against Greek influence, but, on the other hand, Greek influence was the only foreign influence that just at this time the Egyptians would have admitted at all. And, no doubt to their surprise, the Egyptian priests found that the Greeks were not all traders and warriors, but possessed philosophers and wise men who were profoundly interested in Egyptian antiquity. Concerning the history of this period, it is important to observe that the Greeks alone have transmitted a connected account of it, though one composed from their own point of view. The Ionian wise men who visited Egypt, the historiographers like Hecatæus of Miletus, and Herodotus of Halicarnassus after him, were keenly interested in the annals of the land in which so many of their countrymen were settled,

First Contact with Greece

and have left no accounts of the history of this period treated from the Egyptian point of view. Our information upon the state of civilisation, as derived from this source, can be supplemented in certain details by the memorials belonging to the period of the Saïtes.

In general outline the changes which took place within the empire resembled the reorganisation of Greece which was introduced by the removal of Constantine to Byzantium. Upper Egypt rapidly lost the traces of its former importance, which it never in any respect recovered. " Thebes of the hundred gates," notwithstanding the proud and pious recollections of its past, fell into a state of irrevocable decay. The administration was no longer capable of keeping even the vast temples in repair, although during the Persian period rebel kings took a pride in restoring shattered walls or pillars in Karnak and Medinet Habu that they might set their names upon them. Memphis, however, as in antiquity, again became the political centre. Its favourable site at the head of the Delta system gave it geographical advantages over Thebes akin to those possessed by Corinth over Athens. Saïs, the capital of the Psametik kings, though provided with many stately buildings, remained a town of moderate size compared with Memphis.

Decay of Thebes

In conformity with this change in the conditions of government, Ptah and Osiris laid claim to that supremacy which the divinities of Amon had lost, Osiris now rising to be lord of the sky from his previous position as monarch of the dead. Isis maintained herself at his side, though the Libyan Neith imposed some temporary limitations upon her influence. Horus acquired the attributes of Ra. These expressions of the change in religious belief were equivalent to the restoration of the primitive doctrine of the country, and were continued in the conscious choice of customs and types belonging to the old régime. Names and titles from the old kingdom and its language as written and spoken were now revived. The learned classes prided themselves upon that antiquarian knowledge which filled Herodotus with respect. The art of the period naturally underwent a corresponding change. Goose-herds and basket-makers, market and harvesting scenes, were again employed as decorations for the tombs and represented in the rough style of primitive Egyptian art, though touches of the realism of later days are occasionally apparent. This is the archaistic revival in art, mentioned above.

The " history " of the Saïtic rulers comes fresh to us from Greek sources. We have a detailed account of the impossible undertaking of Psametik I. to discover the sources of the Nile and the origin of language ; whereas we have but short references to the fact that he strengthened the frontier forces of Daphne at Pelusium, Marea on the west, and Elephantine on the south ; that he conquered the Philistine town of Ashdod after a struggle extending over twenty-nine years, and drove back from Egypt the Scythians, who had advanced into Palestine. The king died after a long reign at the moment when the fall of Assyria was clearly inevitable, and the supremacy in Further Asia changed hands. Nekau, or Necho, II. (610 to 595 B.C.), the son of Psametik, invaded Palestine in 608 B.C., and induced the former Assyrian vassals to accept his supremacy, though some few of these princes, among them the Jewish king Josiah, continued to defend the cause of the Assyrians. They were defeated at Megiddo, or Migdol, by the mercenaries of Necho, who then captured "the great town of Kadytis," or Kadesh, on the Orontes. The Egyptian headquarters were situated for a time at Ribla, close at hand, and it was from that spot that Necho arranged the succession to the throne of Judah. However, in spite of the footing which he had gained within the country where Thothmes III. had previously begun the conquest of Syria, this new attempt at expansion came to a rapid end. In the year 605

Last of the Asiatic Possessions the army of Necho was utterly routed by Nebuchadnezzar on the Euphrates at Carchemish ; by the year 601 B.C. Egypt had lost the last of her Asiatic possessions. The remarkable story related by Herodotus of the circumnavigation of Africa, which was accomplished in three years by Phœnician sailors at the command of Necho,

QUEEN AMENERITIS
A fine example of the Egyptian art revival from Gizeh.

necessarily implies the supremacy of that king in Phœnicia for a period of years. The supposition that Necho resumed the construction of a canal from the Delta to the Red Sea, but suspended the work after it had cost the lives of one hundred and

A Suez Canal Attempted twenty thousand labourers, is legendary, but must rest upon a historical foundation. Under Psametik II. (594 to 589 B.C.) monuments occur in much greater abundance than during his father's reign. Egypt again attempted expansion southward. The army advanced as far as Abu Simbel if not farther—the mercenaries were commanded by Psamatichos, the son of Theokles—and scratched their names upon the columns of the Rameses temple in Greek and Phœnician and perhaps also in Cypriote letters. " When King Psamatichos came to Elephantine," the chief Greek inscription reads, " those who sailed with Psamatichos, son of Theokles, wrote this. Now, they came above Kerkis as far as the river let them go up. And Potasimto led the foreigners, and Amasis the Egyptians. And Archon, the son of Amoibichos, and Pelekos, the son of nobody, wrote us " (that is, the letters). According to Herodotus the king died before the struggle had been definitely terminated.

He was succeeded by Apries, or Haa-ab-Ra. Once again Egyptian politicians dreamed of conquest upon the disputed ground of Syria - Palestine. About the appearance of Apries in Phœnicia and his operations by sea against Tyre and Sidon our information is scanty. It can, however, be supplemented by the Biblical references to the untrustworthy character of Pharaoh " Hophra " when Jerusalem was reduced to extremities. The surrender of this city and the subjugation of Judah marked the firm establishment of the power of Nebuchadnezzar in West Asia. An inscription of Nsihor, the governor of Elephantine, also refers to disturbances in Upper Egypt, which were apparently suppressed only by means of treachery and cunning. The interference of Apries in the long-continued struggle of the Libyans against the Greek state of Cyrene led to no result. According to Herodotus, it even brought about the overthrow of the Pharaoh. His general, Amasis, availed himself of the refusal of the Egyptian militia to expose themselves to further defeats in the west for the purpose of seizing the throne. Apries then marched against Amasis at the head of his foreign

A Soldier Seizes the Throne mercenaries, but was defeated and captured at Momemphis. For a time he was imprisoned at Saïs and treated kindly ; but eventually the dethroned monarch fell a victim to the popular resentment, and was then given a royal burial.

It has now been established that Amasis was by no means of "low birth," as is asserted by the Greek historian. His mother, Tseneset, was a daughter of Psametik II. It appears to be certain that Amasis and Apries ruled in conjunction for several years. The facts as to the death of Apries are given in an inscription which has been translated by M. Daréssy. The elder king, always friendly to his foreign mercenaries, escaped from Saïs and joined a force of Greeks which was ravaging the Delta. Amasis followed, and defeated him at Andropolis. But later on Apries and his Greeks reappeared, only to be again attacked by Amasis. Apries was then murdered by some country people as he was asleep in the cabin of his boat, and Amasis gave him royal burial, pardoning him his sin against the gods.

Such is Amasis's own account. It is evident that Amasis represented a national Egyptian movement against the too great friendliness of Apries for the foreigners. A fragmentary inscription of Nebuchadnezzar points to the fact that the Babylonians invaded Egypt about 568–567 B.C. Possibly the change in the dynasty is connected with this event. The date 564 given by Herodotus as the end of the reign of Apries appears to be too late. Amasis, who regarded his brother-in-law as a legitimate

Amasis, a Cunning Knave monarch in spite of all their dissensions, probably began his own reign as early as 570, and it was in his third year (567–66 B.C.) that the death of Apries took place.

The reign of Amasis is estimated at forty-four years by contemporary historians. However, the king's foreign policy is characterised by an entire lack of enterprise. Indications are not wanting that Amasis must be regarded as nothing more than a cunning knave, notwith-standing the Greek anecdotes which represent him as the personal friend of Thales, Bias, etc., as the wise law-giver and the humane philanthropist. His sole object was to gain for Egypt a short respite from destruction. He made no effort to save Lydia from her fall, and Xenophon's references to the help lent by Egypt are pure fiction. He occupied the island of Cyprus for a time, but soon evacuated it in favour of the Persians. After the fall of Sardis his chief anxiety was lest the source of his supply of Greek troops should now be closed ; for this reason he entered into negotiations with the towns on the east coast of the Ægean, which still preserved their independence, and presented gifts to their temples, as Necho had once made gifts to the temple of Branchidæ. A typical example of this policy is the well-known story of the alliance between Amasis and Polykrates of Samos—especially typical as regards the extent of the help which the " reed of Egypt " was accustomed to lend to others in their hour of need.

In other respects, however, the Greeks might in every case count upon pre-

A Greek Town in the Delta ferential treatment. Amasis dealt gently even with the turbulent Cyrene. Not far from the later Alexandria, on the Canopic mouth of the Nile, about seven hundred Greek merchants, apparently Ionians from Teos, had already settled. Their factory grew to the size of a foreign settlement, and was given the name of " mighty in ships," Naucratis. After the fall of Lydia— that is, about 545 B.C.—Amasis thought it advisable to oblige the sudden stream of immigrants from the towns of Ionia and Doria to settle in Naucratis by the issue of a decree forbidding them to land elsewhere for trading purposes. The town received the privilege of self-government. Its central shrine was the Hellenion, in the provision of which nine privileged towns and islands took part. It was, however, overshadowed by the fame of the Apollo temple of the Milesians, an offshoot from the temple of Branchidæ. Greek tradition has evinced a spirit of gratitude to King Amasis for his protection of their nationality, which he continued for at least twenty years. Egyptian historians are less laudatory. In fragments of a demotic text of the Ptolemaic period containing a large number of references to past history, Amasis is reproached for diverting the incomes of the temples of Memphis, Heliopolis, Bubastis and Saïs to the payment of his mercenaries. Ultimately, the gods suffered a considerable loss, both of wealth and of landed property.

The army of Cambyses, king of Persia, met with no resistance to its conquest of the country in the summer of 525 B.C., nine months after the death of Amasis. The highly paid mercenaries of Psametik III., the last of the Saïte kings, were defeated by the Persian at Pelusium after a hard struggle. A traitor, Phanes of Halicarnassus, is then said to have betrayed to Cambyses the easiest mode of approach through the desert. Psametik retired to Memphis. The zealous defenders of this town soon lost heart, surrendered after a short siege, and are said to have been treated with severity. Legend reports other cruelties by Cambyses. The destroyer of the Saïte dynasty, which was friendly to the Greeks, is naturally represented by their historians in the worst possible light, and we have no Egyptian confirmation of these stories; rather, Cambyses appears in Egyptian records as interested in the people he had conquered, and in their religion. We must

THE ANIMAL WORSHIP OF EGYPT

During the period of Persian supremacy, which had no influence on Egyptian development, animal worship increased to the point of childishness; it became customary to mummify cats and other animals, as here illustrated.

remember that Cambyses was no monotheistic Persian, like Darius, but an Elamite, and probably a polytheist, like his predecessor, Cyrus. It was the later fanatical Persians who really behaved cruelly to the Egyptians, and persecuted their religion. Psametik III. seems to have sworn allegiance as tributary prince. However, he immediately set a revolt on foot, and his execution became inevitable. Egypt had now lost her native rulers and paid tribute to Susa instead of to Saïs. Naucratis soon lost its commercial privileges, the retention of which was naturally impossible under the Persian government. No further innovations were made during the Persian period, which

The Persian Conquest

lasted for about two hundred years, though interrupted by rebellion. The high officials of Persian origin installed within the country were scanty in number and exercised not the smallest influence upon the nationality, the civilisation, or the religion. Even the permanent garrison maintained in the "white fortress" of Memphis was not necessarily sent out from the distant capital of Iran ; subjects of the great king of other than Egyptian nationality were considered capable of performing this service. Egypt was thus able to continue its development undisturbed. The preference for the old régime displayed by the upper classes seems to have continued for some time.

Egypt Under the Persians

Under the shadow of the Una's pyramid in Sakkara members of prosperous families were laid to their rest as late as the year 540 B.C. ; examples are Psametik and his son Petenisis after him, during the reign of Darius I. The tomb of the admiral Tjanehebu, discovered in 1900, contains a collection of valuable objects displaying high artistic finish. The preference for heavy stone coffins increased. It was considered of special importance to cover

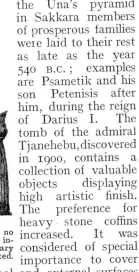

thickly the internal and external surfaces with pictures and written texts. The later kings, Nekhthorheb and Nekhtnebf, left behind sarcophagi displaying twenty thousand hieroglyphics, besides a thousand pictures. The animal worship of this period increased far beyond the limits of the earlier cult of Apis and Mnevis. It became customary to mummify the sparrow-hawk, the ibis, the ram, and the cat ; to envelop them in wrappings, provide them with coffins, etc. In the Ptolemaic and Roman periods crocodiles, snakes, and fishes, as well as dogs, mice, and beetles, became the objects of a piety that had degenerated into childishness.

Saïs had also opened its gates to the Persian kings. Cambyses there appears as a legitimate Pharaoh, with the fore-name Mesut-Ra—literally, child of Ra. He offered solemn sacrifices in the temple of Neith after purging the shrine of intruders, who were apparently members of his own army. Greek historians are our sole sources of information concerning the reported despatch of a division to the western oasis of Amon and the mysterious

Cambyses, a Persian Pharaoh disappearance of these troops in the desert. Cambyses's unsuccessful campaign against the Ethiopians, about 524, is supported by more definite statements. An inscription, belonging probably to Napata, set up by the Ethiopian king Nastesen, or Nastasenen, mentions a certain hostile " Kambasuden " who invaded his country from the sea and was defeated. This is, no doubt, Cambyses. But under Darius the Nubian Kushites are tributary to the Persians and furnish a contingent of troops.

Cambyses endangered his throne by remaining in the Nile valley until 522 B.C. When he was recalled by the revolt of Gaumata he entrusted the government of Egypt to the satrap Aryandes. Events in Persia left this governor in an almost independent position, and he succeeded in subjugating Cyrene ; but Darius I. drove him out in the year 517 B.C., and visited the country in person with the object of subjecting the valuable inheritance of the Pharaohs to the general administrative reforms which he was then introducing. The benefices of the priesthoods were improved, the priestly colleges in Saïs were fully restored, and no doubt the same procedure was followed in Memphis, Heliopolis, and other sacred centres. When Darius had settled the yearly contribution of the Egyptian-Libyan satrapy at 700 talents—about £225,000— and had secured a number of minor sources of income to himself, he was yet able to go to some expense in the construction of temples, as at El-Kharga in the Great

Darius Completes the Canal Oasis. Fragmentary inscriptions also state that the king completed the long projected canal to the Red Sea, and it is not improbable that Indian commerce can have passed to the Mediterranean by this route at that period.

However, these new regulations did not bring peace to the country. About 487–486 B.C., or later, a native chief, by name Khabbash, assumed the title of king, presented a piece of land to the goddess

Buto—since known as the " land of Buto "—and took careful measures to place the coast in a state of defence. Xerxes put an end to this interlude in the year 484 when he restored the satrapy and handed it over to his brother Hakhamanish, or Achæmenes. After the murder of Xerxes, in 465 B.C., disputes arose in Susa concerning the succession, and the revolts of Inarus in 460 and Amyrtaeus in 450 began in Lower Egypt. When the Persians were able to re-establish their supremacy, about 449, Artaxerxes I., " Longimanus," preferred to leave the sons of these revolters, Thannyras and Pausiris, to rule as independent chiefs in their swamps. Darius II. resumed building operations upon a temple in the oasis of Kharga, which the first Darius had founded there. These are practically the last memorials that any Persian king erected in the country.

From the year 415 B.C. Egypt ceased to be a part of the Persian empire, and maintained its independence to the middle of the following century. A Saïte prince, Amyrtaeus (II.), perhaps the grandson of

The Persians Driven Out the previous bearer of the name, enlisted Greek mercenaries, declared himself " lord of both lands," and drove out the Persians, who were prevented from taking the offensive by the outbreak of disturbances in other parts of their enormous empire. The monarchy thus restored certainly gained a breathing space in which to prepare for defence against foreign aggression, but it was impossible to check the autocratic behaviour of the highly paid auxiliaries from Hellas, who were now largely recruited from Greece proper. As far as can be seen, this behaviour was partly due to the reckless payments distributed by Egyptian chiefs who were anxious to seize the throne. A similar phenomenon appeared in the period of the Diadochi, and assumed larger proportions under the prætorian emperors.

About 409 B.C. the mercenaries deposed Amyrtaeus and replaced his dynasty with that of Naifaaurut, or Nepherites, of Mendes. When, however, the new king created his son Nectanebus, or Nekhthorheb, co-regent, " the people " were irritated by this precautionary measure, and forced Nectanebus to retreat to Sebennytos. In 404 B.C. Hakor, or Akhoris, was made king by the troops. He reigned until 391 B.C., and his piety found expression in the construction of temples at different places. Psimut, or Psammuthis, his successor, who had already been the ruling power in the Delta about 400—if he is to be identified with the "King Psametik of Egypt" of Diodorus—was considered a godless ruler ; for this reason his reign lasted only a year, and he was not recognised throughout the country.

Piety returns in the person of "Muthes," who was also able to maintain his position only for a year. Dissensions then divided the mercenaries. After putting a second Nepherites to death, they restored the "old right," apparently by the recall of the king's son Nekhthorheb, or Nectanebus I., about 385 to 363 B.C., who had been formerly driven from the court. Under him Egypt plays a more important part in the revolts of Further Asia. But when the Cyprian

his army melt away, and he himself went over to the great king, by whom he was kindly received. Agesilaus was, in the meantime, obliged to overthrow a new aspirant to the throne from Mendes, and died shortly afterward. With the accession of Artaxerxes III. in Persia, in 358 B.C., the struggle was renewed. An attack of the king on Egypt was repulsed by Diophantus and Lamius, the Greek generals of King Nekhtnebf, but the Persians returned to the attack when Egypt supported the last general insurrection which broke out upon the coast-land of Further Asia. After the capture of Pelusium and Bubastis, Nekhtnebf made a timely escape to Ethiopia with his treasures to avoid being sold into the hands of his enemies. The buildings of Nekhtnebf (361–343

Greece and Persia in Egypt

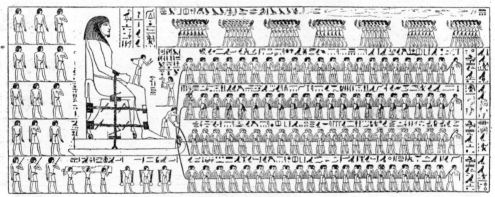

AN ARMY OF LABOURERS MOVING A COLOSSUS FROM THE QUARRIES TO ITS TEMPLE

Evagoras had submitted to the Persians in defiance of his convention with Nectanebus, the danger of reconquest threatened the Nile valley. In the year 374 B.C. a great army appeared from Syria under a Pharnabazus. After the surprise of Mendes by the Athenian Iphicrates, who commanded the Greek mercenaries, the two commanders quarrelled, and Egypt was saved by the rise of the Nile. Tjeho, or Tachos, 363 to 361, the son of Nekhthorheb, availed himself of the next great revolt in Syria to invade that country in force. His careful preparations were, however, ruined by the Greek mercenaries. The Spartan king Agesilaus, who "sailed the sea for gold" in his old age, suddenly declared for the cousin of Tachos, Nekhtnebf, or Nectanebus II. Tachos, who was then in Sidon, saw

Fresh Invasion of Syria

B.C.), far surpassed those of all the other rebel kings. The splendid temple of Isis on the island of Philæ, the construction of which was begun by the Ptolemies, was planned by him.

No memorials survive to mark the short period of the Persian administration (343–332 B.C.). When the Macedonians advanced into Asia and Alexander had won the battle of Issus, he was confronted by a practically new Egyptian kingdom under his compatriot and personal enemy, Amyntas, the son of Antiochus. This partisan of the Persian king occupied Memphis, but the inhabitants of the surrounding country were encouraged by the Persian governor Mazakes to attack his scanty forces, and Amyntas fell in the struggle. Almost exactly a year afterwards, at the end of 332 B.C., Alexander the Great entered Egypt unopposed.

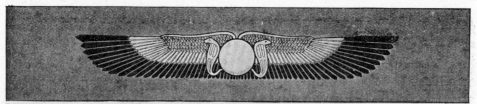

THE DEATH OF CLEOPATRA, THE MOST FAMOUS OF THE PTOLEMY QUEENS
The famous Cleopatra, daughter of Ptolemy XIII. and the seventh of her name on the Egyptian throne, the beloved of
Julius Cæsar and of Marcus Antonius, committed suicide by allowing an asp to bite her when Augustus landed in Egypt.
From the picture by the Hon. J. Collier, by permission of the Oldham Art Gallery.

ANCIENT
EGYPT
VIII

MACEDONIAN
AND ROMAN
DOMINION

FROM ALEXANDER TO MAHOMET

THE development of Egyptian civilisa-tion under the Macedonian supremacy extends over exactly three hundred years, for which period we have a mass of historical material in the shape of papyrus texts. Museums now contain any quantity of evidence upon the life and social customs of every class of the people, the government of the country, of the nomes, temples, and villages, upon the administra-tion of justice, upon beliefs and customs. Only a portion, however, of this material has been examined.

Upon the division of the empire into its provinces after the death of Alexander, Egypt fell to the share of the Macedonian general Ptolemaios, the son of Lagos, who was only forty-four years old and began his rule in 323 B.C. It was not until the year 304 that he assumed the title of king, with the further title of " Deliverer " (Soter), apparently in imitation of Anti-gonus. About the end of 285 Ptolemy Soter abdicated in extreme old age in

Succession of the Ptolemies favour of his son Ptolemy II., Philadelphus (284 to 247 B.C.), and died two years later. This ruler was followed in direct succession by Ptolemy III., Euergetes (247 to 221 B.C.), Ptolemy IV., Philopator (221 to 205 B.C.), and by Ptolemy V., Epiphanes, who did not attain his majority until 198. This ruler left behind him three young children, namely, Ptolemy VI., Philometor, his successor to the throne, a daughter Cleopatra, and Ptolemy Euergetes (II.).

As a result of Syrian interference, the kingdom was divided for the space of a year in the year 170 B.C., as follows : Philometor ruled in Memphis, Euergetes in Alexandria—the latter is now to be entitled Ptolemy VIII., as a son was born to Philometor about 165, who must be reckoned as Ptolemy VII., and who bore the surname of Eupator. From 169 to 164 B.C. all the three members of this family ruled in common as the " Philo-metor gods." Ptolemy VI., who was tem-porarily expelled, returned in the year 163, when the Romans compelled his brother to content himself with Cyrene.

However, in the year 146 B.C. Philometor was killed in Syria. Ptolemy VIII. appeared a few weeks afterwards in Alexandria, killed the young Eupator, and ruled from that time, though with many interruptions, in association with his sister and her niece of the same name, till 116 B.C. In 115 Cleopatra, the niece, appointed

Rule of the Cleopatras her son Ptolemy X., Lathyros, as co-regent—Ptolemy IX. was a son of the elder Cleopatra and of Euergetes, and died in 119 B.C. as king of Cyprus ; in 117 he was obliged to retreat to Cyprus, and evacuated Egypt in favour of his brother Ptolemy XI., Alexander. Alexander murdered his mother in 101 B.C. In the year 88 B.C. he died, and Lathyros returned. He was succeeded by a daughter, Cleopatra Bere-nice. She reigned alone from 81 to 80 B.C. and then married her step-son Ptolemy XII., Alexander II. Their joint rule lasted only nineteen days. They were both mur-dered by Ptolemy XIII., Auletes, literally " the flute-player," a son of Ptolemy X. by a woman of the people ; he ruled from 80 to 58 B.C. After his expulsion and the premature death of his elder daughter, Cleopatra Tryphaena, the younger daugh-ter, Berenice, ascended the throne (58 to 55 B.C), which she then lost, together with her life, at the hands of her father, whom the Romans had helped to return.

Auletes himself left Egypt in the year 51 to his son, who was then ten years old. This ruler, Ptolemy XIV., was con-tinually quarrelling with his sisters Cleo-patra (VII.) and Arsinoe, and was con-quered by Cæsar in the year 47 B.C., and

The Famous Cleopatra drowned in the Nile while in flight. From that date until 44 B.C., Cleopatra VII. (the famous) and her younger brother, Ptolemy XV., ruled in common ; the latter disappeared, and his place was taken by Cleopatra's son, Cæsarion—as Ptolemy XVI.—who was born between the years 36 and 47, and whose putative father was Julius Cæsar the Great. On the collapse of the Ptolemaic kingdom, in the year 30 B.C., both mother and son met their deaths. A daughter of Cleopatra and Antony, named Selene, afterward married Juba, the king of Mauretania, or Morocco. With the son of this couple, Ptolemy, this dynasty finally became extinct in the far west.

Alexandria, the brilliant commercial town, the centre of court life and learning, rises from its obscurity at the outset of the Ptolemaic period, and after a few decades becomes the centre of gravity of the Hellenistic East. Naturally the story of the foundation of this capital by Alexander the Great was repeated without hesitation after a short time. Side by side with the truly fabulous incidents of this Greek account we have the granite "Satrap stele," the date of which is about 317 B.C. This inscription makes it clear that, in the opinion of contemporaries, Alexandria was founded by Ptolemy Soter seven years after the death of the conqueror. Such a piece of evidence, in itself almost irrefutable, can be further supported by a closer examination of the campaigns of Alexander, and also weakens the theory that the other Alexandria, of Issus in Syria, was built upon the initiative of the conqueror whose name it bears. For Egypt Alexander had little time to spare ; his visit to the oasis of Amon was the only long journey he took in the country ; he is known not to have visited Upper Egypt. Alexander entrusted the Delta to Cleomenes of Naucratis, being desirous to confer favours on the old Greek colony. Ptolemy I., however, began his government with the execution of Cleomenes, and reduced Naucratis to the position of a provincial Egyptian parish ; then the fitting opportunity arrived for the foundation of the new capital, the situation of which was determined by his more accurate local knowledge. The town which received its name in honour of the great conqueror contained a splendid tomb of Alexander and his corpse. We have many stories connected with the acquisition of

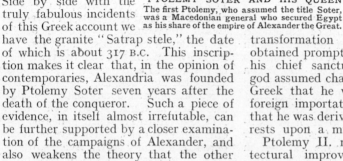

PTOLEMY SOTER AND HIS QUEEN
The first Ptolemy, who assumed the title Soter, was a Macedonian general who secured Egypt as his share of the empire of Alexander the Great.

PTOLEMY II. AND ARSINOE
Ptolemy II. Philadelphus, who reigned from 284 to 247 B.C., married his sister Arsinoe.

the body by Soter. Though he was no general, and cannot be compared with the other great Diadochi, yet the son of Lagos showed himself a clever politician, both in home government and foreign relations. His authority over this foreign country rested necessarily upon the support of bands of Greek mercenaries, the " Macedonians." This fact, however, did not prevent him from asserting his position as successor of the Pharaohs and son of the native gods. The introduction of a new god was highly desirable in order to connect the new capital, the St. Petersburg of Egypt, with the ancient religious districts of the country. For this reason " Serapis," the new transformation of Osiris, naturally obtained prompt recognition ; but within his chief sanctuary at Alexandria the god assumed characteristics so thoroughly Greek that he was always considered a foreign importation, although the theory that he was derived from Sinope in Pontus rests upon a misunderstanding.

Ptolemy II. made many great architectural improvements in Alexandria ; his most famous foundation, the learned society which was maintained at the cost of the state, in the Mouseion, remained purely Greek in character, and achieved no results of importance for Egyptian history. On the other hand, the king proceeded to provide a stricter method of supervision for the Nile valley, the necessity for which had long been forced upon him by the growth of inconvenience and disorder. Colonies of Greek soldiers were settled in two places, which their families soon provided with a population ; these were Ptolemais, in Upper Egypt, and Crocodilopolis in the Fayyum, which was now called Arsinoe after the sister and consort of the king. For marriages of this kind precedents were to be found in Egypt of early date, such as induced the second of the Lagides to marry his own sister, who had been twice a widow. The action of this

Ptolemy stands in contrast to the marriage policy of his father, who allied himself in this way with the courts of most Greek centres of civilisation, though it was a policy that proved as incapable of realising the hopes based upon it as had the system in vogue at the period of the Amarna letters. Ptolemy III. also took his sister Berenice to wife ; his successors, however, considered this custom as valid only for their own family.

Of the first three Ptolemaic kings the warlike Euergetes—the elder—attained the greatest measure of success in foreign affairs ; all, however, opened the path to Greek influence in Egypt so widely that at a later period, even under the most unfavourable circumstances, Hellenism

and Greek writing. With the discovery of the black basalt Rosetta Stone (1799), the science of Egyptology began. This monument was erected in 196 to commemorate the fact that " King Ptolemy, who lives for ever, beloved of Ptah the benefactor, the son of King Ptolemy and Queen Arsinoe, the gods Philopatores, who overwhelm the temples with benefits," had relieved the country of taxes and customs, had remitted arrears and had quashed all prosecutions, on the occasion of the proclamation of his majority.

Unrolling Egypt's Records

Found by the French invaders in a fort at Rosetta, this inscription was, with others, ceded to Great Britain as prize of war two years later, and placed in the

Ptolemy II. Arsinoe II. Ptolemy III. Berenice II. Ptolemy IV.

Ptolemy V. Ptolemy VI. Ptolemy IX. Ptolemy XI. Cleopatra VII.

PORTRAITS OF SOME OF THE PTOLEMY KINGS AND QUEENS FROM THEIR COINS

fully maintained its ground. Egyptian nationalism was forced to accommodate itself to this state of affairs. Relations between the king and the temples now become characterised by a stronger emphasis of the personal element. The payment of thanks to the gods is no longer a prominent feature ; more important is the acknowledgment of the priesthoods of the royal gifts made to them—an instance is the formal decree of honour issued from Canopus in favour of Ptolemy III. and Queen Berenice.

The Rosetta Stone

A resolution on the " Rosetta Stone," regarding Ptolemy V., who was a youth at his accession, as may be seen from his coin portrait, is conceived in a spirit of greater piety. Both of these records were recopied in hieroglyphic, demotic,

British Museum, where it now is. It was the bilingual text of this inscription, when studied by the Englishman Young and the Frenchman Champollion, that yielded to the latter, acting upon suggestions of Young's, the secret of the ancient Egyptian hieroglyphic writing. This we now read with ease ; printed examination-papers are even set in it in the Honour School of Semitic languages at Oxford.

In previous years there seemed but small prospect of duration for the Ptolemaic dynasty. Not only the Greek neighbouring states, but also the Egyptians themselves, had risen in revolt. We hear of a native prince, Horhetep, in Thebes (" year 4 "), and also of a certain Ankhtu, who is said to have ruled fourteen years Hence the revolt in the south must have begun during the second half of the reign of Ptolemy IV., the early years of which had already survived an attempted revolution made by a Greek mercenary of royal rank, Cleomenes III. of Sparta. A fugitive from his native land, he landed a small force in Alexandria, and was there placed in custody; however, he escaped, made a vain attempt to induce the astounded inhabitants to "rise for freedom," and finally fell upon his own sword. The town, which had not hitherto been disturbed by yearnings for this object, fell into a state of wild confusion, Ptolemy Philopator fled, and the rebels seized upon his favourites, who came to a dreadful end. And from that time onward the "delightful rabble of Alexandria" made themselves prominent by recurrent outbursts ending in bloodshed even under the Romans.

"Delightful Rabble of Alexandria"

From the rapid change of rulers after Ptolemy VII., shown by the list of kings, we can easily conclude that the last century and a half of the dynasty of the Lagides forms a sad period of Egyptian history. If, however, we concentrate our attention solely upon the monuments erected at that time, a wholly different impression will be formed; the period of the decadence displays as much of architectural vigour as it does of political weakness, a fact which may well be borne in mind in estimating the importance of earlier periods in the history of Egypt.

The artistic temple of Philæ, the beautiful pylons, and the deep feeling displayed by the halls and columns of Edfu, Esne, and Dendera, which remain the best examples of Egyptian architecture with the exception of Thebes—these all belong to a period of constant disturbances and of continual murders within the royal family, notwithstanding the testimony of such representations as that within the little temple of Der el-Medineh, behind Medinet Habu, where the brothers Ptolemy VI. and VIII., with their sister Cleopatra, can be seen making offerings in common, and dividing their titles with true brotherly love. On the other hand, we have much evidence for the fact that commercial relations were steadily maintained, especially with countries beyond the Red Sea. The "Stele of Pithom," discovered by Naville, tells us of the city which the king founded on the Red Sea shore, and refers to the elephant-hunting

The Art of the Ptolemies

expeditions in the land of the Trogodytes, which supplied elephants for the royal army. These, however, proved remarkably useless at the battle of Raphia against Antiochus III., but were not abandoned for war purposes, nevertheless. An inscription in the British Museum (No. 1207) tells us that Alexandros, son of Syndaios (not "Syndikos" as Professor Mahaffy writes it), the well-known general Charimortos, and a captain named Apoasis, were sent to hunt elephants in Somaliland more than seven years after the battle of Raphia. We hear also of another elephant hunter named Lichas. These hunters added considerably to accurate geographical knowledge in the direction of Ras Hafûn and Cape Gardafui on the way to India. The connection with India remained unshaken; an embassy from that country successfully approached the victorious Augustus shortly after the fall of the Ptolemaic kingdom. Together with the blessings of the Nile floods and the harvests they produced—the lion's share of which the kings during this period, as during all others, were careful to secure to themselves—taxes and harbour duties raised the revenue to the amount of about £2,500,000 yearly, even under the corrupt and careless government of the piper, "Auletes." From the time that a Roman embassy, in the year 168 B.C., had succeeded by mere threats in driving the Seleucid Antiochus (III.) Epiphanes out of Egypt, which he had practically conquered, the house of the Ptolemies had become dependent upon Rome. Ptolemy VIII., Euergetes, whom the meticulous truthfulness of his Alexandrine subjects had named "King Potbelly," or Physkon, had done many a mean and disgraceful action. Under the government of this bloodthirsty buffoon the Egyptian state had missed the opportunity of assuming its due position in juxtaposition to Rome. Physkon, though he did not mind blood, had an aversion to war; he fled before the trouble he had raised, and took refuge at Rome itself. Henceforward there was usually to be found a Ptolemaic pretender to the throne in Rome, or one who sent appeals to the Senate from Cyprus or Cyrene.

Prosperity in an Age of Decay

Lathyros was most probably one of these candidates for the position of Pharaoh, otherwise he would not have been able to appear as a conqueror in Palestine during the twenty years of his

THE REVIVAL OF THE ART OF SCULPTURE UNDER THE PTOLEMIES

Though the period of the Ptolemies was one of constant disturbance, it displayed great architectural and artistic vigour. The first bas-relief represents a Ptolemy with two Cleopatras, and the second the sun-gods crowning a Ptolemy.

authority in the island of Cyprus; from Palestine he was driven out by the Jewish generals of his mother Cleopatra and his brother Alexander. However, in the year 88 the Egyptian throne fell vacant, and he was able to seize it without the consent of the Senate, for Rome was at that time threatened by Mithradates of

An Effort for Independence Pontus, and was even forced, about 86, to make overtures to the Ptolemaic ruler with a view to securing the help of his fleet. Lathyros received Lucullus, the ambassador of Sulla, with extravagant hospitality, but clung tenaciously to his fleet. This attempt to initiate a policy of independence was as ill-timed as it was lacking in enterprise, and led to no successful issue. The cause of Mithradates did not advance as had been expected; party divisions in Rome continued, and Lathyros was obliged to turn his attention to a dangerous revolt in Upper Egypt. Once again the centre of insurrection was Thebes, which was now, as before, the residence of the higher administrative officials of the priestly colleges, and possessed a royal bank, records of the transactions of which have recently been discovered. On this occasion this old and sacred town was not spared; the king devoted it to destruction (about 83), and when the geographer Strabo visited the spot about sixty years later, he found but a few villages scattered in the midst of a large area of ruins.

After the death of Lathyros, stories of scandal are the only evidence to show that the falling Ptolemaic dynasty retained any vitality. The succession invariably followed in the female line. Whenever the occupant of the throne lost his power, the nobles and the population of Alexandria turned forthwith to the nearest female relation, who could choose a brother or a cousin to share her throne after she had been exalted to the position of queen. A natural result of

Ptolemaic Inter-Marriages these endogamous marriages was the fact that legitimacy depended upon relation to the female line. As Dr. Strack has proved, this change of ideas became definitely stereotyped about the time of Physkon — between 145 to 116 B.C. Moreover, the marriages of Queen Berenice, the daughter of Auletes, with two foreigners had proved entirely unfortunate. None the less the last representatives of the Ptolemaic house in Egypt rose to

a certain height of grandeur as compared with their immediate predecessors, and their fall was tragical in the extreme —Arsinoe, Ptolemy XIV., the famous Cleopatra, and her son Cæsarion. The ultimate destiny and the conquest of Hellenised Egypt are treated in other parts of this work.

The dominant characteristic of the Ptolemaic age is its imperial spirit. Under the rule of cosmopolitan Greeks who had inherited the imperialism of Alexander, the old spirit of the Thothmes and the Ramessides revived. Under the Saïtes, the Egyptians, sickened with foreign war, had turned for inspiration to the days of the old kingdom, built pyramids, and fancied themselves once more the isolated contemporaries of Khufu. Greek encroachment and Persian conquest rudely shattered this dream. The accession of the Ptolemies opened a prospect of active reassertion of Egyptian superiority to the Asiatics. Isolation was impossible; conquest and revenge were possible. The humour of the kings tallied with that of their people. Ptolemy Euergetes

Revival of the Imperial Spirit marched into Asia in the grand style of a Rameses, and brought back the images of the gods which had been carried off by Esarhaddon and Ashurbanipal. He was received on his return to Egypt with acclamations as a true successor of the great Pharaohs. The imperial spirit was again in vogue, and the archaistic simplicity of the Saïtes gave place to an archaistic imperialism, the first fruits of which were the repair and building of temples in the Ramesside style. On these we see even Ptolemy the Piper masquerading as Rameses II., and striking down Asiatic enemies in the great Pharaonic style. Lists of conquered peoples were put up which were badly copied from those of Thothmes III., with the addition of modern names, such as Persia, Susa and India (" Hinto," at Kom Ombo), which had been utterly unknown to Thothmes III. Mistakes were made in identifications; thus " Keftiu," the ancient name of Crete, was mistranslated as " Phoenicia," and Asi, properly Cilicia, as Cyprus, for nobody but priestly antiquarians could read the hieroglyphs, and even they were often wrong in their theories, just like modern archæologists. The revived Egyptian spirit eventually resulted in revolts which, as we have seen, were led by native princes such as Harhetep or Irobastos. These attempts at independence were ruthlessly suppressed, and resulted in a complete insistence on Greek supremacy. Conquest was no longer disguised, and Egypt was Hellenised as far as possible. The large discoveries of papyri which have been made of late years, chiefly by Messrs. Grenfell and Hunt at Oxyrhynchus, show us how far, at the end of the Ptolemaic period, Greek control had penetrated into the country. Numbers of the subordinate officials were Greeks ; the Egyptians began to adopt Greek and Græcised names, and the way was paved for the complete Greek administration which existed during the Roman period.

In the Roman period Egypt, like other countries bordering the Mediterranean, was no longer of independent political importance in the history of the world. She was but the granary of Rome, and only when a rebellious general occupied her and cut off the supply of corn from Italy, as a weapon against the home authorities, did she occupy a position of temporary political weight. Hence Egypt was never constituted a senatorial province, but was always regarded by the emperors from the time of Augustus as their peculiar property, and was governed by a knightly prefect of the emperor directly responsible to him. Otherwise, Egypt was not even one of those frontier provinces for the possession of which Rome was forced to struggle : it was only against the Ethiopian kingdom of Meroe that comparatively harmless punitive expeditions were occasionally undertaken. The " Dodekaschoinos " (ninety-six mile land), or upper district

Egypt as the Cæsar's Property between Assouan and Maharraka, was permanently occupied by small divisions of the imperial troops ; here Augustus founded the great temple of Talmis, the modern Kalabsha, to which additions were made by his successors until the time of Septimus Severus. Within the empire Egypt was

THE ROMAN EMPEROR TIBERIUS
A sculpture at Kom Ombo, representing the emperor in Egyptian head-dress.

justly regarded as the " granary "; of its harvest products a considerable proportion was invariably assigned beforehand to the maintenance of the population of Rome. Augustus, who appropriated

Egypt the Granary of Rome the possessions and the property of the Ptolemies as being the heir of Cæsarion, kept the whole country under his personal supervision ; he controlled the food of Rome, and, as Pater Patriæ, " father of the fatherland," he thus made the mistress of the world entirely dependent upon his imperial will.

For administrative purposes Egypt proper was divided into about forty nomes, the chief authority in each being a " strategus," or sheriff and judicial officer : especially populous nomes, such as that of Arsinoe, were supervised by two of these officers. The prefect (Hegemon or Eparchosh in Greek) was chosen by the emperor from the Roman knightly order, not from among the senatorials. This chief official resided in Alexandria, and his duty apparently was to travel through the country throughout the year. Two Epistrategi were created for his relief, one being placed over the seven nomes of Middle Egypt, " Heptanomis," the second over the fifteen of Upper Egypt. For the rest, all Romans of senatorial rank were forbidden by a special decree to visit the country without the emperor's special permission. In 19 A.D. Germanicus disobeyed this regulation to his own detriment.

The Roman emperors did not abandon the divine attributes which the possession of the throne of Horus conferred upon them ; they were thereby provided with an excuse for continuing the architectural labours of the Pharaohs. Tiberius improved the shrines of Medamot and Karnak in Thebes in the name of Osiris, who inclined his " fair countenance " upon him in return. Vespasian, who made an unusually long stay in Alexandria upon the outbreak of the war with the Jews, ordered the work of restoration to be begun upon the temple of Latopolis. It was at that period that the sound given out by the Colossus of Memnon became known to the West. Hadrian, in whose life and travels Egypt holds a place of some importance, also visited the statue in the year 131, as is testified by the Æolic verses on the pediment by the court poetess, Julia Balbilla. The death of the emperor's favourite, Antinous, provided him with an excuse for founding a new nome in his honour in the capital town of Antinoe, not far from El-Amarna. Moreover, in the course of this imperial visit the Egyptian customs of that time seem to have developed a practical activity. The mother country of the Isis worship, which had now invaded Rome, was ready to display its marvels. A quarrel between Memphis and Heliopolis concerning the sacred bull was even brought for decision before the philosophical emperor. The two sacred bulls, Apis of Memphis and Mnevis of Heliopolis, had evidently now become confused. The struggle between the nomes concerning the relative value to be attached to their animals had long become notorious, but was perhaps not wholly displeasing to Roman authority, which acted on the principle "divide et impera." The knowledge of the hieroglyphic writing was then dying out even among the priestly classes, as is shown by many inscriptions in Upper Egypt from the time of Trajan onwards. The hieroglyphs are now used in fanciful ways. On the other hand, the learned society, founded in Alexandria, was in a highly flourishing condition, and at the time of Philadelphus had become the meeting-point for all scientific investigators. The Mouseion continued to flourish under Antoninus Pius, a portrait of whom has been found in Medinet Habu, together

Mansell

GRÆCO-EGYPTIAN MUMMY-CASES
During the Roman period a mixed Græco-Egyptian style of art arose, of which these mummy-cases, with portraits, are good examples

with inscriptions in Dendera, Philæ, Esneh, and the oasis of Khargeh, as well as under his successors, until the time of Septimius Severus, who also succeeded in destroying the resonant properties of the statue of Memnon as a result of his attempts to repair it.

Alexandria remained the great centre for the distribution of Indian products westward. Even the contemporaries of Augustus were astounded at the rapid rise of this trade and the great fleet possessed by Egyptian traders. The hybrid population of Alexandria had become utterly spoiled, and was continually breaking into revolt. Hadrian, in a letter to the consul Servian, says, "The people are, of all others, the most inclined to sedition, vain and insolent. Alexandria is opulent, wealthy, populous, without an idle inhabitant. They have one god, Serapis, whom the Christians, Jews, and Gentiles all worship. I could wish that the city practised a purer morality, and shewed itself worthy of its pre-eminence in size and dignity over the whole of Egypt." This troublesome peculiarity of revolting was definitely checked by a cruel massacre, inflicted upon the town by Caracalla in the year 216. The trenchant measures instituted by this emperor for the government of Alexandria were cut short by his death. To the time of Decius (249 to 251) belongs the last of the hieroglyphic inscriptions in the temples referring to a Roman emperor (at Esne).

Twenty years later Egypt formed part of the conquests of Zenobia for a short period. A decree remains issued in her name and in that of her son Vaballath in favour of a Jewish synagogue. Aurelian wrested the Nile valley from this new oriental empire. But in Egypt, as elsewhere, the signs of approaching disruption became apparent from this time onward. We constantly hear of rebel emperors in Alexandria, and also of incursions made by the neighbouring desert tribes in Upper Egypt. Diocletian himself was ultimately obliged, between 284 and 296, to reconquer the whole country, which had fallen into a state of wild confusion. Even this emperor seems to have abandoned the district to the south of Philæ to the "Nobatæ," or Nubians. Egypt had been converted to Christianity before the accession of Constantine to the sole government—a process reflected in the new administrative measures which he issued. The Patriarch of Alexandria and the bishops, together with the rapidly developing bureaucracy, were the ruling powers under the new constitution.

Several changes were made in the division of the country during the fourth century. Arcadius, the first "East Roman" emperor, divided the Delta and the Nile valley as far as Philæ into three provinces each—Augustamnica, Augusta Secunda, and Ægyptiace (the Eastern, Central, and Western Delta); Arcadia (Heptanomis), the "nearer" and upper Thebaïs. Justinian, whose administrative edicts confirmed the heavy taxation system then in force, had appointed two "duces," or dukes, to Alexandria in addition to the Augustan prefects already existing. In later times, especially under the Mohammedan supremacy, the Egyptian Christians reckoned their chronology from the "era of the martyrs," which began in the year 284, and formed a permanent memorial of the fierce persecution of the professing Christians by Diocletian.

The extensive discoveries of papyri at Arsinoe provide the most valuable material for tracing the development of culture and administration, especially during the imperial period. The province which on

Mansell

THE MUMMY - CASE OF ARTEMIDORUS

A beautiful Græco - Egyptian mummy-case with a portrait of the Greek occupant painted upon it.

account of its extent had been entrusted to two strategi—to the strategus of the Heraclides district, including the capital, and to the strategus of the "Themistes and Polemon district"—remained in exactly the same condition in which the rule of the Ptolemies had left it. This remark applies also to the taxation system and the personal *leitourgiai*, or "liturgies"—that is, the obligations to undertake public duties and positions generally for the whole of one year. Dams had to be repaired or erected by the poor villagers. A money deposit was apparently required before beginning certain liturgies involving greater responsibility. Such was the case for the post of tax collector, which was considered as specially burdensome. Declarations of property for assessment—"Apographæ" are naturally forthcoming. The cattle-breeder Nepheros thus makes a declaration in writing: "On the demand of the officials, how many pigs I possess at this time, I swear by the providence of Commodus our lord that I have 165, which I am fattening for the market of Psenkollechis. If you wish to count them, I will produce them." Taxation receipts also form an extensive collection. Besides the poll-tax, we have mention of taxes on dams, pasture grounds, asses, camels, sheep, trades, rents, and sacrifices. The garland tax, for the golden triumphal wreaths of the Cæsars, was also a burden.

The soil of Egypt was more favourable to the propagation of Christianity than were many other Roman provinces, but the peculiarities of the Egyptian character often produced the most extraordinary conceptions of and additions to the Christian teaching, and such as the fathers of the Church found the greatest difficulty in combating. Hermit life and a kind of monasticism begin from the middle of the Ptolemaic period, and very probably still earlier ; even in 162 B.C. there was a hermit in the Serapeum of Memphis who had voluntarily retired from the world, and was regarded for many years as the advocate of the oppressed. On the other hand, it appears from Coptic texts—that is, texts of a late period—that

Christianity in Ancient Egypt Jesus Christ and his mission could be "expounded" to the people only through the medium of the legend of the winged solar disc ; the Saviour passed from place to place through the Nile valley as a new Horus, everywhere driving out and destroying the enemy.

The development of art during the Roman period is of great interest. During the Ptolemaic age Greek and Egyptian art had pursued separate paths in Egypt, rarely combining to form a mixed style. Ancient Egypt and her traditions were still alive, and the Ptolemies never appeared as Greeks outside Alexandria, which was practically a Greek city ; while the Alexandrian Serapis was a Greek god. But in Roman times, as the knowledge of the hieroglyphs declined, and the Egyptian religion degenerated, a mixed Græco-Egyptian style of art arose, of which we have good examples in sculpture of the time of Hadrian.

To the same period belong the beautiful mummy-portraits from Hawara and the Fayyum found by Petrie and Graf. These are either painted on wood or canvas, or modelled in relief in plaster, and placed over the head of the mummy. The portraits are very lifelike, and are thoroughly Greek in spirit, while the method of use is Egyptian. Tombs of the same age are sculptured with mingled Egyptian and Greek motives, as at Kom-esh-Shugfa, close to " Pompey's Pillar " at Alexandria. A fine specimen of the same mixed art in architecture is a small temple at Naga in the Sudan. Out of this mixed

An Age of Confusion and Change style grew the peculiar mongrel art of the Coptic Christians as we see it on their gravestones. In Egypt, as elsewhere, the age was one of confusion and change. The Egyptians embraced Christianity the more eagerly because they were throwing off a religion which was far lower and more superstitious than the beautiful beliefs of the Greeks. All that was best in Egyptian religion had disappeared when their own living gods,

the Pharaohs—religious foci of national pride and self-confidence—had ceased to reign ; and what was left was merely a fast-decaying superstition of snake and mouse-worship, the derision of the civilised world. Hence they turned from it with loathing when the faith of Christ, with its new hope for the poor and the lowly, the condemned and oppressed, dawned upon them. But the fanaticism with which they embraced Christianity was the cause of further trouble.

Adherence to certain dogmas became a matter of life and death ; also national patriotism impelled the Egyptians to fierce rejection of the Christianity of their masters, the Greeks, and the Egyptian heresy of Monophysitism drew to it the great mass of the people, with the result that in order to get rid of the hated " Melkites," or orthodox Greeks, the "Copts" were willing to ally themselves with the invading Mohammedans. Thus is explained the easy conquest of Egypt by the Arabs. In the year 619 the Persians made their way into the Delta. The

Why Christianity Triumphed Persian supremacy lasted only ten years, during which a stately palace was erected in Alexandria. The victorious Asiatic campaigns of the indefatigable Heraclius forced Khosru's successor to conclude a peace, under the terms of which Egypt was evacuated in 629 by the Persian military governor Shahbaraz.

The restoration of the Byzantine power was not, however, destined to be permanent. The emperor endeavoured to secure religious harmony, but the attempt was made too late. The conciliatory efforts of the patriarch Cyril of Alexandria proved equally fruitless, and were nullified by the cry for " pure doctrine " raised by the school of his predecessor Joannes. Consequently, the appearance of the caliph Omar's troops under Amr in the year 639 was in no way opposed to Egyptian aspirations.. At the end of the year 640, the emperor had lost everything except the western part of the Delta, and his death, in 641, shattered the last hopes of his adherents. The patriarch Cyril obtained a promise from Amr of protection for the Christian churches, and then surrendered Alexandria. On September 17th, 642, the last representatives of the Roman supremacy left the shores of Egypt.

CARL NIEBUHR
H. R. HALL

FROM THE MOHAMMEDAN CONQUEST
TO THE PRESENT TIME
BY STANLEY LANE-POOLE

EGYPT IN THE MIDDLE AGES

FROM 641 to 868 Egypt was a province of the successive caliphates of Medina, Damascus, and Bagdad, and was ruled by a series of ninety-eight governors appointed by the Orthodox, Omayyad, and Abbassid caliphs exactly in the same manner as the other provinces of their empire. The Arab conquest made little difference to the Egyptians, who merely had to pay their taxes to mudirs and mamurs, instead of to epistrategoi and strategoi. The government was decentralised, and the governor interfered as little as possible with the district officers or these with the village sheikhs. The governor was assisted by three great officers of state—the commander-in-chief, the treasurer, and the chief kadi—whom he usually nominated himself, but who were sometimes directly appointed by the caliph. The kadi, or chief justice, often held office under a series of governors, who rarely ventured to overrule him, and the upright and dignified manner in which these chief kadis, men of humble origin and simple life, generally upheld the law was the best feature of Arab administration.

The legal taxes were not so heavy as under Roman rule. The land-tax amounted to two dinars (rather more than £1) per acre, and the poll-tax on nonconformity levied upon all able-bodied male non-Moslems was also two dinars a head. The Moslems had besides to pay a poor-tax, and there were sundry dues on trades, licences, etc. The total revenue varied from £6,000,000 to £7,000,000, and would seem to have been made up of about £4,000,000 poll-tax, £2,000,000 land-tax, and various duties ; but the proportions varied at different times. The land-tax had increased by the first half of the ninth century, owing to the care with which the Arabs developed the irrigation system. It was managed by a special department of state advised by inspectors, and supported by the corvée, or forced labour, which was practised from ancient times to nearly the close of the nineteenth century. The surplus of revenue over the cost of administration was sent by the treasurer to the caliph, except in rare cases, when a governor's unusual services were rewarded by the grant of the whole surplus—amounting in one instance to £1,500,000.

The caliphs, away at Damascus and afterwards at Bagdad, seldom took any interest in Egypt, except as a milch-cow to feed their treasury. " Milk till the udder be dry and let blood to the last drop" was one of their instructions to the officials. Naturally the frequent changes of governors—there were 67 in 118 years under the Abbassid caliphs—encouraged illegal extortion, since the governor had but a brief and uncertain time in which to garner his personal harvest. Except the two Omayyad caliphs, Marwan I. and II., whom civil war brought to Egypt, the only caliph who made an official visit was El-Mamun, in 832.

Egypt Under the Caliphs

The policy of the caliphs at first was not to colonise but to control Egypt, and the Arab tribes who conquered the country were forbidden to acquire land and settle there, because they might be required for other campaigns. For the same reason, as well as because it was the symbol of Roman power, the capital was transferred from Alexandria, which was dismantled in 645 after a brief re-conquest by Manuel, to El-Fostat, "the Tent," a military settlement on the site of Amr's camp, which has slightly shifted and grown into the modern Cairo. The caliph's object was to keep the Arab army of Egypt in touch with his then capital of Medina, and for this purpose Amr cleared and reopened the old canal, which enabled ships to sail from the Nile at Fostat to the Red Sea. The process of Arabising Egypt was undesigned and accidental, and must have been slow. Most of the governors arrived with an escort of several thousand Arab troops, and many of these must have settled and inter-married with the Egyptians ; but the chief organised immigration was the planting of three thousand Arabs of the tribe of Kays in the Hauf district in the Delta, north-east of Fostat, as a precaution against rebellion. Arab tribes, such as the Kenz, also gradually permeated parts of the Said or Upper

DESCENDANTS OF ANCIENT EGYPTIANS
The Coptic Christians are the lineal descendants of the people of the ancient Egyptian empires.

Egypt. The bulk of the population, however, remained Egyptian and Christian (Copt), and they had little to complain of in their treatment by their conquerors, who had relieved them from the oppression of Constantinople and the prosecution of its Orthodox theologians. By treaty they were accorded full liberty of conscience and equal rights with the Moslems, and suffered only the additional poll-tax on nonconformity. Amr invited the exiled Jacobite patriarch Benjamin to return, and no attempt was made to convert the Copts to Islam, which would indeed have involved a heavy loss to the revenue. In practice, the treatment of the Copts depended upon the character of the governor. Wealthy Egyptians were doubtless "squeezed" by grasping collectors, and sometimes humiliating orders were issued imposing vexatious passports, fines, and badges to be worn by monks, especially during the fanatical revival under the caliph Mutavakkil, when, in 850, the Copts were ordered to wear yellow dresses and set up degrading images of apes or dogs over their doors, and were forbidden to ride horses. Now and then a governor would demolish Coptic churches or burn their sacred pictures ; but, on the whole, it cannot be said that the Christians of Egypt were severely persecuted. Occasionally they revolted in the Delta, but this was usually due to the constant insubordination of the Kays Arabs settled there. Indeed, most of the many revolts which distracted Egypt under the Abbassid caliphs were caused by sectarian and political discord among the Moslems themselves. The partisans of the Shia doctrine of the divine right of the descendants of Ali to the caliphate, as well as the Kharigis, a sect of puritans who had largely contributed to Ali's downfall,

Tolerance of the Christians

were both strong in Egypt ; and in 754 we read of 3,000 heads of Kharigi rebels being sent to Fostat. The greatest and last Coptic insurrection occurred in the always disturbed district of the Hauf in 830–832, and was so ruthlessly suppressed by the caliph Mamun, who brought for the first time Turkish troops to Egypt, that we hear no more of national revolts. Many Copts apostatised, and from this time dates the predominance of the Arab population in Egypt, the settling of Moslems on the land and in the villages—and not mainly, as heretofore, in the few towns—and the prevail-ing Mohammedan character of the people.

Up to 856 all the governors of Egypt were Arabs, and many of them were members of the caliphs' families. The last Arab governor was An-basa, an exceptionally strong just man of un-ostentatious and devout character. During his government the East Romans, in 853, suddenly raided the coast and carried off 600 women and children from Damietta; and in order to guard against similar surprises Anbasa built the fort at Damietta which afterwards proved a serious stumbling-block to the Crusaders. Another external attack occurred in his time. The Sudan, or Nubia, which had been subdued by Amr's lieutenant Abdallah ibn Sad, and in 652 had been overrun as far as Dongola and forced to pay an annual tribute of 360 slaves —which was levied for more than six centuries—repudiated this tribute in 854, and the Baga Sudanis invaded Upper Egypt and sacked Esne. With the aid of reinforcements from Bagdad, an Egyptian army crossed the desert from Kus to the Emerald Mines, and, supported by a fleet sent by the caliph to Aydhab on the Red Sea coast, totally defeated the Sudanis near Dongola. The only other external events of importance during this period of provincial rule were the annexation of the province of Barka to Egypt in 766, and the arrival at Alexan-

Invasion from the Sudan

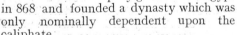

THE NILOMETER AND ITS USE
A graduated pillar on the island of Roda, by which the rise of the Nile is measured, and the amount of the land tax calculated.

dria in 798 of over 15,000 Andalusian refugees from Spain, who became masters of the city from 815 to 827, when they were forced to surrender and exiled to Crete.

The suppression of the Copts' rebellion by Turkish troops marked a vital change. Henceforth Turkish mer-cenaries played an in-creasingly predominant part in the Mohammedan empire. From the middle of the ninth century it became the habit of the caliph to grant Egypt as a fief to a chief of his Turkish bodyguard, who would appoint a deputy to govern the country and to remit the surplus revenue to him at Bagdad. After Aubasa's recall, in 856, these deputies were also Turks, and one of them, Ahmad ibn Tulun, a Turk from beyond the Oxus, but highly educated according to the Moham-medan standard at Bag-dad and Tarsus, became deputy governor of Egypt in 868 and founded a dynasty which was only nominally dependent upon the caliphate.

After suppressing two revolts and sup-planting the overgrown authority of the treasurer Ibn Mudebbir, Ibn Tulun exer-cised kingly power and state in Egypt. Previous governors had lived in the official suburb of El-Askar, or in the summer pavilion called the " Dome of the Air " on Mukattam Hill; but Ibn Tulun built himself a new royal suburb, called El-Katai, between the two, with a splendid palace and hippodrome, and the noble mosque, built in 877–879, which still survives, and is the earliest dated example of the exclusive use of the pointed arch. He also built an aqueduct to bring fresh water to his palace from a spring in the southern desert, and restored the second nilometer on the island of Roda. In 870 the surplus paid to the caliph was £375,000; but as the years went on this tribute was discontinued, and Ibn Tulun refused to pay any more substantial form of allegiance than the inscription of the caliph's name, as well as his own, on his coinage, and the usual homage in the public prayers.

Governor Gains Independence

Firmly established in Egypt, he next occupied Syria in 878 and extended his kingdom from Barka to the Euphrates. The Egyptian army also inflicted a severe defeat on the East Romans under Kesta Stypiotes at Chrysobullon near Tarsus in 883, when 60,000 Christians are said to have fallen and immense booty was captured.

A King Who Left £5,000,000 Ibn Tulun died in 884, leaving £5,000,000 in the treasury, over 30,000 military slaves, and a hundred ships of war. He had reduced the taxes, encouraged the small farmers, beautified his capital, and made Egypt once more a power. His son, Khumaraweyh, after a weak beginning, soon learnt to follow in his father's steps : he regained Syria from the caliph in 886, obtained, for a consideration, his official diploma as governor of Egypt, Syria, and the Roman marches, and sealed the understanding by giving his daughter in marriage to his spiritual suzerain.

Khumaraweyh outdid his father in pomp and display, enlarged the palace, laid out elaborate and fantastic gardens, and wooed sleep on an air-bed floating on a lake of quicksilver, guarded by a tame lion ; notwithstanding which he was murdered by his slaves in 896, and after nine years of anarchy, during which the Turkish troops did as they pleased with Khumaraweyh's two young sons, the caliph in 905 sent an army and reannexed Egypt.

For the next thirty years the country was still nominally a province of the caliphate, under governors appointed from Bagdad, but was really dominated by the Turkish soldiery. An audacious young man named Khalangi seized the government, and held it for eight months in defiance of the caliph ; the great Shia dynasty of the Fatemid caliphs was advancing along the shores of the Mediterranean, and in 914 and again in 919, their generals occupied Alexandria and pushed on into the Fayyum ; their fleet **Caliphs Regain Egypt** of eighty-five sail was destroyed in the harbour of Alexandria, but the invaders were not dislodged from Upper Egypt till 920. The only semblance of order and authority was shown by the successive treasurers of this family of Madarai.

At last, in 935, the governor of Syria, Mohammed " the Ikhshid "—a title held by his ancestors in Ferghana on the Jaxartes—was appointed governor of Egypt. During his firm rule of eleven years there was no rebellion. His army of 400,000 men, largely recruited in Syria, which he also held, kept down the mutinous Turkish troops, and repelled all attacks of the Fatemides. He suffered some losses in Northern Syria, but kept his hold on Damascus, defeated the Hamdanid prince of Aleppo, Seyf-ed-daula, near Kinnesrin, in 945, and obtained from the caliph the hereditary grant of Egypt and Syria with the added glory of the government of the holy cities of Mecca and Medina. His sons were young at the time of his death, in 946, and their regent, the black eunuch Kafur, ruled Egypt and Syria with success, and even recovered Aleppo and Northern Syria as far as Tarsus. He kept a luxurious and cultivated court, surrounded by poets and musicians, upon whom he was almost as lavish as he was upon his kitchen, for which every day, it is said, 100 sheep, 100 lambs, 1,000 pigeons and small birds, 500 fowls, 250 geese, and 100 jars of sweetmeats were supplied. His death, in 968, was followed by the usual turmoil of the troops, and a year later Egypt passed from **Lack of Great Men in Later Egypt** the orthodox eastern caliphate to the heretical Fatemides. Three centuries of Mohammedan rule had blended the Egyptians and Arabs more or less into one people, and turned the great majority into Moslems, but had produced no great men ; Ibn Tulun the Ikhshid and Kafur were neither Arabs nor Egyptians. The country had all along been treated by the caliphs mainly as a source of revenue ; but, with few exceptions, the governors had done little to develop its wealth or productiveness. Only the capital had benefited by the luxury and expenditure of the rulers, and it was still far behind some of the other great cities of the caliphate, such as Cordova and Damascus. It had evoked no poet or writer of the first rank.

The Fatemid revolution had moved fast since the proclamation of Obeydallah El-Mahdi as its first caliph at Kairouan in 908. The impressionable Berber tribes had received the mystical doctrine of the Shias with ecstasy, and the Fatemid power rapidly spread to the shores of the Atlantic on the west, and the borders of Egypt on the east. It had absorbed the old Aglabid princedom of Tunis and annexed Sicily. Egypt itself had been twice invaded and even partly occupied. In the anarchy which followed the death of Kafur the fourth Fatemid caliph El-Moizz found his opportunity. He had for two years been digging wells and building rest-houses on the road to Alexandria, and in 969 he sent the kaid, or general, Gauhar with an army of 100,000 men to Egypt. The oppressed populace received them as deliverers, and after a defeat at Gizeh the Turkish troops submitted. Gauhar entered Misr, as Fostat was usually called, amid acclamations on August 5th, and that same night laid the foundation of a new city, or rather fortified palace, named, after the planet Mars, El-Kahira ("the Martial" or "Victorious"), which gradually supplanted the adjacent Misr, and grew into the modern Cairo. Gauhar ruled the land with energy and justice, until the arrival of Moizz in 973, and founded the great university mosque, El-Azhar, which stands to this day.

The Egyptians accepted the heretical dynasty with indifference, but the Fatemides were careful not to flaunt their extreme sectarian doctrines before the multitude. The Ismailian theology recognised stages of initiation, and was essentially esoteric in its higher **Triumph of the Heretics** planes. In Egypt little more was done than to add the Shia formulas to the usual Mohammedan prayers and ritual. There was no persecution and not much attempt at a propaganda. The majority of the people remained orthodox. On the other hand, every effort was made to conciliate the non-Moslems; a Copt was made head of the customs, and a renegade Jew, Ibn Killis, who had been a favourite of Kafur and had paved the way for the Fatemid occupation, was rewarded with high office, and became a noted patron of belles lettres. The Abbassides were powerless to resist the new aggressors. The Fatemid caliph was acknowledged by the Christian king of Nubia, by the holy cities of Mecca and Medina, by the Hamdanid prince of Aleppo; and in Syria the rump of Ikhshidids was subdued, and the heretical caliph was even proclaimed, most reluctantly, in orthodox Damascus. This last conquest, by diverting a handsome source of blackmail hitherto levied by the Karmati, or Carmathian, sectaries of Arabia, brought their leader Hasan ibn Ahmad into collision with the Fatemides, though both professed the same Shia doctrine. Hasan overran southern Syria and attacked Cairo, where he was beaten back on the very threshold of Gauhar's new city in 971. A second Karmati invasion, in 974, was with difficulty repulsed, with the aid of a heavy bribe, by Moizz himself.

These attacks showed how little the pretensions of the Fatemides to the apostolic succession of the house of Ali were accepted even by fellow Shias, while **By Sword and Gold** their alleged pedigree from the caliph Ali was repeatedly demolished by orthodox theologians. When the leading Shias and Sherifs of Egypt came to demand a formal substantiation of his claims, Moizz is said to have taken a short way with them. Unsheathing his sword, he said, "Here is my pedigree"; and, throwing a shower of gold among the spectators, he added, "There is my proof!" Gold had certainly paved his way to power, and gold was seldom lacking in the Fatemid treasury. The wealth and luxury which prevailed in "the guarded city of Cairo," where the caliphs dwelt behind strong walls in a mysterious pontifical isolation, were prodigious, and the accounts of contemporary historians, if exaggerated, cannot be wholly disbelieved. One of Moizz's daughters is recorded to have left a fortune of 2,700,000 dinars and 12,000 dresses. We read of sacks of emeralds, thousands of chased and inlaid silver vessels, Sicilian embroidery, crystal cups, and all manner of works of art. Great artistic and industrial activity prevailed in Egypt and elsewhere under the new dynasty. Lustred pottery and glass were brought to high perfection, and silks and woollens were manufactured at various Egyptian towns, one of which, Damietta, gave its name to dimity. The Shias did not hold with the usual Mohammedan reprobation of the drawing of human figures, and the arts of painting and sculpture were thereby encouraged. From a financial point of view the people had no cause at first to complain of the new dynasty. Moizz abolished the old system of farming out the **Prosperity Under the Heretics** collection of the revenue, and his chief land administrators, while exacting prompt and full payment of the taxes, appear to have exercised their powers with equity.

The Fatemid rule subsisted in Egypt for two centuries by no special virtues or efforts of the rulers. These maintained a luxurious seclusion, and abandoned the government to vizirs, who were chiefly bent on making their own fortunes and were seldom inspired by any great policy or states-manlike ideas. The empire, which had comprised all North Africa, Sicily, Syria, and the Hijaz, quickly shrank in every part except Egypt and Arabia, and in Egypt itself the dynasty rested upon no popular devotion, no general adhesion to their doctrine or persons, but solely upon the army—the Berber, Turkish, and Sudani mercenaries, who, con-stantly recruited from their native lands, formed a perpetual terror to the unfortunate population. The virility and statesmanship of the early caliphs soon evaporated in a bath of luxury and profligacy.

The Best Caliph

Moizz's son and successor, El-Aziz (975–996), a red-haired, blue-eyed hunter and soldier, was the best of these Egyptian caliphs, and his Christian wife encouraged his natural clemency and tolerance. He was a friend to the Coptic patriarch and to Severus, the bishop of Ushmuneyn, and allowed the rebuilding of Coptic churches. Christians and Jews held high offices and justified their appointment by their ability. The land had rest under this wise and prudent caliph. If he set the fashion in luxury, in gorgeous display and sumptuous palaces, and in the love of costly novelties in dress and food, he repressed the corrupt administration, enforced justice, substi-tuted fixed salaries for gratuities and bribes, and vigorously maintained the defence of his kingdom. In Maks, then the port of Cairo, where his father had built a naval dock, Aziz fitted out the fine fleet of 600 sail which protected Egypt from the Emperor Basil, and though Africa was slip-ping out of his grasp, his name was still recited in the mosques from the Atlantic to the Euphrates.

Unfortunately, his son, El-Hakim, who succeeded in 996 at the age of eleven, was his opposite. He early showed a passion for blood, and one after the other the minis-ters who governed during his minority were assassinated. Once his own master, the young caliph showed a vein of eccentricity which developed into madness. He loved darkness and rode about the streets in the night, spying upon his subjects. Then he turned night into day and ordered the shops to be opened and the houses illumin-ated and all business to begin after sunset. Women were compelled to stay at home and not allowed even to take the air on the flat roofs. Shoemakers were forbidden to

The Mad Caliph

make outdoor shoes for ladies. For seven years no woman was seen in the streets of Cairo. Not only were intoxicating drinks prohibited, in accordance with Islamic rule, but vines were cut down, dried raisins confiscated, and honey poured into the Nile. Games were stopped, dogs were to be killed wherever found, distinguishing badges and other humiliations were revived for Christians and Jews, and churches were demolished and their lands confiscated, though Christians were still appointed to official posts, since the treasury could not do without them. Officials were tortured and executed in numbers with every kind of barbarity, and a special department had to be created for the management of their confiscated estates. At the same time Hakim completed a noble mosque, and erected a " Hall of Science," not merely for the spread of Shia doctrine, but for the encouragement of all learning, and fur-nished it with a rich and varied library.

When the caliph finally proclaimed himself the Incarnation of the God-head—a logical deduction from extreme Shia doctrine—and Darazi and other preachers called upon the people to worship Hakim as divine, the long pent-up hatred burst all bounds, and the mob rose, only to be savagely trampled under foot by the brutal Sudani troops. Happily, the Turkish and Berber soldiery for once made com-mon cause against the blacks, and some degree of order was restored in the miser-able capital. Then, in the midst of the reign of terror, Hakim disappeared in 1021, killed, no doubt, by the avengers of blood ; but to this day the mystery of his vanishing remains, and he is still worshipped as the incarnation of the Divine Reason by the Druses of the Lebanon, who look for his second advent.

Caliph Assumes Divinity

Hakim's son, Ez-Zahir (1021–1036), and grandson, El-Mustansir (1036–1094), did nothing to revive the empire which his madness had shattered. As a Christian wife had guided Aziz, and had borne him the monster Hakim, so the Sitt el-Mulk, or Princess Royal, sister of Hakim, con-trolled the youth of Zahir, who speedily showed himself cruel, like his father ; and a black mother swayed Egypt during the minority of Mustansir, a weak-minded nonentity. The real power was in the hands of the soldiery, and government consisted in appeasing their greed. Palace cliques, disastrous famines, slave revolts, military uproar, and the occasional ascendency of a few of the vizirs, are the chief features of Egyptian history during the eleventh century, though there were intervals of tranquil prosperity, such as the traveller Nasir-i-Khusrau described in 1046. A famine, the worst known in mediæval times, lasted seven years (1066–72), until human flesh was actually sold in public as butcher's meat. The sufferings of the people were indescribable ; great nobles were reduced to menial employment in the public baths, and the caliph sat on a mat in his empty palace, rifled by Turkish troops of all its treasures and jewels, and, worst of all, its magnificent library, in 1068, and was indebted to the daughter of a scholar for the daily dole of two loaves of bread.

The tyranny of the Turks was at last ended by the death of their leader, Nasir-ed-daula, and by the accession to the vizirate of Bedr el-Gemali, the Armenian governor of Akka, or Acre, who brought his Syrian veterans to Cairo in 1073, massacred the Turkish officers, reduced the revolted districts, restored order and prosperity, built a new wall round Cairo with great Norman-like gates, and remained virtual ruler of Egypt for twenty-one years, till 1094, when he was followed by his son, El-Afdal, for twenty-seven more (1094–1121). These two great Armenians gave the land half a century of peace and firm yet humane government. Their chief anxieties were in Syria, which was conquered by the Turkoman Seljuks in 1076, and twenty-two years later became the battlefield of the first crusade. El-Afdal did a little by diplomacy and by arms to retain the vestiges of Fatemid power in Syria, and the Egyptians twice defeated Baldwin ; but, one after the other, the coast

fortresses, Acre, Tripolis, Tyre, fell ; and Askalon remained, until 1153, the last relic of Fatemid dominion in Palestine.

The great vizir was assassinated in 1121 at the instigation of the caliph El-Amir, who had succeeded his father El-Mustali, son of El-Mustansir, in 1101, and was himself murdered in 1130. A curious interregnum followed, when Afdal's son, Abu-Ali, the vizir, ruled Egypt and ordered the prayers and coinage in the name of the predicted Mahdi, or Imam el-Muntazar, "the expected," whose second advent was confidently anticipated by a sect of the Shias. This vizir was in turn assassinated by order of Amir's cousin, El-Hafiz, who became caliph in 1131, and who also appointed Armenians to the vizirate, and, like most of the caliphs of his line, cultivated friendly relations with the Christians and frequented their monasteries and gardens. The Armenian community was naturally most favoured when several of their nation held the government ; but besides these most of the clerkly posts were in the hands of Copts. The excesses of the black soldiers, however, made any sort of orderly government impossible. The next caliph, Ez-Zafir (1149–1153), as well

THE ZAWILA GATE IN OLD CAIRO

The great Zawila gate was built in the 12th century by a Fatemid vizir. The period was remarkable for its architecture, as many other beautiful buildings in Cairo testify.

as his vizir, Ibn es-Salar, was treacherously murdered ; his son, a child four years old, only lived till 1160, when the last Fatemid caliph, El-Adid, aged nine, was set on the nominal throne by the vizir Ibn Ruzzik, who had been the real ruler of Egypt since 1154, and skilfully played off the rival powers in Syria, Nur-ed-din of Damascus, and Amalric of Jerusalem, against each other. He built a beautiful mosque, the ruins of which remain near the great Zawila gate of his great predecessor Bedr el-Gemali. The Fatemid period was remarkable for its architecture, which

2147

has a character of its own, but shows close affinities to Byzantine work. In literature the age was far less notable than in the arts, but this is perhaps accounted for by schismatic isolation.

It had for some time been a question whether Egypt was to fall to the Christian king of Jerusalem or to the Moslem king

Egypt Falls to Damascus of Damascus. After the assassination of Ibn Ruzzik, in 1161, the rivalry of two vizirs at Cairo precipitated the crisis. One called in Nur-ed-din, the other tried to make terms with Amalric. Thrice the opposing armies of Syria and Jerusalem entered Egypt and fought there, under the guise of deliverers. In 1164 and 1167 the honours were divided, but the Christians gained a slight advantage. Amalric's massacres and greed of gold finally drove the Egyptians into the arms of his most powerful enemy, and when, in 1169, Nur-ed-din's general, Shirkuh, appeared for the third time before Cairo the Crusaders withdrew without even offering battle. The deliverer became vizir, and on his death, two months later, was succeeded by his nephew, Salah-ed-din Yusuf ibn Ayyub, the "Saladin" of European writers.

Saladin was a Kurd of Tekrit by birth (1138), but he had been brought up at the Turkish court of Nur-ed-din at Damascus, and his military and political ideas were Turkish. He introduced the system of military fiefs and slave troops which afterwards developed under the Mameluke sultans. He learned soldiership under the best generals, and won his spurs at the battle of Baban, in Upper Egypt (1167), when his tactics routed Amalric he defended Alexandria against heavy odds for seventy-five days, when the Crusaders besieged it in the same year. As vizir of an heretical caliph, and at the same time viceroy of a particularly orthodox king, his position was intolerable; the Fatemid

Saladin in Egypt caliphate was soon abolished (1171), and the death of Nur-ed-din, in 1174, left Saladin the protagonist of Islam against the Crusaders. Most of his career falls outside Egyptian history. Of the twenty-four years of his reign only eight were passed in Egypt; the rest were filled with campaigns in Syria, Mesopotamia, and Palestine. He had already made Egypt safe against further invasion, suppressed a great revolt of the black troops in Cairo,

repelled an attack on Damietta by the combined fleets of the Eastern Emperor and the king of Jerusalem, made a dash upon Gaza, seized the port of Eyla on the Red Sea, carrying his ships overland in sections from Cairo, and sent expeditions to Barka and Gabes on the west, to Ibrim in the Sudan, and to Sana in the Yemen, which his brother Turanshah conquered in 1174.

The repression of a conspiracy at Cairo in favour of the deposed dynasty, the failure of a fleet of 282 ships despatched by the king of Sicily to capture Alexandria, and the deaths of Amalric and Nur-ed-din, removed all fears of external attack and internal rebellion, and Saladin was free to enter upon his great policy—to consolidate the Moslem states of Syria and Mesopotamia with Egypt and to bring the whole force of all to bear upon the supreme task of driving the Christians out of Palestine.

In 1174 he entered Damascus, still nominally the vassal of Nur-ed-din's little son, and in 1176 he defeated the Atabeg of Mosul and all the forces of Mesopotamia and Aleppo at the Turkoman's Wells, and was recognised as sovereign over all Syria.

Saladin's Wise Administration During the comparative peace of the next six years, an interval of strenuous preparations, Cairo was fortified by a new wall, a citadel, and the great dike of Giza. Several theological colleges, or Medresas, were founded for the first time in Egypt for the free teaching of Mohammedan learning according to the Shafite school of Sunnite orthodoxy. In his wise administration Saladin had the devoted counsel of his chancellor, the learned Kadi El-Fadil, whose rigid orthodoxy supported his master in a policy of confiscation, if not actual persecution, against the Christians of Egypt, which contrasted with the lenient indulgence of the Fatemid caliphs.

In 1182 Saladin left Cairo, as it turned out for ever, to muster his forces for the Holy War. He had already, in 1180, formed a general alliance of the Moslem princes from the Persian Gulf to the Black Sea and the Mediterranean, but it needed the sterner lessons of a series of triumphant campaigns to bring the whole of the Mesopotamian lordships to his standards. At last, in 1186, he had secured his northern flank, and could advance boldly on Palestine. The history of his great war (1187–1193) may be read elsewhere. The crushing defeat of the Crusaders at Hittin near Tiberias on July 4th, 1187, was followed by the fall of the whole kingdom of Jerusalem and the honourable capitulation of the holy city itself. Tyre alone of all the fortresses of Palestine defied his assaults, and Saladin vainly tried to dislodge Guy of Lusignan and the Christian army beleaguering Acre, which fell at last, in 1191, to the attack of Richard I. [see page 1964]. When peace was made, in 1192, the Crusaders retained only the strip of coast from Acre to Jaffa. All the rest of Palestine and Syria remained part of the dominions of the great " Soldan," who died six months later (1193). Magnanimous, chivalrous, gentle, sympathetic, pure in heart and life, ascetic and laborious, simple in his habits, fervently devout, and only severe in his zeal for the faith, he has been rightly held to be the type and pattern of Saracen chivalry.

Saladin's successors ruled Egypt for more than half a century, as other members of his family ruled other provinces of his empire, and the various kinsmen were usually fighting with each other. Out of the turmoil his brother El-Adil Serf-ed-din, or " Saphadin," emerged as the true leader,

Saladin's Great Brother second only to his greater brother, whom he had faithfully served for over twenty years ; and by 1200 he was master of most of Saladin's dominions. Much of Adil's reign was taken up with resisting futile efforts of the diminished and disunited Crusaders ; the " Children's Crusade," in 1212, only filled Egypt with prisoners, but the capture of Damietta by John of Brienne in 1218 was a death-blow to the sultan. His able son El-Kamil (1218–1238), however, defeated the invaders, though strongly reinforced, at Mansura in 1219, and they were forced to evacuate Egypt. Kamil, who was as wise and prudent a statesman as his father, kept his hold of Saladin's empire as far as the Euphrates, and did much for Egypt by improving the irrigation, completing the citadel of Cairo, founding colleges, and encouraging learning. He was on friendly terms with the Emperor Frederick II., who sent an embassy to Cairo, and in 1229 a treaty was made by which Jerusalem (except the Hazam esh - Shezif), Bethlehem, and Nazareth were ceded to the emperor in return for a defensive alliance and other friendly agreements, which aroused the indignation of the Pope. Kamil's sons, El-Adil II. (1240–1242) and Es-Salih Ayyub (1242–1249), followed, and then, in the midst of Louis IX's crusade, Salih died, and the saving of Egypt was left to his brilliant cavalry, the famous Mamelukes, or white slaves who ruled Egypt for the next 270 years.

The Ayyubid period had been remarkable chiefly for wars abroad, but it had raised Egypt once more to a pitch of power **Egypt's Symbol of Empire** and prosperity such as it had not known since the days of the Fatemid Aziz. The building of the citadel of Cairo meant much more than the mastery of the city ; it was the symbol of empire. Internal resources were developed, and trading concessions were granted to the Venetians and the Pisans, who had a consul at Alexandria. Learning was encouraged by a series of scholarly sultans, and Kamil was generous and benevolent towards the Christians. Francis of Assisi preached before him, and the Dominicans visited his son Es-Salih ; but the crusade of St. Louis revived the old exasperation between the creeds, and his pious invasion caused the demolition of over a hundred churches.

The men who broke King Louis's French chivalry at the second battle of Mansura, in 1249, and afterwards surrounded, pursued, and made an end of his army, and took the king prisoner, were the Bahri Mamelukes, or " white slaves of the river," so called because, out of several similar brigades, they were quartered on the island of Roda, opposite Cairo. Bodyguards of vigorous young Turkish slaves had long been employed by the Abbassid caliphs, by the Seljuks, by the Atabegs of Mosul, and by Saladin ; but Es-Salih specially organised them as a corps d'élite in Egypt. Their leader at the critical moment happened to be a woman, a widow of Salih, who gave way for three months when her husband's son, Turanshah, arrived and took command. But after his murder, Sheger-ed-durr, who had been the brains **Mameluke Queen of Egypt** of the army during the most anxious period of the crusade, became again the queen of Egypt, and exercised royal authority (1250-57), though nominally associating with herself in the sovereignty El-Ashref, a child of the house of Ayyub. She married one of the chiefs of the Mamelukes, the Emir Aybek, but he was only her generalissimo, and the real power always rested in her hands till, in 1257, she had Aybek murdered out of jealousy and was herself beaten to death by rival women slaves three days afterwards. Aybek's son, who instigated this crime, was a frivolous youth, and was soon deposed by his regent Kutuz. Henceforth the throne belonged to the man with the longest sword. The bravest and richest generals and officers of the court accumulated slave retainers and acquired a power and state almost equal to that of the reigning sultan, and on his death his throne usually fell to the strongest of them, if it did not fall before, for most of the Mameluke sultans came to a violent end. All were alike slaves by origin—sultan, emirs, or military chiefs, soldiers, servants —and the origin brought with it no sense of degradation. Any slave with personal qualifications, courage, skill at arms and sports, good looks and address, had the chance of rising to favour and influence in his master's household, where he might earn his freedom. Thence he would climb to court offices, as cupbearer, taster, polo-master, equerry, mace-bearer, and the like—for the Mameluke court was elaborately organised—and gather a host of slave retainers around him, and keep a miniature court of his own. To grasp the throne was the final step, if he were both strong and diplomatic, and then he would try to hold it as long as he could—usually but a few years—till a stronger man took it from him. Every man was every other man's equal, if he could prove it so. The process of proving it implied constant struggles, and the people of Cairo used to close the great wooden gates of the quarters, sometimes for a whole week, and listen trembling to the turmoil outside. They were repaid in quieter times by the sight of the most splendid pageants that Egypt ever knew ; for the Mameluke sultans and their emirs loved pomp, and their progresses were conducted with dazzling equipment and stately ceremony, while their frequent polo matches, archery, and falconry, showed off their magnificent horsemanship.

The Mamelukes were physically superb : Beybars swam the Nile in his cuirass, dragging after him several great nobles seated on inflated cushions, and on one of his campaigns he swam the Euphrates at the head of his troops. They were a race of born soldiers, bold, dashing horsemen, fighting with mace and sword and bow, and throwing the javelin with extraordinary skill. They were also the most luxurious of men, and filled their great palaces with works of art, costly carpets, carved ivory and woodwork, inlaid gold and silver drinking and washing vessels, porcelain, flowers, perfumes, beautiful stained windows and panelled ceilings. Most of the beautiful mosques of Cairo were built by these truculent soldiers—all foreigners, chiefly Turks, a caste apart, with no thought for the native Egyptians whose lands they received in fief from the sultan ; and no bowels of mercy where ambition called for massacre or secret assassination, yet fastidious in dress, equipment, and manners, laborious in business, and much given to music and poetry, but most of all to wine.

Twenty-four sultans of the Bahri dynasty followed one another between 1250 and 1390, but only three or four stand out from the rest as men of exceptional character. The greatest of all was Beybars (1260–1277), the brilliant cavalry leader, who shattered Louis's knights at Mansura, and afterwards helped Kutuz to crumple up the Mongol hordes of Hulagu Khan at the momentous battle of Ayn Galut, "Goliath's Spring," in Palestine, on September 3rd, 1260, and, then conspiring against his sultan, stepped over his body to the throne. He was the real founder of the Mameluke empire, and consolidated his wide dominions so ably that all the follies and jealousies of his successors could not undo his work. The fabric stood unshaken for two centuries and a half, till the Ottoman Turks flowed over it. He raised the Mameluke army of 12,000 picked troops to the highest pitch of discipline and efficiency, organised the system of military fiefs, built a navy of forty war galleys, dug canals, and made bridges all over Egypt, strengthened Alexandria and other fortresses, built a mosque, college, and hall of justice, and connected Cairo and Damascus by a regular post service of four days, so that he used to play polo in both cities in the same week. He strengthened his position as chief sultan of Islam by importing a representative of the " Abbassids of Bagdad "—whose caliphate was extinguished by the Mongols in 1258—and enthroning him as caliph at Cairo, where this fainéant heir of the Abbassid caliphate subsisted till the

The Slave Sultans

Egypt s Most Splendid Pageants

The Greatest Mameluke

Ottoman conquest. One caliph, El-Mustain, even sat nominally on the Mameluke throne for a few months in 1412. Beybars sent friendly embassies to the emperor at Constantinople, to Manfred of Sicily, to Baraka Khan of the Golden Horde, whose daughter he married, and whose alliance preserved the Mameluke empire from the assaults of the Mongols of Persia. Between 1265 and 1272 he captured most of the Crusader fortresses of Palestine, took all the strongholds of the dreaded sect of Assassins in the Ansariya mountains, defeated the Mongols in Cilicia (1277), and seated

THE SLAVE RULERS OF EGYPT
For two and a half centuries Egypt was ruled by a brilliant series of soldier sultans, famous in history as the Mamelukes, who were slaves by origin and retained their power only by the might of their arms.

himself for the nonce upon the Seljuk throne at Kaisariyeh—he had already annexed Dongola and the Sudan (1275). His unquestioned sway extended from the fourth cataract of the Nile and the holy cities of Arabia to the Pyramus and the Euphrates. He had revived the empire of Saladin. Egypt prospered under his just, firm rule, and the cost of his wars was met from the conquered provinces, while taxes were remitted at home. He strictly prohibited wine, beer, and hashish, and suppressed immorality in the towns. Suspicious and perfidious towards shifty

agents, he was true to loyal officers, and his bravery, munificence, and toleration made him so popular with the people that his exploits were a favourite topic of the Arabic story-tellers in Cairo cafés down to the nineteenth century.

The two sons of Beybars, who were set on the throne successively, did not inherit their father's capacity, and were soon deposed by the emir Kalaun (1279–1290), who emulated his great predecessor in every respect, defeated a Mongol invasion at Hims in Syria (1281), seized several of the few remaining Crusader fortresses, including Tripolis, and maintained close relations with the European Powers; he concluded commercial treaties with Genoa and Castile, and Sicily even entered into a kind of alliance with Egypt. His prudent policy and just rule—though intolerant towards the Copts—preserved the prosperity which Beybars had inaugurated, and the celebrated Maristan, or hospital, at Cairo, with its wards, lecture-rooms, laboratories, dispensary, and the adjoining mosque and exquisite tomb-chapel, testify to the benevolence, piety and architectural taste of Kalaun. His son Khalil (1290–1303) took Acre and all that remained of the Crusaders' fortresses, and proclaimed a holy war with a view to the conquest of the world; but the braggart, whose only virtue was courage, and whose vices were unspeakable, was opportunely murdered by the disgusted emirs before he could do more harm. Khalil's brother, a child of nine years, En-Nasir Mohammed (1293–1341, interrupted 1294–1298, and 1309–1310), held the throne with two intermissions for nearly half a century, chiefly because of the jealousies of rival emirs, who found the claim of an hereditary title, however unrecognised in principle, more tolerable than the risk of civil war. They tried it, indeed, when they had deposed Ketbugha, who from regent of En-Nasir became sultan (1294–1296), and then elected Lagin, the lord armour-bearer of Kalaun, to be their king, but strictly as primus inter pares. He made favourites, who flouted and imprisoned the great nobles; so they murdered him and brought back

En-Nasir, who now found himself a half-starved nonentity in the hands of jealous emirs, whose armed bands were constantly making the streets of Cairo a pandemonium. The wealth of these great lords was prodigious, as may be seen from the numerous mosques they founded and the wonderful development of all the arts and luxuries during this period.

Prodigious Mameluke Wealth It was only by degrees, after a diplomatic retirement in 1309—during which the emir Beybars II. mismanaged the government—and by many executions and treacheries, that En-Nasir established his supremacy. Meanwhile the Mongols of Persia renewed their invasions of Syria, and, after a victory at Hims, in 1299, occupied Damascus, to be handsomely defeated on the Marg es-Suffar by the Mamelukes, who beat them back for the fourth and last time in 1303. Whatever else the Mamelukes left undone, their splendid dash and discipline saved Egypt from the curse of Mongol conquest.

Egypt was exceptionally wealthy, and the trade with Europe and India, and the transit dues, were immense. Christians and Jews indeed suffered much persecution after a long toleration and overgrown authority. The old sumptuary laws were revived in 1301, and renewed in 1321; blue and yellow turbans were enforced, while many churches were demolished or closed, though Copts were still employed in all the government offices. As he grew more absolute the sultan levied more money from the great nobles, and remitted many taxes which burdened the people. His general rule was just but very stern, and he did much to better the conditions of the agriculturists. He was a notable builder—it was the great age of Saracenic architecture in Egypt—and all the high officers vied with each other in founding mosques and medresas. Nasir himself built two

Cairo' Noble Mosques noble mosques, greatly improved the citadel of Cairo, made the canal between Alexandria and the capital, and the aqueduct from the Nile to the citadel, encouraged stock-breeding, farming, falconry, and everything except vice, wine—and kindliness. His reign was the climax of Mohammedan civilisation in Egypt.

So great was the reputation established by Nasir's long reign that eight of his sons, two grandsons, and two great-grandsons succeeded him during the next forty years. But none of them can be said to have ruled, though one son, Sultan Hasan—remembered by his great mosque —had a broken reign of ten years; and one grandson, Shaban, retained the nominal throne for sixteen. The real rulers were the too powerful emirs, Kusun, Aksunkur, Sheykhu, etc., who built exquisite mosques and ruined the country by their extortions and contests. The "Black Death" of 1348-1349 carried off thousands of the people of Cairo in a single day. The king of Cyprus, Peter of Lusignan, raided Alexandria in 1365.

It was inevitable that the race of puppets descended from Nasir should be supplanted by some strong emir, and the man appeared in Barkuk—1382-1399, interrupted by Haggi, 1389-1390—one of the Burgi Mamelukes, or " White Slaves of the Fort," so called because since the time of Kalaun this brigade had been quartered in the Burg, or citadel of Cairo. They were at first chiefly of Circassian race, though recruited later from Greeks, Mongols and Turks; and of the twenty-

Rule of the White Slaves three sultans who formed this dynasty (1382-1517) all were Circassians save two Greeks. They usually had short reigns, and six of them fill 103 out of the total 134 years. Seven of them transmitted the throne to their sons, but the latter were mere temporary stopgaps until the leading emirs fought out the succession.

The Circassian sultan was little more than chief emir, primus inter pares, like Lagin, elected by his peers, and quite easily deposed by them when they were tired of him. The real authority rested with the military oligarchy. The greed and jealousy of the great emirs led to widespread corruption and barbarous cruelty. Governorships and justice were openly sold, and rivals were abominably tortured. So debauched were the Mameluke troops that no woman could be allowed to appear in the streets; and the peasants did not dare to bring their cattle and produce to market at Cairo. Such excesses took place under the best and most devout sultans, like El-Muayyad (1412-1421), a learned and accomplished man of ascetic life, as well as under the venal and grasping Greek, Khushkadam, who took bribes from everybody for the vilest purposes. Famine, plague, risings of starving peasantry, mercilessly stamped out under horses' hoofs, form the staple of the history during this period.

The only good things these villainous rulers did was to build some of the loveliest mosques in and around Cairo, probably in the hope of atoning for their crimes. Their one foreign exploit of importance was the conquest of Cyprus in 1426, long a stronghold of Mediterranean piracy, which remained tributary to Egypt till the close of the dynasty. Barkuk and his son Farag (1399–1412) resisted Timur in Syria with some success, though the great conqueror's death was the chief cause of Egypt's escape. Muayyad and his son Ibrahim reduced a large part of Asia Minor for a time (1418–1419). Bars Bey (1422–1438), the strongest and most oppressive of all, was the conqueror of Cyprus, who held James of Lusignan to ransom at Cairo, and his successor—after the usual farce of setting up his son for three months—Gakmak (1438–1453), a learned theologian, tried to emulate him by several unsuccessful attacks on Rhodes, and emphasised his Moslem correctness by persecuting Christians and Jews and reviving their old humiliations. Kait

The Last Strong Emir Bey (1468–1496) reigned the longest and was the most successful of all the Burgi sultans He had worked his way up in the usual Mameluke way. Bought for £25 by Bars Bey, he was sold to Gakmak, made a lieutenant by Inal (1453–1461), a colonel by Khushkadam (1461–1467), and finally was elected, in 1468, to succeed the well-intentioned but wholly unsuccessful Timurbugha as sultan. He was the last strong ruler of independent Egypt, and he was great in every sense, wise, brave, energetic, and ready. Cairo is full of his monuments and restorations, and his public works extended from Egypt to Syria and even Arabia. He travelled over all his dominions, to Jerusalem and the Euphrates, as well as performing the pilgrimage to Mecca, and wherever he went bridges, roads, mosques, schools, or fortifications bore witness to his progress. His reign rivalled Nasir's in artistic and architectural pre-eminence.

It was attained at the cost of heavy taxation in addition to oppressive government monopolies and high duties on foreign trade. The European trade had grown to vast proportions. The Italian republics found it necessary to keep consular agents at Alexandria. Venice had two funduks, or marts; Genoa, Ancona, Florence had their magazines, and Naples, Narbonne, Marseilles, and Catalonia were represented there. The wealth and influence of Venice is shown by the fact that her consul guaranteed the king of Cyprus's ransom of £100,000 in 1426. The Indian trade was also very

Immense Trade Monopoly valuable. We read of £36,000 paid in customs dues at Gidda on the Red Sea, which was an Egyptian port. The Mameluke sultan took toll on every bale of goods that passed between Europe and India, until Vasco da Gama sailed round the Cape of Good Hope in 1497. It was an immense monopoly, and extortionately used.

Troubles with his nominal vassals, the Turkoman chiefs of Asia Minor, nearly brought about a rupture with the Ottoman sultans who had recently taken Constantinople, and Kait Bey's welcome to the exiled prince Gem was resented by his brother sultan, Bajazet, who retaliated by annexing Tarsus, but was defeated at Adana by the Mameluke emir Ezbek in 1488, and had to restore his conquests when peace was arranged in 1491.

Four incapable successors followed in as many years, and then Kansuh El-Ghuri (1501–1516) restored order, levied ten months' taxes at a stroke, laid hands upon every possible source of revenue, built and fortified, strengthened the army, the citadel, and the coast defences, and even sent a fleet to the Bombay coast and defeated the Portuguese off Chaul in 1508 in the vain hope of preserving the Indian transit trade; but Almaida avenged the Portuguese honour by his victory over the Admiral Hoseyn off Diu in 1509. Kansuh was preparing for the inevitable conflict with Turkey, but he was too late. Selim I. was bent on the conquest of Egypt; there was treachery among the Mamelukes, and Kansuh fell at the head of his gallant army in the fatal battle of Marg Dabik near

Massacre of the Mamelukes Aleppo on August 24th, 1516. His successor, Tuman Bey, refused to become the viceroy of the Turkish sultan; the Mamelukes fought their last desperate battle at the Mukattam hill beside Cairo on January 22nd, 1517; the city was stormed street by street, and after a week's massacre the conquest was complete. The last of the Abbassid caliphs was carried off to Constantinople, where the sultan arrogated to himself the sacred office.

A general view of the native quarter of Cairo, showing the Pyramids in the distance.

The mosque of the Sultan Hassan, the most beautiful in Cairo.

The citadel of Cairo, built in the ninth century, and a portion of the great Mohammedan burial place.

CAIRO: THE CAPITAL OF MEDIÆVAL AND MODERN EGYPT

Cairo was founded at the Arabian conquest in 640 A.D., when Fostat was built, since when it has spread northwards to the present town. Cairo is famous for its beautiful mosques, of which there are over 150.

SINCE THE OTTOMAN CONQUEST

ALTHOUGH from 1517 Egypt was a mere province of Turkey, like Syria or Irak, it was still practically under the domination of the Mamelukes, and remained so up to the invasion of Napoleon. The chief difference was that instead of a sultan elected out of their own ranks, they had a Beglerbeg, called, after 1573, a Pasha, sent from Constantinople. This pasha, whose principal business was to collect as much cash as possible for the Sultan of Turkey—who extorted as much as 800,000 to 1,000,000 ducats a year from Egypt—and for himself, was controlled by a council of Mameluke emirs, soon to be known by the Turkish title of Bey, and the head Mameluke, or Sheikh el-Beled (mayor), had much greater power than the Pasha. The unfortunate tax-gatherer of the sultan, for the pasha, as a rule, was little more than that, shut up in the citadel of Cairo, guarded by the Turkish regiments of Azabs and Janissaries, held but a little brief authority. We hear of **The Sultan's Extortions in Egypt** seven pashas succeeding one another in eighteen months, till the people of Cairo remonstrated, saying that a pasha every three years was change enough. The real power remained with the Mamelukes, and with the commanders of the Azabs and Janissaries, who were practically Mamelukes.

Very little change in the character of Egyptian life and history was brought about by the Turkish conquest. The annals become more monotonous, the stage is smaller, and the actors less distinguished, because with the loss of outside possessions and foreign wars, statesmanship and military prowess degenerated, and politics became provincial. Wealth diminished, of course, by the transference of much of the trade of Alexandria to Constantinople, and by the loss of the Indian trade following upon the discovery of the Cape route, in spite of which the extortions of the sultan of Turkey continued exorbitant. Otherwise, the Mameluke Beys, who controlled Egypt under a nominal Turkish chief, bore a strong family likeness to the Mameluke emirs of earlier days. They were smaller in their aims and achievements, but they did just the same things, fought one another's retainers in the streets, turned mosques into forts, and fired cannon from their roofs at one another, laid siege **Splendour of the Mamelukes** to the Turkish troops in the citadel for months together, kept great state and open house every day to all comers in their palaces on the banks of the Ezbekiyeh, then a lake at high Nile, or by the Birket el-Fil (Lake of the Elephant), supported learning and the arts, and built and restored mosques. Abd-er-Rahman Kihya, who died in 1776, was one of the greatest builders of modern Egypt, erected several mosques and numerous fountains and drinking tanks, and made innumerable restorations of great merit, notably in the Azhar mosque.

Some of the great Mameluke Beys recall the best traditions of the days of En-Nasir. Othman Bey Dhu-l-Fikar, in the first half of the eighteenth century, was the greatest man in Egypt of his time; he made his own Mamelukes emirs, led the pilgrimage to Mecca with great pomp, feasted the pasha in his palace—where he held his own court of justice—punished oppression, fixed the price of the necessaries of life, and waged war against every form of corruption. So noble was his character and just and proud his life, that he created an era, and people used to date events from his banishment. Rudwan el-Gelfi, commander of the Azabs, also in the eighteenth century, was another great figure, and while he held sway plenty reigned—at least in the capital. His hospitality in his great house on the Ezbekiyeh **Flourishing of Literature and Learning** was lavish and his charity unbounded. Like Othman Bey, he fell a victim to the conspiracy of his rivals, the inseparable bane of the Mameluke system. Literature and learning flourished under such rulers, and the zeal for the strict observance of the religious law was so burning that smoking in the streets was sternly forbidden, and anyone found publicly smoking

2155

was compelled to eat his clay pipe-stem. One of the Mameluke emirs, Ali Bey, taking advantage of the Sultan's preoccupation in a war with Russia, actually made himself independent of Turkey (1768–1772), and even took Mecca and invaded Syria, but was defeated at Gaza by Murad Bey. His lieutenant, betrayer, and successor,

Munificence of the Mamelukes Mohammed Bey Abu-Dhahab (Father of Gold, so-called from his munificence), who had distinguished himself in the Syrian campaign, was an admirable ruler, whose memory is preserved by the great collegiate mosque which he founded in 1774 near the Azhar, whose salaried professors, a novelty in the East, in fur hoods expounded the law according to the four schools of teaching.

After the death of Ali and Mohammed, in 1773 and 1775, there was a struggle between rival Mamelukes, and when Murad and Ibrahim had put down the rest, they fell out between themselves. The Porte attempted unsuccessfully to restore order by sending Hasan, the captain-pasha, in 1786, but the rivalry of Murad and Ibrahim Bey was to be ended by the arrival of a new and wholly unexpected master. Napoleon Bonaparte had begun his dream of Eastern Empire.

The connection of the Egyptian campaign with Napoleon's general policy is treated elsewhere. He had conceived the idea of mastering the East, including in the scheme the overthrow of the British power in India. From the East he would turn on the West, and compel Europe to submission. The first step was to be the seizure of Egypt. The true objective of the fleet, which had for some time been in preparation at Toulon, had been more or less disguised by threats of an invasion of England; but, although Bonaparte managed to evade Nelson's watching squadron, the English admiral correctly guessed his destination. It was an accident—as will be elsewhere related—that enabled the great general of the French Republic to reach Alexandria, disembark, and fight the battle of the Pyramids, before Nelson fell upon the French fleet. Undoubtedly the battle of the Pyramids

A GREAT MAMELUKE BEY
Murad was one of the two Mameluke Beys who unsuccessfully opposed Napoleon's invasion.

transformed the "little grape-shot general" into the "Man of Destiny."

Twenty-four hours before the arrival of the French fleet at Alexandria, in 1798, the intentions of General Bonaparte were apparent in Egypt; on the evening of July 1st his army, numbering about 40,000 men, began to disembark; at midday on the 2nd, the city was occupied, and on the 3rd the vanguard set out for the south. When the tops of the great pyramids became visible on the horizon, Bonaparte uttered the famous words : " Forty centuries look down upon you." Murad and Ibrahim had taken up a position between the pyramids and the river ; their centre, the village of Embabeh, surrounded by entrenchments but without artillery, was stormed by the French after a furious onslaught of Murad's cavalry had been repulsed by the infantry squares. This battle of July 21st dispersed the Mameluke army; Ibrahim retreated to the Eastern Delta and Murad to Upper Egypt ; Cairo capitulated four days later. On August 17th, Bonaparte cut off Ibrahim at Salahiyeh and compelled him to seek refuge in Syria. Meantime Nelson had destroyed the French fleet at Abukir on August 1st. Bonaparte and his army were isolated ; the Mediterranean had been transformed into a British lake. Nevertheless, Desaix marched on Upper Egypt at the end of August, arriving at Assouan after two severe engagements; Murad's resistance became a mere guerrilla warfare. The French in Cairo made preparations for a continued occupation. On first landing, Napoleon had announced that he, the destroyer of the Knights of Malta, was a friend of Islam, who only desired to make

Napoleon Becomes Mohammedan war upon the "godless race of the Beys." He adopted the customs of the Moslems with all possible publicity, taking part in the festival of Molid en-Nebi in Arab costume. A proclamation, which has been recovered in the form of a Fetwa of the Cairo divan, dated February 11th, 1799, was drawn up in order that Bonaparte might be declared by the Ulema not only a complete believer in the Prophet, but also sultan of Egypt. Although some of the

NAPOLEON'S ENTRY INTO EGYPT: THE OCCUPATION OF ALEXANDRIA

Napoleon conceived the idea of mastering the East, and, with its aid, to master the West, the first step being the seizure of Egypt. On July 1st, 1798, his army disembarked at Alexandria, and on the 2nd the city was occupied.

conversions were genuine, the confidence of the Orientals was not thus to be taken by storm. Seyyid Bedr el-Mukaddam, a fanatical descendant of Mahomet, roused the population of Cairo to revolt on October 21st, 1798, and three days of street fighting ensued. Bonaparte's bold Syrian enterprise, from the end of January until June, 1790, in spite of several such brilliant successes as the capture of Jaffa and the victory over Ibrahim at Tabor, ended in a complete failure at Acre, where the French forces were opposed by Gezzar Pasha and Sir Sydney Smith. A few weeks

THE BATTLE WHICH MADE NAPOLEON "THE MAN OF DESTINY"

It was the Battle of the Pyramids, fought on July 21st, 1798, before Nelson could attack the French fleet, that transformed the "little grape-shot general" into "the Man of Destiny." The Mameluke army was dispersed and Cairo fell.

after Bonaparte's return, in the middle of July, 1799, 20,000 Turks under Mustafa Pasha landed in Abukir under the protection of the English fleet, but were driven back to their ships with heavy loss by a French force of 8,000 troops on July 25th.

Napoleon Leaves Egypt This event marks the conclusion of Bonaparte's career in Egypt. Tidings from Europe transmitted to him through the British admiral induced him to return thither on August 23rd, with two frigates, which had been saved from the English, and a following of 500 men.

Kléber, upon whom the chief command now devolved, was by no means in love with the undertaking which he was expected to continue ; moreover, the Turkish grand vizir, Yusuf Pasha, was advancing from Syria at the head of an army of 80,000 men. An exaggerated report of Kléber to the Directory upon the bad condition of the French army fell into the hands of the British and led to the opening of negotiations for the evacuation of the country. On January 28th, Desaix signed the convention of El-Arish, a town that had just been occupied by the grand vizir, and immediately left the country. Kléber made every effort to fulfil the heavy conditions of the agreement.

Upper Egypt and Cairo had been already evacuated when the British admirals declared that the French troops must surrender as prisoners of war. Kléber's reply to these demands was issued in his orders for the day : " Soldiers, such demands are to be answered simply by victory; prepare for battle ! " On March 20th, 1800, with scarcely 10,000 men, he defeated the army of the grand vizir, which was eight times as large as his own, at Matariyeh close to Cairo, in the famous " battle of Heliopolis " ; two days later the encampment of Yusuf Pasha with his large supply of stores fell into the hands of the French.

Cairo was retaken after a struggle lasting several days, which began upon the 27th ; Ibrahim was exiled to Syria, but Murad, as the ally of France, was rewarded with the governorship of Upper Egypt. Though it lasted but a short time, Kléber's administration was attended with high success ; the army was also strengthened by the addition of a Coptic and a Greek legion. On June 14th, 1800, the day of the battle of Marengo and the death of Desaix in Europe, Kléber was assassinated by a fanatic. As senior commanding officer, Menou, who had taken an Egyptian wife, now assumed the responsibility of administration ; under the title of " Abdullah Menou " he continued the work of government reform and sought to develop the natural resources of the country with a view

French Government of Egypt

NAPOLEON PARDONING THE LEADERS OF THE REVOLT AT CAIRO IN 1798

NAPOLEON AS A MOHAMMEDAN AT A MOSLEM FESTIVAL IN CAIRO

One of Napoleon's first acts on landing in Egypt was to announce himself a friend of Islam, adopting Moslem customs and taking part in a Mohammedan festival, in order that he might be declared Sultan of Egypt.

to a permanent occupation. However, the Turks advanced from Syria, and the British commander, Sir Ralph Abercrombie, landed at Abukir with 17,000 men and won a victory near Alexandria on March 21st, 1801. A considerable force of sepoys, despatched from India under the command of Sir David Baird, arrived to assist the British operations. Belliard, who had remained in Cairo, where Murad Bey had recently died of the plague, was compelled to capitulate on June 23rd, and Menou at Alexandria on September 22nd. The French army, which still consisted of no less than 24,000 men, was transported to France on English vessels. In March, 1803, the British also evacuated the country, after obtaining an amnesty for the Mamelukes by a convention with the Porte, the Beys promising henceforward to abstain from all interference in the government of Egypt.

The French occupation was transitory but its legacy to science was permanent.

The great " Description of Egypt," published by the savants who accompanied Bonaparte's army, laid the foundations of an exact knowledge of the history, antiquities, and actual conditions of the country. The discovery of the famous " Rosetta Stone " by French sappers at Fort St. Julien paved the way to the decipherment of the hieroglyphic inscriptions first successfully begun by Young and Champollion, whence the science of Egyptology had its birth. Ever since, the supervision and interpretation of the monuments of Egypt has been especially a French charge, ably performed, and in many other ways the influence of French science has been felt in various departments of Egyptian progress.

When Bonaparte drove the Turks into the sea in 1798, one of them was picked up by a boat of Sir Sidney Smith's flagship, H.M.S. Tiger, and thenceforth played the chief part in Egyptian history for the first half of the nineteenth century. This was Mohammed Ali—or in popular spelling,

2159

Mehemet Ali—an Albanian of Kavala, on the Macedonian coast, who was born in 1769, the same year as Wellington and Napoleon. Up to nearly the age of thirty he was merely a small local official who combined tax-gathering with the profits of a tobacconist.

Tobacconist Becomes Ruler of Egypt

When the Porte joined England to turn the French out of Egypt, Mehemet Ali went as second in command of the Kavala levy of 300 Bashibazuks, and, after narrowly escaping drowning at the first attempt, landed a second time in 1801, when the Kapudan pasha combined with Abercrombie. The major of Bashibazuks rose to the supreme command of the 5,000 Albanian troops in Egypt, struggled through a welter of intrigues, anarchy and civil war to the highest office in the land, and held it as pasha of Egypt till 1848. He made his way up in precisely the same way as many of the Mameluke sultans before him, and raised Egypt to a position of power and of territory equal to that which she possessed under Beybars.

For ten years he was climbing to the throne; in the second decade he was conquering Arabia and the Sudan; in the third he was gathering strength for his great struggle with Turkey, which filled most of the fourth; and the last decade was the reaction of a man whose vaulting ambition had overleaped itself.

When the British evacuated Egypt, in May, 1803, they left anarchy. Khusrev Pasha, a slave of the Kapudan pasha, was the nominated governor, with few troops and no money. The Mamelukes, who were bent upon recovering their old power, held the provinces. Mehemet Ali at first threw his weight on the side of the Mamelukes, in order to weaken the authority of the Turkish pasha, whom he made prisoner at Damietta. But he had no intention of letting the Mamelukes

grow too strong, and when Elfi Bey, the ablest of them, arrived in a British man-of-war with assurances of support from the British Government, Mehemet Ali contrived to keep him at a distance from the other Mamelukes, whose leader, Bardisi Bey, was jealous of Elfi and readily fell into the plot. The old recruiting-ground of the Mamelukes in Circassia and Georgia had been cut off by the Porte, and it was manifestly futile to put trust in a decaying and unprolific race which depended upon slaves, no longer forthcoming, for its perpetuation.

So Mehemet Ali soon drove Bardisi into Upper Egypt and took possession of the capital as the representative of the

Mehemet's One Fatal Mistake

Sultan. His one fatal mistake was in liberating Khusrev, and sending him back to Constantinople, where he never ceased to thwart his rival so long as they both lived. Khusrev afterwards became grand vizir, and was still alive at the time of the Crimean War. Khurshid Pasha, who succeeded Khusrev in Egypt in 1804, introduced mutinous Bashibazuks into Cairo, who spread anarchy and weakened the governor's authority.

Hence, Mehemet Ali was able to pose in the curious rôle of protector of the people. In May, 1805, he was elected Pasha by general acclamation, and at once proceeded to bombard Khurshid in the citadel with guns laid on the roof of the opposite mosque of Sultan Hasan, till, in April, 1806, the Sultan's firman arrived, confirming the Albanian as pasha of Egypt. The opportune but suspicious deaths of both Elfi and Bardisi removed his last effective rivals; and

GENERAL KLÉBER
Who was left in chief command in Egypt after Napoleon returned to Europe, and governed the country with considerable success.

the British expedition of 1807 to support the Mamelukes against Turkey, whom Napoleon had succeeded in embroiling with England, ended in humiliating defeat. Master of Egypt, but with a very insubordinate army of 90,000 men, Mehemet Ali had first to get money. He confiscated the whole land of Egypt, destroyed all titles to estates, and made every cultivator his tenant at will ; he took over the vast properties of the Wakfs, or religious and charitable foundations ; he extorted taxes, and forced labour and military service from the wretched fellahin, or peasants, without justice or remorse. So long as he got his full demand, he did not inquire by what iniquitous methods his officials raised the men and money. Egypt had never groaned under a worse tyranny. Finally, in 1811, he lured the Mameluke Beys, to the number of 500, to the citadel of Cairo and massacred them to a man in the steep narrow passage that leads down to the Azab gateway. The incredible story that one of them leaped his horse over the battlements is mere legend. Emin Bey did not arrive till after the massacre, and wisely betook himself to Stambul. About 5,000 Mamelukes were slaughtered throughout Egypt ; the remnant fled into the Sudan and were eventually dispersed as far as Kordofan. They had brought their fate upon themselves by centuries of bad government. The massacre, however, was never forgiven by Europe.

From 1811 to 1818, Mehemet Ali was occupied chiefly on behalf of the Porte in suppressing the Wahabi insurrection in Arabia, which threatened to revive the old Arab caliphate, and from 1820 to 1822 he sent three expeditions to conquer the Sudan as far as Darfur and Kordofan. The leader of one **Conquest of the Sudan** of these, his son Ismail, was burned alive ; but Mohammed, the infamous Defterdar, or treasurer, the pasha's son-in-law, avenged his death by horrible massacres and atrocities. Khartoum was founded in 1823, and thenceforward the Sudan became a hunting-field for slaves, and the chief recruiting-ground of the Egyptian

MEHEMET ALI
The tobacconist who rose to become Pasha of Egypt, its strongest ruler and worst tyrant.

army. The Sudanese troops enabled Mehemet Ali to keep his Albanians in order, but the other object of the Sudan conquest, the search for gold, proved unremunerative.

For some years after this, the pasha was busy organising his dominions. In 1821, his revenue was about £1,200,000, of which the land tax of about 7s. an acre on 2,000,000 acres of cultivated land furnished £660,000, most of which was spent on the army. A system of monopolies, maintained with great vigour, brought in vast profits but discouraged trade ; he also did a large personal trade, bought cereals from the fellahin at his own price, and sold at a profit to Europe, while the peasants were starving. He dug the Mahmudiyeh canal, which connects Alexandria with the Nile, and thus revived the prosperity of the ancient port at the cost of the death of 20,000 out of the 300,000 labourers who were forced to work at it. He encouraged Lieutenant Waghorn and the overland route to India, and **Great Days of Mehemet** used Europeans skilfully for his advantage, and to some extent for the advantage of Egypt, while heartily despising Turks and Egyptians. His attempt to make Egypt a manufacturing country was foredoomed to failure. Nevertheless, by 1833 he had doubled the revenue, and had an army of 150,000, with an efficient fleet.

His assistance to Turkey during the Greek War of Independence is described elsewhere ; the main events were the despatch of his son Ibrahim to the Morea in 1824, the conquest of Modon, Tripolitza, and finally Mesolonghi in April, 1826, and the sinking of the Turco-Egyptian fleet by Codrington in Navarino harbour on October 20th, 1827. The Egyptians evacuated the Peloponnesus under French pressure in 1828. The campaign in Greece cost Mehemet Ali the support of England.

The oppression of the fellahin was driving them in shoals into Syria, and this was made the pretext for another war of aggrandisement. Mehemet Ali had long resolved to try conclusions with his suzerain the Sultan, and in 1832 his army, under his son Ibrahim, descended upon Syria, stormed Acre, and entered Damascus, where it was welcomed as a liberator from Turkish misrule. The Ottoman forces were repeatedly routed with appalling loss —at Homs on July 8th, at the Beilan Pass on July 29th, and at Koniya on December 21st, when 50,000 Turks under the famous Reshid Pasha were put to flight. As D. A. Cameron wrote, "Ibrahim had achieved the impossible. The Egyptian had defeated the Turk in three pitched battles against odds, had out-fought him, out-marched him, out-manœuvred him, and taken him captive." Ibrahim had certainly proved himself a military genius, but intrigues at the Porte had undoubtedly helped him. He now threatened Constantinople itself; but the landing of a Russian army at Hunkiyar Iskelesi barred his way. A peace was made at Kutahiya on May 6th, 1833, by which Mehemet Ali retained the whole of Syria and Cilicia.

But he had conquered too much. His new possessions were five times the size of Egypt, and their mixed population was not to be governed on Egyptian models ; Syrians and Druses would not endure the lash; and when the great pasha tried to levy his taxes in the way which the mild fellahin had suffered patiently, his new subjects revolted again and again, and no massacres or atrocities could subdue them. Moreover, he alienated the one Power that could have saved him. England and France together had forced the Sultan to yield him Syria, but, miscalculating the

SAID PASHA
Who paved the way for French predominance by the concession of the Suez Canal.

TEWFIK PASHA
Who came to the throne when Egypt was under European control, owing to the reckless extravagance of his predecessor.

relative sea-power of the two, he cultivated Louis Philippe, and thus threw Palmerston more than ever on the side of the Anglo-Turkish alliance.

It is true that the great victory of Ibrahim over the Turks at Nezib on June 24th, 1839, followed by the death of Sultan Mahmud II. and the voluntary surrender of the Turkish fleet at Alexandria, seemed to crown the pasha's triumph ; but it was short lived. His empire was founded on sand ; he had alienated his subjects by unexampled tyranny and extortion, and he had made an enemy of the greatest sea-power in the world. Palmerston threatened to "chuck Mehemet Ali into the Nile," and it was practically done. Admirals Stopford and Napier landed troops at Beyrut, defeated Ibrahim, and took Acre on November 3rd, 1840. A few British ships, a handful of Royal Marines, and a small Turkish force, supported by a vengeful population, drove the Egyptians out of Syria with the loss of half their number on the desert march. Napier compelled Mehemet Ali to accept his terms, and after he had surrendered Syria and made submission to the Sultan, he was granted the hereditary pashalik of Egypt in 1841, at the instance of the Western Powers. But he was now a broken man, and, after paying homage to the Sultan at Constantinople, he gradually sank into lethargy and then into imbecility in 1848, and died almost forgotten in his eightieth year, on August 2nd, 1849, leaving behind him the memory of the strongest, shrewdest, and most relentless of all the "illiterate barbarians" that have ruled Egypt. His brilliant son Ibrahim, who had been appointed regent in July, 1848, predeceased him by nine months, and his grandson Abbas, son of Tusun, succeeded. Warned by the tragic collapse of his grandfather's schemes, Abbas turned his back upon Europe and deliberately undid all that had been attempted. His brief reign, till his murder by his slaves in July, 1854, was an interval of mere reaction to old Turkish ways. All Mehemet Ali's so-called reforms, which were largely on paper, were

ARABI PASHA, THE REBEL EGYPTIAN COLONEL
In 1881, in the early days of European control in Egypt, the discontent due to the general distress following on Ismail's extravagance, and jealousy of Turkish officers, resulted in the revolt of Arabi, which had to be suppressed by the British.

abolished, and no connection was permitted with European influence. The railway between Alexandria and Cairo, however, was undertaken, and the overland route was encouraged.

The accession of Said Pasha, on July 12th, 1854, a genial, self-indulgent, weak-minded man, who tried to improve the condition of the fellahin and gave them freehold tenure by the Land Act of 1858, paved the way for French predominance in Egypt, and especially for the influence of Ferdinand de Lesseps. The concession of the Suez

Canal, in 1856, was the event of Said's reign, though the canal was not opened till November 17th, 1869, by his successor. It was to be a purely Egyptian concern, and was to make the pasha master of the situation. As it turned out Egypt spent some £16,000,000 on it, for which she does not get a penny of interest. She gave lands, taxes, and every possible facility, and paid an iniquitous arbitration award delivered by Napoleon III. Lesseps extorted the very last pound of flesh for " my canal," with the logical and inevitable result that thirteen years after its opening Britain, the sea-power that was most interested in it, took possession in 1882. The making of the Suez Canal created an Egyptian Question which constantly embarrassed the relations of Great Britain and France till all sources of disagreement were happily removed by the Anglo-French Agreement of April 8th, 1904.

If Said Pasha's monument is his princely gift of the Canal to the French company, his successor, Ismail's (January 18th, 1863), is the Egyptian debt. Said had indeed begun it with a modest loan of £3,250,000; but Ismail raised it to the disastrous total of £80,000,000—of which it is true he received not much more than half —and contrived to run through about £130,000,000 in twelve years, with very little to show for it. That he was the sport and victim of unscrupulous roguery and unblushing swindling does not excuse his reckless extravagance and muddling finance. This ruinous debt, moreover, was contracted at a time of exceptional prosperity, when the Egyptian cotton market was supplying the loss of American cotton during the Civil War in the United States, and when a vast increase in cultivated land and every source of revenue was observed in Egypt.

An example of Ismail's and his finance minister Ismail Sadik's methods of bankruptcy was his sale of Egypt's 176,602 founder's shares in the Suez Canal to Lord Beaconsfield's Government for £4,000,000, thus depriving Egypt of her only future profit from the canal lease, and sacrificing what is now worth about £20,000,000, and brings in dividends to the amount of £700,000 a year.

Immense sums were spent upon bribery at Constantinople, in return for which Ismail obtained a series of firmans granting him the novel title of Khedive—a Persian word for "prince"—at the cost, apart from secret douceurs, of an increase of the tribute to Turkey from £60,000 to £665,000 a year. He also purchased the ports of Sawakin and Massowa in the Red Sea ; sent Sir S. Baker and afterwards General Gordon to expand and attempt to govern the Sudan ; made war upon Abyssinia in 1876, and was disastrously beaten ; and spent at least £500,000 at the state opening of the Suez Canal.

When bankruptcy stared him in the face, the European Powers intervened, and since 1875 Egypt has been under tutelage. The Goschen and Joubert mission of 1876 created the Dual Control by representatives of Great Britain and France, and established the Commission of the Debt, which controls the payment of interest and sinking fund ; but the full truth did not come out till a commission of inquiry with power to take evidence was appointed in 1878, under the presidency of Sir C. Rivers Wilson, with Lord Cromer—then Major Evelyn Baring —on the board. The result was that, after an attempt to reform the government by the introduction of the European controllers into the Ministry of Nubar Pasha, Ismail was deposed by the Sultan on the advice of the Powers, and quitted Egypt on June 30th, 1879. He was succeeded by his eldest son, Tewfik, an amiable and virtuous gentleman of thoroughly Egyptian education and tastes, who accepted the inevitable subordination of his authority to the

Dittrich

THE PRESENT KHEDIVE ABBAS II.

Who succeeded Tewfik Pasha in 1892, and followed his example of loyal support to the British administrators of Egypt.

necessities of the situation created by his father, and loyally supported the British administrators till his death, on January 7th, 1892, when his son, the present Khedive, Abbas II., followed, on the whole, but less docilely, his example, when once he had grasped the essential conditions.

The history of Egypt from 1875, however, is not the record of Khedives, but of European administrators. The Dual Control, which Ismail had summarily abolished, was revived, and the Law of Liquidation regulating the debt was enacted in July, 1880. Everything, however, was soon thrown into confusion by the Arabi mutiny. The causes of this revolt were many—popular discontent at the general poverty and distress caused by Ismail's extravagance, and set down to European influence ; the germs of national aspirations for self-rule ; discontent among the ill-fed and unpaid fellahin soldiers ; Turkish jealousy and cupidity ; and jealousy of the Circassian and Turkish officers, who were promoted to the highest grades in the army over the heads of their Egyptian comrades—all these contributed to the outbreak. But the military jealousy was the immediate cause of the appearance of a riotous mob of soldiers under Arabi and other colonels at the Abdin Palace on September 9th, 1881, which resulted in the chief mutineer's nomination in January, 1882, to office in the so-called "National" ministry of Mahmud Sami.

They immediately revived the Chamber of Deputies, and gave it the control of the finances. This, of course, brought the European Powers upon the scene, and after ineffectual protests the British and French fleets appeared off Alexandria, on May 20th, 1882, and their consuls presented an ultimatum which included the dismissal of Arabi. At the last moment the French parted company, and their fleet steamed away from Alexandria. It remained for the British to accomplish alone what the Sultan, the Powers, and the Dual Control had declined.

THE BRITISH OCCUPATION

WHEN Arabi persisted in strengthening the defences of Alexandria in defiance of the warning of the British admiral, Sir Beauchamp Seymour opened fire from the fleet on July 11th, 1882, and after ten hours' bombardment silenced the **End of the Arabi Rebellion** forts. For two days Alexandria was at the mercy of the mob, but on the 13th a force of marines and bluejackets restored order. The Khedive proclaimed Arabi a rebel, and Arabi in reply proclaimed a holy war against the " infidels." Neither the Sultan, nor the great Powers, nor France separately, though all were invited, would interfere, and Great Britain accordingly sent an army of about 30,000 men to Alexandria, July 24th, which defeated the undisciplined mob of fellahin which formed Arabi's troops at Kafr Dawar, and then swiftly occupying the Suez Canal, turned his flank, beat back an attack at Kassasin on August 28th, and crushed the rebellion on the field of Tell el-Kebir on September 13th. On the following day, Arabi and 10,000 Egyptian troops laid down their arms before two squadrons of English dragoons. He and his fellow conspirators were tried and condemned to death, but their sentence was commuted to exile to Ceylon. The British army returned home in October, leaving a garrison of 12,000 to restore and maintain order.

The British occupation was from the first intended to be temporary. Its sole object was to restore the authority of the Khedive and set his Government on its legs. There is no doubt whatever of the sincerity of Mr. Gladstone's Government in its assurance that its desire was to withdraw from Egypt as

Russell
THE MAKER OF MODERN EGYPT
Lord Cromer, who, from his appointment as British Minister in Egypt in 1891 to his retirement in 1907, was virtual ruler of Egypt.

soon as its troops were no longer needed in the interests of Egypt herself; and this sincerity was confirmed in 1886, when Lord Salisbury went out of his way to make an agreement with Turkey, fixing the future term of occupation at three years, with the right of re-entry in case events imperatively called for intervention. This agreement fell through, not from any difference between the British and Turkish Governments, but solely owing to the opposition of France and Russia to the conditional right of re-entry. The Anglo-French Agreement of 1904 has removed all sources of friction between the two nations, and British rights and interests in Egypt have been fully recognised **British Permanence in Egypt** by France. There has never been any real doubt at Paris or at Cairo that the British masked protectorate of Egypt is permanent. The first step of the British was to get rid of the Dual Control, which had proved insufficient at the crisis, and to substitute the control of a single British Financial Adviser for all matters connected with the debt and taxation. The real control, however, has rested for the past twenty-four years with the British Minister (Agent and Consul-General), Sir Evelyn Baring, created Lord Cromer in 1891, and advanced to an earldom in 1901.

From September, 1883, to his retirement in May, 1907, Lord Cromer was the virtual ruler of Egypt, and carried out all the invaluable reforms which have raised the country from bankruptcy and universal oppression and corruption to its present high pitch of prosperity and good government. He was aided by a notably able staff of British

THE BATTLE OF TELL EL-KEBIR, WHERE THE REBELLION OF ARABI PASHA WAS CRUSHED

The rebellion of Arabi Pasha was suppressed in three battles, of which Tell el-Kebir, fought on September 13, 1882, was the decisive contest, Arabi and 10,000 troops surrendering.

officials, many of whom had had experience of the most necessary kind in India ; but he was himself the true regenerator of Egypt, at once the mainspring and regulator of the whole complex machine—the man whose will was law on all vital Egyptian affairs, as much in Downing Street as at Abdin Palace, " the man who has made modern Egypt." " In less than twenty-five years, Egypt, under the guiding hand of Lord Cromer, has risen from bankruptcy and abject misery to her present state of opulence and credit. Never in all her long and varied annals have the masses of her people enjoyed as they now enjoy the blessings of a just, an orderly, and

implacable and formidable enemy in the Sudan ; and it was carried to a brilliantly successful issue without any breach of international engagements or any infringement of the Sultan's prerogative.

Lord Cromer was not a " masterful Resident " in the Indian sense. He was bound by every variety of official restriction, and his power was personal and not technically administrative, though all the administrative departments were practically under British officials, who looked to him for policy and instructions. There was, and is, also a national legislative machinery set up by Lord Dufferin, who was sent to Egypt in November, 1882,

ALEXANDRIA: THE SEAPORT OF EGYPT AND ITS OLDEST LIVING CITY

Founded about the time of Alexander the Great's occupation of Egypt, a mighty city of the Ptolemies, temporarily ruined by the Arabs and Turks, and restored to prosperity by Mehemet Ali. It was bombarded by the British in 1882.

an enlightened rule. That rule is the creation of Lord Cromer." (" Times," May 13th, 1907.) This supremely beneficial work was accomplished in the teeth of every possible difficulty—of vacillating British Governments, of constant hindrances on the part of foreign Powers, of the cramping restrictions of the Law of Liquidation—which, though modified in 1885, still kept too tight a hand on legitimate expenditure in Egypt—and gave occasion for selfish niggardliness at the hands of the other Powers, of perpetual intrigues by the Sultan, of the misrepresentations of a venomous so-called " national " Press and the menace of an

to report, and who drew up a Constitution in February, 1883, which was embodied in the Organic Law of April 30th. The Legislative Council thus created, however, is purely consultative and advisory, and the General Assembly possesses the sole but important right of a veto on fresh taxation. The representative element included in these bodies may eventually exert an educative influence, but self-government is still a long way off in Egypt. What was wanted in 1883 was a strong purpose and a clear head. " For at least six years all that could be done was to struggle against bankruptcy, to throw off the incubus of the Sudan, and, by scraping together funds in order to improve the system of irrigation, to lay the foundations of the prosperity which the country now enjoys."

The Mahdi's insurrection will be related further on. Lord Cromer's first step was the extremely unpopular one of insisting on the abandonment for the present of all attempts to regain the Sudan, which the financial position of Egypt rendered hopeless, until British help were forthcoming, and this was persistently refused.

The next step was to reorganise all the departments of government and regenerate the army and police under British officers, so far as the financial exigencies of the treasury permitted. The modification of the Law of Liquidation by the London Convention of 1885, which permitted a fresh loan of £9,000,000, and relaxed in a slight degree the onerous restrictions of the Caisse de la Dette, gave Lord Cromer a freer hand for the most necessary improvements. The repair of Mougel's ineffectual barrage of the Nile was taken in hand by Sir C. Scott Moncrieff and finished in 1890, whereby, at a cost of £420,000, the cotton crop of the Delta—which furnishes about £9,000,000 out of the total £12,000.000 of Egyptian produce annually exported—was increased by the value of nearly a million pounds a year. Scientific irrigation was the prime necessity of the country, and Anglo-Indian engineers were soon hard at work introducing improved drainage, fresh canals, and hydraulic works, and by vigilant inspection securing to every peasant equally with the richest pasha a just share of the fertilising Nile water—a wholly new feature in Egyptian water distribution. In 1898 Messrs. Aird began the great dams across

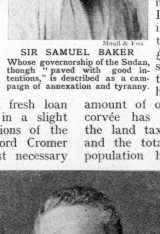

Maull & Fox

SIR SAMUEL BAKER

Whose governorship of the Sudan, though " paved with good intentions," is described as a campaign of annexation and tyranny.

Chalkley Gould

GENERAL CHARLES GORDON

The great reputation which Gordon made during his governorship of the Sudan from 1877 to 1879 led to his reappointment in 1884.

the Nile at Assouan and Asyut, which enable 750,000 acres, hitherto dry and barren in summer, to be profitably watered, with a gain of about £2,500,000 a year to the productive wealth of Egypt. The result of these measures is seen in the fact that the revenue has been growing at the rate of £500,000 a year. In 1881 it was about £9,000,000, and it has risen to £15,337,000 in 1906, leaving a surplus over expenditure of £2,175,000. In 1881 the service of the Debt cost £4,236,000, more than half the total revenue ; in 1906, although £13,000,000 more had been borrowed, the Debt cost under £3,700,000 in interest and sinking fund ; there is a reserve fund of £11,000,000, and Egyptian stock stands as high as any on the market. Yet direct taxes have been remitted to the amount of over £1,000,000 a year, the corvée has been practically abolished, the land tax reduced to 18s. an acre, and the total taxation per head of the population has fallen 20 per cent.—to 17s. 9d. Egypt is now more lightly taxed than any country in Europe.

In the same period the volume of trade has increased between two and three millions, and in 1906 reached £49,000,000, half of which was export. The population, which numbers over 11,000,000—a new census, however, is now being prepared—increased 43 per cent. between 1883 and 1897, and the traffic in passengers and goods on the hundreds of new miles of railways has doubled and trebled. A thousand miles of light railways for agricultural purposes have been widely used by the cultivators. The cotton yield, by far the most important in the country and the best and most profitable cotton crop in the world, has nearly trebled, and so has the sugar. The price of agricultural land has doubled in recent years, reaching as much as £50 an acre when sold in open competition among Egyptian purchasers; while building land in Cairo which was bought for 4s. in 1890 now fetches from £20 to more than £50 per square metre. The whole area of cultivable land is estimated at 6,000,000 acres, of which about 1,000,000 still remain unculti-vated until the irrigation system is complete. About 4,500,000 acres are held by Egyptian cultivators, and there are 1,000,000 holdings of under five acres. A quarter of the land is under cotton, which now produces 7,000,000 kantars (a kantar being roughly 100 lb.), or nearly 450 lb. an acre, and will probably be raised event-ually to 10,000,000 kantars. An Agricultural Bank has done good service in advancing loans to the peasants and rescuing them from greedy usurers. The administration of justice has been reformed by the establish-ment of the Native Tribunals organised by Sir John Scott in 1883, which have gained the respect and confidence of the people; but the Mixed Courts inaugurated in 1876 for civil causes and the Consular Courts held under the capitulations of the Turkish empire still stand in the way of progress and efficient control. Education, though still very backward among the peasantry, is making a consider-able advance. The educational budget in 1888 was only £70,000, but in 1906 it was £362,800. The number of Government schools and colleges in the same period has increased from fourteen to fifty, the teachers from 185 to 849, and pupils from 2,373 to 11,063 ; and Government inspection and grants in aid are now extended to some 4,500 village schools with an attendance of 165,000 pupils. The effects of improved educational facilities are seen in the fact that there are now about 12,000 Egyptians employed in the civil service, an increase of 3,500 in ten years, while the Europeans necessarily employed have increased by only 562, and these chiefly in the railway and irrigation branches, which require special qualifications. The regeneration of

THE TRAGIC DEATH OF GORDON AT KHARTOUM

After the rise of the Sudan Mahdi, Gordon was sent out in 1884 as Governor-General. He relied upon his personal ascendency over the people and the support of the British Government, but both failed him and he was killed by the Mahdi in 1885. From the picture by G. W. Joy, by permission of Messrs. Frost & Reid, Bristol and London.

Egypt under Lord Cromer's wise and tactful management is perhaps the most marvellous reform in Oriental history.

Since Mehemet Ali's conquest in 1820 the Sudan as far south as the Albert and Victoria Nyanza had been loosely held by Egyptian governors and garrisons, who squeezed as much money as they could out of the Sudanese peoples, and gave them nothing in return but abominable oppres-sion and slave raiding. Sir Samuel Baker's governorship in 1869 to 1873, though " paved with good intentions," was a campaign of annexation and tyranny. Gordon did some good work in the Equatorial Provinces from 1874, and when he was appointed Governor-General of the Sudan, 1877–1879, he made a great reputation, which led to his tragic end in 1885. In 1881 a fanatic of Dongola, Mohammed Ahmed, proclaimed himself "the Mahdi," or quasi-Messiah of Islam, as many a fanatic had done before him, and the whole Egyptian Sudan joyfully rose against the tax-gatherers and slave-drivers who had trampled upon them for two generations, and followed the standard of the new prophet.

Soon after the Arabi revolt had been suppressed the Egyptian Government sent General Hicks with 11,000 ill-disciplined and half-mutinous native troops to subdue the Mahdi, and the unfortunate army was annihilated near El-Obeyd in Kordofan in November, 1883. The British authorities, who, with deplorable irresolution, had neither countenanced nor forbidden this ill-starred attempt, now definitely decided that the Sudan must be abandoned, and intimated to the Khedive's Government that when advice was given it was to "be followed."

The policy of abandonment was very unpopular in Egypt and led to a change of ministry; but, in the financial situation of the country, to reconquer the Sudan without British assistance was impossible. The defeat of General Valentine Baker and 3,500 Egyptian troops by Osman Digna, or Othman Dakna, at Tokar in February, 1884, brought into strong relief the untrustworthiness of the army as then organised and the courage and élan of the "dervishes," as the Mahdi's followers were styled; though General Graham's victories at Teb and Tamanieb with British troops on February 29th and March 13th partly retrieved the disaster. In January, 1884, General Gordon was sent out by Mr. Gladstone's Government to see what

VISCOUNT WOLSELEY
When Sir Garnet Wolseley, he was in charge of the expedition sent to relieve General Gordon.

Chancellor

could be done in the Sudan. He was made Governor-General, and ordered to withdraw the Egyptian garrisons. He relied upon his personal ascendency over the people and upon the support of the British Government. Both failed him; his task proved impossible even for him. And when at last, under pressure of public opinion, the Gladstone Government sent a relief expedition in August–September under Wolseley, it started too late and took the tedious Nile route, instead of marching from Souakin to Berber, and after defeating the dervishes at Abu-Tlia on January 17th, 1885, but did not come into touch with Khartoum till it was already just in the possession of the Mahdi, who had killed Gordon on January 26th, after a heroic defence of the capital. The British expedition hastily retired, and for eleven years the Sudan was abandoned to a desolating reign of terror which left it starving, depopulated, devastated, and paralysed with fear. The Mahdi, who was a libertine and an impostor, died in June, 1885, and was succeeded by his lieutenant or Khalifa, Abdallah, who was even a worse tyrant than his master. What happened during those awful years when the Sudan was barred off from the rest of the world in impenetrable darkness we know chiefly from the records of two or three prisoners, like Slatin Pasha, who managed to escape from the Khalifa's prisons or were delivered at the reconquest.

LORD KITCHENER
Bassano
Made Commander-in-Chief of the Egyptian army in 1892. After years of training the Egyptian army he advanced on Dongola and totally destroyed the power of the Khalifa.

Reconquest was inevitable; for whoever rules Egypt must command the sources of the Nile, which forms her wealth; and the reconquest became the more imperative owing to

RESTORING THE SUDAN TO CIVILISATION: BOMBARDMENT OF KHARTOUM

After the failure of the Gordon relief expedition, the Sudan was abandoned to the desolating reign of terror of the Mahdi. Eleven years later Kitchener, advancing on Dongola, captured Khartoum, the capital, and restored it to civilisation.

French movements towards the Upper Nile at Fashoda. For four years, indeed, the utmost that could be done was to hold Wadi Halfa, with a supporting garrison at Assouan, and to improve the military and financial resources of Egypt, with the great goal of reconquest ever in mind. General Grenfell's victory with Egyptian troops over the dervishes at Toski on August 3rd, 1889, marked the beginning of confidence in the Egyptian army, which the incessant labours of Wood, Grenfell, and Kitchener were bringing to a high state of efficiency; and the defeat of Osman Digna at Afafit in 1891 at last relieved Souakin and the Red Sea littoral from pressing danger.

In 1892, Sir Herbert, now Lord, Kitchener became Sirdar or Commander-in-Chief of the Egyptian army, and after four more years of quiet but unrelaxed preparation the advance was made on Dongola in 1896; the dervishes were routed at Firkeh on June 7th, and Dongola occupied in September. A railway was rapidly thrown across the desert to Abu Hamed in 1897, and the dervishes abandoned Berber in a

OSMAN DIGNA

The leader of the Mahdi's Sudanese troops who defeated the Egyptian army under General Baker in 1884. In the reconquest of the Sudan twelve years later he was captured and imprisoned.

panic. In 1898 the Egyptian expeditionary force was stiffened with British regiments, and on April 7th, 16,000 dervishes were stormed and driven out of their entrenched zariba on the Atbara, and on September 2nd, 40,000 were totally defeated, with the loss of half their number, by 22,000 British and Egyptian troops under Kitchener in the final crushing victory of Omdurman. Khartoum was restored to civilisation. The Khalifa escaped, but was at last run to earth at Umme Dubraykat, and killed with his remaining emirs in battle by Sir Reginald Wingate, the present Sirdar, on November 24th, 1899. Kitchener went up the Nile to Fashoda immediately after the conquest of Khartoum, and found that a small expedition under Major Marchand had already hoisted the French flag there. The Egyptian flag was duly displayed, and Marchand evacuated the place in December.

A joint Anglo-Egyptian Condominium was set up in the Sudan by the Agreement of January 19th, 1899, under a Governor-General to be always appointed by the Khedive on the recommendation of the British Government; Lord Kitchener of Khartoum became the first Governor-General, and was succeeded, on his taking up a command in South Africa, by Sir R. Wingate. The reconquest of the Sudan was effected with the Anglo-Egyptian loss of only 536 killed and 1,810 wounded in the seventeen engagements between 1885 and 1899; and the cost of the Dongola and Omdurman campaign, 1896–1898, was £2,350,000, of which half was spent upon railways.

The new administration had to begin its work in a desolated desert, short of men, short of labour, short of communications, short of food. The Sudan embraces nearly a million square miles—equal to France and Germany combined—of which only 1,500 are now cultivated. The population is about 2,000,000, of whom 3,000 are European. In the eight years which have passed since the Khalifa's pandemo-

Maull & Fox

SIR REGINALD WINGATE
The present Sirdar of the Egyptian army, succeeded Lord Kitchener in the command.

nium was abolished much has been done. Railways run to Khartoum and connect Port Sudan on the Red Sea with Berber, and Kereima with Abu-Hamed. Khartoum has been rebuilt, and the Gordon College there has begun to introduce education. Domestic slavery has ceased, but the kidnapping of slaves is not easily repressed, and leads to occasional disturbances. Finances have improved, and the Sudan now costs Egypt only £130,000 a year, and is at present repaying £45,000 of this in interest on loans. In a short time the Sudan will pay its own way, and if irrigation works on a large scale are introduced it may become a valuable corn and cotton field, to say nothing of its possibilities in the way of rubber, gum, and ostrich feathers.

Whether it proves highly productive or not, its control of the upper waters of the Nile render its possession vital to Egypt.

STANLEY LANE-POOLE

THE BATTLE OF OMDURMAN: THE FORCES OF THE MAHDI ADVANCING TO THEIR DOOM

EGYPT IN OUR OWN TIME

BY STANLEY LANE-POOLE

ONE is apt to think of Egypt merely as the land of pyramids and temples, of wonderful painted tombs and mural inscriptions recording the most ancient and vigorous civilisation in the world. That is all in the past. The Egypt of our own times does not build temples, but huge dams ; and the Egypt of the future depends upon agriculture, not archæology. No country is so perfectly and naturally adapted for agriculture. The Nile, which made Egypt by scooping its groove in the desert, makes and re-makes the fecund soil every year, and the fertilising flood needs no help, except to be guided where it should go. The Egyptian might vary the Mohammedan profession of faith, from the material point of view, in the formula : "There is no god but the Nile, and the irrigation engineer is his Prophet." The one necessity in Egypt is "water, water every-**Egypt the** where," and wheresoever the **Gift of** Nile is able to deposit the rich **the Nile** slime it carries along in its 3,300 miles course, there one can sow and reap three crops in the year from the generous earth. The old saying of the Father of History that Egypt is the gift of the Nile is as true to-day as it was two-and-a-half millenniums ago ; the only difference is that the gift is better understood and more abundantly enjoyed. The pity is that the Nile did not bore a wider valley while it was about it, and that so much of its precious water, in spite of dams and canals, runs away to waste in the Mediterranean Sea. For Egypt Proper, from the first cataract at Assouan to Alexandria, is so narrow a strip of cultivable land that it contains but 6,500,000 acres, and the total area of the country is but 12,000 square miles, or little more than a third of the size of Ireland. Yet this little strip of land is so rich that it can not only support its population of 11,000,000, but sends away to foreign countries produce

and goods to the value of close on £25,000,000.

The scenery is monotonous and derives the charm that painters try to catch chiefly from atmospheric effects. But for its historic monuments and its vivifying, **Where** rejuvenating desert air, Egypt **Mud is** would never have become the **Precious** resort of the hordes of tourists who annually flock there. After forcing its passage through the granite and syenite rocks of the first cataract, the river, usually about half a mile wide, pursues a naturally uninterrupted and almost unvaried course down the 700 miles to the sea, save where engineering invention has dammed its waters by the great weirs at Esne and Asyut, and the barrage below Cairo. Sometimes it cuts the valley—never more than ten miles across and often much less—into two equal parts, but more often it hugs the eastern boundary hills and spreads over the western plain its deep alluvial deposit, that famous Nile mud, which is the one reason why Egypt is not as barren as the thirsty desert out of which it was scooped. The scene is always much the same till we reach the Delta. In the midst, the dull, brownish, rapid stream ; on each side the high, brown, mud banks, here and there topped by a ruined temple or rude mud village with its white mosque or saint's tomb ; beyond, the fields of corn or beans or lupin ; and still further the rocky barrier formed by the slopes of the desert edge, long, low, red, grey, and **On the** dun-coloured ranges of bare **Slopes of** sandstone and limestone hills, **the Desert** smooth and tame as the Sussex Downs, but without a trace of vegetation, and only rarely rising, as near Thebes, to something like mountainous height and outline. Beyond these bordering hills lies nothing but the hard rocky plateau of the desert, sprinkled with sand and grit and varied here and there at long distances by green oases fed by infiltration from the same fertilising river.

The striking want in Egyptian scenery is shade. Excepting comparatively recent plantations near towns, palms are the only trees of importance, though sparse sycamores and acacias, and willows and tamarisk, are to be seen, besides occasional

Egypt a Shadeless Land forest trees of different species ; and this lack of cover accounts for the absence of any wild beasts of size. Hyenas, jackals, wolves, foxes, etc., abound in desert spots, but the great beasts of prey are not found. The crocodile has followed the hippopotamus further south, in the vain hope of escaping European rifles ; but Egypt makes up in her plagues of insects, reptiles, and vermin for the loss of the larger man-eaters. The domestic animals are the camel, horse, and ass for burthen, the buffalo and shorthorn cattle for field-

dirty, pot-bellied, blear-eyed little children. It is also the home of the only man who really works in Egypt, outside the over-worked Civil Service, for in these tumbledown mud cabins feeds and sleeps the fellah, the agricultural labourer, who in olden times built all the monuments, and in modern times makes the canals and dikes and dams and roads and railways, and fights dervishes—in short, does almost everything manual that has to be done.

He used to do all this under the corvée system of forced unpaid labour, and often died like a fly in the process ; driven to work by the lash and made to pay extortionate taxes, often his defaulting neighbour's as well as his own, on pain of severe floggings on the soles of the feet. Now he is paid like any other free man, and the only time when forced labour is demanded, to the extent of a few thousands instead of hundreds of thousands of labourers, is

THE GREAT NILE DAM : SOUTH SIDE OF THE ASYUT BARRAGE

work, and the sheep and goat for food. Dogs, like pigs, are held unclean animals, but are a pest to the traveller, and swarm, like the cats, in every town and village.

Towns of any size from a European standard are few, but villages are everywhere and are all very much alike, standing some little way back from the river or a canal, and looking much more ruinous than the oldest temples. They are built of mud or sun-dried brick, and the houses —or rather hovels—are constantly falling, and no one dreams of removing the débris. You climb a mound, or push through a gap between high mud walls, and find yourself in a sort of square, perhaps with a few palm-trees and with mud benches or divans round it, and with the headman or sheikh's house, often a hut, at one side. The rest is a tangle of hovels. The village is the home of smells, mosquitoes, and

when an exceptional flood of the Nile requires exceptional efforts to restrain it from carrying destruction over the land. The British régime has abolished the kurbag, with many other abuses. In the old days the fellah was the serf of the pasha, held his plot of land at the pasha's will, and did not know what tax he had to pay or how much. All he knew was

How Britain Has Helped the Fellahin that he had to pay a great deal more than he possessed, before his crops were ready to be sold, and that he must therefore either sell his corn standing, at a ruinous loss, or borrow from the local money-lender at a fabulous rate of interest. Now he holds his land in fee simple, knows exactly what taxes he has to pay, and that they are not to be paid till after harvest ; and if he finds himself short of money, he has only to go to the Agricultural Bank—

THE GREAT DAM AT ASSOUAN NEAR THE FIRST CATARACT OF THE NILE

one of Lord Cromer's invaluable improvements—and he will get an advance on reasonable terms. In 1906, some 90,000 loans, amounting to £3,500,000, were thus contracted, and the arrears unpaid at the close of the year were only 5 per cent.

The fellah is thus solvent, and if any local official tries extortion of any sort, he knows well enough that an appeal to "Krumar"—*i.e.*, to the embodiment of justice—will protect him. Consequently, he is, as a rule, contented, so far as any Hodge ever was; and as the fellahin, with their families, form four-fifths of the population of Egypt, and a million fellahin now occupy small holdings of less than five acres, the improvement in their status is the best and most important result of recent reforms. The fellah is a fine specimen of a man, and a very hard worker; he does not drink, of course, being a Moslem, and his chief faults are those due to centuries of virtual slavery: he may steal and lie, and cringe, and like all poor men, he is apt to be avaricious. He is extremely obstinate, and firmly believes that his own way is the best. But he is good-natured, kind—except to his beasts— tractable if not rubbed the wrong way, and enjoys a joke and a laugh, and a

A TOWN OF MODERN EGYPT: ASYUT, THE SITE OF A NILE BARRAGE

social evening over the pipes in the village square. The women, who are slightly less numerous than the men, are well-made, slender, and graceful, and do their full share of labour in the fields, and especially in carrying water. Polygamy does not seem to weigh much upon them, partly because it is rare ; comparatively

Certainty of Egypt's Seasons few Egyptians can afford to keep several wives, but easy divorce, for no valid cause, is an unquestionable evil.

The fellah has the immense advantage of knowing exactly what to do in any given month. He is not at the mercy of uncertain seasons, and the only uncertainty that exists for him, a deficiency of the Nile flood, has been almost wholly abolished by the present system of scientific irrigation. The old system of basin irrigation, when whole fields lay under the Nile water in winter and were insufficiently drained, and then left fallow in the summer, or watered only to a small extent by a laborious chain of hand-pump (shadufs, see page 1632) and water-wheels (sakiyehs) has given place, or is giving place, to perennial irrigation of all lands by canals fed from the huge reservoirs of water now dammed up on the Nile, and to a proper system of land drainage. The time is coming when all the land, and not only the flat Delta as usually heretofore, will be capable of bearing its three crops in the year. So long as the Nile reaches the land, there is no difficulty about seasons. They rotate with the regularity of clockwork, or of the river which governs them. The Nile, flooded by the equatorial rains, begins to rise in June, reaches its greatest height (about 36 feet at Thebes) about the autumnal equinox, and gently falls for the remaining nine months. It is more or less high Nile from July to February, and low Nile from February to the end of June. Winds and temperature follow the Nile. From June to February the pre-

The Nile's Fixed Time-table vailing wind is from the north ; from February to June it is generally from the south, sometimes rising to a hurricane and sandstorm (samum) ; but in March and April one may expect the parching dust-winds called Khamasin or Pentecostals. The thermometer gradually rises from low Nile in April, till it reaches 109° Fahr. in the shade in Upper Egypt, and 95° in the Delta, and then slowly cools till it falls to a minimum of 40° and 35°

respectively about Christmas. The dry air renders the heat comparatively inoppressive in the upper country, but it is much less bearable as one descends towards the Mediterranean, where mists and damp become more frequent. Freezing is rare, but the nights are often cold, and a drop of 20° in the temperature in a few hours is not unknown.

Everything proceeds with such regularity that the agricultural calendar may be fixed to a day. The fellah knows exactly when he can sow his great crops of wheat and barley and beans and clover, or his cotton and rice and indigo ; or, again, his broad fields of maize and millet—the dura, which forms the staple of his essentially vegetarian diet. It is true that scientific irrigation has changed some of his ideas, and he finds he can grow more valuable crops and use his land to better advantage than formerly ; yet it is but the change from old style to new style, and the regularity of rotation remains a settled fact which may be implicitly relied upon. The old distinction between *rey* and *sharaki* lands will naturally vanish when

Egypt's Splendid Future perennial irrigation is available everywhere. The wealth of Egypt as an essentially agricultural country will exceed even its present marvellous development, and with a further reduction in his present comparatively light taxation, which must follow the adequate taxation of foreigners as soon as more of the unjust privileges secured by the capitulations are relaxed, the fellah freeholder on his small peasant proprietorship will have nothing to complain of. It is to be hoped that he will eventually learn to read and write, for in 1897 about 98 per cent. of the population were returned as illiterate, and until education has made much more progress among the people of all classes it is idle to talk about representative institutions and national self-government.

In the towns, of course, there is an educated class, though a very small one, and in spite of the efforts of the Education Department under Fakhri and Artin Pashas, and their adviser, Mr. Dunlop, during the past twenty years—struggling, it must be said, with a necessarily inadequate grant—it is well known that the supply of educated young Egyptians for employment in the Civil Service falls far short of the demand. The larger towns and the two cities of Egypt are chiefly the

CAIRO SHOPKEEPERS

LEMONADE SELLERS

The streets and bazaars of the native quarter of Cairo are almost unrivalled in the East for the variety and interest of their scenes of daily life. The types here illustrated are among the most familiar. These lemonade vendors and shopkeepers tolerate and profit by the European invasion of their town but remain at heart true Orientals.

CAIRO CRAFTSMEN ENGAGED ON THE FAMOUS MUSHARABYAH WORK

There is nothing more characteristic of Arab craftsmanship than the beautiful work in ivory and wood of these carvers, who use their left feet to help in the carving operation and are thus known as the "three-handed men."

TYPES OF THE EGYPTIAN PEOPLE OF TO-DAY

creations of Europeans. Even Cairo, the capital, with its history of nearly a thousand years, recalled by a long series of exquisite Saracenic monuments, is now mainly a European city, and tourists are apt to call the true Egyptian quarters

European Character of Cairo "the bazars." One may well regret the progress which has converted the picturesque city of the Mamelukes into what has been, somewhat ambitiously, termed "a bastard Paris," but there can be no question that the change corresponds with the general progress of the country in material prosperity. Without Europeans Egypt would be in the same slough of poverty and backwardness as Asiatic Turkey. It is not merely the horde of tourists who pour money into the country every winter, but the more or less regular winter residents who come to Egypt, and especially to such health resorts as Helwan on the desert border near Cairo, or Luxor up the Nile, for the sake of a warm, dry climate. There is besides a permanent European population, numbering in 1897 about 112,000, of whom a third belonged to the quick-witted commercial class of Levantines—a somewhat notorious element in Egyptian town life. Italians come next in number, and then British and French, the Army of Occupation forming about half the English colony.

The other nationalities are represented in comparatively small numbers, and there were less than 300 resident Americans in Egypt in 1897. The increasing European element, practically an importation (save the Levantines) of the past century, has, of course, profoundly modified the life in the two great cities of Cairo and Alexandria, and has had its influence in most of the fifteen towns that have more than 12,000 inhabitants. Railways, tramcars, post and telegraph offices, have done their part in changing the old Egyptian ways.

Yet one may question whether the Europeanising process has got far beneath the skin as yet. "The East changes very

"The Good Old Days" slowly, and the soul of the Eastern not at all. The Cairo jeweller, who will chaffer with you over a few piastres, though he mixes reluctantly, shrinkingly, in the crazy, bustling twentieth century life of Europe that rushes past him, is not of it. In his heart of hearts he looks back longingly to the glorious old days of the Mamelukes, to which he essentially belongs,

and regrets the excitement of those stirring times. What good, he asks, comes of all this worry ? Justice ? More often a man had a need of a little injustice, and a respectable tradesman could usually buy that from the Kadi before these new tribunals were set up ! As to fixed taxes and no extortion, that is chiefly a matter for the stupid fellahin ; and, after all, the old system worked beautifully when you shirked payment, and your neighbour was bastinadoed for your share. Then all this fiddling with water and drains and streets What is it all for ? When Willcocks or Price Bey have put pipes and patent traps and other godless improvements into the mosques, will one's prayers be any better than they were in the pleasant pervasive odour of the old fetid tanks ? The streets are broader, no doubt, to let the Firingis (Allah blacken their faces !) roll by in their two-horse Arabiyas and splash the Faithful with mud ; but for this wonderful boon they have taken away the comfortable stone benches from before the shops and the Cairo tradesman misses his old seat, where unlimited keyf and the medita-

Sanitation versus Romance tive shibuk once whiled away the leisure of his never-pressing avocations. No ; pure water and drains, and bicycles and tramcars, and a whole array of wretched little black-coated Efendis, pretending to imitate the Kafirs, may be all very well in their place, but they are ugly, uninteresting things, and life at Cairo has been desperately dull since they came in ! Life undoubtedly was interesting in the old unregenerate days. There were events then, something to see and think of, and possibly fly from, plenty of blood and assassination, perhaps ; but then you could always shut and bar the strong gates of the Quarter, when the Mamelukes or the Berbers, or, worst of all, the black Sudanis were on the war-path. Now, the gates are taken away, and there are no cavalcades of romantic troopers, beautiful to behold in their array, to ravish your household and give colour to life. In those days it was possible for any man of brain and luck to rise to power and wealth, such wealth as Cairo could not furnish in these blank and honest times. Promotion was ever at hand, and the way was open to the strong, the cunning, and the rich. What were a holocaust of victims, an orgy of rapine, even the deadly ravages of periodical plague and famine, in comparison with the

ONE OF THE MOST WONDERFUL SIGHTS IN CAIRO: THE ARAB UNIVERSITY

Here Arabs meet in thousands to equip themselves for the priesthood. This picture shows the great courtyard of the University. The hall inside is probably as large as the courtyard, and has hundreds of columns. At the foot of each column sits a professor with students about him. Their education consists almost entirely of reading the Koran.

endless opportunities, the infinite variety of those unruly and tumultuous, but never tedious, days?"

Such are probably the views of a great many old-fashioned townspeople and conservative officials and pashas—of all, in fact, who have been deprived of their old opportunities of corruption and thieving. They are not the views of the "enlightened" Cairene, or of the vast body of the peasantry, who now realise the advantages of British administration. Still, conservatism is the keynote of Eastern character, and he would be a rash man who should prophesy cheerfully concerning the pouring of new wine into old bottles. The outward and material reforms in Egypt are manifest to all, but how far these unquestioned benefits have modified the ideas and prejudices of the natural Cairene it is impossible to judge. There are, in fact, two Cairos—the Cairo of the hotels and tourists and busy progressive European life, and again the Cairo that, not a stone's throw away, branching off at the end of the Muski' street, where you will come across scenes that might occur in "The Thousand and

The Changeless East

One Nights," the same historic costume the same veiled women, the fierce-looking Bedouins, the strings of camels loaded with country produce, the water-carrier, the wedding procession and circumcision pomp —nothing seems to be changed—and the pungent smell of the East—a smell unmistakable — pervades it all. The little cupboard-like shops are still there, only the shopkeeper smokes cigarettes instead of five-foot-long pipes, but he is as lazy and indifferent to business, as calm and impenetrable, as ever. He is exactly the same sort of person as looked upon the caliph Harun al-Rashid when he went rambling at night, or who listened to the Barber's interminable stories, for the "Arabian Nights" are essentially Cairene in their descriptions of life and manners.

Life in Old Cairo

The very aspect of the more out-of-the-way streets has little altered in centuries, though they have lost the awnings which once shaded them, and the beautiful lattice windows (meshrebiyas) are fast disappearing. But they are still narrow and dusty and filthy, and after rain indescribably muddy—and incom-

2179

parably picturesque. Most of Cairo is modern, but there are still some of the older, almost mediæval, houses remaining, and a few ruined palaces of the Mameluke emirs, besides the exquisite mosques and tombs, colleges, convents and sebils, in and around the city which record the munificence and taste, the piety and

Wonderful Saracenic Buildings fear of judgment, of a whole series of lords and sultans, from the mosque of the conqueror Amr in " Old Cairo " to the Turkish minarets of Mehemet Ali's mosque on the citadel. Many of these are mere ruins, and most would have almost disappeared by now but for the resolute efforts of the committee which has watched over them for the past quarter of a century and, under the skilled supervision of its architect, Herz Bey, has expended as much as £8,000 to £12,000 a year on the repair and occasionally the complete restoration of these priceless monuments of Saracenic art. The skill which built and adorned them with carvings and mosaics, plaster mouldings and marble, enamelled glass, and chased metal-work inlaid with silver and gold, has long departed, though there are signs in the restoration that work almost, if not quite, equal to the original, can be executed by Herz Bey's craftsmen ; and it is possible that the European demand may in a measure revive the lost arts of Cairo. As it is, apart from a few workshops in the capital, there is very little of art industry in Egypt. Coarse earthenware, coarse textiles, rude brass and copper work there is in plenty ; but the looms no longer turn out the wondrous iridescent silks of the Fatemid period, and fine ceramic and the damascene art are for the present extinct.

Whatever the future of Egypt may be, it will depend upon its Mohammedan agricultural population directed by British

Decadence of the Copts science. It will not be sensibly affected by the native Christians, who form a very small minority. The Copts scarcely seem to take their full share in the general progress of Egypt. Once they were almost the sole source from which the inferior Government officials were taken, since they alone as a rule possessed the necessary skill in book-keeping. Now, though they are under no disabilities, they are generally supplanted by Mohammedans.

They have the reputation, rightly or wrongly, of being more ignorant and less trustworthy than their Moslem contemporaries, and certainly their priests do not set them a good example in learning or in civilisation. They have extremely interesting churches and monasteries, where the same rites and liturgies are celebrated in the same tongue as in the fifth century ; but the Coptic Church has been torn by factions, and its state is not hopeful.

The future lies with the Moslems, who form 90 per cent. of the population. That these will justify in a material sense the wise expenditure of capital and intelligence which has brought such extraordinary prosperity to their land cannot be doubted. Whether there will be any revival of a really national or at least Arabic culture remains to be seen. There are signs of some such revival in Arabic studies ; but that splendid old monument of Arab learning, in its most restricted and conservative limits, the Azhar University, has not so far favoured an enlargement of its old curriculum, and its prejudice against all European innovations is un-

Future of Egypt diminished. A new university for Egypt might work wonders. The more Egyptians take an interest in culture and in public affairs the better ; and it is only an inevitable part of the movement that some of the half educated but ambitious spirits should jump at power for which they are at present unqualified. The reins must remain firmly in the hands of the tutelary Power, and the really interesting problem of the immediate future is how long Britain will continue to accept her present anomalous position instead of assuming openly the protectorate which she has already exerted under an unofficial mask for a quarter of a century. For a long time the progress of Egypt was held back by the uncertainty of an indefinite British occupation. That uncertainty has been removed by a series of events, and lastly by the Anglo-French Agreement. But international fetters and a few obsolete restrictions still check advance. Egypt has been freed by Britain from bankruptcy and corrupt tyranny and brought to a marvellous pitch of prosperity, justice and order. It remains to be seen whether the last remaining fetters of the old régime cannot be snapped.

STANLEY LANE-POOLE

ESSENTIAL INFORMATION ABOUT EGYPT

AREA. Egypt proper, including the five oases of the Libyan desert and the territory between the Red Sea and the Nile, but excluding the Sudan, is about 400,000 square miles. The Nile valley and the Delta, which are the cultivated districts, have an area of only 12,976 square miles. Egypt is divided into two great districts—Lower Egypt, or Masr-el-Bahri, and Upper Egypt, or El-Said. The area of the Egyptian Sudan is estimated at 950,000 square miles.

POPULATION. The last Egyptian census was taken in 1897 and showed a population of 9,734,405, of whom 9,020,404 were settled natives, 601,427 were Bedouins, and 112,574 were foreigners. The chief elements in the foreign population were 38,175 Greeks, 24,467 Italians, 19,557 British, 14,155 French, 7,117 Austro-Hungarians, and smaller numbers of Russians, Germans, Persians, etc. The principal towns in Egypt proper, with their populations at the census of 1897, are : Cairo, 570,062 ; Alexandria, 319,766 ; Tantah, 57,289 ; Port Said, 42,095 ; Asyut, 42,078 ; Zagazig, 35,715 ; Mansourah, 36,131 ; and Damietta, 31,515. The population of the Egyptian Sudan is estimated at 2,000,000, including 3,104 Europeans. The chief towns are Khartoum, 14,023, and Omdurman, 40,000.

GOVERNMENT. Egypt is nominally dependent on Turkey, and pays an annual tribute of £720,000, but except by receiving yearly payment Turkey does not participate officially in the conduct of Egyptian affairs. Egypt is under a hereditary sovereign known as the Khedive, the present ruler being Abbas Hilmi, who succeeded in 1892, and is the seventh in the dynasty of Mehemet Ali. The administration is conducted by native Ministers subject to the Khedive. Associated in the government of Egypt is a British financial adviser, who has a seat on the council of Ministers and without whose consent no decision can be taken on matters of finance. The British Government, thus having through the resident adviser control of Egyptian finance, is in effect the paramount power, and is responsible for the amazing growth of national prosperity during the last two decades. The Anglo-French agreement of 1904 put the seal of permanency on British influence in Egypt.

REVENUE AND EXPENDITURE. The national revenue for 1906 was £E15,337,294 and the expenditure £E12,124,822. The £E equals £1 0s. 6¼d. sterling. The chief sources of revenue are the land taxes, the railways, customs, and tobacco.

NATIONAL DEBT. The Egyptian National Debt stands at £96,483,880, and the annual charge is £E3,615,857 not including tribute to Turkey.

INDUSTRY AND COMMERCE. Two-thirds of the population of Egypt is engaged in agriculture. The chief products are cotton, sugar, rice, maize, millet, wheat, barley, and other cereals and vegetables. There are usually three crops annually, the chief winter crops being cereals, the chief summer crops being cotton, sugar, and rice, and the chief autumn crops being rice,

cereals and vegetables. Egypt has the largest systems of artificial irrigation in the world, the storage capacity of the Assouan reservoir basin above the dam being 234,000,000 gallons. There has been little done in mining, but the prospects of Egyptian mining are engaging attention. A mining department has been organised, and there is considerable prospecting and some mining, the operations at present employing about 1,500 people. Gold and copper are found, and coal and oil are also being investigated. The exports of Egyptian cotton, which commands a higher price than any other variety, have reached an annual value of over £20,000,000. The other principal exports are cereals and tobacco. The total exports in 1906 reached the value of £24,877,280, and the total imports the value of £24,010,795. Great Britain purchases over 50 per cent. of the exports, and supplies about 33 per cent. of the imports.

CURRENCY. The monetary unit is the gold Egyptian pound of 100 piastres, usually indicated by the sign £E. It weighs 8·5 grammes ·875 fine, thus containing 7·4375 grammes of fine gold, and being of the value of £1 0s. 6¼d. sterling. The piastre is worth 2·46 pence and is subdivided into tenths (ochr'el guerche). The coins in circulation are : bronze, $\frac{1}{40}$ and $\frac{1}{20}$ piastre ; nickel, $\frac{1}{10}$, $\frac{1}{5}$, $\frac{1}{2}$, and 1 piastre ; silver, 1, 2, 5, 10, and 20 piastres ; and gold 1 pound. The gold circulating in Egypt, however, is almost exclusively English sovereigns.

WEIGHTS AND MEASURES. The metrical system of weights and measures is standard, but is compulsory only in public and governmental transactions. The native weights are local and vary greatly.

POSTAGE RATES. Great Britain to Egypt. Conditions and rates for letters and papers are as for New Zealand [see page 1002] except that the limit of weight for printed and commercial papers is 4 lb. and the limit weight of samples 12 oz. For parcel post, per P. and O. direct line, which takes 14 days to Alexandria and 13 days to Port Said, the rate is 1/-, 2/- and 3/- for 3, 7 and 11 lb. respectively. The rate via Italy, which takes 9 days to Alexandria and 8 days to Port Said is 1/- per package more than above rates. Limit of length is 3½ feet and limit of length and girth is 6 feet.

PATENTS. There is no patent act in Egypt, but it is customary for inventors to register the specification with drawings of their inventions at the Mixed Courts in Cairo, Alexandria and Mansourah—preferably in all three. These Courts have jurisdiction in disputes between foreigners and between foreigners and natives. Specification should be in French, or, if in English, should be accompanied by a certified translation in French, Italian, or Arabic.

TRADE MARKS. Trade Marks may be registered at the Mixed Courts in Cairo, Alexandria or Mansourah—preferably in all three. Each registration should be accompanied by a certificate of registration in the country of origin, and a legalised power certified by the Foreign Office of the home country.

Young Moor

A Lady of Morocco

Kabyle of Morocco

Arab Woman of Algeria

Kabyle Woman

Woman of South Morocco

Jews of Tangiers

TYPES OF THE PEOPLES OF MEDITERRANEAN NORTH AFRICA

MEDITERRANEAN NORTH AFRICA

BY DR. HEINRICH SCHURTZ

THE COUNTRY AND ITS INHABITANTS

MEDITERRANEAN Africa is divided into two sharply defined geographical regions, an eastern and a western. In the east the coast line sinks back to the south; in the west it juts out towards the north; and while on the eastern edge the desert regions extend to the sea, in the western and projecting part there rises a country of mighty mountains with snow - covered peaks and foaming torrents, and of fertile valleys and well-watered plains. Here, then, tribes of agriculturists could develop into powerful nations, while the east is the home only of nomads. Only at one point in the eastern coast, in modern Tripoli, just where the tableland

East and West

of Barca projects like a peninsula into the sea, lies a feeble counterpart of the western mountainous region, an agricultural district formerly the possession of the once flourishing Greek colony of Cyrene.

But if the coast-line in the east as an independent country is at a disadvantage compared with the west, it has some counterbalancing features. First, it is situated nearer to the ancient civilised countries and came comparatively earlier under their influence; and, secondly, owing to the deep bays that indent its coast, it is the favoured starting-point and terminus of the entire Sudan trade, which is again facilitated by the convenient position of numerous oases. It is no accident that the two most powerful ancient commercial cities of

North Africa, Carthage and Cyrene, flourished in the vicinity of the Syrtes.

Communication with the Sudan was in ancient times probably less difficult than at present. There is no doubt that

Sahara Not Always a Desert

there has been an unfavourable change in the climate. In the northern Sahara especially, the calcareous deposits of dried-up springs, the traces of a formerly richer flora, but, above all, the remains of human settlements in regions now completely uninhabited, speak only too clear a language and assure us that even the deficiency of water in the Algeria of to-day as compared with that of Roman times is not to be referred merely to the decay of artificial irrigation, but must have deeper causes. But if North Africa and, above all, the desert was once better watered and more habitable than it is to-day, then communication also with negritic Africa must have been easier than now, notwithstanding that in early antiquity the camel was not known to the tribes of North Africa. The commercial position of Carthage, as of Cyrene, rested, indeed, to a great extent on intercourse with the Sudan. In Roman times this traffic appears to lessen or completely to cease; the Arabic era first roused it to fresh activity. Parallel with climatic changes there is in the course of history no lack of topographical changes: the rising of the Tunisian coast, which caused many of the famous harbours of antiquity to be silted up, is to be especially mentioned. On the other hand, the shore of the peninsula of Barca is steadily sinking.

Climatic changes, as well as the passion for hunting, have also exercised great influence on the animal life of North Africa : elephants and hippopotami, which were formerly numerous, have now disappeared. And a plant which once was

Vanished Source of Wealth of the highest importance for a part of North Africa, the famous silphium, which grew in the district of Cyrene, and the juice from the root of which was worth its weight in silver in ancient Rome, is no longer to be found, and has not been rediscovered even in other parts of the world. The silphium was one of the chief sources of the wealth of the ancient Cyreneans. As we see it represented on the coins of the town, we know that it belonged to the group of the umbelliferæ. The writings of the ancients tell us of the manifold uses of this healing juice, which was nowhere prepared so excellently as at Cyrene. Whether the plant has been extirpated or whether it has disappeared before the change of climate can no longer be determined.

The existence of a prehistoric population in the Sahara is demonstrated by numerous stone implements which have often been found in quite isolated and now uninhabitable spots of the desert. In historic times, the first accounts do not, any more than any other results of investigation, justify the assumption that before the invasion of the Phœnicians, Greeks and Romans a homogeneous population filled North Africa. If we collect the different accounts and compare them with the conditions of the present day, we can distinguish no fewer than four old races which were permanently settled there, and their descendants, mixed with subsequent comers, maintain even now for the most part their original homes. In the first place, we must name the light-complexioned, fair-haired

Ancient Peoples of the North Libyans, who are often mentioned by the old geographers and historians as inhabiting both the district bordering on Egypt and the tableland of Barca and the places on Lake Triton. They exercised influence on Egypt itself. Especially at the time of the Ethiopian sovereignty we find fair-haired Libyans as dynasts in the Delta. They seem to have been a physically well-built and intellectually gifted race.

Descendants of these " blonds " are found even at the present day in North Africa especially among the Kabyles of the Rif, or Morocco, in such large numbers that for a long time it was thought that the remnants of the German Vandals had been rediscovered ; although, in reality, the fair-haired population of Africa existed long before the migration of the Germanic nations—indeed, before the beginning of historical tradition. Another remnant of this blond race were the Guanches in Teneriffe.

The Canary Islands have served more than once as a refuge for the population of the continent when hard pressed by newcomers. The Guanches, when they first came into contact with Europeans, were still completely in the Stone Age. They knew the use of the mattock, and bred sheep and goats, but did not use the plough or understand how to make bread. In addition to the Guanches, other races have inhabited the Canaries.

The fair-haired African race does not stand apart from the other races. It is very probably identical with that tall,

Fair-Haired Africans long-headed people which was once settled in Western Europe, and which is usually designated the Cro-Magnon race after the chief place where remains of bones have been found. Assuming, then, the relationship of the fair-haired Libyans with the people of Cro-Magnon to be generally admitted, the original homes of the race may have been in North Africa ; this is the more probable, since the megalithic monuments of North Africa are apparently older than those of Western Europe. The hypothesis which accounts for these races as of Celtic origin hardly demands discussion.

Together with, and perhaps before, the fair-haired race, another light-complexioned, but dark-haired and short-headed, race appears to have existed in North Africa. The earliest inhabitants of the Canary Islands seem, at any rate, to have belonged to this dark-haired people, sometimes referred to as " Armenoides." These, it can hardly be doubted, have close affinities with those dark-haired pre-Aryans of Southern Europe, who were later influenced by the immigrating Aryans and robbed of their individual characteristics, but continued to live among the main body of the population of Southern Europe.

We can mention only briefly the traces which point to the existence in the steppes and oases of North Africa of a stunted race, probably related to the bushmen and the dwarf tribes of the rest of Africa. The inhabitants of the oasis of Tidicelt were expressly described by the ancients as being of small stature. Other tribes, such as Troglodytes and Garamantes, may have intermingled with the pigmy peoples who then, perhaps, roamed about the Sahara, as the Bushmen still do in the Kalahari. In many national types of the present day the last remnants of the dwarf race, greatly changed by intermixture, may still be pointed out.

Far more important for the history of Africa was the effect wrought on racial conditions by another cause. If the Libyans, the "Armenoides," and even the stunted tribes, were comparatively fair complexioned, we now see a ruddy-skinned people appear in Egypt as the possessors of a primitive civilisation, which they develop later in Ethiopia and Abyssinia. In quite early times they spread westward. Ultimately all North Africa receives from them its ethnographical and linguistic characteristics, and a new race is formed—that of the Berbers. This people, then, constitutes the core of the present Hamitic population, which, as the "Atlantic race," it is usual to contrast with the negroes on the one hand, and the Aryans and Semites on the other. The ancient name of "Ethiopians" is the most appropriate for them.

Who are the True Ethiopians?

The Ethiopians must have come later than the previously mentioned races to Northern Africa, with the exception, naturally, of Egypt, where they were settled from the first beginnings of civilisation. A certain affinity of the Ethiopian languages with the Semitic, the accounts handed down of their ancient history, and even the conditions of the people at the present day, make us suppose that the original homes of the Ethiopians may have been in Eastern Africa. There they received the stimulus of Asiatic civilisation, which they carried further westward, together with the acquisitions of Egyptian culture. North Africa became Ethiopian only within the course of authentic history.

But even though the races blend, the population of North Africa will always separate afresh into two, or better into three, component parts, made necessary by the nature of the country itself, and distinct in their characteristics. No contrast of language or bodily structure is so thorough or so indestructible as that between the nomad of the steppe and the agriculturist who inhabits the fertile plains and the mountain valleys ; as civilisation gradually develops, a third distinct type arises—the town-dweller, who makes his livelihood by industry and trade. These contrasts are so effectual that the individual countries of North Africa, to say nothing of the whole region, have never become political unities in the sense of European states. Morocco is, in reality, a marvellous conglomeration of partially or entirely dependent tribal districts, together with others that are practically independent.

Races That Don't Mix

All three elements of the population advanced in civilisation as time went on. The agriculturist, probably under the influence of Ethiopian immigration, exchanged the mattock for the plough. The nomad at an early period made use of the ox ; later, during the dynasty of the Hyksos in Egypt, of the horse ; and, finally, in Roman times, of the camel. The town-dwellers finally received, through trade and traffic, ample materials of culture. But they were recruited by new immigrations and changed their national life and character.

The mere enumeration of the numerous shocks from the outside which North Africa has had to bear patiently explains at once the tremendous changes the country has undergone. As colonisers the Greeks appeared on the eastern, the Phœnicians on the western, coasts ; and the supremacy of the Romans and Byzantines did not fail to influence greatly the mixture of nationalities. Then a stream of fair-haired Germans pressed over the Straits of Gibraltar and held the new possessions for a century. More important and more lasting than all previous influences was that exercised upon the inhabitants of North Africa by the invasion of the Arabs and the spread of Islam. The Arabs were followed by the Turks. Finally, the civilised nations of Europe appeared in the field and undertook to forge anew out of that region sunk in savagery another link in that chain of civilised states which had once circled the Mediterranean and had been snapped by the adherents of Islam.

North Africa's Tremendous Changes

Thus the history of North Africa in its recorded form is little else than the struggle of the native Berbers against foreign intruders. Sometimes they almost succumb ; the lords of the North African coast wear the Carthaginian dress or the burnous of the Arab ; then, again, they show their indestructible vitality, and genuine Berber states arise where formerly foreign colonisers had the power in their hands. In mediæval and modern times have come the Jews, the detested and yet indispensable traders of the kingdom of Morocco and of the old Barbary states, of whose immigration, as almost everywhere else, there is nothing definite to be said, it being sufficient that they are there.

The Detested Jews

They seem fit and ready to play, in their way, an important part in the civilising of North Africa by European nations : in fact, they are the only component part of the population which knows how to conform itself externally to European ideas and to derive profit from the advantages of our culture without acknowledging its moral claims.

Apart from the migrations in Roman times, the stream of European blood which has been poured into the veins of the North Africans is not inconsiderable. When the Moors retreated from Spain a large number of them settled in North Africa and gradually mixed with the natives. But the Moors had just formed in Spain a united nation out of native Iberian, Arabic, Berber, and even North European elements : they were not only in their civilisation but also in their ethnical composition a connecting link between the world of Islam and that of Western Europe. Still more important, perhaps, was the influx of European slaves of both sexes which, from the Middle Ages down to modern times, had been directed into the Barbary states by the constant expeditions of the corsairs inhabiting the North African coasts, an element much more easily absorbed, owing to the Mohammedan institution of the harem. Besides this, many European renegades appear in the military history of North Africa.

The White Slaves of North Africa

If, through the capture of slaves, European blood came into Barbary, still more so did negritic blood. The negroes, whose own homes do not, indeed, extend far into the Sahara, do not voluntarily come to Mediterranean North Africa ; but they flocked in under the crack of the slave whip as despised servants of the ruling peoples. Yet their vital tenacity caused them to take root in the new soil. But they proved fatal to the national life of North Africa. Every drop of negritic blood takes its owner farther from Europe, as well as from the civilisation of the Mediterranean countries, and brings him nearer to the dull, unprogressive peoples of Central Africa. At the present day, after centuries of silent immigration of the dark race, the coast of the Mediterranean is more African than it ever was in the course of its history.

The three non-racial elements of the population which, through natural conditions, are always recreated—nomads, husbandmen, and dwellers in towns— have been, as was inevitable, influenced and technically altered in very different ways by the advancing waves of nations. The agriculturists of the highlands, after the earliest fusion was completed, have best preserved the purity of race : these are essentially genuine Berbers and the pick of the population in Western North Africa. The nomad Berber population was, on the contrary, not able to resist the impact of the Arabs, nomads like themselves, and was compelled to give way to the intruders. They either withdrew into the Sahara or fled to their brethren permanently settled in the highlands, so that in North Africa proper at the present time the terms Arab and nomad almost coincide. The towns, finally, were the proper homes of the mixed nationalities. Foreign merchants and fugitives settled in them by preference ; the Jew built his ghetto here, and the negro his miserable quarter. Notwithstanding the hatred which the nomads and the agriculturists have for each other, they are at one in their contempt for the inhabitants of the towns.

The Three Elements of the Population

We must, first of all, consider the history of the two colonising states, Cyrene and Carthage. Then we must give our attention to Roman times and describe the invasion of the Arabs. Finally, considering how North Africa has been split up into separate states and possessions, we must fix our eyes on the modern development of these states. The encroachments of the European Powers will be briefly touched upon in conclusion.

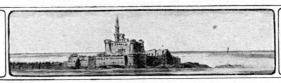
CARTHAGE IN ITS SPLENDOUR
AND ITS DOWNFALL

THE Greek settlements on the peninsula of Barca deserve special notice because they were the only important Hellenic colonies on the coast of North Africa, and because also their isolated position allowed them to develop their individuality in comparative independence. The cultivated territory of Cyrenaica, surrounded by the sea or desert regions, supported a numerous population on the products of the soil ; and the favourable commercial situation, which made Cyrene a depôt on the through trade route to the most varied destinations, must have proved a source of wealth as soon as an energetic people made use of it, and found out, besides, how to make the most of the natural treasures of their own territory, among which the silphium, already referred to, must especially be named.

In the middle of the seventh century B.C. Dorian settlers had come, under the leadership of Battus, from the island of Thera, or Santorin, where a civil war had caused their emigration : at first they settled on a small island in the Gulf of Bomba ; six years later they settled on the mainland and founded Cyrene, the government of which Battus assumed under the title of king. It is characteristic of the country that a copious spring of water, called Cyre, led to the choice of the site and gave its name to the place. The colony was subsequently strengthened by the accession of numerous Dorian Greeks from the Peloponnesus, from Crete, and other islands. The colonists were now in a position to take possession of large tracts in the peninsula of Barca—against the will of the nomad Libyans of those parts, who at last in their distress appealed to the king of Egypt for help. The new colony soon saw itself compelled to assume a hostile attitude towards the

A COIN OF PTOLEMY APION
One of the kings of Cyrene. The reverse of the coin shows the famous silphium plant, now extinct, which was one of the colony's natural treasures.

powerful civilised state on its east frontier. Fortunately for Cyrene, disturbances in Egypt forbade the decisive invasion of a neighbouring people. But finally the Libyans themselves proved to be dangerous opponents. The tribes united and inflicted a severe defeat on the Greeks in a great battle. The large number of Cyreneans killed—seven thousand—and the fact that notwithstanding all this the vitality of the young community was not sapped allows us to conceive how rapid the rise to prosperity of the settlement was.

Its defeat was destined to bring important results in its train. Cyrene, in search of help, turned its eyes to Greece, and was immediately swept along in that transformation of political life which was then going on in the old home. Peacefully, or by force, aristocracy and tyranny were repressed in favour of democracy. Those communities were fortunate where prudent and respected men stood at the head of affairs and accomplished with moderation and fairness the revolution which had become necessary through the growing power of the lower strata of the people. In Cyrene the disastrous issue of the war furnished a reason for similar action ; while another impelling cause was the counsel of the famous oracle at Delphi. Just as the oracle had once commanded Battus to found a colony, so it now counselled the Cyreneans to summon from Mantinea the legislator Demonax, who would arrange the internal affairs of the settlement and enable it to offer a more powerful resistance to external foes. Demonax assigned equal rights to all citizens and limited the royal power of the Battian dynasty, which was still on the throne. This led to new struggles ; King Arcesilaus was exiled in

GENERAL VIEW OF THE PHŒNICIAN TOWN OF UTICA AS IT WAS

The oldest of the Phœnician settlements on the north coast of Africa was Utica, although Carthage politically outstripped it.

530 B.C., but with the help of the foreigners regained power till he was slain by the people, together with the tyrant of Barca, which had been founded before this. As he had previously submitted to the Persians, who, under Cambyses, then occupied Egypt, the Persian governor in Egypt now interfered, destroyed Barca, which, however, soon became prosperous again, and upheld the tottering monarchy. It was not until 450 B.C. that it finally broke down, and Cyrene became a republic.

Notwithstanding all these wars, Cyrene had meantime attained great prosperity. The fertile soil of the country, which, above all, produced the valuable silphium, afforded a secure basis for the power of the state ; and the trade which was carried on, partly by land with Egypt and the Sudan, partly by sea, brought immense wealth to Cyrene, where the citizens were conspicuous among all Hellenes for their luxury, and also for their keen interest in **Luxury and Learning in Cyrene** the artistic and philosophic movements of the Greek people. The restless spirit of the Cyreneans, which manifested itself even after the fall of the monarchy in continuous friction between the nobles and the people, may have been due to their luxurious character. The power and prosperity of the town suffered for the

time very little from these internal feuds. The struggle with its rising rival, Carthage, which broke out soon after the expulsion of the Battidæ, did not end to the disadvantage of Cyrene. The two emporia **Cyrene's Struggle with Carthage** of trade came finally to an understanding as to the limits of their respective influence. The Cyreneans did not come into hostile relations with Alexander the Great, who appeared in Egypt in 332 B.C., since they secured their position in advance by a feigned submission. It was, indeed, fortunate for the town that, owing to their remote position, they were somewhat distant from the paths of political whirlwinds. Only faint gusts of the storm blew over them. The same advantage was enjoyed by the other and smaller city-republics which had sprung up on the coast of Barca and, with Cyrene, were included under the name of the Pentapolis, literally, the five cities.

When, however, after the death of Alexander, the mighty stream of his policy of conquest divided into numerous rivulets—when everywhere his old generals raised their weapons against each other and endeavoured to break off for themselves the greatest possible portion of that enormous inheritance—Cyrenaica did not escape the eyes of the rapacious soldier-

THE REMAINS OF UTICA, THE OLDEST AND LONGEST-LIVED PHŒNICIAN COLONY
Utica, at first the chief city of the African Phœnicians, preserved its existence by going over to Rome in the Punic wars.

kings. As though the external danger were not enough, party struggles blazed up with fresh fury in the republics of Pentapolis, and fugitives from Cyrene summoned the assistance of the Alexandrian general, Timbron, who was then in Crete. Ptolemy, who, in the meantime, had firmly established himself in Egypt, availed himself of the opportunity to interfere : Timbron was defeated, and in 322 B.C. all of Cyrenaica was obliged to recognise the suzerainty of the crafty Egyptian king.

Cyrene Subject to Egypt

With this the decay of the country seems to have begun. Drawn into the family disputes of the Ptolemies, the region sometimes regained its independence temporarily, but remained in essential points under Egyptian influence. Cyrene was no longer able to compete in trade with Carthage, on the one hand, or with Alexandria on the other. Even though the gigantic struggle of the Phœnician colony with the aspiring Roman empire may have brought much passing benefit, and the advantages of its geographical situation could never be quite lost, yet Cyrene, together with its sister towns, undoubtedly sank in importance. This decadence, recognisable in the domain of thought also, stands in a certain con-

nection with the increasing intermixture of populations, by which the old Hellenic spirit was more and more repressed and subdued. The Jews especially, who were intentionally favoured by the Ptolemies, greatly increased in Cyrenaica in the course of time. In the later Ptolemaic period they are said to have composed almost the fourth part of the town population. To what degree the Libyan, Egyptian, and even negritic elements may have increased is not, indeed, known, but may be roughly estimated from the situation and from the trading relations of Pentapolis. The intellectual culture of African Hellenism, which once had its centre in Cyrene, passed entirely to Alexandria.

The Romans, after the death of a prince of the Ptolemies, to whom Pentapolis had fallen as an independent realm, came into the possession of the territory by peaceful means. It was only loosely bound to the Roman empire about 95 B.C., since Cyrenaica had long ceased to be an important factor in international affairs. Disturbances in the new tributary land led to its complete subjugation by Pompey in 67 B.C., and to its union with Crete. In the future Pentapolis comes seldom into notice ; what we do

Decay in Culture and Power

hear of it shows its continued decay. A terrible revolt of the Jewish population in the time of Trajan is said to have cost the lives of 200,000 Greeks and Romans, so that the emperor, after the suppression of the rebellion, founded a new colony, Adrianopolis, in Cyrenaica, in order to revive the depopulated land. But the weak condition of the province had already been seized by the Libyan nomads as an opportunity of occupying part of the fertile land, without its being possible to check their encroachments. The ravages of the Islamitic era of conquest annihilated the last traces of its ancient prosperity.

Cyrene's Prosperity Annihilated

Long before Cyrene, and not through gradual decay, but in a tremendous tragic catastrophe, her proud rival, Phœnician Carthage, had disappeared.

The most important of the Phœnician settlements in the west are well known. On the coast of North Africa there lie, west of the Syrtes, Leptis, Hadrumetum, Carthage, Utica, and the two Hippos. Those that lay on the Mauretanian, or Morroccan, coast had no special significance. In Sicily the western portion particularly was Phœnician; but there, as in other instances, we can never know what was primarily Carthaginian and therefore secondarily Phœnician. We must renounce the attempt to prove very ancient Phœnician pre-Hellenic settlements in Eastern Sicily, since we doubt the applicability of the explanation of names for such purposes. The same holds good of Spain. What we know of Carteïa and Gadir, or Cadiz, is quite uncertain; and the identification of Tartessus with the Biblical Tarshish is very doubtful. Thus, still less information has come down to us of the various Phœnician settlements in Spain than of those in Africa. The town which at a later period was promoted by Hasdrubal to be the seat of government for the Carthaginian dominion under the name of Carthago, or Carthago Nova, seems at a still earlier time to have been a sort of centre. We must abandon even more completely the attempt to prove the existence of any definite points further to the east. In Sardinia alone can we trace with any confidence the existence of Carthaginian influence, although in that case again a previous universal Phœnician occupation of the land is quite probable.

No Phœnician History of Carthage

We have no materials for the history of these settlements and their further development. Our accounts begin where the Western Phœnicians came into contact with the Greeks, when these latter began to dispute the western basin of the Mediterranean and when the struggle between Rome and Carthage was being waged. Carthage was already at the head of these settlements. There were no longer "Phœnicians" there, but only an immense Carthaginian empire to which everything was subordinated. The history of these Western Phœnicians is, therefore, so far as we can follow it, the history of Carthage, and even there it is very incomplete. The Carthaginian documents which are forthcoming have no historical value. We have no accounts of the first settlement of Carthage, and we can deduce the course of events only from some institutions of later date. What legend tells us about the founding of Carthage by Dido, and the transference of this legend to the reign of Pygmalion of Tyre—all this is pure fable. Dido does not belong to history.

The Carthaginians, even in later times, acknowledged Phœnicia as their mother country, and as a proof of this paid an annual tax to the temple of Melkart in Tyre. Carthage has, therefore, been regarded as a Tyrian colony, and the Dido myth is traceable to this idea, or it may have helped to sustain it. We have, however, evidence that the chief gods of Carthage were not Melkart, but Eshmun and Astarte—that is to say, the gods who were worshipped at Sidon. This proves, according to Semitic ideas, that Carthage was not a Tyrian but a Sidonian colony.

Origin of Carthage

What we have clearly seen with regard to the conditions of Phœnicia and the course of its expansion beyond the sea forbids us to look on Carthage as a colony sent out from the city of Sidon; the Phœnician towns as such could never have done that. On the contrary, the migration across the sea originated with the Phœnicians who were still in movement. If, therefore, Carthage worshipped the same gods as Sidon, she did so not because they were the gods of her mother city, but because she did homage to them as the common gods of all Phœnicians. The Carthaginians did not regard Sidon as their mother city, but as the head city of all "Sidonians," just as Tyre and the other states did. When through the destruction of Sidon by Esarhaddon even the religious headship was transferred to Tyre the Carthaginians began to send their offering of homage to Tyre, because the rescued gods of Sidon had found a refuge there. From this time, and only in this sense, Carthage was a "Tyrian colony."

A further clue to the explanation of the conditions of the historical period is given us by the name Carthage itself, and by a remarkable and well-authenticated fact as to its relations with the neighbouring town of Utica. Carthage signifies the "New Town"; it can only have been so called in distinction from an old town. Citium in Cyprus and the subsequent "New Carthage" in Spain received the same name when they were "newly founded"—that is, when they fell under

others are included under the title of "allies"—that is subject and tributary towns. This implies a recognition of the "motherhood" of Utica as much as of Tyre; the religious fame of the former capital had thus been preserved even when Carthage had long possessed the political supremacy, and was strong enough to secure to Utica an exceptional position above the other towns. From this we may deduce the fact for the period on which no accounts throw any light that Utica was formerly the chief city of the African Phœnicians and had been gradually ousted from that position by Carthage. This also explains why Utica in the Third Punic War voluntarily ranged itself on the side of the Romans and was afterwards made by them the capital of a province.

Utica Goes over to Rome

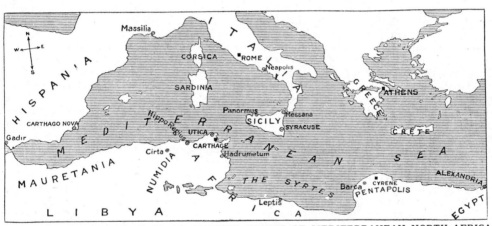

MAP SHOWING RELATIONSHIP OF ANCIENT STATES OF MEDITERRANEAN NORTH AFRICA

the Phœnician and Punic sway. The old name of Carthage was possibly Byrsa, which really belongs to the old quarter of the town, the city, and not merely to the citadel, and is found also, perhaps, in the inscriptions upon coins.

Utica, on the other hand, signifies "Old Town." It must have first received this title in place of its old and unknown name, when the New Town assumed its name and thus politically outstripped it; that is precisely the state of things which is illustrated in the mother country by the struggle between Sidon and Tyre for the "motherhood" or the higher antiquity.

Utica Senior to Carthage

In the second treaty with Rome Utica is expressly named with Carthage and on the same footing as Tyre, while all

In short, at what date Carthage was, in fact, founded, or at what time she had secured the hegemony, or dominion, over the other Phœnician settlements in Spain and Sicily and elsewhere, we do not know. But when we have definite record of rivalry between Phœnicians and Greeks the Phœnician power centres in Carthage.

At the beginning of the seventh century Sicily and the coast of Massilia are in the possession of the Greeks. The Phœnicians had only held their own in Western Sicily, where they were protected by the Carthaginians. Their strongholds were Panormus, Motye, Lilybæum; but what part of them was Phœnician, in other words, a remnant of some old immigration, and what Carthaginian, that is to say founded only from Africa, our information does not enable us to judge.

About the middle of the sixth century the Phocæans attempted to establish a footing in Corsica—according to tradition in 562 B.C.—and founded Alalia. After reinforcements had been sent from the mother city, fear of the threatening growth of the Greek immigration—which had already laid a firm grip on Lower Italy,

Carthage Combines with Etruria the larger part of Sicily, and the coast round Massilia— drove the two great powers of Carthage and Etruria to combine. The Phocæans were totally defeated and expelled from Corsica. Somewhere about the same time are recorded the wearisome wars of the Carthaginians in Sicily and Sardinia under Malchus. All details and even the precise dates it is impossible to fix, but we may clearly infer that here further Greek expansion received a check, and that limits were roughly fixed which were not afterwards overstepped. The Greeks after this did not encroach to any extent on the Carthaginian sphere of interest. The accounts of wars with Massilia—that is, with the chief town of the Greek colonies on the Franco-Spanish coast—are also obscure. These wars bear upon the history of the country we are considering equally with those in Sicily and Sardinia.

Malchus, the general who put a stop to the advance of the Greeks, is reported to have interfered in the home affairs of Carthage in a way which leads us to draw conclusions as to the cause of her earlier weakness. The account is certainly vague, as indeed is everything we learn of Carthage from the records, but still it shows us the same dissensions which combined afterwards to bring about the fall of the city. There had been an unwillingness to receive the general on his return with the army, from fear of the effect of his power on the government of the Families. We therefore infer that he looked to the support of the people against the nobles. In

Dissensions Within the State the end, as he was aspiring to the kingly power, he was defeated and executed. It must be assumed that he attempted to put an end to the rule of the great Families; but when he had obtained possession of the city by means of his army, he miscalculated his power, relinquished the army, and thus fell a victim to a reaction. The accounts suggest that he was not a thoroughgoing "tyrant," who relied upon the

army, but that he tried to obtain the crown by a constitutional revolution.

Our accounts designate as his "successor" Mago, who has left his mark on the subsequent course of events, and whose family was for a long period at the head of affairs. He had made himself the directing mind of the Families, and his house long conducted the government in their spirit. He and his descendants are named as generals of the Carthaginians in the wars in Sicily and in Africa, where the maintenance of the Carthaginian territorial power was at stake.

Meanwhile the Greeks had found in the Sicilian tyrants leaders who could organise the operations against Carthage with greater energy. This chance was very soon appreciably felt, and compelled Carthage to look for assistance in the struggle against her foe where it was voluntarily proffered. Tradition tells us, in an anecdotal and no longer intelligible fashion, of an embassy from Darius to Carthage. Its demands sound somewhat foolish ; but apparently its object was to claim the submission of Carthage, since her mother country was now tributary.

Carthage Joins Persia Against Greece In combination with the Phœnician, the Carthaginian fleet would have made Persia the undisputed mistress of the sea. Carthage rejected this suggestion. Nevertheless, she was soon forced by an identity of interests to work hand in hand with Persia. While Xerxes tried to crush the Greeks in the eastern basin, the Carthaginians made a simultaneous effort in the western. The success, or rather want of success, was the same for the two allies ; Xerxes was defeated at Salamis, and the army of the Carthaginians, under Hamilcar, the son of Hanno, was vanquished by Gelo at Himera. Hellenism, attacked in both halves of the Mediterranean, successfully resisted in both the Semitic civilisation of the Orient.

We have what would be an invaluable piece of evidence from this period if its date were more trustworthy. Polybius mentions a treaty which, in the year of the first consuls, 509 B.C., the new republic of Rome concluded with Carthage. This treaty had been discovered in his time among the Roman archives, and could be deciphered only with difficulty. The entire conception of the development of earlier Roman history depends on the point whether this treaty is to be referred to this

A PANORAMIC VIEW OF THE SITE OF THE ANCIENT PORT OF CARTHAGE

A PUNIC TOMB NEAR CARTHAGE

REMAINS OF THE OLD SEA GATE

RUINS OF THE AQUEDUCT: A MONUMENT OF THE ROMAN SETTLEMENT AT CARTHAGE

THE FRAGMENTARY RUINS OF CARTHAGE, ONCE QUEEN OF THE SEAS

year or, as it has acutely been suggested, to the year 348 B.C. But the data do not permit of a decision. The most weighty provisions were that the Romans and their allies were not to be permitted to undertake raiding expeditions, or to found colonies beyond " the beautiful promontory." Doubt arises whether this

Rome and Carthage at Peace boundary between the Carthaginian and Roman spheres of interest is to be looked for in Africa or in Spain ; the most probable explanation is that by this Mastia and Tarseum—the subsequent Carthago Nova—must be understood as the furthest points to which the protectorate of Rome and the trade of the Roman allies were allowed to extend. Massilia would thus belong to Rome. Sicily, again, so far as it was Carthaginian, would be included by the Romans in the African territory of Carthage. The Carthaginians bound themselves not to make overtures to the Latins, so far as they were subject to the suzerainty of Rome.

Contemporaneously with the development of the African situation at the close of the fifth century we have accounts of a subjugation of the African district by the members of the house of Mago. This can refer only to a subjugation of the native tribes ; their district was occupied by Carthage, and they themselves became subjects of the Carthaginians. From this time Carthage began the system of large estates (*latifundia*) in which Rome was her predecessor and teacher. Hitherto we have been able to represent the African settlements only as towns with a fair-sized territory situated in the coast region ; now there was a province. This became directly Carthaginian, not Punic, since Carthage was already ruler of the remaining Punic towns. These naturally retained their respective civic rights and their territory, but were dependent on Carthage.

The house of Mago held for several generations the conduct of affairs in its own hands. Its influence then seems to have become suspected by the Families, and it was ousted from the exclusive exercise of the governing power. All details are again obscure. The revulsion is said to have followed as a consequence of the battle on the Himera in 480 B.C. From that time the rivalry between two great parties leaves its mark on the internal policy of Carthage. The one party, at

HIERO II.
OF SYRACUSE
Who was the immediate cause of the First Punic War.

whose head we shall soon find the Barcidæ, aimed more at a centralisation of power, had therefore an ultimately monarchical tendency, and was based on the army ; the other represented the interests of the Families. This opposition is strongly emphasised in the Second Punic War, when the fall of Hannibal was due perhaps chiefly to the enmity of his own countrymen.

The Carthaginians were forced by the battle on the Himera to desist from their schemes of conquest in Sicily, and could retain only their strongholds in the west. New attempts at aggrandisement inevitably followed the revival in the next period, since the prosperity of Sicily and of Syracuse in particular must have been a growing source of danger to the Carthaginian trading supremacy. Nevertheless, Carthage had for a comparatively long time looked on passively at the growth of the Syracusan power. That may have been connected with internal conditions— namely, with the overthrow of the house of Mago, which had exclusively conducted the government. The first attack on Syracuse was not made by Carthage ; but the Eastern and Western Greeks allowed her the role of the tertius gaudens. Segesta, hard pressed by Syracuse, appealed to the Athenians for help. The latter used the opportunity to carry out long cherished schemes, of which Themistocles is said to have been the original deviser. But the interference of Athens soon unexpectedly ended in disaster (415–413 B.C.). The Carthaginians were therefore compelled, as regards Syracuse, which was now stronger than before, either to give up their role of the expectant looker-on or to renounce all claims on Sicily. When, therefore, Segesta again turned to them for help they had no option left but to decide on war. Possibly the subsequent vigorous inter-

Carthage and Sicily ference was connected with a change in the government, in so far as the aristocratic régime, having been found lacking in energy, had been supplanted by the rival party. In any case, the war was carried on from the outset with vigour, and, after a preliminary reverse at sea, with success. Selinus, Himera, Agrigentum, and Gela were captured, and Syracuse was compelled to acknowledge the Carthaginian suzerainty over the western half of the island (410–405 B.C.) Peace had been concluded with Dionysius I., to whom the reverses gave a favourable opportunity of making himself master of the situation. But friendly relations did not last long; war was declared for the second time, and for the second time peace was made between the two powers (397–392, 393 B.C.). A third war was begun by Dionysius, and was ended by a treaty with his son. Here we have an obscure account of the revolt of a certain "Hanno the Great" in Carthage; even before this there had been revolts in Libya and in Sardinia. The Sicilian wars were brought to a temporary close by the peace with Timoleon, who, by the victory on the Crimissus in 343 B.C., was able to secure somewhat favourable conditions for the Greeks, and to restrict Carthage once more to the west.

THE CARTHAGINIAN CERES
A splendid mosaic from the Carthaginian temple of Astarte, who was worshipped by all the Phœnicians.

Polybius inserts two new treaties with Rome—in 348 and 343 B.C.—between these events; once more the "beautiful promontory" is fixed as the limit of the respective spheres of interest, and at the same time Sardinia, with Libya, is expressly secured to Carthage.

In Sicily there was no permanent tranquillity, but opportunity was repeatedly offered to Carthage for renewed interference in the various quarrels between 318 and 314 B.C. New complications threatened from the east through Alexander the Great. As lord of Tyre he is said to have followed the example of Darius, and to have claimed the submission of Carthage; moreover, the deputation with the gifts to the temple of Melkart had fallen into his hands. By the founding of Alexandria the danger drew nearer to Carthage; but nothing is reported of any measures taken on either

A PHŒNICIAN PRIESTESS
From a mosaic of a priestess dancing before an altar, found in the excavation of what was probably the temple of Astarte, the goddess of Sidon, at Carthage.

side. If Carthage adopted in this instance a waiting policy, she did so successfully, for with the death of Alexander the danger of a further expansion of Hellenism was past. Both Carthage and Rome escaped by this the otherwise inevitable day of reckoning; but they had received in Alexandria a rival to their commerce. With the Ptolemies, however, who had temporarily occupied Cyrene, there never appear to have been any unfriendly relations; at the beginning of the First Punic War there is actual evidence of a treaty with Ptolemy II., according to the terms of which both parties reciprocally guaranteed their respective territorial possessions and commercial undertakings.

In Sicily, however, fresh complications soon ensued. Agathocles, in his efforts to found a Sicilian empire, was forced first to make an attempt to drive out the Carthaginians. This led to that tedious struggle, with those marvellous vicissitudes, in which Agathocles, driven back on Syracuse, attempted to change the scene of war to Africa, and there on his side besieged Carthage itself, until in the end he was compelled to return to Sicily, having lost his army in Africa, and was forced to make peace with Carthage on the basis of the *status quo* (312–306 B.C.). He died in the midst of preparations for a new expedition against Carthage in 289 B.C. With him disappeared the rival who had once more combined the forces of Western Greece against the Carthaginian dominion. After this time no power was again formed which could have made head there against Carthage.

Agathocles bequeathed an inheritance destined to promote the outbreak of hostilities between the two powers which had survived all these disturbances—that is, between Rome and Carthage. As rivals of Carthage by sea only the Italian Greeks were survivors, and even their power was broken once more, while Carthage, on the whole, played a waiting game. The favourable opportunity to seize possession of Tarentum which was offered her by the one party was let slip, while the Romans were not so foolish. But, after Tarentum had fallen, and Pyrrhus was defeated, the struggle between the last two powers for the supremacy in the Western Mediterranean could no longer be postponed.

First Punic War

The pretext for the rupture with Rome was afforded by the request for help sent by the mercenaries of Agathocles, the Mamertines, who had established themselves strongly in Messana ; being besieged by Hiero II. of Syracuse, one part sought help from Carthage, the other from Rome. The Roman relieving army crossed the straits, unhindered by the Carthaginians, but found a Carthaginian garrison in the citadel and Carthaginian ships in the harbour. Nevertheless, the semblance of peace was still maintained. Carthage, hesitating as ever, was anxious to avoid an open breach. But when the Romans drove out the garrison from the citadel, no course was left to Carthage but to declare war, the First Punic War (264-271 B.C.). Rome was victorious, and Carthage had to renounce all claims on Sicily.

Doubtless Rome before this had forced on the war, but her unblushing policy was soon afterwards unmasked by her action in the occupation of Sardinia. The war with Rome had been far from glorious, except for the valiant defence of Eryx by Hamilcar. On the conclusion of peace his army had to be transferred to Africa ; but there the Carthaginians either would not or could not give the troops their full pay.

Rome's Unblushing Policy

In the end there was a mutiny of the army, which was supported by the Libyan peasant population. Utica and Hippo, or Diarrhytus, were taken by the mutineers and Carthage itself invested, until Hamilcar, appealed to for help, successfully stamped out the revolt. At the same time the Carthaginian mercenaries in Sardinia had mutinied and obtained possession of the island. But being hard pressed by the inhabitants, they de-

manded to be admitted under the Roman overlordship. This was refused them so long as Carthage herself was occupied with the mercenary war in Africa ; when, however, tranquillity was restored there, and signs were shown of an attempt to subjugate Sardinia again, Rome disclosed her real intentions and granted the renewed request of the insurgents for help. In defiance of the conditions of the treaty concluded three years previously, Sardinia was occupied by Rome.

The feud between the two parties in Carthage becomes conspicuously prominent in the period between the first two wars with Rome. A war party, represented by the Barcidæ, did not indeed bring about the war—that was always done by Rome—but wished to protect the actual independence of the state, since it had no doubt as to the views of Rome. The other, with which opposition to the great power of the Barcidæ must have been the real motive, was the Roman party, bribed possibly by money or by hopes held out to them by Rome. It advocated unqualified submission to Rome ;

Carthage Divided Against Itself

in the last resort it waived all claim to self-government. The party of the Barcidæ, the preponderant power of which we must not look for in the person of a Hamilcar or Hasdrubal, but in the vigorous vitality of the state, had always had constitutional right on its side, so long as Carthaginians could hold their own in the field. It was only when, through the difficulties of the war which was threatening before the very gates, no other possibility existed that the Roman party had tried to enforce even constitutional measures for submission to Rome. Hitherto its influence had always consisted merely in clogging any energetic conduct of the war ; and by its policy it had succeeded in accomplishing what it intended. Hannibal, the victorious general, was, strictly speaking, defeated nowhere except in Carthage. The Roman army, needed by the Roman party in order to work the new constitutional machinery in the city, was now before the gates.

After the loss of Sardinia, Hamilcar went to Spain in 237 B.C. and proceeded, by conquering a new Carthaginian province, to replace the loss of Sicily and Sardinia. We know nothing of the conditions of the Phœnicians there. We see from the treaties with Rome that the existing towns belonged to Carthage. What happened now was precisely that which had taken place previously with the Libyans ; the hinterland was subjugated, and a province constituted, while hitherto merely trading towns under Carthaginian overlordship had existed there. Hamilcar fell in battle against the Iberians in 229 B.C. and Hasdrubal took his place. He continued the work of his father - in - law, and made the ancient Mastia the capital of the new province under the name Kartchadast, or Carthago Nova, as it was called by the Romans. After his death, in 221 B.C., the supreme command was entrusted to Hamilcar's son, Hannibal.

HAMILCAR AND HIS SON HANNIBAL
The great Carthaginian generals in the Punic Wars. Hamilcar fell in Spain, and after the death of his son-in-law Hasdrubal, his son Hannibal took over the chief command.

The acquisition of the province of Spain and the second war with Rome seem exclusively to have been the work of the Barcidæ ; in fact, the impression is created that these were really the holders of power in Carthage, and had possessed in substance a monarchical power. This depends, however, to a considerable degree on the nature of our accounts ; these, on the one hand, only describe the war, in which those personalities were naturally more prominent, and, on the other hand, their object was to justify Rome's action towards Carthage. But to do this they were obliged to represent the Roman party at Carthage as the outraged one, while it can admit of no doubt that in reality the Barcidæ were always in harmony with the constitutional authorities. The Roman party were simply practising treachery. It was not Hannibal who governed the authorities in Carthage—he went as a boy with his father to Spain, and came back to Africa only at the close of the war—but it was the majority of the Families which filled the constitutional offices, and he belonged to their party and executed their resolutions. The command of the army had, of course, given Hamilcar and Hannibal a weighty voice in the council of their party, and they doubtless contributed largely to its preponderating power, but they were nothing more than many other generals of whom history tells ; Mago, perhaps, possessed personally greater influence than Hannibal.

The pretext for the war was, as usual, dragged in anyhow by the Romans. Hannibal, when he besieged Saguntum, had in no way infringed the unjustified demand of Rome that the Ebro should not be crossed. The course and result of the Second Punic War are related elsewhere. The Roman party carried its points ; a Roman army appeared in Africa ; pressure was brought upon the government to recall Hannibal, and the matchless leader was vanquished at Zama in 202 B.C. Rome now dictated severe conditions of peace : cession of the Spanish province to Rome and of the tributary state of Numidia to Masinissa, and the loss of independence. Carthage became tributary to Rome, and forfeited even the right of waging war. Carthage as a sovereign state disappears ; politically she could no longer play a part. But commerce gave her an importance which was finally able to win her political power. Rome was bound to take measures against this. Just as the Assyrians always contrived to effect a rebellion on the part of their allies and their tributaries in order to be able to annex their states, so Rome was never at a loss for the means of provoking the last fight of desperation. With this object Masinissa was therefore placed by the side of Carthage. He played, according to instructions, the part assigned to him. The Third Punic War, from 149 to 146 B.C. was the struggle of despair, which was the result of the petty provocations of the Numidian king, and afforded the pretext for getting rid of Rome's rival in peaceful competition. Carthage was destroyed in 146 B.C. In blood and flames sets the sun of the Phœnician city, once the

HANNIBAL THE VICTORIOUS
Hannibal was, strictly speaking, nowhere defeated except in Carthage by pro-Roman treachery.

proud mistress of the seas ; and with it disappears the Carthaginian people as such from the history of mankind. Utica became the capital of the new Roman province of Africa.

The sources of our information as to the internal development of the Carthaginian state are practically worthless. Besides the eulogies which have been lavished on the Carthaginian constitution by Plato, Eratosthenes, Polybius, Cato, and Cicero, we are indebted to Aristotle's " Politics " for a long discussion of it ; but these discussions are for purposes of comparison, and presuppose a familiarity with his lost work on the Carthaginian constitution, lacking which we are reduced to little more than conjecture.

Carthage Disappears From History

The constitution of Carthage was, so far as we know, that of a provincial town— that is, the government was based on the tribal organisation of still unsettled Semites. There was a council, presumably a representation of the citizens and a body of elders, which may originally have corresponded to the leaders or elders (sheikhs) of the Families, but in historical times, according to its nature, may have comprised the administrative magistrates of the state, elected from the aristocracy. The executive heads of these magistrates were the two *Suffetes*, the " Judges." From this dualism we infer that Carthage was mainly a settlement of two tribes, or else that, after the settlement, in the process of forming a citizen class and a patriciate, these two predominant sections of the community each had a representative in the government.

If the Phœnicians, possessors of the best harbours in a large civilised district and limited to a narrow strip of coast, were driven to seafaring and trade, still the settlers in the western basin of the Mediterranean, so soon as they were strengthened in their intercourse with the Eastern civilisation, were enabled to subjugate a larger territory for themselves by defeating the still uncivilised inhabitants of the hinterland. The great merchants of Carthage did not wish to sacrifice the advantage which was obtained by exploiting the productions of the land, and they therefore subdued the Libyan inhabitants of the hinterland. We know little of the actual course of events. The

Government of the Natives

victors must at first have taken only a portion of the land for themselves, while they left the old owners the presumably larger portion in return for a fixed tribute. The introduction of a monetary system, which is essential in a mercantile state, only brought more land into the hands of the Carthaginian lords since the peasants were overwhelmed by debt. Thus a great land-owning class was developed, which employed slave labour for agriculture, and took for its model the Roman system of *latifundia*. It is uncertain what the policy of Carthage was in her foreign provinces. It is well known that the Spanish metal mines were thoroughly exploited. But whether the Carthaginians themselves were the workers, or whether they left the working to the natives and, by a system of taxes, directed the profits into their own coffers, must remain undecided. The latter alternative seems the more probable.

We possess practically no available account of their trade relations generally. With regard to their intercourse with the Eastern civilised world, it is obvious that they must have furnished it with the raw products of the countries of the western basin of the Mediterranean. The Bible calls the most important of these countries Tarshish. It must remain undecided to what country in particular this name was applied ; in any case the Carthaginians were the masters of the Tarshish trade, the track of which bounded the horizon of the civilised nations of Western Asia. The trade which commanded the Spanish coasts must have penetrated beyond the Straits of Gibraltar. There was the famous attempt which, even before Herodotus' time, somewhere about the year 470 B.C., the " elder " Hanno made to acquire the West African coast by planting factories there. His journey took him beyond the mouth of the Senegal, and the record of his achievement is said to have been set up in the temple of " Cronos " at Carthage. The extant Greek account claims to be a translation of it. The counterpart to this journey is found in the Periplus of Himilcus, who is said to have explored the North as far as Britain. We are, however, less well informed as to his report, since it is only known to us by its employment in the " Ora Maritima " of Avienus.

World-wide Commerce of Carthage

ROMANS AND VANDALS IN NORTH AFRICA

ROME entered on the inheritance of Carthage and formed the province of Africa out of the territory of the republic. The region preserved its prosperous condition even in the Roman period. The towns which had stood most loyally by Carthage were destroyed, and others were administered by Roman prefects. Only Utica and Hippo, which in the last war had taken the side of the conquerors, retained the greater part of their privileges. Utica gained greatly by the fall of Carthage, of which it took the place for some time in matters of trade, and could compete with Rhodes and Alexandria in wealth and commerce. But **Carthage Rises From its Ruins** Carthage itself rose from its ruins. The attempt of C. Gracchus to plant a colony on the historic site failed, it is true ; but Cæsar, and after him Augustus, successfully prosecuted the scheme. The new settlements enjoyed for centuries fair prosperity.

But the real inheritance from Carthage was not the rich corn-land and its commanding position on the Mediterranean, so favourable for trade, but the war with nomad peoples, the real sons of North Africa who with restless spirit swarmed round the borders of the rich province. The wise policy of Masinissa had made the Numidian state a formidable power, and its territory extended from the borders of Cyrenaica to Mauretania. After the death of this most loyal ally of the Romans, it required but a slight pretext to renew the old struggle between agriculturists and nomads in the form of a war between Rome and Numidia. Under Micipsa, the successor of Masinissa, friendly relations remained undisturbed. The feud broke out when, after the death of Micipsa, in 118 B.C., and the murder of Hiempsal, the crafty Jugurtha, grandson of Masinissa and nephew of Micipsa, ascended the throne. For the first time a genuine son

MASINISSA
King of Numidia and a loyal ally of Rome in North Africa.

of North Africa came forward in the theatre of war—a man who combined Punic cunning with brigand bravery, and who, as an ally of the Romans, had learnt the art of war among a people who aspired to the dominion of the world. For the first time, too, a people of Aryan race came into conflict with the native genius of North Africa in a struggle **The Wars of Jugurtha** for supremacy on the shores of the Mediterranean. Jugurtha, according to Roman stipulation, had received only the more valuable western part of Micipsa's kingdom —that is, the present Algeria, with the exception of the most easterly portions and of Cirta, the capital—while his adopted brother, Adherbal, was allotted the east, corresponding roughly to the present Tripolis. Adherbal's good fortune was short-lived. In 112 B.C. Jugurtha found a pretext for war ; Adherbal was besieged in his capital, Cirta, and in the storming of the town was killed, together with many of the inhabitants.

Rome had now no choice but to take up arms against the usurper on the trivial pretext that among the slain inhabitants of Cirta were a number of Roman citizens. In reality, the war which now began concerned the security of the province of Africa, which was not only a valuable possession, on account of its natural wealth, but a cornerstone in the fabric of the Roman empire.

The so-called Jugurthine War began in the year 111 B.C., but ended for the time in a shameful peace, for Jugurtha knew how to avail himself artfully of the venality of the senatorial party and of the consul, Calpurnius Bestia, who had been sent out against him. Indeed, when the leader of the popular party, Memmius, succeeded in obtaining the summons of the Numidian king to Rome, the wily African was able to extricate himself from all difficulties, thanks to the corruption of the parties in power, which astounded the king himself. It was only when he carried his audacity to such a pitch as to cause his cousin, Massiva, who was staying in Rome, and had put himself under the protection of Roman hospitality, to be treacherously murdered that he was forced to leave the city and prepare for a new war. The senatorial party once more conducted the war unenergetically and unskilfully. A division of the Roman army was actually cut off by Jugurtha, and had to purchase its liberty from the Numidian king by a shameful submission.

Rome's Fight for North Africa

At last the popular party, which then embraced the more active element of the Roman people, succeeded in breaking the influence of the former leaders in the state, by enforcing the punishment of the chief offenders, and by placing incorruptible generals at the head of the army. Jugurtha, hard pressed by the consul Metellus succeeded in uniting temporarily the whole power of nomad North Africa against the Romans by making an alliance with his father-in-law, King Bocchus of Mauretania. The Mauretanian kingdom already existed in the time of the Second Punic War, and probably included the greater part of Morocco, while in culture it did not stand much behind Numidia, since the old Phœnician influence on the west coast of Morocco must have left some lasting traces. The alliance soon came to an end. Bocchus gave up his son-in-law to the Romans, who adorned their triumphal procession with him, and allowed the miserable captive to die in a subterranean dungeon. The Numidian kingdom was divided—one part was assigned to Bocchus, another joined to the Roman province, the rest was given over to two Numidian princes.

There was no attempt even in later times at a complete subjugation of North Africa by the Romans. If the Roman rule in North Africa did, however, in time secure a stronger position it was due more to the advance of civilisation and the common progress of the agricultural and town classes than to political measures. Where agriculture took hold, there the Roman influence also gained entrance ; and the intellectual ascendency of Rome was followed by a political ascendency, which made the Romans the natural protectors of every

Intellectual Ascendency of Rome

peaceful people in North Africa. While the province of Africa was in time transformed into a genuinely Roman territory, Numidia, too, did not escape the fate of being Romanised. Masinissa had diligently encouraged the settlement of agriculturists in his dominion. By so doing he laid a firm foundation for his power and first rendered a united Numidia possible ; but he at the same time abandoned the standard of pure nomad life, under which alone the Numidians could hope to resist the influence of Rome

The partly accidental circumstance that King Juba of Numidia, in the struggle between Pompey and Cæsar, placed himself on the side of the first and was involved in his fall, led to the change. Augustus annexed the eastern half of Numidia as a " new province " to the Roman empire and left Juba in possession of only the less cultivated west, as well as of Mauretania, which, however, recognised the rule of the king only to the smallest extent. From this time the name of the Numidians begins to be disused and the designation of " Mauri " becomes universal for the inhabitants of North Africa, especially for the nomads. The Romans soon saw themselves compelled to protect the cultivated lands now subject to their rule by lines of fortresses and a sort of military frontier against the nomads, who, driven back into the steppes and mountains, allowed themselves to be won over quite temporarily as fickle allies, but were always ready to make inroads into the corn-growing district. Since after the final decay of the Numidian power no formidable enemy threatened Roman Africa, a comparatively small number of troops was always sufficient to protect the country. Two legions, and later only one, had their permanent station in Africa ; indeed, the military strength of North Africa was trained by Rome to be used in foreign wars. Outside the province only the agricultural districts were under Roman influence ; and as these districts lay like oases in the regions occupied by nomads, there never was any attempt at a complete subjugation of the country. This applies particularly to Mauretania, which never became an integral part of the Roman empire.

The First Moors

The external history of Mediterranean Africa at the time of the Roman emperors presents little worthy of narration. Of all the border countries of the Roman empire, it was the least threatened. At the same time it belonged to those regions which offered little prospect of territorial expansion, and, therefore, never had to serve as the centre of military operations. Such favourable circumstances contributed greatly to the prosperity of the country. Roman Carthage, which had grown up on the site of Rome's annihilated rival, flourished to such a remarkable degree that it could compete in wealth and population with Alexandria. The grain exported from Africa had long become indispensable for Rome and Italy, where the country population steadily diminished; a portion of the stream of gold which poured into Rome was thus diverted to the African province.

The arts and sciences, when they sank from their high place in Rome, enjoyed a second period of prosperity in some provinces, and especially in Africa. But luxury and immorality, the evil associates of wealth, found a splendid soil. Perhaps both phenomena, intellectual development and material luxury, caused Christianity to strike deep root in Africa in a short time and favoured the further spread of the new teaching from this centre. We see the influence of Africa on Christianity embodied in the mighty form of Augustine. An intense and forceful nature, he sought fruitlessly to find the fulness of existence in pleasure, until an hour of true knowledge led him into the path of self-denial, which he trod with the same fiery impetuosity. African Christianity triumphed with Augustine. While it made the culture and wealth of the country of service to its cause, it gave Africa an important place in the civilised world, which, however, it was destined to keep for only a short time and then to lose for ever.

Augustine, the Fiery Bishop Augustine himself in the last year of his life saw hostile armies appear before Hippo, the town of which he was bishop— armies which were destined to tear Africa away from the Roman empire and to reduce it to a condition of misery, from which it did not rise until the time of the Arabs. In the great migratory movement, which had affected all the tribes of East Germany, the Vandals, who were settled in Western Silesia, had not remained quiet. Their relation to other Teutonic peoples is not quite clear; many historians of the period of the migration class them with the Goths; according to other surmises, they would belong to the great Suevian group. Pure Germans in the anthropological sense they could hardly have been. They were largely intermixed with that older population **Coming of the Vandals** which must have settled in Germany before the inroad of closely federated Teutonic tribes. Indeed, it has been concluded from the name of the Vandals that Slavonic or Wendish tribes were merged with them. At any rate, the Vandals are considered the least important of the Teutonic peoples that marched southward, the least courageous, and the most barbarous.

At the time of the wars with the Marcomanni the Vandals had already moved towards the Roman frontier in small hordes, until finally the whole people, moved by a spirit of unrest, began to look for new abodes. Partly as enemies, partly as allies of the Romans, the Vandals, then, as later, a people whose armed strength principally lay in cavalry, appeared on the Danube frontier. Beaten and almost annihilated by the Goths, they at last placed themselves entirely under the protection of Rome and received settlements in Pannonia, until, after a long period of quiet, and aroused apparently by the fortune of their countryman, Stilicho, they moved towards the Rhine; in alliance with the Alans they defeated the Franks on the Main and poured over Gaul, which almost without resistance fell a prey to their predatory hordes.

Three years later the treachery of German frontier guards opened to them the passes of the Pyrenees; and now Spain, which, like Gaul, accepted her fate with dull resignation, learnt all the horrors of a war with barbarians and of a foreign supremacy in 409. After some years of unrest the victors divided the land among themselves, though a part of it still remained Roman. Already better times seemed to be dawning for the vanquished, when the attack of the West Goths brought new disorders into Spain. A part of the Vandals were completely exterminated; the rest retreated towards

JUBA I. and II.
Kings of the State of Numidia during the Roman ascendency in Africa.

the south and once more acquired considerable power there for a time. That they then began definitely to apply themselves to maritime matters and to building a fleet is an important proof that they recognised their situation ; and though we might not be inclined to form too high an opinion of their fleet, it per-

The Vandals Become a Maritime People mitted them not only to undertake predatory expeditions to the neighbouring islands and coasts, but, in case of need, to flee with their families before the onset of enemies. The perfect development of the Vandal fleet was to take place in Africa.

During the feud of the Roman generals, Boniface and Aetius, the former in rage had recourse to the desperate expedient of appealing to Geiserich, king of the Vandals, for help. It was gladly granted. In May, 429, the army of the Vandals landed on the African coast. According to the most trustworthy account, there were, including women, children and old men, some 80,000 souls.

Boniface, who, meantime, had become reconciled with the Roman court, hurled himself against the invaders without avail, although he held Hippo Regius, the seat of the bishopric of Augustine, against the barbarians. After the defeat of Aetius he returned to Rome, where he died of his wounds. Hippo fell, so that in 435 almost the whole of Africa, with the exception of Carthage, the capital, was abandoned to the Vandals. Since nothing was done to ensure the security of this last and most important Roman centre, Geiserich grasped a favourable opportunity and, in 439, took the town by a sudden assault, the effeminate inhabitants offering no serious resistance. After prolonged struggles a new treaty was concluded, which, strangely enough, conceded Mauretania and Western Numidia to the Romans, while the rich east fell entirely to the

The Tide of Vandal Conquest Vandals in 442. In all these wars there is no trace of any serious resistance offered by the inhabitants. Boniface had defended Hippo with Gothic mercenaries, while the native population lent no appreciable assistance, and the nomad tribes of the country either adopted a dubious attitude, or availed themselves of the difficulties of the Roman governor to make attacks and engage in predatory expeditions. This demoralisation resulted from social conditions, the system of *latifundia* in particular, which had, perhaps, developed more favourably in Africa than in other parts of the Roman empire. The free peasants had long ago become the serfs of the great landed proprietors, and were little superior in position to the masses of slaves who were everywhere to be found.

But the great landowners became in their turn easy victims of the policy of extortion followed by unscrupulous governors increasingly as the dignity of the imperial power sank lower. No man who had anything to lose would now take a place in the senate of the large towns, which had once been the goal of the ambitious, for the senators were required to make up those deficiencies in the revenue which, with increasing oppression, became more and more frequent. At last Jews, heretics and criminals were forced into posts of honour and stood at the head of the town government which in Roman times had been so powerful. Bloody insurrections repeatedly broke out, always traceable ultimately to the pressure of taxation. The people had

Demoralisation of Roman Africa long since lost all military efficiency, for while the greatest part of the inhabitants of North Africa had lost all energy of character under the unfavourable social and economic conditions, the citizens of the towns had sunk into extravagance and vice. " Just as all the filth collects in the bottom of a ship," says Salvian, " so the manners of the Africans contain, as it were, the vices of the whole world. All other nations have their particular vices, as they have their peculiar virtues ; but among almost all Africans no single vice is missing."

Only one thing gave a certain stability to the African population and a power of resistance, though only passive resistance, against the Vandals in particular ; and that was religion. The Vandals, during their sojourn in Spain, had developed into fanatical Arians. They cruelly persecuted in its African home the Catholic faith, which Augustine had firmly planted ; but in doing so they planted in the vanquished the feeling of brotherhood, while they themselves remained like a strange body in the conquered land, without entering into permanent relations with the people or the soil of Africa. The fact that the Vandals came into Africa entirely as conquerors forced them immediately to organise their political system without special consideration for the conditions of the defeated. In particular, they did not attempt to draw over to their side, or even to spare, the two most powerful orders—the great landowners and the clergy—but actually proceeded to exterminate them ; and when they had seized for themselves all their property, assumed the position of the former owners of the soil.

But in so doing they were compelled to stop half-way, for the number of the Vandals was too small to enable them to bring the whole conquered territory under their immediate influence ; so that, at least in the more outlying and less fertile regions, old conditions continued, while the richer lands in the vicinity of the capital, Carthage, fell partly to the

of their property. We thus see the Vandals, after a certain state of tranquillity had set in, almost entirely concentrated in the Carthaginian territory. From there, as from the watch-tower of a castle, they observed their African kingdom and kept it in obedience, while in the greatest part **Tranquil** of Africa the Roman institutions **Vandal** remained almost undisturbed, **Rule** and only the revenues were surrendered to the Vandal overlord. There was no sign of any fusion of the conquerors with the old inhabitants of the country or even of the formation of a new race.

The Vandals, however, founded their power on the insecure base of piracy and their marauding rather than on the development of territorial possessions. The spiritual victory of African Christianity signified the tardy triumph of the old

THE AMPHITHEATRE OF EL JEMM, A ROMAN RELIC IN TUNIS
After the fall of Carthage most of North Africa became Roman, only Numidia and Mauretania retaining independence.

king, partly to his army. Even the king saw himself soon compelled to settle Roman farmers on his estates or to leave the old proprietors as serfs on their farms ; and other leading Vandals followed his example. The downfall was, therefore, not so complete as might seem at the first glance ; and a considerable part of the African population, after the first storm of conquest had blown over, might find themselves not **Vandal** worse off under Vandal rule **Conquest** than under the control of **Only Partial** corrupt Roman governors. The Africans had even less to do with military service than in the Roman times. Besides serfs and the slaves there were also the native officials, who were treated by the conquerors almost as equals ; and the caprice of the Vandal ruler left here and there free landowners in the enjoyment

Carthaginian land over Rome, the mistress of the world ; now a fleet was destined to set sail from the harbour of Carthage under the command of the fair-haired Geiserich, which was to bring on Rome all the horrors of devastation.

With this pillage of Rome, in 455, a long succession of Vandal predatory expeditions begins. Almost yearly King Geiserich harassed the coasts of Sicily and Italy with his fleets ; and he knew how to avoid successfully a dangerous blow, planned by the emperor Majorian in 458, in alliance with the West Goths. The confused state of affairs in the western empire constantly afforded him new pretexts for marauding expeditions ; and when the Byzantine emperor interfered the Vandal king welcomed the opportunity for completely devastating his territories on the coast. The campaign of vengeance, which the emperor Leo undertook in 468 with all his forces, absolutely failed, after the Byzantine fleet had been annihilated by a night attack of the Vandals. Some years later Geiserich, whose restless spirit began at last to feel the burden of old age, concluded a peace with Byzantium and soon afterwards with

Power of Geiserich the Fair Rome. This most powerful of the Vandal kings died in 477. His kingdom at his death embraced not merely North Africa as far as Cyrene, but also Sardinia, Corsica, the Balearic Isles, and a part of Sicily. But, indeed, in internal strength it had lost rather than gained, since the numbers of the Vandals necessarily were steadily diminished by their constant predatory expeditions. It is significant that under his successor, Hunerich, a number of the Moorish tribes regained their independence, while Hunerich himself entirely forfeited what popularity he had among the natives through his cruel persecutions of the Catholics. Still more grave was the defection of the Moors under King Gunthamund from 487 to 496.

The efforts of King Thrasamund (496–523), by every means, and wherever possible by conciliatory measures, to establish the supremacy of the Arian faith in his kingdom, and thus to root the Vandal power more firmly in the soil, failed as completely as the previous attempts to do so by violence. Nor was the king successful in the wars against the Moors. An alliance with the East Goths, cemented by the marriage of the king with the Gothic princess Amalafrida might have been of great use to the realm, but it was not lasting. Disturbances arose among the Vandals themselves. And when Hilderich, successor of Thrasamund, who sought to gain the support of Byzantium, and was inclined to Catholicism, was driven from the throne by his general, Gelimer, the Byzantine

Decline of the Vandal Kingdom emperor, Justinian, believed that the time had at length come to reassert his old claims on Africa. The attempt succeeded beyond his expectations. The towns of the Tripolitan coast, which had no Vandal garrison, submitted without demur ; Carthage offered no resistance ; and when Gelimer mustered his Vandals for the decisive battle he sustained, in spite of the enemy's inferior numbers, a crushing defeat.

This ended the Vandal rule. The Catholic population of the country greeted the Byzantine general, Belisarius. as their liberator ; the Moors remained neutral or availed themselves of the confusion to make raids on friends and foes. This was all the more grave, because the Vandals had early begun to form a part of their armies out of Moorish mercenaries, and in particular could no longer dispense with the Moorish archers. King Gelimer, who had thrown himself into a frontier castle, surrendered in the spring of 534. Subsequent risings of the Vandals only brought about the result that the rest of the nation were exterminated or banished from Africa. This fact is important, because the attempt has been made repeatedly to trace back peculiarities of North African peoples to a strong admixture of Vandal blood, while, in reality, even at the time of the Vandal rule, religious differences prevented any widespread amalgamation, and afterwards the Germanic conquering race entirely disappeared from Africa. Even their language and customs have left little trace. The emperor Justinian, after the con-

Disappearance of the Vandals quest of the country, did not find it hard to reintroduce the Roman institutions, which had only partially been superseded by the Vandals, and among them the detested Roman system of taxation. But as the Vandal conquerors had carried on the war of the settled population against the nomads, which they had been forced, as owners of the cultivated land, to take up, difficulties increased for the Byzantine governors, who had to hold the province. An imposing command of Justinian, that the petty Moorish principalities should in the future submit to the Roman laws, made little impression. Continual risings of the Moors depopulated the land ; and, in addition, religious dissensions among the Africans, who were zealous supporters of the faith, found the best soil. Thus the moral and economic forces of North Africa had sunk to the lowest depths when the wave of the Arabian conquest came rolling on.

The West Goths from Spain had temporarily planted foot on the African coast ; but the importance of their possessions can hardly have been greater than that of the present Spanish presidios, which exercise not the slightest influence on the interior.

BARBARY IN THE MIDDLE AGES

NATURALLY, the storm of Arabian invasion fell first on Egypt, which in 641 came under the domination of Islam. In the first ardour of conquest the Arabian armies pressed on further, and, perceiving the feeble resistance of the Byzantines, went beyond Tripoli, without, however, at once attaining any permanent results. The difficulties of communication and of sending reinforcements by land always made it possible for the Byzantines, who were the masters of the sea, to win back what was lost. It is obvious that the settled population was again diminished by these wars ; but at the same time the importance of the nomad Berbers grew, and the contending powers had more and more to reckon with them.

It seemed as if after the founding of Kairuan in the vicinity of the old capital, Carthage, the Arabian supremacy was secured. But in 683 the general Okba was defeated by the united forces of the Byzantines and the Berbers. **Arabs Cross to Spain** The Berbers, who essentially are disposed to extreme political disunion, combined this time to a great extent under the leadership of a heroic priestess, Damia, or Kahinah, defeated the Arabian general, Hassan ibn Noman, in 696, drove the Arabs back into Cyrenaica, and endeavoured to make the return of their opponents impossible by devastating the frontier lands. Hassan's successor, Musa ibn Noseir, first succeeded in conquering North Africa, or at least in driving out the Byzantines ; but he used the hard-won territory as a bridge for passing into Spain. There, in the fertile land that had been cultivated for centuries he founded a strong frontier post of Islam in 712. In this way the victory of the Mohammedan religion in North Africa was assured.

No foreign rule had such far-reaching effects on the coast of North Africa as the Arabian. The Arab invaders were the natural protectors of the settled population, on whose work and tribute their own existence depended. But they were at the same time a people of the desert, who found in the steppes of the conquered land a welcome scope for their love of nomad life. North Africa became a real home to them. While spreading their religion and their language, they assimilated the aborigines to themselves to a continually increasing degree, **The Struggle of Arab and Berber** or drove back the refractory tribes into the mountains and deserts. But by their side rose in rapid growth the native race of the Berbers, to whom the religion of Islam, with its disputes and its infinite sects, gave a new spiritual outlook and supplied the core of a national unity. The struggle between Arabian civilisation and refinement and the rude strength of the Berbers occupied for centuries the history of North Africa, and even to-day the civilisation of the Arabs is not everywhere victorious.

Of the greatest importance, however, for North Africa, and especially for the most westerly and most uncivilised district, Mauretania—the later Morocco—was the conquest of Spain and the close relations which were thus necessarily formed between the Mohammedans in Spain and Morocco. The marvellous blending of Eastern and Western civilisation in Moorish Spain, the pure blossoms of art and science which in the gloomy days of the Middle Ages flowered here in fabulous abundance, of which the memory even now glorifies the ruins of Moorish grandeur, did not fail to make a deep impression on the rude sons of Mauretania. But as the advance of the Christian Spaniards began gradually to reduce the territory of Islam in Spain, bands of Moors, skilled in the fine arts, streamed over the straits, and, finding a refuge in **Spanish Moors in Morocco** the towns of Morocco, transmitted their industry and their skill to the old inhabitants of the land, as later the French refugees brought the germs of industry and skilled production into distant German countries.

Only one famous craft of the Spanish Moors need be mentioned, the dyeing of leather, which, under the name of

Corduan, was formerly exported to all countries, but is now no longer prepared in Cordova, as of old. In Morocco the dyeing of leather is even to-day one of the most important and flourishing industries. Nor merely in Morocco, but also far to the south, on the banks of the Niger and its tributaries, the same craft is practised,

Morocco's Most Important Industry which, introduced probably by emigrant Moors, has found its way thither over the desert. Even direct relations between Spain and the Sudan can be proved, for we find architects, especially from Granada, in the service of Sudanese princes.

Such facts make it plain that intercourse with the countries of the negritic races must have been developed in a quite different and more important fashion than during the Roman and Vandal times. The growth of the Sudanese trade is, in fact, a further and most valuable result of the appearance of the Arabs in North Africa. When numerous Arab tribes scorned to settle in the corn-growing land as lords of the agricultural population, but turned as true nomads to the steppe and the desert, they brought the influence of Islam into the wide desert belt, whose natural dangers and hostile inhabitants had until now restricted all brisk commercial intercourse.

Things were immediately changed when the Arabs began to act as guides for the merchants. The trading spirit of the Arabian race, which showed itself conspicuously in the first centuries after the conquest, helped to surmount all difficulties. Even the political influence of the Arabian power extended further south than that of the Roman empire, for the armies of the conquerors penetrated to the oases of Fezzan and even Kauar—that is to say, half-way to the Central Sudan. And as they then succeeded in spreading Islam in Negroland, North and South were united by a spiritual bond, and the

The Arabs Open up the Sahara severing tract of the Sahara formed no longer a hindrance to the streams of trade and culture. Communication with the Sudan had, however, other results for North Africa than the accumulation of wealth ; those coast towns which lay safe behind their walls and defended harbours showed often an almost republican independence in their dealings with the caliphs. For the treasures of the East and West, which the Arabian merchant forwarded to

the banks of the Niger and of Lake Chad, the Sudan offered in return gold and ostrich feathers and, above all, men, sons of Ham, destined in the eyes of believers to be slaves. In the markets of the north coast black slaves were a staple article of sale ; negro women filled the harems of the wealthy, and negro guards protected the governors of Africa and the Spanish caliphs.

The result was that beneath the original population of the north coast, which, under Arabian influence, was being absorbed into a new Islamitic nationality, there lay a deeper social stratum, a proletariat, which, in undertaking all hard labour, lightened the burdens of the upper classes, but influenced them unfavourably by the unavoidable mixture of blood. This applies chiefly to Morocco, where even the present ruling dynasty has a goodly proportion of negritic blood in its veins, and everywhere marriages with negro women are of ordinary occurrence. This had not been the case in earlier times to at all the same extent. And as the country already possessed in the powerful

Arabs Become Negritic Berbers an element not amenable to culture, the hampering influences on civilisation must inevitably have grown stronger with the rise of the negroes. In Africa the supremacy of the caliphs of Bagdad was maintained for only some hundred years. During this period the greater part of the Berber tribes were won over to Islam, but not without frequent risings, which disturbed the peace. The Berbers, who had already taken part in the conquest of Spain as the picked troops of the army, proved dangerous and obstinate opponents ; and though Islam made continued progress among them, the number of the Arabs diminished to a serious extent in the constant battles. An utter defeat of the Arabs near Tangier in 740 is known as the " Battle of the Nobles," on account of the number of nobles and generals slain.

When, on the overthrow of the Ommayyads, the caliphate went to the Abbassides Africa became temporarily independent, and was not reduced to submission until 772. In the meantime, a prince of the Ommayyad house, Abd ur-Rahman, made himself master of Spain, and all efforts of the Abbassides to win back the land were successfully frustrated. The loss of the African possessions was henceforth only a question of time. Mauretania, the present Morocco, which in early times had always been least accessible to foreign influence, owing to its out-lying position and its geographical conditions, was the first to break away from the world-empire of Islam. Under the leadership of Edris ibn Edris, a descendant of the caliph Ali, the Moors succeeded in finally shaking off the yoke of the Abbassides. It is a significant fact that Berber tribes were the first to join the new rulers. Immediately the zealot trait in the Berber nature employed itself in the forcible conversion of Christians and pagans, who were still numerous in the land. The empire of Morocco has preserved even to the present day the reputation of being a stronghold of Moslem intolerance. The town of Fez was founded in 806 as the centre of the new state, and within its walls a not unimportant civilisation was soon developed.

The rest of Africa was held only a few years longer by the Abbassides. The caliph, Harun al Rashid, thought he had made a good choice when he entrusted the governorship of Africa to **Africa Lost to the Caliphate** the energetic and wise Ibrahim ebn al Aglab; but only too soon the loyal subject was transformed into the ambitious rebel. He found but little opposition, for even the caliph made no serious effort to recover the lost province. The centre of the empire of the Aglabites remained Kairuan ; Tripoli and the greater part of the present Tunis and Algeria formed the most valuable portion of the dominion. Tunis succeeded Carthage as a great commercial town. The Arabian possessions in Sardinia and Sicily naturally fell to the Aglabites, who strengthened their position considerably by the conquest of the important town of Syracuse in 877.

The dynasty of the Aglabites was displaced in 908 by Obeid Allah, who posed as the Mahdi promised by Mahomet. He also dislodged the Edrisites from the throne of Mauretania, and united all North Africa, with the exception of Egypt, under his rule. But Egypt, too, was lost to the Abbassides in the year 968, and fell into the power of the Fatemides. These shifted the centre of their power to Cairo, and in 972 gave their western possessions to the family of the Zeirites to hold in fee. The history of the Zeirites shows how at that time, just as

much as in the Roman period, North Africa was filled with partially and sometimes completely independent petty states and tribal districts, and how in the hands of a brave leader an empire could be formed that might either last or break up again quickly into its component parts. The Zeirites firmly established their power in the struggle with the **Petty States of North Africa** feudal lords of Africa, and now, although nominally they remained dependent on Cairo, completely took the place of the Fatemides. Africa remained united, outwardly at least, for nearly a century, until Morocco once more attained its independence, and began to exercise a decisive influence on the history of the surrounding countries.

Religion gave once again the pretext for a national revolution. Arabs were this time the spiritual leaders of an insurrection, which had, however, mostly to be fought out by the Berbers. An Arabian tribe, whose suddenly awakened religious zeal was sharpened by a famine, under the leadership of its chief, Abu Bekr, took possession of the town of Sejelmesa, and there arose the new dynasty of the Molathemides, or, as it is usually called, of the Almoravides.

Under the second ruler of the line, Yusuf (1069–1109), the greater part of Mauretania was subdued, and a new capital, Morocco, was founded in the south-west, where the pasture grounds of the victorious tribe lay. The forces of a rude, but brave and hardy people, which Yusuf now united under his command, enabled him to prosecute his conquests. While, on the one hand, the empire of the Zeirites had become so disorganised that it finally and irretrievably broke up, on the other hand, the Moorish princes of Spain, who were subject to the rule of the Christians, implored the aid of the African ruler. Nothing could have been more welcome to Yusuf. Received as protector and **Spain Conquered By Africa** saviour, he inflicted a crushing blow on King Alfonso VI. of Castile at Zalaca in 1086 ; but the rulers of Granada and of Seville had in turn to renounce their powers. The cultured Islamitic Spaniards now saw themselves with reluctance ruled by the rude sons of Africa, whose brutal strength they, however, no longer ventured to resist. The conquest was, on the other hand, most advantageous to Yusuf and his African subjects. The overthrow of Islam had been successfully prevented, and Spain had been made a source of strength to Africa ; but the rude Berbers, who crossed the straits, not only found wealth in Spain, but learnt to value in some degree the attractions of a higher civilisation. The age of the Almoravides seems to have been for Africa a period of increasing prosperity and of tolerable internal tranquillity. The second successor of Yusuf was defeated by a genuine Berber from the Atlas, Mohammed Abdallah ibn Tomrut. The proclamation by this successful fanatic of his descent from Hosein was one of the favourite means employed by politico-religious reformers to win universal respect. In reality, his success signified a new victory of the native spirit and a further strengthening of the Berber influence. The sharp antagonism to enlightenment so characteristic of Berber life becomes more distinctly seen in the course of history. After bloody civil wars the new dynasty of the Almohades obtained undisputed sway in Morocco in 1149. On them the task devolved of supporting the Moslem states in Spain, which could not, unaided, hold out against the Christians. Once more the African saviours proved dubious friends, and it was only after numerous conflicts that the greater part of Islamitic Spain consented to acknowledge the supremacy of the Almohades.

Rise of the Berbers

Though the centre of the African power lay in Western Morocco, and the fate of the state was repeatedly decided there, the eastern districts of the north coast stood only in very loose connection with the empire of the Almoravides and Almohades, and maintained—as, for example, the district of Bugia—under their own dynasties almost complete independence. Sicily, the rampart of Africa, had fallen in the eleventh century into the hands of the Normans, who soon afterwards gained possession of several towns on the African coast, as Tunis and Mahadia ; and it may well be imagined that the Berber tribes of the mountains and steppes would hardly recognise a lord over them. It was only in 1159 that Abd al Munen, a prince of the Almohades, succeeded in once more setting foot firmly in the East in conquering Bugia, Tunis, and Mahadia, and in driving out of the land all Christian inhabitants. The claims of the Almohades to Spain

Driving Out the Christians

became in the end fatal to them. By the ever-increasing power of the Christian states they saw themselves driven to incessant wars, in which the flower of their armies was destroyed. Their dominion received, however, the most terrible blow in the battle at Tolosa, in 1212, in which the enormous army they had collected with the greatest exertions was utterly crushed. Their African empire now began to fall to pieces. In 1206 Tunis was lost to an insurgent, who was able to establish his power firmly, and founded the dynasty of the Hafides. The Spanish possessions also regained their independence. And, finally, after civil war the dynasty of the Merinides eventually gained the throne of Morocco in 1269, after the founder of the family had already asserted his independence in the province of Schaus in 1213.

Thus, then, the African empire of Islam was finally destroyed ; and the chief " Barbary " states of subsequent times already begin to develop—Morocco, Algeria, Tunis, and Tripoli. The relations of Islam to the Christian states on the Mediterranean had, meantime, completely changed. The West once more advanced to the attack. The African states soon saw themselves harassed on their own soil by the armies and fleets of the Christian rulers. Then first, and more for defence than for aggression, the fleets of the " Barbary states " were formed, which were destined to remain the scourge of the Mediterranean countries down to the nineteenth century.

Barbary States Develop

The internal development of Morocco offers for centuries nothing worthy of remark. Not until 1588 did the empire of Morocco expand, and then, which is significant, not towards the east or north, but towards the south. A small Moorish army occupied Timbuktu, and the town was in 1680 still in the hands of Morocco. Here and in the western Sudan their influence has been maintained until almost the present day. The opportunity was thus presented to the princes of Morocco of enlisting large numbers of black troops, which were of great service to them in the frequent civil wars, but also continually increased the negritic element in the population of North-west Africa. The negro guards, naturally, found many opportunities to decide the fate of the rulers and of the ruling houses.

MEDI-
TERRANEAN
NORTH AFRICA
V

BARBARY
STATES IN
MODERN TIMES

THE MODERN BARBARY STATES
AND THE FRENCH IN NORTH AFRICA

THE expulsion of the Moors from Granada was of still greater importance for the eastern African states than for Morocco. The small states in Algeria and Tunisia had led up till now an unimportant existence, which had been only temporarily disturbed by the adventurous and completely unsuccessful crusade of King Louis IX. of France against Tunis. With the increasing influx of Moors, who were filled with a burning thirst for vengeance against Spain, and who also had the means to fit out pirate ships, these small states came into hostile relations with Spain, and in the beginning distinctly to their disadvantage. The punitive expedition which Cardinal Ximenez undertook in the year 1509 struck panic into the whole coast region. From that time the Spaniards occupied not merely Oran, Bugia, and a fortress in the harbour of Algiers, but exacted tribute from some petty states, while **A Cardinal Attacks the Pirates** the Berber tribes in the mountains were practically independent. The town of Tripoli, with some other places on the coast, was in the hands of the Knights of Malta, and the Genoese occupied the island of Tabarca. Thus the resistance of the African states was limited to petty acts of privateering, until they in their turn were drawn into that new movement of Islam which started with the Turks, and was destined to send out its offshoots as far as the borders of Morocco.

The man who gave life to the new influence was the renegade Horuk Barbarossa, a Greek from Lesbos. As captain of a privateer, fitted out by traders of Constantinople, he sailed to the Western Mediterranean, and made the town of Tunis the starting-point of successful predatory expeditions. He was soon in possession of a complete fleet of well-equipped ships, the crews of which were, for the most part, Turks. He gradually made himself master of several places on the coast, and at last of the town of Algiers ; the expelled ruler tried in vain to recover his small territory by help of the Spaniards in the year 1517. After the death of Horuk his brother, **Founding a Robber State** Cheireddin, extended the newly formed robber state, and put it on a permanent footing by placing himself under the overlordship of the Porte.

The period of Turkish rule which now begins was, on the whole, a sad time for the countries on the coast of North Africa. The real rulers of the country were the Turkish garrisons. By the side of these the pasha, appointed by the Sultan, enjoyed only the merest semblance of power, while the Arabian and Berber inhabitants of the country were exposed helplessly and unjustly to the caprice of the rude soldiery. Piracy became more and more the only source of wealth for the unhappy countries. The reason why this source was not soon stopped by strong measures was chiefly that Spain, diverted from her design on Africa by the discovery of America, gradually sank into political impotence. Charles V., by the conquest of Tunis in 1535, took the first step towards ending the curse of piracy. But the attack on Algiers failed ; and in 1574 Tunis was finally lost.

There, too, the Turkish military rule was instituted. As in Algiers, the representatives of the soldiers formed a sort of republican government, or " divan," at the head of which a Dey with uncertain influence was usually placed. The relations between Algiers and Tunis were, as **Turkish Vassal States** a rule, unfriendly : in 1757 Tunis was actually conquered and sacked by Algerian troops, and its reigning lord deposed. As compared with Algiers, the third Turkish vassal state of Tripoli fell into the background even more than Tunis. It had been founded in 1551 after the expulsion of the Maltese by an old subordinate officer of Cheireddin Barbarossa, Dragut. Here also the Turkish militia had things completely in their hands. Algiers, Tunis, and Tripoli—nominal vassals of Turkey—

In the Days of the Corsairs all obtained an unenviable reputation for piracy; although, in reality, it was not the nature of privateering itself as practised by them which distinguished them, but only the long persistence of a condition which had been gradually abandoned by the other inhabitants of the Mediterranean. In the Middle Ages the Christian states had fitted out corsairs as much as the Mohammedan states, in order to capture hostile merchantmen and to plunder the coasts of their enemies.

possible victims was much lessened, the sphere of these raids must have been extended. In fact, the corsairs appeared quite early on the other side of the Straits of Gibraltar. In 1617 Madeira was plundered; the Irish coast was devastated in 1631, and Iceland invaded in 1637.

A severe check was inflicted upon them by the English Navy, under the command of Robert Blake, in the time of the Commonwealth; nevertheless, even at the beginning of the nineteenth century Algerian pirates cruised as far as the North Sea. The object of these voyages was not only the seizure of gold and property, but also of men. The sums obtained as ransoms for captive Christians were an important source of income to the rulers

THE PIRATES' STRONGHOLD : THE TOWN OF ALGIERS AS IT WAS ABOUT THE YEAR 1670

Algiers, one of the three great pirate states of Barbary, was organised by a Greek renegade in 1517, and from that time until the French conquest in 1830 subsisted by open piracy, though nominally vassal of Turkey.

There could be no possibility of thoroughly extirpating the curse unless the districts on the coast were brought under the dominion of a Christian state. But for a long time no nation showed any desire for a difficult and thankless undertaking of this kind; and it was thought preferable to secure immunity by treaties. This succeeded partially, and the whole burden of the loss naturally devolved on those states which could not come to an agreement with the corsairs. On the whole, the power of the Barbary states sank steadily in the course of centuries; and petty enterprises took the place of the great predatory expeditions of the earlier times. But as the number of

and inhabitants of the Barbary states. The power of the Turk waned from the time when his advance was finally repulsed by Prince Eugene of Savoy. States which subsist primarily by open piracy cannot be tolerated by civilised maritime powers. Yet the Barbary pirates continued to practise their profession without

End of the Barbary Pirates being definitely suppressed through the eighteenth century. Even severe chastisement inflicted by British and other fleets in the early nineteenth century did not destroy the plague spot. It was France which finally put an end to the pest.

In 1830, the French monarchy of Charles X. was in parlous state. Searching

ALGIERS: THE BASE OF FRENCH EMPIRE-BUILDING IN NORTH AFRICA

Algiers, the capital and only important seaport of Algeria, was occupied by the French in 1830 after three centuries of piracy. Its exquisite climate has made it a favourite winter resort for Europeans, and the consequent growth of the town can be seen in the picture at the top of the page. Inset on the left is a street in the Arab quarter, and on the right a view of the Governor's palace. At the bottom is a view of the principal boulevard.

THE TOWER OF SKULLS AT JERBA IN TUNIS
A ghastly monument of a Christian expedition to the pirates' haunts in 1561 and its defeat by the Arabs.

for some means of recovering popularity without desisting from its reactionary domestic policy, it sought to obtain martial glory. The Dey of Algiers had very flagrantly insulted the French consul, and reparation had never been made. A strong punitive expedition was despatched; it made a rapid conquest. The Dey and his Turks were removed from the country; and to this the Berber population appear to have felt no strong objections. The French had no more intention of staying in Algeria than Europeans ever have of staying in barbaric realms in which they have been compelled by circumstances to make a military demonstration. But the honest intention of retiring is usually frustrated by the sense of responsibility for restoring order and then for maintaining it — since it is commonly manifest that withdrawal will be followed by the recrudescence of anarchy. So it was with the French in Algeria;

and there was a further inducement at the outset to postpone retirement. The Bourbon monarchy fell, and Louis Philippe could hardly venture to signalise his accession by what his enemies would have clamoured against as an example of "the craven fear of being great." So the French stayed—to restore order.

The natives had acquiesced in the ejection of their Turkish governors; they were not equally ready to accept control by the infidels, especially as the latter displayed some want of tact in handling their susceptibilities. They rose in insurrection under Abd el-Kadir, a leader of heroic type, who met with such success that after two years of fighting the French recognised him as sultan of a great part of the country. This, however, did not suffice; and in 1839, two years after the truce, Abd el-Kadir and the French were at war again. This time the relentless vigour of the French attack presently drove the native chief out of the country to Morocco; only to return with fresh forces. Under such circumstances, the emperor had no alternative but to carry the contest through to a finish. The French did so. Abd el-Kadir ultimately found himself compelled to surrender to save his country from destruction. For some time he was held in durance, till Napoleon III. released him.

The whole of Algeria was not, in fact, brought into subjection until 1847. Under the Republic which upset Louis Philippe,

A CONFERENCE WITH THE PIRATE DEY OF ALGIERS IN 1816
The Barbary pirates flourished in the 18th century, and in 1816 a British fleet, under Lord Exmouth, visited Algiers and inflicted severe chastisement, after conference with the Dey.

A GENERAL VIEW OF TUNIS, THE CAPITAL OF THE FRENCH PROTECTORATE
Tunis, the second of the Barbary pirate states, remained a nominal vassal state of Turkey until 1883, when it was placed under French protection, and its government controlled by French administrators.

Algeria was treated as if it had been simply an outlying portion of France. Napoleon III. recognised that European methods of self-government were not adapted to the population. One after another, a series of experiments in the form of military governments, governments more or less modelled on that of the British in India, were attempted, culminating, in 1879, with a reversion to parliamentary methods ; but none have achieved distinguished success. On the other hand, there has been a very large immigration of Europeans from Southern Italy, Malta, and Spain, as well as from Southern France, and these elements seem likely to fuse with the native Algerians, so as to produce a distinct race-modification. Finally, Algeria is a base from which French influence has extended southwards to meet the northward movement from the French Sudan, and the consolidation of a French North African empire is in sight.

On the east of Algeria, Tunis—like Algeria, a nominal vassal-state of Turkey—enjoyed in the nineteenth

ABD EL-KADIR
Who carried on a "holy war" against the French in Algeria.

century a much more enlightened government under the ruling dynasty than her neighbours. France, established at Algiers, was willing enough to extend her ascendency to Tunis ; but Algerian difficulties on the one hand, and British opposition on the other, checked her zeal. In course of time, however, the Tunisian administration degenerated ; European intervention became necessary. The British Government remained inert ; Italy, the other Power mainly interested, hesitated to assume direct rivalry with France ; and France found sufficient excuse for forcing the Dey to place himself under French " protection." From 1883, therefore, Tunis has been recognised as a French Protectorate —that is, like the protected states in India, it retains its dynasty, but its government is practically controlled by French administrators, with excellent effects.

Tripoli, like her western neighbours, owned but a very nominal allegiance to her suzerain at the Porte. But when France was asserting herself in Algeria, Turkey

2213

took the opportunity, in 1835, to reassert her authority in this eastern member of the group of Barbary states. The existing dynasty was removed, and the country administered under a pasha as a vilayet of the Turkish empire ; and so it has remained ever since—not without the occasional revolts which might be regarded as matter of course.

Morocco, though, unlike the other three corsair states, it did not fall under the casually exercised dominion of the Turk, did not establish itself as a consolidated Power till some two centuries after the annihilation of the Moorish power in Spain, when Muley Ismail brought the country under his dominion. Since then it has remained a single kingdom—the type of an Oriental absolutist monarchy. To European influences it continues to oppose an impenetrable screen of what Europeans call fanatical prejudice. The state retains an obstinate power of resistance to the intervention of " infidels," as the Spaniards found in 1859, though their campaign in that year was in form successful. The history of Morocco has been one, not of progress, but of stagnation, if not of retrogression. Its government nominally displays all the worst features of an utterly irresponsible despotism —and its people ask for nothing else. The thing they have is the thing they understand. Individual liberty, in the sense of an absence of government control, flourishes ; in the sense of security of life,

ABDUL AZIZ, SULTAN OF MOROCCO
The present Sultan of Morocco, who is credited with Europeanising tendencies, though they do not seem accompanied by administrative ability.

MULAI HAFID, THE RIVAL SULTAN
Who has derived much support from the anti-foreign agitation due to the Sultan's leanings to Europeanisation.

person, or property against outrage, chains and robbery, it hardly exists. In the interior, the monarch can command no obedience ; nowhere, and at no time is he secure against revolt. The population of Morocco has no idea of accepting the one method by which anything which Europeans recognise as permanent can be established — the assumption of sovereignty by a European Power.

It is not easy to judge how far there is any real probability of such a sovereignty coming effectively into play ; the mutual jealousies of European states always militate against any one of them becoming supreme, and even when a supremacy is established, as with the British in Egypt, it tends to be hampered. Nevertheless, a tendency to mutual accommodation has been displayed. In 1904 France and Great Britain arrived at a convention which was accepted by Spain. French antagonism was withdrawn in Egypt, and France was to be in effect recognised as having paramount interests in Morocco. In other words, apart from reservation of express treaty rights, France was conceded the right of intervention in the administration of the Moorish kingdom. Still, as other Powers were dissatisfied, a further conference of all the Powers interested was held at Algeciras in 1906, resulting in an agreement, of which the fundamental point is the paramount authority and responsibility of France.

On France, therefore, has devolved the lion's share of the troubles which have

TANGIERS AND TETUAN: THE CHIEF CITIES OF MOROCCO

Unlike the other three corsair states of North Africa, Morocco did not come under the vassalage of Turkey, but has remained a single despotic kingdom. A general view of Tangiers, the chief commercial city and diplomatic headquarters, is given at the top of the page, the royal palace being shown in the middle on the left, and a street in the city on the right. Tetuan, the city and seaport next in importance, is seen at the bottom.

Photos by N. P. Edwards

recently disturbed Morocco. The sultan Abdul Aziz is credited with Europeanising tendencies ; but these are not accompanied by administrative vigour or ability. Hence the anti-foreigner agitation has received an additional incentive among the population ; and a rival sultan, Mulai Hafid, was proclaimed in 1907, who has found considerable support. Before Mulai Hafid's appearance the native attitude to the foreigner had found expression in the murder of a French subject, with the result that France found herself compelled to make naval and military demonstrations. These in turn were followed by antiforeigner demonstrations. At one time it seemed that several Powers would cooperate, but finally the management of affairs was left to France. The French troops have had several engagements with native forces, but the spirit of revolt has as yet hardly been checked. In any case, Islam in its rigid North African form will

RAISULI   KAID MACLEAN

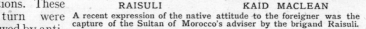

A recent expression of the native attitude to the foreigner was the capture of the Sultan of Morocco's adviser by the brigand Raisuli.

remain a most dangerous and almost invincible foe to European civilisation. How, at the present day, this fanatical antagonism to European influences has acquired overwhelming force in North Africa is shown by the history of the Senussi order, a party of reform, organised in the true North African spirit of hostility to civilisation. The founder, who came from Tlemcen in Algeria, found in the oasis Siwah a continually increasing body of followers. From here the supporters of the order have spun, as it were, a net round North Africa, and have acquired an influence with which every ruler of the separate countries and every European colonial power has seriously to reckon. The death of the original Senussi in the middle of the 'sixties did not harm the movement. Under his successor the oasis of Siwah is still the centre of the Senussi influence and the home of a burning hatred of Christianity.   HEINRICH SCHURTZ

ADMINISTRATION DIFFICULTIES IN MOROCCO : KABYLES DEFYING THE TAXGATHERERS

TROPICAL NORTH AFRICA
ITS NATIVE RACES AND STATES
BY DR. HEINRICH SCHURTZ

PEOPLES OF THE WESTERN SUDAN

BY reason of its climatic conditions and ethnographical character, the Sudan may be considered as a transition zone between the Sahara and the well-watered tropical regions of Central Africa, together with the Guinea Coast.

In its population, the Negro, the Ethiopian, and the Libyan combine in varying proportions, while at a comparatively later period another light-coloured race, the Arabs, influenced the Sudan.

We may assume that the power and importance of the desert tribes of the Sahara and the southern steppes increased considerably in proportion as the growing numbers of their cattle enabled them to derive more profit from the poor soil upon which they lived. At first probably unsettled bands of hunters, they grew to be powerful and warlike tribes. In this course of development were two separate stages, marked by the introduction of cattle at an early period, and the introduction of the camel, which did not

Development of Desert Tribes take place until late in the Roman period. At first the black agricultural tribes of Central Africa were superior to the needy inhabitants of the desert, but the balance of power turned in the opposite direction until the negroes were subjugated or forced to retreat.

At an early stage the negroes seem to have been spread over nearly the whole of the Sudan and far into the desert. In the Western Sahara are also unmistakable remnants of an old negro population. According to the

The State-forming Races Roman historian Sallust (86–34 B.C.) the southern districts of the true desert were in the hands of the negroes in his time; but even then forerunners of those different races from which the Berbers were afterward compounded may have been settled side by side with the negro inhabitants.

In the Western and Central Sudan are two great state-forming races, largely of negro blood, the Mandingo and the Hausa. These are manufacturing and trading peoples by profession. They are thus endowed with the necessary qualities for entering a foreign district, forming small colonies within it, and seizing the government for themselves when occasion offers. The Mandingo are leather-workers, dyers, weavers, and smiths, and extend as far as the west coast. Trade and manual industry have enabled the Hausa to advance to the slave coast, where their support of Mohammedanism has gained them considerable influence. The Soninke, to the south of the Mandingo, are a tribe of similar character. We have examples of involuntary migrations of this kind, especially in the east of the Sudan, to which inhabitants of Bornu and Bagirmi have been transplanted, bringing with them a higher civilisation. It is very possible that the transmission of civilisation by migration of this kind was one of the forces which completed the expansion of the earliest states in the Sudan, the negro finding manufacturing ability to be a new means of overpowering the shepherd tribes of the desert, who were disinclined to labour.

How Negro Civilisation Grew The stimulus given to pilgrimage by Mohammedanism extended the horizon and greatly increased traffic. When the Berber races grew to be powerful tribes, excellently conformed to their special environment, the black races, with their tendency to form petty states, were forced to retreat. By far the most important of these tribes is the great Tuareg people, or, more properly, Imoschagh. Their conformation to the conditions of desert life and their advance southward appear to have been purely involuntary. Though the northern parts of the desert were already in the possession of the Tuareg in Sallust's time, the main body of the people seems to have been settled in the fruitful districts under the mountain chain of North Africa until the Arab conquest drove them gradually to retreat southward. Different Arab tribes pressed after them, and in places divided the new territory with them ; but the negroes, who were settled in the oases on the south of the desert, succumbed to the attacks of the Tuareg. These repeated shocks produced racial movements which were transmitted to the Sudan in southerly and easterly directions.

Even before that period important negro kingdoms existed in the Western Sudan. The history of the kingdom of Ghana, or Gharata—properly Aucar—can be retraced further than any other. This state is said to have been founded about 300 A.D. It was situated on the edge of the desert, west of Timbuktu, and northwest of the Upper Niger valley. It was

Earliest Negro Kingdom not, however, a pure negro kingdom. The ruling house seems to have belonged to a fair race, while the bulk of the population was Mandingo or Malinke. This information is valuable as showing that long before the Mohammedan period the Sudan was a district of mixed population, and that the oft-recurring course of events which brings a fair race to rule over a negro population was not unexampled even at that time. Twenty-two rulers are

said to have reigned in Ghana before the beginning of Mohammedan chronology.

Carthage and Cyrene carried on commercial relations, at any rate indirectly, with the countries beyond the desert, and Mediterranean civilisation had strongly influenced the Sudan when the Arabs overran North Africa. A people thus appeared on the edge of the great desert for whom the inhospitable land had no terrors, and who were spurred on to desperate enterprises by the hope of extending the Mohammedan religion and their own power. The kingdom of Senhagia in the Western Sahara seems to have been the starting-point for the spread of Mohammedan propaganda. The town of Biru, or Whalata, was apparently a centre of trade and of Mohammedan civilisation until it was overshadowed by Timbuktu. In fact, it is at an early period that we find the first traces of Mohammedanism in the Sudan. It was not everywhere that the new religion found favourable soil, and it has not even yet made its way throughout the country ; but it brought with it the greatest mark of a higher civilisation, the art of writing, and thus laid the founda-

What Islam Did for the Sudan tion for a reliable history of the Sudan. The most priceless historical records of this district, the annals of Sonrhay, were composed by Ahmed Baba about 1640.

While Ghana was at the height of its prosperity a new kingdom was developed at no great distance, Sonrhay, where the dynasty of the Saa—apparently also of Berber origin—came to power at the outset of the seventh century. The Saa Alayaman was the first ruler, according to Ahmed Baba, and was succeeded by fourteen kings before the land came under Mohammedan rule. The centre of the kingdom of Sonrhay lay within the great curve of the Niger, south of the modern Timbuktu ; but it also possessed important districts beyond the Niger, further to the east.

Sonrhay was at first of no great importance ; a third and somewhat younger state, the kingdom of Melle, was for a long time predominant in the Western Sudan. The early history of Melle is wholly obscure. It seems to have been founded by the Mandingo, who perhaps first overthrew the Berber supremacy. At the time of its greatest prosperity its power extended northward far beyond

Hausa woman　　　　　Bambara woman　　　　　Woman of Massina

Mandingo musicians　　　　　　　Fulbe of Senegambia

Arab of Yola　　　　　Woman of Segu　　　　　Bambara man

TYPES OF THE VARIED RACES OF THE WESTERN SUDAN

In the Western and Central Sudan the great state-forming races are the Mandingo and the Hausa, who are the traders and manufacturers of the negro peoples. The fair-skinned Fulbe, who first settled in the Senegal valley, are true nomad sons of the steppes. Among the most important of the negro tribes are the Bambara, whose chief centre is Segu.

the curve of the Niger, and it may have made itself felt indirectly as far as the Atlantic Ocean ; its rulers were Mandingo, and consequently belonged to the dark races. The first Mohammedan preachers are said to have come to Melle in the year 990 and to have met with a favourable reception. Mohammedanism had

Founding of Timbuktu
spread among the peoples of the desert, and greatly stimulated their tendencies to political union. As early as the ninth century a Berberchief, Tilutan, had accepted Islam, had converted the neighbouring negro races, and risen to great power. About 1034 most of the Berber tribes of the desert were united under the sceptre of Abu Abdallah. Towards the end of the eleventh century the Tuareg founded the town of Timbuktu in a spot which had been regularly used for holding markets ; the town became an important centre of their influence. About this period the old kingdom of Ghana was conquered for a time by the Almoravides, who became highly important in the history of North Africa and Spain.

Meanwhile the princes of Sonrhay had accepted Mohammedanism about 1009, and become rulers of Ghanata about 1100 ; the chiefs of Melle, on the other hand, a state which was steadily growing in power, do not seem to have followed this example before 1200. Mansa (Sultan) Mussa was the most important of the rulers of Melle. He ruled from 1311 to 1331, raised his kingdom to the position of a first-rate military power, and proceeded to make conquests in all directions. He subdued what remained of the old kingdom of Ghana, which had recovered its independence but had lost most of its territory to Melle in the thirteenth century ; he conquered the Sonrhay kingdom and took the prosperous town of Timbuktu from the Tuareg. His reputation extended far and wide, when he undertook

Mohammedan Kingdom of Melle
a pilgrimage to Mecca with a vast retinue of followers in the year 1326, and showered wealth around him with a liberal hand. An architect was brought from Granada to Timbuktu to build a palace for the king. After the death of Mussa the kingdom was threatened with disruption ; however, Mansa Isliman restored its power about 1335 and recovered Timbuktu, which had been conquered by the heathen prince of Mossi. Melle seems to have

carried on a furious struggle with general success against the southern kingdom of Ginne, or Jinne, the princes of which had accepted Mohammedanism in the thirteenth century. Melle continued at the height of its power for another century, and then began to sink beyond hope of recovery. According to Ahmed Baba, an " army of God," which appeared and disappeared with equal rapidity, destroyed the larger part of the population ; this must refer to some great and fatal revolution or to a devastating epidemic. In the year 1433 the Tuareg recovered possession of Timbuktu while the governors of the different provinces of Melle were at war among themselves.

During the latter half of the fifteenth century Sonrhay rose to a dominating position under the guidance of the cruel but energetic Sunni Ali, a ruler of Berber extraction. One of his ancestors, Ali Kilnu, who had been brought up at the royal court at Melle, fled away with his brother and raised a successful revolt in Sonrhay. At first the rulers of Sonrhay were content to retain their independence ; Sunni Ali was the first to begin conquest

Negroes Assert their Supremacy
on a large scale. He stormed Timbuktu with fearful slaughter in 1469 ; the town at once became a trading centre for the Western Sudan and North Africa. He then acquired most of the former kingdom of Ghana and had considerably increased his power, when he was drowned on an expedition to the Sudan in 1492.

His son, who succeeded him, was soon overthrown by one of the deceased king's generals, Mohammed ben Abu Bakr by name, a pure negro who took the royal title of Askia. Here we meet with an instance of those reactionary movements which frequently occur in the racial struggles of the Western Sudan : the negro population, which formed the main element in the Sudanese kingdoms, succeeds in throwing off the yoke of the fair desert peoples and asserting the supremacy of its own race. As a matter of fact, the racial fusion which took place in most cases makes it as little possible to speak of pure negroes as of pure Berbers, and a change of rulers disturbed neither the Mohammedan religion nor the existing civilisation. The "Askia" soon showed himself a born ruler. He was a capable general, and strengthened the resisting powers of his kingdom by the encouragement

TIMBUKTU: THE GREAT CARAVAN CENTRE OF THE SAHARA DESERT
Founded by the Tuareg in the 11th century in a spot which had been used regularly for holding markets. Later it fell into the hands of the princes of Sonrhay, and in the 16th century became the centre of a Moorish province.

which he gave to domestic industries; a brilliant pilgrimage to Mecca increased the reputation of his country abroad. He seems to have created a standing army, Sunni Ali having been accustomed to lead out merely a general levy of the whole people. After his return from Arabia he conquered the kingdom of Mossi, the ruler and people of which country had displayed an obstinate hostility to Mohammedanism; he then turned upon Melle, took and destroyed the capital of this ancient kingdom, and made the country tributary to himself in 1501. With the peoples dwelling further south and the western tribes he had a more obstinate struggle. Leo Africanus shows that the Askia also extended his power on the east and succeeded in partly subjugating the Hausa states, which were even then in a flourishing condition; his power extended as far as Agades on the north-east, where he drove back the Berbers and planted negro colonies from Sonrhay. This action may also be considered as a counterstroke of negro against Berber. Toward the end of his life dissensions broke out in his family, and in 1529 his son Mussa forced him to abdicate. Sonrhay maintained its power to the

full during a long period of time. Especially glorious was the reign of the Askia Isshak I. (1539–1553), who embarked upon the first of the quarrels with Morocco.

He was succeeded by Daud, who ruled in peace from 1553 to 1582. However, El Hadj, the son of this latter king, was troubled with constant outbreaks of civil war. Shortly after he had ascended the throne ambassadors appeared from Morocco bringing gifts; these were, however, in reality the forerunners and spies of a powerful Moorish army, sent out by the Sultan Mulai Hammed of Morocco, which was advancing through the desert upon the Niger. This monarch had resumed the policy of the Almoravides, who had conquered Ghana from Morocco, and in whose army the Sudanese negroes formed a most valuable contingent. The army of Morocco was overthrown in the desert; but the civil wars continued. In 1587 El Hadj was deposed and died shortly afterward.

Hardly had the Askia Isshak II. put down the revolt and established himself upon the throne when a fresh army advanced from Morocco, seized the capital of Gogo, and then took Timbuktu. The leader of this army entered into negotiations with Isshak instead of continuing his conquests, and was immediately dismissed in consequence by Mulai Hammed, whose ambition had been fired by the example of the Spanish empire of Philip II. His successor, the Basha Mahmud, notwithstanding the scanty numbers of his troops, utterly defeated Isshak's army, which could not stand before the firearms of the Morocco forces. Isshak fled eastward to the heathen tribes upon his frontiers, and met his death among them. Further resistance was in vain, and the powerful kingdom of Sonrhay was no more. It had comprehended all the country on the Upper Niger and Senegal, and had extended its power to the sea-coast and deep into the

certainly felt. Henceforward it moved eastward to the Central Niger and Benue, and to the district contained in the angle of these two streams, the Hausa states. When once civilisation had made an entry into this district it became more strongly rooted there than upon the Upper Niger.

The Hausa States Since the latter area largely consists of steppe lands, nomadic tendencies are predominant, and civilisation is permanent only in the commercial and industrial towns. Now the Hausa states form a country of towns, from which civilisation radiates to the surrounding districts; the inhabitants also are not wandering nomads, but agricultural negroes. It is true that civilisation has not even yet become universal, nor is the country a political whole. Heathen races have their settlements scattered between the territories belonging to the several states, are persecuted by the expeditions of the territorial masters and make raids upon the country in revenge for the tribute of slaves which is constantly exacted from them.

A VILLAGE SCENE IN THE REGION OF THE UPPER NIGER
The area of the Upper Niger consists largely of steppe lands, and it is only in the commercial towns that there is permanent civilisation. This village is inhabited by an industrial tribe.

desert. The immigrants from Morocco formed a new element in the racial fusion; their descendants are now known as Rumat—literally, sharpshooters. The town of Timbuktu became the centre of the new Morocco province, which did not, however, extend as widely as the old Sonrhay kingdom had done—many of the frontier provinces seceded, and individual races conquered additional territory for themselves, such as the Bambara, and especially the Fulbe.

The destruction of the kingdom of Sonrhay led to more important results than these. Hitherto the central point of West Sudanese civilisation had been upon the Upper Niger, where Northern influences made themselves most rapidly and

The ancient history of the Hausa states is even more obscure than that of the western kingdom. All that can be said with certainty is that the Hausa people, to whom the states owe their name and their first political organisation, were originally settled as a whole further to the north, and that they belonged to those negro races which inhabited the southern parts of the Sahara and the neighbouring districts.

Beginnings of the Hausa

The mountain land of Air, or Asben, may once have been in the possession of the Hausa. Thence they were driven south by the Berbers of the desert, having previously received some infusion of Berber blood, and gradually imposed their language upon a countless number of tribes, language and not race thus

VIEW OF THE GREAT CATARACT OF GOUINA ON THE UPPER NIGER

The Niger, the third longest river of Africa, rises near the west coast, and flows right across the bend of Africa into the Gulf of Guinea. Like all the African rivers it is much broken by rapids and cataracts, one of which is seen here.

becoming the bond of unity among them. The Hausa point to Biram as the cradle of their race, a little town lying east of Kano, near the borders of the kingdom of Bornu ; if this tradition be reliable, the greater part of the Hausa civilisation must therefore have come from the Central Sudan, and especially from Bornu rather than from the west through Melle and Sonrhay.

The founder of the town of Biram bore the same name as the place, and from him and his grandson, Banu, it is said that the forefathers of the seven ancient Hausa peoples descended, and also the first kings of those seven states which were bounded collectively by the River Benue and the desert on the one side, and by the Niger and the Bornu frontiers upon the other. But when the Hausa started from the lands on the edge of the desert to found their kingdom, the original

inhabitants on the river banks held out against them for a long period, and are to be found existing in parts even at the present day, just as they defied the attacks of the Sudanese civilisation and its exponents in a thin strip of country on the Atlantic coast, or as they even now maintain their position in the Upper Nile valley. The seven old Hausa states were

Hausa Talent for Trade

Biram, Kano, Daura, Gobir, Katsena, Sofo or Saria, and Rano. Gobir and Daura, together with Biram, may be considered the earliest political creations of the Hausa people. They have a tradition that the mother of the founder of the Hausa kingdoms was a Berber woman, which confirms the opinion that they are not a pure negro people, but have intermingled with the races of the desert.

The Hausa people probably developed their great talents for trade and

LARGE NATIVE VILLAGE AND MOUNTAIN SCENE ON THE UPPER NIGER

Note the stockade and the conical-roofed huts, which are typical of the whole of tropical North Africa.

2223

manufacture at an early period. It was perhaps rather the influence of their civilisation than their military power which extended their language, and to some extent their authority, over a second group of states which are generally known as the illegitimate or bastard Hausa states, from the tradition that they were founded by seven

Antiquity of the Hausa States illegitimate sons of Banu. They are Kebbi, Zanfara, Guari, Yauri, and beyond the Niger and Benue, Nupe, Yoruba, and Kororofa. The legends concerning the founders of the seven Hausa states enable us to form some idea of the political conditions prevailing during their antiquity.

When the Hausa states of Banu were divided among his sons they also received definite posts of responsibility : thus, two of them were appointed overseers of traffic and commerce, two more were to superintend the dyeing industry, a fifth had to make the kidnapping of slaves from hostile districts his special business. Here we have an excellent sketch of the economic conditions of the old Hausa kingdoms. The main sources of the national wealth were the flourishing manufactures, especially the making and dyeing of textile fabrics, which were distributed far and wide by a vigorous trading system. Slave hunting was the means of obtaining cheap labour for the factories, which were, however, generally carried on by the freemen, and slaves were used also for purposes of agriculture, though this again was chiefly in the hands of the half-civilised aboriginal negroes, who lived around the great industrial centres. Slaves were for many reasons a very important article of export, and to this chiefly was due the flourishing character of the trade between the Sudan and the countries round the Mediterranean.

In early times both the rulers and the inhabitants of the Hausa states were in a state of heathenism. It was apparently

Hausa Before Islam in pre-Mohammedan times that the nucleus of the kingdoms was formed upon the southern edge of the desert, even though the Arabs and the racial movements caused by their expeditions provided the real impulse which drove the Hausa southward. States began to be formed at an early period in the territory of the true and half-breed Hausa states, as is proved by the existence of the old kingdom of Fumbina in the modern Adamawa.

In fact, the entry of the Hausa into the districts which they now occupy naturally brought about the retreat of the peoples settled there, who may have been partly civilised and capable of concerted political action ; and an impulse was thus given to the formation of new kingdoms on the border of the modern Hausa land. If it is the fact that the Hausa migrations were connected with the racial changes caused by the advance of Mohammedanism, then the foundation of the Hausa kingdoms may be placed in the ninth or tenth century of our era.

Little is known of the history of the Hausa states previous to the introduction of Mohammedanism, which seems to have been first effected in Katsena about the year 1540. In the sixteenth century Katsena was the most powerful kingdom, and the ruling dynasty can be retraced to about the year 1200. About 1513 it seems to have been conquered by the Askia of Sonrhay, Hadj Mohammed, and forced to pay tribute. When the prince of Kebbi shook off the yoke of Sonrhay, Katsena became dependent upon Kebbi, and at a later time was under the

Rise of Kano influence of Bornu. The first Moslem prince of Katsena was called Ibrahim Maji ; fifty years after his death the Habe dynasty came to the throne, and ruled until the country was conquered by the Fulbe. The town of Kano rose to importance after Katsena ; it was partly inhabited by Bornu people, and repeatedly united to the Bornu kingdom. During a long period the rulers of Bornu and Kororofa struggled for the possession of the town. We have but scanty information upon the condition of the other Hausa states and their relations to one another previous to the beginning of the nineteenth century. The kingdom of Saria, Soso, or Segseg seems to have been temporarily in the possession of the first Askia of Sonrhay.

Our lack of information is due partly to the fact that when the Fulbe conquered the Hausa states they deliberately destroyed all the earlier historical records. Hence continuous history begins only with the victorious invasion of the Fulbe, who have given their name to the whole district for the time being. Where the Fulbe race—also known by neighbouring peoples as Fula, Fellani, Fellatah, and Fullan— has preserved its purity, the slender, sinewy figure and the fair colour of the

TUAREG SLAVE HUNTERS RETURNING WITH THEIR UNHAPPY CAPTIVES FROM A SUCCESSFUL RAID UPON NEGRO VILLAGES

skin mark this people as true sons of the steppes; their habits are those of typical nomads, and for livelihood they depend upon cattle-breeding. Their language shows their connection with the Berber races. Their original settlements were in the Western Sudan, probably in the steppe district north of the Senegal and partly in

True Sons of the Steppes the valley of this river. The conjecture that the Fulbe are the old dominant race of Ghana can be no more proved than the theory, which is not without intrinsic probability, that the ancestors of this people reached the Sudan from Morocco.

It is at a somewhat early period that the Fulbe appear in the history of those states on the Upper Niger and Senegal which were the first to bcome important in the Western Sudan. It is quite possible that they originally settled as a state upon the Central Senegal, soon spreading further eastward, at first almost imperceptibly. About 1300 the Fulbe, who were settled in Melle, sent an embassy to Bornu. Sunni Ali, king of Sonrhay, made an expedition against the Fulbe in the south of his country in 1492, and made them tributary to himself; but about 1500 we hear of the Askia Hadj Mohammed as again struggling against this people, so that they had presumably become powerful and had spread considerably eastward.

This expansion was brought about at that time by the same methods as at a later period. The Fulbe entered the territory of settled peoples in their character of wandering cattle-herds, and seized any opportunity which offered of making themselves masters of the country and founding small independent kingdoms. About 1533 mention is made of wars between the declining kingdom of Melle and those western Fulbe who had settled near their original home. As the Fulbe advanced eastward they naturally incorporated other nomadic races with

Advance of the Fulbe themselves, and also intermarried largely with the negroes, especially with the dark-skinned Jolof, near the old settlements of their race; in this fusion the Torode tribe originated. A development in the direction of a caste system reduced many tribes to the position of manual workers; some portion at least of the Fulbe people abandoned their nomadic life in favour of manufacturing occupations. These migrations gradually brought the

Fulbe into Hausa territory. At first they were merely tolerated, and contemptuously regarded as intruders. In the sixteenth century they had increased considerably, and gained some political influence in certain quarters, especially in Kebbi, where about this time they succeeded in interfering in the dissensions of the Kanta dynasty, which had been founded shortly before. Even then individual bodies had advanced as far as Bagirmi on the east, and perhaps also to Adamawa on the south. At the present day, heathen Fulbe are settled in that district, the rest of the population being distinguished by a fanatical adherence to Mohammedanism.

This same fanaticism was the ultimate cause of a fundamental revolution in the Hausa states. As in most cases, so also in this, the religious movement was nothing else than the natural result of a gradual change of social and racial elements; but the religious movement produced this further consequence—that it roused the Fulbe to consciousness of

Hausa Religious Revolution their own strength, and gave them a common watchword against the Hausa, who approached religious questions in a spirit of tolerance though not of absolute indifferentism.

In the year 1802, in the land of Gobir, a Fulbe sheikh, by name Othman dan Fodio, succeeded in using a religious movement to forward his political designs; his vigorous religious songs roused his compatriots to the height of enthusiasm and excited them to war against the rulers of Gobir. Though at first defeated, he contrived to make head against his adversaries, and upon his death he left a kingdom to his warlike son Mohammed Bello. The latter, though constantly defeated by the kings of Bornu, steadily increased the area of his dominions. The sultans of Sanfara, Gobir, and Nupe formed an alliance with the Tuareg, and strove to drive back the Fulbe, but in vain. At the same time the Fulbe in the river district on the Senegal revolted and founded the kingdom of Futa Jallon in the mountainous country to the south of the river. In 1816 a fanatic from Gando set up the kingdom of Massina, to which Timbuktu was added in 1826. Between the years 1850 and 1860 Segu, which had been founded about 1650 by the heathen Mandingo, suffered a similar fate.

The Hausa states fell entirely into the hands of the Fulbe ; though some states held out for a long time, the Hausa people were forced to surrender their supremacy to the nomadic people they had formerly despised. In other respects political conditions underwent but little change. The chief Fulbe power was centred in the kingdom of Sokoto, Mohammed Bello's inheritance. The king of this state is at the same time spiritual lord of all the Fulbe states on the east, but his influence does not extend to political relations. The lands upon the Central Niger form the kingdom of Gando ; its first ruler was Abd Allahi, Othman's brother. To Gando belong—though only as regards religious matters—the highly civilised Nupe, with its capital, Bida, which was weakened by civil war and fell into the hands of the Fulbe in the first decade of the nineteenth century. Their most southern state is Ilorin, to the north of Yoruba. Finally Adamawa on the southwest, which was conquered by the Fulbe during the years 1820–1830, is now practically independent. The other rulers

Break-up of Hausa States of the former Hausa states are chiefly loosely dependent upon Sokoto ; some of them, such as the sultan of Bautshi, whose dynasty came to the throne about 1800, are not Fulbe, but pure negroes.

The first attack of the Fulbe had shaken the states of the Western Sudan to their foundations and had threatened Bornu itself with destruction, but the kingdom which they founded soon showed signs of disruption. Many of the Fulbe moved into the town, intermarried with the Hausa, and lost their own language and their distinguishing characteristics, with the exception of the Borroro, who clung to their nomadic habits. At the same time their fanatical temper disappeared, and with it their military prowess. The armies raised by the sultans consisted almost exclusively of negroes. In short, the negro element began to assimilate with the dominant race imperceptibly, but irresistibly. Further, the Fulbe rulers were as little masters of the whole district as the Hausa kings had been. Numerous heathen races continued to offer a desperate resistance to the Mohammedan advance ; even when conquered, converted, and made serfs to the Fulbe, they merely helped to swell the numbers of the negroes. One small Hausa kingdom was even able

to preserve its independence. When the Fulbe conquered Saria, the capital of the old state of Soso, the king retreated southward into heathen territory and there founded a new kingdom, with Aguja as its capital, which survived all the attacks of the Fulbe. The Hausa also maintained their position in their early home at Gobir. Thus

Hausa a Universal Language the Fulbe supremacy was nominal rather than real, and extended over a district the population of which a higher civilisation had endowed with indestructible powers of recuperation. Though reduced to the position of an inferior race, the Hausa people were rapidly distributed in the course of trade over all the surrounding districts, and brought their language with them. As far as Kete-Kratji in German Togoland, Hausa is now the universal commercial language, though in a somewhat debased form. The Fulbe kingdom has decayed internally and is on the point of dissolution. Small tribes are able to cut all communications between Kano, Saria, and Sokoto for a long period in the year, or to carry off Hausa people from the very gates of Gando. The only reason why this kingdom has so long survived any foreign attack is the fact that no energetic neighbour is to be found upon its frontiers.

On the south the old Hausa kingdoms were surrounded by a ring of independent heathen states—Korosofa, south of the Central Benue, Fumbina, the predecessor of the modern Adamawa, and others. The whole southern frontier of Adamawa, so named after the first Fulbe ruler, Adama, touches Central Africa with its pure negro population ; hence unbounded possibilities of extension lay before it, and its rulers were enabled to carry on slave hunting upon the largest scale. The soil is, moreover, extremely rich and fertile, and specially adapted for an

Heathen State of Adamawa agricultural people, so that the cattle plague, which impoverished the Fulbe in the other Hausa countries, was but little felt in this kingdom and did not seriously impair the national strength. In Adamawa most of the Fulbe had devoted themselves from an early period to agriculture, and labour for this purpose was always obtainable by slave hunting ; moreover, the immigration from Bornu of industrial families proved highly beneficial to the development of civilisation.

Adamawa is governed by the prince of Yola, who is resident on the north-western frontier, facing the other Hausa states. His influence is weakened by the remote position of his capital, and his supremacy is by no means universally acknowledged throughout the country. Small heathen districts and communities are to be found scattered everywhere among the main centres of the Fulbe power, and most of these are in a state of continual feud both with the Fulbe and among themselves. The organisation of the Fulbe kingdom in general and of Adamawa in particular is exactly parallel to mediæval feudalism. The provinces are placed under separate dignitaries, each of whom commands a large number of vassals, while most of the officers at court are in the hands of the slaves. The most important Fulbe provinces of Adamawa are Bubanjida, Ngaundere, Tibati, and Banyo. Before the entry of Germany, Tibati and Ngaundere extended their frontiers, and were the strongest provinces in the Fulbe kingdom. Near them and to the south of Adamawa is the independent heathen state of Galim, which was formed in comparatively recent times, and has been strengthened by the addition of numerous heathen refugees. In the north the fierce guerrilla chief Mallam Hajato, son of Prince Saidu and grandson of Mohammed Bello, has thrown off the supremacy of Yola. Lower down the Benue the Fulbe have founded new states within the last century. In our own times Germany has entered Adamawa on the south and checked the advance of the Sudan negroes.

Negro Advance Checked

In spite of unfavourable conditions, the small numbers of its army, and the difficulty of providing reinforcements, not to speak of the numerous revolutions in Morocco itself, which cannot have failed to influence the course of events in the Sudan, the supremacy of Morocco over the western districts previously belonging to Sonrhay was maintained, nominally

AHMADU, LAMINE OF SEGU
Ahmadu, "Lord of the Faithful" in Segu, inherited a great kingdom on the Upper Senegal and Niger, created by his father, but was subjugated by the French.

at least, for a surprisingly long period. The reasons for its long continuance are sufficiently simple. The Morocco soldiers, the Rumat, whose muskets had brought the war to a rapid termination, settled in the strongholds and adopted the position of a ruling caste, gained friends and influence by marrying the native women, and eventually became a separate nationality, capable of retaining their hold of the conquered district in independence, though it was against their interests to sever all connection with Morocco.

The connection between the new province of Sonrhay and Morocco thus continued unbroken until the latter kingdom was shaken by the disturbances which broke out after the death of Mulai Hammed in 1603. From that time onward Morocco no longer sent out a pasha as governor, and administration was carried on by the Rumat themselves. Every newly-elected pasha was forced to secure recognition by presents to his supporters, and the system resulted in excesses which surpassed all that Rome had seen under the Pretorian guards. One hundred and fifty-four pashas are known to have ruled within a period of one hundred and fifty years. Civil wars and extortion were the natural consequences of such an unsettled state of affairs. At the same time constant struggles with the different Tuareg races had to be maintained.

In the seventeenth century Sonrhay provided a large number of black soldiers for the Morocco army. These constituted the bodyguard of the sultans, and rendered valuable service against such vassals as attempted revolt. About 1680 a small Morocco army made an expedition against the Sudanese districts which were independent of Morocco, and returned home with rich booty. But from 1682 the sultan of Morocco's name no longer appears in the government documents, the last trace of dependence thus disappearing. The attempt of one ambitious ruler to found a dynasty of his own proved a failure.

End of Moroccan Supremacy

The power of the Rumat, the descendants of the old Morocco army of conquest, gradually declined. In 1737 they were defeated by the Tuareg prince Ogmor, who now became the overlord of Sonrhay for a time, though he did not succeed in entirely subduing the Rumat. About 1770 the town of Gogo, or Gao, on the Niger, was lost to the Tuareg. On the north bank of the river rose the powerful kingdom of Aussa, which cut off all communication with Morocco and seized Timbuktu. Finally, at the beginning of the nineteenth century the Rumat power was utterly destroyed by the **Rise of Fulbe Fanatics** attacks of the Fulbe. Mohammed Lebbo started from Gando, the new Fulbe kingdom on the Central Niger, with an army of fanatics, and in 1816 founded a kingdom on the upper part of the river, the central point of which was the town of Massina. A further period of disturbance began with the rise of a new Fulbe fanatic, Hadji Omar. He set himself up as the founder of a religion, and soon collected a powerful army. After utterly devastating the negro kingdoms on the Senegal and Upper Niger—Bambuk, Kaarta, and Segu—he entered into rivalry, much to his own disadvantage, with the French in Senegambia, and finally gained possession of Timbuktu. When his garrison had been driven out by the Tuaregs he marched upon the town in person, but was severely defeated in 1863. However, he succeeded in uniting the territory on the Upper Senegal and Niger into a great kingdom, which he left to his son Ahmadu, who assumed the title of Emir el-Mumenin, or Lamine, lord of the faithful, as his father had done, chose Segu-Sikoro as his capital, and thus lived among the Bambara negroes, who were **French in Segu** chief among the tribes subject to him. Segu was conquered by the French in 1890, and a year later Ahmadu's kingdom was was completely subjugated. The history of those districts which lie further to the south-west toward the coast and have been visited by Europeans only in recent years, is comparatively obscure. Their economic importance rests chiefly upon their possession of the kola nut, which has become a valuable article of exportation. By no means all of these districts were or are Mohammedan. In many of the south-western kingdoms the numbers of the faithful are extremely scanty, while others cling tenaciously to heathenism. The kingdom of Mossi, lying nearly halfway between Ashanti and Timbuktu, is a stronghold of heathenism, and, what is about the same thing, of a pure negro nationality. After the fall of the kingdom of Melle new states were formed of its southern provinces. Undoubtedly the Mandingo kingdom, mentioned in the sixteenth century, was one of these, as the Mandingo people were the founders of Melle. In this case also large towns became the central point of the kingdom, such as Kong, the importance of which was formerly much exaggerated, owing to the false rumours which reached the coast. In the middle of the nineteenth century Samory founded a powerful kingdom to the south of Segu, which ultimately fell to the attacks of the French in 1898.

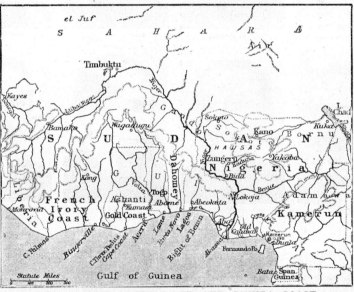

MAP OF THE NIGER RIVER AND GUINEA COAST

David Livingstone   Hugh Clapperton   Mungo Park   Sir H. M. Stanley

V. L. Cameron   J. H. Speke   Captain Grant   James Bruce

Gustave Nachtigal   Captain Wissmann   Sir Richard Burton   Joseph Thomson

Lewis Krapf   Heinrich Barth   George Schweinfurth   Wilhelm Junker

MEN WHO BROUGHT LIGHT TO THE DARK CONTINENT

The first considerable African exploration was begun at the end of the 18th century by Mungo Park, who solved the
Niger problem. In North African exploration Barth, Clapperton and Bruce were prominent. Livingstone discovered
Lake Ngami and the Zambesi, and explored the Congo; his reliever, Stanley, followed the Congo to its mouth, while
Cameron crossed its basin. Schweinfurth, Junker and Nachtigal were the chief explorers of the East Sudan. Speke
and Grant traced the Nile to its source, while in Central Africa Stanley, Thomson, Burton and Wissman discovered much.

Photos: Elliott & Fry and Russell & Sons

2230

THE CENTRAL SUDAN
THE STRUGGLES AND DECAY OF ITS NATIVE STATES

HITHERTO the central districts of the Sudan, extending to the Nile region, have been invaded by European activity far less than the west. The district is by no means uniform but consists of a number of territorial areas more or less self-contained, wherein are to be found a corresponding number of political communities generally independent of one another. On the west we can observe the Chad basin, in the fruitful plains of which the kingdom of Bornu has developed. Next we have the valley of the Shari, with Bagirmi, and finally in the east two mountainous districts with the states of Wadai and Darfur. To the south of these districts begin the pure negro territories, which belong ethnographically to the northern frontier of the Congo basin. As being the source of an unceasing supply of slaves, they have founded the prosperity of the states in the Sudan proper, and have also given rise to continual racial fusions. On the north extends the Central Sahara,

Prosperity Based on Slavery the peoples of which have taken an important part in the history of the Sudan states, and in some cases have decisively influenced their fate. It was from the desert and the North African coast that civilisation was brought into the Central Sudan.

The geographical position of the Central Sudan, especially of the area from Bornu to the North African coast, is of the highest importance. North of Lake Chad the Mediterranean makes its deepest indentation in the African continent, forming the two bays of the Syrtes. The emigrant advancing southward from this point will find rest and repose in a chain of oases, including the land of Fezzan, the greatest of all the oases of the Sahara. Hence the journey from Tripoli to Lake Chad has been a favourite route with European explorers; there are no great mountain chains to be crossed as in Morocco and Algiers, and the dangerous part of the desert is comparatively narrow. So favourable a conjunction of circumstances

must have given rise at an early period to trade and intercourse, which would be only temporarily interrupted by the desert tribes.

The most remarkable people of the Central Sahara are the Tibu, or Teda; the purest types of this race are settled in

A Strange, Unsociable People the mountains of Tibesti, and have apparently dwelt here from very early times. They are a peculiarly unsociable type of humanity, wholly conformed to the conditions of their environment, both in character and physique. A strong, perhaps even a preponderant infusion of negro blood has left unmistakable traces in the race; possibly, also, certain dwarf tribes resembling the Bushmen, of which the old geographers make mention, may have been absorbed by them. Spareness of build, activity, and power of endurance are the chief characteristics of the individual. The colour of the skin is, upon the average, lighter than that of the Sudan negroes, and darker than that of the Berbers. The negro type of face is to be found side by side with features of a more aristocratic cast. Their perseverance and their intellectual quickness enable the Teda to become capable merchants as well as clever robbers and thieves. A further stimulus in these directions is given by the avarice and lack of scruple which has been ingrained in them by years of grinding poverty.

At the present day, in addition to Tibesti, the Teda inhabit the oasis of Kauar on the chief route from Bornu to Tripoli. Antiquity has nothing to tell us

A Race of Merchant Thieves concerning the Teda; nor have they any traditions of their own. It is only a few centuries ago that they seem to have embraced Mohammedanism; yet Arab strongholds appear at an early date in Fezzan and in the Central Sahara. Very little is known of the early history of these Arabs; but at a later period we are able to learn the history of one Arab tribe, which is not only noteworthy in itself, but may also serve as a typical example of nomadic life, and of the influence exerted by nomads upon trade and settled races.

The tribe of the Aulad Soliman once dwelt near the great Syrtes, where the herds of camels found abundant pasture during the winter; in the summer they moved to Fezzan, in order to visit their date plantations and collect the harvest. Dissension with the rulers of Tripoli drove the Aulad Soliman into a temporary exile in Egypt. In 1811 disturbances broke out again in Tripolitania and Fezzan, and the usurper Bey Mohammed el-Mukni séized the town of Mursuk. The tribe then took the opportunity of returning to Fezzan, and laid siege to Mursuk, but was in large part treacherously annihilated in 1815.

Nomad Lords of Fezzan

For twenty years the tribe disappears from the history of Fezzan, while a new generation of warriors was growing up. Then a chieftain's son, who had been brought up at the court of Tripoli, joined in some of the raids from Fezzan into the Sudan, and was struck with the wealth of that country; as his tribe had recovered its strength, he conceived the idea of leading it into this district to acquire riches and power. For the moment he found a sufficient field for his energies in Tripoli and Fezzan, and maintained his position as lord of Fezzan for twelve years.

When he lost his land and life in a decisive battle against the Turks his earlier plan was remembered; and the remnants of the tribe marched southward, first upon Bornu, and afterward to Kanem on the north shore of Lake Chad. They numbered scarce a thousand men capable of bearing arms, but in spite of these scanty numbers they soon spread the terror of their name throughout the district between Lake Chad and Tibesti; they plundered the flocks of the resident tribes, exacted toll from the caravans, and made forays from time to time into the adjacent Sudan states, until, as they extended their sphere of action, they came into collision with the most eastern of the Tuareg tribes, who were accustomed to import Bilma salt to Bornu and the Hausa states from the pits at Garu and Kalala in the oasis of Kauar. The Tuareg are said to have lost fifty

Terrors of the Sudan

thousand camels in a short time. But this warlike people could not be provoked without making reprisals; an army of seven thousand men marched to Kanem, and defeated the Aulad Soliman so utterly that the tribe and its power seemed to be annihilated for the second time, in 1850. However, it recovered itself, and was taken into the service of the king of Bornu as a frontier guard against Wadai. In time the Aulad Soliman regained its position and became the terror of the neighbourhood, which was so utterly devastated that the Arabs were obliged to push their marauding expeditions to a greater distance. Such was the condition of affairs when the German explorer Gustav Nachtigal visited the country in 1871. In earlier times there may have been many a counterpart to this history which shows to what a small extent the steppes and deserts form any real boundary to the Sudan states.

Thanks to its favourable situation, to the fertility of its soil, and to a happy fusion of populations, Bornu for a long period illumined the darkness of the Central Sudan with the light of its civilisation, and was able to transmit the seeds of higher culture to neighbouring kingdoms. Anterior to its partial inclusion in the British protectorate of North Nigeria, at the end of 1899, it comprehended the territory extending from the south-west of Lake Chad and west of the Shari to the frontiers of the Hausa states; it was bounded on the north by the desert and on the south by the settlements of independent heathen tribes. It was a typical Sudan state, a district of transition from the Sahara to negro Africa. On the east and the west its boundaries were determined with some precision; but on the north and south they varied, and were rather lines of decreasing influence than definite frontiers. Kanem in particular, the country to the north-east of Lake Chad, was ultimately almost entirely independent of Bornu, although at one period the most intimate relations had subsisted between these two districts.

Light in the Dark Sudan

It is not until about 900 A.D. that its history becomes reasonably trustworthy. Bornu is an admirable example of the manner in which states which were first formed on the desert frontiers of the Sudan have gradually shifted their centres of gravity further and further south into what was once pure negro territory; thus the origins of the Bornu kingdom were not in the modern Bornu, but in Kanem, further to the north-east, at the present time the raiding district of the Aulad Soliman. The Kanembu, as they are called from their old place of settlement, together with the Kanuri, form the nucleus of the Bornu population. However, Kanem itself does not seem to have been the original home of the Kanembu, who are related to the Teda in point of language and were possibly an early offshoot of this desert people of the Tibesti, inasmuch as their own traditions speak of earlier settlements lying further northward.

or so improved the cavalry, the most dreaded arm of the Sudanese forces, that his successors were able to advance northward and reduce Fezzan, and also to take the first steps toward the subjugation of Bornu on the south, which was at that time inhabited by heathen negro races in a low stage of civilisation. The kingdom of Kanem seems to have attained its greatest area about this period; it was even in friendly relations with Tunis, and consequently in touch with Mediterranean civilisation.

However, shortly afterwards the process of disruption began, and advanced as it usually does in states based upon feudal organisation. Quarrels about the succession, revolts of powerful vassals, conspiracies of every kind, sapped the strength of the kingdom for two centuries. None the less, about 1360 the conquest of the heathen countries on the south was gradually completed in spite of the desperate resistance of the aboriginal inhabitants, the So, who had defeated four kings of Kanem between 1348 and 1351, and take the form of giants in the legends of the Bornu people. Some portion of the inhabitants of Kanem immigrated into this newly acquired territory, but the aboriginal negro inhabitants were not wholly expelled.

TYPES OF THE TUAREGS OF THE NORTHERN SAHARA
The most important of the Berber tribes is the great Tuareg people, originally settled in North Africa, but driven to retreat southward into the Sahara after the Arab conquest.

A great impulse was given to the kingdom of Kanem under King Hume or Ume about 1130 A.D., when Mohammedanism was introduced, and the land was thereby brought into close connection with the Mohammedan civilisation. The strength of this connection is shown by the fact that the ruler of Bornu undertook a pilgrimage to Mecca, in the course of which he died in Egypt in 1151. His son and successor, Dunama II., made three pilgrimages to Mecca, and died in 1205. In the second half of the thirteenth century Dunama III., Dibbalami, became famous as a powerful monarch; he organised the army, and either introduced

It was, moreover, high time for the rulers of Kanem to find and secure for themselves a new district further removed from the steppe-dwellers and their attacks; for not only were Fezzan and Tibesti gradually slipping from the grasp of the shattered kingdom, but it proved impossible to retain possession of Djimi, the capital. In this quarter the Bulala tribe gradually made themselves masters of the land after a long struggle, and, about 1370, forced the rulers of Kanem to retreat southward to Bornu. Wars with the

Bulala began under the rule of King Daud, and continued until the definite abandonment of Kanem, though the cession of this place by no means made an end of the internal dissensions and disunion of what now becomes the kingdom of Bornu. The Bulala also continued their hostilities for a long period. Meanwhile the resources of the new district seem to have been gradually developed, and to have proved favourable to the rise of a second era of power. The impulse was given by the energetic king Ali Dunamami (1465-1492), who checked the excessive growth of feudalism, and created a definite centre for the kingdom by founding a new capital, Oasr Eggomo, and especially by extending his frontiers westward. When his son Idris III. had twice defeated the Bulala, about 1500, Bornu again became the dominant power in the Central Sudan and westward as far as the Niger. Under Mohammed V. (1515-1539) the kingdom reached the highest point of its prosperity. A no less distinguished ruler was the " Sultan " Idris IV., Amsami, who reigned from 1563 to 1614. He secured the military supremacy of his kingdom by the introduction of firearms, subdued the small half-independent heathen tribes within the boundaries of Bornu, then extended his influence over the Hausa states on the west and the desert tribes on the north, and in general established his kingdom so firmly that it enjoyed a period of comparative peace and prosperity under his successors.

But the peace thus acquired was but the prelude to a second fall. In the following period most of the rulers were weak-minded pietists, who allowed the military power of the kingdom to decay. The body politic was internally corrupt, and was saved from destruction only by the absence of any more powerful enemy. The inevitable collapse came at the beginning of the nineteenth century. In 1808 began the Fulbe revolt in the Hausa states, which eventually made this apparently harmless pastoral people the masters of that great district. The Fulbe had also migrated into Bornu about 1560 at latest, and their excitement at the success of their kinsfolk is not surprising. King Ahmed (1793-1810) was, according to the chroniclers, " a learned prince, liberal to the priests, extravagant in

Rise and Fall of Bornu

THE SHEIKH WHO SAVED BORNU

In 1800, during the reign of a weak king, Bornu was overrun by the nomad Fulbe, but was rescued by the efforts of Faki Mohammed el-Kanemi, a petty feudal lord, who assumed the title of sheikh and the real power.

almsgiving, the friend of science and religion, kind and gracious to the poor " ; but energy he had none. When the Fulbe, under their leader, Othman dan Fodio, attacked Bornu, all resistance was in vain, the more so as the country had been depopulated by a fearful plague. Birni was hastily abandoned by King Ahmed, and fell into the power of the nomad race in 1809.

Bornu, however, was not destined to share the fate of the Hausa states. The kingdom displayed unsuspected recuperative powers. The leader of the Kanembu was the Faki Mohammed el-Amin el-Kanemi, a native of Fezzan. He entered into marriage relations with one of the petty feudal lords of Bornu, and drove the Fulbe out of his territory by arousing in his own followers a spirit of religious enthusiasm which proved a match for the fanaticism of the Fulbe. After the death of King Ahmed, in 1810, his son Dunama X. continued the war against the Fulbe, but met with no definite success, until he was driven to place himself under the protection of the victorious Faki. The king attempted afterwards to recover his independence, with the result that Mohammed el-Amin gained all the real power, he

The Saving of Bornu

himself becoming a mere figurehead. At that time a new capital, Kuka, was founded.

Mohammed, who now assumed the title of "sheikh," found himself involved in a severe struggle with the neighbouring kingdom of Bagirmi in 1817, from which he did not emerge in triumph until 1824, after being forced to procure reinforcements from Fezzan. When he died, in 1835, he left to his son Omar, and to the nominal sultan, Ibrahim (1818–1846), a strongly established, though not very extensive, kingdom. Omar succeeded in concluding peace with the Fulbe and in reducing the western provinces to obedience ; but the adherents of the deposed dynasty seized this opportunity of striking a blow at the usurper with the help of the king of Wadai.

Triumph of the Sheikh

Omar gathered a small army, but was defeated at Kusseri in March, 1846. He then had the sultan Ibrahim executed, and retreated to a strong position in Ngornu. The ruler of Wadai had advanced too far from his base of operations and was obliged to retire for reinforcements, leaving Ibrahim's son Ali, whom he had set up as sultan, to continue the struggle. Ali soon met with an honourable death on the field of battle, and his family became thereby extinct.

SUDANESE SOLDIERS OF BORNU

Omar thus became sole ruler of Bornu. He proved a pious, judicious, benevolent, and generally moderate ruler, and the peace of his reign was disturbed only by the revolt of his brother Abd er-Rahman, who temporarily (1853–1854) drove him from the throne. At this time the organisation of Bornu was much like European feudalism in the Middle Ages. The sultan of Bornu theoretically ruled over several other sultans, who were practically independent. The other territories of Bornu proper were either personal property or were held by the ruling dynasty and the nobles of the royal family. However, many of the smaller princes were mediatised and their titles void of real significance. The king was surrounded by a council, or Nokena, composed of his relatives, the representatives of the different tribes and classes of the population and of the military authorities, which met every morning in the palace.

In addition to the members of the council numerous officials and favourites also existed, whose offices were in many cases sinecures, together with many eunuchs and slaves. The sources of national income were the king's landed property and that of his courtiers, and the profits gained by slave-hunting, which was an industry regularly carried on in the heathen districts in the south. Thus slaves were accepted as payment by the

BODYGUARD OF THE SHEIKH OF BORNU

2235

merchants from the north coast, who brought in European wares, guns, horses, etc., and were often forced to await the return of the troops before their accounts could be settled. Such expeditions against the heathen were always a necessary condition of existence for the states of the Sudan. In modern times Bornu has again been

Bornu in Our Own Time thrown into confusion, though on this occasion the disturbing cause has not come from the Fulbe, but from the east. When Sheikh Omar died, in 1882, after a long reign, he was first succeeded by Aba Bu Bekr until 1885, who was followed by Aba Brahim until 1886, and finally Aba Hashim until 1893, a learned but indolent prince. Events in the Eastern Sudan and the results of the Mahdi revolt proved fatal to him.

While the Egyptians were engaged in the conquest of the Upper Nile district, Zebehr, the slave-hunter, had become so powerful that the Egyptian Government determined to remove this disturbing cause, and, after enticing him to Cairo, kept him prisoner. His son Suleiman thereupon revolted, but was several times defeated in 1880 by Romolo Gessi, and finally surrendered to the Egyptians. But one of the subordinate leaders of Zebehr's army, Rabah, a low-born Arab by extraction, refused to surrender, and retreated westward with a division of the troops, consisting of about 3,000 negro soldiers. Here he held out until 1891 in Dar Runga; he did not, however, join the Mahdi kingdom, which had arisen during that time. Slave-hunting was probably his chief source of income, supplies being gained by secret trading with the Mahdi district of the Sudan. When his hunting-ground for slaves became exhausted he was forced to extend his operations further westward and to attack the states of the Central Sudan. He was immediately repulsed by the warlike Wadai; but Bagirmi, being a weaker state, was quickly overcome in 1893. The king evacuated the country almost without a struggle, and threw himself into his fortified capital of Massenya. Bagirmi, however, was regarded by Rabah merely as affording him a passage for attack upon the weak and wealthy kingdom of Bornu. With the help of the Fulbe chieftain, Mallam Hajato of Jamare, who readily joined in the enterprise, he penetrated as far as Kuka, but was there defeated by Kiyari, who had dethroned and executed his weak uncle, King Hashim. However, Rabah's emissaries had previously sown the seeds of treachery and disunion among the nobles of Bornu; Rabah gained the victory in a second battle, slew the king, and subdued his capital in 1894. Dikaua, on the Yaloe river, south-east of Lake Chad, became the capital in place of the unhealthy town of Kuka, which was destroyed.

Conquered by the Slave-hunters Thus it appeared that a new dynasty had been founded, and that this infusion of fresh blood might revive the failing powers of Bornu. As a matter of fact, trade with the north increased, and at the same time the boundaries of the kingdom were extended towards the south and south-west as the result of conflicts with the petty states there situated. However, a struggle with the French led to the overthrow of

OMAR, SULTAN OF BORNU, WITH HIS ESCORT
The son of the sheikh who saved Bornu and established it as a strong kingdom.

the conqueror. Several small French expeditions, striving for the great object of a union of the Congo land with the Western Sudan and Algeria, were beaten back or destroyed altogether at the instigation of Rabah. Finally, however, in February, 1899, Rabah was defeated and killed by the French; and at the beginning of 1900 Kanem, or Halifa Djerab, also recognised the French supremacy. How-

THE SULTAN RABAH OF DIKAUA, THE CAPITAL OF BORNU
Rabah, a leader of the slave-hunter Zebehr's army, conquered Bornu in 1894 and made Dikaua its capital. He was defeated in 1899 by the French, whose supremacy is now recognised.

ever, Rabah's son Fad el Allah continued to hold out with his brother Niebe on Lake Chad with the support of the influential Senussi, made an incursion into Bornu, and at the beginning of 1901 expelled Hashim's second son, the sultan Gerbai, who had been set up by the French; but about the middle of 1901 he was driven back to Gujiba in North Nigeria. In the course of a further attempt to invade the Shari delta, he fell on British soil, on August 25th, 1901, in a conflict with the French. Niebe was taken prisoner. In this way the desired connection of the French colonial districts was brought about, although their control cannot as yet be considered more than nominal.

Bagirmi, the neighbouring state to Bornu, is very similarly situated in point of position, and has suffered a like fate. Bagirmi proper consists of the level districts on the Central and Lower Shari, and its lowest part forms the western frontier of the little kingdom of Logone, which is dependent upon Bornu. In the **The State of Bagirmi** north Bagirmi is separated from the desert by Kanem and the most westerly provinces of Wadai; hence its influence extends further south than that of the states of Bornu or Wadai. Further the civilisation of Bagirmi is of considerably later growth than that of its neighbour Bornu. In the sixteenth century several small heathen kingdoms existed upon the area

of the modern Bagirmi. The country was also overrun by wandering Arabs as well as by the bodies of the Fulbe, who were dependent upon the owners of Kanem, the Bulala. The nucleus of an important state was formed by immigrants **First Prince of Bagirmi** from the east, who can hardly have come from any great distance. The leaders of these foreigners succeeded in shaking off the influence of the Bulala and also in winning the rest of the nomadic population to their own interests. The first prince of Bagirmi, who founded the capital of Massenya, or Massenja, and his immediate successors had not been converted to Mohammedanism. Malo, the last of the heathen kings, was deposed in 1568 by his brother Abdallah, who had accepted the tenets of Islam.

Under the Mohammedan dynasty, which was thus founded, the civilising influences exerted upon Bagirmi came almost exclusively from Bornu. Among Abdallah's successors Mohammed el-Amin is worthy of mention. He extended the area of the kingdom and undertook a pilgrimage to Mecca (1751-1785). At the outset of the nineteenth century Abder-Rahman of Bagirmi revolted against Bornu, which seems to have exercised some kind of suzerainty. He was utterly defeated and slain by Sabun, sultan of Wadai, whom the king of Bornu had summoned to his help. In consequence the country came under the influence of Wadai, and civil war was the result. When Othman, or Burkomanda, eventually gained the throne he was obliged formally to acknowledge the supremacy of Wadai and to submit to the imposition of a tribute. In spite of this, we find him engaged in petty warfare—now with

A War With the Pilgrims Bornu, now with Wadai — and making good his losses by marauding expeditions against his neighbours and the heathen races of the south. His son, Abd-el-Kader (1846-1858), continued this policy until the latter years of his reign, which he was enabled to spend in peace. A curious instance of the Fulbe restlessness, from which Bagirmi had been hitherto spared, proved in its consequences fatal to this monarch. Under the leadership of a fanatic of Fulbe extraction a great caravan of pilgrims marched through Bornu to Bagirmi in complete defiance of the king's regulations. The king attempted to oppose them by force of arms, but was defeated and slain.

His successor, Mohammedu, escaped, and when the band of pilgrims broke up on the death of their leader he took a bloody vengeance on part of them for his predecessor's defeat. For a long time King Ali of Wadai had borne with the unfriendly behaviour of the prince of Bagirmi, his vassal, in silence. In the autumn of 1870 he suddenly appeared with an army before Massenya. After a long siege of this extensive town he succeeded in breaching the walls with a powder-mine, captured the town, and forced the king to fly to the south. Ali had the plunder conveyed to his own capital, settled many of the industrial inhabitants of Bagirmi in Wadai, and about 1885 placed Abd-er-Rahman Gaurang, the son of Abd-el-Kader, on the throne. A fresh outbreak of civil war enabled Rabah to make himself master of the country in

Rise of the State of Wadai 1893. Gaurang held out in the capital of Massenya, and thought himself secure from further attacks after placing himself under French protection in 1897. But in the autumn of 1899 he was again hard pressed by Rabah, until, in 1900, the French attack on the state of and the death of Rabah gave him a breathing space. In later times the state of Wadai became the dominant power in the Central

Sudan as opposed to the older state of Bornu. Its authentic history begins at an even later date than that of Bagirmi. It is an indisputable fact, at any rate during the Mohammedan period, that the kingdom of Bornu, owing to its favourable situation in connection with the Mediterranean states, was the centre whence all the districts on its eastern frontier gained the means of advancing their civilisation. This is also true to some extent of the Hausa states, since not only was the Bornu civilisation spread far and wide by trade and commercial intercourse, but also because parts of the Hausa race migrated voluntarily or involuntarily into the other countries of the Sudan, and there formed the nucleus of a settled industrial population. In this manner the seeds of a higher civilisation were carried westward to Bagirmi, Wadai, and Darfur.

This was not, however, the line of movement invariably followed. As long as the civilisation which had advanced up the Nile from Egypt continued to flourish in the Upper Nile valley, the light of culture came from the east. It is probable

Centre of Sudanese Civilisation that even in antiquity the Central Sudan had received valuable, though not permanent, impulses from this district. Remains of the old civilisation are yet to be found here and there. The Arab traveller Zain el-Abidin, whose narratives are usually trustworthy, visited Wadai in the first quarter of the nineteenth century, and speaks of ruins, stone sarcophagi, and remnants of a sun worship which he affirms that he discovered near the capital. This may be considered an offshoot of Egyptian civilisation in remote antiquity; but we have no means of connecting it with the modern history of the country, which hardly begins before the sixteenth century of our chronology.

Until a short time ago Wadai embraced, speaking generally, the district between Lake Fittri and the mountains of Darfur on the one side, the desert and the tributaries of the Shari on the other. The nucleus of the kingdom is formed by the mountainous country on the east, together with the central district. Here dwell the ruling people; while on the south, as everywhere in the Central Sudan, are districts inhabited by heathen tribes of pure negro blood, cutting off all connection with Central Africa in general and the Congo valley in particular. The inhabitants of the mountains, the Maba, who are now the ruling tribe, seem from their dark colour to have received a strong infusion of negro blood, though they may originally have been closely connected with the Ethiopians. Their country is by no means unfertile, but its wild nature is reflected in the rough and violent, though energetic, character of this people, which has made them superior in the long run to the unsettled nomads of the desert and a standing danger to the neighbouring kingdoms of the Sudan. In many cases the social system of the Maba races shows remnants of ancient institutions — for example, of a matri-archal system, the wife's property being held entirely separate from the husband's. As regards religion, some tribes are more fanatical than others.

The modern civili-sation of Wadai is of Western origin, but the first impulse to constitutional unity came from the east. The Arabs made their influence felt here before the period of the Mohammedan movement, having crossed the southern extremity of the Red Sea, which has never been any real barrier to communication be-tween Arabia and Africa. With this heathen Arab group we may associate the Tunjer, who seem to have previously been settled in Nubia. With the appearance of this Arab race, who are credited with having attained a comparatively advanced stage of civilisation, the history of Wadai begins. The petty mountain tribes of Wadai, constantly at war with one another and sunk in absolute barbarism, were for the first time united into some kind of polity, perhaps from about 1500 – 1600 A.D., by the Tunjer, who insisted upon the recog-nition of their supremacy and upon the payment of tribute. After Darfur had shaken off their yoke the Tunjer continued to rule in Wadai for some time, until

Beginning of History of Wadai

ONE OF THE SULTAN OF BAGIRMI'S LANCERS
Bagirmi, a Shari river state, suffered a fate similar to its neighbour Bornu, coming under French influence in 1900.

their power was also broken in the latter district. It was not a native leader who brought about their overthrow, but Abd el-Kerim, the descendant of a man of Arab extraction, an immigrant from Shendi, on the Nile. Abd el-Kerim had acquired great influence among the native tribes, and here once again a religious movement be-came the cloak for a national revolution. This leader was a Mohammedan, and as such the natural enemy of the heathen dynasty of the Tunjer and their sultan, Daud. He won over the Arab races and the dark-skinned mountain tribes, de-feated the sultan, and forced the Tunjer to the westward. In the new capital of Wara he gathered round him the first Mohammedan con-gregation, the numbers of which increased rapidly. Darfur had freed it-self from the Tunjer rule at an earlier period, and had grown so powerful that it had made the last Tunjer princes of Wadai tributary to itself. Abd el-Kerim, when he seized the inheritance of the Tunjer, was obliged also to accept this dependent position, and, according to custom, a princess was sent to the king of Darfur every three years. Bornu, which was previously in friendly relations with the Tunjer, had also to be appeased by a payment of tribute. Abd el-Kerim is said to have reigned from 1635 to 1655, and his son Charut from 1655 to 1678.

Sudanese Victories of Islam

The power of Wadai gradually increased. In the rude but powerful mountain population the country possessed a race which was indisputably superior in mili-tary prowess to the inhabitants of the neighbouring states. These conditions naturally influenced the relations of Wadai and Darfur. A national opposition was apparently organised against the handing over of a princess to Wadai, a form of tribute which had been placed upon a regular footing by the sultan Yakub Arus (1681–1707). The payment of tribute ceased. The sultan Ahmed Bokkor of Darfur was a man of peace, and hesitated before employing armed force to avenge the insult. Arus himself then advanced to the attack, but was forced to retreat,

Princesses Offered as Tribute and, after reaching Wadai with much difficulty, found himself obliged to conclude peace. However, tribute was not again exacted, and when Omar Sele, Ahmed Bokkor's grandson, attempted to restore the old state of affairs and invaded Wadai he was defeated and taken prisoner by Arus.

Under Charut the younger (1707–1747) the country enjoyed a period of peace and prosperity. But his successor, Djoda (1747–1795), soon found himself involved in war with Darfur. The army of the eastern state was defeated, and a noble, who gave himself out as the sultan, was kept prisoner for a long time in Wadai. Djoda also undertook eight great campaigns against the heathen tribes upon the south, and thus extended his kingdom in this direction. On the west he conquered part of Kanem. Wadai had encroached upon the rights of Bornu by the occupancy of Kanem, but the sultan Abd el-Kerim Sabun (1803–1813) made the attack upon Bagirmi of which the consequences have been already described, and brought this neighbouring kingdom under his influence. Notwithstanding the unfavourable position of his country, he successfully revived the trade with Tripoli and Egypt, and by settling families from Bagirmi in his territory he raised the standard of manufacture, both of these improvements adding largely to the royal income. Campaigns against the independent negroes of the heathen states were almost an annual event. At that period the real wealth of the

Agricultural Prosperity of Wadai country was not derived from trade and manufacture, as at the present day, but from a highly flourishing system of cattle-breeding and from agriculture. From these sources was drawn the sultan's income, all taxes being paid in kind. The land was considered as the sultan's property. It is only in the original Maba districts that landowners in the full sense of the term were to be found. Still, the tenants in the other districts are by no means the sultan's serfs. They are sturdy, independent types of humanity; the comparative ease with which their obedience is secured is due entirely to their social organisation, which seems to be of great antiquity, and is based chiefly upon the division of the members of any one group into old men, youths, and children. Notwithstanding the uncivilised character of the people, religious education is much more advanced than in Bornu or Darfur. In recent times evidence of elementary attempts at scientific inquiry is to be found.

After Wadai had enjoyed prosperity under a succession of capable rulers, Yusef Chorefin came to the throne (1813–1820), the type of a bloodthirsty monarch, conspicuously unsuccessful in all foreign enterprises. The mother of the next sultan, Rakib, who was still a minor, was descended from an Arab slave family; she, together with the numerous representatives of the Arab nationality in Wadai, thought that the opportunity had now come of deciding the old quarrel between the

The Old Nomadic War Revived nomadic and settled tribes in favour of the Arabs. Though the queen-regent resorted to measures of the utmost cruelty to secure her aims, the plan was defeated by the determined resistance of the mountain tribes—Kodoi—who chose as their ruler Abd el-Aziz (1829–1835), a prince of the royal house, stormed the capital of Wara after a severe struggle, and crushed Sultan Rakib and his adherents. However, peace was not restored by this success. The mountain tribes had found that revolt was an occupation very much to their taste, and proceeded to support pretender after pretender to the throne on which they had themselves placed Abd el-Aziz; when he stopped this dangerous amusement by force of arms Wadai was reduced to great extremities by a famine. An army marched south against the heathen countries to procure a supply of corn; the sultan of Darfur at once availed himself of this opportunity of making an incursion into the disturbed frontier districts of Wadai. Exactly at this juncture Abd el-Aziz died.

Mohammed Sherif, a prince who had been forced to flee from Wadai at an earlier period, succeeded in setting himself upon the throne and in securing his position after the retreat of his friend Mohammed el-Fadl of Darfur (1835–1858). Mohammed

Sherif then renewed the war against the sultan of the little mountainous country of Tana, to the east of Wara, which had now become a neighbour of some importance. In 1846 he also interfered in the affairs of Bornu. At Kusseri he crossed the Shari and defeated the sheikh Omar, but was unable to maintain his position in the enemy's country, and ultimately— apparently upon the receipt of 8,000 Maria Theresa thalers—retreated to Wadai. In his own country, of which Abeshe had now become the capital, his avarice absorbed his energies and made him very unpopular. The consequence was a series of revolts and internal dissensions, in the course of which the country of Tana became the invariable place of refuge for the defeated revolutionaries, and ultimately for the eldest son of the sultan Mohammed, whose mother was a Fulbe woman. Mohammed Sherif attempted to punish Ibrahim of Tana for his conduct, and was himself severely defeated.

He was succeeded by Ali, the lawful heir to the throne (1858–1875–76), who deserves credit for the encouragement which he gave to trade and barter, the revival of caravan communication with the Mediterranean, his protection of the learned, and the peaceful character of his relations with neighbouring states. About 1870 a flourishing trade existed with Egypt by way of Darfur and Julo, with Bornu and Benghazi, the harbour of Tripoli, the exports from Wadai being slaves, ostrich feathers, and ivory. The king himself equipped caravans, and made a larger profit than he could gain by taxation and customs duties. This policy contributed to increase the strength of Wadai and to make it a formidable rival to the other Sudan states.

An Admirable Ruler

Latterly Wadai was hard pressed— by the invasion of Rabah, on the one hand, and, on the other, by the rivalry of the European colonising powers, which brought about the Franco-British agreement of March 21st, 1899. Turkey has also claimed that Wadai forms part of the hinterland of Tripoli. The natural conditions of the country have endowed the native peoples of Wadai with the highest degree of tenacity and military prowess. To this day the aboriginal mountain peoples of the Maba group form the flower of the population and the ruling class. No sultan

whose mother was not of Maba extraction could hope to ascend the throne of Wadai. The French protectorate will produce no material change in these conditions.

In the neighbouring district of Darfur the influence of Eastern civilisation is more marked; its history also can be retraced further than that of Wadai, which lies, so to speak, in the dead water between the main streams of civilisation in the Central and Eastern Sudan. Little, however, is known concerning the Darfur of pre-Mohammedan times. The nucleus of this state is a mountainous district, the highest part of which, in the Djebel Marra, may be considered as the cradle of the old heathen state Darfur. Its first rulers came from the East, and, to judge from the majority of the royal titles, were mixed with Arabs, if they were not of pure Arab blood. These were the Dajo, a people of little account, and in a low stage of civilisation at the present day; but at one period they were the most important element of the population, and held the country more or less in subjection to themselves from their station in the Marra mountains. The first Dajo king, Kosber, is said to have resided in Debba, at the eastern foot of the Djebel Marra. Tradition speaks of twenty-one, thirteen, or even so few as five Dajo rulers.

Mountain State of Darfur

We are better informed respecting the Darfur dynasty of the Tunjer. The first Tunjer ruler was Ahmed el-Maqur. The dynasty of the Kera, who brought the Tunjer predominance to an end, sprang from a fusion of native families with the old ruling house. The last Tunjer king was called Shau, the first Kera king was Delil Bahar, or Dali, a half-brother of Shau, the severity of whose rule had provoked a rebellion. Dali availed himself of this favourable opportunity to introduce laws and institutions into the kingdom, which remained in force until Darfur lost its independence. His government may have fallen in the middle of the fifteenth century. The land then seems to have been disturbed by quarrels concerning the succession; continual changes in the government were the natural consequence. Suleman Solon was the first king to grasp the reins of government with real firmness; as a child he had fled to Wadai and had been received by the Massalit, his mother's

Darfur in the 15th Century

relations. He returned to war against his great-uncle Tinsam, established himself in the Marra Mountains, and from this point subdued and extended the territory of Darfur. He is especially noteworthy as the introducer of Mohammedanism. The military strength of the people seems at that time to have been greater than their civilisation. Suleman Solon (1596–1637), by a series of campaigns extended his power eastward beyond the Nile up to the Atbara, thus ruling over the whole of Kordofan and part of Sennar ; he also interfered to some purpose in the affairs of the Eastern Sudan. Less prosperous was the reign of his son Musa (1637–1682). Under his rule a feature peculiar to almost all the Sudan states became very prominent. While remote districts recognised the monarch's authority, tribes which he was unable to subdue were to be found a few miles from his capital. As the inhabitants of the Tama Mountains were a thorn in the side of the kings of Wadai, so the Massabat were a standing menace to Musa ; their sultan Djongol laid claim to the throne on the strength of his relationship to the ruling dynasty. At that period, however, the supremacy of Darfur was undisputed over a wide area ; Wadai, which had been connected with Darfur since the time of the Tunjer, also recognised its suzerainty.

Darfur's Greatest Ruler

This condition of affairs was greatly changed during the reign of the next king, Ahmed Bokkor (1682–1722). His policy aimed at making the kingdom a pure Mohammedan state ; by encouraging the priesthood and founding schools he hoped to crush heathenism and barbarism at the same time. To this end he settled in Darfur colonies of foreigners whose civilisation was more advanced than that of his own people. Together with peoples from the banks of the Nile he chose inhabitants from Bornu and Bagirmi, The next rulers were the tyrannical Mohammed Daura (1722–1732) and his son Omar Lele (1732 to 1739 ; deceased about 1750 in Wadai), whose followers showed their disgust at his military incapacity by deserting him in the decisive battle against Arus of Wadai. He was succeeded by Abul Casim (1739–1752). When he made an attack upon Wadai to avenge the last defeat, the Furaner freemen deserted without striking a blow,

The Rule of the Tyrants

being embittered by the severity of the taxes and the undue preference given to slaves. His brother Tirab (1752–1785) was then elected sultan ; he consolidated his kingdom, undertook numerous campaigns, and enjoyed a high reputation for learning and piety. After a series of disputes as to the succession, he was followed by his brother Abd er-Rahman (1785–1799), whose peaceful government greatly increased the prosperity of the country.

During the reign of his son Mohammed el-Fadl (1799–1839) began that revolution in the Eastern Sudan which was destined to prove fatal to Darfur. Kordofan, which had hitherto been under the supremacy of Darfur, was conquered by the Egyptians. Mohammed el-Fadl correctly appreciated the situation, and attempted to strengthen his powers of resistance by subjugating Wadai, but his plans were wrecked by accidental circumstances. His successor, the sultan Mohammed el-Hasin (1839–1873), was occupied chiefly by wars with the Arabs in the south-east of Darfur, the Risegad, and other almost unconquerable tribes. Hasin's campaigns were almost entirely fruitless of result. With Egypt, on the other hand, he was on excellent terms, though he by no means under-estimated the dangers which threatened him from that quarter, and induced the Turkish sultans Abd ul-Medjid and Abd ul-Aziz to confirm his supremacy. With King Ali of Wadai he also concluded an offensive and defensive alliance.

The End of the Kingdom

On the death of Hasin, his youngest son, Ibrahim Koiko, ascended the throne in 1873, and the kingdom rapidly approached its doom. The Egyptian Government had appointed Zebehr to be governor, or Mudir, of the province of Bahr el-Ghazal, situated upon the southern frontier of Darfur. In this capacity he attacked and conquered the Risegad, who had made a temporary peace with the sultan of Darfur, in view of the approaching danger. Ibrahim was thus forced to enter into war with Zebehr. The campaign was decided late in 1874 by the battle of Menawatji, in which the sultan Ibrahim was killed. Thus Darfur became part of the Egyptian Sudan. Until 1879, descendants of the king held out against the Egyptians in the Marra Mountains, the cradle of the old princely stock. The remainder of the story belongs to Egyptian history.

THE EASTERN SUDAN
THE NUBIAN PEOPLE, ANCIENT AND MODERN

AS regard the broader lines of development, the Eastern Sudan displays many points of affinity with the western districts; but as its geographical character differs in two main points from that of the countries on the southern frontier of the Sahara, its history in these respects ran a course of its own.

The first point of difference is the existence of the Nile, which creates a narrow strip of fruitful land in the midst of a steppe district. The river, being navigable, makes of this fertile territory a connected whole, though its unity is not that of those arable districts situated like oases at some distance from the stream, while the cataracts have effectively prevented the Nile from serving as an open highway to Egypt proper. Still, civilisation spread by this channel to the districts of the Sudan at an earlier period than in other cases. The second special characteristic is the neighbourhood of the Eastern Sudan to the sea and to Arabia. The narrow channel of the Red Sea presents no obstacle to the crossing of a people, like the Arabs of old, whose merchant ships reached India and Zanzibar. The Arab steppe-dwellers hold with reference to the Eastern Sudan that position which was occupied on the west by the desert tribes, who have so often founded and destroyed powerful kingdoms. No enemy of this kind threatened the Eastern Sudan upon the north. Egypt and her ancient civilisation was at times a cause of fear, but more often of reverence for the priceless gifts which she bestowed. Apart from these special features, the general characteristics of the Eastern Sudan correspond to those of the central and western parts.

Characteristics of the East Sudan

During remote antiquity we find that the greater part of the modern Nubia was peopled by a red-skinned race, the Kushites, who were apparently of Hamitic origin and related to the Egyptians. Further, in the desert land right and left of the Nile valley, we find miserable tribes of steppe-dwellers, who were also Hamites or Ethiopians; and fair-complexioned Libyans are also to be found who may have made their way to Nubia from the north coast. While Egypt was developing her civilisation, the Nile valley was uncultivated above the first cataract; its population was on the level of the wandering desert nomads of the neighbourhood. It is hard to say how far northward the negroes extended. Probably negro tribes and Kushites lived side by side where the Nile valley was broader and more fertile, the negroes being in sole possession of the river banks further in the Sudan, perhaps in the same manner as the Shilluks and the Dinka now inhabit the shores of the upper river. The tribute of the land of Kush was always largely paid in slaves.

Remote Antiquity in Nubia

As the Kushites were related to the Egyptians, the different theories upon the origin of the Egyptians apply equally to them, and need not be discussed anew. Commercial enterprise, and the hope of gain, attracted individual Egyptians southward, until the rulers of the country interfered, occupied part of Nubia, and monopolised the profits. Two very valuable articles were exported from Kush—namely, ivory and black slaves—which appear as the regular tribute payment in the Egyptian picture writing. But interest rose to an extraordinary pitch when rich deposits of gold were found in the mountains on the south, which for a long period were to be the sole source whence Egypt drew her supply of this desirable metal. Wood for shipbuilding was also brought from Kush at the time when extensive forests covered the mountains on the banks of the Nile, which are now absolutely bare. The earliest information which we possess

Egypt's Gold Supply

upon the relations of Nubia and Egypt is derived from an inscription of the sixth dynasty, which, among other subjects, describes the preparations of king Pepi I. for a campaign into the Sinaitic peninsula and the south of Palestine. We are told that on this occasion troops were drawn from the negro countries of Aaretet, Zam, Aman, Uaust, Kaau and Tatam. Thus we see that about this period part of the Kushites recognised the full supremacy of Egypt, which had perhaps been already enforced for some considerable time. We have no information for the period subsequent to Pepi's dynasty.

Earliest Relations with Egypt

When Egypt recovered her prosperity, under the eleventh dynasty after the fall of the old kingdom, and Thebes became the capital, Nubia also felt the consequences of the change. The Nubian possessions seem to have been one of the most important sources of the king's revenue ; not only the products of the gold-mines, but also the tribute paid by the subject races, came directly into his coffers. However, the district was not completely subjugated until the era of the twelfth dynasty. The name " Kush" is then for the first time applied to the land in the south, and probably referred at first to the territory of the most powerful among the tribes which were then subdued. This tribe must have belonged to the red-brown Ethiopians. Negroes do not appear in these conflicts before Senusret I. Negro labour also seems to have been employed under compulsion in the gold-mines.

Upon this occasion, as before, the advance of the Egyptian kings was due chiefly to anxiety to get possession of the gold-mines and to ensure the safe arrival of their output. Kush was kept in subjection by a chain of military posts, which also formed little oases of civilisation. Senusret III. built a frontier fortress at Semneh above Wadi Halfa [see page 2058], and forbade the negroes beyond this boundary to pass this point in their boats as they sailed down stream. The king secured the frontier by a second campaign, and Kush was henceforward in close connection with Egypt.

It is obvious from the position of this frontier fortress that only the northern parts of Nubia were in the hands of the Egyptians, and that the modern Dongola never belonged to the kingdom of the Pharaohs. In spite of this fact Egyptian civilisation spread further up the Nile, a development which must have taken place on peaceful lines. Such transmission of civilisation was facilitated by the fact that the Egyptians were in possession of the gold-mines south of the modern Korosko. At Korosko the road branches off into the desert, and, by cutting off a great bend in the Nile, forms the route of quickest communication with the Sudan. It was perhaps at an early period that the beginnings of the later kingdom of Napata on the south came into existence, though the actual foundation of the state is an event which belongs to the period of the Ramessides. This kingdom may, however, have received the seeds of civilisation from another direction. When the prosperity of Egypt revived, under the eleventh dynasty, an unprecedented impulse was given to commercial enterprise, and Egyptian fleets sailed down the Red Sea as far south as the Straits of Bab el - Mandeb. The Egyptians were not skilled seamen, but the desire to

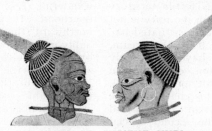

NEGROES OF ANCIENT NUBIA
From a painting in an Egyptian tomb, commemorating one of Egypt's many wars with the Nubians.

secure a supply of that desirable commodity, frankincense, without the inconvenience of dealing with middlemen, had impelled them to venture upon the perilous waters of the Red Sea and the Gulf of Aden, and had thus brought them into communication with the inhabitants of Southern Arabia and Somaliland. The starting-point of the Egyptian voyages must have been somewhere about the latitude of Thebes, where the little harbour of Kossir, or Kosseir, is to be found at the present day. An inscription describes fully how a road with water cisterns was laid from Thebes to the coast through the barren mountain district, and how a ship was built upon the shore which seems to have made a successful voyage to Punt, a name apparently denoting the coasts on each side of the Gulf of Aden. Commercial intercourse eventually became fairly vigorous, and may have

The Egyptian Trade in Frankincense

THE STRIKING RESEMBLANCE OF THE NUBIANS OF TO-DAY TO THE ANCIENT EGYPTIANS

exercised some indirect influence upon the civilisation on the Upper Nile. Under the thirteenth dynasty a prosperous trade with Punt continued. It may then have declined until it was temporarily resumed at the time of the " New Kingdom " ; but it gave so powerful a stimulus to the Arab coast dwellers that they were afterward able to become the carriers of the trade in the Red Sea and the northern Indian Ocean. However, they were much more strongly influenced by the Babylonian-Assyrian civilisation than by the Egyptian. That the Nubian possessions were, at any rate, retained during that period is proved by a dumb but irrefutable

witness, a giant granite figure of King Sebekhotep V., which still rises upon the island of Argo above the third cataract, quite close to the modern Dongola.

Long afterwards, when the Hyksos had been driven out and the military " new kingdom " was founded, the kings set to work to recover the influence which the country had lost in Nubia. At first expeditions were sent out, rather with the object of weakening the Kushite tribes than of making a permanent subjugation, but afterward the kings devoted their energy to this latter task. Thothmes I. advanced by land and water, apparently contrived to transport his ships above the

A GROUP OF MODERN NUBIANS : WARRIORS AND A CHIEF

This picture, together with that above, illustrates the very striking way in which the ancient Egyptian method of doing the hair, as well as certain characteristics of dress adopted from the Egyptians, is continued to this day.

first cataract, and, after defeating the Nubian fleet in a great battle on the Nile, subdued all the country up to the third cataract.

These wars with Nubia do not harmonise with the tradition, which is in any case very doubtful, that the Hyksos were expelled with the help of the Ethiopians. Possibly in **Wars and Alliance With Nubia** the course of the struggle with the northern intruders a temporary alliance was formed with some of the "nine bow-peoples," as the Nubians are called in the Egyptian inscriptions. The consort of the first Egyptian king of the victorious eighteenth dynasty seems to have been an Ethiopian. Under Queen Hatshepsut, who was regent for Thothmes III., the frontiers of the Nubian province were certainly extended further southward; at the same time the trade with Punt was revived, and territory perhaps acquired on the coast of the Red Sea. Pictures belonging to the king's reign show the inhabitants of the Upper Nile valley, the red-brown Kushites, and the dark-skinned negroes bringing cattle, giraffes, the skins of wild animals, gold rings, and precious stones as tribute; but even at that period negro slaves were the most welcome of the presents brought from the south.

In this way negro and Egyptian were commingled, and at the same time Egyptian farmers and craftsmen settled on the Nubian Nile, especially after Rameses II. had caused a number of new towns and temples to be built in that district. The gold-mines continued to yield a rich output. The Nile valley was taxed in the same way as Egypt proper, and the tributary tribes on the south made heavy payments to the royal treasury. Nubia was thus an important and carefully-administered province of the Egyptian kingdom. In any case Egyptian civilisation advanced far into the Sudan, and led to results which **A Second Egypt Attempted** were afterward to react upon the destiny of Egypt. When the royal power began to decline in Egypt, and mercenaries became predominant, the native dynasty held out longest in Thebes, as it had done before on similar occasions. After the loss of this town it retreated, apparently to Kush, and there founded a separate kingdom, the rulers of which continued characteristically enough to assume the royal titles of the Egyptian kings. This is the account usually given of the origin of the Napata kingdom, a

name in general use and derived from the capital situated below the fourth cataract

Napata forms a very remarkable contrast to the Sudan states of modern times. Founded by a fair-complexioned people in a district originally negro, with a civilisation and a religion of northern origin, it seems to have been intended as a second Egypt; upon occasion its rulers even dared to aspire to the throne of the elder state. But its power is not permanent. Its exotic civilisation deteriorates; and the black races, constantly reinforced by fresh infusions of negro blood, lay like a leaden pall upon the state and stifled every upward tendency. The growing strength of the negro races is easily explained. The centre of the Napata kingdom lay at first, as is obvious from its historical development and the position of its capital, in the Nubian Nile valley, and the dominant race were the Kushites, who were commingled with the immigrant Egyptians; but later, when the various attempts to conquer Egypt had definitely failed, the more southerly districts of the Eastern Sudan inhabited by negroes were added **Golden Age of the Priesthood** to the kingdom, in particular the important peninsula between the White and the Blue Nile. During the early period of Ethiopian independence a difference between the condition of Ethiopia and Egypt, proceeding from causes purely ethnical, became more and more pronounced in course of time. In Egypt religion doubtless counted for a great deal; but among the duller Ethiopians it became absolutely predominant, and in Napata the priesthood, which naturally was chiefly recruited from Egypt, lived in a golden age. This was partly due to the fact that the priests in Ethiopia appeared as the chief exponents of civilisation; but a more potent cause was the character of the Kushites and Berbers, which has remained unchanged to the present day. Nowhere has Mohammedanism found such faithful, bigoted, and devoted adherents as among the Berbers; without their help, for example, Islam would never have conquered Spain, nor maintained its hold over the country for so long.

These characteristics of the " blameless" Ethiopian people, which were equally strong in ancient times, were highly valued by the priests, and explain why so many exaggerated accounts of the moral purity of the Ethiopians and the high excellence of their civilisation were current in the ancient world. The Egyptian priests were the source of these rumours, and in this way discharged some part of their obligations to their most loyal adherents.

The confusion prevailing in Egypt upon the downfall of the "new kingdom" not only secured their independence to the Ethiopians, but also enabled the Ethiopian dynasty, which was probably of Egyptian origin, to seize the throne of the old kingdom with the help of Kushite warriors about 840 B.C. This portion of Ethiopian history is again absorbed in that of Egypt, and we can pass on to the time when the Ethiopian dynasty found it necessary to evacuate the territory of the Lower Nile, about 668 B.C.

Our information upon the affairs of the kingdom of Napata after the retreat of the Ethiopians from Egypt is derived from Greek sources and the inscriptions of the Ethiopian rulers. The priesthood had turned the piety of the princes to good account, and had gradually become a directing influence within the state. In the name of their divinity they elected that candidate to the throne whom they pre-

Suicide By Order of the Priests ferred, and if a ruler thwarted their policy he was informed that it was God's will that he should expiate his sins by a voluntary death. However, religious conflicts and bloody disputes about the succession were by no means exceptional events. When Egypt had recovered its independence an unsuccessful attack was made upon Nubia; and, in consequence of internal dissensions, part of the Egyptian warrior caste, which had originated from mercenaries settled in the country, emigrated to Ethiopia.

After the separation from Egypt, the centre of gravity of Ethiopia shifted more and more southward. Napata remained the home of the priests, but the kings built a new capital south of the confluence of the Atbara and the Nile, the town of Meroe, by which name the kingdom was generally known in later times. Thus, Ethiopia was in less danger than before of being involved in the further destinies of Egypt. In the time of the Persian supremacy over Egypt the invaders seized a part of Nubia, and in some degree the events of antiquity were repeated in this frontier land; but the kingdom of Meroe was untouched. The overwhelming influence of the priesthood was broken for a time by King Argamon—the Ergamenes

of the Greek accounts—about 270 B.C. The priests, as usual, had sent the old but vigorous prince the command of God that he should put an end to his life; Argamon answered by cursing the priests.

The monarchy thus gained in independence, but this advantage was counterbalanced by the development of another **The Priests Defied** peculiarity, which recurs in manifold form throughout the world. In Meroe the old matriarchal system, whereby children belong to the mother's and not to the father's family, appears to have held its ground with such tenacity that the queens acquired a position of unusual privilege, acted as regents during the minority of their sons, and eventually, when these latter came of age, declined to resign their authority, but left the son in the position of co-regent. Writers of the classical period invariably speak of these queens by their title of Candace.

Ethiopia was gradually transformed into a pure Sudanese state. Its attention was directed chiefly to the negro lands on the south, and its connection with the north steadily relaxed. Once only did a queen of Meroe attempt to revive the old traditions and to enforce the Ethiopian claims to Egypt by force of arms in 23 B.C.; but Egypt was then a province of the great Roman empire. The Ethiopian attack failed miserably before the resistance of the Roman frontier troops, whose leader, Petronius, replied with a punitive expedition, which ended with the destruction of Napata, the old royal capital. The collision had no further consequences. Meroe remained independent of Rome behind the barrier of the desert and the Nile rapids. In the course of the century the kingdom became weaker and fell into a state of disruption. Previously the information received in the north concerning Meroe had been very scanty, and now all communication **Decay of the Kingdom of Meroe** was cut off by the rude tribe of the Blemmyer, who began their devastating raids in the mountain country to the east of the Nubian Nile, and completely blocked the road down the Nile valley. However, fragments of the Græco-Roman civilisation were carried southward, and prevented Meroe and the Eastern Sudan in general from relapsing into utter barbarism.

It was in full accordance with the religious character of the Ethiopians that the Christian missionaries, who eventually penetrated to their district, should have met with the unexpected success which they obtained. The date of their first appearance in Meroe is unknown ; but it is certain that the disruption of the kingdom and the decay of the old priesthood were events no less favourable to

Greek Culture in Meroe

their efforts than was the support gained from the infiltration of the Greek language and culture. In Nero's time the town of Meroe seems to have been in ruins. The kingdom itself was divided by its configuration into two main parts—a Nubian district, for which the name Napata reappears ; and especially the south-eastern district, the centre of which was in Axum, among the sturdy mountain tribes of Abyssinia, and in close relations with Arabia. Axum had been strongly influenced by Greek civilisation. Moreover, among the people of Napata, the later Nubians, Greek influence had taken the place of Egyptian in a large degree. The only Nubian prince of whom we have any information during a long period, Silkon, who lived in the fifth or sixth century A.D., used the Greek language in an inscription, though in a barbarous form, assumed the title of Basiliskos, and compared himself with Ares, the god of war. However, at that period Axum was by far the more powerful, and in a sense the more civilised, of the two kingdoms.

It must have been shortly after Silkon's time that the conversion of Nubia to Christianity was brought about. When Mohammedanism raised its standard and subdued Egypt, in the year 639, Nubia became a refuge for the fugitive Christians, as it may have been for the Egyptian priests at an earlier age in time of dangerous revolution. Together with Axum it formed a stronghold of the Christian faith which long withstood the assaults of the Arabs. We may reasonably

History of Christianity in Nubia

suppose that it was these refugees who completed the conversion of the people and fanned the flames of their religious zeal. But though Christianity has held its ground to the present day in the mountains of Abyssinia, in Nubia it eventually succumbed to the attack and persecutions of Mohammedanism. By the Arab immigration across the straits, Nubia was not only severed from Axum on the south, but was also cut off from all connection with the negro districts, a connection which is indispensable to the economic prosperity of the Sudan states.

In consequence the centre of gravity of the Christian state of Nubia again shifted northward to the modern Dongola. Its area had now been greatly reduced, and here, protected by deserts and cataracts, the little Christian kingdom offered a successful resistance to the attacks and the propaganda of Mohammedanism for a long period. A remnant of the Græco-Egyptian civilisation survived in this district at a time when elsewhere all traces of antiquity had been swept away by the stream of change. In the year 651 bands of Arabs burst into Nubia and besieged Dongola, but met with so resolute a resistance that they contented themselves with the imposition of a yearly tribute of 360 slaves, promising, moreover, to send a present of corn in return.

This connection with Egypt appears to have continued for a long period with occasional interruptions. In the tenth century we hear of various attacks de-

Christian Kingdom of Dongola

livered by the Nubians upon Egyptian territory. In the year 962 an ambassador of the Ikshid princes of Egypt was received in Dongola by the king of Nubia ; his attempts to convert the king to Mohammedanism proved ineffectual. The king's declaration that his country was more powerful and populous than Egypt seems to show that even then the southern possessions had not been entirely lost. Another source of information speaks of thirteen provinces, which were administered by the high-priests. Even during this later period hereditary rights went in the female line of dscent. This fact, and also the dominating position of the priesthood, is in agreement with the organisation of the old kingdom of Napata.

In the eleventh century the power of Nubia began to decline, although it still successfully resisted the attacks of the sultans of Egypt. During the years 1172–1174 a small Christian buffer state, which had been formed on Egyptian soil about Assouan and Elephantine—that is, north of the first cataract—was overthrown. The Nubian kingdom then seems to have been torn by internal struggles. Eventually the Egyptian sultans found that their attacks were no longer opposed by the united forces of the country. In 1275 the town of Dongola was conquered, and David, the reigning king, expelled. After a series of conflicts which brought the Mohammedan army almost to the southern frontier of Nubia, King David was definitely driven out of the country; his nephew Shekendah became king, and Nubia was made a vassal state of Egypt, and was consequently thrown open to Mohammedan influence.

Yet the strength of the united Christian state had not been entirely broken. Such remnants of Christendom as were left in Egypt looked to Nubia for support. About the middle of the thirteenth century the threatening attitude of the ruling Kyriakos of Nubia put a stop to the Christian persecutions in Egypt; but shortly afterward the ruling dynasty in Dongola accepted Mohammedanism. It was not the old royal house which had adopted the new faith, but a usurper, apparently of the tribe of the Beni Kensy, or Kenz, near Assouan. That Nubia during this period suffered greatly from internal strife and the attacks of foreign enemies, is proved by evidence from many quarters. It seems that one of the pretenders secured the support of Egypt by adopting the Mohammedan faith. The confusion was probably evoked and fostered by the influence of the bands of Arabs who now began to spread in the Nile valley.

When Christianity had thus lost its hold of the country it disappeared imperceptibly but inevitably. The priests diminished in numbers, the churches fell into decay, and the Christian clergy, who seem, to judge from the case of Abyssinia, to have preached a very degraded form of the Gospel, were replaced by Mohammedan missionaries;

Islam Replaces Christianity nor does it anywhere appear that the process of change was attended by any serious conflict. The ties of connection between the Christian congregations were gradually dissolved in consequence of the increased immigration of Arab tribes, and the Arabs themselves became the dominant power. Nubia thus underwent the fate of all the Sudan states—the nomadic overpowered the agricultural people.

Henceforward Nubia can hardly be considered as a self-ruled district, for the ruling power passed from one Arab group to another—changes barren of result. The Shaikiah Arabs eventually

Mamelukes in Dongola proved themselves the most powerful tribe. The general stagnation was at length disturbed by the revolutions in Egypt at the outset of the nineteenth century. In 1812 the remnant of the Egyptian Mamelukes fled to Nubia, prevented all pursuit on the part of Mehemet Ali's troops by devastating the Nile valley, and established themselves in Dongola in 1814. In 1820 the Egyptian troops succeeded in driving the Mamelukes from this retreat. Access to the Sudan proper was thus made possible, and a new and eventful period began for the districts on the Upper Nile.

ZEBEHR PASHA
The most important of the petty trader-princes of the Sudan during the days of the prosperity of the Egyptian slave-trade was Zebehr Pasha, the famous slave-hunter.

Christian states also existed in the southern parts of the old kingdom of Meroe. Aloa, the capital of which must have been situated near the later Khartoum, is mentioned in the tenth century; a smaller state was the kingdom of Mokra, between Aloa and Dongola. At a later period a Mohammedan kingdom was formed, Sennar, which again was conquered and reconstituted about 1500 by the Fundj, a tribe apparently related to the Shilluk. The Fundj extended their influence over Nubia and Darfur, and probably destroyed the last remnants of the Christian states on the Upper Nile. At the same time it seems likely that the Fundj migrations were closely connected with the movements of the Galla, who brought fearful destruction upon the Christian kingdom in Abyssinia about the same period.

As the power of Sennar declined, the kings of Darfur were able to extend their influence beyond Kordofan to the Nile, and even to make Sennar tributary to themselves for some period of time. About twenty small principalities existed on the Nile from Sennar northward toward Dongola, so that Egypt had no great obstacles to surmount when it addressed itself to the task of extending its influence southward. Mehemet Ali, who had conquered the Mamelukes in 1811 and was striving to make himself independent of the Porte, had every reason for employing the wealth and the admirable soldiery of the Sudan for the struggle which lay before him. The first step to this end was the conquest of

Mehemet Ali in the Sudan Dongola. When the Shaikiah Arabs, the real masters of Nubia, recognised the intentions of Egypt, with which they had joined hands against the Mamelukes, they offered a desperate but fruitless resistance. In 1820 the Egyptian troops, under the command of Ismail, a son of Mehemet Ali, renewed their advance southward. One detachment invaded Sennar, another turned upon Kordofan, both attempts being attended with success. However, the country remained in the hands of the Egyptians, was exposed to the rapacity of the officials for ten years, and was shattered by the occasional revolts of the desperate population. The free negro races on the south felt the weight of the new yoke in all its severity. Their land became more than ever an area for the operations of the slave-hunters.

The inexhaustible supply of black slaves and ivory in the Upper Nile districts was not clearly manifest until the Government sent several expeditions up the White Nile and established communication with those districts without much difficulty. Ivory was at first the staple article of trade. Slaves were occasionally captured or purchased, to be given in exchange for the valuable commodities offered for sale by the natives, who themselves without exception were anxious to acquire slaves. By degrees slave-hunting inevitably became the more important occupation. The native tribes, who lived in their usual state of mutual hostility, aroused the avarice of the traders, with whom they allied themselves against their neighbours. By this

Growth and Death of the Slave Trade means they gained a temporary accession of strength, ultimately falling victims to the rapacity of the slave-hunters. By such processes Egyptian influence was steadily extended—at any rate, indirectly—in the negro lands. The Government had only to follow in the tracks of the traders. Among those traders who ruled as petty princes in their own sphere of plunder, and naturally could not remain permanently at peace with the Government, the most important

was Zebehr of Dar Fertit. The ivory and slave trade had enjoyed only a few decades of prosperity when a storm of indignation was aroused by the expostulations of European missionaries and explorers against this destructive system. Egypt was at that time anxious to be considered a civilised state, and was forced to yield to the pressure. The vice-regent, Said Pasha, appeared in person at Khartoum in 1855, curtly prohibited the slave trade, and especially forbade his officials to make their customary raids into negro territory, an edict which cut off the larger part of their income. The consequence was that the slave trade, if more dangerous, was also more lucrative, and that the officials covered their loss of income by bribes and hush-money.

European influence, and therefore opposition to the slave trade, greatly increased in Egypt upon the accession of Ismail Pasha in 1863. He was a man devoted to Western culture, determined, rather out of vanity than from inward conviction, to declare himself in favour of reform and progress in every direction. At that

Gordon's Work in the Sudan moment the Englishman, Samuel Baker, had returned from his journey to the Albert Nyanza by the Upper Nile with the intention of procuring the assistance of the Egyptian Government against the slave-traders. Ismail supported his plans. In 1869 Baker Pasha entered the Upper Nile district with a small army, and by 1873 had succeeded in extending the Egyptian rule to Lake Albert and the frontiers of Unyoro. General Charles Gordon was now called in to reduce the Sudan to order. During the years 1874–1877, Gordon, under the greatest difficulties, was occupied in bringing the undertakings begun by Baker on the Upper Nile to a conclusion. In 1877 he was appointed pasha and governor-general. He was then called to Darfur by a revolt raised by Zebehr's son Sulaiman, who was defeated and killed in 1879–1880 by the Italian Romolo Gessi. Gordon, however, had been very feebly supported from Cairo. He despaired of completing his task and resigned.

And so we reach the last phase in the history of the Egyptian Sudan. It dates from the beginning of the Mahdist revolt in 1881, of which the story has already been told in the concluding chapter of our account of Egypt.

ABYSSINIA'S MOUNTAIN KINGDOM
ITALY'S DREAM OF A COLONIAL EMPIRE

THE highland country of Abyssinia, with its sheer descent to the sea on the east, forms a natural fortress, comparatively easy for hostile access on the southern side alone. The ethnical and political development of the country has entirely conformed to these natural conditions. In the south there is little political union, and the supremacy of the Abyssinian nationality is by no means absolute. In the west the rivers flowing down from the highlands point the way to the Nile and the ancient civilisation of Meroe. Here lie the gates through which some portion of Abyssinian civilisation made its way into the highlands. But the most permanent and decisive influence came from the coast, where the path of the world's commerce passed for thousands of years— a commerce which was almost destroyed for a time by the discovery of the maritime route to India, but has recovered more than its former brilliancy by the opening of the Suez Canal. The various influences which have affected Abyssinia are reflected in the composition of its people. The nucleus of the population, and probably the oldest stock, were Hamitic tribes, related to the Nubians and in a more remote degree to the Egyptians. The inhabitants of Punt, the ancient land of frankincense, also seem to have been Hamites. This people covered all the coastline of the Gulf of Aden and was further in touch with the later Phœnicians. Probably here, as in the rest of the Sudan, the frontiers of the negro races lay further northward than in our own times, though it is possible that the climatic conditions of Abyssinia were unsuitable for the negroes. At the present day pure negro tribes inhabit the central parts of the Blue Nile. To the Hamitic was added a strong Semitic element from the neighbouring land of Arabia. A Semitic language eventually became the universal idiom, the Geez, which is now dead and is used

A Path of the World's Commerce

only in the church services, but is represented by two daughter languages, the Amharish and the Tigrish.

The first seeds of higher civilisation must have come to Abyssinia from Egypt by way of the kingdom of Napata, and naturally developed here at a later time than in Nubia. In the course of years, however, the highlands made greater progress than did Meroe and gave proof of stronger powers of resistance. This is partly accounted for by the configuration of the country, which has produced a sturdier type of humanity than the hot districts on the banks of the Nile, and especially by the neighbourhood of Arabia and of the Red Sea, with its constant stream of traffic. When the connection between Meroe and Egypt came to an end the former naturally relapsed into barbarism and ultimately succumbed to the attacks of its enemies; but in the case of Abyssinia separation from the Nile valley did not imply degeneration, but only obliged the country to strengthen its connection with Arabia and the seafaring races.

Birth of Abyssinian Civilisation

The cradle of the Abyssinian civilisation and ruling power was the modern Tigre; that is to say, the most northerly province and the one nearest to the sea. South-west of Adua are yet to be seen the ruins of the old Ethiopian capital of Axum, with its obelisks and pillars, the style of which plainly points to Egypt, the parent of all early Ethiopian culture. When the kingdom of Axum became an independent power it is impossible to say. It apparently rose as an offshoot of the Arab coast kingdom Habashat, about the beginning of the Christian era. Some information upon the early history of the country is to be gained from the Abyssinian legends. According to these sources, the founder of the town of Axum was a son of Ham, called Cush, so that the kingdom was founded shortly after the Flood. From a son of Cush named Ethiops

Ancient Ethiopian Kingdom

it received the name of Ethiopia, which it divided with Meroe at an earlier period; but to this name it is now the sole claimant, and it appears to the present day in the official title of the Abyssinian ruler. The legend is conjoined with another Biblical

Solomon's Son King of Abyssinia

story, that, in the eleventh century B.C., Maketa, queen of Sheba ruled in Axum, and paid a visit to King Solomon, and their son, Menilek Ebn-Hakim, afterwards known as King David I., became the founder of the Ethiopian dynasty, and from him the rulers trace their descent to the present day.

The truth seems to be that civilisation was not fairly established in Axum until the age when Greek influence became predominant throughout the ancient world. While the Ptolemies ruled over Egypt the coast of the Red Sea was constantly visited by ivory traders and others. A trading station, Adulis, was founded near the modern Massowa, and military expeditions were even made into the interior. Greek was gradually adopted as the language of the court, the Greek mythology was partly borrowed or amalgamated with native beliefs, and Greek art and culture were patronised, at least by the nobility.

Several centuries of the Christian era had elapsed when Abyssinia reached the highest point of its prosperity, which was attained about the period when the first Christian missionaries penetrated to the Abyssinian highlands. To the year 333 belongs the boastful inscription which proclaims the king Uizanas, or Aeizanes, as ruler, not only of Northern Abyssinia, but also of large areas in Southern Arabia, thus showing that the kingdom of Axum was then the dominant power on the Straits of Bab el-Mandeb. In his inscription Uizanas calls himself a son of the war god Ares; but he may himself have favoured the introduction of Christianity and have received baptism from Frumentius, the apostle of the Abyssinians. The introduction of Christianity definitely determined

the course of spiritual development to be followed by Abyssinia. In this case it was no thin veneer of new doctrine to be wiped away by the lapse of time. In spite of all the calamities of fate Christianity remained permanent.

The succeeding period is shrouded in obscurity; tradition has handed down nothing but a list of kings. Abyssinia maintained its influence in Southern Arabia, though with the consequence that it became thoroughly saturated with Semitic civilisation. However, communication was steadily maintained with the Greek world. About the year 532 the emperor Justinian is said to have ordered Caleb, the ruler of Axum, to put a stop to the persecutions of the Christians which the Jews had begun in Southern Arabia. Caleb obeyed, and took the opportunity of greatly extending the Abyssinian power, which seems to have been slowly retrograding In 571, the year of Mahomet's

Abyssinians at the Gates of Mecca

birth, an Abyssinian general made an unsuccessful campaign against Mecca. Southern Arabia was then abandoned, ostensibly in consequence of the ravages of smallpox among the Ethiopian troops. Then came the first waves of the Mohammedan movement, which passed harmlessly by, so far as Abyssinia was concerned. But Christianity was to undergo another trial: the old dynasty known as Solomon's was expelled for centuries by a Jewish family. Jews, known as "Falasha," inhabit Abyssinia at the present day, and there can be no doubt that they originally migrated from Arabia into the African mountains. Israelite nomads are known to have migrated from antiquity to Arabia and to have advanced to the south of the peninsula, and Mahomet's first campaigns were directed against Jewish nomad tribes in the neighbourhood of Medina.

It was during the ninth century of our chronology that king Delnaod of the old Solomon dynasty was driven from the throne by a Jewess. Judith practically exterminated the old royal family and

RUINS OF AXUM, CAPITAL OF ETHIOPIA
According to tradition, Axum was founded after the Flood by a son of Ham. Remains of the king's seat are shown here.

AN ABYSSINIAN PRIEST

ABYSSINIAN COURT LADIES

secured her power in Northern Abyssinia, while the south, and Shoa in particular, probably remained independent under petty Christian rulers. After her death the crown remained in Jewish hands for more than 350 years. The striking weakness of Christianity in Abyssinia at this time is to be explained partly by the Mohammedan conquest of Egypt, which cut off communication with the rest of the Christian world. Formerly the bishops of Abyssinia had been sent out by the Patriarchs of Alexandria, and connection with the religious development of the civilised world had thus been maintained; henceforward the Abyssinians were forced to apply to the Coptic patriarchs in Cairo, whose nominees soon brought the country into a state of religious confusion and discord. It is at this period that the degeneration of Abyssinian Christianity begins.

In the year 1262 the Jewish dynasty was overthrown by a scion of the old royal house of Solomon, the ruler Iquon Amlag of Shoa, who thus united the whole of Abyssinia under his sceptre.
Struggle with Islam The leading spirit of the anti-Jewish movement was the archbishop Tekla Haimanot. It was high time for Christianity to bestir itself. Mohammedanism had long before gained a footing upon African soil, and was preparing to overthrow Nubia and Abyssinia, the two remnants of the Christian Ethiopic kingdom.

Abyssinia was now a united whole, and able to withstand all immediate attacks; but the danger grew ever more menacing. In their isolation the Abyssinian rulers bethought them of their co-religionists in the West. They began to reply to the messages which the popes had continued to send them at intervals. **Embassies to Rome and Portugal** The Negus Constantine (1421–1468) even sent an embassy to Rome, and put the Abyssinians in connection with the Catholic Church. But the Negus was anxious for more than spiritual support from his European fellow-believers; he therefore turned to Portugal, where the spirit of adventurous enterprise inherent in the Western races had then reached its highest activity.

His embassy was enthusiastically received. When we remember that it was the hope of finding the legendary kingdom of Prester John which inspired the Portuguese mariners to fresh enterprises, we can well understand the satisfaction of King Alfonso V. at receiving an embassy directly from this kingdom. It was, however, impossible to send any practical help to the hard-pressed Abyssinians before the circumnavigation of the Cape of Good Hope in 1486; and after the discovery of India, in 1498, the attractions of this new acquisition claimed all the energies of Portugal. In 1514, however, a small fleet was sent to the Straits of Bab el-Mandeb, but was almost at once wrecked in a storm. Thus

2253

Abyssinia found itself entirely alone in the hour of greatest need.

In the year 1527 the Turks had seized the harbour of Massowa, and concluded an alliance with the prince of Harar, Mohammed Ahmed Granj, who thought the time had now come for him to satisfy his inherited hatred of the Abyssinians. He **An Hour of Darkness** equipped an army, which Turkish help enabled him to provide largely with firearms, whereas the Abyssinians at that time were armed only with spear and sword, and advanced through the passes into the highlands of Shoa. Spreading devastation as he went, he continued his victorious career northward, destroyed the old capital of Axum, and shook the Abyssinian nationality to its foundations. From 1537 the Galla tribes poured into the desert district between Shoa and Northern Abyssinia ; their numbers had swelled to a formidable extent, and they had long been menacing the southern frontier.

At length, in 1541, a small Portuguese force under Christoforo da Gama appeared in Massowa and joined the remnants of the Ethiopian army. The Portuguese leader was slain almost immediately ; but Mohammed Abu Granj also fell in the battle. The exiled king Claudius was now able to regain his grasp of the reins of power. His position was not an enviable one ; the Portuguese demanded heavy compensation for the assistance they had given, the Galla were threatening the kingdom on the south, and, as if this were not enough, Rome was beginning to send out missionaries with the object of Catholicising the Abyssinian Church. The first Jesuit mission arrived in Abyssinia in 1555. Upon the death of Claudius, in 1558, civil wars broke out, for which the Jesuits may not have been wholly blameless, although it was not until the beginning of the seventeenth century that they acquired any great influence. Correctly appreciating the situation, they represented Western civilisation, and by many public services won people to Catholicism.

But the Abyssinian Church was thoroughly adapted to the character of the nation, and, in spite of its internal decay, was not thus to be remodelled upon a system adapted to the needs of Western civilisation. This fact the Jesuits failed to appreciate. Fazilidas, the son of King Sosnesos, took the lead of the anti-Romanist party, compelled his father to restore the Ethiopian Church, and after his accession to the throne, in **Why the Jesuits Failed** 1632, destroyed the Jesuits and their adherents in 1634. All later attempts to reintroduce the propaganda of Rome failed entirely. On the contrary, the Ethiopian Church gradually connected itself with the Greek Orthodox Church, whose theology was better suited to the monophysite Abyssinians than the Romans, and thus in course of time entered into friendly relations with Russia.

FACSIMILE OF TWO PAGES FROM AN OLD ABYSSINIAN BIBLE

Christianity was introduced into Abyssinia about 350 A.D., and, in spite of all calamities, has remained permanent, though it degenerated in form, and the Ethiopian Church of Abyssinia has become connected with the Greek Orthodox Church.

RECEPTION OF THE BRITISH COMMISSIONER BY KING THEODORE OF ABYSSINIA
Theodore, Negus of Abyssinia, who fought his way to the crown in 1855, was incapable of reasonable behaviour to his European co-religionists, and missionaries suffered severely from his capricious treatment. When Mr. Rassam was sent by Great Britain to remonstrate, he was imprisoned, necessitating the expedition of Lord Napier to Magdala.

As years went by the disruptive forces within the kingdom grew stronger. The provinces achieved a greater measure of independence. The country was continually devastated by civil war, much to the advantage of the Galla, who became an influential power as the mercenaries of the princes, and nearly succeeded in making themselves supreme. Civilisation relapsed, especially in the little Abyssinian states on the south, which were separated by the Galla from the northern states. About 1750 the ambitious vassal Ras Michael made himself notorious by his bloodthirstiness. After the abdication of the Negus Tekla Haimanot, in 1777, anarchy became rampant. The princes of Tigre made more than one attempt to seize the supreme power, especially Sabagades in 1823, and after him Ubie. The latter gained possession of Tigre after a bloody conflict won by Ras Mario in 1831, and ruled as he pleased in Northern Abyssinia

Civil War and Disruption until 1854. About this time Ras Ali was ruling in Amhara, and acting as the protector of Saglu Denghel, the nominal monarch in Gondar, while the prince Sahela Selassie had made himself independent in Shoa.

But the man who was to restore the unity of Abyssinia had already begun his work. By name Kasai, the son of poor parents, though apparently of noble descent—born about 1820 as the son of the governor Hailu Maryam of Quara—he had won some reputation in true Abyssinian style as a guerrilla leader, and in 1847 became the son-in-law of the Ras Ali

Theodore Reunites the Kingdom of Amhara. Shortly afterward he had a quarrel with his father-in-law, defeated him near Aishal in 1853, and made himself master of Amhara; in 1854 he defeated the Ras Ubie of Tigre near Debraski and thus gained possession of Northern Abyssinia. On February 4th, 1855, Kasai had himself crowned under the name of Theodore as Negus Negesti—literally, king of kings; the ceremony was performed by the Abuna Selama, who had surrendered to him in the church of Deresge Maryam.

The new monarch was soon able to subdue the southern part of the country. The independent Galla princes of the highlands were conquered, and Haila Malakot, the king of Shoa, fled to a monastery in 1856; his son Menelik was allowed to ascend the throne of Shoa as the vassal of the Negus. However, peace was not even then assured to Abyssinia; revolt followed revolt in rapid succession, and the king's troops brought greater misery upon the land than the rebels, for they received neither pay nor supplies and

2255

devastated the country in a frightful manner. The Negus was equally incapable of reasonable behaviour to his European co-religionists. The missionaries in particular suffered from his violent and capricious temper and his distrustful character; whether, like the Catholics, they were definitely excluded from his favour, or whether, as in the case of the Protestants, a temporary display of partiality was followed by treatment correspondingly severe. In 1864 Theodore imprisoned a number of missionaries, together with the French and English consuls. When Britain sent her commissioner Rassam to remonstrate, he also was imprisoned. A British expedition, under Robert Napier— Lord Napier of Magdala— landed at Sula, or Zoulah, south of Massowa, on January 2nd, 1868. The advance into the highlands was beset with difficulty, but the British encountered practically no resistance, with the exception of an unimportant skirmish when they reached the mountain fortress of Magdala, where Theodore had taken refuge (April 10th). The Negus then released his prisoners. When the British advanced to storm the place on April 13th, the Emperor Theodore committed suicide

KING JOHN OF ABYSSINIA
After the suicide of Theodore and the confusion and war following, a prince of Tigre secured the throne, assuming the name John.

on the next day. His son Alemajehu died shortly afterward in England.

Though Theodore had been able to impose only a temporary unity upon the Abyssinian kingdom, he had restored the old prestige of the crown. In Abyssinia, as in different European countries, feudal development had resulted in absolutism. After some years of warfare and confusion, the prince of Tigre, Kasai, who was nearly forty years of age, was able to defeat Gobesie, the prince of Lasta and Gojam, at Adua, on July 14th, 1871, thanks to the support of the British and the munitions of war provided by them; he then secured the chief power, and ascended the throne on January 21st, 1872, under the name of John. Hardly had he reached the goal of his ambition when he found himself involved in a quarrel with Egypt, which desired to carry out its East Sudan policy in the case of Abyssinia also. The Egyptian troops, under Werner Munzinger Bey, the governor of Massowa, occupied in 1872 two districts belonging to Abyssinia— namely, Bogos and Mensa in the North, John was then occupied in suppressing a revolt among his vassal princes and was unable to prevent this encroachment. The Khedive Ismail was emboldened by

GENERAL VIEW OF ADUA, THE CAPITAL OF THE MOUNTAIN STATE OF ABYSSINIA

his success and determined upon the final conquest of Abyssinia in 1875. When he ordered his troops to advance into Tigre, the Negus John collected his forces and utterly destroyed the Egyptian army, who were led by Arakel Bey and Axendroop, a former Danish colonel, in the battle of Gudda-Guddi. Another attempt of the Egyptians in the following year ended in almost equal disaster. Prince Hasan was totally defeated at Gura on March 7th, 1876, and with difficulty escaped to Massowa with a remnant of his troops. Menelik of Shoa then submitted when John marched against him in 1879, and the two princes made peace. In 1880 Ras Adal of Gojam followed the example of Menelik. At that moment a European Power conceived the idea of extending its supremacy over Abyssinia. Before the general rush of the Powers for territory in Africa had begun, Italy had been induced by P. St. Mancini to secure a trading station and a point of ingress to Central Africa on the bay of Assab, near the Straits of Bab el-Mandeb. When the general partition of Africa began, the Italians turned their attention to Abyssinia, whose favourable situation and Alpine climate appeared specially adapted to the needs of European immigrants. The state of affairs in the Sudan, which was then practically in the hands of the Mahdists, was all in favour of the Italian undertaking, since British policy in Egypt was by no means opposed to the appearance of another friendly Power in the neighbourhood. Thus Italy met with no opposition when she sent her fleet to Massowa in February, 1885, and declared an area of about 600 square miles on the coast to be an Italian protectorate. As the climate of the coast proved unhealthy, part of the

KING MENELIK II.
Menelik, who was Prince of Tigre, gained the throne in 1899, and has raised Abyssinia to unprecedented prosperity.

MENELIK'S QUEEN
The queen Taï Tou is Menelik's principal wife. She has the sole right to use a coloured umbrella and gold jewellery.

neighbouring Abyssinian highlands was soon occupied.

By this time the strength of the Ethiopian kingdom had been considerably increased, and in its resistance to Italy it was encouraged by certain of the European states. Russia and France, already anxious to place obstacles before the Triple Alliance, had reasons of their own for opposing any extension of Italian power. France, which had also gained a footing on the coast, looked on Italy as an intruder, and Russia was in relations with the Ethiopian Church. This dual alliance, and the support which it gave to Abyssinia, undoubtedly contributed in no small degree to the ultimate defeat of the Italian plans.

On January 26th, 1887, occurred the first collision between the Italians and the Abyssinian troops under Ras Alula. A small Italian column was destroyed at Dogali, or Saati, but an attack upon the fortified positions was repulsed with heavy loss to the Abyssinians. In the next year the Negus himself marched against the Italians, who had been considerably reinforced, but avoided a battle in view of the favourable position which his enemies had occupied. On March 9th, 1889, the emperor John fell at Metemmeh, fighting against the Mahdists in Galabat. His nephew Ras Mangasha, who should have inherited the kingdom upon the premature death of the crown prince Area, was not recognised.

There was but one possible successor to the Negus John, Menelik II. of Shoa, born in 1844 at Ankober, the son of the then crown prince Ailu Malakot, and the most powerful vassal in the kingdom since 1878. With great foresight he ceded a large part of Tigre to Uccialli on May 2nd, 1889, which, together with the coast line, was formed into the colony of Erythrea.

On September 29th, he accepted the extension of the Italian protectorate over Abyssinia. The districts south of Shoa were then subdued with general success. Harar and Kassa recognised Menelik's supremacy, and Abyssinian outposts were stationed on the Central Juba as far as Berdera. The dangers of Mahdism, which was beating upon the gates, were soon averted, in particular by the Italian occupation of Kassala on June 17th, 1894. Menelik, being now freed in that quarter, could renew his opposition to Italy.

In consequence of the continual outbreak of small disturbances on the frontier, the Italians, under the major-general and civil governor of Erythrea, Oreste Baratieri, crossed the boundary river Mareb in 1894, and at Coatit and Senafe, on January 13th and 16th, 1895, scattered the Abyssinians under Ras Mangasha in Tigre, and garrisoned the important post of Adigrat. They had shortly before strengthened their flank against the Mahdists by the capture of Kassala, already mentioned. Meanwhile, Menelik was making preparations, to which Baratieri replied by occupying Adua on April 1st, and shortly afterward the fortress of Makale, south of Adigrat. But on December 7th, 1895, the Italian outpost—1,050 men—under Major Toselli

was almost destroyed at Amba-Aladji, and Major Galliano, with 1,500 men, was blockaded at Makale. Though additional supplies of money and troops were sent out to Major-General Baratieri, that officer remained incapable of dealing with the state of affairs. Makale was surrendered January 20th, 1896, the garrison stipulating that their withdrawal should be unmolested. Some of the native allies seceded from the Italians, and an Abyssinian army threatened the line of retreat to Adigrat. In this desperate situation Baratieri suffered a defeat on March 1st, 1896, at Adua, which entirely overthrew the Italian power in Abyssinia. In the peace of Addis-Abeba, on October 26th, 1896, Menelik was content to secure the recognition of Abyssinian independence and to limit the colony of Erythrea to the area which it had occupied before 1889.

Thus the dream of a great Italian colonial empire passed away. Meanwhile, Russia and France continued the work of establishing their influence in Abyssinia to their own commerical advantage. Menelik has latterly found time to secure his conquests in the south, to subdue the refractory Ras Mangasha in 1898, to set Ras Makonnen over Tigre in 1899, and to raise the power of Abyssinia to its present height, unprecedented in the history of the country.

Lafayette

RAS MAKONNEN, PRINCE OF THE ABYSSINIAN PROVINCE OF TIGRE, WITH HIS SUITE

THE GOLD COAST AND SLAVE COAST

GEOGRAPHICALLY speaking, Senegambia is a transition point between negritic West Africa and the Sudan. With the latter it is brought into connection by the proximity of the desert and of the desert tribes and the rivers communicating with the interior, while its affinity with the former, is shown by the pure negro substratum of its population. The remnants of several peoples in a low stage of civilisation are now settled upon the coast to the south-west as far as Sierra Leone. The Jolof are the most important race in the country ; when they first become known to us historically, in 1846, we find them thoroughly well organised politically, though already entering upon a period of retrogression. At an earlier period the Jolof had probably extended much farther into the interior. About 1500, the larger part of Senegambia seems to have formed a fairly uniform state under a Burba-Jolof or Great-Wolof, whose district included even the mountain **Tribes Without History** country of Futa ; but shortly afterwards the kingdom falls into a number of petty states, constantly at war with one another—Cayor, Baol, Ualo, Sine, and others—although the tradition of their earlier unity has not even yet entirely faded. It is highly probable that the fall of the Jolof kingdom is to be connected with the rise of the Fulbe military power at that period — in other words, with the events then occurring in the Sudan proper.

With the Jolof we have to mention the Serer, the Barbacin of the Portuguese, the inhabitants of the coast about Cape Verde, who maintained themselves in partial independence of the Jolof and preserved the tradition that they had migrated to the coast from the interior at an early period—in the fifteenth century.

In fact, however, we can hardly speak of the "history" of the scarcely distinguished tribes which have been more or less predominant along the coast. It is not till we come to Ashanti and Dahomeh, behind the actual coastal tribes, that we meet with what can be called states. Although these two states appear to be primordial in their origin, yet it was European influence which brought about their rise. Both are very similar in their manner of development and their customs, **Ashanti and Dahomeh** and both lie behind the belt of forest which protects the interior by impeding any advance from the coast. The power of both Ashanti and Dahomeh is founded upon the same basis, and the final destruction of their independence came to pass very nearly at the same time.

Ashanti does not appear as a historical state before the end of the seventeenth century. The name of the new kingdom was first known on the Gold Coast about 1700. In physique, language, and customs the Ashanti population is closely related to many of the dwellers upon the Gold Coast, among whom the Fanti are the most powerful tribe. They themselves, however, have a tradition that their original home was near the town Inta, or Assienta, north-west of the territory they now occupy. We may, therefore, assume that the Ashantis, together with the later inhabitants of the Gold Coast, undertook one of those migrations to the sea of which we hear in the case of other peoples, and that during their progress part of the original race failed to penetrate to the coast and remained behind the forest belt on the first terraces of the highlands.

Before the rise of Ashanti a state appears to have existed in the interior, the capital of which lay to the south of the modern royal residence of Kumassi ; according to Ashanti tradition the state **Birth of the State of Ashanti** was known as Denkjera. The Ashanti are said to have been exasperated by excessive demands for tribute, to have revolted at the beginning of the eighteenth century, and to have utterly defeated the ruler of Denkjera under their king, Osai Tutu, or Sai Totu, in the year 1719, although the former brought cannon into the field, which he had brought from the

Dutch in exchange for slaves. There is the less doubt about the fact of this victory, as the cannon were preserved in Kumassi until modern times and have been seen there by Europeans. But the real cause of the collision, and the consequent domination of Ashanti, was undoubtedly the exigencies of the slave trade. The Denkjera tried to obtain supplies by raiding the Ashantis; the

determined, in consequence of a sudden demand for slaves, to slaughter comparatively few of the captives taken in war and to send the remainder down to the coast.

Osai Tutu, the founder of the Ashanti kingdom, fell in an expedition against the coast tribe of Axim. His successors, foiled in an attack on Dahomeh, directed their excursions mainly to the north; at

the close of the eighteenth century they defeated the Sudanese cavalry in several engagements. However, the north could not offer a sufficient supply of slaves to meet the existing demand. Hence the energetic Osai Kwamena, who ruled in Kumassi from 1800 to 1824, first reduced the Mohammedan countries upon his northern frontier, and in 1807 led his armies against the

Ashantis overthrew the Denkjera, and took over the business.

The slave trade was largely to blame for those bloody hecatombs in honour of dead kings which were a regular part of a funeral ceremonial in Ashanti and Dahomeh. The custom of sacrificing human beings to the dead is found among many savage peoples of Africa, but in few cases did it grow to such cruel proportions as in Ashanti and Dahomeh; there it is to be referred to the low value set upon human life, which is the inevitable consequence of continual warfare, and also to the fluctuations in the slave trade, which often made it impossible to export all the slaves on hand at a profitable rate. Sometimes a sudden rise in prices saved the victims already doomed to death; for instance, in the year 1791 the king of Dahomeh

HUMAN SACRIFICE AS FORMERLY PRACTISED IN DAHOMEH
In Ashanti and Dahomeh the custom of human sacrifice grew to cruel proportions. These illustrations show the sacrifice of prisoners captured in war by King Gezo.

coast tribes of the Fanti and disturbed the peace of the European forts. In 1811 and 1816 he repeated his invasions with such success that the British agreed to the payment of a subsidy. When the Governor of Sierra Leone, Charles McCarthy, refused payment, he was defeated and killed by Kwamena, on January 21st, 1824. This was the beginning of the hostilities which were inevitably to bring about the fall of Ashanti in course of time. Kwamena's successor again advanced upon the Gold Coast, but the new governor, Niel Campbell, inflicted a terrible defeat upon him, and under the next king, Kwaku Dua (1830–1867), Ashanti remained at peace for a long time. A new war, very much against the will of the peaceful monarch, broke out in 1863, ostensibly against certain of the coast tribes, but also against the British, under whose protection these tribes were living. At first no event of importance took place. In 1868 Kofi, or Kalkalli, ascended the throne of Ashanti, and in 1871–1872 the British took over certain places from the Dutch — Axim, Sekundi, Tshama, Elmina, Anomabo, Apang — and disturbances began upon the coast in consequence. An Ashanti army then appeared in the British protectorate, for the Ashantis looked upon the Gold Coast as a tributary district, where no changes could be made without their sanction. The first campaign ended in long negotiations, until in 1873 the Ashanti army again advanced. This time the British determined to make an end of so undignified a situation. European troops were sent into the country under the command of Sir Garnet Wolseley, as he then was. After a toilsome passage through

KING GEZO OF DAHOMEH
During whose reign the prosperity of Dahomeh began to decay owing to the cessation of the slave-trade, raids being made almost entirely for victims for the infamous human sacrifices.

the region of primeval forest the king's army was totally defeated on January 31st, 1874. On February 4th the capital, Kumassi, was reached and burned on the following day. The Ashanti terror was at an end. The corner of the coast between Ashanti and Dahomeh, the modern Togoland, is inhabited, especially in its mountainous districts, by a very mixed population, which must have suffered greatly in the wars of the neighbour states. But here also greater uniformity is gradually rising by more peaceful methods, as the language and civilisation of the Ewe races, which are related to the Dahomeh people, are steadily spreading. The old languages of the inhabitants are partly retained as " fetish dialects."

The history of Dahomeh is very similar to that of Ashanti, although it begins at an earlier period. It contains, however, noticeable points of difference, arising in great measure from the configuration of the country. In the first place, the influence of Dahomeh upon the coast has been greater than that of Ashanti, as the European settlements on the Slave Coast were of less importance than on the Gold Coast. Moreover, Abomeh, the capital of Dahomeh, is situated far nearer to the sea than Kumassi. In the second

DAHOMEH AMAZON   DAHOMEH WARRIOR
The ferocious soldiers of Dahomeh, especially the famous Amazon Guard, were a terror to all neighbouring races.

place, Dahomeh was for a long period in some way dependent upon a state with Sudanese civilisation, Oyo, which again seems to have been tributary to the kingdom of Nupe, on the Niger. In the country itself the faith of Islam took so strong a hold in course of time that in the year 1855 the Mohammedans actually planned an insurrection.

Among the people of Dahomeh, the Fon, the tradition runs that they had migrated from the interior of the continent to their present territory. Like the Ashanti, they are the most important members of a group of races related by language, the Ewe peoples, or Asigheh, who extended from the Volta as far as Yoruba and the Niger. The pure dialect of Dahomeh is also spoken in certain places on the coast—in Weidah, in Badagry, an old centre of the slave trade, and in the Mohammedan island of Lagos.

The rise of the kingdom of Dahomeh was certainly brought about by a course of events similar to those which occurred

KING BEHANZIN OF DAHOMEH
The last native ruler, who was deposed in 1892, when France took possession.

in Ashanti. The ruling dynasty, to which the foundation of the state must be ascribed, has remained upon the throne until modern times. The first ruler, Takudua, is said to have come forward in 1625. As the line of dead monarchs increased in number, the hecatombs in their honour appear to have become larger and more frequent. The king also had viceroys of a kind, known as " princes of the forest," he himself bearing the title of " prince of the town." In spite of the rather low population the military power of Dahomeh was always important, and became a terror to all neighbouring races in consequence of their constant drill, their incessant campaigns, and their ferocious bravery. Most extraordinary is the fact that even the female part of the population contributed a strong and especially formidable contingent to the army, the " Amazon guard." This institution was no doubt a remnant of the matriarchal stage of society ; the Amazon legends of European

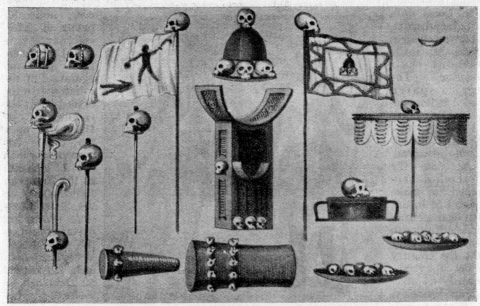

THE MURDER MANIA OF DAHOMEH ILLUSTRATED IN ITS ART
The custom of sacrificing human beings on funeral and other occasions grew in but few cases to such cruel proportions as it did in Dahomeh and Ashanti, where the low value set on human life was a consequence of the continual warfare and fluctuations in the slave trade. The custom is reflected in the decorative use of the skull.

and Asiatic peoples possibly point to a similar state of affairs; but it may have come into use at a period when the male strength of the community had been **The Amazons of Dahomeh** brought very low by endless wars. This is the more probable in view of the fact that the kings of Dahomeh were accustomed to put every one into the field who could stand upright, in order to terrify their enemies with the appearance of overpowering numbers. The enormous losses of men finally brought the kingdom to such a pass that very few pureblooded Dahomeans remained, and their place was taken by the children of slaves belonging to neighbouring races.

For a long time the affairs of Dahomeh attracted very little attention from Europeans, until, in 1723–1724, and again in 1727–1728, the king Guadja Trudo appeared on the coast, conquered the rulers of Popo and Weidah and reduced them to vassalage. Several European factories were destroyed on this expedition, and many Europeans were carried off to the new capital of Allada— which was later exchanged for Abomeh; they were, however, released later on, with the single exception of the English governor of Weidah, who had to pay for his hostility to Dahomeh with his life. After the subjugation of the coast, the slave trade revived considerably; Weidah and the neighbouring harbours were the most important export stations for these black cargoes, and the name "Slave Coast" recalls that disgraceful epoch even today. An attempt of the coast races to reconquer Weidah in 1763 was a total failure. The **The Disgraceful Slave Coast** ruler who succeeded Guadja Trudo (1708– 1730) was greatly his inferior in warlike zeal, and as the coast was now tributary to Dahomeh, he directed his armies against the less known races of the interior. He overran the district of Togo, which lies between Ashanti and Dahomeh; in the first half of the nineteenth century

Ashanti itself is said to have been tributary to him. On the other side his expeditions seem to have penetrated as far as Benin. The gradual cessation of the slave trade by sea naturally had a great effect upon Dahomeh, as the state's existence depended upon this traffic. The continuance of their raids may be partially explained by the fact that some demand for slaves existed in the Mohammedan states on

THE WONDERFUL NEGRO ART OF BENIN
Marvellously carved elephant tusks (3 and 4) and admirably cast bronzes in Benin in 1897. The technical perfection of the casting of a winged negro (1), the panther (2), and the chieftain (5), is extraordinary.

the north, but chiefly by the bloody funeral sacrifices which took place at certain periods of the year, and were almost invariably preceded by a raid into neighbouring territory. Conquest upon a large scale was a thing of the past. Such was the condition of Dahomeh in the last years of Gezo, and under his successors Bahadung, Gelele, and Beharzin, until

Colonel Dodds took possession of the country in the name of France in 1892, and put an end to the bloody rule of the old royal house.

If Ashanti and Dahomeh are to be considered as the head and front of the negro resistance to Sudanese influence, Yoruba is remarkable as being the district **An End to the Reign of Murder** where the civilisation, the religion, and the trade of the Sudan are most deeply rooted even as far as the coast. But it is only the civilisation of the fair Sudanese races, and not their political power, that is a modifying factor in this district. In the north the town of Ibadan is the main bulwark against the Fulbe. In the south the constitutional principality of Abbeokuta is in a flourishing condition; it was founded as a refuge state about 1820–1825, and the population increased rapidly.

On the other hand, the kingdom of Benin, which had been practically inaccessible to Europeans for a long period, forms a parallel to Ashanti and Dahomeh in certain respects. It was not until the British stormed the capital in the spring of 1897 that information was forthcoming upon the bloody sacrificial customs there prevailing; at the same time material evidence of the highest importance both for the history of the country and for negro art was brought to light in the shape of old bronzes and ivory carvings. These productions mark the culminating point of a native West African art, hardly touched by any external influence. The clothing of the different Europeans represented shows that these works were completed in the sixteenth and seventeenth centuries—at any rate, hardly earlier than 1550; therefore the kingdom of Benin must have been at the height of its prosperity and in communication with the Portuguese about that period. It remains uncertain whether it was European influence which **Wonderful Negro Art of Benin** brought the art of brass founding to the high technical perfection which it attained; but in any case the Benin bronzes are evidence for the artistic gifts of the West Africans, and help to point the contrast with the utter lack of artistic talent among the South and East Africans.

At the close of the eighteenth century, when antipathy to the slave trade was rising in England, which had on her hands a number of slaves liberated during the American War of Independence, various attempts were made to settle and to civilise liberated slaves on the coast of Africa; these attempts were by no means unsuccessful in Sierra Leone, where the movement was very sensibly directed by the English Government. A few decades later, Liberia was founded from North America. In that country a society was formed in the year 1816—the American Colonisation Society for colonising the free people of colour of the United States—the object of which was to return liberated negroes to Africa and to form them into an organised colony.

After several failures, the colony was founded on Cape Mesurado, and in 1822 obtained a constitution under the name of Liberia, but was governed for some time longer by a white agent, Ashmun, who may be considered the real founder of Liberia; he succeeded in organising the somewhat helpless elements of the new state, and in considerably extending its area. The number of immigrants steadily increased. In 1835 the temperance party founded a special colony, Maryland, which was joined to Liberia in 1857; other companies were content to **Negro Republic of Liberia** found individual settlements within the Liberian territory. At length the hostility of Britain, who declined to recognise the supremacy of the American Colonisation Company, forced the Liberians to declare their independence on July 26th, 1847; they placed their country under a republican constitution elaborated by Professor Greenleaf, of Harvard University. Roberts, who had hitherto acted as governor, was chosen president, and the first negro governor, Stephen Allen Benson, was elected in 1855. Immigration from America gradually declined, the first hardy colonists died out, and their descendants proved an inferior stock. This deterioration became terribly plain abroad upon the contraction of a loan of £100,000 sterling in 1871, which Liberia obtained upon terms incredibly disadvantageous; the country is even yet suffering from the consequences. At the present day the population consists of 18,000 "Americans," the immigrants from America and their descendants, and of the natives of the coast, who may amount to a million. Christianity has spread to a very small extent among the natives, whereas Mohammedanism is making formidable progress.

TROPICAL
NORTH
AFRICA
VI

NORTH
CENTRAL
AFRICA

FROM THE KAMERUN TO THE HORN OF AFRICA

AS we pass eastwards from the coast still less is known of the tribes which form the transition zone between the Sudan and the Bantu negroes. The first group we meet with are the Niam-Niam, or Makaraka, a name properly applied to the most eastern branch of the race, and sometimes extended to include the whole.

They call themselves Sandeh. Their district lies on the northern tributaries of the Upper Ubangi ; the population is by no means uniform in character, the land being sprinkled with remnants of peoples half or wholly subjugated. When the Niam-Niam were first visited by Europeans they were undoubtedly in the course of a northward advance. Possibly they were originally connected with the Fan of the west coast ; but they must have been in contact with the races of the Congo itself for a long period. This is evidenced by the characteristic throwing-knife of the Niam-Niam—which is wholly unlike that of the Fan, and is found among the dwellers on the Congo about the mouth of the Aruwimi— as also by the fierce cannibal habits which distinguish them sharply from the races on the Upper Nile. To these latter the Niam-Niam were objects of hatred and disgust by reason of their cannibal customs. The name " Niam-Niam " was given them by the Denka, and denotes " devourer."

A Fierce Race of Cannibals

The people of Mangbattu, on the sources of the Ubangi, resemble the Niam-Niam in many points, though they are, or rather were, upon a far higher level of civilisation. They are in many respects a mysterious race. A great deal in their civilisation reminds us of the Wahuma states on the great lakes, especially their use of pounded bark as clothing material. Their general practice of cannibalism connects them with the Congo races. It is however remarkable that the weapon characteristic of this zone of transition, the throwing-knife, is not found among the Mangbattu. Their traditions point to an immigration from the west, and not from the east ; nevertheless they show unmistakable traces of Hamitic blood. George Schweinfurth, the first European to visit the Mangbattu, found them governed in 1871 by two supreme chiefs, Munsa and Degberra. On the north the land was divided by a frontier of desert from the territory of the Niam-Niam.

Hunters Become Hunted

On the south lived pure negro races in a low state of civilisation, known by the Mangbattu as Momsu and Mambode. South-west were the remarkable dwarf people, the Akka, which were partly subject to the chief Munsa. The Mangbattu made constant raids in true Sudanese style into the territory of their southern and south-eastern neighbours, and sold the slaves, whom they captured, to the Nubian merchants, who had even then found their way to the northern tributaries of the Congo, until eventually the Mangbattu became the hunted instead of the hunters. Their power collapsed upon the fall of Munsa in 1873.

A transition to the races of the Nile valley is formed by a group of peoples inhabiting the highlands about the southern tributaries of the Gazelle River, of whom the Bongo are the most important. Their comparatively fair colour and several of their manners and customs seem to connect them with the Niam-Niam, though in other points they rather resemble the true Nile negroes.

When we reach the upper channel of the White Nile and the Bahr el-Ghazal we come upon a chain of pure negro tribes which has found a refuge from the attacks of advancing migrations and has dwelt in security for thousands of years. Pottery

The Races of the Upper Nile

akin to what these tribes make at the present day is found at a depth of seven or eight feet, which points to their having occupied this region since a remote antiquity. This, moreover, is borne out by their peculiar anthropological character; a very definite development in precise adaptation to their environment. Thus the more northern races of the Upper Nile valley have become typical swamp peoples. In comparison with the inhabitants of the rocky highlands which surround the Nile valley, the Shilluk, Nuér and Dinka present the appearance of human flamingoes. Flat feet and long heels are distinguishing marks of their physique. Like swamp birds, they are accustomed to stand motionless for hours on one leg, which is supported by the knee. Their gait is slow, the limbs and neck long and thin. Surely we are here reminded of the legendary cranes with whom the pygmies fought.

The Human Flamingoes of the Nile

So complete a conformation to environment cannot be accomplished in a few centuries ; we have here the results of development lasting throughout an immense period of time. Further, an expedition sent by the emperor Nero to the Upper Nile merely brought back accounts of the people " invariably naked " above Meroe, whose customs correspond exactly to those of the modern swamp-dwellers. In spite of their secluded situation, the peoples of the Nile valley were not wholly untouched by foreign influence, as is shown by the progress among them of cattle-breeding and iron-working, two great achievements of civilisation which certainly did not grow up spontaneously among them.

The existence of the most northerly race of negroes on the White Nile is proof of the fact that even this remote corner of the world is not entirely at rest. The Shilluk, who are settled on the left bank of the Nile from the mouth of the Sobat to nearly the twelfth degree of latitude north, and extended even further northward at an earlier period, are a typical swamp people, entirely conformed to the environment of the district they now inhabit ; for this reason they must have been long settled in the damp lowlands. According to their own traditions, their first home was not upon the Nile itself, but on the Lower Sobat, where a remnant of the race is still to be found. They left their native swamps about 1700, retreating before the advance of the Galla races, and spread in different directions—possibly several successive migrations may have taken place. The main body settled in the district already mentioned upon the left bank of the Nile ; another group, now known as Jur, pushed forward north of the Bongo to the Bahr el-Ghazal on the south ; the Belanda were driven yet

The Swamp People's Migration

further southward between the territories of the Bongo and the Niam-Niam. Finally, tribes related to the Shilluk are now settled where the Nile issues from Lake Albert Nyanza, the Shilu in the Nile valley, and on the heights which come down to the east bank of the river ; and the Lur, who have been strongly influenced by the Niam-Niam, have been settled perhaps for some centuries upon the north-west bank of Lake Albert.

A second people, which has apparently inhabited the marshes from the remotest antiquity, are the Dinka, or Denka. Their numerous tribes occupy the whole of the Nile valley from the sixth to the twelfth degrees of latitude, with the exception of the parts inhabited by the Shilluk ; they are also settled on the Bahr el-Ghazal and its tributaries as far as the highland frontiers. In spite of their large numbers, which must have always been an inducement to colonisation, they have no tradition of any active migratory movements, but only of losses which they have suffered at the hands of the Shilluk in the north and the Bari in the south. They are the real nucleus of the peoples in the Nile valley ; the reason that their name is not mentioned by the ancients is to be found in the fact that their disruption into small tribes concealed their national unity. Until recent times many of their subdivisions, such as the Nuer, or Nuehr, Kitsh, Elyab, Bor, etc., have been considered as independent tribes, before their connection with the great Dinka family was discovered.

The Oldest Swamp Dwellers

South of the Dinka district the ethnographical conditions become more confused. Here the Nile flows through boundless swampy plains, and its banks do not afford so sure a refuge as further northward. The mountains become more prominent, and the immediate result of this local configuration is a confused mixture of races and racial influences. The Bari still hold a self-contained district between the Nile valley and the surrounding mountains from about the fourth to the sixth degree of latitude north. According to their own accounts they have been settled for only a few generations in this district ; they came up from the south and took the land from the Berri, a Dinka race. As a matter of fact, their national type does not wholly correspond to the true Nilotic peoples, the Dinka

FASHODA, THE PRINCIPAL VILLAGE OF THE SWAMP-DWELLING SHILLUK

and Shilluk; but the resemblance is comparatively close, so that their migrations cannot have been very extensive.

Further south, and extending to Lake Albert, side by side with the Shilluk tribes dwell the Madi, a race apparently composed of a fusion of Nilotic negroes with the fair-skinned inhabitants of the frontier district. The fact of this fusion is all the information which we possess concerning their earlier history.

Speaking generally, it may be said that although the negro races have successfully maintained their position in the Nile valley, yet they must at one time have been settled further north. They retreated to the east of the Nile valley before the Hamites, or were absorbed by them.

East Africa displays in miniature the same characteristics as the great Sahara desert, with its civilised states upon its southern boundary oppressed and dominated by the inhabitants of the desert. The Wahuma district on the south corresponds to the kingdoms of Sokoto, Bornu, and Bagirmi; the Sahara is replaced by the extensive and arid district of the east cape, the dreaded Guardafui. At this point the fleets of the seafarers crossed over from early antiquity; here, in the land of incense, settlements were founded upon the barren shores, and trade routes led from the seaboard far into the interior of the continent. The deepest and most lasting influence proceeded from Arabia, which is but a

A VILLAGE OF HUMAN FLAMINGOES, THE SHILLUK OF THE UPPER NILE

The people of three of the tribes of the marshes of the Upper Nile, of whom the Shilluk are the most important, present the appearance of human flamingoes, being accustomed to stand motionless for hours on one leg.

few miles distant from the African coast. But upon this barren district no civilisation could strike its roots deep into the soil. The population was invariably restless and unsettled, " their hand against every man, and every man's hand against them." Nature herself pointed **Why the** the direction for their migra- **Negroes** **Went South** tions and their incursions. Eastward, the ocean thundered upon a harbourless coast ; westward, the swamps of the Nile valley checked their advance. The Abyssinian highland tempted the eyes of the greedy nomads with its wealth ; but the most promising land lay southward, in the district of the black races. Southward stretched away the boundless plains, with no obstacle to stay the passage of the nomads and

A VILLAGE OF THE NIAM-NIAM CANNIBALS
Among the races of the Upper Nile, the Niam-Niam are sharply distinguished by their fierce cannibalism. This view of one of their typical villages is from a drawing by George Schweinfurth, the first European who visited their country.

their herds. The first bands to pass this way were followed by others, and often the conquerors of one age fell victims to their relatives who followed them in the next ; only one of these wandering tribes, the Wahuma, was able to found permanent kingdoms, because they alone found an old civilisation in the lake district, and were protected from later invasions by the configuration of the country. Their development is more conveniently treated in our South African division.

In Northern East Africa at the present day we can distinguish four great groups of Hamitic nomad peoples, more or less mixed with Semites and negroes, the Danakil — plural of Danakli — Galla, Somali, and Massai ; none of these groups

is a uniform whole, with the possible exception of the Danakil. Each of them includes remnants of peoples whose origin is in part doubtful.

The history of the Danakil, or Afar, is very simple. Hemmed n within their old territory in the corner between the Abyssinian highland and the east coast of Massowa up to the Straits of Bab el-Mandeb, the south was the only direction in which they had room to expand. But in this direction the northern Somali races checked them. Possibly the Somali are a mixed people, including a portion of the Danakil within themselves ; at the moment little more can be said as to the relationship of the two races. At any rate the Danakil have exercised less influence upon their neighbours than any of the other North-east African Hamites, as far as their history can be traced. The Galla, or Oromo, appear in a very different character. They appear on the East African battleground with surprising suddenness and in overpowering strength. Their settlements extend over a wide area, and though they have in some cases become persecuted instead of persecutors, they remain a great and powerful people even to-day, though without political unity. Concerning their origin, many theories are extant. Many writers have erroneously connected them with the Masimba people, which begins to disappear from history just at the time when the Galla are first mentioned. Others place the early home of the Galla near the snow-topped mountains Kenia and Kilimanjaro, so that their first migrations would have been from south to north. More recently a contrary theory has found favour, **The Great** that the east cape of Africa **and Powerful** was the cradle of the Galla **Galla People** race, and that in pre-Mohammedan times they were situated to the south of the Gulf of Aden ; their own wandering tendencies and the development of the Somali races then drove the Galla west and south from their early home. But in view of the fact that the Galla certainly have a strong infusion of negro blood in their veins, this theory does not seem wholly satisfactory, although it is undoubtedly true that negroes were once settled much further north than they are found to-day. Finally, they have been **Inroads into Abyssinia** described as "a group of peoples, the central point of which once lay a great deal further north than it does now, probably to the north and perhaps to the west even of Abyssinia; their history, from a general point of view, is the process of their irresistible advance southward."

Part of the Galla under Mohammed Granj acquired a new home in the north at the expense of the Abyssinians in the years 1526–1543; a second wave of migration went south. The vanguard crossed the Tana and reached the Sabaki at its mouth, near Melinde. They seem to have been established in this district at the beginning of the nineteenth century. In the mountainous country to the south of Lake Rudolf were settled races of Hamitic origin, perhaps Galla offshoots, which had been forced into these barren lands under pressure from without, while others retreated southward and attacked the negro peoples of East Africa. The Galla themselves have apparently expelled many negro tribes or taken their territory, as is shown by the existence of pariah tribes among them, which are certainly in part of Hamitic origin, and also by the strong infusion of negro blood which many Galla divisions display. Small tribes of the Bushman type may, perhaps, be referred to this mixture of races.

Historically, the Somali are even later than the Galla. However, it is certain that this people grew up in the east cape of Africa; they were apparently of Hamitic origin and were strongly modified by an influx of Arab blood and civilisation. The Hamitic stock seems to have been of Tir, which is often mentioned in Somali records. The people thus developed were prompt to seek new pastures and advance southward, in which process they certainly assimilated some Bantu negro tribes.

In North Somaliland Arab influence led to the growth of stronger political formations. At the outset of the sixteenth century the Portuguese under Cristoforo da Gama found the kingdom of Adal upon the north coast; it extended from Cape Guardafui to Tadjurra Bay, and was governed by Mohammedan princes, one of whom, Imam Ahmed, conquered Harar about the year 1500. The Somali advance soon led to war with the Galla. In Harar, at any rate, the Galla population appears to have repelled the Somali, which fact seems to point to a Galla migration from west to east; but in all other directions, and especially in the south, where the attractive pasture-land diminishes between the mountains and the sea, the Somali were victorious, and before them even the proud conquerors of the negro races fled like hunted animals. Those Hamites who had advanced furthest to the south, and whose most important offshoot was the shepherd tribe of the Massai, were a far greater terror to the agricultural negroes than the Galla and the Somali. Apparently the Massai were but one of those racial waves which **Storm and Terror of a Racial Wave** storm across the plains of East Africa, finally disappearing in mutual collision. Before their period we find a mixed Hamitic people on the east and south-east of Victoria Lake, especially the Wakwafi and Wataturu, who were overpowered by the invading Massai, shattered, and forced to fly in different directions. All these races

A DANAKLI OF NORTH-EAST AFRICA
The Danakil are the only people of the four great Hamitic groups of North-east Africa who are unmixed.

were largely mixed with the negroes, and apparently to a special degree with those of the Nile valley.

The central point of the Massai diffusion may be placed north-east of Lake Victoria in that district which is now inhabited by other mixtures of Hamites and Nile negroes—Wakikuyu, Burgenedji, Elmolo, Suk, Naudi, Kamassia, Turkana, Karamoyo, and Donyoro. Thence the lust of battle and migration drove them southward. A general picture of East Africa in modern times will show us three nearly parallel lines of movement from north to south followed by the Hamitic peoples— the Somali upon the coast, the Massai in the western undrained highlands, and the Galla between these two. The victims of this invasion were both pure Bantu negroes and older mixed races of Hamitic stock. Before the Massai advanced, a nearly related people, the Wakwafi, or, as they called themselves, the Mbarawui, had already established themselves in the Pare Mountains to the south-east of the Kilimanjaro, and were oppressing the surrounding peoples. Meanwhile the Massia seem to have pressed on to the west of Pare; they now attacked their kinsfolk. The Wakwafi were defeated and scattered. Some of them found refuge among the negro races, and devoted themselves to the pursuit of the agriculture which they had formerly detested; but the main body streamed back in a northwesterly direction to the Naivasha Lake, until they were again defeated and driven away from that district by the Massai. Once again, many joined the agricultural tribes of the highlands; the remainder escaped to Leikipia, east of the Baringo Lake and north-west of Mount Kenia, and there they at length found peace and security. These migrations are invariably instructive; the Massai pour into the south from the north and drive away their forerunners from the rich plunder; the latter then return to the old barren cradle of the race to recover their strength and again to start for the south.

The Hamitic shepherd race of the Wataturu, who were originally settled to the north of Lake Eiassi, were in like manner defeated and ejected; remnants of them now lead a miserable existence in the different districts bordering the riverless highland, and have also in part become tillers of the soil. The devastating effects of the Massai wars arose from the fact that their object was not the conquest of new lands, but cattle raiding and plunder. They even planned, though they did not carry out, attacks upon the coast settlements of Usambara. Districts of Usagara were wasted both by Zulus and Massai; the German station of Mpwapwa, founded by Wissmann in 1889 to protect the caravan route, marks the meeting-point of these marauding races.

The power and mobility of the dwellers upon the steppes are contingent upon the possession of cattle. The nomad of the steppes without cattle and sheep is a miserable creature, a wandering hunter, like the South African Bushman, presenting no terrors for his agricultural neighbours. Remnants of these earlier steppe dwellers are still to be found in East Africa; a people living with the Massai as a kind of pariah caste, the Wandorobbo, are a case in point. So long as this was the condition of all the desert races, no obstacle opposed the northward expansion of the black agricultural races. Hence we have in East Africa the same phenomenon as in the Sahara; traces of a negro distribution spreading far northward, then the growth of the steppe peoples and their predominance, and the consequent formation of a broad zone of mixed races, in which the negroes form the passive element.

At the present time the old conditions tend to recur. The outbreak of rinderpest, especially since 1891, has weakened the offensive powers of the nomads, and unless their herds recover from this plague, the consequence will be a fresh advance of the negroes into the forsaken districts. At the same time the despised hunting races are growing stronger and taking possession of the steppes unsuitable for cultivation; at present the Wandorobbo are stronger than the Massai.

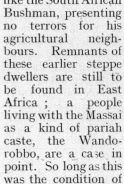

CLAY LAMPS MADE IN NUPE, NIGERIA

THE EUROPEANS IN NORTH AFRICA

THE Portuguese, the circumnavigators of Africa, are the first Europeans to appear upon the scene. Although their voyages were undertaken in the hope of discovering the realm of Prester John, which was placed at one time in India and at another time in Abyssinia, yet they did not despise the work of planting settlements and trading factories from the outset, in order to derive what profit they could from the districts of Africa. Previous to the rounding of Cape Bojador—that is, before the year 1434—but little interest attached to the possession of the barren shores of the Sahara; but when a further advance southward discovered a land of increasing richness and attraction the Portuguese began to tap the resources of this almost unknown country. Gonzales Baldeza, the second mariner to pass Cape Bojador, returned home with a cargo of dogfish skins. After a second voyage, he was able to present the king with the first slaves from Africa and some quantity of gold-dust in the year 1442.

The First Slaves From Africa The slaves were delivered up to Pope Martin V.; in return he granted a decree assigning to Portugal the right to all the African coast between Cape Bojador and the yet undiscovered Indies. For a time the Portuguese were able to extend and enjoy their African possessions in peace. Shortly afterward, trading companies were formed, in the first of which Prince Henry the Navigator seems to have taken a personal share.

It was not, however, until the year 1461 that Portugal began definitely to establish herself; the gulf of Arguin, the first comparatively secure point upon the coast, has invariably attracted the attention of later colonising powers, and at that period a fort was built there, which afforded a good base of operations for a further advance southward. There is no doubt that numerous settlements sprang up in Senegambia also, though historical information on this point is somewhat scanty. But we have clear evidence of the fact in the traces of a strong influence which must have extended far into the interior, and is even yet manifest in the existence of numerous half-breeds in certain parts of the coast. The district where the results of this influence are most apparent, the land about the Rio Grande, is in the hands of the Portuguese at the present day, as also are the Cape Verde Islands. When they ultimately reached the Gold Coast they hastened to assure their possession of this promising district by founding the stronghold of Elmina in 1481. They afterward entered into close relations with the Congo kingdom.

First Fort on the Gold Coast

The first nation to demand a share in the African trade, in spite of all the threats of Portugal, was England. Holland and France soon followed her example. Portugal gradually lost the larger part of her possessions in Guinea, which had, however, greatly decreased in importance after the discovery of India, and in their best period had never included the whole of the coast line. In the district of Senegal, the natives themselves seem to have thrown off the Portuguese yoke at a somewhat earlier date.

At the beginning of the seventeenth century the Dutch were the most dangerous enemies of Portugal in West Africa. Their rise begins in 1621, when the States General gave the "West Indian Company" the exclusive right to all territory that might be conquered between the Tropic of Cancer and the Cape of Good Hope. At that time Portugal was united to Spain and involuntarily involved in her fatal downfall. The Portuguese rule in Senegambia was practically abolished; the Gold Coast was attacked; in the year 1637 the strongest Portuguese fortress, Elmina, was besieged and stormed; and Portugal gradually lost all her possessions in West Africa. At length she secured her independence from Spain in 1640, and recovered some part of her colonies by a compact with the States General; but she had to accept conditions which greatly restricted her trade. The struggle between Holland and Portugal

Portugal Loses West Africa

was finally brought to an end by the conventions of 1662 and 1669. Portugal has retained to the present day nothing but the settlements south of the Gambia on the Rios Cacheo, Geba and Grande, the chief harbour of which is Bolama.

The Dutch, the most energetic rivals of the Portuguese, have, strangely enough, lost every foot of land which **All Dutch** they had ever possessed in **Possessions in** Africa. It is certainly true **Africa Lost** that, with the exception of the Cape, they never made any wide or permanent settlements on that continent. Such coast stations as they took from the Portuguese remained in their possession for only a short period; it was upon the Gold Coast alone, the district which has attracted every seafaring nation, that Dutch forts and factories have remained during any great part of the last century. The first Dutch ships appeared off the African coast about 1595. In the seventeenth century the Dutch became more active, and not only occupied different stations upon the coast, such as Goree, on the Green Mountain range, but also proceeded to place all possible obstacles in the way of other trading peoples. These efforts were systematised by the foundation of the "West India Company" in 1621, the great object of which was the development of the slave trade. We have already indicated the result of the struggles which ensued. Holland remained in possession of her conquests on the Gold Coast and in Senegambia; but a long period was to elapse before the affairs of the district could be brought into order. The encroaching English were gradually repelled, but in the peace of 1667 retained Cape Coast Castle on the Gold Coast, and soon founded many new factories. Eventually the Dutch confined their attention solely to their commercial settlements on the Gold Coast, which exported slaves and gold to a large extent, and proved extremely profitable. **The Rise of** Gradually the trade declined, **Britain in** and the larger part of the **West Africa** factories were abandoned. Finally, in 1871-1872 Great Britain took over by convention the Dutch settlements of Tekundi, Axim, Tshama, Elmina, Anomabo, and Apang.

The condition of the Gold Coast is typical of the earlier methods of European colonisation. No commercial state settling there gains any real possession of the land. Nothing is done but to found

trading stations, which are invariably protected by fortifications, and exercise a certain influence in the neighbourhood. The occupants, however, are obliged to purchase permission to trade from the local chiefs and to allow the tribes upon the coast to act as middlemen. The natives usually consider themselves the real owners of the forts and factories. Hence, upon the revival of English commerce, it was possible to found a large number of English settlements in the immediate neighbourhood of the Dutch, and indeed for the most different European peoples to place their settlements in motley array along the coast line.

The English appear about the middle of the sixteenth century in African waters. A great expedition was equipped in 1553 and purchased a quantity of gold upon the Gold Coast, but met with no great success in other directions. However, such voyages were constantly repeated from this time onward. In consequence the English soon came into conflict with the Portuguese, who considered all intruders into their commercial waters as pirates. The slave trade was vigorously pursued— the famous John Hawkins **African** was its pioneer—and finally **Trading** privileges were granted to **Companies** commercial companies, in 1585 to the Morocco or Berber Company, and in 1588 to the Guinea Company. These, like the Dutch, profited by the unfortunate position of Portugal. The attempts of the British to penetrate into the interior are worthy of note. They made efforts to reach Timbuktu, which was thought to be the source of the gold which reached the coast from the mouth of the Gambia. These attempts were energetically prosecuted by a company founded in 1618.

For a long time the English possessions in West Africa were of little importance, and their extension was further restricted by the opposition of the Dutch, as we have already observed. However, Britain successfully maintained her footing upon the Gold Coast and appreciably extended her influence. She made repeated attempts to settle in Senegambia, and when the close of the seventeenth century brought a period of peace, she possessed a factory on the Gambia, another on Sherboro Island, and perhaps a dozen on the Gold Coast. The first two of these settlements became the nuclei of the present colonies, the territory on the Gambia, with

Danish fort of Frederiksborg, on the Gold Coast, about 1670, afterwards ceded to Great Britain.

The Dutch fort of St. Anthony at Axim about 1670, a Gold Coast stronghold.

Elmina, the first settlement on the Gold Coast, founded by the Portuguese in 1841, afterwards a British fort.

An English castle in a Dutch settlement, Anomabo, in the seventeenth century.

The British fort at Cape Coast Castle about 1670, afterwards capital of the Gold Coast.

EUROPEAN SETTLEMENTS ON THE GOLD COAST IN THE SEVENTEENTH CENTURY

Bathurst and the forts George and Yarbutenda, and the colony of Sierra Leone. At that time they were the property of the " Royal African Company of England," which carried on the slave trade with great energy, though in spite of this it became involved in serious financial difficulties in the course of the eighteenth century. Three hundred thousand negro slaves are said to have been exported during the years 1713–1733. The average increased when a new company was founded after the collapse of the old society in 1749, and the restrictions upon the slave trade removed. The trade was shattered by the secession of the United States in 1776, and the new company was obliged to go into liquidation ; but the exportation of slaves continued as before.

Great Days of the Slave Trade

Meanwhile interest of a less selfish nature concerning this mysterious continent had been gradually increasing in Britain. On June 9th, 1788, the " Association for Promoting the Discovery of the Interior Parts of Africa " was founded ; and at the same time a strong antipathy to the slave trade and its horrors was growing up. These feelings were the prelude to a slow but fundamental revolution of the conditions of the African colonies. During the war between England and the seceding United States (1775–1783) a large number of negroes had contrived to escape from the yoke of their American masters and to enter the British service ; at the close of the war Britain had to deal with the question of providing for these allies. Certain philanthropists persuaded the Government to take the negroes back to Africa, and to settle them on some suitable part of the coast under British protection. In 1787 the first expedition started for Sierra Leone with 400 blacks and about sixty European women of loose character, whom it was intended to get rid of in, this way. The arrival of further contingents, and the foundation of an English company gradually raised to prosperity a colony which had made a somewhat unpromising start ; and even the ravages caused by the descent of a French man-of-war were speedily repaired. In the year 1807, Sierra Leone became a Crown colony ; the population was greatly increased by the liberated slaves brought in by the

Rise of the Colony of Sierra Leone

British and settled on the land, though the first contingent of negroes who had been brought over from America showed a tendency to despise the new arrivals. The country now became self-governing, and on the whole ran a favourable course of development. The British protectorate, though mild, prevented any gradual relapse into barbarism on the part of the negroes. The settlement of Freetown became the central point of the local civilisation ; the rest of the district was inhabited chiefly by indigenous tribes and parts of it were practically unknown.

Upon the Gold Coast, British influence increased, until it became predominant. The native tribes were not disposed to consider themselves as subject to the British, as is shown by the history of the Ashanti War in 1817, the result of which was that the tribute of four ounces of gold per month paid to the Fanti as a kind of rent for the use of the soil was henceforward paid to the Ashantis ; the presence of the British was thus merely tolerated. The Ashanti war in the following decade opened disastrously, but was brought to a successful conclusion, a result which materially strengthened the British power, especially when the Ashantis, in 1831, renounced their supremacy over the allied chieftains of the coast. In the following years Britain exercised little more than a protectorate over the Gold Coast, the notoriously bad climate of which deterred Europeans from making settlements. Disturbances occurred after 1868, due to the fact that Great Britain and Holland had exchanged certain coast settlements with a view to the better delimitation of their territories. Subsequent events are : The short campaign of the year 1874, already narrated ; the proclamation of the chief of Kumassi as King of Ashanti, in the year 1894 ; his degradation after a nearly bloodless war in 1895, which brought the Ashanti kingdom to a well-merited end and marks the beginning of the British protectorate ; and a formidable revolt in 1900, during which Frederic Hodgson, the Governor, was besieged in Kumassi from March to June, and reduced to the greatest straits ; it was not until July that the beleaguered garrison could be relieved.

British Tribute to Ashanti

Much later in date than the Gold Coast possessions, but belonging to the earlier period of colonisation, is the colony of

Lagos, which was founded in 1861, and has been autonomous since 1886; at first an important centre of the palm oil trade, it is now merged in the great British possessions on the Niger and Binue. Friendly relations with the immediate hinterland of Yoruba have been maintained from the outset.

In East Africa, the islands of Mauritius — a French possession from 1712–1810, as the " Ile de France " —and Rodriguez excepted, England had no colonies or forts for a long period. In 1884 certain places on the North Somali coast — British Somali Coast Protectorate, Zeila, Berbera, and others—were occupied from Aden, a base which has been in British hands since 1839; the important position of Harar was given up to Abyssinia under the convention of June 4th, 1897.

The French began their efforts to gain a share in African commerce at the same date as the English and Dutch. In 1541, four ships left the little harbour of La Bouille, near Rouen, to begin commercial relations with Guinea, and mention is made of the Cap à Trois Pointes in documents of 1543 and 1546. At the outset, the attention of French merchants was concentrated chiefly upon the district which has since become the real centre of France's great West African possessions— namely, Senegambia. Attempts have been repeatedly made to penetrate further into the interior from this point, which is one of the most easily accessible parts of the continent, but it is only comparatively lately that results of any great political importance were achieved. In 1626, St. Louis was founded on the lagoon at the mouth of the Senegal, and became the central point of the growing colony; the island of Goree is also deserving of mention as a second important settlement. By degrees numerous commercial settlements and forts were founded along the

TREATY-MAKING ON THE GOLD COAST IN 1672

The Gold Coast was first in the hands of the Portuguese and Dutch. In 1664, however, the English successfully attacked the Dutch defences, and four years later " the new five-pieces of gold, coined by the Guiny Company," were issued.

Senegal river, especially by André Brué about 1700. Senegambia received her first real impulse to development in the latter half of the nineteenth century (1852–1865) from Faidherbe.

The province of " French Guinea," the coastland of Futa Djallon—hitherto known officially as " Rivières du Sud "—has been separated from Senegambia since 1890 by the Portuguese possessions. France has never exercised any great political influence in this district, but by founding numerous factories has assured her position upon the coast, which is valuable as a point of entrance to the interior of the Sudan.

The claims of the French to the Ivory Coast, which has been in their occupation since 1842, and was governed from the Gabun river before that date, were not seriously put forward before 1893; Abidjean-Adjame, now " Bingerville," has taken the place of the unhealthy Grand Bassam, as the capital. Allada and Abomeh, the remnants upon the Slave Coast of the Dahomeh kingdom subjugated in 1892, have recently risen to importance owing to the increased trade of the harbours of Great-Popo, Weidah, and Kotonu. The first settlements on the Gabun river were made in 1830 and 1845; Libreville was founded in 1849. In 1862 and 1868 the district was extended southward to Cape Lopez and to the Ogowe, the claims to territory further northward remaining undecided. France had no possessions south of the Ogowe before the foundation of the Congo State.

Ivory and Slave Coasts

The four great names in the earlier history of African colonisation are Portugal, Holland, England, and France; side by side with these powers other rivals have come forward who have now almost entirely disappeared from the scene. Spain alone has retained something, or to speak more correctly, everything, for her African possessions were never of any great account; for when Pope Alexander VI. declared on appeal that all newly discovered lands were to be divided between the two Iberian colonial Powers, who were the only claimants with a show of legal right by discovery or acquisition, the Portuguese received the whole of Africa in undisputed possession. The claims of Spain were thus confined to the Canary Islands, which are not parts of negro Africa, to the islands of Fernando Po and Annobon in the Gulf of Guinea, and—since 1843—to a small district between Kamerun and Gabun, namely, the strip of coast-line on the Rio Muni and the islands of Corisco, and Great and Little Eloby.

Fernando Po, the most valuable of the possessions on the south, was at first in the hands of the Portuguese, like the whole of West Africa, without rising to any great importance. The few settlements made by the Portuguese failed to prosper, and were entirely destroyed by the Dutch in 1637; it proved impossible to begin friendly relations with the Bube, a Bantu people, who had apparently migrated to the island before its discovery. In 1777–1778 Portugal ceded the islands of Fernando Po and Annobon (south-west of Saõ Thomé), in exchange for territory in South America; the Spaniards failed

Spain's Failure in Africa

in their attempts at colonisation, and abandoned the island. In 1827 the British occupied the favourably situated island, founded Port Clarence—the present Santa Isabel—and settled a number of liberated negro slaves there, who still retain the English language; but all attempts to acquire the island by purchase or exchange were thwarted by the obstinacy of Spain. Since 1841 Spanish officials have been stationed in the island, and a governor was appointed in 1858; but nothing has been done to improve the economic condition of the settlement.

Toward the end of the eighteenth century, Africa attracted the attention of Sweden and Denmark. The efforts of the Swede, Carl Bernhard Wadström (1764–1799) to found an agricultural colony on the West Coast, resulted in total failure; more successful were the efforts of the Danes, who had been trading on the Gold Coast and founding factories at an earlier date. In the nineteenth century they possessed several strongholds in the eastern part of the Gold Coast, of which Christiansborg was the most important, but in 1851 they ceded the entire district to Britain. Ruined settlements are to be found on the Gold Coast over which the flag of a German Power once flew—the old colonies of Brandenburg. A station was procured by treaty on the Gold Coast in 1681, and another on the island of Arjuin in 1684. The king of Prussia, however, sold his possessions to the Dutch in 1717.

Germany's African Colonies

A new phase in the history of European colonisation appeared in the latter half of the nineteenth century. In the scramble for African territory German South-west Africa was established, and not long after the districts on the Slave Coast and at the mouth of the Kamerun river were placed under German protection. Hamburg and Bremen merchants, whose trade upon the yet unclaimed coast districts had been constantly disturbed, were anxious, if not to establish a formal protectorate, to send German men-of-war into those waters, and to conclude compacts with the negro chiefs. The events in South-west Africa, and the growing enthusiasm in Germany for colonisation, induced Prince Bismarck to accede to these desires. The Togo district on the Slave Coast, where the presence of a German warship had been found necessary a short time before, was placed under German protection in 1884. This possession, though certainly the smallest of all Germany's African colonies, has, in comparison with others, developed most successfully. After an agreement with France had been arranged, the British frontier was defined in the Convention of Samoa of 1899, German Togoland thereby advancing to Sansanne Mangu. Hamburg firms had long been active in Kamerun, and trade was increasing. On July 14th, 1884, it was placed under the German flag. The area of the German protectorate on the coast was speedily settled by arrangement with France and Great Britain in 1885. The first occupation was followed by serious collisions with the natives ; but subsequently matters have taken a more satisfactory course.

The new competition for the possession of African territory was raised to fever heat by the advance of Germany ; but the first steps in this direction were made by France ; she very cleverly employed the several coast stations which she had long possessed as bases for a bold advance into the interior, and advanced systematically towards the realisation of the dream of a great French empire in Africa. The first step was the further extension of the possessions in Senegambia. The British territory on the Gambia and that held by Portugal on the Rio Grande were soon so surrounded by districts under French protection that their further development was impossible ; the left bank of the Senegal was entirely under French supremacy, and an advance to the Upper Niger was seriously determined. As early as 1854 the governor Faidherbe had succeeded in checking the advance of a dangerous Mohammedan army which had been collected by the marabout Hadji Omar. Faidherbe raised the siege of Medina in 1857, defeated Hadji Omar, who retired to his capital of Segu-Sikoro on the Niger, and subdued the larger part of Upper Senegambia. Colonisation on a large scale began considerably later, and is nearly contemporary with the events on the Congo, to be related subsequently. In the year 1878 Paul Soleillet made his way to the Upper Niger, and found a friendly reception ; a year later the French Assembly voted funds for the building of a railroad from Medina to Bammako, which was to connect the Upper Senegal with the Niger and thus

French Dream of Empire

attract all the traffic of the Western Sudan to Senegambia. The work of construction was vigorously begun, labourers were imported from China and Morocco ; but in 1884 only some forty miles had been completed, and this at a cost of 30,000,000 francs. The enterprise was thereupon abandoned for the time and has only recently been resumed. Meanwhile Joseph Simon Gallieni had advanced to the Niger in 1880, and had concluded a treaty with the sultan Ahmadu Lamine of Segu, the son of Hadji Omar, whereby the valley of the Upper Niger as far as Timbuktu was placed under French protection in 1881 ; Kita, an important point between the Senegal and the Niger was fortified. In the next year a second expedition defeated the bold guerrilla leader Almamy Samory, the son of a Mandingan merchant of Bankoro, who was born at Sanankoro in 1835 ; this action took place on the Upper Niger, and a fort was built on the river bank at Bammako. Several smaller movements kept open the communications with the Senegal and drove back Samory, until he eventually placed himself under the French protectorate in 1887. The resistance of Ahmadu, who declined to fulfil the obligations of the treaty which he had made, was not broken down until April 6th, 1890, when the town of Segu-Sikoro was captured. In the same year Louis Monteil started from Segu, and went eastward to Kuba in Bornu, making treaties at every point of his journey, and returning by Tripoli to his native land. The French also made a successful advance into the interior from the Ivory Coast. Dahomeh, which was subdued in 1892, was a further possible starting point for expeditions into the Sudan districts. Great Britain had previously agreed with France, on August 5th, 1890, that a line drawn from Say on the Niger to the north-west corner of Lake Chad should form the boundary line of their respective spheres of influence. In 1893, Samory, the ruler of Bissandugu, Kankan, and Sansando was forced to abandon his kingdom of Wassulu to the French, and to retire upon Kong, which lay to the south-east. In the middle of the year 1898 he was driven from this district and fled, accompanied as usual by a numerous body of dependents, to the hinterland of the Liberian republic.

Railway Building in Senegal

Natives Ousted by France

There he was defeated on September 9th, 1898, and twenty days later was driven back upon the sources of the Cavally by the advance of Captain Gouraud, and taken prisoner ; he died in captivity on June 2nd, 1900. From that date the supremacy of France in the west of the Sudan has gained in strength. The vast

French Supremacy in the Sudan project of uniting the north coast and the Western Sudan into a great Franco-African empire has been overshadowed by the yet more comprehensive plan of extending French Congoland to the Central Sudan, and thus uniting into a compact whole all the French possessions in Africa, with the exception of Obok. From the time when Pierre Savorgnan de Brazza transformed the humble colony of Gabun into the huge " Congo Français," between the years 1878 and 1880, France has made unceasing attempts to extend her territory on the north and north-east. In this connection, the Fashoda incident has been referred to elsewhere. The German colony of Kamerun has, among others, been shut out from further expansion by the French movements. The destruction of Rabah, as previously recorded, has removed the chief obstacle to the main French designs, and so a great compact French colonial empire is practically formed.

The British have made use of their position on the Lower Niger to advance into the interior, and have succeeded in bringing the Hausa states under their influence, with the exception of the greater part of Adamawa. Events have developed slowly, and, comparatively speaking, upon a sound basis, for the trader has preceded the politician — a process exactly reversed in most of the French colonies. The fact that Britain has been able thus opportunely to secure the monopoly of the Niger trade and of the products of the Hausa countries is due

British Monopoly on the Niger to the low estimation in which Africa was held by the European Powers until late in the nineteenth century. The Niger in particular, the only waterway to Central Africa navigable by ships of great draught, was practically unused until in 1832, 1854, and afterwards, the Scotchman Macgregor Laird made numerous journeys up stream while trading for ivory. However, it was not until 1870 that the first factories were built upon the river. One of the chief retarding causes was the conformation of the Niger delta, which offers many obstacles to navigation, and is inhabited by hostile tribes. Indeed, at an earlier period no one had supposed that these numerous arms were the estuary of a great river. For this reason, again, the first important settlement of the British in this part of Africa, the town of Lagos, was not made upon the delta, but upon the lagoons further to the west.

In the 'seventies a number of small companies were formed, each of which attempted to embitter the existence of the others, until in 1879 the general agent, MacIntosh, succeeded in incorporating almost the whole number into the United African Company. In 1882 this undertaking was renamed the " National African Company," and extended its operations ; on July 10th, 1886, it received a charter from the British Government, and has since taken the title of the Royal Niger Company. Two French companies now turned their attention to the Niger, but succumbed in 1884 before the competition of the British traders, who now

The Royal Niger Company entirely monopolised the Niger trade. Britain strengthened her political influence, not so much by military operations as by dexterous handling of the native chiefs, who have been very ready to accept yearly subsidies.

Under the deed of transference, executed on June 30th, 1899, which became operative on January 1st, 1900, from the territories of the Royal Niger Company, together with the Niger Coast Protectorate, two new protectorates were formed—Northern and Southern Nigeria. The frontiers were determined as follows : Southern Nigeria extends to the Niger coast of Ogbo to the Cross mouth, is bounded on the west by Lagos, on the north by the sister protectorate, on the east by Kamerun. The chief commissioner has his residence in Old Calabar. The other chief towns are Benin and Akassa. Northern Nigeria is a much larger district, and is bounded on the West by French Dahomeh, on the north by the French Sudan, on the east by the hinterland of the German Kamerun ; thus it embraces the old Fulbe and Hausa States—Sokoto, Nupe, Ilorin, Saria, Bautshi, and Muri—parts of Borgu and Gando, and also of Bornu, as far as Lake Chad.

HEINRICH SCHURTZ

SOUTH AFRICA

THE NATIVE RACES AND STATES
BY DR. HEINRICH SCHURTZ
THE YELLOW RACES OF THE SOUTH-WEST

THROUGHOUT the south-western part of Africa the negro is not the aboriginal inhabitant. Where he has established himself, he has done so by conquest, expelling or in part absorbing his predecessors. Of these earlier yellow-skinned peoples two racial groups can be distinguished : the nomadic Hottentots, and the Bushmen, who are wandering hunters. The Hottentot is of medium stature, the Bushman dwarfish. Their languages appear at first to be related, but display many points of difference, as also do their respective attainments in civilisation. However, their relationship can be confidently asserted upon anthropological grounds. It can be seen in the formation of the head, in the fair colour and rugosity of the skin, and in other points of physical similarity, and in the number of clicks used in their respective languages.

In modern times, light-skinned dwarf races, forming a third group, have been discovered at numerous points of Central Africa, usually dwelling in the seclusion of the primeval forests, and, like the Bushmen, belonging to such primitive types as "garbage-eaters," "hunters of small game," or "unsettled peoples." In respect of language, most of them have adopted the Bantu speech of the neighbours round them ; but their anthropological characteristics, to which may be added, in the case of the Akka, who have been more carefully examined than any others, the

Primitive Races of Pygmies

rugosity of the skin, leave no room for doubt that we have here also relations of the Bushmen and Hottentots, and that consequently the fair South African races and the dwarf peoples belong to a common race. In order to understand the course of the early history of the Hottentots and dwarf peoples, we must briefly examine their settlements and mode of life, as they appeared when European inquiry first shed light upon them.

Discovery of the Hottentots

At the time of their discovery the Hottentots, or Koi-koin as they called themselves, inhabited most of the modern Cape territory. Upon the east, fronting the Kaffir territory, the Kei River formed their boundary. Further northward the Hottentot district extended in an easterly direction to the western part of the Orange River Colony. Even at that period scattered tribes lived north of the Orange River in German South-west Africa, so that no definite northern boundary of the race can be fixed. The people that dwelt in these districts were shepherds by profession, rich in cattle, sheep, and goats, knowing nothing of agriculture or pottery-making, though well acquainted with the art of smelting and forging iron.

It was quite otherwise with the Bushmen, or San. Their districts partly corresponded with those of the Hottentots, for little bands of nomad Bushmen wandered about almost everywhere among the Hottentot settlements, in some cases carrying on the profession of cattle-breeding, though they were more generally hated and persecuted as robbers and cattle-stealers. Similarly upon the east of the steppe district to the bordering mountain ranges, San tribes mingled with the South African negroes, especially with the Bechuanas. The Kalahari desert as far as Lake Ngami is pure Bushman territory.

The Cattle-stealing Bushmen The Bushmen are an unsettled people, collecting the poor possessions of their homes by constant wanderings, hunting the game upon the plains, and also spoiling the herds of the shepherd tribes, and in later times of the European settlers ; low in the scale of civilisation, but extremely hardy and simple in their wants.

Races similar to the Bushmen are also found further north. Such are the Mucassequere, a light-coloured race of hunters, living in the woods in the interior of Benguela, near the negro Ambuella, though they do not approach or mingle with this agricultural people. As regards their mode of life, physical characteristics, and civilisation, they are very similar to the real Bushmen.

The dwarf peoples in the narrow sense of the term inhabit a broad zone stretching obliquely through Central Africa, which corresponds very nearly with the area of the dense forest, and is interrupted only where the forest is replaced by the more open savannah land. In East Africa there is one remarkable exception in the tribes of the Wanege and Wassandani, first discovered and described by Oscar Baumann. The Wanege are a hunting people of diminutive stature, wandering over the plains to the south of the Eyassi Lake ; but the Wassandani, a name which perhaps echoes the national title of San, are a branch of the race which has settled in one spot. Both tribes speak a special language of their own, full of clicks, and utterly unlike the Bantu—the negroes of South Africa

The Dwarfs of Darkest Africa belong to the Bantu races—dialects ; but in other respects, especially in their form of civilisation, they have been greatly influenced by their environment. Yet in such matters as their burial customs they strongly remind us of the customs in use among the Hottentots.

At the same time, it has been shown that there are in Equatorial Africa tribes of the Bushman type who hunt in the plains and are not entirely confined to the forests ;

the dwarf peoples have also been found in the lake district. But the larger portion of the dwarf race appears to cling to the forest, and has entirely conformed to this environment. In some cases they are in subjection to their agricultural neighbours, or to a certain extent upon common terms with them. Here and there a complete fusion has taken place, the traces of which are still visible. But in no case do the dwarfs form tribal communities by themselves, for their character does not incline them to this course, and still less does their mode of life. They draw their sustenance from the resources of wide poverty-stricken districts, and thus tend invariably towards isolation.

Of these dwarf peoples the first group is that on the north-east, the Akka. They live about the sources of the Welle, or Ubangi, and, spreading southward, form a junction with the dwarf inhabitants of primeval forest on the Aruwimi, where Stanley first discovered them ; in fact, dwarf population of unusual density appears to inhabit the country from the Upper Aruwimi to the western

The Pygmies Discovered by Stanley lakes at the source of the Nile, while scattered colonies only are found further south as far as Tanganyika. A second great group is that of the Watwa, or Batwa, in the southern part of the Congo basin, especially in the district of the Baluba. A third group inhabits the rainy forests which cover the rising ground from the coast to the West African tablelands—that is to say, the Kamerun and Gabun interior. People of extraordinarily small stature have been found inhabiting the primeval forest district behind the Batanga coast, not living in settlements as village communities, but existing in the woods by hunting.

Apparently there is another dwarf people, the Doko, living in the forest district south of Kaffa—that is, north of Lake Rudolf, in East Africa. Although their existence, or at any rate their relationship with the Akka and Batwa has not as yet been definitely proved, there is no reason to doubt the veracity of the native accounts of them. At the present time the Doko seem to be the most northerly outpost of the African pygmies. Our knowledge of the racial movements up to the period of present-day discovery clearly shows us that the fair-skinned races of South Africa as a whole, together with the dwarf of the forests, are on the downward grade, or at best are merely holding their own.

In the seventeenth century the Hottentots retreated to the Fish River before the Kaffir or Bantu invasion, and the remnants of Hottentot races left in Natal showed how large a district had even previously been taken from them by the energetic Kaffir race. The dwarf peoples found their territory greatly diminished by the advance of agricultural tribes who penetrated into the primeval forests. Many of them were absorbed by intermarriage with their numerous negro neighbours. Thus, in a general sense at least, the problem of the disruption of this racial group is solved; their early unity was broken by the advance of other peoples; they are the remnants of a population, at one time of wide distribution, which inhabited Central and Southern Africa.

Their migratory character, however, inevitable in a nomadic hunter race, forbids us to infer, from their presence in a given district, that they, and not negroes, were its primeval inhabitants. We must be content to presume that the South African steppes developed a special race in the dwarfs, who have simply accommodated themselves to the conditions of their new home, the tropical forests, whither they were driven when the negroes became an agricultural people and occupied all the ground available for cultivation; with such resources the negroes naturally multiplied far more rapidly than the dwarfs, who had to rely upon Nature's bounty.

The process of expulsion was not carried out without a struggle. It has even been suggested that the wars between the pygmies and the cranes mentioned by Homer refer to a contest between the dwarfs and the swamp-dwellers of the Upper Nile, the Shilluk, Nuer, and Dinka.

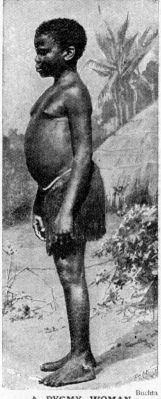

A PYGMY WOMAN   Buchta
A woman of the Akka tribe of dwarfs, a tribe discovered by H. M. Stanley in the dense forests of Central Africa.

Now, as compared with the Bushmen, the Hottentots show sundry affinities with the negro races. Their clothing and that of the Bantu peoples of South Africa, especially their chief garment, the kaross, is entirely similar. The wooden vessels of the Hottentots, in the manufacture of which they show great dexterity, resemble those of the Kaffirs so closely in shape and ornamentation as to be easily confused with them. The same remark applies to their musical instruments. Both races breed the same animals and upon very similar principles. Both understand the art of forging iron. The civil constitution of the Hottentot races corresponds to that of the neighbouring negroes in its main details.

As all these implements and institutions are nowhere to be found among the Bushmen, we may reasonably conclude that the higher civilisation of the Hottentots has been derived from the neighbouring negro races, especially the Kaffirs. If this transference of civilisation followed upon an infusion of negro blood, we have a complete explanation of the anthropological difference between Hottentot and Bushman, and, in particular, of the greater stature of the Hottentot. Moreover, in East Africa a small admixture of Semitic blood may not be wholly inconceivable. At the same time, the Hottentots have not merely taken what the Kaffirs have to give; they also exerted an influence in their turn. Certain figures of Kaffir mythology are undoubtedly derived from Hottentot legends, as is proved by the phonetic changes of words; the custom of mutilating the fingers for superstitious reasons arose in this way, for, generally, when two races come into contact, the weaker is considered as possessing greater magical powers, and thus influences the intellectual life of the stronger.

On the other hand, the point which differentiates the Hottentots from the cattle-breeding negro races is not any one characteristic, a repetition of which may be sought in far North Africa and West Asia ; it is a point of primal and original difference, common to Hottentot and Bushman. Above all, the Hottentot is not a cultivator, like the Kaffir ; he procures his scanty vegetable diet as the Bushman does, by grubbing up edible roots with a stone-weighted stick. Again, he has lost none of his passion for the chase, by which he often procured his chief food-supply, as, like most nomads, he could rarely bring himself to slaughter one of his cattle. His weapons combine the arsenal of the Bushman and the Kaffir. The great intellectual characteristic of the race, a fatal and yet invincible carelessness, makes the final link of the chain uniting Hottentot and Bushman, and has been handed down to him from his unsettled and uncultured ancestors, who abandoned their destinies to the sport of chance and accident.

Fatal Carelessness of the Hottentot

The transformation of the Hottentots to a shepherd people probably took place in East Africa ; perhaps the relatively better physical development of the race may be explained by their stay in this more fruitful district. The Bantu peoples, who first instructed them, soon drove them out. Even within historical times, remnants of the Hottentots were to be found in Natal, though the larger part of the race were then living beyond the Kei River, and were soon forced back as far as the Great Fish River. The Hottentots retreated in some cases northward across the Orange River, while others invaded the western part of the Cape ; this district, previous to these migrations, had been in the possession of the Bushmen, who even at the time of European colonisation were wandering about the country in numerous bands, and were constantly involved in bloody wars with the Hottentots. Such were the respective conditions of the Hottentots and Bushmen when, in 1602, the first Dutch colonists set foot upon South African soil. These formidable European adversaries now appeared upon their western flanks, while in the east the Kaffirs continued their advance, inflexibly, though for the most part in peaceful fashion.

First Europeans in South Africa

Before the year 1652, when Jan van Riebeek founded a Dutch settlement in Table Bay, the Hottentots had come into only temporary and generally hostile contact with Europeans. The first Portuguese viceroy of the Portuguese Indies, Don Francesco d'Almeida, had paid with his life for a landing on the Cape at Saldanha on March 1st, 1510. Misunderstandings also took place with the new Boer settlers, which speedily resulted in open war in 1659. Gradually the Dutch succeeded in driving back their opponents. The fickleness of the Hottentots and the hostility of the separate tribes proved the best allies of the Dutch ; thus in the year 1680 a war broke out between the Namaqua and the Griqua, in which the latter were defeated and sought the protection of the colonists.

The history of the war between the Hottentots and the Dutch settlers is not rich in striking events ; the Hottentots were not destroyed at one blow ; we see them gradually retreating and dwindling in a manner more suggestive of fusion and absorption than of extermination. But as the Hottentots retired, and the settlers with their flocks advanced, a new enemy appeared, who considered the Dutch cattle quite as well worth plundering as those of the native shepherd tribes ; the Bushmen did not vanish as rapidly as the Hottentots, in whose territories they had lived as predatory, hated enemies, but maintained their ground. They soon brought upon themselves the hatred of the colonists. The Dutch had their dealings with the Hottentots, and lived on peaceful terms with them from time to time ; but a ruthless war of extermination was waged against the Bushmen. Thus in a comparatively short time the fate of these related peoples was decided in the Cape itself ; the Hottentots were reduced to poverty, their unity was broken, and they intermingled more and more with the settlers, whereas the Bushmen were exterminated or driven northward across the Orange River.

Early Wars of the Dutch

Relations between the Hottentots and the Kaffirs on the east at that period seem to have been friendly, and produced a mixed race of Kaffirs and Hottentots, the Gonaqua, upon the frontier line. About 1780, their chieftain Ruyter succeeded in collecting a following upon the Fish River and resisting all attacks for some time ; similarly the brothers Stuurman maintained their independence for a considerable period about 1793.

The names of these leaders seem to indicate that these were not movements of pure-blooded Hottentots. Soon after, the Dutch supremacy collapsed, and in 1795 Great Britain first seized the Cape of Good Hope on the absorption of Holland by France, an occupation to become permanent by 1806. After this the Cape Hottentots have no further historical importance, though they performed useful service in the employment of the Government during the different Kaffir wars; the Bushmen had been almost exterminated. The Hottentots who still survived in the Cape were mainly concentrated in the different reservations; the largest of these, in Fort Beaufort district, was originally founded as an outwork against the Kaffir invasions.

AN ABORIGINAL TYPE: THE BUSHMAN
The Bushmen are an unsettled people, extremely hardy, living by cattle breeding and stealing

But in the north a portion of the race remained independent for nearly a century, an age of long and not inglorious struggle. Here, to the north of Cape Colony, lived the Namaqua; the greater part of the race was settled south of the Orange River, although, even at the time of the discovery, they extended as far north-west as the heights of Angra Pequena. Whether they were then attempting to extend their area, or were remaining quietly within their territory, is not known. The southern part of the race had come into contact with the Dutch as early as 1661, had quickly lost their language and distinctive character, and had received a considerable infusion of European blood; the northern group, on the contrary, were hardly affected by these influences. This nation was constantly molested by the

THE WONDERFUL ART OF THE BUSHMEN
No race in South Africa has shown such profound artistic skill as is seen in the drawings of the Bushmen, a fine example of which, representing a raid on Kaffir cattle, is reproduced here.

Dutch upon the south, and became vigorously aggressive, finding an energetic leader in the chieftain Christian Jager. Christian made attacks and marauding expeditions both north and south; when the Korana Hottentots moved down the Orange River in the last decade of the eighteenth century, and entered the territory of his race, he drove them back with great slaughter. The weakest resistance which he experienced was that offered on the north, where the Bantu shepherd tribe of the Herero was situated; they were now plundered and reduced to slavery by the Hottentots. The marauding expeditions of the Namaqua extended to Ovamboland and beyond the Cunene; the tribe had been gradually transformed into a mobile nation of riders.

The rule of Jonker Afrikaner, a son of Christian (1836–1862), is marked by continuous warfare and plundering; he completely subjugated the Herero, and at Windhoek and Okahandja he ruled over Nama, Damara, and (from 1861) Ondonga-Ovambo. Under his successor, Christian, this dominion almost entirely collapsed. The Herero were incited to take up arms by the Swedish traveller, Karl Johan Andersson, whose leg was broken in 1864 in one of these "battles"; Christian was killed in the course of this struggle. But the Hottentot supremacy received its severest blow under Christian's brother, Jan Jonker Afrikaner, when the most powerful of the Herero chiefs, Kamaharero, the son of Ka-Tjamuaha, procured supplies of arms and ammunition and fought

2283

against the Namaqua with general success. Under the influence of German missionaries hostilities were suspended; but when a new war broke out Jan Jonker was so utterly beaten that his power was completely broken.

It was now plain that only the interference of a stronger power could put a

Wars of the Boers and Herero stop to these continual wars. Hardly had Jan Jonker disappeared from the scene, when a new enemy to the Herero appeared in the person of Moses Witbooi, who again troubled the land for another series of years. He was no more successful than his predecessor in thoroughly subduing the Herero; on the contrary, he suffered several serious defeats, and lost the position of leader to the forces of the race, his place being taken by his son, Hendrik Witbooi, who was an even more restless personality.

In the year 1884 Hendrik Witbooi undertook an expedition into the district of the Herero, just at the time when the Germans were making their first attempts at colonisation upon the coast; when he returned, in 1885, he suffered a heavy defeat at the hands of the Herero, and at the same time Kamaharero placed himself under German protection. A troublesome period of confusion and weakness then ensued, and after the death of Kamaharero, in 1890, Witbooi's invasions were pressed with greater ferocity; he made his fortress of Hornkranz the base for these operations, until, in the usual manner of European intervention, the Germans advanced in force, stormed Hornkranz on April 12th, 1893, and at length forced Hendrik Witbooi to surrender unconditionally on September 9th, 1894. Beside the Namaqua, two other Hottentot races are worthy of mention, the Korana and the Griqua, who settled in the north of the Cape and north of the Orange River. The Korana, who origin-

Colonists Displace the Hottentots ally dwelt in the interior, did not come into contact with Europeans until a late period. The advance of the colonists threw them back upon their old settlements on each side of the Middle and Upper Orange River, where they were more closely confined as time went on; they made an attempt to extend their territory down stream, but were defeated with great slaughter by the Namaqua. Since that time the people has been broken up into numerous small tribes and is in a state of hopeless disruption.

As the Namaqua had migrated northward, so the Griqua, a race with a strong infusion of European blood, retreated northward to avoid the pressure of the advancing colonists. The main body, under the leadership of their chieftain Adam Kok, a liberated negro slave from the coast of Mozambique, crossed the Orange River in 1810 a little below its junction with the Vaal, and founded a "Free State." In the year 1820 the Griqua were living in three races under the two Koks and Berend, in a district extending from Daniel's Kuyl to the Riet River. When Nicholas Waterboer was elected in Griquatown in 1822, many of the Griqua withdrew and joined other races; a second exodus under Buys moved toward the mountains on the frontier of Cape Colony, and produced the Bergenaers. In 1826, Adam Kok's Griqua went to the Bushman colony of Philippolis, which had been devastated by the Kaffirs. From 1834 the Griqua chiefs were in receipt of British subsidies,

Doom of the Yellow Races and in 1848-1853 the people were under British suzerainty. After the recognition of the Orange Free State in 1854, the government of that republic pressed yet harder upon the eastern Griqua, who emigrated in 1862 beyond the Drakensberg to "No Man's Land" in Kaffraria. About this time, 1861, the Pondo chieftain Faku, who was threatened by the Kaffirs, resigned his rights in favour of Great Britain, who divided a portion of the territory among the Griqua, Basutos, and Fingos of Adam Kok. This district was united, in 1876, with Cape Colony, as "East Griqualand." Meanwhile, the western Griqua, who were divided from their brethren by the Lower Vaal, had also suffered under the continual advance of the Cape Boers. Finally, on October 27th, 1871, Britain succeeded in persuading Waterboer, the chief, to cede his territory to her, including the newly discovered diamond-fields. Everywhere, by slow degrees and diplomatic skill, a peaceful modus vivendi was attained for Hottentots and European settlers alike. But the yellow races of South Africa must eventually disappear from history. Such hybrid races seem doomed to wear out rapidly, unless saved by strong infusion of new blood.

THE KAFFIR PEOPLES OF THE SOUTH-EAST

THROUGHOUT Southern and Central Africa the negro races speak Bantu dialects. The tribes of the south-east—that is, south of the Zambesi and east of the Hottentots—are generally included under the title of Kaffir, a term of Arab origin, meaning " unbelievers."

It appears that the Kaffirs migrated from the north southward, and, starting from Abyssinian territory, finally arrived at South-east Africa. The extent of these migrations is probably exaggerated. In the tenth century a kingdom of the Zingi, or Sendsh, existed in the interior of Sofala; the king could place 3,000 warriors in the field, who were mounted upon oxen. The kingdom exported a large amount of slaves, gold, iron, and ivory. Races related to the Sendsh seem to have lived some distance away upon the coast; others who were less civilised lived in the interior and appear from descriptions to have been the ancestors of the Jagga and Masimba. The later kingdom of Monomotapa, or more correctly of *the* Monomotapa—the word means " sons of the mines," and is undoubtedly applied to the ruling family —is probably identical with the older state of the Sendsh. The gold of the country, which was also worked by the Kaffirs, gave a splendour to the kingdom of the Monomotapa, which was widely exaggerated by the ancient chroniclers; hence the kingdom was finally represented upon European maps as of fabulous extent.

In modern times two races of the Kaffir people of South Africa can be distinguished : an older race, which dates back to the original conquest of the district in antiquity, and a younger, warlike race,

A ZULU WARRIOR

which, migrating back again from the south, presses upon its peaceful northern relations as well as upon other peoples. The people of Monomotapa belong to the older group, and their descendants now inhabit Mashonaland ; for the modern Mashona call themselves Makalanga, evidently the same name as that of the inhabitants of Monomotapa, who were called Mocaranga. The Portuguese chroniclers tell us that, about 1600, Monomotapa was divided into three states, separate provinces which had made themselves independent—Sakumbe, Manu, and Chicova.

After this disruption of the wealthy Monomotapa no other great political organisation came into being, and a conquering race would have found itself confronted by a very feeble opposition. In process of time such a race arose among the south-eastern Kaffirs. Our information concerning their internal history is extremely scanty previous to their first collisions with the European settlers ; but this is not a serious loss, inasmuch as their great campaigns of conquest, which convulsed Africa as far as the great lakes, were begun at a much later period. Most of the Kaffir races agree in the tradition that they migrated to their territory from the north-east, and the legend is confirmed by the Arab chronicles ; these migrations were not simultaneously undertaken, but were slowly and gradually completed. In the seventeenth century the race of the Kosa Kaffirs were living furthest to the south, and had slowly penetrated into the Hottentot district. The northern group of the south-east Kaffirs were collectively

2285

known as "Zulu" and originally inhabited Natal and its northern coastline; the Swazi, who lived in the district which bears their name, were closely related to them in language.

Before the appearance of Europeans movements seem to have been going on within the Zulu group, resulting in the absorption of smaller tribes and the formation of stronger racial confederacies. Meanwhile the Kosa had to reckon with the advance of white colonists.

The first victims of the merciless war which afterward began fell in the year 1736, when a hunting party which had entered the Kaffir territory was murdered. Small skirmishes continued, especially after 1754, without stopping the advance of the colonists, until, in the year, 1778, the Governor of Cape Colony, Von Plettenburg, laid down the boundary line of the Great Fish River. The Kaffirs,

however, paid not the smallest attention to this delimitation; consequently, in the year 1780, the first Kaffir war broke out, when a small band of ninety-two colonists and forty Hottentots successfully drove the Kaffirs across the Great Fish River. Internal dissension had broken out among the Kaffirs themselves, and the races which fled across the boundary river had already been defeated and weakened, and were now forced to give way once more. In the following year the disturbances continued; in the years 1795-1796 the chief Ndlambe had a desperate struggle with his nephew, Gaika, for the supremacy in the Kosa territory.

In 1797 Gaika was proclaimed king of all the tribes to the west of the Kei by John Barrow, private secretary to Lord Macartney; he remained peaceful during the struggles of the British with the chief Kungwa, who died in 1811, on Algoa Bay, and with Ndlambe on the Great Fish River. In the year 1818 he was driven westward after his defeat on the Amalinde plain on the Chumie River by Ndlambe's party under a man of low rank, the prophet and magician Makanna; but shortly afterwards — in 1819 — before Grahamstown on the Cowie river, Makanna fell into the hands of the colonists he had attacked. The further details of the struggle are closely connected with the development of Cape Colony, and are reserved until we reach that subject.

Meanwhile, undisturbed by European attacks, a warrior state had arisen among the Zulus, for which few parallels are to be found in the whole course of the world's history. The Zulus, whose name is now generally extended to include the whole race, were originally nothing more than a small wandering tribe of little importance; but about the beginning of the

THE BIRTH OF THE COLONY OF NATAL

Lieut. Farewell treating with the chiefs under Chaka, the Zulu king, in 1824.

nineteenth century the immense energy and ruthless tyranny of their chief Chaka gave them undisputed pre-eminence. Chaka's mother had sent him for safety to Dingiswayo, chief of the neighbouring and more powerful tribe of the Tetwa, where he was brought up; then about the year 1818 he returned, at the age of thirty, took up the reins of government, and quickly succeeded in incorporating the Tetwas with the Zulus.

The whole state was now remodelled with a view to war and conquest, and the subject members were organised and systematically trained for this purpose. The smaller racial confederacies disappeared one after the other, and family life within the tribe itself was almost entirely broken up. The nation was henceforward divided into army corps, each under its own warrior chief, or induna ; the women, who were also subjected to this military system, were nothing more than concubines, and were often not permitted to rear their own

ZULU WITCH-DOCTOR MAKING WARRIORS INVULNERABLE

When about to practise their arts these wizards smear their faces with some white pigment. Round their heads they wear fish-bladders. Their bodies are swathed in a dress of bullock's hair. The doctor works himself into a frenzy and dances wildly round the circle of warriors, dashing his switch in their faces and occasionally thrusting a lump of clay and dirt into their mouths

children. The army was constantly rejuvenated by enlisting the youthful members of conquered races ; the obvious result of this system was that constant wars were a vital necessity for the Zulu kingdom, and that its influence upon its neighbours was invariably destructive. When these neighbours were not destroyed, they fell upon other races in their hasty retreat before the advancing Zulus, until at length a considerable part of South Africa was in a state of ferment and commotion. Thus the Mantati, who had been thrust aside by the Zulus, threatened the Cape itself, after crushing some of the weaker races to the north of the Orange River ; however, in 1823, they were defeated by the

Griqua Hottentots, and gradually relapsed into quiescence. Remnants of other races, partly Fingoes from the Tugela, partly Zulus who had shared in revolts against Chaka's cruelty, streamed toward the south-west and finally joined the Fingo tribe ; from 1835, after the war, some 16,000 of them were settled by the British to the east of the Great Fish River.

In the year 1828 Chaka fell a victim to a conspiracy of his two brothers, one of whom, Dingan, seized the power after a hard struggle with his fellow conspirator. He surpassed even Chaka in cruelty and ferocious energy, and completed the organisation of the army. But the enemies were already approaching who were finally to break the Zulu power.

2287

British colonists had settled on the coasts of Natal; in 1837 Boers crossed the mountains and asked permission of Dingan to settle. The Kaffir chief enticed the leader of the Boers, Pieter Retief, with sixty-six of his men, into his encampment, and for their confidence murdered them on February 5th, 1838; then begins a new page in South African history, one of the many which have been written in blood.

For Dingan the cowardly deed brought fatal consequences. The Boers gathered a strong force, marched into Natal under command of Andries Pretorius, and inflicted a bloody defeat

WIFE OF A KAFFIR CHIEF

on Dingan when he attacked their laager with 12,000 men on December 16th, 1838. Dingan fled to the Swazi Kaffirs, and met his death among them shortly afterward, about 1840. His successor, Panda, "Prince of the Zulus," who came to power on February 4th, 1840, was obliged to abandon Natal to the Boers, who were shortly afterwards forcibly incorporated with the British colonial empire. Thus an impassable barrier was set up on the south against the warlike tendencies of the Zulus; their attacks upon the north became all the more frequent.

Panda's reign was a period of peace with the British. This state of affairs continued until Panda's son

THE BURDEN-BEARERS: ZULU WOMEN

Ketchwayo, or Cetewayo, in 1857, succeeded in defeating his brother Umbelasi in a bloody battle upon the Tugela River, and ousting his father, who had

not interfered in the quarrel. In Cetewayo, the typical warrior Zulu prince again came to light, and upon the death of Panda, in 1872, it became plain that the peace between the Zulus and the British Government would be of no long duration. Marauding expeditions upon the frontier increased in frequency, and were further incited by refugees from both parties. Cetewayo, who saw what was coming, had raised his army to the number of 40,000 men. The British insisted that this dangerous force should be disbanded, and declared war upon the refusal of the Zulu ruler. There could be no doubt about the final issue. A British force was, indeed, destroyed by the spears and clubs of the Zulu regiments at Isandlhwana, or Isandula, on January 22nd, 1879, and the base camp at Rorke's Drift, held by 120 men, fiercely attacked by 4,000 Zulus; but as Dingan was ultimately beaten by the Boers, so was Cetewayo by the British on July 4th, at Ulundi; the Kaffir king was forced to surrender unconditionally, in the forest of Ngome on the Black Umvolosi, on August 28th, 1879. The further advance of the British and their gradual occupation of the country are events which belong to European African history.

The crater of this racial war had thus been violently stopped; but bands of warriors were spreading devastation over a wide area. At the time when Chaka rose to be head of the Zulu races a part of his people fled away from his iron rule. Under the leadership of the chief Moselikatse, the band started north-west in 1818, and first came into collision with the race of the Makololo, who were settled in the eastern part of the modern Orange River Colony. The Makololo retired before their attack, marched northward in 1824 under their chief Sebituane, and crossed the Central Zambesi.

Meanwhile, the Matabele, as the people of Moselikatse called themselves after a Zulu tribe that had long been settled in the Transvaal, met with other opponents between the Orange and Vaal rivers—namely, a part of the Korana Hottentots, and also the Basuto people, who were of the Bechuana race. These latter are said to have migrated to their territory at the outset of the seventeenth century, and to have grown considerably in power by absorbing the remnants of other races. The most important of the Basuto chiefs, Moshesh — from about 1820 to 1868 — repelled the Matabele

THE ZULU WAR OF 1879: FUGITIVES FROM ISANDLHWANA
The Zulu state was remodelled with a view to war and conquest about 1820, and the resulting state of ferment in South Africa was brought to a head when Cetewayo destroyed a British force at Isandlhwana, near the Buffalo River, in 1879

attack in 1831, acquiring thereby both reputation and influence. The Matabele were unable to advance further south, and gradually got possession of the modern Transvaal. However, on one side the Boers, trekking across the Vaal River, defeated Moselikatse in 1837, and drove him north of the Limpopo. The Matabele then turned upon Mashonaland, the old Monomotapa. Here the tribes could offer no effective resistance. Plundering and slaughter was carried on in true Zulu fashion; the wives of the conquered race followed their new masters as prisoners, while the young men were enlisted in the army. As all the attempts of the Matabele to cross the Zambesi were fruitless, the main body of the race remained in Mashonaland, a

standing cause of annoyance to their neighbours. After the death of Moselikatse, Lobengula became chief in 1870. About the beginning of the 'eighties there was a constant influx of whites into his kingdom, attracted by its wealth of gold; at the beginning of 1889 and 1894 his territory was taken over by the British South Africa Company. The power of the Matabele was utterly broken by the defeat of Lobengula on November 1st, 1893, on the Bembesi River, to the north-east of his capital of Buluwayo.

Less known to us than the history of the Matabele is that of the other Zulu peoples, whose devastating raids extended eastward and far beyond the Zambesi. In their case we have to proceed more cautiously. In the first place it appears that Kaffirs of an older stock, closely resembling the Zulus in their customs, had been settled in the Zambesi district and the East African highland for centuries —that is, probably since the time of the great migration from the north; the Wayao, who vigorously attacked the Makua on the Rovuma about a decade ago, were probably one of these tribes. But, in the next place, whole races, the so-called Zulu apes, have adopted the manners and military customs of the Zulus, and have consequently helped to confuse the boundaries of the true area of Zulu distribution, overspread by the "later invasion." Now, this same northern group of Kaffirs seems to have been vigorously active several centuries ago, and perhaps played the same part as the Zulus did in our own times; such at least seems to be the true significance of the Jagg and Masimba expeditions, which are worthy of a closer examination.

The Matabele campaign, which convulsed Central South Africa up to the Zambesi, and indirectly beyond it, were in point of influence even surpassed by the warfare and devastation spread by other Zulu bands upon the east coast and upon either side of the Lower Zambesi. The chief Mani-kus is said to have led the first army northward after Chaka's death. Gasaland, the district between the mouth of the Zambesi and Zululand, was first overrun and devastated; the inhabitants, who had previously been a happy and industrious people, were scattered or reduced to slavery, and they now bred dogs for their supply of meat in place of their beloved cattle, which fell into the hands of the Zulus. A similar fate befell

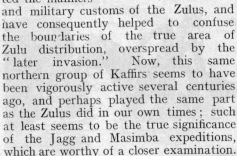

CETEWAYO   LOBENGULA

Two of the most famous native chiefs : Cetewayo, the typical warrior Zulu prince, and Lobengula, the last independent Matabele chief.

LORD CHELMSFORD

Whose force was cut to pieces at Isandlhwana in the Zulu War of 1879.

the races on the Lower Zambesi. The regular export of gold had maintained a certain connection between this district and more advanced races, and the inhabitants had made considerable progress in civilisation. Artistic iron and gold smiths exchanged the products of their industry not only with their fellows, but even with Arabs and Portuguese, and the manufacture of woollen fabrics had spread from the Zambesi far into the interior. The population was composed of very different elements, for slavery had here been a flourishing institution from an early period, and its usual results, the dissolution and fusion of races, were plainly manifest.

The warlike Zulus, under Songondawe, Mpesen, Suru and Mbonan, Mputa and Kidiaonga, attacked this mixture of races with shattering energy. But in this case they no longer appear under their own name; perhaps they had in part emigrated northward to escape Chaka's tyranny at a time when this people was being consolidated under his iron rule, and had not entirely imposed the name of its own little tribe upon the general whole. We find such Zulu offshoots as "Landin" on the Zambesi, as "Wangoni" to the west of the Nyassa, as "Masiti" or "Masitu" between the Nyassa and the east coast of the continent, as "Watuta" to the south of Unyamwesi. All these exercised a terribly destructive influence; their example induced peaceful agricultural tribes to assume the dress and arms of the conquerors (the stabbing spear and the shield covered with oxhide), and in like manner to invade and devastate the territory of their neighbours. Among these "Zulu-apes" may also be included, in a certain sense, the Wahehe, who, as a whole, are closely related to the

THE HEROIC DEFENCE OF RORKE'S DRIFT: 120 MEN AGAINST 4,000 ZULUS

In the beginning of the Zulu War of 1879, Chelmsford's main force advanced to Isandlhwana, leaving a small band to guard communications at Rorke's Drift. The Zulus evaded him, and burst on the camp, and, but for its heroic defence by 120 whites against 4,000 Zulus, would have invaded Natal. From Lady Butler's picture by the artist's permission.

Wasagara. About 1860, and especially from about 1870, they founded several kingdoms upon true Zulu principles under their chiefs Nyugumba, Matshinga, and Mambambe, which were ultimately subdued in 1896 by the advance of German colonisation. Phenomena precisely similar in kind to these modern aggressive military Kaffir communities had presented themselves three centuries before. When the second Portuguese embassy was staying in the year 1490–1491 with Mani-Congo, the king of the Lower Congo, whose court was at Ambasse, news arrived from the interior that the people of the Mundequete, on the lakes at the sources of the Congo, were preparing for war. The Congo king immediately had himself baptised, like Clovis of old, and successfully beat the enemy. This first movement seems to have been the prelude to further struggles and the invasion of the Jagga. Under their king, Simbo, these "Giacas" advanced toward the west coast, defeated the Congo troops, whose king had great difficulty in maintaining his position even with Portuguese help, and subdued part of the Portuguese district of Angola.

They renewed their attack from 1542–1546, and, after bringing Congo to the verge of destruction, were finally defeated; the remainder of them then settled in the district of Kassandje. Their original habitation is said to have been about the sources of the Zambesi and of the Congo; so they may very well have been a Kaffir race. Moreover, the military organisation of the Jagga apparently corresponds in its main features with that of the Zulus. The Jagga also increased their strength by incorporating with their troops the youth of the peoples whom they defeated and generally slaughtered. Of their attainments in civilisation, or of their customs, we know but little; the name Jagga is certainly a Kaffir word, and means "troops," "soldiers," or "bodies of young men."

THE DEFENDERS OF RORKE'S DRIFT

Lieutenants Chard and Bromhead, whose six score men held the camp against 4,000 Zulus, saving Natal from Cetewayo.

THE ARAB SETTLEMENTS ON THE EAST

ALMOST throughout Eastern Africa, evidences are to be found of the presence of an early civilisation of which it may be confidently affirmed that it was not indigenous. From Somaliland as far southward as Mozambique ruined stone buildings are to be found upon

The Ruined Cities of Mashonaland the coast. Many of these doubtless belong to the period of Portuguese and Arabic supremacy; the origin of others, however, is yet unexplained. This chain of ruins is terminated at Mozambique. But further south, beyond the Zambesi, in the interior of Sofala is a large district—Mashonaland—containing a number of extensive ruins, including the famous Simbabwe, the unusual size and solidity of which vividly impress the imagination.

These were stone buildings, all of very similar character; in their simplest form they consist of a circular wall, built of hewn stones without mortar, and often displaying some simple ornamentation of straight lines running round their circumference. Usually a second wall surrounds this first circle, and the intervening space is divided into small rooms by partitions. The entrance is guarded by special fortifications; their whole character indicates that the inhabitants lived in a hostile district in a state of continual war. Strong massive towers, the object of which it is difficult to explain, rose here and there. The ruins are exceptionally poor in objects of civilisation. We may mention a few figures of birds and pots of soapstone, iron implements which perhaps belonged to later inhabitants of the ruins, some porcelain, which may have been brought into the interior by Arab merchants; and this is practically all. In

Fortresses of Ancient Gold-diggers old accounts, especially in those of the Arabs, we hear of strange inscriptions on the gates, which were unintelligible to the visitors; such inscriptions have been discovered in modern times, and appear to be of Semitic origin.

But the reason why those stone castles were built is clear. Everywhere in the neighbourhood of the buildings we find smelting furnaces, dross, pieces of ore, and remnants of crucibles, and in many of these fragments are still to be found traces of gold; there can be no doubt that these old fortresses were built to protect the gold-diggers.

In the next place it is clear from the utter lack of artistic work that the builders were not Indians, Egyptians, or Greeks. In effect, we must attribute the buildings to a Semitic people, with an overwhelming presumption in favour of the Arabs. We are irresistibly led to identify Mashonaland with the Ophir of the Bible.

When and why the district was abandoned it is impossible to say; but the condition of the buildings seems to point to their almost simultaneous destruction by hostile forces. As regards the question of the Arab settlements of Roman times, we have information from writers who belong to European civilisation—namely, the so-called "Peri-

The Real Land of Ophir plus of the Erythræan Sea," and the Geography of Ptolemy. From these sources it appears that in the second century A.D. there were a large number of trading stations upon the east coast of Africa, with which the Arabs maintained a vigorous and profitable trade. It was just at that period that the Arabs began to monopolise the trade by forcing the Egyptian ships to transfer their cargoes to Arab vessels at the exit of the Strait of Bab el-Mandeb. It can hardly be doubted that the settlements had been in existence long before that period. The most southerly point known to Ptolemy was the promontory of Prasum, which he places in 16° 25′ latitude south. This would nearly correspond to the latitude of the modern Mozambique. He also mentions Rhapta, which is to be found upon the coast of Zanzibar, corresponding possibly with the modern Pangani, which lies upon the river Rufu as the old town did upon the Rhaptus; or it is to be identified with Kilwa. Further north lay Tonike, Essina, and other trading stations. Our informants know nothing of any unusually great export of gold or of the gold-mines and towns of Mashonaland. They lay more stress upon the export of resin from Northern East Africa. Possibly the Arabs were careful to hide the source of their gold supply; that their domination in Mashonaland may have already come to ruin is supported by an observation in the Arabic chronicle of Kilwa, stating that it was not before the year 1000 A.D. that the people of Makdishu—that is, Somaliland—rediscovered the gold-mines of Sofala.

According to Arab accounts of later centuries, trade appears to have continued in a flourishing condition, and to have been shared by Indian and at times by Chinese ships. About 908 A.D. Makdishu and Borawa, or Brava, on the Somali coast were founded by Arabs from El-Chasa on the Persian Gulf, as also was Kilwa about 975. The islands of Zanzibar and Pemba had been in the hands of the Arabs long before, and even mixed races of Arabs and negroes were to be found on the coast. In the twelfth century we have mention of Malindi, or Melinde, and also of Momba; but Kilwa seems to have been predominant for a long period—probably because it had the monopoly of gold export—while Makdishu was of chief importance on the north. Islam was early transplanted to Africa and helped to consolidate the Arab settlements. So when the Portuguese finally raised the veil which shrouded these districts, there were a number of flourishing sultanates and rich towns upon the coast, which were in the hands of the Arabs from Sofala as far north as Malindi, while a vigorous communication was kept up by sea between the coasts of East Africa and India. The appearance of the Portuguese was promptly followed by collisions with these Arab settlements. In the south, the Arabs were successfully driven back; but the northern towns, especially Mombasa, though more or less subjugated, were at best a doubtful and expensive acquisition, even during the flourishing period of Portuguese predominance. When Portugal's power declined the strongest and most maritime of the Arab states naturally entered her inheritance.

This Arab state was Oman, which was situated on the eastern point of the Arabian peninsula, a district facing India and Persia; at an early date its geographical situation gave it a dominant position, and the power of the state was increased by the formation of a special Mohammedan sect, the chief of which was the reigning sultan of the land, with the title of Imam of Maskat. Oman was

RUINS OF FORTS OF THE GOLD-DIGGERS OF OPHIR
Throughout Mashonaland are impressive ruins, probably forts of ancient gold-diggers, the district being identified with the Ophir of the Bible. Those of Simbabwe, shown above, are most famous. A model of the ruins is shown in the top right-hand corner; one of the massive tower fortifications at the bottom, the other objects being sculptures found in the ruins.

torn by internal dissensions for a long period; but in 1624 the Jarebite Nasser ben Murdjid made himself sole ruler. He was forthwith obliged to embark upon a war with the Portuguese, who had several coast towns belonging to Oman in their possession; but it was his cousin and successor, Sultan ben Sef (1649–1668), who first succeeded in taking the last Portuguese stronghold, Maskat, in 1650. During the course of this war Oman had become a formidable maritime power. Sultan ben Sef harassed the Portuguese in India and East Africa, and about 1660 temporarily seized the town of Mombasa. In 1698, his son and successor, Sef ben Sultan, succeeded in capturing Mombasa, stirring up the entire population of the coast against the Portuguese, and thus subduing East Africa as far as Cape Delgado.

Rise of the Arab State of Oman

Meanwhile it began to appear that the little state of Oman had undertaken a task beyond its powers. If the coast towns—Kilwa, Zanzibar, Melindi, Patta, Fasa—took advantage of the weakness of Oman to declare themselves independent petty states the Arab dominion would be overthrown. This was precisely what occurred. In 1728 Portugal availed herself of the resulting confusion to make a second attack; Patta fell into her hands again, and on March 16th Mombasa, the last Arab stronghold on the coast, was obliged to open its gates. This was the expiring effort of the Portuguese power. As soon as the inhabitants of the coast again united their forces against the foreigners, the towns were lost in rapid succession—Zanzibar, Masia, Pemba, and on November 26th, 1729, Mombasa.

In Maskat the Jarebite dynasty was replaced by the Abu Saidi family, which rules in Oman and Zanzibar now. The founder of this dynasty was the commander-in-chief Sohar Ahmed ben Said, who ascended the throne in 1744. The change of dynasty led to a second change in the relations between Oman and the African coast towns. Marka, Zanzibar, and Kilwa alone acknowledged the new supremacy; the remaining towns, headed by the ever restless Mombasa, under the brothers Mohammed and Ali ben Osman, declared their independence and found themselves immediately at war with Ahmed ben Said in consequence. At the same time, internal struggles were raging in the several towns, especially in Patta. Ultimately, in 1785, an ingenious manœuvre restored to Maskat the whole coast line, which for a long time bore the mild yoke of the rulers without complaint.

It was not until the governor of Mombasa, Abdallah ben Ahmed (1814–1823) attempted to make himself independent, that the reigning monarch of Maskat, Seyyid Said, was roused to greater energy. After long hesitation, he sent a fleet to East Africa in 1822, and with the assistance of Mohammed ben Nasser, the governor of Zanzibar, who had remained faithful to him, he speedily reduced Mombasa to a desperate condition. As a last resource Seliman ben Ali placed himself under the protection of the Englishman Owen in 1824. But the British Government did not confirm the

Struggles of the Arab States

MOMBASA IN THE DAYS OF THE SLAVE TRADE: BOMBARDMENT BY BRITISH WARSHIPS

Mombasa, the ever restless Arab state on the east coast of Africa, founded before the Portuguese occupation in the fifteenth century, is now the capital of the British East African Protectorate. It was a centre of the slave trade.

convention, and the town was forced to surrender to Seyyid Said, who appeared in 1828 with a fleet of eleven ships of war. Shortly afterwards, however, Mombasa was again in full revolt, until 1837, when Seyyid Said succeeded in recovering possession of the town by treachery and completely expelling the ruling family of the Msara, to which he had previously entrusted some powers of government. In 1840 the victorious sultan determined to transfer his residence permanently to Africa, and chose Zanzibar for this purpose. The connection between Oman and Zanzibar was dissolved by the death of Seyyid Said in 1856, one of his sons, Seyyid Madjid, taking the African dominions, while Seyyid Sueni received the Arabian territory. Great Britain, whose position as dominant Power in the Indian Ocean was now assured, adjusted certain points of vari-

THE END OF SLAVERY IN ZANZIBAR

With the introduction of the clove-tree and the growth of plantations, the old Arab slave trade of Zanzibar revived, and rose to enormous proportions, until the British intervened. This picture shows the destruction of the last of the slavers' stockades.

ance between the two rulers in 1859, by inducing the sultan of Zanzibar to pay his brother in Maskat a yearly subsidy of 40,000 dollars. She also supported the sultan against one of his younger brothers who attempted to revolt, the later sultan Seyyid Bargash. During the closing years of Seyyid Madjid's life Great Britain paid the yearly compensation due from the sultan to Maskat out of her own resources. After Seyyid Madjid's death, in 1870, the power passed to his brother Seyyid Bargash, who died on April 25th, 1888. Under his government those changes began which have effected a fundamental revolution in African affairs.

The wealth of the Arabs dwelling on the coast and the islands was chiefly derived from their landed property. Mombasa,

for instance, was strong enough to offer a long resistance chiefly by reason of its possession of the island of Pemba, with its rich plantations. Since 1818 the clove-tree had been cultivated there with brilliantly successful results. At the beginning of the nineteenth century the commerce of Zanzibar was very unimportant; the export of ivory was comparatively small; the slave trade was carried on in a very modest way, and the traders, chiefly Indians, were few in number. The introduction of the clove-tree produced a great change. Large plantations now sprang up, requiring many hands to work them; slave-hunting and the slave trade revived. The wealth thus acquired enabled enterprising Arabs not only to get slaves from the coast tribes by barter,

2295

but also to fit out strong, well-armed expeditions for the purpose of breaking down the numerous obstacles to trade, and of buying or kidnapping slaves in the interior. Ivory and cheap slaves now came down to the coast in abundance, and the extraordinary profits which were made at the outset were a stimulus to more extensive raids and trading expeditions. Thus Arab influence spread further into the interior, though the idea was never entertained of establishing any permanent political supremacy on the continent, apart from that already existing in the settlements upon the coast. The Zanzibar government certainly claimed the allegiance of the several Arab contractors who made their way into the interior on their own account ; but it could not and would not exercise any control, and generally did not attempt to assert its rights until the return of the caravans.

The increase of the slave trade, and the devastation which it created, compelled the intervention of the British. As early as 1847 they had prohibited the slave trade north of Brava ; in 1873, Sir Bartle Frere was sent out to add his persuasions, which were of a forcible character, to those of the Consul-General, Sir John Kirk, and to impose upon the sultan a treaty whereby the slave trade was officially abolished. The result was inevitably disastrous for the Arab plantation owners, who, deprived of the labour necessary to their work, were reduced to poverty and inspired with fierce hatred of every European. The only course open to these ruined men was to try their fortunes at trading on the continent, to collect ivory and kidnap slaves, which were secretly brought over to Zanzibar. Thus the unfortunate districts of East Africa were sacrificed to marauders of the worst class, and the Arabs became the curse of the country. About the different centres of Arab influence oases of higher culture certainly arose amid the general devastation, which exercised some beneficial influence upon the natives ; but such benefits were far outweighed by the attendant misery. The Arabs began to make plantations at these centres also, a fresh demand for slaves arose, and the raids continued incessantly. The earliest and most important base of operations was Tabora in Unyamwesi, which may be said to mark the first and shortest stage of the Arab advance. Further inland is Ujiji, the harbour of Tanganyika, and also the notorious Nyangwe, on the Upper Congo, whence the Eastern Congo valley was cruelly devastated. Many tribes, such as the Manyema, became the ready helpers of the Arabs, and took to raiding on their own initiative.

Within the few years ensuing, British influence was strengthened by the appointment of several British officials. But other Powers were now alert to appropriate " spheres of influence " in the Dark Continent. Treaty-making began to be actively carried on in the interior, and presently it became imperative that Great Britain and Germany should come to a definite understanding as to their respective areas of ascendency. The matter was finally settled by the Anglo-German Convention of 1890, accompanied by an Anglo-French agreement, which virtually turned the northern half of the Zanzibar sultanate into a British protectorate, Zanzibar and Pemba being included therein.

A VIEW OF ZANZIBAR, ONCE THE CENTRE OF THE SLAVE TRADE
Zanzibar, the capital of the sultanate, on the island of Zanzibar, is the principal port on the east coast of Africa, and is under British protection. It was the centre of the East African slave trade in the days of its greatest prosperity.

TRIBES OF NORTH AND CENTRAL EAST AFRICA

AT the present time in Central East Africa it is possible to distinguish with tolerable clearness several zones of civilisation which display the results of long-continued foreign influence. The coast towns and the larger portion of the sea-board are inhabited by the Suaheli, a mixed people with a certain infusion of Arab and also of Portuguese blood, united by a common language and a uniform civilisation. In the fruitful mountainous country behind the coast-line and in the plain districts further in the interior dwell small races often in a very low stage of civilisation. When we penetrate the highlands between the Victoria Nyanza, Tanganyika, and Nyassa, we reach a district too far from the coast to be demoralised by the influence of the foreigners settled there, and yet sufficiently near to receive all kinds of stimulus. Thus, in this district has arisen a people, the Wanyamwesi, civilised—at least in the African sense of the word—

Civilised People of Moonland admirably distinguished by manufacturing industry and by an inclination for trade, and likely to be highly important in the future of the continent.

This people has apparently maintained a peaceful intercourse with the coast from a very early period. The word Unyamwesi means "Moonland," and originated among the coast population, who may have heard, like the Arabs, their teachers, of the legendary Mountains of the Moon of the ancients : the name was naturally attached to the most important district of the interior, the goal of all trading expeditions. The natural advantages of the locality, and especially the protection afforded by the plains and lakes against attacks from without, contributed to advance the prosperity of Unyamwesi; so too did the caravan trade and the higher civilisation thereby introduced, which helped to consolidate the different races of the district to a closer political unity. The highest prosperity of this state certainly came to pass at a time concerning which we have no direct information ; but its importance can easily be inferred even in its present condition of decay.

The central point of Unyamwesi is Unyanyembe ; even after the disruption of the kingdom, the date of which is unknown, communication with the coast was maintained here, and certain traditions of no great antiquity were preserved. We are probably correct in placing the founder of the present dynasty, Swetu I., at the end of the eighteenth century. Under this ruler the caravan trade, which had probably ceased, must have been reopened—a movement apparently begun by two elephant hunters, Mparangome and Ngogombe, who made their way nearly to the coast and then acted as guides to the caravans of their countrymen about 1825–1830. The Arabs soon availed themselves of the newly opened trade route, and founded Tabora in 1846 as their centre of operations. At this point begins the great modern Arab incursion into Central Africa, with the great revolutions and struggles to which it led.

Beginning of Arab Invasions

Other foreign elements were also to be found in Unyamwesi. An offshoot of the Hamitic Wahuma immigrations from the north appears at an early period but did not attain to any political influence in the country. On the other hand, the Zulu raids brought detachments of this warlike race into the district ; their influence upon the destinies of Unyamwesi was to become important in later times, when these additions were known as Watuta or Wangoni. About 1850 the Watuta separated from the Masitu, the Zulus upon Lakes Schirwa and Nyassa, and, advancing from the north-west end of Lake Nyassa, attacked the Warori, being attracted by their wealth of cattle ; finding them too strong, they passed by Urori and advanced to Udjidji in 1858, the Arab inhabitants taking refuge on the island of Bangwe. The Watuta then attacked Uhha, on Lake Tanganyika, and Urundi, with its capital,

Zulu Raids in Moonland

Muwukeye, without success, marched through Uvinsa, entered Unyamwesi, and arrived by way of Usindja at the Ukerewe Lake. Here they remained some years, and then returned to Sudussukuma, the chief of which prudently became the son-in-law of the Watuta leader and received his land back as dowry. How-

East Africa's Napoleon

ever, part of the Watuta went farther south, and became the most reliable contingent in the service of the powerful Mirambo, the "Napoleon of East Africa." Under him they were gradually transformed from a fierce tribe of wanderers to a state which became highly prosperous in the well-watered pasture lands of Ugomba and Ngalla.

Mirambo himself, born about 1830, was of the race of the Wanyamwesi, probably the son of a petty village chieftain; he was a caravan porter, and, being badly treated by an Arab, escaped into the wilderness and collected a band of robbers about him, which was soon as great a terror to the natives as were the Arabs themselves. Upon the death of the chief of Uyoweh, a small district belonging to Unyamwesi, he seized this territory and terrorised the whole of south-west Unyamwesi by his devastating raids. Conflict with the Arabs was inevitable. Stanley, who was travelling through the country just at that period, 1871, took part in the expedition which the Arabs made against Mirambo; their victorious advance was speedily terminated by a crushing defeat. In the same year Mirambo stormed and burned the town of Tabora. He was then, between 1870 and 1880, at the height of his power.

But the system of conquest which he had adopted from the Zulus was not the method by which permanent empires are formed. Unyamwesi, which had been formerly so powerful, did not rise to new prosperity under Mirambo. His power

The Clutch of Europe in Moonland

was wasted, as it had grown, by continual war. After his death, in 1886, Unyamwesi was more than ever torn by faction, and before a path out of this state of disruption to further development could be found Tabora was garrisoned by the Germans in 1890. This event, together with the defeat of Sikki, chief of Unyanyembe, announced the beginning of a new era for these districts. The clutch of Europe had closed upon the savage region.

Very little is known of the history of the Bantu-speaking peoples settled to the eastward between Unyamwesi and the coast. It is clear that their numbers were once greater and their situation more favourable than now. On the other hand, the state of the Bushman races in the unwatered territory is an argument against assigning the whole of Central East Africa to the Bantu. Here also there was undoubtedly constant migration and fusion of races at an early epoch.

The inhabitants of Usagara, Useguha, Usambara, Ukami and Chutu appear to form a connected group, which, like the Wanyamwesi, has been settled in its territory from an early period. Contrasted with these are those Bantu who have come under Hamitic influence, of whom the chief representatives are the Wagogo, beside numerous smaller tribes further northward, such as the independent Wadchagga at the Kilimanjaro, the tributary Wapokomo on the Tana, etc. The northern races of the Wanyamwesi are originally related to the Wagogo, and the latter have linguistic affinities to the

Bantu Peoples of the East

Bantu people of the Wahuma states, so that a general connection can be made among them, enabling us to draw several conclusions as to their early history. In more recent times Usambara and the district on the Kilimanjaro have been of special historical importance. About halfway through the nineteenth century Usambara was in a comparatively well-ordered condition, under a king named Kmeri. He resided in Wuga, and was the fourth of his dynasty, possessing for the moment only a part of Usambara, until Bondei and also a piece of Wadigo-land, inland from Mombasa, were added by conquest. Useguha, the coast dwellers of which were provided with guns, broke away. His family appear to have been of Arab origin, or at least to have received a large infusion of Arab blood; legend speaks of their immigration from Nguru, or Dshagga. After Kmeri's death, in 1867, the power of the little state declined very rapidly. Simbodja, Kmeri's successor, who resided in Wasinda and ultimately became involved in a quarrel with the Germans, even lost Bondei, where another chief of the Wakilindi family, Kibanga, made himself independent. The historical importance of Usambara may be easily explained by the natural characteristics of the country. A fruitful mountainous district gives protection and security to a strong government until its influence is automatically extended over the surrounding plains, and a state arises with tolerably strong powers of resistance. In this way the power of the races about Kilimanjaro, and especially that of the Wadchagga in the surrounding districts, became noticeable. But the scanty numbers and the disunion of these mountain tribes have invariably hindered the formation of a greater kingdom.

Every district in North-east Africa, inhabited by Bantu tribes, with the possible exception of the little states about Kilimanjaro, has been subjected to the disintegrating and destructive influence of Hamitic races, who advanced from the north. Unyamwesi was one of those East African districts which are so far distant from the coast that the influences of trade

exercised a beneficent rather than a disturbing influence. The same is true to a far greater extent of the lake district, which is surpassed by few parts of the continent in the advantages of its situation. Protected by the lakes, rivers, and steep mountain ranges, without being utterly cut off from communication with the outer world, the several states were here in possession of a fruitful and well-watered soil, and could develop a true negro civilisation. Africa can show but few parallels to the firmness of their structure and external power. Bantu peoples founded these kingdoms in antiquity, and still form the main stock of the population, though they have certainly been greatly changed by intermarriage with other negro races. They have been the real founders of the local civilisation ; not only do they till the soil, but they also manufacture those tasteful objects which have been praised by all European visitors to the country. The civilisation of the coast has touched more lightly upon the lake district than upon Unyamwesi, where cotton is planted and woven. In the Wahuma states, as they are generally called collectively, the older art of making cloth from the bark of trees has been brought to unusual perfection.

We know nothing of the political condition of the lake district in that earlier period when the Bantu were at the same time the rulers and the owners of the land ; but it is highly probable that there was a settled constitution even then. This constitution did not take its present form until immigrants of Hamitic blood came into the land from the north-east. These immigrants are the Wahuma. The rulers of Uganda were probably not of Wahuma race, but were in any case of Hamitic origin, and must therefore have entered the country from the north-east, as the eastern

THE DEATH OF BISHOP HANNINGTON IN UGANDA

After the appearance of Europeans and Arabs in Uganda, the conflict of foreign ideas provoked great confusion, and both Christians and Mohammedans were persecuted, King Mwanga even ordering the murder of Bishop Hannington.

side is protected by the Victoria Nyanza. The date of the invasion is very uncertain; but on the whole the probabilities are that it took place about the fifteenth century. The Wahuma not only spread over the lake district, they also penetrated into Unyamwesi on the north, where they led a nomadic life in separate groups under the name of Watussi. Their fair complexion and the tradition of their origin mark their connection with the Galla and the other Hamitic peoples of North-east Africa. In Unyoro Emin Pasha heard the following story: Unyoro, together with Uganda, Ussoga, Udda, and Karagwe once formed a large territory, inhabited by the Witshwesi, a black agricultural race. Then many fair people came out of the north who were cannibals. When they crossed the Nile, the Witshwesi fled westward. At Matjum, south-east of Mruli, the invaders, the Wawitu—people of Witu, the "land of the princes" lying in the east — divided into two groups, one of which advanced to Uganda, the other to Unyoro. The remnant of the Witshwesi, who named their oppressors Wahuma, literally Northmen—in Uganda they were also known as Walindi, in Karagwe as Wahinda—went about the country as minstrels or magicians, or were reduced to slavery. From that time the name Witshwesi has been synonymous for serf in Unyoro. The Wahuma now intermarried closely with the Bantu peoples, as is related in their own extraordinary tradition communicated to Speke by King Kamrasi: "Formerly our race was half white and half black, with straight hair on one side and curly on the other." Whether the word Wawitu is to be referred to the country of Witu or to the old name for Mombasa, Omwita, is extremely doubtful. Philological arguments will not help us here, as the Wahuma have adopted the language of the subject Bantu in nearly every case. The Wahuma seem to have founded a kingdom which was at first more or less self-contained, the kingdom of Kitara; it extended southward to the Kagera, its centre of gravity lying in the later Unyoro. Internal dissensions led to the despatch southward of further expeditions, and to the foundation of new

Invasion of the Fair Peoples

Half White and Half Black

states. Of these Ihangiro seems to have been the first; afterwards, twenty generations ago, a Wahuma chief Ruhinda is said to have fled to the country of Wanyambo, situated to the south of Kagera; there he won over the favour of the King, Nono, treacherously murdered him and seized the power.

Such was the origin of the kingdom of Karagwe, which was more or less dependent upon Uganda in later times. Later, however, we find princes of the Ruhinda family in Ihangiro and Ussuwi, or Ussui; for a time the whole group of states formed one kingdom under the name of Ukanga, Ushirombo being also included. Uha was also a powerful and extensive state for some time, and formed the southernmost outpost of the Wahuma power on the north-east coast of Lake Tanganyika. Upon the disruption of this kingdom the power of the Wahuma collapsed utterly in the south, though it was maintained in Karagwe and Ihangiro. When the first Europeans, Speke and Grant, arrived at Karagwe at the beginning of the 'sixties, the benevolent Rumanika was in power. After his death there were disputes about the succession. The country is now within the sphere of German interests. The history of the south-western Wahuma state Ruanda is uncertain. It cannot be determined whether it originally belonged to Kitara or whether it was connected with Ukanga; the only certain fact is that the supremacy of the Wahuma, who were here known as Wasamboni, was established over the Wavira, and that the power of the kingdom in course of time has rather increased than diminished. The population of Kissakka is dependent upon Ruanda.

Speke and Grant in Wahuma

The seat of the highest Wahuma civilisation is in the north; here are situated the districts of Uganda and Unyoro, which developed into independent, closely organised states from the earlier kingdom of Kitara.

The early history of Uganda is wholly legendary. Kintu, the first king, marched from the north into the uninhabited lake district, peopled it with his descendants and the produce of the cattle which he had brought with him, and ruled as patriarch over the land. When his people plunged into all kinds of depravity he mysteriously disappeared, and was succeeded by his son, Tchwa. Of the following kings the fourth, Kimera, stands out more clearly in the mist of legend. He is depicted as a man of superhuman size and strength, and passionately devoted to hunting; but we are also told that it was he who emigrated from Unyoro and founded an independent kingdom in Uganda, after subjugating the native Wiru or Waddu. Kitara appears to have collapsed about that period.

Several kings followed Kimera, of whom legend has but little to relate. Nakivingi, the tenth king, is the first personality of any importance; he is said to have conquered and subjugated Unyoro, so that the northern province of the old Kitara kingdom was again unified for a short period. The legendary winged warrior Kibaga is said to have been very useful to him during this struggle. Of a long succession of rulers who followed we know practically nothing. Then followed the conquest of Usoga, under the twenty-seventh king Tchabagu, whose reign dates back probably not more than a century. After two more unimportant rulers, Djundju Yunya and Wasedje, Kamanya ascended the throne, the grandfather of Mtesa, the first king visited by Europeans. We have the most divergent accounts of his struggles with the Wakidi in Usoga. These Wakidi are related to the Galla, and are therefore a Hamitic people; the manner of their attacks shows that they had the same wandering tendencies as the Wahuma formerly displayed. The king seems to have repelled the incursions of this race, and to have finally reduced them to subjection.

Under Sunna II., the successor to Kamanya, new influences were brought to bear upon the country by the Arab traders who made their way from the coast to Uganda. Sunna was born abut 1820, came to the throne in 1836, and

THE YOUNG KING OF UGANDA
Daudi Chwa, who came to the throne in 1903.

died in 1860. He was a typical example of the despotic Uganda prince, careless of human life, ever ready to make war and inclined to cruelty, but benevolent and hospitable to strangers. Under his rule the power of the kingdom greatly increased. Ihangiro was conquered, the ruler of Unyoro was humbled, and the ruler of Ruanda beaten. A powerful fleet terrorised Victoria Lake, and even the warlike population of the island of Uvuma was forced to submit. The most formidable sea-fight took place when Usoga revolted and Sunna advanced to reconquer the country with 500 large ships, after the Wasoga had retired before his land forces to one of the islands of the lake and had mustered a fleet of equal strength. The rebels were blockaded in their island, were ultimately forced to surrender, and were partly massacred in the most ruthless manner. Many marauding expeditions were also made by the chiefs of the frontier provinces, who were constantly seeking to aggrandise themselves at the expense of their neighbours.

Sunna had named the prince Kadjumba as his successor; however, after his death, the chiefs elected Mtesa, who appeared to be of milder character than his tyrannical brother. They soon discovered that they had made a terrible mistake. There were certain elements of greatness in Mtesa's character, but many more repulsive features, which became very apparent in the first years of the government to which he had been elected with too little consideration. After a great victory over the Wasoga, he named himself Mkavya (he who causes weeping). He was capricious and cruel; at times he seemed inspired with the lust for slaughter, though at the same time he was by no means incapable of appreciating the higher civilisation of Arabs and Europeans. Shortly after his accession the first Europeans, Speke and

Grant, entered his capital of Banda—afterwards Rubaga and Nebula-galla were Mtesa's residences—which had already been visited by Arab merchants ; they obtained an excellent reception. The different ideas of these foreign visitors soon came into conflict, and wrought endless confusion in Uganda. At first Arab influence was predominant : as early as 1862 Mtesa adopted the Arab costume instead of the native Mbugu, began to read the Koran, and allowed some part of his people to embrace the Mohammedan faith. Then Christian missionaries came into the country, at first Protestants in 1877, followed by the Catholics in 1879. Both persuasions found ready acceptance, in spite of the capricious cruelty of Mtesa. who at one time executed a number of Mohammedans, and at another instituted a regular persecution of the Christians (1881 and 1883), without himself deciding in favour of either of the new beliefs.

Religious Confusion in Uganda

Mtesa died in October, 1884. His son Mwanga, who succeeded him, at first showed no special favour to either of the new religions, and followed the example of his father's capricious and bloodthirsty behaviour. Under his persecutions Christians and Mohammedans suffered alike, and he even ordered the murder of a European, Bishop Hannington, in October, 1885. At length Mwanga formed the wild project of massacring his bodyguard, which was composed of Christians and Mohammedans ; a general insurrection then broke out, and he was forced to flee to the south. This movement was, however, only the prelude to further disturbance. The adherents of the Bible and the Koran divided the land peacefully between themselves, and elected Mwanga's brother Kiwewa as king. A war then broke out, which ended in the victory of Islam ; some of the Christian chiefs were slain, others fled with the missionaries to the frontier lands in the south. As the king Kiwewa had not shown sufficient consideration toward the Arabs, he was replaced by Karema, another of Mwanga's brothers, who now made public profession of Islam. Meanwhile Mwanga, who had been in exile at Bukumbi, had been won over to Christianity by the French missionaries, who had given him a hospitable reception. With the help of the Christian party he succeeded in establishing himself on the

Murder of Bishop Hannington

island of Shassa, and after several failures at length defeated Karema in a decisive battle. On October 11th, 1889, he re-entered his capital of Mengo, most of the Arabs taking refuge in Unyoro.

But even now the land was not at peace. The points of dispute existing between the Protestants and Catholics resulted in an open breach, and the exasperation was increased by British attempts to gain a footing in Uganda. Eventually the country was divided among the adherents of the several religions, the Protestants receiving four-sixths, and the Catholics and Mohammedans one-sixth each. Since 1890 the much devastated and depopulated Uganda has been entirely under British influence.

There is but little to be said of the history of Unyoro, except in so far as it comes into connection with the other Wahuma states. Unyoro was undoubtedly the earliest home of the Wahuma and the centre from which they afterward spread ; but it was not the centre of the civilisation of the states in the lake district, for the original civilisation of that region belonged to the earlier Bantu inhabitants and not to the Wahuma. The marauding armies of the country are the curse of the surrounding districts. The unusual force of these nomadic instincts may be partially explained by the fact that Unyoro received a later immigration from the north-east at a comparatively late period ; at any rate, according to Emin Pasha, the Wawitu, who are now in possession, did not enter the country before 1800 ; they have readily coalesced with the cognate Wahuma or Wahinda probably the original name of the people.

Marauders of Unyoro

South of Unyoro, and east and south-east of Lake Albert Edward lie two other smaller Wahuma states, Nkole, or Ankore, of which the capital is Katwe, and Mpororo, which have only recently been discovered. Here also we meet with the tradition that Wahuma, or Wassamwo, invaded the country from the north and subjugated the original inhabitants. In Nkole the predecessor of Ntali, the present ruler, was called Mutambuka. Under the king Rokay, Mpororo had risen to considerable power, but has decayed greatly under his daughter and successor Nyawingi, and is now hard pressed by the inhabitants of Nkole.

THE TRIBES OF THE CENTRE AND WEST

IN the Upper Zambesi region the most important race is that of the Barotse, who display many characteristics denoting their close relationship to those peoples who founded states in the south of the Congo basin and on the West Coast, which borders that district. The Barotse, extending along both banks of the Zambesi inhabit the central part of the kingdom ; they suffered some temporary humiliation at the hands of the Makololo, but soon regained their position as the dominant race among the other inhabitants of the kingdom. The smaller tribes were considered by the Barotse as their slaves. But in 1870-1890, when Holub and Selous visited them, the Barotse were themselves living under an absolutely despotic government. This state of affairs cannot have been of long duration ; the existence of a small and of a great council shows that the institutions characteristic of Africa have been handed down from **Barotse** antiquity in this case also— **Councils** institutions which are powerless **of State** against a strong ruler, but speedily grow beyond the control of a weak monarch. The very different manner in which the civilisation of the several tribes has developed induces the conjecture that the kingdom did not always cover the area which it now occupies.

Much more strongly marked in the states of Central South Africa than in the other kingdoms of the Dark Continent is the peculiar fact that they are surrounded by boundary zones and not by sharply defined frontier lines. The power of the state is at its strongest in the centre and declines in proportion as the frontiers are approached. The tribes living nearest to the dominant race may be nothing more than slaves, while those at a greater distance merely pay tribute and are generally inclined to shake off the yoke upon any signs of weakness in the supreme power. Hence it is impossible to say how far the influence of the old Barotse kingdom extended previous to its temporary conquest by the Makololo Kaffirs.

The Makololo belong to the western group of Kaffirs, the east Bechuanas, the remnants of which now bear the general name " Basuto." Until the year 1820 they lived in the eastern part of what is now the Orange River Colony. It was about this time that Moselikatse came upon the scene with his Matabele. **The** This event, and a defeat which **Basuto** they suffered in 1823, together **Kaffirs** with the Mantati—a branch of the Batlokua who belonged to the north-eastern Bechuanas — near Lithaku, at the hands of the Griqua under Andries Waterboer, forced the Makololo to abandon their old settlements in 1824 and to migrate northward. The Bangwaketse, whose chief village was Makabe, first of all made a fruitless attempt at opposition ; then the Makololo found an opportunity of interfering in the internal dissensions of the Bakwena, one of the most powerful of the Bechuana races ; they raised to the rulership of the people, Setshele, the son of a chief who had been overthrown by his subjects.

The Makololo chief at this period was Sebituane, a born leader of men, and one of the strongest and most attractive personalities of whom we hear in the whole history of Africa. According to Livingstone he was accustomed to lead his troops into battle in person, unlike Moselikatse, Dingan, and other generals. Setshele's support enabled the Makololo to settle in the neighbourhood of the Bakwena. But a quarrel with the Boers obliged them to retreat northward. The **A South** history of Sebituane's advance **African** into Northern Bechuanaland is **Odyssey** an Odyssey of battles, privations, and sudden changes of fortune. Harassed by the advancing Matabele, he turned westward to the district of the Herero, and then again eastward to the Zambesi. Menaced by the treachery of the island Batoka, he nevertheless succeeded in crossing the river and defeated his enemies in the neighbourhood of the Victoria Falls ;

the capture of countless herds of cattle enabled his people to resume their pastoral life in the rich pastures of the district. Sebituane was then able to turn his attention to the organisation and extension of the kingdom, which he ruled in his "capitals" of Seseke on the Zambesi and Linyanti on the Chobe,

Death of Africa's Finest Ruler the north-east point of the modern German South-west Africa. Sebituane died in 1851. He was succeeded by his daughter Mamotshisane and his son Seketetu, who reigned until about 1856. Upon the extinction of the Makololo the Barotse people again became predominant in the kingdom, while at the same time the Mambunda people became an influential power. At this period a new native family gained possession of the throne, which prided itself upon the pure Makololo blood in its veins, although it was founded by Letshulatebe, the conqueror of the last of the Makololo. He had originally resided at Lesotsilebe, east of Lake Ngami. Of these princes Sepopo, who removed his capital from the Barotse towards the Masupia district, became notorious for his cruelty. He succeeded in placing himself upon the throne of the Mambunda kingdom, which was governed by a dynasty related to his own and reverted to one of his daughters upon the death of the last queen. He thus completely unified the Barotse-Mambunda kingdom. He was murdered in 1876, and his kingdom fell into confusion.

His successor, Nwana-Wana, destroyed such slight independence as had been left to the kingdom of Mambunda by forcing the queen to resign the throne in her own name and that of her descendants. However, he speedily fell from his position, owing to the discovery of a plan which he had conceived for the murder of the most important chiefs. In his stead

Barotse Under Lewanika Leboshe was elected king, much against his own desire. However, the struggle with Nwana-Wana ended in the defeat and death of the latter. The peace policy which Leboshe inaugurated was not to the liking of his people, who had been demoralised by revolts and battles. After the murder of Leboshe, about 1880, Lewanika waged war in the north-east, in 1882, against the Mashikulumbwe, from whom he took 40,000 cattle, though

his subjugation of this people was not really complete. In the year 1884 disturbances again broke out; the king was driven into exile with his more vigorous sister and co-regent, and Waga-Funa temporarily ascended the throne. In 1886 Lewanika made a successful return, but stained his victory by ingratitude and cruelty. He afterwards maintained his position upon the throne in spite of neighbouring British, Portuguese, and Belgian influences.

To the north-west of the Barotse kingdom, from which it is divided by a stretch of independent territory, lies the second great political state of Central Africa, the kingdom of Lunda, more generally known as the kingdom of the Muata Yamwo. Here, again, there are no permanent or sharply defined boundaries. The central part of the kingdom lies on the Upper Kassai and the rivers flowing parallel to it in a northerly direction. On the west the influence of the king extends nearly to the Kwango, on the south to the watershed between the Congo and the Zambesi; on the north and east the boundary lines

Character of the Kingdom of Lunda vary even during the short period over which our accurate knowledge of the Lunda kingdom extends. The Kalunda are the dominant race, a pure negro people speaking a Bantu language. Their civilisation is certainly poorer than that of the Barotse-Mambunda kingdom. It is very remarkable that neither the palm-fibre cloth of the true Congo valley nor the cotton fabrics of the Zambesi district are produced here; nor has the art of iron-working attained any high development. Agriculture is assiduously practised, while cattle-breeding is somewhat neglected.

The political institutions of the country are of the highest importance for its history. In Lunda we also find the king, here known as Muata Yamwo, at the head of the state, with absolutely unlimited powers, surrounded by a body of councillors whose influence varies according to the character of the ruler. Moreover, we find the country separated into a number of small districts, which are divided among individual chieftains, who govern them quite after the manner of the feudal system. These chieftains enjoy complete independence as regards the internal administration of their districts so long as the monarch chooses to refrain from interference, but are obliged to pay tribute and provide contingents of troops for the army. Naturally, most of these small districts have not been made by a process of arbitrary division, but are of historical origin, and thus have an additional stimulus to cling to their independence; the result being that, as in the Barotse kingdom, the outlying portions are kept to their allegiance solely by the exertions of the ruler for the time being, while the extent and power of the kingdom is continually changing.

A very remarkable feature in the constitution of the state, and one that doubtless goes back to some older type, is the queen-consort, the Lukokesha. This female ruler is not the king's wife, but is a member of the royal house, possessing her own court and her own income, and the power of deciding the election of a new Muata Yamwo. She is allowed to marry, but her husbands are officially known as " wives," and, generally speaking, have no influence. Thus in the Lunda kingdom the government has two heads in existence, which are neither mutually exclusive nor in mutual hostility.

Such a state of affairs cannot but be the outcome of previous historical development. In this case we probably have before us the remnant of a matriarchal system of government. At a certain stage of tribal development kinship is recognised through the females, not through the males; and consequently the mother, not the father, becomes of primary authority. Hence arises a female sovereignty. In spite of its inevitable replacement in course of time by a male sovereignty, similar instances remain of its formal survival. In the case of Lunda, tradition declares that the present system had its origin when a Lunda princess married an immigrant prince, and associated him with herself in the rulership. The existence of the Lunda kingdom was known upon the coast as **Governed by Women** early as the end of the sixteenth century, from the slaves who brought descriptions of it from the interior. Very little, however is known of the internal history of the country, although Portuguese traders must have penetrated to Lunda at an early period.

The extent of the kingdom varied under different rulers, as also did the position of the capital, Mussumba (great encampment). Its site was altered with every **An Ever-changing Capital** change in the succession, though it was never removed beyond the fruitful plain lying between the Kalangi and Luisa, tributaries of the Lulua. A short time ago (1896–1897) it was situated on the left bank of the Luele. The burial-place of the royal dynasty is Nsai, on the Kallanji.

Although, generally speaking, the Lunda kingdom is but little troubled by foreign enemies, this advantage is somewhat discounted by the slow growth of an element of danger within the state, which will produce a complete revolution of affairs unless disturbed by European interference. To the south-west of the Lunda kingdom is the race of the Kioko, which has lived in a forest district from an early period, and forms a contrast to the plain-dwelling people of the Kalunda. The Kioko show a preference for settlements in the forest, are excellent hunters, collect indiarubber, keep bees, but also understand the art of agriculture and have strongly marked inclinations for trade; this latter tendency has been the reason of their slow but continuous migration northward. The true home of the Kioko is tributary to the

LEWANIKA
The king of the Barotse, who has retained his independence in spite of neighbouring European influences.

Muata Yamwo, and is divided into numerous departments. But for a long period this restless people has been advancing upon its original habitat in two main streams, one on the Kuillu and Loange, the other northward on the Luatshim; everywhere they are outstripping the Kalunda by their industry. About 1860 they had not passed beyond the tenth degree of latitude south; in 1880 they were found upon the seventh degree. The Kalunda eyed them suspiciously, and hinted boastfully of a war to wipe out the unwelcome intruders; but the Kioko had even then become necessary to them for their trading habits and their industrious pursuit of agriculture and metal-work. Moreover, manners and customs were so rapidly exchanged at every point of contact between the two races that any sharp lines of demarcation disappeared rapidly. In the event of war between the Kioko and the Kalunda, the former would probably become the dominant race ; at any rate, a new independent state would be formed in the west of the Lunda kingdom, which is even now upon the point of severance.

In addition to the land of the Kioko, the Muata Yamwo possess a number of districts, some of which are loosely con-

Kingdom of Kasembe nected with Lunda, and at times break away from it entirely. By far the most important of these is the kingdom of the Kasembe, the capital of which lies between the Lakes Mweru and Bangweolo and changes its situation almost as frequently as the capital of the Lunda kingdom. In other respects also the country is a counterpart of Lunda, except that it is not governed by a Lukokesha. There is no permanent connection between the kingdom of the Muata Yamwo and that of Kasembe ; the power of the latter has diminished greatly within recent times, and the connection between the two states appears to have been maintained not so much by fear of the military power of Lunda as by other influences, perhaps of a superstitious nature. At any rate, when Kasembe resumed the payment of tribute—copper, slaves, and salt—to Lunda in the year 1875, this action is said to have been taken upon the advice of the court magician, who referred several unfortunate occurrences to the interruption of this traditional homage. The Muata Yamwo were considered by many of their neighbours as endowed with special magical powers which made them invincible.

The Kasembe power dwindled more rapidly after the immigration of Msiri ; his tribe came from Unyamwesi, and rose to supreme power in Katanga, or properly Garenganja, of which the capital is Mukurru, Bunkea, or Kimpatu, a district further to the west between the Luapula on the east and the Lualaba in

Tribute to the Magician the west on the Lusira. About the middle of the year 1880 Msiri possessed from two to three thousand warriors armed with flint-lock guns, and perhaps three times as many archers ; but they paid tribute to the magical Muata Yamwo. Msiri's trading caravans went as far as Benguela, and at the same time he maintained commercial relations with the east coast. In December, 1891, he was shot in an affair with the Belgian captain Bodson.

The kingdom of Kasongo in Urua is tributary to the Muata Yamwo. Here again the ruler demands and receives a superstitious veneration. The founder of the kingdom, Kungwe a Banza, is considered as the most powerful deity and invariably receives a sister of the ruling chieftain to wife. Further, the Kasongo, in their own opinion, are related to the Muata Yamwo. But in the last decade of the nineteenth century this district has shown clear evidence of the wide disruption caused by the collapse of the once flourishing negro states of Central Africa, a disaster due to the far-reaching operation of the Belgian Congo State.

When we leave the kingdom of the Muata Yamwo and turn northward to the mighty valley of the Congo, we reach the most mysterious and unexplored district of Central Africa. Even from an ethnographical point of view it has a uniformity and a character of its own, though nowhere does any sharp line of demarcation separate it from the outer world. It belongs wholly to the district of the Bantu languages, and possesses a population

Most Mysterious District purely negro, with the exception of the dwarf peoples in the forest depths. In the Congo valley the right-angled type of hut with ridged roof takes the place of the round beehive shape and its varieties. The huts are not placed in a circle or in disorderly confusion, but in long, straight streets. But this style of building is also found on the negro west coast, which belongs only in part to the Bantu-speaking region. Moreover, a remarkable similarity exists between many of the examples of ironwork produced in the two districts. The work of the Congo valley has a fairly uniform style of its own. Knives, spearheads, etc., are broad, stumpy, and severely symmetrical. Many knives from the west coast show the same style of workmanship.

On the other hand, the west coast has no knowledge of the Congo valley palm fibre and grass fabrics which are to be found in scattered districts of East Africa and especially in Malay Madagascar. Possibly we have here the traces of an advance from east to west of a civilisation of which the most deeply rooted remnants must be sought in Indonesia.

Cannibalism is found prevailing under the most varied forms in the Central Congo valley. Endocannibalism and exocannibalism are alike practised—that is, some races eat their own dead, others their defeated enemies. Some eat both.

The Congo valley is connected with West Africa not only by the practice of cannibalism, but also by the custom of skull worship. The whole group of ideas attaching to this subject is not nearly so developed in Africa as in Indonesia, where head-hunting is an "authorised peculiarity" among many island races, and is pursued with true fanatical enthusiasm. None the less, many survivals of the custom are to be found in Congoland. On the west coast it has greatly developed in certain places, and recalls the typical Malay usage.

Many isolated features thus show the Congo valley as the most untrodden and secluded part of Africa—as being, in a sense, a world apart. Yet this isolation has not prevented the general distribution of the American garden plants—maize, manioc, and tobacco, which were introduced by Europeans—and also of the Indian hemp, a narcotic well known in the most central part of the Congo valley.

The Untrodden Congo The knowledge of iron smelting and forging may have been carried over the continent in a similar manner at some earlier period, and certain domestic animals may have found a new home among the races of the interior. The extent to which the land had been opened up by trade in earlier centuries is indicated by the ancient European glass beads in the possession of many Congo tribes, who are now unable to give any account of the source whence these treasures came. Still more notable is the information given by the curious swords of Congoland. Their cutting edge lies upon the inner curve, and in their broad, flat points they conform to the laws of style observed in the ironwork of the Congo. But on a closer examination the type it appears already strangely familiar; it is in fact the same crooked weapon which we find in Arabia, India, and Abyssinia, but has been altered and modified upon its inclusion within the armoury of the Congo races. Its shape, even to-day is evidence of that stream of civilisation which brought it from the north-east coast into the interior.

Another piece of early African history is revealed to us by an examination of the distribution of the throwing knife. This remarkable weapon is found among the heathen races of the Central Sudan in a characteristic and fairly simple form, and was most probably at one time in use throughout this district. In Bornu at the present time those troops which are armed with the throwing knife form a contingent enjoying special privileges; in Darfur the sultan possesses a number of these weapons, which his **History of the Throwing Knife** people no longer use. The Teda in the Sahara show a preference for them to the present day. The weapon is a product of pure Sudanese civilisation anterior to the Mohammedan period; it has passed southward, changing its shape in the most marvellously varied manner. During earlier and later times we can trace its movements, which are partly confirmed by other evidence, and which show us that the southern portion of the Central Sudan has been a point of departure for many important racial movements. The Fan carried the throwing knife westward to the Gabun coast. On the east the Niam-Niam brought it to the neighbourhood of the Upper Nile valley. An isolated example on the Upper Blue Nile shows the probability of earlier and even more extensive migrations. Finally, in the Sudan it was brought to the Ubangi, downward as far as the Congo, and was further distributed along the banks of this great river. Here, then, we have traces of a migration into the Congo valley from the north. On the other hand, there is a tradition among the Bateke on Stanley Pool that the ancient home of their race was in the north-west, in the highlands of the Ogowe. This, together with many other indications, points to the fact that the pressure exerted by the negro advance from the Sudan brought about migration into the Congo valley from Adamawa also.

Beside the immigration from the north there is a very remarkable movement from the south-east, and of this the **Remarkable Baluba Migration** Bashilange at least have preserved a trustworthy tradition. This people dwells on the Lower Lulua between the Central Kassai and Sankuru—that is to say, on the northern frontier of the Lunda kingdom. In reality they are a mixed people composed of an earlier peaceful settled race and the warlike Baluba, who came in from the south-east. Whether this migration was connected with the great racial movements in Africa during the sixteenth and seventeenth centuries must remain an undecided question in default of any trustworthy evidence. It is probable that there was some connection between Kalunda and Baluba ; one of the leaders of the Baluba migration, Kapuku-Muluba —the other two were called Katana and Kanyoka—was, according to the legend,

Religion of Hemp Worship a son of that chief Kasongo who lived in the east, and from whom the tribe of the Muata Yamwo is descended. Their possession of the characteristic Kaffir shield and many other special features invited the conjecture that the Baluba and also the Babunda were a mixed Kaffir race, or, at any rate, under Kaffir influence. East of the Bashilange district as far as Lake Tanganyika are situated pure, unmixed Baluba, differing in many respects from the Bashilange.

Intellectually the Bashilange are better developed than the average negro type ; they are readier to learn and are less inclined to blind superstition, though singularly imitative. Among them there has been developed a very peculiar religion, of most inexplicable origin.

The central point of this new religion is hemp worship, and its beginning therefore probably goes back to the time when the custom of hemp-smoking spread from the east coast to the interior of the Congo valley. The adoration and veneration of a narcotic or stupefying drug, and the growth of a conventional worship round such a centre, is a peculiarity by no means exclusively confined to the Bashilange. In the Soma offerings of the Indian Aryans, in the reverence with which tobacco is regarded by many Indian tribes, we have a similar class of phenomena. At first small groups and societies of hemp-smokers appear to have been formed, who not only formed a close bond of friendship with one another but enlisted new members with passionate zeal, until they

A State of Hemp Smokers attained a preponderating power. In this way friendly relations within the state were maintained and strengthened. The hemp-smokers promulgated decrees of a mildness wholly exceptional in Africa. Their manifestations of friendship were not confined to the members of their society, but were also extended to foreigners —not always to their own advantage. The keen, industrious Kioko took advantage of the inexperience of the Bashilange

to plunder them in every possible way. They sold into slavery whole trading caravans which had entered the Kioko territory in unsuspicious confidence. They themselves brought powder and guns to the Bashilange, and thus enabled individual chieftains to increase their influence. When Pogge and Wissmann, the first Europeans to visit the land of the hemp-smokers, entered the country, they found two rival chieftains in predominance, Kalamba and Tshingenge. Meta, a sister of Kalamba, occupied a position analogous to that of the Lukokesha in the Lunda kingdom.

In recent times the raids of the Arabs and their native allies, especially the notorious chieftain Zefu bin Mohammed, or Zappu-Zapp, the son of Hammed ben Mohammed, or Tippu-Tibb, have thrown the Eastern Congo valley into total confusion, depopulated entire districts, and shattered the civilisation of the interior. There were, however, migratory movements in constant progress at an earlier period. The inhabitants of Uregga on the south still preserve a definite tradition of

East Congo Civilisation Shattered their immigration from the north to their present settlements towards the end of the eighteenth century. In the Arab wars the tribe of the Manyema adopted the profession of raiders, and not only provided the Arabs with their most valuable auxiliary troops, but entered the business of slave-catching on their own account. Consequently, other races, such as the Bassonge, to the east of the Bashilange, were broken up and partly destroyed. At the expense of the civilisation and culture of wide districts, those Arab settlements have been formed which on a cursory glance appear to be the starting-points of a new and higher manner of life. European interference betokens all the introduction of further change, and change, let us hope, of a more beneficial nature.

In the central part of the Congo valley the peoples settle most thickly upon the river, which exercises a power of attraction like that of the ocean. It affords an abundant supply of fish, easy communication between the settlements, and, in case of hostile attacks, a secure refuge in the thickets on its banks, in the islands, and the opposite shores. The same remarks apply on a smaller scale to the navigable tributaries of the Congo, which in some cases have set a limit to the marauders' raids, and are consequently thickly populated on one bank, the other being barren and deserted. The tendency to advance towards the stream, the shocks of great racial movements transmitted from the outer world, are impulses felt even by the inhabitants of the most central part of Africa. But there is no general connection in these migrations; none of those huge and rapidly constructed states could be formed here as they were in other parts of Africa. The boundless forests, the numerous broad streams, are so many obstacles in the way of any impetuous advance; on the river itself, intercommunication, the first great incentive to the peaceful formation of states, never attained any high stage of development.

now become the trade language for the district above the falls. European influence early made itself felt in the lower part of the Central Congo, with the result that the river banks in this district became in **Yearning** a measure a zone of attrac- **for** tion for unsettled tribes. The **the Sea** yearning for the sea seems to have been equally prevalent among the races about the lower falls. The kings of Loango were in constant warfare with the Anzig; the coincidence of sound in the names Anzig and Banyansi is probably wholly fortuitous, for the latter are more properly called Babangi, and gained the name by which they are now known, which means "fleas," from the parasitic manner in which they gained their livelihood

SÃO SALVADOR, THE CAPITAL OF THE NATIVE KINGDOM OF CONGO, ABOUT 1670
In the 16th century the Portuguese entered the great kingdom of the Congo and induced the rulers to embrace Christianity, Portuguese customs also being adopted and the name of the capital being changed to São Salvador.

Stanley alone was able with the help of European weapons to fight his way through the fierce cannibal tribes. To the natives the inviting waterway is a closed path beyond the boundaries of their own tribes.

These conditions have certainly undergone a fundamental change since the arrival of Europeans. In particular, the small fishing tribes who lived on the islands **Opening** and banks of the river have **the Congo** extended their journeys, and **to Traffic** in some cases have become enterprising traders, founding colonies among other tribes. In the lower reaches of the river beginnings had been made in this direction at an earlier period. The Bayansi especially have become a typical trading people. Their dialect has

In the forest districts, and especially among the negro races who have inhabited their settlements for a long period, an important ethnical transposition has been brought to pass. These negroes could not fail to come into contact with the dwarf peoples, and, finally, perhaps after long struggles, they arrived at a common modus vivendi which was bound to have its effect upon each race. Such a community of existence must have resulted in course of time in a more or less extensive fusion of races which led here and there to the formation of actual mixed tribes. We have already mentioned the Bashilange, who had probably received a strong infusion of pygmy blood; but the most numerous settlements of this mixed race are to be found in the forests of the Upper Aruwimi—that is, near the smaller lakes at the sources of the Nile, where the ancients laid the scene of the war between the pygmies and the cranes. From a purely philological point of view, the west coast tribes form a special group of Bantus. Physically, they give the impression of a very mixed race, united only by the tie of language.

State of Loango

A large number of petty states originally existed upon the coast of Loango, until a prince belonging to Zerri in Kacongo subjugated the larger portion of these states and made Loango his capital. The town is said to have had a population of 15,000. In the south, Kacongo, or Maïimba, and Ngoyo, or Kabinda, maintained their independence in certain respects; but the other parts of the country were in no very close connection with their suzerain. The power of the rulers varied with the prestige which they were able to maintain, and a strongly centralised organisation was rather the exception than the rule. At some period in the last part of the sixteenth century, at any rate before 1648, the date of the arrival of the Portuguese, Loango is said to have been a province of Congo, though we have no certain information as to the nature of the relationship. The influence of the Portuguese and of Christianity did not make itself felt until a comparatively late period. The king of Loango was certainly converted about the middle of the seventeenth century by a zealous missionary; but as both missionary and convert died shortly afterward, no permanent result was effected. It was not until the year 1766 that missionaries again entered the country. On this occasion they were a French party, and settled in Kacongo.

Meanwhile, the kingdom of Loango was entirely overshadowed by its powerful and prosperous neighbour, Congo. For a time, indeed, it appeared as if Congo was to be a Christian state, and to become the starting-point whence Christianity and European civilisation were not so much to conquer as to overspread the Dark Continent. But it became apparent only too quickly that the seed which had so rapidly sprung up could bring forth no fruit; it was in turn choked and destroyed by the growth of native weeds.

When Diego Cao, with Martin Behaim, anchored in the mouth of the Congo in 1484, he found the country south of the river to a point nearly reaching Angola under the supremacy of one prince, the Mani-Congo, whose capital was at Ambasse, in the interior of the coastland.

Mansell

NATIVE CARVINGS OF LOANGO
Beautiful ivory carvings showing traces of the influence of the Portuguese who entered Loango in the 17th century.

The Portuguese at once perceived that if they could gain over this ruler to their side, and succeed in converting him to Christianity, they would be able rapidly to extend their influence over a considerable part of the country. They took some of the Congo inhabitants back to Lisbon, and in 1490 sent a formal embassy to Ambasse, obtaining permission to build a Christian church. Certain special causes made the success of the embassy even more brilliant, and led to the complete conversion of the king and of his people. One of these causes was to be found in the state of political affairs within the Congo kingdom. It was a kingdom characterised by a lack of solidarity. Beside the central portion, whence it took its name, there were other provinces governed according to the invariable negro custom by their own semi-independent princes. Any temporary weakness on the part of the overlord enabled the provinces to acquire a further measure

BANZA LOVANGIRI, THE CAPITAL OF THE KINGDOM OF LOANGO, ABOUT 1670

About the beginning of the 16th century, a native prince subjugated a large number of the petty states on the coast of Loango, making Loango his capital. In the upper part of this engraving are seen the royal buildings and market-place.

of independence. Complete defection occasionally resulted, when the solidarity of the kingdom had to be maintained by force of arms. Of the provinces in this relation to the kingdom, the most important was Songo, a district immediately south of the mouth of the Congo; after its chieftain had come into contact with the Portuguese, he was accustomed to call himself "count," and later "great prince." The count of Songo was always an untrustworthy vassal, especially during the period when the Congo power began to decline. In 1631 the count succeeded in conquering Kacongo and Ngoyo, whereupon he felt himself strong enough to throw off his allegiance to Congo.

At the same time the Congo king had attempted to hand over Songo to the Portuguese as a reward for services rendered by them. On two occasions, in 1636 and 1641, the king of Congo was utterly defeated. Even at the time when the Portuguese were beginning their missionary **Counts of Songo and Congo** labours, a certain jealousy existed between Songo and Congo, in consequence of which the Songo prince, who was the weaker of the two, entered into close relations with the dreaded foreign arrivals, and embraced Christianity in the year 1491. At the very time when the Portuguese were laying the foundations of their church in Ambasse those great migratory movements began of which the attack of the Mundequete upon Congo may be considered as the prelude. Portuguese narratives would make it appear that the **The Magic of the Portuguese** Mundequete were settled on the great lakes in the far interior and had "revolted" against Congo, thus giving an incredible area of extension to the Congo kingdom. The truth is that we meet in this case with one more instance of those constant migrations to the coast, probably occasioned by the beginning of upheavals elsewhere, which were to devastate districts in Africa far remote from any visited by the warrior Mundequete.

However this may be, the unexpected incursion of their outnumbering foes placed the king of Congo in a most embarrassing situation. His glance fell involuntarily upon the Portuguese. They, with their crosses, their rose wreaths and bells, their admonitions and preachings, seemed to be proclaiming a new magic which would assure victory; and they may very well have promised the king more practical assistance in the last extremity. The defection of the ruler of Songo was not without its influence; the king had himself baptised his whole court under the name of Dom Joao da Silva, and countless numbers of his subjects hastened to follow his example. The army, sprinkled with holy water and protected by the banners of the Cross, utterly routed the Mundequete in a fierce battle, and the victory of Christianity was thereby assured. Numerous churches arose, priests and monks found a wide field open for their efforts, and in 1534 a

Influence of Christianity on the Congo
bishop was consecrated for the newly acquired province. Congo itself was more powerful than ever ; its influence must have extended far into the interior, and, under the protection of the Portuguese king, is said at that time to have reached even the great lakes.

This state of affairs was rudely interrupted by the invasion of an even more formidable enemy, the Jagga. In the year 1542 this cannibal tribe of warriors first appeared on the borders of the Congo kingdom, spreading terror and panic before them as they came. The Congo army was utterly defeated ; the capital, which had been called São Salvador since the conversion of the people, was stormed and burnt to the ground with its cathedral and chapels ; the ancient civilisation of Congoland was almost destroyed, together with the carefully ingrafted European culture which it supported. The king, Dom Alvaro I., whose palace had come to ape the style and manners of the court at Lisbon, deserted its capital, and fled to an island of the Congo, where he passed several miserable years. After four years of war, the utmost efforts of his people and the valuable assistance of Portuguese troops drove the Jagga out of the land in 1546. The country recovered its prosperity, and its connection with Portugal was naturally even closer than before.

Loango suffered from the incursions of the Anzig, with their little bows bound with lizard-skin, even as Congo had been troubled by the Jagga ; but these two

Cannibals Devastate the Congo
peoples seem to have been of different origin. For a long time the Jagga were the terror of all the land about the Congo estuary. Angola was devastated ; the town of Loanda is said to have been in their possession for seven years. Between 1590 and 1600 Benguela was the object of their marauding raids ; Battel, who visited their encampment at that period, estimates their fighting strength at 16,000. Eventually they abandoned the pursuit of

war and settled in the district of Kassanje near the Upper Kwango, where remnants of them are said to have survived up to the present day.

The weakness of the civilisation founded in the Congo kingdom and the superficial character of its conversion to Christianity were soon to become apparent. In the year 1636 began the unfortunate struggle with Songo already mentioned, which weakened the kingdom to a considerable extent. These internal weaknesses finally led to an open breach ; the king, Antonio I., threw off his allegiance, and drove the clergy out of the country, obliging the transference of the bishop's see to São Paolo de Loanda, which had been founded in 1574. A Portuguese army made a successful invasion of the Congo kingdom, but it was henceforward left entirely to itself. Further struggles with Songo in 1667 and with Bamba, which also declared its independence in 1687, brought about the final collapse of the Congo kingdom. Angola now became the centre of the Portuguese power. It had originally been

Congo Kingdom Collapses
a province of Congo with its "capital" Mapungo, under the name of Dongo, or Ambonde, had been raised by Portuguese interest to a considerable height of importance, and, after a revolt in 1578, had become partly dependent upon Portugal. The power of Congo, on the other hand, rapidly declined. It was not until 1882 that the missionaries again entered the country and made some 2,000 converts. But the once powerful ruler of Congo remains, and has remained throughout the nineteenth century, the helpless chieftain of the fallen town of São Salvador. Christianity, which was apparently deeply rooted in Congo, also disappeared entirely in course of time.

It was only by slow degress that the Portuguese gained possession of the whole of Angola. The rising of 1578, or 1580, cost the lives of many Portuguese, and was followed by many lesser struggles, in which the advantage generally remained with the whites. Most tedious of all were the wars with the queen Ginga Bandi ; after poisoning her brother she received baptism, but then continued for thirty years in hostility to Portugal. Eventually, in 1648, the Portuguese firmly established their supremacy. HEINRICH SCHURTZ

BRITISH & DUTCH IN SOUTH AFRICA

BY ARTHUR D. INNES, M.A.

CAPE COLONY AND ITS EXPANSION

THE story of European colonisation in South Africa before the last quarter of the nineteenth century was, with one exception, a story of coastal settlements, never extending an organised government into the interior. None of these has been established on a basis such that an autonomous state could be constructed thereon : none of them have been colonies in the full British sense of the term, any more than Madras and Calcutta and Bombay were colonies.

But there has been one exception. In the extreme south a European group established itself at the Cape, and formed itself into an agricultural as well as a trading community. For more than a hundred and eighty years expansion was slow enough. Then, not eighty years ago, began a great movement northwards and eastwards, extending past the **Beginnings** Orange River, past the Vaal **of Dutch** River, on to the Limpopo: **Expansion** always to the east of the junction of the Orange and the Vaal. Then the expansion spread from its old starting point in the south to the north, till it reached the Zambesi and passed beyond it into Central Africa.

In this movement, wholly distinct from other colonial movements in Africa— though not, in its last stages, uninfluenced by them—two peoples were concerned, Dutch and British. On the harmonious fusion of those two peoples in the future depends the successful development of a great African state analogous to the Canadian Dominion in another continent ; a Dominion where also the harmonious fusion of the British with another race has been the condition of success.

It was the Portuguese who first discovered the Cape of Storms, re-christened the Cape of Good Hope. But for more than a century and a half no practical attempt was made by any European power to treat the place as anything more than a port of call for the East India trade. At last, in 1652, the Dutch East India Company took possession, and planted a station at Table Bay under the command of Van Riebeek. Although for the next **First** twenty-five years England and **Dutch** Holland were intermittently at **Station** war, and some years elapsed before France ceased to be a rival to these two Powers in the contest for the empire of the seas, the Dutch position at the Cape was unchallenged. France was satisfied with the Mauritius, and England with St. Helena, which she took from the Dutch. In France, England or Holland no one as yet was thinking of establishing an African dominion.

For nearly another hundred and fifty years, then—from 1652 to 1795—the Dutch were left to themselves. Emigrants did not flock from Holland ; but the settlers made their homes in the new country and imported Dutch wives. In 1685 the whole Dutch population was under 1,000. But in that year Louis XIV. revoked the Edict of Nantes ; the Huguenots were driven from France, and some hundreds of them found a refuge **Huguenots** at the Cape, where they amal- **at** gamated with and materially **the Cape** modified the Dutch stock. This was the easier because in matters of religion both Dutch and Huguenots were rigid Calvinists.

The white population increased and multiplied ; by 1770 it numbered some 10,000. There were the inevitable occasional collisions with the Hottentots, who were more or less in occupation of the country ; as yet the Bantu negroes had not approached near enough to bring on conflicts. The system of negro slavery was established, but these negroes were imported, as also were Malays. It was not till 1778 that the gradual expansion of the Dutch colony brought it into touch with a Bantu tribe. Then the attempt to open friendly relations was promptly

Cape Ruled from Holland accepted as a sign of conscious weakness, and was followed by a Bantu raid. At this time, the Great Fish River was fixed as the eastern boundary of the Dutch colony. Settlers had moved inland, northwards, but were only just reaching as far as Graaf Reinet. The colony was administered in a highly arbitrary manner by the Dutch company; and the idea that citizens of a colony have the same rights and privileges as citizens of the mother country had not dawned in Holland any more than it was then accepted at Westminster. The hunter and farmer " Boer " population had remained untouched by the intellectual movement of the eighteenth century in Europe, while intercourse with the Hottentots and the practice of slavery tended on the one hand to lower moral standards, and on the other to intensify the peculiar Old Testament religiosity which has been a common characteristic of Calvinistic puritanism—and incidentally an extraordinary source of strength and confidence to puritan armies.

But the régime of the Dutch company was coming to an end. The French Revolution sent the French Monarchy toppling and then the Republic challenged all the monarchies of Europe in the name of Liberty, Equality, and Fraternity. Presently the French overran the Netherlands. The hereditary Stadtholder, William of Orange, took ship to England, to which Power, in 1795, he transferred the colony, in order to preserve it from falling into the hands of France, which proceeded to convert Holland into the

Cape Transferred to Britain " Batavian Republic." Accordingly, in June of that year a British squadron arrived at the Cape. The authorities there, uncertain as to their allegiance, disputed the occupation, but after some show of resistance capitulated to superior force. A subsequent attempt of the Batavian Republic to recover possession was frustrated without difficulty, and the Cape remained under the British administration till the

Peace of Amiens in 1802. It was then restored to the Dutch Republic, which took over the administration, and conducted it on new and excellent lines for nearly three years. But the exigencies of the renewed war produced a fresh British expedition to secure a point of such importance to naval strategy ; the authorities were again unable to offer more than a nominal resistance, and on January 18th, 1806, they capitulated. With the downfall of Napoleon, in 1814, the European monarchies were restored and William formally ceded the colony to Great Britain, receiving £6,000,000 as compensation. The Cape had already changed hands by right of conquest ; that was now permanently confirmed by right of purchase. Holland's direct interest in it was at an end.

It is the business of the historian not merely to narrate events, but to investigate problems of causation ; the last hundred years of South African history afford him a peculiarly interesting subject. Great Britain takes over the administration of a large territory, in which a population

Problems of Empire numbering perhaps 25,000 of Low German stock, with an admixture of French Huguenot blood, dominate an immensely larger servile or semi-servile native population. Pressing on their borders are hordes of militant negro tribes, quite distinct from those under their rule : not the indigenous inhabitants, but no less emphatically invading conquerors than the Europeans themselves.

The Briton entering upon the task of ruling a new dependency must always be satisfied that he is possessed of an indefeasible legal title, for his conscience will not endure illegality. He enters upon it with a firm and justifiable conviction that English ideas about government are the best in the world, and that English officials as a class are the most disinterested, the most incorruptible, the most fairminded in the world. He has a conscientious determination to " keep troth," to " be just and fear not." Hence, no subject - populations in the world have enjoyed such security of person and property, such immunity from extortion and positive oppression as the subject-populations of the British Empire.

But the rectitude of which he is somewhat aggressively conscious is not always so obvious to others ; to them, the legal indefeasibility of his title to rule may not be equally convincing. They mistrust professions of disinterestedness which issue in territorial annexations. They are not equally assured that English methods of government are superior to those for which they have a traditional predilection. They do not see any benefit to themselves in the absorption of all higher official posts by Englishmen. And when Englishmen set about ruling over races which are near akin to them, this spirit of antagonism becomes intensified. It completely wrecked their attempts to dominate Scotland. It has made the government of Ireland an eternal struggle. It lost them the American colonies. It has played a disastrous part in South Africa. Nevertheless, this spirit of antagonism has

THE FIRST EUROPEAN STRONGHOLD IN SOUTH AFRICA
The Portuguese were the first to discover the Cape of Storms, re-christened the Cape of Good Hope; but it was not until 1652 that the first Dutch fort was built, a picture of which, as it was in 1687, is given here.

habitually presented itself to the English mind as preposterous and unreasonable.

In the matter of race, even the Scot is—or was a hundred years ago—hardly nearer akin than the Hollander to the Englishman. The Huguenot admixture in the South African Boer rather increases the similarity than otherwise; but his Puritanism is of the Scottish rather than the English type, and, broadly speaking, the antagonism of the Boer to the Englishman—whom he is apt to differentiate from the Scot—is closely analogous to the ancient antagonism of the Scot to the Englishman. At length, however, Englishman and Scot realised that amalgamation was better than antagonism. The time has at last come when we may hope that Briton and Boer are realising the same truth in South Africa; but in the nineteenth century it had not come.

Title by right of conquest pure and simple is always liable to be challenged if the conquered become strong enough to rebel. Between 1806 and 1814, that was the nature of the British rights at the Cape. After 1814, the title was no longer open to any such challenge, the cession having been made by a friendly Government for adequate consideration. That question at least did not arise till another score of years had elapsed. Moreover, at the outset, the actual British population was very small, while the character of the government was such as the circumstances obviously demanded. The governors were practically absolute; but they did not materially interfere with the established system of local government, the established customs of the population, or the established relations between Boers and natives within the colony. Boers and natives were probably quite as well content as they would have been as a Dutch colony under the Dutch system. Nevertheless, a primary source of friction soon made itself felt in the disposition of the Government to intervene between Boer and Hottentot, generally in favour of the Hottentot. About 1820 an important change was inaugurated. The governor, Lord Charles Somerset, obtained the support of the Home Government in obtaining a supply of British immigrants, who were planted in the eastern portion of the colony, hitherto unoccupied. Hence it came about that a substantial British element was added to the Boer population, and predominated in the eastern section, much as, after the American War of Independence, Lower Canada remained French while Upper Canada became British.

In this decade the racial grievance began to develop; the Government, adopting a series of Anglicising measures, which, if they had been cheerfully accepted by the burghers, would have tended to the early fusion of the races, and would have improved the system generally. But, unhappily, they were not so accepted.

Absolute British Governors

The First Boer Grievances

The Dutch, who formed five-sixths of the white population, objected to having English imposed as the official language, and to the abolition of the traditional system of local government in favour of English methods. They objected also to an ordinance which placed Hottentots and whites on the same legal footing, and they found no consolation in the appointment of a small advisory council which was supposed to be a check on the absolute power of the Governor.

Freedom for the Slaves

Then came a measure, excellent in itself, which entirely exasperated the old inhabitants. Already, in 1807, Great Britain had declared against the slave trade; now, in 1833, she resolved on the total abolition of slavery in all British territory, the people in the British Isles voting the huge sum of £20,000,000 to compensate the slave owners. But of that sum only about £1,250,000 was allotted to South Africa, where the official valuation of the slaves amounted to £3,000,000. Moreover, it was impossible immediately to replace the slave labour by free labour. The pastoral employments of the great bulk of the Dutch population were worked by slave labour, and to immense numbers of them emancipation meant something like ruin. It was not yet known that the compensation would be so inadequate, and exasperation had not yet reached its height when Sir Benjamin Durban arrived as governor in 1834, to find himself confronted with the additional problem of dealing with the Bantu Kaffirs on the borders.

For fifty years past there had been periodical collisions with the Kaffir tribes beyond the Fish River; two of these Kaffir wars had taken place since the establishment of British rule. Practically the whole population, official and other, held a single view with regard to the Kaffirs; with the exception of one element —the missionaries. In the view of these the Kaffir was a peaceable and simple person, who became troublesome only when goaded by the whites. In the view of the rest the Kaffir was a born marauder, who abstained from robbery and murder only so long as he feared superior force. At this time, the Zulu Tamerlane, Chaka, and the kindred armies of the Matabele, had for many years been devastating and slaughtering on the east and north; the

Missionary View of the Kaffirs

Kaffir closer at hand had been feeling the pressure. Whatever might be thought in England, where the missionaries had the ear of the public, to men in Africa it was obvious that the Kaffir tribes were a serious menace.

The Governor then sent the principal representative of the missionary societies as a commissioner to obtain from the chiefs assurances of their peaceful intentions. They gave the assurances, but took the fact that they had been invited as an indication of fear, and therefore of weakness. While Sir Benjamin Durban was giving an official Christmas entertainment news came to him that the Kaffirs were across the Fish River, raiding, robbing, and slaughtering. Thus a new Kaffir war opened. The operations were ably conducted by Sir Henry Smith—who became Governor some years later—but nearly a year passed before the Kaffirs fairly submitted. Sir Benjamin then planted in the belt of territory across the Fish River a number of tribesmen whose hostility to the group, with whom the war had been going on, would prevent a dangerous coalition, so that, in fact, these would serve as a buffer. The territory beyond these was to be under British military control, though the chiefs were to retain much of their powers. The whole scheme was regarded as generally wise and satisfactory. But it had to be submitted to the home authorities.

Early Kaffir Wars

The home authorities listened to the missionary societies, and to no one else. The theory of the missionaries was that the Kaffirs were a harmless and persecuted people, who should be left independent under their own chiefs, wherever the chiefs were well disposed to missionaries. Consequently, an astonishing despatch reversed Durban's arrangement, and signified that the missionary theory was to be carried out. The dwellers in the eastern districts, exposed to the Kaffir attacks, saw no possible prospect before them but anarchy and chaos. The Governor protested, and was thereupon recalled.

This was precisely at the moment when the colony was realising the full extent of the losses entailed by the abolition of slavery. Deprived of the labour by which their farms had been run, and faced by the fact that the wisest and most moderate of governors was unable to provide against the Black peril so long as the missionary societies remained all-powerful in London, great numbers of the Boers resolved to shake off their feet the dust of the British colony, and to seek new pastures beyond its borders. There was nothing to prevent them from doing so; the law-officers of the Crown declared that there was no power to prevent British subjects from emigrating out of British territory. Thus began the Great Trek. The emigrants were only later to realise that the Crown declined to admit that, in passing out of British territory, they ceased to be British subjects. Whither should the stalwarts make their pilgrimage? Virtually, the limits of the colony were the Orange River on the north, and the Fish River on the east. To trek into the Kaffir country between the mountains and the sea, beyond the

Fish River, would obviously be worse than useless. The warrior Matabele had crossed the mountains; they had raided and depopulated most of the country between the Orange and Vaal rivers; but for the most part they had settled beyond the Vaal. Here, then, between the Vaal and the Orange, the emigrants had the best chance of making a new home.

But the first adventurous caravans were determined to betake themselves as far as might be from British territory. These passed the Vaal; far northward, the bulk of them were trapped and slaughtered by the Matabele. A remnant struggled through to the Portuguese at Delagoa Bay.

The next group, a larger body, stopped short of the Vaal, and made friends with a local chief who was living in fear of Moselikatse and his Matabele. A few members of the party, including their "commandant," Hendrik Potgieter, went exploring across the Vaal, and almost to the Limpopo. They returned to find that the Matabele had already cut off and massacred a party of twenty-five, and, having been repulsed by others, were likely to return in force. Potgieter chose his ground, drew his whole company—forty guns, and their women and children —into laager—that is, constructed a fortified position with the waggons — and awaited the attack. The Boer fire proved too much for the Matabele, whose rushes were repeatedly broken by the hail of bullets. The laager was not entered, but the cattle were carried off. The party was extricated from its dangerous position by a third band under Gert Maritz, who had arrived at Thaba Nchu, and sent up cattle to draw the waggons, in place of those which the Matabele had carried off.

Maritz and Potgieter having joined forces, were nowise daunted by these experiences. On the contrary,

THE BIRTH OF CAPE COLONY
When the French overran the Netherlands in 1795, William of Orange transferred the colony at the Cape to Great Britain; a British squadron was sent there, and the British flag hoisted, to preserve it from the hands of France.

2317

they took the offensive, marched, 150 strong — including some half-breeds — to smite the Philistines, surprised a kraal, or military village, routed the "regiment" which occupied it with considerable slaughter, drove home a mighty herd of cattle, and fortified themselves at Winberg —so named in memory of the victory.

Boer Wars on the Matabele There they were reinforced by a number of fresh emigrant families; and there, in June, 1837, they drew up for themselves a republican constitution, naming Pieter Retief, one of the recent arrivals, their "commandant-general."

The next step was a second attack on Moselikatse; 135 Boers marched into the heart of the Matabele country, found the chief at the head of a force outnumbering their own by not much less than a hundred to one, fought him for nine days, and wrought such immense havoc that the Matabele threw up the struggle, fled north across the Limpopo, and turned their attention to the peaceful Mashonas. The entire country from the Orange to the Limpopo having been thus evacuated by the Matabele, who had succeeded in very nearly wiping out the previous inhabitants, the new republic proceeded to proclaim itself lord of the whole— which corresponds approximately to what afterwards became the Orange Free State and the South African or Transvaal Republic.

While Potgieter had been occupied in the expulsion of the Matabele, Retief and others were investigating the possibility of crossing the mountains and effecting a settlement nearer the sea— in what is now Natal, and was then dominated by Dingan, the successor of Chaka, the ruler of the Zulu military state. By grace of Dingan there were a few British residing at Port Natal, but the Cape Government exercised no sovereignty in that region. The natives, up to

First Settlement in Natal the Tugela, regarded these Britons as their chiefs, while recognising perforce the supremacy of the Zulu king. Retief and his comrades, with the approval of the English at Port Natal, sought and were granted an interview with Dingan, in order to treat with him for a grant of land. Dingan received them hospitably, promised them the land, then suddenly, at the moment of parting, turned on them and slaughtered every man of them. Then he despatched a host against the most advanced of the Boer camps, and massacred its occupants— men, women and children, whites and Hottentot servants—to the number of over 400. One youth alone had time to spring on horseback, ride for his life, and give the alarm at other camps. At each one, the waggons were promptly laagered, and when the Zulu hosts appeared they were met with so fierce a resistance that they failed to carry a single one. Next day the scattered camps were able to concentrate. The resolve was promptly taken not to budge, but to exact vengeance for the massacre.

The commandos from over the mountains came down to join their comrades; the British at Port Natal made common cause with them. But they could not unite under any one leader. British and Dutch advanced against Dingan in two separate columns. The Dutch were drawn into an ambush, from which they fought their way out with difficulty. The British column—seventeen whites and some 1,500 natives—was trapped by a Zulu force of

Zulus Defeat Dutch and British five times its strength, and was cut to pieces after a terrific struggle, only a third of the whole number escaping (April, 1838). For a time further offensive action was paralysed.

The arrival of Andries Pretorius in November provided a new and capable leader. Leaving a garrison in the camp, Pretorius, with a force 460 strong, marched against the Zulus, scouting constantly and forming laager at every halt. Through captured Zulus, messages were sent offering to treat for peace. Dingan sent not envoys, but an army. On December 16th, "Dingan's Day," they fell upon the Boer laager, to meet with an overwhelming defeat. Four of the Boers were killed; 3,000 Zulu corpses were left dead on the field; the stream that flows hard by has been known from that day as the Blood River; Dingan's Day has been celebrated annually ever since.

Though Dingan had to flee from his chief kraal for the time, he was not yet crushed; hence, instead of scattering over the district, the Boers concentrated at Pietermaritzburg. It was not till Panda, a half-brother of Dingan, rebelled and allied himself to the white men that Dingan's power was finally broken. It was Panda's force that actually inflicted the decisive defeat in January, 1840, on the king, who was shortly afterwards assassinated. Panda was established in his place, as a vassal of the new republic, which proclaimed its dominion over Natal—a dominion which it might fairly claim to have acquired by right of conquest in a war whose justification was quite indisputable.

The new Government, however, was inexperienced in administration ; moreover, it made arbitrary regulations concerning its Bantu subjects, and it attacked a native chief in the territory which lay

was besieged. There the British held out behind their entrenchments till a relieving force arrived. The Boers then withdrew their resistance. The assertion of British supremacy was accepted as an accomplished fact, the British action being warranted mainly by the theory that the

British Supremacy Asserted Boer conquerors were British subjects, who could not on their own responsibility set up a dominion free from the British allegiance. The bulk of the emigrants withdrew westwards across the Drakensberg Mountains to the lands where

THE SECOND OCCUPATION OF THE CAPE: BRITISH TROOPS IN CAPE TOWN IN 1814
After the Peace of Amiens, of 1802, the Cape was restored to the Dutch, but was re-conquered by the British in 1806, and formally and permanently ceded for £6,000,000 to Great Britain in 1814.

between Natal and the Cape Colony. British sentiment, still guided by the missionaries, demanded protection for the natives, and the demand cannot be regarded as unreasonable. There was an

British War With the Boers agitation to compel the emigrant Boers to return to the colony. The Dutch volksraad continued its arbitrary course, and presently the British Governor ordered Port Natal to be occupied.

The military operations took the regular course. British troops were marched on Port Natal, a party of them was met in arms by the Boers, was defeated, and was driven into the camp, where the force

as yet the British made no claim to extend control. Three years later a British government was definitely established in Natal.

The experiment was now tried of establishing border states under British influence and protection between the British colony and the interior—not without some expectation that the Boers would thus find themselves cut off, and would be compelled to return to British territory. To this end, the Basuto chief Moshesh was recognised as ruler over a great part of the upper Orange River basin ; and west of Moshesh a Griqua state was recognised under Adam Kok. But in both these

2319

regions there were now a considerable number of the emigrants planted, who had no mind to submit to the sovereignty either of a Basuto or a Griqua. Under these conditions it was natural that troubles should soon break out in the treaty-states, where Adam Kok, assured of British support, asserted the authority which the Boer settlers repudiated. British intervention had as its only practical result the withdrawal of most of the farmers to a more remote district. A general conference of the various parties interested brought about a new arrangement : a portion of Adam Kok's territory was allotted to the emigrants under a British Governor, who were to pay a sort of tribute to the Griqua chief.

Basuto and Griqua States

Meanwhile, affairs on the Kaffir frontier were in an unsatisfactory condition ; Kaffir raids were not duly checked by the chief, and presently the friction developed into a new Kaffir war—counted as the seventh. The operations, though costly, demand no special record. But the war itself had at last the effect of inducing the Ministers in England to recognise the folly of governing the Cape according to a priori theories affected in London instead of in accordance with the judgment of the men who really knew the conditions. Hence Sir Harry Smith was sent out as Governor.

Sir Harry at once took up the policy in which Durban had been checked. The belt of Kaffir territory on the near side of the Kei River was made a British province, Kaffraria, the chiefs in general retaining much of their authority. The nominal authority of the Griqua Adam Kok over the settled district was abolished, the chief receiving practical compensation. The Boers made no demur at first to the proclamation of the " Orange River Sovereignty " as a province under British administration. Presently, when the farmers to the northward, headed by Andries Pretorius, rose in arms to resist, they were defeated in the field at Boomplaats, and withdrew beyond the Vaal. Then, in 1850, the Kaffirs again revolted. This eighth Kaffir war was long and bloody. After two years it was concluded, practically by the exhaustion of the tribes.

Eighth Kaffir War

The Orange River Sovereignty found itself in difficulties—primarily because Moshesh was dissatisfied with the existing arrangements. He permitted or encouraged disturbances among the minor chiefs. Sir Harry Smith instructed the Governor, Major Warden, to intervene by force when expostulation failed. Moshesh at once dropped the pretence of submission. The section of colonists who continued disaffected to British rule made a compact of neutrality with him, and then invited the intervention of Pretorius and the Boers across the Vaal. Pretorius, technically a rebel against the British, but now residing beyond their formal jurisdiction, informed Major Warden that he would not intervene if the independence of the Transvaal territory were guaranteed ; otherwise he would. Major Warden could not deal with so strong a combination as that which threatened : Sir Harry Smith could not reinforce him in the thick of the Kaffir war. The Governor of the Cape, seeing no alternative, arranged a conference between the Transvaal leaders and British commissioners ; and the result was the Sand River Convention in January, 1852, guaranteeing to the Transvaal—thereafter acknowledged as the South African Republic—the independent control of its own affairs. About this time, Sir Harry Smith was replaced by Sir George Cathcart, who before long was able to employ troops released from the Kaffir contest to restore order. Moshesh made prompt submission before it was too late, while his prestige was at its height. The submission was accepted, Cathcart withdrew, and immediately afterwards the Home Government made up its mind to retire from the Orange River Sovereignty altogether. By a convention signed at Bloemfontein in February, 1854, the Orange River Sovereignty was transformed into the Orange Free State, with a guarantee of independence.

Independence of the Transvaal

Nearly twelve months earlier the Cape Colony had been granted a new constitution. The first ineffective limitation on the Governor's arbitrary powers had been made a little, but not much, more effective by the appointment of a nominated Council in 1834. In 1853, the Cape Colony was given two elected Assemblies, which had practically complete control of legislation. Full responsible government did not arrive until eighteen years later. Natal, as well as Kaffraria, continued to be governed in connection with Cape Colony, but Natal was separated in 1856, when it received more restricted representative institutions.

RISE OF THE SOUTH AFRICAN STATES
A GENERATION OF DEVELOPMENT

AT this time it was the prevalent conviction among politicians of all parties in England that colonies inevitably separate from the mother country as soon as may be after they are strong enough to stand by themselves. The old notion that they are to be treated as mere dependencies existing for the convenience of the parent state, to whom they must remain subservient, had been virtually destroyed in the British mind by the American War of Independence. The modern conception of colonies as forming a group of states whose common interest it is to stand fast together on terms of practical equality, under a single flag, had hardly come into existence. The outcome of the intermediate attitude was that the mother country was generally anxious to avoid responsibilities herself, and willing to leave the colonies to manage their own affairs—provided that they did not irritate humanitarian sentiment, or entail expenditure at home.

Thus the recognition of the South African Republic and of the Orange Free **Cutting Loose the Colonies** State appeared to be a convenient method of creating responsibilities on the north of the Orange River. The recognition was so nearly unconditional as to make any subsequent attempt to assert British authority exceedingly difficult in fact, and questionable in law. In other words, the way in which the thing was done very gravely complicated the South African problem for those whose larger imagination pictured the ideal of a homogeneous South African state or federation.

The problem, as we have already noted, bore a strong analogy to that which, before the eighteenth century, confronted those statesmen in England and Scotland, from the days of Edward I., who realised the immense advantage which unification would bring to both countries, subject always to the conditions that there should be no subordination of the one to the other, and that the union should be accepted with goodwill by the bulk of both populations.

In Africa, indeed, there was no danger of the subjection which the Scots had feared, but rather of absorption. Unification could come only under the British flag, as in Canada, unless Great Britain altogether lost her place among the nations.

Primarily, what Ministers in London effected was to establish one state half Dutch and half British south of the Orange **The South African States in 1854** River; a second British state in Natal, with the subject native territory of Kaffraria intervening; a practically independent native state in Zululand beyond the Tugela; another in Basutoland, flanking the new Orange Free State; and between the Orange and the Limpopo, with the Drakensberg for their eastern boundary, the Boer Orange Free State, which rapidly developed an excellent organisation; and the Boer South African Republic, which was hardly organised at all. Each of these developed on its own lines, until the complication of their mutual relations attained a degree of entanglement for which politicians could find no solution save the arbitrament of war.

The Governor who was placed at the head of Cape Colony in 1854 was Sir George Grey, who had already won high distinction as an administrator in Australasia, and notably in New Zealand. Had Sir George been given a perfectly free hand the history of South Africa during the last fifty years would have been less disturbed, for **A Governor of Large Imagination** he was possessed of the large imagination which looks far into the future, and also of the resolution, the tact, and the sympathy, without which it is not possible to carry out a policy wherein the opposing interests of rival races have to be reconciled. He recognised in Africa the necessity, repeatedly demonstrated in British-Indian history, of exercising a constant influence over native communities through the presence of British Residents and Agents. He saw also the need of fusion between the two white races—of unification as opposed to the political disintegration consequent upon the breaking up of South Africa into a number of independent states. But he was debarred from giving his policy effect in any high degree. The

Union With Dutch Checked
existence of the Boer republics checked, though it did not altogether prevent, the amalgamation of the Cape Dutch and British. The principle of non-intervention was maintained, with the result that, as in India, intervention was ultimately forced on the Government at the cost of bloody wars.

Grey's time Kaffraria became the scene of a gigantic tragedy, a psychological phenomenon of a very remarkable character. Grey introduced excellent schemes calculated to civilise the natives ; but the benefits therefrom were not immediately apparent—much as, almost contemporaneously, Dalhousie's measures for the advancement of the natives of India were viewed by them with the most grotesque suspicion—and it is clear that in Africa there was a great undercurrent of hostility to the white man's rule. As skilful agitators in India played upon the superstitious terrors or the religious

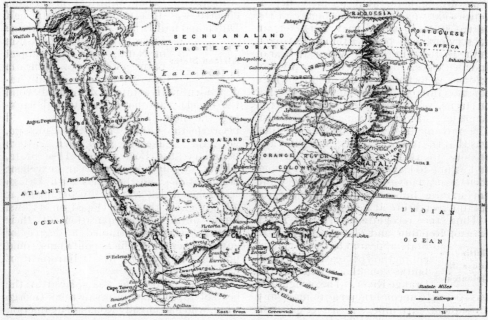

GREAT BRITAIN IN SOUTH AFRICA: MAP OF THE BRITISH STATES AND PROTECTORATES
Beginning with the half British and half Dutch State of Cape Colony, British influence in South Africa has expanded, through the anti-colonial period, when the Boer and native states were established, until the whole of South Africa south of the Limpopo river, with the exception of German South-west Africa, has come under British rule or protection.

Internally, the premier colony progressed. The same may be said of Natal and of the Orange Free State. But the Cape had its troubles with the native dependency of Kaffraria, as the Free State had in its turn with the Basuto power, and Natal with Bantus within her own borders, and ultimately with the Zulu state on the north-east.

British Kaffraria did not form a part of Cape Colony. It was administered on different lines, the population being practically entirely black ; but it was under the Governor of the Cape in his capacity as High Commissioner. During Sir George

prejudices of the uneducated classes and of the sepoys, so in Africa superstition was the lever by which conspirators or fanatics sought to let loose a black avalanche upon the alien which should destroy him. The bulk of the population of Kaffraria

A Gigantic Kaffir Tragedy
belonged to the Kosa tribes, against whom the series of Kaffir wars had been waged. Suddenly among them, beyond the British border, there came a prophet, Umhlakaze, who claimed that he and his niece Nongkause, were mediums, mouthpieces, through whom the spirits of departed Kosa heroes spoke their bidding.

Umhlakaze had seen them in the flesh, spoken with them, heard their message. In due time, the white men were to be wiped out utterly ; but there was to be a time of preparation. When the great day arrived, the heroes would come back to earth, and lead the faithful to victory ; crops, in plenty unheard of, would spring from the soil in a day ; cattle would cover the pastures. Meanwhile, the faithful were bidden to slaughter cattle and destroy crops—in effect, to clear the land of all means of obtaining a food supply. The principal Kosa chiefs took up the cause with enthusiasm ; the European observer more than suspects that what was really hoped for was that when the population suddenly found themselves utterly destitute they would hurl themselves upon the white man and the white man's lands in sheer desperation. Certainly, nothing but a frenzy of superstition could have made the masses deliberately destroy all they had to live on.

HENDRIK BRAND
President of the Orange Free State during the litigation as to the ownership of the diamond fields.

The Cape Government, through the early months of 1857, when it had appreciated the nature of the hideous illusion which had taken possession of the Kosas, made every preparation to resist the anticipated onslaught, and to accumulate stores to alleviate the terrible destitution, which was daily becoming more inevitable as the Kaffirs continued to slay cattle and to destroy grain. It must be supposed that among the leaders many had veritably persuaded themselves of the prophet's truth. At any rate, nothing

else, it would seem, can explain the fact that no measures were taken to gather the fighting men in arms, so that when the day arrived they might be launched at once against their foe, or upon their prey. The day came. The grain was gone ; the cattle were gone ; the warriors were not assembled. And the fresh grain did not sprout nor the divine cattle appear ; nor did the dead return to lead the living. Proclamation went forth that the "day of resurrection" was—postponed. But it was vain to attempt to organise war after the process of starvation had begun, when the illusion of superstition was already shattered to fragments. There was no war, other than where starving Kaffirs fought each other for scraps of anything edible that could be found. Driven by famine, they poured in streams over the border, crying for food. But the destitution was more overwhelming than the available resources could cope with; 25,000 at least perished, possibly even double that number. At the end of 1857 the Kaffir population was but one-third of what it had been when the year opened. On the deserted lands settlers were planted from the Cape, from home, from Germany. The white immigration changed the character of the district, and seven years later—in 1865—Kaffraria was formally incorporated with Cape Colony.

Meanwhile, the Orange Free State was organising itself on lines which showed the marked political capacity of its citizens.

Edwards
THE CAPITAL OF ORANGE RIVER COLONY: THE MARKET SQUARE, BLOEMFONTEIN

The chief authority lay in the Volksraad, elected by all full citizens and naturalised citizens with a property qualification. The executive functions were vested in an elected president and an executive council. Coloured inhabitants might be accorded the vote by a resolution of the Volksraad. A high standard of efficiency was attained in administration, but the conditions under which the Republic had been established made it inevitable that there should be difficulties with the Basuto Moshesh, who aspired to recover for the Basuto kingdom

as President. He renewed the appeal for arbitration to the Governor of the Cape, Sir Philip Wodehouse. Wodehouse, after careful and impartial examination, restored the old line of demarcation claimed by the Free State. The Basutos refused to withdraw from the territory they had occupied, and the second Basuto war began with savage raids on the part of the Basutos, from whom, on the other hand, the burghers captured several positions. Moshesh, who wanted a delay, obtained terms of peace; but fifteen months later he again challenged the Free State. This time victory lay more decisively with the Republic, and Moshesh begged the British to assume sovereignty and extend him their protection. The request was granted, and the Free State was in part deprived of what it had a strong title to regard as the legitimate fruits of victory in a war which it had not sought. Basutoland became a British Protectorate in 1869. While the Basuto war was in progress a discovery was made

KIMBERLEY, THE DIAMOND TOWN

the widest area of ascendency which it had held in the past—an area which included a portion of what the Free State claimed as its own territory, and quite accurately regarded as essential to its existence. In 1858, disagreement reached a head, and the Boers invaded Basutoland with little success. With an uncertain prospect of the Free State being joined by the South African or Transvaal Republic, the President invited, and Moshesh accepted, the mediation of Sir George Grey, whose award was in the main favourable to the Basuto. On the other hand, the Griqua sold their territory to the Free State, and removed themselves to Griqualand East, on the south of Natal.

Moshesh, however, made it evident that he meant to grasp even more than had been conceded by the Grey award. The friction again went on until, in 1865, Hendrik Brand succeeded Martin Pretorius

Edwards

THE EARLY DIAMOND MINES OF KIMBERLEY
In 1869 diamonds began to be found in lands claimed by the Griquas, who sold them to Great Britain, though the Orange Free State had the legal title, afterwards recognised by compensation. Since that time the mines have become the world's most important diamond supply.

which was vitally to affect the attitude of the British Government towards South Africa. First a few stray diamonds and then, in 1869, a very magnificent stone were found. The war was hardly over when digging for diamonds began in earnest. The diamond fields were on the west of the two republics, on lands which no one had

VIEWS OF CAPE TOWN AND ITS OVERSHADOWING MOUNTAIN

Cape Town, the seat of the first European settlement in South Africa, in 1652, has always maintained its supremacy among South African towns and its importance as the seat of British influence. The general views of the town and its harbour, and of Table Mountain, at the top and bottom of the page, give an idea of the beauty of its situation, while the photos of the Houses of Parliament and the General Post Office, on the left and right, indicate the importance of its public buildings.

Photos, N. P. Edwards and Underwood & Underwood, London

hitherto very definitely claimed. The Griqua chief, Nicholas Waterboer, asserting his ownership of the most valuable fields, sold them to the British Government. Waterboer's title was disputed by the Transvaal and by the Free State. The dispute between Waterboer and the Transvaal was referred to the arbitration of the Governor of Natal; and on the evidence laid before him Mr. Keate gave judgment entirely in favour of Waterboer. The Free State, however, declined to recognise an award to which it had not been a party. Great Britain claimed the land by right of purchase. But then, under the British flag, disputes as to title arose, and the courts, after examining all claims, rejected Waterboer's. President Brand appealed to England. British courts had now found that the land claimed by Waterboer had never been his to sell.

Legal Fight for the Diamond Fields

In this dilemma the British Government, deprived of its technical claim, fell back on the principles of high policy, and affirmed that its responsibilities as paramount power in South Africa compelled it to retain the diamond districts in its own hands; but it presently recognised that the Free State, in being thus deprived of territories to which they had a legal title, had a legitimate grievance. Compensation, therefore, was offered, and the republic accepted £90,000. The transaction amounted in effect to this : that the Paramount Power claimed the right of compulsory purchase on its own terms when reasons of state should make such purchase practically necessary. The claim, of course, rests on the principle that the Paramount Power acknowledges obligations to the maintenance of the security of the minor states which make the reservation of corresponding rights imperative. On the other, the Free State would in this case have found the control of the mines and the mining population so serious a task that the bargain was a better one than appears prima facie. In this connection, the Transvaal Republic was in a different position from the Free State. The Keate award had been made on the understanding that the President was authorised to pledge the republic to abide by the award ; and the authorities were entitled to regard the question as having been thereby definitely settled. But the Boers repudiated their

The Free State's Bargain

President's pledge, in consequence of which he resigned. Thus the point remained one as to which it was obviously possible that fresh dispute might arise in the future. It was to become evident, however, that something of more importance was involved for the Paramount Power than the mere possession of the diamond mines, since it thereby secured access to the interior, with possibilities of development which had not hitherto been taken into consideration.

The development of the diamond industry reacted curiously upon Natal, which now demands our attention. The relations here between the whites and the Bantu natives differed somewhat from the position in other colonies, the whites forming only some eight per cent. of the population ; hence the necessity for a strict limitation of the black man's opportunities of acquiring a vote. A degree of representative government had been granted shortly after the recognition of Natal as a separate colony, but responsible government did not arrive till the last decade of the century.

There was one quite necessary restrictive law in Natal—that all Bantu owners of guns should be registered. A portion of the country had been settled by Hlubi tribesmen, who had withdrawn from Zulu territory. Their chief, Langalibalela—or more briefly, Langa— allowed some of his young men to betake themselves to the diamond fields ; and they, with the money thus earned, purchased firearms, with which they returned to Langa's country, evading registration. In fact, it became clear that Langa's people were arming surreptitiously. The Government summoned Langa to answer for his people ; his replies were evasive ; in fact, he was concocting plans for defying the British. An armed force was sent to compel obedience to the Government demands ; an advance party narrowly escaped being cut off, and in doing so half a dozen lives were lost.

Diamonds and Zulu Risings

Every European in South Africa knew that nothing but a very convincing demonstration of superior force would prevent a general rising. The Boer Republic promised aid if needed ; Natal and Cape Colony were prompt to take decisive measures. Langa hoped to raise the Basutos as allies ; but he himself was caught and compelled to surrender, while his forces were scattered after a hot skirmish, before he had succeeded in effecting his object. He was removed from the colony, after full trial, and detained in a very comfortable captivity for some twelve years, while the Hlubi settlement was broken up, and the land transferred to fresh occupants. All danger of further insurrection was averted. The colonists, however, were—according to the standing rule—irritated by the intervention of the Home Government on behalf of the insurgent tribe.

A source of future difficulties for other parts of South Africa as well as Natal was created by the importation to that colony of coolie labour from India, the Bantu proving themselves wholly impracticable as plantation-workers. The measure was successful enough commercially; but it resulted in the permanent settlement of considerable numbers of Indians, whose presence is now regarded with aversion by the whites—both as an industrial danger, and as complicating the native question. On the other hand, the Imperial Government can hardly approve the exclusion of British subjects, as the Indians are, from free access to British dominions. Some observers are in favour of diverting the immigration, which tends to continue, to the more tropical region, where it would, at any rate, not affect the prospects of the white labourer or tradesman.

In 1877 Sir Bartle Frere arrived as Governor of the Cape and High Commissioner, having been appointed by Disraeli's Government with a view to the carrying out of Lord Carnarvon's aims for the unification of South Africa. Native questions, however, demanded his immediate attention. Prompt measures rendered a Kaffir rising abortive; but beyond Natal, still graver dangers threatened from the Zulu power, with its capital at Ulundi. The great military organisation of Chaka had met with a set-back when his successor, Dingan, was overthrown, and his place taken by the comparatively lethargic Panda. But Panda himself had been followed by his son, Cetewayo, who

Sir Bartle Frere Appointed

SIR BARTLE FRERE
Appointed Governor of the Cape in 1877 and made the scapegoat of the disastrous Zulu War of 1879.
Photo: London Stereoscopic

inherited not a few of Chaka's qualities. Under his sway the systematic development of a polity organised exclusively for military purposes was revived. Disagreements between this formidable potentate and the South African Republic threatened to issue in open war. In 1878, Frere as High Commissioner intervened to arbitrate on the points in dispute. But the Zulu menace was found to be so serious that his award, favourable enough to the Zulus, was joined to what was in effect an ultimatum to Cetewayo, requiring not only reparation for injuries of which his people had been guilty, but also the disbanding of his army, and the admission of a British Resident at Ulundi, Cetewayo's capital. The demands passed unheeded. An attack by Cetewayo would almost certainly mean a general Basuto rising in Natal. Sir Bartle Frere judged that the attack must be forestalled. A powerful force was dispatched against the Zulu king, in three divisions. Two advanced, successfully repulsing the forces sent against them, till the fate of the third division compelled them to halt and maintain a defensive attitude. The main body, under Lord Chelmsford, advanced to Isandlhwana, leaving a small band to guard communications at Rorke's Drift. Chelmsford moved with the bulk of his force to attack a Zulu kraal, leaving some 1,300 men, more than half being whites, in an unfortified camp. On that camp suddenly burst the Zulu torrent: 15,000 warriors. They had evaded Lord Chelmsford, and encircled the downward force before the situation was realised. The British were cut to pieces. But for the heroic defence of Rorke's Drift, where six score men under Chard and Bromhead held at bay 4,000 Zulus on that same night, Cetewayo's men would have been into Natal.

For the moment, the invading forces were compelled to mark time; but reinforcements were pushed up. Within six months of Isandlhwana, Lord Chelmsford had shattered Cetewayo's army at Ulundi, and the king was a fugitive. When presently he fell into the hands of the

Beginning of Zulu War of 1879

British, he was detained under surveillance till, in 1883, he was allowed to return to Zululand as a vassal monarch, an experimental form of government in the interval having proved quite unsuccessful. The restoration was contested. On his death next year, his son, Dinizulu secured the succession, with assistance—in return for a cession of territory—from the Transvaal. Continued disorders made annexation imperative in 1887, when the recalcitrance of Dinizulu and other chiefs necessitated his deportation. Subsequently his return was permitted ; but the Natal authorities have since obtained evidence on which he has been charged with fomenting fresh disturbances. The issue of his trial is still uncertain at the time of writing.

By a common perversion of reasoning processes, it was held that Sir Bartle Frere's policy was wrong because a British force had been cut up. He was recalled in 1881, the victim of wholly unmerited censure ; and there was a general reaction in England against the "forward" doctrines of the Beaconsfield Cabinet.

The story of Zululand has carried us out of our chronological course, and we have now to revert to the career of the South African or Transvaal Republic. This had been chequered enough, ever since the recognition in 1852. The Transvaalers were the extremists, the stalwarts among those Boer families which had resented control ; they had no disposition to adopt, even among themselves, any government of so carefully organised a type as that of the Free State. Their attitude to the native races was derived from their Old Testament conception of the relations ordained between the children of Japhet and the children of Ham. For some time after 1852 they were broken up into four communities ; it was not till 1860 that these managed to unite as a single state with a single President. They found themselves engaged in desultory hostilities now with one great Basuto tribe, now with another, and habitually without funds sufficient for decisive action. These quarrels were in part dealt with by arbitration under the Keate award mentioned already.

PAUL KRUGER
Elected with Pretorius and Joubert to the government of the Transvaal Republic at the rebellion of 1880, later made President.

Then, under President Burgers, new complications arose with the natives. But a rigid puritanism made the Boers believe that their arms could not prosper under a President who was an avowed Freethinker ; and when they took the field, the voice went forth : " To your tents, O Israel," and the burghers departed to their own homes, though they knew well enough how to fight when they had a mind. The situation demanded energetic measures—and money. And they had no money.

On this scene of anarchy appeared Sir Theophilus Shepstone as British Commissioner, with extensive powers from the Government. To him it appeared—though not to the Boers—that they were doomed to destruction at the hands of the Zulus, and much more would be involved in that than their own ruin. Moreover, such residents as were not themselves Boers saw their only refuge from anarchy in a British annexation. No open opposition was offered, and the Transvaal was annexed by proclamation, in April 1877. At the moment, Imperialism, sane or otherwise, was dominant in England. The successful unification of British North America had inspired hopes of an equally successful unification of South Africa, despite the antagonism of the Dutch element within Cape Colony as well as outside it. The annexation of the Transvaal, supposed to have been accomplished with the assent of its inhabitants, was accepted as a step in this desirable direction. The awakening was rude.

PIET JOUBERT
Commander-in-Chief of the Boer army and Vice-President of the South African Republic, 1896-1900.

Although the new order was accompanied by an access of unwonted prosperity, the Boers sent successive deputations to London to urge the cancellation

PRETORIA AND JOHANNESBURG, CHIEF CITIES OF THE TRANSVAAL

The Transvaal was founded about 1833 by Boers who trekked from British territory on the abolition of slavery. The market square at Pretoria, the capital of the Transvaal, is seen at the top of the page, and the Courts of Justice and the interior of the Legislature immediately below on the left and right. Below, Johannesburg, the goldfield capital, in the early days of the mines, is contrasted with the city of to-day, while above, in the centre, one of the large mine workings is shown.

Photos, N. P. Edwards and Underwood & Underwood, London

of the annexation. Their protests fell on deaf ears. The fall of the Beaconsfield Cabinet gave them new hopes, but Mr. Gladstone declared against a retrocession. Then the burghers bade defiance to Great Britain, elected Kruger, Pretorius, and Joubert to conduct the government, called the old Volksraad together, and, on December 6th, 1880, hoisted again the flag of the South African Republic. On the same day a collision between a party of Boers and the military at Potchefstrom opened hostilities. Four days later a small detachment was attacked, and forced to surrender at Bronkhorst Spruit. Sir George Colley marched from Natal

SIR GEORGE COLLEY
Whose force was defeated by the Boers in 1880 at Laing's Nek and Majuba, where he was killed.
Photo: Maull & Fox

pression had suddenly become dominant that Great Britain had arrogantly and without sufficient consideration annexed a free state ; that the state was justified in taking arms in defence of its liberty ; and that justice forbade the obviously mightier Power to penalise the smaller one for its courage. Where the discrepancy between the resources of the two nations was so enormous, the giant could surely afford to be magnanimous to the pygmy, and any well-conducted pygmy would recognise the generosity with which it had been treated. Such at least was the hypothesis which obtained from the British nation a somewhat

with a force of 1,000 men, but was beaten back with considerable loss at Laing's Nek. On the night of February 26th he occupied the summit of Majuba Hill, commanding the Nek ; but a small party of Boer volunteers climbed the hill, the Regulars were seized with panic, and Sir George himself was killed.

THE FATAL HILL ON THE BATTLEFIELD OF MAJUBA

Although a large force was by this time collected under Sir Evelyn Wood, orders had been sent from England in accordance with which first an armistice was arranged, and then a peace, restoring in terms not too free from ambiguity the independence of the South African Republic under British suzerainty. The retrocession has been the subject of stormy controversy ; but when it is treated as a party question in England it is as well to remember that if Gladstone was the prime mover, the most trusted and brilliant leaders of advanced Imperialism at the present day were at least consenting parties. The im-

KHAMA
The enlightened native chief of the Bechuanaland Protectorate.

dubious assent to the action of Ministers. Unhappily, events showed that the pygmy had not taken a correct view of the giant's conduct. The mass of the Boer population, as distinct from a very few intelligent men among the leaders, attributed the British action to a despicable pusillanimity ; and contempt proved an unsatisfactory basis for the new and pleasanter relations which it had been hoped to establish. But for the time at least the truth was not realised at Westminster ; and when, in 1884, a deputation arrived in London to procure modifications in the Convention of 1881, a revised Convention was conceded, of which the wording was so careless as to leave it open to question whether any tangible suzerainty was left to the British at all.

About the same time the inaction of the British and Cape Governments enabled Germany to establish a protectorate in south-west Africa.

THE PRINCIPAL STREET IN BULUWAYO, CAPITAL OF RHODESIA

Now, however, a reaction set in ; the disposition to concede every demand was giving way to an inclination to extend the area of British activity, of which the first fruits were the Bechuanaland settlement. This great district, lying on the west of the Transvaal, formed the highway into the interior. In this field the great explorer, Dr. Livingstone, had laboured as a missionary, and had successfully foiled the efforts of the Boers to bring it under their sway. Here for some years past there had been much unrest and internal discussion between the tribes, which began to call in to their support the aid of groups of white adventurers. As a natural result it soon became

CECIL RHODES   Russell

As a young politician of the Cape, he dreamed the vast dreams out of which grew Rhodesia.

evident that the adventurers would practically partition Bechuanaland among themselves. The apparent inertness of the British Government led the Transvaal President, Paul Kruger, to proclaim the protectorate of the South African Republic over the disturbed districts in September, 1884. But the districts were under the general authority of the High Commissioner, though the first efforts to bring them into order had been only tentative in character and ineffective in result. The Imperial Government declined to recognise the validity of Kruger's proclamation, and a force was sent up to Bechuanaland under Sir Charles Warren. The adventurers, who had constituted themselves into the so-called Republics of Goschen and Stellaland, found themselves manœuvered out of any possibility of resistance ; they were removed, the natives reinstated on the soil, and Bechuanaland was organised as a Crown Colony, the more remote territory, under its particularly enlightened chief Khama, forming a protectorate.

There now ensued a period of expansion. Already in the Transvaal discoveries of gold were being made which were entirely to transform the character of that republic—a subject to which we shall shortly revert. Beyond

RHODESIA'S GEM: THE VICTORIA FALLS

Bechuanaland and on the north of the Transvaal were established the Matabele under Lobengula, with his headquarters at Buluwayo, with the peaceful Mashona beyond, up to the Zambesi.

In Cape Colony, Cecil Rhodes, a young Englishman who had already achieved political prominence, was dreaming vast dreams, and watching with an exceedingly practical eye for stepping-stones to their realisation. The Germans from the west were beginning to turn acquisitive glances towards the unappropriated lands. From Lobengula Rhodes obtained mining concessions; by patient organisation he bought out or absorbed rival syndicates, whose aims were limited to a desire for gold-mines. The High Commissioner was induced to declare Matabeleland under British protection ; and, in 1889, Rhodes's company obtained a charter from the British Government which placed in its hands the administration of the territory up to and beyond the Zambesi — to be known afterwards as Rhodesia. It was not long then before the Chartered Company extended its administrative sphere across the Zambesi, and included therein Barotseland. Meanwhile, on the south and west of the great Lake Nyassa, British

MAP OF THE BASIN OF THE ZAMBESI

settlements, primarily of a missionary character, had been taking root for some years past. Now the definite organisation of a British protectorate in those regions was resolved on. Negotiations with the native chiefs were conducted through agents, of whom the most notable was Sir Harry Johnston, and extended its control as far north as Lake Tanganyika ; and the whole of the territory north of the Zambesi up to that lake and west of what was recognised as Portuguese was divided between the Chartered Company and the Imperial British Central Africa (or Nyassaland) Protectorate.

South of the Zambesi the Chartered Company had a more serious task in some respects than on the north, for there the territory included Matabeleland, where Lobengula ruled those warlike tribes who

had been the terror of their more peaceful neighbours further south, till the advance of the Boers had driven them over the Limpopo. The Matabele in their present quarters had been in the habit of raiding their neighbours as of old—neighbours whom they had dispossessed and robbed. After the coming of the British, Lobengula was to all appearance friendly. But he fell a victim to the delusion that because the British displayed no violence, they too might be bullied and defied. In 1893 he dropped the mask. Careful inquiry subsequently proved that the company had no alternative except war or evacuation. They chose war. The military Matabele were crushed by the company's administrative chief, Dr. Jameson, and the peaceful Mashonas were relieved from an intolerable tyranny. Buluwayo — the name meaning the place of killing— became the capital of Rhodesia. It must be borne in mind that the Matabele were not the old possessors of the soil, but a conquering horde which had only recently taken possession.

Hitherto we have found the British colonisation in South Africa always in some sort taking the form of expansion from the Cape. But the general scramble in the 'eighties among the European Powers for African territory led to the establishment of another British protectorate in equatorial regions, which are included in our South African division. We have already seen that affairs in Zanzibar brought about a critical partition of that state and of its hinterland as " spheres of influence " mainly between Britain and Germany. British East Africa lies north of German East Africa. In 1888 administrative control over what was so far recognised as the definitely British sphere was placed in the hands of the Chartered British East Africa Company— that is, from Mombasa inland to the Victoria Nyanza. On the west of this lay the kingdom of Uganda, under King Mwanga, which was declared a British protectorate in 1895 and reorganised in 1901.

THE WAR AND RECONSTRUCTION
THE NEW CONDITIONS IN SOUTH AFRICA

WHILE the British dominion was expanding northward and setting a girdle round the two Boer states, so that all prospect of their extending their territory inland or acquiring an oceanic outlet disappeared, the Orange Free State continued to prosper on its own lines, and to present to the world something of the character of a model republic. Prosperity in the shape of material wealth was also descending upon the sister state ; but there her best friends could not admire the system of government.

As a simple community of farmers the people of the Transvaal had excited in England a certain sympathy—with an element of patronage about it—resulting in the Conventions of 1881 and 1884. But just after the latter it was realised that in parts of the Transvaal territory there were rich gold-mines. The usual influx of settlers in the gold districts followed. The town of Johannesburg grew up, and **Birth of the Gold City of Johannesburg** its population was mostly British—politically, if not racially. The Uitlanders were soon, in numbers, a formidably large proportion of the white men in the territories of the republic. The simple farmers turned the new state of affairs to account. They taxed the mining industry to its utmost capacity; they required the Uitlanders to hold themselves liable to military service ; the once empty coffers of the state treasury were comfortably filled. But the Uitlanders were as firmly barred from citizen rights as the aliens whom an ancient Greek city admitted within its gates. Years had to pass before naturalisation was granted, and the community from which the state drew nearly all its wealth was in effect refused any voice in the control of its expenditure, and any share in the administration.

Now, the government was not without a certain excuse for this attitude. If full citizenship had been placed within easy grasp of the Uitlanders, there was reason to fear that their numbers would soon enable them to become the controlling political factor. The Boers saw no sufficient reason for allowing themselves to be politically swamped in their own territory. The Uitlanders might come into the country if they **Isolating the Transvaal** chose to accept the conditions ; if not they might stay away. The Transvaal wished to remain isolated, and carried the principle to such a pitch that the cost of importing foreign goods by what was virtually the State railway became prohibitive, and even the Cape Dutch took to sending their merchandise by waggons across the drifts or fords on the frontier, instead of by rail. When the President proposed to go the length of closing the drifts, he found that his isolation from even Dutch sympathy, as well as from foreign intercourse, would be more dangerously complete than he had expected. That attempt was a failure.

Granted the existence of excuse for this policy, the grievance of the Uitlanders must equally be admitted. Civilised nations do not treat industries established by aliens within their boundaries as inexhaustible fountains of taxation ; and they permit the alien himself to acquire citizenship on reasonable terms. That is, if we use the term civilised in the European sense. Non-European states which adopt such an attitude are apt to find the wall of isolation forcibly broken through, if the incentive is strong enough. Englishmen conceived that they had a right to **Grievance of the Uitlanders** expect from a White State the normal conduct of a White State ; all the more when Great Britain claimed a suzerainty, however ill-defined, over the state in question. Least of all did it seem tolerable that a state which would not have been in existence at all but for the British reverence for the conception of freedom should treat free Britons as a subject population.

To reconcile such irreconcilables was a sufficiently difficult problem; but the difficulty did not end even here. In some form or other a South Africa united under one flag, and under free governments, was the ideal of every far-seeing states-man, however remote its realisa-

Ideal South Africa tion might be. To that end Cecil Rhodes, now Premier at the Cape, had been working with promise of success. The race antagonism of British and Dutch in that colony was already becoming mitigated, and yielding to the idea of a South African patriotism. It did not seem vain to hope that the enlightened Government of the Orange Free State would shake off the prejudices

secure public sympathy for unofficial intervention on their behalf. A Trans-vaal Government reorganised, with the rule of the stalwarts at an end, would simplify the whole situation. Rhodes and his administrator in Rhodesia, Dr. Jameson, lent themselves to the scheme; but to meet with success, absolute unan-imity was necessary, every detail must be agreed upon. But there were hitches. Before the hitches were removed, the official administrator of Rhodesia made a dash for Johannesburg at the head of a troop of mounted police on December 30th, 1895. It was the wrong moment for the Uitlanders; as things stood, an attempt at insurrection would only have made

THE AMAZING BLUNDER: DR. JAMESON'S RAIDERS CAPTIVES OF THE BOERS
The extraordinary action of Dr. Jameson, whose portrait is inset in the above picture, in making a dash for Johannes-burg in 1895 alienated official sympathy from the Uitlanders, who had genuine grievances against the Transvaal

created in the past, and fall in with the ideal. But while the northern republic maintained its attitude of dogged, ob-stinate antagonism, it was not merely a passive obstacle, but served to quicken the race-hostility outside its own borders.

The action of the Transvaal Govern-ment in the affair of the drifts had gone far to alienate even Dutch sentiment, when an amazing blunder turned the tables. The Uitlanders in Johannesburg were meditating the feasibility of bringing about a revolution by some means more active than constitutional agitation. To that end they would need outside help. Their case seemed strong enough to

matters worse. The raiders found them-selves in a trap and had to surrender.

Nothing could better have served the purposes of the Transvaal President; from being in a distinctly critical position he had suddenly become complete master

The Tables Turned of the situation. The official position of Dr. Jameson could not be ignored, nor was it possible to deny that Mr. Rhodes was more or less implicated in the plot. The home authorities repudiated any suggestion of complicity; but the official inquiry which followed gave a certain speciousness to the allegation that there was more behind. The Uitlanders had gone quite far enough to warrant any Government in turning a deaf ear to their appeals. Mr. Kruger's position had been rendered technically impregnable, while a situation that was practically intolerable was prolonged. Perhaps from the British point of view the most serious result was the revulsion of Dutch feeling in favour of the attitude of the republic.

Instead of the pressure on the Uitlanders being relaxed, it was intensified; to all protests the raid was a sufficient answer. The President began to act as if the conventions had established the republic as a sovereign state. The imputation to the British Government of sinister designs, against which precautions were warranted, was made plausible by the fiasco of the raid inquiry. Sir Alfred Milner, sent out as High Commissioner in 1897, came very definitely to the conclusion that if Great Britain was to remain a power in South Africa she must assert her title **The Boer War Declared** resolutely, and bring pressure to bear for the remedying of grievances. The very question of suzerainty under the 1884 Convention was disputed. The Colonial Office expressed itself vigorously; the President was immovable, and the Free State, under a new President, Steyn, gave him moral support and the promise of material assistance. Before, as well as since, the raid, the Transvaal had been arming. Now British troops began to concentrate. Negotiations failed to produce any basis for agreement. Then the President sent an ultimatum on October 9th, 1899, demanding an undertaking to withdraw the British forces within forty-eight hours. On October 12th the Boer commandos were over the frontier, and war had begun. In England and among the British at the Cape the conviction had gained ground that President Kruger was actuated by something more than the determination to preserve the independence of

LORD MILNER
Who was sent out to Cape Colony in 1897 as High Commissioner.
Barnett

the Transvaal. There is no doubt that in certain quarters among the Dutch of South Africa the idea had taken root that a Dutch ascendency might replace that of the British. It is not to be supposed that intelligent Dutchmen imagined that they could overthrow the British supremacy single-handed. If any such plot had been formulated at all, it rested on the expectation that Britain would find her powers so fettered by European complications that the obvious odds in her favour would be made nugatory. Nor is it, in fact, clear that such an ambition was widespread, or was anything more than the dream of a few politicians. But as the enormous expenditure of the republic on the secret accumulation of munitions of war for some years past came to be revealed, Englishmen refused to credit that these had been dictated by considerations merely of self-defence **Dream of a Dutch Ascendency** against hypothetical British aggression. It was believed that Kruger had deliberately sought occasion to fling down the gage of combat at a moment which he regarded as favourable. The great bulk of the population was satisfied that no diplomacy, no concessions which could be made with honour, would have averted the war; nor did the vigorous protests of a minority affect the practical unanimity with which the challenge was accepted and the struggle fought out to the end.

No less doggedly did the Boers set about their task, whether with the more ambitious aim attributed to them, or with merely a stern determination to fight to the last for the independence which, since the use they made of the concessions after Majuba, they could hope to preserve only by decisive victory. There could be no more similar experiments in magnanimity. The British Government and the British nation entered upon the war under an extraordinary misconception of the nature

PRESIDENT STEYN
President of the Orange Free State, who supported President Kruger at the declaration of war in 1899.

of the problem before them. It was estimated that the whole Boer population capable of bearing arms in the two republics did not exceed 30,000. Obviously, however, the whole adult male population could not take the field, deserting the avocations on which their livelihood depended. Fifty thousand regular troops, then, should have no sort of difficulty in demonstrating that any resistance the farmers could offer must be futile.

For misconception as to the relative value of the burgher troops and British Regulars there was perhaps some excuse, such disasters as those of Laing's Nek

consummate horse-masters and dead shots. What history taught, expert military advisers on the spot emphasised; but their warning was disregarded. It was, indeed, true that in the impending contest the odds were so overwhelming that if Britain proved determined the Boer resistance must at last fail, if only because the Boer population would be ultimately eliminated. But the British nation conceived that it had only to give a clear demonstration of superior strength, and the affair would be comfortably over.

The Boers, too, had doubtless miscalculated. Majuba had made common a quite erroneous estimate of the British

ELANDSLAAGTE, THE SECOND BATTLE OF THE CAMPAIGN, FOUGHT FROM LADYSMITH
One of the first objects of the Boer campaign was the investment of Ladysmith, during which Sir George White was forced to fall back on Ladysmith, fighting the battles of Talana Hill, Elandslaagte, and Nicholson's Nek on the way.

and Majuba appearing in the light of accidents. But, in fact, the British had to deal with a people solidly determined to fight to a finish, occupying a huge territory, with a mountainous frontier eminently adapted for defence, and containing large districts peculiarly suited for guerrilla warfare. History has proved repeatedly that the subjugation of such a country is a matter of enormous difficulty if the local levies avoid concentration and refuse pitched battles. Scotland of old had defied England, Switzerland had defied the Empire, Spain had defied Napoleon. The men, moreover, were

soldiery and of British persistency. Very few realised that the retrocession of the Transvaal had been accepted by the British people in a spirit not of pusillanimity, but of generosity; it was imagined that a few reverses would make the British Government eager to find an excuse for coming to terms. It was believed, too, that other European Powers would intervene, and that no great masses of troops could be spared for South Africa. It was not understood that until England's sea-power can be effectively challenged she has no vulnerable point except India, though she herself is equally unable to attack except by sea. It was imagined, too, that the Dutch south of the Orange River would convert the Cape itself into practically hostile territory. President Kruger had timed his defence skilfully, so that the Boers could immediately assume the offensive while the British forces in South Africa were still wholly inadequate.

Additional forces were, indeed, to be expected very shortly. But at the moment, the regulars in South Africa numbered only about 22,000. Half of them were for political reasons gathered at Ladysmith and Dundee in the north angle of Natal —strategically, about as bad a position as could have been occupied, both sides of the angle being exposed to attack, while Ladysmith, topographically speaking, was peculiarly ill-fitted for defence. On the opposite side of the Free State a small British force held Kimberley, and to the north, on the Transvaal border, Mafeking. Fortunately for the British, Mr. Rhodes quartered himself at Kimberley. Now, until reinforcements arrived, it was impossible for the British to do anything but stand on the defensive ; the attack lay with the Boers.

Between Ladysmith on one side, and Kimberley on the other, the Free State ran south into British territory like a half-sausage. Thus, the British had an immense frontier to guard, with their posts hundreds of miles apart ; the Boers at the centre could strike on one side at Ladysmith, on the other at Kimberley, or make a direct invasion of Cape Colony southward, and could transfer forces from one to another of these fields of operation with great rapidity, which the British could not. And the Boers could at the moment send to the front two, or perhaps three times as many men as the whole of the British forces. If they had sent merely

"containing" forces to keep Ladysmith and Kimberley in check, and had thrown themselves in force into Cape Colony, they would probably have brought the bulk of the Cape Dutch to their standard, and the British would have had to reconquer the whole country, just as with the Ganges Provinces in the Indian Mutiny.

They did not realise their opportunity, however, but expended the whole of their energies in investing the towns of Ladysmith, Kimberley, and Mafeking.

THE TRAGEDY OF THE SPION KOP VICTORY
The Dublin Fusiliers, rushing the Boer trenches at Spion Kop, near Ladysmith, on the bitter day when the British won the Kop, did not know it was won, and so lost it.

Sir George White's force at Ladysmith held an advance post at Glencoe, close to Dundee. The campaign opened with an attack at this point. On October 20th was fought the battle of Talana Hill—a British success. But it revealed the fact that the Boer artillery commanded a longer range, and that the Glencoe position would soon be untenable. The only chance was to fall back on Ladysmith before retreat was cut off. The Boers were multiplying fast. White, from Lady-smith, engaged them in the battle of Elandslaagte, and the difficult march from Dundee was successfully completed on October 26th. On the 30th followed the battle of Ladysmith, terminated by

The Siege of Ladysmith
the disaster of Nicholson's Nek. A detachment had been sent to occupy that position. In the night the mules stam-peded. On their backs were not only the ammunition but portions of the guns. The artillery was made useless. The force held on, knowing that it was its business to cover White's flank in the impending battle. No help came to it. All through the 30th it was the object of a concentrated attack ; finally it found itself with no alternative but surrender. In the main battle, after much hard fighting, White had been obliged to withdraw his troops into Ladysmith, and the investment began. But one touch of good fortune had befallen ; a naval detachment with naval guns had been sent up from the coast, and joined the defenders of Ladysmith.

Meanwhile, on the west, large forces were investing Mafeking and Kimberley, since the Boers were pos-sessed with an over-mastering desire to capture Cecil Rhodes at all costs. But no invasion of Cape Colony proper was taking place. With November, the reinforcements from home began to assemble, and soon the attack passed from the Boers to the British. As the Boers had divided their attack, so now did the British. Sir Redvers Buller, with the main army was to advance from Natal, and join forces with the Ladysmith garri-son ; on the west Lord Methuen with a second army was to proceed to the relief of Kimberley. The new troops were strengthened by volunteer detachments which the loyalty of the Colonies had sent to the aid of the

mother country. To reach Kimberley and raise the siege, Lord Methuen had first to pass the Orange River and then the Modder, and then fight his way up to the besieger's lines. To reach Ladysmith, Buller had to force his way over the Tugela, and then through a mountainous region eminently adapted for defence. In the former region the Boers had neglected any attempt on the British line

British Advance Begun
of communications. In the latter, they had secured the north bank of the Tugela, and made a belated raid into Natal, but not until the accumulation of troops there had already made the operation ineffective.

The British, holding the passage of the Orange River, made their advance in the middle of November. Between them and the besieging force lay General Cronje.

THE APPARENT RETREAT OVER THE TUGELA

General Buller's last, and successful, move in the campaign for the relief of Lady-smith was a flanking movement which involved re-crossing the Tugela, apparently a retreat, but in reality an enveloping movement which compelled the retreat of the Boers investing Ladysmith. Inset is a portrait of General Buller.

THE RELIEF OF LADYSMITH BY GENERAL BULLER
After a fierce siege of four months, during which the garrison was reduced to sore straits, Ladysmith was relieved by the success of General Buller's flank attack across the Tugela river on the Boer position. This picture shows the meeting of the relievers and the besieged, a photo of Sir George White being inset.

on the enemy's lines, though unaware of their extreme proximity, while they were advancing in the close quarter-column formation—deployment can take place only at the last moment in a night attack —suddenly out of the darkness where the Boers lay in perfect cover, belched a devastating storm of fire. Over 600 men fell in some three minutes. The Highlanders broke—no mortal troops could have done otherwise. The moment they reached cover they rallied, but a fresh advance was impossible. With the day came help, and all day the struggle continued; but the Boer position proved impregnable. The repulse was decisive. It is remarkable that of the 1,000 casualties on that day, two-thirds occurred in the few minutes described. Meanwhile, to the south, Boer forces were at last entering Cape Colony in the district where there were many disaffected Dutch. Here, on December 9th, General Gatacre made an unfortunate attempt to take the offensive. Warning reached the Boers of the surprise contemplated. The tables were turned at Stormberg. Half the attacking force was cut off from the rest, and 600 men were obliged to surrender. It was fortunate that the enemy took no further advantage of the victory. The news of Stormberg and Magersfontein opened the "black week." The next news was that of the battle of Colenso, where the Boers held the north bank of the Tugela. The river was to be crossed at two points by Hart's and Hildyard's brigades. The former was led to a loop in the river where it was exposed to a cross fire, and efforts to discover a supposed ford proved fruitless. Hildyard's brigade made its attack at Colenso itself, and made good progress. But the artillery which should have supported it

The Black Week

On November 23rd a small Boer force, skilfully entrenched, gave the British a hard task in dislodging them at Belmont. And now Methuen was to face Cronje himself on the Modder. And with Cronje was Delarey. It was not anticipated that material resistance would be offered at the river, and Lord Methuen unexpectedly found himself involved in a very hot struggle to force the passage. But the thing was done at last. Another step had been gained. Cronje, however, had only fallen back to a new and very strong position at Magersfontein. To face that position Methuen made the arrangements on the night of December 10th. The Highland Brigade was to effect a night surprise; but the Boers were prepared for that. At the end of a long march, as the Highlanders were almost

Tragedy of the Battle of Magersfontein

met with disaster. The guns dashed forward to attack Fort Wylie; but, exposed to the full fury of the rifle-fire from the trenches, men and horses dropped—the guns could neither be withdrawn nor worked. In spite of desperate attempts to recover the guns, in which the only son of Lord Roberts lost his life, they had to be abandoned. The infantry attack, unsupported by artillery, could not be carried through. The first attempt to cross the Tugela had been disastrously repulsed on December 15th. For reasons unexplained, Buller's movement was made two days before the date he had notified to White in Ladysmith, so that nothing was done by way of co-operation in that quarter. On the other hand, White entirely declined to consider Buller's suggestion that he should surrender on the best terms he could get. The British nation was roused only to a sterner resolution by the week of disaster. From every quarter of the empire volunteers flocked to add fresh regiments to the increasing army in South Africa. Roberts and Kitchener, the two generals whose reputation stood highest in the British Army, were given the task of turning the tide of war. But before they arrived on the scene Ladysmith had victoriously repelled a determined attack, and the relieving force had been beaten back a second time. Never has a more splendid display of stubborn valour—on both sides—been made than on January 6th, when the Boers stormed the posts known as Waggon Hill and Cæsar's Camp, and the British hurled them back in rout. Yet hardly less splendid was the conduct of the troops on the bitter day when the British won Spion Kop, did not know that they had won it, and so lost it again.

Two divisions had been added to Buller's army since Colenso. In the third week of January a series of skilfully-designed movements enabled Buller to carry a large

LORD ROBERTS
Who, with Lord Kitchener, was given the task of turning the tide of the war after the "black week."

part of his force over the river at a point higher up, and the Boers had to re-entrench to face a flank attack. On the 19th and 20th, Sir Charles Warren, who was in command, carried through the next stages of the turning movement. On the night of the 22nd picked regiments climbed Spion Kop. There all day they held their ground under constant fire—waiting for guns. No guns came. Woodgate was shot; Thornycroft was placed in command. Hour by hour the men held on, till it seemed to their commander that before the next morning came there would be no men left to fight or to retire. He gave the order to retreat. It is said that the Boers were actually preparing to retreat themselves when they discovered what was going on. On the next morning Spion Kop was still held by the Boers.

Once again the relief failed, when a new key to the Boer position was found in Vaalkranz. The Boers were beguiled by a feint, and Vaalkranz was carried. Then it was found that the key did not fit the lock, and Vaalkranz was abandoned

And still Ladysmith held out grimly, and far away Kimberley and Mafeking maintained the one a stubborn and the other a light-hearted defiance; and General French in the neighbourhood of Colesberg held the Boers in that region in check, though in the perpetual skirmishes which took place fortune distributed her favours pretty evenly between the combatants.

But by the second week in February the newly-arrived commander-in-chief had his new plan of campaign in order, and new hosts were accumulating on the line of advance to Kimberley. The army had been drawn back south of the Modder. While he kept the Boers alert to resist an advance on the west, General French had been placed in command of a large cavalry force which was to circumvent them on the east. Starting on February 12th, through

CHRISTIAN DE WET
Whose genius for guerrilla warfare was mainly responsible for the long continuance of the struggle.

CRONJE'S MEN MARCHED AWAY CAPTIVES AFTER THE BATTLE OF PAARDEBERG
The last days of February, 1900, definitely decided the British supremacy in the theatres of war. The Boers investing Ladysmith were ousted from their position, and General Cronje, whose portrait is inset above, entrapped at Paardeberg.

four days of hard riding, here rushing a drift, there sweeping off an outpost, French raced round to Kimberley, meeting with no check which could stay him. On the evening of the 15th his force was encamped triumphantly in the neighbourhood of the beleaguered town, the Boers decamped, and the siege was raised.

Not at such speed could Roberts move the main force, whose extended lines were now intended to encircle Cronje in a net. In that enveloping movement, Cronje saw his doom, and he made a sudden and furious dash to escape before the net closed round him.

He passed the gap behind French, yet not so quickly but that a detachment was able to hang on his rear, and detain his retreat. It sufficed to give French time **Cronje** from Kimberley to head off the **Trapped at** course of his march. Cronje **Paardeberg** was trapped. On February 28th was fought the battle of Paardeberg, one of the hottest encounters in the war, often criticised as a superfluous waste of life, since the doom of the Boer force was already sealed, and was hardly even hastened by that engagement. The next day the British battalions were

gathering round the position where he had entrenched—one might say buried—himself. But it was still necessary that he should be crushed before the Boers could gather all their forces to come to his relief. The preparations were carried out steadily **The March** and without haste. The move-**Towards** ment which was to bring the **Bloemfontein** trenches under an enfilading fire was effected on the night of the 26th. On the 27th Cronje's whole force had no alternative but surrender.

Lord Roberts began preparations for the march upon Bloemfontein.

Meanwhile, Buller had made his final and decisive move. This time he was going to try turning the Boer's left flank, which meant first clearing them from the positions they held on the south of the Tugela. The new attack began within forty-eight hours of the relief of Kimberley. On that day the flanking movement was completed. By the 20th the whole south bank was secured. On the 23rd the Irish Brigade did not succeed in capturing Railway Hill, but carried and held the slopes. Then there seemed to be a deadlock, and men saw with bitterness that British troops were passing back over the Tugela. But it was only to carry out a further enveloping movement. The right wing held its ground, serving as a pivot on which the army swung. The fresh move converted it into the left wing. On the 28th the Boer position was practically carried. The enemy now no longer hoped to prevent the relief of Ladysmith, and were soon in full retreat. The long endurance of the worn-out garrison

The Relief of Ladysmith

had found its reward at last. It may be that the events of those days on the west had drawn off a substantial proportion of the Free Staters to oppose Roberts. In any case, those last days of February definitely established the British supremacy in both the theatres of war.

On March 6th began the advance on Bloemfontein, with an intervening force commanded by Christian De Wet, who now showed his extraordinary genius for exciting envelopment. The Boers never again fought a pitched battle with the main British army, though they fought skilful rearguard actions and harassed the advancing foe, who never got them in his grip. Such actions were those of Poplar's Grove and Driefontein. On March 13th Lord Roberts was in Bloemfontein. There a six weeks' pause was necessary before the advance on the Transvaal and Pretoria could be made in force, while the army suffered severely from an epidemic of typhoid fever. In the interval, the annexation of the Free State was proclaimed— following the example of the Boers, who had formally " annexed " every district which they occupied in force. Before Pretoria itself was reached the sportsmanlike defenders of Mafeking had been relieved by a small detachment, to the natural if somewhat delirious delight of the British public.

The Free State, however, still had an active force in being, while General Botha commanded the Transvaal army which lay in the neighbourhood of Pretoria. By

Fight to the Finish

September the old President had finally taken flight, and the British had carried their arms to Komatipoort. Technically, the conquest was completed. Yet the desperate struggle continued for another eighteen months. Nothing short of a European war could have altered the ultimate issue, but as long as it was possible to fight at all, the Boers fought. The English have emerged successfully from innumerable conflicts, simply through the dogged

tenacity which refuses to know when it is beaten ; the Boers showed the same quality, though with results less fortunate for them.

Hence, on the one hand, the whole period was full of incident. Mobile Boer forces, flashing from point to point, would snap up an outpost here and ambush a convoy there. British garrisons holding remote posts, or small bodies of troops on the march, would find themselves suddenly cut off, and conduct sometimes a brilliant and successful defence for days or weeks till relief arrived, sometimes find themselves forced to surrender because food or water or ammunition had given out. The brilliant dashes of the irrepressible Christian De Wet excited the sporting admiration of the foes, through whose enclosing forces he repeatedly ran the gauntlet, escaping time after time by the skin of his teeth. On the other hand, extended movements swept several bodies of Boers into the British nets. The regrettable frequency of breaches of parole and of abuse of the white flag, coupled with the conduct of the occupants of farms in contravention of what may be called the recognised rules

The Guerrilla War

of the game, necessitated a vast amount of destruction which otherwise would also have been against the rules of the game ; and led further to the establishment of " concentration camps," in which the families of the Boers were maintained by their adversaries.

But the struggle was vain. Lord Kitchener, left in charge after the departure of Lord Roberts, steadily and persistently perfected the system of blockhouses, which formed a barrier increasingly difficult to penetrate : the lines drew closer and closer. The time approached when the Boers would find themselves pressed into a corner from which there would be no escape, by a force now immensely superior in numbers and in equipment, which had, moreover, thoroughly learnt those conditions of warfare which at the outset had been so completely misapprehended. President Kruger, now in the Hague, still fulminated ; but in Africa the facts of the situation became too palpable. At last the Boer leaders made up their minds to recognise that they had fought to a finish and had been beaten. More than once during the eighteen months they had been offered terms, but had refused to treat on any basis save that of recognition of complete independence for the two republics. Now at length, at the end of March, 1902, they opened negotiations. For two months discussion continued. On the last day of May they signed the treaty which ended the long strife.

The republics lost their independence, or partial independence, and were definitely incorporated in the British Empire. To begin with, they were to be governed as Crown Colonies, an obvious necessity; but, in course of time, it was the desire of the victors that they should receive responsible government on the same basis as the other states comprised in the British dominions. Great Britain was to provide three millions of money to place them once more on a working financial footing; the Dutch language was to be allowed in the schools and law courts. Such were the main provisions of the Peace.

The principle was clear. There were two lines open : either the Boers were to be treated as a vanquished but still hostile people, who had brought their own doom on themselves at the cost of an immense expenditure of blood and treasure to the conquerors, and were to be held under ; or they were to be offered the right hand of fellowship and something more, on the hypothesis that they would grasp it in a frank and loyal spirit. That there were dangers in this course, risks that loyalty was merely assumed, was obvious ; but, on the other hand, it was the one condition without which the concord of the two races in South Africa was clearly impossible. So long as there could be talk of " top-dog " and " bottom-dog " the bottom-dog would eternally seek every occasion to reverse the positions. The bolder course of autonomous government was adopted.

SOUTH AFRICA TO-DAY

SINCE the British Empire at the Present Day will form the subject of detailed treatment in a later volume, we may here confine ourselves to rounding off the narrative of South African history.

Pacification, the calming of the waters which had been so troubled, the harmonising of the races which had been so fiercely at feud, was no easy task. The British population of Cape Colony had suffered heavily, directly and indirectly; and not a little natural animosity was felt towards rebels—those of the Cape Dutch who had taken part with the Boers. There were many outcries—very much in the nature of the Royalist complaints when the Merry Monarch was brought back to England in 1660—that the Act of pacification was one of " Indemnity for the King's enemies and oblivion for the King's friends." Adjustments where generosity in one quarter looks like injustice in another are always peculiarly difficult ; but where goodwill subsists at bottom, such heart-burnings gradually lose their bitterness.

The work, first in the hands of Sir Alfred Milner as High Commissioner, was entrusted in 1905 to Lord Selborne. The

Haines

LORD SELBORNE
Who, as High Commissioner for South Africa at the conclusion of war, had the task of pacification.

governorship of the Cape was separated from the commissionership, and during the Crown Colony period the control both of the Transvaal and the Orange River Colony was vested in the High Commissioner. The rehabilitation of the country after the damage and losses of the war has offered serious problems. The great common peril to the whites —that of a native rising during the war—had been successfully averted; but in the general disorganisation native labour became much more difficult to obtain, and white labour in the mines is costly. Hence a scheme was carried out for obtaining coolie labour from China, which involved the application of extremely strict regulations and conditions of contract. A storm arose over this question, the argument being, on the one side, that coolie labour was necessary to the development of the industry, and the coolie was better off than in China ; while, on the other, it was held that if the mines could only be worked under these conditions— and " free " Chinese labour was an obvious impossibility—it would be better for the community that they should not be worked at all; although it was not admitted that the exclusion of Chinese labour need, in fact, prevent the mines from being worked.

The preponderant sentiment, however, in a short time definitely declared itself against Chinese labour, and

The Chinese Labour Problem steps were taken to bring the system to an end. Again, politics were perpetually complicated by suspicions and accusations of racial or class intrigues to capture the machinery of government in the Cape Colony, and in the two newly-organised states, so soon as representative government should be established; while hot controversy raged as to the wisdom or folly of granting responsible government for some years to come. Nevertheless, the Transvaal received its constitution at the end of 1906, and the Orange River Colony some months later. It is a healthy omen that the opponents of that policy have shown a frank readiness to make the best, instead of the worst, of a situation which they feared; and, on the other hand, there has been no sign that the Dutch element—ably led now in the Transvaal in politics, as formerly in war, by Louis Botha—will use its weight in the political scales in a spirit hostile to the British. Traces of the war are not to be effaced in a day; but under shrewd and broad-minded guidance the prospects of harmony appear to be satisfactory.

In Natal native questions have inevitably a peculiar prominence. Now, as always, there is a section of the British public which is particularly alert to any suggestion of injustice to natives, and ready to demand the interposition of the Home Government; now, as always, the men on the spot claim that such interposition is invariably harmful. In the nature of things, therefore, friction is exceptionally apt to arise in this quarter. The trial of Dinizulu on a charge of conspiracy was fraught with combustible elements; but at the time of writing there seems to be no serious danger of disagreement. Passing northwards, it is to be remarked that the control

Native Question in Natal of the military force in Rhodesia was withdrawn from the Chartered Company after the Jameson Raid. The general administration of the territories remains in its hands, general development is proceeding, and the Pax Britannica is regarded with general approbation by the natives.

A. D. INNES

SWEARING-IN THE MINISTERS OF THE TRANSVAAL'S FIRST PARLIAMENT

INFORMATION ABOUT BRITISH SOUTH AFRICA

British South Africa consists of Cape Colony, Natal (including Zululand), Transvaal, Orange River Colony, Southern Rhodesia, Basutoland, the Bechuanaland Protectorate and Swaziland. The resident High Commissioner, the present holder of office being the Rt. Hon. the Earl of Selborne, exercises supervision on behalf of the British Colonial Office. He is empowered to arrange conferences between the governments of the various colonies. He is also Governor of the Transvaal, Basutoland, and Swaziland, and has supervision of the Bechuanaland Protectorate, of the administration of the British South Africa Company in Southern Rhodesia, and also of Barotseland, which is not in South Africa proper.

CAPE COLONY. Cape Colony, or the Cape of Good Hope, as the territory is officially named, has an area of 206,860 square miles, and a total population of 1,489,691, including 553,452 European or white, and 936,239 native or coloured. But including the native territories administered under the colony—East Griqualand, Tembuland, Transkei, Walfish Bay, Pondoland, and Bechuanaland—the total area is 276,995 square miles, and the population 2,409,804, of whom 579,741 are European or white. The chief towns in Cape Colony are: Cape Town, 77,668, or, with suburbs 169,641 ; Kimberley, 34,331 ; Port Elizabeth, 32,959 ; East London, 25,220 ; Graham's Town, 13,877 ; Uitenhage, 12,193 ; Paarl, 11,293. The government is vested in a Governor—the present holder of office being the Hon. Sir Walter F. Hely-Hutchinson—a Legislative Council, and a House of Assembly. The Legislative Council has 26 members elected for seven years, and the House of Assembly has 107 members elected for five years. Members of both houses are elected by the same voters and are paid. In 1906 the revenue of Cape Colony was £8,236,880, the public debt £43,980,112, the value of imported merchandise £18,102,872, and of exports £40,048,693. The principal industries are wool and wine, stock breeding (horses and cattle), ostrich farming, cereals, diamonds, copper and coal.

NATAL. Natal, including Zululand, has an estimated area of 35,371 square miles, and a population of 1,108,754, including 97,109 Europeans or whites, 100,918 Indians or Asiatics, and 910,727 natives and half-breeds. The chief towns are Durban, with a population of 69,903, of whom 32,925 are white, and Pietermaritzburg, the capital, with 31,199, of whom 15,086 are whites. Government is vested in a Governor —the present Governor being H. E. Lt.-Col. Sir Matthew Nathan—a Legislative Council (13 members), and a Legislative Assembly (43 members). In 1906 the revenue was £3,665,989, the expenditure £3,670,608, the public debt £19,484,143, the imports of the value of £8,409,311, and the exports of the value of £9,036,386. The principal industries are the cultivation of maize, sugar, tea, wattle, coffee, arrow-root, ginger, tobacco, bananas, and pineapples, sheep-farming, and horse and cattle breeding. Coal-mining is important and coal is exported.

TRANSVAAL. The Transvaal has an area of 111,196 square miles, and the population in 1904 was 1,268,716 of whom 299,327 were European or white. The largest town is Johannesburg, with a population of 158,580, of whom 83,902 are white, and Pretoria, the capital, with a population of 36,700 of whom 21,161 are white. Administrative power is vested in a Governor—the present Governor being the Rt. Hon. the Earl of Selborne—a Legislative Council of 15 members, and a Legislative Assembly of 69 members. Members are paid. During the financial year 1906-7 the revenue was £4,387,175, the expenditure £4,432,767, the imports of the value of £15,881,268, and the exports of the value of £26,607,776. The chief industry is gold-mining, but diamond and coal mining are also important. Copper, tin and iron have been found. Apart from mining the chief industry is stock raising. Agriculturally, the colony is not so well suited or developed as the sister South African colonies.

ORANGE RIVER COLONY. The area of Orange River Colony is 50,393 square miles, and the population 387,315, of whom 142,679 are white. The chief towns are Bloemfontein, the capital, with a white population of 13,512 ; Kroonstad, 2,454 ; Ladybrand, 2,333 ; and Harrismith, 2,238. The Government consists of a Governor—the present Governor being H. E. Major Sir Hamilton John Goold-Adams—a Legislative Council of 11 members, and a Legislative Assembly of 38 members. In the year 1906-7 the revenue was £787,328, the expenditure £774,586, the value of the imports £3,761,171, and the value of the exports £3,655,009. The colony is a rich pastoral and agricultural district, and scientific farming is prosecuted under Government assistance. Diamonds and coal are the only minerals worked to any extent.

SOUTHERN RHODESIA. Southern Rhodesia has an area of about 144,000 square miles, and is divided into the provinces of Matabeleland and Mashonaland. The white population of the former province is 7,706, and of the latter 4,917. The entire native population is about 620,000. The capital is Salisbury, with a white population of 1,726, and the commercial centre is Bulawayo, with a white population of 3,840. Southern Rhodesia is administered by the British South Africa Company under powers conferred by special charter. The administrator—the present holder of office being Sir. W. H. Milton—is advised by an Executive Council of not fewer than four members, and there is a Legislative Council of 14 members, half of whom are elected by the registered voters and half nominated by the Company with the approval of the Secretary of State for the Colonies. The chief industry is gold-mining, but stock raising and agriculture are making progress. The revenue in 1906-7 was £554,937, and the expenditure £501,473.

POSTAGE. Conditions generally as for New Zealand [see page 1002]. Parcels post to Cape Colony and Natal, 9d. per lb.; to Transvaal and Orange River Colony, 1/- per lb.; to Rhodesia via Cape Town, 1/9 per lb.; and to Rhodesia via Beira, 3/-, 6/-, and 9/-, up to 3 lb., 7 lb. and 11 lb. respectively.

TELEGRAMS. To Southern Rhodesia, 2/8 per word ; to other parts of South Africa 2/6 per word.

THE NON-BRITISH EUROPEAN NATIONS IN SOUTH AFRICA
PORTUGAL, BELGIUM, AND GERMANY

UNTIL the last quarter of the nineteenth century the European nations had not started on the scramble for African territory. Only one Power had preceded the Dutch in the attempt to establish permanent stations in the southern half of the continent. Except for the French in Madagascar, the Portuguese efforts alone have a history before 1876.

Portugal First in South Africa

Portugal, however, was taking the lead in maritime exploration as early as the fifteenth century. Before that century closed, 150 years earlier than Riebeek's Dutch settlement at the Cape, Vasco da Gama rounded the southern point of Africa in his search for a new route to India, and failed to secure a footing at Mombasa and at Mozambique.

In 1502, however, he was more successful in Sofala; and during the ensuing year several fortified posts were established on the east coast—such stations being of the utmost importance to the Portuguese dominion over the Indian waters. The first fort was planted at Kilwa in 1505. Henceforward the coast was kept under the surveillance of a flying squadron. In the year 1512 the fort at Kilwa was abandoned, and the settlement in Mozambique which had been begun in 1507, now became the chief base of the Portuguese power in East Africa. At the beginning of 1507 the admiral Tristão da Cunha made a punitive expedition against the enemies of the sheikh of Malindi, and at the end of March burnt the town of Brava, which had hitherto been consistently hostile; he made, however, no attempt upon Makdishu. As every fleet sailing to India or Eastern Asia touched at the East African coast, the Portuguese predominance was rapidly assured, to the great advantage of the nation, which drew a considerable income from the coast trade and the gold-mines of Sofala.

But at no period was there an absolute cessation of disturbances and struggles, which were especially frequent in the north.

By the end of the sixteenth century the Portuguese were in occupation of several coastal positions from Sofala northward, but had made no attempt to take possession of the interior. Mining operations in search of silver were set on foot, but with disappointing results. The power of Portugal had collapsed with her absorption by Spain, and was not recovered with her independence in the middle of the seventeenth century. She found herself unable to overcome the Arab resistance; she was driven from Maskat, and then from Zanzibar, and in the eighteenth century retained only a somewhat vague command of the coast from Cape Delgado on the north to Lorenço Marquez on the south.

In the meanwhile, a somewhat similar fate had attended the Portuguese efforts at colonisation on the west coast. Portuguese influence was early established in the Congo kingdom, where the native monarchs adopted Christianity, were baptised with Portuguese names, and in other matters sought to imitate the Portuguese example. Towards the end of the sixteenth century a Portuguese station was secured in Angola, which developed into the city of São Paulo, and some unsuccessful attempts were made to penetrate into the interior and to reach the settlements on the east coast. But in the disastrous period of her subjection to Spain, Portugal could do little beyond maintaining her ground against hostile native rulers. And when emancipated Holland attacked her as a member of the Spanish empire, her chances of effectively extending diminion practically disappeared, and she retained her ascendency in Angola

Dark Days of Portugal in Africa

only with great difficulty. It was not till near the close of the eighteenth century that Portuguese colonial activity revived in Africa; even then it was doomed to receive an early check from the cruel burden thrown upon Portugal during the Napoleonic wars. After that troublous time, however, she gradually extended her dominion and the sphere of her influence from Angola. Both in that province and on the east coast administration progressed, though few will question that the rigid enforcement of economic isolation was a serious drawback to commercial development. Later jealousies arose over the prospect of the British dominion extending itself into Central Africa, and permanently separating the eastern Portuguese dominion from the western; also over British claims to rights in Delagoa Bay, the southern limit of Portuguese East Africa.

The latter question was settled by the arbitration of Marshal McMahon, at the time President of the French Republic. His award was wholly in favour of the Portuguese claims; but British interests had been safeguarded as against rival Powers by a preliminary convention securing a right of pre-emption to whichever party should be defeated in the arbitration. The Central African question was settled by an altogether distinct agreement on the delimitation of the respective spheres of influence of the two Powers, which has been productive of a satisfactorily harmonious spirit between them—viewed not without some acrimony by a rival colonising Power. **Progress in Portuguese East Africa** This agreement took final form in the convention of 1891. Angola is fairly entitled to be called prosperous, while the commercial prospects of the eastern colony have been distinctly improved by the activity and enterprise of the British in Rhodesia. In the last quarter of the nineteenth century Central Africa began to engage

the serious attention of the European Powers. The history of the Congo State begins on September 15th, 1876, with the foundation by King Leopold II. of Belgium of the "Association Africaine Internationale." Its chief objects were the exploration of Central Africa, **Foundation of the Congo State** the civilisation of the natives, and the suppression of the slave trade; the foundation of permanent settlements was therefore an essential part of its policy. Meanwhile the Congo problem had been solved by H. M. Stanley. Not content with the accomplishment of purely scientific achievements, the great explorer saw plainly that the Congo river offered the only possible route by which a large part of Africa could be opened up without loss of time and with resources comparatively scanty. Full of bold schemes, he returned to Europe in August, 1877, and gained a friendly reception from the new company and King Leopold. The company determined to work the recently discovered district for itself.

It was high time. France, in the person of the Count Pierre Savorgnan de Brazza, had already seized a part of Congoland. On November 25th, 1878, Stanley founded the branch company in Brussels, "Comité d'Etudes du Haut-Congo," returned to the Congo in 1879, founded the settlement of Vivi, and began to make a road from the river's mouth to Stanley Pool, or Leopoldville, in 1882. He also concluded many conventions with the negro chiefs, thus forestalling De Brazza, who had founded or was preparing to found the stations of Franceville, Brazzaville, and Poste de l'Alima between 1880 and 1881. Meanwhile Portugal, supported by Great Britain, with whom she made a convention on February 26th, 1884, laid claims to the territory at the mouth of the Congo, which were vigorously resisted by most of the other states. With the object of relieving this state of tension, Germany invited the Powers to a conference.

MAP OF THE BASIN OF THE CONGO

The practical result was the recognition of the Congo Free State under the sovereignty of the King of the Belgians, the theory being that the administration was to be cosmopolitan. Cosmopolitanism did not prevail for long ; by degrees, all the official posts were absorbed by Belgians. In the last decade of the century

Belgian King's Oppression of the Congo a sharp conflict with the Arabs terminated with the total expulsion of the Arab power from the Congo territory. The effective conversion of what had been intended to be a state under international management into a private estate of the Belgian king proved by no means satisfactory to other Powers. The trade of the Upper Congo regions, instead of being kept open, was virtually made a Belgian monopoly. Very evil reports were made by Protestant missionaries of various nationalities as to the malpractices, the oppression, and the violence of the administration. British feelings were further outraged by the quasi-judicial murder of a trader, Mr. Stokes, without trial, on a charge of supplying the Arabs with powder, and by the repeated acquittals of the official who sentenced him.

The stories of administrative atrocities were virtually confirmed in all their ugliest features by the official report made at the instance of the British Government by the British Consul, Mr. Casement. Hence a continuous agitation has been maintained, more especially in Great Britain, for a vigorous intervention, while the King of the Belgians emulates the example of the Sublime Porte when the concert of Europe starts the tune of Armenian or other atrocities. There are indications that the patience of at least one Power is nearly exhausted. A solution may perhaps be found by transferring the sovereignty—and the responsibility—to the Belgian nation instead of the Belgian monarch, a process in course of being

Germany in South Africa carried out at the time of writing, in 1908.

The history of the German colonies in Southern Africa begins officially on April 24th, 1884, when Prince Bismarck proclaimed a German protectorate in South-west Africa. On August 7th of the same year the German flag was hoisted in Angra Pequena, and at other points of the coast shortly afterward. By slow degrees, the British Government was induced to recognise the German protectorate.

Great Britain retained possession of Walfish Bay and the adjacent territory, and also of the islands on the coast, to which she had priority of claim. Namaland and Damaraland were gradually brought under German supremacy, a process which ultimately led to a definite arrangement with Great Britain on July 1st, 1890. By the terms of this agreement, the lower course of the Orange River was to be the southern boundary of the German territory, the eastern boundary was the twentieth degree of longitude east (of Greenwich), but from the twenty-second degree of latitude south the frontier was to extend to the twenty-first degree of longitude east. On the north a small strip of German territory was to be run as far as the Zambesi.

The compact with Portugal of December 30th, 1886, determined the Lower Cunene as the northern frontier, and thus placed Ovamboland under German protection. German South-west Africa is undoubtedly the most important German acquisition in Africa, and the only one which is capable of being gradually transformed into an entirely German district. The Herero, however, continue to be restive, and assured tranquillity in the

German East Africa German colony appears still somewhat remote. The existence of a German sphere of ascendency in East Africa originated with the "German Colonisation Company," which was founded on April 3rd, 1884

It conceived the idea of sending an expedition into the hinterland of the Zanzibar coast, acquiring territory there, and awaiting the further results of its action. Karl Peters, who had started the company, and was the leader of the little expedition, concluded a number of treaties in November, 1884, with different chieftains in Usagara, Nguru, etc., which were officially confirmed on February 27th, 1885. At the same time the company obtained an imperial charter. Seyyid Bargash, sultan of Zanzibar, endeavoured to put legal obstacles in the way of the settlement, and to assert his rights to the hinterland of the coast by the despatch of troops to that district—action which was attributed in Germany to British intrigue.

When Germany vigorously rejected these claims, the French Government declared their intention of abstaining from any interference. On August 13th, 1885, the parties interested came to a temporary understanding. By the agreement between

Great Britain and Germany of October 29th, 1886, the coast remained the property of the sultan ; but the harbours of Dar es Salaam and Pangani were to be at the disposal of the German East African Company, which was formed on September 7th, 1885.

The company at once set to work, extended its territory further inland, began experimental plantations, and founded stations. When the custom-houses of the coast were leased to the company on April 8th, 1888, and a permanent income was thus definitely assured, it appeared as if no obstacle now remained to check the course of a sound development.

Unfortunately the actual resources of the company were totally inadequate to meet the claims upon them, or to provide against the dangers of the situation. The whole of the Arab power raised the standard of opposition. The occupation of the coast settlements had dealt the slave trade a deadly blow, and had thereby destroyed the second chief source of Arab wealth —the plantations, which were worked by means of the cheap labour brought down from the interior. Utter ruin was now threatening the once prosperous Arabs of the coast. Their profession of slave-hunters and slave-traders had made them fierce and lawless, and inspired them with a passionate hatred of foreigners.

Ruin of the Slave-Traders

The most formidable opponent of the Germans was the Arab Bushiri, who had stirred up the revolt in Pangani, and from this point guided the movements upon the coast. Moreover, he found allies in the Masiti and advanced with them against Bagamoyo from the south-west. He was defeated, however, and ultimately captured and executed in December, 1889. The administration has certainly been painfully lacking in efficiency. Notwithstanding this, the capital Dar es Salaam has developed satisfactorily, and plantations of considerable extent have been made in the Tanga hinterland, which has been partly opened up by a railway.

Zanzibar Under British Control

The final delimitation of the colony was under the Anglo-German convention of July 1st, 1890, whereby Zanzibar was placed under the British protectorate, an agreement which dealt a heavy blow to the development of the German protectorate district, and, according to German views, was extravagantly favourable to Great Britain. The coast from Umba to Rovuma was left entirely to Germany ; the sultan Seyyid Ali of Zanzibar received the sum of four millions of marks as compensation. Of late years the colony has developed fairly satisfactorily in spite of bad harvests.

HEINRICH SCHURTZ
A. D. INNES

Edwards

ANTANANARIVO, THE CAPITAL OF THE ISLAND KINGDOM OF MADAGASCAR
Inset is a view of the palace where the Hova queens of Madagascar reigned before it became a French colony.

MADAGASCAR AND THE MASCARENES
By Dr. Heinrich Schurtz

MADAGASCAR, with the Mascarenes, must be associated with Africa, though ethnologically its connection is much closer with Malaysia. Its dark-skinned inhabitants, like its fauna, seem much more closely related to the Melanesians than to the negroes, though it is impossible to say positively that they are not of African origin. The Malays **Madagascar's** were clearly brought to Ma- **Connection** dagascar by more than one of **With Malaysia** those marvellous migrations which have become of paramount import- ance for the history of Indonesia and Oceania. Certain similarities favour the view that Sumatra was the point from which the colonisation of Madagascar started. The date of the most important immigrations cannot be satisfactorily determined, but, considering the compara- tively high culture of the immigrants, we should not venture to place the be- ginning of the migration in a very remote age. The immigrants brought with them the art of iron-working, but do not seem to have been acquainted with cattle-breeding, since the Hova word for ox is borrowed from the East African Swahili language. They were not unfamiliar with the loom, but apparently employed it to weave palm fibre, not cotton. Their social divisions were hereditary nobles, or Andrianes, free men, and slaves.

Since, on the arrival of the Europeans, the Mascarenes, which lie to the east of Madagascar, were found uninhabited, these migrations could not have reached Madagascar through these islands. It is possible that the seafaring Malays, who by piracy and trade commanded the shores of the Indian Ocean before the Christian era and until the beginning of the Hindu trading expeditions to Malacca and Java, may have reached the coasts of Madagascar in this way from the north, and founded settlements there in course of time. All connection with their eastern home was then aban- doned, and the settlers on Madagascar

continued to develop independently of the mother country, but not without experiencing in a considerable degree the influence of Africa. Among the Hovas, who must be regarded as the latest im- migrants, the legend is still current that their forefathers came from a distant island on a marvellous road of lotus leaves to the coasts of Madagascar; and that then, to escape the malarial fever, they penetrated far into the hill country. The legend says nothing of any aboriginal inhabitants.

The most pure-blooded Malays are the Hovas, who live in the central province of Imerina, and number at present about a million souls. The Betsileo, some 1,200,000 strong, who inhabit the hill country south of Imerina, seem to be more contaminated by negro blood. The Bet- simisaraka, on the east coast, are more nearly allied to the negroes than to the Malays. Besides the light-complexioned races of Madagascar and the remnants of an undersized primitive people there are also, especially on the coasts and in the south, dark inhabitants of a negro type, although at present no hard and fast line can be drawn between the races.

The negritian portion of the Malagasy population speaks Malay dialects, and must have been long subject to a distinct Malay influence. The main body of the dark population, whose most important branch are the Sakalavas, inhabit the west coast of the island opposite Africa, which points to an African origin for them. On the other **Influence of** hand, their skill as naviga- **the Arabs in** tors has its parallels in **Madagascar** Melanesia, but not in Africa. The Arabs made their in- fluence felt on the coasts of Madagascar at a comparatively early period, possibly long before the growth of Islam, and evidently owing to the vicinity of the gold-mines of Sofala.

The name Madagascar is first mentioned by Marco Polo, who derived exact information about the island from the

Arabian navigators, and heard in this connection of a gigantic bird, the roc. The fabulously exaggerated account may refer to those gigantic ostrich-like birds which clearly inhabited Madagascar down to historical times.

The religious controversies after Mahomet led to further Arabian immigrations, principally of sectaries, such as the Zeidites, a branch of the house of Ali, who may have partly come to Madagascar at the close of the eighth century; also about the same time a number of Ishmaelites immigrated. We know in any case that Sunnite and Shiite Persians emigrated to East Africa. Descendants of all these immigrants can still be identified in Madagascar.

The Portuguese, after the circumnavigation of South Africa, reached Madagascar also. The first of them to do so was Fernando Soarez, on February 1st, 1506, St. Laurence's day, from which circumstance the island received the name of San Lourenço. It was repeatedly visited by Portuguese afterward, but no permanent settlements were founded. The Dutch also soon abandoned their attempts at colonisation, which were made in the years 1595–1598.

At the end of the sixteenth century, as an indirect consequence of Arabian influence, the great Sakalvan kingdom of Menabe arose, which, in the course of the seventeenth and eighteenth centuries, planted many offshoots, especially Iboina. The real founder of the power of Menabe was Andriandahifotch, who died in 1680. These conditions were first changed by the appearance of the Hovas, a genuine Malay people, in the heart of the island. The eighteenth century saw the completion of the national union of the Hovas, who gradually realised their own strength and became a menace to the surrounding tribes. King Andrianimpoina began the first campaigns against the Betsileo, who lived in the south. His son Radama I. (1810–1828) continued the operations with still more success, became master of the greater part of the northern highlands, and pressed on to the east coast, where he

QUEEN RANAVALONA III
Deposed by the French, who made Madagascar first a French protectorate, and then a colony.

Rise of the Malay Hovas

made a treaty with the British. Provided with firearms by the latter, he then commenced war on the Sakalvas, compelled them to recognise his suzerainty, nominally at least, and proceeded to assert his claim to the dominion over the whole of Madagascar, a claim which was still absolutely opposed to the actual state of affairs. The sovereignty of the Hovas was never really acknowledged in the south and south-west districts of Madagascar. Radama soon quarrelled with the European Power which had long cast envious eyes on Madagascar—that is, France. The early French settlement, Fort Dauphin, had been founded in the year 1642, on the south-east coast of the island. An attempt of Colbert to form an immense colonial empire out of Madagascar and the surrounding islands, and to raise the necessary funds by founding an East India Company in 1664, seemed to promise success at first, but in consequence of the arrogant behaviour of the governor, La Haye, it ended with the massacre of all the French settlers and the destruction of Fort Dauphin in the year 1672. All plans for the time being were thus stopped. In 1750 the island of Sainte Marie was acquired, and the ruined Fort Dauphin regarrisoned in 1768. Soon afterward Count Benjowski appeared as French governor of the possessions in Madagascar. He was an enterprising but untrustworthy character, who obtained from some chiefs on the coast the concession of the entire island, and, when he laid down his office, regarded himself as owner of Madagascar, which he repeatedly but vainly offered to the French Government.

France Casts Envious Eyes on Madagascar

The wish to occupy the island could not fail to clash unpleasantly with the budding hopes of the Hovas for the overlordship. Under the reign of Queen Ranavalona matters came to open hostilities, which did not end gloriously for the French. Fortunately for France, the queen, who conquered parts of the south-east of the island, roused Great Britain—whose competition in the island had made itself felt by the occupation of Tamatave, in 1810 —also against her by her passionate

Po.l.

hatred of foreigners and by her expulsion of the English missionaries in 1835. In the years 1838–1841 the French occupied some more points on the north-west coast, particularly the island Nossi Bé, and in this way consolidated their influence among the Sakalavas. But for the time being there was no idea of a decisive and consistent policy.

A Feeble Copy of New Japan The intolerable misgovernment of Queen Ranavalona finally forced the Hovas themselves to seek help from without. Once more the French and British began to intrigue one against the other, and dangerous complications had already arisen when the sudden death of the queen, in 1861, and the accession of Radama II., who was friendly to France, completely changed the aspect of affairs. An age of reforms then set in, which presents a feeble counterpart to the similar and almost contemporary process in Japan. Even when Radama had been murdered, on May 12, by the reactionary party, reforms were continued by his widow and successor, Rasoaherina. The real power lay, however, in the hands of her husband, Rainitaiarivoy, the first Minister, a member of the Hova family Rainiharo, which founded a sort of palace government. The " reforms " gradually assumed a character which was very serious for France.

When Rasoaherina died, on April 1st, 1868, Ranavalona II. mounted the throne. On February 21st, 1869, she, together with her husband, again, of course, the chief Minister, adopted Christianity, and joined the Anglican Church, which had been in the meanwhile extending its influence among the Hovas, and now acquired complete ascendency. The news of the French defeats in the war of 1870–1871 naturally caused a further diminution of the influence of France in Madagascar.

France Asserts Her Claims The pretensions of the Hovas finally compelled the French Government, after long and unprofitable negotiations, to assert by force of arms their claims to Madagascar, which was more and more inclining to the side of Great Britain. On June 13th, 1883, Tamatave, on the east coast, was occupied. The death of the reigning queen, on July 13th, and the accession of Ranavalona III. Manyuake were followed by an abortive French expedition into the interior. But a treaty favourable to the French was concluded on December 17th, 1885. By this treaty Madagascar became a French protectorate ; a resident-general was placed in the capital, Antananarivo, to control the foreign relations of the state. This treaty was not, however, regarded very seriously by the Hovas until, in 1895, a new expedition, starting from the north-west coast, under Lieutenant-General Duchesne, took the capital on September 30th, after a singularly feeble resistance on the part of the Hovas, and then asserted the French protectorate by force of arms.

Madagascar was declared a French colony on August 6th, 1896. Rainilairivony, the husband of the queen, was banished to Algiers ; she herself was left for a time in possession of her title, but in 1897 she, too, was deposed and brought to Réunion. In this way the kingdom of the Hovas has been brought under French influence ; but the island as a whole has yet to be subdued. Under the rule of France the trade of Madagascar

The French in the Mascarenes has greatly improved, and a preferential tariff has succeeded in checking the British imports in favour of the French ; the exports, of which the most important articles are gold, vanilla, and indiarubber, are now sent chiefly to France.

The history of the French claims on Madagascar is closely connected with the fact that on the Mascarenes, in Mauritius and Réunion, French colonies were founded and plantations opened, with considerable success. The islands when discovered by the Portuguese Pero Mascarenhas in 1505 were totally uninhabited. Mauritius was for some time in possession of the Dutch (1640–1712), and was colonised in 1715 by the French, who had held settlements since 1646 on Réunion. Between 1734 and 1746 Bourdonnais, whom we have already met in India, was French governor here. For seventy years its position as a naval station made it a thorn in the side of the British on Indian waters. The introduction of the remunerative industry of coffee-planting increased the prosperity and the population of the Mascarenes during the course of the eighteenth century ; afterwards sugar-growing was extensively introduced. HEINRICH SCHURTZ

END OF THIRD VOLUME

41